P9-CCU-804

Property of

THOMAS J. ESPENSHADE
Office of Population Research
Princeton University
Wallace Hall, Second Floor
Princeton, NJ. 08544

How College Affects Students

Volume 2

A Third Decade of Research

Ernest T. Pascarella
Patrick T. Terenzini

JOSSEY-BASS
A Wiley Imprint
www.josseybass.com

Copyright © 2005 by John Wiley & Sons, Inc. All rights reserved.

Published by Jossey-Bass
A Wiley Imprint
989 Market Street, San Francisco, CA 94103-1741   www.josseybass.com

No part of this publication may be reproduced, stored in a retrieval system, or transmitted in any form or by any means, electronic, mechanical, photocopying, recording, scanning, or otherwise, except as permitted under Section 107 or 108 of the 1976 United States Copyright Act, without either the prior written permission of the Publisher, or authorization through payment of the appropriate per-copy fee to the Copyright Clearance Center, Inc., 222 Rosewood Drive, Danvers, MA 01923, 978-750-8400, fax 978-750-4470, or on the web at www.copyright.com. Requests to the Publisher for permission should be addressed to the Permissions Department, John Wiley & Sons, Inc., 111 River Street, Hoboken, NJ 07030, 201-748-6011, fax 201-748-6008, e-mail: permcoordinator@wiley.com.

Jossey-Bass books and products are available through most bookstores. To contact Jossey-Bass directly call our Customer Care Department within the U.S. at 800-956-7739, outside the U.S. at 317-572-3986 or fax 317-572-4002.

Jossey-Bass also publishes its books in a variety of electronic formats. Some content that appears in print may not be available in electronic books.

Library of Congress Cataloging-in-Publication Data

Pascarella, Ernest T.
    How college affects students : a third decade of research / Ernest T. Pascarella, Patrick T. Terenzini.— 2nd ed.
        p. cm.
    Includes bibliographical references and index.
    ISBN 0-7879-1044-9 (alk. paper)
    1. College students—United States—Longitudinal studies. 2. College graduates—United States—Longitudinal studies. I. Terenzini, Patrick T. II. Title.
    LA229.P34 2005
    378.1'98'0973—dc22   2004021981

Printed in the United States of America
FIRST EDITION
PB Printing   10 9 8 7 6 5 4

The Jossey-Bass
Higher and Adult Education Series

CONTENTS

LIST OF FIGURES AND TABLES

FIGURES

TABLES

To Caroline
and
In Memoriam
Mary Evelyn Dewey
A valued mentor, dissertation chair, and friend to us both

PREFACE

*If one believes in the cumulative nature of science, then periodic
stocktaking becomes essential for any particular arena of scientific endeavor.
The cumulation of knowledge may, of course, occur more or less haphazardly—
but this does not and should not preclude more systematic attempts by laborers
in the field to determine where they have arrived and where they might go.*

With these words, Kenneth Feldman and Theodore Newcomb (1969)
opened the Preface to their landmark work, *The Impact of College on
Students,* in which they reviewed more than 1,500 studies conducted
over four decades on the influence of college on students. Feldman and Newcomb
were pioneering explorers in essentially uncharted territory. More than two
decades later, encouraged by Ken Feldman, we ventured into this vast empirical
expanse, and in 1991 published a synthesis of more than 2,600 studies on college
impact entitled *How College Affects Students.* We assumed at the time of its publication that the volume would be something of a summary statement on the field
of college impact research. We soon realized, however, that we had just concluded
an intellectual task that was roughly the equivalent of painting the Golden Gate
Bridge from one end to the other. By the time you are finished at one end, you
have to start all over again at the other. On the day *How College Affects Students*
went into production, a new body of research began to accumulate, and the
product of about eight person-years of intensive work began a slow, inexorable
transformation to, if not exactly obsolescence, at least "dated scholarship."

Given the veritable explosion of research on college students in the past
15 years, the fact that our earlier volume was published over a decade ago would
be sufficient warrant for an update. However, the warrant for this update also
rests on the fact that *How College Affects Students* was published at a time (1991)
when the "ground rules" of American postsecondary education were changing,
and it was inevitable that a new and different body of research would reflect
these changes. We discuss these changes and how they are presented in the literature in greater detail in Chapter One. Suffice it to say here that the literature
beginning in the 1990s was characterized by an expanded notion of the kinds of

students and institutions worthy of study, a broader vision of how students learn, an expanded use of innovative instructional approaches and information technologies in the classroom, a more comprehensive set of policy concerns, and an expanding repertoire of research approaches for estimating college impact.

To be sure, a new and somewhat differently oriented body of research did not lead us to abandon the framework we used to organize the literature in the original *How College Affects Students.* We ask the same six questions of the evidence, and we organize our categories of outcomes in essentially the same way. We believe that this continuity of intellectual and organizational structure in the two books will make it easier for readers to understand similarities and differences in the conclusions we draw. To facilitate this understanding further, we have included sections in each chapter of the present book that briefly review the main conclusions from the first edition.

AUDIENCE

Based on the response to *How College Affects Students,* we believe our findings here will be useful to a wide spectrum of people involved in or responsible for postsecondary education. The full range of academic and student affairs administrators and staff—from middle-level administrators to vice presidents and presidents—will find in this volume the current empirical foundations for many of their institutions' student-related activities, programs, and policies. Graduate students preparing for administrative or research positions in postsecondary education, as well as researchers in such fields as psychology, sociology, anthropology, economics, public administration, and business administration who have an interest in the effects of college on students, will find a comprehensive analysis of the literature for a wide variety of student outcome areas, identification of areas in this literature where research is most needed, a conceptual framework (provided by the six questions we pose) for thinking about college effects, and a comprehensive bibliography. State and federal policymakers and their staffs—perhaps better able than we to extract policy significance from this literature—will gain insight into the sources of influence on student change and what we consider to be the main implications of this body of evidence for administrative practice and public and institutional policy. Anyone interested in postsecondary education in America and its effects on students will, we hope, find this a useful reference book and a guide to understanding one of America's most important social institutions.

OVERVIEW OF THE CONTENTS

The introductory chapter (Chapter One) provides a detailed discussion of how the literature has changed since the 1991 publication of *How College Affects Students.* It also outlines the conceptual framework that guided our present synthesis of the literature (as well as our previous review) and explains each of the six questions we pose in each college impact area. These questions, we believe, provide a useful way to think about college effects, whether retrospectively (as we have done) or in planning future research. This first chapter also describes how we have organized the outcomes we consider as well as our search and review methods, and defines key terms used throughout the book.

Chapter Two updates our earlier review of the most significant student development and college impact theories and models underlying much of the research on college effects. The chapter also incorporates refinements that have appeared in the theories and models put forward before 1990 and summarizes new theories and models that have appeared since then. Finally, the chapter examines the different perspectives afforded by developmental and sociological models of how college students change and why.

Chapters Three and Four examine the influence of postsecondary education on learning and cognitive development. Chapter Three focuses on academic subject matter and skills learned during college, whereas Chapter Four is concerned with the development of more general intellectual skills and analytical competencies.

Chapters Five through Seven address the influence of college on various dimensions of personal growth and change. Chapter Five focuses on psychosocial changes in students' self systems and relational systems. Self systems include sense of identity (both general and specific in such dimensions as race-ethnicity and sexual orientation) and self-concepts. Relational systems focus on the ways in which individuals relate to people and institutions beyond the self, and includes such topics as autonomy, locus of control, interpersonal relations, leadership, and overall personal adjustment. Chapter Six examines changes in students' sociopolitical views and activities; civic and community involvement; attitudes relating to race-ethnicity, gender roles, and nontraditional sexual orientations; educational and occupational values; and religious attitudes and values. Chapter Seven assesses the impact of postsecondary education on moral development.

Chapters Eight and Nine deal with the influence of postsecondary education on the socioeconomic attainment process, primarily for educational, occupational, and economic attainments. Chapter Eight examines the impact of college on educational attainment, focusing on factors that influence educational aspirations, persistence, completion of college, and earning graduate and professional degrees. Chapter Nine synthesizes the contributions of postsecondary education to career choice, the noneconomic aspects of career achievement and progression, and the economic returns from college attendance and various collegiate experiences.

Chapter Ten synthesizes recent evidence concerning the long-term impact of postsecondary education on quality of life, including such factors as subjective well-being, health status, health-related behaviors, welfare of children, and community and civic involvement.

Chapter Eleven summarizes the entire body of evidence on college impact reviewed for this book. In the process, the chapter emphasizes the extent to which the evidence corroborates, amplifies, or conflicts with the conclusions of our 1991 synthesis in *How College Affects Students*. The chapter also delineates some of the ways in which certain evidence supports theoretical models of student development and the impact of college. Chapter Twelve discusses implications of the evidence for theory and research, institutional practices, and public policy.

LEVELS OF DETAIL IN EACH CHAPTER

Chapters Three through Nine, devoted to a synthesis of the evidence, are written on two levels of detail. On one level, we review the literature within the framework of our six guiding questions, giving attention to theoretical and methodological considerations that often determine the reliability and validity of findings. This detailed presentation of the evidence constitutes the major portion of each chapter. On a second level, we provide a comprehensive summary of our conclusions about the evidence, generally purged of methodological discussion. That summary appears at the end of each chapter.

Although many readers will approach each chapter by reading first the detailed synthesis of studies and then the summary, that is by no means the only effective way to digest the large amount of information in this book. Some may find that they gain more from reading the detailed discussion of studies *after* they read the comprehensive summary. We also recognize that many readers may be most interested in the comprehensive summary and will use the detailed discussion of evidence in each chapter primarily as an elaborative selective reference. For this group of readers, we have taken pains to ensure that the summary section is in fact a comprehensive rather than a cursory review of our conclusions.

January 2005   Ernest T. Pascarella
                                                       Iowa City, Iowa
                                                       Patrick T. Terenzini
                                                       State College, Pennsylvania

ACKNOWLEDGMENTS

Publication of this volume represents the culmination of more than a dozen person-years of work, but its completion would have been impossible without the assistance of a large number of people. We are indebted to all the people who helped us in one way or another, such as the several million students who agreed to participate in the nearly 2,500 studies we reviewed; our graduate students who understood what we were about and respected our need for time and privacy; and the many scholars in the field who supplied us not only with encouragement but also with conference papers, technical reports, unpublished papers, and original data for our review.

Some, however, have helped us in ways that require special recognition. We benefited immensely from the generous financial support of the National Association of Student Personnel Administrators and the American College Personnel Association. This support underwrote a major segment of our early library research and greatly reduced our copying costs. We are also deeply indebted to the Department of Educational Policy and Leadership Studies at The University of Iowa and to the Center for the Study of Higher Education and the Higher Education Program at The Pennsylvania State University for their sustained financial and other forms of support for our efforts. We highly value and appreciate the exceptional quality of the staff they made available to us at various times and in various capacities. Without the competent secretarial and technical support of Mary Struzynski and Jan Latta at The University of Iowa and Sally Kelley at Penn State, this book would not have been possible.

We are also deeply grateful to our graduate research assistants: Becki Elkins-Nesheim, Lamont Flowers, Christopher Pierson, Rachel Truckenmiller, and Gregory Wolniak of The University of Iowa, and Heidi Cuthbertson, Lisa Shibley,

Kathleen Sherman, Melissa Gorman Salvia, and Samuel Palmer of Penn State. Collectively, they spent thousands of hours locating, copying, and abstracting journal articles, setting up and maintaining computerized bibliographic systems, verifying references, editing chapters, and even conducting some of the research we review in the book. We appreciate their enthusiasm for our project, their patience, and their good humor as much as their ability and competence.

The excellent libraries of The University of Iowa and The Pennsylvania State University played a major, if quiet, role in supporting both these young scholars and us. The resources of these two fine research libraries are exceeded only by the competence and patience of their staffs, and on behalf of both our graduate assistants and ourselves we gratefully applaud them.

We wish to thank all our colleagues who study the effects of college on students. The breadth and depth of the scholarship they have collectively produced is an enormous contribution to America's college students, the institutions they attend, and the higher education programs and public policies that affect their lives and futures. In particular, we recognize the friendship and support both in this effort and over the years of Alexander Astin, Len Baird, Stephen DesJardins, Kenneth Feldman, Don Heller, Robert Hendrickson, Larry Jones, George Kuh, Deb Liddell, Robert Pace, Gary Pike, John Smart, Vincent Tinto, Lee Upcraft, Fredricks Volkwein, and Liz Whitt. Finally, we offer a simple but profound thank you for the editorial and limitless personal support of Caroline Terenzini.

E.T.P.
P.T.T.

THE AUTHORS

Ernest T. Pascarella is the Mary Louise Petersen Professor of Higher Education at The University of Iowa. He received his A.B. degree from Princeton University (1965), his master's degree from The University of Pennsylvania (1970), and his Ph.D. (1973) from Syracuse University. Before coming to Iowa in 1997 he spent 20 years as a faculty member at the University of Illinois at Chicago.

He has focused his research and writing for the past 25 years on the impact of college on students and student persistence in higher education. He is a consulting editor for the *Journal of Higher Education* and has been on the editorial boards of the *Review of Higher Education* and the *Journal of College Student Development*. He has received a number of awards from national associations for his research. These include the research awards of the Association for Institutional Research, Division J of the American Educational Research Association, the Association for the Study of Higher Education, the American College Personnel Association, and the National Association of Student Personnel Administrators. In 1990, he served as president of the Association for the Study of Higher Education and in 2003 received the Howard R. Bowen Distinguished Career Award from ASHE.

Patrick T. Terenzini is distinguished professor and senior scientist in the Center for the Study of Higher Education at The Pennsylvania State University. He received his A.B. degree in English from Dartmouth College (1964), his M.A.T. degree in English education from Harvard University (1965), and his Ph.D. degree (1972) in higher education from Syracuse University. Before coming to Penn State, he served as a faculty member and administrator at Dean College (Massachusetts), Syracuse University, the State University of New York at Albany, and the University of Georgia.

For more than 30 years he has studied the effects of college on student learning and development, persistence and educational attainment, and low-income and first-generation students. He has published more than 100 articles in refereed journals and made more than 170 presentations at scholarly and professional conferences. He has been a consulting editor for *Research in Higher Education* for more than twenty-five years and served as editor in chief of *New Directions for Institutional Research* for over a decade. He has also been an associate editor of *Higher Education: Handbook of Theory and Research* and an editorial board member for the *Review of Higher Education.* He has received the research awards of the Association for the Study of Higher Education, the Association for Institutional Research, the American Society for Engineering Education, the American College Personnel Association, and the National Association of Student Personnel Administrators. He also received the Outstanding Service Award from the Association for Institutional Research and is a three-time winner of the AIR Forum Best Paper Award. He is a past president of the Association for the Study of Higher Education.

How College Affects Students

CHAPTER ONE

Studying College Outcomes in the 1990s

Overview and Organization of the Research

W hen we completed and published our synthesis of nearly 2,600 studies on the impact of college conducted primarily during the 1970s and 1980s (Pascarella & Terenzini, 1991), we believed that we were in a position to draw a fairly large number of conclusions about the institutional and programmatic factors that facilitate student growth and development across a wide range of outcomes. At the same time, however, we also grappled with the vague feeling that we had completed our synthesis at the front edge of a major period of demographic transformation in American postsecondary education (Adelman, 1998b; Astin, 1998; Callan, 1997; Henderson, 1995; Levine & Cureton, 1998b; National Center for Education Statistics, 1996, 1998; O'Brien, 1993; Rhoads, 1995c; Silverman & Casazza, 1999). As a result, over time we (along with others) began to question seriously the extent to which the conclusions drawn from research done in the 1970s and 1980s would help us understand the impact of college on students as we move into the 21st century (Kuh, 1992; Pascarella & Terenzini, 1998; Stage, 1993). Indeed, as we reviewed the research on the impact of college conducted since the 1991 publication of *How College Affects Students* we realized that the "ground rules" of American postsecondary education were being rewritten and that the research, with some natural lag time, was beginning to reflect these changes.

HOW THE LITERATURE HAS CHANGED

If there is a single adjective that describes the body of research on the impact of college conducted during the decade of the 1990s it is *expansive,* and this expansiveness is manifest along a number of different dimensions. First, there has been an expansion of the notion of who constitutes the students worthy of study in the American postsecondary system. With some notable exceptions, the research base for the first volume of *How College Affects Students* was strongly biased toward "traditional" White undergraduates, ages 18 to 22, who attended four-year institutions full-time, lived on campus, did not work, and had few, if any, family responsibilities. To some extent, this bias still exists in the research base of the 1990s, perhaps reflecting characteristic student populations at those institutions that employ the majority of scholars doing research on college impact. Yet it is also true that the literature of the 1990s has shifted its focus in important ways to reflect the changing, and increasingly diverse, national undergraduate student body.

Thus, we witness an appreciably greater volume of evidence in the 1990s that attempts to account for variations in many factors—such as age, work responsibilities, ethnicity, sex, full- or part-time (or even interrupted) attendance, and resident versus commuter status—in estimating the impact of college. In short, compared with the body of evidence synthesized in the first volume of *How College Affects Students,* the literature of the 1990s appears more sensitive to an important implication of the growing diversity of American undergraduates—namely, that not all students will necessarily benefit to the same extent, or perhaps even in the same direction, from the postsecondary experience. When different kinds of students benefit differently from the same experience, social scientists usually refer to this difference as a *conditional* (or *interaction*) *effect.* (This effect is often contrasted with a general effect in which all students appear to benefit about the same from a given experience.) We found an increased, if not universal, concern for the estimation of conditional effects in the literature of the 1990s that we believe represents an expanded vision of the impact of college that is consistent with the growing diversity of American undergraduate students.

Second, the literature of the 1990s evidenced an expanded notion of the kinds of postsecondary institutions worthy of study. This phenomenon is certainly reflected in a continuing and more sophisticated body of evidence on women's colleges and historically Black institutions, but it is perhaps most pronounced in the case of two-year, community colleges. The dramatic increase in student diversity in American postsecondary education has been paralleled by the equally dramatic growth in the importance of two-year colleges. For example, between 1978 and 1991, enrollments in community colleges increased by 31 percent (versus 23 percent for four-year institutions), and two-year college enrollments were expected to increase another 11 percent by 2003 (Chronicle of Higher Education: Almanac Issue, 1995). In 1996, community colleges constituted about 28 percent of all U.S. colleges and universities and about 39 percent of all public institutions, and these colleges enrolled about 37 percent of all U.S. undergraduates and about 50 percent of all undergraduates in public institutions (Callan, 1997; Terenzini, 1996).

Although community colleges are clearly major players in the national system of postsecondary education, they were largely ignored, with a few notable exceptions, in the literature base we synthesized for the first volume. A liberal estimate is that only about 5 to 10 percent of the literature we reviewed focused on community college students. Fortunately, that trend changed substantially in the literature we reviewed for this book. Though community colleges are still significantly underrepresented in the total body of evidence on college impacts, there is a growing body of evidence, conducted largely in the 1990s, that greatly contributes to our understanding of how these important educational institutions influence students (Pascarella, 1999).

Third, there is an expanded vision of how students learn that is clearly evident in the literature base of the 1990s. Scholars no longer regard learning solely as an act of acquiring or absorbing a set of objectively verifiable facts and concepts and, subsequently, incorporating them into long-term memory. Instead, they argue that a substantial amount of knowledge is actively constructed by the learner. There are a number of excellent, and detailed, discussions of the psychological and philosophical foundations for such constructivist approaches to student learning (Baxter Magolda, 1993; Baxter Magolda & Buckley, 1997; Cross, 1999; Dykstra, 1996; Fassinger, 1995, 1996; Felder, 1995; Mayer, 1999; Stage, Muller, Kinzie, & Simmons, 1998; Twomey Fosnet, 1996). What appears central to all of these discussions, however, is that the learner does not just passively receive knowledge or "truth" from others—that is, faculty members. Rather, students work actively and collaboratively with faculty members and student peers to create their own knowledge by trying to make personal sense out of the material that is presented to them (Brooks & Brooks, 1993).

Accompanying this expanded view of how students learn and develop intellectually has been an expanded use of innovative instructional approaches in postsecondary education, many of which incorporate the underlying assumptions of constructivist learning in their pedagogy. Research on instructional approaches such as collaborative and cooperative learning, learning communities, freshman interest groups, supplemental instruction, problem-based learning, and service learning was largely absent, or in its embryonic form, in the literature we reviewed for the first volume of *How College Affects Students*. Findings pertaining to the effectiveness of these instructional innovations, however, are quite evident in the literature we reviewed for this book.

Fourth, the research on college impact from the decade of the 1990s reflects an expanded set of policy concerns that were not particularly evident in the literature we reviewed for the first volume of this book. In many ways, these policy concerns reflect societal changes and technological advances that have come to fruition in the last 10 to 15 years. Whatever their cause, however, they are playing a major role in reshaping the policy research environment of American postsecondary education. For example, the increasing racial diversity of American society in general has been paralleled by a line of research that focuses not only on how college changes students' attitudes toward, or openness to, diversity but also on how experiencing diversity during college influences the outcomes of college itself. Similarly, recent national concern with the rapidly increasing costs of attending college ("College Affordability Concerns of College Freshmen," 1996; McPherson & Shapiro, 1991; Morganthau & Nayyar, 1996) has

been reflected in a line of inquiry that focuses on the costs as well as the benefits not only of attending college but also of attending colleges that differ in their
tuition structures.

In addition to societal changes and economic concerns, technological
advances have played a significant role in creating new policy issues that have
shaped the research agenda of the past decade. None of these advances has
been more significant than the availability of a rapidly expanding and increasingly powerful array of computer and information technologies. It would appear
that, although there is not uniform adoption across institutional types (Gladieux & Swail, 1999), postsecondary institutions in general have embraced these
new technologies with great fervor. For example, a recent report issued by the
Institute for Higher Education Policy (1999) indicated the extent to which computer use in postsecondary education increased during the second half of the
last decade. Based on data from the 1998 National Survey of Information Technology in Higher Education, the report indicated that in 1994 about 8 percent
of postsecondary classes used electronic mail (e-mail). This proportion increased
to 44 percent by 1998. Similarly, the percentage of classes reporting that they
used Internet resources increased from 15 percent in 1996 to 30 percent in 1998.
By 1998, it was estimated that 46 percent of all institutions had a mandatory
student information technology (computer use) fee.

When used appropriately the power of these technologies for enhancing student learning and cognitive growth in college is, indeed, substantial (for example, Ehrmann, 1995; Green, 1996; Kuh & Vesper, 1999; Upcraft, Terenzini, &
Kruger, 1999; West, 1996). This potential has not been lost on scholars concerned with the impact of college. Although there was some research focusing
on the cognitive impacts of computers in the literature we reviewed for the earlier *How College Affects Students,* that line of research has grown substantially
and is far more evident in the body of literature we reviewed for this book.
Moreover, the growing sophistication of information technologies such as tele-
conferencing, computer conferencing, the World Wide Web, gophers, file transfer protocols, listservs, and bulletin boards has enhanced the potential for
off-campus or remote site instruction. The relative impact of such "distance education" on learning is another line of research that is markedly more evident in
the literature we reviewed for this book than it was in the literature we reviewed
for the earlier edition.

Fifth, and finally, the literature we reviewed for this book evidences a more
expanded repertoire of research approaches for estimating the impact of college than did the literature we synthesized for the 1991 volume. To be sure the
positivist, quantitative paradigm still dominates the total body of research we
reviewed, with true experiments, quasi experiments, and correlational designs
with statistical controls for salient confounding variables being the methodological tools of choice. Most of what we learned in our present synthesis of
evidence is based on such approaches. At the same time, however, we also
noted an increased use of naturalistic, qualitative methodologies in the total

body of literature. Our prediction toward the conclusion of the last volume "that in the next decade important contributions to our understanding of college impact will be yielded by naturalistic investigations" (Pascarella & Terenzini, 1991, p. 634) has certainly been borne out, although this was probably more a case of reading the writing on the wall than of any great prescience on our part. In addition to the increased importance of naturalistic, qualitative studies, the current body of evidence also reflects an expanded repertoire of sophisticated statistical approaches that have helped refine and extend our understanding of college impact. These include hierarchical linear modeling, structural equation modeling, correction for selection procedures, and the estimation of effect sizes.

The warrant for this book stems largely from the confluence of the trends and changes noted in the preceding paragraphs: (1) a rapid increase in student diversity and an accompanying expansion of the notion of the students who should be studied in American postsecondary education; (2) an expanded interest in the impacts of postsecondary institutions that were largely ignored in previous research, particularly community colleges; (3) an expanded and evolving vision of how students learn that has been accompanied by new bodies of evidence on teaching, instruction, and learning; (4) an expanded set of policy issues, such as college costs and the impacts of student diversity and new information technologies, that have spawned new lines of research; and (5) an expanded repertoire of methodological approaches for estimating and understanding the impact of college on students. These five influences had a large role in shaping a body of literature between 1989 and 2000 that is substantially more diverse and complex, and nearly as extensive in sheer number of studies, as the 20-plus years of research—that is, 1967 to 1989—that we synthesized for our earlier volume.

This book is an attempt to synthesize comprehensively the new research evidence on the impact of college on students that has accumulated since the 1991 publication of *How College Affects Students.* As we already noted, it covers primarily the body of research produced from about 1989 through the end of 1999, although at times we cite studies done earlier than 1989, either because they are important to an understanding of the total body of evidence or because we somehow overlooked them in our previous synthesis. Because the body of research is an ever-expanding entity, we have also tried, when possible, to include important studies produced during the 2000 to 2002 period. To be sure, there have been important and well-conducted research syntheses on the impact of college on students since the 1991 publication of *How College Affects Students* (Gardiner, 1994, 1998; Kuh, Vesper, & Krehbiel, 1994; Love & Goodsell Love, 1995; Stage et al., 1998). However, these syntheses have been focused on relatively specific dimensions of impact, such as teaching and learning or the developmental impact of students' out-of-class involvement. None of them is—nor do any make the claim to be—an attempt at a comprehensive review of the research on college impact.

CONCEPTUAL FRAMEWORK

Much of the heavy lifting in terms of developing a conceptual framework, or set of organizing principles, for this synthesis was done when we wrote the first edition of this volume. (It should be noted that in the rest of this chapter, and throughout the book, we use the title *How College Affects Students* to refer to the first volume published in 1991, not the current one.) We employ the same general conceptual framework in this book that we did in its predecessor. There are two reasons for this decision. First, although any conceptual framework for organizing such a vast and complex body of evidence clearly has weaknesses, the one we used in *How College Affects Students* seemed to work reasonably well (Baird, 1992). Second, using the same conceptual framework gives us a measure of continuity and consistency with our previous synthesis. We reasoned that a consistent conceptual framework across the two volumes would facilitate comparison of the dimensions along which the literature has advanced and where new findings have changed or reinforced previous conclusions. This conceptual continuity between volumes not only helped us organize and conduct the present synthesis of evidence but, we believe, will also help readers see clearer connections between the conclusions of this synthesis and the conclusions of *How College Affects Students.*

In this synthesis, as in the earlier volume, we organize the evidence in terms of different types of outcomes (for example, cognitive development, values and attitudes, career) rather than in terms of the potential sources of influence on college outcomes (for example, major field, place of residence, interactions with peers). Astin's (1973) taxonomy of outcomes was particularly influential in defining the content and scope of our synthesis in *How College Affects Students,* and it continues its strong influence in this volume. Astin reasoned that college outcomes can be organized along three dimensions: type of outcome, type of data, and time span. The first two dimensions can be thought of as a 2 x 2 matrix where type of outcome tends to be either cognitive or affective and type of data tends to be either psychological or behavioral. It makes less sense to consider the temporal dimension as a dichotomy. Rather, it can be considered a continuous variable tapping the time span over which outcomes are assessed (for example, during college, 10 years after graduation from college). Under the first dimension, cognitive outcomes have to do with the utilization of higher-order intellectual processes such as knowledge acquisition, decision making, application, and reasoning. Affective outcomes are attitudes, values, self-concepts, aspirations, and personality dispositions. The second dimension of Astin's taxonomy refers to the operations required to assess the cognitive or affective outcomes under consideration. Psychological data reflect the internal states or traits of the individual and are usually assessed indirectly by means of a test or examination. Thus, an individual's level of skill in evaluating arguments or critical thinking is typically inferred from responses to a set of questions. Behavior measures, in contrast, are based on direct observation of, or reporting by, the individual. Consequently, there is much less to infer.

Astin's (1973) 2 x 2 taxonomy of college outcomes permits us to look at four different general clusters of outcomes based on the intersection of the two dimensions: *cognitive-psychological* (for example, subject matter knowledge, critical thinking), *cognitive-behavioral* (level of educational attainment, occupational attainment, income, and the like), *affective-psychological* (attitudes, values, personality orientations), and *affective-behavioral* (leadership, choice of a major, career choice, use of leisure time, and so on). Using Astin's model as an organizing principle and guide for defining the parameters of the evidence to be considered, the chapters of this book address different broad categories of college outcomes designed to provide coverage of the four taxonomic cells. Some chapters fit rather neatly into a single cell. For example, chapters on the acquisition of subject matter knowledge and academic skills and on the development of general cognitive competencies and skills (Chapters Three and Four) fall into the cognitive-psychological cell, chapters on psychosocial development and values and attitudes (Chapters Five and Six) fit generally into the affective-psychological cell, and the chapter on educational attainment (Chapter Eight) falls into the cognitive-behavioral cell. Other chapters, however, cover more than one cell. The chapter on moral development (Chapter Seven) probably taps both the cognitive-psychological and affective-psychological cells. Similarly, the chapters on career and economic returns and quality of life (Chapters Nine and Ten) tap both the cognitive-behavioral and affective-behavioral cells.

It is important to state explicitly that the focus of this volume, as with *How College Affects Students,* is on the outcomes of college for individual students. Certainly, the impact of postsecondary education on society is a scholarly topic worthy of attention. However, as in its predecessor, we judged a synthesis of the societal benefits of postsecondary education to be beyond the scope of this volume.

Obviously, some artificiality is inherent in any separation of the outcomes of postsecondary education into discrete categories. We know from the evidence we reviewed for *How College Affects Students,* as well as from other research and research reviews (Buczynski, 1991a; Davis & Murrell, 1993; Kuh, Schuh, Whitt, et al., 1991; Love & Goodsell Love, 1995), that a student does not develop in discrete, unrelated pieces but rather grows as an integrated whole. Indeed, one of our most significant conclusions in *How College Affects Students* was that student growth along any one dimension is often highly related to, and perhaps even dependent on, growth along other dimensions. For example, principled moral judgment may develop with, and perhaps even depend on, growth in formal or abstract reasoning. Still, the daunting size, diversity, and complexity of the existing literature makes some reasonable taxonomy or categorization necessary if one is to make sense of the evidence.

One might also reasonably take issue with our organizing the chapters of this book around outcomes rather than influences. Indeed, the seminal work in this area of inquiry, Feldman and Newcomb's (1969) *The Impact of College on Students,* takes the latter approach with considerable success. However, attempting to isolate the discrete influences of postsecondary education on students (for example, residence, peers, faculty, college environment, work experiences,

instructional and classroom experiences) is probably fraught with the same limitations of artificial categorization as an organizing scheme built around different outcomes. Certain aspects of students' intellectual development during
college, for example, may result from the intersection and interaction of a number of influences (interactions with peers, classroom experiences, work experiences) whose separate effects cannot be clearly disaggregated. Irrespective of
the conceptual structure one might use to organize the immense body of evidence on college impact, there are trade-offs to be made and limitations within
which one has to work. We acknowledge that focusing the chapters in the present volume on outcomes is only one of several equally valid ways of conceptually organizing the evidence.

The second main dimension of the conceptual framework of the present synthesis concerned critical questions to be asked of the evidence in each of the
broad categories of outcomes. Here, we once again adopted the framework
employed in *How College Affects Students.* This framework, which developed
out of previous work by G. Gurin (1971), Nucci and Pascarella (1987), and Pascarella (1985), asks six basic questions in each category of outcomes:

1. *What evidence is there that individuals change during the time in which
they are attending college?* In many ways this is frequently regarded as the most
fundamental question and one on which the relevance of many subsequent
questions that might be asked concerning the impact of college hinges. It is
tempting to believe that if individuals fail to change during college, then other
questions regarding effects of college versus noncollege or the effects of institutional environments are essentially moot. As we observed frequently in *How
College Affects Students,* however, it is more complicated than that. Put simply,
the presence of change during college is no guarantee that college is having an
impact. Other influences such as simply growing older (maturation), or the natural improvement that may occur when one takes the same test or instrument
twice (practice effect), could account for much or all of the change we attribute
to exposure to postsecondary education. Conversely, the absence of change during college does not always mean that college is failing to have an impact. In
How College Affects Students, we observed a number of instances when average change or growth during college was either nonexistent or trivial. That is,
college seniors were about at the same level as, or only slightly higher than,
freshmen. Yet students not exposed to postsecondary education tended to retrogress substantially (that is, change in a negative direction) during the same
period of time. In short, college had an impact by anchoring development and
preventing its retrogression. In this volume, we continue to summarize new evidence on documented change that occurs during college. In terms of estimating the actual impact of postsecondary education on students, however, it is
perhaps the least relevant of the six questions that guide our synthesis. A shorthand expression for the question will be "change during college."

2. *What evidence is there that change or development during college is the
result of college attendance?* This question is more specific and, therefore, more

difficult to answer than our first one. It is not concerned merely with whether change or growth occurs during college. It focuses instead on the extent to which whatever change does occur can be attributed to college attendance rather than other causes or influences (for example, normal maturation, differences in background traits between those who attend and do not attend college). In different contexts and different disciplines this has been referred to as the "unique," "value-added," or "net" effects of college. Our shorthand for this question is "net effects of college."

3. *What evidence is there that different kinds of postsecondary institutions have a differential influence on student change or development during college?* This question is essentially asking whether discernible differences in student development or the outcomes of college are attributable to the characteristics of the particular institution attended (institutional type, student body selectivity, size, financial resources, and so on). Because this question is primarily concerned with differential impacts between and among institutions, the shorthand phrase for this question will be "between-college effects."

4. *What evidence exists on effects of different experiences in the same institution?* This question is concerned with identifying different subenvironments or experiences inside the institution (for example, residence arrangement, academic major, quality of instruction, peer group involvement, extracurricular activities, interaction with faculty) that may have influences on student change or development. The shorthand expression will be "within-college effects."

5. *What evidence is there that the collegiate experience produces conditional, as opposed to general, effects on student change or development?* The question essentially asks whether various influential collegiate experiences have the same aggregate or general effect for all students or whether these experiences vary in their influence for different kinds of students (for example, men versus women, minority versus nonminority, low-aptitude versus high-aptitude students). As we mentioned earlier, although a general effect suggests that a particular experience is the same in magnitude and direction for all students, a conditional effect suggests that the magnitude or direction of the effect is conditioned by or varies according to the specific characteristics of the individuals being considered. Thus, for example, a particular experience may have stronger developmental effects for male than for female students. Conditional effects are sometimes referred to as interaction effects because individual subject differences are said to interact with the particular experience or exposure thought to influence the outcome. Our shorthand label will be "conditional effects of college."

6. *What are the long-term effects of college?* This question addresses the durability or permanence of the collegiate experience, or differences in that experience, on students' postcollege activities, attitudes, beliefs, and behaviors. Our shorthand phrase will be "long-term effects of college."

Obviously, and as in our previous synthesis, not all six questions will be meaningful to each category of college outcome considered. The influence of postsecondary education, for example, is manifest much earlier on such outcomes as cognitive or moral development than on occupational or economic attainments. Indeed, for the latter two outcomes it makes little sense to talk about development or changes during college.

SCOPE OF THE EVIDENCE REVIEWED

In *How College Affects Students,* we reviewed evidence generally covering the time period 1967 to 1989. The temporal, chronological focus for the present synthesis is from 1989–90 to 2001–02. In several instances, however, as already noted, we review studies conducted prior to 1989–90. We do this for two basic reasons: first, to help us place the synthesis of more recent evidence in context, and second, to include significant studies we missed in our previous synthesis. To identify applicable investigations, we initially conducted searches of various abstracting documents and databases (for example, *Sociological Abstracts, Psychological Abstracts, Dissertation Abstracts, Higher Education Abstracts*). We also reviewed conference proceedings from such scholarly and professional associations as the American Educational Research Association, the Association for the Study of Higher Education, the American Sociological Association, and the Association for Institutional Research. This strategy allowed us to obtain studies that had yet to be published or that had never been published. Finally, we also used an extensive network of colleagues to obtain unpublished papers and technical reports that dealt with college impact.

It would be foolhardy to claim that the results of our literature search were exhaustive. In *How College Affects Students,* we reviewed in the neighborhood of 2,600 studies and discovered over the last decade that we missed some studies. If anything, the literature of the last decade is even more complex and extensive, sometimes to the point of being overwhelming. With such a mass of literature to screen we know that some studies were missed. Nevertheless, we believe our search methodology has been thorough and extensive and that the studies we synthesize here comprise a comprehensive representation of the existing evidence.

ANALYSIS OF THE EVIDENCE

This volume continues the tradition of the three most comprehensive previous syntheses of evidence on the impact of college—those of Feldman and Newcomb (1969), Bowen (1977), and Pascarella and Terenzini (1991)—by being a narrative or explanatory literature review. That is, the synthesis and conclusions are based on a logical explanatory analysis of the literature and presented in narrative form. That this type of literature review or research synthesis has a strong and lengthy tradition in education and the social and behavioral sciences is evidenced by scanning such journals as *Review of Educational Research* and *Psychological Bulletin* and annual reviews such as *Review of Research in Educa-*

tion, Annual Review of Sociology, and *Higher Education*: *Handbook of Theory and Research.*

To be sure, there are some advantages to using more quantitative techniques, such as meta-analysis, to synthesize a large body of literature. Among these are greater standardization in reporting results, ease of comparability across different bodies of research, and an objective method for resolving conflicting findings in a body of evidence. Despite these advantages, we did not employ meta-analysis as the primary method for synthesizing the literature we review here for one important reason: the remarkable diversity of ways in which inquiry on the impact of college is conducted and reported made meta-analysis, with its strict requirements for information from each study, an unwieldy tool for synthesizing the full range of existing evidence. This diversity perhaps reflects the multidisciplinary nature of research on college impact. Different disciplines often take very different approaches in the conceptual models they employ, the analytical methods they use, and the statistical detail they report. As a result, in any particular category of outcomes one can frequently confront a mass of diverse statistical information. This information not only may be in different form (for example, partial correlations, increases in explained variance, unstandardized regression weights, standardized regression weights, logistic regression coefficients, adjusted means, or total, direct, and indirect effects in structural equation models) but may also have different meanings depending on how prediction equations are specified (that is, what controls are effected) or on the form of the outcome itself (for example, actual versus natural logarithmic transformations of wages or income). Furthermore, a substantial percentage of studies simply did not report adequate information (for example, standard deviations) for computing effect sizes—the sine qua non for meta-analysis.

Confronted with such overwhelming complexity and diversity in the studies reviewed, we judged it virtually impossible to compute comparable study effect sizes or to aggregate them in a manner that would produce meaningful conclusions. Related to this issue was our concern that the meta-analytic requirement of quantifying study results in a comparable metric exclude studies based on naturalistic inquiry or other relevant investigations whose results were simply not amenable to the computation of effect sizes.

In using a narrative explanatory synthesis as our primary approach to the analysis of evidence, we are, as in our predecessor volume, guided by the criterion of "weight of evidence." That is, given a logical analysis of the studies conducted, what does the weight of evidence allow us to conclude about the impact of college or the influence of different aspects of the collegiate experience? When operationalized as "box scores" or "vote counts" (that is, the percentage or proportion of studies that show positive results versus those that do not), the simple criterion of weight of evidence has been found to yield conclusions quite similar to those based on effect sizes computed in meta-analysis. Indeed, there is evidence that the correlations between the two approaches are in the .77 to .87 range (Walberg, 1985).

Our own operationalization of the weight of evidence criterion, although not always in the form of box scores or vote counts, nevertheless has two important characteristics. First, it is not exclusionary in that we try to synthesize all the available studies pertaining to an outcome, not just those that report a certain level of statistical detail. Second, we attempt to take into account variations in the methodological characteristics of studies and to place a greater inferential burden on those investigations that are the most methodologically sound. This effort is particularly important in those instances where findings conflict or where findings from one or two methodologically sound studies conflict with findings from a larger number of less well-conducted investigations.

Although we have continued the narrative, explanatory approach that characterized *How College Affects Students* in this volume, we have still made supplementary use of meta-analytic techniques and results. In several of our chapters we review the results of meta-analytic work and in several cases have employed meta-analytic techniques to corroborate findings or estimate the magnitude of an effect. We have also used subsets of studies in other syntheses to conduct our own meta-analysis of studies in those areas that pertain directly to postsecondary education. In short, wherever we can estimate the magnitude of an effect with reasonable accuracy we try to do so.

A BRIEF NOTE ON METHODOLOGY

What we can confidently conclude about the influence of college or the influence of different collegiate experiences on students is highly dependent on methodological rigor. There is simply no escaping this fact. Throughout our present synthesis, we attempt to deal with issues of research design, measurement, and data analysis as they arise and then as simply and benignly as possible. Nevertheless, because we employ several terms frequently throughout the book, it is important to define them here.

The first of these terms is *net effect*. The easiest way to explain net effect is through an example. Suppose one wishes to estimate the effect of attending versus not attending college on critical thinking while at the same time controlling for the confounding influence of differences in initial intelligence between college and noncollege groups. If one were to compute the association or correlation between college attendance and a measure of critical thinking while statistically controlling for (or statistically removing) the effect of intelligence, the result would be an estimate of the effect of college on critical thinking *net* of (or independent of) the confounding influence of initial intelligence. Thus, the term *net effect* has a relative meaning depending on what potentially confounding variables are controlled or taken into account.

The second term is *direct effect*. A direct effect can be thought of as the unmediated influence of one variable on another (that is, the impact is direct and does not pass through an intervening variable). Although the descriptor *direct* is only occasionally used in the literature we reviewed, direct effects are by far the most frequently estimated effects in educational and social science research. Using our previous example, if going to college has a significant association with critical thinking when initial intelligence is controlled, then it can be said to have a direct effect on critical thinking net of intelligence. Throughout the text we periodically employ the complete descriptor *direct effect*. For purposes of brevity and variety, however, we also use the shorthand (and more common) term *effect* to stand for direct effect. Thus, whenever the term *effect* is used without an antecedent modifier, it signifies the direct or unmediated effect of a variable.

Although it is estimated less often than direct effects, a variable may also have an indirect or mediated effect on an outcome. An *indirect effect* occurs when the effect is transmitted through an intervening variable or variables. For example, it is possible that college attendance (versus nonattendance) may have a substantial indirect effect on adult critical thinking by influencing a person's reading habits. Thus, the path of indirect influence would be college attendance directly influencing reading habits, and reading habits, in turn, directly affecting adult critical thinking. In this and similar ways, college could have a significant indirect impact on a range of outcomes in addition to having a direct effect on them—or even without having a direct effect on them.

A final term is *total effect*. This term means nothing more than the sum of the direct and indirect effects of one variable on another. In some instances the total effect of a variable will consist largely of its direct effect on an outcome. In other instances most of the total effect may be indirect. In still other cases a variable may have substantial direct and indirect impacts.

Our brief introduction of these terms should afford readers a basic understanding of them when they are used in the remainder of the book. For a more detailed discussion of each, including their statistical estimation, readers are referred to the Appendix of the 1991 edition of *How College Affects Students*. We attempt to provide a brief working definition of each new statistical or methodological term as it is introduced in the text.

Finally, it is important to make a distinction between the causal meaning of the term *effect* when it is derived from experimental rather than correlational studies. The simple fact is that we can make stronger causal statements from the results of experimental studies than we can from correlational studies. The easiest way to illustrate this distinction is through an admittedly contrived example adopted from Pascarella and Terenzini (1991). Suppose we randomly provide half the entering students in a small liberal arts college with a dictionary-thesaurus combination and withhold it from the remaining half. At the end of the first year of college we give the entire class a test of vocabulary and find that those who received the dictionary-thesaurus score a statistically significant 15 percent higher than the nonrecipients. Given this randomized, true experiment, we could conclude that the typical improvement in vocabulary achievement we could routinely get by purposefully providing incoming students with a dictionary-thesaurus is around 15 percent. In short, we can be reasonably confident that the 15 percent advantage in vocabulary achievement is attributable to (or caused by) the college's providing students with a dictionary-thesaurus.

Conversely, suppose in a correlational study we find that, with precollege level of vocabulary achievement controlled statistically, having a dictionary-thesaurus (versus not having one) is associated with a statistically significant 15 percent advantage on the same measure of vocabulary achievement at the end of the first year of college. In this situation we have not been able to manipulate and control the conditions under which the relationship between having a dictionary-thesaurus and end-of-first-year vocabulary achievement is observed. Consequently, the 15 percent advantage is only an estimate of the average difference in vocabulary knowledge between students who own a dictionary-thesaurus and those who do not, net of precollege vocabulary achievement. We cannot conclude to the same degree we can in the randomized experiment that purposefully providing students with a dictionary-thesaurus will produce the same effect.

In short, even though the terms *effect* or *causal effect* are often used in correlational research, they do not have the same meaning with respect to causal certitude as they do in experimental investigations. In the correlational study described in the preceding paragraph, the strongest inference we can make from the findings is that *a causal link between having a dictionary-thesaurus and improved vocabulary cannot be ruled out.* Correlational investigations that introduce controls for salient confounding influences are extremely useful in identifying plausible causal associations among variables. In the majority of investigations on the influence of college, however, statistically significant net associations from correlational research are a necessary but not sufficient condition for inferring causality (Light, Singer, & Willett, 1990).

A BRIEF NOTE ON THE EVIDENCE

Evidence on such a diverse topic as the impact of postsecondary education on students varies not only in methodological approach and rigor but also in the focus of research, the characteristics of the samples, and the operational definitions of variables. Consequently, it may be useful for readers to be aware of several general limitations or problems in the overall body of evidence. Most of these problems were evident in the literature we reviewed for *How College Affects Students* and remain problems in the literature we reviewed for the present synthesis.

The first problem with the evidence is that the characteristics of samples in the research vary dramatically, from single-institution samples with only a few students to multi-institutional, nationally representative samples with hundreds and even thousands of students. In some areas of research, such as the impact of college on moral development or the impacts of instructional interventions on content acquisition, synthesizing the evidence is primarily a task of finding common threads among many small-sample, single-institution, or single-course studies. Here the key problem, and one that is not always resolved, is the generalizability of the findings. In other areas of research, such as attitudes and values, psychosocial characteristics, educational attainment, economic returns, and personal health, we rely more on findings from secondary analyses of large, nationally representative samples. Such samples increase generalizability but may also come with a price. Secondary analysis often requires the construction of scales from items that may not have been intended for the purpose to which they are subsequently put in a particular investigation. Consequently, the items may end up having only a marginal or surface relationship with the construct they are purported to measure. In short, the price one often pays for the generalizability inherent in national samples is problematic measurement of salient variables.

A second and related problem is that a number of national data sets, which produce a substantial portion of the evidence on the impact of college on students, have become targets of opportunity for large numbers of social scientists. Although this was clearly the original purpose of creating such nationally representative databases, there is an additional price to be paid in terms of interpreting the findings from different studies. For example, the National Longitudinal Study of the High School Class of 1972 (NLS-72) has been used by large numbers of economists, sociologists, and other social scientists to estimate the economic returns to postsecondary education of attendance at different kinds of postsecondary institutions. Much of this work appears to have been done in relative isolation with minimal communication between individual scholars and even less between scholars in different disciplines. The result is a body of findings based on the same data set and focusing on the same general outcomes but with different samples, different variables represented (or specified) in the prediction equations, different operational definitions of variables, different analytical procedures, and quite frequently, different results. We do our best to resolve such conflicts in our synthesis, but it is not clear that complete resolution is always possible.

Third, researchers and lay readers alike should be wary of the potential in large national studies for identifying statistically significant (that is, with low probability of being due to chance) differences or changes that may or may not have discernible educational, administrative, or policy significance. This potential is an artifact of the sensitivity of tests of statistical significance to large sample sizes: the larger the sample size, the more likely one is to detect statistically significant associations between and among variables. To minimize the risk of inferring a mountain from a molehill, wherever possible we try to estimate the magnitude of the effects observed in an area of study.

Fourth, with a few exceptions, such as the research on moral reasoning, reflective judgment, and cooperative learning, studies often differ substantially in their operational measurement of the same construct. For example, variables such as critical thinking, college quality, liberalism, formal education, career success, and subjective well-being are measured in a number of different ways in different studies. Such multiple assessment versions of the same construct present a challenge not unlike that of the problematic measurement of constructs in secondary analysis. The challenge is essentially one of determining replicability of results. Is it possible to uncover consistent findings across studies that differ in the instruments used or the operational definitions of the same construct?

Fifth, in some areas of study, particularly those assessing change in cognitive development, psychosocial development, or attitudes and values, the evidence is sometimes derived from instruments that place a premium on stability of measurement. Consequently, some of these instruments may have a built-in bias *against* reflecting change due to education. Thus, evidence that suggests no shifts in certain student traits may not necessarily mean that no growth or development did in fact occur. There is at least the possibility that instruments emphasizing measurement stability may underestimate student growth during college.

Finally, it is important to place some parameters around the evidence we review in this synthesis. As with *How College Affects Students,* this book limits its focus to the various impacts of postsecondary education on the individual. We certainly acknowledge that education in general, and postsecondary education in particular, provide a wide range of benefits to society. For example, the positive impact of education on health may have important societal implications in areas such as employee productivity and health care costs. But as we mentioned earlier, although such social benefits may be a potentially important outcome of postsecondary education, they fall outside the primary focus of our synthesis. Similarly, as with its predecessor volume, this book focuses, in its entirety, on the *impact* of college or the *impact* of different college experiences on students. It is not intended to be a book about student cultures, or what college students do, or what it is like to be a college student. These topics are certainly important areas for the best inquiry we can produce, but they too are, in and of themselves, beyond the scope of this synthesis. Consequently, many very important and newsworthy studies that describe the experience of college or trends in college student behaviors for different student groups or subcultures are not reviewed, or even cited, in this book. It is not that we think such investigations are unimportant. Rather, they simply do not focus on college impact and, therefore, fall outside what we consider to be the primary concern of our work in this book.

CHAPTER TWO

Theories and Models of Student Change in College[1]

Many of the theories highlighted in our 1991 review continue to guide the study of college's impact on students, and some of the more recent writings refine these theories. This chapter updates the discussion, reviewing the theoretical ground on which the study and practice of undergraduate education presently stands. Subsequent chapters examine the research of the past decade and shed light on the conceptual validity of many of the theories reviewed. This review, however, makes no attempt to develop a comprehensive, integrated theory or to evaluate the conceptual adequacy of current theories and models.

The overall organization of this discussion derives from distinctions between development and change. The concept of *development* has generated considerable philosophical and theoretical debate for some time. We make no attempt to settle the matter here, although Learner (1986) believes some agreement exists on the basic characteristics of development, regardless of the disciplinary lens. According to Learner, development involves changes in an organism that are "systematic, [organized, and] successive . . . and are thought to serve an adaptive function, i.e., to enhance survival" (p. 41). Intrapersonal changes may be due to physical maturation, environmental forces, or the combined effects of interactions between person and environment. The concept usually implies or presumes growth, or the potential for growth, toward maturity or toward greater complexity through differentiation and integration. Developmental growth is typically valued and pursued as a desirable psychological or educational end, perhaps even as a moral end (Perry, 1970). *Change,* in contrast, refers only to alterations over time in students' cognitive skills, affective characteristics, attitudes, values, or behaviors. Change is a descriptive term and may be quantitative or qualitative. The term implies no directionality, whether regression or progression. It means simply that a condition at Time$_2$ is different from what it was at Time$_1$.

CATEGORIES OF THEORIES OF COLLEGE STUDENT CHANGE

The majority of post-1990 studies of change in college, like those published earlier, focus on traditional-age undergraduates. Similarly, the theories and models relating to college students that have emerged or evolved also deal primarily with change or growth in adolescents and young adults. Thus, our review discusses theories and models targeting that age group. This emphasis does not mean that older students are unimportant in higher education or that theories of change over the full life span lack value for understanding the effects of postsecondary education. Indeed, the increase in the number of older adults attending college has generated a large and wide-ranging theoretical literature on change or growth in the adult years, although much of that literature concerns "adult" development rather than "student" development.[2] A meaningful review of that literature is beyond the scope of this chapter, and summaries are available elsewhere (Merriam & Caffarella, 1999; Tennant & Pogson, 1995).

As in our earlier book, we group theories and models of student development and change into two broad families. One cluster, labeled *developmental* theories or models, addresses the nature, structure, and processes of individual human growth. These theories focus primarily on the nature and content of *intra*individual change, although interpersonal experiences are often salient components of these models. These theories usually describe one or more of the dimensions of student development and the stages, phases, or other movements along a given dimension. This family of theories has been dominated by psychological *stage* theories, which posit one or another level of development through which individuals pass in a largely invariant and hierarchical sequence, although recent theories place less emphasis on stage progression than was the case earlier.

The second family of models for the study of change among college students focuses less on intraindividual development than on the environmental and *inter*individual origins of student change, which need not be seen as developmental. These *college impact* models emphasize change associated with the characteristics of the institutions students attend (between-college effects) or with the experiences students have while enrolled (within-college effects). These models tend to be eclectic and to identify and evaluate several sets of variables presumed to influence one or more aspects of change. These sets may be student-related (such as gender, academic achievement, socioeconomic status, race-ethnicity), structural and organizational (such as institutional size, type of control, selectivity, curricular mission), or environmental (for example, the academic, cultural, social, or political climate created by faculty and students on a campus).

As will become clear in the following discussion, however, the social and cultural norms, the people with whom an individual interacts, and other environmental factors figure with varying degrees of prominence in both families of theories. Individual characteristics, such as gender, race-ethnicity, and sexual orientation, can also be important factors in both developmental and change theories. The primary difference between the two families of theories lies in the relative degree of attention they give to *what* changes in college students versus *how* these changes come about. Whereas student-centered developmental models concentrate on the nature or content of student change (for example, identity formation, moral or cognitive development), college impact models focus on the sources of change (such as different institutional characteristics, programs and services, student experiences, and interactions with students and faculty members).

DEVELOPMENTAL THEORIES OF STUDENT CHANGE

Although developmental theorists disagree on the characteristics or features of the developmental process, most writers view development as a general movement toward greater differentiation, integration, and complexity in the ways that individuals think and behave. This movement is usually seen as orderly, sequential, and hierarchical (often across the life span), passing through ever higher and more complex levels or stages that are to some extent age-related. Developmental theorists disagree over whether the progression is irreversible and whether it is continuous and gradual or disjunctive and abrupt. Developmental change may be due to biological and psychological maturation, to individual experiences, to the environment, or to the interaction of individual and environment.

Several taxonomies of developmental theories or models of college student change exist, each with its own merits.[3] In this chapter, we adopt essentially the four-category structure originated by Knefelkamp, Widick, and Parker (1978) and modified by Rodgers (1989), with revisions to accommodate the growth in identity theories since the mid-1980s. The clusters of theories and models deal with (1) psychosocial development, including identity formation, (2) cognitive-structural theories, (3) typological models, and (4) person-environment interaction theories and models.[4] It is important to bear in mind that some of these categories overlap to varying degrees. For example, King and Baxter Magolda (1996) suggest that the cognitive and affective dimensions of development are really parts of the same process. Finally, the typological and person-environment categories of models describe characteristics that seek to differentiate among groups of people or settings rather than to describe the nature or processes of change. Because this book examines change or development in college students, we discuss only the broad characteristics of type or person-environment models and call readers' attention to the most prominent ones in each category.

Psychosocial Theories

Psychosocial theories view individual development as the accomplishment of a series of "developmental tasks." Partly through growing older and partly through sociocultural or environmental influences, individuals over their life span face several developmental challenges. The nature of the challenge varies with age and developmental status. Although these developmental tasks tend to be presented in a sequence heavily influenced by age-related biological, psychological, or sociocultural influences, the individual may not resolve these challenges in the order they are encountered, and the pattern may vary by gender and culture. In addition, most psychosocial theories assert that the individual's success in resolving each task can significantly affect the resolution of succeeding tasks and, consequently, the rate and extent of psychosocial development (Rodgers, 1989).

Psychosocial theories of development fall into two categories. The first group, which deals with overall development, has been dominated by Arthur Chickering's seven vectors model since it first appeared (Chickering, 1969). The second cluster of psychosocial theories deals specifically with identity formation overall or with specific aspects of identity, such as those relating to gender, race-ethnicity, or sexual orientation.[5]

The psychosocial theory literature builds to a large extent on the work of Erik Erikson (1959, 1963, 1968), whom Chickering and Reisser (1993) refer to as "the progenitor of the psychosocial models" (p. 21). Three elements are apparent in Erikson's work and that of others who followed in his footsteps. The first is the *epigenetic principle*, which states that "anything that grows has a ground plan, and that out of this ground plan the parts arise, each part having its time of special ascendancy, until all parts have arisen to form a functioning whole" (Erikson, 1968, p. 92). The principle implies not only sequential, age-related, biological and psychological development but also the view that the individual's environment shapes the particular character and extent of development in important ways. Second, according to Erikson, development occurs through a series of *crises,* when biological and psychological changes interact with sociocultural demands to present a distinctive challenge or threat characteristic of a given stage. For Erikson, a crisis does not mean a physical or psychological emergency, but rather a time for decision requiring significant choices among alternative courses of action. The result is developmental progression, regression, or stasis. Embedded in this conception is the view that developmental change involves stimulus (or challenge) and response, with development (or the lack thereof) determined by the nature of the response (see Sanford, 1967). Third, Erikson considered the *identity versus identity confusion* crisis (Stage 5) as the dominant developmental task for people of traditional college age. As discussed in the following paragraphs, identity development is a prominent issue in most psychosocial theories of change among college students.

Chickering's Seven Vectors of Student Development. Probably no psychosocial theorist has had more influence on the research on college student development or administrative efforts to promote it than Arthur Chickering (1969; Chickering & Reisser, 1993). Recognizing the absence of any systematic framework for integrating or synthesizing the abundant empirical evidence on college students (almost exclusively traditional age and enrolled at four-year institutions) and based on his review of that literature, Chickering (1969) identified seven *vectors of development,* each of which has several subcomponents. He labeled his seven dimensions vectors "because each seems to have direction and magnitude—even though the direction may be expressed more appropriately by a spiral or by steps than by a straight line" (p. 8). Identity development occupies a central place in Chickering's theory, and his seven vectors both give greater specificity to this central construct and describe the developmental dynamics that lead to and follow from it. For Chickering, development involves differentiation and integration as students encounter increasing complexity in ideas, values, and other people and struggle to reconcile these new positions with their own ideas, values, and beliefs.

Chickering and Linda Reisser (1993) subsequently revised and reordered the vectors and their specifications in light of the substantial volume of research completed since the model appeared in 1969.[6] The revised model is presumed to apply to college students of all ages, and Chickering and Reisser "tried to use language that is gender free and appropriate for persons of diverse backgrounds" (p. 44). The rate of movement along any of the vectors may vary, and progress is not stagelike; movement on one vector may be simultaneous with change on another. Progress "from 'lower' to 'higher' brings more awareness, skill, confidence, complexity, stability, and integration" (p. 34), but moving backward and retracing steps are possible. The vectors are "major highways for journeying toward individuation—the discovery and refinement of one's unique way of being—and also toward communion with other individuals and groups, including the larger national and global society" (p. 35).

The seven vectors are as follows:

1. *Achieving competence.* According to Chickering, the college years lead to increased competence in intellectual areas, physical and manual skills, and interpersonal relations with both individuals and groups. Increases in intellectual competence are particularly important and involve knowledge acquisition; increased intellectual, aesthetic, and cultural sophistication; and development of higher-order cognitive skills. Increased intellectual competence enables development along other vectors inasmuch as it entails the symbolic expression of "the events and objects of our experience" (Chickering & Reisser, 1993, p. 62).

2. *Managing emotions.* Students of any age must recognize and wrestle with emotions that can interfere with the educational process, including "anger, fear and anxiety, depression, guilt, shame, and dysfunctional sexual or romantic attraction" (Reisser, 1995). Development occurs when students learn to control impulses and to develop appropriate responses (both immediate and long-term) for handling intense, potentially disruptive, emotions. Not all emotions are negative, however, and movement along this vector includes increased capacity to experience feelings such as wonder, sympathy, relief, caring, and optimism.

Growth comes with learning to balance tendencies to assertiveness with tendencies toward participation.

3. *Moving through autonomy toward interdependence.* The redefinition of this vector, originally labeled "developing autonomy," retains the importance initially ascribed to developing independence and also attributes more developmental prominence to gains in *inter*dependence, a component less prominent in the original statement of the vector. Development involves increased emotional freedom from the need for reassurance and the approval of others as well as greater instrumental independence, the self-sufficiency evident in individuals' ability to organize their own affairs, solve problems, and make decisions. Movement on this vector may take different gender-related forms but is generally toward interpersonal relations that rest on equality and reciprocity and that occur in a broader theater involving community and society. Balance emerges between the need to be independent and the need to belong.

4. *Developing mature interpersonal relationships.* Conceived originally as the fifth vector and as an outcome that follows establishment of identity, this vector's updated placement and definition reflect the view that students' interactions with peers provide powerful learning experiences and help shape the emerging sense of self. Maturing interpersonal relationships reflect an increasing awareness of and openness to differences in ideas, people, backgrounds, and values. "At its heart is the ability to respond to people in their own right" (Chickering & Reisser, 1993, p. 48), respecting differences. Movement along this vector also entails an increased capacity for healthy intimacy and commitment, for relationships that are increasingly independent and founded on mutual interdependence. The vector involves the complex interplay "between autonomy, interdependence, and intimacy" (Reisser, 1995, p. 508).

5. *Establishing identity.* This vector, shaped by movement on the previous vectors and influencing progress on subsequent ones, is pivotal. It retains some of the original vector's elements relating to conceptions of physical characteristics and personal appearance, but extends beyond them to a broader age range and to comfort with self-conceptions relating to gender and sexual orientation. Identity formation also involves a developing sense of self in a context shaped by historical events and social and cultural conditions and by issues emanating from family and ethnic heritage. Self-esteem and stability grow. "A solid sense of self emerges, and it becomes more apparent that there is an *I* who coordinates the facets of personality, who 'owns' the house of self and is comfortable in all of its rooms" (Chickering & Reisser, 1993, p. 49).

6. *Developing purpose.* According to Chickering and Reisser, expanding competencies, developing interpersonal relationships, and clarifying identity require some sense of direction and purpose. Development along the sixth vector occurs as an individual answers not only the question "Who am I?" but also "Who am I going to be?" and not just "Where am I?" but "Where am I going?" Growth requires increasing intentionality—developing plans that integrate priorities in vocational goals and aspirations, interpersonal interests, and family. The emerging identity and values help guide decision making.

7. *Developing integrity.* Growth along the seventh vector involves clarification and rebalancing of personal values and beliefs. An absolutistic reliance on rules yields to a relativistic consideration of rules and the purposes they are intended to serve as well as recognition of the interests and values of others. Values previously taken on authority are reviewed, and those found consistent with the emerging identity are retained, personalized, and internalized. Finally, the emerging values and identity find expression in ways that are internally consistent and manifest themselves in socially responsible behavior. Evans, Forney, and Guido-DiBrito (1998) discuss the model's assessment techniques; its validity for women, students of color, and gay, lesbian, and bisexual students; and its educational programming applications.

In both the original and revised models, Chickering tries to bring knowledge and practice closer together. To do so, he and Reisser (1993) identify seven (six in the original) primary areas where they believe colleges and universities can encourage student development along each of the seven vectors. These areas of influence are (1) clarity of institutional objectives and the internal consistency of policies, practices, and activities; (2) an institutional size that does not restrict opportunities for participation; (3) frequent student-faculty relationships in diverse settings; (4) curricula oriented to integration in both content and processes; (5) teaching that is flexible, varied in instructional styles and modes, and aimed at encouraging active student involvement in learning; (6) friendships and student communities that become meaningful subcultures marked by diversity in attitudes and backgrounds and by significant interpersonal exchanges; and (7) student development programs and services characterized by their educational content and purpose and offered collaboratively with faculty.

Chickering and Reisser (1993) also suggest that educationally powerful environments reflect several "principles" or characteristics: (1) a view of education as systemic, comprising interrelated parts; (2) a willingness to re-evaluate existing assumptions; (3) the integration of work and learning; (4) recognition and respect for individual differences; and (5) an understanding of learning and development as "cycles of challenge and response, differentiation and integration, disequilibrium and regained equilibrium" (p. 280).

Identity Development: General. Although Chickering's work has attracted more attention and inspired more research and administrative programming than other psychosocial theories or models, several other models merit attention. These include theories or models relating to identity formation, whether global or specific to a particular dimension of identity (usually gender, race-ethnicity, and sexual orientation).[7] By and large, identity development models describe a process of increasing differentiation in the sense of self and the integration of that growing complexity into a coherent whole (Sanford, 1967). McEwen (2003b) discusses models relating to identity formation in multiple dimensions.

Building on Erikson's (1959, 1963, 1968) proposition that defining one's identity constitutes the central "crisis" of adolescence, James Marcia (1966, 1980) reasoned that identity status formation involves resolution of two psychosocial tasks. Whereas Erikson viewed development as movement through a hierarchical set of stages, Marcia's adaptation is less linear, allowing movement in both task areas simultaneously. The first task, *exploration,* involves the search for and choice among meaningful competing alternatives. The second task, *commitment,* refers to the level of an individual's personal investment in each of three areas—occupational, religious, and political. Shortly after the model's initial explication and early testing, a fourth area—sexual values—was added so that its theoretical and operational forms could apply to women as well as to men. Exploration and resolution of the crisis are presumed to lead to differentiation and individualization, whereas commitment is assumed to promote stability, continuity, and comfort.

Juxtaposing these two psychosocial tasks, Marcia's model of identity status describes four different responses to the need for identity and to the process of identity formation. "Identity-diffused" individuals have neither experienced the crisis of the search for identity nor made commitments to an identity in any of the occupational or value areas. These individuals tend either to be uninterested in occupational or ideological matters or to accept all positions as more or less equal. "Foreclosed" individuals have not undergone any crisis, but they have made commitments without question or examination, usually to identities encouraged by others, chiefly their parents. People in "moratorium" status are actively searching for a defining identity and evaluating alternatives. These individuals differ from those who are identity-diffused by the fact of their conscious search, although their commitments remain unformed, or at best, emergent. "Identity-achieved" individuals have successfully weathered a crisis and made personal occupational, religious, political, and sex-role commitments. These commitments, independently arrived at, provide a basis for independent action and may be at variance with those encouraged by parents or others. Marcia notes, however, that identity achievement probably is not a permanent state and that individuals shift through various statuses as they accommodate changes associated with the life cycle.[8]

Identity Development: Gender. Ruthellen Josselson (1973, 1987, 1996) adapted Marcia's model to her *theory of identity development among women* only.[9] Josselson's work began with a series of interviews with 60 women when they were in college and again with 30 of the women when they were in their early 30s and 40s. Josselson classified her informants in the four groups suggested by Marcia based on "the pathway they seemed to be taking toward identity—a pathway of decision-making rather than one defined by content" (1996, p. 12). Josselson describes the various manifestations of the exploration process (or lack thereof) and resulting personal commitments in the four areas specified in Marcia's theory. Josselson concludes, however, that for her informants, social, sexual, and religious issues are less often the grounds on which the struggle for identity takes place than a woman's sense of how she is effective in the world and how she is linked to others (1996, p. 179). In addition, relationships are suggested as particularly fertile areas in engendering the "crises" that may lead to identity formation. For Josselson, identity "cannot be simply named, for it resides in the pattern that emerges as a woman stitches together an array of aspects of herself and her investments in others" (1996, p. 9).

Identity Development: Racial and Ethnic. Much of the early research and theory on college student change and development assumed that the nature and processes of identity development among Black and other non-White students were essentially the same as for Whites. During the two decades covered in our earlier review, however, a literature examining Black identity development and proposing models of it emerged; most of these models view racial identity primarily as a sociopolitical or cultural construction (Helms, 1995).[10] Much of this thinking and writing focuses on counseling and psychotherapeutic applications, although it directs some attention to the programmatic implications of group-specific student development models. The utility of these models for research on the psychosocial development of students over time remains unexamined.

Helms (1990b, p. 5) identifies three components of any racial identity: (1) a personal identity (consisting of "one's attitudes and feelings about oneself"), (2) a reference group orientation (using a particular racial group to define personal identity, reflected in one's values, attitudes, and behaviors), and (3) an ascribed identity ("the individual's deliberate affiliation or commitment to a racial group"). Racial identity is presumed to derive from the particular weightings the individual assigns to these three components. The possible variations in weightings give rise to different models or racial identity "resolutions" (Helms, 1990b). Space constraints preclude even a brief description of the various models dealing with racial or ethnic identity development, a task complicated by varying definitions of race and ethnicity (Helms, 1994, 1995; Helms & Talleyrand, 1997; Sodowsky, Kwan, & Pannu, 1995), by differences across groups, and by multiple models for each of several racial, ethnic, or cultural groups.[11] Thus, we limit discussion to the four models that have attracted the most attention.

Cross's model of Nigrescence. William Cross (1971a, 1971b, 1980, 1991, 1995) offers a theory of African-American identity, or "Nigrescence." In the first statement of his views, Cross referred to Black identity change as a "Negro-to-Black conversion experience" (1991, p. 189), "a *resocializing* experience" that "transforms a preexisting identity" (p. 190). In its current form, the model is far more nuanced and fully explicated, and Cross examines its sociohistorical and conceptual roots. Cross continues to view Black identity as taking shape through five hierarchical stages. In Stage 1, *Preencounter,* the individual's worldview is frequently Eurocentric, and being Black is either not a salient factor or is seen as social stigma. Although some African Americans at this stage may hold actively anti-Black attitudes, most preencounter Blacks avoid internalizing these negative views. In any event, "the scene is set for a possible identity conversion experience" (1995, p. 198). Stage 2, *Encounter,* involves an experience (such as the assassination of Martin Luther King, Jr.) or an accumulation of experiences (such as legal difficulties) that threaten the individual's understanding of the place of Blacks in the world, engenders a range of emotions, and triggers a reinterpretation of initial views and beliefs. Stage 3, *Immersion-Emersion,* is "the vortex of identity change" (1991, p. 190). The individual is "in between" and searches for a new understanding of self as Black. Immersion in "the world of Blackness" (p. 203) involves a turning inward and the view that everything of value must be Black. In the emersion phase, the individual emerges from "the emotionality and dead-end, either/or, racist, oversimplified aspects of the immersion experience" (p. 207), beginning to "level off" and regain control of emotions and intellect. It can be a time both of personal growth and recognition that Black role models "operate from a more advanced state of identity development" (p. 207). The individual is ready to move toward a new identity.

In Stage 4, *Internalization,* the dissonance is resolved, a new worldview emerges, and the individual returns to a personality more stable and calm than that in Stage 3. Personal conceptions of Blackness replace the views of others, and concern over whether one is sufficiently Black recedes. The individual is freed to deal with matters "that presuppose a basic identification with Blackness" (p. 210) and that conception is more open and expansive than at any previous stage. The impact, however, may be greater on the reference group dimension of the individual's identity than on personality more globally. The individual redefines relationships with others of different races or ethnicities, adopting bicultural or multicultural perspectives. Stage 5, *Internalization-Commitment,* marks the pinnacle of Nigrescence when the individual's sense of Blackness is translated into a course of action and commitment to deal with issues and problems shared with African Americans and other groups. To some extent, this stage represents the habituation of Stage 4, although Cross acknowledges that the two stages differ only slightly, and whether the identity and commitments of Stage 5 are sustained over time awaits further empirical examination (1995). Although Cross's stages suggest a onetime cycle, he speculates that the cycle may repeat across the life span.

Helms's people of color racial identity model. Adapting the Cross model (1971a, 1971b) and Atkinson, Morten, and Sue's (1989) theory of minority identity development, Janet Helms (1990a, 1990c, 1994, 1995; Helms & Piper, 1994) offers a framework that purports to describe the racial identity development of Latinos, Asians, and Native Americans as well as African Americans. For Helms, the racial identity of all socioracial groups, regardless of race, takes shape through a series of experiences that comprise different "statuses," a term selected to avoid the suggestion of stasis inherent in her earlier use of "stages." Each status reflects beliefs and behaviors that primarily govern racial reactions. Although the developmental process may be common to many racial groups, the content of each status varies according to the sociohistorical and economic conditions and socialization processes each group has experienced. "The central racial identity developmental theme of all people of color is to recognize and overcome the psychological manifestations of internalized racism" (1995, p. 189).

Helms's model consists of six statuses. In Status 1, *Conformity,* people of color hold identities derived and internalized from Whites, devaluing their own group by accepting stereotypes and either seeking to resemble Whites and assimilate into the dominant society or deprecating themselves and their group. In this status, socioracial issues are of little concern. According to Helms (1995, p. 186), "maturation is triggered by need" when the individual encounters racially meaningful materials or conditions that require adaptation or adjustment of the current identity. Status 2, *Dissonance,* reflects the beginning of these readjustments, recognition that one cannot be fully a part of White society, and efforts to resolve the dissonance. Status 3, *Immersion,* constitutes the early phases of what is essentially a reeducation process. It is a time of struggle for a different racial identity and involves rejection of whatever is "White" along with idealization of one's own socioracial group. In Status 4, *Emersion,* individuals more fully embrace the values, beliefs, and behaviors of their racial group, and affective commitments to the group emerge. Helms (1995) has noted that although Statuses 3 and 4 are conceptually distinct, the differences remain empirically unconfirmed. In Status 5, *Internalization,* individuals commit themselves to their racial group, and racial attributes are internally defined. The capacity to critique both one's own and the dominant racial group emerges. Individuals also develop the ability to respond objectively to members of the dominant group. Status 6, *Integrated Awareness,* constitutes the most sophisticated identity level and permits expression of a positive racial identity. The individual now has the ability "to recognize and resist the multiplicity of practices that exist in one's environment to discourage positive racial self-conceptions and group expression" (1995, p. 190).

Helms's White racial identity model.[12] Until the decade of the 1990s, White racial identity formation had attracted little scholarly attention perhaps, Helms suggests, because of assumptions of racial group superiority and entitlement. According to Helms (1990c, 1990d, 1993, 1995), however, a healthy identity for Whites requires recognition and understanding of the role of race, of Whites' perpetuation of race as a significant social feature, and of efforts to confront racism in oneself and society. For Whites, the issue in racial identity development is the recognition and abandonment of beliefs in White superiority and privilege and the rejection of normative White strategies for dealing with race.

According to Helms, racial identity formation among Whites, as for people of color, proceeds through six statuses, three in each of two phases. The first phase involves recognition and abandonment of racism in both one's own racial group and oneself, while the second phase entails development of a nonracist White identity. Phase 1, the abandonment of racism, begins in Status 1, *Contact,* when a White individual lives in color-blind obliviousness or denial of racism and any participation in it. Formation of a healthy White racial identity begins when awareness dawns regarding the benefits membership in the dominant group confers. Obliviousness and denial give way to recognition of the moral dilemmas inherent in a privilege based on race rather than merit. The emerging recognition leads to the disorientation and anxiety of Status 2, *Disintegration,* in which the individual struggles to resolve the contradictions between beliefs about racial and social equality and race-related differences in social and economic conditions. Consideration of the possibility that one's group may bear some responsibility for race-based inequities can lead to anxiety, suppression of that idea, and avoidance of people of color in order to reconcile the conflicts and resolve the dissonance. In Status 3, *Reintegration*, the individual also accepts Whiteness and beliefs about Whites' superiority and earned entitlement. The individual accepts stereotypes of racial out-groups, and anger and intolerance build. Perceptions are selective. This point in the process can be pivotal: the individual may either fixate in this status or begin (perhaps because of some obviously race-related event) to question the meaning and role of race, the legitimacy of White entitlement, and the justification for racist behaviors or policies.

Phase 2, the movement toward a nonracist identity, begins with the *Pseudo-independence* of Status 4. In this state, the individual's commitment to White society is intellectualized through various forms of acceptance of persons of color or through curiosity about them. A deceptive tolerance develops as the individual begins to question beliefs about the inferiority of non-White racial groups and to explore the possibility that Whites bear some responsibility for perceived injustices. Individuals may seek ways to "help" other racial groups. Status 5, *Immersion-Emersion*, entails a search for the meaning of racism and how one benefits from it. Stereotypes are abandoned and questions of racial identity arise. The individual confronts the possibility that a Black "problem" may in fact be a White problem and may engage in various forms of racial activism. A White identity slowly begins to develop as individuals explore racism through reading and discussions with others, recognize and acknowledge their own racism, and develop a sense of responsibility for fighting racism in society. In the *Autonomy* of Status 6, individuals have developed a positive White identity that is defined internally, no longer feel threatened by race, and reject racially based privilege and behaviors. The individual is open to information about other races, seeks greater racial understanding personally and in others, and values racial and cultural similarities and differences.[13]

Phinney's model of ethnic identity development. Based on her review of 70 ethnic identity studies published since 1972, Jean Phinney (1990, 1992) developed a model of ethnic identity development grounded conceptually in Erikson's theory of identity formation and Marcia's operationalization of that theory (see earlier sections). For Phinney, self-identification as a member of and a sense of belonging to a particular ethnic group are necessary conditions for an ethnic identity. She maintains that an ethnic identity is one dimension of a person's social identity and that individuals may have both negative and positive views of their group. According to Phinney (1989, 1992; Phinney & Alipuria, 1990), "a sense of identification with, or belonging to, one's own group, is common to all human beings" (1992, p. 158) despite group differences in history, traditions, language, religion, and values that are shared within groups and bind members together. These issues are more salient among minority groups than among Whites because differences in these areas are the basis for these groups' subordinate place in society. Ethnic identity is not static but rather changes with the individual's accumulation of experiences, personal development, and shifts in the social and historical context (Phinney, 1992).

Following Erikson and Marcia, Phinney maintains that a member of an ethnic minority group faces two conflicts, one involving the individual's sense of self and self-esteem when confronted with the presence of prejudice and discrimination, the other between minority and majority values and the need to find a balance in order to live in a bi- or multicultural society. Phinney concluded from her research that "ethnic identity formation appears to involve an exploration of the meaning of one's ethnicity (e.g., its history and tradition) that [when successfully concluded] leads to a secure sense of oneself as a member of a minority group" (1992, p. 160).

For Phinney, identity development proceeds in three stages. In the first stage, *Diffusion-Foreclosure* (a consolidation of two of Marcia's four stages), neither a search for nor a commitment to an individual ethnic identity has taken place. Indeed, individuals at this stage may show little interest in ethnic beliefs, values, or feelings. Instead, they have uncritically accepted their present views from family. Individuals who also accept uncritically the dominant society's negative evaluations of minority group members are at some risk of internalizing those views and foreclosing further development of an ethnic identity. Examination of these views, however, may initiate the search for refined ethnic understanding. The *Moratorium* of Stage 2 reflects a growing awareness of ethnic issues, which may cause distress as the individual learns about the majority group's views, beliefs in their superiority, treatment of minority group members as second-class citizens, and overt racism. Such heightened consciousness can produce anger directed at the dominant group and embarrassment at not having noticed racial-ethnic conflicts earlier. The anger and embarrassment grow as the individual explores the history and traditions of his or her ethnic origins and considers the meaning of that ethnicity and its implications for the individual's future. As the search for an ethnic identification continues, movement to Stage 3, *Identity Achievement,* can begin. In this stage, which is the optimal outcome, the individual resolves the bicultural conflicts of Stage 2 and finds relative calm and confidence in "a secure sense of oneself as a member of a minority group" (1992, p. 160). Phinney's research suggests that ethnic identity is to some degree age-related, may stabilize over time, and does not vary with gender or socioeconomic status (1992).

Identity Development: Gay, Lesbian, and Bisexual. Early studies of homosexuality began with the premise that same-sex attraction was pathological. The search was for "cures," and studies hunted for "causes" in early childhood experiences, stimulus-response conditioning, biological origins, hormonal imbalances or genetic mutations, and psychosocially generated feelings, attitudes, and behaviors. The recent theoretical and empirical literatures have focused on gay or lesbian identity formation (Evans & Wall, 1991), but both theory development and research are complicated by the sexual nature of

the topic and political and ideological agendas, as gay activists advance biological determinism and opponents argue that sexual orientation is voluntary
(D'Augelli, 1994b). Moreover, definitions vary, complicating theory descriptions
(Cass, 1983–84). Broido (2000) suggests that *gay* and *lesbian* refer to an
individual's identity, whereas *homosexual* describes behavior. *Bisexual* and
heterosexual often describe both identity and behavior. The conceptual models
we discuss apply to gays, lesbians, and (in D'Augelli's model) bisexuals.

The literature addresses sexual identity formation in the United States and
generally views this area of development as one dimension of an individual's
overall identity. Theorists have offered both social models, which emphasize
the salience of an individual's social interactions and the role of the gay community, and psychological frameworks (Evans & Wall, 1991). Vivienne Cass proposed the most frequently referenced framework, although Anthony D'Augelli's
life span model has also attracted attention. We focus on those two models,
although others are available, including ones concerning bisexual, transgendered, and heterosexual identity.[14]

Cass's psychosocial model of sexual identity formation.[15] Vivienne Cass (1979,
1983–84) assumes that identity evolves in a developmental process and that
psychosocial stability and change depend on interactions between individuals
and their environments, a concept that gives individuals an active hand in shaping whatever identity develops. Dissonance within the individual concerning
beliefs and actions, or between the individual and others, can trigger a response
leading to a higher developmental stage or result in foreclosure at any point
in the process. The model proposes a progression from self-identification as a
heterosexual to perception of oneself as gay or lesbian, and the time needed to
move through Cass's six stages will vary. Although the model is presumed to
apply to males and females, sex-role socialization will lead individuals to follow different paths. The conflict between private identity and public or social
aspects of identity drives the developmental process, depending on how the
individual responds to the conflict.

In Cass's first stage, *Identity Confusion,* the individual holds an unexamined
belief in his or her heterosexuality but slowly begins to be aware that gay or lesbian feelings or behaviors may be relevant to his or her life. Awareness of a gay
or lesbian orientation in others is by itself insufficient to stimulate development.
The individual becomes conscious of feelings, thoughts, and behaviors that are
at odds with beliefs about his or her sexual identity and with the perceptions
of others of the individual as heterosexual. The resulting conflict leads to movement to Stage 2, *Identity Comparison,* provided repression has not foreclosed a
developmental response. In the comparison stage, the individual begins to consider the possibility of being gay or lesbian. Although increasing acceptance of
that possibility may reduce confusion and anxiety, it also leads to awareness
of the potential for (perhaps reality of) social alienation from the larger society
and also from family and friends. The individual realizes that the guidelines for
a future identity as a heterosexual no longer apply. Alternatives are not yet in

sight, but the individual increasingly accepts the proposition of "difference." Again presuming no identity foreclosure, the growing commitments of Stage 2 lead to the *Identity Tolerance* of Stage 3. But the freedom that comes with making commitments to the possibility of a gay or lesbian identity engenders a keener awareness of the incongruence between the individual's beliefs and the views of others. Feelings of isolation and alienation from the larger society lead to increased contact with the gay or lesbian community and, in turn, to growing strength and confidence in a gay or lesbian identity, although the individual is not yet ready to reveal that identity to heterosexuals. This stage appears to represent a bridge between the individual's private internal world and the more public social world of openly gay, lesbian, and bisexual individuals. According to Cass (1979), the individual's perceptions of the supportive or unsupportive quality of the contacts with this new community can be decisive in whether movement to the next stage occurs.

In Stage 4, *Identity Acceptance,* contacts with other gay or lesbian individuals and the larger gay community increase to the extent that the community validates the individual's gay or lesbian identity. More frequent contact leads to a preference for the gay community, and friends and friendship networks are redefined and restructured, although at the cost of increased tension within the individual concerning what the individual knows and what others believe. Reduction in that tension may come from "passing as 'straight,' limit[ing] contact with heterosexuals, or selectively disclosing to significant (heterosexual) others" (Evans & Wall, 1991, p. 9). Those who find the tension too strong move toward Stage 5, *Identity Pride,* a position in which the individual reconciles the differences between identifying as gay or lesbian and society's rejection of that identity. The reconciliation manifests itself in "gay pride" and rejection of heterosexual beliefs and values. The individual accepts a new identity and "comes out," but anger and resentment of rejection by the heterosexual society prompt action against the heterosexism. If others respond positively to the individual's newly acknowledged identity, the individual may move to Stage 6, *Identity Synthesis,* in which the previous "us-versus-them" stance is no longer needed. Support from heterosexuals leads the individual to trust them more and to view them more positively. In this stage, the individual finds comfort in the congruence that now exists between the private inner world and the public social world, "personal and public sexual identities [are] synthesized into one image of self receiving considerable support" (Cass, 1979, p. 234). Individuals in this stage now view their sexual identity as part of their overall identity.

D'Augelli's model of lesbian, gay, and bisexual development. Anthony D'Augelli (1994a) disagrees with the view taken in traditional, essentialist models of both global and sexual identity development that identity develops along normative guidelines, and once achieved (usually in late adolescence or early adulthood) remains relatively stable and enduring. Instead, he offers a view of sexual identity as a social construction, as something malleable and variable over time, shaped by customs and sociohistorical conditions. For D'Augelli, gay, lesbian, and bisexual individuals must assume multiple identities in a predominantly heterosexual society. Self-definition as lesbian, gay, or bisexual involves two processes: a conscious and purposeful rejection of the heterosexist identity and behavior required by mainstream society and creation of "a new identity oriented around homosocial and homosexual dimensions. Constructing a complex 'essence' is the task" (p. 313).

In the development of a lesbian, gay, or bisexual identity, individuals confront the twin barriers of the "social invisibility" of being lesbian, gay, or bisexual and the social and legal proscriptions against expression of that identity. In place of traditional, essentialist theories, D'Augelli proposes a life span, human development view involving multiple factors that interact over time. Individual stability and change take shape in the context of the social networks, community, and institutional settings the individual inhabits. From a human development perspective, sexual identity development is plastic, responding to environmental influences, including family, as well as to physical and biological factors, but it is also shaped in important ways by the individual, "out of necessity, due to a heterosexist culture that provides no routine socialization for lesbian and gay development" (D'Augelli, 1994b, p. 127).

D'Augelli maintains that three factors influence lesbian, gay, and bisexual identity formation: "personal subjectivities and actions," which include feelings and beliefs about sexual identity throughout the life span; "interactive intimacies" with parents, family, peers, and partners; and "sociohistorical connections," including social customs, public policies, laws, and cultures. These factors comprise a system that entails movement through six identity "processes mediated by the cultural and sociopolitical contexts in which they occur" (D'Augelli, 1994a, p. 324):

1. *Exiting heterosexual identity* entails recognizing that one's sexual orientation is not heterosexual and understanding the attraction to others of the same gender, although the full meaning may yet be unclear. This process includes coming out to others, a process that will continue throughout the individual's life. Devising means to assert one's nonheterosexuality is essential.

2. *Developing a personal lesbian-gay-bisexual identity status* requires challenging internalized stereotypes and myths about what it means to be lesbian, gay, or bisexual and developing a sense of stability in one's feelings, thoughts, and desires. The process also impels the individual toward social interaction with others who share the same affectional identity. These interactions both affirm the individual's sexual orientation and aid in learning to be gay, lesbian, or bisexual.

3. *Developing a lesbian-gay-bisexual social identity* involves creating a network of others who know one's sexual orientation and support it. This process is also lifelong, requiring time for the individual to understand others' reactions and to recognize the differences between a potentially harmful tolerance and genuine acceptance and support as well as to deal with others' reactions that may change over time.

4. *Becoming a lesbian-gay-bisexual offspring* requires disclosing one's sexual orientation to parents. Parental and sibling reactions and adaptations may be complex and vary over time. Reintegration into the family depends on the family's supportiveness.

5. *Developing a lesbian-gay-bisexual intimacy status* in the identity formation process is complicated by the invisibility of same-sex couples in society and by social myths about the durability of such relationships. The absence of cultural guidelines for developing intimate lesbian-gay-bisexual relationships produces "ambiguity and uncertainty, but it also forces the emergence of personal, couple-specific, and community norms, which should be more personally adaptive" (D'Augelli, 1994a, p. 327).

6. *Entering a lesbian-gay-bisexual community* involves engagement in social and political action. Although this process may never happen for those who believe sexual orientation should be a private matter, for others it can lead to risky confrontations with legal, social, and political barriers. "The inequities become clearer as the person becomes more and more open or learns how much hiding is needed and why. . . . It also, generally, leads to an appreciation of how the oppression continues, and a commitment to resisting it" (p. 328).

Cognitive-Structural Theories

If Erik Erikson is the progenitor of many psychosocial theories and models, virtually all cognitive-structural theories of student development have their origins in Jean Piaget (1964). Whereas psychosocial theorists focus on the content of development (for example, vectors, identity statuses, dimensions), cognitive-structural theorists seek to describe the nature and processes of change, concentrating on the epistemological structures individuals construct to give meaning to their worlds. Indeed, the psychosocial and cognitive-structural categories appear to be complementary. "One describes what students will be concerned about and what decisions will be primary; the other suggests how students will think about those issues and what shifts in reasoning will occur" (Knefelkamp et al., 1978, p. xii). As noted earlier, King and Baxter Magolda (1996) suggest that these two dimensions are really parts of the same developmental process.

Cognitive-structural theories have several elements in common. All propose a series of stages through which an individual passes in the developmental process. In most theories, these stages are hierarchical, with the successful attainment of one presumed to be a prerequisite for movement to the next. In most theories, the progression tends to be irreversible, although most theorists believe some movement backward and forward can occur. By and large, however, because of personal development's foundations in cognition, the individual simply "can't go home again" because development alters perceptions and the structures that give meaning to the world. In addition, because "meaning making" is so fundamental, cognitive-structural stages are believed to be universal, occurring in all cultures. All such theories focus on *how* meaning is structured, not on what is known or believed.

Finally, as with psychosocial models, cognitive-structural theories assume that developmental change involves a chain of stimulus and response. Encounters with new information or experiences that conflict with or challenge the validity of current cognitive structures trigger adaptive responses. These reactions may involve either *assimilation* or *accommodation*. In assimilation, the individual perceptually reorders or reinterprets the challenge to make it consistent with current knowledge, belief, or value structures. In accommodation, the individual changes current epistemological or belief structures to admit or be consistent with the new experience. The developmental process is seen as a series of constructions and reconstructions. The individual may deny the presence of any challenge, but such a response is not considered developmental. "Healthy" responses to cognitive or affective dissonance lead to a reformation of existing structures incorporating old and new knowledge, attitudes, values, and self-concepts in revised, coherent, integrated perceptual structures at a more advanced stage or developmental condition. William Perry, Lawrence Kohlberg, and Carol Gilligan have been among the most influential of the cognitive-structural developmental theorists in the study of college students. Patricia King, Karen Kitchener, and Marcia Baxter Magolda have offered more recent models of cognitive development among college students. Although other cognitive-structural theories exist (for example, Belenky et al., 1986; Kegan, 1982, 1994), because of space constraints, we will limit our discussion to those mentioned here. Baxter Magolda and King and Kitchener, for example, draw on the work of Belenky et al. and Kegan. Evans, Forney, and Guido-DiBrito (1998) and King (2003) also summarize these and other theories.

Perry's Scheme of Intellectual and Ethical Development. On the basis of an extensive series of interviews with Harvard College students, William Perry (1970, 1981) sought to map conceptually the development he observed clinically in the "structures which the students explicitly or implicitly impute to the world, especially those structures in which they construe the nature and origins of knowledge, of value, and of responsibility" (1970, p. 1). Perry maintains that such structures transcend content and thus are unlikely to be socially, culturally, or otherwise temporally dependent. Although his theory is clearly a stage model, Perry prefers the term *position* because it implies no assumptions about duration and is "happily appropriate to the image of 'point of outlook' or 'position from which a person views his world'" (1970, p. 48).

Perry's model, or "scheme," asserts that the developmental sequence "manifests a logical order—an order in which one form leads to another through differentiations and reorganizations required for the meaningful interpretation of increasingly complex experience" (1970, p. 3). Perry identified nine positions. The progression is not entirely linear, however, and he identifies three "deflections" or temporary suspensions in developmental movement. At the broadest conceptual level, he asserts that development comprises two major parts, with the pivotal stage (Position 5) being the perception of all knowledge and values (including those of authorities) as relative.

Prior to Position 5, a dualistic perception dominates cognitive structures or ways of perceiving one's world—right or wrong, good or bad. Knowledge of this kind comes from authorities. The dichotomous categories include knowledge, values, and people, and knowledge in each area is absolute. At Position 5, the individual begins to perceive not only multiple points of view but also the indeterminacy of "Truth." The individual recognizes the relative character of knowledge and values. The individual then progresses through the last four positions, moving toward higher developmental levels depending on the ability to cope with a relativistic world and to develop personal commitments (1970, p. 57). Perry (1981, p. 79) grouped his original nine positions into three groups. King (1978) suggested the following four clusters.

- *Dualism* (Positions 1–2). In the early positions, individuals order their worlds in dualistic and absolute categories. Alternative opinions or differing perspectives on the same phenomenon create discomfort. For students at these levels, classroom learning means catching whatever the instructor pitches. In Position 2, uncertainty about what is or is not true creeps in, although the uncertainty an authority might introduce is sometimes seen as merely a heuristic device to prod students to learn on their own.

- *Multiplicity* (Positions 3–4). In these positions, the existence of multiple perspectives on any given issue is recognized, although alternative perspectives may be considered temporary in areas where authorities still search for the answers. In Position 4, others holding an opinion contrary to one's own are no longer seen as simply wrong but rather as entitled to their views. Indeed, all opinions are seen as having comparable claims on correctness.

- *Relativism* (Positions 5–6). Recognition of multiplicity in the world leads to understanding that "knowledge is contextual and relative" (King, 1978, p. 38). The shift is transformational. Analytical thinking skills emerge, and in critiquing their own ideas and those of others, students recognize that not all positions are equally valid. This stage may be problematic, however, because the discovery of relativism in ideas and values can engender resistance to choosing among presumably equal alternatives. Development may be delayed at this stage.

- *Commitments in relativism* (Positions 7–9). Students moving through Positions 7 to 9 test various propositions and truth claims, eventually making "an active affirmation of themselves and their responsibilities in a pluralistic world, establishing their identities in the process" (King, 1978, p. 39). The individual makes commitments to ideas, values, behaviors, and other people (for example, in marriage and careers).

Like students' cognitive structures, their commitments are dynamic and changeable, not capriciously but as a series of constructions and reconstructions, "differentiations and reorganizations" (Perry, 1970, p. 3). Commitments may be made, but they are not immutable; they are alterable in the face of new evidence and understanding about who one is and how the world is, and such alterations may continue throughout an individual's life.

By 1981, Perry attached greater significance to the transitions between positions: "Positions are by definition static, and development is by definition movement" (p. 78). He stressed that each position "both includes and transcends earlier positions, as the earlier ones cannot do with the later [ones]. This fact defines the movement as *development* rather than mere changes or 'phases'" (p. 78). Perry also suggested that development is recurrent: the discovery and reconstruction of "forms" that characterize the development of college students can also be experienced at later points in the life span. He concluded: "Perhaps the best model for growth is neither the straight line nor the circle, but a helix, perhaps with an expanding radius to show that when we face the 'same' old issues we do so from a different and broader perspective" (p. 97).

King (1978) noted a shift in the scheme's focus between Positions 5 and 6 from cognitive and intellectual growth to identity formation and contextual considerations, although the cognitive processes and commitments to values presumed to be involved at the higher positions are consistent with Perry's use of the phrase *ethical development* in the title of his book.

King and Kitchener's Reflective Judgment Model. Patricia King and Karen Kitchener (King & Kitchener, 1994, 2002; Kitchener & King, 1981, 1990) offer a model of "reflective judgment" that has conceptual roots in the writings of John Dewey, Jean Piaget, Lawrence Kohlberg (see following section), William Perry, and others. The model also rests on considerable empirical evidence (see Chapter Four of this book). King and Kitchener define a hierarchical, increasingly complex seven-stage sequence relating to what people "know" or believe and how they justify their knowledge claims and beliefs. Although the term *reflective judgment* is sometimes used interchangeably with *critical thinking*, these authors differentiate the two on the basis of the epistemological assumptions that an individual holds and the degree of structure of the problem confronted. Reflective judgment is needed when a problem is real and "ill-structured," having no known or "right" answer or solution. Such problems are sometimes referred to as unstructured or ill-defined, and applying the formal rules of logic, mathematical formulas, or other guidelines cannot solve them. With unstructured problems (such as pollution, inflation, or whether to withhold life-sustaining treatment from a patient in a coma), information or knowledge may be incomplete or contradictory, and multiple solutions are possible. Solutions vary in parsimony, cost, and effectiveness, and selection from the alternative possibilities requires evaluation of knowledge claims and of the validity of the evidence supporting them.

Development of reflective judgment proceeds through seven stages, each characterized by a distinctive set of assumptions about knowledge and how it is acquired, with each set accompanied by a cluster of stage-related problem-solving strategies. Each stage builds on the assumptions and strategies of preceding stages and lays the foundation for higher stages. As an individual's "epistemic" assumptions and problem-solving strategies become more complex, they "allow greater differentiation between ill-structured and well-structured problems and allow more complex and complete data to be integrated into a solution" (King & Kitchener, 1994, p. 13). Individuals are not presumed to be at one stage at a time but rather to operate "within a developmental range of stages" (King, 2003, p. 239). King and Kitchener (1994) cluster their seven stages into three categories.

- *Prereflective thinking* (Stages 1–3). In these stages, individuals may not even be aware that knowledge is uncertain, that problems exist for which there is no definite answer. No need exists to muster evidence to support a conclusion. In Stage 1, knowledge is assumed to be concrete, absolute, and observable, and, therefore, beliefs require no justification. "The thinking [at this stage] is the epitome of cognitive simplicity" (King & Kitchener, 1994, p. 50). In Stage 2, the individual still assumes knowledge is absolute and certain but may concede that it is not always available to everyone. Some knowledge belongs only to authorities who know the truth. Beliefs remain unexamined and aligned with the pronouncements of authorities. The individual's views appear dogmatic because the belief in a clear truth or "right" solution persists, and the individual continues to rely on authorities for knowledge. In Stage 3, the individual maintains the certainty of knowledge but may admit to temporary uncertainty in some areas in the belief that the truth will eventually be known. In uncertain knowledge areas, personal opinions guide learning "since the link between evidence and beliefs is unclear" (King & Kitchener, 1994, p. 14). The recognition that knowledge is sometimes uncertain and the increasing need to justify beliefs reflect a growing ability to differentiate categories of thought and signal movement toward more complex stages of thinking.
- *Quasi reflective thinking* (Stages 4–5). Individuals in these stages of cognitive development "recognize that some problems are ill-structured and that knowledge claims about them contain an element of uncertainty" (King & Kitchener, 1994, p. 58), but reasoned conclusions based on evidence remain elusive. In Stage 4, belief in the temporariness of uncertainty diminishes, and knowledge is increasingly recognized as uncertain and abstract. The conviction that knowledge is concrete, which characterized earlier stages, begins to dissipate. Knowledge claims come to be seen as requiring justification and evidence and as idiosyncratic to the individual making the claim. Reasoning and evidence are offered in support of beliefs, but the individual begins to realize that others' views may be more strongly reasoned and supported, requiring better justification for one's own beliefs. In Stage 5, knowledge is considered subjective, context-specific, shaped by the individual's perceptions and interpretations of the evidence and criteria for judging, and thus idiosyncratic to the individual making the claim. In accepting knowledge as contextual, the individual recognizes the legitimacy of other views and conclusions. Developing the ability to

relate abstractions to one another and to see knowledge as related to evidence and argument mark the primary achievement in this stage.

- *Reflective thinking* (Stages 6–7). At its highest stages, reflective judgment rests on recognition that knowledge is neither "given" nor found but constructed and that knowledge claims are linked to the contexts in which they were developed. These claims, moreover, should remain open to re-evaluation. In Stage 6, the individual recognizes that knowing requires action and draws on information from multiple domains or contexts to develop knowledge and reach conclusions about ill-structured problems. Beliefs are grounded on evaluations of the opinions of authorities and on information from different domains. Beliefs and solutions are evaluated on criteria such as utility, preponderance of evidence, or need for action. Individuals reasoning at Stage 7 recognize that knowledge is never a given but rather the outcome of inquiry, synthesis of evidence and opinion, evaluation of evidence and arguments, and recognition that some judgments are more solidly grounded and defensible than others. Beliefs are judged with respect to their reasonableness, consistency with the evidence, plausibility of the argument, and probability in light of the assembled information. The individual also recognizes that judgments may be reviewed and altered on the basis of new information, perspectives, or tools for inquiry.

Baxter Magolda's Epistemological Reflection Model. Marcia Baxter Magolda (1992b) was influenced by Perry but also by Belenky, Clinchy, Goldberger, and Tarule (1986), who like her found evidence that the progression of women's "ways of knowing" did not conform well with Perry's positions. She launched a five-year qualitative study of 101 randomly selected students entering Miami University of Ohio in 1986. Women and men were equally represented, but only three participants were students of color. Drawing on her interviews with these students over their college careers and one year later (70 students stayed in the study throughout), Baxter Magolda developed a model of *epistemological reflection.*

Influenced also by the work of King and Kitchener (see preceding section), Baxter Magolda (1992b) identified four ways in which college students "make meaning." Although these ways could suggest a hierarchical sequence in epistemological development, she avoids the term *stage* and the rigidity it implies. She is clear that more similarities than differences exist in men and women's ways of knowing, but she finds gender-related differences in reasoning, referring to them as *patterns,* a term borrowed from Frye (1990) to help "make sense of experience but stop[s] short of characterizing it in static and generalizable ways" (p. 17). These reasoning patterns are "used more often by one gender than the other but not exclusively by either" (Baxter Magolda, 1992b, pp. 81–82). For Baxter Magolda, students come to know through the complex interplay of instructors, peers, and the individual learner.

- *Absolute knowing.* People using this way of knowing consider knowledge absolute, and any uncertainty reflects the conviction that the individual just does not know the right answer. Instructors are expected to transmit knowledge and make sure students receive and understand it. The student's role is to acquire what the instructor and other authorities already know.

Although Baxter Magolda found that absolute knowers share these assumptions about the nature of knowledge and how to acquire it, she also identified gender-related differences in approaches to acquiring the knowledge being presented. Among absolute knowers, women tend more than men to manifest a "receiving pattern" of knowing, taking a private approach to learning that relies on listening and recording information rather than on talking and asking questions. Receiving-pattern learners rely on peers to help maintain a comfortable learning environment by asking the questions and helping others to acquire the important information. Although in this pattern knowledge is considered absolute and certain, varying perspectives on knowledge are apparent in students' reliance on personal interpretation to resolve conflicts in what is presumably known. Baxter Magolda notes that these individual interpretations do not yet reflect any perception of the possibility that the learner may be an active participant in the construction of what is known.

The "mastery pattern," in contrast, is more often apparent in men than women and reflects a verbal and interactionist approach to learning. These learners ask questions both as a way of acquiring information and as a vehicle for developing knowledge mastery. Discussions of course information and debating points with peers are a means to learning, and instructors are expected to provide material in ways that interest students and provide an incentive for attending class. Baxter Magolda found differences between receiving- and mastery-pattern learners relating to "voice" (remaining largely silent versus asking questions and engaging in discussions and debates), identification with authority (detachment versus an imitative, apprenticelike relationship to the instructor), and relationships with peers (as sources of comfort and support in the classroom versus partners in learning and testing knowledge to enhance achievement).

• *Transitional knowing.* Encounters with alternative points of view appear to spark the shift from absolute to transitional knowing. Transitional knowers acknowledge that although some knowledge may be certain, some is not. Reliance on authority begins to recede as students come to accept that the learner's role is to understand rather than simply acquire. The individual becomes a more active learner, expecting instructors to provide opportunities for active understanding and to demonstrate life applications of what is being learned. Peers become active participants and collaborators in the search for understanding by challenging one another's views.

Like absolute knowers, transitional knowers share the earlier assumptions about the nature of knowledge and the roles of others, but gender-related differences in the patterns of knowing are also apparent among transitional knowers as they seek understanding in areas where knowledge is uncertain. "Interpersonal-pattern" knowers (more often women than men) tend to view their role in learning as gathering the ideas of others. This pattern for learning is interactional, and relationships are central to the process because peers provide exposure to new ideas and alternate views. These learners expect instructors to be supportive and to allow students to become involved and to express their views in a safe learning environment. Recognition of uncertainty appears to encourage these learners both to become more involved and to make some judgments in learning.

"Impersonal-pattern" knowers (more often men than women) value interaction with others, but primarily as a prod to clarifying individual understanding. Other learners provide opportunities to debate, requiring thinking, which leads to understanding. Knowledge mastery, however, remains the objective. Where relationships play an important role in interpersonal-pattern knowers, "challenge is more important than the relationships" for impersonal knowers (Baxter Magolda, 1992b, p. 134). Where interpersonal-pattern knowers display some willingness to move away from authorities as the source of knowledge, impersonal-pattern learners are less disposed to do so.

• *Independent knowing.* The view of knowledge as uncertain, which had been recognized tentatively in the transitional pattern, becomes a basic assumption for independent knowers. "Differences among authorities represent the variety of views possible in an uncertain world" (Baxter Magolda, 1992b, p. 137), and with authorities seen as only one source of knowledge, independent knowers come to recognize themselves as participants and their own views as legitimate. They expect instructors to encourage independent thought and to provide opportunities for students to explore and to exercise their emerging intellectual independence. Independent-knowing pattern students value open-mindedness and recognize the rights of others to their own opinions. This openness also changes these students' relationships with peers and authorities.

As with the two previous ways of knowing, gender-related patterns are apparent here. "Interindividual-pattern" knowers (primarily women) develop closer connections to peers and authorities, but not at the expense of having their own ideas. Articulating their own views and weighing them against those put forward by peers and others helps clarify their own views. As independent-pattern knowers gain confidence in their own views, the importance of the reactions of others diminishes. These learners are finding their own "voice."

For "individual-pattern" knowers, however, the changing relationships move somewhat more toward separation than connection with peers and authorities. These students acknowledge the legitimacy of the views of others, but find it difficult to pay attention to those views, concentrating instead on their own thinking. Acknowledging the legitimacy of others' views, however, appears to free individual-pattern learners from authority, enabling pursuit of their own views.

• *Contextual knowing.* The importance of thinking for oneself that characterizes independent knowers persists in contextual knowing but with a difference: independent thought now occurs in the context of knowledge generated by others and the relationship of one's ideas to those of others. Contextual knowing requires judgments of the evidence supporting truth claims. Knowledge now comes from integrating the ideas of others with one's own. Contextual knowers have come to recognize that some truth claims are better than others, and they judge the validity of truth claims on the basis of the supporting evidence. Other people's ideas continue to be important, but no longer simply as a source of ideas that coexist with the learner's; rather, they are potential elements that, when judged to be valid, can be incorporated into the learner's own thinking and views. Experts are still sources of knowledge or supporting evidence, but anyone, including a peer, who has gained special expertise that is judged to be valid in a particular context or topic area is considered an expert. Contextual knowers' emphasis on evaluating knowledge claims extends into decision making. These knowers identify available options, evaluate the evidence supporting each option, marshal specifiable criteria for guiding decisions, and balance the risks against priorities. Baxter Magolda found only a few students who were contextual knowers, however, even a year after college. She therefore deferred judgment about whether gender-related differences exist, although she speculated that earlier differences in patterns within the other ways of knowing converge in contextual knowing.

Baxter Magolda also takes care at the outset of the description of her own views to acknowledge the homogeneity of participants in her study in terms of age, race-ethnicity, and socioeconomic status as well as their institution's selectivity and emphasis on academic values. Thus, the ways of knowing Baxter Magolda identified may not generalize to other, traditional college-age adults. She does, however, call attention to three "story lines" that she suggests provide grounds for extending the insights gained from her research to other young adults: (1) the development of "voice" (the movement from reciting the knowledge of others to articulating an individual perspective), (2) shifting relationships with authority (the progression from relying on authority to moving away from it and then to developing one's own sense of authority), and (3) evolving relationships with peers (who were initially vehicles for support or testing and learning knowledge to being knowers with ideas to be incorporated into one's own thinking).

Baxter Magolda (2001) continued to study the development of participants in her study, interviewing 39 of them over the decade following their graduation. In the process, her interests broadened to encompass participants' evolving sense of identity, their interactions with others, and how intra- and interpersonal aspects of these individuals' lives shaped their development. She concluded that during their 20s young adults pass through four phases[16] on their way to "self-authorship," or "the capacity to internally define their own beliefs, identity, and relationships" (p. xvi). The passage is characterized by complex interactions among three dimensions of development, each with a driving question: epistemological ("How do I know?"), intrapersonal ("Who am I?"), and interpersonal ("What relationships do I want with others?"). In both of her books, Baxter Magolda, like Chickering and King and Kitchener, offers an extensive discussion of the implications of her work for faculty and academic and student affairs administrators (see also Baxter Magolda, 1999d).

Kohlberg's Theory of Moral Development. Although both Perry and King and Kitchener recognize the linkage between cognitive development and moral reasoning,[17] they focus primarily on cognition and learning broadly defined. Lawrence Kohlberg, in contrast, focused specifically on moral development (Kohlberg, 1969, 1971, 1972, 1975, 1981a, 1981b, 1984; Kohlberg & Candee, 1984; Kohlberg, Levine, & Hewer, 1984).[18] Kohlberg sought to delineate the nature and sequence of progressive changes in individuals' cognitive structures and the rules these individuals use to process information when making moral judgments. His principal concern was not with the content of moral choice (which may be socially or culturally determined) but with modes of reasoning, with the cognitive *processes* (thought to be universal) by which moral choices are made.

Kohlberg's is a cognitive "stage" theory that identifies three general levels of moral reasoning. The model has two stages at each level, although in his later writings Kohlberg dropped the sixth stage because of the lack of empirical evidence to support it (Kohlberg et al., 1984). At each stage, the primary concern is with the principle of justice. Kohlberg (1972) distinguishes between a *rule,* which prescribes action, and a *principle,* which guides choice among alternative behaviors. Passage through the presumably invariant sequence of stages leads to an increasingly refined, differentiated set of principles and sense of justice. Self-interest and material advantage dominate the earlier stages, whereas an internalized, conscience-based set of moral principles guide decision making at the far end of the moral development continuum.

- *Level I: Preconventional.* At Stage 1 ("Obedience and Punishment Orientation"), likely physical consequences determine whether behavior is "good" or "bad." The individual recognizes and defers to superior power or physical strength out of self-interest. Any concern for laws or rules is based on the consequences for violations of those rules. At Stage 2 ("Naively Egoistic Orientation"), "right" actions are those that satisfy one's needs, but signs of an emerging relativism are apparent. The needs of others might be acknowledged, but any reciprocity is based not on a sense of the rights of others but on a pragmatic "You-scratch-my-back-and-I'll-scratch-yours" bargain.
- *Level II: Conventional.* At Stage 3 ("The 'Good Boy' Orientation"), the expectations of others are recognized as valuable in their own right, not merely for what obedience to them will return to the individual. Behavior is guided by a need for approval, particularly from those closest to the individual such as parents and peers. "Intention" is important. At Stage 4 (the "Authority and Social-Order Maintaining Orientation"), respect for authority as a social obligation emerges. Concern for maintaining the social order and meeting the expectations of others governs moral judgments, and laws are recognized as necessary for the protection and maintenance of the group as a whole. Kohlberg (1975, p. 671) also characterized this stage as the "'Law and Order' Orientation."
- *Level III: Postconventional.* At Stage 5 ("Contractual Legalistic Orientation"), duty is seen as a social contract acknowledged to have an arbitrary starting

point, with an emphasis on democratically agreed-upon mutual obligations. Violations of the rights of others or the will of the majority are avoided. Because this third level emphasizes "equality and mutual obligation within a democratically established order," Kohlberg (1972, p. 15) referred to the guiding philosophy at this stage as "the morality of the American Constitution." Principles thought to be logical and universal, not social rules, govern behavior at Stage 6 ("Conscience or Principle Orientation"), the highest level. "Highest value [is] placed on human life, equality, and dignity" (Kohlberg, 1972, p. 15). Right action is guided by personally chosen ethical principles and the dictates of conscience. As noted earlier, however, this stage has been dropped from more recent formal statements of the theory for lack of empirical evidence of its existence. Moreover, in the decade following the initial proposition of the theory, evidence accumulated to challenge Kohlberg's assumption that the tenets of his theory of moral development applied to women as well as men (Gilligan, 1977, 1979). (Studies of change in principled moral reasoning during college, most of which are based on Kohlberg's theory, are reviewed in Chapter Seven.)

Gilligan's Model of Women's Moral Development. For some time, analyses of interviews done using instruments operationalizing Kohlberg's theory had indicated that women consistently scored at lower stages of development than men, a finding interpreted as evidence of a problem in women's development. In her research, however, Carol Gilligan, a student and research assistant of Kohlberg, observed persistent discrepancies between women's concepts of self and morality and the major theories of human and moral development, including those of Piaget, Erikson, and particularly Kohlberg (Gilligan, 1977, 1979, 1981, 1982, 1986a, 1986b). She suggested that the problem lay not with women's development but with gender-biased theoretical conceptions and studies of moral development that relied almost exclusively on male subjects. Although the accepted theories purported to explain a universal developmental sequence, Gilligan argued that they did not accurately describe women's experience, sense of self, or the bases of their moral reasoning.

Gilligan's (1977) critique of Kohlberg's theory focuses on its "subordination of the interpersonal to the societal definition of the good" (p. 489). The problem, says Gilligan, is that women's perceptions of self are "tenaciously embedded in relationships with others," and women's judgments of what is moral are "insistently contextual" (1977, p. 482). The values of justice and autonomy that dominate Kohlberg's theory "imply a view of the individual as separate and of relationships as either hierarchical or contractual, bound by the alternatives of constraint and cooperation. In contrast, the values of care and connection that emerge saliently in women's thinking imply a view of self and others as interdependent and of relationships as networks sustained by activities of caregiving and response" (Gilligan, 1986a, p. 40). For Gilligan, women's concern with others' well-being constitutes a "different voice" from that of males. Whereas men tend to reason in the "justice" voice, women's moral reasoning is in the "care" voice. Similar observations of the central importance of interpersonal relations in women's sense of themselves are reported by Douvan and Adelson (1966), Belenky, Clinchy, Goldberger, and Tarule (1986), and Josselson (1987, 1996).

For Gilligan, women's moral reasoning develops in three stages, moving "from an egocentric through a societal to a universal perspective" (1977, p. 483) with two transition periods. Level I, or *Orientation to Individual Survival,* focuses clearly and squarely on the self and the individual's desires or needs, an emphasis that can preclude recognition of or engagement with moral dilemmas. Isolation from others may accompany the emphasis on self. Development begins in the first transition period ("From Selfishness to Responsibility") with the discovery of connections to others and a sense of responsibility to care for others as well as oneself. This discovery provides a new basis for defining relations between self and others as care and responsibility become criteria for moral decision making.

In the second level, *Goodness as Self-Sacrifice,* caring and responsibility for others become the basis for acceptance. Subordination of the individual's needs or wishes to those of others is central to maintaining connections to others. At this stage, "the feminine voice" emerges clearly, and "the good is equated with caring for others" (Gilligan, 1977, p. 492). The inherent inequality between self and others, however, leads the individual to question whether her own interests should always be secondary, and she enters the second transition period ("From Goodness to Truth"). In the transition, the individual seeks to resolve the conflict between selfishness, which means "hurting" others, and responsibility, which means "caring" and subordination. The search can lead to reconsideration and redefinition of responsibility so as to include caring for others and oneself. Resolution is achieved at the third level, *The Morality of Nonviolence,* when equilibrium is found between individual needs and the expectations of conformity and caring in conventional notions of womanhood. That equilibrium lies in nonviolence as a moral principle as well as a basis for decision making. "Judgment remains psychological in its concern with the intention and consequences of action, but it now becomes universal in its condemnation of exploitation and hurt" (Gilligan, 1977, p. 492).

The differences between Kohlberg and Gilligan are the differences between the morality of rights and the morality of responsibility, between concepts of autonomy and separation and concepts of connectedness and relationships. Gilligan, however, does not see these differences as reflecting any conflict; it is not a case of one theory being more or less adequate than the other. Rather, she believes they represent two different ways of viewing the world. Moreover, despite her focus on women, she asserts that both "justice" and "care" voices are inherent in the life cycle, constituting alternative grounds on which to evaluate the moral. She believes all individuals reason in both voices, although one tends to be predominant in any single individual. The care voice is more frequently found among women and the justice voice among men. Gilligan asserts that emphasizing one dimension tends to neglect the other, leading "to the casting of all problems as problems of dominance and subordination" (Gilligan, 1986a, p. 54).[19]

Other Models. Other cognitive-structural theories or models are available. Kegan (1982, 1994) initially offered a "constructive-developmental" framework for ego development that focuses on the processes by which individuals simultaneously "make meaning" of their world and define themselves in subject-object relationships. For Kegan, developmental stages are less interesting than the often painful and disorienting transitions that mark the end of one stage and the beginning of the next. In his more recent work, Kegan proposed five "orders of consciousness" that span the lifetime, each providing an organizational framework for making sense of the demands of the world. Each "order" contains components relating to cognition, self-concept, and interpersonal relations. As in other cognitive-structural models, the orders are not strictly hierarchical, although they do define a progression of increasingly complex states of being. Reflection and construction of one's self, or self-authorship, are important components of the model.

Other cognitive-structural models deal with faith or spiritual development.[20] James Fowler (1981, 1991, 1996), drawing on the theories of Piaget and Kohlberg, proposed a model to describe spiritual development, viewing meaning making as a spiritual as well as cognitive process. His model is concerned not with the particular beliefs the individual holds but with the process by which the individual comes to subscribe to them. For Fowler, the relational nature of that meaning making involves the individual not only with others but also with beliefs in and commitments to a higher being as the origin of meaning and purpose. Like its conceptual predecessors, this model is hierarchical, with each stage more differentiated and complex than the previous one and with a challenge to current beliefs that may originate internally or externally triggering the advance to a higher stage.

Sharon Daloz Parks (2000), in contrast, examines the development of a sense of purpose in life as the development of an understanding of faith. According to Parks, this development proceeds through four stages, each "shaped by forms of knowing (cognitive processes), dependence (affective aspects focusing on relationships), and community (social and cultural contexts)" (Evans, 2003, p. 192), and each form contributes to a more differentiated understanding of faith. The stages of faith development are labeled "Adolescent or Conventional," "Young Adult," "Tested Adult," and "Mature Adult," with each stage influenced by acts of imagination that contain elements of conflict, reflection, insight, reintegration, and interpretation. Parks considers colleges and universities as settings that can affect faith positively or negatively.[21]

Typological Models

Psychosocial and cognitive-structural theories focus, respectively, on the nature and processes of change, whereas a third family of theories or models emphasizes relatively stable differences among individuals and categorizes individuals according to these distinctive characteristics. These "type" models focus on differences in the ways individuals perceive their world or respond to it.

Type models share several features (Rodgers, 1989). First, the styles or preferences that characterize people and differentiate them are believed to develop relatively early in life and to remain comparatively stable, although not invariant, over time. Second, an individual may demonstrate characteristics indicative of other types within the taxonomy but tend to think or behave in ways consistent with the distinctive characteristics or preferences of the dominant type. Third, type categories describe areas of preference or tendencies that people have in common, but they do not explain idiosyncratic differences. Rather, they constitute "various tracks to wholeness, 'zip code' areas within which we grow and develop" (Rodgers, 1989, p. 153). Finally, these models generally do not attempt to explain either the content or processes of change or development in students. If change is considered at all, it is marginal to the typology's defining characteristics.

Nonetheless, typological models can be useful in understanding differences between college students and in illuminating why students may respond in different ways to the same college setting or experience. Indeed, as will be seen in subsequent chapters in this book, although we are beginning to identify and understand how certain experiences have differing effects related to differences in students' personal characteristics, much remains unknown. Individual differences shape both cognitive and affective learning, and typological models remind us to take these differences into account in studies and in academic and nonacademic policies and practices. The models can also be helpful in guiding selection of potentially important, theoretically grounded variables. Type models do not explain changes in students, however, so we will simply call readers' attention to the most prominent ones among them.

Perhaps the most widely known and used type theories are those of David Kolb, dealing with learning styles and experiential learning (Kolb, 1976, 1981, 1984); John Holland, relating to vocational preferences and environments (1997), and Katherine Briggs and her daughter, Isabel Briggs Myers, describing personality types (Lawrence, 1982, 1984; Myers, 1980a, 1980b; Myers & McCaulley, 1985). Others include Witkin's cognitive styles (Witkin, 1962, 1976) and Gardner's multiple intelligences (Gardner, 1983, 1987, 1993). Evans, Forney, and Guido-DiBrito (1998) devote a chapter to the origins, theory, assessment techniques, research, and programmatic applications of the leading type theories.

Person-Environment Interaction Theories and Models

To various degrees, the theories and models discussed in the previous paragraphs acknowledge the role of the individual's environment in shaping student behavior and development. Person-environment theories and models, however, focus in detail on the environment and how it influences behavior through its interactions with characteristics of the individual. Person-environment models, like typological models, make no attempt to explain either the nature or specific processes of student development or growth, but we include them here because they attempt to identify some origins of behavior and provide frameworks for discussing student change and college effects.

Several clusters are identifiable in this category of models. Some of the distinctions among clusters derive from writers' decisions about whether the environment should be defined objectively, as an external reality, or perceptually, with reality defined as whatever the individual perceives it to be. Baird (1988) provides an extensive discussion and critique of a number of models that fall into this category, as well as of some of the important theoretical and technical issues involved in assessing person-environment interactions and their effects (see also Huebner, 1989).

In the following discussion, we use the structure devised by Strange and Banning (2001), who group person-environment models into four categories: physical, human aggregate, organizational, and constructed (see also Strange, 2003).

Physical Models. Physical theories and models focus on the external environment, whether natural or man-made, and on how it shapes behavior by permitting some activities while limiting or preventing others. The physical environment may be specific and bounded, as in the architectural features of residence halls (for example, Heilweil, 1973; Schroeder, 1980), or broad and extended, as in urban settings (Gaines, 1991; Michelson, 1970; Sommer, 1969). Several disciplines provide theories of the physical environment's influences on people, including architecture (Dober, 1992; Gaines, 1991), social psychology (Barker, 1968; Barker & Associates, 1978), and cultural anthropology (Moffatt, 1989; Rhoads, 1994). In these models, physical surroundings encourage or constrain certain kinds of behavior depending on the physical and symbolic characteristics of the setting as well as on the number and kinds of individuals in it.

Human Aggregate Models. Authors of human aggregate models describe an environment and its influence in terms of the aggregate characteristics (for example, sociodemographic traits, goals, values, attitudes) of its occupants. According to this view, individuals create or define environments even as these environments attract other individuals and help socialize them to maintain the interests, attitudes, values, and behaviors of all occupants. Astin (1968, 1993b), Holland (1997), and Kuh, Hu, and Vesper (2000) provide examples of human aggregate models. Strange (2003) suggests these models fall into two groups: subcultures, typologies, and styles models and person-environment interaction models. Elements of human aggregate theories and models often appear in the psychosocial and typological models discussed previously.

Organizational Environment Models. According to Strange (2003), environments can also be viewed as systems influenced by an organization's goals, values, and activities, which, in turn, shape the organizational structures and designs. Organizational environments may be static or dynamic, depending on their resistance or responsiveness to change. The nature of the environment depends to some extent on an organization's complexity, centralization, formalization, stratification, production, and efficiency (Hage & Aiken, cited in Strange, 2003).[22]

Constructed Environments. Some person-environment models have deep roots in social psychology and cultural anthropology, defining and characterizing an environment in terms of its occupants' perceptions of the setting's characteristics. In our earlier book, we grouped these models into a single category called *perceptual models*. Strange (2003) organizes them into three categories, grouped according to environmental press (such as Pace, 1969; Pace & Stern, 1958; Stern, 1970), social climate (Moos, 1979, 1986), and campus cultures (for example, Horowitz, 1987; Kuh & Hall, 1993).

Commonalities in Developmental Theories

Even the foregoing brief summaries make it clear that the most prominent and influential theories of college student growth differ in important ways, including the structure of the developmental process, its end points, the number of developmental stages or dimensions, the origins of developmental growth or stage change, and the characterization and labeling of each dimension or stage. At the same time, most of these theories and models have certain commonalities in both substance and process. Rodgers (1980) gives a similar but more extensive analysis than is possible here.

Similarities in Substance. Several substantive themes run through many developmental theories and models. Common to several of the psychosocial theories is the emergence during the college years of self-understanding and awareness of self as a participant in learning. As the individual gains experience and confidence, external controls on behavior slowly give way to internal controls. This theme is identifiable, for example, in Chickering's managing emotions vector and in virtually all of the identity development models, whether general or specific to gender, race-ethnicity, or sexual orientation.

Several theories take the view that growth in self-awareness during the college years and an emergent understanding of and appreciation for the roles of other people and obligations to them are central features of development. Increased individuality is accompanied by expanded interpersonal horizons and by a growing appreciation for the paradoxical merger of dependence and independence in the concept of interdependence.

Developmental theories, at their highest stages, share some conception of a culminating stage of self-definition and self-direction. Although the specification of the developmental end point varies across psychosocial and cognitive-structural theories, the progression is invariably toward greater differentiation and complexity accompanied by greater integration. A number of progressive developmental sequences are apparent: from cognitive and affective simplicity to complexity, from personal nonresponsibility to responsibility, from dependence through autonomy to interdependence, from impulsiveness to self-control, from immaturity to maturity, from external controls to internal controls and self-determination, from self-interestedness to a sense of fairness and responsibility for others, from instinctual to principled action.

Similarities in Process. Developmental theories and models also share similar conceptions of the processes of student development. Miller and Winston (1990) identify five "fundamental developmental principles that recur throughout the literature on human development" (p. 101).[23] According to these two writers: *psychosocial development is continuous,* with maturation following a certain course regardless of the environment but not independent of it; *psychosocial development is cumulative,* with each experience or stage providing part of the foundation for the next; *development progresses from a simple to a more complex state; developmental progress is orderly,* with one state or stage leading to the next; and *developmental progress depends on the satisfactory completion of developmental tasks* (Miller & Winston, 1990, p. 102).

Other process commonalities are apparent in developmental theories of student growth:

Cognitive readiness is a necessary but not sufficient condition for development. Sanford (1962) stated that for change to occur a student must be biologically and psychologically *ready* to change, although psychological readiness is probably most important. Most of the developmental theories reviewed here share that view implicitly or explicitly by assuming that for development to occur, the individual must be capable of recognizing the conflict(s) inherent in retaining epistemological structures or beliefs in the face of evidence that doing so is intellectually untenable. The individual may be ready to change but choose *not* to do so, although the intellectual ability to recognize the possible need for change and revise cognitive structures must exist in order for growth to occur.

Recognition of complexity precedes higher-level developmental change. Cognitive capacity and readiness for change are intimately related to development because they are necessary for recognizing the complexity of one's world as well as one's place in it. Epistemological skills and readiness to apply them provide the foundation for making choices among truth claims, values, and behaviors. Together, growing awareness of complexity and cognitive readiness for change constitute the developmental trigger. Both are necessary but not sufficient conditions for growth.

Developmental movement originates in a challenge to the current state of development. If cognitive readiness and the perception of complexity are the trigger, then cognitive or affective conflict is the finger that pulls it. The proposition that forward movement requires an encounter with conflict, or the awareness of a challenge to the integrity and stability of the current developmental stage or condition, is fundamental to virtually all developmental theories. In the resulting disequilibrium, the individual "strives to reduce the tension caused by a challenge and thus to restore equilibrium" (Sanford, 1967, p. 49). Most developmental theories hold a Newtonian view of change: a structure at rest will remain at rest unless confronted by experiences or perceptions that challenge its ability to remain internally consistent by explaining them.

If the challenge is too great, the individual may simply deny its existence or relevance. Or the individual may alter the content of the new knowledge or experience in order to assimilate it into current structures and beliefs. Such a response, like denial or rejection, is unlikely to lead to developmental change. The individual may, however, recognize the magnitude of the conflict and accommodate to it by restructuring existing beliefs or knowledge structures. Such reconstructions are the essential developmental act. Whether growth occurs depends on the nature of the individual's response to the challenge and the level of support received from others for working through the disequilibrium.

The capacity for detachment from self and for empathy controls access to higher developmental levels. Recognition of the pluralism of knowledge and values, the ability to differentiate among alternatives, and the capacity to deal with the conflicts that may exist among alternatives are preconditions for another important process common to developmental models: the ability to separate from self and empathize with others. For most developmental writers, the capacity for empathy with others is an important determinant of higher-level individual development. Most importantly, the capacity for empathy is presumed to lead not only to a better understanding of self and a wider appreciation of the ideas and rights of others but also to the development of more mature interpersonal relationships and, ultimately, commitments.

SOCIOLOGICAL PERSPECTIVES

Developmental explanations for changes in college students face theoretical challenges from sociologists and others who seek the origins of change in students' external rather than internal worlds. Feldman (1972), for example, identifies several troublesome problems in the adoption of developmental models for understanding the change process. According to Feldman, much of the research based on a developmental theory of change is not neutral. Evidence of change tends to be interpreted in developmental terms, as reflecting movement toward a more advanced stage of growth even when the changes are not in expected directions. Although regressive changes may in fact occur, the positive, developmental bias militates against such interpretations of the evidence. Heath (1968), for example, found that entering freshmen scored higher on various measures of autonomy and emotional independence when they entered college than they did seven months later. Despite this evidence, however, he concluded that "the apparent 'regression' in autonomy was necessary to become more autonomous. Similarly, the apparent 'integration' of the entering freshmen's talents, values, and interests may have been a less mature form of integration than the 'disintegration' the same men experienced later in the year" (p. 253).

Feldman (1972) believes that in addition to the tendency to "psychologize" student change, developmental models also ignore a variety of other changes that college students experience. He suggests that "some (many?) of the imputed or actual changes in students, prompted by their moving into new [social and preoccupational] positions in college or by their anticipation of future roles, imply little or nothing about development; these changes simply may lie outside the developmental [growth] framework" (p. 17).

Dannefer (1984a), although writing specifically about adult development, offers a similar but even sharper critique. Dannefer believes the entire developmental approach is flawed. The developmentalist propositions of "sequentiality, unidirectionality, an end state, irreversibility, qualitative-structural transformation, and universality" (p. 103) do not take into account the influence exerted by the environment. Dannefer charges that, although developmentalists acknowledge environmental influences, their role is usually considered a supporting, instrumental one, a necessary but not sufficient condition for opportunities that trigger internal, growth-determining mechanisms. Moreover, even when environmental and social structural characteristics are included in analyses, "they tend to be considered only insofar as they are seen as *immediately* impinging on personality development, cognitive development, attitudinal development, or the like" (Feldman, 1994b, p. xix), and their potential indirect influences are overlooked or ignored.

Dannefer (1984a) suggests that environmental structures influence the social organization of developmental opportunities at each of three levels: at the societal level (for example, through stratification patterns based on social class, sex, race, or age), at the organizational level (for example, in bureaucracies, schools, and social service agencies), and at the micro level, where peer and other small-group dynamics operate through a variety of mechanisms. In the traditional microlevel view, educational institutions socialize students through a series of experiences in a wide variety of environmental settings that instill knowledge, attitudes, values, and skills through the influences of faculty, other students, and other socializing agents. In these ways, schools shape the content and direction of student change and growth.

A common sociological perspective on organizations (see, for example, Clark, 1960; Feldman, 1972, 1994b) conceives of colleges and universities as "gatekeepers" conferring socioeconomic and occupational status, position, and benefits and controlling who is certified for access. Institutions therefore are also presumed to exert considerable influence on students' present and future behaviors, attitudes, values, beliefs, interests, and even cognitive preferences. Through their social "charters" to produce certain kinds of students (Kamens, 1971, 1974), colleges not only "allocate" students to various and select adult roles but also thereby induce adoption of behaviors, attitudes, goals, and values appropriate to the roles and expectations of the station and status assigned by their education (Meyer, 1977). Bourdieu (1977a, 1977b, 1986; Bourdieu & Passeron, 1990) provides an extended discussion of education's contributions to the social forces at work in the development of social and cultural capital.[24] Kaufman and Feldman (2004), for example, taking a sociological perspective, find the college experience plays a constitutive role in the formation of student identity in three "domains": intelligence and knowledgeability (including thinking critically and "talking smart"), occupation, and cosmopolitanism (developing more sophisticated cultural interests and tastes).

Traditional approaches to individual development, these critics say, do not take adequate account of "(1) the malleability of the human organism in relation to environments; (2) the structural complexity and diversity of the social environment; [or] (3) the role of the symbolic—of social knowledge and human intentionality—as factors mediating development" (Dannefer, 1984a, pp. 106–107). According to Dannefer (1984b, p. 847), developmental theories fall into the trap of "ontogenetic reductionism—the practice of treating socially produced and patterned phenomena as rooted in the characteristics of the individual organism . . . view[ing] the social environment as [little] more than a setting that facilitates maturational unfolding" (p. 847).

Smart, Feldman, and Ethington (2000) illustrate the potential for error in applying a developmental perspective uncritically to studies of the impacts of college on students. These scholars note the apparent discrepancy between the evidence reviewed by Feldman and Newcomb (1969) and what we reviewed in our earlier book concerning the contributions of academic departments to patterns of student stability, change, or development. Feldman and Newcomb, as well as Smart et al. (2000), find considerable evidence that these "academic tribes" exert a net influence on students' abilities, skills, attitudes, beliefs, and behaviors. Our earlier review of the literature on the effects of academic departments on students led us to conclude that their impact was small compared with the impact of other factors. Smart et al. suggest that the discrepancy can be traced to differences in both the conceptual underpinnings and associated measures adopted by the primarily psychological, developmental research that dominated the literature we reviewed. The root explanation, they argue, lies in the emphasis given by "sociological social psychologists" to *processes* versus the concentration of "psychological social psychologists" on *effects* (see Smart et al., 2000, pp. 16–20 and 236–246).

The overriding point is that the developmental conception of student change is only one of several possible conceptual paradigms. The various theories and models reviewed here, as well as those proposed by nondevelopmentalists, differ in their propositions, assumptions, structures, dynamics, and inferences. As Feldman (1972) notes, however, the two orientations are neither completely distinct nor incompatible; the important lesson is to understand what the constraints are on any approach and to bear in mind that relying solely on developmental or sociological models may lead to misstatements concerning the origins of student change and growth. "Each [approach] may be necessary to the study of student change and stability during college, but none of them is sufficient" (p. 21).

COLLEGE IMPACT MODELS OF STUDENT CHANGE

Theories concerning the environmental or sociological origins of change in college students constitute a second family of models of student change. These impact models concentrate not so much on any particular intraindividual process or dimension of student change as on the origins and processes of change. These models are less specific than theories of individual development in their explication of the particular changes students undergo, less detailed in their overall exposition, and less explicit about their grounding in the work of other theorists, whether in sociology, organizational impact, or industrial psychology.

Astin's I-E-O Model and Theory of Involvement

Astin (1970a, 1970b, 1991) proposed one of the first and most durable and influential college impact models, the now familiar input-environment-outcome (I-E-O) model. This construction differs from models discussed earlier in this chapter in that it is less an effort to explain theoretically why or how students change than a conceptual and methodological guide to the study of college effects. According to this model, college outcomes are viewed as functions of three sets of elements: *inputs,* the demographic characteristics, family backgrounds, and academic and social experiences that students bring to college; *environment,* the full range of people, programs, policies, cultures, and experiences that students encounter in college, whether on or off campus; and *outcomes,* students' characteristics, knowledge, skills, attitudes, values, beliefs, and behaviors as they exist after college. The inputs are presumed to shape outcomes directly but also indirectly through the ways in which students engage with the multifaceted institutional environment. Studies adopting this conceptual approach attempt to explain the effects of environmental influences (in the aggregate or individually) on student change or growth, focusing on factors over which college faculty and administrators have some programmatic and policy control.

In addition to his interests in explaining the influences of college on student outcomes net of other noncollege factors, Astin (1985, 1993c) has also come to view the purpose of higher education as one of talent development. Based on his own research, and consistent with Pace's (1988) work on the quality of student effort, Astin proposed a "theory of involvement" to explain the dynamics of how students change or develop. According to Astin (1985), his theory "can be stated simply: *Students learn by becoming involved*" (p. 133). He sees in his theory elements of the Freudian notion of cathexis (the investment of psychological energy) as well as the learning theory concept of time-on-task. He suggests five basic postulates: (1) involvement requires the investment of psychological and physical energy in "objects" of one sort or another (such as tasks, people, or activities), whether specific or general; (2) involvement is a continuous concept; different students will invest varying amounts of energy in different objects; (3) involvement has both quantitative and qualitative features; (4) the amount of learning or development is directly proportional to the quality and quantity of involvement; and (5) educational effectiveness of any policy or practice is related to its capacity to induce student involvement (Astin, 1985, pp. 135–136).

Astin's (1984, 1985, 1991) conception occupies the middle ground between psychological and sociological explanations of student change. He assigns the institutional environment a critical role in that it offers students a wide variety of academic and social opportunities to become involved with new ideas, people, and experiences. The student, however, plays the lead role inasmuch as change is likely to occur only to the extent that the student capitalizes on opportunities and becomes involved, actively exploiting the opportunities to change or grow that the environment presents. Thus, development or change is not merely the consequence of college's impact on a student but rather a function of the quality of student effort or involvement with the resources provided by the institution.

Whether Astin's propositions constitute a theory, however, is open to question. They probably do not meet generally accepted definitions of theory. Kerlinger (1986), for example, defines a theory as "a set of interrelated constructs (concepts), definitions, and propositions that present a systematic view of phenomena by specifying relations among variables, with the purpose of explaining and predicting the phenomena" (p. 9). Astin offers a general dynamic, a principle, rather than any detailed, systemic description of the behaviors or phenomena being predicted, the variables presumed to influence involvement, the mechanisms by which those variables relate to and influence one another, or the precise nature of the process by which growth or change occurs. It is clear, however, that Astin's concept of involvement and I-E-O model provide the conceptual and analytic underpinnings of an extraordinary volume of research (see Chapters Five, Six, and Eight) and have provided faculty members and administrators with a useful way of thinking about college impacts.

Tinto's Theory of Student Departure

Tinto (1975, 1987, 1993) has given a more explicit, longitudinal, and interactional model of institutional impact that is similar to Astin's in its underlying dynamics but specifically seeks to explain the college student withdrawal process (see Figure 2.1). Adapting Durkheim's (1951) theory of suicide and building on Spady's work (1970), Tinto describes his model as an "interactive model of student departure" (1993, p. 112) and as "primarily sociological in character" (p. 113). He theorizes that students enter a college or university with a variety of patterns of personal, family, and academic characteristics and skills, including initial dispositions and intentions with respect to college attendance and personal goals. These intentions and commitments are subsequently modified and reformulated on a continuing basis through a longitudinal series of interactions between the individual and the structures and members of the academic and social systems of the institution. The academic and social communities within an institution are seen as nested inside an external environment of family, friends, and other commitments that places its demands on students in ways largely beyond the students' institutional worlds. (Bean and Metzner, 1985, offer a more detailed model of the effects of students' noninstitutional lives on persistence.)

Rewarding encounters with the formal and informal academic and social systems of the institution presumably lead to greater student integration in these systems and thus to persistence. *Integration* is the extent to which the individual shares the normative attitudes and values of peers and faculty in the institution and abides by the formal and informal structural requirements for membership in that community or in subgroups of it. As integration increases, it strengthens students' commitments to both their personal goals and to the institution through which these goals may be achieved. Negative interactions

Figure 2.1. A Longitudinal Model of Institutional Departure

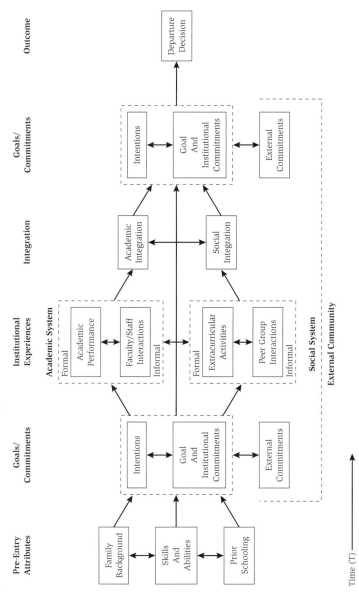

Source: Tinto, 1993, p. 114. Copyright 1987, 1993 by the University of Chicago. Used by permission.

and experiences, however, tend to impede integration and distance the individual from the academic and social communities of the institution, thereby reducing commitments to both goals and institution and promoting the individual's marginality and ultimate withdrawal.[25]

Some scholars consider the concepts of academic and social integration, as well as the operational forms they commonly take, to be inappropriate, either in general (for example, Corman, Barr, & Caputo, 1992), or for various racial and ethnic minority groups (Attinasi, 1992; Biggs, Torres, & Washington, 1998; Francis & Kelly, 1990; Kraemer, 1997; Murguia, Padilla, & Pavel, 1991; Rendon, Jalomo, & Nora, 2000; Velasquez, 1997), or for adult populations (Bills, n.d.; MacKinnon-Slaney, 1994; Spanard, 1990) and, indeed, to rest on a flawed epistemological foundation (Tierney, 1992). Some evidence, however, suggests that the dynamics underlying Tinto's concepts of academic and social integration operate in substantially the same way to explain the persistence decisions of both Whites and minority students (see, for example, Cabrera & Nora, 1994; Cabrera, Nora, Terenzini, Pascarella, & Hagedorn, 1999; Eimers & Pike, 1997; Nora, Cabrera, Hagedorn, & Pascarella, 1996). Braxton, Sullivan, and Johnson (1997) provide a comprehensive examination of the validity of Tinto's model, and Braxton (2000) presents essays on alternative conceptualizations of students' persistence behaviors.

Although Tinto focuses on the college attrition process, his model has been successfully employed to study other student outcomes. Indeed, the underlying dynamic of Tinto's theory of departure—student integration into the academic and social systems of an institution—is similar to Astin's (1985) "involvement" and Pace's (1988) "quality of effort," although the importance of the investment of physical and psychological energy postulated by Astin and Pace is only implied in Tinto's concept of integration. Tinto's comparatively more explicit theoretical structure, however, offers guidance in variable selection to researchers who wish to study the college student change process and to administrators who seek to design academic and social programs and experiences intended to promote students' educational growth.

Pascarella's General Model for Assessing Change

Tinto's (1975, 1987, 1993) model is largely (although not exclusively) concerned with intrainstitutional influences on students, particularly those exerted by other individuals, primarily students and faculty members but also family and non-college peers. He devotes less attention to specifying the nature or strength of the influences of an institution's structural and organizational characteristics or to the role of individual student effort.

Pascarella (1985) suggests a general causal model that includes explicit consideration of both an institution's structural characteristics and its environment, providing a conceptual foundation for multi-institutional studies of collegiate impact. Drawing on his own work (Pascarella, 1980), as well as that of Lacy (1978), Pace (1979), Weidman (1984b), and others, Pascarella suggests that growth is a function of the direct and indirect effects of five main sets of variables (see Figure 2.2). Two of these sets, students' background and precollege characteristics and the structural and organizational features of the institution (such as size, selectivity, and residential character), together shape the third variable set—a college's or university's environment.

These three sets of variables, in turn, influence a fourth set that includes both the frequency and content of students' interactions with the major socializing agents on campus (the faculty and other students). The fifth set of variables, quality of effort, is shaped by students' background traits, by the institutional environment, and by the normative influences of peers and faculty members. Change, then, is a function of students' background characteristics, interactions with major socializing agents, and the quality of effort invested in learning and developing. The structural features of an institution are believed to have an indirect rather than a direct influence on student development, with their impact mediated through the institution's environment, the quality of student effort, and students' interactions with peers and faculty members. Although initially designed to explain changes in students' learning and cognitive development, Pascarella's model is equally appropriate for the study of other student outcomes.

Figure 2.2. A General Causal Model for Assessing the Effects of Differential Environments on Student Learning and Cognitive Development

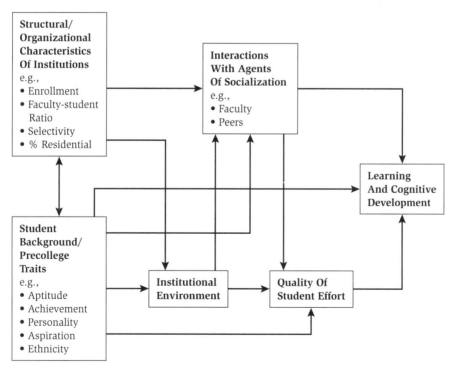

Source: Pascarella, 1985, p. 10. Copyright © 1985 Agathon Press, Inc., with kind permission of Kluwer Academic Publishers.

Weidman's Model of Undergraduate Socialization

Weidman (1989) has proposed a model of undergraduate socialization that incorporates both psychological and social-structural influences on student change. Reflecting its sociological roots, the model pays particular attention to noncognitive changes, such as those involving career choices, lifestyle preferences, values, and aspirations (see Figure 2.3). Weidman's model is more explicit than the three already summarized in its explication of the process of undergraduate socialization—the acquisition of the knowledge, attitudes, and skills that are valued by the society or by important subgroups involving the individual.

Weidman's model is based primarily on his own research (Weidman, 1984a, 1984b, 1985) as well as the models of Chickering (1969), Astin (1977, 1984), and the sociological literature on adult socialization (Brim & Wheeler, 1966; Mortimer & Simmons, 1978). Like Tinto and Pascarella, Weidman hypothesizes that students bring to college a set of important background characteristics (such as socioeconomic status, aptitudes, career preferences, aspirations, and values) as well as normative pressures from parents and other noncollege reference groups (for example, peers, employers, community). These characteristics and shaping forces constitute predisposing and, to a certain extent, constraining forces on students' choices in the college's structural and organizational settings. These contexts, formal or informal, expose students to the normative pressures of the settings. The mechanisms underlying these normative pressures include interpersonal interactions, intrapersonal processes and changes, and the normative order and expectations expressed in various ways by an institution's mission and faculty.

To a greater extent than either Tinto or Pascarella, Weidman hypothesizes important noncollege influences on students. The model explicitly posits a continuing socializing role for parents (even when students live away from home) and for other noncollege reference groups such as peers, current and possible future employers, and community organizations.

According to Weidman, the socialization process encourages students to evaluate and balance these various normative influences in order to attain personal goals. The process also requires decisions about maintaining or changing values, attitudes, or aspirations held at the time of matriculation. This process is both longitudinal and reciprocal, with the salience of segments of the model varying over time and both influencing and being influenced by other components of the socialization structure.

Commonalities in College Impact Models

Like the developmental models reviewed earlier, the primarily sociological impact models share several characteristics. For example, compared with the developmental frameworks, each of these sociological models assigns a much more prominent and specific role to the context in which a student acts and thinks. Institutional structures, policies, programs, and services, as well as the attitudes, values, and behaviors of others who occupy (and to some extent

Figure 2.3. A Conceptual Model of Undergraduate Socialization

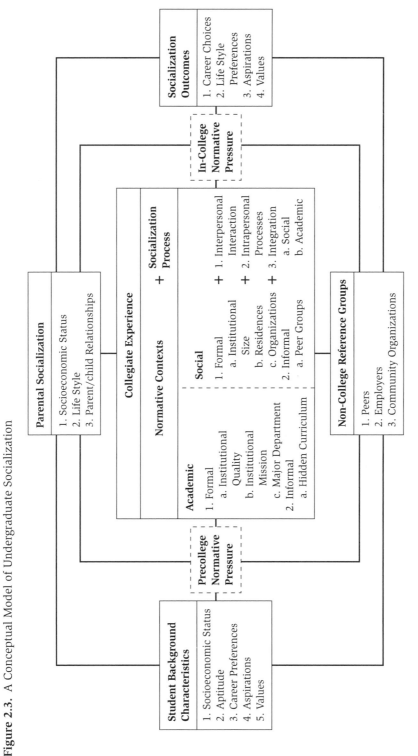

Source: Weidman, 1989, p. 299. Copyright © 1989 Agathon Press, with kind permission of Kluwer Academic Publishers.

define) institutional environments, are all potential influences for change. These sociological models resemble the developmental theories in that students are active participants in the change process, but these models also see the environment as an active force that not only affords opportunities for change-inducing encounters but also can induce particular kinds of responses. Thus, change is influenced not only by whether and how the student responds but also by the nature and intensity of the environmental stimulus. Specification of potential areas of variation in institutional environments (both within and across institutions) is a more salient characteristic of sociological models than of developmental models.

At the same time, sociological impact models' specification of the student characteristics that are considered important tends to be general. To be sure, variations in student change attributable to such characteristics as gender, race or ethnicity, socioeconomic status, and academic aptitude and achievement have been empirically established, but developmental theories and the research based on them suggest that other, more complex student traits may be overlooked if the perspective is strictly sociological. For example, sociological models may not give enough attention to such student traits as cognitive and emotional readiness for intellectual, academic, or psychosocial change; to the individual's current levels of intellectual or occupational motivation; or to students' capacities for empathy. At the least, the student traits considered in studies of student change probably should extend beyond demographic and background characteristics.

CONCLUSIONS

This chapter has summarized the most prominent theories and models of the origins, nature, and processes of student change. These theories and models and their commonalities provide a useful backdrop for our review of the research on college impacts that has appeared in the past dozen years. An understanding of the general nature of change in college students is also fundamental to the design and development of academic and nonacademic policies, programs, and practices as well as to useful research on student change during the college years.

The theoretical and conceptual foundations for the study of college's effects on students vary, and judgments about what factors are significant and what dynamics underlie the process depend in large part on the theoretical perspective one takes. As Smart, Feldman, and Ethington (2000) suggest, "What scholars find in their inquiries may be influenced by what they look for" (p. 238). For some writers, the college years are a developmental testing ground between adolescence and adulthood, a time to try out new roles, attitudes, beliefs, and behaviors. In Erikson's (1968) view, college offers the traditional-age student a *psychosocial moratorium*, providing some breathing room as well as a psychosocially safe place to experiment.

For other researchers, the transition to college provides a form of culture shock requiring significant social and psychological relearning in the face of encounters with new ideas; new teachers and friends with different values and beliefs; new freedoms and opportunities; and new academic, personal, and social demands. Feldman and Newcomb (1969) characterize the freshman year as a combination of *desocialization*—pressures to unlearn certain attitudes, values, beliefs, and behaviors, and *socialization*—pressures to learn new attitudes, values, and beliefs and participate in a new culture and social order. From the perspective of the theories and models of institutional impact summarized here, the potency of colleges and universities for influencing student change and growth appears to lie in their ability to expose students to diversity (broadly defined), opportunities to explore, peer and adult models to emulate or reject, and experiences that challenge currently held values, attitudes, and beliefs.

Although much remains to be done to validate many of these theories in different settings with different groups of students, as well as to consolidate psychological and sociological perspectives, each of the two approaches to the study of change among college students—developmental and sociological—has much to offer. Focusing on one to the exclusion of the other is likely to result not only in misunderstanding the college student change process but also in poor theory and inadequate research and practice.

Notes

1. The distinctions between a theory and a conceptual model are elusive, and the terms are frequently used interchangeably. Kerlinger (1986) defines a theory as "a set of interrelated constructs (concepts), definitions, and propositions that present a systematic view of phenomena by specifying relations among variables, with the purpose of explaining and predicting the phenomena" (p. 9). We use the term *theory* with that definition in mind. Model, as used here, denotes a specification of variables and the relations between them that is less precise and detailed than the theories described by Kerlinger.

2. Merriam and Caffarella (1999) suggest that theories of adult development and learning fall into four categories: biological and psychological development, sociocultural and integrative perspectives, cognitive development, and intelligence. Psychological development theory has three strands, depending on whether a theory focuses on sequential stages (such as Gould, 1978; Levinson, 1978; Levinson & Levinson, 1996; Sheehy, 1976, 1995; Vaillant, 1977), life events and transitions (Fiske & Chiriboga, 1990; Schlossberg, 1981; Schlossberg, Waters, & Goodman, 1995), or relationships (Belenky, Clinchy, Goldberger, & Tarule, 1986; Brown & Gilligan, 1992; Gilligan, 1982; Jordan, 1997). Sociocultural models view adult development as largely a function of the individual's historical, social, and economic context rather than internal processes or principles. These models view social roles, gender, race-ethnicity, and sexual orientation as social constructions, and they take evidence from cross-cultural studies into account. Integrative models rest on the premise that the other categories of theory are conceptually too narrow, and integrative models seek to combine concepts from two or more other

categories (Baltes, 1982; Magnusson, 1995). Clark and Caffarella (1999) and Merriam (2001) provide discussions of recent theoretical issues. Kasworm (1990) discusses both conceptual and methodological issues in studying adult undergraduates.

3. See, for example, Evans, Forney, and Guido-DiBrito (1998), Knefelkamp, Widick, and Parker (1978), Learner (1986), McEwen (2003a), Rodgers (1990), Widick, Knefelkamp, and Parker (1980). Evans et al. also summarize the historical roots, assessment procedures, relevant research relating to a theory's validity, as well as applications and critiques of most of the major developmental theories. See also Komives and Woodard (2003, Chapters Eight through Fourteen) and Love and Guthrie (1999). Thomas (2001) discusses more than three dozen theories and models that emerged in the last two decades of the twentieth century.

4. Tanaka (2002) proposes an "intercultural theory of student development" that seeks to augment current student development theory with considerations of students' social histories, cultures, and power relationships. The goal is to understand power issues inherent in the interactions between students, faculty, and institutional cultures and how they shape student development. Tanaka also proposes ways to incorporate such considerations into higher education research methods.

5. Renn, Dilley, and Prentice (2003) review the identity research as it relates to people and their roles in higher education, including students, faculty members, and administrators. They describe three "seasons" of such research, examining the concepts and dynamics underlying each season and how they have changed over time.

6. Thomas and Chickering (1984) contains Chickering's reflections on the original vectors 15 years after their initial appearance.

7. Some authors differentiate between religious identity and spiritual or faith development. In these discussions, religious identity includes elements of denominational membership, the beliefs to which the individual subscribes, religiosity, and the centrality of religion to the individual's overall identity. Spiritual and faith development, in contrast, are considered to be closer to cognitive-structural models of how one finds and makes meaning than to religious identity. See Love (2001, 2002), Love and Talbot (1999), and McEwen (2003b).

8. Bourne (1978) provides a conceptual and methodological critique of Marcia's model.

9. Belenky, Clinchy, Goldberger, and Tarule (1986), Brown and Gilligan (1992), Downing and Roush (1985), Gilligan (1982), Jordan (1997), O'Neil, Egan, Owen, and Murry (1992), Ossana, Helms, and Leonard (1992) offer other views of women's identity and psychosocial development. O'Neil et al. propose a gender identity development model applicable to men as well as women. Downing and Roush, O'Neil et al., and Ossana et al. view gender development as a function of the societal positions women and men occupy. Given the historically dominant roles assumed by men, these theorists argue that gender identity formation follows a path similar to that of other subordinated groups, particularly those based on race-ethnicity, although the models' correspondence with views on racial-ethnic oppression and its impacts on identity development is imperfect.

10. See Pascarella and Terenzini (1991, p. 25) for a list of models offered in the literature before 1990.

11. See, for example, models concerning Asians (Kim, 2001; Kodama, McEwen, Liang, & Lee, 2001; Sodowsky et al., 1995; Sue & Sue, 1990), Latinos (Bernal & Knight, 1993; Casas & Pytluk, 1995; Ferdman & Gallegos, 2001; Martinez, 1988; Padilla, 1995; Ruiz, 1990; Torres, 1999), and Native Americans (Choney, Berryhill-Paapke, & Robbins, 1995; Horse, 2001). Kerwin and Ponterotto (1995), Reynolds and Pope (1991), Root (1990), and Wijeyesinghe (2001) discuss biracial and multiracial identity. Jones and McEwen (2000) propose a multidimensional model of identity formation that takes into account considerations of gender, race, sexual orientation, social class, religion, and culture as well as contextual influences such as family background, sociocultural conditions, and experience.

12. Mercer and Cunningham (2003), Ortiz and Rhoads (2000), Rowe, Behrens, and Leach (1995), and Rowe, Bennett, and Atkinson (1994) also consider existing models and issues of White racial identity.

13. Helms and Carter (1990) developed the White Racial Identity Attitude Scale (WRIAS) to operationalize Helms's conceptual model. The instrument has been adopted more often than any other measure of White racial identity formation, and a considerable literature exists on its psychometric characteristics. See Behrens (1997), Behrens and Rowe (1997), Helms (1997, 1999), Helms and Carter (1990), Mercer and Cunningham (2003), Pope-Davis, Vandiver, and Stone (1999), Swanson, Tokar, and Davis (1994), Tokar and Swanson (1991), some questioning its validity.

14. See, for example, D'Augelli (1995), Evans and Wall (1991), McEwen (2003a), and Reynolds and Hanjorgiris (2000), and Troiden (1989). Brown (1995) and Gonsiorek (1995) review central concepts in lesbian and gay male identity formation.

15. When Cass (1979) first offered her conceptual framework, she labeled it a model of "homosexual identity formation" (p. 219).

16. Baxter Magolda (2001) characterizes these phases as "following external formulas, the crossroads, becoming authors of their own lives, and [finding] the internal foundation" (p. xxiii).

17. In King and Kitchener (1994), see Chapter Eight.

18. Schrader (1990) provides an anthology on Kohlberg's contributions.

19. Kohlberg (1984) rejected the need for two structures, asserting that differences in the two voices merely constituted different styles of moral reasoning. Despite these theoretical disagreements, the evidence does not support the view that women and men use different criteria to reach moral decisions (see note 3 in Chapter Seven).

20. See Helminiak (1987) for another model of faith or spiritual development. The remainder of the discussion in this section relies heavily on Evans (2003).

21. Love (2001; see also Love & Guthrie, 1999) discusses theoretical issues in spirituality and student development. Jablonski (2001) provides a collection of essays on spiritual exploration and development in college settings.

22. See also Kuh (2003).

23. Miller and Winston use a broader definition of *psychosocial* than we do in this chapter.

24. Bieber (1999) examines the applications of Bourdieu and the cultural capital framework to the study of faculty life.

25. In his 1987 and 1993 books, Tinto suggests that students' transitions to the college environment and their subsequent decisions to persist or withdraw are conditioned by their passage through three stages analogous to those described by Van Gennep (1960) in his studies of the rites of passage employed by tribal groups to signal and support the movement of individuals and groups from one state or status to another. The stages describe the processes of *separation* as the individual leaves family, friends, and other past associations behind, *transition* as the individual seeks and adapts to new relationships with members of the new group, and *incorporation* as the individual develops new interaction patterns and establishes *competent membership* in the new group. Tinto's adaptation of Van Gennep to the college setting has drawn criticism from Tierney (1992, 1999, 2000) and others (see, for example, Rendon, Jalomo, & Nora, 2000) as a misinterpretation and misapplication of the social anthropological concept of rites of passage. Tierney (1999) challenges the adaptation for its "implicit suggestions that [students of color] must assimilate into the cultural mainstream and abandon their ethnic identities to succeed on predominantly White campuses" (p. 80).

CHAPTER THREE

Development of Verbal, Quantitative, and Subject Matter Competence

Consistent with the structure and organization of the first edition of *How College Affects Students,* this chapter reviews the evidence from the 1990s pertaining to the influence of college on the acquisition of subject matter knowledge and academic skills. (Chapter Four focuses on more general cognitive development and intellectual skills less directly, or specifically, tied to the academic program.) Our notion of subject matter knowledge and academic skills casts a wide net that reflects the often diverse ways in which the knowledge and skill outcomes of college have been assessed. Examples include, but are not limited to, the general and specific academic knowledge and skills assessed by standardized tests (such as the Graduate Record Examination, the College Basic Academic Subjects Examination, and specific subtests of the Collegiate Assessment of Academic Proficiency), measures of content learning in specific courses, level of verbal and mathematical competence, and individual self-reports of gains in general and specific dimensions of academic knowledge and skills.

Our review in this chapter synthesizes the findings of studies that employ these and related measures of knowledge and academic skills. We do not include cumulative grade point average, or college grades, in this rubric. To be sure, there is evidence to suggest that college grades in some disciplines have moderate correlations (in the .35 to .50 range) with standardized measures of achievement such as the Graduate Record Examination (Smith, 1992) and that grades remain a statistically significant predictor of GRE scores when controls are in effect for important confounding influences (Astin & Astin, 1993). Other research, however, suggests that the associations between college grades and standardized measures are so small that they call into question the validity of grades as an objective measure of learning (Bridgeman & Lewis, 1994). We acknowledge that in certain circumstances grades may well reflect learning. At the same time, it is also clear that grades are influenced by many factors essentially extraneous to how much one learns during college. These factors include the type and selectivity of the institution attended (Astin & Astin, 1993; Kuh & Hu, 1998), the student's major field of study or academic discipline (Barnes, Bull, Campbell, & Perry, 1998; Cheng & Chen, 1999; Ekstrom & Villegas, 1994; Kuh & Hu, 1998; Menec, Perry, & Hunter, 1996; Pollio, 1996; Thompson & Smart, 1998), situational constraints such as stress and workload (Hatcher, Prus, Englehard, & Farmer, 1991), faculty cognitive style (O'Brien & Thompson, 1994), faculty attitudes toward testing and grading (Cross, Frary, & Weber, 1993), and the specific type of course or coursework being taken (Kuh & Hu, 1998; Sabot & Wakeman-Linn, 1991). Because of these potential confounding influences, as well as others identified by Pascarella and Terenzini (1991), we concluded that it is extremely hazardous to make comparisons of student learning based on cumulative grades across different courses, different academic disciplines, or different institutions. Consequently, as in our predecessor volume, we treat student grades not as an outcome of college that stands for how much is learned but rather as an indicator of the extent to which a student successfully complies with the academic norms or requirements of the institution. Thus, grades are viewed as one among a number of dimensions of the college experience (both academic and nonacademic) where the student may demonstrate different levels of involvement, competence, or achievement. In subsequent chapters, we review the evidence pertaining to the influence of college grades on various dimensions of postcollege achievement.

CHANGE DURING COLLEGE

Conclusions from *How College Affects Students*

In our 1991 synthesis, we uncovered 17 studies conducted between 1934 and 1981 that estimated the extent to which students made gains during college on standardized tests of subject matter knowledge or academic skills. The findings were markedly consistent across five decades of research. Our best estimate of freshman-to-senior gains from this body of evidence was that they averaged approximately .56 of a standard deviation for general verbal skills, .24 of a standard deviation for general mathematical or quantitative skills, and .87 of a standard deviation for specific subject matter knowledge.[1] These numbers represented improvements over entering student competencies of approximately 21 percentile points, 9.5 percentile points, and 30.8 percentile points, respectively.

The second main conclusion was that the evidence was unclear as to when during the postsecondary experience these changes or gains in subject matter knowledge and academic skills are most likely to occur. Some evidence suggested that the greatest gains occurred during the first two years of college, while other evidence suggested that students continue to make important gains through their senior year.

Evidence from the 1990s

With a few exceptions, the literature of the 1990s paid relatively little attention to estimating the gains in subject matter knowledge or academic skills that occurred during college. The modest literature that does exist consists largely of cross-sectional studies (for example, comparing current freshmen with current seniors) using standardized instruments or student self-reports of gains made during college. Indeed, we uncovered only two longitudinal studies, both of which were conducted at single institutions. Thorndike and Andrieu-Parker (1992) gave the College Basic Academic Subjects Examination (CBASE) to a sample of 197 students in October of their first year of college and then tested them again with the same instrument 18 months later, in May of their second year of college. The CBASE is a standardized, criterion-referenced achievement test focusing on the degree to which students have mastered particular skills and competencies consistent with completion of general education coursework. It consists of four general subject areas, each of which has either two or three subareas (Osterlind & Merz, 1990): English (reading and literature, writing), mathematics (general mathematics proficiency, algebra, geometry), science (laboratory and fieldwork, understanding fundamental concepts), and social studies (history, social sciences). On average, students demonstrated gains in all four subject areas of about .25 of a standard deviation. This number converts to a 10 percentile point gain. In other words, if incoming students at the institution were functioning at the 50th percentile, after about two years of exposure to college they were functioning at the 60th percentile.

Underwood, Maes, Alstadt, and Boivin (1996) administered the College Outcome Measures Program (COMP) Objective Test to 41 students when they were beginning freshmen and then again when they were seniors. The COMP is a standardized test that assesses so-called liberal arts competencies, such as using science, using art, and solving problems. The freshman-to-senior growth on the COMP total score was 9.6 points. No standard deviations were reported, however, so we could not directly compute an effect size. Our readings of other studies that have used the COMP suggest that the typical standard deviation is in the neighborhood of 12 points. From this we indirectly inferred an increase on the COMP total score from the freshman to senior year of about .80 of a standard deviation, or 29 percentile points.

Although the Thorndike and Andrieu-Parker (1992) and the Underwood et al. (1996) studies have the advantage of being longitudinal (that is, following the same students over time), they are substantially limited in generalizability by their small, single-institution samples. Evidence with greater generalizability is reported in a cross-sectional study (students of different class standing measured at the same time) by Osterlind (1996, 1997). Osterlind administered the CBASE to nearly 75,000 students in 56 colleges and universities located in 13 different states. The institutions included research universities, regional universities, and liberal arts colleges. We employed the statistical information reported by Oster-lind to compute effect sizes estimating the CBASE advantages of seniors over freshmen. The assumption of such cross-sectional comparisons is that the senior-freshman comparison reflects the influence of college. On the English test seniors had an advantage over freshmen of .77 of a standard deviation (a 27.9 percentile point advantage), for mathematics the advantage was .55 of a standard deviation (20.9 percentile points), on the science test the advantage was .62 of a standard deviation (23.2 percentile points), and on the social studies test the advantage of seniors over freshmen was .73 of a standard deviation (26.7 percentile points).

Because it reports CBASE scores for each class level, the Osterlind (1996, 1997) study also permits one to estimate the pattern or timing of changes that occur during college. Using his reported class level means and the pooled standard deviations, we estimated the advantage of sophomores over freshmen on the four CBASE subject areas to be as follows: English, .66 of a standard deviation; mathematics, .72 of a standard deviation; science, .58 of a standard deviation; and social studies, .60 of a standard deviation. Thus, based on estimates from the CBASE data, it would appear that the majority of changes in subject matter knowledge or academic skills that take place during college occur during the first two years. Indeed, the estimated advantages of sophomores over freshmen on the CBASE English, science, and social studies tests were 86 percent, 94 percent, and 82 percent, respectively, of the corresponding advantages of seniors over freshmen on the same tests. On the mathematics test, the estimated advantage of sophomores over freshmen was actually about 1.3 times as large as the corresponding advantage of seniors over freshmen.

It may well be that the pattern or timing of estimated changes suggested by Osterlind's (1996, 1997) extensive data reflects in part the nature of the instrument employed. Recall that the CBASE is a standardized test designed to measure mastery of skills and competencies imparted in general education coursework. Because much of this coursework may be taken during the first two years of college, one might expect the majority of advances in CBASE subject areas to occur by the sophomore year. The fact that the growth in mathematics skills estimated during the first two years of college is larger by about a third than the corresponding difference between freshmen and seniors may also reflect the fact that most mathematics courses required as part of general education coursework are taken early during college. Subsequently, students who do not major in quantitative or scientific fields may actually regress somewhat in mathematics skills by their senior year (Flowers, Osterlind, Pascarella, & Pierson, 1999; Wolfle, 1983).

In addition to estimated changes or growth on standardized measures of subject matter knowledge, there is also a body of literature that documents student self-reports of gains in these areas. Not surprisingly, findings from this research are generally consistent with those reported from studies using objective, standardized instruments. Employing a variety of self-report instruments, the evidence is consistent in suggesting that the higher one's class standing (for example, seniors versus freshmen), the greater the gains one reports. Also, students attending college full-time and completing more credit hours report significantly greater gains than students attending part-time who complete fewer credit hours (Bauer, 1995; Conklin, 1990; Feldman, 1994a; Greer, Weston, & Alm, 1991; Knight, 1994; Kuh & Hu, 1999a; Lincoln, 1991; Pettit, 1992; Tan, 1995; Williams, 1996). Because of the nature of the self-report instruments used and because many studies do not report the requisite statistical information (that is, group standard deviations as well as group means), however, it is difficult to estimate effect sizes from this literature.

Although the evidence on gains in subject matter knowledge and academic skills appears much less extensive in the 1990s than it was in the literature we reviewed for *How College Affects Students,* we observed little that would change the general, and quite unsurprising, conclusion from our predecessor volume: students on average do, in fact, make statistically significant and, in some areas, substantial gains in subject matter knowledge and academic skills during college.

This conclusion, however, needs to be understood in the context of two additional, and important, lines of work conducted during the 1990s. The first of these is rather sobering. Barton and LaPointe (1995) report the results of a massive national study of literacy conducted by the Educational Testing Service. The sample of over 26,000 individuals was representative of American adults 16 years of age and older. Three types of literacy were considered—prose, document, and quantitative—with each type having five levels of competence, level 5 being the highest. Consistent with the evidence on gains reviewed in the preceding paragraphs, Barton and LaPointe found out that the *relative* level of all three types of literacy was strongly related to degree of exposure to postsecondary education. College graduates had higher levels of literacy than those with some college, who, in turn, had higher levels of literacy than those who had never attended college. In terms of *absolute* levels of literacy, however, the performance of college graduates ranged, in the words of Barton and LaPointe (1995, p. 2), "from a lot less than impressive to mediocre to near alarming, depending on who is making the judgment." For example, only 53 percent of college graduates performed at level 4 or 5 in prose literacy, where they could integrate and synthesize information from complex passages or make high-level inferences based on text. Similarly, only 47 percent of college graduates performed at level 4 or 5 in document literacy, where they were required to make high-level inferences from complex documents that contain distracting information. Finally, in quantitative literacy only 53 percent of college graduates were functioning at levels 4 or 5, where they could handle two or more arithmetic operations in a sequence or where they could perform multiple arithmetic operations.

The sobering conclusions of the Barton and LaPointe (1995) study are significant in their own right. However, their study is also important because it moves beyond simply documenting how much change occurs during college to estimating the functioning of college graduates (as well as those with less exposure to postsecondary education) against absolute criteria of performance. As such, it suggests an important direction for future inquiry. Knowing the specifics of how well college graduates can function in an absolute sense on salient dimensions of subject matter competence and academic skills may be equally, if not more, important than knowing how much they change or grow during college.

The second line of work leads to a somewhat more optimistic conclusion. Semb and Ellis (1994) synthesized the results of nearly 100 individual studies of knowledge retention (long-term memory) of subject matter content commonly taught to adult or near-adult populations. Their synthesis attempted to estimate the average relative percentage of loss of the content originally learned in terms of three types of tasks: recognition, recall, and cognitive skills (for example, concept identification, prediction, explanation, comprehension). Across all studies the mean percent loss scores were 16.17 percent for recognition, 28.25 percent for recall, and 13.32 percent for cognitive skills. In short, students can apparently retain much of the knowledge taught in classrooms. Perhaps even more significant, it was found that increasing the level of original learning increases later retention performance (Semb & Ellis, 1992; Semb, Ellis, & Araujo, 1993). In subsequent sections of this chapter and in the following chapter on cognitive skills and intellectual growth, we will review evidence concerning the effectiveness of different instructional approaches in enhancing student learning.

NET EFFECTS OF COLLEGE

It is one thing to conclude that increases in subject matter knowledge and academic skills occur *during college.* It is quite another to conclude that these increases occur *because of college.* Problems inherent to both the longitudinal and cross-sectional designs of the studies reviewed in the previous section make it risky to assume that the amount students change during college or the average advantage of seniors over freshmen reflects the unique or net impact of college. For example, in longitudinal studies that follow the same individuals over time, the difference between scores in the first and fourth years of college might at least partially reflect the fact that students are growing older. The natural process of maturation could lead to a certain amount of increased knowledge and skill acquisition between the first and fourth years of college that is independent of the effects of college. This growth might occur through such mechanisms as work, travel, or personal reading, quite apart from one's normal course of study. To the extent that gains between the first and fourth years of college capture normal maturation as well as the influence of college itself, they may spuriously overestimate the latter.

Threats to the internal validity of longitudinal studies are discussed in considerable detail in the technical appendix and pages 66 and 67 of *How College Affects Students.* (By internal validity we mean the extent to which gains in learning can be attributed to the impact of college and not other influences.) Suffice it to say that, in the absence of a comparison group of similar individuals who have less or perhaps even no exposure to college, it is extremely difficult to determine how much of the documented freshman-to-senior gain is due to the impact of college and how much is due to other influences.

In cross-sectional studies (for example, those comparing test scores of separate samples of freshmen and seniors at the same time), differential institutional recruiting standards for successive comparison classes and the natural attrition of less capable students from freshman to senior year might yield a markedly more selective population of seniors than the population of freshmen with whom they are compared. Consequently, the differences observed between freshmen and seniors could simply be the result of comparing samples from populations differing in ability or motivation rather than reflecting the influence of college.

Studies that attempt to determine whether differences in subject matter knowledge and skill acquisition are attributable to differences in exposure to postsecondary education (that is, the net effect of college) are by necessity more complex in scope and design than investigations that simply document change during college or the advantage of seniors over freshmen. Typically, they involve comparing groups with different levels of exposure to postsecondary education and the use of various statistical procedures (for example, multiple regression, analysis of covariance) to control or adjust for the influence of salient confounding variables such as academic ability or motivation.

Conclusions from *How College Affects Students*

In our 1991 synthesis, we found relatively little research that focused on the net effects of college on subject matter knowledge and skills. The research we did uncover was concerned largely with verbal and quantitative skills. For verbal skills, the estimated net effect of graduating from college compared with not attending college was between .26 and .32 of a standard deviation. This estimation converts to an advantage of between 10.3 and 12.6 percentile points. For mathematical skills, the estimated net effect of college was between .29 and .32 of a standard deviation, which converts to an advantage of between 11.4 and 12.6 percentile points. The instruments used to assess verbal skills and mathematical knowledge in this body of research were far from comprehensive. Consequently, they probably did not fully capture the impact of college.

Evidence from the 1990s

As in our 1991 synthesis, we did not uncover a large body of research that estimated the net effects of college on subject matter knowledge and academic skills. Indeed, we uncovered only two studies that focused primarily on this issue: Flowers, Osterlind, Pascarella, and Pierson (1999) and Myerson, Rank, Raines, and Schnitzler (1998). Flowers, Osterlind, Pascarella, and Pierson (1999) reanalyzed a subset of Osterlind's (1996, 1997) extensive sample of students who took the College Basic Academic Subjects Examination (CBASE). Their sample consisted of between 18,500 and 20,500 students at 56 four-year colleges and universities located in 16 different states. They weighted the sample to make it more representative and introduced statistical controls for student precollege academic ability (composite verbal and quantitative ACT score or the

SAT equivalent), race, sex, college grades, cumulative credits taken in postsecondary education, and the average ACT score of the sample of students at the institution attended. With statistical adjustments made for these control variables, they reported senior advantages over freshmen on the four CBASE subject areas as follows: English = .59 of a standard deviation, or 22 percentile points; mathematics = .32 of a standard deviation, or 13 percentile points; science = .47 of a standard deviation, or 18 percentile points; and social studies = .46 of a standard deviation, or 18 percentile points. The addition of age as a control variable had only a trivial influence on these estimates.

The results of the Flowers, Osterlind, Pascarella, and Pierson (1999) analyses lead to two additional observations. First, their estimates of the net effects of college (that is, the senior-freshman comparisons adjusted for the set of confounding variables) are markedly smaller than the unadjusted senior-freshman differences reported by Osterlind (1996, 1997). Using our estimates of effect sizes from Osterlind, it would appear that the introduction of statistical controls by Flowers et al. reduced the senior advantage over freshmen by about 23 percent on the English test, about 42 percent on the mathematics test, 24 percent on the science test, and about 37 percent on the social studies test. This finding is not particularly surprising given the potentially higher rates of attrition of the least academically able students during college. The senior advantage over freshmen on CBASE competencies estimated from the Osterlind (1996, 1997) investigation likely reflects in part the uncontrolled or unadjusted differences between freshmen and seniors in academic ability.

A second observation concerns the consistency of findings from the Flowers, Osterlind, Pascarella, and Pierson (1999) investigation and our 1991 conclusions from *How College Affects Students.* Recall that in our previous synthesis we concluded that college had a net positive impact on quantitative skills of between .29 and .32 of a standard deviation. This reported advantage is remarkably similar to the net senior advantage over freshmen of .32 of a standard deviation on the CBASE mathematics test reported by Flowers et al. Our 1991 conclusion concerning verbal skills was that college had a positive net impact of between .26 and .32 of a standard deviation. This advantage is somewhat smaller than the senior advantage over freshmen on the CBASE English test of .59 of a standard deviation reported in the Flowers et al. investigation. This inconsistency may be explainable in large part by the instruments used. The studies we reviewed for our 1991 synthesis focused primarily on vocabulary development, whereas the CBASE English test covers a much more wide-ranging set of skills, such as literature comprehension and evaluation, and writing skills. As such, the latter is more likely to capture the comprehensive impact of a postsecondary program of study than instruments that simply measure vocabulary development.

Myerson, Rank, Raines, and Schnitzler (1998) analyzed data from a cohort of the nationally representative National Longitudinal Study of Youth to estimate the net impact of exposure to postsecondary education on the Armed Forces Qualification Test (AFQT). The AFQT score represents a composite of scores on verbal and quantitative tests consisting of word knowledge, paragraph completion, arithmetic reasoning, and mathematics knowledge. Using a creative cross-sectional design, they controlled for selective attrition by conducting analyses only on those who ultimately completed a bachelor's degree but had no postgraduate work and who had completed either 12, 13, 14, 15, or 16 years of formal schooling at the time they took the AFQT in 1980. In addition to controlling for selective attrition through their design, Myerson et al. also introduced statistical controls for race, age, and socioeconomic status. With these controls in place, they found that years of postsecondary education completed had a statistically significant, positive effect on AFQT scores. The statistical detail they report makes it difficult to determine the size of the effect. However, using the graphs and the sample characteristics they present, we estimate for their entire sample that having a bachelor's degree (that is, 16 years of education) produced an advantage compared with 12 years of education of about .25 of a standard deviation (about 10 percentile points). Although it should be noted that this number is a less precise effect-size estimate than others reported in this section, it deviates only slightly from our conclusions about the net effects of college on verbal and quantitative skills in *How College Affects Students.* (Recall that we estimated the impact on verbal skills to be between .26 and .32 of a standard deviation and the impact on quantitative skills to be between .29 and .32 of a standard deviation.) Since the AFQT consists largely of tests measuring verbal and quantitative competencies, the similarities are perhaps not too surprising.

Although not nearly as comprehensive in scope or as focused on estimating the net effects of college as the Flowers, Osterlind, Pascarella, and Pierson (1999) or the Myerson, Rank, Raines, and Schnitzler (1998) investigations, there are nevertheless several additional studies with findings that bear on the influence of college on the acquisition of subject matter knowledge and skills. Hagedorn, Siadat, Nora, and Pascarella (1997) analyzed data from the National Study of Student Learning (NSSL) to determine the factors leading to gains in mathematics during the first year of college. NSSL was a longitudinal study focusing on the factors influencing learning and cognitive development in college. It traced the growth of students from 23 two- and four-year colleges located in 16 states through their third year of postsecondary education. The study dependent variable was change during the first year of college on a 35-item mathematics test from the Collegiate Assessment of Academic Proficiency (CAAP). The CAAP mathematics test measured students' ability to solve mathematical problems typical to college curricula while emphasizing quantitative reasoning over formula memorization. With statistical controls in place for such factors as gender, race, study involvement, extracurricular involvement, work responsibilities, and type of math courses taken, number of enrolled credit hours had a significant positive effect on gains in all analyses conducted. On average, students enrolled for between 21 and 24 semester hours had about a .30 of a standard deviation (11.8 percentile points) advantage in first-year mathematics gains over students enrolled for six or fewer hours.

Another investigation analyzing data from the National Study of Student Learning sought to determine the institutional factors and college experiences that influenced reading comprehension through the third year of college for African-American students (Flowers & Pascarella, 1999a). The dependent measure was the CAAP reading comprehension test, a 36-item standardized test that assesses reading comprehension as a product of skill in inferring, reasoning, and generalizing. With statistical controls for level of precollege reading comprehension, academic motivation, socioeconomic status, age, the average cognitive ability of students at the institution attended, study and work involvement, and the pattern of coursework taken, number of credit hours completed had a significant positive effect on third-year reading comprehension. After three years of postsecondary education, African-American students who had completed between 60 and 72 credit hours had a reading comprehension advantage of about .45 of a standard deviation (17.4 percentile points) over students who had completed less than 20 credit hours.

In addition to studies employing standardized measures such as the CBASE or the CAAP, a number of investigations have estimated the net impact of college on subject matter knowledge and skills using student self-reports (Knight, 1994; Knox, Lindsay, & Kolb, 1992; Williams, 1996). Consistent with findings from those studies using objective, standardized measures, the results of these investigations clearly suggest that students with greater exposure to postsecondary education report learning more or experiencing greater gains in science and technology, general education, and the arts and humanities than those with less exposure. These statistically significant advantages favoring those individuals with more exposure to college persist in the presence of statistical controls for such factors as age, gender, race, family and job responsibilities, socioeconomic status, major, campus involvement, and academic ability. Because of the nature of the instruments employed and the statistical data reported, however, estimating effect sizes for these studies is problematic.

We uncovered only one study (Flowers, Osterlind, Pascarella, & Pierson, 1999) that permitted estimation of the timing of the net effects of college on subject matter knowledge and skills. In addition to reporting the CBASE advantages of seniors over freshmen (that is, the estimate of the overall effect of college), these authors reported the corresponding net advantages of sophomores over freshmen. (In both analyses, statistical controls were made for individual precollege academic ability, race, sex, college grades, postsecondary credits taken, and the average ACT score of the students at the institution attended.) Their findings suggest that in mathematics and science, virtually all of the net effects of college take place by the sophomore year. In English, approximately 75 percent of the net effect of college and in social studies about 85 percent of the net effect of college was evident by the sophomore year. It is worth reiterating that this pattern may reflect the fact that the instrument used in the study (the College Basic Academic Subjects Examination) is designed to assess academic competencies imparted in general education coursework—much of which is typically designed to be taken in the first two years of college. Instruments not so focused on measuring the effects of general education might have yielded a different pattern of effects.

BETWEEN-COLLEGE EFFECTS

In estimating the net effects of college attendance on learning in general, the problem was one of distinguishing the unique impact of differential exposure to postsecondary education from differences in the characteristics or traits of individuals that might influence the learning outcomes being assessed. Students who attend college full-time, for example, may have substantially different levels of academic ability, secondary school preparation, and academic motivation than those with less or no exposure to postsecondary education. In trying to estimate between-college effects, one is confronted with an analogous methodological problem—namely, how does one identify the unique or net influence of attending different kinds of postsecondary institutions given the fact that different kinds of institutions recruit and enroll substantially different kinds of students (Astin, 1991; Astin & Astin, 1993; Pascarella & Terenzini, 1991)? Because students who attend college are not distributed randomly across different postsecondary institutions, it is likely that the achievement, as well as the other outcomes associated with different types of postsecondary institutions, is confounded by differences in the motivations, academic aptitudes, secondary school experiences, and aspirations of the students they enroll. Sometimes the shorthand for this ubiquitous and irksome methodological problem is separating the socialization effect from the recruitment effect (Pascarella & Terenzini, 1991). We will confront this socialization versus recruitment issue, albeit in different forms, repeatedly throughout the book.

Attempts to separate the socialization effects of different institutions from the effects of the differences in background characteristics among the students they recruit and enroll usually entail the use of reasonably complex statistical controls (for example, regression analysis, path analysis, analysis of covariance). Although there are a number of variations, the typical study we reviewed used some form of regression analysis to estimate the extent to which institutional characteristics or environments affected learning outcomes above and beyond the influence of individual student characteristics. (For a more detailed presentation and discussion of these methods see Ethington, 1997; Pascarella & Terenzini, 1991, Appendix).

The study of between-college effects has been complicated by a major student demographic trend that has grown more pronounced over the last quarter of a century but that has become particularly identifiable in the literature of the last 10 years. Both Adelman (1994, 1998a, 1998b) and McCormick (1997b) provide substantial evidence from nationally representative data sets, such as the National Longitudinal Study of the High School Class of 1972 (NLS-72), High School and Beyond (HS&B), and the Beginning Postsecondary Survey (BPS), indicating that, as a group, American undergraduates have become highly mobile consumers of postsecondary education. For example, during the period 1972 to 1984, 38.8 percent of individuals in the NLS-72 sample who started at a four-year college eventually attended two or more undergraduate institutions. Although it is not always clear just how much of one's undergraduate experience is spent at more than one institution, the corresponding population parameter estimates for the 1982 to 1993 period from the HS&B sample and for the 1989 to 1994 period from the BPS sample are 52.3 percent and 50.1 percent, respectively (Adelman, 1998a).

Given such a national rate of multi-institutional attendance, one might reasonably question both the interpretability and generalizability of studies that estimate institutional effects on such outcomes as learning and cognitive growth (as well as other outcomes such as values, attitudes, psychosocial development, or moral development). How does one estimate institutional effects when the effects are both multiple and, quite likely, take place over varying lengths of time? Not surprisingly, we uncovered no investigation that even attempts this extremely complex and daunting task. Rather, the body of evidence on between-college effects gets around this issue essentially by ignoring it in one of two usual ways. The first is composed of studies that estimate institutional effects over a comparatively short period, such as the first year of college. The second involves studies that follow students for an extended period of time but confine their analyses to the subsample who attend only one postsecondary institution. When properly conducted, such investigations can provide important insights into the nature and magnitude of institutional effects on students. Indeed, given the penchant for nationally visible periodicals to use institutional resources and "selectivity" as proxies for the quality of the education one supposedly receives, insights based on rigorously collected and analyzed data are a valuable counterbalance. Nevertheless, it is important to underscore that the findings of the majority of between-college studies may not necessarily generalize to the substantial numbers of American students who attend more than one undergraduate institution.

Conclusions from *How College Affects Students*

Our 1991 synthesis found little consistent evidence indicating that measures of institutional quality or environmental characteristics had more than small, and generally trivial, net influences on how much a student learns during college. When student precollege traits were controlled statistically, only three variables had statistically significant, positive associations with standardized measures of achievement across at least two independent samples: frequency of student-faculty interaction, degree of curricular flexibility, and faculty members' formal educational level. It is important, however, to underscore that the magnitude of these associations was quite small and perhaps of questionable practical importance. Given the persistent conventional wisdom of major differences in educational quality among American postsecondary institutions (Ewell, 1989; Gilmore, 1990; Grunig, 1997; Lewis & Kingston, 1989; Schmitz, 1993), we conceded that the weight of evidence was counterintuitive. However, we also underscored the distinct possibility, consistent with the evidence, that with differences in the academic capabilities of student bodies taken into account, four-year institutions with substantial differences in their stock of human, financial, and educational resources may have essentially similar impacts on how much students learn as undergraduates. We also suggested the possibility of a diminishing return relationship between institutional resources (for example, library size) and learning that may at least explain why increases in level of resources beyond a certain threshold level are not similarly matched by a proportional increase in measured student learning.

Evidence from the 1990s

Compared with our previous synthesis, we uncovered a substantial body of evidence focusing on between-college effects on the development of verbal, quantitative, and subject matter competence. This evidence falls generally into three categories: institutional characteristics, institutional type, and institutional environment.

Institutional Characteristics. Of all the institutional characteristics that one might study in relation to between-college effects, the one considered most consistently in the studies we reviewed was institutional student body selectivity. This characteristic was most often defined operationally as the average scores of entering students, or in some cases the entire undergraduate student body, on standardized tests such as the SAT, the ACT, or their equivalent. There are at least two reasons why institutional selectivity is such a prominent variable in research on between-college effects. First, as compared with measures of the institutional environment, which can at times be somewhat subjective and contain abstract concepts, institutional selectivity is a relatively easy-to-obtain, straightforward, low-inference measure. It can be communicated by a single number (for example, an average SAT of 1200 or an average ACT of 26.5) that is both reasonably recognizable and understandable by large numbers of people. Second, and certainly not unrelated, is the fact that institutional selectivity is often used as a proxy for institutional "quality," both by scholars who study the impact of college (Brewer, Eide, & Ehrenberg, 1996; Dale & Krueger, 1999; Daniel, Black, & Smith, 1996b; Hagedorn et al., 1999; Hilmer, 1997; Katchadourian & Boli, 1994; Lillard & Gerner, 1999; Rumberger & Thomas, 1993) and by the more general public (consider college rankings in such outlets as *U.S. News & World Report*). It is almost as if it were axiomatic that if the college you attend is difficult to get into you must be getting a better education there.

We uncovered 10 studies based on three independent samples that investigated the impact of college selectivity on various standardized measures of academic achievement. Consistent with our 1991 synthesis, the weight of evidence from these studies provides little support for the premise that attendance at a selective institution has a consistent and substantial positive influence on how much one learns—at least as measured by standardized tests. One series of important studies analyzed longitudinal data from the 1985 cohort of the Cooperative Institutional Research Program (CIRP). This sample of students in slightly more than 200 four-year institutions was followed up in 1989 with analyses focusing on individuals who took various standardized tests typically used in the admissions process for graduate or professional school, such as the verbal and quantitative portions of the Graduate Record Examination, the Medical College Admissions Test, the Law School Admissions Test, and the National Teachers Examination (Anaya, 1992, 1996, 1999a, 1999b, 1999c, 2001; Astin & Astin, 1993; Opp, 1991). Although the specified prediction equations differ across studies, the general approach taken in the various analyses was first to control statistically for important student precollege variables (for example, SAT-ACT scores, high school achievement, aspirations, family background) and college experiences (major, interactions with faculty and peers, measures of academic and social engagement, and so on). With these controls in place, estimates were then made of the net influence of different institutional characteristics on the various standardized tests. Institutional selectivity (that is, the average SAT-ACT score of entering students) had trivial and statistically nonsignificant effects on the quantitative score of the Graduate Record Exam, the Medical College Admissions Test, the Law School Admissions Test, and all three subscores of the National Teachers Examination (communication, general knowledge, and professional knowledge).[2] Anaya (1999b) found a very small positive effect of institutional selectivity on GRE verbal scores. However, in an earlier series of analyses using the same data but a more extensive set of controls, the effect of institutional selectivity on GRE verbal scores was nonsignificant (Anaya, 1996).

It is important to note that standardized tests, such as the Graduate Record Examination, are taken by a relatively small percentage of students while they are actually in college. For example, extrapolating from the description of Astin's (1993c) national Cooperative Institutional Research Program sample, we estimate that roughly 20 to 25 percent of all students in four-year colleges actually took the GRE while in college between 1985 and 1989. Thus, estimates of the impact of institutional selectivity taken from the 1985 to 1989 CIRP data may have limited generalizability to the entire population of college students. However, other investigations, based on independent samples, report evidence that is quite consistent with that yielded by the extensive analyses of the 1985 to 1989 CIRP sample. In their cross-sectional analyses of the College Basic Academic Subjects Examination, described in the previous section of this chapter on the net effects of college, Flowers, Osterlind, Pascarella, and Pierson (1999) sought to determine if the net difference on CBASE tests between freshmen and seniors differed in magnitude at institutions differing in student body selectively (estimated by the average ACT score of the student body at the 56 institutions in the sample). With controls in place for such factors as individual ACT scores, college grades, race, and gender, institutional selectivity had a trivial and statistically nonsignificant impact on freshman-senior differences across all four tests (English, mathematics, science, and social studies). Similarly, analyzing longitudinal data from 23 two- and four-year colleges, Edison, Doyle, and Pascarella (1998) and Whitt, Pascarella, Pierson, Elkins, and Marth (in press) found that institutional selectivity (operationally defined as the average reading comprehension, mathematics, and critical thinking levels of entering students) had no statistically significant general effects across gender (that is, for both men and women) on standardized measures of writing skills or science reasoning at the end of the second year of college or on reading comprehension at the end of the third year of college.

Evidence from studies using self-reports of student learning is generally consistent with evidence from studies employing standardized tests.[3] Knox, Lindsay, and Kolb (1992) analyzed data from the National Longitudinal Study of the High School Class of 1972. With controls in effect for such factors as academic ability, race, gender, major, and place of residence, institutional selectivity was essentially unrelated to how much respondents reported having learned during college. Consistent findings are reported by Astin (1993a) and Toutkoushian and Smart (2001) in the prediction of student self-reports of gains along dimensions such as general knowledge, knowledge of a field or discipline, problem solving, and writing skills. Similarly, Kuh and Hu (1999b) found that student body selectivity among 33 research universities was essentially unrelated to the size of gains seniors reported they made during college in 23 areas of learning and personal development. Hayek and Kuh (1998) did find that seniors from selective liberal arts colleges reported making greater gains on a measure of "capacity for lifelong learning" (consisting of academic skills, thinking skills, and functioning in groups) than did seniors from doctoral-granting universities, comprehensive colleges, and less selective liberal arts colleges. However, the only control in effect in their analyses was student socioeconomic status. Given the absence of more salient controls for the background characteristics of the students reporting the extent of gains during college, it is problematic to interpret this finding as being the result of the impact of selective liberal arts colleges. It may simply be that such colleges recruit and enroll students who are more open to the impacts of postsecondary education to begin with. Similar students attending other institutions in Hayek and Kuh's sample might report learning gains of essentially the same magnitude.

Understanding just why selectivity tells us so little about an institution's net impact on how much students learn is a complicated issue. Probably the most useful research in this regard is provided in a creative study of course examination rigor at 40 research universities differing in undergraduate student body selectivity (Braxton, 1993; Nordvall & Braxton, 1996). A sample of 115 final examinations from the institutions were categorized by the percentage of questions asked in four areas, reflecting ascending levels of complexity and sophistication: knowledge (simple recall or recognition of course content), comprehension (ability to grasp meaning of course content so that one can explain or summarize course material), application (ability to apply course content to new or real situations), and critical thinking (ability to analyze, synthesize, and evaluate). Controlling for course level, the discipline in which the course was offered, whether or not it was intended for major, and class size, institutional selectivity did have a small negative association with the percentage of knowledge-level questions asked. This finding is seemingly consistent with Astin's (1993b) finding that institutional selectivity is negatively associated with the use of multiple-choice questions on tests. More importantly, however, selectivity had no significant relationship with the percentage of examination questions asked at the higher-order levels of comprehension, application, or critical thinking levels. This finding suggests that more selective research universities tend not to give any more rigorous examinations than less selective ones. To the extent that rigor in course examinations reflects similar rigor in the instruction received (an association that cannot be determined from the study), it may be that undergraduate selectivity alone is simply not a particularly effective way of identifying universities that have demanding academic programs.

To be sure, there is other work on the relationship between institutional characteristics and student learning in the literature of the 1990s. For example, net of student background characteristics and other influences, institutional size was found to have small, but statistically significant, positive effects on Graduate Record Examination quantitative scores as well as on National Teachers Examination communications skills and professional knowledge scores (Astin & Astin, 1993; Opp, 1991). Similarly, the percent of undergraduate students who are Asian had statistically significant, positive net effects on both the verbal and quantitative scores of the GRE (Anaya, 1996). Finally, and perhaps not surprisingly, Astin's (1993c) analyses found that, even when controls are made for SAT scores and other important variables, there is some evidence that different standardized test scores are influenced by the dominance of certain academic majors in an institution. For example, GRE verbal scores were positively influenced by the percentage of history or political science majors, whereas scores on the Law School Admissions Test were positively influenced by the percentage of majors in the social sciences. Unfortunately, all of these findings are based on a single sample—the 1985 to 1989 CIRP data discussed previously. We found little in the way of attempts by other scholars to verify the robustness of the findings through replication on independent samples.

Institutional Type. A small body of literature attempts to estimate the net influence of attendance at different types of institutions on students' acquisition of subject matter knowledge and academic skills. The majority of this research focuses on comparisons of two-year community colleges with four-year institutions, historically Black colleges with predominantly White colleges, women's institutions with coeducational institutions, and on comparisons among institutions differing in classifications that might include several dimensions such as public universities, private four-year colleges, comprehensive universities, and so on.

A series of studies analyzing data from the National Study of Student Learning (NSSL) sought to estimate the comparative effects of attending two-year versus four-year institutions. In the initial study, Bohr et al. (1994) compared samples of students from a single two-year college and a large research university, both located in the same urban area, on first-year gains in standardized measures of reading comprehension and mathematics. With controls for pre-college scores on the two standardized tests, residence, age, work responsibilities, and full- or part-time enrollment, first-year gains made by two-year college students were essentially the same in magnitude as gains made by four-year college students. Employing a similar analytic model, this finding was replicated in an independent sample of students from five two-year and six four-year institutions located in eight different states (Pascarella, Bohr, Nora, & Terenzini, 1995a). When this second sample was followed through the second year of postsecondary education and with controls made for such factors as precollege academic ability, age, race, and full- versus part-time enrollment, there were only trivial and statistically nonsignificant differences between two- and four-year college students on standardized measures of writing skills and science reasoning. This parity persisted no matter whether the comparison group was the 6 four-year colleges used in the Pascarella et al. (1995a) study or a more varied and academically selective group of 18 four-year institutions (Pascarella, Edison, Nora, Hagedorn, & Terenzini, 1995–96). Though not using standardized measures of learning, other investigations comparing the academic performance of two- and four-year college students, or the quality of instruction they receive, report findings that are consistent with those yielded by the National Study of Student Learning (Banta & Associates, 1993; Conklin, 1990; Montondon & Eikner, 1997). Thus, the small body of evidence we reviewed suggests that two-year colleges, which enroll nearly 40 percent of all students in postsecondary education nationally, may be fostering learning along such basic dimensions as reading comprehension, mathematics, writing skills, and scientific reasoning with about the same level of proficiency as a substantial segment of four-year institutions (Pascarella, 1999).

Another small, but important, body of research in the 1990s focused on the extent to which college racial composition influences the acquisition of subject matter competence and academic skills of African-American students. There are about 100 historically Black colleges (HBCs) and universities in the United States (Roebuck & Murty, 1993), which educate about 27 percent of all African-American college students (Higgins, Cook, Ekeler, Sawyer, & Prichard, 1993; Nettles, Perna, & Freeman, 1999). Although these institutions have been an important source of the country's African-American leaders and professionals, it is clear that, compared with predominantly White institutions (PWIs), HBCs as a group function at a distinct disadvantage in terms of financial and educational resources (Gladieux & Swail, 1999; "Vital Signs," 1996). Despite this resource disadvantage, the evidence we reviewed suggests that HBCs may be at least as proficient as PWIs, if not more so, in fostering the learning of African-American students.

A series of analyses of the National Study of Student Learning (NSSL) database followed a sample of African-American students attending two HBCs (one public and one private) and 16 public and private PWIs for three years (Bohr, Pascarella, Nora, & Terenzini, 1995; Flowers & Pascarella, 1999a; Pascarella, Edison, Hagedorn, Nora, & Terenzini, 1996). With controls in place for such factors as precollege academic ability, sex, academic motivation, age, socioeconomic status, and the average academic ability of the entering students at each institution, differences between African-American students at HBCs and PWIs on standardized measures of end-of-first-year reading comprehension and mathematics and end-of-second-year science reasoning were trivial in magnitude and statistically nonsignificant. But on standardized measures of end-of-second-year writing skills and end-of-third-year reading comprehension, African-American students at HBCs had a statistically significant advantage over their counterparts at PWIs of about .33 of a standard deviation (13 percentile points). Similar results have been reported when student learning is measured by student self-reports rather than objective, standardized tests. African-American students at HBCs typically report learning gains that are equal to (Kim, 2002b; Watson & Kuh, 1996) or greater in magnitude than (DeSousa & Kuh, 1996; Flowers & Pascarella, 1999a) their counterparts attending PWIs.

It is not entirely clear how historically Black colleges are able to provide educational experiences that compensate for their relative lack of educational resources. However, some clues are available. A fairly extensive body of literature suggests that HBCs provide a social-psychological climate that is more conducive to the academic adjustment and comfort of African-American students than do PWIs. (For a brief review of these studies, see Bohr et al., 1995.) Consistent with this, DeSousa and Kuh (1996) found that African-American students attending HBCs had a distinct advantage (about .70 of a standard deviation) over their counterparts attending PWIs in a scale measuring their level of effort and involvement in such academic activities as writing experiences, course learning, interaction with faculty, library use, science learning, and interactions with peers based on course content. Such differences in academic effort and involvement may at least partially explain why comparative outcomes between HBCs and PWIs on various measures of student learning do not reflect differences in educational resources.

Although women's institutions educate only a very small percentage (about 2 percent) of women in American postsecondary education (Ricci, 1994), they have been the focus of considerable scholarly attention. This attention is likely due to the fact that graduates of these institutions are remarkably overrepresented in professional achievement and leadership positions (Astin & Leland, 1991; Tidball, Smith, Tidball, & Wolf-Wendel, 1999). (We will review this literature in greater detail in a subsequent chapter on career and economic returns to college.) Compared with the literature linking attendance at women's institutions with career achievement, there is only a very small body of evidence on the net impact of women's institutions on student learning in college. The evidence is mixed but overall does not support the notion that single-sex institutions foster women's acquisition of subject matter competence or academic skills any more proficiently than coeducational institutions. For example, analyzing the 1985 to 1989 CIRP data, Anaya (1992, 1996) found that when controls were in effect for such factors as SAT scores, sex, secondary school grades, and whether a student majored in engineering or the physical sciences, attending a women's institution had a small but statistically significant negative impact on GRE quantitative scores and essentially no impact on GRE verbal scores. Similarly, analyzing the same data and with essentially the same analytical approach, Astin (1993c) found that attendance at a women's institution had a small negative influence on Medical College Admissions Test scores. Findings reported by Smith, Wolf, and Morrison (1995), based on the 1986 to 1990 CIRP data, are somewhat at odds with those reported by Anaya and Astin. However, this incongruence may be attributable in large measure to the fact that their dependent variable, a scale termed "learning goals and outcomes," was a composite of self-reported items that tapped women's gains in preparation for graduate school and academic self-confidence as well as gains in general and specific knowledge. Net of such factors as SAT scores, high school grades, and socioeconomic status, attendance at a women's institution had essentially no direct influence on "learning goals and outcomes" but did have a small, positive indirect effect, mediated primarily through increased academic involvement.

Finally, there is a small body of research that attempts to estimate the net effects of institutional classifications, such as public university, private four-year college, and the like, on student acquisition of subject matter competence and academic skills. The findings from this research are confusing and, at times, seem contradictory. For example, Anaya (1999b) found that, even when controls were made for such factors as SAT scores and academic major, attending a public four-year college negatively influenced GRE verbal scores, whereas attending a private four-year college negatively influenced GRE quantitative scores. Conversely, employing a similar analytic model with a subsample of the same data, Anaya (1999c) found that attending either a public or private university had positive effects on Medical College Admissions Test scores. Similarly equivocal findings are reported in studies using various student self-reports of how much they learned during college. Kuh and Hu (1999b) found that students at private research universities report greater gains than their counterparts at public research universities, but when Knox, Lindsay, and Kolb (1992) introduced controls for such factors as student academic ability and major field of study, the effect of attending a private institution became small and statistically nonsignificant. Smart (1996, 1997) found that attendance at a research or doctoral-granting university, a comprehensive college or university, or a liberal arts college was unrelated to self-reports of learning gains when controls were made for precollege dispositions to enter different fields of study.[4] The most recent and comprehensive study by Pike, Kuh, and Gonyea (2003) found no meaningful link between students' self-reported learning gains and the type of institution attended based on the Carnegie classification.

That such broad classifications tell us little that is consistent or definitive about institutional effects on student learning should not come as too great a surprise. Classifications such as public research university, comprehensive college or university, or private liberal arts college are so general that each might include institutions differing substantially on other characteristics that have more immediate and important implications for how much students learn. Put differently, there may be so much within-classification variability among institutions that it washes out between-classification influences.

Institutional Environment. Although institutional characteristics such as student body selectivity and size, and institutional classifications such as two-year college or historically Black college, are relatively straightforward indicators of institutional traits requiring little inference, the same cannot always be said of measures of the institutional environment. In the research we reviewed, the nature of institutional environments is often inferred from aggregate student (or faculty) responses on items, either about themselves or about their experiences at the institution that cluster into internally consistent (that is, reliable) scales. Scholars then attempt to name the scale in a way that accurately reflects or signifies the underlying construct being measured by the cluster of items. Thus, for example, Arnold, Kuh, Vesper, and Schuh (1991) used student perceptions of the nature of their interactions with peers, faculty, administrators, and professional staff at their institutions to form an environmental measure that they termed supportive personal relationships. Similarly, Astin (1993c) used a cluster of items measuring faculty goals for themselves and undergraduates that he termed faculty commitment to the student's personal development/altruism.

This method is certainly a very legitimate, and often creative, means for assessing different dimensions of the environmental emphasis of an institution. However, one is often presented with a nontrivial challenge when attempting to synthesize the results of different investigations that measure institutional environments in this way. Whereas low-inference characteristics such as student academic selectivity or size are relatively objective and interpretable across studies, different scholars often measure institutional environments in substantially different ways or from a very different perspective. This difference means that obtaining comparable findings of environmental effects across different investigations is frequently problematic. Consequently, in an attempt to make some sense of the different findings, we have chosen to group them into the following general categories or general environmental emphases: scholarship and learning; relationships among students, faculty, and professional staff; vocational-professional training; and racial-gender equity.

The most extensive and useful work on the impact of institutional environments on academic learning has been conducted by Astin (1993c, 1996a) and by Kuh and his colleagues (Arnold et al., 1991; Arnold, Kuh, Vesper, & Schuh, 1993; Kuh, Arnold, & Vesper, 1990, 1991; Kuh, Pace, & Vesper, 1997; Kuh & Vesper, 1992; Watson & Kuh, 1996). Although the estimated environmental effects they report appear to be generally quite small, both report consistent, and perhaps not surprising, evidence to suggest that the acquisition of subject matter knowledge and academic skills is enhanced by institutional environments that emphasize scholarship and learning. For example, in analyses of several different independent samples, a scale measuring the strength of an institution's emphasis on scholarly, intellectual, and aesthetic matters had statistically significant, positive relationships with students' self-reported gains in areas such as general education, understanding science and technology, and understanding the arts, literature, and humanities (Arnold et al., 1993; Davis & Murrell, 1993; Kuh et al., 1997; Kuh, Schuh et al., 1991; Kuh & Vesper, 1992). These relationships persisted even with controls in different studies for confounding influences such as academic preparation, educational aspirations, socioeconomic status, race, work responsibilities, and other dimensions of the institutional environment. Corroborating evidence is reported by Whitt et al. (in press). With controls for student ability, institutional selectivity, and measures of academic effort and involvement, they found that the same scale used by Kuh and his colleagues had statistically significant positive effects on an objective, standardized measure of writing skills. Astin (1993c) takes a somewhat different approach in that he looks at environmental characteristics from a faculty as well as a student perspective. Nevertheless, the results he reports are also consistent with those of Kuh and colleagues. Controlling for student academic ability and a battery of other confounding influences, Astin found that the average scholarly orientation of an institution's faculty had statistically significant, positive effects on scores on the Law School Admissions Test and on both the verbal and quantitative scores of the Graduate Record Examination.

There is also a body of evidence to suggest that the nature of an institution's social or relational environment has implications for student learning. This evidence, however, is not totally consistent, and the direction of the findings appears to depend on whether one measures learning with student self-reports or objective, standardized measures. In a series of studies carried out primarily by Kuh and his colleagues, an environmental measure was employed that taps the extent to which students regard their relationships with peers, faculty, and administrators at their institution as friendly, approachable, and helpful (Kuh et al., 1997). (The negative end is competitive, remote, and rigid.) Across the different studies conducted, this scale has usually had statistically significant, positive effects on students' self-reports of gains in such areas as general education skills and understanding the arts, literature, and humanities. Moreover, these effects persisted even in the presence of controls for confounding influences such as students' academic preparation, socioeconomic status, work responsibilities, and other dimensions of the institutional environment (Arnold et al., 1993; Davis & Murrell, 1993; Kuh et al., 1997; Kuh, Schuh, et al., 1991; Watson & Kuh, 1996). Using somewhat different measures of the social-relational environment of the institution, similar results are reported by Glover (1996) for two-year colleges and Graham (1997, 1998) for both two- and four-year colleges.

Related investigations by Kuh, Arnold, and Vesper (1990) and Hayek and Kuh (1998) have disaggregated this overall measure of an institution's social environment and report that it is the extent to which peers and student groups are seen as friendly and supportive and to which faculty are seen as approachable, helpful, and encouraging that have the most important positive implications for how much students report learning during college. Using a different approach to the measurement of institutional environments, Astin (1993c) reports generally similar findings in his analyses of the 1985 to 1989 CIRP data. With controls for important student precollege traits and other potentially confounding influences, a scale termed "student orientation of faculty," which measured the extent to which an institution's faculty were accessible to students and concerned with them as individuals, had a statistically significant, positive impact on students' self-reported growth in writing skills. More generally, the student orientation of the institution, as indicated by the percentage of the institutional budget spent on student services, also positively influenced self-reported writing skill gains.

Although they are perhaps not directly comparable, somewhat different results are obtained when the acquisition of subject matter competence and academic skills is assessed with objective, standardized measures rather than student self-reports. For example, Astin (1993c) found that faculty perceptions of the extent to which an institution's environment was characterized by competition among students had net positive impacts on both Graduate Record Examination quantitative scores and scores on the Medical College Admissions Test. Similarly, the percentage of an institution's budget spent on student services, which positively influenced self-reported writing gains, had a negative impact on the general knowledge score of the National Teachers Examination.

A third body of evidence has focused on whether an institution's environmental emphasis on vocational preparation influences the acquisition of subject matter knowledge or academic skills. Nearly all of the research in this area has employed a two-item scale, developed by Kuh and colleagues, that taps students' perceptions of the practical value of the coursework at their institution and the extent to which their institution emphasizes the development of vocational and occupational competence (Kuh et al., 1990). There is replicated evidence on different samples to suggest that an institution's practical-vocational emphasis, as measured by this scale, has statistically significant positive effects on students' self-reported gains in understanding science and technology. This effect persists even in the presence of controls for institutional type, individual student academic and social involvement, and measures of the scholarly and social environment of the institution (Arnold et al., 1991, 1993; Kuh et al., 1990; Kuh, Arnold, & Vesper, 1991; Watson & Kuh, 1996). There is less consistent evidence to suggest that an institution's practical-vocational emphasis has a net influence on more general education gains, such as students' self-reported growth in understanding literature and the arts or in writing skills. Some investigations suggest that it does (Hayek & Kuh, 1999), some suggest that it does not (Arnold et al., 1993; Davis & Murrell, 1993; Watson & Kuh, 1996), and still others suggest that the effects are positive in some institutional types and negative in others (Kuh et al., 1997).

When the criterion is objective standardized tests rather than student self-reports, there is little evidence to suggest that the practical-vocational emphasis of an institution has consistent net effects on student learning. Using the scale developed by Kuh et al. (1990), and controlling for student academic ability, measures of student academic and social involvement during college, and other measures of the institutional environment, Whitt et al. (in press) found that the practical-vocational emphasis of a community college environment had a statistically significant, positive effect on reading comprehension. However, this effect did not hold for four-year colleges, and the same environmental dimension had only trivial, nonsignificant impacts on other learning outcomes such as mathematics, writing skills, or science reasoning.

Finally, there is a body of literature arguing that an institutional environment that is relatively free of racial or gender bias may foster the learning of students of color and women (Gallos, 1995; Hayes & Flannery, 1997; Kraft, 1991; Sandler, Silverberg, & Hall, 1996). There is some evidence to support this contention, although in the case of gender equity the evidence is complicated by how one defines the institutional environment. Analyzing data from the National Study of Student Learning, Cabrera, Nora, Terenzini, Pascarella, and Hagedorn (1999) sought to determine if a measure of perceived racial discrimination inhibited the self-reported learning gains of both Caucasian and African-American students. The measure of discrimination in the institutional environment was based on students' perceptions of such things as witnessing discriminating gestures or words directed at minorities or witnessing acts of racism or prejudice. With statistical controls in place for such factors as secondary school and college grades, parental encouragement, and measures of the social and academic experience of college, the level of prejudice or discrimination in the institutional environment had a statistically significant and negative total impact on the self-reported gains of African-American students in quantitative skills, analytical thinking, and understanding the fine arts. About two-thirds of the effect was indirect, mediated through the negative influence of prejudice-discrimination on the quality of African-American students' academic and social experiences. The environmental prejudice-discrimination scale had little or no impact on the self-reported learning gains of Caucasian students.

Similar findings are reported by Hagedorn, Siadat, Nora, and Pascarella (1997) using essentially the same sample and measure of environmental prejudice-discrimination as Cabrera et al. (1999) but with gains on an objective measure of mathematics skills as the dependent variable. With controls for such factors as full- or part-time enrollment, quality of teaching received, study habits, work responsibilities, and social involvement, environmental prejudice-discrimination negatively influenced gains in mathematics skills made by students of color. In contrast to Cabrera et al., however, Hagedorn, Siadat, Nora, and Pascarella also found environmental prejudice-discrimination negatively influenced the gains in mathematics skills made by Caucasian students.

Both the Cabrera et al. (1999) and Hagedorn, Siadat, Nora, and Pascarella (1997) investigations were conducted on the same sample, and we failed to uncover research based on an independent sample that directly replicates their findings.[5] However, Astin's (1993c) extensive analyses on the 1985 to 1989 CIRP data provide evidence that is not inconsistent with their findings. With controls for student academic ability and a large number of other potentially confounding influences, Astin found that the diversity emphasis of an institution had a significant, positive effect on the quantitative score of the Graduate Record Examination.

A number of scholars have posited that American coeducational postsecondary institutions often create a "chilly climate" for women that can be detrimental to their intellectual and personal development (Allen & Niss, 1990; Boyer, 1987; Hall & Sandler, 1982, 1984; Holland & Eisenhart, 1990; Sandler et al., 1996). Although the presence of such a chilly climate has been challenged by observational studies of classroom behaviors (Brady & Eisler, 1996; Cornelius, Gray, & Constantinople, 1990; Fassinger, 1995; Williams, 1990), other researchers have attempted to determine if women's perceptions of gender inequity in an institution's environment inhibit their learning (Hagedorn, Siadat, Nora, & Pascarella, 1997; Pascarella et al., 1997; Whitt, Edison, Pascarella, Nora, & Terenzini, 1999b). This latter body of research is based on analyses of a single sample (the National Study of Student Learning), and gender inequity (or the chilly climate) is assessed by a scale measuring women's perceptions of the extent to which they have experienced such things as being singled out in class for their gender, being treated differently by faculty because they are women, or observing prejudice against women by other students at the institution.

The findings from this research are mixed. When the institutional environment is assessed from the level of individual women's perceptions of gender inequity, the weight of evidence supports the contention that gender inequity has a negative impact on how much women learn during college. Controlling for such factors as precollege academic ability, the type of coursework taken, and other measures of academic and social involvement, the gender inequity or chilly climate scale had statistically significant, negative impacts on a standardized measure of learning consisting of reading, mathematics, and critical thinking for two-year college women (Pascarella et al., 1997); gains on a standardized measure of mathematics skills for women at both two- and four-year colleges (Hagedorn, Siadat, Nora, & Pascarella, 1997); and self-reported gains in writing and thinking skills, understanding science, and understanding the arts and humanities for women at both two- and four-year colleges (Whitt et al., 1999b). The only exception to this was a small, positive influence of institutional gender inequity on reading comprehension for women at four-year colleges (Whitt et al., 1999b).

When environmental gender equity was assessed at the aggregate institutional level, however, the nature of the findings was markedly different. Whitt et al. (in press) redefined the gender inequity environment as the average responses on the gender inequity–chilly climate scale by the sample of women at each institution. Subsequently, this aggregate measure of institutional-level gender inequity was found to have positive associations with women's gains on a standardized measure of mathematics skills. This positive association persisted even in the presence of statistical controls for factors such as a student's precollege academic ability, extensive measures of a student's academic and social effort and involvement, and other measures of the aggregate institutional environment.

A Final Thought on Between-College Effects. If there is one thing that characterizes the research on between-college effects on the acquisition of subject matter knowledge and academic skills it is that in the most internally valid studies, even the statistically significant effects tend to be quite small and often trivial in magnitude. (For excellent examples of studies that estimate the size of between-college effects relative to other influences, see Angoff & Johnson, 1990; Ethington, 1998; Kuh & Hu, 1999a.) There may, of course, be some methodological and measurement reasons for this phenomenon (see, for example, Pascarella & Terenzini, 1991, pp. 80–83). However, perhaps the most useful explanation from a substantive standpoint is one argued cogently by Baird (1988, 1991) and Pace (1997) and supported empirically in creative studies by Smart and his colleagues (Smart, 1997; Smart & Feldman, 1998). Specifically, we find few major between-college influences because aggregation of characteristics or environmental stimuli at the institutional level provides indexes that are simply too remote from the actual social and intellectual forces that shape individual learning in college. Though it likely varies by institutional size and mission, the majority of colleges and universities in the American postsecondary system have important subenvironments with more immediate and powerful impacts on individual students. Because of these subenvironments we should probably anticipate a greater diversity of impacts within than between institutions. We turn to a synthesis of the impact of some of these subenvironments in the next section on within-college effects.

WITHIN-COLLEGE EFFECTS

Conclusions from *How College Affects Students*

In our 1991 synthesis, we came to the following general conclusions:

1. Although it is likely that students learn the most during college in the subject matter specific to their major, we found little methodologically sound evidence to indicate that academic major had a differential influence on the acquisition of subject matter knowledge or academic skills outside the major.

2. What is learned during college is differentially influenced by the pattern of courses taken, even when student ability is controlled. This research is in its nascent stages, however, and we cannot yet determine if replicable patterns of differential coursework effects on learning exist across institutions.

3. There is little consistent evidence to suggest that factual subject matter content is mastered any more efficiently in small, discussion-oriented classrooms than in large, lecture-oriented classrooms. However, the evidence does suggest that the former may be preferable when the goal of instruction is affective or higher-order cognitive skills.

4. Considerable evidence exists to suggest that certain individualized instructional approaches or systems emphasizing small, modularized

units of content, mastery of one unit before moving to the next, timely and frequent feedback to students on their progress, and active student involvement in the process of learning are consistently effective in improving subject matter learning over more traditional instructional formats such as lecture and recitation. Of the five individualized instructional approaches reviewed, four of them (audio-tutorial, computer-based, programmed, and visual-based instruction) showed statistically significant modest learning advantages over traditional approaches of from 6 to 10 percentile points. The typical advantage attributable to the personalized system of instruction (PSI, or the Keller Plan) was 19 percentile points.

5. Given the nature of the evidence, it is probably an overstatement to say that we know what causes effective teaching. However, we do know what effective teachers do and how they behave in the classroom. Student subject matter learning appears to be enhanced when teachers: (1) structure and organize class time well, (2) are clear in their explanation of concepts, (3) have a good command of the subject matter and are enthusiastic in its presentation, (4) present unambiguous learning stimuli to students (for example, using examples and analogies to identify key points, signal a topic transition clearly), (5) avoid vague terms and language mazes, and (6) have good rapport with students in class (are open to student opinions and encourage class discussion and the like) and are accessible to students outside of class. Perhaps the most important finding in research on teacher behaviors that are associated with student learning is that some behaviors may themselves be learnable (for example, structuring and organizing class time efficiently, teacher clarity).

6. Not all subject matter learning in college is simply a function of what the institution does to the student in instructional settings. Rather, much depends on the quality of the student's effort in making use of the range of learning opportunities provided by the institution. Instructional strategies such as tutoring and studying material for the purpose of teaching it to someone else appear to enhance student involvement or effort in learning, thereby enhancing subject matter mastery. Coursework, however, may not be the only arena where student involvement or effort is associated with increased learning. Though not as methodologically sound as that from instructional experiments, there is nevertheless a considerable body of correlational evidence to suggest that how much a student perceives himself or herself as having learned in college is a function of his or her effort in the social as well as the academic system of the institution. Such effort seems to be independently and positively influenced by living on campus (versus commuting to college) and by attending a small institution.

Evidence from the 1990s

Evidence in the 1990s pertaining to within-college effects on the acquisition of verbal, quantitative, and subject matter competence is both extensive and varied. Indeed, we uncovered literally hundreds of relevant studies and scores more that were marginally relevant. In order to make sense of this voluminous literature, we have grouped the studies into the following eight general topics or clusters: academic major, coursework patterns, class size, general pedagogical approaches, focused classroom instructional techniques, teacher behaviors, academic effort-involvement, and social and extracurricular effort-involvement. Within these general clusters, we have limited our review to specific areas of inquiry where there is a reasonable body of evidence upon which to base conclusions. Thus, we have tended to exclude evidence based on the findings of single studies that lack replication or, at least, the attempt at replication.

Academic Major. We found little in the research from the 1990s that is at odds with the conclusions from our previous synthesis concerning the impact of academic major. Net of precollege ability and other potential confounding influences, undergraduates tended to make the greatest gains in subject matter areas consistent with their major area of study. This finding was particularly true of majors that place a premium on quantitative competencies. For example, analyzing the 1985 to 1989 CIRP data, Astin (1993c) and Anaya (1992, 1996) found that majoring in physical science, engineering, and technical fields had small positive effects on GRE quantitative scores. Similar findings for the physical and biological sciences are reported by Angoff and Johnson (1990) with an independent sample of over 20,000 students who took both the SAT and the GRE. The evidence is less clear-cut for the acquisition of verbal skills. Astin (1993c) found that majoring in the social sciences positively influenced GRE verbal scores, but this was not replicated by Anaya (1992, 1996) working with the same data or by Angoff and Johnson (1990) analyzing an independent sample. Similarly, Lehman and Nisbett (1990) found that gains in verbal reasoning during college were essentially unrelated to whether a student majored in the natural sciences, humanities, social sciences, or psychology.

The evidence with respect to the impact of major on professionally related knowledge is at best mixed and, therefore, less than convincing. Analyzing the same data, Astin (1993c) and Opp (1991) report somewhat different findings with respect to the net impact of majoring in education on National Teachers Examination scores. Controlling for academic ability and other confounding influences, Astin found that majoring in education negatively influenced the general knowledge score on the NTE but positively influenced the NTE professional knowledge score. Opp, however, reported that majoring in education (versus another major) neither facilitated nor inhibited scores on any of the NTE area tests. We suspect that this difference in findings from the same sample reflects differences between the two studies in the confounding influences taken into account.

There is also evidence to suggest that academic major may have little consistent net impact on scores on the Medical College Admissions Test. Net of confounding influences Astin (1993c) found that no specific major enhanced scores on the MCAT, although scores were negatively influenced by majoring in the allied health fields. Anaya's (1999a) analyses suggest that, with the possible exception of a very small, positive influence of majoring in the physical sciences, undergraduate major field of study is essentially unrelated to MCAT scores. Consistent with the conclusion that academic major has little or no impact on MCAT scores is a body of recent research suggesting that performance in medical school—as measured by such criteria as clinical science grades, scores on the National Board of Medical Examiners Examination, or U.S. Medical Licensing Examination scores—is largely unrelated to undergraduate major when undergraduate grades and other confounding influences are taken into account (Hall & Stocks, 1995; Smith, 1998; Sorenson & Jackson, 1997).[6]

Coursework Patterns.[7] It seems logical, perhaps even axiomatic, that what students learn in college is related to the coursework they take as undergraduates (Jones & Ratcliff, 1990, 1991; Pike, 1992a; Ratcliff, Jones, Guthrie, & Oehler, 1991; Ratcliff & Yaeger, 1994). Not surprisingly, there is a substantial body of knowledge to support this contention, even when student academic ability is controlled. However, beyond the unsurprising conclusion that students tend to acquire the most knowledge and the highest level of academic skills in areas where they take the most courses, it has been difficult to uncover consistent patterns of effects across institutions. This difficulty in itself is not particularly surprising because even courses with the same name or topic may differ substantially across institutions in both the content covered and the level at which they are taught.

The most focused research in this area has been conducted by Ratcliff and colleagues (Jones & Ratcliff, 1991; Ratcliff, 1993; Ratcliff & Jones, 1993; Ratcliff & Yaeger, 1994). This body of research has most often used the Graduate Record Examination as the dependent variable and has generally attempted to control for student precollege academic ability, usually in the form of SAT or ACT scores. The method is empirically driven and essentially consists of calculating residual GRE scores—that is, the difference between one's actual GRE score and the GRE score one is predicted to get based on precollege academic ability scores. Subsequently, student transcripts are examined, and the courses reported on them are clustered into patterns based on the residual scores of the students who enrolled. In this way, clusters of courses associated with the greatest net learning (that is, the largest positive residual scores) can be identified (Ratcliff & Jones, 1993). This "Coursework Cluster Analysis Model" (Ratcliff, 1993) has been applied at a number of different institutions, and it would appear that there are two basic generalizations from the findings: students who took different patterns of coursework learned different things and developed different academic skills, at least as measured by different item types on the Graduate Record Examination; and the structure of general education or a core curriculum in institutions did not produce important impacts on learning as measured by the GRE. For example, quantitative skills were linked to upper-division coursework in economics, music, physical therapy, and business as well as general mathematics courses. Because the coursework cluster analytic model is empirically rather than theoretically driven, however, the findings concerning general education may have an alternative explanation. The linking of nonquantitative courses with high mathematics residuals may be correlational rather than causal. Students who develop strong quantitative abilities in general education courses may simply be more likely to subsequently enroll in specific nonquantitative courses.

It is also quite possible that the Graduate Record Examination is not the most content-valid instrument for assessing the impact of a general education curriculum. Indeed, analyses of data from a national sample and a single institution sample of seniors who took the College Basic Academic Subjects Examination— a test specifically designed to measure the outcomes of general education— found that whether or not students took general education courses in physical sciences–engineering, business-accounting-economics-statistics, or liberal arts significantly predicted their scores on the four CBASE subtests (English, mathematics, science, and social studies), even in the presence of controls for precollege academic ability (Pike, 1992b). In a more focused single-institution study, Olsen (1991) reported similar results for the impact of general education science-oriented coursework on sophomores' scores on the science reasoning module of the Collegiate Assessment of Academic Proficiency. Unfortunately, a somewhat counterintuitive finding reported by Knight (1993a, 1993b) increases ambiguity about the effects of general education coursework. Using the College Outcome Measures Project (COMP) Objective Test (another measure of general education skills) as the dependent measure, Knight found just the reverse of what might be anticipated. With institutional type and entering academic ability taken into account, students attending institutions where less than 40 percent of undergraduate curricular requirements were devoted to general education and where there was not equal distribution of courses within the general education requirement had significantly higher gains on the COMP than students at institutions where 40 percent or more of the undergraduate curriculum was devoted to general education and where there was equal distribution of courses within the general education requirement. This finding seems more consistent with those of Ratcliff (1993) than with those of either Pike or Olsen.

Although it is often not the primary focus of inquiry, evidence pertaining to the impact of coursework on the acquisition of subject matter competence and academic skills is reported in a substantial number of additional studies. These topics include the following: historical knowledge (Grossweiler & Slevin, 1995), mathematics skills (Gray & Taylor, 1989), reading comprehension (Bohr, 1994–95), writing skills (Edison et al., 1998), verbal and quantitative scores on the Graduate Record Examination (Anaya, 1992, 1996; Astin, 1993c; Hurtado, 1990), general academic knowledge and skills (Pike, 1991b), the Medical College Admissions Test (Anaya, 1999c; Astin, 1993c), the Law School Admissions Test (Astin, 1993c), and the National Teachers Examination (Astin, 1993c).

Nearly all of the studies introduce controls for precollege academic ability (SAT-ACT scores) and, in some cases, other important confounding influences such as race, gender, academic motivation, and full- or part-time enrollment. Although there are one or two unexpected findings and exceptions (Pike, 1991b), the weight of evidence from this body of studies is quite clear in suggesting that scores on each of the outcome instruments are significantly, if modestly, improved by taking undergraduate courses that emphasize content or the acquisition of skills consistent with what the instrument measures. Put differently, other things being equal, undergraduates learn and become skilled in what they study. Thus, history knowledge is improved by the number of history courses taken; mathematics and quantitative skills by the number of mathematics and science courses taken; reading comprehension and verbal ability by the number of literature, English, foreign-language, and writing skills courses (and somewhat surprisingly, by the number of science courses taken); writing skills by the number of courses taken in the arts and humanities; Medical College Admissions Test scores by the number of science courses taken; and scores on the Law School Admissions Test and the National Teachers Examination by the number of interdisciplinary courses taken.[8, 9]

Class Size. The literature we reviewed from the decade of the 1990s suggests that we may need to revise, at least to a certain extent, our 1991 conclusion that subject matter knowledge is acquired with equal proficiency in both large and small classes. We uncovered 10 studies that focus on the effects of class size on course learning. All of the investigations are quasi-experimental or correlational in design, and with some variation across studies, each attempts to control for important confounding influences such as academic ability or prior achievement, instructor experience, amount of homework, and the like. Unfortunately, five of the studies used course grade as the measure of learning, one study used both course grade and a common final examination, and four studies (all in the field of economics) employed an objective standardized measure—the Test for Understanding of College Economics (TUCE).

The weight of evidence from the body of research using course grade as the dependent measure is reasonably clear in suggesting that, other factors being equal, increasing class size has a statistically significant, negative influence on subject matter learning. This finding held in five of the six studies that used course grade as a measure of learning (Biner, Welsh, Barone, Summers, & Dean, 1997; Keil & Partell, 1998; Raimondo, Esposito, & Gershenberg, 1990; Scheck, Kinicki, & Webster, 1994; Thompson, 1991). The sixth study (Goldfinch, 1996) found no difference in course grades between students in small classes and students in large classes, but the former had significantly higher scores than the latter on a common final examination.

In the four studies of economics classes using the same standardized measure of economics knowledge (TUCE) as the dependent variable, the weight of evidence is less clear. This lack of clarity may be attributable to the use of different samples from the same data or different operational definitions of class size. In the most extensive of the three investigations, Zietz and Cochran (1997) analyzed data from 189 separate economics courses taught at 53 separate institutions. The institutions included community colleges, liberal arts colleges, comprehensive universities, and doctoral granting institutions. With controls for such factors as institutional control and type, precourse TUCE score, cumulative college grades, gender, interest in economics, course meetings per week, amount of homework, and instructor experience and professional preparation, Zietz and Cochran found that increasing class size beyond 30 students negatively influenced individual student scores on the postcourse administration of the TUCE. However, a study of a subsample of the same data, but using classes rather than individuals as the unit of analysis, failed to find that class size negatively influenced achievement on the TUCE (Kennedy & Siegfried, 1997). Similarly, a third study of 12 economics sections at a single institution (Lopus & Maxwell, 1995) found that class size had a statistically nonsignificant impact on course achievement when controls were in effect for a battery of potential confounding influences, including precourse TUCE scores, college grades, and course instructor characteristics. Most recently, Becker and Powers (2001) suggest that when a statistical adjustment is made for sample attrition, initial class size has a negative influence on pre- to postcourse gains on the TUCE. However, they caution that their results are only suggestive and tentative. The conflicting evidence and continuing methodological problems surrounding this small body of research make it difficult to form a firm conclusion.

Taken as a body of research it would appear that, when learning is measured by course grade, class size may have a negative influence. However, when learning is assessed by a standardized measure, the evidence is not as compelling that class size has a negative influence, at least in the field of economics.

General Pedagogical Approaches. In this section, we attempt to synthesize a vast literature on the learning impacts of general or broad-based pedagogical-instructional approaches. The following approaches are discussed: learning for mastery, computer and information technology, distance learning, active learning, collaborative learning, cooperative learning, small-group learning, supplemental instruction, constructivist-oriented approaches (for example, constructivist teaching, problem-based learning), and learning communities. Because of the literally hundreds of studies that have been conducted on these general instructional approaches we cannot review each investigation in detail. Rather, we will attempt to provide an overall assessment of what the weight of evidence suggests, citing as many relevant studies as we can. In some areas we benefit from the results of research syntheses that have already been conducted.

Learning for mastery. In our 1991 synthesis, we reviewed the accumulated evidence pertaining to the effects on the acquisition of subject matter knowledge of the personalized system of instruction (PSI, or the Keller Plan). In addition to concluding that PSI resulted in an average course content achievement advantage (over conventional methods) of about 19 percentile points, we also concluded that the instructional feature accounting for the majority of PSI's impact was the requirement that students demonstrate mastery of one unit of course content before moving on to the next. Mastery learning is not the exclusive domain of the personalized system of instruction, however. There is also a body of evidence on an instructional procedure termed "learning for mastery" (LFM), or group-based mastery learning (Bloom, 1968; Guskey, 1985), that we overlooked in our 1991 synthesis. Like PSI, learning for mastery requires students to demonstrate mastery of course content against an absolute criterion. However, as explicated by Guskey and Pigott (1988), it differs from PSI in that PSI requires students to pace themselves through self-instructional materials while the instructor provides support and individual assistance only when needed. In contrast, the mastery learning model relies primarily on a group-based and instructor-paced approach to instruction. As such, mastery learning is generally more conveniently adapted to classroom situations where a single teacher has charge of 25 or more students and both instructional time and the curriculum are relatively fixed. In a mastery learning class, the teacher determines the pace of the original instruction and directs accompanying feedback and corrective procedures (Guskey & Pigott, 1988). Students who fail unit quizzes in learning for mastery courses usually receive individual or group tutorial help on the unit before moving on to the new material or before being allowed to take the course final examination (Kulik, Kulik, & Bangert-Drowns, 1990). (Excellent, detailed discussions of the implementation of learning for mastery are provided by Bloom, 1968; Guskey, 1985; Guskey & Pigott, 1988; Kulik et al., 1990.)

We uncovered two meta-analyses of learning for mastery at the postsecondary level. Guskey and Pigott (1988) synthesized the results of 12 college-level studies, while Kulik, Kulik, and Bangert-Drowns (1990) based their conclusions on a synthesis of 19 studies conducted with college samples. Our best estimate is that there is about a 60 to 65 percent overlap in the two groups of studies considered. Both meta-analyses considered only experimental or quasi-experimental studies, and the subject areas were algebra, history, education, biology, reading, psychology, and English. Guskey and Pigott found that group-based mastery learning approaches had an average course achievement advantage over conventional (nonmastery) approaches of .41 of a standard deviation (16 percentile points), whereas Kulik, Kulik, and Bangert-Drowns report a corresponding achievement advantage of .68 of a standard deviation (25 percentile points). It would also appear, in comparison to nonmastery approaches, that students in mastery-taught classes spend more class time on task or engaged in learning and that instructors in mastery-taught classes use class time more efficiently (Guskey & Pigott, 1988), both of which may account for its impact on knowledge acquisition.

Interestingly, there is not a great deal of evidence to suggest that group-based mastery learning is any less effective than mastery learning in the PSI self-paced model. For example, Kulik, Kulik, and Bangert-Drowns (1990) report an achievement advantage based on 67 college-level PSI studies of .48 of a standard deviation compared with .68 for group-based mastery learning studies. Moreover, Semb, Ellis, and Araujo (1993) present experimental evidence suggesting parity between introductory psychology students taught by PSI or group-based mastery approaches, not only in end-of-course achievement but also in course content retained 4 and 11 months after the end of the course.

Computers and information technology. It appears to be widely accepted that computers and related information technologies have the potential to transform fundamentally the nature of teaching and learning in postsecondary education (for example, Green, 1996; Kozma & Johnston, 1991; Kuh & Vesper, 1999; Upcraft, Terenzini, & Kruger, 1999; West, 1996). The promise is, indeed, substantial. "Used appropriately and in concert with powerful pedagogical approaches, technology is supposed to enhance student learning productivity. It does this by enriching synchronous classroom activities and providing students with engaging self-paced and asynchronous learning opportunities that enable students to learn more than they would otherwise at costs ultimately equal to or below that of traditional classroom based instruction" (Kuh & Vesper, 1999, p. 1).

Not surprisingly, during the decade of the 1990s there was an extensive body of inquiry on the use of computers and related technologies to assist or augment postsecondary instruction. We found little in this literature that would lead us to alter our 1991 conclusion that computer-assisted instruction is linked to modest increases in course-level achievement. In the early 1990s, a number of scholars produced either narrative or quantitative (meta-analytic) research reviews suggesting that computer-based instruction leads to modest improvements in subject matter acquisition with a decrease in instructional time (Cartright, 1993; Cohen & Daganay, 1992; Kulik & Kulik, 1991; Leonard, 1990; Liao & Bright, 1991; McComb, 1994; Teich, 1991; Weller, 1997).

The most comprehensive of these research syntheses is the meta-analysis of Kulik and Kulik (1991). They synthesized the results of 149 experimental and quasi-experimental studies conducted from 1984 to 1991 with postsecondary samples. The course content was in mathematics, science, social science, reading and language, and vocational training. Of these studies, 91 were classified as computer-assisted instruction (CAI), where the computer provides (a) drill-and-practice exercises but not new material or (b) tutorial instruction that includes new material; 17 of the studies were classified as computer-managed instruction (CMI), where the computer evaluates student test performance, then guides students to appropriate instructional resources and keeps records of student progress; and 35 of the studies were classified as computer-enriched instruction (CEI), where the computer (a) serves as a problem-solving tool, (b) generates data at the student's request to illustrate relationships in models of social or physical reality, or (c) executes programs developed by the student. In all three categories, computer-based instruction (versus traditional instructional approaches such as lecture, discussion, and text) produced average improvements in tested understanding of course content that were statistically significant. The average effect sizes were as follows: CAI: .27 of a standard deviation (11 percentile points), CMI: .43 of a standard deviation (17 percentile points), and CEI: .34 of a standard deviation (13 percentile points). Overall, only chance differences in effect sizes were found for studies based on true experiments and those based on quasi experiments. Weighting the effect sizes by the number of studies in each category, we computed an effect size across all three types of computer-based instruction of .31 of a standard deviation (12 percentile points).

Of the 149 postsecondary studies reviewed by Kulik and Kulik (1991), 32 also compared the instructional time for students in computer-based and traditional classes. The ratio of instructional time for computer-based students to instructional time for students in traditional classes averaged .70 across all comparisons. In other words, students in computer-based classes required about two-thirds as much instructional time as their counterparts in traditionally taught classes.

Since the publication of Kulik and Kulik's (1991) meta-analysis, the impact of computer-based instruction on learning has continued to be the focus of substantial inquiry. Most of this research employs true experimental or quasi-experimental designs in which various forms of computer-based instruction are compared with traditional or conventional instructional approaches such as lecture, discussion, or text. The weight of evidence from this more recent body of research is quite consistent in suggesting that, compared with similar students taught by traditional instructional methods, the knowledge acquisition of students in computer-based courses is either significantly better (Agarwal & Day, 1998; Alavi, 1994; Askar & Koksal, 1993; Connolly, Eisenberg, Hunt, & Wiseman, 1991; Faryniarz & Lockwood, 1992; Gregor & Cuskelly, 1994; Huang & Aloi, 1991; Lowe & Bickel, 1993; Marttunen, 1997; Mose & Maney, 1993; Reisman, 1993; Riding & Chambers, 1992; Vitale & Romance, 1992; Williamson & Abraham, 1995) or not significantly different (Adams, Kandt, Thronmartin, & Waldrop, 1991; Billings & Cobb, 1992; Carlsen & Andre, 1992; Guy & Frisby, 1992; Marrison & Frick, 1993; Murphy & Davidson, 1991; Smeaton & Keogh, 1999; Taraban & Rynearson, 1998; Tjaden & Martin, 1995; White, 1999). There was only isolated evidence in which students taught by traditional methods significantly outperformed students receiving computer-based instruction (Watkins, 1998). We computed an effect size for all of the studies in this recent body of literature that provided the requisite statistical information. The average effect size favoring computer-based instruction was .28 of a standard deviation (11 percentile points). There appeared to be little or no difference in the mean effect sizes of studies using true experiments or quasi experiments. Though admittedly this is a rougher estimate, it is nevertheless quite consistent with the overall effect size of .31 of a standard deviation that we derived from Kulik and Kulik's (1991) comprehensive meta-analysis. Also consistent with Kulik and Kulik's conclusions was evidence suggesting that students in computer-based classes require less instructional time than their counterparts in traditionally taught classes (Leonard, 1992; Taraban & Rynearson, 1998; Tjaden & Martin, 1995).[10]

Although our synthesis found extensive work focusing on computer use in individual courses, we uncovered only two studies of the impact of computer use during college on student learning. Possibly because they use different measures of computer use, different institutional samples, and different measures of student learning, the results of the two studies are only partially consistent.

Kuh and Vesper (1999) analyzed data from over 125,000 students at 205 four-year institutions. With controls for such factors as college grades, age, gender, work responsibilities, parental education, and educational aspirations, a measure of the extent to which students felt they gained a familiarity with computers was significantly and positively associated with self-reported gains in such areas as writing clearly, problem solving, and self-directed learning.

Flowers, Pascarella, and Pierson (1999) considered the impact of both e-mail and different types of computer use on objective, standardized measures of end-of-first-year reading comprehension and mathematics. Their sample was drawn from the 5 two-year and 18 four-year institutions participating in the National Study of Student Learning. With controls in place for such factors as precollege reading and mathematics achievement, academic motivation, patterns of coursework taken, the academic selectivity of the institution attended, and the quality of instruction received, they found differences in the impact of computer use between the two- and four-year samples. Electronic mail use had no significant impact on either reading comprehension or mathematics for the four-year sample but had statistically significant, if modest, negative impacts on both outcomes in the two-year sample. Consistent with the literature on computer-based classroom instruction, the use of computers for class assignments had a net positive impact on reading comprehension for two-year college students. The corresponding effect for four-year college students, however, was trivial and statistically nonsignificant. Engaging in computer word processing had a small but statistically significant, positive impact on reading comprehension for the four-year sample that persisted even when additional controls were introduced for students' first-year writing experiences.

Interestingly, the extensive body of research indicating consistent, albeit modest, positive impacts of computer-based instructional approaches on student learning appears to have initiated an ongoing and vigorously contested debate in the educational technology field. Clark (1991, 1994) has argued that the results of such research and of research syntheses such as those by Kulik and Kulik (1991) are questionable because the medium of instruction does not influence learning—the quality of teaching and instruction does. The essence of his argument appears to be that studies comparing the relative advantage for student learning of one instructional medium (for example, computers) over another (for example, lecture) will inevitably confound the instructional medium with the quality or type of instruction received. Consequently, all the supposed learning benefits attributed to computer-based instruction could just as easily be explained by the specific instructional methods they support or augment (Ehrmann, 1995; Weller, 1996).

On the other, or at least different, side of this debate, Kozma (1991, 1994a, 1994b) and Reiser (1994) have argued that the specific ways computers or instructional technology are employed are not irrelevant to instruction or student learning. Indeed, certain technological attributes make certain kinds of instructional approaches possible or enhance their impact. Moreover, some types of computer applications may be particularly effective in supporting some kinds of instructional approaches or learning goals with some kinds of learners. In effect, computer or information technology approaches may interact with learner characteristics. The essence of these arguments would appear to be that it is probably fruitless to focus on computers as a conveyer of some type of instructional approach. Rather, what counts is how information technology or visual media integrated with instructional approaches can facilitate knowledge construction and meaning making and thereby increase learning on the part of students (Kozma, 1994a, 1994b).[11]

Distance learning. Paralleling, and indeed dependent on, the growth and development of information and media technologies has been the dramatic growth of distance or remote-site instructional offerings in postsecondary education (El-Khawas, 1995; Keegan, 1993; Moore & Thompson, 1997; Walsh & Reese, 1995). For example, a 1997 report by the National Center for Education Statistics found that about 60 percent of American public two- and four-year institutions offered distance education courses, usually in the form of either one-way prerecorded courses or two-way interactive video courses (Lewis, Farris, & Alexander, 1997). Distance education has been used to deliver remote-site or off-campus courses in a variety of fields such as religious education, business, library science, teacher education, general studies, medicine and nursing, social sciences, social work, and scientific and technical fields (Burgess, 1994).

Literally hundreds of studies have addressed the issue of whether instruction delivered to remote sites, via various media technologies, is as effective as conventional on-campus, face-to-face instruction. In most instances, this research question is essentially the same as asking whether instructional media, such as television, videotapes, two-way interactive video, or computer conferencing, positively or negatively influence student learning. In the context of on-campus versus remote-site instruction, the clear weight of evidence from this research appears to support the contention of Clark and others that the specific medium of instruction has little impact on how much students learn (Carter, 1996; Clark, 1991, 1994; Schlosser & Anderson, 1994). Students who study via distance education approaches appear to learn as much course content as do their counterparts in conventional on-campus classroom settings. This conclusion is the consensus of numerous syntheses of the research evidence (Barker, Frisbie, & Patrick, 1989; Jones, Simonson, Kemis, & Sorensen, 1992; Machtmes & Asher, 2000; Moore & Thompson, 1990, 1997; Olcott, 1992; Pittman, 1991; Russell, 1995, 1999; Schlosser & Anderson, 1994; Wetzel, Radtke, & Stern, 1994; Zigerell, 1991).[12] Moreover, the weight of evidence that does exist also suggests that per-student costs of courses offered in a distance education format are not appreciably different from those offered in a conventional format on campus (Wetzel et al., 1994).

Despite apparent consensus in the evidence, there are some inescapable methodological problems in the body of research. A recent report outlines a number of these problems (Institute for Higher Education Policy, 1999; Merisotis & Phipps, 1999). Perhaps the most important problem is that geographical constraints make it virtually impossible to conduct either true experiments, with random assignment of individual learners to treatments, or quasi experiments, with random assignment of preexisting or intact class sections to treatments. Rather, nearly every study is, understandably, characterized by students self-selecting themselves into on-campus and remote-site instructional groups. Thus, the body of evidence on distance (versus on-campus) instruction and student learning tends to be flawed by a major threat to causal inference (or internal validity)— the interaction of self-selection and course achievement (Pascarella & Terenzini, 1991). The reasons why students take courses on campus or at distant sites in the first place may represent a constellation of uncontrolled influences that bias the findings on distance learning and student achievement in unknown ways.

Active learning. Slightly more than a decade ago, Chickering and Gamson (1987, 1991) published an influential list of principles for good practice in undergraduate education. These practices were grounded in research on student development and college teaching and included, among others, such things as student involvement in active learning activities, student involvement in cooperative learning activities, faculty and student interaction in and out of class, and prompt feedback to students on their performance. Some of these principles for good practice were the focus of considerable research in the 1990s. In this section, we attempt to summarize the evidence on student involvement in active learning experiences.

Consistent with our previous synthesis, the evidence we reviewed for the 1990s suggests that lecturing is still by far the modal instructional approach most often used in postsecondary education (Bonwell & Eison, 1991; Carlson & Schodt, 1995). In the hands of a skilled instructor, lecturing can often be an effective method for presenting major aspects of course content. Yet it is usually the case that lecturing requires students to assume the role of passive learners— absorbing concepts and facts and, ideally, incorporating them into some form of long-term memory. Lecturing is not a particularly effective approach for exploiting the potential efficacy of the learning that occurs when students are actively engaged in processing information in new and personally relevant ways and, in a very real sense, "constructing" their own knowledge (Baxter Magolda, 1998; Baxter Magolda & Buckley, 1997; Gagne, Yekovich, & Yekovich, 1994; Meyers & Jones, 1993; Nunn, 1996; Reynolds & Nunn, 1997).

A substantial amount of both experimental and correlational evidence suggests that active student involvement in learning has a positive impact on the acquisition of course content. For example, Lang (1996), reported in Murray and Lang (1997), conducted an experiment in which course topics in an undergraduate psychology course were randomly assigned to be taught by either an active participation method or a control lecture-only method. For the topics taught by the active participation method, at least 75 percent of class time was spent in activities requiring active participation (for example, small-group discussion, question-answer dialogue, case study debates). At the end of the course, mean student performance on both multiple-choice and essay examination questions was significantly better for topics taught by active participation than for topics taught by lecture. (From the graphic information reported in Murray & Lang, we could not compute an effect size.)

On balance, the weight of evidence from other experimental or quasi-experimental research tends to be consistent with the findings reported by Murray and Lang (1997). Studies either report that students demonstrate significantly better mastery of course content when actively engaged in learning (Doran, 1994; Dori & Yochim, 1994; Hake, 1998; Hall & McCurdy, 1990; Kritch, Bostow, & Dedrick, 1995; McBroom & Reed, 1994; McCarthy & Anderson, 2000; Terenzini, Cabrera, Parente, & Bjorklund, 1998; Tudor & Bostow, 1991; Van Heuvelen, 1991) or they find no significant learning differences or mixed learning effects when comparing active to passive lecture instructional approaches (Bin & Lee, 1992; Carlson & Schodt, 1995; DeNeve & Heppner, 1997; Etemad, 1994; Ferguson & Hegarty, 1995; Hilligoss, 1992). Not all of the studies cited here provide the requisite statistical data to compute an effect size. However, using the data provided by those studies that do, we estimated that active learning approaches provide a learning advantage over passive approaches of about .25 of a standard deviation (10 percentile points). This estimate should be interpreted with extreme caution because it is not clear that the studies we used to compute an effect size are representative of the entire body of evidence.

Evidence from the correlational research on the impacts of active learning is quite consistent with that from the body of experimental research. We uncovered four relevant correlational studies, three of which measured knowledge acquisition with student self-reports (Grayson, 1999; Kuh et al., 1997; Kuh & Vesper, 1997a) and one of which measured it with objective tests (Murray & Lang, 1997). All of the investigations attempted to control statistically for various important confounding influences such as socioeconomic status, high school or college grades, institutional environments, and gender. In the presence of these controls, each of the studies reported a statistically significant, positive association between active involvement in various learning experiences (for example, participated in class discussions, made outlines from class notes, did additional readings on topics introduced in class, considered practical applications of the material) and various indicators of learning, either at the class level or for the student's overall college experience.

Collaborative learning. Another of Chickering and Gamson's (1987, 1991) principles of good practice in undergraduate education is that student learning is enhanced when it occurs in a context in which students work with and teach each other. One approach to such interactive instruction is collaborative learning. There are a number of excellent and detailed descriptions of collaborative learning (Bruffee, 1993; Cottell, 1996; Cuseo, 1992; Kadel & Keehner, 1994; Matthews, Cooper, Davidson, & Hawkes, 1995; Palinscar, Stevens, & Gavelek, 1989). Smith and MacGregor (1992) offer a representative definition: "'Collaborative learning' is an umbrella term for a variety of educational approaches involving joint intellectual effort by students, or students and teachers together. In most collaborative learning situations students are working in groups of two or more, mutually searching for understanding, solutions or meanings, or creating a product. There is wide variability in collaborative learning activities, but most center on the students' exploration or application of the course material, not simply the teacher's presentation or explication of it" (p. 10).

The intellectual and philosophical justification for collaborative learning would appear to be that knowledge is more a socially held or socially based phenomenon than it is a body of information and concepts transmitted from expert to novice. Consequently, it is most effectively acquired through social or group interactions and activities in which peers actively engage in knowledge construction (Palinscar et al., 1989). Collaborative learning is often used interchangeably with cooperative learning. However, along with others (Cottell, 1996; Cuseo, 1992; Millis & Cottell, 1998), we make a distinction between the two and regard cooperative learning as a distinct and highly structured version of collaborative learning. (Evidence on the impact of cooperative learning is reviewed in the next section of this chapter.)

The body of research on collaborative learning embraces a broad spectrum of approaches to inquiry—from relatively brief and highly controlled laboratory experiments, to more generalizable instructional experiments and quasi experiments, to correlational studies. With some exceptions (Hagedorn, Siadat, Fogel, Nora, & Pascarella, 1997), the weight of evidence from this research is reasonably consistent in suggesting that collaborative learning approaches can significantly enhance learning. For example, a brief but creative experiment by Okada and Simon (1997) compared pairs of postsecondary subjects working in collaboration with single subjects in a task of discovering scientific laws with the aid of experiments. The collaborative pairs condition was not only significantly more successful than subjects working alone in discovery tasks but also led to more active participation in explanatory activities (that is, entertaining hypotheses and considering alternative ideas and justifications). Similar results are reported in an experiment that compared the mathematics problem solving of students working in groups with those working alone (Stasson, Kameda, Parks, Zimmerman, & Davis, 1991). The results of these laboratory-type learning experiments appear to generalize to postsecondary instructional settings. Although we could not estimate an effect size from the findings, it would nevertheless appear that learning in a collaborative context can significantly improve the acquisition of course content over learning on one's own in statistics and research methods (Bonsangue, 1991; Leppel, 1998; Stearns, 1996), sociology (Rau & Sherman Heyl, 1990; Son & Van Sickle, 1993), biology (Sokolove & Marbach-Ad, 2000), and college algebra (Thomas & Higbee, 1996).

There is also a small body of correlational research that suggests that student participation in collaborative learning activities in an engineering design course (for example, collaborate with other students on assignments, students teach and learn from one another) has a significant, positive influence on self-reported gains in both problem solving and design skills (Cabrera, Colbeck, & Terenzini, 1998; Terenzini, Cabrera, Colbeck, Bjorklund, & Parente, 1999; Terenzini, Cabrera, Colbeck, Parente, & Bjorklund, 2001) and that participation in collaborative learning activities during college has a significant, positive influence on self-reported, end-of-first-year gains in understanding science and technology, understanding the arts and humanities, and acquiring general education knowledge and skills (Astin, 1993c; Cabrera, Nora, Bernal, Terenzini, & Pascarella, 1998; Kuh et al., 1997; Kuh & Vesper, 1997a). These positive impacts of involvement in collaborative learning activities persisted even in the presence of controls for such potential confounding influences as student precollege academic ability, secondary school grades, gender, ethnicity, and parental education. Similar results are reported by Light (1990, 1991, 2001), though without controls for potential confounding influences.

Cooperative learning. Cooperative learning is usually considered the most operationally well-defined and procedurally structured form of collaborative learning (Cuseo, 1992; Johnson, Johnson, & Smith, 1998b; Slavin, 1996; Smith & Waller, 1997). It is a systematic instructional strategy in which small groups of students work together cooperatively to accomplish shared learning goals, and each student achieves his or her learning goals only if other members achieve theirs (Cooper, Robinson, & McKinney, 1994; Johnson, Johnson, & Smith, 1998a). Although there are a range of different versions or forms of cooperative learning (Kagan, 1992), it would appear that there are several common attributes: a common task or learning activity suitable for group work, learning in small groups, positive interdependence and cooperative behavior among group members, and individual accountability and responsibility (Millis & Cottell, 1998).

The research on the impact of cooperative learning in postsecondary education is extensive. Fortunately, in the 1990s several comprehensive meta-analyses attempted to synthesize this literature. Johnson and Johnson (1993a) conducted a meta-analysis of about 120 experimental and quasi-experimental studies that compared the relative efficacy of cooperative, competitive, and individualistic learning on the individual achievement or knowledge acquisition of postsecondary students. Cooperative learning provided an advantage of .54 of a standard deviation (21 percentile points) over competitive learning and .51 of a standard deviation (19 percentile points) over students learning on their own. An update of that metanalysis (Johnson et al., 1998a, 1998b) incorporated research conducted through 1996–97 on some 45 to 50 additional studies, but the findings changed in only trivial ways. In this more extensive analysis, cooperative learning produced an achievement advantage of .49 of a standard deviation (19 percentile points) over competitive learning and .53 of a standard deviation (20 percentile points) over students learning on their own. These meta-analytic results held for verbal tasks (such as reading, writing, and oral presentation), quantitative tasks, and procedural tasks (such as swimming). Moreover, across the entire body of evidence, the effect sizes do not appear to be seriously influenced by the methodological rigor of the studies. Although there are some exceptions (DePree, 1998), there is little to suggest that these estimates of positive achievement effects of cooperative learning would be substantially altered by more recent evidence (Giraud, 1997; Kim, Cohen, Booske, & Derry, 1998; Miller & Groccia, 1997; Mourtos, 1997; Potthast, 1999; Tom, 1997).[13]

There is also a lesser-known variation on cooperative learning known as *academic controversy* (Johnson & Johnson, 1993b; Johnson, Johnson, & Smith,

1996). Academic controversy involves dividing a cooperative group of four students into two pairs and assigning them opposing positions on a major topic of controversy in a discipline or field of study. "The pairs then develop their position, present it to the other pair, listen to the opposing position, engage in a discussion in which they attempt to refute the other side, and then drop all advocacy and seek a synthesis that takes both perspectives and positions into account" (Johnson & Johnson, 1993b, p. 40). Johnson and Johnson (1995) and Johnson, Johnson, and Smith (1996) present the evidence of a meta-analysis of the effects of academic controversy based on 26 published studies, 75 percent of which were randomized, true experiments and about 42 percent of which were conducted with postsecondary samples. Unfortunately, no separation of effect sizes is made for postsecondary and nonpostsecondary studies. Nevertheless, they report that, compared with approaches in which the student learns on his or her own, academic controversy produced a demonstrated content knowledge advantage of .87 of a standard deviation (31 percentile points).

Small-group learning. Small-group learning is a term that has been applied to a range of instructional approaches that incorporate elements of collaborative or cooperative learning in various combinations. As such, small-group learning also frequently includes elements of active learning (Cooper & Robinson, 1997; Springer, Millar, Kosciuk, Penberthy, & Wright, 1997). This flexible repertoire of pedagogical approaches has been used frequently in undergraduate science, mathematics, engineering, and technology instruction (Bonsangue, 1994; Borresen, 1990; DeClute & Ladyshewsky, 1993; Hall, 1992; Jones & Brickner, 1996; Keeler & Anson, 1995; Koch, 1992; Mehta, 1993).

Recently, Springer and colleagues (Springer, Stanne, & Donovan, 1999) conducted a detailed meta-analysis of the published and unpublished research on small-group learning in science, mathematics, and related areas. The meta-analysis was based on 49 separate samples from 37 studies in which the outcomes of small-group learning procedures were compared with those of instruction where students did not work cooperatively or collaboratively. (Unfortunately, it was not possible to determine the extent of overlap between this meta-analysis and the body of studies considered by Johnson, Johnson, and Smith [1998a, 1998b] in their meta-analysis of cooperative learning.) Across all studies, the course achievement of students working in small groups was .51 of a standard deviation (19 percentile points) greater than that of students who did not work cooperatively or collaboratively, a result markedly similar to that of Johnson, Johnson, and Smith. No statistically significant differences in course achievement effect sizes were noted whether the instruction was primarily cooperative, primarily collaborative, or mixed; whether there was randomized or nonrandomized placement of students into small-group or control conditions; in different disciplines (for example, science, mathematics, allied health); or based on the amount of time spent in groups. Conversely, some factors did moderate achievement effect sizes in statistically significant ways. For example, the average achievement advantage for small-group learning was larger when achievement was measured with a locally developed course examination or grade (.59 of a standard deviation) rather than with a standardized test (.33 SD); the instructor was one of the study investigators (.73 SD) rather than when he or she was not (.41 SD); cooperative-collaborative groups met outside of class, usually in study sessions (.65 SD) rather than when they met in class (.44 SD); and in four-year institutions (.54 SD) rather than in two-year institutions (.21 SD). In all cases except one, however, these effect sizes represent statistically significant achievement advantages for the small-group learning condition. Only the effect size for studies conducted in two-year colleges was not statistically significant, and this may be attributable to the fact that it is based on only seven independent samples.[14]

There is also evidence from a comprehensive meta-analysis by Lou, Abrami, and d'Apollonia (2001) indicating that students may derive greater individual learning benefits from using computer technology when they work in small groups rather than alone. Extracting only those studies from their meta-analysis that were based on college samples, we estimate that learning with computers in small groups provided an average individual-level content achievement advantage of .27 of a standard deviation (11 percentile points) over learning with computers on one's own.

Supplemental instruction. Supplemental instruction (SI) is a structured program designed to increase mastery of course content in "high-risk" courses through the use of collaborative learning strategies. High-risk courses are those that typically have 30 percent or more D or F grades or withdrawals. SI provides regularly scheduled, out-of-class, peer-facilitated sessions offering students the chance to discuss and process course content (Arendale, 1994; Burmeister, 1995; Eig, 1997). The leaders of these peer-facilitated sessions are other students who have previously taken the course and are trained to help current students develop strategies for learning and understanding course content (Arendale & Martin, 1997; Congos, Langsam, & Schoeps, 1997).

In the last 25 years, supplemental instruction has seen wide use throughout the country and has produced an extensive literature of comparative studies focusing on its impact. Fortunately, Arendale and Martin (1997) have synthesized the results of these studies, which were conducted between 1982 and 1996 and are based on data from nearly 5,000 courses in 270 institutions. The studies were conducted in a broad range of disciplines, including biology, chemistry, history, economics, statistics, calculus, physics, and government. Course grades on a five-point scale, where 0 = F and 4 = A, are the measure of content mastery in all studies. Across all studies, students participating in SI had about one-third (.33) of a final course grade advantage over control group students not participating in SI. Unfortunately, Arendale and Martin do not report standard deviations. Consequently, one cannot directly compute an effect size from their synthesis. However, it would appear that course grade standard deviations in a sample of the studies they reviewed average about .85. Using this as our standard deviation estimate, we would conclude from their data that participating in SI leads to about .39 of a standard deviation (15 percentile points) advantage in course content mastery over nonparticipation—although we would caution that this is a rough estimate based on imputed values. An additional finding reported by Arendale and Martin is that, across all studies, SI students averaged a significantly lower percentage of D, F, and course withdrawal grades (23.1 percent) than did non-SI students (37.1 percent). There appears to be little evidence in studies not covered by the Arendale and Martin synthesis, or in more recent research, that would change their conclusions (Congos et al., 1997; Hensen & Shelley, 2003; Kochenour et al., 1997; Warren, 1997–98; Wittig & Thomerson, 1996). Moreover, qualitative analyses have suggested that SI's emphasis on connected knowing, realized through collaborative peer instruction, may be a particularly salient determinant of women's success in science courses (Lundeberg & Moch, 1995).

As pointed out by Arendale and Martin (1997), in the majority of comparative studies on supplemental instruction there were only chance differences between SI and non-SI students on such potentially important confounding influences as age, gender, ethnicity, secondary school rank in class, work responsibilities, or standardized test scores such as the ACT or SAT. However, an important problem with most studies is that students self-select themselves into involvement or noninvolvement in SI, and there is evidence that more motivated and academically confident students choose SI involvement (Visor, Johnson, & Cole, 1992a; Visor, Johnson, Schollaet, Good-Majah, & Davenport, 1995). Recent SI studies, however, have controlled for self-selection either by randomly assigning intact class sections to SI or non-SI conditions (Peled & Kim, 1996) or by building a measure of academic motivation (that is, cumulative grades) into the design of the study (Ramirez, 1997). In the presence of these controls for self-selection effects, SI students still significantly outperformed their non-SI counterparts on measures of course achievement.

A second rival hypothesis is that supplemental instruction merely provides "double exposure" to the course content, once in a lecture and for a second time in the SI session. However, a quasi-experimental study conducted by Kenny (1989) found that students who attended course lectures and SI sessions still had significantly higher levels of final course achievement than similar students who attended lectures and special question-and-answer sessions led by a graduate student. Thus, given equal exposure in terms of instructional time, SI students still outperformed their non-SI peers.

Constructivist-oriented approaches. There is an additional group of related instructional approaches that do not fit neatly into single categories such as active learning, collaborative learning, or cooperative learning. Instead, they usually combine elements of each of these approaches in various ways and are based on the premise that students learn best when they actively construct knowledge in socially interactive contexts rather than receiving it from an "expert." For lack of a better term, we refer to these approaches as *constructivist-oriented.* Examples include constructivist teaching (Lord, 1997), new-wave methods (Hofer, 1994, 1998–99), and problem-based learning (Arambula-Greenfield, 1996; Schumow, 1999).

Constructivist teaching emphasizes active discovery of new knowledge, working in small groups, sharing with others what the group has discovered, and the self-assessment of learning. Lord (1997) conducted a quasi-experimental study of constructivist teaching in an introductory biology course where some sections of the course studied the material presented under the constructivist teaching format, and control group sections studied the same material in a traditional lecture-laboratory format. The two groups had the same instructor, but since they took the class in a different semester did not self-select themselves into different instructional formats. They also differed in only chance ways in previous science courses taken and a measure of precollege academic aptitude. Students in the constructivist teaching format, however, had significantly higher scores on all four unit examinations in the course. Using the statistical data provided by Lord, constructivist teaching had an achievement advantage across all four unit tests of about .40 of a standard deviation (16 percentile points).

As with constructivist teaching, new-wave approaches emphasize active and collaborative learning, but they also focus on solving complex problems. Hofer (1994, 1998–99) conducted a quasi experiment in which sections of a calculus course were randomly assigned to a new-wave and a traditional approach. Thus, students could not self-select the instructional method they preferred. The new-wave approach emphasized active and collaborative learning activities in and out of class, the use of graphing calculators, and a curriculum based on a new text that was largely a collection of complex word problems for which answers were not provided. The traditional sections used a standard calculus text that proceeded sequentially, and instructors covered the material primarily through lecture and presentation. The new-wave and traditional students differed in only chance ways in such potentially confounding influences as gender, ethnicity, high school calculus background and grades, and tested mathematics ability. At the end of the course, however, the new-wave students had a statistically significant advantage in course grade that was .32 of a standard deviation in magnitude (13 percentile points) as well as a statistically significant advantage on a common final examination that was .14 of a standard deviation (6 percentile points). Hofer is quite candid in pointing out that differences in instructor experience might confound these results. It is also unclear how much the results reflect between-group differences in the text employed rather than involvement in active, collaborative learning.

Another variation of what we have termed constructivist-oriented approaches is problem-based learning (PBL). As its name implies, PBL is learning organized around solutions to a complex problem in the discipline or field. However, as with other constructivist approaches it also emphasizes active, collaborative learning where the instructor is a facilitator or guide rather than an information provider (Barrows, 1996). Problem-based learning has had reasonably extensive use in medical education with somewhat mixed results (Albanese & Mitchell, 1993; Vernon & Blake, 1993). Evaluation of the use of PBL in undergraduate settings appears to be in its nascent stages. Recently, however, Schumow (1999) conducted a quasi experiment in which two sections of an educational psychology class were taught the same material, with the same instructor, but in different formats. In the first half of the semester, section one learned in a PBL approach, while the second section learned in a regular class discussion format. In the second half of the semester the approaches were switched—section one receiving traditional instruction and section two the PBL approach. At the end of the first half of the semester, there were no significant differences between the two groups in either tested content knowledge or problem solving. However, at the end of the second half of the semester, the PBL group had a statistically significant advantage in problem solving of .41 of a standard deviation (16 percentile points) and a marginally significant advantage in content knowledge of .38 of a standard deviation (15 percentile points).

Learning communities. Learning communities are an attempt to move collaborative learning beyond the classroom and into broader aspects of a college student's life. Although there are many variations on the theme (Cross, 1998; Matthews, 1993; Tinto, Goodsell Love, & Russo, 1994), learning communities in their most basic form appear to have two common elements: shared or collaborative learning, and connected learning. Shared or collaborative learning comes from the learning communities' enrollment of the same students in several common courses, thereby increasing the likelihood of an integrated social and academic experience. Connected learning comes from the shared courses' organization or link around a theme or single large topic (Tinto, Goodsell Love, & Russo, 1994; Tinto, Russo, & Kadel, 1994)—"Individual and Society" (Pike, Schroeder, & Berry, 1996) or "Society and Science" ("A Student Success Story," 1996), for example. When implemented in the first year of college such learning communities have also been referred to as freshman interest groups (Tinto & Goodsell, 1993). As suggested by Cross (1998), the purpose of structured learning communities is to facilitate active over passive learning, collaboration and cooperation as opposed to competition, and community instead of isolation.

Research on the outcomes of learning communities is in its nascent stages and has measured student learning almost exclusively with student self-reported gains. Nevertheless, there is at least some evidence to suggest that participation in learning communities is linked with student perceptions that they are deriving greater benefit from their academic experiences during college. Tinto and Russo (1994) found that students participating in a community college learning community (the Coordinated Studies Program) not only reported significantly greater academic involvement during the first year of college in such areas as library use, writing, course involvement, and interaction with faculty and students but also reported significantly higher learning gains than did their counterparts not in the learning community. Similar results are reported for freshman interest groups at a residential university ("A Student Success Story," 1996). In both of these studies, however, it is not clear that controls were in effect for background differences between students who elected to participate in learning communities and those who did not. Thus, it is possible that they overestimate the direct effect of learning communities on student learning.

Additional analyses of the effects of learning communities are mixed. Walker (2002) reported that participation in learning communities appeared to enhance students' self-reported gains in problem-solving skills, reading ability, and writing ability. However, Pike, Schroeder, and Berry (1996) failed to uncover statistically significant differences between learning community and non-learning-community students in self-reported first-year gains in such areas as science and mathematics, communication skills, or general education (for example, literature, arts, writing). Moreover, in what is perhaps the most rigorous and informative published study in this small body of research, Pike (1999a) found that any direct effects of residential learning communities on self-reported general education gains disappeared in the presence of controls for important background characteristics (for example, ACT scores, secondary school class rank, major, gender, ethnicity). However, participation in the learning communities had a positive indirect effect on general education gains. This effect was due largely to the fact that being in the learning communities enhanced students' involvement in art, music, and theater; their interaction with peers; and the intellectual content of their peer interactions. In turn, these involvement and interaction dimensions positively influenced general education gains. (For unpublished work generally supporting this evidence with regard to living-learning programs, see Inkelas, 1999, and Scholnick, 1996. For a recent supportive published study, see Inkelas and Weisman, 2003.)

Focused Classroom Instructional Techniques. In the preceding paragraphs, we focused on the learning impacts of general pedagogical approaches. In this section, we turn our attention to more focused classroom instructional techniques and their impacts on course content acquisition. The techniques we discuss here are peer tutoring, reciprocal teaching, attributional retraining, concept-knowledge maps, and the one-minute paper.

Peer tutoring. Although highly structured general pedagogical approaches such as the personalized system of instruction and supplemental instruction rely heavily on students being tutored by their peers, peer tutoring is a frequently used instructional technique in its own right (Topping, 1996). There is a small body of research on the impact of peer tutoring on learning. Much of the evidence is reviewed in an informative paper by Topping (1996). Of the different types of peer tutoring, the most tightly structured learning format appears to be reciprocal peer tutoring. In reciprocal peer tutoring each student is paired with another in the class. In each tutoring session the pair reciprocates roles: creating short tests on course content for each other before the session, administering them to each other, scoring them, discussing the outcomes, and coaching their partner as necessary (Fantuzzo, Dimeff, & Fox, 1989). The body of experimental and quasi-experimental evidence on reciprocal peer tutoring suggests either that it produces significantly better course achievement than conducting the same or similar learning tasks and studying on one's own (Fantuzzo, Dimeff, & Fox, 1989; Fantuzzo, Riggio, Connelly, & Dimeff, 1989; Riggio, Fantuzzo, Connelly, & Dimeff, 1991; Topping, Watson, Jarvis, & Hill, 1996) or that it produces essentially the same learning as working on one's own (Griffin & Griffin, 1995; Topping et al., 1997). Because not all studies provide usable statistical data, we could not estimate an effect size.

Additional findings suggest that it is the combination of peer teaching (both the preparation for and the actual teaching itself) and the highly structured learning format that is essential to the impact of reciprocal peer tutoring (Fantuzzo, Riggio, Connelly, & Dimeff, 1989; King, 1990; Riggio et al., 1991). However, there is also quasi-experimental evidence to suggest that brief (two-minute), unstructured reciprocal peer tutoring sessions during lectures can also significantly enhance course learning, at least in the short run (Hollingsworth, 1995). This finding, however, awaits replication.

Aside from reciprocal peer tutoring there are other forms of peer tutoring that may have positive impacts on knowledge acquisition at the course level (Groccia & Miller, 1996; Landrum & Chastain, 1998; Lidren, Meier, & Brigham, 1991; Longuevan & Shoemaker, 1991). However, there is sufficient variation in both the tutoring interventions and the quality of the research designs of these investigations that we are hesitant to form a conclusion.

One additional point needs to be made with respect to the relationship between peer tutoring and learning. There is both experimental evidence (Semb et al., 1993) and correlational evidence with appropriate controls for ability (Astin, 1993c) to suggest that tutoring itself can have an important, positive impact on knowledge retention. Thus, learning the material to teach another student may be a particularly effective way to increase content mastery.

Reciprocal teaching. Reciprocal teaching was developed in the 1980s by Palinscar and Brown (1984). It involves students working in dialogue with classroom teachers to learn a set of strategies for fostering comprehension of textual material. The dialogue is structured to incorporate four crucial components: generating questions, summarizing, clarifying difficult or ambiguous words or ideas, and predicting upcoming content from cues in the material and from prior knowledge of the topic (Beyler & Raftery, 1998). As they become more adept at using the strategies, students take on more difficult content, and the focus of dialogue shifts from student with teacher to student with student (Simpson, Hynd, Nist, & Burrell, 1997). A synthesis of reciprocal teaching that combined studies from all educational levels concluded that reciprocal teaching was significantly superior to traditional methods in about 80 percent of the studies when experimenter-constructed tests were the dependent variable. When standardized tests were the dependent variable, reciprocal teaching was significantly superior to traditional methods about 20 percent of the time (Rosenshine & Meister, 1994; Simpson et al., 1997).

Most research on reciprocal teaching and text comprehension is conducted with elementary and secondary school samples. There is, however, a small body of experimental and quasi-experimental research with postsecondary students that has reasonably strong internal validity. Several of these postsecondary studies focus on improving the reading comprehension of poor readers or students at risk for academic failure (Hart & Speece, 1998; Hodge, Palmer, & Scott, 1992; Rich, 1989). Others estimate the effects of reciprocal teaching on course achievement or the reading comprehension of readers at all levels of proficiency (Al-Hilawani, Merchant, & Poteet, 1993; Beyler & Raftery, 1998; Rush & Milburn,

1988). The evidence from this research suggests that students in reciprocal teaching conditions either significantly outperform their peers who are not receiving reciprocal teaching (Hart & Speece, 1998; Hodge et al., 1992; Rich, 1989), perform at essentially the same level as their counterparts who are not receiving reciprocal teaching, or show substantial improvement in achievement when reciprocal teaching is introduced during a course (Beyler & Raftery, 1998). Moreover, in those studies where students receiving reciprocal teaching exhibited significantly higher performance, the dependent measures have been both experimenter-constructed tests (Rich, 1989) and standardized tests (Hart & Speece, 1998; Hodge et al., 1992).

The weight of evidence, then, suggests that reciprocal teaching is an instructional technique that can foster significant improvement in the comprehension of textual material, particularly when used with poor readers. Not all of the studies we reviewed reported adequate information for estimating effect sizes, and the control conditions differed substantially across studies. Thus, we are hesitant to estimate an effect size for the body of evidence.

Attributional retraining. Attributional retraining is an intervention strategy designed to enhance motivation and achievement striving by changing how students think about the causes underlying their success or failure (Perry, Menec, & Struthers, 1996; Perry & Struthers, 1994). For example, one such desirable change might be to move students from regarding academic failure as attributable to lack of ability to regarding it as attributable to lack of effort. Another might be to move from regarding academic success as due to luck to regarding it as due to high ability. As such, it is expected that attributional retraining would produce an increased expectancy of success and increased motivation and mastery strivings. These increases, in turn, should lead to better classroom performance and increased learning (Perry, Hechter, Menec, & Weinberg, 1992). Generally, the appropriate attribution is presented to students directly (often through a short videotape) or by modeling the attribution in a structured interview (Perry, Hechter, Menec, & Weinberg, 1993).

A substantial body of integrated and sequential experimental research has focused on attributional retraining and its effects. Much of this research is beyond the scope and purpose of this book. However, the pioneering research of Perry and his colleagues on the effects of attributional retraining on learning have led to two important conclusions. First, it would appear that the positive achievement effects of attributional retraining are selective. Evidence suggests that it is most effective in improving the learning of students who have experienced past failure or who tend toward an external locus of attribution for success—that is, attribute it to luck (Menec et al., 1994; Perry & Penner, 1990). Second, retraining interventions to increase internal attributions (such as effort or hard work) may have their largest positive impact on learning when students are faced with poor or ineffective instruction. Attributions appear to make little difference when instruction is effective (Menec, Perry, Struthers, Schonwetter, & Hechter, 1992; Perry & Magnusson, 1989a, 1989b; Perry, Schonwetter, Magnusson, & Struthers, 1994). Thus, the evidence suggests that positive attributions (for example, effort, hard work) can provide a "buffer" against the consequences of ineffective teaching (Perry & Struthers, 1994). (In all of these studies effective instruction was operationally defined as *expressive instruction*. We will review the evidence on expressive instruction, along with other dimensions of instruction, in a subsequent section of this chapter.)

Concept-knowledge maps. A concept-knowledge map (hereafter c-k map) is a visual tool for representing conceptual knowledge in a discipline or area of study. It is usually constructed as a scheme to represent knowledge in hierarchical graphical networks. As such, a c-k map is structured around "nodes," which identify key concepts, and links (lines between nodes) labeled in ways that indicate the meaningful relationships between two or more concepts (Briscoe & LaMaster, 1991; Dansereau, 1995; Santhanam, Leach, & Dawson, 1998). As pointed out by Romance and Vitale (1999), c-k maps form propositional networks that display key concepts and the networks of functional relationships among them and model the accessibility of knowledge in ways that may become part of the student's long-term memory. Examples of how c-k maps are constructed can be found in detailed discussions by Dansereau and Newbern (1997), Evans and Dansereau (1991), and Santhanam, Leach, and Dawson (1998). C-k maps have the potential to become effective learning tools because they can be constructed and revised using the considerable flexibility and power of computer graphics.

There is a small but remarkably consistent body of experimental and quasi-experimental evidence on the impact of c-k maps on student learning in post-secondary settings. With some exceptions (Cliburn, 1990), the weight of evidence is quite clear in suggesting that use of c-k maps significantly enhances comprehension of text and knowledge acquisition and retention over control methods of instruction where c-k maps are not used (Amundsen, Gryspeerdt, & Moxness, 1992; Chmielewski & Dansereau, 1998; Hirumi & Bowers, 1991; Lambiotte & Dansereau, 1992; McCagg & Dansereau, 1991; Ruddell & Boyle, 1989). (For evidence of significant increases in understanding using concept maps, though without a control group, see also Zeilik et al., 1997.) Moreover, there is also evidence from two independent experiments to suggest that training students in the construction and use of c-k maps positively transfers to recall information from text when a c-k mapping strategy is not used (Chmielewski & Dansereau, 1998).

Not all of the studies in this body of evidence report the statistical data required for computing an effect size. However, based on those studies that do, we estimated that use of c-k mapping produced a knowledge acquisition advantage of .43 of a standard deviation (17 percentile points).[15]

The one-minute paper. The one-minute paper is a modest, relatively simple, low-tech pedagogical procedure designed to obtain regular feedback from students (Angelo & Cross, 1993; Light, 1990). In the final few minutes of the class the instructor asks students to respond to two questions: *What was the most important thing you learned today? What questions remain uppermost in your mind as we conclude this class session?*

The idea of the one-minute paper is that it can be used by instructors on a regular basis to review and clarify misunderstanding of key points. It also permits students somewhat greater input and control of the class, which in turn can foster increased motivation to learn (Chizmar & Ostrosky, 1998).

Hypothesizing that regular use of the one-minute paper, along with clarification of misunderstood course content, would improve student learning, Chizmar and Ostrosky (1998) conducted a large-scale quasi experiment in a course on economic principles. Course sections were assigned either to an experimental condition that employed the one-minute paper or to a control condition that did not. The same instructors taught both the experimental and control sections. With statistical controls in place for precourse scores on the Test of Understanding of College Economics (TUCE—a standardized measure of economics knowledge), college grades, and dummy variables representing different instructors, the one-minute paper condition produced a statistically significant advantage in posttest scores on the TUCE of .12 of a standard deviation (5 percentile points). Although this is not a particularly dramatic effect, neither is the one-minute paper a particularly difficult pedagogical procedure to implement. Moreover, the magnitude of the one-minute paper effect was the same for different instructors and for students with different college grades. Results consistent with those of Chizmar and Ostrosky have been reported for the use of the one-minute paper in an introductory accounting course (Almer, Jones, & Moeckel, 1998). Unfortunately, the Almer, Jones, and Moeckel investigation did not provide sufficient statistical information to estimate an effect size.

Teacher Behaviors. Differences in teacher behaviors have important implications for the acquisition of subject matter knowledge by students. With the exceptions of predicting college grades and student persistence-withdrawal decisions, perhaps no other topic in postsecondary education has elicited so much empirical inquiry. As with the research through 1990, the majority of the more recent work is correlational. However, the decade of the 1990s also saw an increase in experimental studies that augment those on teacher clarity reported in our 1991 synthesis.

Correlational studies. Literally hundreds of correlational investigations have been conducted to determine the extent to which student perceptions of teacher behaviors such as instructional clarity, expressiveness, rapport with students, feedback to students, and organization and structure are related to various measures of course-related knowledge acquisition. Fortunately, there have been a substantial number of excellent summaries of this research (Braskamp & Ory, 1994; Cashin, 1999; Cashin, Downey, & Sixbury, 1994; d'Apollonia & Abrami, 1997a; d'Apollonia, Abrami, & Rosenfield, 1993; Feldman, 1996, 1997; Greenwald, 1997; Marsh, 1987; Marsh & Dunkin, 1997; Marsh & Roche, 1997; McKeachie, 1997; Wachtel, 1998). The bottom line on these meta-analyses and narrative syntheses is that student perceptions of teacher behaviors are multidimensional, have reasonable reliability and stability, and have moderate positive correlations with various measures of course-related knowledge acquisition (for example, course grade, course final examination). For example, Feldman's (1997) synthesis of meta-analytic studies suggests that student course achievement has average correlations of .57 with teacher preparation-organization, .56 with teacher clarity and understandability, and .49 with the extent to which course objectives were met. More modest average correlations with course achievement were found for such dimensions of teacher behavior as stimulation of interest in the course and subject matter (.38), teacher's availability and helpfulness (.36), quality and frequency of feedback from teacher to student (.23), and teacher concern for and rapport with students (.23).

An additional study that attempts to estimate the underlying constructs of the different dimensions of teacher behavior found that these various dimensions can be further reduced to three: delivering instruction, facilitating interactions, and evaluating student learning. Together these dimensions formed a component termed "general instructional skill" that had an average correlation across 17 different student instructional rating forms of .33 with student achievement (d'Apollonia & Abrami, 1997a).

Although the evidence is clear that student perceptions of teacher behaviors are linked in nonchance ways with how much students learn in a course, there is also evidence to suggest that student perceptions of teaching behavior themselves are influenced by a number of instructor and course characteristics. These factors include expected or actual grade (Greenwald, 1997; Krautmann & Sander, 1999; Marsh & Roche, 1997), academic discipline (Cashin, 1990; Franklin & Theall, 1992; Murray, Jelley, & Renaud, 1996; Murray & Renaud, 1995), class size (Ludlow, 1996; Wachtel, 1998), faculty age (Renaud & Murray, 1996), whether the study is a published article or dissertation (Brodie, 1999), and grading leniency (Greenwald & Gillmore, 1997; McKeachie, 1997).[16] Such influences may be troublesome factors, or at least factors that need to be taken into account, when student perceptions or evaluations of teaching are used in faculty promotion, tenure, or salary decisions. However, they may have little impact on the extent to which student perceptions of teacher behavior can help us understand teaching actions that, at least in the aggregate, enhance student learning (Aleamoni, 1999).

Simply because a variable biases student perceptions of teaching does not necessarily mean that it biases or speciously inflates the relationship between perceptions of teacher behavior and student knowledge acquisition. This notion is suggested by d'Apollonia and Abrami (1997a, 1997b), who reanalyzed data from 43 multisection studies to estimate the unique contribution of instructor effectiveness to student learning with statistical controls for potentially important confounding or biasing influences (for example, published articles or theses, student knowledge of final grade, faculty rank, student ability differences). They concluded that "under appropriate conditions (all instructors are faculty members, evaluation is carried out prior to students knowing their grade, sections are equivalent in terms of student prior ability or equivalence is experimentally controlled) and when the validity coefficient is corrected for attenuation, more than 45 percent of the variation in student learning among sections can be explained by student perceptions of instructor effectiveness" (d'Apollonia & Abrami, 1997a, p. 1203). In short, the association between teacher behaviors and student learning was not explained away by potentially confounding influences.

Nearly all the correlational research on the relationship between student perceptions of teaching behaviors and student knowledge acquisition has been conducted at the course level. The latter half of the 1990s, however, saw initiation of a small body of research seeking to estimate the relationship between teaching behaviors and student learning at the program or institution level. For example, various analyses of the National Study of Student Learning data have asked students to indicate the extent to which the overall instruction they received at their institution was characterized by *pedagogical skill and clarity* (for example, instructors give clear explanations, instructors make good use of examples) and by *organization and preparation* (for example, presentation of material is well organized, class time is used effectively). These two scales had the highest correlations with student course-level learning in Feldman's (1997) meta-analysis. With statistical controls in place for such factors as precollege test scores, race, academic motivation, patterns of coursework taken, place of residence, work responsibilities, and full- or part-time enrollment, perceived instructional organization-preparation had modest but statistically significant positive effects on the following: end-of-first-year scores on standardized tests of reading comprehension and mathematics (Pascarella, Edison, Nora, Hagedorn, & Braxton, 1996), end-of-second-year scores on a standardized measure of writing skills (Edison et al., 1998), and end-of-third-year scores in reading comprehension (Edison et al., 1998; Whitt et al., in press). It also had modest but statistically significant, positive effects on student self-reported gains in writing and thinking skills at the end of the second and third years of college (Whitt et al., in press). No significant net effects were found for the skill-clarity variable. Taken in total, these findings support Svinicki's (1991) theoretical proposition that when instruction is presented in an organized fashion it increases the probability that students will exploit that organizational structure to understand and store content. Furthermore, the correlational evidence from the National Study of Student Learning suggests that the positive link between teacher organization and preparation and course-level achievement might extend to more general literacy skills and quantitative proficiencies.

Another group of scholars has looked at the relationship between student perceptions of teaching behavior and student learning (assessed with self-reports) in an engineering curriculum (Cabrera, Colbeck, & Terenzini, 1998, 2001; Terenzini et al., 1999). The dimensions of teaching behavior considered were these: instructor interaction and feedback (for example, interaction with the instructor is part of a course, instructor gives frequent feedback on work) and clarity and organization (for example, assignments and class activities are clearly explained, assignments and class activities are interrelated). With statistical controls for such factors as academic ability, gender, ethnicity, and year in college, both measures of teacher behavior had significant, positive effects on self-reported gains in engineering design skills and problem-solving skills.

Experimental studies. It is one thing to say that teacher behaviors (as perceived by students) are significantly correlated with student learning and quite another to say that teacher behaviors cause student learning. In order to make the strongest possible causal statements about the link between teacher behaviors and student achievement, that link needs to be observed under experimental conditions. In our 1991 synthesis, we reported that only teacher clarity (for example, clear explanations, avoidance of vague terms, and use of concrete examples) was found to influence student content acquisition positively under experimental conditions. In the 1990s, however, additional experimental work was conducted that focused on teacher expressiveness and organization.

Teacher expressiveness, sometimes referred to as teacher enthusiasm, consists of behaviors such as speaking expressively or emphatically, using humor, maintaining eye contact, and physical movement (Murray, 1991; Schonwetter, 1993). Expressiveness is thought to enhance learning in classroom situations by engaging the learners' attention, both generally and to specific course content or topics (Murray, 1991). Despite some skepticism (Williams & Ceci, 1997), experimental investigations have consistently shown that expressiveness significantly enhances student content learning. For example, Schonwetter, Perry, and Struthers (1994) randomly assigned college students to two comparison groups. The intervention was two videotaped lectures of expressive or unexpressive instruction. Specific instructor characteristics distinguishing expressive from unexpressive instruction included continuous eye contact versus no eye contact, voice inflection in the delivery of the lecture versus a monotonal presentation, physical movement defined as appropriate hand gestures and physical relocation of the presenter around and in front of the lectern versus no hand gestures and remaining in one position behind the lectern, and appropriate humor reflecting the lecture content versus no humor. The amount of material presented was held constant by equating the two lectures for the number of teaching points. Students receiving expressive instruction scored approximately one standard deviation higher (34 percentile points) than their counterparts receiving unexpressive instruction on a 30-item posttest designed to assess retention and conceptual understanding of the content presented. Similar impacts for expressive or enthusiastic instruction are reported in other experimental studies (Menec et al., 1992; Perry, 1991; Perry et al., 1994; Wood & Murray, 1999).

Other experimental work indicates that expressive instruction also increases motivation to learn (Schonwetter, Perry, Menec, Struthers, & Hechter, 1993). However, an important experiment by Wood and Murray (1999) suggests that three mediating processes may be involved in the link between teacher expressiveness-enthusiasm and student learning: selective attention to academic content, motivation to learn, and signaling of topic structure for memory encoding. Of those processes, memory encoding plays a more decisive role in student learning than either selective attention or motivation.

Teacher organization embraces the organization of subject matter and the planning of course content. Typical behaviors might be putting the outline of a lecture on the blackboard, giving a preliminary overview of the lecture, and signaling transition to a new topic (Murray, 1991). As with teacher clarity, teacher organization is expected to increase student learning by facilitating information processing and recall of the material presented (Schonwetter, 1993). Organization may also improve achievement by eliciting attention to specific material that is cued by outlines, headings, and serial connection of relevant topics. Thus, like expressiveness, organization is thought to influence learning by enhancing student attention.

There appears to be less experimental work on teacher organization than on teacher expressiveness. However, Schonwetter, Menec, and Perry (1995) conducted an important large-scale experiment with students in an introductory psychology course that combined both factors. There were two main interventions in the study: expressive and unexpressive instruction, operationally defined in essentially the same way as in the Schonwetter, Perry, and Struthers (1994) experiment described in the preceding paragraph, and high versus low organization. The high organization condition consisted of such behaviors as giving a preliminary overview of the lecture, providing an outline of the lecture, using headings and subheadings, and signaling transitions to new topics. These behaviors were decreased or eliminated in the low organization condition. Students were assigned to one of four conditions where they watched a videotape lecture characterized by one of the following combinations: high expressiveness–high organization, high expressiveness–low organization, low expressiveness–high organization, and low expressiveness–low organization. All four lectures were given by the same instructor, and lecture content was held constant by having the instructor use the identical set of notes in all lectures. Irrespective of level of expressiveness, students receiving the highly organized instruction had significantly higher scores on posttests of recall, recognition, and self-perceived learning than their counterparts in the low instructional organization condition. The advantages for highly organized instruction were about .55 of a standard deviation (21 percentile points) on recall, .58 of a standard deviation (22 percentile points) on recognition, and .45 of a standard deviation (17 percentile points) on perceived learning. A marginally significant advantage on content application averaged about .20 of a standard deviation (8 percentile points). The most effective combination of teacher behaviors across achievement outcomes was the high organization–high expressiveness condition. However, high organization appeared the more important in that high organization–low expressiveness resulted in significantly greater recall achievement than either low organization–high expressiveness or low organization–low expressiveness.

Improving teaching effectiveness. The interesting thing about teaching behaviors such as clarity, expressiveness, and organization is that they themselves appear to be eminently learnable by college teachers. This suggests that we may be able to improve faculty teaching effectiveness through purposeful interventions. There is an extensive body of literature suggesting that this may, indeed, be possible. Over 20 years ago, Cohen (1980) conducted a meta-analysis of 22 field experiments (not cited in our 1991 synthesis) and concluded that feedback from student perceptions of teaching alone led to modest improvements in faculty teaching performance, whereas student feedback supplemented by competent consultation aimed at weak areas of teaching led to more substantial gains in the quality of teaching. In all cases, teaching effectiveness or the quality of teaching was measured by subsequent student perceptions. Murray and Smith (1989) and Marsh and Roche (1993) have further refined this conclusion with evidence suggesting that feedback from student perceptions on specific behaviors resulted in greater improvement than perceptions on more general characteristics. Other studies, or syntheses of studies, have consistently supported the notion that feedback from student perceptions of specific teaching behaviors coupled with competent consultation leads to the greatest gains in effective teaching (L'Hommedieu, Menges, & Brinko, 1988, 1990; Marsh & Roche, 1997; Menges & Brinko, 1986; Waltman & Cook, 1997; Weimer & Lenze, 1997; Wilson, 1986).

Unfortunately, all of the research we reviewed on feedback, consultation, and improved teaching effectiveness used student perceptions of teacher behaviors and the quality of instruction received as the measure of effective instruction. We found no evidence that linked feedback and consultation, based on student perceptions of teacher behaviors, directly with actual measures of student learning or content acquisition.

Academic Effort-Involvement. It is quite clear from the preceding sections that a student's coursework and classroom experiences shape both the nature and extent of his or her acquisition of subject matter knowledge and academic skills in college. It would be surprising indeed if this were not the case. What has been made particularly clear in the research from the 1990s, however, is that what the student does to exploit the academic opportunities provided by the institution may have an equal, if not greater, influence (Astin, 1993c; Kuh, Schuh, et al., 1991).

Since the 1991 publication of the first edition of *How College Affects Students,* a substantial amount of research has focused on estimating the net impact on knowledge acquisition of a student's level of academic effort or involvement. The weight of evidence from this research clearly suggests that, other things being equal, the more the student is psychologically engaged in activities and tasks that reinforce and extend the formal academic experience, the more he or she will learn. Most, though by no means all, of this research measures academic effort-involvement with various scales from the College Student Experiences Questionnaire—CSEQ (Pace, 1987, 1988, 1990) or the Community College Student Experiences Questionnaire—CCSEQ (Friedlander, Pace, & Lehman, 1990). Both instruments assess involvement by asking students to indicate how often they engage in a range of specific activities clustered into different areas such as Library Experiences; Course Learning; Art, Music, and Theater; Experiences in Writing; Science; and the like.

A recent typical example of this type of research is found in Whitt et al. (in press). Analyzing data from the National Study of Student Learning, they sought to determine the extent to which involvement in academic or academic-related activities uniquely influenced both standardized and self-reported measures of knowledge and academic skill acquisition during college. In order to estimate accurately the net impact of different measures of academic involvement, statistical controls were introduced for an extensive set of variables. These variables included tested precollege ability, academic motivation, and demographic characteristics; the academic selectivity and other characteristics of the institution attended; and measures of the academic and social experience of college (for example, patterns of coursework taken, perceived quality of instruction received, full- or part-time enrollment, work responsibilities, on- or off-campus residence, extracurricular involvement). In the presence of these controls, a global measure of academic involvement (that is, library experiences, writing experiences, and course learning) had statistically significant, positive effects on student self-reported gains in writing and thinking skills and in understanding the arts and humanities; a measure of science effort had positive effects on self-reported gains in understanding science; and a measure of involvement in nonassigned reading positively influenced standardized measures of reading comprehension, writing skills, and science reasoning. Astin (1993c) reports a markedly similar effect for nonassigned reading on the verbal score of the Graduate Record Examination.

Other studies employ different operational definitions of academic effort-involvement and vary in their ability to control for potential confounding influences. However, the results they report are quite consistent with those of Whitt et al. (in press). Net of other influences, a student's level of engagement in academic and academic-related tasks and activities positively influences knowledge acquisition and academic skill development. This holds when knowledge acquisition is measured by student self-reported gains in both community college samples (Douzenis, 1996; Ethington, 1998; Friedlander & MacDougall, 1992; Glover, 1996; Knight, 1994; Lipetzky & Ammentorp, 1991) and four-year college samples (Arnold et al., 1993; Davis & Murrell, 1993; Kuh, Arnold, & Vesper, 1991; Kuh & Hu, 1999a; Pike, 1991a; Watson & Kuh, 1996; Williams, 1996). It also holds when academic skill development or knowledge acquisition is assessed by objective measures (Johnstone, Ashbaugh, & Warfield, 2002) and when the sample combines students from community colleges and four-year colleges (Hagedorn, Siadat, Nora, & Pascarella, 1997). Moreover, as with Whitt et al. (in press), the great majority of these studies also control for the level of student social involvement during college.

Social and Extracurricular Effort-Involvement. As we observed from the evidence on collaborative learning, cooperative learning, supplementary instruction, and peer tutoring, peers can play a central role in how much students learn in formal classroom settings. A growing number of scholars have suggested that this peer influence on learning extends into nonclassroom situations, and that if much learning is socially based, then students' social and extracurricular involvements have important implications for what is learned in college (Aleman, 1994, 1997; Baxter Magolda, 1992a; Kuh, 1995; Lamport, 1994; Love & Goodsell Love, 1995; Moffatt, 1991; Rendon, 1994; Rendon & Jalomo, 1993;

Terenzini, Pascarella, & Blimling, 1996). In this section, we review the evidence on the ways in which student social and extracurricular involvement influences learning. We will focus on interactions with peers, interactions with faculty, Greek affiliation, intercollegiate athletic involvement, service involvement, diversity experiences, work responsibilities, and on- or off-campus residence.

Interactions with peers. Perhaps because of the wide availability and use of the College Student Experiences Questionnaire and similar instruments, the 1990s witnessed a substantial amount of research on how student interaction with peers influences learning. The weight of evidence from this research is quite clear in suggesting that certain kinds of nonclassroom interactions with peers have a net positive impact on learning. Not surprisingly, the most influential peer interactions appear to be those that reinforce the ethos of the formal academic program and extend it into nonclassroom settings. That is, they are interactions among students that include such things as discussing policies and issues related to campus activities; having serious discussions about religious, philosophical, or political beliefs; discussing personal problems; discussing the arts, science, technology, or international relations; and talking about an idea brought up in class. For example, Whitt, Edison, Pascarella, Nora, and Terenzini (1999a) constructed a scale from CSEQ responses in the National Study of Student Learning data that measured the extent to which students were involved in many of these, and similar types of, peer interactions. They were interested in the net impact of this nonclassroom peer interaction scale on various standardized and self-report measures of learning. Consequently, they introduced statistical controls for such potential confounding influences as precollege ability test scores, academic motivation, demographic characteristics and family background, full- or part-time enrollment, work responsibilities, on- or off-campus residence, time spent studying, and patterns of coursework taken in five areas. With these controls in place, the nonclassroom peer interaction scale had significant, positive effects on self-reported gains in writing and thinking skills and in understanding the arts and humanities across all three years of the study. It also had significant, positive effects on end-of-first-year scores on a standardized measure of reading comprehension and on a standardized measure of composite learning consisting of reading, mathematics, and critical thinking.

Other studies have employed somewhat different measures of peer interaction and have effected varying levels of control for confounding influences, but their results have been quite consistent with those of Whitt et al. (1999a). Peer interactions, particularly those that extend and reinforce what happens in the academic program, appear to influence positively knowledge acquisition and academic skill development during college. This conclusion holds when knowledge acquisition is assessed by student self-reported gains in both community college samples (Douzenis, 1996; Ethington, 1998; Knight, 1994) and four-year college samples (Arnold et al., 1993; Astin, 1993c; Cabrera et al., 1999; Davis & Murrell, 1993; Kuh, Arnold, & Vesper, 1991; Volkwein & Carbone, 1994; Watson & Kuh, 1996; Whitt et al., in press; Williams, 1996). It also holds when learning is measured by standardized tests such as the National Teachers

Examination (Astin, 1993c) or the verbal score on the Graduate Record Examination (Anaya, 1999b). In the great majority of these studies, the positive impact of involvement in peer interactions persists even in the presence of controls for students' level of academic effort or involvement. Thus, it is unlikely that the statistically significant impact of peer interactions on learning is merely a proxy for a high level of academic effort or involvement. Substantial evidence indicates a strong positive correlation between academic and social involvement (Bryant & Bradley, 1993; see also Pascarella & Terenzini, 1991, pp. 98–101). Students with a high level of engagement in their academic experience during college also tend to be highly engaged in nonclassroom pursuits.

Not all student involvement with peers, however, has positive implications for learning. Student extracurricular involvement that may have little to do with extending and reinforcing the academic program can, at times, inhibit knowledge acquisition and the development of academic skills. For example, in analyses of the 1984 to 1989 Cooperative Institutional Research Program data, Anaya (1992, 1996) found that even in the presence of controls for precollege ability, student demographic characteristics and high school experiences, institutional characteristics, and measures of academic involvement, participation in student clubs and organizations had small but statistically significant, negative effects on Graduate Record Examination verbal scores. Similar results are reported by Astin (1993c) and Anaya (1999c) for scores on the Medical College Admissions Test, by Whitt et al. (in press) for community college students' scores on a standardized measure of writing skills, and by Williams (1996) for self-reported gains in general education knowledge and skills. The only exception to this weight of evidence is a positive effect of participation in clubs and organizations on end-of-first-year scores on a standardized measure of mathematics skills by Hagedorn, Siadat, Nora, and Pascarella (1997). Using a more extensive set of controls with the same sample, however, this finding was not replicated by Whitt et al. (in press).

Interactions with faculty. As suggested in an important recent work by Kuh and Hu (1999a, 2001), frequent student-faculty interaction outside the classroom has become something of an assumed characteristic of an undergraduate education that makes an impact. In our 1991 synthesis, we found a modicum of evidence to support this notion. However, in terms of impact on student learning, the frequency of informal interaction between students and faculty may not be as important as the focus of that interaction. Interactions having an intellectual or substantive focus may have greater impact than simple social exchange (Kuh & Hu, 1999a; Pascarella & Terenzini, 1991).

By far the most comprehensive and focused study of the impact of student interaction with faculty was conducted by Kuh and Hu (1999a, 2001). Their sample was nearly 55,000 full-time enrolled undergraduates from 201 four-year institutions who completed the College Student Experiences Questionnaire between 1990 and 1997. They used factor analysis to divide students' reported interactions with faculty into three types: *substantive interaction* (for example, asked for information related to a course, made an office appointment with faculty, asked for comments-criticisms about work), *out-of-class contact* (for example, had coffee, cakes, snacks with faculty; discussed personal problems with faculty), and *writing improvement* (for example, asked instructor for advice on writing, made appointment to talk about criticism). In the presence of statistical controls for gender, race, socioeconomic status, academic major, measures of academic effort and involvement, and institutional characteristics (selectivity, type, public or private control, and so on), only substantive interaction with faculty had a consistently significant and positive (though modest) impact on a measure of self-reported gains during college that was highly loaded with items assessing knowledge acquisition and academic skill development. The positive effect was reduced to near zero, and became statistically nonsignificant, when measures of the institutional environment were added to the prediction equation. This suggests that the impact on learning of substantive interaction with faculty is transmitted through the institutional environment. Substantive interaction with faculty influences elements of students' perceptions of the environment such as the scholarly-intellectual emphasis and the relational emphasis, which, as we observed in the between-college effects section of this chapter, has direct, positive impacts on learning.

A second important finding from the Kuh and Hu (1999a) study was that only two specific student-faculty interaction items had significant, positive effects on gains reported by seniors when both environmental perceptions and all of the other control variables specified earlier were represented in the prediction equation. These items were "talked with a faculty member" and "worked with faculty on a research project." Thus, both of these specific interactions could be said to have direct, positive impacts on self-reported gains. Unfortunately, the measure of gains employed by Kuh and Hu combines learning items with other dimensions of student growth in college such as work skills, values and ethical standards, and teamwork skills. Consequently, it is not clear that the impacts of student interaction with faculty are unequivocally on student learning. However, a recent study by Anaya (1999c) using a standardized measure of learning essentially replicates this aspect of Kuh and Hu's findings. Controlling for student precollege academic ability, demographic characteristics, institutional characteristics, and other measures of the academic and social experience of college, both talking with faculty outside of class and working on a professor's research project had modest but statistically significant, positive effects on scores on the Medical College Admissions Test.

Other studies on the impact of student-faculty interaction on learning are consistent in using student self-reported gains as the measure of learning. However, they vary dramatically in sample, research design, control of potential confounding influences, and, perhaps most importantly, operational definition of student interaction with faculty. It should not be overly surprising, then, that they also differ somewhat in their results. Some studies find that student interaction with faculty has rather consistent positive effects on student self-reported learning (Cabrera, Nora, Terenzini, Pascarella, & Hagedorn, 1998; Douzenis, 1996; Volkwein, 1991; Volkwein & Carbone, 1994), some find more isolated positive effects (Kuh et al., 1997; Pike, 1991a), and some find no significant impact (Ethington, 1998). There is little in this body of evidence to suggest that differences in findings are attributable to the methodological quality of the study. However, one possible explanation may be in the operational definitions of student-faculty interaction. Two of the four studies that reported generally consistent, positive effects on learning (Cabrera et al., 1999; Volkwein, 1991) employed measures of student interaction with faculty that focused largely on academic-intellectual issues. Considered in concert with the findings of both Kuh and Hu (1999a) and Anaya (1999c), the results of the Volkwein and Cabrera et al. studies appear reasonably consistent in suggesting that student interactions with faculty that focus mainly on academic or related issues may be the most salient in terms of facilitating student learning.

Greek affiliation. Social fraternities and sororities, commonly called Greek organizations, are a visible, if sometimes controversial, aspect of student life at many colleges and universities. Although it is clear that Greek organizations contribute to a student's psychological sense of community, particularly on large campuses (Lounsbury & DeNeui, 1995), and tend to increase levels of social involvement (Pike & Askew, 1990), there has been some question as to their contribution to the academic mission of an institution (Pike, 1999b). The 1990s witnessed the inception of a small but growing body of inquiry that has attempted to estimate the impact of Greek affiliation on student knowledge acquisition and academic skill development. The results of that research depend to some extent on whether one measures learning with student self-reported gains or with objective, standardized measures.

Two single-institution studies assessed the impact of Greek affiliation on learning using students' self-reported gains as the criterion measure. In the first study, there were no significant differences in general education gains between first-year students who joined fraternities or sororities and those who remained independent. However, Greek-affiliated seniors reported significantly higher general education gains than did their counterparts who remained independent ("The Influence of Greek Affiliation," 1997). Because this study did not control for potential confounding differences between seniors who joined Greek organizations and those who remained independent, however, it is difficult to tell if these results reflect differential socialization or differential recruitment effects. A second study at the same institution corrected for this limitation by statistically controlling for such factors as gender, academic ability, and measures of students' social and academic involvement (Pike, 1999b). In the presence of these controls, Greek affiliation had no significant effect on either self-reported gains in general learned abilities or self-reported gains in math, science, and technology. However, Greek affiliation (versus remaining independent) did have a positive indirect effect on gains in general learned abilities, transmitted through social involvement. Unfortunately, the general learned abilities scale combined learning outcomes with such dimensions as gains in interpersonal skills. Consequently, it is difficult to determine if Greek affiliation influenced the learning or the interpersonal skills part of the scale.

Multi-institutional studies employing objective, standardized measures of learning present a somewhat different perspective on the impact of Greek affiliation. For example, analyzing the National Study of Student Learning data, Pascarella, Edison, Whitt, Nora, Hagedorn, and Terenzini (1996) sought to determine the impact of Greek affiliation on end-of-first-year scores on standardized measures of reading comprehension and mathematics. With controls for precollege reading or math scores, academic motivation, race, full- or part-time enrollment, work responsibilities, on- or off-campus residence, patterns of coursework taken, and the academic selectivity of the institution attended, fraternity membership (versus remaining independent) led to modest but statistically significant disadvantages for men of .17 of a standard deviation in reading comprehension and .14 of a standard deviation in mathematics (7 and 6 percentile points, respectively). Sorority membership led to a statistically significant disadvantage for women of .20 of a standard deviation in reading comprehension (8 percentile points).

Following the same sample into their second and third years of college, Pascarella, Flowers, and Whitt (1999) found that the overall negative impacts of Greek affiliation on standardized learning measures tended to diminish in magnitude by about one-third. With the same set of controls as in the first-year study, Greek affiliation had only small and statistically nonsignificant, negative effects on standardized tests of end-of-second-year writing skills and science reasoning for both men and women. Similarly, sorority membership had only a small and statistically nonsignificant impact on end-of-third-year reading comprehension. The only exception to this trend was that fraternity membership led to a significant disadvantage in third-year reading comprehension of .22 of a standard deviation (9 percentile points). Additional analyses employing student self-reported gains found that fraternity members also reported significantly lower gains than independents in end-of-second-year understanding of the arts and humanities. Conversely, sorority members reported significantly greater gains than independents in second-year understanding of science and in third-year writing and thinking skills. The comparison groups in all of these analyses were students who were members of Greek organizations through the first two or the first three years of college, respectively, versus students who remained independent during the same respective time periods. For those students who joined fraternities or sororities after the first year of college, the implications for learning were trivial across all measures used. Taken together, both NSSL analyses suggest that the negative learning effects of Greek affiliation are somewhat more pronounced for men than for women and may diminish in magnitude, though not totally disappear for men, after the first year of college.

The Pascarella et al. (1996, 1999) investigations with the National Study of Student Learning data cited in the preceding paragraphs are not alone in finding negative effects of Greek affiliation on standardized measures of learning. Analyzing the multi-institutional 1985 to 1989 Cooperative Institutional Research Program data, Anaya (1992) found that being a fraternity or sorority member had a very small, but statistically significant, negative effect on the composite score of the Graduate Record Examination. This negative effect could not be explained away by differences in student precollege ability, demographic characteristics, motivations, institutional characteristics, major, and involvement in academic and social experiences during college. Similar results are reported by Pike and Askew (1990) in a single-institution study of college seniors that controlled for precollege academic ability (ACT scores) and used the College Outcome Measures Project (COMP) Objective Test to assess learning. Somewhat in contrast with the NSSL analyses by Pascarella et al., the findings of Anaya, as well as Pike and Askew, suggest that Greek affiliation has a significant, albeit small, negative impact on standardized measures of learning through the senior year of college. Neither Anaya nor Pike and Askew, however, appear to have disaggregated the effects of Greek affiliation for men and women.

Intercollegiate athletic involvement. Intercollegiate athletics is one of the salient filters through which the public views American postsecondary education. Often the public's image of an institution, as well as its attractiveness to prospective students, is, for better or worse, shaped by the performance of its athletic teams (Toma, 1998; Toma & Cross, 1996). Paralleling the visibility of an institution through its athletic teams, however, has been a general concern about the contribution of intercollegiate athletics to an individual's education (Diaz, Gonyea, Junck, & Ward, 1998; Jordan & Denson, 1990; Lewis, 1993; Parham, 1993; Sperber, 2000; Telander, 1996). There is a small but consistent body of evidence to suggest that intercollegiate athletes, and, in particular, those participating in football and basketball, may not be deriving the same cognitive benefits from college as their nonathlete peers. There is also evidence to suggest that any negative influence of athletic participation is more pronounced for men than for women. All of the evidence in this body of research is based on standardized measures of student learning.

Both Anaya (1999b) and Astin (1993c) conducted analyses of the 1985 to 1989 Cooperative Institutional Research Project data, which are based on student samples from over 200 four-year institutions. In their studies, they introduced statistical controls for an extensive battery of potential confounding influences, including tested academic ability (for example, SAT scores), secondary school performance, demographic and family background characteristics, academic major, measures of academic and social involvement in college, and characteristics of the institution attended. In the presence of these controls, participation in intercollegiate athletics was found to have a modest, but statistically significant, negative effect on scores on the verbal test of the Graduate Record Examination and the Law School Admissions Test. Participation in intercollegiate football or basketball negatively influenced general knowledge scores on the National Teachers Examination.

Quite similar findings are reported in two studies that analyzed data from the 18 four-year colleges and universities participating in the National Study of Student Learning (Pascarella, Bohr, Nora, & Terenzini, 1995b; Pascarella, Truckenmiller, et al., 1999). Where the findings from Anaya (1999b) and Astin (1993c) appear to be based on combined samples of women and men, the NSSL findings disaggregated the impact of athletic participation for men and women. The NSSL studies also separated intercollegiate athletic participation for men into "revenue-generating" sports (football and basketball) and "non-revenue-generating" sports (all others). With statistical controls in place for precollege test scores in reading comprehension and mathematics, ethnicity, family socio-economic status, precollege academic motivation, age, full- or part-time enrollment, on- or off-campus residence, the academic selectivity of the institution attended, and whether or not the institution's athletic program was in Division I, Pascarella, Bohr, Nora, and Terenzini (1995b) found that men participating in intercollegiate football and basketball were significantly disadvantaged, relative to both male nonathletes and male athletes in other sports, on end-of-first-year reading comprehension and mathematics. In reading comprehension, the disadvantage was .24 of a standard deviation (10 percentile points) relative to nonathletes and .19 of a standard deviation (8 percentile points) relative to athletes in other sports. In mathematics, the disadvantage for male participants in revenue sports was .20 of a standard deviation (8 percentile points) relative to nonathletes and .17 of a standard deviation (7 percentile points) relative to athletes in nonrevenue sports. Differences between male nonathletes and athletes in nonrevenue sports were trivial and nonsignificant in both reading comprehension and mathematics.

Because of ambiguity in defining revenue-producing sports for women, Pascarella, Bohr, Nora, & Terenzini (1995b) grouped all female athletes together regardless of their sport. They found virtual parity between female athletes and nonathletes in first-year mathematics and only a small, though statistically significant, disadvantage for female athletes in first-year reading comprehension. Net of the control variables, female athletes had a disadvantage in reading comprehension of .10 of a standard deviation (4 percentile points).

A follow-up of the same sample, using essentially the same research design and analytical model, found that the learning disadvantages for male football and basketball players persisted into the second and third years of college and became somewhat more pronounced (Pascarella, Truckenmiller, et al., 1999). For example, at the end of the second year of college, male football and basketball players had statistically significant disadvantages on a standardized test of writing skills of .27 of a standard deviation (11 percentile points) relative to male nonathletes and .33 of a standard deviation (13 percentile points) relative to male athletes in nonrevenue sports. Similarly, male football and basketball players were also disadvantaged relative to athletes in other sports on a standardized measure of science reasoning (.21 of a standard deviation, 8 percentile points). At the end of the third year of college, male football and basketball players had significant disadvantages in reading comprehension of .27 of a standard deviation (11 percentile points) relative to male nonathletes and .36 of a standard deviation (14 percentile points) relative to male athletes in other intercollegiate sports. Once again, there was virtual parity across all measures of learning between male nonathletes and males participating in nonrevenue intercollegiate sports. For women, intercollegiate athletic participation had only one significant negative effect. Relative to their nonathlete counterparts, women athletes had a disadvantage in third-year reading comprehension of .23 of a standard deviation (9 percentile points).

Both of the investigations based on the National Study of Student Learning data also found that the negative learning effects for men participating in intercollegiate football and basketball were similar in magnitude, irrespective of their levels of precollege test scores, academic motivation, socioeconomic status, or ethnicity. In short, no particular type of male student received greater learning penalties from participating in intercollegiate football or basketball than any other. Similarly, no evidence was uncovered to indicate that the learning disadvantages accruing to male football and basketball players differed in magnitude at NCAA Division I or non-Division I institutions or at institutions differing in the academic selectivity of their undergraduate student bodies (Pascarella et al., 1995a; Pascarella, Truckenmiller, et al., 1999). It is also interesting to note that the negative learning impacts on men of participation in intercollegiate football and basketball were not explainable by differences between these athletes and other men in their experience of college (for example, amount studied, credit hours completed, work responsibilities, or patterns of coursework taken). This finding suggests that it may be necessary to look elsewhere—perhaps to the time requirements and the culture of revenue-producing sports themselves—to understand just why football and basketball players are not deriving the same knowledge acquisition and academic skill benefits from college as other men.

Service involvement. A growing number of postsecondary institutions in the United States have become actively engaged in encouraging undergraduates to involve themselves in some form of volunteer service (Astin, 1996b; Astin, Sax, & Avalos, 1999; Eyler & Giles, 1997, 1999; Eyler, Giles, & Braxton, 1995, 1996, 1997b). As reported by Astin, Sax, and Avalos (1999) the importance that higher education leaders place on volunteer service as part of the undergraduate curriculum can be seen in the growth of a consortium of colleges known as the Campus Compact, which seeks to promote service among students and faculty. This consortium currently has over 500 member institutions. Paralleling growth in postsecondary education's interest in service experiences has been an interest in assessing the educational impacts of service. In short, what do students learn from volunteer service?

One line of inquiry into the impact of service experiences compares the learning or knowledge acquisition of students who participate in service experiences with those who do not. For example, Markus, Howard, and King (1993) conducted a quasi experiment in which sections of a political science course were randomly assigned to two instructional conditions: community service and control. Students had no knowledge during course registration about the intended experiment or which sections were to be the treatment or control groups. In the community service sections students were assigned to engage in 20 hours of service over the 13-week semester. The service opportunities included working in a homeless shelter, a women's crisis center, and an ecology center and tutoring at-risk primary or secondary school students. Discussions about what students were learning from their service experiences and how those experiences related to course readings and lectures were built into section meetings. Students also wrote short papers and presented brief oral reports on their experiences. The control sections used a traditional format, in which section meetings were devoted to discussion of readings and lectures. Students in the control sections wrote longer term papers based on library research intended to take an amount of time and effort equivalent to that expended by students in the service sections. Both the community service and control sections were taught by doctoral student graduate teaching assistants with comparable levels of teaching experience. The students in the community service and control sections did not differ in sex, race, year in school, measures of personal attitudes and values, or strength of desire to take the course. At the end of the course, however, the students in the community service sections had a statistically significant advantage in final course grade based on common midterm and final examinations of course content. Using the statistics they provided, we estimated the learning advantage accruing to the community service students to be .29 of a standard deviation (11 percentile points). Students in the community service sections were also significantly more likely than control students to say that they learned to apply principles from the course to new situations.

The results of the Markus et al. (1993) study were essentially replicated in a quasi experiment with random assignment of course sections conducted by Berson and Younkin (1998). Students participating in a 20-hour service activity as part of their course experience had a statistically significant advantage in course grade, based largely on the same course examination, over students not participating in the service activity. The learning advantage was .24 of a standard deviation (9 percentile points). Similar results are also reported in a quasi-experimental study by Strage (2000), but with a smaller estimated effect size (.10 of a standard deviation, or 4 percentile points).

Findings consistent with those of Markus et al. (1993), Berson and Younkin (1998), and Strage (2000) have also been reported in large-scale correlational studies, employing extensive statistical controls, by Astin and Sax (1998), Gray et al. (1996), and Whitt et al. (in press). Other, smaller-scale quasi-experimental studies report that, even though they do not always demonstrate greater achievement (Miller, 1994), students in courses with a service component demonstrate a greater ability to apply course concepts to new situations than do their counterparts in parallel courses without the service component (Kendrick, 1996; Miller, 1994).

A second line of inquiry tests the general, and seemingly reasonable, hypothesis that greater learning will occur in courses or curricula where the service component is an integral part of the course content and activities and where there is a regular reflective component linking the two (that is, service learning) than in courses that simply contain a service component (Eyler, 1993; Eyler & Giles, 1997; Giles, Honnet, & Migliore, 1991). Although the dependent variables employed are often indirect measures of knowledge and academic skill acquisition, the weight of evidence would nevertheless support this hypothesis (Eyler, 1993, 1995; Eyler et al., 1995; Ikeda, 2000; Myers-Lipton, 1994).

Diversity experiences. Paralleling trends in the larger society, it would appear that racial and cultural diversity are a central aspect of the future for American postsecondary institutions (Astin, 1998; National Center for Education Statistics, 1998). A number of university presidents have argued that this is a fortuitous trend because a diverse undergraduate student body is more educationally effective than a homogeneous one (for example, Rudenstine, 1999; Schmidt, 1998). To what extent, however, are these claims supported by evidence?

The 1990s witnessed a growing body of research that attempted to assess the extent to which involvement in diversity experiences influences student learning in college. The majority of work in this area employed the longitudinal data sets of the Cooperative Institutional Research Program—CIRP (Astin, 1993a; Gurin, 1999; Hurtado, 1997, 1999). A basic hypothesis of this research is that institutional diversity (for example, the percentage of undergraduates and faculty who are persons of color) will lead to the greater likelihood of students being exposed to diversity experiences both in the classroom (for example, taking an ethnic studies course, reading about ethnic or gender issues) and in informal, nonclassroom settings (for example, discussing racial issues, attending a racial-cultural awareness workshop, socializing with someone from a different racial-ethnic group, proportion of close friends in college who are not of one's race-ethnicity). In turn, it is hypothesized that involvement in diversity experiences will enhance learning (Gurin, 1999). Thus, a diverse student body in an institution will have an indirect, positive influence on student learning by increasing the likelihood of student exposure to, and involvement in, diversity experiences.

Not surprisingly, perhaps, there is strong support for the first hypothesis in this indirect causal sequence. Analyzing data from students at 184 four-year institutions in the CIRP 1985 to 1989 data, Gurin (1999) found that student body diversity (which she refers to as structural diversity) at an institution significantly and positively predicted level of student involvement in a range of diversity experiences. Similarly, in analyses of faculty at 159 four-year institutions from the CIRP 1989–90 Faculty Survey, Hurtado (1999) found that faculty of color tended to introduce diversity experiences into the curriculum significantly more often than White faculty.

Although all the findings are based solely on student self-reports of learning or academic skill gains, there is also consistent evidence to support the second hypothesis in the causal sequence—involvement in diversity experiences positively influencing student learning. For example, Astin's (1993a) analyses of the multi-institutional 1985 to 1989 CIRP data found that diversity experiences such as attending a racial-cultural awareness workshop, discussing racial or ethnic issues, and socializing with someone from another racial-ethnic group had modest, but statistically significant, positive effects on specific self-reported gains in knowledge and skill acquisition. These gains included general knowledge, knowledge of a field or discipline, and writing skills. These positive effects persisted even in the presence of statistical controls for an extensive battery of potential confounding influences such as student precollege ability, secondary school experiences, demographic characteristics, and institutional characteristics.

Quite consistent results are reported by Hurtado (1999) in analyses of the multi-institutional 1987 to 1991 iteration of the CIRP data. With controls for students' academic self-concept, secondary school grades, hours per week spent studying, and the selectivity of the institution attended, enrolling in an ethnic studies course had small, statistically significant, positive associations with self-reported gains in general knowledge, foreign-language ability, and writing skills. Similarly, studying with someone from a different racial-ethnic background had positive and significant, though modest, net associations with gains in general knowledge, knowledge of a particular field, foreign-language ability, and writing skills.

Although the findings of Astin (1993a) and Hurtado (1999) appear to be based on samples that pool students with different racial-ethnic identities, Gurin (1999) attempted to disaggregate the effects of involvement in diversity experiences for African-American, Latino, and White students, respectively. Her analyses of the 1985 to 1989 CIRP data used essentially the same extensive set of statistical controls as Astin's (1993a) analyses of the data. All three racial groups derived learning benefits from involvement in diversity experiences. However, the positive effects appeared to accrue in a more broad-based and comprehensive way for White students. Thus, one conclusion from Gurin's findings is that White students may derive greater benefits from involvement in diversity experiences than African-American or Latino students. A reasonable competing explanation, however, is that the substantially smaller samples of African-American and Latino students may simply have made it more unlikely to uncover statistically significant effects for those groups.

A somewhat different approach to the study of the learning impacts of diversity experiences was taken in a study of problem solving in engineering in 49 course sections at seven institutions by Terenzini, Cabrera, Colbeck, Bjorklund, and Parente (1999). They sought to determine if classroom racial diversity had a unique impact on students' self-reported growth in engineering problem-solving skills (for example, ability to design, solve an unstructured problem, clearly describe a problem orally or in writing, and the like). Classroom diversity was operationally defined as the ratio of students of color to White students. A .50 ratio was treated as the most diverse class, while .00 was the least diverse. Statistical controls were introduced for academic ability (combined SAT scores), individual race-ethnicity, sex, and measures of the extent to which class instruction was characterized by collaborative learning activities, instructor clarity and organization, and the extent to which the instructor interacted with students and gave detailed and frequent feedback on student progress. In the presence of these controls, classroom racial diversity had a small, but statistically significant, positive impact on students' self-reported gains in engineering design skills. Additional evidence suggested that there may be a curvilinear relationship between classroom diversity and growth in design skill competencies. A ratio of minority to majority race students of between 33 and 39 percent appeared to be most conducive to design skill gains, net of other influences. Levels of class diversity below and above that interval had less positive effects.

Work responsibilities. It has become increasingly clear that a substantial percentage of the students entering American postsecondary education will work while attending college (Hexter, 1990; Luzzo, McWhirter, & Hutcheson, 1997; O'Brien, 1993). The National Center for Education Statistics (1996) estimates that 14.5 percent of all postsecondary students work 34 or more hours per week while enrolled, 43.4 percent work between 15 and 33 hours per week, 31.2 percent work less than 15 hours per week, and only 10.9 percent do not work. In short, working while in college has become the norm, and better than half of all undergraduates are, on average, working 15 hours or more per week. What implications does this fact have for the impacts of postsecondary education on working students? Because time is a finite commodity, it seems reasonable that the more one works, the less discretionary time one has available for academic work or study. Although there are some exceptions (Wade, 1991), most evidence does in fact suggest that work has a significant negative association with academic effort-involvement and time spent studying (Douzenis & Murrell, 1992; Pascarella, Bohr, Nora, Desler, & Zusman, 1994; Pascarella, Edison, Nora, Hagedorn, & Terenzini, 1998a). Conceivably, then, one might anticipate that work would have a negative net impact on student knowledge and academic skill acquisition during college. When such learning is measured either with standardized tests or student self-reported gains, however, this may not necessarily be the case.

For example, two analyses of data from the National Study of Student Learning found that, with a few notable exceptions, amount of on- or off-campus work had only trivial and statistically nonsignificant effects on standardized measures of learning. In the first study, based on a single-institution sample, Pascarella, Bohr, Nora, Desler, and Zusman (1994) found that when controls were introduced for precollege test scores, academic motivation, age, full- or part-time enrollment, on- or off-campus residence, and hours studied, hours worked on or off campus had no significant effects on end-of-first-year scores on standardized measures of reading comprehension and mathematics. A follow-up study (Pascarella et al., 1998a) analyzed longitudinal data from five community colleges and 18 four-year institutions. They used essentially the same set of control variables and analytical model as the Pascarella et al. (1994) study, but they also added controls for socioeconomic status, amount of coursework taken in five general areas, and the average academic ability of students at the institution attended. Controlling for this battery of variables, amount of either on- or off-campus work had no significant linear or curvilinear effects on end-of-first-year scores on a standardized measure of learning consisting of a composite of reading comprehension, mathematics, and critical thinking. In the second year of college, on-campus work had a small, negative impact on a standardized measure of science reasoning, but off-campus work had no effect. Neither form of work had a significant impact on a standardized measure of second-year writing skills. Both forms of work had a significant curvilinear relationship with a composite measure of end-of-third-year learning consisting of reading comprehension and critical thinking. Part-time on- or off-campus work had a significant, positive influence, but on-campus work in excess of 15 hours per week and off-campus work in excess of 20 hours per week had a negative impact. Finally, across all years of the study the impacts of work on learning appeared to be essentially the same irrespective of student characteristics (for example, ethnicity, gender, age, precollege ability, full- or part time enrollment) and whether the student attended a community college or a four-year college.

In addition to the results of the National Study of Student Learning analyses (Pascarella et al., 1994; Pascarella et al., 1998a), a number of other studies have assessed the impact of work responsibilities on learning. The weight of evidence from this body of research, however, would not appear to change fundamentally the basic conclusions to be drawn from the NSSL data—namely, that work during college, particularly if it is only part-time, may not consistently or seriously inhibit student learning. Some studies find that work has no significant effects on measures of learning (Graham & Long, 1998; Kuh, 1993; Lundberg, 2002; Steele, 1999; Volkwein, Schmonsky, & Im, 1989), some find that the effects are mixed (Hagedorn, Siadat, Nora, & Pascarella, 1997), and some find that the effects are generally positive (Penny & White, 1998; Terenzini, Yaeger, Pascarella, & Nora, 1996).

Because work during college probably does reduce the discretionary time available for academic involvement and study, it is not entirely clear why it does not have a negative influence on measures of learning during college. It may well be that, by absorbing discretionary time, work (and in particular off-campus work) has its greatest negative influence on one's ability to meet the normative requirements of successful progress through college such as persistence, grades, and degree completion (Astin, 1993c). This, however, may not necessarily translate into a negative influence on the actual gains in knowledge acquisition or academic skills one makes during college. It may be that, for a substantial number of students who work during college, employment provides a context in which they acquire efficient organizational skills and work habits. As a result, they may be able to compensate for less study time by using the study time available more efficiently. Indeed, the organizational skills and normative work habits acquired from employment during college may in part explain why, as we shall see in the chapter on career and economic impacts of college, it is often positively linked with measures of job success.

On- or off-campus residence. A small body of research has attempted to assess the net learning effects of living on campus versus living off campus and commuting to college. Because living on campus significantly enhances effort and involvement in both the academic and social experiences of college (Pascarella & Terenzini, 1991), it seems reasonable to hypothesize that it might also enhance learning. With a few isolated exceptions, however, there is little consistent evidence to support this hypothesis.

A number of analyses of the multi-institutional National Study of Student Learning have considered living on campus (versus off campus and commuting to college) as a salient influence on both standardized tests and self-reported measures of knowledge acquisition and academic skill development (Flowers & Pascarella, 1999a; Pascarella et al., 1993; Pascarella et al., 1997; Whitt et al., in press). Generally, these studies introduced statistical controls for such factors as precollege test scores, academic motivation, age, socioeconomic status, race, gender, full- or part-time enrollment, and the like. In the presence of such controls, there were generally no statistically significant, positive or negative direct effects of residence on either standardized measures of learning (that is, first-year reading comprehension and mathematics, second-year science reasoning and writing skills, third-year reading comprehension) or on first-, second-, or third-year self-reported gains in writing and thinking skills, understanding science, and understanding the arts and humanities. Similar findings are reported by Kuh (1993) and Shorter (1993). The only exceptions to this finding were positive effects of residing on campus on African-American students, end-of-third-year reading comprehension (Flowers & Pascarella, 1999a), and women's end-of-first-year self-reported gains in writing and thinking skills (Pascarella et al., 1997).

Such evidence suggests that living on campus versus commuting to college may have little consistent, direct influence on student learning. However, it is entirely possible that it does exert an indirect, positive influence on learning by means of its enhancement of student academic and social engagement (for example, Ballou, Reavill, & Schultz, 1995). We uncovered no investigation, however, that tested this hypothesis.

CONDITIONAL EFFECTS OF COLLEGE

Conclusions from *How College Affects Students*

In our 1991 synthesis, we concluded that there was little consistent evidence to suggest that either postsecondary education in general or the type of institution attended in particular had a differential effect on knowledge acquisition for different kinds of students. In the area of instructional research, in contrast, there was a reasonably consistent body of evidence to suggest that certain kinds of students learn more from one instructional approach than from another. Students high in need for independent achievement or internal locus of control appear to learn more from instructional approaches that stress student independence, self-direction, and participation than from more structured or teacher-directed approaches. Conversely, students high in need for conforming or dependent achievement, or external locus of control, appear to benefit more from structured, teacher-directed instructional formats than from approaches that emphasize independent learning.

Evidence from the 1990s

The decade of the 1990s witnessed a substantial focus on estimating the conditional (or interaction) effects of college. Accordingly, in our current literature review we uncovered many more statistically significant conditional effects than we did in our 1991 synthesis. These conditional effects appear to cluster into three general types: student by net effects of college, student by between-college effects, and student by within-college effects. Unfortunately, as we indicated in our 1991 synthesis, specific conditional effects do not necessarily replicate well, particularly in correlational or nonexperimental research. In fact, a clear majority of the larger number of conditional effects we uncovered in the literature of the 1990s is based on a single finding and have yet to be replicated on an independent sample. Although we do not totally ignore single-finding conditional effects, their great number has necessitated that we be selective in reporting them. We judged it counterproductive (not to mention tedious) to report and describe every statistically significant conditional effect that we uncovered in our review of the literature. In correlational research many of these conditional effects have a high probability of being artifacts of anomalies in the data (Pascarella & Terenzini, 1991). Consequently, in selecting what to report we placed greatest emphasis on areas of research where there has been a reasonably concerted effort to determine the presence of conditional effects, conditional effects that are replicated, and conditional effects that have either strong theoretical rationales or potentially important policy implications or both.

Student by Net Effects of College. Unlike the literature from our 1991 synthesis, the research from the decade of the 1990s presents evidence to suggest that the net effect of college on dimensions of verbal, quantitative, and subject matter competence may differ in magnitude by gender. Evidence with respect to differences by race or ethnicity is not compelling.

Gender. In their analysis of the multi-institutional 1986 to 1990 Cooperative Institutional Research Program data, Smith, Morrison, and Wolf (1994) concluded that college was largely a "gendered experience" (p. 696) and that we might well expect differences between men and women, not only in the experience of college but also potentially in the impact of college. Although the evidence is not unequivocal, recent studies based on two multi-institutional data sets have supported this conclusion (Flowers, Osterlind, Pascarella, & Pierson, 1999; Whitt et al., in press). Flowers et al. examined the 56-institution, cross-sectional College Basic Academic Subjects Examination (CBASE) data set to determine if there were differences between men and women in the magnitude of the impact of college. The impact of college was operationally defined as the difference between freshmen and seniors on the four CBASE scores: English, mathematics, science, and social studies. With statistical controls for individual ACT score, race, college grades, number of credit hours completed, and the average ACT score of students at the institution attended, the magnitude of the freshman-senior difference was significantly larger for men (compared with women) on all four CBASE tests. Across all four CBASE tests the average net freshman-senior difference for men was about 1.5 times as large as the corresponding difference for women. On the individual CBASE tests, the ratio of the male to female freshman-senior differences were: English = 1.27, mathematics = 2.46, science = 1.46, and social studies = 1.42. In short, it would appear that women were deriving smaller learning benefits from college than men across all four subject areas.

Such conditional effects involving gender in the areas of mathematics and science knowledge may be largely a function of men and women taking different patterns of courses related to their major field of study (Jacobs, 1995, 1996a). However, it is harder to explain away the larger male freshman-senior differences in English and social studies as being simply the result of different gender-dominated majors. Furthermore, there is also evidence to suggest the possibility that coursework during college cannot explain why significantly greater benefits in mathematics and science knowledge accrue to men. Analyzing the National Study of Student Learning data, Whitt et al. (in press) found that, compared with men, women in both two- and four-year colleges had significantly lower scores on a standardized measure of end-of-first-year mathematics knowledge. Similarly, women in four-year colleges also had significantly lower scores on a standardized measure of science reasoning after two years of college. These conditional effects persisted in the presence of controls, not only for patterns of coursework taken in mathematics and science but also for precollege test scores, academic motivation, student demographic characteristics, the academic selectivity of the institution attended, credit hours completed in college, and extensive measures of academic effort and social involvement during college.

We uncovered only one conditional effect related to gender in which women demonstrated greater net learning on a standardized measure than men. With controls for precollege ability, academic motivation, demographic characteristics, institutional selectivity, number of credit hours completed, patterns of coursework taken, and measures of academic effort and social involvement, women in both two- and four-year colleges had significantly higher levels of writing skills after two years of college than did men (Whitt et al., in press).

Race. Evidence that the verbal, quantitative, or subject matter competence benefits of college accrue differentially to students from different racial or ethnic groups is inconsistent to the point of being contradictory. For example, in their analysis of a cohort from the National Longitudinal Study of Youth, Myerson, Rank, Raines, and Schnitzler (1998) found that, with controls for socioeconomic status, age, and educational attainment, African-American students made gains during college on the Armed Forces Qualification Test (a composite of standardized verbal and quantitative test scores) that were approximately four times as large as those for European-American (that is, White) students.

Such results, however, are not supported by Flowers's (2000) analyses of two multi-institutional data sets: the National Study of Student Learning and the College Basic Academic Subjects Examination (Osterlind, 1996, 1997). In analyses of the NSSL data, Flowers introduced statistical controls for such factors as precollege test scores, academic motivation, demographic characteristics, institutional selectivity, number of credit hours completed, patterns of coursework taken, and extensive measures of student academic effort and social involvement. With these controls in effect, African-American students made significantly smaller gains during college across a range of standardized tests than did similar White students, a finding almost exactly the opposite of that reported by Myerson et al. (1998). The disadvantages for African-American students, relative to their White counterparts, were as follows: first-year mathematics = .19 of a standard deviation (8 percentile points); second-year science reasoning = .40 of a standard deviation (16 percentile points); second-year writing skills = .51 of a standard deviation (19 percentile points); and third-year reading comprehension = .55 of a standard deviation (21 percentile points). Muddying the waters even further is Flowers's additional finding with the 56-institution CBASE data. With controls in place for sex, ACT score, cumulative credits taken, college grades, and the average ACT score at the institution attended, the freshman-senior difference across all four CBASE tests was essentially the same for African-American and White students.

An additional analysis of a national sample of community college students by Swigart and Ethington (1998) found significant differences between African-American, Asian-American, Hispanic-American, and Euro-American students in self-reported gains during college in such areas as arts and humanities, communication skills math, science, and technology. However, because of the self-report nature of the dependent variables and the apparent absence of controls for potentially confounding influences, it is difficult to determine if these group differences reflect differences in the impact of college or merely differences in reporting tendencies among students from different racial-ethnic groups.

Student by Between-College Effects. Conditional between-college effects involve institutional selectivity and type.

Institutional selectivity. Consistent with conclusions from our 1991 synthesis, we found little consistent evidence to suggest that attending an academically selective institution has a differential impact on gains in verbal, quantitative, or subject matter competence for different kinds of students. For example, Flowers's (2000) analyses of the National Study of Student Learning and the College Basic Academic Subjects Examination data sets also sought to determine if institutional selectivity (operationally defined as the average tested academic ability of the students at the institution attended) had a differential impact on different dimensions of learning for African-American versus White students. In both data sets analyzed, the cross-product terms representing this race by institutional selectivity conditional effect failed to account for a statistically significant increase in explained variance. This finding indicated that attending a selective institution did not benefit African-American or White students differently in terms of learning gains in such areas as mathematics, science and science reasoning, English, social studies, reading comprehension, and writing skills.

Analyzing the same two data sets, and using essentially the same variables and analytic design as Flowers (2000), Whitt, Pascarella, Elkins-Nesheim, Marth, and Pierson (2003), and Whitt et al. (in press) sought to determine if attendance at a selective institution had differential learning impacts for men versus women. Like Flowers, their analyses of the CBASE data indicated that any effects of institutional selectivity on freshman-to-senior gains were essentially the same for men and women across all four tests (that is, English, mathematics, science, and social studies). Analyses of the NSSL data did yield some significant sex by institutional selectivity effects, but they were isolated and inconsistent. For example, net of other factors, institutional selectivity had a significant, positive effect on first-year reading comprehension for men but a small, significant, negative effect for women. Conversely, the net effect of institutional selectivity on second-year writing skills was positive for women and modestly negative for men. In areas such as first-year mathematics, second-year science reasoning, and third-year reading comprehension, attending a selective institution did not benefit either sex more or less than the other.

Institutional type. In an earlier section of this chapter ("Between-College Effects"), we saw that when controls were made for precollege ability and other confounding influences, students in two-year colleges made gains of essentially the same magnitude as their four-year college counterparts in first-year reading comprehension and mathematics and second-year science reasoning and writing skills. Although it is based on analyses of a single sample and has yet to be replicated, there is also evidence, however, to suggest that different kinds of students may benefit in different ways by spending their first two years of postsecondary education at a two-year rather than a four-year college. Specifically, students of color appeared to derive significantly larger benefits in terms of first-year reading comprehension and mathematics competencies from attendance at a community college (versus a four-year college). For their White counterparts, however, the reverse was true. White students appeared to benefit more, in terms of first-year reading comprehension and mathematics competencies, from attending a four-year (rather than a two-year) college (Pascarella et al., 1995a). Similarly, students of color who were relatively older and from relatively low socioeconomic backgrounds tended to benefit more in terms of second-year writing skills from attendance at a community college (rather than a four-year institution). Conversely, their counterparts who were White, relatively younger, and from relatively high socioeconomic backgrounds benefited more from attendance at a four-year college (rather than a two-year, community college) (Pascarella et al., 1995–96). In short, the kinds of students appearing to derive the greater learning benefits from attendance at a community college tended to be those students of color, older students, and less affluent students who were most likely to attend a community college, rather than a four-year institution, in the first place.

Student by Within-College Effects. Conditional within-college effects involve student learning styles, student characteristics, and academic and social effort and involvement.

Student learning styles. In our 1991 synthesis, we saw that students with different levels of conforming versus independent learning orientations and with external versus internal locus of control learned more efficiently from different types of instruction. The research of the 1990s would reinforce and extend this finding into a more general conclusion about matching student learning style to appropriate instruction or learning experiences. A number of scholars have suggested that students exhibit a rather broad range of ways in which they either enjoy learning or actually learn new material most efficiently. The typical name given these preferred approaches or orientations to learning is *learning style* (Cook, 1991; Dunn & Dunn, 1993; Dunn, Dunn, & Price, 1990; Grimes, 1995; Matthews, 1994). Learning style can be thought of as the "way each individual begins to concentrate on, process, internalize, and remember new and difficult academic information or skills" (Dunn & Stevenson, 1997, p. 333). Learning style can be measured by a number of existing instruments, examples of which are the Productivity Environmental Preference Survey and the Learning Style Inventory (Dunn & Dunn, 1993; Dunn, Dunn, & Price, 1990). Both instruments elicit student self-diagnostic responses that yield a profile of preferred learning style based on dimensions such as cognitive, environmental, emotional, sociological, and physiological (Dunn & Stevenson, 1997). The idea appears to be that, once preferred learning style is profiled, instructional experiences can be matched to learning style to maximize content acquisition and learning.

The weight of evidence from research attempting to estimate the impact of fit between instructional approaches and learning style suggests that college students demonstrate significantly higher levels of knowledge acquisition when they are exposed to instruction that matches their preferred learning style than when they are exposed to instruction that does not. For example, Lenehan, Dunn, Ingham, Signer, and Murray (1994) conducted an experiment in which students in an entry-level science class completed the Learning Style Inventory and then were assigned to either an experimental or control group. In the experimental group prescriptions for studying and doing homework were matched to students' preferred learning style as indicated by the Learning Style Inventory, whereas in the control group there was no such matching. Although the two groups were essentially equal in tested precollege verbal and mathematics ability, at the end of the course the experimental group demonstrated significantly higher course achievement and curiosity about science and significantly lower anxiety about science. Consistent results are reported in other experimental or quasi-experimental studies (Clark-Thayer, 1987; Cook, 1991; Dunn, Dunn, Deckinger, Withers, & Katzenstein, 1990; Dunn, Bruno, Sklar, Zenhausern, & Beaudry, 1990; Klein & Pridemore, 1992; Lichtenberg & Moffitt, 1994).

A meta-analysis of studies testing the general model of matching instruction to diagnosed learning style was conducted by Dunn, Griggs, Olson, Beasley, and Gorman (1995). Their meta-analysis was based on 36 experimental studies at all educational levels that were judged to have minimal threats to internal validity. Their findings clearly suggest that students with different learning styles learn most efficiently from different instructional approaches. Across all 36 studies, students who were exposed to instruction that accommodated their learning styles demonstrated an achievement advantage of .75 of a standard deviation relative to students who had not had their learning styles accommodated. Of the 36 experimental studies, 8 were conducted with college-level samples.

Across these 8 studies, students who received instruction matched to their learning style demonstrated an achievement advantage of .91 of a standard deviation (32 percentile points) over their counterparts who had no attempt made to provide instruction accommodating their preferred learning style.

Student characteristics. Beyond the research on student learning styles there is also evidence to suggest that different kinds of students benefit differentially from the same instructional experience. These conditional effects include the following: students with low tested academic ability and prior academic performance may derive greater learning benefits from participation in supplemental instruction than students with high academic ability and prior academic performance (Kochenour et al., 1997); students of color may benefit more from cooperative learning approaches than White students (Posner & Markstein, 1994); knowledge maps may be most effective in facilitating the learning of students with low levels of prior content knowledge (Lambiotte & Dansereau, 1992); cooperative learning with knowledge map supplements may be most effective in fostering the content recall of low ability students (Rewey, Dansereau, Dees, Skaggs, & Pitre, 1992); and high verbal ability students may derive greater learning benefits from assuming a learner's role in cooperative learning dyads, whereas low verbal ability students may derive greater benefits from assuming a teacher's role (Wiegmann, Dansereau, & Patterson, 1992). It is important to note, however, that these conditional effects appear to be based on single studies, and although it may exist, we failed to uncover evidence of their replication on independent samples.

Academic and social effort and involvement. Substantial research in the decade of the 1990s attempted to determine the extent to which dimensions of academic and social effort-involvement in college have differential impacts on verbal, quantitative, and subject matter competence for different kinds of students. Although an impressive number of statistically significant conditional effects were uncovered, few were replicated. One possible exception is in the area of computer and information technology use. In analyzing the potential impact of instructional technology on student learning, Kozma (1991, 1994a, 1994b) has argued that we should expect conditional or interaction effects; some types of computer applications or uses may be particularly effective in supporting some kinds of instructional approaches or learning goals with some kinds of students. A recent meta-analysis of the learning outcomes of hypermedia has supported Kozma's argument (Dillon & Garbard, 1998). Hypermedia or hypertext is a computer-enabled technology that permits random access to great volumes of information. It allows for substantial student control over the pace and timing of access as opposed to a structured, linear scheme of access. An example is the World Wide Web. Dillon and Gabard's synthesis of the experimental studies with undergraduate samples found small and statistically nonsignificant learning differences between hypermedia- and text-based (paper-based) instruction. However, consistent with Kozma's prediction, the effectiveness of hypermedia interacted with learner characteristics. Specifically, the largest learning benefits accrued to the highest-ability students, suggesting that these students were most able to manipulate hypertext effectively to construct new knowledge.

Findings generally consistent with those of Dillon and Gabard (1998) are reported in an analysis of the National Study of Student Learning data by Flowers, Pascarella, and Pierson (1999). For four-year college students in the upper half of precollege academic ability, unstructured electronic mail use had significant, positive net effects on a standardized measure of composite first-year achievement (consisting of reading, mathematics, and critical thinking). For students in the lower half of precollege academic ability, however, the corresponding effect of e-mail was negative. In short, it appeared that the highest-ability students were able to manipulate or convert unstructured e-mail use, and attendant skills, into the largest learning gains during the first year of college.

In addition to research on the interaction of student ability and information technology use, evidence also suggests that the impact on learning of different dimensions of academic and social effort differs by sex, race, academic ability, and instructional context. Examples of such conditional effects are as follows: engaging in volunteer work may have more positive impacts on reading comprehension for men than for women (Flowers, 2000; Whitt et al., 2003); social or non-course-related interactions with peers may have larger positive effects on self-reported gains in both writing and thinking skills and in understanding the arts and humanities for high-ability students than it does for lower-ability students (Whitt et al., 1999a); African-American students in four-year colleges may derive greater first-year reading comprehension benefits from computer use than other students (for example, White, Latino, Asian-American), whereas, conversely, for Latino students in four-year colleges, unstructured e-mail use may have stronger negative effects on first-year reading comprehension than it does for other students (Flowers, Pascarella, & Pierson, 1999); the differential effects of coursework in college on standardized measures of learning may be greater in magnitude for students with relatively lower levels of precollege academic ability than for students with relatively higher levels of ability (Pike, 1992a); the negative first-year impacts of fraternity membership on reading comprehension and mathematics competencies may be larger in magnitude for White men than for men of color (Pascarella, Edison, Whitt, et al., 1996); first-generation college students may derive significantly greater first-year reading comprehension benefits from extent of study effort and off-campus work than students whose parents went to college (Terenzini, Springer, Yaeger, Pascarella, & Nora, 1996); and computer use may have significantly larger positive effects, and unstructured e-mail use significantly larger negative effects, on students' first-year reading comprehension in community colleges than in four-year institutions (Flowers, Pascarella, & Pierson, 1999).[17, 18] As with the majority of conditional effects we uncovered, however, each of these findings appears to be based on a single sample and, as far as we can tell, has not been replicated. Because several of the conditional effects may not be easily explainable and thus are quite possibly an artifact of the particular sample, replication is particularly salient. At the same time, it should also be pointed out that there is no requirement that an effect has to be understood to be real.

LONG-TERM EFFECTS OF COLLEGE

Conclusions from *How College Affects Students*

Although it had several serious methodological problems, we uncovered a comprehensive body of evidence to indicate that college graduates have a more substantial factual knowledge base than those whose formal education ends with secondary school. This difference remained statistically significant over a fairly wide age range. Moreover, there was additional consistent evidence to suggest that college graduates are much more inclined than high school graduates to engage in activities that are likely to add to their knowledge (for example, serious reading, continuing education) after graduation. The implication of these findings is that the total effect of college on knowledge acquisition is not simply limited to what occurs while the student is in attendance. Rather, by influencing postcollege interests and activities that enhance learning, college may also have an important indirect effect on one's knowledge that extends well into adult life.

Evidence from the 1990s

The literature of the 1990s provides substantial reinforcement for the conclusions from our 1991 synthesis. This is particularly true with respect to involvement in postgraduation activities that add to one's knowledge base and repertoire of lifelong learning skills. Analyses of U.S. Census Bureau *Current Population Reports* and *Statistical Abstracts of the United States* ("Private Correlates of Educational Attainment," 1995; "Why College?" 1999) show a number of marked differences between high school graduates and those with at least a bachelor's degree in activities, such as these: using the Internet (high school = 10.8 percent, bachelor's = 48.7 percent), participation in continuing education (high school = 30.7 percent, bachelor's = 58.2 percent), leisure reading (high school = 49 percent, bachelor's = 71 percent), creative writing (high school = 4 percent, bachelor's = 14 percent), reading any book in the last six months (high school = 57 percent, bachelor's = 83 percent), and reading a national newspaper or magazine every day (high school = 27 percent, bachelor's = 42 percent).

Of course, the link between these activities and educational level might be substantially confounded by differences between high school graduates and college graduates in such areas as occupation or income. College graduates as a group, for example, would likely have more family discretionary income ("Family Income by Educational Attainment," 1999) than high school graduates, and having more discretionary income might allow them to purchase more books, magazines, newspapers, or computer access. There is, however, evidence to suggest that the more highly educated are also more likely to participate in activities that increase their fund of knowledge and continuing learning competencies even when such factors as income, occupation, and other confounding influences are taken into account. For example, in a study of public library use, Marchant (1991, 1994) found that even when statistical controls were introduced for such factors as age, number of children, income or occupation, sex, and motivation for using the library, formal education was still a significant, positive predictor of both library use and having a library card. College graduates had nearly 2.5 times as many visits to the library in a three-month period as high school graduates and were almost 1.7 times as likely to have a library card.

Level of formal education not only predicts level of engagement in knowledge- or skill-producing activities but also appears to influence positively one's proficiency in acquiring useful knowledge. Most of the evidence in this area treats years of formal education as a continuous variable and does not permit direct comparison between high school and college graduates. It does, however, suggest the ways in which those with more advanced education are more efficient at acquiring information. For example, Drew and Weaver (1991) conducted a study of voter understanding of candidates' positions in the 1988 presidential election. With statistical controls for political affiliation, age, sex, and campaign interest, formal education was a strong, positive predictor of accurate knowledge about the candidates' positions on current issues. When additional statistical controls were introduced for dimensions of exposure to the media and actual exposure to the presidential debates, the positive effect of formal education on knowledge of candidates' positions was reduced by a little over one-third but was still substantial and statistically significant.

Such a finding suggests that at least two causal mechanisms may be at work in explaining the positive link between level of formal education and knowledge of candidates' positions in the Drew and Weaver (1991) investigation. The first is that the more educated probably had greater exposure or access to sources of information about the candidates. This possibility is indicated by the one-third reduction in the magnitude of the net education effect when measures of media and debate exposure were added to the prediction equation. The second is that the more educated appear to be able to extract more accurate or useful knowledge from equal exposure to the same sources of information as those with less education. This mechanism is suggested by the fact that the net positive effect for years of formal education remained statistically significant even when levels of exposure to information sources were taken into account. Irrespective of whether one or both mechanisms are at work, findings similar to those of Drew and Weaver (1991) have been found for knowledge about energy issues (Griffin, 1990) and knowledge about environmental resources and hazards (Smith, 1997).

Finally, there is also some new evidence in the literature of the 1990s to suggest that postsecondary education may have a long-term impact on knowledge acquisition in the form of an intergenerational benefit or legacy. That is, a parent's exposure to postsecondary education may enhance knowledge acquisition in a daughter or son. We uncovered three studies that address this issue (Chaney, Burgdorf, & Atash, 1997; Sheehan-Holt & Smith, 2000; Terenzini, Springer, et al., 1996). Using data from the 1990 National Assessment of Educational Progress (NAEP), Chaney, Burgdorf, and Atash found that having a parent who attended college significantly and positively influenced high school seniors' scores on both the NAEP standardized science and mathematics tests. This positive effect persisted even in the presence of statistical controls for such variables as grade point average, race, sex, attitudes toward math and science, secondary school graduation requirements in math and science, school priority given to math and science, region of the county and level of urbanicity, and whether the school was public or private. Generally, if not totally, consistent results are reported by Terenzini et al. for first-year college students and by Sheehan-Holt and Smith for adult readers. Analyzing the National Study of Student Learning data, Terenzini et al. reported that, even in the presence of statistical controls for an extensive array of confounding influences such as precollege test scores, race, age, sex, family income, educational aspirations, and family support, having a parent who attended college had a positive influence on first-year gains on a standardized measure of reading comprehension. Similarly, in their analyses of the 1992 National Adult Literacy Survey, Sheehan-Holt and Smith found that parents' education had a significant, positive effect on an individual's level of prose literacy, even when controls were in effect for age, race, years of education, occupational status and income, disability status, neighborhood context, and amount of newspaper reading, though not for ability.

The causal mechanisms underlying the findings of Chaney, Burgdorf, and Atash (1997), Sheehan-Holt and Smith (2000), and Terenzini, Springer, Yaeger, Pascarella, and Nora (1996) are not readily apparent. A partial explanation, however, may lie in the quality of the home environment fostered by parents with different levels of formal education. As we concluded from the evidence on quality of life after college that we reviewed in our 1991 synthesis, college-educated parents tend to spend more time with their children than do high school–educated parents on developmentally enriching activities such as reading, talking, and transportation to various lessons (for example, music and dance). Furthermore, they also tend to spend more of their income on such things as education, books, magazines, and other reading materials (Pascarella & Terenzini, 1991). The result is that, compared with their high school–educated counterparts, college-educated parents may simply be creating a home environment that fosters a stronger orientation toward learning, or greater "learning capital," in their children. Consequently, other things being equal, children of college-educated parents may enjoy a marked advantage in their proficiency as learners.

SUMMARY

Change During College

Although the evidence on gains during college in subject matter knowledge and academic skills appears much less extensive in the 1990s than it was in the literature we reviewed for our 1991 synthesis, we observed little that would change the general, and quite unsurprising, conclusion from our predecessor volume. Students on average make statistically significant and, in some areas, substantial gains in subject matter knowledge and academic skills during college. Our best estimate of freshman-to-senior gains is that they average .77 of a standard deviation in English (reading and literature, writing), .55 of a standard deviation in mathematics (general mathematics proficiency, algebra, geometry), .62 of a standard deviation in science (laboratory and fieldwork, understanding fundamental concepts), .73 of a standard deviation in social studies (history, social sciences), and .80 of a standard deviation in liberal arts competencies (for example, using science, using art, solving problems). These represent improvements over entering student competencies of 28 percentile points in English, 21 percentile points in mathematics, 23 percentile points in science, 27 percentile points in social studies, and 29 percentile points in liberal arts competencies. In English, mathematics, science, and social studies, about 90 percent of the total advantage of seniors over entering students occurred during the first two years of postsecondary education. This finding, however, may reflect the fact that the instrument used was a standardized test designed to measure skills and competencies important in general education coursework, much of which may be taken during the first two years of college.

This conclusion about the relative advantage of seniors over first-year students in subject matter knowledge and academic skills needs to be understood in the context of two additional findings from work conducted in the 1990s. The first indicates that college graduates as a group are not performing particularly well in terms of an *absolute* standard of knowledge acquisition. For example, only about 50 percent of all college graduates appear to be functioning at the most proficient levels of prose, document, or quantitative literacy. Such a finding suggests an important direction for future research. Understanding the proficiency of college graduates on absolute standards of subject matter competence and academic skills may be equally if not more important than knowing how much they change or grow during college.

A second line of inquiry leads to a more optimistic conclusion. It appears that students can retain somewhere between 70 and 85 percent of the subject matter content usually introduced in postsecondary settings. Perhaps even more important, increasing the level of original learning also increases later retention.

Net Effects of College

As in our 1991 synthesis, we did not uncover a large body of evidence on the net effects of college on subject matter knowledge and academic skills. What evidence we did uncover, however, was not inconsistent with the conclusions from our previous synthesis. We estimated that the net impact of a bachelor's degree (compared to a high school degree) on verbal and quantitative skills was about .25 of a standard deviation (10 percentile points), quite similar to our 1991 estimates. We further estimated that the net effects of college on English, mathematics, science, and social studies ranged from about 60 percent to 75 percent of the simple freshman-to-senior difference. (The estimated net effect of college on these tests was the freshman-senior difference statistically adjusted for academic ability, race, age, sex, credit hours taken, college grades, and institutional selectivity.) The estimated net effects of college were as follows: English = .59 of a standard deviation, mathematics = .32 of a standard deviation, science = .47 of a standard deviation, and social studies = .46 of a standard deviation. These numbers represent estimated improvements of 22 percentile points in English, 13 percentile points in mathematics, 18 percentile points in science, and 18 percentile points in social studies. Once again, most (75 percent or more) of this estimated net impact occurred during the first two years of college. This occurrence likely reflects the focus of the instruments used on assessing general education competencies that are usually taught in the first two years of college. Consequently, the assessment instruments, and our estimated net effects based on them, may actually underestimate the full net effects of college in these content areas.

Between-College Effects

The study of between-college effects has been complicated by an important student demographic trend that has grown more pronounced over the last quarter century. Based on analyses of nationally representative samples, it would appear that since the late 1980s, 50 percent or more of the students who initially enrolled at a four-year college eventually attended two or more undergraduate institutions. This phenomenon makes the estimation of between-college effects on such outcomes as learning and cognitive growth somewhat problematic. Moreover, findings of the research in this area may not generalize to the substantial numbers of American students who attend more than one institution as undergraduates.

This caveat not withstanding, we still uncovered substantially more evidence pertaining to between-college effects in the 1990s than we did for our previous synthesis. The new body of evidence, however, did little to change our main conclusion: between-college effects on the acquisition of subject matter knowledge and academic skills are generally inconsistent and quite small in magnitude. For example, as in our 1991 synthesis, we uncovered little support, in a fairly large body of research, for the premise that attendance at an academically selective institution has a consistent, discernible, positive influence on how much one learns. Similarly, little evidence indicated that single-sex institutions had a stronger impact on women's learning than coeducational institutions, and there was an essential parity in learning gains during the first two years of college between students attending community colleges and those enrolled in four-year institutions. There was also evidence to suggest that, despite relative disadvantages in financial and educational resources, historically Black colleges may be as proficient as primarily White institutions, if not more so, in fostering the learning of African-American students.

Although the unique effects are quite modest in magnitude, there is consistent evidence to suggest that the acquisition of subject matter knowledge and academic skills is enhanced by institutional environments that emphasize scholarship and learning, and such environmental impacts appear to occur independent of institutional selectivity. Finally, there is also evidence indicating that institutional environments supportive of diversity and relatively free of racial bias may facilitate the learning of students of color.

In the most methodologically sound studies, even the statistically significant between-college effects are quite small and often trivial in magnitude. We have suggested that this is due to the fact that aggregation of characteristics or environmental stimuli at the institutional level yields indexes that are simply too remote from the actual social and intellectual forces that shape learning in college. The majority of colleges and universities in the American postsecondary system have important subenvironments with more immediate and powerful impacts on individual students. Because of these subenvironments, we should probably anticipate a greater diversity of impacts within than between institutions.

Within-College Effects

Although the vast literature (literally hundreds of studies) pertaining to within-college effects on the acquisition of subject matter knowledge and academic skills did not lead to major changes from our 1991 conclusions, it did provide evidence in an extensive number of areas that were not addressed in our previous synthesis. The following general conclusions appear warranted from the evidence of the 1990s:

1. Consistent with our previous synthesis, the evidence indicates that undergraduates tend to make the greatest knowledge gains in subject matter areas consistent with their major field of study.

2. Consistent with our previous synthesis, what students learn in college is related to the coursework they take as undergraduates. However, beyond the unsurprising conclusion that students tend to acquire the most knowledge and the highest level of academic skills in areas where they take the most courses, it is difficult to detect consistent patterns of effects across institutions.

3. The research from the 1990s suggests that we may need to revise modestly our previous conclusion that subject matter knowledge is acquired with equal proficiency in large and small classes. When learning is measured by course grades, the weight of evidence is reasonably clear in suggesting that greater class size has a negative impact. However, when learning is assessed by a standardized measure, there is little consistent evidence to suggest that class size has a negative influence, at least in the field of economics.

4. We uncovered reasonably consistent experimental and quasi-experimental evidence that a number of innovative pedagogical approaches appear to improve subject matter learning over more traditional methods. These include the following:

   Learning for mastery: Between .41 and .68 of a standard deviation advantage (16 to 25 percentile points) over traditional methods.

   Computer-assisted instruction: About .30 of a standard deviation advantage (12 percentile points) over traditional methods.

Active learning: About .25 of a standard deviation advantage (10 percentile points) over traditional methods.

Collaborative learning: The weight of evidence indicates a significant advantage over traditional methods, but an effect size could not be estimated.

Cooperative learning: About .51 of a standard deviation advantage (19 percentile points) over traditional methods.

Small-group learning: About .51 of a standard deviation advantage (19 percentile points) over traditional methods.

Supplemental instruction: Participation associated with about .39 of a standard deviation advantage (15 percentile points) over nonparticipation.

Constructivist-oriented approaches: Based on two studies, constructivist-oriented approaches appear to confer a learning advantage of between .14 and .40 of a standard deviation (6 to 16 percentile points).

5. Methodologically sound research on problem-based learning and learning communities is in its nascent stages. However, both approaches show some promise as interventions that foster improved learning.

6. A massive body of research suggests that students who study via distance education approaches learn as much course content as do their counterparts in conventional, on-campus settings. However, this research is plagued by major threats to internal validity inherent in the fact that individuals self-select themselves into on-campus and remote instructional sites.

7. There are also a number of focused classroom instructional techniques that appear to be effective tools for enhancing student course learning, including peer tutoring, reciprocal teaching, attributional retraining, concept-knowledge maps, and the one-minute paper.

8. Consistent with our previous synthesis, a large body of correlational research in the 1990s indicated that differences in teacher behaviors have important implications for the acquisition of subject matter knowledge by students. Such factors as teacher preparation-organization, teacher clarity and comprehensibility, teacher availability and helpfulness, quality of and frequency of feedback from teacher to student, and teacher concern for and rapport with students continued to have significant, positive correlations with measures of student learning of course content. Moreover, teacher preparation and organization also appear to have positive impacts on more general measures of learning not tied to specific courses.

9. Experimental validation of the effects of teacher clarity was discussed in our 1991 synthesis. The literature from the 1990s presents additional experimental evidence validating the positive impact on student con-

tent acquisition of both teacher expressiveness-enthusiasm and teacher organization. It is likely that all of these enabling teacher behaviors may themselves be learnable.

10. Consistent with our previous synthesis, we found that a substantial part of subject matter learning depends not just on what the institution does in instructional settings but also on the quality of the student's engagement or effort in making use of the range of learning opportunities provided by the institution. Other things being equal, the more the student is psychologically engaged in activities that reinforce and extend the formal academic experience (for example, library experiences, writing experiences, science effort, course learning), the more he or she will learn.

11. Also consistent with our 1991 synthesis, there is a substantial body of evidence suggesting that the nature of students' social and extracurricular involvement has a unique impact on learning. Nonclassroom interactions with peers and faculty that extend and reinforce what happens in one's academic experience appear to have the most consistent positive impact. Similarly, there is reasonably consistent evidence that interaction with racially and culturally diverse peers and involvement in academically integrated service learning experiences enhance subject matter knowledge. Not all types of social or extracurricular involvement have positive effects on learning, however. Intercollegiate athletic participation, particularly for men in revenue-producing sports (that is, football and basketball), appears to have an inhibiting influence. Similarly, Greek affiliation may have a negative impact during the first year of college, although this appears to diminish in magnitude in subsequent years.

12. Finally, given the substantial numbers of undergraduates who work during college, it is perhaps noteworthy that the weight of evidence indicates that on- or off-campus work during college, particularly if it is only part-time, may not consistently or seriously inhibit student learning. Similarly, we found no consistent evidence to suggest that living off campus and commuting to college (versus living on campus) directly inhibited the acquisition of subject matter knowledge. At the same time, however, we hypothesize that living on campus may exert an indirect, positive influence on learning by means of its enhancement of student academic and social engagement.

Conditional Effects of College

We uncovered substantially more evidence pertaining to conditional (or interaction) effects of college in the literature of the 1990s than we did in our previous synthesis. Unfortunately, many of the findings are based on single samples and await replication. Unlike our 1991 conclusions, the evidence from our present synthesis suggests that the net effects of college on dimensions of verbal, quantitative, and subject matter competence may differ in magnitude by gender. In the great majority of cases, men appeared to be deriving larger learning benefits from college than women. Evidence with respect to differences by race or ethnicity was not consistent or compelling. Consistent with conclusions from our 1991 synthesis, there was little evidence to suggest that attending an academically selective institution had a differential impact on gains in verbal, quantitative, or subject matter competence for different kinds of students.

The most consistent evidence pertaining to conditional effects was in the area of student learning style, and it essentially extended findings from our 1991 synthesis into a more general conclusion about matching student learning style to appropriate instruction or learning experiences. Replicated experimental and quasi-experimental evidence clearly suggests that college students demonstrate significantly higher levels of knowledge acquisition when they are exposed to instruction that matches their preferred learning style than when they receive instruction that does not. There is also substantial evidence to suggest the following: first, students with different racial identities or levels of academic ability derive different size learning benefits from instructional approaches such as supplemental instruction, cooperative learning, and the use of knowledge maps, and second, dimensions of academic and social engagement such as using computers and electronic mail, engaging in volunteer work, interacting socially with peers, and joining a fraternity differ in the magnitude of their effects on subject matter knowledge for students differing on such characteristics as gender, race, and academic ability. Nearly all of these conditional effects, however, are based on single-sample findings that await replication.

Long-Term Effects of College

One of our most significant conclusions from our 1991 synthesis was that part of the long-term impact of college is realized through college graduates' increased likelihood (when compared with high school graduates) to engage in postgraduation activities that add to their fund of knowledge (for example, serious reading, continuing education). The literature of the 1990s would tend to reinforce this conclusion. However, level of formal education not only has a net positive effect on level of engagement in knowledge- or skill-producing activities but also appears to influence positively one's proficiency in acquiring new and useful knowledge. The evidence suggests two causal mechanisms at work. Compared with those with less education, the more educated probably have greater access to sources of information. However, the more educated also appear to be able to extract more accurate knowledge when exposure to the critical sources of information is equal. There is also replicated evidence of an intergenerational benefit or legacy—that is, a parent's exposure to postsecondary education may enhance a son's or daughter's knowledge acquisition. This tendency is likely attributable to the fostering of greater learning capital in the offspring of the college educated, much of which is transmitted through the quality of the home environment.

Notes

1. Whenever possible through the remainder of the book, we will attempt to esti-
    mate the size of an effect between two or more groups. This effect size is usually
    estimated as the average (across studies) changes or difference in group scores
    calculated in terms of standard deviation units. More specifically, for any individ-
    ual study an effect size was estimated (according to Hays, 1994) by subtracting
    one group mean from the other (for example, the mean of first-year students sub-
    tracted from the mean of seniors) and then dividing that difference by the pooled
    standard deviation or, if that was not available, the standard deviation of the
    comparison or control group (for example, first-year students). The effect sizes
    from each study for a given outcome variable were then averaged across studies.
    Although there is some disagreement about what constitutes a practically signifi-
    cant effect size, the consensus seems to be that effect sizes less than .30 are con-
    sidered small, those between .30 and .70 moderate, and those above .70 large
    (Bowen, 1977; Cohen, 1988; Gall, Borg, & Gall, 1996; Sprinthall, Schmutte,
    & Sirois, 1991). Interestingly, a synthesis of over 300 meta-analyses, combining
    school and college samples, found that the typical effect size of an educational
    intervention is .40 for achievement-cognitive outcomes and .28 for affective out-
    comes (Hattie, Marsh, Neill, & Richards, 1997). When expressed in standard devi-
    ation units, effect sizes can be converted (using the area under the normal curve)
    to an estimate of the percentile point change or advantage. For example, given an
    estimated effect size equal to one standard deviation, the area under the normal
    curve extends from the 50th to the 84th percentile, indicating a change, or advan-
    tage of one group over another, of 34 percentile points. Where possible and appro-
    priate in the remainder of the book, we report estimated effect sizes in terms of
    both standard deviation and percentile point units. Because percentile points are
    not equidistant under different parts of the normal curve, this estimate should be
    used with caution. However, in our previous synthesis we found it to be more
    comprehensible to readers with limited statistical background than an effect size
    expressed as a fraction of a standard deviation.

2. Astin (1993c) did find that the "intellectual self-esteem" of entering students had
    positive net effects on a number of standardized achievement tests. It might be
    argued that student intellectual self-esteem is merely a proxy for student body
    selectivity. In the multiple regression procedure employed by Astin, when intellec-
    tual self-esteem is in the equation, institutional selectivity would in all probability
    be excluded. However, other analyses of the same data set by Anaya (1992, 1996,
    1999c) and Opp (1991) did not consider student intellectual self-esteem as an
    institutional-level predictor variable, and institutional selectivity still did not sig-
    nificantly influence scores on the Graduate Record Exam, the Medical College
    Admissions Test, or the National Teachers Examination. Thus, Astin may be cor-
    rect when he points out that scores on standardized tests such as the GRE, MCAT,
    or NTE can be enhanced by a competitive academic environment. However, an
    academically competitive environment may not always be easily identified simply
    by the academic selectivity of the undergraduate student body.

3. No matter whether one uses student self-reports or objective, standardized mea-
    sures of learning, separating the net influence of different institutions from the
    influence of the background characteristics of the students attending the institu-
    tions is a particularly thorny problem in all between-college effects studies. We

would argue, however, that it is a more severe problem in studies employing self-reports than in those employing objective, standardized measures. The issue here is not so much what is being measured by the two different approaches, although that issue has been the concern of a number of scholars (Bradburn & Sudman, 1988; Pike, 1995, 1996, 1999b). Rather, the issue is in identifying and adjusting for that part of the outcome score that is attributable to student background traits. It is usually possible to find a very strong predictor (that is, correlations in the .70 to .75 range) of standardized outcome measures if one employs scores on a parallel pretest or a similar precollege measure. Consequently, when one uses standardized outcomes such as the Graduate Record Examination, the SAT or ACT score provides an excellent estimate of the contribution of student precollege traits to the outcome score. Statistically significant associations between institutional characteristics and GRE scores, above and beyond the contribution of SAT-ACT scores, have a reasonably good chance of reflecting institutional impacts. Nearly all of the studies employing students' self-reported learning gains, however, fail to explain much variance in the magnitude of the gains with student precollege traits. Thus, the net associations found between institutional characteristics and gains are substantially more likely to be confounded by unmeasured variations in student characteristics. (See Pascarella, 2001, for a fuller discussion of this problem.) This is a persistent problem when one uses self-reports, not only in trying to identify between-college effects but also in trying to estimate within-college effects. The relationship between college experiences and self-reported gains may also be artificially influenced or inflated by other factors. These factors include a halo effect (Pike, 1999b) and, because measures of experiences and gains are often completed by students on the same questionnaire at the same time, a response set. Thus, although we certainly acknowledge the validity of student self-reports of gains or growth during college, we nevertheless place greater interpretative weight on evidence derived from objective measures.

4. Kuh (1993) found that students at liberal arts colleges tended to have significantly higher scores on a measure of self-reported gains in knowledge and academic skills than students at comprehensive or metropolitan universities. In the absence of controls for student background characteristics, however, this could simply reflect student recruitment factors rather than any distinctive socialization occurring at liberal arts colleges.

5. A single-institution study found that a measure of perceived discrimination negatively influenced self-reported gains in mathematics, net of such factors as ability, race, and sex ("Factors Influencing Senior Students' Gains," 1997). However, the nature of the perceived discrimination variable was not clear.

6. Davis and Murrell (1993) present evidence suggesting that majoring in the liberal arts (versus professions) has a positive influence on self-reported gains in general education. However, in contrast to other investigations of college major, their data did not permit them to control for important precollege variables such as student ability. Thus, it is unclear if the effects of major reflect differential socialization or merely differential recruitment.

7. In this section, we omit findings that indicate the *negative* impact of taking certain courses or patterns of courses on specific outcomes. We do this because we are skeptical that negative associations in the body of evidence necessarily represent negative causal effects. Thus, for example, if the number of mathematics courses

taken is negatively related to verbal skills, it may represent not a negative causal effect of taking math courses but rather the simple fact that taking numerous mathematics courses prevents one from taking courses in other areas, such as literature, English, and the humanities, that may positively influence verbal skills.

8. Interestingly, variation in the scheduling format of coursework (that is, traditional scheduling, daily versus weekly scheduling, intensive courses, modular courses, weekend courses, compressed summer courses) does not appear to have a pronounced impact on student learning (Caskey, 1994; Cullivan, 1990; Daniel, 2000; Scott, 1996; Woodruff & Mollise, 1995).

9. There is also a small body of research on the impact of learning skills classes or interventions on student learning. A useful metanalysis of this literature was conducted by Hattie, Biggs, & Purdie (1996). We took the statistical detail they provided and computed an effect size for 11 studies with postsecondary samples where we could isolate the impact of learning skills classes on test performance or content learning. This included three types of learning skills interventions: *structural aids,* designed to help the learner interact with content to define structural and high-level meaning (for example, note taking, summarizing, organizers); *study skills,* designed to diminish use of ineffective study behaviors and train students to use one or more effective skills; and *memory,* designed to improve recall of specific factual material. Our estimate is that these learning interventions were, on average, linked to an improvement in learning or performance of about .27 standard deviation (11 percentile points).

10. There is also a small body of related recent research on the learning outcomes of hypermedia. Hypermedia or hypertext is a computer-enabled technology that permits random access to great volumes of information. It allows for substantial learner control over the pace and timing of access as opposed to a structured, organized, linear scheme or access. The World Wide Web is an example. A synthesis of six experimental studies conducted with undergraduate samples found small and statistically nonsignificant learning differences between hypermedia-based and text-based (paper-based) instruction (Dillon & Gabard, 1998).

11. For example, excellent demonstrations of how multiple presentations of visual and textual material can be coordinated or synchronized to increase student learning and knowledge transfer can be seen in an interesting and creative series of experimental studies with postsecondary samples by Mayer and colleagues (Mayer, 1997; Mayer & Anderson, 1991, 1992; Mayer & Gallini, 1990; Mayer & Sims, 1994; Mayer, Steinhoff, Bower, & Mars, 1995).

12. For examples of representative individual studies comparing the learning of on-campus and remote-site students in the same course see Bothan (1998), Cheng, Lehman, and Armstrong (1991), Collins (2002), Dexter (1995), Glascott and Stone (1998), Haynes and Dillon (1992), Hodge-Hardin (1995), Johnson (1991), Knight and Zhai (1996), McCleary and Egan (1995), Neuhauser (2002), Pirrong and Lathen (1990), Stanton, Floyd, and Aultman (1995), Verduin and Clark (1991). All but one (Glascott & Stone, 1998) found no significant differences between the course learning of students in distance education and on-campus classes.

13. In addition to achievement effects, cooperative learning also appears to facilitate greater interpersonal attraction among students as well as perceptions of greater social support from peers and instructors than do either competitive or individualistic approaches to learning (Johnson et al., 1998a, 1998b).

14. There is also modest evidence suggesting that forming student groups in a class to take advantage of peer influences can have modestly positive effects on learning, even when group interactions may not be structured as they are in cooperative learning. This comes from a comprehensive meta-analysis of within-class grouping by Lou et al. (1996). We took data from seven studies included in their review that used postsecondary samples and found that within-class grouping led to an estimated achievement advantage of .19 of a standard deviation (8 percentile points) over classes where student groups were not used. Because of the small number of studies, this effect size was not statistically significant at $p < .05$ but was at $p < .10$.

15. Closely related to concept-knowledge maps is the matrix representation system (MRS). The MRS displays structural knowledge spatially using patterns of hierarchy, sequence, and matrix, the last being the cornerstone of the system. It can be used as a guide for taking notes from lecture material. (See Kiewra, 1997, for a detailed discussion and examples of MRS.) A series of experiments comparing it with text or differently structured outlines suggest, in general, that the matrix representation system may enhance both short- and long-term memory for factual detail (Kiewra, DuBois, Staley, & Robinson, 1992), memory for relationships (Kiewra, DuBois, Christian, & McShane, 1988; Kiewra et al., 1991), and the organization of written discourse (Benton, Kiewra, Whitfall, & Dennison, 1993).

16. Teaching behavior or instructional effectiveness appears to have only a very weak relationship with faculty scholarly productivity (Centra, 1993; Feldman, 1987; Kremer, 1990, 1991; Noser, Manakyan, & Tanner, 1996; Olsen & Simmons, 1996; Reich, Rosch, & Catania, 1988). The most comprehensive synthesis of this research (498 correlations from 58 studies conducted between 1949 and 1992) is a metanalysis by Hattie and Marsh (1996). They reported an average weighted correlation of .06 between teaching behaviors (measured by student perceptions, self-ratings, or peer ratings) and research productivity (measured by number of publications, citations, or grants; a measure of research quality; or a composite of these factors). There was little or no difference in the correlation when teaching effectiveness was measured by student perceptions (.071) or faculty peer ratings (.083). Though statistically significant, a correlation of .06 means that teaching effectiveness and research productivity have less than 1 percent of their variability in common. Thus, although the evidence does not suggest that either research productivity or teaching effectiveness is achieved at the price of the other, it does clearly suggest that they may be independent domains of academic work.

17. Analyses by Hayek and Kuh (1999) and MacKay and Kuh (1994) also found that dimensions of social and academic effort differed in their effects on student self-reported learning gains by such factors as race, sex, and socioeconomic status. However, because we were not certain from these studies that actual tests for the presence of statistically significant, conditional effects were conducted, we are unsure as to which are statistically reliable and which are merely chance differences. Consequently, we hesitate to report them as conditional effects.

18. A qualitative study of older (30 or over) undergraduates by Kasworm (1997) also suggests that the influential learning experiences for such students resided largely in the classroom and interactions with instructors. Compared with their younger undergraduate counterparts, the learning of older students is not powerfully influenced by interaction with peers.

CHAPTER FOUR

Cognitive Skills and Intellectual Growth

In Chapter Three we focused on the learning outcomes generally thought to be directly, or at least purposefully, related to the curriculum or academic program of a college—namely, the acquisition of subject matter knowledge and academic (usually verbal and quantitative) skills. In this chapter we turn to the acquisition of more general intellectual or cognitive competencies and skills, which, if they are not so directly tied to a particular curriculum or course of study, are nevertheless thought to be salient outcomes of postsecondary education (Jones, 1994; Jones, Dougherty, Fantaske, & Hoffman, 1997; Jones et al., 1995). As we pointed out in our 1991 synthesis, these cognitive skills go by a number of different names—critical thinking, reflective judgment, epistemological development, and so on—and they differ somewhat in conceptual definition and the types of problems or issues they address. They do, however, have as a common theme the notion of applicability and utility across a wide range of different content areas. These cognitive competencies and skills represent the general intellectual outcomes of postsecondary education that permit individuals to "process and utilize new information; communicate effectively; reason objectively and draw objective conclusions from various types of data; evaluate new ideas and techniques efficiently; become more objective about beliefs, attitudes, and values; evaluate arguments and claims critically; and make reasonable decisions in the face of imperfect information. These and related general cognitive skills are a particularly important resource for the individual in a society and world where factual knowledge is becoming obsolete at an accelerated rate" (Pascarella & Terenzini, 1991, pp. 114–115).

CHANGE DURING COLLEGE

Conclusions from *How College Affects Students*

In our 1991 synthesis, we concluded that, compared with freshmen, college seniors have better oral and written communication skills, are better abstract reasoners or critical thinkers, are more skilled at using reason and evidence to address ill-structured problems for which there are no verifiably correct answers, have greater intellectual flexibility in that they are better able to understand more than one side of a complex issue, and can develop more sophisticated abstract frameworks to deal with complexity. Our best estimates of the magnitudes of the gains, or the advantage of seniors over freshmen, were as follows: oral communication, .60 of a standard deviation (a 23 percentile point advantage); written communication, .50 of a standard deviation (a 19 percentile point advantage); Piagetian formal (abstract) reasoning, .33 of a standard deviation (a 13 percentile point advantage); critical thinking, 1 standard deviation (a 34 percentile point advantage); using reason and evidence to address ill-structured problems, 1 standard deviation (a 34 percentile point advantage); and ability to deal with conceptual complexity, 1.2 standard deviations (a 38 percentile point advantage). These estimates were based on a large and extensive body of studies.

Evidence from the 1990s

Compared with the literature base we reviewed for our 1991 synthesis, we found relatively few studies focusing on change or gains in general cognitive skills and intellectual growth during college. The literature we did find is focused largely in two broad areas that we term *critical thinking* and *postformal reasoning*.

Critical Thinking. There are many different definitions of, and ways of measuring, critical thinking (Ennis, 1985; Erwin, 1997; Moore & Parker, 1989; Paul, 1987, 1992; Sternberg, 1985; Tsui, 1999). However, it would appear that most attempts to define and measure critical thinking operationally focus on an individual's capability to do some or all of the following: identify central issues and assumptions in an argument, recognize important relationships, make correct references from the data, deduce conclusions from information or data provided, interpret whether conclusions are warranted based on given data, evaluate evidence or authority, make self-corrections, and solve problems (Erwin, 1997). Typical in the measurement of these dimensions of critical thinking is the notion that some answers or solutions are more verifiably correct than others.

It comes as no surprise that the generally accepted dimensions of critical thinking identified here have a strong cognitive component. Recently, however, a number of scholars have argued that, in addition to the cognitive ability to use or apply critical thinking skills, there is also a motivational dimension to critical thinking. They term this dimension the *disposition to think critically* (Erwin, 1997; Facione, Facione, & Giancarlo, 1996; Facione, Sanchez, Facione, & Gainen, 1995; Jones, 1993, 1995; Taube, 1997). Thus, critical thinking as a broad concept involves both cognitive skills and the dispositional openness or willingness to apply those skills. Disposition to think critically involves, among other traits, such factors as the inclination to ask challenging questions and follow the reasons and evidence wherever they lead, tolerance for new ideas, willingness to use reason and evidence to solve problems, and willingness to see complexity in problems (Facione, Facione, & Giancarlo, 1994; Facione et al., 1995). In our synthesis we will review research on both critical thinking skills and critical thinking disposition.

The most extensive research in the 1990s on gains in critical thinking skills during college appears to have been conducted by Facione (1997). His findings are based on an aggregate sample of over 6,000 students in nearly 150 undergraduate samples from 50 nursing programs throughout the United States. Employing a cross-sectional design, Facione administered the California Critical Thinking Skills Test (CCTST) (Facione, 1990a, 1990b, 1991) to separate samples of freshmen, sophomores, juniors, and seniors in each of the institutions. The CCTST is an objective, standardized test of critical thinking that measures an individual's skills in analysis, evaluation, inference, deduction, and induction. The results suggest that scores on the CCTST increase steadily with year in college. Using the descriptive statistics reported by Facione, we estimated that the sophomore advantage over freshmen was .34 of a standard deviation (13 percentile points), the junior advantage over freshmen was .45 of a standard deviation (17 percentile points), and the senior advantage over freshmen was .54 of a standard deviation (21 percentile points). Thus, based on Facione's cross-sectional results, about 63 percent of the change in critical thinking skills that occurs during college happens by the sophomore year.

Facione's (1997) results are of course limited because they are based on samples of nursing students rather than on broader samples of undergraduates. Nevertheless, with some exceptions (Criner, 1992; Marr, 1995), the weight of evidence from other cross-sectional studies, using various standardized measures of critical thinking such as the Watson-Glaser Critical Thinking Appraisal or the California Critical Thinking Test, is generally consistent with Facione's findings in suggesting that the greater one's exposure to postsecondary education, the more advanced one's level of critical thinking skills (Beck, Bennett, McLeod, & Molyneaux, 1992; Brooks & Shepard, 1990; Drouin, 1992; Hill, 1995; McDonough, 1997; Mines, King, Hood, & Wood, 1990; Pearson, 1991). Although not all studies provide requisite statistical data, our best estimate from this group of cross-sectional studies is that seniors have an advantage over freshmen of between .55 and .65 of a standard deviation (21 to 24 percentile points).

A remarkably similar trend is reported by Ennis, Millman, and Tomko (in press) in a summary of evidence using the Cornell Critical Thinking Tests. Increased exposure to postsecondary education was clearly linked to higher levels of critical thinking. However, it is difficult to estimate the exact size of the freshman-senior difference from the summary statistics they report.

The longitudinal research on gains in critical thinking skills is less extensive than the cross-sectional research. Moreover, only one study (Mentkowski et al.,

1991) traces growth in critical thinking for more than three years. Mentkowski et al. administered the inference, assumptions, and deductions scales of the Watson-Glaser Critical Thinking Appraisal to 135 undergraduates upon entrance to a small liberal arts college and again toward the end of their senior year. The gain across all three scales from entrance to college through the senior year averaged .25 of a standard deviation (10 percentile points). Facione (1997) and Hagedorn, Pascarella, Edison, Braxton, Nora, and Terenzini (1999) both report critical thinking gains based on multi-institutional samples but only for a three-year period. Facione traced the growth of 625 nursing students at eight institutions from their sophomore through their senior year with the California Critical Thinking Skills Test and reported an average gain of .15 of a standard deviation (6 percentile points). Hagedorn et al. analyzed data from a sample of over 1,000 students attending 18 four-year colleges located in 15 different states. From the time they entered college until the end of their junior year the students in the sample made an average gain of .37 of a standard deviation (14 percentile points) on the critical thinking module of the Collegiate Assessment of Academic Proficiency (CAAP). The CAAP critical thinking module is an objective, standardized test of critical thinking skills that correlates in the .75 range with the Watson-Glaser Critical Thinking Appraisal (Pascarella, Edison, Nora, Hagedorn, & Braxton, 1995).

We uncovered only one additional study that looked at change in critical thinking during college using an objective, standardized instrument. Saucier (1995) administered the Watson-Glaser Critical Thinking Appraisal to several small, convenience samples of nursing students when they entered the program, either in their sophomore or junior year of college. The samples were then followed up with the same test one month before graduation. Saucier reports average gains in two of the three consecutive years covered by the study, but in only one year was the gain statistically significant. The failure to find statistically significant gains in the study is likely due to the very small sample sizes, ranging from 7 to 18. Moreover, because standard deviations were not reported we could not compute effect sizes for the critical thinking gains.

Although change during college is quite often an inaccurate estimate of the actual impact of college, the evidence from the 1990s nevertheless suggests that students are making gains in critical thinking skills during college that are appreciably smaller in magnitude than the gains we observed in our previous synthesis. It is not readily apparent from the evidence why this is the case. However, the more modest evidence of change in the 1990s does underscore an important point. Not all students develop as critical thinkers during college. For example, Keeley (1992) had samples of freshmen and seniors at a single institution read and evaluate two essays to identify the underlying assumptions of the argument put forth. Although seniors were, on average, more proficient than freshmen in identifying assumptions, between 58 and 78 percent of seniors made the mistake of restating at least one premise as an assumption, and between 21 and 58 percent of seniors made the mistake of restating at least three premises as assumptions.

Our synthesis uncovered four studies that estimate growth in the disposition to think critically during college. Three of these studies were cross-sectional (Bers, McGowan, & Rubin, 1996; Facione, 1997; Giancarlo & Facione, 1997) and one was longitudinal (Giancarlo & Facione, 2001). All four studies estimated growth in the disposition to think critically with the California Critical Thinking Dispositions Inventory (CCTDI). The CCTDI (Facione & Facione, 1992; Facione, Facione, Blohm, Howard, & Giancarlo, 1998) is a standardized measure that assesses the extent of one's internal motivation to engage problems, seek answers to questions, and make decisions using critical thinking skills. It measures this disposition along seven dimensions or subscales—truth seeking, open-mindedness, analyticity, systematicity, critical thinking self-confidence, inquisitiveness, and maturity of judgment—and also reports a total score.

Using the same large multi-institutional sample of undergraduate nursing programs previously described, Facione (1997) administered the CCTDI to a sample of over 2,600 undergraduates, consisting of freshmen, sophomores, juniors, and seniors. Using the descriptive statistics reported by Facione, we estimate that the seniors in the sample had an advantage in critical thinking disposition over freshmen of about .50 of a standard deviation (19 percentile points). However, most of the change appeared to have occurred by the second year of college. The estimated critical thinking disposition advantage of sophomores over freshmen was .46 of a standard deviation (18 percentile points), or about 90 percent as large as the corresponding advantage of seniors over freshmen.

Once again, because the Facione (1997) sample is limited to students in a single professional program there may be some question about the generalizability of the results. However, two additional cross-sectional studies, one at a private liberal arts university and one at a community college, report findings generally consistent with those reported in Facione's analyses with undergraduate nursing samples. Giancarlo and Facione (1997) administered the CCTDI to a sample of over 1,100 students in all four class levels at a private university. Using an estimated freshman standard deviation on the CCTDI from a subsample of students attending the same institution, we computed a senior advantage over freshmen in critical thinking disposition of .45 of a standard deviation (17 percentile points). Once again, the sophomore advantage over freshmen was almost as large as the senior advantage, but because the sophomore average was not reported numerically we hesitated to compute an effect size.

Bers, McGowan, and Rubin (1996) administered the CCTDI to a sample of 224 community college students and found that disposition to think critically had a statistically significant positive relationship with exposure to postsecondary education, operationally defined as number of credit hours completed. Using the descriptive statistics reported by Bers et al., we estimated that the difference in overall critical thinking disposition between students who had completed 30 or more credits and those who had completed 12 or fewer credits was .68 of a standard deviation, a 25 percentile point advantage for the former group.

The longitudinal study of gains in critical thinking disposition was conducted by Giancarlo and Facione (2001) at the same private university where they conducted their cross-sectional investigation. A sample of 147 students took the CCTDI as beginning freshmen and then again as seniors. From the first to the second testing, the sample increased a statistically significant 7.43 points in critical thinking disposition. This translated into a gain from freshman to senior year of .28 of a standard deviation (11 percentile points).

Postformal Reasoning. Critical thinking (as it has usually been assessed) focuses to a great extent on an individual's ability to solve intellectual puzzles or problems. These puzzles or problems come in many forms and require the application of complex reasoning and information processing, yet they usually have the common trait of a verifiably correct, or at least a more valid, answer. The critical thinking, information processing, and formal reasoning skills involved in puzzle or problem solving are an important acquisition in the development of intellectual resources. However, there are other kinds of real-world adult problems that require a somewhat different approach to reasoning than the intellectual skills typically included under the rubric of critical thinking. These are "ill-structured" or "wicked" problems for which there is likely to be conflicting or incomplete information, unspecifiable problem parameters, and a number of plausible solutions, none of which may be verifiably correct (King & Kitchener, 1994). Examples of such problems are gun control, safety of food additives, waste disposal, objectivity of the press, reducing poverty, teaching evolution in the schools, and the like. In addressing these and similar problems, formal rules of logic may not suffice, and tentative answers or solutions usually need to be "constructed" rather than "discovered." Descriptions of successful entrepreneurs, managers, researchers, and educators often include references to strong abilities for framing and resolving ill-structured problems (Lynch, 1996; Sherman, 1994). Several scholars and cognitive development theorists (Basseches, 1984; Perry, 1970; Wood, 1997) have argued that constructing tentative solutions to such real-world problems requires a set of intellectual capabilities beyond those usually included in the concepts of critical thinking or formal reasoning (hence, the term *postformal reasoning*). These intellectual capabilities have been operationally defined in a number of ways but the most well known, and those that have dominated the measurement of postformal reasoning, are the Reflective Judgment Interview (King & Kitchener, 1994), the Measure of Epistemological Reflection (Baxter Magolda, 1990; Taylor, 1983), and the Measure of Intellectual Development (Knefelkamp, 1974; Moore, 1991a; Widick, 1975).

The Reflective Judgment Interview (RJI) measures reasoning along a multi-level continuum of seven stages. Each level is characterized by a person's view of knowledge and his or her concept of justification of belief. To paraphrase King and Kitchener (1994), at the lowest stages (prereflective thinking), knowledge is gained either by direct, personal observation or through the word of authority and is absolute and certain. Reasoning at the middle stages (quasi-reflective thinking) recognizes that knowledge claims about ill-structured problems contain elements of uncertainty. However, the quasi-reflective individual has difficulty successfully addressing ill-structured problems because of a lack of understanding of their inherent ambiguity. At the highest stages (reflective thinking), it is understood that knowledge useful in addressing ill-structured problems must be actively constructed. Beliefs are justifiable to the extent that they are based on a rational process involving appropriate forms of inquiry and use of evidence. The RJI consists of four dilemmas and a set of standardized probe questions designed to tap level of reasoning. Each dilemma is defined by two contradictory points of view and represents an ill-structured problem. Subjects are asked to state and justify their points of view about the issues in each dilemma. The four dilemmas represent different content domains: science, current events, religion, and history.

In our current synthesis we uncovered only one published study in the first half of the decade that estimated gains during college in reflective judgment. Employing a cross-sectional design, Mines, King, Hood, and Wood (1990) tested 20 freshmen and 40 seniors at a large research university with the RJI. Their descriptive statistics indicate that seniors had an advantage over freshmen of about 2.08 standard deviations, which converts to a 48 percentile point advantage. Fortunately, our current synthesis of gains during college in reflective judgment was augmented by two comprehensive literature reviews of research using the RJI with postsecondary samples (King & Kitchener, 1994; Wood, 1997). It is apparent from these reviews that our 1991 synthesis missed several unpublished studies and that our current synthesis would also have overlooked several unpublished studies. Consequently, we used the results of the work of King, Kitchener, and Wood (King & Kitchener, 1994; Kitchener, Wood, & Jensen, 1999; Wood, 1997) to reestimate the overall relationship between exposure to postsecondary education and level of reflective judgment.

King and Kitchener (1994) report the individual results for 20 cross-sectional studies of 966 traditional-age (for example, 18-year-old freshmen and 22-year-old seniors) college students using the RJI. The studies were conducted between 1978 and 1993. The evidence suggests a strong positive relationship between exposure to postsecondary education and reflective thinking. Using the individual study data they report in an appendix, we estimated the average reflective thinking advantage of seniors over freshmen across all studies to be .68 of a standard deviation (25 percentile points). Similar summary data reported by Wood (1997) yielded a senior advantage over freshmen of .79 of a standard deviation (29 percentile points). King and Kitchener also report data from five cross-sectional studies of 135 nontraditional-age college students (for example, 22-year-old freshmen and 26-year-old seniors). Using the information they report, we estimate the senior advantage over freshmen across all studies to be .98 of a standard deviation in reflective thinking, or a 34 percentile point advantage.

In their 1994 summary, King and Kitchener also report the results of a smaller number of longitudinal investigations of change during college in reflective thinking. From the data they report, we weighted the studies by sample size and estimated the gain in reflective judgment from the freshman to the junior year to be .65 of a standard deviation (a 24 percentile point gain) and from the freshman to the senior year to be about 1.90 standard deviations (a 47 percentile point gain). These estimates have to be viewed with extreme caution, however, because they are based on only two studies with a combined sample of only 60 students.

More recent research on reflective judgment not included in either the King and Kitchener (1994) or the Wood (1997) summaries would nevertheless appear to be quite consistent with their conclusions. In what is probably the most comprehensive study of reflective judgment or reflective thinking to date, Kitchener, Wood, and Jensen (1999) administered the Reflective Judgment Interview (RJI) and the Reasoning About Current Issues Test (RCI; an objective paper-and-pencil measure of reflective thinking) to 1,588 freshmen, 141 sophomores, 135 juniors, and 265 seniors at four different institutions. Of the total sample, 34 freshmen and 29 juniors at two of the institutions completed the RJI, while the remainder at all four institutions completed the RCI. On both measures there was a statistically significant class effect, and using the descriptive statistics reported we estimated the junior advantage over freshmen on the RJI to be .86 of a standard deviation (a 31 percentile point advantage), while the senior advantage over freshmen on the RCI was estimated at .71 of a standard deviation (a 26 percentile point advantage).

Perhaps more important than a quantitative estimate of the gains in reflective judgment that occur during college is an understanding of the qualitative change in thinking processes that appears to happen between the freshman and senior years. Results of both cross-sectional and longitudinal studies using the RJI are quite consistent in indicating that the typical change in reflective judgment between the freshman and senior years is a movement of about half a stage on the reflective judgment conceptual model from stage 3, the end of pre-reflective thinking, to stage 4, the beginning of quasi-reflective thinking. The modest size of this advance may be deceiving in that it represents a qualitative shift from a style of reasoning based on personal beliefs to one that explicitly uses reason and evidence in forming judgments. As such, it may represent an important prerequisite for the development of a reasoned approach to addressing ill-structured problems.

Another line of inquiry on change or growth in postformal reasoning during college has employed the Measure of Epistemological Reflection (MER). The MER was designed to measure development on the first five stages of Perry's (1970) scheme of intellectual and ethical development. In the first five stages of the Perry scheme the individual moves from an understanding of knowledge that is presumed to be dualistic, absolute, and obtainable only from authorities to an understanding of knowledge that assumes multiplicity, that is contextual and relative, and where analytical skills enable the individual to critique ideas—his or her own and others. The MER is a written instrument that assesses the respondent's views in six domains of thinking related to learning and elicits specific justification for the respondent's thinking. In a longitudinal study at a single institution, Baxter Magolda (1990) employed the MER, along with a semi-structured interview that also addressed the same six domains, to estimate growth during two years of college on the Perry scheme. On both instruments, progression through college was associated with statistically significant gains on the Perry scheme. Using the descriptive statistics reported by Baxter Magolda, we estimated the change from the beginning of the freshman to the beginning of the junior year to be about 1.37 standard deviations (41 percentile points) on the MER and 1.73 standard deviations (46 percentile points) on the semistructured interview. Gains from the freshman to the sophomore year were also statistically significant and were about 70 percent and 35 percent as large as the two-year gains on the MER and the semistructured interview, respectively.

Similar results are reported in another single-institution, longitudinal study by Kube and Thorndike (1991). They also employed the MER, but their study differs from Baxter Magolda's (1990) investigation in that they traced growth from the beginning of the freshman year through the end of the senior year. Using the descriptive statistics they report, we estimated the freshman-to-senior gain on the MER to be 2.54 standard deviations, which translates to an average gain of 49 percentile points.

A final line of research on growth in postformal reasoning during college uses one of several versions of the Measure of Intellectual Development (MID), or the Scale of Intellectual Development (SID). Like the Measure of Epistemological Reflection, the MID is a written instrument that attempts to capture development across the first five positions of the Perry scheme. The somewhat lesser-used SID is a multiple-choice measure. Results of research using these instruments have generally not reported change in terms of average scores. Rather, the evidence is usually reported in terms of differences in group (for example, freshman versus senior) distributions across the different stages of the Perry model. With the exception of one study that reports mixed results (Durham, Hays, & Martinez, 1994), the weight of evidence from both longitudinal and cross-sectional investigations constituting this body of research is generally consistent in suggesting a statistically significant, positive relationship between extent of exposure to postsecondary education and level of intellectual development (Hart, Rickards, & Mentkowski, 1995; May, 1990; Moore, 1991b; Pearson & Rodgers, 1998; Thompson, 1991; Zhang & Richarde, 1998). Although there is some variation among studies, generally it would appear that freshmen are functioning intellectually in the transition from Perry stages 2 and 3, whereas seniors are functioning intellectually between stages 3 and 4. In short, the growth during college in intellectual development defined by the Perry scheme is largely a movement from a dualistic, right-wrong notion of knowledge to one embracing the potential legitimacy of multiple perspectives and the importance of context.[1]

In addition to the evidence based on standardized measures, there is also a small body of research that attempts to estimate growth in cognitive skills and intellectual development during college using student or alumni self-reports (Bauer, 1992, 1995, 1996, 1998; Bauer, Mitchell, & Bauer, 1991; Dollar, 1991; Graham & Cockriel, 1989; Kelley, 1994). Consistent with the findings from studies employing standardized measures reviewed earlier, the weight of evidence from this body of research suggests that the majority of students and alumni perceive that they made moderate to substantial growth during college in such areas as analytical thinking, synthesis of ideas, critical thinking, and independent learning.

NET EFFECTS OF COLLEGE

Conclusions from *How College Affects Students*

In the 1991 synthesis, we made the following general conclusions with respect to the net impact of college on general cognitive skills and intellectual growth.

1. Seniors in college have significantly better written and oral communication skills than freshmen, even when controls are made for age and academic ability.

2. Graduates of community colleges score significantly higher than incoming freshmen on a measure of general intellectual and analytical skill development even in the presence of controls for age, verbal ability, and mathematical ability.

3. There is reasonably sound and consistent evidence to suggest that exposure to postsecondary education has a statistically significant, positive effect on critical thinking even when controls are in effect for precollege level of critical thinking, academic aptitude, maturation, family socioeconomic origins, and aspirations. The positive net influence of postsecondary education, at least in the initial years of exposure, however, appears to be concentrated in the enhancement of one's ability to determine the validity of data-based conclusions and to evaluate the strength or weakness of arguments.

4. Those who attend college make significantly greater gains in reflective judgment—one's ability to use reason and evidence in making judgments about controversial issues—than those who do not attend college. This difference persists even when controls are made for differences in academic ability.

5. Net of age, intelligence, and academic ability, exposure to postsecondary education appears to have a statistically significant, positive influence on one's intellectual flexibility (that is, ability to comprehend and effectively argue both sides of a complex or controversial issue).

Evidence from the 1990s

Although we did not find studies in the current synthesis that spoke to the net effect of college on written or oral communication skills, or intellectual flexibility, the evidence we did uncover is quite consistent with our 1991 synthesis in suggesting that exposure to postsecondary education does, in fact, have a statistically significant, positive effect on both critical thinking skills and postformal reasoning. Moreover, the literature of the 1990s provides a somewhat greater opportunity for estimating the magnitude of the net effect of college on critical thinking and, to a lesser extent, postformal reasoning.

Critical Thinking. A number of cross-sectional and longitudinal investigations have attempted to estimate the net impact of differential exposure to postsecondary education on critical thinking. The majority of these studies employ objective, standardized measures. Rykiel (1995) administered the Watson-Glaser Critical Thinking Appraisal to independent samples of incoming freshmen and outgoing sophomores at a single community college. The sophomores had completed at least 43 of the 64 credits required for graduation. Introducing statistical controls for a measure of verbal aptitude, Rykiel found that sophomores scored significantly higher on the Watson-Glaser total score and on the evaluation of arguments subscale. Using the group standard deviations and adjusted group means reported by Rykiel, we estimated that sophomores in her study had a net advantage over incoming freshmen in total critical thinking of .34 of a standard deviation (13 percentile points). Because we could not find group standard deviations for the Watson-Glaser evaluation of arguments subscale, we could not estimate an effect size for this group comparison. However, Rykiel's finding on this subscale is partially consistent with the conclusion from our 1991 synthesis that the effect of the early years of college on critical thinking skills appears to be largely one of fostering the ability to determine the validity of data-based conclusions and to evaluate the strength or weakness of arguments.

Although Rykiel's (1995) findings might be confounded by age or maturation, they are nevertheless also consistent with longitudinal research in which maturation is controlled. Analyzing longitudinal data from 13 four-year and 4 two-year colleges participating in the National Study of Student Learning, Pascarella, Bohr, Nora, and Terenzini (1996) sought to determine the effects of exposure to postsecondary education, operationally defined as credit hours taken, on end-of-first-year critical thinking. Critical thinking was assessed with the critical thinking module from the Collegiate Assessment of Academic Proficiency, which is a standardized test quite similar to the Watson-Glaser Critical Thinking Appraisal. In the presence of statistical controls for level of precollege critical thinking, race, gender, age, academic motivation, work responsibilities, the average critical thinking level of students at the institution attended, and type of coursework taken, four-year college students taking 24 or more credit hours during the first year of college had a statistically significant advantage in end-of-first-year critical thinking over students taking 6 or fewer credit hours of about .41 of a standard deviation. This number converts to an advantage of 16 percentile points. The corresponding advantage for two-year college students was also statistically significant and was estimated at .24 of a standard deviation, or 10 percentile points (see also Klassen, 2001).

The Pascarella et al. (1996) estimate of the net effect of postsecondary education on critical thinking for two-year colleges (.24 of a standard deviation) is somewhat smaller than the estimated effect from Rykiel's (1995) two-year college study (.34 of a standard deviation). However, the smaller effect reported by

Pascarella et al. is based on one year of exposure to postsecondary education, while Rykiel's study encompasses nearly two years. The effect on critical thinking of one year of exposure to postsecondary education reported by Pascarella et al. in their four-year college sample (.41 of a standard deviation) is quite consistent with the results of an earlier study (Pascarella, 1989) included in our 1991 synthesis. In that study, Pascarella matched samples of secondary school seniors who attended and did not attend college on the Watson-Glaser and followed them for an entire academic year. Net of such factors as initial level of critical thinking, academic ability, secondary school grades, and educational aspirations, those students with one year of exposure to college had an advantage of .44 of a standard deviation in critical thinking over those students who did not attend college during the first year after graduation from secondary school.

Other research has attempted to estimate the net impact of college on critical thinking beyond the first year. In the Mines, King, Hood, and Wood (1990) study reviewed in the previous section on change during college, samples of seniors and freshmen at a single institution were administered both the Watson-Glaser Critical Thinking Appraisal and the Cornell Critical Thinking Test. In an attempt to determine if the freshman-senior differences noted on these tests were confounded by academic ability, Mines et al. adjusted the group differences for composite ACT score. Net of this measure of academic ability, seniors still had a statistically significant advantage over freshmen on both measures of critical thinking. Because no adjusted means are reported, however, we could not estimate an effect size.

Although the results of the Mines et al. study might be confounded by maturation, other research that controls for the differential effects of age, among other factors, reports similar results. Doyle, Edison, and Pascarella (1998) followed students from 18 four-year colleges and universities in the National Study of Student Learning through the end of their third year of college. With controls in effect for a battery of confounding influences such as precollege level of critical thinking, academic motivation, race, gender, work responsibilities, socioeconomic status, campus residence, coursework taken, and the quality of instruction received, the number of credit hours taken still had a statistically significant, positive effect on end-of-third-year scores on the critical thinking module of the Collegiate Assessment of Academic Proficiency. Using descriptive statistics available from the National Study of Student Learning (Hagedorn et al., 1999), we estimated that students who had completed 72 or more credit hours had a net advantage in critical thinking over students who had completed 18 or fewer hours of .55 of a standard deviation, or 21 percentile points. Because this estimate of the net effect of three years of college is actually larger in magnitude than our previous estimate of simple change during four years of college, we suspect the latter estimate is overly conservative.

Postformal Reasoning. We uncovered four cross-sectional studies that attempt to estimate the net effects of college on postformal reasoning using the Reflective Judgment Interview. Because of the interview nature of the RJI each of the studies is based on relatively small samples, ranging from 38 to 63. Thus, they have only limited statistical power to detect significant reflective thinking differences between students with different levels of exposure to college. Nevertheless, the weight of evidence from these studies supports the conclusion that undergraduate education probably does have a net positive impact on the development of reflective thinking. Evans (1988) and Mines, King, Hood, and Wood (1990) each administered the RJI to small samples of freshmen and seniors at a single institution. Evans matched the two groups with respect to gender, college grades, and academic aptitude (ACT composite scores) and found that seniors had a statistically significant advantage over freshmen of about .9 of a standard deviation (32 percentile points). Mines et al. statistically controlled for ACT composite and likewise found that seniors had a statistically significant advantage over freshmen in reflective thinking. A more recent study by Jensen, Kitchener, and Wood (1999) found that the senior advantage over freshmen on the RJI became statistically nonsignificant when the effects of verbal ability were controlled. However, analyzing data from what appears to be a different sample, Kitchener, Wood, and Jensen (1999) found that, even when statistical controls were made for ACT composite scores, juniors still had a statistically significant advantage over freshmen in reflective thinking. Because the last three studies (that is, Mines et al., 1990; Jensen et al., 1999; and Kitchener et al., 1999) do not report statistically adjusted group means, we were unable to estimate net effect sizes from their results.

A fourth study attempting to estimate the net impact of college on reflective judgment employed the recently developed objective measure of reflective thinking called the Reasoning About Current Issues Test (RCI). In the Kitchener et al. (1999) investigation reviewed in the previous section on change during college, the authors introduced a statistical control for ACT composite score. With this control in place, the senior advantage over freshmen in reflective thinking remained statistically significant, although we could not estimate a net effect size because ACT-adjusted means were not reported. Most recently, however, Wood (2000) presented additional evidence on the RCI that permitted estimation of a net senior-freshman effect size. Using an expanded sample of students from seven institutions, Wood had comparison groups of freshmen and seniors that were essentially matched on ACT composite score. Freshman ACT scores averaged 25, whereas the average ACT of his seniors was 24.72. Despite ACT score parity, however, the median performance of seniors was about 18 to 20 percentile points higher than the median performance of freshmen across the discrimination and endorsement of judgment sections of the RCI.

The weight of evidence from these studies suggests that freshman-senior differences in reflective thinking, whether measured by the RJI or the RCI, cannot generally be explained away by differences in academic ability. It is still possible, of course, that such net effects are confounded by age (King & Kitchener, 1994).

Evidence Based on Self-Reports. The small body of research that estimates the net impact of college on general cognitive skills and intellectual development employing student self-reports is generally consistent with the evidence based on objective, standardized measures. For example, Whitmire and Lawrence (1996) analyzed data from a sample of over 9,000 undergraduates in different types of institutions using a measure of student self-reported intellectual development consisting of estimates of gains in such areas as ability to think analytically, ability to put ideas together, ability to learn on one's own, and quantitative thinking. With statistical controls in place for age, college grades, academic major, and measures of the college environment, year in college had a statistically significant, positive impact on self-reported gains in intellectual development, although it was not possible to compute an effect size. Similarly, in a single-institution study by Grayson (1996), graduating seniors had a statistically significant advantage in analytical and communication skills over entering students that persisted in the presence of controls for gender, race, and language spoken in the house. The net advantage of graduating seniors over entering freshmen was approximately .65 of a standard deviation, or 24 percentile points.

BETWEEN-COLLEGE EFFECTS

Conclusions from *How College Affects Students*

In our 1991 synthesis, we found only very limited evidence to suggest that the development of general cognitive skills was influenced by institutional characteristics. When general cognitive growth was assessed by self-reports there was some evidence to suggest it is positively influenced by attendance at an institution with an academically selective undergraduate student body. However, this relationship generally disappeared in studies using objective, standardized measures of cognitive growth or controlling for important precollege characteristics. We concluded that student body selectivity in and of itself may tell us little about institutional influences on general cognitive skills and intellectual growth. Rather, selectivity may only have a discernible impact on student general cognitive development if it is combined with other institutional factors, such as small size and an institutional ethos that encourages a high level of student academic effort and involvement.

There was some cross-sectional evidence paired with statistical controls suggesting that African-American students demonstrate greater development in measures of critical thinking and concept attainment at historically Black institutions than at predominantly White ones. However, this finding was based on a single study.

The only area where we found replicated evidence with respect to between-college effects on general cognitive skills (and it was based on two studies conducted nearly 30 years apart) was in the influence of institutional curricular emphasis. Despite some methodological limitations, the findings suggested that students at institutions with a strong and balanced commitment to general education demonstrated particularly marked gains in measures of critical thinking and adult reasoning skills.

Evidence from the 1990s

Compared to our previous synthesis we uncovered a relatively larger body of evidence focusing on between-college effects on general cognitive skills and intellectual growth. This evidence falls generally into three categories: institutional characteristics, institutional type, and institutional environment.

Institutional Characteristics. As with our synthesis of the evidence on the development of verbal, quantitative, and subject matter competence in the preceding chapter, undergraduate student body selectivity was by far the dominant institutional characteristic considered in research on between-college effects on general cognitive skills and intellectual growth. The weight of evidence from this body of research is quite consistent with the conclusions from our 1991 synthesis. For example, a series of studies analyzing the National Study of Student Learning database attempted to determine if the average student body academic ability (measured in various, but highly correlated ways) had a net impact on the development of individual students' critical thinking (Doyle et al., 1998; Edison, Doyle, & Pascarella, 1998; Hagedorn et al., 1999; Prendergast, 1998). The sample consisted of 5 two-year colleges and 18 four-year colleges. Although the sample was small, the four-year colleges ranged from essentially open-admission institutions to some of the most selective liberal arts colleges and research universities in the country. When statistical controls were made for such factors as individual precollege critical thinking, race, gender, family social origins, and age, the average critical thinking level of incoming students at each of the four-year institutions had only trivial and nonsignificant effects on scores on a standardized measure of critical thinking after three years of college (Hagedorn et al., 1999; Prendergast, 1998). When operationally defined as the average score on a composite of objective tests of precollege reading comprehension, mathematics, and critical thinking, institutional selectivity actually had a small but statistically significant, negative effect on end-of-third-year critical thinking. This negative impact persisted in the presence of controls for individual precollege critical thinking, socioeconomic origins, age, race, gender, and full- or part-time enrollment (Doyle et al., 1998; Edison et al., 1998).

Although based on only five institutions, there is some evidence in the Hagedorn et al. (1999) study to suggest that institutional selectivity positively influences the end-of-first-year critical thinking of two-year college students. However, this was not replicated by Whitt et al. (in press) employing a more extensive set of individual- and institution-level controls.

Results quite consistent with those yielded by the National Study of Student Learning data have been reported in analyses of a much more comprehensive sample of about 200 institutions in the Cooperative Institutional Research Program 1985 to 1989 database. When controls were made for precollege academic ability and an extensive set of other potential confounding influences, student body selectivity (the average SAT or ACT score of the incoming students) had no statistically significant impact on the analytic score of the Graduate Record Examination (Anaya, 1992; Astin, 1993a; Dey, 1991).

When gains in general cognitive development are based on student self-reports rather than on objective, standardized measures, evidence concerning the impact of institutional selectivity is mixed and generally inconclusive. Most of the research in this area is based on various longitudinal iterations of the Cooperative Institutional Research Program data, and with one exception (Volkwein, Valle, Parmely, Blose, & Zhou, 2000), each study estimates the net impact of selectivity after controlling for important precollege confounding influences. Kim (1995, 2002a), Tsui (1998b), and Volkwein et al. (2000) report small positive net effects of institutional selectivity on self-reported gains in such dimensions of cognitive development as critical thinking and analytic and problem-solving skills. However, analyses predicting self-reported gains on the same or very similar cognitive dimensions by Astin (1993c), Dey (1991), Franklin (1993), and Strauss and Volkwein (2001a) report no statistically significant impact for institutional selectivity. Most recently, selectivity was found to have a negative impact on a measure of self-reported intellectual development (Hu & Kuh, 2003a).

The effects on general cognitive skills of institutional characteristics other than student body selectivity have been estimated. For example, Dey (1991) reported that institutional size negatively influenced at least two of three measures of gains in critical thinking skills, and he hypothesizes that this negative effect may be due to the inhibiting influence that institutional size has on interaction with peers and faculty. This finding, however, is based on a single sample and awaits replication.

Institutional Type. The overall weight of evidence suggests that the net effects of institutional type on students' general cognitive development are generally trivial in magnitude or inconsistent. For example, research based on two independent samples found that when student precollege characteristics and other potential confounding influences are taken into account, attendance at a two-year community college versus a four-year college or university has no statistically significant impact on end-of-first-year scores on a standardized, objective measure of critical thinking skills (Bohr et al., 1994; Pascarella, Bohr, Nora, & Terenzini, 1995a; Terenzini, Springer, Yaeger, Pascarella, & Nora, 1994). Similar results are reported with respect to the impact of attending an historically Black college (HBC) or predominantly White institution (PWI) on the development of critical thinking skills in African-American students. When level of precollege critical thinking and other important confounding influences were controlled statistically, African-American students attending HBCs had end-of-first-year and end-of-third-year scores on a standardized, objective measure of critical thinking that were essentially indistinguishable from those of their counterparts attending PWIs (Bohr et al., 1995; Flowers & Pascarella, 1999a). Evidence more supportive of the cognitive benefits of attendance at an HBC is reported by DeSousa & Kuh (1996), Kim (1995, 2002a), and Flowers (2002a). All of these studies found that African-American students attending HBCs reported significantly greater progress on self-reported measures of gains in critical thinking or analytical skills than African-American students at PWIs, although only Kim and Flowers introduced controls for potential confounding influences. Thus, when cognitive outcomes are assessed with self-report measures there is some support for the tentative conclusion from our 1991 synthesis that attendance at an HBC may foster increased levels of critical thinking in African-American students. This was not the case, however, when outcomes are assessed with objective measures.

Other institutional typologies have been considered with respect to their impact on students' general cognitive development. These typologies include private versus public control (Franklin, 1993; Terenzini, Springer, Yaeger, Pascarella, & Nora, 1994); women's versus coeducational institutions (Kim, 1995, 2002a); and Carnegie, or similar, classification (for example, research university, doctoral university, comprehensive college, liberal arts college) (Franklin, 1993; Whitmire & Lawrence, 1996). The results of these investigations suggest either trivial and statistically nonsignificant or inconsistent effects. Kuh (1993) did find that students at liberal arts colleges reported greater gains in cognitive complexity than their counterparts at comprehensive or metropolitan institutions; however, without controls for student background characteristics it is difficult to determine just how much of this difference is simply attributable to differential recruitment effects rather than to institutional impacts. Furthermore, a recent analysis of 120 institutions participating in the National Survey of Student Engagement suggested that attendance at a selective liberal arts college actually had an inhibiting influence on self-reported intellectual development (Hu & Kuh, 2003a).

Institutional Environment. As with our synthesis in the preceding chapter, research on the impact of institutional environment on the development of general cognitive skills and intellectual growth is characterized by a wide range of approaches and operational definitions of "institutional environment." We believe the evidence, however, can be generally grouped into the following three general environmental emphases: scholarship and learning, close student-faculty relationships, and vocational-professional training.

A small body of research has focused on the extent to which an institution's emphasis on scholarship or learning has a net influence on students' intellectual growth and development of general cognitive skills. The clear weight of evidence from this research indicates that the stronger an institution's scholarly emphasis, the greater the growth in intellectual skills. This relationship holds irrespective of whether intellectual skills are measured with objective tests or student self-reports and even with controls for other institutional characteristics or environmental emphases. For example, Prendergast (1998), analyzing the National Study of Student Learning data, used a three-item measure estimating the extent to which students perceived the institutional environment as placing an emphasis on being critical, evaluative, and analytical as well as emphasizing the development of scholarly and intellectual qualities and of expressive, aesthetic, and creative qualities. Controlling for an extensive battery of confounding influences, including student precollege critical thinking and institutional selectivity, this measure of an institution's scholarly emphasis had a modest but statistically significant, positive influence on end-of-third-year scores on an objective measure of critical thinking. Analyzing the same data and employing a similar analytic design, Terenzini, Springer, Yaeger, Pascarella, and Nora (1994) reported similar findings for end-of-first-year critical thinking, but in their analyses it was the institution's emphasis on being critical, evaluative, and analytical that accounted for the influence. The findings of Prendergast and Terenzini et al. with an objective measure of critical thinking are essentially replicated in studies using the same environmental scale but student self-reports of their gains in intellectual and analytic competencies (Arnold, Kuh, Vesper, & Schuh, 1993; Hu & Kuh, 2003a; Kuh, Arnold, & Vesper, 1991; Whitmire & Lawrence, 1996).

Although based on studies that employ diverse measures, there is nevertheless a body of evidence to suggest that the extent to which an institution emphasizes close relationships and frequent interaction between faculty and students has implications for students' general intellectual-cognitive development. For example, analyses by Terenzini, Springer, Yaeger, Pascarella, and Nora (1994) found that students' end-of-first-year scores on an objective measure of critical thinking were positively and significantly (if modestly) influenced by the extent to which they perceived that the faculty at their institution were accessible to students and concerned about student development and teaching. This positive effect persisted even in the presence of controls for an extensive battery of potential confounding influences, including student level of precollege critical thinking, institutional control, and the scholarly emphasis of the institutional environment. Generally consistent findings are yielded when general cognitive growth is measured by student self-reports. After controlling for important confounding influences, Astin (1993c), Graham (1998), and Kuh, Arnold, and Vesper (1990) all provide evidence to suggest that student self-reported gains in critical thinking, analytical skills, or general intellectual development are significantly enhanced when the institution's faculty are oriented toward students or when faculty are accessible to students and concerned about student growth and development during college.[2]

Finally, there is a small body of literature that considers the impact on students' general cognitive development of an institutional environment that emphasizes vocational preparation. The findings of this body of research are contradictory, and the direction of effects depends on use of objective or student self-report measures of cognitive outcomes. Both Arnold et al. (1993) and Kuh et al. (1991) report that student self-reports of their gains on a measure of intellectual skills that includes analysis, synthesis, and learning on one's own are positively influenced by an institutional environment that stresses professional-occupational competence and the practical value of one's course of study. This relationship persisted in the presence of controls for students' levels of social and academic involvement and other measures of the institutional environment. Conversely, using an objective measure of critical thinking after three years of college as the dependent variable, Prendergast (1998) found that the same scale used by Arnold et al. and Kuh et al. to assess an institution's emphasis on vocational preparation had a statistically significant, negative influence. This relationship also persisted when controls were made for such influences as level of precollege critical thinking, measures of academic and social involvement, institutional selectivity, and other measures of the institutional environment.[3]

WITHIN-COLLEGE EFFECTS

Conclusions from *How College Affects Students*

In our 1991 synthesis, we made the following general conclusions about within-college effects on general cognitive skills and intellectual growth.

1. One's major course of study has a selective impact on the development of general cognitive skills. A student's cognitive growth is greatest on measures where the content is most consistent with his or her academic major. On general measures of critical thinking (for example, the Watson-Glaser Critical Thinking Appraisal) or postformal reasoning (for example, reflective judgment), one's academic major has little consistent relationship with gains.

2. The learning cycle–inquiry approach to instruction has been shown to enhance the development of formal (abstract) reasoning and conceptual complexity. This approach stresses an active, inductive learning process in which learner involvement in actual experiments or other concrete activities is used to introduce concepts and abstractions.

3. We found no single instructional or curricular approach that consistently and significantly facilitated the growth of critical thinking when critical thinking was measured by general instruments such as the Watson-Glaser Critical Thinking Appraisal. There was statistically nonsignificant evidence to suggest that instruction that stresses student discussion at a relatively high level of cognitive activity or instruction that emphasizes problem-solving procedures and methods may enhance critical thinking.

4. There is evidence that a curriculum experience that requires the integration of ideas and themes across courses and disciplines enhances critical thinking over simply taking a distribution of courses without an integrative rationale.

5. Specifically structured course interventions may enhance the development of postformal reasoning—specifically, stage movement on the Perry continuum. These interventions, which have been termed

cognitive developmental instruction, focus on providing challenges to the individual's initial cognitive and value structures paired with instructional supports appropriate for the individual's initial level of cognitive development.

6. The estimated magnitude of instructional or curricular effects on measures of general cognitive skills tends to be smaller than that of the effect of the overall college experience. Put another way, a single instructional or curricular experience over a limited period may not provide the developmental impact of a cumulative set of mutually reinforcing experiences over an extended period of time.

7. Extent of growth in general cognitive skills during college appears to be a direct result of a student's quality of effort or involvement in college. Involvement in intellectual and cultural activities may be more important to general cognitive development than other types of involvement (social, athletics, and so on). Yet it also appears that the nature and quality of social interactions with faculty members and student peers play a role of some consequence in one's cognitive growth. These interactions are of particular salience if they focus on ideas or intellectual matters. The weight of evidence suggests that the more one's social experience reflects and reinforces one's academic experience, the greater will be the possibilities for intellectual development.

Evidence from the 1990s

As with the evidence pertaining to within-college effects on the acquisition of verbal, quantitative, and subject matter competence, the corresponding evidence from the 1990s on more general cognitive skills and intellectual growth is extensive. Again, in an attempt to make organizational sense of this vast literature we have grouped the studies into the following six general clusters: academic major, coursework-curricular patterns, general pedagogical approaches, teacher behaviors, academic effort-involvement, and social and extracurricular effort-involvement.

Academic Major. We found that academic major affects critical thinking and reasoning skills as follows.

Critical thinking. It is difficult to form any firm conclusion concerning the impact of academic major on critical thinking. A substantial number of studies find no statistically significant differences in scores on standardized critical thinking measures among students from different academic fields of study (McDonough, 1997; Money, 1997; Sebrell & Erwin, 1998; Spaulding & Kleiner, 1992). In those studies that do find significant critical thinking differences among students in different academic majors (Gadzella & Masten, 1998; Gunn, 1993), it is difficult to determine if academic or other experiences in the major cause differences in critical thinking or if different academic fields of study simply tend to attract students with different levels of critical thinking ability to begin with (Tsui, 1999).

Studies that attempt to separate the recruitment effects from the socialization effects of different academic majors produce similarly inconsistent results. For example, Beckett (1996) found that health science majors made significantly greater gains than liberal arts or business majors on the Watson-Glaser Critical Thinking Appraisal. Because the health science majors started out with higher scores, this is just the opposite of what would happen if the differences in gains were simply the result of regression artifacts (Pascarella & Terenzini, 1991). Conversely, King, Wood, and Mines (1990) found that differences among seniors in different academic majors on the Watson-Glaser Critical Thinking Appraisal and the Cornell Critical Thinking Test essentially disappeared when controls were introduced for academic aptitude. Similarly inconsistent results are reported when the dependent measure is self-reported gains in the ability to think critically rather than objective, standardized tests of critical thinking skills. Some studies find net differences due to academic major (Smart, Feldman, & Ethington, 2000; Whitmire & Lawrence, 1996), whereas others do not (Li, Long, & Simpson, 1998, 1999). Characteristic of this body of studies is the use of different operational definitions of academic major, which likely contributes to the inconsistent findings. Even with this taken into account, however, we find little consistent evidence to suggest that one's major field of study, in and of itself, leads to different effects on general measures of critical thinking.

Reasoning skills. We found very little research that focused on the impact of academic major on reasoning skills. The research that we did find, however, clearly underscores the notion that intellectual training in different fields of study leads to the development of different reasoning skills. For example, a longitudinal study by Lehman and Nisbett (1990) followed a sample of undergraduate students from the first semester of their initial year in college through the second semester of their senior year. The sample was divided into four groups, based on their eventual major: natural science, humanities, social science, and psychology. There were only chance differences among the groups in first-semester scores on measures of verbal reasoning, statistical-methodological reasoning, conditional reasoning, and academic ability. At the end of four years of college, however, there was a distinct pattern of differences in reasoning gains made that reflected one's major field of study. Students majoring in the social sciences and psychology demonstrated substantially greater gains in the ability to solve real-world or scientific problems requiring statistical or methodological reasoning (average gain about 65 percent) than did natural science or humanities majors (average gain about 25 percent). Conversely, natural science and humanities majors made substantial and statistically significant gains in the ability to solve real-world or scientific problems requiring conditional reasoning (average gain about 63 percent), while their counterparts majoring in the social sciences or psychology made essentially no improvement in conditional reasoning during four years of college. With the exception of the impact of majoring in humanities on conditional reasoning, for which Lehman and Nisbett candidly admit they have no explanation, the differential impact of academic major on different reasoning skills would appear to reflect the type of inductive reasoning emphasized in different undergraduate academic fields (that is, conditional reasoning in the natural sciences and statistical-methodological reasoning in the social sciences).

Other investigations have also found significant differences in reasoning or metacognitive skills among students in different academic majors (for example, Zhang & Richarde, 1998). There is little to suggest, however, that anything but chance differences exist among students in these academic majors in the magnitude of the freshman-to-senior gains in reasoning skills.

Coursework-Curricular Patterns. We found that coursework-curricular patterns affect critical thinking and reasoning skills as follows.

Critical thinking. One reason why major field of study may demonstrate little consistent impact on growth in critical thinking skills is that it is too broad a representation of the formal academic experience one has during college. Thus, it is not particularly surprising that a number of investigations have focused on the impact on critical thinking of specific patterns of courses taken. Unfortunately, there is only limited consistency in the findings of these studies. A series of analyses of the National Study of Student Learning data found that, even when such factors as precollege critical thinking, institutional characteristics, and other types of course exposure are taken into account, the number of science or engineering courses taken in the first year of college has a modest, but statistically significant, positive impact on end-of-first-year scores on the critical thinking test of the Collegiate Assessment of Academic Proficiency (Doyle et al., 1998; Terenzini, Springer, Yaeger, Pascarella, & Nora, 1994). Similar results are reported by Olsen (1990) in a single-institution study using the same standardized measure of critical thinking and by Tsui (1999) in a large multi-institutional study using students' self-reported growth in critical thinking. Olsen found that the number of science courses taken had a positive effect on critical thinking scores after two years of college, even when controls were made for academic aptitude, though not for other types of coursework taken. Tsui (1999) reported that number of science courses taken positively influenced seniors' self-reported growth in critical thinking even in the presence of controls for level of exposure to other types of coursework and several instructional variables, though not for precollege academic aptitude.

There is also evidence, using objective, standardized measures to suggest that the number of arts and humanities courses taken may enhance end-of-first-year critical thinking (Terenzini et al., 1994), the number of literature courses taken may foster critical thinking after two years of college (Olsen, 1990), and the number of social science courses taken may have positive effects on critical thinking measured after the third year of college (Edison et al., 1998). In contrast to the effects of natural science courses, however, we uncovered no replication of these findings on independent samples.

A different approach has been taken by Smith-Sanders and Twale (1997, 1998) in a single-institution study that sought to determine if degree of exposure to a required general education or core curriculum influenced scores on a standardized test of critical thinking. The general education or core curriculum included courses in the social sciences, natural sciences, mathematics, English composition, history, fine arts, philosophy, and the "great books." The findings are somewhat difficult to interpret. With statistical controls for precollege academic ability, degree of exposure to the core curriculum had a significant curvilinear relationship with critical thinking skills. Generally, the greater one's exposure to the institution's core curriculum, the higher one's critical thinking skills, but for reasons that were not entirely clear, students with the highest level of core curriculum hours completed had somewhat lower levels of critical thinking than students with less core curriculum hours completed. This finding, however, is based on a single sample and awaits replication.

Postformal reasoning. A small number of studies have attempted to determine the impact of coursework or curricular organization on growth in various measures of postformal reasoning. At first glance it is difficult to find any basic commonality among the studies in terms of how they conceptualize or organize the notion of coursework or curricular experiences. However, there does appear to be a common thread running through investigations by Schilling (1991) and Wright (1989, 1992). Both studies report the impact on students' growth in postformal reasoning of exposure to an interdisciplinary or integrated core curriculum that emphasized making explicit connections across courses and among ideas and disciplines. Courses were generally designed, often by faculty teams, to be integrative in content and to stress synthesis of relationships and connections among different academic disciplines.

In the Schilling (1991) study, a sample of seniors who enrolled in the integrated, or interdisciplinary, core curriculum was matched with a group of seniors who were not exposed to it on entering academic ability (ACT score), sex, and area of academic interest. Both groups took the Measure of Epistemological Reflection (recall that the MER measures reasoning development along the first five stages of Perry's [1970] continuum of intellectual and ethical development). Although there were not sufficient statistical data reported to estimate an effect size, Schilling reported that seniors enrolled in the interdisciplinary core curriculum scored at a significantly more advanced stage on the MER than did the matched seniors who were not enrolled. Generally consistent results are reported by Wright (1992) for growth along the Perry continuum during the first year of college. A sample of first-year students took the Learning Context Questionnaire (LCQ), another measure of development on the Perry continuum, when they first entered college and again at the end of their freshman year. With statistical controls introduced for initial LCQ scores and SAT mathematics scores, the number of interdisciplinary general education courses completed had a statistically significant, positive association with development in reasoning, as measured by gain scores on the LCQ during the first year of college.

Both the Schilling (1991) and the Wright (1992) studies appear to be potentially confounded by the interaction of student self-selection and change. Moreover, in the Wright study, the interdisciplinary courses also introduced several nontraditional pedagogical approaches such as collaborative projects and dialogues. Consequently, it is not clear how much of the positive impact of interdisciplinary courses on informal reasoning was confounded by pedagogical practices. Despite these methodological problems, however, the Schilling and Wright investigations are potentially important in that they represent replicated evidence linking integrated, interdisciplinary general education coursework with development or growth in postformal reasoning.[4]

Other scholars have also sought to assess the impact of innovative courses or curricula on postformal reasoning. For example, Pavelich and colleagues (Pavelich, 1996; Pavelich & Moore, 1996; Pavelich, Olds, & Miller, 1995) have investigated changes in engineering students' position on the Perry continuum during exposure to an innovative curriculum that stresses an experiential, problem-solving approach to engineering education. The centerpiece of the curriculum appears to be a series of courses that emphasize real-world open-ended problem solving, team building, and oral and written technical communication skills. The assumption is that these experiences will help students mature toward more complex thinking as well as foster increased capabilities for more effective decisions about ambiguous, real-world engineering problems. Using an interview approach to measuring position on the Perry continuum, Pavelich and colleagues report that seniors exposed to the curriculum have a statistically significant advantage of about 2.30 standard deviations (49 percentile points) in reasoning development over freshmen with little or no exposure to the curriculum. In the absence of a control group, however, it is difficult to determine just how much of the senior advantage in reasoning is uniquely attributable to the innovative coursework and curriculum versus how much would occur simply by four years of postsecondary education without exposure to the innovation. (For example, recall from the earlier section of this chapter on change during college that Kube and Thorndike [1991] reported a simple freshman-to-senior gain on the Measure of Epistemological Reflection of 2.54 standard deviations.) In this regard, it is worth noting that a generally similar curricular innovation in nursing education was not significantly linked to students' growth in reflective judgment (Nickerson, 1991).

General Pedagogical Approaches. There is substantially less evidence with respect to the impact of general or broad-based pedagogical approaches on cognitive skills and intellectual growth than there is with respect to their impact on verbal, quantitative, and subject matter competence. Nevertheless, some research does exist, and we have organized it into the following three categories: computer and information technology, collaborative-cooperative learning, and interventions designed to increase cognitive growth.

Computer and information technology. Interestingly, the most extensive research we uncovered on computers and the development of general cognitive skills and intellectual growth focused on the impact of learning a computer program language. A fairly large number of studies have addressed this issue. Fortunately, Liao and Bright (1991) have conducted a meta-analysis of some 65 of these studies. Their criteria for inclusion of a study were as follows: (1) it had to assess the relation between computer programming and general cognitive skills such as planning skills, thinking skills, reasoning skills, and metacognitive skills (all cognitive skills were measured by standardized tests); (2) it had to take place in an actual classroom setting; and (3) it had to have a control group that did not require students to learn a computer language. Of the 65 studies in their meta-analysis, only 9 were conducted with postsecondary samples. Those 9 studies yielded 20 effect sizes. We took the raw statistical data provided by Liao and Bright for the postsecondary studies and estimated that college students required to learn a computer program language had an advantage of .35 of a standard deviation (14 percentile points) in various general cognitive skills over their counterparts who did not learn a computer program language. This effect size was statistically significant at $p < .05$. Thus, it would appear that the impact of learning a computer language may extend beyond the specific computer language to the development of general cognitive capabilities.

Although they do not focus specifically on learning a computer program language, reasonably consistent results are reported in correlational studies by Flowers, Pascarella, and Pierson (1999) and Kuh and Hu (2000). Analyzing the National Study of Student Learning data, Flowers et al. sought to determine if different types of computer use influenced critical thinking during the first year of college. To this end, they introduced controls for an extensive series of confounding influences such as precollege critical thinking, academic motivation, full- or part-time enrollment, coursework taken, and quality of instruction received. In the presence of these controls, the extent to which coursework required students to learn to use computers had a modest, but significant, positive relationship with end-of-first-year scores on a standardized critical thinking measure for students in five community colleges. The corresponding effect for students at four-year colleges was not significant. In analysis of data from over 70 four-year colleges, Kuh and Hu found that using computers for such learning activities as searching the Internet for course material, analyzing data, and making visual displays each had small, positive effects on student self-reported gains in intellectual development (for example, synthesizing, thinking analytically and logically). These positive effects persisted even in the presence of statistical controls for such factors as sex, race, socioeconomic background, grades and educational aspirations, academic major, work responsibilities, and institutional characteristics.

We also uncovered one study that focused on the use of electronic mail as a pedagogical tool for influencing aspects of general cognitive development. Marttunen (1997) conducted a study in which undergraduates practiced informal argumentation with each other using e-mail. Argumentation was based on ideas presented in two books, and level of argumentation was determined by the extent to which an argument was grounded in reason or evidence. Over a six-week period, the student groups did not have face-to-face meetings, but there was a significant increase in the level of their argumentation in e-mail messages. The absence of a control group of individuals who engaged in the same type of argumentation, but without using e-mail, makes it difficult to determine the unique effects of e-mail itself. Nevertheless, the results do suggest the possibility that electronic mail is a feasible tool in practicing and improving one's level of argumentation.

Collaborative-cooperative learning. An interesting correlational study by Karabenick and Collins-Eaglin (1996) suggests why one might expect collaborative or cooperative learning approaches to foster general cognitive skills and intellectual growth. Using data from over 1,000 students in 57 classes, they found that the greater the class emphasis on collaborative learning and the lower the emphasis on grades, the more likely students were to use higher-order learning strategies of elaboration, comprehension monitoring, and critical thinking. (Elaboration is the attempt to relate ideas in one's class to ideas in other courses, comprehension monitoring is the attempt to try to figure out a point when one becomes confused, and critical thinking refers to consideration of alternatives to a conclusion or point made in class.) To the extent that use of higher-order learning strategies leads to the development of higher-order thinking skills, one might then expect collaborative and cooperative approaches to learning to facilitate the development of general cognitive skills and intellectual development during college. Although not unequivocal, there is a body of evidence to support this expectation.

Qin, Johnson, and Johnson (1995) conducted a meta-analysis of 43 experimental and quasi-experimental studies that considered the effects of cooperative versus individualistic or competitive learning approaches on general problem-solving skills. Problem solving was operationally defined as "a process that required participants to form a cognitive representation of a task, plan a procedure for solving it, and execute the procedure and check the results" (Qin et al., 1995, p. 131). Four types of problems were considered: linguistic problems, which are primarily solved in written or oral languages; nonlinguistic problems, which are primarily represented and solved in pictures, graphs, mazes, symbols, or formulas; well-defined problems, which have well-defined operational procedures and solutions (for example, a chess problem); and ill-defined problems, which have uncertainty with regard to operational procedures and ultimate solutions (for example, real-world problems such as deciding which car to buy). We took the raw statistical data provided by Qin, Johnson, and Johnson for 20 of the 43 studies that were carried out with postsecondary samples and conducted our own (secondary) meta-analysis. We estimate that, compared with their counterparts not learning in a cooperative format, college students learning in cooperative groups had a statistically significant advantage in overall problem solving of .47 of a standard deviation (18 percentile points). The magnitude of this advantage was largely unchanged by differences in the methodological quality of studies. (Estimates of the methodological rigor of each study were provided in the Qin, Johnson, and Johnson meta-analysis.) Similarly, it appeared that the advantage in problem solving accruing to students engaged in cooperative learning was essentially the same for both well-defined problems (.46 of a standard deviation) and ill-defined problems (.49 of a standard deviation).

Additional secondary analysis of the studies conducted with postsecondary samples provided in the Qin, Johnson, and Johnson (1995) meta-analysis suggested a substantial difference in the magnitude of the cooperative learning advantage in solving linguistic problems (.31 of a standard deviation) versus nonlinguistic problems (.96 of a standard deviation). This finding with college students paralleled Qin, Johnson, and Johnson's results when studies were aggregated across all education levels. They suggest that one reason for this difference in problem-solving advantages accruing to cooperative learning is that there may be more ways to solve nonlinguistic problems than linguistic problems. Thus, cooperative group discussion, "which may result in a great number of strategies being suggested may give cooperators a greater advantage over competitors on nonlinguistic than on linguistic problems" (Qin et al., 1995, p. 139).

Johnson, Johnson, and Smith (1996) conducted an additional meta-analysis of the effects of academic controversy on the development of cognitive reasoning skills. Recall from our more detailed description in Chapter Three that academic controversy is a variation of cooperative learning in which a cooperative group of four students is divided into two pairs and then assigned to opposing positions on a significant topic of controversy in a discipline or field of study. As previously indicated in Chapter Three, their meta-analysis was based on 26 published studies, 75 percent of which were randomized true experiments and about 42 percent of which were conducted with postsecondary samples. No separation of effect sizes is made for postsecondary and nonpostsecondary studies. Nevertheless, they found that, compared with approaches in which the student learns on his or her own, academic controversy produced an advantage of .90 of a standard deviation (32 percentile points) in measures of cognitive reasoning.

Results from the National Study of Student Learning pertaining to the net effects of collaborative-cooperative learning experiences on students' self-reported gains in analytical skills (Cabrera, Nora, Bernal, Terenzini, & Pascarella, 1998) are quite consistent with the postsecondary-level findings derived from the Qin, Johnson, and Johnson (1995) and the Johnson, Johnson, and Smith (1996) meta-analyses. Evidence with respect to the impact of collaborative-cooperative learning on critical thinking, however, is less consistent and depends largely on whether critical thinking is assessed with student self-reports or objective, standardized measures. For example, analyzing the 1985 to 1989 Cooperative Institutional Research Program data, Tsui (1999) found that participating in group learning projects had a significant, positive influence on seniors' self-reported growth in critical thinking. This effect persisted even in the presence of controls for coursework taken and other instructional variables. Conversely, a class-level quasi experiment (Miller & Groccia, 1997) and a multi-institutional correlational study with statistical controls for precollege critical thinking and a battery of other confounding influences (Doyle et al., 1998) found that cooperative learning experiences had only small and chance effects on standardized measures of critical thinking skills.

Interventions designed to increase cognitive growth. A substantial body of research in the 1990s sought to determine if purposefully designed instructional interventions during college can positively influence general cognitive skills and intellectual growth. The majority of this research focused on critical thinking skills (Dale, Ballotti, Handa, & Zych, 1997; Gadzella, Ginther, & Bryant, 1996) or the disposition to think critically (Bers et al., 1996). Although some studies employ self-report measures of critical thinking strategies or critical thinking gains (Logan & Salisbury-Glennon, 1999; Peterson, 1996; Reiter, 1994), the preponderance of investigations employ objective, standardized tests of critical thinking such as the Watson-Glaser Critical Thinking Appraisal, the Cornell Critical Thinking Test, and the California Critical Thinking Skills Test (Dale et al., 1997; Forbes, 1997; Gadzella et al., 1996; Gadzella, Hartsoe, & Harper, 1989; Inlow & Chovan, 1993; Langer & Chiszar, 1993; West, 1994) or essay measures of critical thinking (MacPherson, 1999; Price, Wilmes, & Turmel, 1994; Weast, 1996). The clear majority of studies describe the experimental intervention as one in which students are explicitly or implicitly taught critical thinking or problem-solving skills, usually embedded in a semester-long or quarter-long course, but there does not appear to be a clear operational consensus on just exactly what that means pedagogically. Put another way, it is not particularly clear that instruction or practice in critical thinking skills means anywhere near the same thing across studies. As a result, it is not surprising that the body of evidence from this research is far from unequivocal. (Tsui [1998a] reached a similar conclusion, though based on a substantially smaller sample of studies.)

All of the studies we uncovered using pretest-posttest designs *without* a control group report that students exposed to critical thinking skills interventions make statistically significant gains in measured critical thinking skills (Gadzella et al., 1996; Logan & Salisbury-Glennon, 1999; MacPherson, 1999; Peterson, 1996). The absence of a control group, however, makes it difficult if not impossible to determine what part of these gains is uniquely attributable to instruction in critical thinking skills and what part is due to confounding factors, such as maturation, taking the same test twice, or simple exposure to the academic content in which critical thinking instruction might be embedded. The results of experimental and quasi-experimental investigations that *include* a control group of students not receiving explicit instruction in critical thinking skills are more equivocal than studies without a control group. Some find that critical thinking interventions confer a statistically significant advantage in critical thinking skills on students exposed to them (Dale et al., 1997; Facione et al., 1998; Weast, 1996), some report mixed effects (Bers et al., 1996; Langer & Chiszar, 1993; Reiter, 1994; West, 1994), and some report no statistically significant advantage associated with exposure to critical thinking interventions (Forbes, 1997; Gadzella et al., 1989; Inlow & Chovan, 1993; Price et al., 1994). The methodological rigor of the studies does not appear to be associated with whether or not they find positive, mixed, or chance results. Not all of the studies provide the requisite statistical information to compute effect sizes. However, using the statistical information from those studies that do, we estimate that purposeful instruction in critical thinking skills, broadly defined, leads to an advantage in students' measured critical thinking skills of approximately .23 of a standard deviation (9 percentile points). We would caution, however, that this is a rough estimate.

Consistent with the conclusions of Halpern (1993), we would conclude from the evidence we reviewed that development in critical thinking can be enhanced by purposeful instruction and practice in critical thinking and problem-solving skills. We would amend that conclusion, however, by pointing out that the effects may be widely variable and, therefore, not particularly large. We suspect that, in large measure, this may be due to the general absence of a consensus across studies with respect to the operational definition of what constitutes instruction in critical thinking.

In addition to the research on critical thinking, a smaller body of studies has focused on the impact of purposefully designed course or instructional interventions on the development of postformal reasoning (Kronholm, 1996; Marra, Palmer, & Litzinger, 2000; McAdams & Foster, 1998; Thompson, 1995). Postformal reasoning in these studies is measured either in terms of reflective thinking (King & Kitchener, 1994) or the Perry (1970) continuum. Overall, this body of research is based on carefully conducted experiments or quasi experiments with relatively sound internal validity. Moreover, there is a general, if not total, consistency of findings across studies. Students experiencing instructional interventions designed to increase their intellectual development and skills in addressing ill-structured problems tend to score at more advanced levels on measures of reflective thinking or intellectual development than their counterparts not exposed to the interventions.

For example, Kronholm (1996) conducted an experiment to determine if a one-semester instructional intervention would positively influence students' reflective thinking. Students in two general education science courses were assigned to one of three groups: an intervention group and two control groups. Students in all three groups were assessed with the Reflective Judgment Interview (RJI) at the beginning and end of the course. The intervention group was taught according to King and Kitchener's (1994) reflective judgment–developmental instruction model, whereas the two control groups received course instruction without the reflective judgment–developmental instruction emphasis. Reflective judgment–developmental instruction begins with the introduction of an ill-structured problem or issue and progresses to an exploration of the problem or issue. This is accomplished by very focused questions and activities aimed at encouraging students to think about epistemological assumptions, or how they come to know (King & Kitchener, 1994). With statistical controls for initial RJI position, Kronholm found that students exposed to reflective judgment–developmental instruction made significantly greater average gains in reflective thinking than the average of the students in the two control groups.

Generally, if not totally, consistent results are reported by Thompson (1995) in a quasi-experimental assessment of the impact of a similar intervention emphasizing reflective judgment–developmental instruction on gains in reflective thinking. Students exposed to the intervention scored significantly higher at the end of the study on the Reflective Thinking Appraisal (a written measure of reflective thinking or judgment) than did their counterparts not receiving the intervention. (The two groups demonstrated only chance differences in ACT scores and RTA scores at the beginning of the study.) The difference between the two groups at the end of the study on the Reflective Judgment Interview was in the same direction but not statistically significant.

Slightly different approaches were taken by Marra, Palmer, and Litzinger (2000) and by McAdams and Foster (1998). Marra et al. investigated the impact of a project-focused, active-learning, team problem-solving course in engineering design, while McAdams and Foster estimated the effects of Deliberate Psychological Education (DPE). DPE stresses active practice in problem solving related to actual role-taking experiences and augmented interactive exchanges with peers. With controls introduced for sex, academic aptitude, prior grades, class standing, and honors program participation, Marra et al. found that students who had completed the engineering design course had significantly more advanced positions on the Perry (1970) continuum, as measured by a semistructured interview, than students who were yet to take the course. McAdams and Foster reported that students randomly assigned to Deliberate Psychological Education instruction made positive, though not statistically significant, advances on the Perry continuum, whereas their counterparts not receiving DPE instruction actually retrogressed slightly. Similarly, the DPE students made a significant gain on a measure of conceptual complexity, whereas the control students did not.

The McAdams and Foster (1998) study did not report sufficient statistical information to compute an effect size. However, the other three studies did (Kronholm, 1996; Marra et al., 2000; Thompson, 1995). Using the information they provided, we estimated that interventions designed to improve intellectual development, in terms of postformal reasoning skills, provide an average advantage in the development of postformal reasoning of about .65 of a standard deviation (24 percentile points). We would caution, however, that because it is based on only three studies, this estimate may not be particularly robust.

Finally, there is some evidence that constructivist-oriented pedagogy can facilitate students' movement toward more sophisticated and complex epistemological beliefs. For example, recall from Chapter Three the quasi-experimental study conducted by Hofer (1994, 1998–99) in which sections of a calculus course were randomly assigned to a constructivist-oriented approach called *new wave* and a traditional approach. The new-wave sections emphasized active and collaborative learning activities in and out of class, use of graphing calculators, and a curriculum based on textual material that was largely a collection of complex work problems for which answers were not provided. The traditional sections used a standard calculus text that proceeded sequentially, and material was covered primarily through lecture and presentation by the instructor. The new-wave and traditional students differed in only chance ways in potentially confounding influences such as gender, ethnicity, high school calculus background and grades, and tested mathematics ability. At the end of the course, however, the new-wave students were significantly more likely to hold more sophisticated epistemological beliefs about mathematics knowledge (for example, math problems may have more than one right answer) than the traditionally taught students. The advantage accruing to the students in the constructivist-oriented, new-wave sections was about .16 of a standard deviation (6 percentile points).

Generally consistent findings are reported by Baxter Magolda (1992b) in an intricately detailed qualitative investigation that analyzed the experiences of a sample of students during their four years of college. In the course of periodic interviews, students reported a number of factors that promoted their epistemological development. One of the important factors was teachers defining learning as mutually constructed meaning and thereby encouraging students to engage in thought processes much like critical thinking.

Teacher Behaviors. We uncovered only a smattering of evidence concerning the impact of teacher behaviors on general cognitive skills and intellectual development. The research that speaks to this issue most directly comes from analyses of the National Study of Student Learning data. Pascarella, Edison, Nora, Hagedorn, and Braxton (1996) and Edison, Doyle, and Pascarella (1998) sought to determine if students' perceptions of the extent of teacher organization and preparation (for example, class time is used effectively) and instructional skill and clarity (for example, instructors give clear explanations) in the overall teaching they receive at their institution significantly influenced critical thinking. In both studies critical thinking was assessed with an objective, standardized measure, and each introduced statistical controls for an extensive set of confounding influences such as precollege critical thinking, academic motivation, race, sex, age, full- or part-time enrollment, patterns of coursework taken, and work responsibilities. In the presence of these controls, extent of teacher organization and preparation had modest but statistically significant, positive effects on critical thinking at the end of the first and third years of college. The net effects on critical thinking of teacher instructional skill and clarity were nonsignificant. Thus, it would appear that a teacher behavior (that is, organization and preparation) that, as was seen in Chapter Three, has been shown to influence positively course-level content mastery may also have implications for students' development of more general cognitive skills during college.

Somewhat more indirect evidence of the impact of teacher behaviors or orientations to teaching is suggested in a single-institution study conducted by Kember and Gow (1994). They sought to determine how two teaching orientations termed *knowledge transmission* and *learning facilitation* influenced the ways in which students approached learning. Teachers with a knowledge transmission orientation tended to think that disciplinary or subject matter knowledge is most important, to be imparted by clear presentation of information to students. Conversely, teachers who were oriented toward a learning facilitation approach emphasized the development of problem-solving skills, critical thinking, and independent learning; they believed that good teaching should motivate students and be an interactive process. The findings suggested that departments with faculty who exhibited a greater use of learning facilitation were significantly more likely to have students who took a *deep approach* to learning. A deep approach characterizes learners who have an intrinsic interest in the subject and search for personal meaning in learning activities. In contrast, where a knowledge transmission approach predominated, students tended not only to engage in surface learning but also to change more in the direction of surface learning. Students who utilize a *surface approach* to learning are extrinsically motivated and therefore concentrate on memorizing content that might appear in examinations. Generally consistent results are reported by Tsui (2000) in a four-institution study that uses self-reported gains in critical thinking as the dependent measure.[5]

Academic Effort-Involvement. In the preceding chapter we saw that the development of verbal, quantitative, and subject matter competence was determined not only by a student's formal coursework and instructional experiences but also by his or her individual level of academic effort or involvement. How much students learn is determined to a great extent by how much personal effort and time they are willing to invest in the process of learning itself. It should come as no great surprise that level of academic effort and involvement also weighs in as a substantial influence on the growth of general cognitive skills and intellectual development during college.

For example, a series of analyses of the National Study of Student Learning have attempted to determine the factors influencing critical thinking during college (Doyle et al., 1998; Terenzini, Springer, Pascarella, & Nora, 1995a). Both of these studies assessed critical thinking with an objective, standardized measure (the critical thinking module of the Collegiate Assessment of Academic Proficiency), and both introduced statistical controls for an extensive battery of potential confounding influences, such as precollege critical thinking, academic motivation, student demographic variables, full- or part-time enrollment, work responsibilities, patterns of coursework taken, and measures of student social involvement. In the presence of such controls, factors such as hours studied per week, number of nonassigned books read, and an academic effort-involvement scale (for example, "took detailed notes in class," "did additional readings," "participated in class discussions") had statistically significant, positive effects on critical thinking skills at the end of the first year of college.

Similar results are reported for measures of postformal reasoning in studies by Kitchener, Wood, and Jensen (1999) and May (1990). Kitchener et al. found that first-year growth in reflective thinking or judgment, as measured by the Reasoning About Current Issues Test (an objective test of reflective thinking), was significantly linked with the extent to which students were actively involved in learning experiences. This included such dimensions as involvement in writing experiences and engagement in course learning. The more students actively processed information and ideas acquired in class, the greater their gains in reflective thinking. May reported that freshman-to-senior advances in intellectual development on the Perry (1970) continuum were significantly and positively correlated with a scholarly-intellectual involvement scale that assessed students' effort in such areas as use of the library, writing experiences, and course learning.

The most recent evidence supporting the positive influence of academic engagement on cognitive growth is reported by Carini and Kuh (2003). Analyzing multi-institutional data collected by the RAND Corporation (Klein, Kuh, Chun, Hamilton, & Shavelson, 2003), they found that different measures of student academic engagement and effort were positively linked to both GRE scores and a measure of general cognitive development or critical thinking even when student SAT scores were taken into account.

In addition to those studies that measure general intellectual or cognitive development with standardized assessment instruments, there is also a substantial body of evidence to suggest that level of academic effort-involvement has a positive net influence on student self-reported gains in critical thinking and intellectual development during college. Although the research designs of these studies are variable, nearly all attempt to control statistically for important confounding influences. Not all factors are controlled in each study, but the controls in different studies include such factors as precollege academic ability, race, sex, educational aspirations, family socioeconomic status, institutional characteristics, and extracurricular involvement. In the presence of such controls, measures of student self-reported gains in critical thinking and intellectual development appear to be positively influenced by such specific factors as amount studied (Astin, 1993c; Cabrera et al., 1998, Volkwein, Valle, Parmely, Blose, & Zhou, 2000), participation in honors programs (Kim, 1996), library use and involvement (Whitmire, 1998; Whitmire & Lawrence, 1996; Williams, 1996), engagement in course learning activities (Whitmire, 1998; Williams, 1996), and more global measures of academic effort and engagement that combine specific dimensions such as studying, reading for pleasure, involvement in library experiences, involvement in course learning, and involvement in writing experiences (Arnold et al., 1993; Franklin, 1995; Grayson, 1995a; Kaufman & Creamer, 1991; Kuh et al., 1991; Li et al., 1999; Watson & Kuh, 1996).

Social and Extracurricular Effort-Involvement. As with the preceding chapter on the development of verbal, quantitative, and subject matter competence, there is a substantial amount of evidence pertaining to the ways in which student social and extracurricular involvement influence general cognitive skills and intellectual growth. To maintain a parallel organization with Chapter Three, we review that evidence with respect to interactions with peers, interactions with faculty, Greek affiliation, intercollegiate athletic involvement, service involvement, diversity experiences, work responsibilities, and on- or off-campus residence.

Interactions with peers. A modest but relatively consistent body of research indicates that students' peers play a substantial role in their general cognitive growth and intellectual development in college. Indeed, some studies suggest that one's peers may be an influence that is equal to, and in some cases perhaps even greater than, one's formal classroom experience (Astin, 1993c; Terenzini et al., 1995a; Terenzini, Springer, Yaeger, Pascarella, & Nora, 1994). The majority of studies are correlational and typically attempt to determine the net impact of peer interactions on various measures of general cognitive development while statistically controlling for important confounding influences.

For example, analyzing data from the National Study of Student Learning, Whitt, Edison, Pascarella, Nora, and Terenzini (1999a), sought to determine the unique, or net, impact of out-of-class interactions with peers on an objective, standardized measure of critical thinking. To do this, they introduced statistical controls for an extensive set of potential confounding factors such as precollege critical thinking, academic motivation, student demographic characteristics, full- or part-time enrollment, hours spent studying, work responsibilities, patterns of coursework taken, and the average academic ability of the first-year students at the institution attended. In the presence of these controls, a scale measuring the nature and level of involvement in out-of-class-interactions with peers (for example, discussions about art, music, and theater; discussions with students whose personal values, political beliefs, religious beliefs, or national origin were different from one's own) had a modest, but statistically significant, positive impact on critical thinking skills at the end of the first year of college. Analyzing essentially the same sample, and employing much the same set of statistical controls, Prendergast (1998) found that a somewhat expanded version of the out-of-class interactions scale used by Whitt et al. had a significant, positive net effect on critical thinking skills at the end of the third year of college. Generally consistent findings with independent samples have been reported for scores on the analytical section of the Graduate Record Examination (Astin, 1993c); for critical thinking skills, as measured by the critical thinking module of the Collegiate Assessment of Academic Proficiency (Twale & Sanders, 1999); for women's freshman-to-senior growth on the Perry (1970) continuum, as assessed by the Measure of Intellectual Development (May, 1990); and for first-year gains on the recognition dimension of reflective thinking or judgment, as measured by the Reasoning About Current Issues Test (Kitchener et al., 1999; Kitchener, Wood, & Jensen, 2000). Examples of items measuring students' interactions with peers from this research included socializing with peers; hours spent outside of class discussing current issues with peers; having serious discussions with peers whose interests, values, and philosophy of life were different from one's own; and having conversations with peers that referred to knowledge acquired in classes or readings.

Although less extensive than evidence pertaining to the impact of student interactions with peers, there is related evidence to suggest that student extracurricular or cocurricular involvement may also have positive implications for cognitive development. Analyzing data from a subsample of six National Study of Student Learning institutions, in which approximately half the students commuted to college, Inman and Pascarella (1998) found that a measure of involvement in college clubs and organizations positively influenced end-of-first-year scores on a standardized measure of critical thinking skills. (The same net effect is also reported by Terenzini, Springer, Yaeger, Pascarella, and Nora [1994] with the complete NSSL sample of 23 institutions.) This positive effect could not be explained away by differences in such confounding influences as precollege critical thinking level, academic motivation, student demographic characteristics, full- or part-time enrollment, work responsibilities, measures of academic involvement, and institutional selectivity. Similar findings are also reported by Baxter Magolda (1992a, 1992b) in her detailed qualitative investigation of growth in students' epistemological sophistication and reasoning skills over four years of college. As suggested by one of the participants in her study: "I think some of my best experiences were outside the classroom, where I could take what I learned in the classroom and apply it" (Baxter Magolda, 1992b, p. 296).

In addition to those studies that employ objective, standardized measures, there is also a body of research that estimates the net impact of interactions with peers on student self-reports of their intellectual or cognitive growth. These studies are also largely correlational in design and tend to introduce statistical controls to adjust for the influence of potential confounding factors. The weight of evidence from this research is also consistent in suggesting that various measures of students' interactions with peers outside of class have modest, but statistically significant, positive effects on self-reported gains during college in general cognitive, analytical, or intellectual competencies (Arnold et al., 1993; Franklin, 1995; Kaufman & Creamer, 1991; Kim, 2002a; Kuh et al., 1991; Li et al., 1999; Volkwein & Carbone, 1994; Watson & Kuh, 1996).

Interactions with faculty. A modest body of research permits one to estimate the net impact of student interactions with faculty on general cognitive skills and intellectual development. Although there are exceptions (Doyle et al., 1998; Inman & Pascarella, 1998), the weight of evidence from this body of research suggests that student-faculty interactions that tend to reinforce or extend the intellectual ethos of the classroom or that focus on issues of student development can have positive implications for general cognitive development during college (Astin, 1993c; Dey, 1991; Franklin, 1993; Frost, 1991; Ishiyama, 2002; Kim, 1996, 2002a; Kitchener et al., 1999; Kuh, 1995; Terenzini, Springer, Yaeger, Pascarella, & Nora, 1994; Tsui, 1999).

For example, Kitchener, Wood, and Jensen (1999) measured gains in reflective thinking during the first year of college with the Reasoning About Current Issues Test. They found that gain scores on two dimensions of reflective thinking—recognition and discrimination—were both significantly and positively associated with a scale that measured students' out-of-class interactions with faculty focusing on such things as course issues, work on a faculty research project, career choice, and personal development. Similar findings are reported in multi-institution sample, correlational studies that use standardized measures of cognitive development such as the analytic score of the Graduate Record Examination (Dey, 1991) or that employ student self-reports of growth in critical thinking, intellectual development, or problem-solving skills as the dependent variable (Astin, 1993c; Franklin, 1995; Kim, 1995, 1996). In all of these studies, the effect of student-faculty interaction persists even in the presence of controls for confounding influences such as precollege academic ability, student demographic characteristics, and institutional selectivity.

There is also evidence to suggest that general cognitive skills may be enhanced when student-faculty interactions focus on, or emphasize, student development. In analyses of the National Study of Student Learning data, Terenzini, Springer, Yaeger, Pascarella, and Nora (1994) found that a scale measuring the extent to which faculty were perceived as being concerned with student development and teaching had a significant, positive effect on end-of-first-year scores on a standardized measure of critical thinking skills. This positive effect persisted even in the presence of statistical controls for an extensive list of potential confounding influences that included precollege critical thinking scores, academic motivation, student demographic characteristics, institutional characteristics, coursework taken, full- or part-time enrollment, and measures of academic effort-involvement. The findings of the Terenzini et al. investigation are generally consistent with those of Frost (1991). Frost uncovered evidence in one of two institutional samples that the developmental emphasis of female students' advising contacts with faculty had a significant, positive effect on both the recognition of assumptions scale and the deductions scale of the Watson-Glaser Critical Thinking Appraisal. These effects persisted even with statistical controls for prior level of critical thinking, SAT scores, high school grades, and family income. Developmental advising (Winston & Sandor, 1984) regards the advising process as developmental education, not just providing information. Consequently, it emphasizes activities designed to help students assume responsibilities for problem solving and decision making.

Greek affiliation. We uncovered only two studies that investigate the impact of fraternity or sorority membership on the development of general cognitive skills during college (Pascarella, Edison, Whitt, et al., 1996; Pascarella, Flowers, & Whitt, 1999). Both are based on analyses of the National Study of Student Learning data, and both employ a standardized test of critical thinking skills (the critical thinking module from the Collegiate Assessment of Academic Proficiency) as the dependent variable. The first study (Pascarella, Edison, Whitt, et al., 1996) considered the impact of Greek affiliation during the first year of college at 18 four-year institutions. Statistical controls were introduced for an extensive set of potential confounding influences, including precollege level of critical thinking, academic motivation, student demographic characteristics, full- or part-time enrollment, work responsibilities, patterns of coursework taken, and the academic selectivity of the institution attended. In the presence of these controls, Greek-affiliated men, compared with their male counterparts who remained independent, had a statistically significant disadvantage of .27 of a standard deviation (11 percentile points) in end-of-first-year critical thinking. The corresponding critical thinking disadvantage for Greek-affiliated women was only about 40 percent as large as that found for Greek-affiliated men and was not statistically significant.

Pascarella, Flowers, and Whitt (1999) followed the same NSSL sample through the end of the third year of college to determine if the critical thinking disadvantage accruing to Greek-affiliated men persisted beyond the first year. Thus, critical thinking scores at the end of the third year of college were the dependent variable. With statistical controls introduced for the same set of confounding influences as the earlier (Pascarella, Edison, Whitt, et al., 1996) study, the negative effect of fraternity membership on critical thinking found after one year of college was reduced by about 50 percent and became statistically nonsignificant. Similarly, the small, nonsignificant negative effect of sorority membership on critical thinking after one year of college remained small and statistically nonsignificant through the end of the third year.

Taken together, the NSSL-based studies suggest that any substantive negative effects of fraternity membership on male critical thinking occur during the initial year of college. Thereafter, the impact of fraternity membership on critical thinking becomes small and statistically nonsignificant. There is little evidence that being a member of a sorority has anything but small and nonsignificant effects on critical thinking skills. These conclusions are based on analyses of a single sample, however, and await replication.[6]

Intercollegiate athletic involvement. A small body of research has addressed the impact of intercollegiate athletic participation on objective, standardized tests of critical thinking. Although limited by the small number of studies, this research suggests, first, that intercollegiate athletes may not be as predisposed as their nonathlete counterparts to think critically, and second, that male football and basketball players (that is, those involved in revenue-producing sports) may not be making the same gains in critical thinking skills as either nonathletes or athletes in nonrevenue sports.

McBride and Reed (1998) administered the New Jersey Test of Reasoning Skills (a standardized test purporting to measure critical thinking) and the California Critical Thinking Dispositions Inventory (which assesses the disposition to actually employ critical thinking skills) to small samples of intercollegiate athletes and nonathletes attending a university with a national-level athletic program. Irrespective of gender, athletes scored significantly lower on both tests than did nonathletes. Thus, intercollegiate athletes not only had significantly lower critical thinking skills but also demonstrated a significantly lower disposition to actually utilize critical thinking skills than nonathletes.

The design of the McBride and Reed (1998) study makes it difficult to determine if the differences in critical thinking between athletes and nonathletes are attributable to participation in intercollegiate athletics during college or simply reflect differences on these traits that the two groups bring to college. To address just this type of methodological issue a series of analyses were conducted with the National Study of Student Learning (NSSL) data (Pascarella, Bohr, Nora, & Terenzini, 1995b; Pascarella, Truckenmiller, et al., 1999). These analyses were based on student samples from 18 four-year institutions and employed the standardized critical thinking test from the Collegiate Assessment of Academic Proficiency as the dependent variable. Separate effects of intercollegiate athletic participation were estimated for men and women, with male athletes being further divided into those involved in revenue sports (football and basketball) and those involved in nonrevenue sports (all others). In the first study (Pascarella et al., 1995b), statistical controls were made for precollege level of critical thinking, academic motivation, student demographic characteristics, full- or part-time enrollment, on- or off-campus residence, the academic selectivity of the institution attended, and whether the institution attended fielded an NCAA Division I or a non-Division I athletic program. In the presence of these controls, there were only trivial and nonsignificant differences in end-of-first-year critical thinking scores between women athletes and women nonathletes and among male athletes in revenue sports, male athletes in nonrevenue sports, and male nonathletes.

A follow-up study of the same NSSL sample was conducted to determine if the same parity among intercollegiate athletes and nonathletes in critical thinking extended beyond the first year of college (Pascarella, Truckenmiller, et al., 1999). The dependent variable was critical thinking scores at the end of three years of college, and in addition to controlling for the same variables as in the earlier study (Pascarella et al., 1995b), statistical controls were also introduced for work responsibilities, time spent studying, and patterns of coursework taken. In the presence of these controls there were still only trivial and statistically nonsignificant differences between women intercollegiate athletes and their nonathlete counterparts on critical thinking after three years of college. There were also only small and nonsignificant critical thinking differences between male athletes participating in nonrevenue sports and male nonathletes. However, male revenue athletes (that is, those participating in intercollegiate football and basketball) had significantly lower end-of-third-year critical thinking scores than either male nonrevenue athletes or male nonathletes. Compared with male athletes participating in nonrevenue sports, male football and basketball players had a net critical thinking disadvantage after three years of college of about .35 of a standard deviation (14 percentile points). The corresponding third-year critical thinking skills disadvantage for football and basketball players relative to nonathletes was about .39 of a standard deviation (15 percentile points).

As with previously reviewed findings from the Pascarella et al. studies (Pascarella, Bohr, Nora, & Terenzini, 1995b; Pascarella, Truckenmiller, et al., 1999), summarized in Chapter Three, the negative effects on end-of-third-year critical thinking of participation in intercollegiate football and basketball were similar in magnitude, irrespective of levels of precollege critical thinking, academic motivation, socioeconomic status, or ethnicity. In short, no particular type of male student received greater critical thinking penalties from participating in revenue-producing sports than any other. Furthermore, no evidence was found to indicate that the disadvantage in third-year critical thinking skills accruing to male football and basketball players differed in magnitude at NCAA Division I or non-Division I institutions or at institutions differing in the academic selectivity of their undergraduate student bodies. It is worth noting, however, that all the findings pertaining to the impact of intercollegiate athletic participation on critical thinking are based on analyses of a single sample and await replication.

Service involvement. In Chapter Three we reviewed evidence suggesting that service experiences, particularly when integrated with course activities through a reflective component (that is, service learning), may foster increased acquisition of subject matter knowledge. There is also evidence to suggest that such service learning experiences can contribute in positive ways to the development of students' general cognitive skills and intellectual growth. For example, Batchelder and Root (1994) conducted a quasi experiment in which experimental sections of a course were taught with an integrated service learning component, and the control sections were taught without the integrated service learning component. Both the experimental and control sections were similar in content and were taught by the same instructors, although it was not clear if students self-selected themselves into the service learning sections. At the beginning and at the end of the course, students wrote a 30-minute essay on how they would respond to two situations (for example, child abuse, alcoholism, initiating a community recycling program) that were designed to assess their dimensions of thinking about a social problem. With statistical controls for pretest scores, students in the service learning sections demonstrated a significantly greater increase in use of complex and multidimensional perspectives in their essays than did students in the course sections without a service learning component. We converted the partial correlations reported by Batchelder and Root to an effect size and estimate that the advantage in more complex and multidimensional perspectives accruing to the service learning students was approximately .25 of a standard deviation (10 percentile points).

An important series of multi-institutional studies by Eyler and her colleagues corroborate and extend the Batchelder and Root (1994) findings (Eyler & Giles, 1999; Eyler, Giles, Lynch, & Gray, 1997; Eyler, Giles, Root, & Price, 1997). However, these basically quasi-experimental investigations take a somewhat more fine-grained approach to understanding the impact of service learning on different dimensions of cognitive development. Instead of simply comparing service learning with a control group, Eyler and her colleagues hypothesized that student cognitive development is influenced by the degree to which service learning classes are well integrated and highly reflective. Integrated and reflective service learning classes tend to integrate service experiences with course content, provide for reflection about the service experience, and permit students to apply subject matter learning to the service experience and vice versa. The results of their program of research tend to support this hypothesis. The greater the extent to which service learning courses met the criteria for being highly integrative and reflective, the stronger the positive effects of service learning on such outcomes as reflective judgment (Eyler & Giles, 1999; Eyler, Giles, Lynch, & Gray, 1997) and the use of complex and multiple perspectives in identifying the causes of and formulating the solutions to specific social problems (Eyler, Giles, Root, & Price, 1997). The simple addition of service experiences to a course generally had little impact on cognitive outcomes. To have an impact these experiences had to be highly integrated into course content and provisions made for continuous reflection. The effects reported by Eyler and colleagues tended to persist even in the presence of statistical controls for precourse measures of the specific cognitive outcomes. Because the studies do not report all the requisite statistical information, however, we could not estimate an effect size.

There is also quasi-experimental evidence from undergraduate samples at 42 institutions that students involved in four different types of service experiences (education, human services, environment, and public safety) indicated greater self-reported gains in critical thinking skills than their counterparts not involved in service experiences (Astin, 1996b; Astin & Sax, 1996). This effect persisted even when statistical controls were introduced for such factors as volunteering in high school, precollege leadership ability, commitment to participating in community action programs, tutoring other students in high school, gender, and monetary orientation. Consistent results are also reported in a more recent study by Vogelgesang and Astin (2000).

Diversity experiences. In the preceding chapter we presented evidence that involvement in diversity experiences (for example, taking ethnic or gender studies courses, discussing racial issues, attending a racial-cultural awareness workshop, socializing with someone from a different racial-ethnic group) can have a positive influence on students' academic skill development and knowledge acquisition during college. There is also replicated evidence, based on both standardized measures and students' self-reports, suggesting that involvement in diversity experiences can modestly enhance more general cognitive skills and intellectual development. For example, analyzing the multi-institutional 1985 to 1989 Cooperative Institutional Research Program data, Dey (1991) sought to identify experiences that influenced three measures of cognitive development: the analytical subtest score on the Graduate Record Examination, self-reported growth in critical thinking ability, and self-reported growth in analytical and problem-solving skills. With statistical controls introduced for such factors as SAT verbal scores, secondary school experiences, intellectual self-esteem, self-rated mathematics ability, and institutional characteristics, discussing racial-ethnic issues during the past year had a statistically significant, positive effect on all three measures of cognitive development. Markedly consistent results are reported by Terenzini, Springer, Yaeger, Pascarella, and Nora (1994) in their analyses of data from the 23 two- and four-year institutions participating in the National Study of Student Learning. Attending a racial-cultural awareness workshop had a small but significant, positive impact on end-of-first-year scores on a standardized test of critical thinking skills. This effect could not be explained away by differences in such factors as precollege critical thinking level, student demographic characteristics and aspirations, characteristics of the institution attended, full- or part-time enrollment, work responsibilities, patterns of coursework taken, or extracurricular involvement. Similarly, Kitchener, Wood, and Jensen (2000) found that growth on the endorsement scale of the Reasoning About Current Issues Test, a measure of reflective thinking, was significantly and positively related to making friends and having discussions with students whose race was different from one's own. The effect persisted even when initial scores on the RCI endorsement scale were taken into account.

Analyses of a different iteration of the Cooperative Institutional Research Program data from that analyzed by Dey (1991) have also yielded evidence supporting the positive impact of involvement in diversity experiences on general cognitive development. Both Hurtado (1999) and Kim (1995, 1996, 2002a) analyzed data from the multi-institutional 1987 to 1991 CIRP sample, with Kim restricting the focus of her investigation to women. Both investigators introduced statistical controls for such factors as institutional selectivity, secondary school achievement, academic self-concept, study involvement, and leadership experiences during college. In the presence of such controls, measures of involvement in diversity experiences (for example, studied with someone from a different racial-ethnic background, enrolled in an ethnic studies course, attended a racial-cultural awareness workshop) tended to have significant, positive impacts on self-reported growth in critical thinking (Hurtado, 1999) and on a measure combining self-reported growth in both critical thinking and problem-solving skills (Kim, 1995, 1996, 2002a) (See also Hu and Kuh, 2003a, for recent supportive findings using student self-reported gains.)

A more focused approach is reported by Gurin (1999) in two related single-institution studies. The first was essentially a quasi experiment that compared students who took and did not take an introductory course in a program termed "Intergroup Relations, Community, and Conflict" (IRCC). The IRCC course covered the history of group experiences in the United States; a contemporary analysis of group inequalities in economic, political, and educational arenas; and an analysis of political issues and policies (for example, immigration, bilingual education, affirmative action, sexual harassment, Middle East peace initiatives, and so on) that are contested by various groups in American society. In addition to lectures and discussion sections, students who took the IRCC course also took part in an ongoing dialogue group designed to examine between-group and within-group differences on a contested issue, identify and negotiate group conflicts, and find a basis for joint action on an issue. Students who took the IRCC course and the control group who did not were matched in such areas as first-year residence hall, race-ethnicity, gender, and in-state and out-of-state residency prior to college. At entrance to college and at the time of graduation, both groups completed a self-report index designed to measure complexity of thinking (for example, prefer complex rather than simple explanations, enjoy discussions of causes of behaviors). With statistical controls for precollege level of complexity of thinking, students who completed the IRCC course had significantly higher complexity of thinking levels at the end of college than the control group students who did not. (An effect size could not be estimated from the results reported.) Similar results are reported by Adams and Zhou-McGovern (1994) with respect to a social and cultural diversity course that focused on such topics as racism, sexism, and social justice. Students exposed to the course made advances of about one standard deviation (34 percentile points) on the Perry (1970) continuum, but there was no control group.[7]

The second study conducted by Gurin (1999) attempted to determine what diversity experiences other than the IRCC course influenced the complexity of thinking index. A more comprehensive sample was employed, and it was assessed when it entered the institution (1990) and once again prior to graduation. Statistical controls were introduced for such factors as entering level of thinking complexity, SAT-ACT score, high school grades, gender, and racial composition of one's high school and home neighborhood. With these factors taken into account, a number of diversity experiences had significant, positive effects on complexity of thinking at the end of college for White students. These experiences included classroom diversity (extent to which students reported they had been exposed to diversity issues in classes), personal interactions (extent to which interactions with other racial-ethnic groups involved "honest discussions about race" and "sharing of personal feelings and problems"), number of multicultural events attended (for example, Black History Month, Hispanic Heritage Celebration, and so on), and participation in dialogue groups (an ongoing program of intergroup dialogue and conflict resolution at the institution). Diversity experiences had no significant effects on thinking complexity at the end of college for African-American students. This may not mean that African-American students receive smaller cognitive benefits from diversity experiences than White students, however. As far as we could tell, Gurin did not report statistically significant differences between regression coefficients for White and African-American students. Thus, the failure to find significant diversity experience effects on thinking complexity for African-American students may be attributable in large measure to the weak statistical power associated with the relatively small number of African-American students in the sample.

Work responsibilities. The body of evidence concerning the impact of work during college on the development of general cognitive skills and intellectual growth is inconsistent. Some analyses of the National Study of Student Learning data have found small, negative effects of hours worked per week on a standardized measure of end-of-first-year critical thinking (Inman & Pascarella, 1998; Terenzini, Springer, Yaeger, Pascarella, & Nora, 1994). Other analyses of the same data, introducing somewhat different statistical controls, have found that extent of on- or off-campus work is essentially unrelated to first- or third-year critical thinking (Pascarella, Bohr, Nora, & Terenzini, 1996; Pascarella, Edison, Nora, Hagedorn, & Terenzini, 1998a; Prendergast, 1998). Results of investigations on other samples tend to support the contention that work during college has little or no impact on general cognitive development, and this finding holds irrespective of whether cognitive growth is measured with standardized tests (Criner, 1992) or student self-reports (Graham & Long, 1998; Kuh, 1995; Strauss & Volkwein, 2001a).

We uncovered two studies suggesting the possibility that work can, at times, have a positive impact on critical thinking skills. However, the pattern of effects in the two studies was in marked contrast. Rykiel (1995) found that when a measure of verbal aptitude was taken into account, community college students who worked 25 hours or more per week had scores on the Watson-Glaser Critical Thinking Appraisal that were about .27 of a standard deviation (11 percentile points) higher than their counterparts who worked 20 hours or less per week. Conversely, Pascarella, Edison, Nora, Hagedorn, and Terenzini (1998a) found essentially the opposite with a sample of four-year college students. With controls for precollege critical thinking, demographic characteristics, institutional selectivity, coursework taken, and other factors, part-time on- or off-campus work (that is, 15 to 20 hours per week) during college had positive effects on end-of-third-year scores on the critical thinking module of the Collegiate Assessment of Academic Proficiency. Working more than 15 to 20 hours per week, however, had a negative impact. It is not clear how the potentially different meaning of work for students in community colleges and four-year colleges might have shaped these contrasting findings.

We found little in the total body of evidence on work and cognitive development to indicate that the nature of the findings depended on the methodological rigor of the study. Thus, given the general inconsistency of results across studies, we conclude that there is little compelling empirical evidence to suggest that on- or off-campus work in general has anything more than a trivial impact on cognitive or intellectual development during college. However, it may be, as suggested by Aper (1994, 1997), that work during college has a more salient impact on a student's cognitive or intellectual development when it is related to his or her academic field of study or intended career. The literature on cognitive development during college is largely silent with respect to this type of inquiry. As we shall see in the chapter on career, however, work related to one's major or career can have important implications for early career success.

On- or off-campus residence. As with the impact of work, the evidence pertaining to the direct effects on general cognitive growth of living on campus (versus off campus and commuting to college) is mixed and generally inconclusive. For example, a single-institution study by Pascarella, Bohr, Nora, Zusman, Inman, and Desler (1993) found that students living on campus made significantly larger first-year gains in critical thinking skills (as measured by the critical thinking module of the Collegiate Assessment of Academic Proficiency) than their counterparts who commuted to college. The greater gains of resident students persisted even in the presence of controls for precollege critical thinking level, academic motivation, age, work responsibilities, and full- or part-time enrollment. There is little support, however, for a corresponding positive impact on critical thinking in investigations based on multi-institutional samples (Doyle et al., 1998; Inman & Pascarella, 1998; Whitt et al., in press). Each of these studies used a somewhat different subsample from the National Study of Student Learning data, and each introduces controls for somewhat different sets of confounding variables. At a minimum, however, each controlled for precollege critical thinking, the academic selectivity of the institution attended, full- or part-time enrollment, academic motivation, and work responsibilities. Both the Inman and Pascarella (1998) and the Whitt et al. (in press) investigations uncovered no significant net effect of living on campus on end-of-first-year scores on the critical thinking module of the Collegiate Assessment of Academic Proficiency. Doyle, Edison, and Pascarella (1998) actually found a significant negative effect, although this may be due in large measure to their combining four-year college samples with two-year college samples that had very few resident students.

Studies that follow students beyond the first year of college have generally found that living on campus (versus off campus and commuting to college) has little or no net impact on standardized measures of critical thinking (Prendergast, 1998; Whitt et al., in press). The only exception to this finding is reported by Flowers and Pascarella (1999a) in a study that was limited to a relatively small sample of African-American students. With controls for such factors as precollege critical thinking, demographic characteristics, academic motivation, full- or part-time enrollment, patterns of coursework taken, and the academic selectivity and racial composition of the institution attended, living on campus had a small, positive impact on African-American students' critical thinking skills at the end of three years of college. This finding is based on a single study, however, and has yet to be replicated.

Overall, we found little consistent evidence that living on campus directly influences general cognitive growth during college—at least in terms of critical thinking. However, consistent with our conclusions in Chapter Three, we suspect that it probably does exert an indirect, positive influence on general cognitive growth and intellectual development by virtue of its enhancement of student academic and social-interpersonal engagement (Ballou, Reavill, & Schultz, 1995). Once again, however, we found no empirical test of this hypothesis.

CONDITIONAL EFFECTS OF COLLEGE

Conclusions from *How College Affects Students*

In our 1991 synthesis, we found little consistent evidence to indicate that the effects of college on general cognitive skills differed for different kinds of students. Similarly, little evidence existed to suggest that the characteristics of the college attended had a differential influence on general cognitive skills for different kinds of students. A small body of evidence suggested that learning cycle–inquiry instruction had its most pronounced influence on the development of Piagetian formal reasoning either for students who are initially at the concrete reasoning stage or for students grouped with others at the same initial Piagetian reasoning level.

Evidence from the 1990s

We uncovered substantially more research in the 1990s that estimates the conditional effects of college on general cognitive skills and intellectual development. As with the great majority of research on conditional effects, however, nearly all of the findings are based on single samples, with little or no evidence of independent replication. This caveat having been stated, there is evidence of conditional effects that cluster into four general types: student by net effects of college, student by between-college effects, student by within-college effects, and instructional approaches.

Student by Net Effects of College. In contrast to our 1991 synthesis, evidence from the 1990s suggests that the net effects of college on critical thinking skills may vary in magnitude by student race and gender. All of this evidence comes from analyses of the National Study of Student Learning data. For example, with statistical controls in place for such factors as precollege critical thinking level, academic motivation, socioeconomic status, sex, institutional selectivity, total credit hours completed, study effort, patterns of coursework taken, work responsibilities, and extensive measures of academic and social involvement, African-American students made significantly smaller gains in critical thinking through the first and third years of college than did Euro-American (White) students (Flowers, 2000; Terenzini, Springer, Yaeger, Pascarella, & Nora, 1994). The net disadvantage in critical thinking for African-American students was modest, about .16 of a standard deviation (6 percentile points) in the first year of college and about .18 of a standard deviation (7 percentile points) after three years of college (Flowers, 2000). Similarly, compared to their White counterparts, Latino students derived significantly smaller critical thinking benefits during the first year of college (Terenzini et al., 1994). The net disadvantage accruing to Latino students, relative to White students, was about .15 of a standard deviation (6 percentile points).

The conditional effects based on sex present a somewhat more complex picture because there is evidence that the effects vary in direction at community colleges versus four-year colleges. Controlling for essentially the same variables as Flowers (2000), but adding race, Whitt et al. (in press) found that in community colleges women had a statistically significant disadvantage in first-year critical thinking gains (relative to men) of about .16 of a standard deviation (6 percentile points). Conversely, although there was no significant conditional effect after one year, at the end of three years of college women in four-year institutions demonstrated a statistically significant advantage in critical thinking gains over men of .20 of a standard deviation (8 percentile points).

Student by Between-College Effects. As with our 1991 synthesis, we found little to suggest that institutional characteristics such as selectivity, size, or private versus public control had a differential impact on dimensions of general cognitive skills or intellectual development for different kinds of students (see, for example, Flowers, 2000, and Whitt et al., in press). The one possible exception to this is reported in analyses of the community college sample of the National Study of Student Learning data by Hagedorn, Pascarella, Edison, Braxton, Nora, and Terenzini (1999). They found that the average precollege critical thinking level of students at a community college had a compensatory effect on individual students' first-year gains in critical thinking skills. That is, the benefit of attending a community college where one's peers had a relatively advanced level of critical thinking was somewhat more pronounced for a student who started postsecondary education with a relatively low level of critical thinking skills. For the student who entered a community college with a relatively high level of critical thinking, the average critical thinking level of his or her peers was less important. This finding, however, is based on a sample of only five community colleges. Thus, it is suggestive at best. The same compensatory conditional effect was not uncovered in the NSSL four-year college sample.

Other student by between-college conditional effects are likewise based on somewhat isolated findings, and they are not always easily explainable. For example, in analyses of the four-year college sample from the National Study of Student Learning data, Whitt et al. (2003) found that the average socioeconomic status of students at the institution attended was essentially unrelated to third-year critical thinking for men but had a significant, negative impact for women. Other analyses of the NSSL data by Terenzini, Springer, Yaeger, Pascarella, and Nora (1994) have suggested that although an institution's environmental emphasis on being critical, evaluative, and analytical has a positive net impact on first-year critical thinking for all students, the impact is most pronounced for Latino students. In contrast, elements of "covert discrimination" in the college environment appear to affect the growth of critical thinking skills in Latino students more adversely than in other students. (Examples of covert discrimination were "people feeling uncomfortable around me" and "concerns-thinking about safety on campus.")

There is also evidence to suggest that the impact of the institutional environment on self-reported gains in intellectual development and problem-solving skills may vary in magnitude for older versus traditional-age college students. Graham (1998) analyzed data from over 20,000 students at 154 colleges and universities throughout the country to determine the effects of the "educational ethos" in the campus environment. Educational ethos in the environment included items measuring such things as faculty respect for students, the quality of instruction, the availability of faculty, informal contact with faculty, and sense of belonging on campus. The educational ethos measure was positively linked to self-reported gains in both intellectual development and problem-solving skills, but the impact was significantly stronger for students age 27 or older than it was for traditional-age students between 18 and 22. However, because Graham was not able to control for student background traits that might have predicted both self-reported gains and perceptions of educational ethos, this conditional effect may be a proxy for other influences not specified in his analytic model.

Student by Within-College Effects. We uncovered a substantial number of student by within-college conditional effects. Most are based on findings from the National Study of Student Learning data (Pascarella, Edison, Nora, Hagedorn, & Terenzini, 1996; Pascarella, Palmer, Moye, & Pierson, 2001; Terenzini, Springer, Yaeger, Pascarella, & Nora, 1994; Whitt et al., 2003). In these studies a standardized measure of critical thinking skills is the dependent variable, and the studies each introduce statistical controls for an extensive array of potential confounding variables such as precollege critical thinking, academic motivation, student demographic characteristics, the academic selectivity of the institution attended, full- or part-time enrollment, work responsibilities, patterns of course-work taken, and other measures of academic and social involvement in college. A second sample of students from two institutions investigated growth on the discrimination and endorsement scales of the Reasoning About Current Issues Test (RCI). The RCI is an objective, paper-and-pencil measure of reflective think-ing or judgment (Kitchener et al., 2000). A final sample considered the effects of academic and social engagement during college on a measure of general cog-nitive development for students with different levels of tested academic ability (SAT scores) (Carini & Kuh, 2003).

The significant student by within-college conditional effects uncovered from this series of studies include the following: (1) the number of courses taken in the natural sciences and engineering had a stronger positive influence on first-year critical thinking for White (versus African-American) students and for women (versus men) (Terenzini, Springer, Yaeger, Pascarella, & Nora, 1994; Whitt et al., 2003); (2) the number of courses taken in the humanities and fine arts had a stronger positive effect on first-year critical thinking for men than for women (Terenzini, Springer, Yaeger, Pascarella, & Nora, 1994); (3) fraternity membership had a significant, negative influence on the first-year critical think-ing of White men but a modest, positive influence for non-White men—for example, African-American, Asian-American, Latino (Pascarella, Edison, Whitt, et al., 1996); (4) Greek affiliation had a significantly stronger negative impact on first-year critical thinking gains for men than for women (Whitt et al., in press); (5) studying with peers had a net positive effect on first-year critical thinking for African-American students but a negative effect for White students (Terenzini et al., 1994); (6) engaging in volunteer work had a significantly stronger positive effect on both first- and third-year critical thinking skills for men than for women (Whitt et al., 2003); (7) full-time enrollment in college had a significantly stronger positive influence on first-year critical thinking for first-generation college students than for students whose parents attended college (Terenzini, Springer, Yaeger, Pascarella, & Nora, 1996); (8) involvement in diver-sity activities (for example, attending a racial-cultural awareness workshop, making friends with someone of a different race) had significantly stronger effects on first- and third-year critical thinking for White than for non-White students (Pascarella, Palmer, Moye, & Pierson, 2001); (9) working off campus was negatively related to growth in reflective thinking for men but working on campus, or cumulative hours worked either on or off campus, was positively related to growth in reflective thinking for women (Kitchener et al., 2000); and (10) academic and social engagement may have stronger positive effects on gen-eral cognitive development for students with relatively low SAT scores than for their peers with higher tested academic ability (Carini & Kuh, 2003).

There is also evidence from analyses by Whitt et al. (2003) to suggest that men in four-year colleges generally convert various dimensions of coursework and academic and social engagement into significantly stronger impacts on three-year gains in critical thinking than do women. For men, such factors as cumulative credit hours completed, number of social science and mathematics courses taken, computer use, social interactions with peers, and extent of involvement in volunteer work had significantly stronger positive impacts on gains in critical thinking through the third year of college than they did for women. In contrast, living on campus (versus living off campus and commuting to college) had a stronger positive impact on end-of-third-year critical thinking skills for women than it did for men.

Instructional Approaches. Earlier in this book we reviewed evidence to suggest that cooperative learning may provide a general advantage over traditional, individualistic learning approaches in such areas as knowledge acquisition and the development of problem-solving skills. There is also evidence, however, to suggest that the positive effects of cooperative learning may be more pronounced for complex, versus less complex, levels of cognitive functioning. A well-conducted quasi experiment by Garside (1996) randomly assigned intact classes in an introductory interpersonal communication course to two instructional approaches: lecture and small-group cooperative discussion. Both conditions were taught by instructors with equal teaching experience. At the beginning and end of the experiment, students took a test of course content that assessed cognitive functioning at both lower levels (knowledge, comprehension, and application) and higher levels (analysis, synthesis, and evaluation) of skill development. The lecture condition produced gains in knowledge at the lower level of cognitive functioning that were about three times as large as the gains for the small-group cooperative discussion condition. Conversely, the small-group cooperative discussion condition produced gains in knowledge at the higher level of cognitive functioning that were about 1.7 times as large as the gains for the lecture condition.

LONG-TERM EFFECTS OF COLLEGE

Conclusions from *How College Affects Students*

Although the evidence (from national samples) on long-term effects of college was based largely on alumni self-reports, its clear weight indicated that the undergraduate experience is regarded as having had an important influence on general cognitive development and thinking skills. These perceptions of alumni did not appear to be a function of time elapsed since graduation. There was a slight trend for alumni from academically selective institutions to report greater impact than alumni from less selective institutions. However, the nature of the evidence made differential student recruitment by selective and less selective colleges as plausible an explanation for these findings as any differential socialization that might take place in colleges of varying selectivity.

There was also evidence to suggest that intellectually and socially stimulating work environments made an independent contribution to cognitive development in adult life. We suggested that a major, though indirect, long-term effect of college on cognitive development comes through its power to position graduates in intellectually demanding and socially stimulating employment.

Evidence from the 1990s

We uncovered only a small body of research that speaks, either directly or indirectly, to the long-term effects of college on general cognitive skills and intellectual development. Alumni self-reports, although not based on nationally representative samples, tend to reinforce the conclusions from our 1991 synthesis that the undergraduate experience has a substantial impact on general cognitive development and thinking skills (for example, Kelley, 1994; Pettit, 1992). Moreover, there is also evidence to suggest that the undergraduate experience provides cognitive skills that increase one's capacity for lifelong learning and continuing intellectual growth. Analyzing data from the self-reports of over 17,000 seniors at 106 four-year institutions, Hayek and Kuh (1999) focused on the acquisition of skills during college that conceivably provide individuals with a repertoire of lifelong learning competencies (for example, learning on one's own, analytical skills, synthesizing information, using computers). Out of four possible responses—"very little," "some," "quite a bit," and "very much"— seniors in the sample indicated that during college they had made, on average, "quite a bit" of progress across all items constituting the scale of lifelong learning competencies.

Consistent with the findings of Hayek and Kuh (1999) that students tend to acquire lifelong learning skills during college, there is also evidence to suggest that the trends in intellectual growth shaped by the undergraduate experience tend to continue on the same trajectory after college. Perhaps the most comprehensive work in this area has been conducted by Mentkowski and Associates (2000) with samples of women from a small, single-sex, liberal arts college with a strong assessment tradition. A number of different measures of general intellectual development were administered to samples of women when they entered the institution, periodically during college, and five and a half years subsequent to graduation. The measures included the Measure of Intellectual Development (MID), which assesses epistemological development on the Perry (1970) scheme; the Test of Cognitive Development (TCD), which measures the development of abstract or formal operations reasoning; and the inference, recognition of assumptions, and deductions subscales of the Watson-Glaser Critical Thinking Appraisal (WGCTA). The results with respect to growth during college on these measures is summarized in our previous (1991) synthesis, but Mentkowski and Associates (2000) report additional information on alumni performance. What is clear from their results is that general cognitive or intellectual development did not cease after college graduation. Across all these measures the estimated average gain occurring during the five years after college (.26 of a standard deviation) was nearly 80 percent as large as the estimated average gain occurring during college (.33 of a standard deviation). Thus, the intellectual growth put in motion during college appeared to continue for alumni subsequent to graduation.

Additional analyses of what appears to be the same data employed in the Mentkowski and Associates (2000) study, however, suggest some complexities in the overall pattern of intellectual growth during and subsequent to college. Hart, Rickards, and Mentkowski (1995) examined periodic changes in essay scores on the Measure of Intellectual Development. Their analyses of the overall sample indicated a typical pattern of growth during college from the transition position between dualism and multiplicity to the transition between multiplicity and relativism. Five years after college, the alumnae as a group were well past multiplicity and into relativism. This general pattern, however, masked several different patterns of progress, and a small percentage of the women showed continuous decline over the period of the study. Such a finding suggests that although the undergraduate experience may set in motion a general trajectory of intellectual growth, continual growth after college may depend in large measure on the degree of intellectual stimulation and challenge characterizing the postcollege lives of alumni. We suspect that this synergistic combination of what happens during college and what happens in one's postcollege life underlies the finding by Glenn and Eklund (1991) that retired college professors have substantially higher levels of reflective thinking than do high school graduates of essentially the same age and tested intelligence. Similarly, Mentkowski and Associates report that breadth of involvement after graduation in 12 areas (for example, cultural activities, volunteer work, reading, discussing current issues and events, continuing education) had a significant, positive effect on five-year alumna scores on a composite measure of intellectual-epistemological and ego development. This effect persisted even in the presence of statistical controls for scores on the same composite measure at the time of graduation, level of critical thinking at graduation, and a measure of curricular preparation during college.

As we saw in the preceding chapter, there was replicated evidence to suggest an intergenerational impact of parental exposure to postsecondary education on sons' and daughters' learning in such areas as mathematics, science, and reading comprehension. Evidence pertaining to a parallel intergenerational impact on general cognitive skills is less compelling. In a single-institution pilot study for the National Study of Student Learning, Terenzini, Springer, Pascarella, and Nora (1995a) found parents' education had a significant, positive impact on first-year gains on a standardized measure of critical thinking, and this effect persisted even in the presence of controls for precollege critical thinking, family income, race, sex, educational aspirations, measures of class and nonclass experiences, and patterns of coursework taken. However, in analyses of the full, 23-institution sample from the National Study of Student Learning, Terenzini and colleagues (Terenzini, Springer, Yaeger, Pascarella, & Nora, 1996) reported that, when controls were made for important confounding variables, the first-year gains in critical thinking made by students whose parents had attended college were essentially the same as those made by students whose parents had not attended college.

SUMMARY

Change During College

Compared with the literature base we reviewed for our 1991 synthesis, we found relatively few studies on change or gains in general cognitive skills and intellectual growth during college. The literature we did uncover focused on the areas of critical thinking and postformal reasoning. Overall, our best estimate is that seniors had a critical thinking skills advantage over incoming students of about .50 of a standard deviation (19 percentile points). This number is substantially less than our 1991 estimate of one standard deviation (34 percentile points). The reason for this difference is unclear and may represent sample or instrument differences. However, the evidence of more modest change in the 1990s does underscore an important point: on an absolute standard, not all college graduates are proficient critical thinkers.

In addition to critical thinking skills, a new line of inquiry in the 1990s estimated the extent to which students develop during college in the disposition to think critically. Across the studies we uncovered, the senior advantage over first-year students in critical thinking disposition was also about .50 of a standard deviation (19 percentile points).

In the area of postformal reasoning, our conclusion is quite similar to that of our 1991 synthesis. Our best estimate is that seniors have an advantage over freshmen of about .90 of a standard deviation (32 percentile points) in reflective thinking, or the ability to use reason and evidence to address ill-structured problems, and about 2 standard deviations (48 percentile points) in epistemological sophistication or maturity.

Net Effects of College

Research on the net effects of college on general cognitive skills and intellectual growth focused largely on the areas of critical thinking and postformal reasoning. Consistent with our 1991 synthesis, the evidence suggests that a statistically significant part of the gain during college noted in both critical thinking and postformal reasoning is uniquely attributable to exposure to postsecondary education. Our best estimate is that the first three years of college provide an improvement in critical thinking skills of about .55 of a standard deviation, or 20 percentile points. Because this estimate of the net effect of three years of college is actually larger than our previous estimate of simple change or growth during four years of college, we suspect that the latter estimate is overly conservative. Only one of the four studies estimating the net effect of college on postformal reasoning provided sufficient information to compute an effect size. In that study, seniors had an advantage in reflective thinking skills over freshmen of about .90 of standard deviation (32 percentile points). This rather tentative estimate of the net effect of college suggests that most, if not all, of the observed gain during college in reflective thinking is uniquely attributable to the college experience itself. At the same time, it should be noted that the research estimating the net effects of college on postformal reasoning, including reflective thinking, may be confounded by student age.

Between-College Effects

With the possible exception of research on institutional environments, we found little to suggest substantial or consistent between-college effects on students' general cognitive development. In our 1991 synthesis, we concluded that student body selectivity in and of itself may tell us little about institutional influences on general cognitive skills and intellectual growth. The clear weight of evidence from our present synthesis would support this conclusion once again. (Although there is some evidence from a single sample to suggest a positive effect of student body selectivity on critical thinking after one year of college, this effect essentially disappeared by the end of the third year of college.) Similarly, little evidence indicated that single-sex institutions had a stronger impact on women's general cognitive growth than coeducational institutions, and there was essential parity in the first-year critical thinking gains made by students attending community colleges and those attending four-year institutions. Some evidence suggests that institutional size may inhibit critical thinking skills, but this is based on a single-sample finding and awaits replication.

In our 1991 synthesis, we concluded that there was evidence from a single sample to suggest that African-American students demonstrate greater development in critical thinking and concept attainment at historically Black institutions than at predominantly White ones. This is partially supported by evidence uncovered in our present synthesis. When standardized measures were the dependent variable, African-American students attending historically Black colleges had gains in critical thinking that were indistinguishable from those demonstrated by their African-American counterparts enrolled in predominantly White colleges. However, when the dependent variable was self-reported gains in critical thinking or analytical skills, African-American students reported significantly greater progress when they attended historically Black colleges.

The area of institutional environments provided the most consistent evidence we uncovered with respect to between-college effects on students' general cognitive growth. There is replicated evidence to indicate that an institutional environment with a scholarly, aesthetic, and critical-analytical emphasis has modest, positive net effects on student growth in critical thinking and analytical competencies. Moreover, this impact appears to occur independently of institutional selectivity. There is also replicated evidence to suggest that student critical thinking, analytical competencies, and general intellectual development are enhanced by an institutional environment that stresses close relationships and frequent interaction between faculty and students and faculty concern about student growth and development during college. This environmental emphasis appeared to have an influence on general cognitive growth that operated independently of an institution's scholarly environment.

Within-College Effects

As with the evidence pertaining to within-college effects on the acquisition of verbal, quantitative, and subject matter competence, the corresponding evidence from the 1990s on more general cognitive skills and intellectual growth is extensive. The following conclusions appear to be warranted:

1. Consistent with our 1991 conclusion, we found little consistent evidence to suggest that one's major field of study, in and of itself, leads to different effects on general measures of critical thinking. We did find evidence that the intellectual training in different fields of study leads to the development of different reasoning skills, which is also consistent with our 1991 conclusion that academic major has a selective impact on cognitive growth.

2. There is replicated evidence that exposure to natural science courses may positively influence growth in critical thinking skills, but evidence with respect to other concentrations of coursework is either inconclusive or awaits replication.

3. In our 1991 synthesis, we concluded that critical thinking was enhanced by curricular experiences that require integration of ideas and themes across courses and disciplines. Consistent with this conclusion, we found replicated quasi-experimental evidence in our present synthesis that an interdisciplinary or integrated core curriculum that emphasized making explicit connections across courses, and among ideas and disciplines, positively influenced growth in measures of postformal reasoning.

4. Replicated experimental or quasi-experimental evidence suggests that learning a computer program language provided an advantage of .35 of a standard deviation (14 percentile points) in general cognitive skills such as planning, reasoning, and metacognition. Consistent correlational evidence also suggests that critical thinking and general reasoning skills may be enhanced by coursework requiring students to learn the use of computers; using computers in such learning activities as analyzing data, making visual displays, and searching the Internet for course material; and using electronic mail to practice argumentation.

5. Replicated experimental and quasi-experimental evidence exists to suggest that students learning in cooperative groups gain an average advantage in problem-solving skills of .47 of a standard deviation (18 percentile points) over their counterparts not learning in a cooperative format. The positive effect of cooperative learning, however, was larger in the solution of nonlinguistic problems (.96 of a standard deviation) than in the solution of linguistic problems (.31 of a standard deviation).

6. Evidence suggests that critical thinking can be taught, although the average effect is based on a rough estimate and is quite modest in magnitude. Students who receive purposeful instruction and practice

in critical thinking or problem-solving skills appear, on average, to gain an advantage in critical thinking skills of .23 of a standard deviation (9 percentile points) over students not receiving such instruction. We hypothesize that the small effect is due primarily to the general absence of a consensus across studies with respect to the operational definition of what constitutes instruction in critical thinking.

7. Results of a small number of experimental or quasi-experimental studies suggest that postformal reasoning can be enhanced by three loosely related innovative instructional approaches: reflective judgment–developmental instruction, active learning–team problem-solving instruction, and deliberate psychological instruction. We estimate that, on average, students exposed to these instructional approaches gain an advantage in postformal reasoning of about .65 of a standard deviation (24 percentile points) over students not receiving this type of instruction. This estimated effect size, however, is based on only three studies and may not be particularly robust.

8. We uncovered very little evidence pertaining to the impact of teaching behaviors on students' general cognitive development. Though it awaits replication and experimental validation, there is correlational evidence, paired with extensive statistical controls, to suggest that extent of teacher organization and preparation in the overall instruction received at an institution positively influences growth in critical thinking skills through the first and third years of college.

9. Not surprisingly, quite apart from courses taken and instruction received, a student's level of academic effort and involvement has an important net influence on his or her growth in general cognitive and intellectual development during college. This conclusion is quite consistent with that from our 1991 synthesis. Level of individual effort or engagement in such areas as hours studied per week, number of nonassigned books read, writing experiences, library use, and course learning activities appears to have unique, positive impacts on standardized measures of critical thinking and reflective thinking as well as on self-reported gains in critical thinking–intellectual development.

10. Also generally consistent with our 1991 synthesis, we uncovered a substantial body of evidence indicating that the nature of students' social and cocurricular involvement plays a unique role of some consequence in their general cognitive development during college. Interactions with peers that extend and reinforce broad ideas introduced in one's academic experience and that confront the individual with diverse interests, values, political beliefs, and cultural norms appear the most salient in positive impact on critical thinking, analytical skills, and postformal reasoning. Somewhat less extensive evidence also suggests that cocurricular activities such as involvement in clubs and organizations may foster critical thinking.

11. The weight of evidence suggests that student-faculty nonclassroom interactions that tend to reinforce or extend the intellectual ethos of the classroom or formal academic experience or that focus on issues of student development can have positive effects on dimensions of general cognitive development such as postformal reasoning, analytical ability, and critical thinking skills.

12. In addition to their positive effects on the acquisition of subject matter knowledge, there is also consistent evidence to suggest that involvement in diversity experiences and service learning experiences has a unique, positive impact on dimensions of general cognitive development such as critical thinking, analytical competencies, and thinking complexity. The most salient diversity experiences appear to be informal interactions with racially and culturally diverse peers and involvement in more formal programs such as racial-cultural awareness workshops and coursework focusing on social-cultural diversity and intergroup relations. The most effective service learning experiences appear to be those that integrate service experiences with course content, provide for reflection about the service experience, and permit the student to apply subject matter learning to the service experience and vice versa.

13. Though it is based on single-sample findings that await replication, there is evidence to suggest that participation by men in revenue-producing intercollegiate sports (that is, football and basketball) has a negative impact on the development of critical thinking during college. Similarly, joining a fraternity may inhibit critical thinking growth in first-year college men, although this negative impact appears to diminish in magnitude after the first year of college.

14. Given the general inconsistency of results across studies, we conclude that there is little compelling evidence to suggest that on- or off-campus work in general has more than a trivial impact on cognitive or intellectual development during college. Similarly, we found little consistent evidence to suggest that living on campus (versus off campus and commuting to college) directly influences general cognitive growth during college, at least in terms of critical thinking. Consistent with our conclusions in Chapter Three, however, we suspect that it probably does exert an indirect, positive influence on general cognitive growth and intellectual development through its enhancement of academic and social engagement. But, once again, we found no empirical test of this hypothesis.

Conditional Effects of College

Compared to our 1991 synthesis, we uncovered substantially more research in the 1990s that estimated the conditional effects of college on general cognitive skills and intellectual development. As with the great majority of research on conditional effects, however, nearly all of the findings are based on single samples, with little or no evidence of independent replication. In contrast to our 1991 synthesis, evidence from the 1990s suggests that the net effects of college on critical thinking skills may vary in magnitude by student race and gender. African-American students made smaller gains in critical thinking during the first and third years of college than did White students, whereas Latino students made smaller gains than White students in the first year. The conditional effects based on sex present a more complex picture because the effects vary in direction at community colleges and four-year colleges. Women in community colleges appeared to make smaller gains in critical thinking skills during the first year of college than did men, but in four-year institutions women made larger critical thinking gains across three years of college than did men.

As with our 1991 synthesis, we found little consistent evidence to suggest that institutional characteristics such as selectivity, size, or private versus public control had a differential impact on dimensions of general cognitive skills or intellectual development for different kinds of students. There was some evidence, however, that institutional environments may play a stronger role in the growth of critical thinking skills for Latino students than for other students. An environmental emphasis on being critical, evaluative, and analytical had a stronger positive net impact on growth in first-year critical thinking skills for Latino students than it did for other students, while covert discrimination had a stronger negative net impact on critical thinking for Latinos than for other students.

There was also substantial evidence to indicate that the effects on first-year growth in critical thinking skills of such factors as course-taking patterns, Greek affiliation, studying with peers, engaging in volunteer work, involvement in diversity activities, and full- versus part-time enrollment differed in magnitude for African-American (or non-White) versus White students, for men versus women, and for first-generation college students versus students whose parents attended college. Also, men in four-year colleges generally convert various dimensions of coursework and academic and social involvement into stronger impacts on three-year gains in critical thinking than do women. In the latter case, such factors as cumulative credit hours completed, number of social science and mathematics courses taken, computer use, social interactions with peers, and extent of involvement in volunteer work had stronger positive impacts on gains in critical thinking through the third year of college for men than they did for women. Conversely, living on campus (versus off campus and commuting to college) had a stronger positive impact on end-of-third-year critical thinking skills for women than for men.

Finally, there is also evidence based on single samples to suggest that the positive effects of cooperative learning may be more pronounced for higher or more complex levels of cognitive functioning (for example, analysis, synthesis, evaluation) than for lower or less complex levels of cognitive functioning (for example, knowledge, comprehension, application) and that academic-social engagement in college may have stronger positive effects on general cognitive development for students with relatively low tested academic ability than for their counterparts with relatively higher academic ability.

Long-Term Effects of College

An important conclusion from our 1991 synthesis was that the undergraduate experience is regarded by alumni as having had an important influence on general cognitive development and thinking skills. Though based on less extensive evidence, the conclusion from our present synthesis tends to reinforce this. Moreover, there is also evidence to suggest that the undergraduate experience provides cognitive skills that increase one's capacity for lifelong learning and continuing intellectual development. Overall, the trends in intellectual growth shaped by the undergraduate experience continue on the same trajectory after college. However, continued intellectual and cognitive development after graduation also depends to a substantial extent on the degree of intellectual stimulation and challenge in the postcollege lives of alumni. Although there was replicated evidence suggesting an intergenerational impact of parental exposure to postsecondary education on sons' and daughters' knowledge acquisition in mathematics, science, and reading comprehension, the evidence for a similar intergenerational impact on general cognitive skills is not compelling.

Notes

1. For additional studies providing evidence that level of exposure to postsecondary education is positively related to increased complexity or sophistication of epistemological development or beliefs about knowledge see Collins, White, and O'Brien (1992), Mansfield and Clinchy (1990), and Schommer (1990, 1993). Less convincing findings, though in the same direction, are reported by Jehng, Johnson, and Anderson (1993) and Paulsen and Wells (1998). Zhang and Richarde (1998) also report related evidence to suggest that male students make gains in dimensions of metacognitive development (that is, knowing what one knows and using consistent but adaptive strategies in problem solving) during college.

2. This body of evidence is perhaps further supported by Facione's (1997) finding that nursing students' critical thinking skill levels are positively associated with low student-faculty ratios in the programs in which they are enrolled. This association, however, is not adjusted for level of precollege critical thinking.

3. There are additional studies that look at environmental influences on the growth of general cognitive skills. For example, Terenzini et al. (1994) found that perceived covert racism on campus positively influenced critical thinking, and Whitt et al. (2003) found that critical thinking in women was positively influenced by institutions that had a strong "chilly climate for women." These somewhat counterintuitive findings, however, are based on a single sample and await replication. Tsui's (2000) qualitative study of four campuses found that student self-reported gains in critical thinking were maximized by a campus culture that stressed active and collaborative learning experiences and fostered social and political awareness.

4. In this regard, it is worth noting that Astin (1993c) found that taking interdisciplinary courses had a positive net effect on seniors' self-reported gains in critical

thinking skills. Similarly, although their findings may be confounded by sample mortality and absence of a control group, Avens and Zelley (1992) found that community college students participating in an interdisciplinary learning community made gains on the Perry (1970) continuum of intellectual and ethical development that were somewhat larger than national norms.

5. See Graham and Gisi (1999) for evidence from a national sample that alumni retrospective reports of their satisfaction with the instruction they received in college are positively associated with self-reported cognitive gains (for example, analyzing and drawing conclusions from various types of data). Similarly, a 20-college study by Volkwein, Valle, Parmely, Blose, and Zhou (2000) reports a strong, positive association between the perceived quality of the classroom experience and seniors' self-reported intellectual growth (for example, ideas, concepts, analytical reasoning).

6. As this book was being completed, a study by Hayek, Carini, O'Day, and Kuh (2002) found that Greek-affiliated students reported greater general education gains during college than did their counterparts who were not Greek affiliated. However, there was no control for how students responded on the dependent measure when they entered college, so it is difficult to determine the internal validity of the results. What appears to be an "effect" of Greek affiliation could simply be the tendency of students who join fraternities and sororities to respond differently on self-reported gains instruments than other students (Pascarella, 2001).

7. For evidence of growth in cognitive complexity and postformal reasoning associated with a multiethnic, multicultural immersion experience in a foreign country, see Vendley (1998). See also MacPhee, Kreutzer, and Fritz (1994) with regard to the positive impact of diversity perspectives on critical thinking and Adams (2002) for evidence of the influence of a social diversity and justice class on changes from dualistic to multiplistic and relativistic thinking.

CHAPTER FIVE

Psychosocial Change

America's colleges and universities have historically focused on students' intellectual development and occupational preparation. At the same time, most institutions have sought to provide students with a liberal education: promoting self-understanding; expanding personal, intellectual, cultural, and social interests; confronting dogma and prejudice; and developing personal moral and ethical standards while preparing students for participation in a democratic society.

In this and the next two chapters, we review the changes in students' psychosocial development, attitudes and values, and moral reasoning that are associated with college attendance.

Our earlier review of students' psychosocial development took its organizational cue from the two components embedded in the term *psychosocial* and examined first the research on student change in areas Inkeles (1966) characterized as the *self system*—the various dimensions along which a sense of self is defined. That body of research fell rather clearly into four categories: identity status and ego development, academic self-concept, social self-concept, and generalized self-esteem.

We then reviewed the research concerning the impact of college on what Inkeles called *relational systems*—the ways in which students interpret and respond to the people, conditions, and institutions in their external world. These topics include students' relations with peers and their orientations to authority figures, intimates, and others. This research examined changes in six general areas: autonomy, independence, and locus of control; authoritarianism, dogmatism, and ethnocentrism; intellectual orientation; interpersonal relations; personal adjustment and psychological well-being; and maturity and general personal development.

CHANGE DURING COLLEGE

Conclusions from *How College Affects Students*

Despite some ambiguous constructs and terms and some methodological constraints such as small samples and uncontrolled variables, the research on identity development, academic and social self-concepts, and self-esteem consistently indicated that students change during their college years. In general, as students progress through college, they become more positive about their academic and social competencies and develop an enhanced sense of self-worth. With rare exceptions, the identity status literature prior to 1990 reported that over time students resolve identity issues and forge commitments to a personal identity, although with considerable variation across identity domains.

Studies of students' ego stage development (with *ego* understood as a central organizing framework providing structure and meaning for the self and world) produced less consistent results. More often than not these studies found little or no change during the college years—at best, half a stage or less. In addition, few researchers focused on racial identity formation, and those who did generally produced conceptual rather than empirical work. The paucity of studies of racial identity formation constituted a major weakness in our knowledge of the effects of college on students, and we forecast that the need for such research would become more pressing as the number of students of color in America's colleges and universities increased. And indeed, more researchers have since examined racial identity formation, although questions about college's impact remain.

Pre-1990 studies consistently found increases in students' academic and social self-concepts and self-esteem during their college years. Students gained confidence in their writing and mathematical abilities, grew in achievement motivation, and developed stronger intellectual orientations. They also became more confident about their leadership abilities and more positive concerning their popularity in general and specifically with the opposite sex, reporting greater social self-confidence and understanding of others. In both academic and social self-concepts, however, the positive changes were small. Gains in general self-esteem were more substantial, on average about .60 of a standard deviation (22 percentile points) from freshman to senior year.

Changes in students' relational systems were more apparent. With few exceptions, both large- and small-scale studies found increases in students' freedom from the influence of others over time. Gains in independence from parental influence exceeded gains in peer independence, where increases were small or statistically nonsignificant. The largest freshman-to-senior changes were away from authoritarian, dogmatic, and ethnocentric thinking and behavior. Declines in authoritarianism and dogmatism averaged .70 to .90 of a standard deviation (SD) (that is, they declined by 26 to 32 percentile points), while declines in ethnocentrism were more modest (.40 SD, or 15 percentile points). Researchers found intermediate increases in intellectual orientation (.33 SD, or 13 percentile points), personal adjustment and psychological well-being (about .40 SD, or 15 percentile points), general autonomy (.59 SD, or 22 percentile points), and family independence (.60 SD, or 22 percentile points). The smallest shifts were in locus of control (increases in internality of .25 to .30 SD, or 10 to 12 percentile points), peer independence (.20 SD, or 8 percentile points), and interpersonal relations (.16 SD, or 6 percentile points). We suggested that some of the variability in these estimates probably derived from the measures used and the roughness of our estimates, but like Feldman and Newcomb (1969) we noted that variation across areas of change would occur at least in part because students come to college with different personal characteristics, including levels of development, readiness to learn, and openness to change.

Evidence from the 1990s

Identity Development. Many of the studies of identity formation in our earlier review used models with theoretical roots in Erik Erikson's conceptions of psychosocial development (Erikson, 1963, 1968). For Erikson, developmental tasks or *crises* were a central dynamic in identity formation. He theorized eight stages or periods of the life cycle[1] when biological and psychological changes interact with sociocultural demands to present the individual with a crisis that is characteristic of that particular stage. For Erikson, a *crisis* is not a physical or psychological emergency but rather a period requiring serious consideration of and choices among possible courses of action. How the individual handles the crisis at each stage determines developmental progress, regression, or stasis. Erikson's fifth stage—*identity versus identity confusion*—is the dominant developmental task for people of traditional college age, including nonstudents. Erikson's thinking continues to exert significant influence on theory-based research concerning identity development during the college years.

Theoretical rather than empirical writings dominate the post-1990 literature on identity development, whether defined broadly or with respect to a particular dimension of an individual's sense of self such as race-ethnicity, gender, or sexual orientation (Renn, Dilley, & Prentice, 2003). Most publications offer varying conceptions of identity and the underlying processes relating to identity formation. Relatively few studies explored the degree of identity change that takes place during the college years. Among the pre-1990 studies of identity formation, the clearest evidence came from Constantinople (1969), who used a measure of Erikson's fourth, fifth, and sixth stages of psychosocial development (see again note 1) in both cross-sectional and longitudinal designs. Her research involved nearly 1,000 students in all four class years at a small, private university in the mid-1960s. She found consistent increases in the successful resolution of identity issues from freshman through senior years across subjects and from one year to the next within subjects. Whitbourne, Jelsma, and Waterman (1982) partially replicated the longitudinal portions of that study 10 years later, but their findings cast doubt on Constantinople's findings of sex-related differences derived from her cross-sectional samples. Zuschlag and Whitbourne (1994) expanded the Whitbourne et al. study with a sample of students attending the same university in 1988. They found statistically significant main effects for class year and gender but not for measurement period. In each measurement period and for most of Erikson's stages, seniors generally displayed higher levels of identity development than juniors or sophomores, although those cohorts did not differ significantly from one another. This finding suggests that identity development occurs in ways that are relatively unaffected by the sociohistorical times—in this case, periods of varying social and political turbulence in recent U.S. history (the 1960s, 1970s, and 1980s). The findings support the proposition that college may play a role in students' identity development, although the impact may not occur, or be apparent, until the later college years. In any event, the conclusion must be considered tentative because age and college exposure remain confounded in this study.

Of the three other theory-based studies of identity or ego development we identified, two (Buier, Butman, Burwell, & Van Wicklin, 1989; Giesbrecht & Walker, 2000) report findings consistent with those of Zuschlag and Whitbourne. Surething (1999), in contrast, found no evidence of freshman-to-senior differences in identity formation. Although Surething's study involved about 160 students, the Buier et al. and Giesbrecht and Walker studies are based on fewer than 100 subjects. All four of the studies reviewed thus far, moreover, are cross-sectional; three of the four are based on students at single institutions, and three (excepting Zuschlag and Whitbourne) of the institutions are church-related. None of the studies controls for differences among students on potentially confounding variables, such as academic ability or socioeconomic status. Thus, although the evidence suggests that identity development does occur during college, caution is warranted inasmuch as that conclusion rests more firmly on the consistency of the findings than on the methodological rigor of the designs or analytical procedures.

A handful of other studies, generally atheoretical and relying on individual items rather than scales, examine students' reports of changes in their "self-understanding." Overall, these studies' findings are consistent with those of the more theoretically based studies (Bauer, 1992, 1995; Buczynski, 1991a; Cress, Astin, Zimmerman-Oster, & Burkhardt, 2001; Flowers, 2002b; Kuh, 1999; Soller, 2001a). Data from the Bauer, Flowers, and Kuh studies come from the College Student Experiences Questionnaire (CSEQ) (Pace, 1984), which asks respondents about gains they believe they have made in several areas since entering college. The CSEQ estimate-of-gains items ask about increases "up to now" in students' college years.

Kuh (1999) analyzed gains in "personal development" reported by students surveyed in four time periods (1969, 1979 to 1981, 1990 to 1991, and 1996 to 1997; juniors in the first cohort, seniors in the other three samples). Personal development was defined as including "understanding one's abilities, interests, and personality" (p. 102). Kuh found consistently that more than three-quarters of the students reported making "quite a bit" or "very much" progress in self-understanding during college. The percentages across periods reporting gains decline from a high of 84 percent in the 1969 sample (nearly 7,400 juniors at 79 colleges and universities) to 77 percent in the most recent sample (8,647 seniors at 49 institutions). Using cross-sectional data from the 2000 National Survey of Student Engagement reported by Kuh and his colleagues (Kuh, Hayek, Carini, Ouimet, Gonyea, & Kennedy, 2001), we estimate freshman-to-senior gains in "understanding yourself" of .17 of a standard deviation (7 percentile points). Other evidence, however, suggests that students may decline in self-understanding somewhat in the first year, recovering in the second (Loeb & Magee, 1992), or even report first- to senior-year declines on a measure of personal identity (Lapsley, Rice, & FitzGerald, 1990). As with self-confidence (see the following section), the initial college experience may be a period of self-reflection and reevaluation that generates more doubt than certitude. With the exceptions of the studies by Kuh and his colleagues, however, all of these investigations are single-campus studies with relatively small samples.

Racial identity. Our earlier review found that most of the pre-1990 literature dealing with college students' racial identity development was theoretical, proposing conceptual models of the constructs and dynamics. Few studies addressed identity development or change specifically during the college years. The degree of scholarly attention focused on racial identity has increased sharply since 1990, but overall it remains more descriptive than analytical, characterizing differences between and among groups or testing bivariate relations between racial identity and psychosocial dimensions.[2]

We identified only two studies that examined changes in racial identity status during the college years, both dealing with identity shifts among African-American students (Cokley, 1999; McCowen & Alston, 1998). Cokley replicated a cross-sectional study by Cheatham, Slaney, and Coleman (1990) that found no differences between freshmen and seniors on a measure of the stages in Cross's model of Black identity formation (see Cross, 1980, 1991; the stages are described in Chapter Two). Cokley studied 206 lower- and upper-division African-American students using the Multidimensional Inventory of Black Identity and the African Self-Consciousness Scale and, like Cheatham et al., found no significant differences between the two groups. McCowen also reports finding no significant freshman-to-senior differences on a measure of African self-consciousness between African-American women at either an historically Black or predominantly White institution and no class year differences in racial identity among the women at the predominantly White institution. Seniors at the historically Black institution, however, showed significantly higher scores than the first-year women on a measure of racial identity formation. The latter finding suggests that the influences on racial identity development may vary according to the racial composition of the institution, although Cokley also looked for such differences and found none.

Gay and lesbian identity. According to Kim (1998), several factors have elevated scholarly interest in issues, including identity development, relating to gays, lesbians, and bisexuals. These circumstances include the growing willingness of gays, lesbians, and bisexuals to be open about their sexual orientations, their readiness to confront harassment and discrimination against them, the HIV-AIDS epidemic, and increased legal and social visibility and acceptance of gays, lesbians, and bisexuals. At the same time, however, researchers face a number of constraints, including the lack of a widely accepted theory of gay-lesbian identity formation, social and religious disapproval both inside and outside the academy, and the difficulties of identifying and securing the cooperation of study participants who may wish not to be identified in terms of their sexual orientation. Consequently, Evans and Wall (1991) found little in the empirical literature before 1990 on the extent of gay, lesbian, or bisexual identity development during the college years, and we found little published since then. Although small, nonrandom samples tend to complicate clear identification of the salient dimensions and dynamics, some aspects of the process of gay-lesbian identity formation are nevertheless beginning to emerge.[3]

The educational research does indicate that, as with identity development more generally, sexual identity may begin to take shape as early as age three, by some estimates, and it can be a slow process (D'Augelli, 1991; Sears, 1991). Although it remains unclear whether maturation or location is at work, attending college may indeed play a role in nonheterosexual students achieving a major psychological milestone: "coming out," or revelation of sexual orientation. The research indicates that this developmental event often takes place during the college years (D'Augelli, 1991; Evans & Broido, 1999; Rhoads, 1994, 1995b; Sears, 1991), but because studies of sexual identity development in college students rarely include control groups of noncollege, same-age, gay-lesbian individuals, the roles of age and college attendance are confounded. Thus, it remains unclear whether coming out in particular or gay-lesbian identity development more generally are related to chronological age and maturation or to the greater freedom that college attendance affords. Moreover, some evidence suggests that the developmental process may be different for lesbians than for gays (Kahn, 1991). The limited evidence available suggests that although both factors may be involved, the freedom to explore and to experiment at college, as well as the more supportive campus environment, may be more important.

Religious identity. A small body of research published since 1990 concerning development of religious identity during college suggests the process may be more subtle and complex than previously thought. The pre-1990 research indicated that the importance of religion in students' lives tended to decline during the college years. More recent studies indicate that college students may not reject religious identity or values but rather refine and reinterpret previously held beliefs into more complex, personalized, and internalized concepts (Anderson, 1995; Bryant, Choi, & Yasuno, 2003; Bussema, 1999; Cherry, DeBerg, & Porterfield, 2001; Lee, 2002a). The Anderson and Lee studies found changes in religious identity in a single year, and Bussema reported freshman- to senior-year growth in faith development. Bryant et al., however, found slight declines in self-rated spirituality after one year of college but also increased student intentions to integrate spirituality into their lives. Strausbaugh (2003) found no differences in faith maturity between first-year and senior students.

Despite the general consistency in these studies, we are wary of firm conclusions. The studies are limited in their generalizability because they rely on small samples (Bryant et al., 2003, is an exception) at church-related institutions. (Chapter Six reviews studies of changes in religious values and attitudes during college.)

Self-Concept and Self-Esteem. In our earlier review we quoted Hansford and Hattie (1982), who described the self-concept research as "a somewhat ill-disciplined field" but noted "it is clear that the area cannot be ignored" (p. 123). Although the volume of research in the 1990s concerning changes in students' self-concepts during the college years is smaller than that produced in previous decades, it nonetheless constitutes a notable segment of the larger body of research on psychosocial change. But problems in reviewing this literature persist. *Self-concept* and *self-esteem* are slippery terms rarely defined in any consistent way. Indeed, the terms are used almost interchangeably. Thus, as previously, our uses of self-concept and self-esteem should not be taken to imply an assertion that the two terms have clearly different theoretical foundations. Rather, we will distinguish between the two terms empirically, according to their operational expression in the studies we review.

Self-concept is generally considered to be one's self-perceptions, formed through experience with the environment, particularly significant others (Shavelson, Burstein, & Keesling, 1977; Shavelson, Hubner, & Stanton, 1976). Writers on the topic appear to agree that self-concept is also multifaceted (an individual's general self-concept can be theoretically and empirically differentiated from one's academic self-concept or social self-concept) and hierarchical (from general self-concept at the top of a pyramidal structure to individual experiences in specific situations at the base) (Byrne, 1984; Shavelson & Bolus, 1982; Shavelson et al., 1976). The literature we reviewed treats self-concept as a relational term, generally denoting students' perceptions of their competence *compared to that of other students.*

Self-esteem, in contrast, has a more internal referent based on the individual's comparison of a "real" and "ideal" self. It reveals an evaluation with general and personalized connotations. Self-esteem as operationalized usually is not specific to a particular dimension of the self and is based on internal, rather than external, standards. Self-esteem "expresses an attitude of approval or disapproval, and indicates the extent to which the individual believes himself to be capable, significant, successful, and worthy" (Coopersmith, 1967, pp. 4–5). Knox, Lindsay, and Kolb (1993) note the extensive literature on these two concepts and that many scholars treat self-concept as an effect, whereas self-esteem is considered a cause, when, as Knox et al. put it, "Indeed, both concepts can be both cause and consequence" (p. 132). The basic orientation of this book leads us to examine the research that treats both concepts as educational outcomes.

Academic self-concept. The research indicates with modest consistency that students' evaluations of their academic abilities become more positive during their college years. The passage is marked by some interesting turns, however, and the growing confidence is far from total. To address this topic, Astin (1993c) drew on data from nearly 25,000 students in the Cooperative Institutional Research Program (CIRP) who enrolled in more than 200 four-year colleges or universities in the fall of 1985 and responded to a survey again four years later. He found statistically significant gains on a factorially derived "scholar" dimension reflecting academic ability, intellectual self-confidence, and plans for graduate school. In 1985, 37.4 percent of the students met the criteria for this label, and by 1989 that percentage had grown to 39.8 percent. That modest growth, however, masked some shifting about: more than 13 percent moved from "not-type to type," while nearly 11 percent shifted in the opposite direction. On the type's component items, the largest freshman-to-senior gains were in students' ratings of their "academic ability," with the percentage rating themselves "above average" or in "the highest 10 percent" rising 7.4 points. On the "intellectual self-confidence" item, the percentage rating themselves at or near the top increased by 5 points. Other studies, based on other CIRP cohorts or cross-sectional studies of other national samples in the late 1980s, report findings of positive gains consistent with those of Astin (Graham & Cockriel, 1997; Kezar & Moriarty, 2000; Kim & Alvarez, 1995; Smith, Morrison, & Wolf, 1994). Some studies, however, report shifts in percentages, and others report differences in means without their associated standard deviations, so a precise estimation of the magnitudes of the first- to senior-year differences is difficult. From a visual inspection of the data provided, it is clear that the changes are small. Smart and Feldman (1998), however, report evidence indicating that both the degree and direction of the change can vary, depending to some extent on the major field a student chooses (see the "Within-College Effects" section of this chapter).

If students gain in their academic and intellectual self-confidence between their first and senior years in college, the path is probably not linear. One might expect some decline in academic self-confidence as students move from high school to the more competitive college environment, and some evidence suggests that is the case (Hesse-Biber & Marino, 1991), perhaps particularly among high-ability women (Arnold, 1993). These studies suggest that students' intellectual self-concepts may actually decline between high school and the sophomore year of college, rebounding modestly by the senior year, although small samples in these studies make it difficult to estimate the extent of any rebound. These findings are consistent with ample evidence reported in our earlier review indicating initial declines in academic self-image during the first year of college, followed by more positive self-concepts in succeeding years. It remains unclear, however, whether the shifts up or down are a function of students' adjusting the comparison points (their estimates of their abilities compared with those of others), or of increased determination and efforts to succeed, accompanied by greater self-confidence when these efforts pay off.

More clear is the general decline in students' mathematics self-concepts, one of the few areas in which self-concept seems to decline in the overall student population during the college years. Astin (1993c) found a drop of 1.4 points in the percentage of students rating their mathematical abilities "very high" or in the top 10 percent, a figure comparable to the drop of 2.2 percentage points we reported in our earlier review. That small, but statistically significant, decline, however, hides somewhat more movement. Between freshman and senior year, the percentage of students moving from low to high estimates of their math skills rose by 8 percentage points, while 9.9 percent of the students' self-ratings in mathematics moved in the opposite direction. Other studies using different, large, nationally representative samples report drops in students' ratings of their math abilities similar in magnitude to those reported by Astin (Astin, Keup, & Lindholm, 2002; Sax, 1994d, 1994e; Smith et al., 1994). Smaller-scale studies are consistent with the national evidence (Hesse-Biber & Marino, 1991; Jackson, Hodge, & Ingram, 1994). Smith and her colleagues, as well as Sax, found the declines in math self-concepts common to both men and women. Although these studies offer no explanations for the declines in students' evaluations of their math skills, the drops may be due in part to the likelihood that students outside math-intensive major fields will not take additional math courses while in college, with the consequent degeneration in their math skills.

Social self-concept. Relatively fewer studies published in the past decade examined changes during the college years in students' social self-concepts, but researchers who tackled this question reported patterns of change highly similar to those relating to students' academic self-concepts. Students' views of their social skills (popularity in general and with the opposite sex, social skills and self-confidence, leadership skills) may suffer in the transition from high school to college but then rebound between the sophomore and senior year (Hesse-Biber & Marino, 1991).

In the main, it appears that students' social self-concepts generally become more positive during the college years. Astin (1993c) found that the number of students reporting their social self-confidence as above average or in the top 10 percent rose by nearly 5 percentage points between freshman and senior year. As with academic self-concepts, that modest increase reflects net growth and masks the movement of nearly 18 percent of the students from "low to high" self-concept ratings and 13 percent from "high to low." Kezar and Moriarty (2000), using a national cohort that entered four-year institutions in 1987, report first- to senior-year gains in social self-confidence of 7.5 percent and 10 percent among White men and women, respectively, and shifts of 7 percent and 8.5 percent among African-American men and women, respectively. Other studies using independent national samples show similar patterns (Jackson et al., 1994; Kim & Alvarez, 1995; Smith et al., 1994).

Overall self-concept. A number of studies that make no distinctions in students' self-concepts across academic, social, or other facets of the sense of self are consistent in indicating positive changes in students' self-images and self-confidence. The evidence comes from large, nationally representative samples of students in the United States (Graham & Cockriel, 1996) and the United Kingdom (Belfield, Bullock, & Fielding, 1999), from smaller-scale studies (Bauer, Mitchell, & Bauer, 1991; Kuh, 1993; Mather & Winston, 1998; Miller-Bernal, 2000), and from studies of adult students (Cupp, 1991; Graham & Donaldson,

1996). Interpretation of any changes in self-concept, whether general or more specific, is complicated by the fact that the students' reference group is becoming increasingly competent over time and also changing in composition as some students withdraw from higher education.

Self-esteem. As noted earlier, *self-esteem*, as used in this review, is an empirically based term reflecting students' generalized judgments of their own worth or merit, evaluated not by their position relative to others but with reference to an internal, personal standard. Compared with earlier decades, studies published since 1990 devoted much less empirical attention to changes in students' self-esteem, and the studies themselves are (with one exception) smaller in scale. Knox, Lindsay, and Kolb (1993) analyzed data from a sample of nearly 5,500 high school seniors randomly selected in the National Longitudinal Study of the High School Class of 1972. Students were surveyed in their senior year and again 2 and 14 years later. The Knox et al. study is noteworthy not only for its large, nationally representative sample but also for its inclusion of a control group of students with only a high school diploma. Most of the studies of academic and social self-concept discussed earlier relied on student responses to single-item reflections of the traits under study. Knox and his colleagues, however, used a multi-item, factorially derived scale with selected items from Rosenberg's (1979) self-esteem scale, a widely used measure. The selected items dealt with "feeling oneself to be a person of worth, taking a positive attitude toward oneself, feeling oneself to be as capable as others, and feeling satisfied with oneself" (Knox et al., 1993, p. 212).

Knox et al. (1993) found educational attainment and self-esteem were highly correlated, with self-esteem scores increasing at each level of education above high school. Findings from smaller-scale studies of first- to senior-year changes are generally consistent with those of Knox et al. (Brand & Dodd, 1998; Cheng, 2001; Kelava, 1993; Miller-Bernal, 2000; Monzon & Maramba, 1998; Munoz-Dunbar & Snyder, 1993; Sawyer, Pinciaro, & Bedwell, 1997, is an exception). In the only study examining year-to-year shifts in self-concepts, Brand and Dodd found some evidence of a decline in lower-division students' self-esteem, a finding similar to the drop in academic and social self-concept from freshman to sophomore year noted earlier.

Autonomy, Independence, Locus of Control, and Self-Efficacy. Studies concerning autonomy, independence, locus of control, and self-efficacy explore the extent to which college students' susceptibility to external influences changes over time. Various theoretical or conceptual perspectives guide the research, resulting in the use of different constructs, terminologies, and instrumentation. Rather than attempt to differentiate the various constructs or parse sometimes fine differences in terminology, we will note that the guiding constructs share a focus on the extent to which students believe themselves to be in control of their lives.

Autonomy or *independence* refers to the degree of freedom students feel from the influence of others in their choices of attitudes, values, and behaviors. Others include peers, parents, or institutions (such as a church or government).

Locus of control, based on social learning theory, refers to the extent to which individuals are self-directed, believing themselves to be in control of their fate. Internally directed people tend to believe they can control what happens to them, whereas externally directed individuals believe their destiny is determined more by others, luck, chance, or fate (Rotter, 1966, 1975). This concept has spawned numerous studies whose findings show that locus of control is related to learning and cognitive growth at all educational levels. Students who attribute their academic success to their own efforts (those who are internally directed) are more likely to score at higher levels on various measures of academic achievement and motivation than are similar students who believe their success is a function of something other than their own ability, motivation, or effort (Perry, 1991). Locus of control may also influence learning in other areas as well. *Attribution* is a closely related variant of locus of control that refers to the reasons students give for their successes or failures, including luck, timing, motivation, effort, or health (Weiner, 1980).

More recently, studies have explored changes in students' *self-efficacy,* a concept similar to locus of control. Bandura (1994, 1997) defines self-efficacy as individuals' "beliefs about their capabilities to produce designated levels of performance that exercise influence over events that affect their lives" (1994, p. 71). Self-efficacy is a product of multiple personal and comparative factors, including students' conceptions of their intellectual and social abilities and their successes and failures in previous academic settings, all tempered by comparisons with others. The term is usually used in the context of learning, and as with locus of control, the evidence indicates self-efficacy correlates positively with academic performance. In a meta-analysis of 11 studies of the relation between college students' sense of self-efficacy and their academic performance, Multon, Brown, and Lent (1991) report an average effect size (unbiased correlation) of .35. More recently, the term self-efficacy has come into vogue (see Chapter Six, on attitudes and values) as it applies to students' beliefs about their abilities to "make a difference" through sociopolitical or civic action.

Several researchers examined changes in students' attachment to or dependence on their parents over the college years (Baier & Whipple, 1990; Lapsley, Rice, & Shadid, 1989; Mather & Winston, 1998; Rice, 1992; Rice, FitzGerald, Whaley, & Gibbs, 1995). With one exception, all found evidence of increases in independence from parents from freshman to junior or senior years. The Rice et al. study found no such shifts. The fact that Rice's 1992 study was longitudinal lends somewhat more weight to its findings compared with the other studies, which were cross-sectional. But because all five studies are based on small, single-institution, primarily opportunity samples, it is inadvisable to draw firm conclusions from these findings.

The evidence on student autonomy or independence from peers includes Wilder and McKeegan's (1999) thorough review of the research dealing with Greek-letter social organizations, which provides some insight into changes in student autonomy during the college years. They found generally consistent evidence that both fraternity or sorority members and nonmembers gained on measures of independence from peers. Most of the studies reviewed, however, were done before 1990.

Studies of changes in student autonomy published in the 1990s, in contrast to those published earlier, provide less clear evidence on which to base conclusions, primarily because of the limited samples. Three single-campus investigations using all-women samples (Jones & Watt, 2001; Taub, 1995; Taub & McEwen, 1991) report freshman- to senior-year (or upper division) increases in student autonomy. Taub and McEwen's 1991 study suggests gains on the order of .71 of a standard deviation (26 percentile points), an effect size about 50 percent larger than what we found on average in our earlier review. Other studies (Baier & Whipple, 1990; Cooper, Healy, & Simpson, 1994; Mather & Winston, 1998) also report evidence of increased autonomy and independence from peer influence during college, although the Mather and Winston study is a qualitative study with limited generalizability. Johnson (1995), however, reports declines after one year in "academic autonomy" (ability to deal with ambiguity and to attain educational goals without extensive direction from others) among 77 students at a large, private university in the Northeast.

Greater clarity exists with respect to shifts during the college years in students' locus of control, both general and academic. Although the body of evidence is small, it is methodologically strong and based on large, longitudinal, nationally representative samples of students in different time periods. Knox, Lindsay, and Kolb (1993), using the National Longitudinal Study of the High School Class of 1972 database, studied shifts in locus of control in 5,409 individuals who were followed up 2 and 14 years after high school graduation. Although these authors use the term *self-direction* rather than locus of control, the items in their factorially derived scale reflect the locus of control concept. Overall, these researchers found that students' "internality" was more strongly related to educational attainment than was self-esteem. Knox and his colleagues found educational attainment reliably associated with belief in self-direction at each education level, with the progression generally upward. However, those in the sample with two or more years of higher education but no bachelor's or advanced degree bucked that trend, experiencing a net loss in internality compared with respondents with no postsecondary education exposure. The authors speculate that respondents working toward an as yet unattained degree may feel some loss of control over their lives.

Pascarella and his colleagues undertook four longitudinal studies of students' "internal locus of attribution for academic success." One was a study of students in a community college and a four-year, commuter university (Pascarella, Bohr, Nora, Raganathan, Desler, & Bulakowski, 1994) and three were studies of several thousand students who entered 18 four-year institutions or five community colleges in 16 states in fall 1992 and were surveyed one, two, and three years later (Pascarella, Edison, Hagedorn, Nora, & Terenzini, 1996; Pascarella, Pierson, Wolniak, & Terenzini, 2004; Pierson, Wolniak, Pascarella, & Flowers, 2003). The criterion measure in each of these studies was a four-item, factorially developed, Likert-type scale reflecting the extent to which students believe their academic performance is a function of hard work rather than the instructor's grading standards, luck, intelligence, or quality of instruction. These studies focused on within- and between-college effects rather than simple shifts in students' internal locus of attribution for academic success during the college years, but they provide clear evidence of increased internality over the periods of time studied. Kanoy, Wester, and Latta (1990) also report statistically significant shifts toward internality in locus of control for academic work. They found that during their first year at private, liberal arts women's colleges, both high- and low-ability students gained .38 and .31 of a standard deviation (15 and 12 percentile points), respectively, in willingness to take responsibility for their own academic performance.

Interpersonal Relations and Leadership Skills. The post-1990 research on changes in students' interpersonal skills during college paints an incomplete picture, but some general outlines are discernible. Perhaps the clearest evidence comes from an analysis by Kuh (1999) of successive cross-sectional samples across three decades using the College Student Experiences Questionnaire (Pace, 1984). As already noted in an earlier section, the CSEQ asks students to report the gains they believe they have made since entering college in various academic and psychosocial areas, including experience and skills in relating to and getting along with others. In each of four periods (1969, 1979 to 1981, 1990 to 1991, and 1996 to 1997), the percentage of students reporting "quite a bit" or "very much progress" in their interpersonal skills ranged from 75 to 79 percent. The percentage increased from 77 percent to 79 percent from the first to the second period, stabilized in the third period, and then declined to 75 percent in the most recent sample. Findings from other CSEQ-based studies are consistent with Kuh's (Bauer, 1995; Flowers, 2002b). Grayson (1999) reports a freshman- to junior-year increase of .23 of a standard deviation (9 percentile points) in a sample of 1,300 students at the University of Toronto. Grayson's instrument assessed changes in (among other things) students' ability to sense others' feelings, assuage a friend the student may have annoyed, and admit being wrong.

A second group of studies (Johnson, 1995; Jones & Watt, 2001; Martin, 2000; Niles, Sowa, & Laden, 1994; Taub & McEwen, 1991) relies on the Developing Mature Interpersonal Relationships (MIR) scale of the Student Development Task Inventory (Winston & Miller, 1987), a composite of three subscales that reflect students' peer relationships, tolerance, and emotional autonomy. No clear pattern emerges from the findings; however, Martin found freshman- to senior-year declines on the MIR; Johnson reports small one-year increases; Jones and Watt, like Taub and McEwen, report senior women scoring significantly higher than first-year women; and Niles et al. report finding no relation between college exposure and interpersonal skills.

A handful of other studies yield evidence on changes in students' interpersonal skills during the college years (Cheng, 2001; Ryan, 1989; Soller, 2001; Volkwein, 1991). All point to increases in social competence, but none permits an estimation of the magnitude of the change.

The picture is clearer regarding changes during college in students' leadership skills, indicating fairly consistently that students improve their leadership skills during the college years. Although the average increase may be small, a closer look shows considerably more change—in both directions—among individuals. Astin (1993c), in a longitudinal study of more than 4,000 students he surveyed on their enrollment in four-year colleges and universities in 1985 and again in 1989, developed a factorially derived set of personality types, one of which he labeled "leadership." Students fitting this characterization rated themselves "above average" or "in the top 10 percent" in leadership, popularity, and social self-confidence. Between the freshman and senior years, the percentage of students in this category rose from 35.3 percent to 35.9 percent, a shift suggesting virtually no movement. Examination of the scale's component items, however, revealed net increases in leadership (+5.4 percent), popularity (+2.2 percent), and social self-confidence (+4.7 percent) over the time period. In addition, these small increases masked shifts from low to high scores of 15.8 to 16.8 percentage points. Similarly, Astin found moves from high to low scores of 10.8 to 13.8 percentage points in these same three areas.

The reasons for these shifts are not readily apparent, but it seems clear that more movement on leadership measures takes place between freshman and senior year than is suggested by the net percentage shifts. Sax and Astin (1998) report similar results in somewhat different analyses based on the same sample as Astin's earlier study, and other large, independent, national samples (Astin & Cress, 1998; Bowen & Bok, 1998; Cress, Astin, Zimmerman-Oster, & Burkhardt, 2001; Graham & Cockriel, 1997) and smaller-scale studies (Webb, 2001) also record similar results. Both Cress and her colleagues (using a CIRP cohort subsample of students who entered 10 four-year schools in 1994 and were surveyed four years later) and Graham and Cockriel report somewhat greater increases in leadership skills than does Astin. Cress et al. found that more than 70 percent of their respondents reported in the follow-up that their leadership skills on six items were "stronger" or "much stronger" than when they entered college (the gains were above 80 percent on four of those items). In their study of more than 9,000 students (from all class years) on 75 two- and four-year campuses in 27 states, Graham and Cockriel found the mean contribution of the institution to students' growth on a factorially derived scale reflecting "social leadership development" was 3.3 on a 5-point scale where 1 = "none" and 5 = "very much."

General Personal Development. A number of researchers examine changes during the college years on a general measure of "personal-social development" taken from the College Student Experiences Questionnaire (Pace, 1984). This five-item composite scale assesses the gains students believe they have made since entering college in developing values and ethical standards, understanding themselves (abilities, interests, personality), understanding others, getting along with others, and developing good health habits and physical fitness. Without exception, these studies indicate that the students surveyed believed they had made progress in their personal-social development since entering college

(Flowers, 2002b; Kaufman & Creamer, 1991; Kuh & Hu, 2001; Kuh & Vesper, 1997b; Watson & Kuh, 1996). However, some of these studies use random samples of students in all class years without reporting the means and standard deviations by class year, precluding estimation of the magnitude of the growth students in each class year believe they experienced. Kaufman and Creamer reported an average gain among first-year students on this scale that is more than "some" but less than "quite a bit."[4] Evidence in Kuh and Hu, however, indicates the reported gains rise consistently across class years. Findings based on the community college version of the CSEQ are consistent with those from four-year institutions (Glover, 1996; Plomin, 1997).

NET EFFECTS OF COLLEGE

Conclusions from *How College Affects Students*

Isolating college's effects from the impact of other influences, such as normal maturation or cohort effects, may be most difficult when some dimension of students' psychosocial development is the outcome under study. Erikson (1968) and other developmental psychologists maintain that individuals develop psychosocially in large part according to ontogenetic laws that to some extent operate independently of environmental and sociohistorical influences. Sociological theories, in contrast, maintain that people adapt and change in response to socializing forces exerted by family, peers, schools, churches, and other social agencies. No one claims that either source of influence alone produces change, but the assignment of degrees of influence is problematic, particularly in self-system areas, where the evidence remains methodologically weak.

In our earlier review, we could say little with confidence about college's effects on identity status and ego development beyond the influences of normal maturation or other forces outside the academy. Researchers seemed preoccupied with operationalizing identity structures and compiling evidence for or against the existence of hypothesized statuses or stages. Only a few studies examined the forces that led to status-stage change; fewer still investigated college's role, and these by and large lacked methodological rigor.

The evidence concerning college's net effects on students' academic and social self-concepts was also limited but methodologically stronger than that dealing with identity formation. Educational attainment appeared to have a positive and independent impact on students' ratings of themselves relative to their peers in both academic and social areas and abilities, although the effect appeared to be more indirect than direct—that is, mediated by college experiences. The more rigorously controlled studies also found statistically significant and positive net college effects on students' self-esteem, although the impact was small and intertwined with family background and students' previous achievements.

The evidence supported popular beliefs about the effects of college in reducing authoritarianism, dogmatism, and possibly ethnocentrism as well as in increasing students' intellectual orientation, personal psychosocial adjustment, and sense of psychological well-being. But evidence concerning whether college had any net influence on students' autonomy and independence, maturity in their interpersonal relations, or general maturity and personal development was absent or inconsistent.

Evidence from the 1990s

Identity Formation. Since 1990, a number of theoretical pieces and a few studies have dealt with various forms of identity development. Most of the scholarship has examined racial-ethnic identity formation, but the characteristics and underlying processes of identity development related to sexual orientation and religion also attracted attention. Nonetheless, we identified no studies that examined the extent to which such development could be attributed to the college experience rather than to other maturational or sociocultural forces.

The picture is somewhat different for identity formation more generally. In the previous section we noted studies by Constantinople (1969) based on a measure of Erikson's fourth, fifth, and sixth stages of psychosocial development. She found cross-sectional evidence from the freshman through senior years of the successful resolution of Erikson's fifth stage (identity) crisis, and analyses of her longitudinal evidence over two- and three-year periods supported her interindividual comparisons. Whitbourne, Jelsma, and Waterman (1982) replicated Constantinople's study a decade later, but the clearest evidence of net college effects on identity formation we found is Zuschlag and Whitbourne's (1994) 1988 replication of these two studies with a third sample of students. These two researchers found statistically significant main effects for class year and gender, although not for period, a finding that suggests the absence of sociohistorical effects. But the Zuschlag and Whitbourne study was cross-sectional and left students' age and precollege identity level uncontrolled; thus, the effects of college experience and normal maturation remain confounded. In addition, the Zuschlag and Whitbourne study is the only attempt reported since 1990 that we identified that examines whether college facilitates identity development beyond the process of maturation.

Self-Concept and Self-Esteem. The evidence relating to net changes in students' perceptions of themselves and their abilities, whether compared with their peers or some personal standard, is generally more extensive and persuasive than that relating to identity development.

Academic and social self-concept. Clearer evidence indicates that college, net of other factors, enhances students' perceptions of their academic and social skills. Astin (1993c) found a modest increase from first to senior year in the number of students who qualified as "scholars," and several other measures in this study indicate that college has an effect independent of students' precollege academic self-concepts and an array of other potentially confounding influences. In lieu of a control group of individuals similar to the college students but who did not go to college, Astin relied on measures of the intensity and extensity of students' exposure to college. If college has an effect net of other factors, then students who remain in college longer (extensity) and who are more deeply engaged in college experiences (intensity) can be expected to show greater changes than those with less exposure or involvement. And that is what he found. After controlling for an extensive list of students' precollege self-concepts and other characteristics, as well as for institutional environments, Astin found that the number of years of college completed had a modest, positive net effect on students' senior-year scholarship scores. Other intensity factors, such as the frequency of interaction with faculty members and other students, also showed positive net effects. Other studies using large, multi-institutional samples report findings consistent with Astin's (Belfield et al., 1999; Kim & Alvarez, 1995). The evidence also suggests that the statistically significant declines noted previously in students' mathematical self-concepts are due in part to the college experience (Sax, 1994d, 1994e).

Self-esteem. Few studies examine the net effects of college on students' self-esteem, but the findings of those that do suggest college may have some net impact on self-esteem. Monzon and Maramba (1998), using a cross-sectional design, studied 339 Filipino-American students at a large Southern California university. They found that, after controlling precollege academic ability and achievement, family environment, gender, and age, class year was positively related to reported self-esteem. This study is noteworthy for having controlled age. Although Monzon and Maramba did not take into account precollege level of self-esteem, the fact that the positive relation between class year and self-esteem in their study persists in the presence of controls for age suggests that the relation is not attributable to maturational forces. However, the study's cross-sectional design and the lack of controls for precollege self-esteem, as well as the small, single-campus sample, warrant caution in drawing conclusions.

Such caution is supported by Knox, Lindsay, and Kolb (1993), who report findings from a more rigorous study (although one based on a dated sample). Using data from the National Longitudinal Study of the High School Class of 1972, which included respondents who did and did not go to college, Knox and his colleagues controlled for gender, race-ethnicity, socioeconomic status, academic ability, and a precollege measure of self-esteem. They found educational attainment statistically unrelated to self-esteem a dozen years after high school graduation, although their findings did indicate small increases in reported self-esteem with each successively higher level of education completed.

Autonomy and Locus of Control. What few studies address the net effects of college on student autonomy or internal versus external locus of control examine these psychosocial traits generally or focus on their academic manifestations.

We identified only one study of net college effects on general autonomy. Jones and Watt (2001) found upper-division students scored higher than their first-year counterparts on a measure of emotional autonomy, reflecting such traits as the respondents' trust of their own ideas and feelings, self-assurance, confidence they would be competent decision makers, and ability to voice dissenting opinions.

That statistically significant difference disappeared, however, when age and gender were controlled, suggesting that the univariate differences may be more a function of maturational level or even gender than college impact. Johnson (1995), in contrast, found a net drop on a measure of students "academic autonomy" during the first year in a small sample, single-institution study.

Knox, Lindsay, and Kolb's (1993) analyses of data from the National Longitudinal Study of the High School Class of 1972 provide the only nationally representative evidence published since 1990 on the net effects of college on students' locus of control. Knox and his colleagues used a four-item scale to measure self-direction, a concept they define as similar to locus of control. The items reflected the extent of respondents' belief that planning seldom pays off, that someone or something usually keeps one from getting ahead, that one is happiest when accepting one's condition in life, and that good luck is more important than hard work for success. The net differences these researchers found are statistically significant but small. After adjusting for gender, race-ethnicity, socioeconomic status, and ability, Knox et al. found that students with two or more years of college have a .07 of a standard deviation (about 3 percentile points) advantage in self-direction over students with only a high school diploma, whereas those with baccalaureate or advanced degrees have an advantage on the order of .09 of a standard deviation (4 percentile points). Pascarella and his colleagues (Pascarella, Edison, Hagedorn, Nora, & Terenzini, 1996; Pascarella, Wolniak, & Pierson, 2003) report more recent evidence consistent with that of Knox et al. In their 1996 study, Pascarella et al. found the extensity of exposure to college (as reflected in the total number of course hours taken) had a statistically significant and positive effect on students' end-of-first-year beliefs about their control over their academic performance. The study controlled for initial beliefs and other factors (including ability and age). The statistical controls for age in these studies rule out normal maturation as an alternative explanation for the changes observed.

Interpersonal Relations and Leadership Skills. A number of studies suggest that college experiences appear to have a positive effect on students' interpersonal skills, although no studies examine how much of any change in students' interpersonal skills during college might be due to the general college experience itself rather than to other factors such as maturation.

More evidence speaks to the effects of college on students' leadership skills. Astin (1993c) based his analyses on data from nearly 25,000 students who entered four-year colleges and universities in 1985 and who were surveyed again four years later. With leadership defined in terms of three self-ratings (leadership ability, popularity, and social self-confidence) and whether the student held an elective student office during college, Astin's findings on several measures of college attendance indicated consistently that students' leadership skills increased during the college years in ways not attributable to a battery of precollege characteristics, including students' initial evaluations of their leadership skills and their academic abilities, race-ethnicity, gender, socioeconomic status, and other relevant factors. Net of these and other environmental factors, Astin found the number of years in college significantly and positively related to increases in leadership skills, as were experiences not available to same-age, noncollege individuals, including living on campus and the frequency of interactions with faculty members and other students. Moreover, because age was statistically unrelated to changes in leadership scores, Astin ruled out maturation as an alternative hypothesis to explain the changes. Drawing on a smaller independent sample of 875 students surveyed when they were first-year students at 10 colleges in 1994 and again four years later, Astin and Cress (1998) report corroborating findings based on a different measure of leadership skills.

Kuh and Hu (2001) also provide evidence of net college effects on a measure of overall personal development. The content of this CSEQ-based, five-item scale is conceptually broad, including development of values and ethics, self-understanding, and good health habits. Two of the scale's five items, however, deal with selected aspects of interpersonal relations, including understanding and getting along with different kinds of people and functioning as a team member. In their study of more than 54,000 randomly selected undergraduates from 126 colleges and universities, Kuh and Hu found class year significantly and positively related to students' reported gains in social and personal development even when controlling for gender, race-ethnicity, socioeconomic status, high school preparation, major field, and institutional type. Precollege levels of personal and social development, however, remained uncontrolled.

BETWEEN-COLLEGE EFFECTS

Conclusions from *How College Affects Students*

In our earlier book, we found little to say about the differential effects of college characteristics on students' identity status or ego development. Only a few pre-1990 studies of identity formation used samples from more than one institution, precluding any reliable or meaningful generalization. The weight of the evidence concerning the effects of between-college differences on students' academic and social self-concepts was reasonably consistent in indicating that when various prematriculation characteristics were held constant, what happens to students after they enroll had more impact than the type of institution where they enrolled. Several large, methodologically sound studies reported few direct effects of college size, type of control, predominant race, single-sex versus coed status, or academic selectivity on students' self-evaluations in either academic or social spheres. Some evidence suggested selectivity had a negative, indirect effect on self-concept (via the kinds of academic and social experiences students had, which were in turn positively related to academic self-concept). Large, public institutions also appeared to have a negative, indirect effect on students' social self-concepts by inhibiting social interaction with faculty members and peers. Although the evidentiary base was small, institutional characteristics such as selectivity, cohesion, vocational emphasis, size, proportion of freshmen employed, and type of control were unrelated to differences in students' self-esteem once a variety of student precollege characteristics were taken into account.

Research published before 1990 was virtually silent on between-college effects on changes in maturity or overall personal development. What evidence existed suggested that institutional characteristics had little impact on intellectual dispositions once students' precollege characteristics were taken into account. The pre-1990 evidence generally indicated that changes in the ways students relate to others are inadequately captured by differences among institutions relating to size, type of control, or selectivity. Instead, with students' entering characteristics controlled, increases on measures of internal locus of control, personal adjustment, and general psychological health, and declines in authoritarianism and dogmatism, were more consistently associated with campus environments and students' interpersonal interactions with both peers and faculty members. Those environments and experiences may vary substantially among institutions of similar size, type, or selectivity.

Evidence from the 1990s

Identity Development. Review of the post-1990 research on between-college effects on identity formation leads to the same conclusion as our previous review: little can be said with confidence because so little evidence exists. We found no studies examining differences in general identity status change at different kinds of institutions. The studies we located dealt with racial identity development among students at historically Black colleges and universities (HBCUs) versus predominantly White institutions (PWIs) (Cokley, 1999; McCowen & Alston, 1998). These investigations are cross-sectional contrasts in freshman- to senior-year identity formation among students at one HBCU and one PWI. Cokley found a main effect for institutional racial-ethnic mix, with HBCU students scoring higher than PWI respondents on a measure of racial centrality, racial ideology, and racial regard. At the same time, he found the lower- versus upper-division differences to be about the same at both institutions. McCowen and Alston also found no institutionally related differences between first-year and senior-year women students at an HBCU and a PWI on a measure of African self-consciousness. The two also reported that seniors at the HBCU scored higher than those at the PWI on a measure of racial identity as reflected in Cross's model of psychological Nigrescence (1991). The authors suggest that although the groups may show no differences in African self-consciousness, the environment (at least for women) at this HBCU may have permitted them not only to immerse themselves more fully in African-American culture but also to move beyond the internalization level of racial identity to an appreciation of other cultures.

Self-Concept and Self-Esteem. Our earlier review led to the conclusion that the conventional variables American higher education uses to differentiate among institutions (such as size, type of control, mission, selectivity) are not good predictors of psychosocial change among students, and post-1990 research supports that conclusion. The evidence published since 1990 suggests institutional environments may be more influential than structural or organizational characteristics.

Academic self-concept. When Astin (1993c) found any statistically significant net effects of institutional characteristics on students' academic self-concept or scholarly orientations, these effects were generally small. Sax (1994d, 1994e) reports finding some evidence that institutional selectivity, net of students' precollege characteristics (including ability and math self-concepts), may be negatively related to students' math self-concepts, but that effect disappeared when specific aspects of the educational environments on selective campuses were included in the analysis.[5] Sax, like Astin, found that enrollment in a public university had a slight negative net effect but that other conventional institutional variables had no significant impact. However, Kim and Alvarez (1995) found, in a sample of more than 3,200 women enrolled in 274 coeducational institutions and 387 women attending 34 women's colleges from 1987 to 1991, that the women's college students showed greater increases in academic self-concept than did respondents at coeducational institutions. The advantage persisted after adjusting for the effects of background characteristics (including precollege academic self-concept), college environmental features, and student experiences during college.

Studies of potential differential effects for African-American students associated with attending an historically Black college or university (HBCU) versus a predominantly White institution (PWI) yield findings generally similar to but less clear than those related to attending a women's college or a coeducational institution. Berger (2000a) examined the effects of institutional racial-ethnic mix on freshman- to senior-year changes in various measures of academic self-concept or self-confidence and found greater increases for African-American students enrolled at two church-affiliated HBCUs than for similar students attending six sectarian PWIs. The HBCU advantage persisted even when controlling for differences in precollege self-concept and other student characteristics as well as for a variety of student experiences during college. Kim (1999), however, found that institutional-level variables, including selectivity, size, student-faculty ratio, selected expenditure variables, and HBCU-PWI status, were statistically unrelated to academic self-confidence in the senior year after controlling for a battery of student-related variables, including precollege academic self-concept. According to Kim, the sole significant net predictor of senior-year self-confidence was the peer environment of the institution attended. Both the Kim and Berger studies, which are well designed and control for most relevant factors, suggest that for African-American students any HBCU advantage may be indirect rather than direct, but whether HBCUs have a stronger impact on African-American students than do PWIs remains unclear. Considerable research indicates that African-American students enrolled in HBCUs are more likely to be actively involved in the academic and social systems of their institutions than are similar Black students attending PWIs (Berger, 1997, 2000b; DeSousa & King, 1992; MacKay & Kuh, 1994; Watson & Kuh, 1996).

The weight of evidence post-1990 points more clearly to the effects of institutional cultures and environments, rather than organizational or structural characteristics, as forces shaping academic self-concepts. Chang (1996, 1997, 1999a) found that campus structural diversity (the proportion of students of different races-ethnicities) was significantly and positively related to freshman- to senior-year increases in academic self-concept among more than 11,000 students surveyed in 1985 when they enrolled at more than 300 institutions and again in 1989. These effects were indirect rather than direct, operating through the multicultural orientations of the institutions and the socializing effects of students' interactions with peers and faculty members. Contacts with peers of a different race and discussions of racial issues with others were particularly influential. Szelenyi (2002), using a sample of more than 12,000 students attending 91 institutions from 1996 to 2000, reports findings similar to Chang's, with the refinement that, net of many other student and institutional factors, respondents on campuses where they encounter diverse viewpoints gained more in intellectual self-confidence than did similar students on campuses characterized by less diverse points of view. The peer group context, moreover, may vary by the race-ethnicity of the students (Antonio, 1995). In addition, Berger (2002) found differences in the degree of change in students' academic self-concept dependent on organizational cultures.[6]

Social self-concept. The research on social self-concept comes from some of the same studies that dealt with academic self-concept. Chang (1996, 1997, 1999a) found that a campus's structural diversity had an indirect effect on increases in students' social self-concepts, working primarily through its effects on an institution's multicultural- or diversity-oriented institutional practices and the kinds of experience students have on campus. In Chang's studies, structural diversity positively affected White students' disposition to socialize with peers of different ethnic or cultural backgrounds and to discuss racial issues. These effects were discernible even when controlling for a number of student precollege characteristics (including precollege social self-concept) and such other institutional traits as type and control, location, size, and selectivity. Chang, however, does not report data to indicate whether any of these other institutional characteristics also had any statistically significant impact.

HBCUs and women's colleges may have a stronger positive effect on their students' social self-concepts than do more heterogeneous campuses. Berger and Milem (2000a) found that, net of a number of students' precollege traits (including social self-concept) and students' experience during college, African Americans enrolled at two church-affiliated HBCUs showed greater freshman- to senior-year gains in social self-concept than did similar students enrolled at six church-related predominantly White institutions. Kim and Alvarez (1995) report similar net freshman-to-senior gains in social self-concept among women who attended a women's college compared with peers at a coeducational college or university. The institutional effect, however, was only marginally noteworthy ($p < .09$), indicating that the impact of attending a women's college, like that of enrolling at an HBCU, was probably indirect, mediated through the greater opportunities for women at these institutions to become involved in student organizations, leadership classes, and other activities that lead to increased social self-confidence.

Self-esteem. With one exception (Knox et al., 1993), the research dealing with differential institutional influences on self-esteem is limited to the effects on women's self-evaluations of attending a women's college versus a coeducational institution (Kelava, 1993; Miller-Bernal, 2000; Riordan, 1990, 1992, 1995). Knox and his colleagues found no statistically significant effects of institutional characteristics on self-esteem once other factors were controlled. For his 1990 study of the impact of women's college attendance, Riordan relied on data from the National Longitudinal Study of the High School Class of 1972; the 1992 study draws on the High School and Beyond database. Both studies show clear patterns of greater gains in self-esteem among women's college students than among similar students at coed institutions, but the institutional effect becomes statistically nonsignificant when controls are introduced for socioeconomic status and cognitive ability. The Kelava and Miller-Bernal studies, both smaller in scale than Riordan's, show no particular net advantage in increased self-esteem to women students at all-women colleges compared with women at a coed school.

Locus of Control. Only a few studies published since 1990 examined whether institutional characteristics had any discernible effect on changes in students' locus of control. When Pascarella and his colleagues examined shifts in students' locus of attribution for academic success, they used a four-item, factorially developed scale reflecting the extent to which students believe their academic performance is a function of hard work rather than luck, intelligence, the instructor's grading standards, or poor teaching. In a study that amounted to a pilot test of that measure with first-year students at a community college and at a four-year, commuter university, Pascarella et al. (Pascarella, Bohr, Nora, Raganathan, Desler, & Bulakowski, 1994), after adjusting for other variables, found no statistically significant difference one year later in the two groups' internal locus of attribution for academic success. Knox, Lindsay, and Kolb (1993) report similar findings from a study of a nationally representative sample. They found no relation between the residential-commuter character of institutions and changes in students' locus of control (self-direction). The findings of both studies cast doubt on popular beliefs that these two kinds of institutions differ in their educational effectiveness.

However, two subsequent studies using the same criterion measure but larger and more recent national samples that varied during the years studied from 1,800 to 2,700 students at five community colleges and 18 four-year institutions point in a different direction with respect to type of institutional control (Pascarella, Edison, Hagedorn, Nora, & Terenzini, 1996; Pierson et al., 2003). These studies identified statistically significant net differences in locus of attribution for academic success between two- and four-year institutions, with community college students showing greater gains than similar students at four-year institutions. The community college advantage, however, was apparent only at the end of the first academic year. This finding suggests not only that the effect may be variable over time but also that the impact is greatest when it is perhaps educationally most important—during the first year. McLure and McClanahan

(1999) report findings from a cross-sectional study of nearly 16,000 community college students and more than 36,000 students at four-year institutions indicating that two-year students are more likely to report their general education courses helped them become more independent and self-directed learners.

Riordan (1990, 1992) provides the only other evidence of differential effects on self-esteem associated with institutional characteristics. As with his analyses of the impact on women's self-esteem of attending an all-women's college rather than a coeducational institution, he found some indications that women's colleges had more positive effects on women's internal locus of control, although the impact of institutional type disappeared once differences in students' socioeconomic status and academic ability were taken into account.

Interpersonal Relations and Leadership Skills. The research before 1990 on the effects of institutional characteristics on students' abilities to interact with others relied heavily on psychological constructs and measures (for example, measures of dominance and extroversion). Few studies examined institutional effects on leadership skills. In contrast, the post-1990 research has largely ignored interpersonal relations in favor of examining the influences of institutional characteristics on students' self-reported abilities in areas related to leadership. These skills are often measured by composite scales reflecting such traits as self-confidence, ability to get along with others, popularity, or leadership positions held. As with studies of other forms of psychosocial change, the variables generally used to differentiate among institutions appear to have little predictive value. Most studies find few, if any, independent effects on freshman- to senior-year changes linked to institutional type, control, or size after adjusting for students' precollege traits (usually including their initial evaluations of their leadership talents) and experiences during college (Antonio, 1998, 2000; Astin, 1993c; Sax & Astin, 1998; Smart, 1997; Smart, Ethington, Riggs, & Thompson, 2002). Whether selectivity plays a role remains unclear. Some evidence suggests it does (Bowen & Bok, 1998), and other evidence indicates it does not (Antonio, 2000). Bowen and Bok, however, did not control for other institutional characteristics or for the kinds of experiences students had while in college. The Bowen and Bok study also indicates that any selectivity effect may vary with the area in which leadership is manifested. Graduates of less selective institutions are more likely to take leadership roles in youth and educational groups (perhaps because these respondents are more likely to have children), whereas their counterparts from more selective institutions are more likely to lead cultural or alumni organizations or social and community groups. Most of these studies suggest that various aspects of a campus's climate or the experiences students have while enrolled are more powerful predictors of leadership development than an institution's structural or organizational characteristics.

A few studies explore the effects of other institutional dimensions on leadership skills. Kimbrough and Hutcheson (1998) searched for net effects on leadership skills among African-American students that might be associated with attending an historically Black college or university rather than a predominantly White institution, and Langdon (1997) searched for differences in leadership skills among women who had attended a women's college rather than a coed school. Neither study found statistically significant net effects (positive or negative) related to the type of institution.

A number of researchers report little or no association between expenditure patterns and learning outcomes in K–12 education (Hanushek, 1997), but similar studies of higher education institutions are rare. Smart et al. (2002) reports evidence suggesting that gains in freshman- to senior-year leadership skills may be affected by institutional expenditure patterns in ways unattributable to students' precollege characteristics and leadership talents or college experiences, including leadership activities. Net of these other factors, Smart and his colleagues found instructional expenditures had a negative effect, and student service expenditures a positive impact, on a five-item leadership scale reflecting ability, drive to achieve, popularity, and intellectual and social self-confidence. The effects of expenditure patterns in both areas, however, were indirect, being mediated through students' leadership activities and perceptions of campus priorities. This finding is consistent with the proposition put forward earlier and in our discussion of other psychosocial outcomes that dimensions of a campus environment and the kinds of experiences students have there are more powerful determinants of student leadership development than are expenditures.

General Personal Development. The importance of an institution's environment as opposed to its structural features is also apparent in studies using general measures of personal development, although limited evidence suggests that the effect on African-American students of attending an HBCU rather than a predominantly White institution persists even after adjusting for students' backgrounds and on-campus experiences (Flowers, 2002b; Watson & Kuh, 1996). Most likely, the statistically significant, institutional-type effects in these studies are indirect, exerting their influence through the kinds of environments they provide. If so, these findings are consistent with the proposition that institutional environments and cultures are more powerful shapers of students' personal development than are the standard institutional descriptors.

In a study of nearly 5,500 randomly selected undergraduates at 126 colleges and universities, Kuh and Hu (2001) found no statistically significant differences in reported gains in personal development associated with institutional type or control, although there was a hint that selectivity might have negative effects. Kuh and his colleagues report similar findings in other studies based on independent samples, suggesting that conventional institutional descriptors are largely unrelated to educational effects (Hu & Kuh, 2003a; Kuh & Vesper, 1997b). Studies of the impacts of organizational cultures support the conclusion that student experiences, and personal and institutional environments and cultures, are more salient factors in how students change than are structural features (Berger & Milem, 2000b; Smart & Hamm, 1993).

WITHIN-COLLEGE EFFECTS

Conclusions from *How College Affects Students*

The few studies we found in the pre-1990 literature concerning the kinds of college experiences that might be associated with changes in students' identity status, ego development stage, or self-esteem were generally weak methodologically with inconsistent results. Some evidence suggested that majoring in math, the sciences, or technical fields tended to bolster students' academic self-concepts but not their social ones. Living on campus rather than commuting seemed to increase the likelihood that students would gain in both academic and social self-concept. When controlling for confounding factors, these studies suggested the residential effects were indirect rather than direct, less a function of place than of living environment and associated activities and experiences. The frequency and nature of students' interpersonal experiences with peers and faculty members were the more likely sources of influence. A larger and more consistent body of evidence indicated that, net of other factors including pre-college self-concepts, the levels of academic and social integration (manifested in many forms but particularly in the degree of involvement with peers and faculty members) were positively associated with enhanced academic and social self-concepts. These effects, particularly those associated with peer involvement, were both direct and substantial in terms of academic and social outcomes.

Studies of within-college effects on students' "relational systems" (governing how they related to others and to their world) led to conclusions similar to those associated with "self-system" changes. Academic major seemed not to be a factor, but there were hints that departmental environments, rather than specific disciplines, might be influential. Similarly, researchers found that residing in a living-learning center, net of other factors, was consistently linked to increases in autonomy and independence, intellectual disposition and orientation, and overall personal development as well as to declines in authoritarianism and dogmatism. The impact of a living-learning center's structural, organizational, and programmatic features appeared to be indirect, mediated through interpersonal relations fostered among students and faculty members. The influence of such interactions varied by outcome, with faculty members' influence greater in intellectual areas and peer influences dominating the noncognitive spheres.

Evidence from the 1990s

Identity Development. Post-1990 studies of the effects of college experiences on identity formation focused on the influences of various kinds of courses. One subset of this research studied the identity-related outcomes of participation in service-learning courses or community service (Batchelder & Root, 1994; Eyler & Giles, 1999; Jordan, 1994; Malone, Jones, & Stallings, 2001; Rhoads, 1998). In a qualitative study of more than 200 students who participated in various university-sponsored community service projects from 1991 to 1996, Rhoads concluded that such activities promoted change by bringing students into contact with people from diverse backgrounds and forcing them to confront their own generalizations and stereotypes. Service also provided a context for identity clarification. Malone et al. also found evidence of increased self-understanding in the essays of teacher education students who were tutoring disadvantaged elementary pupils. Batchelder and Root, Eyler and Giles, and Jordan adopted quantitative or mixed designs. Batchelder and Root reported bivariate statistical evidence suggesting greater reflection on occupational identity issues among service-learning students, but the differences disappeared when controls were added for precourse occupational identity. Jordan (1994) found only nonsignificant differences among three groups of students, one with no volunteer activity and the other two in a service-learning course with and without reflection. Like Malone et al., Jordan reported evidence of increased self-awareness in some of the journal entries of students in the "with reflection" group. In the largest of these studies (more than 1,500 students in 20 colleges and universities), Eyler and Root reported positive effects in both their qualitative analyses and the pre- and posttest quantitative portion of their study.

Musil (1992) indicates majoring in women's studies may be a transformational experience, at least for some students. In a study of graduates of 10 women's studies programs, Musil and her colleagues found that "no single refrain was heard more clearly in the reports than that women's studies courses gave students a voice and empowered them" (p. 201). The impact, however, appeared to be more a function of course content than of the pedagogies adopted. Although the instructional methods used in a number of the courses resembled instructional methods in other active learning courses, the important difference seemed to be "gender-focused" content that explored gender issues systematically rather than "gender-balanced" content that integrated gender issues into other curricular content. Luebke and Reilly (1995) report that many of the 89 women's studies program graduates they interviewed described their studies as a time of self-discovery and a personal journey. Bargad and Hyde (1991) report quantitative evidence of the development of higher levels of feminist identity among women enrolled in women's studies classes than among a control group of women who had expressed interest in those courses but did not enroll. The study reports nothing more concerning controls for possible self-selection effects. Thus, although these studies are consistent in reporting evidence of identity development, self-selection remains a plausible alternative explanation for the changes observed.

Researchers who examined other kinds of academic experiences each concentrated on a different source of influence, making synthesis problematic. The findings include some evidence of a positive influence on identity formation from taking a senior capstone course (Collier, 2000), learning in supportive multiracial-multiethnic classrooms (Marin, 2000), taking diversity courses (Palmer, 2000; Palmer, 1999), taking courses taught by supportive faculty who encourage self-discovery (Keller-Wolff, Eason, & Hinda, 2000), and studying abroad (Bates, 1997). All but the Palmer studies use qualitative methods and, consequently, small, single-campus samples, limiting generalizability. The consistency of the findings, however, suggest not only that course or academically related experiences may be a factor in identity formation but also that this area of investigation merits more attention.

Few studies of within-college effects on student identity development have concentrated on the impacts of out-of-class experiences. Kilgannon and Erwin (1992), after controlling for students' precollege scores on measures of Chickering's identity vector, found that members of fraternities and sororities, when compared with independents, showed no statistically significant differences in level of identity development after two years. The researchers did find that fraternity and sorority members showed significantly lower levels of development on the instrument's confidence subscale. Rhoads (1997b) found indications that identity formation may be associated with student activism for issues relating to race-ethnicity, gender, or sexual orientation.

Racial identity. Several studies that explore possible links between students' college experiences and racial identity and consciousness offer noteworthy but unreplicated findings. These studies have in common the investigation of formal academic experiences and identity formation. Gurin, Peng, Lopez, and Nagda (1999), for example, found that participation in the Intergroup Relations, Conflict, and Community Program at the University of Michigan was associated with both opportunities for racial identity development and more positive intergroup racial-ethnic attitudes. This intergroup program provided carefully balanced, racially-ethnically mixed groups of first-year students with reading materials, lectures, and discussions about the histories of ethnic and racial groups in the United States, theories of group conflict, and strategies for conflict management. Over the 10-week period of the program and subsequently throughout their college years, participants showed significantly more positive intergroup perceptions than did nonparticipants, even after controlling race-ethnicity, gender, college residence hall, and precourse psychological openness to others. The findings suggest that the program may also have provided students of color with particular opportunities for later-stage identity development through the inclusion of others of a different race-ethnicity.

Other research reports that membership in racial-ethnic organizations also appears to promote racial identity development and comfort with that identity (Hurtado, Milem, Clayton-Pedersen, & Allen, 1999; Mitchell & Dell, 1992) and that White students may derive racial identity benefits through participation in multicultural training activities (Parker, Moore, & Neimeyer, 1998).

Self-Concept and Self-Esteem. Ample evidence suggests that students develop more positive self-concepts and greater self-confidence during the college years and that institutional environments and cultures shape student change more powerfully than conventional structural or organizational characteristics such as type, control, size, or selectivity. The considerable evidence on the effects of different college experiences on student self-concepts supports these conclusions.

Academic self-concept. Studies of freshman- to senior-year changes in students' academic or intellectual self-concepts point to the importance of student interactions with the primary agents of socialization during college—peers and faculty members—as well as to the settings where those encounters occur. Few studies examined whether peers or faculty members were the more influential group, but there can be little doubt that student contact with peers plays a central role in how students think about themselves. Most of these studies rely on data from surveys for the Cooperative Institutional Research Program at the University of California at Los Angeles' Higher Education Research Institute. These databases are made up of large, nationally representative samples of students surveyed on entry at several hundred four-year institutions and again four years later. The criterion variables are usually either individual items based on self-reports of characteristics such as their academic ability, intellectual self-confidence, or mathematical ability or composite scales of these or similar items.

Whatever the measure, the evidence consistently indicates freshman- to senior-year increases in academic self-confidence are positively associated with student-student interactions, even after adjusting for a battery of background characteristics, including initial academic self-concept, institutional characteristics, and other college experiences (Astin, 1993c; Szelenyi, 2002). With a few exceptions (such as Berger & Milem, 2000a), studies consistently show that socializing with peers, regardless of the setting, enhances students' academic self-concepts. Studies report positive effects on academic self-concept associated with tutoring another student, discussing course content with other students, participating in student government or other organized activities, and participating in a campus protest as well as working part-time on campus (Astin, 1993c; Berger, 2000a; Sax, 1994d, 1994e; Szelenyi, 2002). The effects may be particularly powerful when the interactions involve discussions with peers of another racial-ethnic group or conversations with peers on issues relating to race and ethnicity (Chang, 1996, 1997, 1999a, 2001; Gurin, 1999). These interactions mediate the effects of an institution's structural diversity, which influences the extent of students' contacts and conversations with peers of different racial-ethnic and cultural backgrounds. Although the evidence consistently indicates the presence of direct effects of social interactions, the impact is small. Antonio (1995; Antonio & Lopez, 1999) traced the peer effects to students' immediate friendship groups, although his evidence suggested the effects may vary depending on students' race-ethnicity and the racial composition of their friendship groups.

According to the research, the consequences of students' contacts with faculty members are similar to those stemming from student-peer interactions. Students derive statistically significant and net benefits from talking with faculty members outside class, interacting with faculty they perceive to be supportive and intellectually challenging, being a guest in a faculty member's home, helping teach a course, and working on a faculty member's research project (Astin, 1993c; Berger & Milem, 2000a; Chang, 1997; Szelenyi, 2002).

Several carefully designed studies have examined the effects of the environment in various academic disciplines on psychosocial outcomes (Feldman, Ethington, & Smart, 2001; Feldman, Smart, & Ethington, 1999; Smart, Feldman, & Ethington,

2000; Smart & Feldman, 1998). These studies are based on Holland's theory of careers and occupational choice (Holland, 1997), which holds that the intersection and degree of congruence between and among six personality types and six analogous environments shape occupational and other outcomes.[7] Applying Holland's theory to academic disciplines, Feldman and his colleagues found that "investigative" students (identified by using a composite measure reflecting students' self-assessments of their intellectual self-confidence, academic ability, math ability, drive to achieve, and expectations of making a contribution to science) majoring in investigative disciplinary environments not only entered college scoring higher on measures of these interests and abilities but also gained more in those same areas than did noninvestigative students in other environments. The evidence also indicates a socialization effect: students who enter an incongruent environment may enter with lower levels of interest and ability in the areas that are central to that particular environment than do students whose interests and abilities are congruent with those environments, but over time incongruent students appear to increase in those same interest and ability areas at about the same rates as congruent students. This finding holds in four of the six Holland environments tested (Feldman et al., 2001) and are consistent with the proposition that students' interactions with faculty members and other students are a significant influence on the kinds of changes students experience.

One aspect of this academic climate issue concerns whether students will be adversely affected when other members of their gender are underrepresented in a major. The question has attracted particular attention as it relates to women in the sciences and engineering. In a series of well-executed studies using nationally representative databases, Sax (1994a, 1994b, 1996b) found that, after controlling students' background characteristics (including academic self-concept), major field, and other college involvement variables, the proportion of women in a major had minimal impact on academic self-concepts. Where an effect was identified, it was positive for both males and females. In addition, majoring in engineering and business had modest and positive net effects on women's math self-concepts (Sax, 1994d).

The nature of the processes underlying the beneficial outcomes associated with students' contact with their peers and with faculty members has not been clearly explicated. Nonetheless, the interactions that seem to lead to enhanced academic self-concept all involve students' encounters with people different from themselves or those with different knowledge, ideas, or beliefs. These encounters have the potential to stimulate reflection on students' knowledge and currently held beliefs and values and, perhaps, lead to new ways of thinking about and understanding the world and others.

Net gains in students' positive academic self-concepts have also been linked to other college experiences, including participation in both generic community service and service learning (Astin & Sax, 1998), participation in ethnic studies courses and cultural awareness workshops (Chang, 1996), involvement in cocurricular activities (Berger, 2002; Kezar & Moriarty, 2000; Kim & Alvarez,

1995), and instructors' use of active and collaborative instructional methods and the frequency and nature of their feedback to students (Colbeck, Cabrera, & Terenzini, 2001). Participation in intercollegiate athletics has no apparent effects, positive or negative, direct or indirect, on students' intellectual self-confidence (Pascarella & Smart, 1991).

Social self-concept. Although somewhat smaller in volume, the research on within-college effects on students' social self-concept leads generally to the same conclusions as studies of shifts in academic self-concept. Both academic and nonacademic experiences are factors in shaping students' self-concepts.

Numerous college experiences appear to have positive net impacts on students' social self-confidence and perceptions of their popularity. Studies of academic-related factors suggest that participating in "educating for success" programs (Betz & Schifano, 2000; Swell, 1992), working on group projects in courses (Kezar & Moriarty, 2000), and the percentage of women in one's major field all have positive net effects on students' social self-concepts (Sax, 1994b, 1996b). One study found no social self-concept benefits from study abroad (Laubscher, 1994). Where positive effects are found, however, they tend to be small.

Out-of-class experiences and activities are also linked to enhanced social self-concepts. For example, after adjusting for students' initial self-concepts and other precollege characteristics, as well as for institutional characteristics and other college involvement variables, socializing with peers has a significant, positive, and direct (if small) effect on freshman- to senior-year increases in social self-concepts (Chang, 1997, 1999a, 2001; Kezar & Moriarty, 2000). Chang's studies suggest that discussing racial-ethnic topics also has a positive but indirect effect on social self-concept as well as on academic self-concept (Chang, 1997, 1999a, 2001). Other out-of-class activities that promote positive social self-concept include interactions with faculty members (Kezar & Moriarty, 2000), community service and volunteer work (Astin & Sax, 1998; Kezar & Moriarty, 2000), leadership experiences (Whitt, 1994), and participation in intercollegiate athletics (Kezar & Moriarty, 2000; Pascarella & Smart, 1991).

Self-esteem. Knox, Lindsay, and Kolb (1993) was the only study we identified that tested for within-college effects on overall self-esteem in a large, nationally representative sample. Using data from more than 5,000 participants in the National Longitudinal Study of the High School Class of 1972, who were surveyed at high school graduation and again 2 and 14 years later, Knox and his colleagues found no statistically significant net effect of selected college experiences on self-esteem. The factors examined included academic major, living on campus, and grade performance during college. Knox et al. did report a strong correlation between pre- and postcollege self-esteem scores, indicating considerable stability over time.

Other studies report a positive association between other college experiences and increased self-esteem, including generally consistent evidence that service learning enhances self-esteem and a sense of self-worth (Rama, Ravenscroft, Wolcott, & Zlotkowski, 2000; Shumer & Belbas, 1996). Using an experimental design, however, Osborne and colleagues (Osborne, Hammerich, & Hensley,

1998) found that students randomly assigned to a service-learning project as part of a course showed statistically significant declines in their scores on Rosenberg's Self-Esteem Scale compared with students assigned to another, non–service-learning project. The researchers suggest their findings may reflect "realistic" self-assessments on the part of students.

Studies of whether instructional approaches influence self-esteem also yield mixed findings. Some evidence indicates that students enrolled in clustered courses (the same group of students taking the same two or more related courses) derived no statistically significant advantages in self-esteem compared with students in unclustered courses. Indeed, some evidence suggests that cluster course enrollment may even depress self-esteem scores (Toth, 1996). An explanation for this finding does not come immediately to mind, although students who consider themselves less capable or successful than other students in one course would be likely to feel similarly when in another course with the same students. Other studies indicate no significant gains in self-esteem accruing to students in Supplemental Instruction courses versus those in other courses once precollege self-evaluations have been taken into account (Visor, Johnson, & Cole, 1992b). Two meta-analyses suggest that students taught using active and collaborative or other small-group pedagogical methods show significantly larger net gains on measures of self-worth than do similar students exposed to traditional pedagogies (Johnson, Johnson, & Smith, 1998a; Springer, Stanne, & Donovan, 1999). Johnson et al. estimate that students taught using cooperative learning approaches gain in self-esteem by .47 of a standard deviation (18 percentile points) more than similar students taught by instructors who use more competitive approaches and by .27 of a standard deviation (11 percentile points) more than students in individual learning settings. These studies suggest that cooperative and group approaches boost self-esteem by increasing student interest in learning and the quality of their social adjustment and support. Informal faculty contact—a likely consequence of such instructional approaches—also promotes student feelings of self-affirmation, confidence, and self-worth (Kuh, 1995).

Autonomy and Locus of Control. Several studies that examined the within-college effects on student autonomy and locus of control report mixed findings. Most explored the effects of volunteer activities and service-learning courses. In their two-year study of nearly 1,800 students on 18 four-year campuses, Pierson and Pascarella (2002) found that volunteer activities had no statistically significant effect on internal locus of attribution for academic success after taking into account a battery of precollege characteristics (including initial locus of attribution score), institutional characteristics, and measures of other forms of academic and social engagement. Astin, Vogelgesang, Ideka, and Yee (2000), however, report that community service has a positive net effect on students' sense of self-efficacy.

Service activities that are well integrated into an academic course may have greater impact than generic volunteer activities, but even for such service-learning courses the evidence is mixed. Some studies report no statistically significant service learning effects on self-efficacy (Astin et al., 2000; Kendrick, 1996), whereas others report finding effects. Eyler and Giles (1999), for example, in a study of more than 1,100 students on 20 college and university campuses found significantly greater increases in self-efficacy among students in service-learning courses than among students with no service-learning experiences. The effects persisted even after statistical adjustments for precourse differences in age, gender, race-ethnicity, family income, and other community service while in college. The differences in these findings may be due at least in part to their different methodologies. Astin et al.'s students reported whether they had had service-learning experiences, but these experiences were not linked to specific courses, as they were in the Eyler and Giles study. Moreover, the net effect of the service-learning experiences in the Astin et al. study was minimal ($p < .05$) in a study with a large sample, making detection of small effects more likely. Also, Astin and his colleagues had set their standard for significance at $p < .01$. The evidence appears to suggest that service-learning courses have an impact on students' sense of control over their lives, but that conclusion must be considered tentative.

Other studies point to positive influences from other aspects of students' academic experiences on different dimensions of independence. Visor et al. (1992b) cast some doubt on whether Supplemental Instruction has a net impact on students' locus of control, at least in an introductory psychology course. A larger nationally representative and well-controlled study did find statistically significant and positive net effects after one year associated with the number of courses taken (Pascarella, Edison, Hagedorn, Nora, & Terenzini, 1996). This study also found that the quality of the instruction received had a positive net impact on students' internal locus of attribution for academic success. This finding suggests that effective teaching may not only enhance student learning but also bolster students' belief that they are capable and can control their own academic performance. Volkwein (1991) also reports finding positive net effects of students' classroom experiences on students' sense of responsibility, self-discipline, and self-reliance. Other researchers found evidence of positive impacts of study abroad on students' independence and self-reliance (Laubscher, 1994) and of leadership experiences on students' sense of self-efficacy (Whitt, 1994).

Studies of the effects of peer relations and participation in extracurricular activities indicate these factors have a positive influence on students' sense of autonomy, as measured by the Student Development Task and Lifestyle Inventory and the Iowa Developing Autonomy Inventory (Cooper, Healy, & Simpson, 1994; Smith & Griffin, 1993; Taub, 1995). In the Cooper et al. and Taub studies, these effects persisted even with controls for such other factors as age, race-ethnicity, residence status (on campus versus commuting), and (in Cooper et al.) precollege level of autonomy.

Membership in a Greek-letter social society appears not to have any statistically significant net effect on measures of peer independence (Baier & Whipple, 1990; Wilder & McKeegan, 1999) or on internal locus of attribution for academic success (Pascarella, Edison, Hagedorn, Nora, & Terenzini, 1996). The Baier and Whipple study does contain evidence suggesting that in the early years independents may be less susceptible to the influence of their families than are fraternity and sorority members, although the gap disappears in the later college years. The authors do not report whether that finding is statistically significant.

Whether living on or off campus affects locus of control remains uncertain. Students living off campus in Greek society housing showed greater freshman-to junior-year increases in measures of locus of control than other off-campus residents but no greater gains than independents living on campus (Erwin & Love, 1989). Knox, Lindsay, and Kolb (1993) found no statistically significant net effect of on-campus living on locus of control, but their posttest measure was taken 10 years after college graduation, leaving open the possibility that any effects of place of residence during college could be attenuated by time and other postcollege experiences.

After both one year (Pascarella, Edison, Hagedorn, Nora, & Terenzini, 1996) and three years (Wolniak, Pierson, & Pascarella, 2001), male intercollegiate athletes show net gains in internal locus of attribution for academic success that are equivalent to gains of similar students who are not intercollegiate athletes. In both of these nationally representative, multicampus, longitudinal samples, it seemed not to matter whether the athletes were involved in revenue-producing or other sports.

Interpersonal Relations and Leadership Skills. More studies examined within-college effects on the development of students' interpersonal relations during the 1990s than before, but inconsistent findings leave the picture clouded. For example, three well-done, large, nationally representative studies that examined the effects of participation in community activities and service learning reached different conclusions. Astin (1998) found that community service enhanced all but one measure of "life skills," including interpersonal skills, among a cohort of students surveyed when they entered college in 1990 and again four years later. The effects of service were evident even after adjustments for students' initial interpersonal skills and other precollege characteristics, features of the institutions attended, and other college experiences. Gray and her associates (1999, 2000), using a sample of more than 1,300 students on 28 campuses, found fairly clear evidence of the positive net effects of service-learning (versus traditional) courses on several measures of life skills, including interpersonal relations. Vogelgesang and Astin (2000), in contrast, using another large, representative sample, report that participation in service-learning courses showed no greater impact after four years than did generic forms of service. The variations in findings are difficult to explain, but differences in samples, designs, and the measures of service, service learning, and criterion variables are all possibilities.

It may also be that college's impacts on students' interpersonal skills are cumulative rather than specific to a single course or other short-term experience. Some evidence indicates, for example, that fraternity or sorority members may experience greater gains in interpersonal skills than nonmembers (Hunt &

Rentz, 1994; Pike, 2000), although the effects of membership net of other considerations, while small, are statistically significant. Similar benefits may accrue to intercollegiate athletes (Ryan, 1989), but Cooper, Healy, and Simpson (1994) found no evidence over a three-year period of any association between involvement in other cocurricular activities and students' interpersonal skills.

Studies of within-college effects defined more broadly report generally consistent and positive findings (Grayson, 1999; Hurtado, 2001; Kuh, 1995; Martin, 2000). These investigations all indicate that the frequency of students' interactions with other students is associated with reported gains in interpersonal skills, even after other influences are taken into account. Grayson found peer interactions more influential than interactions involving faculty members. The nature of these interactions and their settings, moreover, vary across studies, prompting speculation that gains in interpersonal skills may be due more to the cumulative effect of interpersonal contacts than to specific forms or settings for such contacts.

Studies of within-college effects on students' leadership skills, including the effects of community service in general and service learning in particular, have produced mixed results. Among the largest investigations with the best controls, most report finding a positive influence of some kind of service on leadership, even when controlling for a wide range of other personal, institutional, and experiential influences (Astin, 1993c, 1996b; Astin & Sax, 1998; Astin et al., 2000). Other well-done studies, however, report finding positive effects of service learning on a variety of attitudes but that service-learning experiences afforded no particular advantages over generic service activities in leadership skill development (Astin et al., 2000; Vogelgesang & Astin, 2000). The explanation may lie in the details of students' generic and service learning activities and experiences. For example, the nature or level of responsibility in the two forms of service may have been too similar to produce differences in leadership skills.

Studies of programs or educational experiences specifically designed to promote leadership skills consistently show that such interventions are successful (Astin & Cress, 1998; Cress et al., 2001; Kezar & Moriarty, 2000; Whitt, 1994). These studies examine the effectiveness of various classes, programs, or experiences on such outcomes as decision-making skills, willingness to take risks, tolerance for ambiguity and complexity, conflict resolution skills, program planning and implementation abilities, understanding leadership theories, and self-assessed leadership skills. Leadership classes had a statistically significant, positive net impact on gains in leadership for both males and females, and for students of color as well as Whites, although some evidence suggests that men may derive greater benefits from such classes than women.

Although the public in general, and collegiate sports backers in particular, may believe that participation in intercollegiate athletics promotes leadership skills, the jury is still out on this claim. Ryan (1989) found that, even with pre-college leadership abilities and 49 other variables controlled, participation in intercollegiate athletics was positively, although modestly, associated with leadership development. But more recent evidence, also from a large, national study,

concluded that any inclinations to leadership on the part of intercollegiate athletes were not reflected subsequently on any of several measures of actual leadership (Shulman & Bowen, 2001). Studies of the impact of club or intramural
athletic participation on leadership skills also show mixed results. One investigation revealed no relation between sports involvement and development of
leadership skills (Cornelius, 1995), while a national study reported statistically
significant and positive net effects from playing intramural sports (Astin, 1993c).

A small body of evidence suggests that membership in Black fraternities and
sororities may have a positive influence on leadership development (Kimbrough,
1995; Kimbrough & Hutcheson, 1998). These studies are cross-sectional, however, and employ no controls for the effects of self-selection. Controlled studies of
the effects of participation in ethnic-racial student organizations on the leadership skills of students of color find only weak evidence after one year (Trevino,
1992) and stronger signs after four years (Antonio, 1998, 2000), suggesting that
such participation contributes directly to leadership skill development. Most of
the four-year differences relating to level of participation, however, were attributable to students' precollege leadership and related abilities.

Studies of leadership skill development suggest that college's impacts, with the
exception of leadership programs, are more likely general than specific. The effects
may also be a product of students' overall contact with peers, although no study
explores that possibility directly. In his study of over 4,000 students in four-year
institutions over a four-year period, and net of a host of students' precollege characteristics (including initial leadership skills) as well as institutional characteristics,
Astin (1993c) found the strongest effects on leadership skill formation associated
with students' interactions with peers. The forms and locations of such interactions varied, including fraternity or sorority membership, intramural sports participation, and active involvement in the classroom, such as making presentations
and working on group projects. Other studies report findings consistent with
Astin's regarding students' peer interaction and fraternity or sorority membership
(Sax & Astin, 1998), discussing racial-ethnic topics and studying with others of a
different race-ethnicity (Antonio, 1998, 2000; Astin, 1992; Hurtado, 2001), participating in cultural awareness workshops (Antonio, 1998, 2000), majoring in
"enterprising" disciplines that emphasize goal achievement or economic gain,
speaking and persuasion skills, or leadership abilities (Kezar & Moriarty, 2000;
Smart, 1997; Smart et al., 2000), and holding a leadership position while in college (Antonio, 2000; Astin & Cress, 1998; Smart et al., 2002). Studies indicate
that students' interactions with faculty members also have statistically significant and positive net effects (Astin, 1993c; Sax & Astin, 1998). By one estimate,
however, the impact of peer contact may be as much as twice that of students'
interactions with faculty members outside the classroom (Astin, 1992).

General Personal Development. With a few exceptions, most of the studies of
students' gains in their personal development are based on Pace's College Student Experiences Questionnaire (Pace, 1984), which contains a five-item scale
reflecting the progress students report making since they enrolled at an insti-

tution. The component items deal with gains in developing values and ethical standards, self-understanding, ability to get along with different kinds of people, functioning effectively in a group, and developing good health habits and physical fitness. Even after adjusting for an array of other factors (students' initial level of personal development is frequently missing), these studies consistently find that the effort invested in various academic and social activities is positively related to gains in personal development whether the students attend a two-year institution (Glover, 1996; Plomin, 1997) or a four-year college or university (Arnold, Kuh, Vesper, & Schuh, 1993; Davis & Murrell, 1993; Kaufman & Creamer, 1991; Kuh & Hu, 2001; MacKay & Kuh, 1994). Moreover, these studies indicate that students' interactions with their peers are the dominant force involved. The impact of student-faculty contact is less clear: some studies report that such contact has a significant and positive net effect on students' personal development (Berger & Milem, 2000a; Pace, 1995), whereas other analyses find no link (Kuh & Hu, 2001).

More specific aspects of students' college experiences also appear to affect personal development. Although only a few studies have examined the relation between personal development and students' exposure to active and collaborative instructional practices in their courses, the findings all point to the presence of such an impact (Berger & Milem, 2000a; Cabrera, Nora, Bernal, Terenzini, & Pascarella, 1998; Pace, 1995). The effects of these instructional procedures persist after adjustments for a number of potentially confounding variables. Other positive sources of influence on social and personal development include on-campus residence (Blimling, 1993), fraternity or sorority membership (Hayek, Carini, O'Day, & Kuh, 2002), and study abroad (Ryan & Twibell, 2000; Zorn, 1996). As a group, these studies controlled for a number of potentially confounding factors, but only Berger and Milem also took into account the students' level of personal development at the time they entered college. Consequently, it remains unclear whether the effects discussed here are, in fact, the effects of colleges or reflections of students' readiness for psychosocial change.

CONDITIONAL EFFECTS OF COLLEGE

Conclusions from *How College Affects Students*

Pre-1990 studies of conditional college effects on psychosocial changes focused almost exclusively on gender-related differences, leaving aside the questions of whether sex is differentially related to the degree of change in students' identity status or ego development. Some studies suggested that males experience greater gains than females during the traditional college years, whereas other inquiries reported no differential effects. The evidence more consistently suggested that, with salient student background and institutional characteristics held constant, college's effects on academic and social self-concepts were general, being about the same for all students, rather than conditional and varying by gender. Differences by sex and by race-ethnicity in rates of change in social (but not academic) self-concept appeared to be associated with certain college experiences. Social leadership or involvement, for example, had a stronger positive effect for African-American men than for White men and for African-American men compared with African-American women. Academic integration appeared to have a greater impact on Black women than Black men, and majoring in a scientific or technical field was linked to greater declines in social self-concepts among White men than among White women. What limited evidence existed hinted at no gender-related difference in self-esteem related to educational attainment.

We found nothing to support confident conclusions about conditional college effects on such dimensions of students' relational systems as autonomy, independence, or locus of control; authoritarianism, dogmatism, or ethnocentrism; intellectual orientation; interpersonal relations; psychological adjustment and well-being; or general personal development. Numerous studies examined changes in these areas among women and men, but few tested whether the *degree* of change differed at a statistically significant level by gender. Studies that tested such interaction effects concentrated on changes in autonomy or locus of control. The only nationally representative study on this topic found that women made slightly larger gains than men during college, but a number of single-institution studies produced conflicting findings. Some found no gender differences, whereas others reported larger gains among males; still others found larger gains among females. We concluded that the study of conditional college effects in these areas was largely uncharted research territory.

Evidence from the 1990s

Identity Development. Constantinople (1969) found that men displayed greater gains in identity development during four years of college than did women. When Whitbourne, Jelsma, and Waterman (1982) reanalyzed Constantinople's data, along with information from another cohort, they concluded that the differences Constantinople observed between the sexes across the college years were more likely due to cohort effects than to gender. Zuschlag and Whitbourne (1994) studied a third cohort in a replication of the earlier investigations, thus working with a three-wave, cross-sectional design. In all three studies, the criterion variable was level of identity development using a measure of the successful resolution of Erikson's fourth, fifth, and sixth crises, the fifth being identity versus identity confusion. Although finding statistically significant differences across the three cohorts relating to class year (seniors generally had higher scores than younger students) and gender (women showed generally higher development than men), the sex-by-year interaction, which would show differential, gender-related effects, was nonsignificant. The finding suggests that the effects of the overall college experience are general rather than conditional on gender. Cokley (1999), in a study of African-American identity development, also found no differential, gender-related effects across college years.

We identified only one study of differential effects associated with specific college experiences. Kilgannon and Erwin (1992) tested for conditional effects associated with membership in a fraternity or sorority. After adjusting for precollege level of identity development, they found that after two years fraternity members scored lower than male nonmembers, sorority members, and female independents on the "confidence" component of a measure of identity.

Overall, it appears that although men and women may enter college at different levels of identity development, they probably change to about the same degree during the college years. But this conclusion is tentative because few studies examine this process, and those that do are based on small, single-institution samples. In addition, most leave students' initial identity development status uncontrolled. Thus, as in our previous review, whether college's effects on students' identity development vary with either gender or race-ethnicity remains largely an unanswered question.

Self-Concept and Self-Esteem. Four studies examined conditional effects associated with various dimensions of students' academic or intellectual self-concept, but any synthesis is difficult because each study explored the potential conditional impacts of different college experiences. Nonetheless, we summarize them here to emphasize that, even if we cannot say with confidence which student trait or experience may have a differential impact on a particular outcome, there is good reason to believe that at least some college experiences may affect different kinds of students differently. Only replication can help separate artifacts from real effects.

In a two-year study of the influences of friendship groups on students' intellectual self-confidence, Antonio (1999) found that the racial-ethnic diversity of a student's immediate friendship group had a different impact on the intellectual self-confidence of African-American and of White students. As the friendship group's diversity increased, White students' intellectual self-evaluations declined at a marginally significant rate, whereas the self-confidence of minority students rose significantly. These effects were apparent even with controls in place for students' precollege intellectual self-confidence, other background characteristics, and other group experiences.

Analyses of major field–related conditional effects provide evidence of gender-related differences (Sax, 1994e; Smart et al., 2000; Smart & Feldman, 1998). Sax studied both major field– and gender-related differences on students' math self-concepts. Although students majoring in math and science generally begin college highly confident in their math skills and maintain that confidence during college, students in other fields both enter with less math self-confidence and lose much of the precollege confidence they had in those skills while in college. Women majoring in math-intensive fields, however, appear to gain in math self-confidence during college at higher rates than men, with the initial male-female confidence gap among math and science majors nearly disappearing after four years. This finding is probably attributable both to practice and to an environment that reinforces women students' initial interests and abilities and where those interests and abilities are shared and valued by others.

The studies by Smart and his colleagues (Smart et al., 2000; Smart & Feldman, 1998) point precisely to such environmental effects in several (but not all) academic disciplinary environments categorized according to Holland's theory of career choice, described in an earlier section of this chapter. The theoretical expectation is that academic environments exhibit distinctive patterns of values, abilities, and behaviors, that students seek out and enter the environments most congruent with their interests and abilities, and that those initial differences are accentuated over time, even when precollege differences on a number of relevant variables (including initial interests and abilities) are controlled. The Smart group's analyses generally support these expectations, and the effects appear by and large to be general, rather than conditional on gender, with one exception: Smart et al. (2000) found the weakest support for Holland's theory as it relates to "social" academic environments. These disciplines emphasize mentoring, helping others, interpersonal skills, friendliness, and sensitivity to others. Over a four-year period in such settings, men change as Holland's theory would predict, showing net gains in these interest and skill areas relative to peers in other environments. In contrast, women in these social environments show much weaker gains when compared with similar women in other disciplines. The difference between women in social environments and those in other environments was small initially, and the separation increased only slightly over the four years of the study.

In the only other study found that looked for differential effects of a college experience on students' self-concept, Pascarella and Smart (1991) explored whether intercollegiate athletic participation might have a different effect on the intellectual and social self-concepts of White and minority male students. In this study of male students from the time they entered college to five years after graduation, these researchers controlled for 11 precollege characteristics, including initial self-concepts, socioeconomic status, degree aspirations, and various attitudes and values, as well as admissions selectivity and other institutional characteristics, and measures of postcollege status attainment and social and political values. After adjustments for these factors, Pascarella and Smart found, with one exception, no statistically significant interactions between intercollegiate sports participation and any of the precollege student characteristics or institutional selectivity within groups of White and African-American students. They did find a significant interaction between race-ethnicity and intercollegiate athletic participation, with significantly stronger positive direct and indirect effects on both social and academic self-concepts for African Americans than for Caucasians.

A search identified only one study that explored conditional college effects on self-esteem (Knox et al., 1993). Our earlier review concluded that college appeared to have no appreciably different impact on the self-esteem of women versus men. Knox and his colleagues, however, suggest otherwise. Although the net effect is small, they found that 14 years after graduating from high school, women with two or more years of college showed significantly greater gains in self-esteem than did men. The trend was similar but statistically nonsignificant at other levels of education. Relaxing the criterion for statistical significance to $p < .10$, however, it appears that earning an advanced degree provides a slightly greater boost in self-esteem to women than to men. But Knox and his colleagues left postcollege experiences (such as employment) uncontrolled, and thus the advantages of college that appear to accrue to women may also reflect those influences.

Locus of Control. A number of studies done since 1990 examine conditional college effects on students' locus of control. These studies use nationally representative samples, a battery of relevant variables and sound measures, and appropriate analytical procedures. Despite these advantages, however, the research highlights the difficulty not only of identifying conditional effects but also of replicating them with different samples or somewhat different measures. Knox, Lindsay, and Kolb (1993), for example, analyzed data from the National Longitudinal Study of the High School Class of 1972. With controls in place for gender, race-ethnicity, high school rank in class, academic ability, and family socioeconomic status, Knox et al. found no appreciable difference at each successive level of postsecondary education in the rates at which men and women moved toward an internal locus of control over the 14-year period after high school. Whites and Blacks also gained in internal locus of control at about the same rate as they achieved successively higher levels of education. These findings, however, have not been replicated.

Studies by Pascarella and various colleagues provide an extended look at differential effects on locus of attribution for academic success associated with student characteristics and with attendance at two-year versus four-year institutions. Although the findings vary, some consistency is discernible. Pascarella, Bohr, Nora, Raganathan, Desler, and Bulakowski (1994) first examined whether the type of institution students attend has an effect after one year on their internal locus of attribution, which varies depending on a number of precollege characteristics including students' initial locus of attribution for academic success. Despite differences in students' precollege traits and the kind of institution they attended, two-year and four-year students showed about the same degree of movement toward greater internality. In addition, the effects of institutional type were the same for students of different precollege levels of internality, ability, and age as well as for the number of courses they took and hours they worked. In an approximate replication of that study, Pierson, Wolniak, Pascarella, and Flowers (2003) used a design and instrumentation similar to the Pascarella et al. study (1994) but surveyed a nationally representative sample of more than 1,700 students from 18 four-year institutions and five community colleges over a two-year period. Like Pascarella et al., Pierson and his colleagues found no differences in the effects of attending a two-year or a four-year institution on internal attribution that varied with students' gender, race-ethnicity, socioeconomic status, age, or precollege academic motivation and ability. Thus, replicated evidence indicates that two-year and four-year institutions have about the same impact on internal locus of attribution for academic success during the first two years of college regardless of students' precollege locus of attribution, academic ability, or age.

Although student traits may not interact with the type of institution, some evidence suggests that the experiences students have at two-year and four-year schools may well vary in their impact on students' internal locus of attribution for academic success. Pascarella and colleagues (Pascarella, Edison, Hagedorn, Nora, & Terenzini, 1996), using the same data set as Pierson et al. (2003), found several college experiences common to both two-year and four-year institutions that produced more positive effects on two-year students than on similar students at four-year schools. In some cases, the two-year institutional advantages were substantially greater. Honors program participation, fraternity or sorority membership, hours worked, and teachers' instructional skills and clarity all had more positive first-year effects on community college students. Instructor skill and clarity, for example, was nearly eight times more positive for two-year students than for their four-year counterparts. Only in the number of essays written did four-year institutions produce more positive effects than two-year colleges on students' internal attributions. Such assignments had a negative effect after one year on community college students' locus of attribution for academic performance. Pascarella and his colleagues had no ready explanation for the more positive associations between community college attendance and internal attributions, although they posit that the explanation may lie in differences in the quality of the teaching reported by students at the two kinds of institutions.

Pascarella, Edison, Hagedorn, Nora, and Terenzini (1996) also report evidence indicating that different kinds of students may respond differently to selected college experiences during their first year and that these varied reactions may differentially shape internal locus of attribution for academic success. Race-related differential net effects were linked to credit hours taken and number of hours worked per week (in both instances, non-White students derived greater benefits than White students from the hours invested). Men gained greater internality than women from active participation in the classroom, and younger students gained more than older ones from being in an honors program. Fraternity or sorority membership negatively affected the internality of younger students but had the opposite impact on older students. An explanation for these findings is elusive.

Some evidence suggests that students who are the first generation in their families to attend college respond differently to certain college experiences than do similar students with one or both parents who have had some college experience or hold a bachelor's degree. After taking into account an array of students' precollege characteristics (including level of internal locus of attribution for academic success, cognitive development, parents' income, degree aspirations, academic motivation, secondary school achievement, gender, and age), Pascarella, Pierson, Wolniak, and Terenzini (2004) found that first-generation students gained more than other students in internal locus of attribution from a number of second- and third-year experiences. The number of courses taken in mathematics, the social sciences, and the arts and humanities had significantly more positive impact after two years on the internal locus of attribution for academic success among first-generation students than on their non-first-generation peers. First-generation students also derived more positive benefits in internal attribution than other students from their academic effort and involvement in the third year and from extracurricular involvement in both their second and third years. London (1996) concluded from interviews with first-generation students that "the most commonly reported change, regardless of age, gender, or race, is an enhanced self-esteem . . . born of a growing sense of competence and mastery" (p. 12).

Not all first-year experiences had differentially positive effects. Pascarella, Pierson, Wolniak, and Terenzini (2004) also reported that in both the second and third years the number of hours students worked had a statistically significant and negative impact on internal locus of attribution for academic success among first-generation students but not on similar non-first-generation students. Likewise, doing volunteer work had a negative impact on internal attribution among first-generation students but a positive effect on other students during the third year. It may be that the hours spent working and doing volunteer work reduces both the time available and the level of involvement of first-generation students in on-campus academic and nonacademic activities, perhaps isolating them from broad exposure to other students and to the larger campus culture. One of the most striking features of Pascarella et al.'s findings is that first-generation students derived greater benefits in terms of their sense of control over their own academic fate *despite* their tendency, on average, to be less involved in campus activities than other students.

LONG-TERM COLLEGE EFFECTS

Conclusions from *How College Affects Students*

Few studies before 1990 looked at the long-term effects of college on ego or identity development. What evidence existed indicated that the net effects of college on academic and social self-concept were still apparent nearly a decade after graduation, even when holding constant students' precollege characteristics, various features of the institutions attended, and postcollege occupational status. College's long-term impact on academic self-concept appeared to be indirect rather than direct and to apply more to White than to minority students. College's influences on social self-concept were only marginally more general or direct. The indirect effects appeared to be mediated through postcollege occupational status. Statistically significant, if small, beneficial net college effects in self-esteem were also found in the pre-1990 research, with the greatest benefits going to students who persisted into the upper-division years or went on to graduate or professional school.

Positive long-term effects of college, although small, were still apparent 7 and 14 years after graduation. We also identified evidence of stability in graduates' levels of authoritarianism 3, 5, and 10 years after graduation, with limited evidence hinting at drops in intellectual orientation, somewhat higher levels of personal integration, and lower levels of stress and anxiety compared with measures in these graduates' senior year. Controls for occupational status reduced but did not eliminate these long-term educational effects on psychological well-being overall.

Evidence from the 1990s

A review of the long-term effects of college attendance on identity formation (and other aspects of psychosocial development) draws one toward the intimidatingly extensive literature on adult development. The number of nontraditional-age students and life span theories of development have increased dramatically over the past three decades (see Merriam & Caffarella, 1999; Tennant & Pogson, 1995). The adult development literature, however, covers broad developmental issues extending well beyond the purpose of this book, drawing on theory and research in biology, education, philosophy, psychology, sociology, and other fields as well as on the web of their interconnections. The focus of much of that literature, moreover, is on human development per se during the adult years. Although some of the research necessarily (or opportunistically) examines the development of people who have attended college, the effects of people's college experiences is generally not a central point of interest. Thus, our review of the literature will focus on studies dealing specifically with the long-term effects of college, insofar as they can be discerned, on various dimensions of psychosocial development.

Identity Development. The evidence concerning identity development among college students in their postcollege years comes primarily from Baxter Magolda (2001) and Josselson (1996), both of whom trace the identity development of a limited number of individuals (women only in Josselson's study), all college graduates. Thus, partitioning the effects of college from those of normal adult maturation or sociohistorical events in these studies is problematic. Josselson articulates the challenge: "People, of course, grow within a culture. Identity is what we make of ourselves within a society that is making something of us" (p. 28).

Baxter Magolda's research began in 1986 with 101 first-year students (51 of them male) entering Miami University of Ohio, a selective public institution with a liberal arts orientation (see Baxter Magolda, 1992b). She interviewed these students in succeeding years, and the 39 students who continued to participate in the project through Year 14 are the subjects of a series of qualitative studies of their postcollege years (Baxter Magolda, 1995, 1998, 1999a, 1999b, 1999c, 2000, 2001). These studies are noteworthy for the light they shine on how changes begun in college shape postcollege development and because they highlight the interconnections among the intellectual, intrapersonal, and interpersonal facets of development.

Baxter Magolda identified three questions that appear to frame progress toward what she calls "self-authorship," or "the capacity to internally define [one's] own beliefs, identity, and relationships" (Baxter Magolda, 2001, p. xvi; subsequent page and chapter references are to this book). These questions—"How do I know?" "Who am I?" "What relationships do I want with others?" (p. 4)—reflect cognitive, intrapersonal, and interpersonal dimensions of development that evolve to varying degrees and in interconnected ways during and after college.

According to Baxter Magolda, graduates pass through four phases as they move toward self-authorship. In the first phase, labeled "following external formulas," graduates persisted largely as they had during college, shaping their views of their worlds and themselves according to the views of others. In the second phase, "the crossroads," participants began to recognize the drawbacks of relying on others and the need to rely on themselves to answer the driving questions. In the third phase, "becoming the author of one's life," participants started making their own decisions about identity and how to interact with others. As "self-authoring" abilities developed, participants moved into the fourth phase, finding an "internal foundation" or sense of control over themselves and their world, a phase that generally had not stabilized by age 30. The experiences of Baxter Magolda's respondents suggest that college may launch complex interactions among the epistemological, intrapersonal, and interpersonal dimensions of psychosocial development that persist into early adulthood.[8]

Josselson interviewed 30 randomly selected women in 1972 when they were seniors on four different campuses and again when they were in their early 30s (Josselson, 1973) and in their 40s (Josselson, 1996). Josselson categorized her participants along two dimensions drawn from James Marcia's theory about how people resolve Erik Erikson's developmental fifth crisis (identity versus identity confusion). According to Marcia (1966, 1980), identity development is a function of whether an individual has undergone a period of identity exploration and made any firm commitments to an identity. Josselson found that the resulting identity statuses placed her seniors on one of four "path(s) to identity formation" (p. 35). As college seniors, "Guardians" had made largely unexamined commitments to an identity framed by their parents and found as adults that their earlier commitments had closed them off from themselves. Over time, Guardians grew more adventuresome and confident and more open to self as well as to new experiences. As seniors, "Pathmakers" had also made commitments to identities but only after passing through a period of identity exploration. As these graduates aged, they continued to explore and to grow, remaining fairly close to the identity they had achieved while in college but open to changes in their lives and sense of self. For "Searchers," who as seniors were actively engaged in identity exploration but had not yet internalized a more advanced sense of self, the searching and self-reflection continued into the adult years, often at the emotional expense of failing to achieve resolution. By their senior year, "Drifters" had neither actively explored their identities nor made any commitments. For them the adult years consisted of "quests for structure and stability" (p. 177).

Josselson notes that although resolution of Erikson's identity stage crisis is the central task of adolescence, when identity may be far more malleable than later in life, identity does not remain fixed. The underlying dynamic, as Josselson sees it, is "revision." Although the women she studied left college on different paths toward identity, Josselson found that whatever identity her participants defined, each achieved it by determining "both her competence—the regions where she can be effective and do things of value—and her connection—the people whom she chooses to make important in her life" (p. 178). The relevance of other people in this process is consistent with the salience of interpersonal relations in the postcollege identity development process that Baxter Magolda observed.

Self-Concept and Self-Esteem. Before 1990, several studies based on representative national samples produced evidence that college's impact on self-concepts was, indeed, durable, and further research since 1990 reports evidence of statistically significant, positive, and net effects of college on intellectual self-confidence five years after college graduation (Gurin, 1999) and on overall self-confidence 11 years out (Belfield et al., 1999). Gurin's findings are based on more than 9,000 students surveyed when they enrolled in nearly 200 four-year institutions and again four and nine years later. With controls in place for precollege student characteristics and institutional traits, Gurin found that college's long-term impact may be a function, at least in part, of students' interactions with peers from a racial-ethnic or cultural background different from their own. She found that institutional structural diversity (the proportional mix of students by racial-ethnic origins) positively, but indirectly, shaped the likelihood that students would interact with diverse peers. Such interactions, in turn, were positively linked to intellectual self-confidence five years after graduation. Some evidence, consistent with Gurin's concerning peer interactions and contact with people from different cultural backgrounds, indicates positive effects on self-concept 10 years after participation in a "semester-at-sea" program (Dukes, Johnson, & Newton, 1991). Pascarella and Smart (1991) found a positive and statistically significant total effect of intercollegiate participation on social self-concept among both African-American and White students nine years after college entry, although there were subtle differences related to race-ethnicity. For African-American students, the influence appears to be largely but not exclusively indirect through social involvement during college. Among White students, only the total effect was significant. Intercollegiate sports had no appreciable impact of any kind on the intellectual self-concepts of either African-American or White students. Only the Pascarella and Smart study took into account postcollege educational and occupational status attainment or income. The other studies thus leave open the possibility that the postbaccalaureate levels of self-concept and self-confidence observed may have been mediated, if not directly shaped, by students' academic, social, and occupational experiences and attainment after leaving college.

Knox, Lindsay, and Kolb (1993) studied the long-term impact of college on self-esteem using information from nearly 5,500 students in a representative, national sample of high school graduates surveyed when they graduated in 1972 and again in 1974 and 1986 when most participants were 32 years old. With controls in place for gender, race-ethnicity, academic ability, family socioeconomic status, and precollege self-esteem, Knox and his colleagues found no statistically significant relation between respondents' level of self-esteem and any of successively higher levels of educational attainment. The authors note, however, that the direction of the relationship was positive. They also noted that women were more likely than men to have shifted in a negative direction, and they suggest this finding may be attributable in part to the fact that the "emergence into adulthood in America in many respects favors men in contrast to women" (p. 125). When they restricted their analyses to those 1972 high school graduates who went on to college, Knox et al. found neither the characteristics of the institutions attended (including type, control, size, selectivity, percent residential, and mission) nor students' experiences while enrolled (including major field, living on campus, and academic performance) had any impact on self-esteem 14 years after leaving high school.

Several researchers examined the long-term effects on women's self-esteem from enrollment in a women's college (Miller-Bernal, 2000; Riordan, 1990). Relying on the same data set as Knox et al. (1993), Riordan found some evidence of a positive, institutional impact, but that effect disappeared when adjusted for academic ability and socioeconomic status. In a follow-up study of individuals who had been studied while they were in college, Miller-Bernal found high levels of self-esteem six years after graduation among all the alumnae of four liberal arts colleges, suggesting at least no postcollege declines. She found no differences across the institutions, which varied in their gender mixes.

Schuster, Langland, and Smith (1993) report links between attendance at women's colleges and levels of self-esteem and self-confidence 30 years later. Brown and Pacini (1993a) found high levels of self-esteem among a dozen female octogenarians who participated in studies prior to their graduation from Vassar College in the late 1920s and early 1930s. These post-1990 studies concentrated on women college graduates in their adult years, however, and provide no basis for linking self-esteem or other psychosocial developmental levels in the adult years to the college experience. Indeed, college attendance was a condition for participation in the study. Moreover, a central and compelling theme in these and other more recent studies of women college graduates in their adult years is the interlaced influences of college, maturation, and sociohistorical conditions during the periods studied (Schuster et al., 1993). The emphasis is on women's experiences and changes in their adult years, not on college's effects on these changes.

Based on the findings reviewed here, it appears that college has some durable impact on students' views of themselves, although the evidence is not compelling. The studies with the most controls report somewhat conflicting findings, although the differences might be a function of the cohorts studied or the time periods. Whether college triggers any postcollege shifts, or whether self-concepts stabilize after graduation, also remains unclear. More likely, college influences on postbaccalaureate levels of self-concept or self-esteem are mediated in as yet unexplored ways by subsequent personal, social, and occupational experiences.

Locus of Control. Some evidence from large, representative, national samples indicates that college may have durable effects on students' sense that they have some control over their lives. In addition to studying college's long-term effects on self-esteem, Knox, Lindsay, and Kolb (1993) tested for evidence of college influences 14 years after respondents had left high school. Their criterion measure was a four-item scale reflecting respondents' sense of what the authors label *self-direction,* which, as noted earlier, is a term similar to locus of control. After controlling for students' precollege gender, race-ethnicity, academic ability, family socioeconomic status, and level of self-direction as well as selected institutional characteristics, the authors found educational attainment significantly and positively related to internal locus of control. Compared to respondents with only a high school education, those with two or more years of college, those with a bachelor's degree, and those with an advanced degree showed progressively higher levels of self-direction. Educational attainment, moreover, had a stronger impact on levels of internal locus of control than on self-esteem. Among those who went to college, however, Knox and his colleagues found no relation between sense of direction and any particular educational factor, whether individual or institutional. This finding suggests that college effects are cumulative and not attributable to differences in college experiences or institutional characteristics. Riordan (1990) provides evidence consistent with this proposition.

Astin (1996b) and Sax and Astin (1997) report findings consistent with those of Knox et al. (1993) and Riordan (1990) in pointing to the beneficial net overall influence of college on students' self-perceptions. The studies by Astin and Sax, however, also suggest that specific college experiences have appreciable impact on students' long-term sense of control over their affairs. The evidence indicates that participation in community service and service-learning experiences during college leads nine years later to higher levels of self-efficacy, or the sense that one "can make a difference." Service-related gains in self-efficacy, moreover, are apparent after adjusting for the influences of an array of students' precollege characteristics, including service activities in high school, characteristics of their institution, and a range of student experiences after they had enrolled in college.

Leadership Skills. The few studies that examined any long-term college effects on leadership indicate that the influences of college on leadership skill development are measurable 5 and 15 years after graduation (Bowen & Bok, 1998; Langdon, 1997; Shulman & Bowen, 2001). For example, Bowen and Bok found that 15 years after earning a bachelor's degree, having an advanced degree was more highly related to civic leadership than were family circumstances or the selectivity of one's undergraduate institution. The level of service involvement was notably higher among African-American graduates than among their White counterparts. Shulman and Bowen, working with the same database, found no differences 15 years later between those who had been intercollegiate athletes and those who had not in terms of the proportion of graduates serving as business or corporate chief executive officers. Indeed, these researchers concluded that reports of the advantages of sports in developing leadership "may have outrun their translation into actual leadership" (p. 198).

Langdon (1997) found no statistically significant, long-term advantage to women's leadership skill development from attending a women's college rather than a coeducational institution. Five years after graduation, however, leadership skills were positively associated, net of other factors, with having had opportunities during college to participate in various activities, a condition more likely to have been available to women's college alumnae than to their coed college sisters. This finding suggests that any leadership-related benefits for women of attending a women's college rather than a coed institution are probably indirect rather than direct, being mediated by the greater number of leadership opportunities and experiences women have at the institutions they attend.

SUMMARY

Our attention in this chapter focused on changes among college students in two general areas of psychosocial development identified by Inkeles as the self system and the relational system (Inkeles, 1966). The self system concerns the sense of self, personal identity, academic and social self-concepts, and self-esteem. Relational systems cover students' interactions with others and with institutions.

Change During College

The post-1990 research on students' psychosocial development falls into five general areas: identity formation, self-concept and self-esteem, autonomy and locus of control, interpersonal relations and leadership skills, and general personal development.

Among the small number of studies published since 1990 on overall identity development, only a handful have clear, theoretical underpinnings, and these have limited generalizability because they are based on small samples of students at single institutions. Nonetheless, these studies are generally consistent with the earlier research in finding movement among students during the college years toward higher levels of identity development. More numerous studies with larger samples based on student reports of changes in "self-understanding" produce similar findings, although they are less conceptually sophisticated and based on psychometrically weaker measures. That these conceptually and methodologically varied studies consistently indicate that students develop their identities during college leads to greater confidence in concluding that students probably make important progress in this facet of their psychosocial development during the college years.

Although the level of attention to general identity development has declined since 1990, exploration of selected dimensions of identity has expanded, including identity formation as it relates to race-ethnicity, sexual orientation, and religion. More researchers have examined racial (largely African-American) identity development since 1990 than before, but these studies continued to focus on the presence or absence of various theorized stages of identity development and the characteristics of individuals at each stage rather than on whether change occurs during the college years. The few studies of changing racial identity replicate earlier research in finding no evidence of freshman- to senior-year changes in Black racial identity. Research on the development of gay, lesbian, and bisexual identity more consistently reports evidence of changes taking place during the college years. These studies consistently indicate that coming out—revealing to others one's gay-lesbian-bisexual affectional orientation—is a developmental event that commonly occurs during the college years. Authors speculate that the college environment may provide more opportunities and support for individuals to explore identity issues. Studies of religious identity formation suggest that, during college, students refine and reinterpret previously held beliefs into more complex, personalized, and internalized positions.

The evidence from post-1990 studies of changes in students' self-concepts (defined operationally here as students' self-evaluations in comparison with others) reinforces the conclusions reached in our earlier review. In the aggregate, students gain intellectual and academic self-confidence during college, although the changes are not always in the same direction. A net freshman- to senior-year increase of about 2.5 percent in the number of students classified in one study as "scholars" masked the movement of 13 percent of the participants into that category and 11 percent out of it. Other research suggests considerable variation within samples, with the overall direction sometimes nonlinear. As in the pre-1990 research, some evidence indicates that students' academic self-concepts may decline initially before recovering in the later college years. Students' social self-concepts, including self-confidence and perceptions of popularity, follow a similar although less apparent pattern to that of their academic self-concepts. Studies of overall self-concept, as well as the limited evidence on shifts in students' self-esteem, consistently point to growth in positive self-perceptions over the college years.

Another segment of the research on psychosocial shifts during the college years examines changes in students' autonomy (beliefs about their degree of freedom from the influence of others), locus of control (whether internal, with control by oneself, or external, with control exerted by other people or events), or self-efficacy (the belief that one "can make a difference" in the world). A few studies point to increases in students' independence from their parents, but the evidence is not strong. More studies have examined shifts in independence from peers, but the findings are mixed. Although generally consistent with the research before 1990 that found increased freedom from peer influence, more recent evidence is less compelling. The body of research on changes in academic or general locus of control, although small, is more methodologically rigorous and clearer than that concerning autonomy. Studies of locus of control consistently point to increases in internality during the college years.

Fairly consistent evidence indicates that students also gain (in some studies substantially) in their interpersonal skills. One series of analyses, for example, found that more than three-quarters of the respondents in large, national samples of seniors from three different decades reported "quite a bit" or "very much" progress in developing social competence. Smaller-scale studies may suggest less dramatic changes, but the evidence is generally positive. As with the research on changes in students' academic self-concepts, studies of leadership skills point to freshman- to senior-year gains, although the aggregate increases in leadership talents may hide more movement, perhaps shifts of as much as 12 to 15 percentage points in both directions. Studies of personal development broadly defined also indicate gains during the college years.

Net Effects of College

Researchers paid little attention to the net effects of college on identity development before 1990, and the small volume of research in this area remains a problem a decade later. Greater attention has been given since 1990 to identity formation related to race-ethnicity and sexual orientation, but scholarship on the presence or absence of theorized developmental levels or on the characteristics of individuals at each stage of development continues to outstrip exploration of college effects. In the post-1990 studies, age and the college years remain confounded, leaving unanswered the question of whether the observed changes are maturational or college-related. Some evidence suggests the observed shifts cannot be ascribed to cohort or period effects.

Carefully controlled studies using large, representative, national samples indicate that college has effects on students' self-concepts independent of effects attributable to precollege characteristics and to normal maturation. These net effects reveal positive changes in both academic and social self-concepts. The studies of net college influences on changes in students' self-esteem, however, are contradictory and afford no basis for a confident conclusion.

Greater confidence can be invested in the few methodologically rigorous studies that generally indicate statistically significant, if small, freshman- to senior-year increases on measures of students' internal locus of control or belief that they can influence what happens to them. By one estimate, students may experience net increases of .07 to .09 of a standard deviation (3 to 4 percentile points) over a 10-year period. These estimates may be attenuated by noncollege experiences over the period of study. Several methodologically sound national studies also point to first-year increases in students' beliefs that good academic performance is a function of their abilities and hard work rather than luck or the quality of instruction.

Solid evidence indicates that students make statistically significant freshman- to senior-year gains in leadership abilities, popularity, and social self-confidence. These gains are apparent in longitudinal studies of large, nationally representative samples, even when controls are in place for students' precollege characteristics, including self-reported leadership skills, and variations in the characteristics of the institutions students attended.

Between-College Effects

In our earlier review, we found little that could be said about changes in identity formation that could be attributed to the characteristics of the institutions students attended. A decade or more later, we are no further along in answering this question as it applies to overall identity development because few researchers have examined it. Studies of institutional effects on racial identity development among African-American students who attend an historically Black college or university compared with those at a predominantly White institution suggest that HBCUs enroll students at higher levels of racial centrality, ideology, and regard, but first- to senior-year changes among Black students appear to be about the same at both kinds of institutions. HBCUs may, however, have an indirect effect through the stronger emphasis their environments place on Black culture.

Both our earlier review and this one lead us to conclude that the variables commonly used to differentiate between or among institutions, such as size, type, control, or selectivity, are poor predictors of student change or development. Although institutional selectivity was occasionally found to have an impact on students' self-concepts net of other factors, the impact was always small and occasionally negative, as with students' math self-concepts.

One notable exception relates to a campus's structural diversity, or the mix of students by race-ethnicity or cultural origins. Several studies done since 1990 suggest that structural diversity has an indirect, positive impact on self-concepts by influencing the frequency with which students interact with peers of a different race-ethnicity, discuss issues of race, or encounter different points of view. The homogeneous student bodies at HBCUs or women's colleges, however, promote positive academic and social self-concepts and self-esteem among their students. For the members of underrepresented or socially disadvantaged groups, the company of others like themselves may provide a safe environment where experimentation, risk taking, and development can occur.

Other structural or organizational institutional characteristics appear to have no role in changing students' academic or social self-concepts, a conclusion supported by research on within-college effects, which consistently indicates that students' interactions with peers and faculty members—the primary agents of socialization—are more influential than institutional characteristics in shaping students' academic and social self-concepts.

The few studies of college-related changes in students' locus of control, or the sense that they have some influence over what happens to them, tend to concentrate on the academic dimensions of such control, or what has been called the locus of attribution for academic success. Evidence suggests that institutional characteristics are unrelated to any changes in locus of control. A recent and growing body of evidence, however, indicates that students who attend a community college may experience greater increases in internal locus of attribution than do students in four-year institutions. These differences persist even when adjustments are made for students' initial levels of internality and other precollege characteristics. There is some reason to believe, however, that the advantage accrues to community college students only in the first year. The difference is nonetheless noteworthy because gains in students' sense of control over their academic success may play an important role in their subsequent academic confidence and success.

Research after 1990 shifted from an earlier focus on interpersonal relations as an individual psychological phenomenon toward a more specific, group-oriented, sociopsychological focus on leadership skills, reflected in such traits as self-confidence and ability to get along with others as well as popularity and leadership positions held. As with other dimensions of psychosocial change, most studies find few independent effects on changes in this area related to institutional size, type, control, or selectivity. We found no evidence of net advantages in this area for African-American students from attending an HBCU rather than a predominantly White institution (although HBCU students may gain greater benefits in terms of personal development in general). Women's colleges, compared with coeducational institutions, may have a positive but indirect effect on women's internal sense of control over their academic performance. Campuses with expenditure levels on the higher end of the scale for student services and toward the lower end for instructional services may also contribute indirectly to enhanced student leadership skills. A small body of evidence indicates that varying organizational cultures may also play a role, a finding consistent with the proposition that in shaping students' psychosocial development, an institution's environmental conditions are more powerful forces than its formal structural features.

Within-College Effects

Research after 1990 on how various college experiences influence changes in identity formation have focused primarily on the effects of community service and various kinds of coursework. Qualitative studies of volunteer service and service-learning courses consistently point to positive effects, but quantitative results are mixed. Based on available evidence, it is impossible to say whether these courses have positive effects on identity formation. It may be that the impact of any college experience may manifest itself only over longer periods of time. We located no studies of longer-term effects of service-learning courses on identity formation. Studies suggest that other academic experiences may play a positive role, including majoring in women's studies, taking senior capstone courses, learning in multiracial-ethnic classrooms, taking "diversity" courses, and studying abroad. The evidence is most persuasive as it relates to majoring in women's studies and taking diversity courses. Membership in racial-ethnic organizations or clubs may also promote racial identity development.

Both pre- and post-1990 research on within-college effects on students' self-concepts points fairly clearly to the importance of students' interactions with peers and faculty members. Studies indicate consistently that students' interactions with their peers, net of other relevant factors, promote positive academic and intellectual self-concepts and self-confidence. Interactions with peers of a different race-ethnicity may be particularly influential in this regard. Although the effects appear to be statistically significant and direct, they are also relatively small.

The picture is largely the same as it relates to students' interactions with faculty members. The fact of contact appears to be more important than where it occurs, although methodologically rigorous evidence indicates that varying environments in different academic disciplines tend to reinforce and reward different student interests and abilities. Students' intellectual self-confidence, academic self-concepts, and expectations about contributing to science are more likely to be nourished in academic major fields with "investigative" environments than in other disciplinary environments. This literature is consistent with our earlier conclusion that departmental environments may be more salient influences than specific academic fields. Other college experiences that appear to promote students' academic self-concepts include generic community service, service-learning courses, exposure to active and collaborative instructional practices, participation in ethnic studies courses and cultural awareness workshops, and participation in most cocurricular activities, although intercollegiate athletics appears to be an exception.

Peer interactions also have a positive, net effect on students' social self-concepts, although their impact, as with academic self-concepts, seems to be small. Other college experiences that appear to bolster students' social self-confidence include "educating for success" programs, working on group projects, interacting with faculty members outside of class, leadership experiences, and participation in intercollegiate athletics. The evidence concerning within-college effects on self-esteem is mixed, but studies generally report positive net influences associated with service learning courses, active and collaborative instructional approaches, and cooperative learning techniques. Studies of the effects of Supplemental Instruction, living on campus, and clustered courses find no significant impacts on self-esteem.

The research indicates that generic volunteer service has little or no effect on students' internal locus of attribution for academic success, net of initial level and other college experiences. Service-learning courses, with their more structured, course-linked experiences, and student reflection on these experiences appear to enhance students' sense of control over their lives. Although some evidence suggests that Supplemental Instruction may not affect students' internal locus of control, the quality of the instruction to which students are exposed and other classroom experiences appear to influence changes in their internal attribution and sense of self-control. Students also appear to gain in their internal locus of control from study abroad, leadership experiences, and participation in cocurricular activities. Males who participate in intercollegiate athletics show about the same net gains as nonathletes in internal locus of attribution for academic success, but fraternity or sorority membership appears to have no net impact on peer independence or internal locus of attribution.

Students' experiences during college appear to have a positive impact on their interpersonal skills, but the picture is not entirely clear. Studies consistently find that volunteer service has a statistically significant, positive net effect on interpersonal skills, but it is unclear whether service-learning courses confer any additional benefits. The evidence indicates that fraternity or sorority membership promotes social skills, but well-controlled studies suggest any advantage is small. Research on the effects of cocurricular activities, in the aggregate, presents a mixed picture. More clear is the positive net effects on interpersonal skills associated with students' interactions with their peers, regardless of the setting.

The evidence relating to students' leadership skills is also mixed. Whether service learning contributes more than conventional volunteer service remains something of an open question, although it seems clear that community service does enhance leadership abilities. Even after adjusting for other factors, the research consistently indicates that leadership development courses and programs are effective. Despite public perception that intercollegiate sports participation promotes leadership, however, little evidence supports this belief. Similarly, leadership skill development among African-American students who belong to Black fraternities and sororities appears to be more closely related to students' precollege dispositions than to their membership in these organizations. As with research on the development of students' interpersonal skills, evidence suggests that gains in leadership skill formation derive from interaction with peers in any setting rather than from any particular form or location.

The environment within students' major field may be an exception to that conclusion. Findings from studies using general measures of personal development consistently support the proposition that peer interactions are the dominant influence on the development of students' interpersonal and leadership skills as well as on other aspects of psychosocial growth. The impact of student-faculty contact in these areas is less clear. Other specific aspects of students' college experiences also play a role, including exposure to active and collaborative instructional practices and study abroad. Most of these studies, however, do not control for students' overall level of psychosocial development when they entered college, leaving open the possibility that the students showing growth may have been the most ready to change when they first arrived on campus.

Conditional Effects of College

What evidence exists suggests that the impact of college on students' identity development is general rather than conditional on gender or race-ethnicity. This small body of research, however, lacks rigor and generalizability.

More researchers studied the differential effects of student experiences or institutional characteristics on academic and social self-concepts after 1990 than before, but the studies cover a broad array of experiences. For example, the racial-ethnic diversity of students' friendship groups appears to have a highly positive net impact on African-American students' intellectual self-confidence but a small negative impact on the same trait among White students. Mathematical self-concept becomes increasingly positive over the college years among women majoring in math and math-intensive fields, closing a precollege gap between themselves and their male peers majoring in the same fields. Among all other students, math self-confidence declines during the college years. Other academic environments appear to shape students in ways that vary little by gender with one exception: males majoring in "social" academic disciplines appear to experience growth in their interests and perceptions of their abilities in these areas, while women majors show little or no effects from such environments.

Some evidence suggests that African-American males participating in intercollegiate athletics may gain more in both academic and social self-concept than their White counterparts. Otherwise, participation in intercollegiate sports appears to have the same impact on athletes' intellectual and social self-concepts regardless of socioeconomic status, degree aspirations, or attitudes and values as well as the selectivity of institutions they attend. College appears to have a marginally greater impact on the self-esteem of women than men, net of pre-college level of self-esteem, ability, and socioeconomic status. The findings relating to conditional college effects on students' self-concepts and self-esteem await replication. Nonetheless, the number of such statistically significant, conditional effects alone suggests that college effects, at least in some areas, are probably not the same for all students.

Stronger but unreplicated evidence indicates that particular college experiences may have a differential impact on students' locus of control depending on whether they attend a two-year or a four-year institution. Participating in an honors program, joining a fraternity or sorority, employment, and teachers' instructional skills have significantly more positive effects on the internal locus of attribution for academic success among community college students than among similar students attending a four-year institution. Given that community colleges are more likely to enroll first-generation and underprepared students, these findings suggest that positive academic experiences may be particularly important to the academic success of such students. Evidence consistent with this proposition indicates that, even though they are less likely to become involved in a variety of college experiences, first-generation students derive greater benefits from these experiences—particularly academically related ones—than do similar students whose parents have had some exposure to college or hold a bachelor's degree. The effect of such involvement on first-generation students' beliefs about their capacity to control their academic performance, moreover, appears particularly important in the first year of college.

Long-Term College Effects

The long-term impact of college attendance on identity development remains largely unexplored, primarily because studies of students' identity development in the postcollege years concentrate on the nature and processes of changes without linking these changes to the college experience. The evidence clearly indicates that identity formation begun in the college years continues to age 30 and beyond. The difficulty lies in differentiating colleges' effects from those of normal maturation or sociohistorical developments. Although the gains students make in their cognitive and interpersonal development while in college are probably linked to changes in the ways graduates think about themselves, these connections are not explicitly examined. The research on identity formation is more properly characterized as studies of human development or life cycle changes among a subset of the population who happened to attend college rather than studies of long-term college impact.

College's influence on academic self-concept, however, is apparent, in at least one study, a decade later. The collegiate experience's effects on academic self-concept appear to be more indirect than direct, and their influence on social self-concept seems to depend to some extent on race-ethnicity. Participation in intercollegiate sports may be one of the mechanisms shaping long-term college effects, influencing participants' social self-concepts but not their academic self-images. The effects appear to vary with race-ethnicity, having a greater (although indirect) impact on African-American than on White students. Although these findings persist after adjustments for other precollege factors and college experiences, they remain unreplicated. Studies of long-term college effects on students' self-esteem, whether in the general student population or among women attending a women's college versus a coeducational institution, found no statistically significant links between educational attainment and self-esteem.

A small but well-executed series of studies of college's long-term impact on students' internal locus of control consistently finds durable, positive effects. These studies suggest that college's influence is undifferentiated by the characteristics of the institution attended and cumulative across a variety of college experiences. The one exception may be students' involvement during their college years in community service and service-learning activities, which appears to have a net positive and durable impact on participants' sense that they can make a difference in their world.

Little evidence exists on whether college's influence on students' development of their leadership skills is apparent in the years following college, although the studies that do explore the topic suggest that college makes a positive difference. The impact, at least with respect to women attending a women's college rather than a coeducational college or university, appears to be indirect rather than direct, mediated by the kinds of opportunities women students have to engage in leadership-related activities at the two kinds of institutions.

Notes

1. Erikson's eight stage-crises in their theorized developmental order and approximate age ranges are as follows: (1) basic trust versus mistrust (birth to age 2), (2) autonomy versus shame and doubt (ages 3 to 6), (3) initiative versus guilt (ages 6 to 10), (4) industry versus inferiority (ages 10 to 14), (5) identity versus identity confusion (ages 14 to 20), (6) intimacy versus isolation (ages 20 to 40), (7) generativity versus stagnation (ages 40 to 65), and (8) integrity versus despair (ages 65 and older) (Rodgers, 1989).

2. A number of studies examine relationships between racial identity (for various combinations of Asians, African Americans, and Latinos-Latinas) and gender (Jackson, 1998; Poindexter-Cameron & Robinson, 1997; Taub & McEwen, 1992); membership in Greek social societies (Taylor & Howard-Hamilton, 1995); various measures of psychosocial development, including developing and establishing a sense of purpose, autonomy, and interpersonal relationships (Pope, 1998, 2000; Sheehan & Pearson, 1995) and self-esteem (Phinney, Chavira, & Williamson, 1992; Poindexter-Cameron & Robinson, 1997; Rowley, Sellers, Chavous, & Smith, 1998; Taylor & Howard-Hamilton, 1995); and the factors and processes that shape racial identity formation during the early adolescent and college years (Murguia, Padilla, & Pavel, 1991; Renn, 2000; Tatum, 1999; Torres, 2003). Phinney (1990) reviewed 70 refereed journal articles published between 1972 and 1990 dealing with racial identity in adolescents and adults and noted that the theoretical writing far outweighs the empirical. Her review includes papers about White ethnic groups as well as historically underrepresented groups.

3. See D'Augelli (1991), Evans and Broido (1999), Rhoads (1993, 1994, 1995a, 1995b, 1997a), and Sears (1991).

4. Each of the scale's five items offers a 4-point response option, where 1 = "very little," 2 = "some," 3 = "quite a bit," and 4 = "very much."

5. Sax (1994d, 1994e) interprets her findings as providing some support for the "relative deprivation" position of the "frog pond" hypothesis. Davis (1966), in his classic study of career aspirations and choices, posed the metaphorical question of whether it was better to be a large frog in a small pond or vice versa. Two opposing theories offer a framework for an answer. One school of thought (see Davis) offers the relative deprivation explanation, hypothesizing that students' self-concepts will suffer in the presence of many others they consider more skilled or talented than themselves. The contrary position, the environmental press hypothesis (Thistlethwaite & Wheeler, 1966), holds that selectivity has a positive effect on academic self-concept through the context it creates, with students spurred to higher achievement by the presence of high-ability peers and confirmed in their positive self-image that accompanied their admission into the company of intellectually talented students and faculty. Our earlier review (1991, pp. 186–188) provides a more extended discussion of this debate and the studies that have tried to settle it.

6. Berger and Milem (2000b) review the literature on organizational behavior in higher education as it relates to various student outcomes.

7. Holland's six personality types and their characteristics (from Smart, Feldman, and Ethington, 2000, pp. 35–36) are as follows: *Realistic* (prefers activities involving use of machines, tools, and objects; disinclined to educational and interpersonal activities), *Investigative* (inclined to exploration, understanding, knowledge acquisition), *Artistic* (drawn to literary, musical, and artistic activities), *Social* (prefers helping others, values social service, and promotes the welfare of others), *Enterprising* (enjoys activities involving persuasion, manipulation, or direction of others to attain organizational goals), and *Conventional* (prefers establishing and maintaining order, routines, and standards).

8. The self-authorship achieved at this stage resembles Chickering's concept of interdependence, in which the perspectives and needs of others are taken into account but do not dominate decisions about what one thinks, values, or does (1969; Chickering & Reisser, 1993). Other studies also point to linkages among different dimensions of students' cognitive and psychosocial development. For example, the development of ego identity and principled moral reasoning may be positively associated (Blimling, 1990), and first-year students' levels of identity development may positively shape intellectual development as measured at the end of the sophomore year (Buczynski, 1991a). Those two constructs, however, may be inversely related during the early college years (Buczynski, 1991b). First-year students with higher levels of intellectual development displayed a less certain sense of identity. Buczynski suggests that more intellectually developed students, compared with their less intellectual peers, may be more aware of their new environments and thus also more inclined to question who they are and who they might become. One can only speculate whether an early disposition to question may lead to a clearer, more developed sense of identity. Although Buczynski found no such relation after two years, such development may emerge later in students' college careers.

CHAPTER SIX

Attitudes and Values

Since the founding of Harvard College in 1636, American higher education has been deeply involved in shaping student attitudes, values, and beliefs. Although differences of opinion exist both inside and outside the academy over *which* values colleges and universities should teach (or how energetically), stakeholders agree that the development of these attributes is an appropriate role for America's colleges and universities. The hundreds of studies of college's effects on student attitudes and values reviewed in both Feldman and Newcomb (1969) and Pascarella and Terenzini (1991) provide ample evidence of the abiding interest in this topic.

As in the decades before 1990, three difficult issues confront meaningful study of college's effects on students' attitudes, values, and beliefs. First, conceptions and measurement definitions vary, and too often the terms are used interchangeably. Decades ago, Rokeach (1960) sought to draw the distinction, specifying that "an attitude represents an organization of interrelated beliefs that are all focused on a specific object or situation, while . . . values are generalized standards of the means and ends of human existence that transcend attitudes toward specific objects and situations" (p. 453). But most researchers in this area are not so precise. Thus, to accommodate usage, we cluster studies that generally deal with either of these concepts.

The second persistent difficulty in this area of research is the correspondence (or lack thereof) between the attitudes and values held and their influence (if any) on behavior. Establishing links or disconnects between attitudes, values, or beliefs and subsequent action is beyond the purpose and scope of this review, but as our earlier study indicated, any correspondence apparently is far from perfect. In this review, as previously, we consider together studies based on measures of what students report as important to them, what they assert as their opinions and beliefs, and what they claim to value as reflections of attitudes and values. Similarly, some studies focus on student behaviors (such as voting or participating in religious activities) that both researchers and casual observers alike would probably accept as operational manifestations of underlying attitudes, values, and beliefs.

Third, the study of college effects on attitude and value change is complicated by attributional problems. Do differences in student attitudes and values between Time 1 and Time 2 reflect the influence of the college experience? Or are those changes more directly related to students' normal maturation (aging)? Perhaps the changes are attributable to generational (cohort) effects originating in the particular formative experiences of a group or cohort of individuals who have shared "the same significant life event within a given period of time" (Glenn, 1980, p. 598). Usually, that "event" is being a member of a particular birth cohort (usually defined by 10-year periods) and growing up and being socialized under a set of economic, social, and political conditions different from that of another birth cohort. Or might the changes be ascribed to the influence of historical (period) changes occurring in the larger society? Such influences are more difficult to identify, although they are usually the consequences of wars or major economic or social upheavals.[1] Research on college's effects on attitude and value change thus confronts the reality that one cannot simultaneously control for the confounding effects of aging, cohort, and period. As Glenn (1980) put it: "Since age is a perfect function of cohort and period, since cohort is a perfect function of age and period, and since period is a perfect function of cohort and age, it is impossible to hold two of these variables constant and vary the third" (p. 601). Thus, in analyses based on cross-sectional data, cohort and aging effects are confounded, and in longitudinal studies, aging and period effects are confounded. The problems of such confounding for interpreting results of studies of net college effects are obvious, and readers should be aware of this interpretive problem.

CHANGE DURING COLLEGE

Conclusions from *How College Affects Students*

Our earlier review found a number of consistencies in the evidence indicating that those who attend college change their value and attitudinal positions in a number of different areas. The evidence in each of five value and attitudinal areas (cultural, aesthetic, and intellectual; educational and occupational; sociopolitical; gender roles; and religion) was moderately to highly consistent. Students gained on the order of .25 to .40 of a standard deviation (about 10 to 15 percentile points) in their cultural, aesthetic, and intellectual sophistication while expanding their interests in the visual and performing arts in general. We observed increases of about 20 to 30 percentage points in the proportion of seniors (compared with themselves as first-year students) who found intrinsic value in a liberal education and exposure to new ideas. The value seniors (compared with themselves as freshmen) attached to the instrumental and extrinsic outcomes of an education declined somewhat (by 10 to 20 percentage points). We found similar but somewhat smaller shifts in students' occupational values over time. The importance of the intrinsic benefits of employment (such as opportunities for creativity, freedom from supervision, and intellectual challenge) increased, accompanied by declines in the importance of extrinsic benefits (such as income, security, and opportunities for advancement).

Students' sociopolitical attitudes and values also changed modestly (8 percentile points, and shifts of 15 to 25 percentage points) but consistently. Students became increasingly open and "other-person" oriented and displayed increases in humanitarian and altruistic values, political tolerance and liberalism, and civil libertarianism. Religious beliefs became more individual and less doctrinaire; tolerance for the religious views of others increased, and with somewhat less consistency, students became more accepting of the equality of men and women socially, educationally, occupationally, and in the family.

In all cases the research pointed to movement toward greater individual freedom, whether artistic and cultural, intellectual, political, social, racial, educational, occupational, personal, or behavioral.

Evidence from the 1990s

Our review of the more recent research on college effects on student attitudes and values suggests a larger and somewhat different set of categories as well as clear new directions in the empirical emphasis on those topics. Studies in the 1990s showed waning interest in college-related shifts in students' religious values and activities, their educational and occupational values, and their cultural and aesthetic interests. The major shifts have been increased interest in college's effects on students' community and civic involvement and on their attitudes toward members of other races-ethnicities and cultures. Sociologists, of course, have long been interested in how sociopolitical views and behaviors are shaped and why they change, and that interest shows no signs of abating.

For that reason, our review in each section of this chapter begins with an examination of the research on college's effects on students' awareness of and participation in the sociopolitical arena. This category includes studies relating to knowledge of government, political attitudes and activities, and attitudes toward individuals' civil liberties. Second, we examine the burgeoning literature on another segment of societal roles and activities—specifically, community service and civic engagement. In the 1990s, the growing racial-ethnic heterogeneity of the students on America's campuses and the national debate over federal affirmative action policies and regulations focused intense scrutiny on college and university affirmative action–based admissions policies. That interest spawned a third substantial subset of research examining the influence of various kinds of college experiences on multiple aspects of student learning and development. This review covers that segment of the literature dealing with students' attitudes and values toward people of different races, ethnicities, and cultural backgrounds.

Fourth, each section of this chapter examines what the research of the 1990s has to say about college's effects on student attitudes toward gender roles in general (a topic in which interest has continued to grow) and, more specifically, student attitudes toward date rape and sexual harassment. Reflecting the larger society perhaps, studies of college effects on students' attitudes toward lesbians, gays, and bisexuals have also grown in number and are reviewed next in each section of the chapter. The concluding parts of the sections update our previous reviews of student attitudes and values as they relate to education, occupations, religion, and artistic and cultural activities, as applicable.

Sociopolitical Attitudes and Values. The empirical literature examining the effects of educational attainment on various sociopolitical attitudes and values is both voluminous and consistent. This category includes studies that relate to individuals' understanding of the democratic process, their participation in that process, their subscription to the values that operationalize it, and broader student social and political orientations.

Voting is probably the most basic and closely monitored indicator of participation in a democratic society, and evidence from the 1990s on the relationship between voting and educational attainment is consistent with the research published previously. Although estimates vary depending on how the question is asked, the findings concur: the more formal schooling a person has had, the more likely that individual is to be registered and to vote. One set of estimates, based on the National Center for Education Statistics National Household Education Survey for 1996 (Nolin & Chapman, 1997), found that 9 in 10 Americans with a bachelor's degree or higher, compared with half of those with less than a high school diploma, reported voting in a national or state election in the past five years. The likelihood of voting increased monotonically with each additional level of formal education. Although voting presumes having registered to vote, ballot-casting rates naturally lag somewhat behind registration rates. The gap, however, is itself related to education, diminishing as educational level increases. Among citizens with less than a high school diploma, the registered-versus-voted gap is about 15 percentage points. Among those with a bachelor's degree or higher, the difference dwindles to about eight points ("Private Correlates of Educational Attainment," 1997; "Why College?" 1999). Other studies, most also based on independent, nationally representative samples, point to the same conclusion: as educational level increases, the probability of voting increases (Bowen & Bok, 1998; "Private Correlates of Educational Attainment," 1995; Tuma & Geis, 1995). By one estimate based on cross-sectional data from the 2000 National Survey of Student Engagement, the cross-sectional freshman-to-senior difference in the average of students' reports of their institution's contribution to their voting in local, state, or national elections was statistically significant but small (+ .08 of a standard deviation, or three percentile points) (Kuh et al., 2001).

Registering and voting take relatively little time and effort, of course, and casting a ballot, at least in a national election, is a biennial event. Other evidence of education-linked involvement in the democratic process, however, is consistent with that relating to voting, and this evidence points to both more varied and demanding forms of involvement and to greater intellectual engagement with political and governmental issues. As educational attainment rises, so does political participation that extends beyond voting to such activities as working in a political campaign, writing to public officials, and attending public meetings (Berkner, Berker, Rooney, & Peter, 2002; Ingels, Curtin, Kaufman, Alt, & Chen, 2002; "Why College?" 1999). Moreover, studies of citizens' knowledge of government (such as who holds office, constitutional facts, governmental rules and procedures) consistently show a positive association with educational level (Nie, Junn, & Stehlik-Barry, 1996; Nolin & Chapman, 1997; "Private Correlates of Educational Attainment," 1997; "Why College?" 1999). Over a series of 10 government-related questions, for example, the percentage of correct answers provided by those with only a high school diploma lagged, on average, 34 percentage points behind that of individuals with a bachelor's degree or higher (Nolin & Chapman, 1997). The better educated someone is, the less likely that person is to believe that politics and government are too complex to understand, to believe that one's family has no say in what the federal government does, and to be reluctant to express an opinion or to speak at a public meeting. People with more education are also more likely to pay attention to political life, to read about and follow the national news on television, to discuss politics and national issues, to contribute to candidates and political parties, to work for a political candidate or group, to attend public meetings, and to write letters or sign petitions on public issues (Nie et al., 1996; Nolin & Chapman, 1997; "Private Correlates of Educational Attainment," 1997; "Why College?" 1999).

These and other studies of the nation's citizenry also point to a positive relation between educational level and knowledge of, and support for, civil liberties. Nie et al. (1996) found that as education level increases, so does the level of agreement with the proposition that speaking out against religion and the expression of unpopular political views are acceptable behaviors.

Other evidence of the "liberalization" of students' sociopolitical attitudes and values during the college years comes from analyses of several large, nationally representative, longitudinal databases. With a few exceptions, these databases were developed under the guidance of Alexander W. Astin as part of the Cooperative Institutional Research Program (CIRP) of the University of California at Los Angeles Higher Education Research Institute (HERI) (see Astin, 1993c).

In an analysis of nearly 25,000 students who provided information when they entered four-year institutions in the fall of 1985 and again as seniors in 1989, Astin (1993c) found that the percentage of students he characterized as "social activists" increased from 14 percent to 22 percent between their first and senior years. That increase represents net change, however, and masks to some extent movement in both directions on items included in the social activist scale. These shifts include 13 to 26 percent of the students moving from "low to high scores" and 9 to 14 percent moving from "high to low scores" (Astin, 1993c, Table 4.1). Astin also reports a sizable difference between the percentage of 1985 freshmen who predicted there was "a good chance" that they would participate in a campus protest and the percentage as seniors reporting that they had actually done so (7 percent and 25 percent, respectively). Although the extent of social or political unrest nationally is likely to have a bearing on student behaviors in this area, not all campus protests focus on national issues. In addition, "protest" casts a rather large net. Both conditions make interpretation of the significance of this finding problematic.

Studies done in the 1990s of changes in students' social liberalism during the college years report smaller shifts over time than those reported in earlier, more activist decades. For example, the proportion of students who as first-year students in 1985 identified themselves as "liberal" or "far left" increased over the next four years but by only 3.8 percentage points (Astin, 1993c). Similarly, the proportion of students identifying themselves as "conservative" also grew but by only 4.4 percentage points. The percentages on the far left and right remained virtually unchanged, with shifts left or right coming from the "middle-of-the-road" group, which lost about 8 percent of its members. Astin and others (Dey, 1996; Schiff, 1993a, 1993b) see such shifts as reflecting increased political polarization among students. The largest shifts toward liberal attitudes (although slight to modest in an absolute sense) were on such items as support for national health care (+9 percentage points), for government control of pollution (+8 percentage points), and for raising taxes to reduce the national deficit (+5 percentage points) (Astin, 1993c). Dey (1996) also found shifts toward the liberal in students' views on abortion rights. Other evidence, also based on large, nationally representative samples of students attending four-year institutions, points to freshman-to-senior increases in students' commitment to influencing social values and the political structure (Rhee & Dey, 1996; Sax, 2000; Smart, Feldman, & Ethington, 2000; Smith, Morrison, & Wolf, 1994; Vogelgesang, 2000a, 2000b, 2001). The upward shifts in the percentage of students subscribing to these attitudes and values, however, are modest (in the 10 to 15 percentage-point range), and the sizes of the within-cohort shifts appear to have been declining since the late 1960s (Dey, 1997). Single-institution studies (whether cross-sectional or longitudinal) also provide evidence of increased liberalism in students' sociopolitical attitudes (Baier & Whipple, 1990; Buier, Butman, Burwell, & Van Wicklin, 1989; Cupp, 1991; Loeb & Magee, 1992; Lottes & Kuriloff, 1994a; Underwood, Maes, Alstadt, & Boivin, 1996), increased awareness of social justice issues, and increases on measures of social conscience (Anderson & Bryjak, 1989; Baier & Whipple, 1990; Lottes & Kuriloff, 1994a; Moes, Bussema, & Eigenbrood, 1999).

Seniors (compared with themselves four years earlier) shifted toward the conservative end of the sociopolitical continuum on some topics. Astin (1993c), for example, found freshman- to senior-year declines in student support for busing to achieve integration and for abolition of the death penalty (down 4 percentage points and 3 percentage points, respectively), a finding consistent with those reported in some single-campus studies (Baier & Whipple, 1990; Dey, 1996; Guimond, 1999; Guimond & Palmer, 1989; Underwood et al., 1996). Some evidence also suggests that shifts toward conservative views may have occurred more among male than female students (Matney & Wiley Kelly, 1997).

This same 1985 to 1989 cohort of CIRP students reported increased libertarianism over their college careers. The proportion of seniors supporting abortion rights, for example, grew by 18 percentage points (from 55 percent to 73 percent). The percentage of students opposing their institution's right to ban persons with extreme views from speaking on campus also grew, gaining 4 percentage points from an existing high of 79 percent. Astin reported little change over the four-year period in students' already high level of opposition to their institution's right to regulate off-campus behavior (90 percent opposed) or in student support for legalizing marijuana (20 percent in favor) (Astin, 1993c; Dey, 1996). Findings from single-institution studies are generally consistent with the national sample evidence in finding modest increases in support for civil liberties (Biddle, Bank, & Slavings, 1990; Guimond & Palmer, 1989, 1990; Murray & Adams, 1998).

Civic and Community Attitudes and Involvement. Political awareness or activity and sociopolitical views are part of a larger domain that might be characterized as "participating in a democratic society." A third sector, and one that requires a specific and more sustained level of commitment and energy, involves students' attitudes, values, and behaviors relating to the social and civic life of their communities, largely through roles as volunteers in community groups. Indeed, Alexis de Tocqueville (1835/1966), after visiting America in the 1830s, wrote: "Americans of all ages, all stations in life, and all types of disposition are forever forming associations . . . of a thousand different types—religious, moral, serious, futile, very general and very limited, immensely large and very minute" (p. 485). Some contemporary observers, however, believe Americans' interest in joining and contributing to civic and other associations is waning (Putnam, 1995) and that America's college students believe conventional politics are irrelevant to social change and so reject traditional political activities such as voting, petitioning, and social activism (Creighton & Harwood, 1993).

Not everyone agrees with that proposition (see Ladd, 1996), but some observers do see evidence of such disassociation on America's campuses and have called for the regeneration of civic engagement and social responsibility. Numerous stakeholders have called on the higher education community to promote civic engagement among students, staff, and institutions (American Association of Colleges and Universities, 2002; Boyte, 2000; Campus Compact, 1999; Carnegie Foundation for the Advancement of Teaching, 1991; Colby, Ehrlich, Beaumont, & Stephens, 2003; Ehrlich, 2000; Levine, 1994; National Education Goals Panel, 1992; Schneider, 2001; see also Wellman, 1999).

The literature of the 1990s relating to the influence of college on students' civic and community involvement shows clearly that such involvement is *far* more prevalent than nonvoting forms of political engagement (Ingels et al., 2002; Knox, Lindsay, & Kolb, 1993). In their 12-year follow-up of students who were eighth graders in 1988, Ingels and his colleagues found that political campaign involvement ranged from only 2.3 percent to 5.1 percent across educational attainment levels. Among the same educational groups, however, rates of volunteering for youth, civic, or other community organizations ranged from 12 to 32 percent, with those holding bachelor's or higher degrees being two to three times more likely to volunteer than their fellow citizens with no exposure to college.

A number of studies draw on nationally representative and independent data sets to provide estimates of community service participation by educational attainment level (Berkner, He, & Cataldi, 2002; Bowen & Bok, 1998; Graham & Cockriel, 1997; Ingels et al., 2002; Kuh et al., 2001; Nolin & Chapman, 1997; "Why College?" 1999). The considerable variety of forms of community service and the varying nature of the samples make it difficult to develop precise estimates, but our analyses suggest that individuals with a bachelor's degree or higher are, on average, perhaps 30 percentage points more likely than those with no postsecondary education to volunteer for a community service group. Based on evidence from the National Survey of Student Engagement (NSSE) reported in Kuh et al., we estimate college seniors were about .20 of a standard deviation (8 percentile points) more likely than first-year students to report that their college education had contributed to their knowledge, skills, and interests in promoting the welfare of their community. However, both absolute participation rates and differences across educational attainment levels can vary considerably by type of community service in question. In some instances, education level may even be inversely related to volunteer involvement (for example, in church or other religious organizations); for other areas or groups (such as hospitals, social welfare organizations, or sports or recreation groups) few education-related differences are apparent ("Why College?" 1999). With few exceptions (for example, Stage & Williams, 1990), however, the association between educational level and community service is positive, linear, and consistent.

Such cross-sectional evidence is supported by several large, nationally representative, longitudinal studies that tracked students from their first college year to their senior year. The panel study findings are consistent with those from cross-sectional studies in indicating increased willingness on the part of students to become engaged in their communities. The measures adopted reflect increased commitment to helping others and other forms of community service (Huang & Healy, 1997; Sax, 2000; Smith et al., 1994), involvement in environmental cleanup projects (Sax & Astin, 1998; Smith et al., 1994), increased commitment to "other-oriented" life goals or values, an amalgam of "social" interests (Smart et al., 2000), and a career in some form of community service (Villalpando, 1996). The proportion of seniors who report their commitment to or actual involvement in community service is 10 to 15 percentage points higher than these same students reported when they first entered college. Among Chicano and White students, Villalpando found freshman-to-senior increases in "commitment to other-oriented life goals and values" about .26 and .31 of a standard deviation (10 to 12 percentile points), respectively.

Just as students' commitment to and involvement in community service increase during their college years, so too, it appears, does their sense of "empowerment" or "social efficacy"—that is, their belief that they can make a difference in their communities or in the larger sociopolitical sphere. Although studies examining this issue are limited in number and report modest impact, they gain credibility by drawing on data from a large and nationally representative sample and for their agreement in finding slight freshman-to-senior increases in students' sense of social efficacy (Astin, 1993c; Sax, 2000; Sax & Astin, 1998).

Racial-Ethnic Attitudes. In our earlier review of the effect of college on students' attitudes and values, we examined a large number of studies dealing with changes relating to civil rights, civil liberties, racism, anti-Semitism, or tolerance for nonconformity. We found uniform shifts toward social, racial, ethnic, and political tolerance and increased support for the rights of individuals. The post-1990 evidence reviewed in the previous sections is consistent with the earlier findings.

The research on changes in student attitudes and values published during the 1990s, however, focuses far more narrowly on racial-ethnic attitudes, no doubt in response to the growing diversity on campuses and the fact that the national spotlight has been trained over the past decade on federal affirmative action policies, particularly as they relate to college and university admissions. Much of the earlier college effects research dealing with questions of race-ethnicity and discrimination had a legal and governmental focus and examined attitudes and views concerning equality for all individuals. The more recent research on college's effects has a personal, interactional quality. The focus seems to have shifted from attitudes concerning philosophical or theoretical matters to a more down-to-earth, "How-do-we-relate-to-one-another?" examination of interracial interaction.

The evidence points to higher education–related increases in positive attitudes toward racial equality and tolerance as well as increases in awareness and understanding of, and interactions with, people of different racial-ethnic or cultural backgrounds. The evidence comes from multicampus qualitative studies (Kuh, 1993) and from large, nationally representative, independent samples of students and citizens. College's influence on racial-ethnic attitudes is reflected in increases in students' egalitarianism and reductions in prejudice (Case & Greeley, 1990), freshman-to-senior increases in racial-cultural awareness (Milem, 1999a), declines (over the first two years) in race-related social distance (Loeb & Magee, 1992), greater understanding of people of other racial and ethnic backgrounds (Kuh et al., 2001), increased commitment to promoting racial understanding and increasing diversity, and reductions in students' beliefs that racial discrimination is no longer a problem (Hyun, 1996; Milem, 1991, 1999a; Smith et al., 1994). These changes during the college years, however, were not dramatic. By one estimate, the percentage of 1985 freshmen who reported promotion of racial understanding as an important goal had increased by only about 4 percentage points by their senior year, a change consistent with that discussed earlier relating to student shifts toward social liberalism (Astin, 1993c). In addition, Kuh (1999) reports that the proportion of upper-division students reporting "substantial" progress in gaining awareness of different cultures, philosophies, and ways of life has declined over the past four decades (from 69 percent in 1969 to 58 percent in 1996). Based on cross-sectional data from the National Survey of Student Engagement reported elsewhere by Kuh and his colleagues (2001), we estimate freshman-to-senior increases of .09 of a standard deviation (4 percentile points) in students' understanding of people of other racial and ethnic backgrounds.

The evidence from smaller sample or single-institution studies is more mixed. Several investigations, for example, report finding no class year–related associations with measures of social distance (McClelland & Auster, 1990) or scores on the Modern Racism Scale (Chang, 2000a). Most studies, however, find freshman-to-senior (or first- to second-year) changes consistent with those reported in the national investigations. These campus-specific studies point to increases in multicultural perspective (Bauer, 1992; Graham & Gisi, 2000; Kuh & Vesper, 1997b; Moes et al., 1999), increased acceptance of close interpersonal interactions with minority students and declines in negative stereotyping of minority group members (Muir, 1991; Wood & Chesser, 1994), greater support for affirmative action practices and educational equity (Lopez, 1993; K. Smith, 1992), greater support for multicultural education and opposition to racial quotas (Seltzer, Frazier, & Ricks, 1995), and increased openness to human differences (Taylor, 1998).

Even so, some research suggests that, although freshman-to-senior shifts in racial-ethnic attitudes and values trend toward the positive, these shifts may mask variations within subsets of undergraduates that are related to gender, race-ethnicity, and social class. These differences are discussed in the "Conditional Effects of College" section of this chapter.

Gender-Role Attitudes. During the 1970s and 1980s, scholarly interest in the effects of college attendance on students' views concerning the appropriate marital and occupational roles of women grew sharply (Etaugh, 1986), a reflection at least in part of the growing national debate about feminism and women's roles in a modern society. Since 1990, however, scholars have focused less attention on how students' attitudes toward gender roles change during the college years. As reported in the "Within-College Effects" section of this chapter, scholarly attention appears to have shifted from *whether* gender-role attitudes change to *why* they change, a topic that required but two paragraphs to review in our earlier book.

Astin's study (1993c) is the most extensive examination of changes in students' views on the equality of the sexes. He found "the most consistent and strongest increases" (p. 143) in students' social attitudes and values on a dimension he labeled "feminism." This factor consisted of three items reflecting student support for "sex equity in pay, . . . a very strong stance on the issue of 'date rape,' and reject[ion of] the proposition that married women should remain in the home" (p. 142). Among the students forming a large, nationally representative sample entering four-year institutions in the fall of 1985 who were studied again as seniors four years later, Astin found that on all three items the proportion of students espousing "egalitarian" gender views had increased.

The shifts toward more egalitarian attitudes and values ranged from 4 percentage points (on the pay equity item) to 8 percentage points (opposing the proposition that a woman's place is in the home) to 11 percentage points (opposing the position that a male's belief he has been "led on" by his date entitles him to unwanted sex) (see also Korn, 1993). Perhaps most striking of all is that these increases in "feminism" were not only the largest shifts in students' social attitudes but that 80 to 92 percent of these students already held "liberal" views on these matters when they enrolled as first-year students.

We identified four other studies with samples more limited than Astin's (1993c) but that also monitored freshman-to-senior changes in this area (Lottes & Kuriloff, 1994a; Miller-Bernal, 1993, 2000; Underwood et al., 1996). Three of the four (Underwood et al. was the exception) report findings consistent with Astin's, including the magnitude of the shifts toward more liberal views on appropriate gender roles. Lottes and Kuriloff studied more than 300 students as freshmen and again as seniors and found a shift of .16 of a standard deviation (or 6 percentile points) toward more "feminist" attitudes and a decline of .23 of a standard deviation (9 percentile points) in attitudes about male dominance. Our analysis of the changes reported by Miller-Bernal among women students at four institutions, both single-sex and coeducational, suggests a shift of .26 of a standard deviation (10 percentile points) toward egalitarian views of gender roles from the freshman to sophomore year, although the more recent of the Miller-Bernal studies suggests considerable attitudinal instability in the first year or two. By the end of the senior year, however, the shift toward "modern" sex-role attitudes had reached .60 of a standard deviation (23 percentile points). The shifts, however, appear not to be monolithic. At least one study points to considerable differentiation in college women's attitudes and views about women's roles (Greeley, 1991).

Attitudes Toward Homosexuality. Scholarly interest in attitudes related to sexual orientation has grown in the past decade for a number of reasons, including increased willingness on the part of gays, lesbians, and bisexual individuals to be open about their sexuality and to confront discrimination and prejudice and growing social and legal acceptance of gays, lesbians, and bisexuals (Kim, D'Andrea, Sahu, & Gaughen, 1998). Yet homophobic attitudes persist. By one estimate, more than one-third of the students who identified themselves as gay, lesbian, bisexual, or transgendered reported having experienced harassment in the preceding year. Of these, 9 in 10 incidents involved derogatory remarks, with other students the most frequently cited source of the harassment. One in five of all respondents (some of whom were faculty members) reported fearing for their physical safety because of such attitudes (Rankin, 2003).

We identified only a handful of studies relating to changes during the college years in students' attitudes toward lesbians, gays, or bisexuals, virtually all limited to single-campus samples. Five of these studies yielded consistent findings pointing to increases in students' knowledge and acceptance of different sexual orientations and to declines in homophobia. These studies used both cross-sectional (B. Kim et al., 1998; Simoni, 1996) and longitudinal designs (Geller, 1991; Kardia, 1996; Loeb & Magee, 1992; Lottes & Kuriloff, 1994a). Loeb and Magee, for example, followed about 100 first-year commuter students over three semesters and found a statistically significant drop during that time in prejudicial attitudes toward members of 14 groups, including homosexuals. Negative attitudes toward all groups except nonheterosexuals dropped most sharply during the first semester; the decline in negative attitudes toward nonheterosexuals took longer, occurring between the start of the second semester and midway through the third term. Lottes and Kuriloff, and Kim et al., found freshman-to-senior reductions of .66 and .53 of a standard deviation (or 25 and 20 percentile points), respectively, in measures of intolerance toward homosexuality. In the Lottes and Kuriloff study, the drop in homophobic attitudes accompanied increased opposition to attitudes supporting male dominance as well as increases in liberalism and feminism. The reduction in homophobic attitudes, however, was more than twice the size of the shifts in other attitudes and values.

Malaney, Williams, and Geller (1997), in contrast, using a cross-sectional, two-institution sample, report somewhat different findings. Despite seniors' reports of greater exposure to gay-lesbian-bisexual issues in their classes, and despite their being more aware of anti-gay-lesbian-bisexual attitudes on campus, seniors (compared with first-year students) were no more likely to report having a gay, lesbian, or bisexual friend, to have a greater interest in gay-lesbian-bisexual history or culture, or to take action upon witnessing an incident of gay-lesbian-bisexual harassment on campus.

Educational and Occupational Values. The weight of the evidence published before 1990 pointed to increases (on the order of 20 to 30 percentage points) in the proportion of seniors (compared with themselves as first-year students) who found intrinsic value in a liberal education and in exposure to new ideas. Researchers then also reported declines in the proportion of students attaching a high value to the instrumental and extrinsic values (such as career preparation) of a college education.

Studies published since 1990 are generally consistent with earlier research. Knox, Lindsay, and Kolb (1993), in their study of nearly 5,500 students who graduated from high school in 1972 (drawn from the NLS-72 database), found level of educational attainment highly and positively related to the value attached to "having a good education." Fourteen years after graduating from high school, the proportion of respondents with a bachelor's degree who said having a good education was "very important" was 24 percentage points higher than that of their peers having only a high school diploma (69 percent versus 45 percent, respectively). Knox and his colleagues acknowledge the possibility of multiple interpretations of the phrase "having a good education" but argue that the item's wording led respondents to understand it as a reference to "education [as] more an end than a means to more instrumental goals" (p. 66).

Study of a nationally representative cohort of students entering higher education in 1985 supports Knox and his colleagues' assumption about the meaning students' attached to "having a good education." Astin (1992, 1993c) found a net freshman- to senior-year drop of 17 percentage points in the proportion of students subscribing to the belief that "the chief benefit of a college education is that it increases one's earning power" (1993c, p. 145). Although 11 percent of the freshmen increased their support for that value by the time they were seniors, 28 percent of their peers who initially had high scores on that item rated it low in importance by the end of their senior year. This finding is consistent with other evidence Astin reports indicating freshman-to-senior declines in materialistic and status needs as well as an 8 percentage point increase from freshman to senior year in the number of students valuing "developing a meaningful philosophy of life" as an educational goal. Over the four-year period, nearly 23 percent of student participants shifted from "low" to "high" in the value they attached to that goal, while 15 percent moved from "high" to "low."

Wilder and his colleagues (Wilder, McKeegan, Midkiff, Skelton, & Dunkerly, 1997; Wilder, Midkiff, Dunkerly, & Skelton, 1996) supply evidence of a different sort, but their findings are consistent with those of Knox et al. (1993) and Astin (Astin, 1992, 1993c). The Wilder group studied freshman- to senior-year changes in the level of endorsement of the four Clark-Trow educational philosophies endorsed by some 4,000 students entering a selective, medium-size, private residential liberal arts college during three periods in the 1960s, 1970s, and 1980s. In both studies, they found that as seniors, students gave significantly higher ratings to "academic" and "nonconformist" philosophies and lower ratings to "collegiate" and "vocational" philosophies than they did as freshmen.[2] The magnitudes of the shifts were greatest for the nonconformist philosophy (+.40 standard deviations, or about 16 percentile points, across the two studies) and the vocational philosophy (-.38 SD, or 15 percentile points). The increase in support for the academic philosophy and the decrease in support for the collegiate philosophy were much smaller (on the order of +.07 and -.03 SD, or +3 and -1 percentile points, respectively). Other studies have produced evidence consistent with the proposition that during the college years, students tend to increase their support for the intrinsic values they find in education and to decrease the extrinsic values they attach to education (Clark & Anderson, 1992; Flowers & Pascarella, 1999b; Hayek & Kuh, 1999; Soller, 2001).

Our 1991 review found similar (but smaller) shifts during the college years in how students judge occupational values. From freshman to senior year, students were increasingly more likely to report intrinsic occupational rewards as important (work being valued as an end in itself with rewards seen as inhering in the work, which in itself might provide intellectual variety and stimulation, autonomy, and opportunities to use one's talents). In contrast, the value students attached to instrumental and extrinsic occupational rewards (such as salary, social status, and security) declined. These shifts, however, were smaller than those relating to the value students attached to their education.

Similar shifts are reported in studies published in the 1990s, and again the work of Knox, Lindsay, and Kolb (1993) provides the clearest evidence. These researchers found that, in 1986, 70 percent of 1972 high school graduates who earned only a high school diploma rated opportunities for advancement as "very important," compared with 62 percent of bachelor's degree recipients and 56 percent of advanced degree holders. Similar splits were apparent on the value attached to job security and providing opportunities for their children. The importance of having a lot of money, however, did not vary by education level. Interestingly, most respondents at all educational levels rejected this goal, only 12 to 16 percent reporting they considered it "very important." A longitudinal study of a nationally representative sample of students who entered four-year colleges and universities in 1985 also suggests a subsequent decline in the value students assign to the extrinsic rewards of an occupation (Astin, 1993c).

Religious Attitudes and Values. Our earlier review found limited but consistent evidence of declines (by about 10 percentage points) in students' traditional religious affiliations during their college years and in their general religious orientations (perhaps 20 percentile points over four years). Religious beliefs became more individual and less doctrinaire, and tolerance for the religious views of others appeared to increase.

The evidence from the 1990s is both more sparse and more mixed. We identified only five studies that drew on nationally representative samples to explore changes in religious values during the college years (Bryant, Choi, & Yasuno, 2003; Graham & Cockriel, 1996, 1997; Graham & Donaldson, 1996; Lee, 2002b). All point to *increases* (or refinements) in the value students attach to religion, although the shifts are generally small. Lee studied 4,000 students on 76 four-year campuses as freshmen in 1994 and again as seniors in 1998. Nearly half (48 percent) of the students in her study reported no change in their religious values between their freshman and senior years. Although 14 percent reported declines in the strength of their religious convictions, nearly three times that number (38 percent) reported increases in the strength of their convictions. The nearly 10,000 two- and four-year students nearing the end of their programs in Graham and Cockriel's cross-sectional study also reported slight increases in the strength of their religious convictions. Bryant et al. found declines in students' religious behaviors after one year but also evidence of students' efforts to integrate spirituality into their lives.

Single-institution studies provide a more mixed picture. One investigation, consistent with the national studies, found freshman- to senior-year increases on a measure of "religious Christian character" (Underwood et al., 1996). Other studies, however, point to declines in religious values (Baird, 1990a) or to little or no change (Serow & Taylor, 1990; Strausbaugh, 2003; Terry, 1992). In addition to being restricted to a small number of institutions or to single campuses, some of these latter studies have other, nontrivial methodological limitations.

Some of this evidence (Baird, 1990a; Bryant et al., 2003; Cherry, DeBerg, & Porterfield, 2001; Strausbaugh, 2003) suggests that studies of religious values during the college years may be overlooking subtle shifts not so much in the saliency of students' religious values as in the ways in which students think about religion. Evidence is mounting to suggest that students' commitments to religious values during the college years may not so much increase or decrease as become reexamined, refined, and incorporated in subtle ways with other beliefs and philosophical dispositions (Bryant et al., 2003; Cherry et al., 2001; Lee, 2002a). Cherry et al., for example, in their qualitative study of four campuses, found students constructing their own religious values quite apart from any of the traditional denominations.

Understanding and Interest in the Arts. We identified only a handful of studies published in the 1990s that examined changes during college in students' cultural and aesthetic interests. Using factor analytic procedures, Astin (1993c) identified a half-dozen "personality types," one of which was the "artist." This appellation includes students interested in the arts as a career, students who rate their artistic abilities highly, or students for whom becoming accomplished in one of the performing arts is a life goal. Although the number of students in this cluster was small initially and increased only slightly between freshman and senior years (from 6.7 percent to 8.3 percent), more than 5 percent of this population moved from "not-type to type," although 3.5 percent switched from "type to not-type." Astin also found, however, a freshman-to-senior drop of 8 points in the percentage of students reporting that they had attended a recital or concert during the past year (from 82 percent to 74 percent) and mixed evidence of shifts (some positive and some negative) in the percentage of students displaying artistic inclinations. Knox, Lindsay, and Kolb (1993) found steady education-related increments in the proportion of individuals interested in participating in "a literary, art, discussion, music, or study group" (p. 67), although the absolute proportions, like those reported by Astin, were all small (less than 10 percent). Other studies (most using national samples) found reported increases during the college years in students' interest in the arts and cultural activities (Baier & Whipple, 1990; DeSousa & Kuh, 1996; Flowers, 2002b; Kuh, 1993; Placier, Moss, & Blockus, 1992; "Private Correlates of Educational Attainment," 1995, 1997; Smart et al., 2000). In his study of the gains reported made by college seniors in each of four periods from the late 1960s to the mid-1990s, Kuh found a decline from 57 percent in 1969 to 36 percent in 1996 of students reporting "quite a bit" or "very much" growth in their "literary acquaintance and appreciation" since entering college. Among those same students, reported growth in their aesthetic sensitivities (appreciation and enjoyment of art, music, and drama) also declined over the period from 53 percent to 30 percent (Kuh, 1999).

NET EFFECTS OF COLLEGE

The question of whether students change during the college years is the most general one we pose in our review, and the answers to that question should not be taken as evidence that students change *because* of their college experiences. As we pointed out at the start of this chapter, normal maturation, cohort, and historical phenomena may be factors shaping students' attitudes and values. In this section, we examine the evidence regarding the extent to which attending college—and not other forces—accounts for observed changes in student attitudes and values.

Conclusions from *How College Affects Students*

Our earlier review led to the conclusion—reassuring in view of widespread popular beliefs and institutional claims about the benefits of higher education—that college does indeed have a number of impacts (albeit rather modest) on students' attitudes and beliefs. More important, these effects appeared to be a consequence of attending a college or university and not simply artifacts of the characteristics, attitudes, and values students brought with them to college, or of normal, maturational processes, or of historical, social, or political trends of the time.

We found that the nature and direction of the net effects of college were, in the main, toward more open, liberal, and tolerant attitudes and values. The evidence we reviewed, moreover, particularly that dealing with political, social, and gender-role attitudes, suggested that any changes were more than mere reflections of changes occurring in the larger society over the preceding 20 years. Even with age and selected other relevant variables taken into account, college-related changes in attitudes and values were consistently apparent both within and across age cohorts.

Evidence from the 1990s

Sociopolitical Attitudes and Values. The evidence published since 1990 concerning whether college has an effect on students' sociopolitical orientations *net of other factors* (such as maturation or societal changes) is more mixed than earlier findings and seems to depend at least in part on the outcome measure chosen. The limited changes in students' political orientation between their first and senior years were noted earlier. When Astin (1993c) explored these changes while controlling for a wide array of students' entering characteristics (including their political identification when first entering college as well as gender, race-ethnicity, ability, socioeconomic status, and other factors), he found no evidence to support the proposition that changes in political orientation were attributable to maturation (age). Nor did the evidence suggest societal changes were a factor (in fact, no trends were apparent in the political identification of freshmen entering in successive years between 1985 and 1989). Astin also found, however, no evidence suggesting that attending college was a factor in changing political orientation: the number of years completed was unrelated to changes in political identification when other considerations were controlled, a finding also reported by Dey (1997) across four cohorts of students who entered college between 1966 and 1987. Astin concluded that his analyses provided no reason to believe that attending college had any significant, systematic effect on student preferences for one end or the other of the political spectrum. Astin and others did, however, find that freshman-to-senior shifts in political identification were associated with the peer and faculty environments of the institutions attended. This relationship, discussed in greater detail in the "Within-College

Effects" section, does suggest that the college experience may have some hand in shaping at least one aspect of students' political dispositions.

The marginal net shifts in political identification are mirrored in studies that use other measures of student social and political attitudes. As noted in the previous section, Astin (1993c) found generally modest (and sometimes inconsistent) increases in a set of items reflecting student "liberalism." These items described traditionally "liberal" policies, including support for greater government involvement in issues relating to disarmament, pollution, taxation, busing, and national health care. The overall freshman-to-senior differences were again slight and toward the liberal end of the rating scale, and Astin concluded (in contrast to shifts in students' political identification) that these shifts toward liberalism may be entirely due to societal changes. On the items showing the greatest movement toward liberalism, the differences between the values of entering freshmen in 1985 and 1989 were all larger than the differences between the 1985 entrants compared with themselves four years later. Astin reports clear evidence, however, of college effects on the likelihood that students will participate in protests. Participation rates were positively associated with each of several indicators of college exposure, including years completed, living on campus, and student-student and student-faculty interactions.

All of these results, suggesting as they do relatively small net college effects on various aspects of students' sociopolitical attitudes, are consistent with Astin, Keup, and Lindholm's (2002) findings indicating that the higher education *system's* capacity to affect these outcomes may have declined between the mid-1980s and mid-1990s. Astin and his colleagues found that, with controls in place for 43 precollege student characteristics (including measures of the outcome variables under study), four-year colleges and universities fell short of statistically derived expectations with respect to increases in student activism and commitment to environmental cleanup. The shortfalls were estimated to be .22 and .39 of a standard deviation (9 and 15 percentile points), respectively, for the two outcomes.

Analyzing the association between senior-year liberalism and students' college experiences, Astin (1993c) did find (as he had with political identification) that, after controlling for a variety of students' precollege characteristics (including liberalism), increases in students' liberal and social activist orientations were associated with the character of the peer and faculty climate at the institutions studied as well as with a wide variety of "involvement" experiences unique to the collegiate setting. These experiences include enrollment in ethnic and women's studies courses, part-time campus employment, discussions of racial or ethnic issues with other students, and participation in campus-based racial or cultural awareness workshops. Astin reports similar findings based on a measure of "social activism." He concluded that neither maturation nor social change appeared to be significant factors in shaping these changes. Other studies report net effects similar to Astin's (Astin, 1992; Dey, 1996, 1997; M. Kim, 1998, 2001; Schiff, 1993a, 1993b; Smart et al., 2000). Both Dey studies, however, also provide evidence suggesting that the net freshman-to-senior changes observed during college are consistent with changes in the external social context, as reflected in changes across student cohorts over time and in studies of 18- to 23-year-olds in the general U.S. population reported in the national General Social Survey for 1985 and 1989. He suggests that the social context may be as important as and statistically independent of the normative peer group influence.

Other studies point more clearly to educational effects on sociopolitical dispositions net of other potentially confounding factors. Knox, Lindsay, and Kolb (1993), in their study of the High School Class of 1972 14 years after high school, for example, found educational attainment has statistically significant and substantial independent effects on several measures of sociopolitical involvement. Compared to their peers with only a high school education, participants who held bachelor's degrees were two and a half times more likely to vote, and people with advanced degrees were three times more likely. Similarly, those with a bachelor's degree were 52 percent more likely to engage in political discussions, and advanced degree holders were more than twice as likely. Although the undergraduate years appeared to confer no advantage over high school graduation in terms of commitment to social justice, those with graduate degrees were 54 percent more likely to display such commitment. Astin (1993c) concluded that freshman-to-senior increases in students' libertarian values were attributable "in part, but not entirely, to social change" (p. 149). More recent studies also show statistically significant effects of education on knowledge of governmental, political, and social issues. These effects persisted even in the presence of controls for such factors as age, race-ethnicity, gender, religious involvement, family income, political party affiliation, and position on selected social and political issues (Anderson & Bryjak, 1989; Drew & Weaver, 1991; Griffin, 1990).

Nie and his colleagues (1996), however, provide evidence that the dynamics behind education's significant net impact on "enlightened political engagement" are more complex than has typically been thought and documented. This careful study, using data from the 1990 Citizen Participation Study and two ongoing surveys of political behavior and attitudes,[3] suggests that the conventional view of educational attainment as an "additive mechanism" (more is better) is not entirely adequate. The researchers found that "education can be thought of as the engine of two separate life trains that . . . combine to shape the configuration of democratic citizenship" (p. 57). Although the additive model of education is not without merit, Nie et al. argue that educational attainment also has indirect net effects on political attitudes and behaviors. These effects are associated with the social and occupational networks to which educational attainment provides entry. Nie and his colleagues identify education-related "positional outcomes," including occupational performance, family income and wealth, and voluntary associational memberships, that also shape political orientations and activities.

Civic and Community Attitudes and Involvement. Few researchers have studied the net effects of college on changes in students' civic and community involvement. Such engagement is more often treated as an independent, or "college experience," variable, of interest for its possible effects on some other college outcome. What evidence exists on civic and community involvement as an outcome is mixed, although the overall findings suggest that attending college has a positive effect above and beyond the influence of other variables. In a Cooperative Institutional Research Program–based study of more than 18,000 students who enrolled as freshmen in 1985 and were surveyed four years later, Huang and Healy (1997) found that students characterized as belonging to Holland's "social" type showed slight, but statistically significant, four-year gains in their attitudes toward "helping others who are in difficulty."[4] This effect persisted after controlling for gender, race-ethnicity, academic ability, age, and precollege attitudes about helping others. The effects of being any of the other five Holland types, however, were significant and negatively related to attitudes about helping.

Knox, Lindsay, and Kolb (1993) provide perhaps the most rigorous evidence of the influence of college on students' involvement in civic and community affairs. After controlling for gender, race-ethnicity, socioeconomic status, and students' precollege attitudes and values, these researchers found that educational attainment was linearly related to involvement in a variety of civic activities. Although postsecondary experience of *any* duration or level of attainment was not always related to civic involvement at statistically significant levels, the trends were clear and consistent: individuals with more education were (net of other factors) more likely to be involved in civic and community activities. Compared to their peers with only a high school education, bachelor's degree holders were significantly and substantially (82 percent) more likely to be involved 14 years later in community groups and more than two and a half times more likely to be doing volunteer work and to be committed to community leadership. Perhaps reflecting the breadth of the concept of "civic involvement," however, educational attainment proved to be *un*related to nonworship church activities and to be negatively related to involvement with youth organizations (with baccalaureate degree recipients about half as likely to be involved in such activities as their high school classmates without postsecondary education experience). Putnam (1995) and others have suggested that involvement in youth activities may be more closely related to having children than to educational attainment, with individuals who do not go on to college starting their families earlier than their college-enrolled peers.

The National Longitudinal Study of the High School Class of 1972 data set on which Knox and his colleagues (1993) relied is dated, but several studies of more recent national (or multi-institutional) samples lead to conclusions consistent with those reached by Knox et al. (see, for example, Astin et al., 2002). These later investigations do not seek to estimate the magnitude of any freshman-to senior-year changes on various measures of civic attitudes, values, or activities, but they produce consistent findings of college effects that are independent of other influences. The evidence is indirect, however, inasmuch as these studies do not treat college attendance as a unitary or generic experience. Rather, they demonstrate that after controlling for precollege differences on such factors as gender, race-ethnicity, ability, socioeconomic status, and precollege measures of the outcome under study, various college experiences shape students' senior-year attitudes and values related to civic involvement. These attitudes and values range from the importance attached to community action, helping others, cleaning up the environment, and influencing the political structure (Rhee & Dey, 1996) to humanistic values and engaging in community service clubs and organizations (Berger, 2000b), altruism (Kuh, 1993), sense of civic responsibility (Astin & Antonio, 1999, 2000), and social activism and commitment to community involvement (Sax, 2000; Sax & Astin, 1998).

Racial-Ethnic Attitudes. The weight of the evidence relating to the net effects of college attendance on students' racial-ethnic attitudes is conclusive. Indeed, Astin (1993c) reports that some of the most persuasive evidence he uncovered relating to the effects of college concerned students' increased commitment to promoting racial understanding. After controlling for a daunting array of precollege characteristics, including the racial-ethnic attitudes students brought with them to college, Astin found that virtually every indicator of college impact—including the number of years of college completed—was a statistically significant predictor of senior-year attitudes toward race. Findings from other independent samples point in the same direction. Using data from four decades (the 1950s, 1960s, 1970s, and 1980s), Case and Greeley (1990) concluded that "the most clear, and surprising, finding as to the nature of the effect of education on egalitarian attitudes is its constancy" (p. 80). Equally important, they also concluded that the changes they observed were not attributable to cohort or social context effects.

Other studies using nationally representative samples point to college effects on other more racial-ethnic attitudes and values. These studies report net effects of a variety of college experiences on freshman-to-senior increases in students' cultural awareness and acceptance of other races and cultures (Astin, 1992); commitment to promoting racial understanding, acceptance of busing as a solution to racial imbalances, and viewing racism as a continuing problem (Milem, 1991, 1992, 1994); and first-year increases in openness to diversity and challenge (Pascarella, Edison, Nora, Hagedorn, & Terenzini, 1996). Each of these studies controls for the effects of a variety of students' precollege characteristics, including their initial racial-ethnic attitudes. Astin, Keup, and Lindholm (2002), however, provide evidence suggesting that higher education's ability to promote racial understanding and acceptance of other races and cultures may have declined between the mid-1980s and mid-1990s, perhaps by .21 to .22 of a standard deviation (or 8 to 9 percentile points).

The findings from single-campus studies are mixed. One study found class year unrelated to acceptance of multicultural education once controls were in place for other variables (Asada, Swank, & Goldey, 2003), and another reports evidence suggesting the possibility of a maturation effect (Pope-Davis & Ottavi, 1994). Other small-scale studies point to positive net effects of education on support for multicultural education, attribution of the difficulties African Americans experience to societal mechanisms rather than to Blacks as individuals (Seltzer et al., 1995), declines in negative racial stereotyping (Wood & Chesser, 1994), increased openness to human differences (Taylor, 1998), and cultural openness and tolerance (Volkwein, 1991). The latter two studies are both longitudinal and control for students' precollege racial-ethnic attitudes as well as for other initial differences.

Gender-Role Attitudes. We identified only a few studies that provide information on the net effects of college on students' gender role attitudes or values (Astin, 1993c; Korn, 1993; Miller-Bernal, 1993). But although limited in number, these studies concur that college probably promotes increased gender egalitarianism to a degree not attributable to other factors. Astin analyzed data from a nationally representative sample of some 20,000 students who entered more than 200 four-year institutions in 1985 and were surveyed four years later. After controlling for some 140 precollege student characteristics, including their gender role attitudes when they arrived on campus, Astin found that the number of years of college completed was significantly and positively associated with each of three measures of "feminism." Net of other influences, seniors (compared with themselves as freshmen) were more likely to agree that women are entitled to receive the same salaries and opportunities for advancement as men in comparable positions and to disagree with the assertions that a man who feels "led on" by a woman is entitled to have sex with her and that married women's responsibilities lie primarily with home and family.

Educational and Occupational Values. Although we uncovered only three studies concerning the independent effects of college on the values students attach to education, the studies are all methodologically sound and lead to the same conclusions. Each investigation finds that college attendance promotes increases in student perceptions of the intrinsic value of education and declines in their perceptions of the importance of instrumental and extrinsic values. Over the period of the studies, respondents also reported declines in their belief that the chief benefits of a college education are monetary, and as seniors they attached less importance to the goal of becoming very well-off financially than they had four years earlier (Astin, 1993c). These shifts persist even after controlling for a large number of students' precollege characteristics and their initial views on the value of education and the importance of being financially well-off. Astin also reports finding little evidence that this decline reflects social change rather than the impact of college.

Wilder and his colleagues (Wilder et al., 1997; Wilder et al., 1996) report findings consistent with Astin's, identifying statistically significant freshman- to senior-year shifts in educational values, or "philosophies," among students entering a selective, residential, liberal arts college during three different time periods ("eras"). The researchers found increases in student support for "academic" and "nonconformist" educational philosophies and declines in student support for "collegiate" and "vocational" philosophies. These shifts were statistically significant even when controlling for initial attitudes and values, academic ability, and motivation. In addition, the freshman- to senior-year increases in support for both the academic and nonconformist philosophies were more pronounced in the more recent eras, and support for the nonconformist philosophy increased more sharply than it did for the academic philosophy.

Knox, Lindsay, and Kolb (1993) provide persuasive evidence on net college effects on students' occupational values. After controlling for race-ethnicity, gender, socioeconomic status, and academic ability, these researchers found that each increment in college exposure increased by 36 to 41 percent the odds that students would value "getting ahead" compared to their peers with only a high school diploma. Completing a bachelor's or advanced degree, however, had no statistically significant net effect on the importance attached to job security, success, or money. Educational attainment also had significant and substantial effects on the importance attached to intrinsic occupational values, such as the freedom to make one's own decisions and doing work considered to be interesting and important. Net of other factors, individuals with two or more years of college, compared to their high school classmates with only a secondary school diploma, were nearly twice as likely to subscribe to those values, while bachelor's degree and advanced degree holders were two and a half and four and a half times, respectively, more likely to value such intrinsic occupational features (Table 2.4, p. 39).

Religious Attitudes and Values. We identified only two studies that dealt with net college effects on student religious attitudes and values (Graham & Cockriel, 1996; Graham & Donaldson, 1996). Both were based on the responses of more than 9,300 respondents to a 1993–94 ACT survey of students nearing the end of an associate or bachelor's degree program. Neither study controlled statistically for students' precollege religious attitudes or values, relying instead on self-reports of how much effect college had on them in selected areas of development. Students reported that both their growth and college's contributions to that growth were smallest in areas relating to the development of religious values. Because of the lack of controls we are not inclined to attach much importance to these findings, but they do call attention to an area of the scholarship on college effects that needs more empirical attention.

Understanding and Interest in the Arts. Studies by Astin (1993c) and Smart, Feldman, and Ethington (2000) provide evidence of the net effects of college on students' cultural and aesthetic interests, but that evidence is mixed. Smart and his colleagues find clear evidence of net four-year increases in the artistic interests of students who expressed such interest upon enrollment as well as later in the college years. Astin found a wide variety of college "involvement" factors positively related to freshman-to-senior increases in the likelihood that students would attend recitals and concerts. Those factors included the liberalism of the faculty, the percentage of peers majoring in the fine arts, and having been a guest in a faculty member's home. Astin concluded, however, that involvement in musical and cultural events reflected a more general tendency toward involvement in college. Astin also reported both increases and decreases in students' "artistic inclinations" depending on whether the analyses were based on a weighted or unweighted sample. Attributing his findings to a mix of college peer group and maturational effects, Astin concluded: "Whatever the explanation, the college experience appears to cause, at best, only a small increase in the artistic inclinations of young people (weighted data) and, at worst, a decrease (unweighted data)" (1993c, p. 118).

BETWEEN-COLLEGE EFFECTS

Conclusions from *How College Affects Students*

We concluded from our earlier review that the structural characteristics of an institution, with one exception, were relatively independent of changes in student attitudes and values. Such institutional features as size, type of control (excepting the influence of denominational schools on religious values), mission, and curricular emphasis appeared to be unrelated to attitudinal and value change in any consistent way. Where influences were found, they were small. Only institutional selectivity appeared to exert any consistent effect on changes in students' aesthetic and cultural values and interests, their political and social values, and their degree of religiousness (the direction of the effects was positive on the first two and negative on the third). Evidence on the effects of selectivity on educational and occupational values was mixed or missing. Overall, the weight of evidence relating to selectivity was modest and occasionally inconsistent.

Evidence from the 1990s

Sociopolitical Attitudes and Values. The past decade saw fewer studies of college effects attributable to the characteristics of the institutions students attend, but, as before, these studies consistently indicate that the kind of college a student attends continues to make a difference. And consistent with previous research, most recent studies lead to the conclusion that the characteristics typically used to differentiate among institutions, and that are widely associated with institution quality (such as type of control, mission, size, curricular emphasis, and selectivity), have little or no relation to changes in students' political orientations, dispositions toward social activism, or support for libertarian values.

We uncovered little evidence suggesting that structural institutional characteristics might shape students' sociopolitical values (Bowen & Bok, 1998; Dey, 1996). Dey analyzed information from nearly 25,000 students on more than 140 four-year campuses who participated in the freshman- (1985) and senior-year (1989) data collections that were part of the University of California at Los Angeles Higher Education Research Institute's Cooperative Institutional Research Program (CIRP). After controlling for the gender, race, ability, and parental income and education of entering students, as well as for indicators of the peer and faculty sociopolitical context on campus, Dey examined the effects on four measures of political attitudes of such institutional characteristics as selectivity, type, size, whether the institution was an historically Black college or university (HBCU), or whether it was a women's college. He found that attending a private college or university was positively related to freshman-to-senior increases in support for a woman's right to an abortion, and admissions selectivity was positively related to increases in students' liberal political orientation and their opposition to the death penalty. In both instances, the selectivity beta weights were less than .10. Dey found no consistent pattern in these findings, however, and the net effects of all other institutional characteristics (excluding measures of the peer and faculty contexts) were statistically nonsignificant. Bowen and Bok found educational attainment, but not institutional selectivity, related to voting behaviors. Some evidence suggests that the emphasis an institution places on diversity, at least as perceived by faculty members, for example, may affect students' electoral participation (Astin, 1992).

In a similar study of freshman- to senior-year change, this one using four panel studies of students entering four-year institutions and extending over the periods 1966 to 1970, 1971 to 1980 (a nine-year panel), 1983 to 1987, and 1987 to 1991, Dey (1997) again found limited evidence of effects associated with conventional, structural institutional features. Attending a women's college was positively related to more liberal political orientations in the first panel, and the same was true of attending an historically Black college in the first two cohorts. Neither type of institution was a significant factor in changing sociopolitical orientations among students in the most recent two cohorts Dey studied. Selectivity was also a positive predictor of increased liberalism in the first three cohorts but not in the most recent one (1987 to 1991). In these samples, measures of type of control and curricular mission were unrelated to any observed changes.

Astin (1993c) reports findings consistent with Dey's. Net of a range of other factors, Astin found that virtually none of 31 institutional and curricular characteristics (including selectivity) had significant effects on assorted measures of freshman- to senior-year changes in students' political identification, social activism, liberalism, or libertarianism. Milem (1998) reports similar results, and M. Kim (1998, 2001) found that modest positive net effects of attending a women's college (versus a coeducational institution) on freshman-to-senior changes in women students' desires to influence social conditions disappeared when measures of the peer and faculty context on a campus were taken into account. Kim also found that once the peer group emphasis on social activism and altruism was taken into account, other institutional characteristics, such as student-faculty ratio and a diversity-oriented curriculum, were unrelated to women students' interest in reshaping the political structure or in helping change social values.

Each of these studies points instead to the power of the sociopolitical environment on a campus. Peer and faculty contexts are commonly operationalized as the arithmetic average of the perceptions of a given environmental dimension among the students in an institution's entering cohort or among faculty members on that campus. The evidence from several independent national samples indicates positive net effects of the peer context on freshman- to senior-year increases in the likelihood of voting (Sax & Astin, 1998), commitment to social activism (Sax, 2000), liberal political orientations (Antonio, 1995; Astin, 1993c; Dey, 1996, 1997), libertarianism (Astin, 1993c), support for abortion rights and public-funded health care, opposition to the death penalty (Dey, 1996), support for higher taxation of the wealthy to reduce the national debt (Milem, 1998), and the importance women attach to influencing social conditions (M. Kim, 1998, 2001; Langdon, 1997). The peer context, however, can work in other directions. Campuses on which students in general attach a high value to material possessions and social status can militate against freshman-to-senior increases in liberalism (Astin, 1993c; Milem, 1998).

Similar, although less extensive, evidence points to statistically significant net effects of faculty attitudes and values on students' sociopolitical views. The faculty effects, moreover, are independent of the peer group influences and other factors, with faculty attitudes toward social activism, liberalism, and libertarianism (Astin, 1993c; Sax & Astin, 1998), social liberalism (Milem, 1998), and support for abortion rights (Dey, 1996) positively related to freshman-to-senior shifts among students toward the more "liberal" in each of these areas. Not all of these studies report statistics for both faculty and peer group effect sizes, but those that do suggest that the peer group exerts a somewhat stronger effect than does the faculty context.

Civic and Community Attitudes and Involvement. The weight of the evidence concerning between-college effects on students' civic and community engagement is consistent with that relating to sociopolitical attitudes. After controlling for characteristics (including students' precollege civic and community values), most of the standard variables used to differentiate among colleges and universities (and frequently for identifying institutional quality) fail as statistically reliable predictors of changes in students' civic and community involvement. There are, of course, exceptions. Some studies (both quantitative and qualitative) suggest that students on private and small campuses are more likely than their peers at larger and public institutions to report increases in altruistic values (Astin, 1996b; Kuh, 1993). Other studies indicate that attendance at both Catholic and Protestant colleges (versus nonsectarian institutions) has direct and positive effects over a four-year period on the importance students attach to civic responsibility, volunteerism, and civic and social values (Astin, Vogelgesang, Ikeda, & Yee, 2000; Rhee & Dey, 1996).

But other institutional characteristics were generally found to be unrelated to these outcomes. Astin (1996b) found that institutional selectivity had a statistically significant, negative effect on civic values, but it may have been indirect, mediated through the culture and kinds of activities encouraged on the campuses studied. Other research suggests that admissions selectivity has no measurable impact on students' civic values above and beyond that attributable to factors such as students' precollege traits and attitudes (Knox et al., 1993; Rhee & Dey, 1996). Neither of these latter two studies, moreover, found any link between institutional size and civic values. Nor, after taking other considerations into account, could Knox and his colleagues find a connection between an institution's type of control, percentage of full-time students, vocational emphasis, or proportion of students living on campus and any changes in student participation in community groups, volunteer work, youth organizations, or nonworship church activities.

Some research suggests—consistent with findings relating to between-college effects on students' sociopolitical attitudes—that the values held by students' peers and other aspects of an institution's organizational environment and behaviors can have important influences on civic and community attitudes and humanistic values (Berger, 2000b; Sax, 2000). Sax, for example, found that after taking into account characteristics students brought with them to college and the kinds of experiences they had once enrolled, the only institutional characteristic related to changes in students' commitments to community involvement was the positive effect of the peer group's concern for social activism.

We identified very few studies that examine the effects of attending a women's college on students' civic values or attitudes toward community service (Langdon, 1997; Smith, Wolf, & Morrison, 1995). Langdon, when controlling for student background characteristics and college experiences, found no relation between enrollment in a women's college and participation in community service. Smith and her colleagues, however, found that attending a women's college may *indirectly* shape net freshman-to-senior changes in civic involvement.

Racial-Ethnic Attitudes. The national debate over the past decade concerning the legality of state and federal affirmative action policies spawned a substantial research literature on students' racial-ethnic attitudes and other educational outcomes. The proportion dealing with between-institutional effects, however, is small.

One segment of the research on between-college effects on racial-ethnic attitudes focuses on the influence of what is frequently called *structural diversity,* or the proportional mix of students of different racial-ethnic or cultural origins. Some studies examine the effects of an institution's ethnic mix on student perceptions of the racial climate on their campus rather than on changes in individual student attitudes. But because student perceptions can be powerful shapers of attitudes and behaviors, it is important to examine how students view the racial climate on their campus.

Some studies indicate that, net of their entering characteristics, students on more racially diverse campuses perceive more racism or racial conflict than similar students on less diverse campuses (Hurtado, 1992, 1994). Other studies suggest just the opposite (Rothman, Lipset, & Nevitte, 2003; Springer, Terenzini, Pascarella, & Nora, 1995b). Studies based on two different samples also indicate that perceptions of campus racial tensions, even after controlling for student characteristics (including academic ability and political views), are positively related to institutional selectivity (regardless of students' race-ethnicity) and to institutional size (among Whites but not among other ethnic groups) (Hurtado, 1992, 1994).

These various studies, however, differ in so many ways (design, sample, instruments, and analytical procedures) that it is difficult to draw any firm conclusions. The Hurtado evidence clearly points to perceptual variations related to students' racial-ethnic origins. Perhaps more importantly, the belief that the racial mix of an institution—by itself—will have a direct effect on attitudes or values may seriously oversimplify the dynamics at work. For example, studies indicate that the structural diversity of a campus is (net of other factors) positively related to the likelihood that students will socialize with someone of a different race, discuss racial issues with peers, develop interracial friendships, and develop greater tolerance and awareness of different racial-ethnic groups (Antonio, 1998, 2000; Chang, 1996, 2001; Springer et al., 1995b; Toutkoushian & Smart, 2001). Convincing evidence suggests a positive, indirect effect of structural diversity both on greater multicultural diversity in the curriculum and on students' informal interactions with peers of a race-ethnicity different from their own, whether in friendship groups or in general (Gurin, 1999; Hurtado, Milem, Clayton-Pedersen, & Allen, 1999). At least one study, however, finds a negative net relation between campus diversity and White students' commitment to promoting racial understanding (Vogelgesang, 2001).

With one exception (Kim, 2000), other research suggests that institutional selectivity also has a slight negative influence on more specific dimensions of students' racial and ethnic attitudes. Even when controlling for other factors, evidence from nearly 9,000 students entering 115 four-year institutions in 1985 who were surveyed again four years later as seniors indicates that admissions selectivity had a statistically significant and negative (but small) effect on students' knowledge of people of different races and cultures as well as on their estimates of their abilities to get along with students whose ethnic origins differed from their own (Antonio, 1998, 2000; Toutkoushian & Smart, 2001). Other studies fail to find statistically significant relations between changes in racial-ethnic orientations and such other standard measures of institutional characteristics as size, type of control, proportion of full- and part-time students, highest degree offered, student-faculty ratios, and faculty salaries (Astin, 1993a, 1993c).

A small but rigorous body of research examines differences in orientation to diverse ideas, people, and cultures associated with attending two-year versus four-year colleges. Pascarella and his colleagues (Pascarella, Bohr, Nora, Raganathan, Desler, & Bulakowski, 1994), after controlling for precollege dispositions, ability, place of residence, and other factors, found no differences after one year between students enrolled in a two-year community college and a four-year, public commuter university in their openness to diversity and challenge. The criterion variable was a factorially derived scale reflecting students' orientation to intellectual challenges and their openness to encounters with diverse people, cultures, and ideas. A similarly structured and controlled study (using the same dependent variable) examined a much larger, nationally representative sample of students entering 5 two-year and 18 four-year institutions who were surveyed again two years after matriculation (Pierson, Wolniak, Pascarella, & Flowers, 2003). That inquiry, however, found that attending a two-year college had statistically significant and positive direct and indirect effects on students' openness to diversity (the same scale used in the previous study) in each of the students' first two years. Net of other factors, including precollege openness to diversity and challenge, community college students (compared with similar students at four-year institutions) gained a total advantage of .21 of a standard deviation after one year and a total advantage of .22 of a standard deviation after two years. Those effect sizes are the equivalent of 8 and 9 percentile point advantages, respectively, and suggest that most of college's impact occurs in students' first year. Pierson and his colleagues also report evidence indicating that two-thirds or more of the total effects of attending two-year colleges were direct rather than indirect.

We identified three studies that examined the effects of attending an all-women's college (versus a coeducational institution) on racial-ethnic attitudes and values (Kim, 2000; Smith, 1990; Smith et al., 1995). Using first- through senior-year data from three independent and nationally representative samples of women, these studies are generally consistent in finding that women's colleges have a positive influence on cultural awareness and appreciation, multicultural goals, and tolerance for the beliefs of others. These small but statistically significant effects persist beyond the influences of a wide array of students' precollege traits, academic involvement while in college, and also institutional size, location, and institutional and curricular emphasis on diversity. This evidence, however, also suggests that these institutions' effects may be indirect rather than direct, operating through their positive influence on women students' perceptions that their institution values multicultural objectives. Those perceptions, in turn, are positively related to higher levels of engagement and the importance attached to multicultural goals.

Flowers and Pascarella (1999a) found no such net changes in a national sample of African-American students who enrolled in historically Black colleges and universities rather than predominantly White institutions. These researchers studied shifts in students' "openness to diversity" using an eight-item scale reflecting openness to various forms of racial, cultural, and value diversity. After taking into account a range of students' precollege traits (including their socioeconomic status, ability, and openness) as well as numerous other institutional characteristics and students' experiences during college, Flowers and Pascarella found year-to-year changes in openness to diversity during the first three years of college unrelated to the racial-ethnic mix of the institution attended. They note that this finding does not support the views of some that HBCUs may inhibit the development of African-American students' openness to racial and ethnic diversity.

Although the weight of evidence indicates that most of the variables typically used to differentiate among postsecondary institutions are weakly (if at all) related to changes in students' freshman- to senior-year racial and ethnic attitudes (a finding consistent with the research examining such effects on other student outcomes), an emerging body of research consistently indicates that other institutional features, such as students' perceptions of an institution's peer and faculty climate, may be significant factors. These studies (all controlling for a variety of potentially confounding variables) indicate that student perceptions that faculty members are concerned about students, that administrators are open and inclusive of people of differing cultural backgrounds, and that their institution is committed to diversity are all associated with perceptions of lower racial tensions on campus (Hurtado, 1992, 1994).

Most institutional characteristics have little influence on one-year and freshman-to-senior net shifts in students' cultural awareness and commitment to promoting racial understanding, but one stands out: an institution's emphasis on promoting diversity (Astin, 1993a, 1993c; K. Smith, 1993; Whitt, Edison, Pascarella, Terenzini, & Nora, 2001). Other evidence, consistent with these findings, shows year-to-year gains in openness to diversity in each of the first three years of college among African-American students who believe their campus has a nondiscriminatory racial climate (Flowers & Pascarella, 1999) and among women who believe their institutions value multiculturalism (Smith et al., 1995) as well as among women exposed to peers and a general campus climate that they perceive to value social activism and altruism (Kim, 2000). The study by Smith and her colleagues suggests that the effects of these perceptions may be indirect (at least for women), mediated by attending an all-women's college, which shapes women's academic and extracurricular involvements and successes, leading in turn to changes in racial-ethnic attitudes.

The role of the peer context remains unclear. Three large, nationally representative, well-controlled studies found no statistically significant net effects of the peer environment on students' openness to diversity (Pascarella, Edison, Nora, Hagedorn, & Terenzini, 1996) or the importance they attach to promoting racial understanding (Astin, 1993c) or understanding differences in cultures and philosophies of life (Ethington, 2000).

The nature of differential institutional effects on students' racial and ethnic views and values is complex. Indeed, although Hurtado (1992) studied perceptions of racial tensions on campus, she may have spoken as well for influences that shape students' racial-ethnic attitudes when she concluded that no single element of a campus environment may be the dominant force. Instead, the dynamics more likely reflect an amalgam of forces, including external influences (such as historical and contemporary conditions), structural characteristics, group relations, and institutional philosophies and ideologies.

Gender-Role Attitudes. We identified six studies that examined the net effects of various college characteristics on students' attitudes toward gender roles or "feminist" orientations, but the findings are inconclusive. Astin (1993c) reported the political liberalism of a campus's faculty positively related to freshman- to senior-year changes in three measures of students' feminism. Langdon (1997) reports a similar finding on the diversity orientation of faculty, although Korn (1993) found no relation between faculty liberalism and changes in student attitudes toward date rape. Besides the faculty's liberalism, however, neither Astin nor Korn found any of a wide array of other institutional characteristics or environmental measures statistically related to gender-role attitudes beyond the effects of student background characteristics and various forms of involvement in college.

Miller-Bernal (2000) provides some evidence that women's colleges may promote adoption of feminist views, but the differences were unadjusted for initial differences in views or other potentially confounding factors. Three studies that did control for such factors as academic ability, religious preferences or religiosity, degree aspirations, parents' socioeconomic status, or mother's role in family decision making (Langdon, 1997; Miller-Bernal, 1993; Riordan, 1990) found no link between attendance at a women's college and first- to senior-year changes on various measures of women's views on gender inequalities. Riordan did find that among college *graduates,* the women's college effect was more substantial and diminished only slightly when controlling for students' socioeconomic status and academic ability.

Educational and Occupational Values. We uncovered only a handful of studies that examined institution-related effects on changes in students' educational and occupational values, but all are methodologically sound and thus relatively persuasive. Knox, Lindsay, and Kolb (1993), after controlling for the race-ethnicity, gender, socioeconomic status, and academic abilities of entering students, as well as for the value they attached to getting a good education, found no college characteristics that had any statistically significant effect on subsequent educational values. The institutional traits examined but found wanting as predictors included enrollment, selectivity, private control, percentage of full-time students, vocational emphasis of the institution, and its being mainly residential.

Pascarella and his colleagues found no net effect on students' interest in learning for self-understanding from attending a four- versus a two-year institution for one year (Pascarella, Bohr, Nora, Raganathan, Desler, & Bulakowski, 1994). A larger, similarly designed study replicating Pascarella et al. with a nationally representative sample, however, found that community college attendance at the end of two years had significant, positive total and direct effects on students' orientation to learning for self-understanding (Pierson et al., 2003). As with the findings relating to the effects of two- versus four-year attendance on openness to diversity, community college students had an advantage at the end of their second year of .22 of a standard deviation (about 9 percentile points), almost all of which was direct rather than indirect. This finding suggests that the positive influence of community college attendance on learning orientation is not totally explained by differences in the academic and nonacademic experiences of two-year and four-year students. The effect persists when controlling for differences in the kinds of students enrolled and in their academic and nonacademic experiences while enrolled.

Among African-American students, some research suggests that the racial composition of an institution can influence educational values. After controlling for a number of other factors, Flowers and Pascarella (1999b) found that African-American students enrolled in an historically Black college or university (compared with similar Black students attending a predominantly White institution) attached greater value after one year to learning for self-understanding. The study, however, has still to be replicated.

Between-college effects on students' occupational values have received little attention since 1990. Knox and his colleagues (1993) found evidence indicating that shifts in both the intrinsic and extrinsic occupational values students hold were "entirely unaffected by the college context" (p. 48), including size, selectivity, control, proportion of full-time students, vocational emphasis, or residential character. As noted earlier, however, more recent studies indicate that students attending an institution where the peer culture values material possessions and status are more likely than their peers on less materialistic campuses to report an increase in the value they attach to being well-off financially (Astin, 1993c; Milem, 1998).

Religious Attitudes and Values. Only a very few studies over the past decade have examined the effects of institutional characteristics on students' religious values, but these are based on large, independent, nationally representative samples of students (Astin & Antonio, 1999, 2000; Lee, 2002b; Railsback, 1994). Astin and Antonio and Lee examined the impact of selectivity, but they found different effects. Astin and Antonio reported selectivity negatively related to changes in religious beliefs and convictions, whereas Lee found no statistically significant selectivity effect, net of other student and institutional characteristics. Lee also reported finding no net effects attributable to institutional type or location. Some limited evidence, consistent with the research we reviewed in our earlier book, indicates that church-related schools (at least Christian College Coalition institutions) may strengthen or maintain their students' evangelical religious commitments more than non-church-related institutions (Railsback, 1994).

Understanding and Interest in the Arts. Few researchers have examined differential institutional effects on students' interests in, or appreciation for, culture and the visual and performing arts. In a large, comprehensive, and well-controlled national study, Astin (1993c) found virtually no institutional characteristics related to freshman- to senior-year changes in student artistic inclinations. He did find, however, a positive association between artistic interests and leaving school or transferring to another institution, and he speculated that artistically inclined students may leave or transfer in order to find an environment more supportive of their interests. This proposition is supported by evidence summarized in Chapter Eight suggesting that institutional climate can be a powerful force in students' decisions to persist or withdraw. In addition, such speculation is supported by evidence from Smart and his colleagues (Smart & Feldman, 1998; Smart et al., 2000).

Two generally well-controlled studies point to a statistically significant and positive net effect on African-American students' interest in, and understanding of, the arts and humanities associated with attending an historically Black college or university rather than a predominantly White institution (DeSousa & Kuh, 1996; Flowers, 2002b).

WITHIN-COLLEGE EFFECTS

Conclusions from *How College Affects Students*

The pre-1990s research suggested that the dominant factors in attitudinal and value changes across topical areas were students' interpersonal associations with both peers and faculty members, often in the departmental context but more frequently in the residence halls. Although the effects were modest, where students lived clearly influenced their occupational, political, and religious attitudes and values. Compared with students living at home or elsewhere off campus, students living on campus showed greater increases in sociopolitical liberalism and in valuing intrinsic occupational rewards and greater declines in religiosity over the periods studied. Researchers reported mixed results when examining residential effects on cultural and aesthetic value change, and residential effects on gender role attitudes were largely unexplored. Students' academic major field was generally unrelated to attitudinal changes, according to the research, but the degree of value consensus and homogeneity among students and faculty members appeared to exert an important contextual influence on student socialization and value change. It is likely that the residential, peer, and contextual effects are mutually reinforcing, but the dynamics underlying these effects remained unclear. Little could be said with certainty about whether the effects observed were a function of the frequency and/or nature of students' individual contacts with peers and faculty members or were due to a more generalized context created by a combination of students and faculty members who shared a certain set of attitudes or values toward which new students gravitated over time.

Evidence from the 1990s

Sociopolitical Attitudes and Values. The within-college forces shaping changes in students' sociopolitical attitudes and orientations fall into four categories: major field and course-taking experiences, service to their communities, peer group and faculty interactions, and membership in Greek social organizations.

Major field and other courses. The academic major field stands out as a potentially important area of college impact, representing as it does a constellation of factors that are part of students' daily experience, shaped by the peers and faculty members with whom they interact and the cultures they create. In the aggregate, however, the evidence relating to the effects of major field on various measures of social activism, social concern, and attitudes toward certain public policies (such as welfare) is specific to a small number of major fields and largely inconclusive. In a study of more than 12,000 new students enrolling in more than 200 four-year colleges in 1985 who were surveyed four years later, Sax (2000) found that the seniors majoring in engineering expressed significantly lower levels of commitment to social activism than did their peers in other academic majors. This finding persisted even after taking into account students' precollege characteristics (including initial commitment to social activism and other social values), institutional characteristics, and a wide array of students' experiences during college. This finding is consistent with other similar analyses of this same database, which suggested that the larger the number of math and other quantitative courses taken, the more likely students were to hold conservative views (Astin, 1993c). Analyses of the NLS-72 database found no net effects of majoring in business, education, or the arts and sciences on students' voting behavior, engagement in political discussions, or the importance they attached to working for social and economic justice (Knox et al., 1993). With some exceptions (such as Royse & Riffe, 1999), other studies provide corroborating evidence (Biddle et al., 1990; Feldman, Smart, & Ethington, 1999; Smart et al., 2000; Smart & Feldman, 1998). Smart, Feldman, and Ethington (2000), for example, found support for the proposition that most academic environments congruent with students' interests and abilities promoted greater increases in those areas than incongruent major environments. Using the same database as Sax, Smart et al. found that "social" Holland-type students in "social" environments showed some increase in their social interests and abilities, while similar students in nonsocial environments displayed some declines, although the changes were slight.

These studies suggest that major field effects tend to be value-specific and most apparent in those areas of value change that are closely related to the fields of study (in this instance, the social sciences and social major field types in Holland's typology). They also indicate that those environmental effects are stronger in some fields (for example, the arts) than in others.

Researchers have also found that specific course topics have a net impact on relevant student attitudes. For example, women's studies courses appear to have demonstrable net effects on student views about egalitarianism and activism for social causes as well as student intentions to engage in social activism (Stake & Hoffmann, 2001). In addition, courses exploring oppression may affect social justice attitudes (Van Soest, 1996). These studies, together with the evidence indicating few if any specific-major field effects, suggest that the impact of academic environments and activities on students' sociopolitical views are a function of the attitudes and values of the people with whom students associate in these academic enclaves, as well as the academic experiences they have, rather than of the particular major field or discipline. With some of the exceptions already noted, it would appear that major field effects may be more variable *within* specific fields than between them. The research on academic majors also examines the impacts of specific disciplines, and Smart, Feldman, and Ethington (2000) provide strong evidence that major field effects are more clearly discernible when academic majors are clustered according to disciplinary traits (not content) consistent with Holland's theory of careers (Holland, 1997). Smart and his colleagues, for example, clustered 76 disciplines into six Holland-based environments. The absence of strong effects associated with specific departments may also be due in part to the fluidity of students' initial and subsequent selection of major fields (Smart et al., 2000).

Community service and service learning. Earlier in this chapter we discussed the research relating to students' social and civic values as reflected in their willingness to engage in various forms of community service, with volunteering viewed as an outcome of the college experience. Here we examine some of the influences of community service on related learning outcomes, such as sociopolitical attitudes, social activism orientations, and attitudes toward individual rights.

We noted earlier the emerging concern about perceived growth in student cynicism and estrangement from the formal political system and its processes. Perhaps the most visible and widespread response has been the increased emphasis on service learning, "a form of experiential education in which students engage in activities that address human and community needs together with structured opportunities intentionally designed to promote learning and development" (Jacoby & Associates, 1996). Service learning goes significantly beyond including community service opportunities for extra credit in a traditional course. Service learning incorporates features found in both long established and more recent philosophical, curricular, and pedagogical literatures, such as "problem-based learning, collaborative learning, undergraduate research, critical thinking, multiculturalism and diversity, civic awareness, leadership skills, and professional and social responsibility . . . just a few items on the contemporary academic agenda that naturally ally themselves with service-learning programs" (Zlotkowski, 1998, p. 4).[5]

The weight of evidence shows—conclusively, we think—that participation in community service in general, and service learning in particular, has statistically significant and positive net effects on students' sociopolitical attitudes and beliefs. Astin (1993c) reports that community volunteer work, net of other variables, most strongly influenced students' disposition to social activism. Other controlled, multivariate analyses of CIRP data from more than 22,000 students entering 117 four-year colleges and universities in 1994 and followed up four years later tested for differences in the effects of varying forms of community service. After controlling for a wide array of students' precollege characteristics (including race-ethnicity, gender, socioeconomic status, religious preferences, high school volunteer work, and pretest scores on the outcome measure), as well as characteristics of the institution attended, the researchers found both service learning and generic community volunteer service produced statistically significant, positive, and independent effects on students' commitment to social activism (Astin et al., 2000; Vogelgesang & Astin, 2000). Sax (2000) reports similar findings based on analyses of a 1985 to 1989 national cohort of students. Some evidence suggests that service learning may have stronger effects on some attitudes than on others (Kendrick, 1996; Vogelgesang & Astin, 2000).

Some studies also suggest that different dimensions of a service-learning course shape the extent of the learning outcomes. These dimensions (more is better on each) include the amount of time spent in service-learning activities (Mabry, 1998); the amount of "reflection" on the experience, such as keeping a journal, writing reflective essays, formal and informal discussion with faculty and peers (Astin et al., 2000; Conrad & Hedin, 1991; Eyler & Giles, 1999; Gray, Ondaatje, Fricker, & Geschwind, 2000; Jordan, 1994; Levesque & Prosser, 1996;

Mabry, 1998; Shumer & Belbas, 1996); the "quality of the placement," such as the challenge and variety of the work, level of responsibility, sense of being appreciated by those with whom the student works (Eyler, Giles, & Braxton, 1997b); the alignment of the service provided with course objectives and content (Cohen & Kinsey, 1994; Eyler et al., 1997b; Gray et al., 2000); and the preparation students receive to ready them psychologically for their service experiences and the benefits they can derive from them (Rhoads, 1998).

Studies smaller in scale and scope than those from the Cooperative Institutional Research Program point with equal consistency (both among themselves and in relation to the large-scale national investigations) to the conclusion that service learning has significant, positive, and independent effects on a variety of sociopolitical outcomes. With a few exceptions (Parker-Gwin & Mabry, 1998) these studies find that, after controlling precollege characteristics including the social or political attitude and value outcomes under study, students who have had a service-learning course (compared with similar students who have not) show postcourse increases on an array of sociopolitical attitudes and values (Cress, Astin, Zimmerman-Oster, & Burkhardt, 2001; Eyler, Giles, & Braxton, 1997a, 1997b; Eyler & Giles, 1999; Giles & Eyler, 1994; Hesser, 1995; Kendrick, 1996; Mabry, 1998). The evidence also suggests that the positive effects of service-learning experiences increase as the number of service hours increases (Cress et al., 2001, for example).

One might reasonably hypothesize that the contributions to their communities that students perceive they are making through their service-learning experience might enhance their perceptions of their social efficacy, the belief that they can make a difference in their communities or their world. But the empirical evidence is mixed. Several controlled studies using independent samples report service learning is related to gains in students' "citizenship confidence" and intentions to include service to others in their career plans (Eyler et al., 1997a, 1997b; Myers-Lipton, 1998).[6] More studies, after controlling for other factors, including precourse measures of self-efficacy, find little or no statistically significant increase in students' perceptions of self-efficacy (Giles & Eyler, 1994; Hudson, 1996; Kendrick, 1996; Markus, Howard, & King, 1993; Sax, 2000; Serow, Ciechalski, & Daye, 1990) or even a decline (Miller, 1997). Miller suggests the decline might reflect a loss of idealism, a regression-to-the-mean effect associated with an initially high sense of self-efficacy, or a larger sense of decline in the ability to control one's world that comes with increasing maturity. The latter two effects could reflect a statistical artifact or a maturational change rather than any college effect.

Skeptics suggest, however, that service learning's outcomes may not always be positive. Kozeracki (2000), for example, thinks that some of the reported positive outcomes of service learning may be attributable to a halo effect or to a "honeymoon period" during which this approach to instruction has not yet been held up to critical scrutiny. Moreover, Jones (2002) has suggested that, for some students, service learning may actually reinforce negative stereotypes and assumptions students bring with them to college.

Peer and faculty interactions. In the "Between-College Effects" section of this chapter we examined the evidence on the effects of an institution's peer and faculty contexts. These contexts had been treated analytically as institutionwide influences on individual students. Here we look at the effects on students' sociopolitical attitudes of personal interactions with other students and with faculty members.

With one exception (Dey, 1996), the weight of evidence clearly indicates that students' interactions with their peers have statistically significant effects on changes in various dimensions of their sociopolitical orientations (Astin, 1992, 1993c; Gurin, 1999; Gurin, Dey, Hurtado, & Gurin, 2002; Gurin, Peng, Lopez, & Nagda, 1999). Studies of the college experiences students have and their impacts on an array of attitudes and orientations are varied, but across measures of cause and consequence their findings share a high degree of consistency. These findings, moreover, all persist in the presence of controls for a daunting variety of pre-college characteristics (including gender, race-ethnicity, socioeconomic status, ability, and students' initial attitude or value), institutional characteristics (such as type, size, selectivity, and measures of peer and faculty contexts), and other variables relating to students' college experiences (such as residence arrangement, employment status, enrollment status, major, coursework, and involvement in various college activities). In several instances, as one might expect, college experiences shape more than one sociopolitical attitude or value outcome.

Participating in campus demonstrations and discussing racial-ethnic topics with peers are positively associated with freshman-to-senior increases in support for more government involvement in disarmament, pollution control, national debt reduction, national health care, and opposition to the death penalty. Students with more frequent interaction with peers are more likely to place themselves toward the left on the liberal-conservative spectrum, although the shifts are slight (Astin, 1993c). Seniors (compared with themselves as freshmen) who interact frequently with peers and with faculty members are also more likely than their less interactive peers to attach importance to influencing social values, participating in community action programs, and influencing the political structure; they are also more likely to vote (Astin, 1992, 1993c; Gurin, 1999; Gurin et al., 2002).

These same activities appear to lead to freshman- to senior-year changes in libertarian views. As seniors, students are more likely to support such policies as liberal divorce laws and to oppose institutional or governmental regulation of individual rights in such areas as cohabitation before marriage, abortion, marijuana use, and selection of campus speakers (Astin, 1993c).

Other factors. Other college experiences that shape freshman-to-senior changes in democratic and sociopolitical attitudes and values seem to be associated with levels of activism and engagement with diversity in many forms. Participation in a racial or cultural awareness workshop and enrollment in ethnic or women's studies courses, for example, are both likely to nudge students' political orientations toward the left side of the liberal-conservative spectrum and increase their support for social activism (Astin, 1993c). The classroom effects appear to be more closely related to courses and their content than to the offering department or program (Gurin et al., 2002), although it is clear that courses dealing with social oppression, diversity, or women's issues are more likely to be offered in ethnic and women's studies programs than in the general curriculum. These effects persist in the presence of controls for students' backgrounds and college experiences as well as for their institutions' structural and environmental characteristics. Participation in intercollegiate athletics appears, nine years after entering college, to have had no impact on students' political and social dispositions once other factors were taken into account (Pascarella & Smart, 1991).

Whether membership in a Greek social organization has any net effect on students' sociopolitical leanings remains an open question. Astin (1993c), studying close to 25,000 freshmen in 1985 and again in 1989 when they were seniors, and after controlling for a large number of student, institutional, environmental, and involvement measures, found that seniors who were members of Greek social organizations were more likely than nonmembers to be conservative in their sociopolitical identification and views. Interestingly, Astin also found that fraternity or sorority members were more likely than independents to show increases on several measures of libertarianism. He speculated that Greek social organization members may support personal and individual freedoms but oppose the views on government and social policy inherent in social and political liberalism.

Other studies, most of them smaller in size and scope than Astin's, uncovered few if any statistically significant effects relating to fraternity or sorority membership. Lottes and Kuriloff (1994a) report small and negative net effects of Greek affiliation on measures of liberalism and social conscience, but other evidence points to no links between fraternity and sorority involvement and political orientation (Matney & Wiley Kelly, 1997), liberalism, or social conscience (Baier & Whipple, 1990). Wilder and McKeegan (1999), after their thorough review of the literature dealing with the effects of fraternity and sorority membership on various student outcomes, concluded that the senior-year differences between Greeks and independents in measures of civic and social values more likely reflected precollege conditions than Greek affiliation.

Civic and Community Attitudes and Engagement. Most post-1990 studies of college's impact on students' civic and community-related attitudes and values focused on the effects of students' experiences as volunteers in their communities,[7] and the effects of service-learning courses drew particular attention. Many entering college students bring previous volunteer and service-learning experience with them, perhaps as many as three-quarters of them by one estimate (Astin, 1996b). Even when previous volunteer community service experience and other self-selection factors are accounted for, however, and with a few exceptions (Hudson, 1996; Jordan, 1994; Parker-Gwin & Mabry, 1998), the weight of evidence indicates that participation in community service activities has statistically significant and, in some studies, substantial positive effects on a wide array of civic values and activities. The operational forms these concepts take vary, but the relation between community service and civic and community-oriented or "other-oriented" attitudes and values is clear.

Studies suggest that *any* form of community service has beneficial effects on students' civic attitudes and orientations. By as much as a two-to-one margin, students who participate in some form of community service (compared with those who do not) are more likely to report an increase in their sense of responsibility and obligation to contribute to their communities, and participants are more than four times as likely to say they plan to volunteer in succeeding semesters and years (Astin, 1993c; Sax & Astin, 1997; Villalpando, 1996).

The net influences of the more systematic, structured, and integrated experiences that typically constitute service learning appear to be stronger yet. When volunteer community service is taken into account, controlled analyses of independent samples indicate that participation in a service-related course provides additional benefits on each of a dozen measures of civic responsibility. These measures include students' commitment to community service, to helping others, to understanding community problems, to helping clean up the environment, and to continuing volunteer work in the future (Astin & Sax, 1998; Gray et al., 2000; Sax & Astin, 1997).[8]

Smaller-scale studies (both quantitative and qualitative) also find significant and positive net effects of community service, particularly service-learning experiences, on students' orientations toward their communities. The studies find service learning promotes citizenship confidence (efficacy), values, and skills (Eyler et al., 1997a, 1997b; Myers-Lipton, 1998); community involvement and commitment to providing service in the future (Giles & Eyler, 1994); and several measures of civic responsibility (Battistani, 1996; Myers-Lipton, 1998; Rhoads, 1998). One series of estimates, based on a quasi-experimental study of about 90 University of Michigan students in service and nonservice-learning courses, reported the benefits of service learning courses ranged from .40 of a standard deviation (about 16 percentile points) on students' orientation toward others and away from self to 1.09 standard deviations (36 percentile points) on the belief that one has a social responsibility to help others (Markus, Howard, & King, 1993). A small body of evidence, however, suggests that *mandatory* volunteerism may reduce the impact of such experiences on civic and community values (Stukas, Snyder, & Clary, 1999).

Evidence from a large, national, controlled study of the levels and areas of engagement among more than 42,000 students indicates that membership in a fraternity or sorority (versus remaining independent) has a positive effect on community service (Hayek, Carini, O'Day, & Kuh, 2002; Thorson, 1997). Thorson also found evidence that Greek alumni, after controlling precollege socioeconomic status and postgraduate income, are more likely than independents to contribute to religious organizations and (marginally) to other nonprofit organizations. Participation in historically Black Greek-letter organizations also appears to increase involvement in service projects (Schuh, Triponey, Heim, & Nishimura, 1992).

Other collegiate experiences that appear to have a positive influence on students' civic values and community orientations include majoring in the social sciences (Berger, 2000b) or in the social Holland-type academic fields (Huang & Healy, 1997; Sergent & Sedlacek, 1990) but not in the sciences (Rhee & Dey, 1996); attending a racial or cultural awareness workshop (Sax, 2000); discussing political and social issues and socializing with students from another racial-ethnic background (Sax, 2000; Villalpando, 1996); interacting with peers in general (Kuh, 1995); participating in learning communities and collaborative learning (Tinto, 1995) or intercollegiate athletics (Shulman & Bowen, 2001); and receiving financial aid in the form of work-study assistance (U.S. Department of Education, 2000).

Racial-Ethnic Attitudes. With the possible exception of students' sociopolitical orientations and behaviors, probably no set of attitudes and values has attracted more attention over the past decade than that relating to race-ethnicity and national and cultural origins. Considering how issues of race and cultural differences have shaped America's history, this attention is warranted.[9]

Over the past half-century, much of the research on race relations, racial-ethnic attitudes, and prejudice has been influenced by Gordon Allport's book *The Nature of Prejudice* (Allport, [1954] 1979). According to Allport, prejudice is conditioned largely by the nature of the contact among individuals of different racial-ethnic groups. This "contact hypothesis" holds that interracial contact is more likely to lead to positive attitudes if it involves people of equal status, occurs under cooperative conditions, and has the active support of powerful authorities (of various kinds).[10, 11]

Since 1990, the research exploring the within-college effects on students' attitudes and values concerning people of different races and cultural backgrounds falls into eight categories relating to the form or location of students' contacts with others whose race-ethnicity differs from their own: academic major field, residence, fraternity or sorority membership, peer and faculty interactions, interventions specifically designed to change attitudes, volunteer work, study abroad experiences, and intercollegiate athletics.

Major field. Our earlier review indicated that majoring in the humanities and social sciences had positive effects on students' sociopolitical attitudes (including racial-ethnic attitudes). Findings from the few studies published since 1990 that examine major field effects, however, are mixed. One found no significant shifts in attitudes toward affirmative action practices once precollege attitudes were controlled (K. Smith, 1993), whereas other analyses were more consistent with the earlier evidence. Astin (1993c), for example, found that net of other factors, freshman- to senior-year changes in students' commitment to promoting racial understanding were negatively affected by majoring in business, nursing, science, or engineering. Other controlled studies based on independent samples report findings consistent with those of Astin (Flowers & Pascarella, 1999a; Guimond, 1999; Guimond & Palmer, 1989, 1990; Springer, 1996).

Residence. With a few noteworthy exceptions (Asada et al., 2003; Knox et al., 1993; K. Smith, 1993), the studies we reviewed generally point to the positive net effects of living in a residence hall (versus off campus) on shifts toward more positive and inclusive racial-ethnic attitudes and openness to diversity broadly defined. These effects are observable in independent, large-scale, national studies even after taking into account students' initial racial-ethnic attitudes, other precollege characteristics, and a wide array of other institutional and college experience variables (Astin, 1993c; Pascarella, Edison, Nora, Hagedorn, & Terenzini, 1996; Whitt et al., 2001). And evidence from single-campus studies leads to the same conclusion (Molla & Westbrook, 1990; Nesdale & Todd, 2000; Pike, 2002), suggesting the multiple effects of living on campus. Pike, for example, found on-campus living positively related to openness to diversity regardless of the kind of housing. Both the Pike and the Nesdale studies also suggest, however, that the magnitude of the impact of a year of on-campus residence is not uniform in all residential settings. Both studies found the residential impact greater when students lived in a residence purposely structured to encourage students' engagement with one another in systematic learning environments focused on academic or social issues or themes or specifically on students' intercultural knowledge and openness. Both of these studies, of course, support the contact hypothesis.

Fraternity and sorority membership. With the exception of Asada, Swank, and Goldey (2003), the weight of evidence indicates that fraternity or sorority membership shapes student views on racial-ethnic diversity, and the effect is probably negative. Pascarella, Edison, Nora, Hagedorn, and Terenzini (1996), for example, in perhaps the most rigorous examination of this question, studied nearly 2,300 students during their first year at 18 four-year colleges and universities around the country. They controlled for student scores on an eight-item scale tapping openness to diversity as well as numerous other precollege student traits, institutional environments, and a range of students' academic and social experiences. Net of all those factors, Greek membership was negatively related to students' openness to diversity at the end of the students' first year. Other studies using independent samples and different measures of racial attitudes, as well as fewer and somewhat less rigorous controls for self-selection factors, yield findings consistent with those of Pascarella et al. (Antonio, 2001; Milem, 1994; Wood & Chesser, 1994).

Peer and faculty interactions. One might reasonably expect that students' college experiences will shape their attitudes toward members of racial-ethnic groups and cultures different from their own, particularly given the lack of ethnic and cultural awareness and understanding many students bring with them to college (Hurtado, Enberg, Ponjuan, & Landreman, 2002; Saddlemire, 1996). A small body of evidence also suggests that the greater the structural diversity (or racial-ethnic mix of students) on a campus, the more likely students are both to socialize with someone of another race-ethnicity and to discuss racial issues as well as to have a variety of other encounters with diverse people (Chang, 2001; Gurin, 1999; Springer, 1996). The direct relation between structural diversity and encounters with people of different cultural origins is not strong, but it is statistically significant even when a number of student background traits, institutional characteristics, and other college experiences are taken into account.

In the overall population, the evidence is mixed about the effects on racial-ethnic attitudes of having friends from a different group. Some studies indicate that such friendships have no appreciable effect once other factors are taken into account (Sigelman & Welch, 1991). Other studies, however, provide support for the contact hypothesis, indicating that among African Americans, at least, having friends of another race may be one of the strongest predictors of racial attitudes even when other considerations are taken into account (Ellison & Powers, 1994; Powers & Ellison, 1995).

In studies of college students, the weight of evidence is reasonably clear and consistent in suggesting that, across racial-ethnic groups, having friends of another race and being a member of an interracial friendship group has significant and positive net effects on racial-ethnic attitudes and values (Antonio, 1998, 1999, 2000, 2001; Asada et al., 2003; Hurtado, Carter, & Sharp, 1995; K. Smith, 1993; Wright, Aron, McLaughlin-Volpe, & Ropp, 1997). Antonio (2000) estimated that students in friendship groups that were diverse were two to five times more likely to interact with students of a different race than were their peers, "most" or "all" of whose friends were of the same race-ethnicity as they. He also found that the percentage of same-race friends was significantly and inversely related to measures of cultural knowledge, interest, and understanding as well as the importance attached to promoting racial understanding. The relation was the same among both Whites and students of color, and it held in the presence of controls for differences in students' backgrounds and precollege knowledge and understanding, institutional characteristics, and a variety of college experiences. It also may be true, however, that living in an environment where interracial social contact is common does not guarantee that either people of color or Whites will see race relations as amicable (Sigelman & Welch, 1993).

Considerable research indicates that students' more casual interactions with members of a racial-ethnic group different from their own (compared to interactions within multiracial friendship groups) also have statistically significant and positive net effects on these attitudes and values. Well-controlled studies using different national samples of students show, for example, that discussing racial issues and socializing with members of a racial-ethnic group different from one's own have positive net effects on such outcomes as increases in students' knowledge and acceptance of persons of other races and cultures, the importance students give to promoting racial understanding, and their acceptance of busing as a means of achieving racial balance in the schools as well as on declines in students' beliefs that racial discrimination is no longer a social problem (Antonio, 1998; Astin, 1993a, 1993c; Friedlander & MacDougall, 1992; Milem, 1991, 1994; Sax & Astin, 1998). Other studies link informal student interactions (net of other factors) to increases on other measures of racial-ethnic awareness and engagement (Gurin et al., 2002), to openness to various forms or manifestations of diversity (Globetti, Globetti, Brown, & Smith, 1993; Lopez, 1993; Pascarella, Edison, Nora, Hagedorn, & Terenzini, 1996; Springer et al., 1995b; Volkwein, 1991;

Whitt et al., 2001; Wolniak, Pierson, & Pascarella, 2001), and to declines in racial prejudice (Chang, 2000a). As was the case with the outcomes cited just previously, these effects generally hold across racial-ethnic groups.

Although some evidence indicates that student-faculty interaction does not increase openness to diversity beyond the effects of peer interaction (Pike, 2002), the pattern of effects of student-faculty contact largely parallels that of student-student interactions. With respect to students' racial-ethnic attitudes and values, student-faculty contact appears to have a significant and net positive impact on promoting racial understanding and other measures of racial-ethnic attitudes (Astin, 1993a, 1993c; Milem, 1994, 1999b).

Curricular, classroom, and other formal interventions. Students' encounters with diversity can, of course, take many forms and occur in many settings, and personal friendships or more casual interpersonal interactions constitute only two of those mechanisms. Over the past decade, colleges and universities have moved to encourage students' encounters with diversity through more formal, often curricular approaches. One such vehicle, widely adopted, has been the implementation of "diversity requirements" mandating that students take one or more courses dealing specifically with issues of race-ethnicity, national or historical cultures, gender, social class, sexual orientation, age, disabilities, and so on. Indeed, by the end of the 1990s, 54 percent of all accredited colleges and universities in the United States had formally adopted such a requirement, and another 8 percent were in the process of doing so. Of the institutions having or planning such requirements, 75 percent have instituted them within the past 10 years and 30 percent within the past 5 years (Humphreys, 2000). Faculty members across disciplinary fields have also revamped courses to incorporate diverse perspectives.

The research is often unclear whether the courses studied are required or elective, offered by a "traditional" program or by one with a specific mission to treat diversity issues (such as women's or ethnic studies programs), address specific diversity-related topics (such as culture or social inequality), or offer traditional materials from diverse perspectives. We will not attempt to unscramble that mixture but will note that the evidence from the 1990s indicates overwhelmingly that participation in such courses has statistically significant and positive effects on students' "multicultural competence," including awareness of other ethnicities and cultures, openness to diversity, and the importance attached to promoting racial understanding.

One segment of this research comprises studies examining course-taking in general, quantifying, for example, the number of diversity courses taken over a given period of time with no particular attention to the details of the courses taken. These studies are usually based on large, national samples of students and employ controls for precollege measures of the outcome variables and a number of other potentially confounding self-selection factors as well as for the characteristics of the institutions attended and a variety of other student experiences. These studies find that such course-taking is associated with increased tolerance and with more inclusive racial-ethnic attitudes, whether the changes are monitored over four years of college (Astin, 1993a, 1993c; Astin & Antonio, 1999, 2000; Gurin, 1999; Gurin et al., 2002; Gurin et al., 1999; Hurtado, 2001; Sax & Astin, 1998) or shorter periods of time (Antonio, 1999, 2001; Lopez, 1993; Milem, 1992, 1994; Moran, 1989; K. Smith, 1992; Springer, Palmer, Terenzini, Pascarella, & Nora, 1997). Some studies suggest that enrollment in women's studies courses also has statistically significant net effects on students' racial-ethnic attitudes and a more general openness to diversity (Hurtado, 2001; Palmer, 1999; Springer et al., 1997), although Palmer's (1999) well-controlled single-campus study indicated no such crossover effects.

Studies of the effects of specific courses lead to the same conclusion as the more nationally representative, larger-sample studies. Most of these inquiries rely on quasi-experimental, pre- and posttest designs and control to varying degrees for precourse self-selection factors. Although both the content empha-sized in the courses and the outcomes measures adopted vary across studies, the findings point consistently to decreased racial prejudice, keener under-standing of social and racial discrimination, greater multicultural understand-ing, increased racial tolerance, and increased interracial comfort (Asada et al., 2003; Chang, 1999b, 2000b; Gurin et al., 1999; Henderson-King & Kaleta, 2000; Martin & Koppelman, 1991; Palmer, 2000; Palmer, 1999; Parker, Moore, & Neimeyer, 1998). The research also suggests that the more such courses stu-dents take, the greater their attitude shifts (Chang, 1999b, 2000b; Palmer, 1999).

Students are often uncomfortable discussing multicultural (especially racial-ethnic) issues and may avoid such conversations (Levine & Cureton, 1998a), and some evidence suggests that diversity-oriented courses, like service-learning experiences, may have negative consequences. According to one review of the literature, although race-related discussions can promote more tolerant racial attitudes, participants may experience emotions ranging from guilt and shame to anger and despair (Tatum, 1992). Such a finding is consistent with evidence from a well-controlled study on one campus indicating that not all diversity courses are equally effective. Indeed, courses offered under an ethnic or women's studies rubric appeared to be more effective at promoting understanding than diversity courses offered in other academic departments, suggesting the possi-bility that some instructors may be more experienced and adept than others in facilitating discussions of sensitive topics (Palmer, 1999). Other research points to emotional and intellectual complexity in discussions of sensitive topics, such as racism and sexism (Trosset, 1998). These findings are consistent with evi-dence discussed in the following paragraphs indicating that *how* the diversity curriculum is delivered may be more important than its structure.

Researchers have found that students' racial and ethnic attitudes and values may be shaped by academic experiences less specific than the content of the courses they take. These other dimensions include faculty values and beliefs, instructional styles, and the kinds of research faculty members undertake. These findings, which suggest that classroom experiences exert a subtle influence, are consistent with research showing that faculty members in different clusters of disciplines create predictable environments that promote skills, preferences, and orientations consistent with Holland's theory of careers and occupational environments. Patterns of longitudinal change and stability in students' choices of majors, moreover, are at least in part a function of the norms and values of their academic departments (Smart et al., 2000; Thompson & Smart, 1999). For example, the evidence indicates that faculty who are women or members of historically underrepresented minority groups are more likely than males or Whites and Asians to do research and to teach about issues of race and ethnicity (Hurtado, 2001) as well as to place greater value on improving race relations and other social conditions (Milem, 1999b). To effect attitudinal changes, some research suggests, the multiracial or multiethnic classroom must provide a supportive and inclusive climate (Marin, 2000).[12]

Such views and orientations are reflected in faculty members' classroom practices, and a growing number of studies indicates that classroom diversity, expressed in such forms as inclusion of content and research on diverse groups as part of the coursework, has a significant and positive net effect on measures of students' cultural awareness and appreciation and acceptance of others of different races and ethnic backgrounds as well as increases in their abilities to empathize with others and in their perception that diversity is not divisive (Gurin, 1999; Gurin et al., 2002; Lopez, 1993; K. Smith, 1993).

Still other studies indicate that classroom experiences are among the most powerful influences on students' reports of their freshman- to senior-year growth on measures of intellectual and cultural openness (Volkwein, 1991).[13] Studies also link multicultural awareness and positive racial-ethnic attitudes and values to having a woman instructor (Hurtado, 2001) or an instructor of color (Molla & Westbrook, 1990), to general satisfaction with one's instructor (Graham & Gisi, 2000), and to an instructor's use of active and collaborative and other pedagogical methods (Cabrera, Nora, Bernal, Terenzini, & Pascarella, 1998; Hurtado, 2001; Hurtado et al., 1999). Taken together, these studies suggest that *how* or *by whom* a program or course curriculum is delivered may be as important as its formal structure (Astin, 1992).

Other formal (but shorter) interventions also have statistically significant, positive net effects on measures of students' racial-ethnic attitudes and values. A substantial and methodologically rigorous collection of studies clearly and consistently indicates that students who participate in a racial-ethnic or cultural awareness workshop (compared with similar students who do not) show heightened cultural awareness, increased tolerance for differences, acceptance of others from racial-ethnic backgrounds different from their own, increased commitment to promoting racial understanding, and openness to diversity broadly defined (Antonio, 1998, 2000; Astin, 1993a, 1993c; Pascarella, Edison, Nora, Hagedorn, & Terenzini, 1996; Sax & Astin, 1998; Whitt et al., 2001; Zuniga, Berger, Kluge, & Williams, 2001). Some evidence suggests that leadership training courses or workshops also increase multicultural awareness (Astin & Antonio, 1999, 2000; Astin & Cress, 1998; Cress et al., 2001). These effects are apparent across independent samples and when controlling for students' precollege attitudes on the outcome measure of interest as well as for a wide range of other precollege characteristics, institutional traits and environments, and other experiences students had during college in addition to their participation in a racial-ethnic or cultural awareness workshop. Whitt et al. found significant workshop effects on a cohort of students in each of three successive years, indicating that this particular intervention cannot come "too late" and that the benefits are both net of other factors and cumulative over time.

Volunteer work. College students' volunteer work frequently brings them into contact with people different from themselves with respect to such characteristics as race-ethnicity, national and cultural origin, social class, and age. Research published since 1990 indicates overwhelmingly that these encounters change students' awareness of and attitudes toward other groups.

We identified only one study that raised any doubts about that conclusion (Pierson & Pascarella, 2002). Although the nationally representative sample, tight controls, and psychometric qualities of the dependent measure in Pierson et al. lead us not to dismiss the study's findings, equally well-controlled studies based on two large, independent national samples did find volunteer work reliably related to freshman- to senior-year increases in students' knowledge and acceptance of different races and cultures, greater awareness and understanding of the world around them (Astin & Sax, 1998; Sax & Astin, 1997), and also stronger commitment to promoting racial understanding as well as shifts in perceptions of the locus of social problems from individuals to systemic origins (Astin et al., 2000; Vogelgesang & Astin, 2000). These studies suggest, however, that the effects may be small when those of other college experiences are taken into account. Smaller-scale research also provides evidence of the positive effects of volunteer service (Rhoads, 1998).

Research on students' experiences in specific service-learning courses leads to the same conclusions as studies of the effects of volunteer work in general or of service that is only loosely linked to coursework. Gray and her colleagues (Gray et al., 2000; Gray et al., 1999), in a well-constructed study of some 1,300 students on 28 campuses, found participation in a service-learning course had statistically significant and positive net effects on students' understanding of people from backgrounds different from their own. Consistent with the findings from studies by Astin and his colleagues, the Gray studies also indicated that the service-learning effects are small, suggesting that other dimensions of students' college experiences may influence attitudes. Other studies find service-learning experiences have statistically significant net effects greater than those of volunteer service in general (and compared with no service at all) on increased racial-ethnic tolerance and reduced stereotyping (Eyler et al., 1997b; Eyler & Giles, 1999; Markus et al., 1993), reduced racism (Myers-Lipton, 1996b), increased international understanding (Myers-Lipton, 1996a), and an increased likelihood of seeing the world from another's perspective (Bringle & Kremer, 1993; Green & Diehn, 1995; McElhaney, 1997).

Study abroad. Colleges and universities have a long history of providing students with opportunities to study abroad, where the contact hypothesis also comes into play. In a socially, economically, and politically interdependent world, international awareness and competence are increasingly important (Carlson, Burn, Useem, & Yachimovicz, 1990; Laubscher, 1994).

With an occasional exception (such as Kalunian, 1997), most research on study abroad finds increases in students' intercultural awareness and tolerance despite wide programmatic variations in kind, duration, and location. Study in another country also appears to promote positive attitudes toward cultural pluralism and "world-mindedness" (Bates, 1997; Geelhoed, Abe, & Talbot, 2003; McCabe, 1994; Sharma & Mulka, 1993), greater tolerance and acceptance of others, including both the settings and the people of another land (Laubscher, 1994), and increased likelihood of perceiving the members of other national groups in personal terms (versus such "nonpersonal" attributes as their national foods and geographical characteristics) (Drew, Meyer, & Peregrine, 1996). Study abroad also increased appreciation of what it means to be different or a minority, and increased critical objectivity (but with no loss of patriotism) toward the United States (Laubscher, 1994), increased interest in international economic, political, and cross-cultural issues (Ryan & Twibell, 2000; Sachdev, 1997), decreased use of stereotypes and negative myths (Sachdev, 1997), promoted greater empathy for others (Ryan & Twibell, 2000), increased friendliness for visiting foreign nationals (Nesdale & Todd, 1993), and promoted other outcomes (Cash, 1993; Nash, 1991; Zorn, 1996).

It is not clear, however, whether attitude changes follow a temporal pattern. One study found an initial openness to others followed by a decline and then a recovery (Nesdale & Todd, 1993); another found no support for such a "U-shaped curve hypothesis" as it relates to study abroad students' sense of adjustment and well-being (Nash, 1991). But Sharma and Mulka (1993) supply evidence from a six-campus study suggesting that students who have been on campus for one to five semesters exhibit more cultural acceptance and world-mindedness than students who were on campus for six or more semesters. They attribute these differences to the fact that lower-division students are more likely than their upper-division peers to interact with international students and to participate in study-abroad programs. Limited evidence suggests that longer terms of study abroad may have greater effects than shorter periods (Zorn, 1996).

All these studies are small-scale and leave uncontrolled numerous factors on which students who study abroad are known to differ from those who do not. The most carefully constructed analyses come from a multi-institutional, multinational database developed for the Study Abroad Evaluation Project (SAEP) (Carlson, Burn, Useem, & Yachimovicz, 1991; Opper, Teichler, & Carlson, 1990). This project gathered data from college juniors (pretest $n = 890$; posttest $n = 439$) participating in 82 study abroad programs in the United Kingdom, France, Germany, Sweden, and the United States during the 1984–85 academic year. Pre- and postexperience comparisons indicate statistically significant and substantial increases in students' knowledge of their host countries' culture, politics, and society. These knowledge gains were apparent even in the presence of statistical controls for more than 30 variables, including age, gender, socioeconomic status, academic ability, motives, and past international experience as well as a number of the structural characteristics of their programs. Such gains apparently did not influence student values relating to international issues, such as the need for greater international cooperation or the desire to interact with people from another country. There was, however, some evidence of the dissolution of stereotypes and of considerable other individual changes that were masked by group averages. Although the researchers did not formally test for statistical interactions, some of their analyses suggested that what significant changes in values they observed were among those students who were initially less internationally oriented (Opper et al., 1990). Opper and his colleagues concluded: "The most remarkable result [was] that altogether, differences between student characteristics, programme [sic] characteristics, students' experiences, and problems abroad have relatively weak explanatory value for the different academic, foreign language, cultural, and professional 'outcomes'" (p. 202). They speculated that complex settings more than single, isolated characteristics of individuals, programs, or experiences are more likely to shape learning outcomes.

Carlson and his colleagues (Carlson et al., 1990, 1991) analyzed data from the larger SAEP study that were provided by 204 U.S. students from four institutions who studied in the four European countries cited previously and contrasted their attitude changes with those of a comparison group of 153 students (most from University of California campuses) who spent their junior year in the United States. The findings largely parallel those of the larger SAEP project, with study-abroad students (versus the comparison group) showing higher scores on measures of cultural interests and the importance attached to promoting peace and international cooperation. Because program characteristics were uncontrolled, however, the possibility remains that the observed differences may have been due to self-selection rather than program effects.[14]

Intercollegiate athletics. Only a couple of studies examine the effects of participation in intercollegiate athletics on students' racial-ethnic attitudes (Wolf-Wendel, Toma, & Morphew, 2000; Wolniak et al., 2001). Wolniak and his colleagues analyzed data from a three-year study of nearly 800 males enrolled in 18 four-year institutions and employed extensive controls for precollege characteristics (including initial openness to diversity) as well as other college experiences. Net of these other factors, they found that participation in *non*-revenue-producing intercollegiate athletics negatively affected students' openness to diversity after both two and three years. Over the period of the study, the net openness disadvantage to males in non-revenue-producing sports compared with nonathletes ranged from .25 and .30 of a standard deviation (about 10 to 12 percentile points). Football and male basketball players showed gains in openness to diversity about equal to those of nonathletes. Wolf-Wendel and her colleagues, however, in a qualitative study of athletes, coaches, and administrators involved in five intercollegiate sports at five institutions, identified several features of men's and women's teams that promoted a strong sense of community among members of groups that were highly diverse, both racially and socioeconomically.[15] Levine and Cureton (1998a) also found self-segregation on campuses to be least apparent among members of athletic teams (and theater groups).

Gender-Role Attitudes. As noted, the post-1990 research on changes in students' gender-role attitudes is smaller in volume than what appeared between 1970 and 1990. Substantive interest has also shifted somewhat from a focus on *whether* gender-role attitudes change and how individual courses affect these attitudes to a broader and stronger concentration on what influences change in gender-role attitudes. Studies fall into three general categories: coursework, interventions to reduce date rape, and fraternity or sorority membership.

Coursework. As with the literature published before 1990, most of the recent research on gender attitudes has focused on how courses offered by women's studies programs[16] affect students' views on gender issues. Research on this topic has grown in both volume and methodological rigor over the past decade. Although findings suggest that not all courses are equally effective, and indeed, some may even produce more negative than positive outcomes (Palmer, 1999), we, like Macalister (1999), conclude that students taking women's studies courses tend to show increased gender-related egalitarianism and awareness of discrimination, knowledge of diversity issues, feminist consciousness, willingness to adopt new gender-related roles and behaviors, involvement in various forms of women's rights activism during the semester, and stronger intentions to engage in feminist activism in the future (Henderson-King, 1993; Henderson-King & Kaleta, 2000; Henderson-King & Stewart, 1999; Miller-Bernal, 1993; Palmer, 2000; Palmer, 1999; Stake & Hoffmann, 2001; Stake, Roades, Rose, Ellis, & West, 1994; Stake & Rose, 1994; Thomsen, Basu, & Reinitz, 1995). These findings remain statistically significant even with controls in place for self-selection factors, including gender, race-ethnicity, academic ability, and students' precourse gender-related attitudes and a variety of other college experiences. Less well-controlled studies yield results consistent with those from the more rigorous designs (Black, 1994; Martin & Koppelman, 1991). Some evidence, moreover, indicates that women's studies (and ethnic studies) courses may promote intellectual curiosity and interest in examining an issue from different points of view that generalize to courses in other disciplines (Palmer, 2000; Palmer, 1999).

Although fewer researchers have examined the effects of participating in workshops designed to alter students' gender-related attitudes than have examined the impact of workshops on racial-ethnic awareness and attitudes, the findings in both cases point to changes toward more egalitarian views (Brooks-Harris, Heesacker, & Mejia-Milan, 1996; Palmer, 2000; Palmer, 1999).

Date-rape workshops. Negative attitudes toward women can manifest themselves in many ways, and campuses are not immune to the issues permeating the larger society. Research indicates that some of the myths and stereotypes associated with racism have analogues in men's (and sometimes women's) attitudes toward women and gender roles, particularly as they relate to sexual roles and date rape (Blumberg & Lester, 1991; Burt, 1980; Lottes, 1991; Nelson & Torgler, 1990; Osman & Davis, 1999). As with other attitudes and values that conflict with the goals of education and a civilized society, colleges and universities have intervened to change student (primarily male) attitudes toward rape and other forms of sexual harassment and aggression. Although the nature and duration of these interventions vary considerably, they usually include workshops that rely on audio- and videotapes, role playing or dramatic presentations, interactive discussions, reading materials, or combinations of these methods.

Three studies on this topic used true experimental designs. One found that none of three different interventions had any statistically significant effect on 54 men, randomly assigned to treatment groups, with respect to attitudes toward rape, rape-specific empathy, or general empathy (Berg, Lonsway, & Fitzgerald, 1999). The two other studies (Heppner, Humphrey, Hillenbrand-Gunn, & DeBord, 1995; Lenihan, Rawlins, Eberly, Buckley, & Masters, 1992) reported effective interventions, but the results are ambiguous. Heppner et al. found that an interactive drama activity and a didactic video both produced significant attitude shifts among the subjects (compared with no intervention), with the drama having somewhat greater impact than the video. The changes, however, varied depending on the constructs and measures examined. The Lenihan et al. study found significant changes only among the women in the experiment.

Several quasi-experimental studies of intact groups (with controls for pre-workshop attitudes and a small number of other variables) suggest that interventions to change attitudes toward date rape are generally effective (Anderson et al., 1998; Bonate & Jessell, 1996; Frazier, Valtinson, & Candell, 1994; Harrison, Downes, & Williams, 1991; Shultz, Scherman, & Marshall, 2000; Williamson & Mellott, 1997). Other studies, however, show mixed results (Earle, 1996) or nonsignificant differences associated with the intervention (Nelson & Torgler, 1990; Schaeffer & Nelson, 1993). It appears that involving students in a workshop actively through, for example, interactive dramas or a talk-show format may have greater impact than more passive approaches, such as watching videos.

Reaching a conclusion is complicated, moreover, because one of the true experimental studies (Lenihan et al., 1992) and one of the quasi-experimental designs (Harrison et al., 1991) contain evidence of testing effects: pretest participants may have been sensitized to the topic under study and thus showed greater declines than nonpretest participants in their acceptance of rape myths and willingness to blame the victim. A third quasi-experimental design study that looked for testing effects, however, found none (Shultz et al., 2000). Finally, a small but consistent group of studies indicates that the positive effects of such interventions in changing attitudes may be short-lived, lasting perhaps only a month or two before students' initial attitudes appear to "rebound" (Anderson et al., 1998; Frazier et al., 1994; Heppner et al., 1995).

Fraternity and sorority membership. The research is clear that fraternities and sororities attract students whose attitudes and values are significantly more conservative and traditional than those of their peers who remain "independents" and that these differences extend to Greeks' and independents' attitudes toward gender roles (Kalof & Cargill, 1991; Lottes & Kuriloff, 1994b; Sanday, 1990; Wilder & McKeegan, 1999). Many of these differences, moreover, persist into the senior year, although it is not clear whether these senior-year differences are a function of the gender-related attitudes and values students brought with them to college or to their having or not having been exposed to the socialization processes that are part of fraternity or sorority membership.

Recent research on this topic is mixed. Sanday's (1990) ethnographic study of fraternities found evidence of these organizations' capacities to promote and reinforce attitudes and actions reflecting a clear dominant-submissive orientation to male-female relations. Some quantitative evidence supports the view that fraternity members, as seniors, are less supportive of gender equality and feminism and more disposed to male dominance and sexual aggression than independent students, even after taking into account precollege attitudinal differences (as well as other background and college experiences) (Korn, 1993). Palmer (2000) found participation in women's studies and other diversity courses had significantly less impact on students who were members of Greek social societies than on similar independent students. Other evidence, however, suggests that both Greeks and independents show freshman- to senior-year increases in feminism and declines in male-dominant attitudes, and the degree of change was about the same for both independents and Greeks (Lottes & Kuriloff, 1994a, 1994b).

Attitudes Toward Homosexuality. Studies published before 1991 sought primarily to describe the extent to which students held positive or negative attitudes toward homosexuality and to portray these students; much of the research published since that time has had a similar focus.[17] Although few studies have examined the within-college dynamics underlying changes in attitudes toward gays, lesbians, and bisexuals, those that have been published do provide some insight.

Considerable evidence reviewed earlier in this chapter supported the contact hypothesis as it applies to students of different racial-ethnic backgrounds. Consistent with that research, some evidence from studies of attitudes toward homosexuality suggests that contact with gays, lesbians, and bisexuals may also be a primary mechanism in reducing negative attitudes toward these individuals (Geller, 1991; Herek, 1994; Kardia, 1996). One study, however, failed to find this relation among males (Green, Dixon, & Gold-Neil, 1993).

We identified two studies concerning the effects of fraternity or sorority membership on attitudes toward individuals with nontraditional sexual orientations (Kardia, 1996; Lottes & Kuriloff, 1994a). Both relied on longitudinal, single-institution samples with modest controls for self-selection, but each reached a different conclusion. Kardia reported that fraternities discourage acceptance of different sexual orientations, and Lottes and Kuriloff, despite finding substantial four-year increases in tolerance for homosexuality, found no statistically significant difference in the rates of change between Greeks and independents.

As with the evidence reviewed earlier on the effectiveness of interventions designed to change gender-role attitudes, the studies we reviewed suggest that such interventions may also be effective in altering students' attitudes toward gays and lesbians. But the jury is still out. The research in this area is largely confined to studies of the effects of speaker panels. Reviewing the research published before 1992, Croteau and Kusek (1992) identified six studies of the effectiveness of such panels. All but one study produced evidence of favorable effects of gay or lesbian speaker panels on student homophobia, but significant methodological limitations afflict all these studies.

More recent studies also endorse the effectiveness of speaker panels in promoting more positive attitudes toward gays and lesbians, but again methodological limitations persist. In the strongest of the three studies we identified, Green, Dixon, and Gold-Neil (1993) examined the impact of a gay-lesbian panel discussion offered as part of a human sexuality class. Controlling for preintervention attitudes, they found the panel presentation had a statistically significant and positive effect on females, although males showed no significant change from pre- to posttest. Nelson and Krieger (1997) found pre- to posttest declines in homophobic attitudes, but the study was done without a control group. Geasler, Croteau, Heineman, and Edlund (1995) analyzed more than 400 pages of text written by 260 students who attended a panel presentation by gay, lesbian, and bisexual speakers and reported finding almost exclusively positive responses.

Educational and Occupational Values. The post-1990 studies we identified that explored within-college effects on the value students attach to education were limited largely to the effects of major field and fraternity and sorority membership. Although few in number, all of the studies examined freshman- to senior-year net effects, and all controlled for students' precollege educational values and other potentially confounding factors.

Wilder and his colleagues (1996) studied freshman-to-senior changes in nearly 4,000 students who entered a selective, medium-size private college in three different eras. Between their first and final years, students majoring in the humanities, social sciences, and physical sciences showed statistically significant declines in the importance they attached to the Clark-Trow "vocational" philosophy of education. The decreases among humanities majors, however, exceeded decreases among their social science counterparts, who in turn declined more than physical science majors in their subscription to the vocational value of a college education. The pattern was reflected in increases in students' endorsements for a "nonconformist" philosophy of education: on this value, the humanities majors outpaced their peers in the social sciences, who in turn reported changes greater than those of physical science majors. Both humanities and social science majors also showed greater increases than physical science majors in the value they placed on an "academic" philosophy, and humanities majors showed significantly sharper declines than the others in their endorsement of a "collegiate" philosophy of education. Wilder and his colleagues report similar patterns from another set of analyses (Wilder et al., 1997). One can only speculate on the underlying dynamics involved in these shifts, but a possibility might be the extent to which disciplines address topics that are relevant to the personal attitudes and values of students.

Three studies using national samples in two different time periods produced as a group no clear patterns (Astin, 1993c; Knox et al., 1993; Springer, Terenzini,

Pascarella, & Nora, 1995a). Knox et al. found that majoring in business tended to reduce the odds of a student's attaching importance to "getting a good education," but the differences were statistically nonsignificant. Majoring in business also reduced the odds of a student's participating in groups interested in literature, art, music, or discussion. Astin found that the number of writing or foreign-language courses was inversely related to the belief that increasing earnings was the primary value of a college education, but Springer and his colleagues found that after one year of college both the number of courses taken and course-related experiences were unrelated to students' interest in learning for self-understanding. Net of other factors, including precollege learning orientations, students' out-of-class experiences, particularly conversations with peers, were much more influential.

Membership in a Greek social organization tends to increase the extrinsic values students attach to an education, while remaining independent tends to promote intrinsic educational values (Astin, 1993c; McCabe & Bowers, 1996; Wilder et al., 1997). Similarly, Astin (1993c) found that, net of a host of other student characteristics (including precollege educational values), as well as the traits of the institutions attended and a wide variety of students' other college experiences, Greek membership was positively related to the support seniors expressed for the proposition that increasing one's earnings is the primary value of a college education. In addition, evidence indicates that living in a residence hall tends to reduce the importance students attach to being financially well-off (Milem, 1998). Other evidence suggests that some fraternities may promote academic dishonesty, "engag[ing] in organizational behaviors that at least condone, if not directly support, questionable academic behaviors among their members" (McCabe & Bowers, 1996, p. 290).

Terenzini and his colleagues (1995b) found that students' class-related and out-of-class-related experiences contributed uniquely and about equally to one-year gains on a measure of the intrinsic values students find in learning. These effects persisted when controlling for precollege learning values, ability, gender, race-ethnicity, family socioeconomic status, and degree aspirations.

One study examined the effects of male students' participation in intercollegiate athletics on the value they attached to learning and academic experiences that increased self-understanding (Wolniak et al., 2001). With controls in place for a variety of students' precollege characteristics (including educational attitudes), other academic and nonacademic experiences during college, and the NCAA division in which they played, Wolniak et al. found that males participating over a three-year period in revenue-producing sports on 18 four-year campuses made net gains in the value they ascribed to learning for self-understanding that were about equal to those of nonathletes. Athletes in non-revenue-producing sports, however, made significantly smaller gains than similar students in revenue-producing sports or nonathletes. Over the three-year period, differences ranged from .21 to .51 standard deviations (8 to 19 percentile points). These findings suggest not only that men's participation in football or basketball may not have negative effects on the value these athletes attach to self-understanding but also, compared with other intercollegiate athletes, that they may actually derive some benefits. The reasons for these differences are unclear.

Understanding and Interest in the Arts. The evidence specifically addressing within-college effects on students' interest in culture and the arts is limited. Smart and his colleagues (2000), however, did a rigorous study that found freshman- to senior-year increases or decreases in these interests were clearly related to the academic environments of the major fields selected. They found that students characterized as "Artistic" in Holland's scheme showed greater net increases in those interests and dispositions if they chose an educational environment congruent with their interests than if they occupied one dominated by a different Holland type. The differences were dramatic: Artistic students in a congruent environment increased their arts-related abilities and interests by .65 of a standard deviation (the equivalent of nearly 24 percentile points), while Artistic students in incongruent environments experienced declines in their abilities and interests in those areas by .24 of a standard deviation (nearly 10 percentile points) (see also Smart, 1997; Smart et al., 2000). Smart and his colleagues also found that nonartistic students (and "Investigative" and "Enterprising" students) who majored in Artistic disciplines gained to about the same degree as artistic individuals in the interests, values, and skills one would expect to be promoted and reinforced in study disciplines. This latter finding supports the view that each discipline socializes its student members to the discipline's values and interests whether or not the student's personality type is congruent with the environment initially. Feldman and his colleagues (2001) acknowledge that these findings may appear to contradict the "person-environment fit" proposition that students gain most in environments congruent with their interests and values, but they note that these studies address two different questions. A previous study (Feldman et al., 1999) found support for the congruence hypothesis in its application to students who enter a congruent environment where their interests and values are indeed enhanced. In that study, Artistic students who entered and remained in nonartistic disciplines showed little growth and even some declines in their artistic interests and values. The later study, however, examined disciplinary effects on *in*congruent students in a particular discipline (in this case an Artistic one). An Artistic environment also enhanced the artistic interests and values of nonartistic students as they became socialized to the values and interests of the discipline.

CONDITIONAL EFFECTS OF COLLEGE

Conclusions from *How College Affects Students*

A number of pre-1990 studies examined differences in attitudinal and value changes between males and females, and somewhat fewer explored differences in the degree of change between White students and students of color. Only a handful of studies, however, examined whether the *degree of change* varied by gender or race-ethnicity. Finding that, say, women change significantly in one way or another while men do not is different from determining whether the *differences in the degree* of change for women and men are statistically significant. Studies that examined such gender-by-time statistical interactions were few and far between. We concluded in our previous book that "the literature has little to say about the differential effects of college on values and attitudes for different kinds of students" (Pascarella & Terenzini, 1991, p. 329).

Evidence from the 1990s

The number of studies of conditional effects published since the 1990s is substantially higher than in the preceding two decades, with the focus largely on differential effects on students' racial-ethnic attitudes or openness to diversity broadly defined. Although the findings are sometimes inconsistent, these studies offer some clarity, particularly with respect to gender-related differences.

A handful of studies formally tested for differential rates of change during college, and the evidence suggests that college's effects on sociopolitical dispositions are general rather than related to students' gender. Although females enter college with somewhat more liberal sociopolitical attitudes than males, after taking selected other factors into account, three studies found no statistically significant differences in the rates at which males and females gained on measures of their social and political orientations whether using measures of liberalism and social conscience (Lottes & Kuriloff, 1994a), voting or involvement in political discussions (Knox et al., 1993), or sensitivity to race and social class (Martin & Koppelman, 1991). Although they did not formally test for gender-by-time effects, Smith and her colleagues (1994) also found that males' and females' sociopolitical views and social involvement goals increased at about the same rate.

Whether college affects the sociopolitical dispositions of men and women differently seems to depend in part on the attitudes being studied, particularly as they involve gender roles and race-ethnicity issues. Some evidence suggests that male support for a selective, public research university's affirmative action practices declined after one year, whereas female support increased (K. Smith, 1992, 1993). Another study estimated that, over a two-year period and net of other factors (including precollege racial-ethnic attitudes), women gained in their acceptance of human differences at a rate about three times that of men (Taylor, 1998).

Studies of differential effects of specific college experiences on the diversity attitudes of males and females produced mixed results. Pascarella, Edison, Nora, Hagedorn, and Terenzini (1996), followed nearly 2,300 students entering 18 four-year institutions in 15 states, specifically testing for gender-related conditional effects while controlling for a wide array of precollege characteristics (including initial openness to diversity), institutional traits and environments, and academic and social experiences during the students' first year of college. The experiences examined included living on campus, participating in a racial-ethnic awareness workshop, number of hours worked, fraternity or sorority membership, and peer interactions. The researchers found that the net effects of those experiences on openness to diversity were largely the same for males and females. Wolniak, Pierson, and Pascarella (2001) found the effects of intercollegiate sports participation on openness to diversity to be similar for men from different backgrounds and with different college experiences. Springer, Palmer, Terenzini, Pascarella, and Nora (1996) studied more than 1,000 White students in the Pascarella et al. sample two years later (1998a) and also found that the effects of participating in a racial or cultural awareness workshop were not conditional on gender. Limited evidence does suggest that first-generation college students (that is, students whose parents have no college experience) may derive significantly greater benefits from certain of their college experiences than do their non-first-generation peers. The number of hours studied, the amount of writing done, and the level of academic effort and involvement all may have more impact on first-generation students, particularly with respect to their openness to diversity broadly defined (including exposure to new ideas) and learning for self-understanding (Pascarella, Pierson, Wolniak, & Terenzini, 2004).

Limited evidence indicates that the general level of openness to diversity among entering students on a campus, or students' perceptions of their institution's support for diversity, may have positive effects on women but negative impacts on men after one year (K. Smith, 1992); Whitt and her colleagues (2001) found the same to be true after two years. Both studies also suggest that males and females may respond differently to different features of the college experience. Although the racial-ethnic or diversity attitudes of both men and women are positively affected (to about the same degree) by having friends of color, men may be affected more by their interpersonal relations (including contacts with faculty members) and being socialized toward individualism, whereas women appear more responsive to institutional efforts to reshape the environment for diverse individuals or to participation in clubs or organizations.

Overall, the evidence suggests that college may well have differential effects on women and men but also that the nature of these effects probably varies both by attitude or value area (as specification of the attitude under study becomes sharper, more conditional effects may come into play) and by the particular experiences students have, women being more responsive to general contextual forces and men more attuned to interpersonal interactions. These conjectures await additional study and verification.

As with findings concerning gender-related conditional effects, tests for differential influences of college experiences relating to the race-ethnicity of the student indicate that perceptions of an ethnically or culturally nondiscriminatory campus environment have a positive net impact on the racial-ethnic attitudes and general openness to diversity of all students. After three years that net effect is significantly more positive for students of color than for White students (Whitt et al., 2001). Racial-cultural awareness workshops appear to be one way to promote a multiculturally accommodating environment. Evidence from two independent samples indicates that, although participation in such workshops has a statistically significant and positive net effect on both White and minority students' racial understanding and openness to diversity, those effects are significantly greater for White students (Hyun, 1996; Pascarella, Edison, Nora, Hagedorn, & Terenzini, 1996).

Limited evidence suggests that the effects of fraternity or sorority membership on students' openness to diversity may vary depending on the students' race-ethnicity, being negative for White students but positive for students of color (Pascarella, Edison, Nora, Hagedorn, & Terenzini, 1996). The finding, which awaits replication, comes from a study of nearly 2,300 students on 18 four-year campuses and persists in the presence of controls for an impressive array of potential self-selection factors (including students' precollege openness to diversity), institutional characteristics, and other academic and social experiences during the first year of college. The study did not differentiate membership in predominantly White and predominantly Black fraternities and sororities, leaving open the question of whether the effects for students of color are independent of the racial-ethnic mix of the fraternity or sorority.

Some evidence suggests that academic majors differentially shape students' attitudes, interests, and abilities in ways consistent with Holland's "social" types and environments (Smart, 1997; Smart et al., 2000; Smart & Feldman, 1998). Smart and his colleagues (Smart, 1997; Smart et al., 2000; Smart & Feldman, 1998) provide the most convincing evidence that academic environments (major fields clustered in ways consistent with the characteristics of Holland's six environments) differentially reward and reinforce different interests and abilities, accentuating initial differences. The changes in students' abilities and interests are greatest when students enter an academic environment congruent with their initial interests. For example, as already noted earlier in this chapter, "Artistic" students entering an artistic academic environment will develop their artistic interests and abilities to a far greater extent than will artistic types who enter a nonartistic environment. That pattern, however, did not hold true for "social" Holland types in social environments. Guimond and his colleague report evidence of discipline-related socialization effects, and that effect appeared not to vary by gender (Guimond & Palmer, 1989, 1990).

Several studies searched for conditional effects shaping students' gender role attitudes, but no patterns are discernible across the studies. Of the five studies we identified, only one examined male-female differences in the rates of gender-role attitude change over time, and that study found no differences in the trends toward greater support for feminist attitudes and declines in support for "male dominance" points of view (Lottes & Kuriloff, 1994a). The remaining studies examined whether the effects of taking a women's studies course had a differential impact on gender role attitudes of males and females. Two of these studies found no differential effects on students' sensitivity to gender issues or their support for feminist activism (Martin & Koppelman, 1991; Stake et al., 1994). Of the remaining two studies, one found a slight increase in male recognition of sexism as a problem (versus no change in women's views) (Henderson-King & Kaleta, 2000), and the other found some suggestion that participation in a women's studies course increased women's feminist attitudes but reduced such attitudes among men (Thomsen et al., 1995).

Wilder and his colleagues report finding conditional effects on students' educational values reflected in the importance they attach to different Clark-Trow philosophies of education (Wilder et al., 1997; Wilder et al., 1996). In the 1996 study, Wilder et al. found decreases in the value attached to "vocational" education and growth in students' "nonconformist" educational values, with both changes being greater among males than females. The latter study produced evidence of significant interaction effects between major field and fraternity or sorority membership. Fraternity and sorority members majoring in the humanities showed significantly and substantially larger increases in their endorsement of an "academic" philosophy of education than their counterparts in engineering, who showed significant declines. Similarly, freshman-to-senior differences in the degree of the increase in support for a "nonconformist" educational philosophy were smallest between Greeks and independents in engineering and largest between fraternity-sorority members versus independents majoring in the humanities, indicating that independents showed greater changes than Greeks in this area, except among those in engineering.

We conclude from this review that, although more is known now than a decade ago about the differential impacts of certain college experiences on the attitudes and values of different kinds of students, our understanding of these differences is still circumscribed. More studies of conditional effects are needed to inform program planning, resource allocation, and public policy. Whether college has differential impacts remains one of the unexplored frontiers in the research on college effects on students.

LONG-TERM EFFECTS OF COLLEGE

Conclusions from *How College Affects Students*

We concluded in 1991 that, although the literature on the durability of college effects on attitude and value change was small, it was also relatively consistent across outcome areas. Overall, the evidence indicated that attitudinal changes occurring during college do, indeed, persist into the adult years. Most of the research done between the late 1960s and 1990 focused on students' humanitarian, political, racial, and civil libertarian values. That body of research strongly suggested that the increases in sociopolitical liberalism that emerged during college appeared to continue in students' later years, although at a reduced rate. Perhaps more important in a discussion of college's effects, the evidence of long-term college-related sociopolitical attitudinal changes was consistent across studies, samples, historical contexts, and analytical designs. Except for a few changes after age 60, the research produced little evidence that social and political values and attitudes held at the time of college graduation reverted to precollege levels. Some evidence suggested that the attitudinal stability was probably attributable, at least in part, to reinforcement by an individual's family, friends, and colleagues, who were likely to be similarly educated and to hold at least somewhat similar attitudes and values.

Cultural and aesthetic values and interests appeared to level off after graduation, as did shifts in religious values, although some findings suggested postcollege declines in the latter area. We concluded that research on changes in sex-role attitudes was "too young a field of study for there to be any convincing evidence on the durability of college effects in this area" (Pascarella & Terenzini, 1991, p. 329). Based on the moderately strong correlations between sociopolitical and sex-role attitudes, however, we also speculated that the long-term effects of college on changes in gender-role attitudes would parallel graduates' sociopolitical shifts.

Evidence from the 1990s

Sociopolitical Attitudes and Behaviors. For this review we identified eight studies that speak to somewhat different topics but whose findings consistently suggest that college-related changes in sociopolitical dispositions and behaviors are lifelong. The evidence indicates that the more education one has, the more likely one is to vote and to participate in various ways in the political process. The finding is apparent (across cohorts and databases) eight years after high school in a national panel study that began in 1988 when participants were eighth graders (Ingels et al., 2002), 10 years after most students in two independent national cohorts of high school graduates entered college (NLS-72 and HS&B:80, sophomore cohort; Knox et al., 1993; Tuma & Geis, 1995), 15 years after graduation among nearly 20,000 individuals in the College and Beyond database who entered 28 academically selective colleges and universities in the fall of 1976 (Bowen & Bok, 1998) as well as in statistics supplied in other national reports ("Private Correlates of Educational Attainment," 1995). After controlling for gender, race, socioeconomic status, and precollege political orientations, Knox et al. estimated that 14 years after leaving high school, and net of background characteristics and previous sociopolitical participation, bachelor's degree recipients were 50 percent more likely to discuss political issues and to participate in political activities and two and one-half times more likely to vote than were their high school classmates who never attended college. Individuals holding advanced degrees were half again more likely than their high school peers without college experience to report a commitment to rectifying social and economic inequities. Bowen and Bok found that more than 90 percent of their responding bachelor's degree holders reported voting in 1992, with White graduates being marginally more likely to vote than their Black counterparts (94 percent versus 90 percent, respectively). The voting rates in both groups were considerably higher than the 78 percent rate in a control group of people who never attended college. The rates among the alumni in this survey, moreover, did not differ appreciably from those of college graduates in a national control group based on the 1980 High School and Beyond (senior cohort) survey. Some evidence, however, suggests modest contractions in the first five years after college in the gains observed during college on measures of commitment to social activism. Postbaccalaureate declines in the importance attached to influencing social values and the political structure tend to be smaller than the gains between students' initial enrollment in college and their senior year (Sax, 2000).

Equally persuasive long-term evidence links education to more knowledgeable participation in a democratic society. These studies indicate that education produces substantially greater understanding of the principles of democratic government, greater ability to identify incumbent local and national leaders, more knowledge of current political facts (Nie et al., 1996), stronger sociopolitical orientation (Alwin, Cohen, & Newcomb, 1991; Alwin & Krosnick, 1991; Cohen & Alwin, 1993), and increased social activism, including efforts to influence social values and the political structure (Sax, 2000). The study by Alwin, Cohen, and Newcomb provides evidence most directly related to the durability of college effects. They undertook the third in a series of studies, notable for their continuity, of the sociopolitical orientations of a group of women who attended Bennington College in the 1930s and 1940s. The original study (Newcomb, 1943) documented the socializing influence of peers on the development of college students' sociopolitical orientations during the college years. The second study in this series (Newcomb, Koenig, Flacks, & Warwick, 1967) demonstrated not only that the political orientations these women developed while in college remained relatively stable even 25 years later but also that the attitudinal stability observed was affected in important ways by the presence or absence of supportive social environments. Women whose attitudes remained stable a quarter century after graduating from college shared social environments with spouses, friends, and colleagues who held similar attitudes. Graduates whose sociopolitical orientations changed the most inhabited less congruent environments.

The most recent study in this series (Alwin et al., 1991; see also Cohen & Alwin, 1993) traced the trajectories of participants' sociopolitical orientations into old age. Alwin and his colleagues[18] report evidence suggesting that the period of "vulnerability" to change, demonstrated to exist in the early years of human development, may for some areas of change persist into late adolescence or early adulthood, which correspond to the traditional college years. They found that the sociopolitical attitudes that had changed so strikingly during college and then appeared to stabilize in the adult years persisted into old age. Basic ideological orientations displayed more stability than less fundamental, "object-specific attitudes tied to particular political issues or actors" (p. 255), but the overall picture showed a high degree of stability. Moreover, and consistent with the earlier Bennington studies, Alwin et al. found additional and substantial evidence that attitude stability was closely linked to a supportive social environment. Findings consistent with these are reported in a study of Vassar College graduates who had reached their mid-50s (Brown & Pacini, 1993b).

More important to the question of college-related effects, Alwin and his colleagues (1991) used data from the National Election Study (NES) series done biennially since 1952 to create "synthetic" cohort models. Using these models, they found evidence of greater *intra-* than *inter*cohort variability, suggesting that, although each new cohort is shaped in important ways by its parents' generation, and may experience its own era differently from other cohorts (depending on sociohistorical conditions and events), each experiences an early period of influence and change, after which attitudes crystallize and become increasingly stable. A related series of analyses of changes in political party identification led to similar conclusions (Alwin & Krosnick, 1991).

Nie, Junn, and Stehlik-Barry (1996) not only found evidence of the long-term effects of education on measures of democratic citizenship but also found that these effects may be both direct and indirect. Nie and his colleagues studied how formal education influenced such things as knowledge of social and political issues and structures, "attentiveness" to such topics, understanding of the principles of democratic government, level of involvement in voting and political activities, and support for civil liberties. They found that the relation between education and democratic citizenship is not simply additive (more education leads to more informed and active citizenship). Rather, the relation is complex, involving both greater knowledge and understanding of sociopolitical issues and processes and greater access to participation in political life, including access to public officials, places on local boards, and working on other local committees. They suggest that education has a direct effect on the cognitive aspects of sociopolitical attitude formation and change but also an indirect one through a series of "positional outcomes" (including occupational prominence, family, and wealth) and through the access education provides to social networks and voluntary, associational memberships that shape sociopolitical attitudes and behaviors.

Civic and Community Attitudes and Involvement. The research also indicates that college's effects on graduates' involvement in their communities endure well beyond graduation. Most of the evidence comes from nationally representative samples monitoring students' commitments and behaviors from 4 to 15 years after graduation (Astin, 1996b; Astin, Sax, & Avalos, 1999; Bowen & Bok, 1998; Gurin, 1999; Ingels et al., 2002; Katchadourian & Boli, 1994; Knox et al., 1993; Sax, 2000; Sax & Astin, 1997; Villalpando, 1996). The results are strikingly consistent across a broad array of outcome measures, including involvement in community groups (relating to youth, neighborhood improvement, social action associations, nonreligious church activities, and environmental action and conservation), commitment to "other-oriented" goals, planning or working in service-related careers, and interest in and commitment to community leadership. The findings are also consistent across studies with and without controls for students' precollege characteristics and dispositions toward community service or involvement, the characteristics of the institutions they attended, or the experiences they had while in college. Knox and his colleagues estimated that 14 years after high school graduation, and net of gender, race-ethnicity, socioeconomic status, and precollege dispositions to community involvement, bachelor's degree holders (compared with their high school peers with no college experience) are 80 percent more likely to be committed to community leadership and to be involved in community groups and nearly two and one-half times more likely to be doing volunteer work. The only departure from the trends they observed involved participation in youth groups, an activity they believe is more related to marital status and number and age of children than to educational attainment.

Consistent with studies of postcollege changes in student activism, some research suggests that the relation between college enrollment and subsequent civic and community engagement may not be linear. These studies, based on follow-up of CIRP samples five years after graduation, indicate a small decline in students' commitment to "other-oriented" values and life goals (Villalpando, 1996) and in their commitment to and involvement in community service (Sax, 2000). The declines are small, however, and may reflect temporary, time-allocation decisions related to jobs, families, graduate study, or other personal commitments and investments of time. These and other studies also indicate the presence of longer-term commitments to community involvement, suggesting that any declines may be temporary (Astin, 1996b; Astin et al., 1999; Gurin, 1999; Sax & Astin, 1997).

Particularly interesting is the evidence suggesting that it is the receipt of an academic credential (primarily the bachelor's degree), rather than the kind of institution attended or experiences while enrolled, that appears to enhance community engagement (Knox et al., 1993). It would appear that the acquisition of educational status in and of itself promotes such involvement. Why this relation might be so is unclear, but Knox and his colleagues speculate that such status carries with it certain roles and expectations that graduates embrace. This hypothesis is consistent with the findings of Nie et al. (1996) indicating that college's effects on subsequent sociopolitical orientations and activities are both direct (through increased awareness and understanding of such issues) and indirect (through the social and occupational networks to which education affords access) and to the corresponding normative attitudes and behaviors accompanying those positions. Thus, educational attainment may be related to community involvement in both the short and long term as the college experience increases understanding of social and economic inequities and thereby interest in action to redress those inequities. But attainment may also put graduates in a position where personal advancement is closely linked with community and sociopolitical participation, visibility, and leadership.

Studies of the graduates of highly selective institutions (Bowen & Bok, 1998; Katchadourian & Boli, 1994) provide evidence consistent with Knox et al.'s speculation concerning community engagement. Katchadourian and Boli found a high degree of social involvement (community and otherwise) among Stanford graduates 10 years after earning their degrees, but their activities tended to be "self-oriented" (exercise, sports, hobbies). Graduates devoted less than a third of their leisure time to helping others or to political action. The graduates of the selective institutions Bowen and Bok studied (15 years after graduation) were more likely than a control sample of same-age graduates to be involved in non-work-related leadership positions and to participate in professional or trade groups, college alumni activities (recruiting, fund-raising), cultural activities and the arts, and environmental or conservation groups. Graduates in the control group, by comparison, were more likely to be involved in community and social service activities, youth groups, nonreligious church activities, and school groups.

Gender-Role Attitudes. We found little research relating to the long-term effects of college on students' attitudes and values concerning women and gender roles, and what we uncovered does not lend itself to confident conclusions, although some of it raises interesting theoretical questions. In a study of more than 1,000 males and females who were surveyed first in 1947 as high school sophomores in Pennsylvania and then three more times between the ages of 40 and 61, Palmer and Willits (1996), after controlling for age, race, and childhood residence (because of the homogeneity of the sample), found evidence more supportive of the "lifelong openness to change" hypothesis than the "aging-stability" proposition. The researchers found education positively related to sex role attitudes in the first follow-up, but between the ages of 40 and 61, educational attainment was negatively related to changes in attitudes. Participants with less formal education were more likely to develop nontraditional sex role attitudes than their better-educated counterparts. The evidence also suggested that such effects were themselves gender-related, with women showing attitudinal changes while men did not. Indeed, among the women in the sample, education was inversely related to the development of nontraditional attitudes toward sex roles, and employment was positively and independently related to attitude change among women, although the effect was small.

The comparative stability of the sex-role attitudes of the better-educated women in the Palmer and Willits study is consistent with the findings of Alwin and his colleagues regarding a pattern of change during the college years followed by stability in the later years (Alwin et al., 1991; Alwin & Krosnick, 1991). Both suggest that, among women at least, higher education appears to lead to earlier formation of liberal attitudes. The Palmer and Willits study, however, raises a question about whether that pattern holds for less educated women. The increase in nontraditional views among less well-educated women is more difficult to explain. This study examined attitude changes during a period of considerable ferment in the larger society with respect to gender roles, and it seems reasonable to suggest that the study's findings may be associated not only with a possible ceiling effect among better-educated women but also with possible cohort effects.

The other studies we identified dealing with the long-term effects of college on gender-role attitudes all address the durability of the impact of taking women's studies courses (Stake & Hoffmann, 2001; Stake & Rose, 1994) or of majoring in women's studies (Luebke & Reilly, 1995). Stake and her colleagues found evidence that, net of precourse attitudes, the effects of women's studies courses on egalitarian attitudes toward women, awareness of sexism and other forms of discrimination, and activism for social causes did persist, at least for six months (Stake & Hoffmann, 2001) and nine months after the course (Stake & Rose, 1994). Although one might dispute whether six and nine months constitute a "long-term" period, the nearly 90 graduates of women's studies programs studied by Luebke and Reilly (1995) reported substantial, or in some cases "revolutionary" (p. 22), outcomes relating to personal development and attitude changes as well as to occupational selections ranging "From Aviator to Union Organizer" (the title of Chapter Three, p. 24). Riordan (1990) reports that the significantly more positive sex-role attitudes held at graduation by degree earners at women's college (versus coed institutions) persisted for three years, even in the face of controls for precollege socioeconomic status and academic ability. He also found that, although the direct effect of attending a single-sex college may be small, the indirect effect (through its impact on attitudes) is strong.

Educational and Occupational Values. We identified only two studies that focused on the long-term effects of college on graduates' educational values (Adelman, 1991; Knox et al., 1993). Both drew on the large, nationally representative database of the National Longitudinal Study of the High School Class of 1972 (NLS-72), and both provide reliable evidence of durable college impacts. Adelman tracked respondents until they were 32 years old, finding that from age 18 to 32, women developed more positive attitudes toward education than did men and came to believe more strongly than men that they had benefited from college. Knox and his colleagues identified a clear, linear trend among NLS-72 graduates in the relation between educational attainment and the value attached to "getting a good education." Even after taking into account any effects of gender, race-ethnicity, socioeconomic status, academic ability, and initial educational values, as well as the characteristics of the institutions attended and selected college experiences, 14 years after leaving high school bachelor's degree holders were still more than twice as likely as their counterparts with only a high school diploma to consider it "very important" to get a good education. Knox et al. also found persistent, positive net effects of educational attainment on participation in artistic and cultural groups.

Knox and his colleagues (1993) provide the only evidence we uncovered examining the long-term effects of college on occupational values. As with college's impact on educational values, these researchers found that educational attainment was positively related to the intrinsic value sample members looked for in their occupations. In general, the importance of extrinsic rewards (such as wages or salary, social status, or security) tended to decline as postsecondary education experience increased, whereas the importance of intrinsic occupational rewards (for example, having opportunities to use one's talents, having variety in the tasks performed, autonomy, and responsibility) increased. After controlling for gender, race-ethnicity, socioeconomic status, and academic ability, the characteristics of the institutions attended, and selected college experiences (grades, major field, and living on campus), bachelor's degree holders were nearly twice as likely (and advanced degree holders three and one-half times as likely) to stress the importance of intrinsic work values as were their peers with only a high school diploma. The intrinsic rewards of an occupation, however, are not the only consideration. Net of other factors, educational attainment was still marginally (but not at traditional statistically significant levels) related to the importance attached to such extrinsic occupational values as the importance of being successful, making money, and having opportunities for advancement.

SUMMARY

Change During College

Studies of college's effects on student attitudes and values fall generally into eight categories: sociopolitical dispositions, civic and community involvement, racial-ethnic attitudes, gender roles, attitudes toward homosexuality, religious attitudes and values, interest in culture and the arts, and educational and occupational values. As can be seen, the first five categories (which contain most of the studies) deal with social issues, several of them controversial ones.

The research on sociopolitical attitudes and values includes studies of changes in students' general understanding of democratic processes and sociopolitical issues, including voting, participation in the political process, and support for civil liberties. We found little to contradict the well-established relation between educational attainment and such outcomes as knowledge of social and political issues and participants, voting, and engaging in political activities. On average, the voting rates of persons with only a high school education and ability to answer correctly questions about government lagged 30 to 40 percentage points behind the rates of bachelor's degree holders. College attendance is also reliably associated with increases on a variety of measures of sociopolitical liberalism, social activism, and support for civil liberties, but the freshman-to-senior shifts on these measures during the past decade are notably smaller than those reported in studies done between the late 1960s and 1990.

By contrast, the research of the past decade points to far greater student involvement than previously in other forms of social engagement. Bachelor's degree holders are two to three times more likely to volunteer for community service than are their peers with no exposure to college. Both the absolute participation rates and the differences across levels of educational attainment, however, vary considerably according to the type of community service. Some evidence (which is not altogether consistent) suggests that community engagement may also engender a sense of "social efficacy" or empowerment as well as students' beliefs that they are "making a difference" in the community.

Studies on changes in college students' racial-ethnic attitudes and values published during the 1990s are both more intense and extensive than those published in the preceding two decades. The post-1990 studies consistently find increases during the college years in positive attitudes toward racial equality and tolerance, greater awareness and understanding of other cultures, more interactions with people of an ethnic or cultural background different from one's own, declines in racial "distance," and increased commitment to fostering racial understanding.

Post-1990 studies of gender-role attitude changes during college mirror the earlier research in finding general increases in "feminism" and support for egalitarian sex-role attitudes. The shifts toward "modern" attitudes and values ranged from 5 to 10 percentage points in the proportion of students supporting gender equity. First- to senior-year gains on other measures of gender attitudes were on the order of a quarter of a standard deviation (or about 10 percentile points).

The increased willingness of gays, lesbians, and bisexual individuals to be open about their sexuality and to confront prejudice and discrimination, as well as the growing social and legal visibility and acceptance of lesbians, gays, and bisexuals, have spurred a small body of research examining changes during the college years in students' attitudes toward homosexuality. These single-campus studies report increases in students' knowledge and acceptance of nontraditional sexual orientations and to declines in intolerance of homosexuality. Two studies suggest the magnitude of the shifts may be on the order of half to two-thirds of a standard deviation (20 to 25 percentile points).

Studies done since 1990 of shifts in students' educational and occupational values report findings similar to those published before 1990. The weight of evidence indicates four-year increases in the importance students attach to "getting a good education" and in their support for "academic" philosophies of education. Similarly, the percentage of students who subscribe to the proposition that increased earning power is the chief benefit of a college education declines from the first to the senior year among nationally representative samples of students. Students' values relating to occupations also shift and in ways consistent with their educational views. By their senior year, college students are less likely to endorse extrinsic and instrumental rewards (such as social status, opportunities for advancement, and security) as important and are more likely to subscribe to intrinsic occupational values, such as on-the-job autonomy, responsibility, and opportunity to use their talents. The importance attached to making a lot of money, however, appears not to vary much by educational level.

The few studies published since 1990 dealing with changes in religious attitudes during college present a less clear or consistent picture than earlier evidence. Whereas pre-1990 studies indicated that students' religious activities and religiosity declined somewhat during the college years, the more recent evidence (although limited) points to *increases* or refinements in students' religious values during college. Some of this evidence suggests (and at this point, it is little more than a suggestion) that studies of changing religious values may be using measures that fail to detect subtle changes in how students think about religion, raising the possibility that students' religious values become incorporated in subtle ways with other beliefs and values.

Only a handful of studies published since 1990 touched on students' interest in culture and the arts, a topic that attracted far greater attention in the previous two decades. The more recent studies concurred with those published earlier: students' interest in the arts does increase over the college years.

Net Effects of College

In contrast to the consistent findings published before 1990 on the effects of college on students' sociopolitical attitudes, the evidence that appeared since then is mixed. Indeed, the findings seem to depend to some extent on the measures used. Net of the attitudes and other characteristics students bring with them to college, the small changes reported in students' political orientations (on a continuum from left to right) virtually disappear. The small net increases in liberalism that are seen parallel societal changes. Although the weight of evidence suggests that college attendance as a global variable has limited net power in predicting attitudinal changes, stronger evidence suggests that college attendance has a positive net effect on increases in students' knowledge of government and social and political issues.

Overall, the evidence consistently indicates that college attendance has a positive effect on students' civic and community involvements beyond the influence of other variables, including precollege attitudes and volunteer experience. The net impact, however, appears to vary by level of education and type of civic involvement. In some areas, educational attainment is unrelated to involvement (such as in nonworship church activities) or even negatively related (as with youth organizations).

The evidence from national studies consistently indicates that attending college has a statistically significant, positive net effect on students' racial, ethnic, and multicultural attitudes and values. The link persists in the presence of a wide array of controls, including those reflecting students' precollege attitudes and values, and across various outcome measures, including cultural awareness, acceptance of different races and cultures, commitment to promoting racial understanding, support for busing, viewing racism as a continuing problem, and increases in openness to diversity broadly defined. Single-campus studies present a somewhat more mixed picture, although they generally support the same conclusion indicated in the national studies.

Studies of the net impact of college on students' gender attitudes are limited in number, but they are consistent in suggesting the presence of college impacts beyond the influences of other factors on increases in support for women having the same salaries and opportunities for advancement as men in similar positions and in opposition to the propositions that a woman's place is in the home and that being "led on" is an acceptable defense for date rape.

We found little research on which to base any firm conclusions with respect to college's net effects on students' religious attitudes and values or on their understanding of or interest in the visual and performing arts.

Although only a handful of studies examined college's impacts on educational and occupational values, the evidence is consistent. Post-1990 studies identify freshman- to senior-year increases in the value attached to getting a good education and declines in the belief that the most important benefits of a college education are monetary. The net effects of college on students' occupational values are more complex, suggesting a "both/and" orientation. Educational attainment has a net and positive impact on the value attached to "getting ahead," although the impact appears to be unrelated to the importance attached to job security, success, or salaries when other factors are controlled. Attainment is clearly linked, however, to increases in the intrinsic values students look for in an occupation, including interesting work, having the freedom to use one's talents, and being able to make one's own decisions.

Between-College Effects

Net of the characteristics students bring with them to college, little evidence suggests any relation between the structural characteristics of an institution (such as size, type of control, curricular mission) and students' sociopolitical attitudes and behaviors. Private and selective institutions, as well as single-sex or historically Black institutions, may have some positive net impact on student support for liberal and libertarian views, but the effects are slight. The weight of evidence is clear, however, in pointing to the significant influence of the sociopolitical environment among students and faculty members on a campus. Students on campuses with a liberal sociopolitical peer context (compared with similar students on more conservative campuses) show greater increases in the likelihood of voting and in commitment to social activism, liberal sociopolitical orientations, and support for civil liberties.

As with the research relating to sociopolitical attitudes and values, differences in the structural characteristics of institutions are at best weak predictors of changes in students' civic and community involvement or in their sense of responsibility for contributing to community improvement. With a few exceptions, such institutional characteristics as size, type of control, or selectivity are not strong influences. The few studies relating to the differential impact on civic engagement of varying peer and faculty contexts across institutions are less conclusive than studies relating to sociopolitical attitudes and values. The general tendencies appear to be in the same direction, with changes in attitudes likely to conform to the dominant peer and faculty attitudes. Women at all-women's colleges (compared with women at coeducational institutions) appear to be marginally more disposed to engage in their communities, even when other factors are controlled.

Whether the "structural diversity" of an institution (that is, the proportional mix of students by race-ethnicity or cultural origin) directly influences students' racial-ethnic attitudes and values remains something of an open question. The evidence more clearly suggests that structural diversity has significant but indirect effects on student attitudes, operating through the frequency and nature of the interactions students are likely to have with peers from racial, ethnic, or cultural backgrounds different from their own as well as through the likelihood that the institution's curriculum will reflect the diversity of the campus. Once again, the descriptors typically used to differentiate among institutions (size, type, selectivity) appear to be largely unrelated to racial-ethnic attitudinal changes among students. Although women's colleges appear to have a small but significantly (statistically) greater impact on racial-ethnic attitudes of women than do coeducational colleges and universities, we found no evidence of such an effect on African-American students attending an HBCU compared with Black students at a predominantly White college or university. Although limited in volume, some evidence suggests that students' perceptions of the support among faculty members at their institution for diversity and multiculturalism and students' perception that their campus has a nondiscriminatory racial climate are both positively related to increases in cultural awareness, commitment to promoting racial understanding, and openness to diversity.

Generally, the research done since 1990 finds few between-college effects on freshman- to senior-year changes in gender-role attitudes. Perceived liberalism among the faculty may have some impact, but the evidence is equivocal. We identified no studies that found statistically significant net effects from attending a women's (versus a coeducational) institution on shifts in women's gender role attitudes once other factors were taken into account.

Studies of between-college impacts on students' educational and occupational values have found few interinstitutional differences, and none of these were associated with the conventional descriptors of institutional differences. Some evidence suggests that attending an HBCU (versus a predominantly White institution) may influence the value African-American students attach to learning for self-understanding and that the value peers attach to material possessions and comforts may elevate the value students' attach to being financially well-off.

Some evidence indicates that attending an HBCU rather than a predominantly White college or university may promote African-American students' interest in the arts and literature. Differential impacts on student attitudes and values concerning the arts, and in their religious attitudes and values, appear to be unaffected by across-institutional differences in selectivity and other structural characteristics. Studies of changes in religious attitudes or values associated with attending sectarian or nonsectarian institutions are too few in number to support a conclusion.

Within-College Effects

With the exception of studies suggesting that majoring in engineering or taking math and other quantitative courses tend to be inversely related to increases in measures of social activism, social concern, and liberal stances on public policy issues, the effects of academic major appear to be largely unrelated to sociopolitical attitudes and values beyond those immediately relevant to a field (such as women's or ethnic studies). These findings suggest that academic environments may be more influential than a particular major field or discipline. The evidence is clear, however, that service learning courses (those in which the service performed is integrally related to course content) have statistically significant and positive independent effects on students' commitment to social activism and to changing the political system, their perceptions of social and economic inequities, their inclinations to attribute those inequities to the system rather than to individuals, and their sense of social responsibility. It remains unclear, however, whether these experiences increase or reduce students' sense of empowerment and social efficacy. Participation in women's and ethnic studies courses and participation in racial, ethnic, and cultural awareness workshops appear to promote movement during college from the conservative toward the liberal end of the sociopolitical spectrum. The causal direction of these relations, however, remains ambiguous, even with controls for precourse or preworkshop attitudes.

Students' interactions with their peers have clear, statistically significant net effects on changes in various aspects of students' sociopolitical orientations, voting, social activism, liberalism, and support for civil liberties. The evidence provides only a limited basis, however, for resolving questions about the net effects of fraternity or sorority membership on changes in sociopolitical attitudes. Although some research points to an inverse relation between fraternity or sorority membership and social and political liberalism, other studies suggest the differences are more likely antecedent conditions rather than consequences of membership.

With few exceptions, the research clearly indicates that volunteer community service has statistically significant, positive effects on civic and community-oriented or "other-oriented" attitudes and values. Participation in service-learning courses has even greater impact on students' commitment to community service, to helping others, to understanding community problems, and to volunteer work in the future. Required service may reduce the positive benefits, however, and some evidence suggests that such service may in some instances confirm negative stereotypes. Fraternity or sorority membership, majoring in the social sciences, attending a racial or cultural awareness workshop, discussing political and social issues with peers, socializing with students from a different racial-ethnic or cultural background, and participating in learning communities and collaborative learning also increase students' community orientation and commitment to civic engagement.

A student's academic major appears to have some effect on changes in racial-ethnic attitudes and values, with freshman-to-senior shifts in the importance of promoting racial understanding being inversely related to majoring in business, nursing, science, or engineering. The effects of major appear to vary, however, depending on the field and the group toward which the attitudes are being studied. Living in an on-campus residence also appears, net of other influences, to promote more positive and inclusive racial-ethnic attitudes and openness to diversity. Although the evidence is far from conclusive, it does suggest that fraternity and sorority membership is negatively related to students' openness to diversity even when other factors (including precollege attitudes) are taken into account. It also appears that the greater a campus's structural diversity, the more likely students are both to socialize with someone of a different racial-ethnic background and to discuss racial issues. Structural diversity also appears to increase the likelihood that interracial personal friendships will form, and these friendships, in turn, have positive net effects on racial awareness, understanding, and attitudes. The causal direction of these relations, however, remains cloudy.

Students may encounter diversity in many settings, and taking women's and ethnic studies courses, as well as satisfying specific diversity-related curricular requirements, both appear to promote increased awareness of other ethnic groups and cultures, openness to diversity, and the importance students attach to promoting racial understanding. More general classroom characteristics also appear to be related to racial-ethnic attitude change, including the race-ethnicity and gender of the instructor, the inclusion of content and research that is diversity-related, and instructional practices that encourage discussion of racial and cultural issues. Other formal interventions, such as participation in service learning courses, in racial and cultural awareness workshops, and in leadership training courses, also have positive (if small) effects on cultural awareness, increased tolerance for differences, greater acceptance of others whose cultural origins differ from one's own, and greater openness to diversity broadly defined. Study abroad experiences appear to promote intercultural and international awareness, knowledge, and understanding, but the research is not particularly strong methodologically. Some of the stronger evidence suggests that the impacts of study abroad may be somewhat smaller on students' attitudes and values than on their intercultural knowledge and understanding.

Our review finds generally consistent (if sometimes methodologically flawed) evidence indicating that women's studies courses have a net positive impact on the modernity of students' gender-role attitudes. Although some research points to more negative than positive effects, most studies find that women's studies courses, even in the presence of controls for other factors (including precourse attitudes), produce increases in gender-related egalitarianism and awareness of discrimination, knowledge of diversity issues, feminist consciousness, and willingness to adopt new gender-role attitudes. Participation in workshops dealing with date rape and less violent forms of sexual harassment and aggression also appears to be effective, although their impact may be short-lived. The influence of fraternity and sorority membership on gender-role attitudes remains cloudy. The evidence suggests that fraternity and sorority members, as seniors, are more supportive of male dominance and sexual aggression than their independent peers, even when precollege attitudes and other factors are controlled.

Some of the research on changing attitudes toward gays, lesbians, and bisexual individuals is consistent with that reviewed earlier dealing with changes in racial-ethnic and gender role attitudes and provides support for the contact hypothesis. Interpersonal interaction may be a primary mechanism in reducing negative attitudes toward gays and lesbians, but the evidence on the effects of fraternity and sorority membership on such attitudes is limited and inconsistent. Specific interventions, such as workshops and speaker panels, appear to reduce student homophobia, but the evidence is not methodologically strong, and nothing is known about the durability of any effects.

Studies of within-college effects on students' educational values are few in number but generally methodologically sound. Majoring in the humanities appears to produce greater freshman-to-senior declines in the extrinsic values students assign to education than does majoring in the social sciences; the declines are smallest in the sciences and business. Humanities and social science majors also appear to experience greater net increases than do science majors in their endorsement of an "academic" philosophy of education. Net of other influences, including precollege educational values and other college experiences, fraternity and sorority membership (compared with nonmembership) appears to increase the extrinsic value members attach to education and to dampen students' intellectual orientations. Remaining "independent" tends to promote intrinsic educational values.

Conditional Effects of College

Compared to earlier decades, the 1990s produced more studies examining whether college in general or specific college experiences had differential effects on attitudes and values of different kinds of students. Studies that tested for gender-related conditional effects on students' social and political attitudes and values found that males and females tended to grow in their liberal dispositions to about the same (small) degree. The matter may depend to some extent, however, on the particular sociopolitical issue in question. When the shifts examined involved gender role or racial-ethnic issues, women experienced greater shifts than men toward the liberal end of the sociopolitical continuum, even after taking into account precollege differences in attitudes and other factors.

On the question of whether specific college experiences differentially affect different kinds of students, the research is limited but consistent. These studies find that a number of experiences (like living on campus, participating in a racial-ethnic awareness workshop, hours worked, fraternity or sorority membership, and peer interactions) had largely the same effects on women as men, both after one year and after two years.

Some well-controlled research, however, indicates that males and females may respond differently to their collegiate context. It appears, for example, that women's openness to diversity may be affected positively to a greater degree than that of men by their perceptions of their institution's support for diversity. In contrast, the racial-ethnic attitudes of men (compared with women) appear to be influenced in positive directions more by interpersonal relations than by institutional environments.

Studies of whether college may affect students differently depending on their race-ethnicity have produced evidence of differential impacts. Perceptions of a campus's environment as ethnically or culturally nondiscriminatory has a positive and statistically significant net impact on the racial-ethnic attitudes of *both* Whites and students of color but with the impact appearing to be significantly greater for minority students. Similarly, participation in a racial-ethnic or cultural awareness workshop contributes to increases in both White and minority students' racial understanding and openness to diversity, with the impacts significantly greater for White students. And fraternity or sorority membership may also differentially influence students' racial-ethnic attitudes, negatively affecting White students' openness to diversity while increasing such openness among students of color.

It remains unclear whether the college experience differentially shapes men's and women's gender-role attitudes, although the few studies we uncovered concerning this issue suggest the impact is general rather than conditional. The evidence is mixed concerning whether participation in a women's studies course has different effects on men and women. Two studies find no differential course impacts on men and women, a third finds an increase in men's recognition of sexism as a problem (but no change among women), and the fourth finds that course participation reduces male support for feminist views while increasing such support among women.

It seems safe to say that the increase in the number of studies exploring whether college has a differential impact on students depending on their personal backgrounds and characteristics constitutes one of the most important advances over the past decade in research on college students' attitudes and values. That such studies do not clearly identify which experiences affect what kinds of students and how should not be a cause for concern, at least not yet. The evidence is significant in confirming speculation in our earlier book that the effects of college, at least in some areas, appear to be conditional on certain student characteristics and therefore not the same for all students. Conditional college effects, however, remain largely unexplored territory.

Long-Term Effects of College

The evidence consistently indicates that the net changes that college attendance promotes in students' sociopolitical attitudes and values and civic and community engagement endure well into the adult years and even into old age. College's long-term impacts on students' postgraduate sociopolitical orientations are manifested in their voting behavior, awareness and discussion of social and political issues, and involvement in aspects of the political process. College's long-term effects are also apparent in graduates' involvement in civic and community groups, commitment to "other-oriented" goals, and promotion of racial understanding. Similarly, the net during-college increases in students' tendencies to value the intrinsic and decreases in their tendencies to value the extrinsic rewards of education and occupations also endure into the adult years, although the effects on extrinsic occupational rewards are most salient.

At least with respect to sociopolitical and gender-role attitudes, it appears that the influence of education is, in general, greatest during the college years and that attitudes and values tend to stabilize after college. Long-term attitudinal stability appears to be a function in part of the social and occupational environments graduates enter. Environments inhabited by spouses, friends, and colleagues with similar sociopolitical attitudes and values are more likely to promote attitudinal stability than are less supportive environments.

It also appears that college's impacts are both direct and indirect. The college experience seems to shape attitudes not only by contributing to students' knowledge and understanding of society, the political process, and social issues but also indirectly by providing greater access to influential social networks and associational memberships by means of the social and occupational status—the social capital—education confers.

Notes

1. The complexity and interplay of college, maturational, and sociohistorical influences on personal development and attitude and value formation is a central theme in the collection of 15 studies assembled by Hulbert and Schuster (1993). The chapters in this volume report findings from studies of successive generations of college women during their college years and often well into their adult years. The volume categorizes the studies into four eras spanning the twentieth century.

2. Individuals endorsing the "academic" philosophy value the pursuit of knowledge and understanding and are willing to follow wherever it leads. Subscribers to the "non-conformist" philosophy emphasize individuality, personal interests and styles, and a measure of disdain for traditional society. People holding the "collegiate" philosophy value the extracurricular aspects of the college experience. Those embracing the "vocational" philosophy value education primarily for its occupational benefits.

3. The two ongoing surveys of political behavior and attitudes are the General Social Survey and the National Election Study, both conducted repeatedly over the past 20 years.

4. Holland (1997) developed a theory of person-environment fit based on six personality types and six analogous vocational environments. The six personality types and their characteristics (from Smart, Feldman, and Ethington, 2000, pp. 35–36) are *realistic* (prefers activities involving use of machines, tools, and objects; disinclined to educational and interpersonal activities), *investigative* (is inclined to exploration, understanding, knowledge acquisition), *artistic* (is drawn to literary, musical, and artistic activities), *social* (prefers helping others, values social service and promotes the welfare of others), *enterprising* (enjoys activities involving persuasion, manipulation, or direction of others to attain organizational goals), and *conventional* (prefers establishing and maintaining order, routines, and standards).

5. Other definitions and discussions of service learning can be found in Bringle and Hatcher (1996), Eyler and Giles (1999), Howard (1998), Jacoby and Associates (1996), McEwen (1996), Shumer and Belbas (1996), and Zlotkowski (1998, 2002). Rama, Ravenscroft, Wolcott, and Zlotkowski (2000) review the research literature, and Conrad and Hedin (1991) review the literature and research relating to community service in the secondary schools.

6. Marks (1994) found similar effects among secondary school students.

7. Colby, Ehrlich, Beaumont, and Stephens (2003) discuss the interlaced dimensions of moral and civic development (Chapter Four) and summarize instructional practices for promoting civic engagement (Chapter Five). See also Colby, Ehrlich, Beaumont, and Stephens (2002).

8. Eyler, Giles, Stenson, and Gray (2001) provide an extensive, annotated bibliography of studies of the effects of service learning on students, faculty members, institutions, and communities. The document provides an outcome-specific key to relevant references. The bibliography was retrieved from http://www.compact.org/resource/aag.pdf.

9. Appel, Cartwright, Smith, and Wolf (1996), Hurtado, Milem, Clayton-Pedersen, and Allen (1999), Milem and Hakuta (2000), and Smith (1997) provide useful reviews of the research on the effects of racial-ethnic diversity as well as discussions of programmatic and policy actions to promote campus environments that are responsive to the learning needs of all students.

10. According to Allport ([1954] 1979), the "contact" conditions that shape prejudice (for better or worse) have at least six different "aspects": (1) quantitative aspects (such as the frequency, duration, number of people involved, and the situations in which prejudice occurs); (2) status aspects (of the individuals involved and the groups from which they come, whether the contact was a case of superordinate-subordinate or of equal status, prejudice being more likely to be reduced in the latter instance); (3) role aspects (competitive versus cooperative, with common

goals); (4) the social atmosphere of the contact (whether voluntary or involuntary, real or artificial, important and intimate or trivial and transient); (5) the personalities of the individuals involved (such as their initial level of, and previous experience with, prejudice); and (6) the areas of contact (such as casual, residential, occupational, recreational, religious) (pp. 261–282).

11. The research support for the contact hypothesis has been ambiguous and limited in generalizability (Nesdale & Todd, 2000; Sigelman & Welch, 1993; Springer, 1996). Springer provides a good review of the evolution of the theory and research on the contact hypothesis across three periods stretching from the 1940s into the 1990s. He found that the concepts of "intergroup proximity, attitudes, and friendships reappear continually in the literature, although theorists disagree on how they interrelate" (p. 44). Springer also found reason to believe that the "relationships among these constructs may be moderated by personal, environmental, and societal factors" (p. 44).

12. A third to half of the respondents in one study of some 570 faculty members in five academic areas (not including the natural-physical sciences, math, or engineering) expressed the view that *they* learn from diverse classrooms and research teams and believe that diversity has positive benefits in the classroom (Maruyama & Moreno, 2000).

13. Banks (1995) reviews the literature on the effects of classroom materials, instructional practices, reinforcement techniques, and other curricular experiences on elementary and secondary school students' racial and gender role attitudes.

14. Weaver (1989) provides a comprehensive bibliography of the literature published between 1951 and 1988 on U.S. students studying abroad. The bibliography draws from a variety of disciplines and includes a section on impact studies.

15. Important community-building characteristics of these groups included their shared goals, frequent interaction, shared adversity, a common "enemy," mutual support, recognition that their team was a meritocracy in which only performance mattered, and being held accountable for their actions on and off the field.

16. The National Women's Studies Association Task Force for the Association of American Colleges (1991) reports a detailed national study of women's studies programs' philosophies, designs, curricula, pedagogies, and related matters.

17. Negative attitudes toward gays and lesbians tend to correlate positively with being sociopolitically conservative and having a religious affiliation (Young, Belasco, Barr, Gallaher, & Webber, 1991), with holding traditional gender role attitudes (Herek, 1994), with being male (D'Augelli & Rose, 1990; Engstrom & Sedlacek, 1997; Green, Dixon, & Gold-Neil, 1993; Herek, 1994; Nelson & Krieger, 1997; Simoni, 1996), with fearing HIV/AIDS (D'Augelli & Hershberger, 1995), and with being younger, having lower self-esteem, and having less educated parents (Herek, 1994; Simoni, 1996). Although some evidence indicates the attitudes toward gay men, lesbians, and bisexuals became more positive between 1986 and 1988 (Sheehan, Ambrosio, McDevitt, & Lennon, 1990), D'Augelli and Hershberger (1995) suggest that, on one campus at least, the prevalence of homophobic attitudes remained relatively unchanged from 1985 to 1992.

18. Newcomb died before the research was completed, but his colleagues honored him for his contributions to this study, as well as for his earlier work, by listing him as a coauthor.

CHAPTER SEVEN

Moral Development[1]

American postsecondary education traditionally has had a clearly articulated role in the development of citizens who both think and act morally. The religiously affiliated liberal arts colleges of the early 1800s attempted to integrate curricular and noncurricular experiences in such a way that students graduated into the larger world both wiser and more sensitive to their moral and ethical responsibilities. The rise of public research universities and the attendant fragmentation of knowledge that accompanied the development of academic disciplines undoubtedly functioned to shift the focus of the curriculum and the faculty away from the development of student character. Yet despite this evolutionary change in the structure of institutions, the tradition of liberal education and its concern with developing the whole person persist as important themes in American postsecondary education. It is widely expected that the college experience should contribute not only to cognitive growth but also to the capacity to apply reason and intellect to interpersonal, social, political, and ethical questions (Ignelzi, 1990; Ikenberry, 1997; King, 1997; Mathiasen, 1998; Pascarella, 1997a). In this chapter, we attempt to synthesize the accumulated evidence on the impact of postsecondary education on both principled moral reasoning and moral behavior.

CHANGE DURING COLLEGE

Conclusions from *How College Affects Students*

The weight of evidence from a large number of studies that used different instruments and were conducted in different cultures clearly indicates that college is linked with statistically significant increases in the use of principled reasoning to judge moral issues. Upperclassmen tend to show higher levels of principled reasoning than freshmen or sophomores, but students also make statistically significant increases in the use of moral reasoning during college The relative magnitude of these gains was difficult to determine from the evidence presented. However, the exact magnitude of the gain may not be as important as the movement from conventional to postconventional or principled judgment during college, which in itself is an important event in moral development.

Evidence from the 1990s

As with our previous synthesis, nearly all the evidence from the 1990s pertaining to change during college has focused on students' principled moral reasoning or judgment, as conceptualized by Lawrence Kohlberg (1981b, 1984). Kohlberg's theoretical framework is certainly not the only valid model of moral or ethical development, but it appears to be, by far, the dominant theoretical framework guiding inquiry into the impact of postsecondary education on such development. His theory can be briefly summarized in the following way:

> Development is described as proceeding through six stages embedded within three levels. The first two stages (Level I) are considered preconventional. At this level, moral reasoning is highly egocentric in that it is based on the person's concerns for his or her own interests and for those of specific others the individual might care about. At Level II (Stages 3 and 4), conventional moral reasoning takes over. This reasoning is based on a concern with maintaining the social order. Moral judgments are guided by obedience to rules and meeting the expectations of others, particularly those in positions of authority. The orientation toward maintaining the system is replaced at Level III (Stages 5 and 6) by a postconventional or principled perspective. The basis of this kind of reasoning is a view of morality as a set of universal principles for making choices among alternative courses of action that would be held by any rational moral individual. These are considered first principles in that they exist independently of and prior to societal codification. Hence, a central emphasis in the postconventional stage is on principles for choosing the most just arrangement for individuals within society. [Pascarella, 1997a, pp. 48–49]

Kohlberg's (1981b, 1984) theoretical work has led to the development of a number of instruments designed to estimate an individual's level of principled moral reasoning or judgment. (Although the terms *principled moral reasoning* and *principled moral judgment* appear to be used interchangeably by scholars in the field, for purposes of consistency we will use *principled moral reasoning*.[2]) The two most visible instruments in the body of research are probably the Moral Judgment Interview (MJI) (Colby, Kohlberg, Gibbs, & Lieberman, 1983) and the Defining Issues Test (DIT) (Rest, 1979, 1986). Each instrument presents a series of moral dilemmas and attempts to determine the extent to which an individual uses principled reasoning or prefers principled considerations in making a judgment or decision about each dilemma. Clearly, there is a cognitive component to moral development as measured by both the MJI and the DIT. For example, both Hill (1995) and McNeel and Granstrom (1995) present evidence to suggest that moral reasoning measured by either the MJI or the DIT has significant, positive correlations with standardized measures of critical thinking.[3]

In our previous synthesis, we concluded that the extent or level of principled moral reasoning was positively associated with level of formal postsecondary education and that students generally made statistically significant gains in principled moral reasoning during college. Unfortunately, because many studies failed to report complete statistical data, an estimate of the actual magnitude of the growth in principled reasoning made during college could not be made. However, McNeel (1994a) conducted a valuable meta-analysis of 13 cross-sectional and 9 longitudinal studies of student moral development as measured by the Defining Issues Test. The individual samples in his synthesis were from 12 different colleges and universities (7 liberal arts colleges, 3 universities, and 2 Bible colleges). We took McNeel's raw data and conducted a reanalysis of his results, weighting each individual study by the size of its sample. The results of our reanalysis differed in only trivial ways from those reported by McNeel. For both cross-sectional studies (that is, comparing different samples of freshmen and seniors at the same time) and longitudinal studies (comparing a sample of freshmen with themselves as seniors four years later), the average advantage of seniors over freshmen in principled moral reasoning was about .77 of a standard deviation (28 percentile points). Moreover, the greatest change that took place during college was that students shifted from using moral reasoning that concedes to societal authority (conventional moral reasoning) to reasoning that is based on the application of universal moral principles (principled moral reasoning). We found little in the results of studies not included in McNeel's meta-analysis that would conflict with his findings of a strong association between principled moral reasoning and extent of exposure to postsecondary education (for example, Duckett et al., 1992; Duckett & Ryden, 1994; Foster & La Force, 1999; Galotti, Kozberg, & Farmer, 1991; Gielen & Markoulis, 1994; Good & Cartwright, 1998; Hill, 1995; Icerman, Karcher, & Kennelley, 1991; Jeffrey, 1993; Lind, 1997; Loviscky, 2000; Paradice & Dejoie, 1991; Thoma, 1994).

NET EFFECTS OF COLLEGE

Conclusions from *How College Affects Students*

The weight of evidence indicated that the college experience itself has a unique positive influence on increases in principled moral reasoning. This influence appeared to be substantially greater in magnitude than that due merely to maturation and could not be attributed solely to initial differences in moral reasoning, intelligence, or social status between those who attend and those who do not attend college. Of course, even with these important variables controlled statistically, one cannot be certain that all confounding influences have been taken into account. Individual differences between students related to their likelihood of attending or not attending college may be the true causal influences underlying differential change in moral reasoning rather than the college experience itself. This particular confounding influence is a potential threat to the internal validity of even the most carefully conducted longitudinal studies of the effect of college on moral reasoning.

It is also important to note that the evidence suggesting a net positive influence of college on the development of principled moral reasoning is consistent with more broadly based findings on the effects of college on values. These findings, from an extensive series of national samples, suggested that college attendance is associated with a humanizing of values and attitudes concerning the rights and welfare of others.

Evidence from the 1990s

Principled Moral Reasoning. As we have seen for previous outcomes, the fact that students demonstrate substantial growth in principled moral reasoning during college does not necessarily mean that exposure to postsecondary education causes that growth. A number of rival hypotheses (for example, cohort differences between freshmen and seniors in cross-sectional studies; maturation or growing older in longitudinal studies) could account for the observed difference between freshmen and seniors. However, consistent with the conclusions from our previous synthesis, there is evidence from the 1990s to suggest that exposure to postsecondary education has a statistically significant net positive influence on principled moral reasoning.

For example, Wilson, Rest, Boldizar, and Deemer (1992) followed a sample of 102 high school graduates for nearly a decade to determine the effects of educational attainment on principled moral reasoning, as measured by the Defining Issues Test (DIT). The DIT was administered at the beginning of the study and approximately 10 years later when the study participants were between 26 and 27 years old. With statistical controls for initial DIT score and a measure of dedication to career or education (for example, motivation to do well in career or amount of time devoted to educational pursuits), level of postsecondary educational attainment had a strong, positive total effect on DIT scores 10 years later of .34. (This can be interpreted as a one standard deviation increase in educational attainment leading to about a third of a standard deviation increase in principled moral reasoning, net of high school DIT score and level of dedication to career or education.) The addition of controls for occupational status and the extent to which the individual was in a career that was personally meaningful and challenging reduced the net effect of educational attainment on young adult moral reasoning but only to about .28. Thus, even in the presence of controls for precollege moral reasoning, dedication to career-education, occupational status, and sense of fulfilling work, an increase of one standard deviation in postsecondary educational attainment led directly to between a quarter and a third of a standard deviation increase in principled reasoning at age 26 to 27. There was, however, also a small indirect, positive effect of postsecondary educational attainment on young adult principled reasoning, transmitted through the positive effect of educational attainment on occupational status and fulfilling work.

Results quite consistent with those of Wilson, Rest, Boldizar, and Deemer (1992) have also been reported in cross-sectional studies by Rykiel (1995), with a single community college sample, and by Finger, Borduin, and Baumstark (1992), with a single four-year college sample. With statistical controls for a standardized measure of verbal aptitude, Rykiel found that graduating second-year students had a statistically significant advantage over incoming first-year students of about .35 of a standard deviation (14 percentile points) in DIT principled moral reasoning scores. (Since Rykiel's results are reported in terms of differences between statistically adjusted means and those of Wilson et al., 1992, are reported in terms of standardized regression coefficients, the results of the two studies are not directly comparable.) Finger, Borduin, and Baumstark found that of all the predictors they considered (year in college, involvement in social activities, age, socioeconomic status, parental control, and parental warmth), year in college was by far the strongest predictor of principled moral reasoning—accounting for 13 percent of the variance in DIT scores. Moreover, consistent with the conclusions of our previous synthesis, they also reported that age was not as strong a predictor of moral reasoning as level of postsecondary education completed. (See also Paradice & Dejoie, 1991.)

Inconsistencies in the way in which the evidence is reported in different investigations makes it difficult to estimate the magnitude of the net impact of college on growth in principled moral reasoning. However, the weight of evidence suggests that at least a substantial part of the growth in principled moral reasoning that occurs during college is uniquely attributable to the college experience. The significant, positive association between extent of exposure to postsecondary education and level of principled moral reasoning persisted even in the presence of controls for potentially important confounding influences such as level of pre-college moral reasoning, verbal ability, maturation, family socioeconomic status, and occupational level. The reasons why postsecondary education may facilitate growth in principled moral reasoning are not completely clear. However, Rest (1994) and Rest and Narvaez (1991) suggest that part of the explanation may be that college provides a relatively challenging and stimulating environment that leads students to overhaul and rethink the fundamental ways in which they form moral judgments. College may do this in large measure because it encourages students to think about the larger social contexts of history, institutions, and broad intellectual and cultural trends—many of which involve moral and ethical issues. Consistent with such an explanation is evidence reported by Mason and Gibbs (1993) that academic perspective taking (that is, exposure to broad perspectives concerning intellectual or social issues) is a strong predictor of advanced levels of moral reasoning among college students.

Despite rather consistent findings in support of a net positive impact of postsecondary education on growth in principled moral reasoning, it is possible that the evidence we reviewed is still confounded by other threats to internal validity, such as the interaction of selection and change. For example, compared to their counterparts with less exposure to college, individuals with relatively high levels of postsecondary educational attainment might simply be more open to the influence of the college experience to begin with. This difference in receptiveness to the impact of education on moral reasoning, more so than the college experience itself, might underlie the positive link between postsecondary educational attainment and level of principled moral reasoning. Thus, as we cautioned in our previous synthesis, differences between individuals related to their likelihood of attending college persist as a threat to the internal validity of studies estimating the net impact of postsecondary education on principled moral reasoning.

Moral Reasoning and Moral Action. The primary instruments used to measure growth during college in principled moral reasoning, as well as the net impact of college on that growth (that is, the Defining Issues Test and the Moral Judgment Interview), estimate the extent to which a person uses principled reasoning in making a judgment or decision about a moral dilemma. These instruments are not, in and of themselves, assessments of an individual's actual moral action or behavior. Nevertheless, although some inconsistencies exist between reasoning and behavior (for example, Crow, Fok, Hartman, & Payne, 1991), we found clear evidence in our previous synthesis of a statistically significant and positive association between principled moral reasoning (as measured by the DIT and MJI) and principled moral behavior, such as resistance to cheating, peer pressure, and unlawful or oppressive authority; whistle-blowing on corruption; the keeping of contractual promises; political and social activism; nonaggression; and helping behavior. (For a review of these studies, see Pascarella & Terenzini, 1991, pp. 363–364.) In research published during the 1990s, level of principled moral reasoning has been found to be positively linked to community involvement and a sense of civic responsibility (Rest, Thoma, & Edwards, 1997); voluntary community service (Hudec, 2002); ethical behavior in professions such as accounting (Arnold & Ponemon, 1991; Bernardi, 1991; Ponemon, 1992; Ponemon & Gabhart, 1990, 1993), dentistry (Bebeau, 1994), and medicine (Baldwin, Adamson, Sheehan, Self, & Oppenberg, 1996; Self & Baldwin, 1994); and the independent clinical performance of undergraduate nursing students (Duckett & Ryden, 1994). There is also evidence suggesting level of principled reasoning is negatively associated with student self-reported academic misconduct (Cummings, Dyas, & Maddux, 2001) and that college students involved in disciplinary matters exhibit lower levels of principled moral reasoning on the DIT than typical college students in normative research samples (Mullane, 1999).

Thus, it would appear that principled moral reasoning does not simply measure an individual's ability to make sophisticated responses to hypothetical moral dilemmas but is also systematically associated with, and perhaps even a precursor to, principled moral action. Growth in principled moral reasoning during college, therefore, should, at least indirectly, enhance the possibility of principled moral action. As Rest and Narvaez (1991) caution, however, although principled moral reasoning may positively influence moral behavior, alone it is not sufficient to determine moral behavior. Rest (1994) further suggests that using principled reasoning to judge moral issues is only one of four components leading to moral action. The other three components are moral sensitivity (being aware that a situation has a moral dimension to it and how one's action could affect others involved), moral motivation (prioritizing moral considerations relative to other situations), and moral character (the capacity to implement and persist in one's moral course of action). Unfortunately, compared with principled moral reasoning, we uncovered little or no systematic evidence concerning the influence of postsecondary education on these other three enabling precursors of moral behavior.

BETWEEN-COLLEGE EFFECTS

Conclusions from *How College Affects Students*

Evidence concerning between-college effects on moral reasoning was nearly nonexistent. Our own reanalysis of available data suggested that such differences may indeed exist. However, differences in student recruitment and selection standards among institutions make any causal conclusion drawn from such analysis highly tentative. Findings from one study were consistent with the notion that the student peer context may function to accentuate initial differences among colleges in terms of gains in principled moral reasoning. However, this finding awaited replication.

Evidence from the 1990s

Principled Moral Reasoning. Credible evidence concerning the impact of different kinds of colleges on the development of principled moral reasoning in students was virtually nonexistent until the early 1990s, when McNeel (1994a) constructed an informative 12-institution data set that provides some tantalizing hints about between-college effects. This data set is essentially the same as the one we reanalyzed in the previous section on change during college. However, McNeel also took the results from the 21 individual samples in his original meta-analysis and aggregated them according to institutional type (liberal arts colleges, Bible colleges, or universities) and study design (longitudinal or cross-sectional). Once again we weighted the studies according to sample size and reanalyzed McNeel's raw data. The results with the weighted samples differ only slightly from those originally reported by him and suggest interesting differences between institutional types. The largest freshman-to-senior gains or differences in principled moral reasoning were made at the private liberal arts colleges (average weighted senior advantage over freshmen across longitudinal and cross-sectional studies = .87 of a standard deviation, 31 percentile points). Somewhat smaller but still substantial gains were made at large public universities (average weighted senior advantage over freshmen across studies = .62 of a standard deviation, 23 percentile points), and the smallest gains were made at the Bible colleges (average weighted senior advantage over freshmen across studies = .13 of a standard deviation, 6 percentile points). Strikingly similar results are reported by Good and Cartwright (1998) with a smaller sample of three institutions—one of each type.

Such findings are, of course, limited by a small sample of institutions and by potential rival explanations for the differences found between institutional types. For example, liberal arts and Bible colleges might simply enroll populations of students characterized by strong differences in their receptivity to those collegiate experiences that facilitate a shift from a conventional to a principled perspective about moral issues. At the same time, however, it is important to note that in the longitudinal investigations, the liberal arts colleges in McNeel's (1994a) sample started out with the highest entering freshman scores in principled moral reasoning and made the largest freshman-to-senior gains. Conversely, students at the Bible colleges started out with the lowest entering principled reasoning scores and exhibited the smallest freshman-to-senior gains. These two trends are just the opposite of what one would expect from regression artifacts (that is, the artificial tendency for samples that have lower initial scores on a test to show greater gains on that test than samples that start out with initially higher scores on the same test). As such, it argues for the possibility that the between-college differences found in principled moral reasoning gains represent actual institutional effects. Traditional liberal arts education, combined with the unique social-psychological environments of small liberal arts colleges, may, in fact, be particularly conducive to the fostering of growth in principled moral reasoning. Findings consistent with this conclusion are also reported by Ponemon and Glazer (1990).

It is also worth noting that, although McNeel's (1994a) data suggest that a conservative religious ideology may sometimes inhibit growth in principled moral reasoning (for example, the Bible colleges), this is by no means an inevitability. As McNeel points out, most of the liberal arts colleges in his sample were also religiously affiliated, with a strong commitment to developing students' personal Christian faith. This was also the case with the single liberal arts college in the Good and Cartwright (1998) study. Yet what apparently counts in terms of their strong impact on students' growth in principled moral reasoning is that the religious orientation of these colleges was integrated within a genuine focus on liberal arts education.

Moral Behavior. A modest body of research has focused on the institutional characteristics that appear to inhibit academic dishonesty or academic cheating. Nearly all of this research has been conducted by McCabe and his colleagues (McCabe & Trevino, 1993, 1996, 1997; McCabe, Trevino, & Butterfield, 1996, 1999). Of particular relevance has been their concern with the contextual factors that influence student cheating behavior. Analyzing a number of multi-institutional samples, they found that peer behavior formed a normative context for cheating. A student was significantly more likely to admit (anonymously) to academic dishonesty if he or she observed another student cheating on an exam and significantly less likely to admit to academic dishonesty if he or she perceived that close student acquaintances would disapprove of cheating behavior. These associations remained statistically significant even in the presence of controls for such factors as age, sex, college grades, parental education, extracurricular involvement, involvement in intercollegiate athletics, and fraternity or sorority membership (McCabe & Trevino, 1993, 1996, 1997). Consistent with these findings, McCabe and his colleagues also found that, irrespective of size and academic selectivity, institutions with honor codes or honor systems that were enforced by students also had significantly less student self-reported academic dishonesty than institutions without such honor codes or systems (McCabe & Trevino, 1993, 1997; McCabe et al., 1996). They suggested three possibilities to account for this difference: students at honor code schools are responsible for reporting academic dishonesty, not the faculty or administration; academic integrity expectations are clearly defined to students at the start of their careers at honor code schools; and students at honor code schools usually receive the privilege of unproctored examinations, which they wish to preserve.

Although these findings suggest that the implementation of academic honor codes can foster a culture of academic integrity that functions to reduce cheating behavior, a degree of caution is appropriate in accepting the causal influences that underlie their results. An equally plausible competing hypothesis is that schools with publicly proclaimed academic honor codes simply attract and enroll students for whom academic integrity is a higher personal priority when they enter college.

WITHIN-COLLEGE EFFECTS

Conclusions from *How College Affects Students*

The evidence pertaining to the influence of different college experiences on principled moral reasoning was somewhat equivocal in terms of offering consistent, replicable findings. This may not be too surprising in that developmental theory in no way guarantees that one particular type of life experience is the preeminent cause of development in principled moral reasoning. A certain specific experience, then, might foster development if it happens to a receptive and reflective individual and if it is accompanied by other experiences in a cumulative and mutually reinforcing pattern. The key role of college in fostering principled moral reasoning may therefore lie in providing a range of intellectual, cultural, and social experiences from which a range of different students might potentially benefit.

From this perspective there was modest support for what, according to Kohlberg's theories, are salient experiences in the fostering of growth in moral development. College experiences in which an individual is exposed to divergent perspectives (for example, living away from home, having intellectual interactions with roommates) or is confronted with cognitive moral conflict (for example, taking courses that present issues from different perspectives) were reported by students as having a salient influence on their moral development. Also consistent with Kohlberg's expectations were students' specification of the importance of interactions with upperclassmen in residential facilities (that is, exposure to more advanced stages of moral reasoning) and assuming new personal responsibilities, such as social role taking. These experiences form a major part of the intellectual and interpersonal opportunities that characterize residential colleges and universities. However, it appeared that the extent to which an individual takes advantage of these opportunities, particularly those having an intellectual or academic content, was the key determinant of growth in moral reasoning during college.

Little consistent evidence existed to suggest that academic major or broad curricular categorizations are systematically associated with differences in the development of moral judgment. Certain specific curricular or course interventions with college students, however, did appear to foster the increased use of principled reasoning in judging moral issues. The most consistently effective interventions appeared to be those that emphasized moral dilemma discussion or personality development. This conclusion seemed to hold regardless of the methodological rigor of the study. Although these academic interventions would appear to enhance moral development, it was clear from the evidence reviewed that their effect, as well as the effect of any specific college experience, was smaller than the effect that could be reasonably attributed to four years of college. One possible explanation for this finding is that, similar to its impact on cognitive development, the influence of college on principled moral reasoning is the result not so much of any single experience but rather of the cumulative impact of a set of mutually reinforcing experiences. Another possibility is that the influence of different course interventions or specific college experiences on moral reasoning is conditional rather than general (that is, the magnitude of the influence varies for different kinds of students).

Evidence from the 1990s

The decade of the 1990s saw a continuation of rigorous attempts to isolate and identify the within-college academic and nonacademic experiences that influence growth in principled moral reasoning. In addition, researchers also sought to estimate the within-college experiences linked to several forms of moral behavior. We have organized our synthesis of this body of evidence into the following general categories: moral development interventions, service learning, major field of study, extracurricular-peer involvement, intercollegiate athletic involvement, off-campus learning, off-campus employment, and interaction with faculty.

Moral Development Interventions. We organize the evidence on moral development interventions into five categories: didactic courses, ethics courses, ethics in the curriculum, ability-based curricula, and other inventions.

Didactic courses. As indicated from the conclusions of our previous synthesis, two types of moral development interventions—those focusing on dilemma discussion and those emphasizing personality development—appear to be particularly effective in fostering the use of principled moral reasoning. As pointed out by Rest and Narvaez (1991), the role of the instructor in both of these types of interventions is more as facilitator than as information provider. However, a subsequent quasi experiment by Penn (1990) suggests that growth in the use of principled moral reasoning is even greater when students are exposed to direct instruction in philosophical methods of ethical analysis as well as to dilemma discussion and personality development. Classes that had all three elements, or all three elements plus instruction in formal logic, demonstrated one-semester growth in principled moral reasoning (as measured by the DIT) that averaged about .92 of a standard deviation (32 percentile points). This average effect size was more than twice as large as those for dilemma discussion and personality development interventions (.41 and .36, respectively) noted in our previous synthesis. A replication of Penn's didactic approach in a general education course by McNeel (1994b) yielded one-semester growth in principled moral reasoning of .65 of a standard deviation, still substantially larger than the typical effect sizes for dilemma discussion and personality development. Such evidence suggests that growth in principled moral reasoning is not always achieved most efficiently through the process of self-discovering the appropriateness and power of such reasoning from discussion of controversial moral dilemmas with one's peers. Rather, the impact of moral problem solving with one's peers may be an even more powerful inducement to growth in principled thinking if one is first taught the basic component skills of moral reasoning (for example, formal logic, role taking, justice operations) (McNeel, 1994b).

Ethics courses. Another purposeful intervention designed to facilitate growth in principled moral reasoning is a course focusing on ethics. This approach has been particularly visible in undergraduate business curricula (for example, Armstrong, 1993; Bonawitz, 2002; Ponemon, 1993; Shaub, 1994; St. Pierre, Nelson, & Gabbin, 1990). The weight of evidence from these studies is somewhat equivocal. Armstrong (1993), Bonawitz (2002), and Shaub (1994) report findings suggesting that business students exposed to courses or interventions having a purposeful focus on professional ethics and ethical issues show significantly greater growth in the use of principled moral reasoning (as measured by the DIT) than similar students not exposed to such courses or interventions. However, both Ponemon (1993) and St. Pierre, Nelson, and Gabbin (1990) found that the inclusion of ethical content in courses, or exposure to a specific course in ethics during college, had a trivial impact on growth in the use of principled moral reasoning. Similarly, Smith and Oakley (1996) reported that completion of a course in business ethics had no significant effect on students' attitudes toward ethical business behavior. We suspect that the mixed findings for this body of evidence reflect to some extent the fact that the ethics interventions in the various studies differed substantially in their content, emphasis, and implementation. On balance, across all studies the effect on principled moral reasoning of exposure to either ethics courses or interventions is probably positive, though quite modest in magnitude. Beyond this rather tentative speculation, however, we hesitate to offer a firm conclusion.

Ethics in the curriculum. There is also evidence from two independent, longitudinal studies to suggest that purposefully integrating ethical content into an undergraduate professional curriculum (that is, nursing) may foster increased growth in principled moral reasoning (Duckett & Ryden, 1994; McNeel, Schaffer, & Juarez, 1997). Duckett and Ryden estimated the impact of a nursing curriculum at a public university that built ethics content vertically into the curriculum and provided ethically focused learning experiences in existing courses across all levels. Across four cohorts of students exposed to the curriculum, they found growth in principled moral reasoning during what appeared to be the last half of college to average about .41 of a standard deviation (16 percentile points). The absence of a control group, however, made it difficult to determine just what part of that growth was attributable to the purposefully enhanced ethics curriculum.

A somewhat less ambiguous estimate of the unique impact of an ethics-oriented curriculum on principled reasoning was presented by McNeel, Schaffer, and Juarez (1997) in a study of undergraduate nursing students at a small liberal arts college. The intervention integrated ethical content and ethical growth experiences into both the general education and nursing program curricula. For example, the general education curriculum included several required courses with a significant ethics component. The nursing curriculum implemented such things as an ethics seminar, specific ethics content in senior courses, and small-group meetings with a faculty member focusing on ethical issues and relationships. Employing a variation on a time-series design, McNeel and colleagues compared the freshman-to-senior growth in principled moral reasoning of three cohorts of students prior to, and three cohorts of students after, the implementation of the ethics-oriented curriculum. Both the preceding and subsequent cohorts entered college with about the same levels of principled reasoning on the DIT. However, the three cohorts entering after the ethics-oriented curriculum was implemented demonstrated average freshman-to-senior growth in principled reasoning that was significantly larger in magnitude (1.54 of a standard deviation, 44 percentile points) than the average corresponding growth in principled reasoning shown by the three cohorts entering prior to the implementation of the curriculum (1.34 of a standard deviation, 41 percentile points). Thus, principled reasoning growth was more pronounced among the cohorts that experienced the ethics-enriched curriculum.[4]

Ability-based curricula. Although it is not experimental in design, and awaits replication, Mentkowski and Associates' (2000) assessment of the impact of Alverno College's Ability-Based Curriculum suggests that student progress through that curriculum may enhance the development of principled moral reasoning. The Ability-Based Curriculum is an integrated set of general education and disciplinary courses constructed according to a common developmental framework. It attempts to provide connected liberal arts learning experiences in courses that increase student competencies in eight broad areas (communication, analysis, problem solving, valuing and decision making, and the like) and at six increasingly complex developmental levels in each competency or ability category. For example, in the valuing and decision-making competency, developmental growth proceeds from identifying one's own values, to engaging in valuing and decision making in multiple contexts, to applying one's own values in an area of knowledge in a professional context. Progress through the curriculum appeared to be measured by a cumulative record of evaluations that students complete. As students completed courses they were evaluated in terms of their developmental level within the eight ability or competency dimensions. Mentkowski and her associates found that, even in the presence of statistical controls for age, entering intellectual development and critical thinking levels, and entering levels of principled moral reasoning (as measured by the DIT), the measure of progress through the developmentally sequenced curriculum had a modest but statistically significant and positive direct effect on women's levels of principled reasoning after two years of college.

One reasonable conclusion from this finding is that Alverno's ability-based and developmentally oriented curriculum is particularly effective in promoting students' use of principled reasoning. However, because of the absence of a control condition (for example, a traditional and less integrated and developmentally based liberal arts curriculum), such a conclusion involves a degree of risk. As Mentkowski and Associates (2000) point out, although there are some clear logical links between the experiences fostered by the Ability-Based Curriculum and growth in principled moral reasoning, the design of their investigation makes it difficult to determine the magnitude of the unique advantage of such a curriculum over other less purposefully structured and integrated approaches to liberal arts education.

Other interventions. To be sure, other studies have estimated the impact of purposeful interventions designed to foster growth in moral reasoning or moral development during college. It is difficult, however, to fit these studies into a larger body of evidence. As a group, they differ substantially from one another in the focus and content of their intervention and, with one exception, are single studies that await replication. Nevertheless, they are of some interest and deserve at least brief mention. For example, Beller and Stoll (1992) reported the results of a rigorously conducted true experiment that estimated the impact of a moral reasoning intervention designed for undergraduate student athletes. Student athletes at a single institution were randomly assigned to two conditions: a "moral reasoning for sports" course and a control group that did not take the course. The moral reasoning course focused on analyzing four values (honesty, responsibility, justice, and beneficence) and was integrated with readings on moral and ethical issues in sports (for example, drug testing, gambling, rule violations, winning, and the like). Compared with their counterparts in the control condition, student athletes exposed to the semester-long intervention demonstrated significantly larger gains on the Hahm-Beller Values Choice Inventory (a measure of principled moral judgment correlating .82 with the DIT) and larger, though only marginally significant, gains in principled reasoning as measured by the DIT.

Similarly, Mustapha and Seybert (1990) sought to determine if two different approaches to general education led to differences in students' principled moral reasoning. The traditional (control) curriculum provided liberal arts studies through separate departmental courses. The experimental curriculum consisted of an integrated six-course, six-semester sequence. Each course combined the study of two or three subjects, was multidisciplinary, and was organized around the central idea of decision making. Instructional methods sought to implement Kohlberg's theory that moral decision making is a cognitive developmental process learned through open Socratic inquiry and active learning participation. Students were confronted with situations requiring moral decision making throughout the curriculum. With statistical controls for a standardized measure of intelligence, students in the experimental general education curriculum had a statistically significant advantage in principled moral reasoning over their counterparts in the traditional general education curriculum of about .50 of a standard deviation (19 percentile points). Though potentially confounded by the fact that individuals could self-select themselves into the experimental curriculum, the results are nevertheless consistent with the conclusions of our previous synthesis that learning to make decisions about moral dilemmas (dilemma discussion) positively influences growth in principled moral reasoning. Indeed, the Mustapha and Seybert findings suggest that this conclusion holds at the curricular as well as the course intervention level.

In addition to interventions based on moral decision making, there has been an attempt to estimate how course interventions that infuse diversity-related issues into the course content influence growth in moral reasoning (Gurin, Dey, Hurtado, & Gurin, 2002; Hurtado, Mayhew, & Engberg, 2003). Students who enrolled in courses that exposed them to diversity-related issues such as racism, sexism, and classism demonstrated gains on the DIT that were nearly 2.5 times larger than their counterparts in a course that did not expose them to such issues. Similar results have been reported by Adams and Zhou-McGovern (1990, 1994) for a social diversity course that focused on such topics as racism, sexism, homophobia, and disability oppression.[5]

Service Learning. A modest body of research has attempted to estimate the net impact of service learning on various dimensions of moral development. The results of this research suggest that involvement in service learning has a somewhat inconsistent impact on growth in principled moral reasoning. We uncovered two independent and rigorously conducted quasi experiments that address this issue. Both Boss (1994) and Cram (1998) randomly assigned two intact classes to different sections of one-semester undergraduate ethics courses, each of which included extensive discussion of moral dilemmas and ethical issues. The experimental section in each study also included an active community service component that was integrated into the course content, whereas the control section had no service-learning component. Boss found that the section with the service-learning component demonstrated significantly greater growth in principled moral reasoning (as measured by the DIT) than did the section without the service-learning component. However, Cram reported that growth in DIT principled reasoning scores was almost identical between the experimental (service-learning) and control sections. Because the two studies are quite similar in both methodological rigor and treatment implementation, it is difficult to choose one set of results as more valid than the other.[6]

Evidence pertaining to the impact of service learning on aspects of moral-ethical development other than principled moral reasoning tends to be consistent with the findings of Boss (1994). For example, in their comprehensive, multi-institutional evaluation of students in service-learning courses, Eyler and Giles (1999) found that, even with controls for age, gender, race, socioeconomic status, other service involvement, and dependent variable scores at the start of the semester, exposure to service-learning courses had a modest but statistically significant, positive effect on the end-of-semester importance students placed on social justice. Similar results are reported by Astin and Sax (1998) and Gray et al. (1996) for the net impact of service learning or service involvement on sense of civic responsibility and the importance of service to the community. Consistent with the cognitive impacts of service learning, Eyler and Giles also report evidence suggesting that the net positive effect of service-learning experiences on growth in the importance students place on social justice is even further enhanced when the service experience is integrated into the course content and provides opportunities for reflection through discussion and writing. Evidence consistent with this aspect of the Eyler and Giles investigation is also reported by Myers-Lipton (1994). Students in a program that closely integrated service and reflective learning showed greater two-year increases in civic responsibility and decreases in social prejudice than their counterparts involved in service without the reflective learning component.[7]

Major Field of Study. The small body of evidence pertaining to the net impact of major field of study on principled moral reasoning is inconsistent and provides little basis for an unambiguous conclusion. McNeel and colleagues (McNeel, 1994a, McNeel et al., 1996) summarize a series of longitudinal analyses from a single-college sample suggesting that major field of study is significantly linked to differences in freshman-to-senior growth in principled reasoning (as measured by the DIT). Specifically, somewhat smaller principled reasoning growth appeared to accrue to students in certain vocational majors (for example, education and business) than in other disciplines or fields of study (for example, psychology, English, nursing, social work, humanities). In contrast, however, Jeffrey's (1993) single-institution, cross-sectional investigation reported that differences between lower-division and senior students in principled moral reasoning were essentially the same for business and accounting majors as they were for liberal arts majors. Similar inconsistent results have been reported by Cummings et al. (2001), St. Pierre, Nelson, and Gabbin (1990) and Snodgrass and Behling (1996). Given the small body of evidence and the generally inconsistent findings, we believe that any conclusion about the impact of major field of study on principled moral reasoning is premature.

Extracurricular-Peer Involvement. In their cogent discussion of the factors that influence growth in principled moral reasoning during college, Rest and Narvaez (1991) argue that the extracurricular milieu of college may play a potentially significant role in moral and ethical development. There is a modicum of evidence to support their argument. For example, Finger, Borduin, and Baumstark (1992) employed a regression approach to determine which among a range of factors was significantly linked to students' level of principled moral reasoning. The factors included year in college, age, socioeconomic status, relationship with parents, and frequency of informal social-extracurricular activities during college. After year in college, level of social-extracurricular involvement during college was the next best predictor of principled reasoning, accounting for 5 percent of the variance in students' DIT scores. Consistent results are reported by Lind (1997), who suggests that the role-taking opportunities that often accompany extracurricular involvement are an important catalyst in the development of principled moral reasoning.

In contrast with the evidence pertaining to the development of principled moral reasoning, the effects of extracurricular involvement on what might be considered ethical behavior are contradictory. For example, Berger's (1998) analysis of eight religiously affiliated colleges from the 1992 to 1996 iteration of the Cooperative Institutional Research Program data sought to determine the factors explaining students' community service involvement during college. With statistical controls for such factors as previous community service, demographic characteristics, academic major, socioeconomic background, residence on campus, and high school grades, level of involvement in clubs and organizations had generally significant and positive effects on students' community service involvement. Conversely, McCabe and Trevino (1997) found that level of extracurricular involvement during college was significantly and positively linked with self-reported academic dishonesty. This positive relationship between extracurricular activities and cheating behavior persisted in the presence of statistical controls for such potentially confounding influences as age, gender, college grades, severity of institutional penalties for cheating, faculty support for academic integrity, perceived peer academic dishonesty, and perceived peer disapproval of cheating.

Although the Berger (1998) and McCabe and Trevino (1997) investigations consider different kinds of moral behavior, with different regression specifications, it is still difficult to account for their diametrically opposed findings. One possible explanation is that different kinds of extracurricular or social involvement can have different impacts on moral reasoning and moral behavior. Consistent with this notion is recent evidence reported by Derryberry and Thoma (2000). They found that students' principled moral reasoning levels were inversely related to the density of their friendship networks in college. Highly dense networks are those in which each person is known by each other. An example might be a fraternity or sorority. Low-density friendship networks are those characterized by multiple independent friendships with a diversity of different kinds of individuals who don't typically interact with one another (for example, friends from a residence facility, friends from one's major, friends from on-campus work, and the like). Low-density friendship networks provide a more diverse social environment during college than high-density networks and, therefore, greater exposure to different ideas, values, and experiences.

Derryberry and Thoma (2000) point out that their findings could reflect the fact that individuals with high levels of principled reasoning may simply be more open to diverse (low-density) friendship networks and tend to enter into them more frequently. However, other investigations with more extensive controls for confounding influences tend to suggest a causal link between diverse friendship networks during college and both principled moral reasoning and principled behavior. For example, Kilgannon and Erwin (1992) sought to determine the impact of fraternity or sorority membership (compared with not being Greek-affiliated) on growth in principled moral reasoning (as measured by the DIT) during the first two years of college. According to Derryberry and Thoma, Greek-affiliated students would be more likely than those not joining fraternities and sororities to have high-density friendship networks that tend to insulate individuals from exposure to the kinds of divergent sociopolitical and cultural perspectives that have been shown to foster growth in principled moral reasoning. One might therefore expect these students to demonstrate less growth in principled reasoning than their counterparts who do not join fraternities or sororities. This is generally what Kilgannon and Erwin found. In the presence of statistical controls for precollege level of principled moral reasoning, women who joined sororities demonstrated significantly lower principled reasoning after two years than did women who were not sorority members. The corresponding comparison for men was in the same direction, though not statistically significant.

Evidence suggesting that fraternity or sorority membership inhibits growth in principled moral reasoning is not an isolated finding. There is also evidence indicating a negative relationship between Greek affiliation and moral or ethical behavior. For example, it appears that fraternity and sorority members are more likely to admit to academic dishonesty during college than their counterparts who are not Greek-affiliated (Kirkvliet, 1994; McCabe & Bowers, 1996; Storch, 2002). Of course, this could to some extent reflect the possibility that individuals who choose to join fraternities and sororities have a stronger disposition toward academic dishonesty when they enter college. Nevertheless, when McCabe and Trevino (1997) controlled for important individual and contextual influences such as age, sex, college grades, parental education, extracurricular and athletic involvement, and the peer environment with regard to cheating at the institution attended, fraternity and sorority members still reported being involved in a significantly higher level of academic dishonesty than their non-Greek-affiliated counterparts.

From a different perspective, there is also evidence suggesting that low-density, diverse friendship networks may have a positive impact on what might be considered other ethically oriented behaviors. In Berger's (1998) eight-institution analysis of the factors influencing community service involvement, both interaction with different racial-ethnic groups and involvement in multicultural activities tended to enhance significantly the likelihood of participating in community service during college. These positive effects remained statistically significant even in the presence of statistical controls for salient confounding influences, such as prior community service involvement, campus residence, academic major, extracurricular involvement, race, sex, socioeconomic status, humanistic values at entry to college, and high school academic achievement. With the same set of controls in effect, being a member of a fraternity or sorority had a significant, negative impact on community service involvement in one of the three analyses conducted. However, there is evidence that conflicts with Berger's latter finding. Pierson (2002) found that Greek affiliation actually increased the likelihood of volunteer work in college, even with controls for secondary school volunteerism, individual background traits, and other academic and nonacademic experiences during college.

Intercollegiate Athletic Involvement. A small body of research has focused, either directly or indirectly, on the relationship between intercollegiate athletic participation during college and moral development. This literature provides little convincing evidence that involvement in intercollegiate athletics has a causal influence on either principled moral reasoning or moral behavior. Baldizan and Frey (1995) found only small, chance differences between male and female intercollegiate athletes and male and female nonathletes in DIT principled reasoning scores. Similarly, Beller, Stoll, Burwell, and Cole (1996) found no significant difference in the use of principled reasoning between intercollegiate athletes participating in individual sports and nonathletes. Intercollegiate athletes participating in team sports had significantly lower principled reasoning scores than either athletes in individual sports or nonathletes. However, this may simply reflect recruitment rather than a socialization effect, in that athletes participating in team sports might have started college with lower levels of principled moral reasoning. The design of the Beller et al. study makes it difficult to determine which of the two effects is more probable.

The same inconclusiveness holds for the relationship between intercollegiate athletic participation and moral-ethical behavior. Nixon (1997) found that, irrespective of sex, intercollegiate athletes are no more likely to demonstrate aggressive behavior (injuring another person) outside of their sport than nonathletes. Similarly, the results of McCabe and Trevino's (1997) multi-institutional study of academic dishonesty indicate that participation in intercollegiate athletics has only a small and nonsignificant effect on cheating behavior when important confounding influences are taken into account.

Off-Campus Learning Experiences. Consistent with Derryberry and Thoma's (2000) contention that interaction with diverse peers and divergent intellectual and social perspectives tends to enhance students' growth in principled moral reasoning, there is single-study evidence to suggest that participation in off-campus learning experiences positively influences such growth. McNeel (1994a) compared the freshman-to-senior growth in principled moral reasoning of students who participated in off-campus learning (for example, study in foreign countries, study in Washington, D.C., or other unspecified off-campus experiences) with students not participating in such programs. Students participating in off-campus learning experiences demonstrated gains in the use of principled moral reasoning during college that were, on average, about 1.7 times as large as the corresponding gains shown by their counterparts who did not have such experiences. As McNeel points out, the causal inferences from such a finding are tenuous at best. For example, those who choose to participate in off-campus learning experiences may simply be on a particularly strong growth trajectory during college because they are especially receptive to the developmental impacts of liberal arts education. At the same time, it is worth noting that those participating and those not participating in off-campus learning experiences started college with only trivial and chance differences in their levels of principled moral reasoning. Consequently, it is unlikely that the results reported by McNeel are simply a reflection of regression artifacts.

Off-Campus Employment. The small body of evidence we uncovered suggests that off-campus employment during college has a negative influence on both principled moral reasoning and moral-ethical behavior. Rykiel's (1995) study of community college students found that, net of verbal ability, individuals working off campus 25 hours or more per week had significantly lower DIT principled reasoning scores than did their counterparts employed off campus for less than 20 hours per week. Similarly, Berger (1998) reported that hours of off-campus work per week tended to influence community service involvement negatively during college, even when confounding influences such as student demographic characteristics, prior community service involvement, place of residence, and academic major were taken into account. It may well be that extensive involvement in off-campus work simply diminishes the time one has available either to commit to community service or to be involved in the social and academic experiences of college that contribute to growth in principled reasoning. At the same time, however, both the Rykiel and Berger studies tell us only that the more hours one works off campus per week, the lower the level of moral reasoning or probability of participating in what might be regarded as moral-ethical behavior. The studies do not inform us with regard to differences between students who work off campus during college and those who do not, the impact of off-campus work related to academic major or intended career, or how on-campus work might influence dimensions of moral or ethical development.

Interaction with Faculty. One of the conclusions from our previous synthesis was that principled moral reasoning was enhanced by exposure to and interaction with individuals at more advanced stages of principled reasoning. Although this interaction might be most likely with upper-division peers, it could also occur through interactions with faculty. Although based on a single-sample finding that awaits replication, there is evidence to support the contention that out-of-class contact with faculty members in a small liberal arts college is linked to growth in principled moral reasoning. McNeel (1994a) found that students who reported at least some out-of-class contact with faculty during college had freshman-to-senior gains in DIT principled reasoning scores that were about three times as large as their counterparts who reported no such contact during college. Furthermore, the two groups differed in only trivial, chance ways in level of principled reasoning when they entered college, so it is unlikely that the finding simply reflects regression artifacts. McNeel speculates that informal, out-of-class interactions with faculty may have a strong impact on students' principled reasoning because such interactions provide a setting in which faculty maturity in reasoning about moral issues with which students may be struggling can be modeled for students in a personal and nonthreatening way. Because of the nonexperimental design of McNeel's study, however, the causal direction of the results is somewhat ambiguous. A reasonable alternative explanation for his finding is that students who are the most receptive to the impacts of liberal arts education, and who are experiencing the greatest changes in how they reason about moral issues during college, may simply be the most strongly oriented toward interaction with faculty outside of class.

A related investigation by Nevins and McNeel (1992) at the same small liberal arts college suggests that it may be possible to develop faculty teaching workshops that enhance a professor's influence on students' growth in principled reasoning. In each of three separate years, a yearlong faculty development program was implemented that sought to introduce faculty to concepts of developmentally based instruction that could be used in their classes. The faculty who chose to participate studied a range of different models of how students develop during college (for example, Erikson, Gilligan, King and Kitchener, Kolb, Perry). In addition, general concepts such as maturational levels, developmental transformations, individual differences (including learning style), and a balance between challenge and support were presented and discussed. Each faculty participant chose a target course to revise in light of what he or she had learned and was given release time to carry out the revision. In order to determine the impact of the program, Nevins and McNeel divided students into groups according to the amount of contact they had with the workshop-trained faculty and then compared their growth in DIT principled reasoning during the first two years of college. Students with moderate or high levels of exposure to the workshop-trained faculty in the professors' target courses demonstrated growth in principled moral reasoning during the first two years of college that was, on average, about 2.9 times as large as the corresponding growth shown by students with little or no such exposure. A similar trend in DIT scores was shown for students with different levels of exposure to the workshop faculty in their nontarget courses. As Nevins and McNeel candidly admit, there are plausible alternative explanations for their findings, not the least of which is that the faculty development program may have attracted the most effective teachers. Despite this limitation, however, the faculty development workshop they describe and assess represents a potentially significant, if yet unreplicated, intervention for enhancing the impact of faculty and their courses on student moral development.

CONDITIONAL EFFECTS OF COLLEGE

Conclusions from *How College Affects Students*

Almost no research systematically looked for conditional effects. The little evidence that did exist suggested that an instructional intervention that stresses exposure to intensive moral arguments and discussion had more positive effects on principled moral judgment for subjects at higher levels of cognitive development (formal reasoners) than for subjects at lower levels (concrete reasoners). This conditional effect underscored the notion that moral development does not occur in isolation from other areas of student development during college but rather is a part of a network of mutually supporting changes.

Evidence from the 1990s

Once again we uncovered relatively little in the way of research that systematically investigated the conditional effects of postsecondary education on moral development. However, consistent with the conclusions of our previous synthesis, we found evidence indicating that a certain level of formal reasoning may be required for students to realize maximum benefits from instructional interventions designed to increase principled reasoning. In an eight-week interpersonal skills training class, Santilli and Hudson (1992) found that only those students with relatively high (consolidated) formal reasoning scores showed gains in DIT principled moral reasoning. Students with relatively low (early basic) formal reasoning levels demonstrated only chance gains in principled reasoning.

There is also evidence to suggest that the impact on principled moral reasoning of hours per week employed off campus varies in magnitude for students of different ages. Recall from Rykiel's (1995) longitudinal study of community college students that, net of tested verbal ability, students working fewer than 20 hours per week had higher DIT principled reasoning scores than their counterparts employed off campus for 25 or more hours per week. The positive effect on principled reasoning of working under 20 hours per week was larger for older (nontraditional-age) students than it was for younger (traditional-age) students. However, we uncovered no independent study replicating this finding, so it is difficult to interpret its meaning in the context of other evidence.

LONG-TERM EFFECTS OF COLLEGE

Conclusions from *How College Affects Students*

Evidence from 10- and 20-year longitudinal studies was clear in identifying the positive, long-term influence of college on principled moral reasoning. The estimated advantages that accrue to those who attend college (versus those who do not) do not diminish over time but tend to increase. In large measure, this may be due to the tendency for college to channel individuals into posteducation occupations and lifestyles characterized by a level of continuing intellectual stimulation and challenge that either maintains or further enhances principled moral reasoning. Conversely, having only a high school diploma may tend to channel people into occupational or lifestyle environments characterized by a relatively low level of intellectual stimulation. Thus, level of principled moral reasoning may actually regress over time.

Evidence from the 1990s

We did not find the kind of longitudinal evidence in the research of the 1990s that permitted long-term comparison of trends in principled moral reasoning growth among individuals completing different amounts of postsecondary education. However, the scant evidence we did uncover is generally consistent with the conclusions of our previous synthesis in suggesting that level of principled reasoning tends to persist or increase modestly among college graduates over the years immediately following graduation.

The most useful investigation in this regard is Mentkowski and Associates' (2000) longitudinal assessment of a sample of women attending Alverno College, a small, single-sex liberal arts college. Mentkowski and her colleagues assessed the sample with the Defining Issues Test (DIT) at four different times: when they entered college, after the first two years of college, at graduation from college, and about five years subsequent to graduation. (The results of the first three assessments were incorporated in the results of our earlier synthesis [Pascarella & Terenzini, 1991] and our reanalysis of McNeel's [1994a] meta-analysis.) They found that during the five years after graduating from college, women's growth in principled moral reasoning on the DIT tended to plateau (although it showed a very small growth trend). The DIT mean score of the alumna was only slightly higher than it was when they were graduating seniors, suggesting that the rather dramatic principled reasoning growth that occurred during college (about .80 of a standard deviation in the Alverno sample) was maintained during the five years subsequent to graduation. A smaller sample of women completed the Moral Judgment Interview (MJI) during the same four assessments and actually showed a modest increase in principled reasoning between graduation and the five-year follow-up (about .18 of a standard deviation). Such evidence reinforces the conclusion that the developmental trends in principled moral reasoning that occur during college do not retrogress afterward. As suggested in our previous synthesis, this is probably attributable in no small way to the particular occupations and lifestyle choices that are characteristic of, or available to, college graduates.

Results generally consistent with those of Mentkowski and Associates (2000) are reported by Astin, Sax, and Avalos (1999) in their longitudinal study of factors influencing community service involvement among alumni nine years after enrolling in college. With controls for service involvement in high school, as well as other relevant confounding influences, engagement in volunteer community service during college had a significant, positive effect on hours spent in voluntary community service activities as alumni. Thus, as with increases in the use of principled reasoning that occurs during college and persists into the early postgraduation years, engaging in what might be considered ethically oriented behavior during college tends to continue when one leaves college.

SUMMARY

Change During College

As with our previous synthesis, nearly all the evidence pertaining to change during college concerns students' use of principled reasoning in judging moral issues. Also consistent with our previous synthesis, the evidence suggests that level of principled moral reasoning is positively associated with level of post-secondary educational attainment and that students generally make statistically significant gains in principled reasoning during college. The primary contribution of the research of the 1990s was that it permitted us to compute an effect size. We estimate that the average advantage of seniors over freshmen in principled moral reasoning is about .77 of a standard deviation (28 percentile points). It is also the case that the main change that takes place during college is a shift from using moral reasoning that concedes to societal authority (conventional moral reasoning) to reasoning that is based on the application of universal moral principles (principled moral reasoning).

Net Effects of College

Inconsistencies in the way in which the evidence is reported in different studies makes it difficult to estimate the magnitude of the net impact of college on growth in principled moral reasoning. The weight of evidence, however, suggests that at least a substantial part of the growth in principled reasoning that occurs during college is uniquely attributable to the college experience itself. The reasons why postsecondary education may be particularly effective in facilitating growth in principled moral reasoning are not completely clear. However, the explanation may be at least in part that college provides a relatively challenging and stimulating environment that leads students to overhaul and reconsider the ways in which they formulate moral judgments. Despite generally consistent findings in support of a net positive impact of postsecondary education on growth in principled reasoning, it is still possible that the body of evidence is confounded by threats to internal validity such as the interaction of selection and change (that is, differences between individuals related to their likelihood of attending college that also predict growth in principled reasoning).

Consistent with our previous synthesis, we found extensive evidence of a positive relationship between level of principled moral reasoning and the likelihood of principled behavior. Thus, growth in principled reasoning during college should, at least indirectly, increase the probability of principled action. However, principled reasoning in and of itself is probably insufficient to determine principled behavior because it is only one of several individual influences on moral action. Others are such things as moral sensitivity, moral motivation, and moral character. Compared with principled moral reasoning, we know relatively little about the impact of college on these other precursors of moral behavior.

Between-College Effects

Despite being based on a small sample of institutions, and the presence of some competing explanations for the results, we uncovered evidence suggesting discernible between-college effects on student growth in principled moral reasoning. Specifically, the greatest increase appeared to occur at small, private liberal arts colleges, a somewhat more modest increase occurred at public universities, and the lowest increase was at Bible colleges. The findings suggest that traditional liberal arts education, combined with the unique social psychological environments of small liberal arts colleges, may be particularly conducive to fostering growth in principled moral reasoning.

In addition to principled reasoning, we uncovered evidence suggesting between-college effects on principled moral behavior. Irrespective of size and academic selectivity, institutions with honor codes or honor systems that are enforced by students tend to have lower levels of student self-reported academic dishonesty than institutions without such honor codes or systems. One interpretation of this finding is that the presence of such honor codes or systems helps foster a culture of academic integrity that functions to reduce cheating behavior. However, it is also possible that schools with visible academic honor codes tend to attract and enroll students for whom academic integrity is a higher personal priority when they enter college.

Within-College Effects

The relatively extensive literature on within-college effects on moral development suggests the following general conclusions:

1. In our previous synthesis, we found meta-analytic evidence indicating that moral development interventions focusing on moral dilemma discussion and personality development are particularly effective in fostering the use of principled moral reasoning. The role of the instructor in these types of interventions is more as facilitator than information provider. However, quasi-experimental evidence from the 1990s suggests that growth in principled moral reasoning is enhanced even further when students are exposed to direct instruction in philosophical methods of ethical analysis as well as to dilemma discussion and personality development.

2. Evidence regarding the effect of exposure to ethics courses or ethics interventions on principled moral reasoning is somewhat mixed. On balance, we conclude that there is probably a very modest positive effect.

3. Evidence from two independently conducted longitudinal studies suggests that purposefully integrating ethical content into an undergraduate professional curriculum in nursing may foster increased growth in principled moral reasoning.

4. Although not experimental in design and based on a single sample, there is evidence suggesting that progress through Alverno College's liberal arts Ability-Based Curriculum may enhance the development of principled moral reasoning. However, the absence of a comparison or control curriculum makes it difficult to determine the net advantage of the Ability-Based Curriculum over other, less purposefully structured and integrated approaches to liberal arts education.

5. Single-sample, quasi-experimental evidence suggests that principled moral reasoning may also be significantly enhanced by a general education curriculum that integrates moral and ethical decision making

throughout a multidisciplinary six-course sequence. Though potentially limited by student self-selection into the experimental curriculum, the results are consistent with our 1991 conclusion that learning to make decisions about moral dilemmas (dilemma discussion) positively influences growth in principled reasoning.

6. Generally consistent findings from separate quasi-experimental studies suggest that coursework that exposes students to diversity-related issues such as racism, sexism, classism, and homophobia positively influences growth in principled moral reasoning.

7. Quasi-experimental evidence on the impact of service learning on principled moral reasoning is mixed. However, additional evidence suggests that service learning or service involvement positively influences such college outcomes as the importance students place on social justice, sense of civic responsibility, and importance of service to the community. It would also appear that the impact of service experiences on these and similar outcomes is enhanced when the service experience is integrated into course content and provides opportunities for reflection through discussion and writing.

8. We found little evidence across studies to indicate that major field of study has a consistent impact on growth in principled moral reasoning.

9. Although we found some evidence to support the contention that the role-taking opportunities that accompany extracurricular-peer involvement in college have positive impacts on growth in principled reasoning, evidence with regard to their impact on actual moral behavior is mixed. Different kinds of social or extracurricular involvement may well have different impacts on moral development. For example, there is clear evidence supporting the hypothesis that involvement in low-density peer networks, which expose one to a diverse intellectual and social environment during college, fosters greater growth in moral development than involvement in high-density, relatively homogeneous peer networks, such as fraternities or sororities. Indeed, the evidence we uncovered suggests that Greek affiliation may inhibit growth in principled reasoning and increase the likelihood of academic dishonesty during college.

10. We found little convincing evidence to suggest that intercollegiate athletic participation had more than a trivial, chance impact on either principled moral reasoning or academic dishonesty.

11. Consistent with the contention that interaction with diverse peers and divergent intellectual and social perspectives tends to enhance growth in principled moral reasoning, we found single-study evidence that students participating in off-campus learning programs (for example, study in foreign countries) showed greater growth in principled reasoning during college than their counterparts who did not participate in off-campus learning experiences.

12. A small body of evidence suggests that off-campus employment during college has a negative influence on both principled moral reasoning and involvement in community service. This may be because extensive off-campus work simply diminishes the time available either to commit to community service or to become involved in the social and academic experiences in college that contribute to growth in principled reasoning.

13. Although based on a single sample, there is evidence to support the contention that out-of-class contact with faculty members has a positive influence on growth in principled moral reasoning. A related finding suggests that it is possible to develop yearlong teaching workshops to introduce the concepts of developmentally based instruction to faculty that enhance these professors' influence on students' growth in principled reasoning.

Conditional Effects of College

Consistent with the conclusions of our previous synthesis, we found evidence supporting the contention that a certain level of formal reasoning may be required for students to realize significant benefits from instructional interventions designed to increase principled moral reasoning.

Long-Term Effects of College

Consistent with the conclusions of our previous synthesis, we found evidence suggesting that increases in the use of principled moral reasoning that occur during college tend to persist into the years immediately following graduation. Similarly, involvement in voluntary community service during college tends to continue when one leaves college.

Notes

1. Parts of this chapter draw heavily on an earlier article, "College's Influence on Principled Moral Reasoning" (Pascarella, 1997a), and on an excellent review by King and Mayhew (2002).

2. Recently the "principled" part of principled moral reasoning has come under criticism by moral philosophers who object to principalism (Rest, Narvaez, Bebeau, and Thoma, 1999). In response to this, some scholars have replaced the term *principled moral reasoning* with *postconventional moral reasoning* (Rest, Narvaez, Bebeau, and Thoma, 1999). Although we recognize this concern, most of the research literature we reviewed still uses the term principled moral reasoning or judgment. Because of this, and for purposes of continuity with our previous synthesis, we continue to employ the term principled moral reasoning in this chapter.

3. However, despite some theoretical arguments to the contrary (Gilligan, 1982; Gilligan & Attanucci, 1988), there is little empirical support for the notion that principled moral reasoning is significantly related to gender (Baldizan & Frey, 1995; Crandall, Tsang, Goldman, & Pennington, 1999; Flanagan, 1982; Galotti,

Kozberg, & Farmer, 1991; Knox, Fagley, & Miller, 1998; McNeel, Schaffer, & Juarez, 1997; Walker, 1984, 1991).

4. There was also a tendency for students who transferred into the program in their junior year to show significantly greater growth in DIT principled reasoning test scores during the last two years of college than students already in the program. However, because the former group began their junior year with nearly a one standard deviation deficit in principled reasoning relative to the latter group, it is likely that this comparison may be confounded by regression artifacts.

5. Other quasi-experimental research has been less successful in finding significant effects of moral development interventions on principled moral reasoning. See, for example, studies estimating the impact of an intergroup dialogue course (Katz, 2001).

6. Results reported by Gorman, Duffy, and Heffernan (1994) tend to support those of Boss (1994). However, the study design is not as rigorous as that of either Boss (1994) or Cram (1998).

7. Batchelder and Root (1994) also found that students in highly integrated service learning courses made statistically significant increases in prosocial reasoning (reasoning reflecting empathy, concern for societal justice, importance of contractual obligations) during a semester. However, their analysis did not provide for a control group, so it is unclear how much of the growth is attributable to service learning.

CHAPTER EIGHT

Educational Attainment and Persistence

Considerable and consistent evidence attests to the vital role educational attainment plays in shaping subsequent occupational, social, and economic status. In our earlier book (Pascarella & Terenzini, 1991, Chapter Nine), we described the seminal models of occupational attainment developed by Blau and Duncan (1967) and of status attainment developed by Sewell, Hauser, and their colleagues (Sewell, Haller, & Portes, 1969; Sewell & Hauser, 1975) and briefly traced the evolutionary use of these frameworks in expanding understanding of social mobility as a lifelong process. Considerable research (Carnevale & Fry, 2000; Knox, Lindsay, & Kolb, 1993, also review this literature) indicates that social mobility and status attainment are a function not simply of family social status and individual ability but also of intervening experiences, including educational experiences and attainment.

Educational attainment—usually defined as the number of years of schooling completed or degrees earned—plays two roles. First, education serves an indirect role by mediating the influence of an individual's background resources (such as family socioeconomic status) on subsequent occupational status and income. At the same time, because family socioeconomic status shapes college enrollment independent of an individual's abilities or prior achievements, education serves to extend advantages an individual already holds in those areas. Second, education's role in the status attainment process can be *direct* through its enhancement of status attainment in ways and to degrees unrelated to socioeconomic origins. Indeed, our earlier book reviewed a substantial body of literature indicating that completion of the baccalaureate degree is a central determinant of occupational status and income. This chapter extends that discussion, reviewing more recent research on educational attainment.

We examine how the characteristics of colleges and universities and the nature of students' experiences while enrolled influence educational attainment. Moreover, although the status and educational attainment research typically focuses on completion of a degree or certificate (whether associate, bachelor's, or advanced degree), we cannot ignore student persistence and the factors that shape it. (For our purposes, *persistence* is understood to be the progressive reenrollment in college, whether continuous from one term to the next or temporarily interrupted and then resumed. We do not consider here the literature on persistence as course completion.) As we noted in our earlier review, persistence "can legitimately be considered a necessary, if not sufficient, condition for degree attainment" (Pascarella & Terenzini, 1991, p. 370). Given the inseparability of persistence and attainment, we again selectively review the large number of studies published over the past decade dealing with student persistence behaviors.[1]

BETWEEN-COLLEGE EFFECTS

Inasmuch as it makes little sense to ask about change during college or net effects of college in this chapter, we begin our review of the research on educational attainment with the evidence concerning between-college effects. We will then review the research on within-college effects, conditional effects, and long-term effects. First, however, it is important to summarize what we learned in our earlier review about educational attainment.

Conclusions from *How College Affects Students*

The pre-1990 evidence clearly indicated that where one begins a college career influences subsequent educational attainment, even after taking into account precollege characteristics known to promote degree completion (for example, ability, socioeconomic status, and motivation or degree aspirations). In addition, the most consistent evidence suggested that beginning pursuit of the baccalaureate degree at a four-year rather than a two-year institution confers an advantage of 15 to 20 percentage points in the odds of completing that degree within a given period of time. Initial enrollment in a four-year (versus two-year) institution also increases the likelihood that a student will subsequently enroll in graduate or professional school.

Attending a private (versus a public) college or a small college promotes educational attainment, each factor having a positive effect independent of the other. The advantages of private control and small size persist when controlling for differences in the precollege characteristics of the students entering those institutions and for other institutional differences, such as admissions selectivity. The effect of size, however, appears to be indirect, with attendance at a smaller college promoting involvement with faculty members and peers, which, in turn, promotes persistence, degree completion, and graduate school enrollment.

African-American students attending a predominantly Black institution and women at a women's college appeared to gain in educational attainment beyond what might be the case at predominantly White or coeducational institutions, respectively. As with college size, however, these advantages are indirect, being mediated largely through the positive effects of these institutions on academic performance.

Some research also suggested that certain college environmental conditions exert independent effects on educational attainment. These conditions include a cohesive peer environment, frequent participation in college-sponsored activities, and a perception that the institution is concerned about students as individuals.

Finally, any interruption in the continuity of students' enrollment (for example, by transfer from one four-year institution to another) appeared to inhibit educational attainment. This effect persisted even after controlling for a variety of students' precollege traits and for selected characteristics of the institution of initial enrollment (such as selectivity, size, control, and predominant race).

In most cases, however, the effects of these other between-college differences were small, explaining not more than 1 to 2 percent of the variance in different measures of educational attainment. The effect of initially attending a two-year versus a four-year college is a possible exception to this conclusion.

Evidence from the 1990s

Two-Year Versus Four-Year Institutions. For at least four decades, proponents and critics of community colleges have debated whether these public two-year institutions democratize or divert educational attainment opportunities. Both camps agree that the growth of the community college sector has reduced the enrollment pressures exerted by an expanding population on the top four-year institutions, permitting them to maintain selective admissions standards (Dougherty, 1994). Supporters argue that community colleges responded, when four-year institutions did not, to growing recognition of social and economic inequalities and demands for equitable treatment of all applicants. Supporters' largely functionalist defense maintains that the proximity, low cost, multipurpose missions, and heterogeneous curricula of the community college brought—and continues to bring—postsecondary education and social mobility within the reach of people who would otherwise be left out, particularly individuals from low-income and racial-ethnic minority groups (Cohen & Brawer, 1996; Grubb, 1989).

But the opening door, critics maintain, was largely illusory. Burton Clark (1960) characterized a "cooling-out" process by which community colleges divert opportunity rather than democratize it. Socializing agents (faculty and student peers), administrative functions (for example, academic advising), and the two-year curriculum, according to this argument, channel students not so much toward a bachelor's degree as toward an associate degree and vocational certificates. The same features of proximity, low cost, and vocational programs through which community colleges offer many students postsecondary opportunities they might not otherwise have also divert many of these same students from pursuit of a bachelor's degree. In addition, because those served are disproportionately working-class and lower-middle-class students, often from racial-ethnic minority groups, some critics maintain that the community colleges preserve social stratification by reducing the opportunities for lower socioeconomic class students to enter bachelor's degree programs (Brint & Karabel, 1989; Dougherty, 1994).

In *How College Affects Students,* we reported some evidence suggesting that the argument that community colleges help maintain existing class differences may underestimate their contributions to social mobility. In the end, however, we concluded that even after taking into account students' precollege degree goals, abilities, and other relevant characteristics, initial attendance at a two-year (versus a four-year) institution reduced the likelihood of bachelor's degree completion by 15 to 20 percent.

The evidence of the 1990s tends to reinforce that conclusion, but it also brings the complexity of the issue into sharper focus. Community college proponents argue that public two-year institutions provide an alternate route to the baccalaureate, offering a "second chance" to students who, for whatever reason, do not begin their studies at a four-year institution (see, for example, Cohen & Brawer, 1996; Grubb, 1991). The argument has a respectable empirical foundation (Berkner, He, & Cataldi, 2002). Surette (1997) reports evidence suggesting that two-year colleges "play an important role as intermediaries between the completion of high school and attendance at a four-year college" (p. 3). After controlling for employment status, hours worked, labor experience, earnings, enrollment in training programs, race-ethnicity, age, parents' education, and a measure of intellectual ability, Surette found that "one cannot reject the hypothesis that a year of two-year college credits and a year of four-year credits raise equally the probability of subsequently attending a four-year college" (p. 18). Possession of an associate degree raised the probability of subsequent four-year attendance even further.

Many students who seek a bachelor's degree but begin at a two-year institution never transfer (Berkner, He, & Cataldi, 2002). Some evidence suggests that those who *do* make the move to a four-year institution show no difference in their rates of persistence to the bachelor's degree. Entry at a two-year institution *is,* however, associated with time-to-degree. Bachelor's degree seekers who begin their college careers at a two-year institution are less likely than their counterparts starting at a four-year school to complete a bachelor's degree within five years (8 percent versus 57 percent, respectively). Two-year matriculants who make the transfer are as likely as four-year matriculants to persist overall (76 percent versus 78 percent). However, baccalaureate degree recipients who begin at a two-year institution are more than twice as likely as their four-year peers to take more than six years to complete their degrees (Cuccaro-Alamin, 1997).

The Cuccaro-Alamin (1997) evidence reflects "persistence" toward a bachelor's degree over a five-year period and requires a leap of faith to conclude that the similarity in five-year persistence rates among two- and four-year matriculants will eventually translate into similar degree completion rates. Adelman (1998a) and Lee, Mackie-Lewis, and Marks (1993), both using data from the national High School and Beyond study, provide some support for that conclusion. For example, after taking into account students' background characteristics (gender, race-ethnicity, and socioeconomic status), college experiences (such as living on campus, full- or part-time attendance, academic and social satisfaction, major field, and college GPA), and institutional characteristics (such as control, location, size, and selectivity), Lee and his colleagues found that six years after graduating from high school, community college students who made the transition to a four-year institution suffered no disadvantage (compared with similar students who first enrolled in a four-year school) on any of three measures of educational attainment. Net of other relevant variables, former community college students were as likely as their four-year counterparts to graduate from a baccalaureate degree–granting institution, to aspire to attend graduate school, and to enroll in graduate school. Adelman (1999) also found that, net of students' precollege academic resources, socioeconomic status, race-ethnicity, and gender, transferring from a two-year to a four-year institution was positively associated with degree completion. It is important to note, however, that Adelman defined "transfer" as an attendance pattern followed by students who earned at least 10 credits from the community college and subsequently earned more than 10 credits from a four-year college. That path to the baccalaureate degree is clearly more direct than most other attendance patterns. Indeed, students displaying this pattern earned bachelor's degrees at a higher rate (71 percent) over the 11-year period than did students who began their postsecondary careers at a four-year institution (66 percent). He also found, however, that students who transferred with 10 or fewer credits were less likely to complete a bachelor's degree (38 percent). Other studies report findings generally consistent with those summarized here (Anglin, Davis, & Mooradian, 1995; DesJardins, Ahlburg, & McCall, 1999b; Eimers & Mullen, 1997), although these latter studies use single-institution or state system samples.

Several studies suggest that the students who transfer from a two-year to a four-year institution are academically distinctive, resembling more their counterparts who initially enroll in four-year schools than their community college peers who do not transfer. These studies indicate that the transfer students (compared with nontransfers) are more likely to come from families in higher socioeconomic brackets; to be younger, white, and male; to have been on an academic track in high school; to have higher degree expectations and be more academically oriented; to have attended school during the day and reached higher academic achievement levels (although somewhat below those of students who went directly to four-year institutions); to have been more academically and socially integrated in the institutions from which they were transferring; and to have been continuously enrolled (Bradburn, Hurst, & Peng, 2001; Cohen & Brawer, 1996; Dey & Astin, 1989; Lee & Frank, 1990; Nora & Rendon, 1990; Townsend, McNerny, & Arnold, 1993). Evidence from the 2001 follow-up of the 1996 national Beginning Postsecondary Students Longitudinal Study (BPS-96–01) indicates that of the bachelor's degree recipients who transferred from a public, two-year institution, more than half (56 percent) were "traditional" students with no "risk factors" when they entered community college (Berkner, He, & Cataldi, 2002). Bradburn, Hurst, and Peng, however, note that as the specifications of the characteristics of successful transfers become more restrictive, the percentage of actual transfers declines. This finding, they argue, indicates that attempts to include in comparative studies only those students most likely to transfer overlook a sizable proportion of the students (perhaps four out of five) who transfer without meeting the criteria.

Some evidence based on the nationally representative samples of the 1980 High School and Beyond (HS&B:80) studies, both sophomore and senior cohorts, suggests that community college attendance and transfer may, in fact, make it easier for some students to enter a higher-quality four-year institution (quality being measured in various ways) than would have been possible had they enrolled initially in a four-year institution (Eide, Goldhaber, & Hilmer, 2000; Hilmer, 1996, 1997; Townsend et al., 1993). The advantages may be particularly strong for students from poor families, those with low measured ability, or those who performed poorly in high school. These advantages persist for these students even after controlling for parents' income and education, institutional costs of attendance, gender, race-ethnicity, high school preparation and performance, and geographic region. Some evidence, however, suggests that the small difference in quality of the schools awarding their baccalaureate degrees between two-year transfers and those who enrolled initially at a four-year college or university may apply primarily to four-year schools in the bottom or middle-quality ranges. Large and statistically significant differences between students using the two different points of entry still persist at institutions of the highest quality (Eide et al., 2000).

Other studies using nationally representative samples and focused more precisely on bachelor's degree completion yield evidence consistent with the conclusions in our earlier review that the net effect on educational attainment of enrolling initially at a two-year rather than four-year institution is negative and nontrivial. Whitaker and Pascarella (1994), for example, using data from the National Longitudinal Study of the High School Class of 1972 (NLS-72), and after accounting for precollege differences in students' gender, race-ethnicity, age, family socioeconomic status, high school achievement, extracurricular involvement, self-esteem, educational and occupational aspirations at the time of college entry, and college grades, found that enrolling initially in a two-year institution had a statistically significant, negative effect on educational attainment measured 14 years after high school graduation. Using more recent data, Christie (1999) studied 1,574 high school sophomores in the HS&B:80-92 surveys who graduated from high school and enrolled in a nonprofit college on a full-time basis during that same year. He excluded students who had claimed as seniors that they would be satisfied with something less than a bachelor's degree as well as "experimenters" (that is, those who earned less than 12 credit hours). Christie tracked these "traditional" baccalaureate degree–seeking students over a 12-year period (10 years following their high school graduation), and after controlling for a wide array of potentially confounding variables, he found that traditional students entering a two-year college before transferring (compared with their counterparts who enrolled initially in a four-year institution) had a statistically significant net decrease of 9 percent in the probability of earning a baccalaureate degree over the 10-year period.

Ganderton and Santos (1995) and Rouse (1995) based their studies on the HS&B senior cohort and reached conclusions similar to Christie's. Ganderton and Santos estimated that entering a two-year institution and then transferring (versus initially enrolling at a four-year institution) decreased the adjusted probability of graduating with a bachelor's degree within a six-year period by 10 to 22 percent. The researchers noted that the disadvantage varied by race-ethnicity. White students incurred the greatest disadvantage (-22 percent) and Hispanic students the least (-10 percent); Black students were disadvantaged by 13 percent. Rouse concluded that community colleges may increase the number of years of postsecondary schooling but not the odds of completing a baccalaureate degree. Lavin and Crook (1990; see also Crook & Lavin, 1989) over a 14-year period tracked nearly 5,000 students who entered the City University of New York in 1971 and 1972. After adjusting for a wide array of students' precollege characteristics, Lavin and Crook estimated that students beginning their college careers in a community college were 19 percentage points less likely to complete a bachelor's degree than similar students who entered a four-year institution (Crook & Lavin, 1989, put that estimate at 21 percentage points). For those completing a bachelor's degree, and net of these same variables, Lavin and Crook estimated that initial community college (versus four-year) enrollment also added about four-fifths of a year to time-to-degree. Community college entrants' longer time-to-baccalaureate-degree also reduced the likelihood (compared with similar students who entered a four-year institution) of earning a postgraduate degree.

These studies, like others reviewed earlier, concentrate on a fairly general and structural difference between two-year and four-year institutions—namely, their highest degree offered. This focus leaves unexamined any differences in the kinds of experiences students at these institutions may have or any of the causal mechanisms that may be in play. Compared with the pre-1990s literature, the evidence of the 1990s sheds a somewhat brighter light on at least one of these potential underlying explanatory mechanisms, what critics call a "cooling out." As noted earlier, cooling out in part moderates the educational degree aspirations or expectations of working-class and lower-middle-class students, guiding them into less-than-baccalaureate-degree or vocational certificate programs.

Degree aspirations are strongly and positively related to subsequent educational attainment levels (Camburn, 1990; Carter, 2002; Pascarella & Terenzini, 1991), perhaps more so for women than for men (Adelman, 1991). Aspirations also are highly variable over time (Ingels, Curtin, Kaufman, Alt, & Chen, 2002) and perhaps poorly understood by students and badly defined by researchers (who confuse them with "plans" and "expectations") (Adelman, 1992). Although limited in number, several recent methodologically sound studies explore the validity of the underlying premise of the cooling-out argument by explicitly examining the effects of two-year college attendance on students' educational aspirations. Pascarella, Edison, Nora, Hagedorn, and Terenzini (1998b), for example, studied changes in educational plans by asking nearly 1,700 students who entered 18 four-year institutions and five community colleges in 1992, "What is the highest degree you intend to earn in your lifetime?" After statistically adjusting for an assortment of students' precollege characteristics (including academic abilities, initial educational plans, academic motivation, socioeconomic status, and college grades), Pascarella and his colleagues found that community college students who entered with plans to complete a bachelor's degree were, after two years of college, 20 to 30 percent more likely than their four-year counterparts to have reduced their degree aspirations below a bachelor's degree. The same net trend, although not statistically significant, was apparent after the first year of college. Other studies report findings consistent with those of Pascarella and his colleagues (Carter, 2001; McCormick, 1990, 1996, 1997a). Indeed, McCormick reports even more dramatic downward shifts than those reported by Pascarella et al. Using data from the large nationally representative High School and Beyond study of graduating seniors in 1980 (HS&B:80-84), and after controlling for a variety of demographic and family characteristics, precollege educational plans, and high school preparation and ability, he found that the odds that students starting at a two-year institution would adopt or maintain bachelor's degree expectations were after two years about 40 percent lower than those of similar students starting at a four-year institution (McCormick, 1990) and about 60 percent lower after four years (McCormick, 1997a).

Pascarella (1999) has noted both the scarcity of such replicated results in the social science literature and the consequent "temptation to accept these results at face value" (pp. 10–11). He questions whether the educational expectations of traditional-age entering college students are clearly defined and certain enough to be meaningful predictors. Researchers have noted the growth in multi-institutional enrollment (Adelman, 1999; Berkner, He, & Cataldi, 2002) and the evidence of a "swirl" in the attendance patterns of two-year college students (Bach et al., 2000; see also Borden, 2004). Others have noted the role community colleges play in providing a "testing" ground for students experimenting with their tastes and abilities for college (Grubb, 1996). Pascarella speculates that "for these students, community college attendance may function not so much to cool out genuinely held aspirations or plans, but rather to assist them in clarifying aspirations or plans that may be undeveloped, unclear, or perhaps even unrealistic" (p. 11). (We discuss some evidence to support this speculation in the "Conditional Effects of College" section of this chapter.)

The nature of the underlying forces that induce changes in students' degree goals, as well as the appropriate comparison groups, has drawn closer scrutiny. Swanson (2002) believes that studies of changes in students' degree plans that contrast only two- and four-year environments are needlessly narrow. To understand fully the effects of attending community college, he argues, one must also compare two-year enrollment with other types of postsecondary experience and in addition study the duration of attendance (as contrasted with the more common independent variable, the dichotomous "did-didn't attend"). Using data from both the High School and Beyond (HS&B:80 sophomore cohort) study and the 1989–90 Beginning Postsecondary Student Survey (BPS:90-94), Swanson contrasted the effects of the amount of time (in months) spent in four different postsecondary environments: not enrolled, less-than-two-year institutions (including proprietary schools), community colleges, and four-year colleges and universities. Compared with having no postsecondary education experience or with attending a vocational/proprietary institution, and net of other factors, community college attendance appeared to "warm"—rather than cool—students' educational aspirations. The warming effect of community college enrollment was not as strong as the effect of attending a four-year institution, but the findings on this topic are decidedly different, at least metaphorically, from what has previously been reported.

"Different," however, does not mean "contradictory." Although Swanson's (2002) study suggests community college attendance has a warming influence on students' degree aspirations or plans and Pascarella, Edison, Nora, Hagedorn, and Terenzini's (1998b) and McCormick's (1990, 1997a) findings indicate a cooling effect, the seeming contradiction is directly related to the comparison group. Swanson included individuals with no postsecondary education experience, whereas for Pascarella et al. and McCormick the comparison group was four-year enrollees. Whether the community college glass is viewed as half empty or half full, these studies are consistent in pointing to some degree of disadvantage among students who enroll initially in a two-year institution when compared with similar students who begin their postsecondary education careers in four-year institutions. Perhaps more importantly, both the similarities and differences in these studies suggest, as Swanson (2002) puts it, "that future research should . . . move beyond generic institutional traits (such as level) and explore in more detail the internal workings of these organizations and more subtle characteristics of the postsecondary student experience. These may be the more proximate mechanisms through which the general institutional effects and their differential influence on particular student populations operate" (p. 26). Pascarella et al. share this view.

Overall, the evidence leads us to conclude that students seeking a bachelor's degree who begin their college careers in a two-year public institution continue to be at a disadvantage in reaching their education goals compared with similar students entering a four-year college or university. Part of that disadvantage, however, appears to be related to whether students in fact transfer to a four-year institution, the greater amount of time needed to complete a baccalaureate degree program, and other factors such as economic conditions and state policies and structures affecting two- and four-year institutions.

State Policies and System Structures. Some researchers have explored the effects of state policies and higher education system structures on whether community colleges facilitate bachelor's degree attainment (Grubb, 1989; Orfield & Paul, 1992; Wellman, 2002). Wellman examined the effects of state higher education policies in six states, three that received high marks and three that received low grades in the retention and degree completion area from the National Center for Public Policy and Higher Education (2000). She found few differences between the two groups in many of their basic approaches to transfer policies, including the academic policies on transfers, core curriculum requirements, articulation agreements, transfer credit policies, and statewide transfer guides. Wellman found that the key difference lay in states' higher education governance structures. High performers have statewide governance capacities, whereas low performers rely on institutional governing structures. High-performing states also made better use of data as a tool to improve transfer performance, including state-level feedback to campuses about their performance relative to other institutions in the state.

Grubb (1989) also examined state educational systems' performance regarding educational attainment and found that "two-year colleges provide opportunities for educational advancement over high school for men while they appear to decrease the likelihood of completing four years of college for women" (p. 369). He found, however, that state educational structures and institutional characteristics provide only a partial picture of the dynamics of educational attainment; state labor market characteristics (particularly as they affect women) also shape educational attainment. Orfield and Paul studied the effects of six states' choices of educational structures and reported that the states with the least reliance on community colleges had higher freshman baccalaureate enrollment and higher bachelor's degree completion rates than those with a heavy reliance on community colleges. The study, however, employed no controls for entering students' abilities, socioeconomic status, motivation or aspirations, or degree plans.[2]

Interruptions in Attendance. As already noted, multi-institutional enrollment rates have risen dramatically over the past two decades, with students following a variety of attendance patterns. One involves delaying entry into college after graduating from high school, a tactic low-income students frequently adopt in order to earn money for their college expenses (Terenzini, Cabrera, & Bernal, 2001). Although not a "college effect" or experience, delayed entry clearly affects educational attainment. The research consistently shows that delaying postsecondary enrollment, for whatever reason, reduces the likelihood that the student will persist and complete a degree program. Indeed, delayed entry is one of the seven major risk factors identified by the National Center for Education Statistics as threats to persistence and graduation (Berkner, Cuccaro-Alamin, & McCormick, 1996; Carroll, 1989; Horn & Premo, 1995; McCormick & Horn, 1996).[3]

A second common attendance pattern is *stopping out,* or interrupting enrollment temporarily. Like other breaks in attendance, stopping out not only increases time-to-degree but also reduces the likelihood of degree completion, whether an associate or baccalaureate degree (Carroll, 1989; Ganderton & Santos, 1995; Guerin, 1997; Hanniford & Sagoria, 1994; Horn, 1998a; Porter, 1990).

In these studies, delaying entry or stopping out reduces the odds of persisting or completing a degree even in the presence of controls for a variety of precollege characteristics.

Another type of transfer also reduces the odds of earning a bachelor's degree. Earlier we discussed the effects on educational attainment of *vertical transfer,* or initially enrolling in a two-year college followed by transfer to a four-year institution. *Horizontal transfer,* or moving from one four-year college or university to another, is also common. Nearly 30 percent of the students who begin their postsecondary education careers in a four-year college or university will leave that institution for another one within a four-year period. About half of those making such a move (16 percent) will transfer to another four-year institution, whereas 13 percent will *reverse transfer* to a two-year institution (McCormick, 1997b).

Only a few studies address the consequences of such transfers, but the findings consistently suggest that such moves reduce the odds of earning a baccalaureate degree. Adelman (1999), using the large and nationally representative HS&B (sophomore cohort) study that included both transcript and survey data, found that students who attended more than one school and did not return to their first institution were less likely than transfers who did return to their first institution to complete a bachelor's degree within 11 years of entering college. This effect was apparent even when controlling for the students' precollege academic resources, socioeconomic status, race-ethnicity, gender, degree expectations, financial aid, and the selectivity of the first institution attended. This finding is attributable in part to the fact that Adelman's "nonreturners" included students who transferred from four-year to two-year institutions, thus moving away from the possibility of baccalaureate degree completion. Other studies yield findings similar to Adelman's concerning the negative effects of transferring from one four-year institution to another (Berkner, He, & Cataldi, 2002; Eimers & Mullen, 1997; McCormick, 1997b). These results, moreover, are consistent with those reviewed in *How College Affects Students.* Together they provide convincing evidence that institutional continuity increases the likelihood that students will complete a bachelor's degree program. Although transferring from one four-year institution to another may benefit some students, generally the impact of such movement appears to be deleterious. These findings underscore the importance of the fit between students and the institutions in which they initially enroll.

Institutional Control: Public Versus Private. Research during the 1990s on differences in bachelor's degree completion rates among students attending a public versus a private college or university supports the findings of earlier studies. Comparisons of public versus private institution persistence or degree completion rates unadjusted for students' precollege characteristics consistently find higher rates at private institutions. These findings appear in rate comparisons at both the institutional and individual level of analysis, and they apply both to persistence into the second year and to degree completion over varying periods of time. When controls are put in place for students' precollege characteristics, however, the differences, if any, are more muted.

Institutional retention rates. National surveys of four-year institutions indicate that the average unadjusted rates of student persistence into the second year range from 72 to 79 percent at public institutions and from 75 to 79 percent at private colleges and universities. The variations in estimates are a function of several factors, including the mix of institutions surveyed, the definitions of the populations, and the census periods used in the calculations. Even more variation is apparent when the highest degree an institution offers is taken into account. Compared with baccalaureate-only institutions, doctoral degree–granting institutions report rates of persistence into the second year ranging from 8 to 15 percentage points higher among public institutions and from 8 to 12 percentage points higher among private colleges and universities (ACT, 2002; Consortium for Student Retention Data Exchange, 2002).

The effects of type of control on institutional graduation rates are consistent with those for persistence into the second year. Studies relying on the five-year degree-completion rates reported by institutions participating in the annual ACT surveys report consistently higher unadjusted institutional graduation rates in the private (versus public) sector ("Five-Year Institutional Graduation Rates," 1997; "Institutional Graduation Rates by Academic Selectivity," 1999; "Institutional Graduation Rates by Degree Level," 1996). These studies also consistently indicate that the private institution unadjusted advantage persists at all levels of institutional selectivity, being about 10 percentage points generally but somewhat higher at the highest selectivity level. They also found, however, that standard deviations within the selectivity levels varied widely for public and private institution groups. This finding suggests that, at each selectivity level, some public institutions have higher institutional five-year completion rates than private institutions at the same selectivity level.

Saupe, Smith, and Xin (1999) provide support for this proposition. Using data from the Consortium for Student Retention Data Exchange, they found no differences in institutional six-year degree-completion rates related to type of institutional control after taking into account such other institutional characteristics as the average admissions test scores of entering students, size, percent of part-time enrollment, and percent of first-time enrollment made up of minority students.

Individual persistence and attainment. The same public-private pattern is apparent when degree-completion studies focus longitudinally on individual students rather than institutional averages. Private college or university students have a modest but statistically significant five percentage point advantage over their counterparts at public institutions. Among students entering a four-year college or university in 1989, 87.5 percent of those entering a private institution persisted into their second year compared with 82.5 percent of those at a public institution (Horn, 1998a, Table 8). These individual persistence rates are higher than the institutional averages reported earlier because of differences in the unit of analysis. Individual student rates come from studies that track individual student persistence regardless of the institution a student attends. Thus, students who enroll in one institution for their first year and transfer to a different institution for the following academic year are considered persisters. Institutional rates, in contrast, are based on only those students who return to the same institution for the second year.

Studies using different nationally representative samples of students and varying census periods (such as four, five, and six years) for estimating graduation rates find that students attending private (versus public) colleges or universities are more likely to complete their bachelor's degree or to enroll in graduate school (Astin, Tsui, & Avalos, 1996; Berkner, He, & Cataldi, 2002; Cuccaro-Alamin, 1997; Dey, 1990; Dey & Astin, 1989; McCormick & Horn, 1996; Porter, 1990). Cuccaro-Alamin, as well as others (such as Dey & Astin and McCormick & Horn), also found that graduates of public four-year institutions took longer to complete their bachelor's degrees than did their peers at private institutions.

When studies of individual persistence into the second year take into account students' preenrollment characteristics, however, a different picture emerges. After adjustments for gender, race-ethnicity, age, first-generation status, hours employed, socioeconomic status, delayed college entry, college performance, financial aid packages, and measures of academic integration during college, the persistence advantage among students in private institutions virtually disappears. The private students' unadjusted five-point advantage drops to a statistically nonsignificant 0.7 percentage point edge, with 84.6 and 83.9 percent of the private and public institution students, respectively, persisting into their second year (Horn, 1998a, Table 8).

The evidence from studies of bachelor's degree completion is mixed. Some studies find that students enrolled at private (versus public) institutions have a statistically significant and positive (if small) net advantage in the likelihood of completing their bachelor's degree. For example, two studies using a large nationally representative sample of students entering four-year institutions controlled for a wide array of precollege student characteristics, college experiences, institutional size and selectivity, and characteristics of the faculty and peer environments (Astin, 1993c; Astin et al., 1996). Net of these factors, public university students were less likely than their counterparts at public colleges, private colleges, or private universities (both sectarian and nonsectarian) to complete a bachelor's degree in four years (at the institutions where they first enrolled) and less likely to enter graduate school. Ethington (1997), using data on more than 3,000 students who entered 173 four-year institutions in 1970 and were surveyed nine years later, also found that private college and university students had a statistically significant advantage over their counterparts at public institutions. The institutional control effect was unattributable to institutional selectivity, per-student expenditures, percent graduate enrollment, size of the institution, or student-faculty ratios. Indeed, the effect of type of control far exceeded that of selectivity and expenditures. Nonetheless, student academic and social background characteristics had substantially larger effects on educational attainment than did institutional characteristics.

Other studies using nationally representative samples find no statistically significant net advantage for private college or university students compared with their public institution counterparts. Although Astin (1993c) reported statistically significant, positive net effects on degree completion from attendance at three kinds of private institutions (independent, Protestant, and Roman Catholic), he suggested that these effects may be indirect and more closely related to other institutional characteristics such as size, research emphasis, commitment to student development, faculty characteristics, and peer effects. After controlling for students' gender, race-ethnicity, socioeconomic status, transfer status, selected college experiences, as well as institutional size, selectivity, location, minority enrollment, and whether the institution awards graduate degrees, Lee, Mackie-Lewis, and Marks (1993) found type of institutional control had no statistically significant effect on students' chances of completing their baccalaureate degree within four years, on their aspirations concerning graduate school, or on whether they enrolled in a graduate or professional school.

We conclude, with Astin (1993c), that institutional control probably has little net effect on whether students earn a baccalaureate degree. Evidence reported in *How College Affects Students* and elsewhere in this volume clearly indicates that what happens to students on any given campus is far more determinant of educational outcomes, including educational attainment, than is institutional control (and most other institutional characteristics; see the following sections).

Institutional Size. The research done before 1990 relating to the influence of institutional size (meaning "number of students") on educational attainment was, we concluded, "inconsistent and at times contradictory" (Pascarella & Terenzini, 1991, p. 378). Although size is more often used as a control variable than as a factor of substantive interest in studies of institutional effects, nothing in the literature since 1990 warrants a different conclusion. Indeed, more recent literature reinforces it.

Astin (1993c) used a large, nationally representative sample of students who entered four-year institutions in 1985 and were surveyed four years later. Holding constant an extensive battery of student precollege characteristics and institutional variables, including mission, control, student-faculty ratio, emphasis on graduate education, expenditures on student services and instruction, and faculty salaries, Astin found that "the largest effect of any institutional characteristic" (p. 195) on educational attainment was size, and its impact was negative.

Other studies, however, suggest that although size negatively affects educational attainment, its direct effect is probably small, possibly trivial. Astin, Tsui, and Avalos (1996), for example, found size was a statistically significant predictor of degree completion for White and Mexican American–Chicano students but not for other racial-ethnic student groups. Size was also less influential on attainment than either type of institutional control or selectivity. Studies focused on women found institution size to be a statistically significant and negative factor but less influential than institutional gender and race-ethnicity (Wolf-

Wendel, Baker, & Morphew, 2000) or than the average SAT verbal scores of entering students (Crosby et al., 1994).

Still other research suggests institution size has no statistically significant, direct effect on educational attainment (Ethington, 1997; Saupe et al., 1999; Stoecker & Pascarella, 1991), although size may play an indirect (and negative) role. Ethington as well as Stoecker and Pascarella used the same nine-year panel study from the University of California at Los Angeles Cooperative Institutional Research Program (CIRP), but the latter examined only the women in that sample, whereas the former included both males and females. The two studies also controlled for different sets of confounding variables and used different multivariate analytical procedures. The results, however, were the same: both studies found institutional size was not a statistically significant factor in students' degree completion. Both studies, however, identified students' social involvement in college as a significant and positive determinant of attainment, a finding supported by other research (Pascarella & Terenzini, 1991). Stoecker and Pascarella also found that institutional size was a statistically significant and negative predictor of social involvement. This finding reveals something of the underlying mechanisms that may be involved in student degree completion. Insofar as size is a factor, the Stoecker and Pascarella study suggests its influence may be negative but indirect, with larger enrollments tending to suppress students' level of social integration, which in turn has a positive influence on educational attainment. Thus, it appears that institutional size may be more important in its mediation of the effects of other, more influential aspects of students' college experiences.

Institutional Quality. Research during the 1990s regarding the influences of institutional quality relies almost exclusively on admissions selectivity as a proxy for academic "quality." Although some studies summarized in *How College Affects Students* relied on measures of institutional prestige or resources, the most recent studies by and large have used measures of the academic abilities of entering students, usually as reflected in admission test scores, high school grade-point average, class rank or percentile rank, or on evaluative rankings based on such statistics. The findings regarding the effects of selectivity on educational attainment, however, are much like those relating to type of institutional control in their consistency across not only analyses of institutional graduation rates but also longitudinal panel studies of cohorts of entering students. Both categories of studies point consistently to higher probabilities of degree completion as institutional selectivity rises.

Studies relying on various data sources for institutional graduation rates, for example, consistently reported that rates are highest for institutions with the most selective admissions policies and lowest among those with the most forgiving standards. That relation holds when institutions are categorized by type of control, although selectivity appears to be the more reliable of the two predictors ("Five-Year Institutional Graduation Rates," 1997; "Institutional Graduation Rates by Academic Selectivity," 1999; "Institutional Graduation Rates by

Degree Level," 1996). In fact, some evidence suggests that selectivity is a statistically significant and positive predictor of institutions' six-year graduation rates even after controlling for such other institutional characteristics as Carnegie type, size, percent of part-time enrollment, percent of first-time enrollment made up of minority students, and other variables (Saupe et al., 1999).

Longitudinal studies of individual students' educational attainment led to the same conclusion as those that examined institutional graduation rates: the higher the selectivity of an institution, the greater the odds an enrolling student has of completing a bachelor's degree. The more selective institutions have a distinct advantage—almost by definition—over less selective colleges and universities in that they tend to attract and enroll students with higher academic abilities, better elementary and secondary school preparation, higher degree aspirations, clearer and higher occupational goals, and greater family economic and other resources (Pascarella & Terenzini, 1991). Even when a variety of the academic and social background characteristics of entering students are taken into account, institutional selectivity remains a positive, albeit small, factor in students' educational attainment, a factor that declines in importance as students' college experiences are taken into account (Adelman, 1999; Astin et al., 1996; Dey & Astin, 1989; Dolan & Schmidt, 1994; Ethington, 1997; Mullen, Goyette, & Soares, 2003; Stoecker & Pascarella, 1991). Some evidence suggests that, although selectivity of one's undergraduate college has a statistically significant and positive net effect on the quality of the graduate school a student attends, that advantage has been declining over time, dropping from 12 percent in the NLS-72 cohort to about 5 percent in the two cohorts of the High School and Beyond studies. The effect of graduating from a top public institution has remained nonsignificant over time (Eide, Brewer, & Ehrenberg, 1998).

Other research, however, clouds the picture by suggesting that other institutional characteristics, such as faculty quality, academic expenditures, and faculty-student ratios, may be more powerful than selectivity in predicting completion of a graduate or professional degree (Dolan & Schmidt, 1994). Lee, Mackie-Lewis, and Marks (1993), after controlling for relevant student background characteristics, selected college experiences, and other institutional characteristics, found selectivity unrelated to degree completion six years after high school graduation. They did find, however, that selectivity had a statistically significant and positive net effect on students' aspirations for graduate school as well as on actual enrollment. For both of these measures of educational attainment, the selectivity effects were small. In addition, the researchers found other institutional characteristics, such as size, percentage of minority students enrolled, and whether the institution awarded graduate-professional degrees, were more influential than selectivity on graduate school aspirations and enrollment.

Thus, the weight of evidence suggests that institutional selectivity may contribute to students' chances of completing a baccalaureate degree independent of the characteristics students bring with them, although studies done before 1990 suggest that effect is probably small and intertwined with the kinds of experiences students have on academically selective campuses. The underlying causal mechanisms are difficult to parse. In *How College Affects Students,* we suggested several possible explanations, including increased student commitment to the institution and to degree completion as the institution's perceived prestige increases, the accentuation of initial educational and career aspirations and plans for graduate education, higher faculty expectations, and a generally direct, positive environmental effect of attending a selective institution (which we found outweighed the indirect negative effect of selectivity on college grades). With the exception of the hypothesis that institutional selectivity promotes increased graduate school aspirations, which is supported by the Lee, Mackie-Lewis, and Marks study (1993), the literature of the 1990s on between-college effects is largely silent concerning which hypothesis best explains the net positive impact of institutional selectivity on educational attainment. As previously, however, recent studies suggest that the effect is modest.

Institutional Gender Composition. Although only a relative handful of women's colleges remain,[4] debate continues over whether attendance at these institutions provides greater educational advantages for women than do coeducational institutions. The debate is fueled, in part, by the underrepresentation of women (and women of color) in the senior faculty ranks and in administrative positions in America's colleges and universities, in the professions, and in senior management positions in the nation's corporations and governmental agencies. Proponents of women's colleges maintain that these institutions play a major role in developing women's talents and, indeed, are more effective in that role than are coeducational colleges and universities that offer women students fewer women faculty members as role models and mentors, generally less supportive climates, and fewer opportunities to develop (see Miller-Bernal, 2000; Riordan, 1994, lists 10 "theoretical rationales" why women's colleges might be more effective for women than are coeducational institutions; Tidball, Smith, Tidball, & Wolf-Wendel, 1999).

The evidence also suggests that women at coeducational institutions have different educational experiences and encounter more potential obstacles to success than do their male peers or their counterparts at women's colleges (Miller-Bernal, 1993; Smith, 1990; Smith, Morrison, & Wolf, 1994). Others, however, have questioned whether the success of women's colleges in helping women achieve reflects the educational effectiveness of these institutions or simply their ability to enroll women with most of the characteristics that predict achievement (Crosby et al., 1994; Riordan, 1992; Stoecker & Pascarella, 1991).

Pre-1990 research indicated that women's colleges afford their students some modest net advantages in terms of educational attainment. But the nature of the effect remained uncertain, apparently being more indirect than direct, operating through the generally higher academic achievement of women in single-sex institutions compared with their coeducational counterparts. More recent evidence tends to support the earlier conclusions concerning a modest educational advantage associated with attendance at a women's college, although the dynamics of how any influences exert themselves remains unclear.

Studies on this topic fall generally into two categories that are based largely on the sampling design selected. The larger set, called *baccalaureate origins* studies, seeks to identify the characteristics of institutions from which successful women have graduated (Tidball et al., 1999, provide a review and listing of these studies), with *success* defined as entering medical school, earning a doctoral degree, or being listed in *Who's Who*. With one exception (Crosby et al., 1994), researchers have found that, for women students, women's colleges outperform coeducational institutions whether the measure of success is entering medical school, earning a doctorate, or gaining a *Who's Who* listing. Wolf-Wendel (1998), for example, identified women who earned doctoral degrees between 1975 and 1991 or who had earned baccalaureate degrees after 1965 and were listed in one of three 1992–93 *Who's Who* books (one for Black Americans, one for Hispanic Americans, and one not specific to race-ethnicity). She used as her criterion variables two "productivity ratios" (the number of women earning doctorates and the number of women graduates listed in *Who's Who* divided by their institution's size) and performed separate analyses for European women, African-American women, and Latinas. She found that women's colleges dominated lists of the most productive institutions in terms of both doctoral degree recipients and *Who's Who* achievers (see also Sharpe & Fuller, 1995). Productive institutions, however, were not equally successful with all three groups of students. When using institutional gender, race, control, selectivity, size, and average enrollment of women of color as the institutional predictors in three multiple regressions (one for each of the three racial-ethnic groups), Wolf-Wendel found that, net of other institutional characteristics, an institution's gender emphasis was the best predictor of its production of successful European women. Institutional selectivity was a close second (beta weights of .42 and .39, respectively). For African-American women and Latinas, however, institutional race was the most powerful predictor (particularly among African-American women), although institutional gender continued to be a statistically significant factor for both groups. Wolf-Wendel, Baker, and Morphew (2000), after controlling for institutional selectivity and other relevant variables, report findings generally consistent with those of Wolf-Wendel; Solorzano (1995), controlling only for institutional size, reports findings consistent with Wolf-Wendel's for doctoral degree achievement among Chicanas.

A reanalysis of the data in Tidball's (1985) study of the comparative productivity of women's colleges with respect to graduates entering medical school, however, pointed to a lesser role for institutional gender. Although gender remained statistically significant net of other institutional characteristics (including selectivity and size), other institutional characteristics (particularly entering students' SAT verbal scores) explained six times more of the variance in medical school student productivity than did institutional gender (Crosby et al., 1994).

Summarizing baccalaureate origins studies during three decades, Tidball et al. (1999) concluded that successful women are most likely to be produced by small, all-women institutions that have a history of educating women, an environment with a large number of adult women and few male students, and a broad selection of major fields.

The second category of studies of the effects of attending a women's college on educational attainment (and other outcomes) focuses on the characteristics of the individual students enrolling. These studies proceed from the argument that baccalaureate origins studies, while controlling for *institutional* selectivity (for example, the average admissions tests scores of first-year students), do not adequately take into account other important characteristics of the students who enroll in these institutions. According to this line of argument, enrolling students bring with them a variety of personal, social, and academic background characteristics (such as motivation, socioeconomic status, and degree aspirations) that are known to shape an array of educational outcomes, including educational attainment. Without adequate student-level controls for these initial differences among students, the argument goes, it is difficult to assess the extent to which the apparent success of women's colleges in graduating high-achieving women is a function of the students enrolled or the education they received.

Studies adopting this approach, compared with most baccalaureate origins studies, commonly draw on nationally representative samples of entering students and apply statistical controls for a wider array of students' precollege characteristics. These studies also produce findings that lead (albeit without perfect consistency) to conclusions different from those suggested by the baccalaureate origins studies. In a typical study, Stoecker and Pascarella (1991) examined the educational attainment of nearly 2,500 women who participated in the 1971 Cooperative Institutional Research Program (CIRP). These women were a nationally representative sample of first-year students who attended only one four-year institution and who responded to a follow-up survey in 1980. Educational attainment was measured on a six-point scale based on highest degree achieved. The study took into account differences in students' background characteristics (including socioeconomic status, high school grades, and high school social accomplishments); precollege degree and occupational aspirations; selected institutional characteristics, including gender, size, and selectivity (a composite scale reflecting SAT/ACT scores, general educational expenditures per student, and perceived prestige of the institution); measures of students' college experiences (major, grades, and social involvement); and marital status. Net of the effects of these variables, Stoecker and Pascarella found that institutional gender had only a small, statistically nonsignificant effect on women's educational attainment.

Astin (1993c) reports a similar study based on more recent CIRP data. Using data from students who entered college in the fall of 1985 and were surveyed four years later, and after adjusting for a number of student and institutional characteristics, Astin found that attending a women's college had a statistically significant and positive net effect on women students' completion of the bachelor's degree. Smith and her colleagues, in two studies that also use CIRP data, found results consistent with Astin's. In both sets of analyses, these researchers found a positive net effect of attending a women's (versus coeducational) college on degree aspirations after four years and on degree completion (Smith, 1990; Smith, Wolf, & Morrison, 1995). The role of institutional gender, however, was indirect, mediated in one study through women students' academic involvement and in the other study by their perception of the value their institutions attached to student learning, civic involvement, and multicultural objectives, which, in turn, were related to educational aspirations. For women, these findings imply potentially important differences in climate and opportunities for academic engagement between women's and coeducational institutions, and they support the proposition that women's colleges have distinctive institutional effects on educational attainment independent of the characteristics of the students they enroll.

Riordan (1992, 1994, 1995), in contrast, using two large, nationally representative samples (NLS-72 and HS&B:80-86) and controlling for a more limited set of potentially confounding variables than the two CIRP-based studies, found results similar to those reported by Stoecker and Pascarella (1991). Riordan defined attendance as a continuous variable (number of years enrolled in a women's college) as opposed to the dichotomous criterion (graduated/not graduated) that is usually used. In his 1992 study, Riordan found that after six years, and net of women's precollege socioeconomic status, cognitive ability, and geographical region, attending a women's college conferred a statistically significant advantage for women students of about three-quarters (.73) of a year in educational attainment over enrollment in a coeducational institution. But when the analysis was limited to women who had graduated from a women's college (and thus presumably benefited fully from attending a women's college), the findings indicated these women had achieved slightly lower educational attainment levels than graduates of coed institutions. Women graduates of coed institutions were also significantly more likely to earn a graduate degree than were their counterparts who graduated from women's colleges. Riordan (1990, 1992) suggests that graduates of women's colleges may be less likely than their counterparts graduating from coeducational institutions to earn advanced degrees because graduates of the former are less likely to work full-time following graduation and are more likely to plan to have more children. Whether this finding is now dated remains an open question.

In his 1994 study, Riordan found that attending a women's college for a single year conferred an educational attainment advantage (of about .22 of a year) compared with women who attended coed institutions, suggesting that any advantage of attending a women's college may accrue in the early years of enrollment. The two earlier studies were based on data from NLS-72. For the 1995 study, Riordan used the High School and Beyond (1980 to 1986) data set and controlled for high school type and program, leadership involvement, parental socioeconomic status, educational expectations, race, gender, and senior-year academic test scores. In this investigation, he found "insufficient evidence to conclude that women [at women's colleges] are any more likely to pursue further schooling than their counterparts who attended only coeducational colleges" (p. 20). Other evidence from a nationally representative sample is consistent with Riordan's, indicating that attending a women's college confers no advantage in terms of preparation for graduate or professional school (Kim & Alvarez, 1995). In each succeeding year of attendance at a women's college, however, Riordan found that students' educational expectations were higher than those of similar women enrolled in coeducational institutions. Overall, these results indicate that college type does not consistently shape educational attainment.

The Riordan studies do, however, provide evidence that, after adjusting for students' precollege characteristics and experiences, women's college graduates develop significantly more of several forms of "human capital." These outcomes include increased egalitarian attitudes toward women's roles, advantages in postcollege occupational aspirations and status (see Chapter Nine), a consistent (but statistically nonsignificant) pattern of enhanced self-esteem and self-control, and for every year of attendance at a women's college, statistically significant advantages in the form of higher educational degree *expectations,* a finding also reported by Astin (1993c). Riordan (1992) notes that when asking questions about the most effective forms of education for women, answers should address multiple outcomes, including "occupational choice and attainment, educational attainment, marital outcomes, cognitive outcomes, and attitudinal outcomes" (p. 329).

Institutional Racial-Ethnic Composition. As with the debate over the relative effectiveness of women's colleges in promoting educational attainment among women, a similar but perhaps more empirically muted discussion continues with respect to the degree completion prospects of African-American students who attend historically Black colleges and universities (HBCUs) versus predominantly White institutions (PWIs). HBCU supporters argue along lines similar to those offered by backers of women's colleges: the institutions' faculty and staff, mission, student orientation, peer climate, and general culture provide a more supportive and effective educational experience than is available to African Americans at PWIs (see, for example, Berger, 2000b). Indeed, considerable evidence indicates that African Americans on PWI campuses confront significantly more social isolation, alienation, dissatisfaction, and overt racism than their counterparts at HBCUs (Allen, 1992; Allen, Epps, & Haniff, 1991; Bennett, 1995; Feagin, 1992; Feagin, Vera, & Imani, 1996; Outcalt & Skewes-Cox, 2002; Watson, Terrell, Wright, & Associates, 2002). The pre-1990s research we summarized in *How College Affects Students* suggested a modest net advantage in terms of persistence and degree completion for Black Americans attending HBCUs versus their African American counterparts at PWIs. That advantage, however, appeared to be more indirect (through academic achievement) than direct. Moreover, although the underlying dynamic is unclear, the evidence suggests that the indirect advantage is related not so much to any differences in the academic standards of HBCUs or PWIs as to the more supportive social environments at HBCUs.

Research published in the 1990s is consistent with earlier studies. When students' precollege characteristics are held constant, African Americans attending

HBCUs are more likely to complete their bachelor's degrees than are similarly qualified Black students enrolled at PWIs (Astin et al., 1996; Ehrenberg & Rothstein, 1994). However, estimates of the magnitude of the benefit to Black students of attending an HBCU (versus a predominantly White institution) vary. Astin et al. found the advantage to be about 6 percentage points; Ehrenberg and Rothstein estimated the advantage to be between 9 and 29 percentage points, depending on the model used. Some evidence also suggests that, for African Americans, attendance at an HBCU (versus a predominantly White institution) has a net positive effect on degree aspirations and the likelihood of enrolling in graduate school (Carter, 1999; Heath, 1992; Weiler, 1993). One multi-institutional study found no relationship with degree aspirations net of student's gender, father's education, family income, or precollege achievement (Springer, Terenzini, Pascarella, & Nora, 1996).

Although the underlying mechanisms remain largely unexamined, the evidence tends to buttress the supportive environment hypothesis. The research consistently indicates that, net of their precollege characteristics, Black students attending HBCUs are more likely than their peers at PWIs to report a positive and supportive environment on their campuses, including perceptions of a student-oriented faculty, and satisfaction with the overall college experience. The matter, however, may be more complex than that. When Astin and his colleagues controlled for institutional size, the HBCU effect disappeared, returning when institutional selectivity was added to the analysis. With student backgrounds and institutional size and selectivity held constant, attending an HBCU increased African-American students' chances of completing a bachelor's degree by perhaps 17 percentage points (Astin et al., 1996). The authors caution against concluding from their findings that the typical African-American student will improve his or her chances of completing a bachelor's degree by attending an HBCU rather than a PWI. This outcome, they maintain, must be estimated in terms of attending an HBCU of, for example, a certain size and selectivity versus a PWI of similar size and selectivity. Differences in the institutional profiles may in fact affect the chances of degree completion.

Although Astin (1993c) found enrollment in an HBCU had a positive effect on an African-American student's chance of graduating with honors (versus simply earning a bachelor's degree), he noted that other characteristics of HBCUs (including their low selectivity and having faculty who emphasized diversity) were more influential. Moreover, as described earlier, institutional race-ethnicity appears to have more influence on the development of successful African-American women (as it was for Latinas attending Hispanic-serving institutions) than either the gender or selectivity of the institutions they attended (Wolf-Wendel, 1998). Heath (1992) found that for Black students, attending a predominantly Black institution had an indirect positive effect (through grade performance) on expectations for graduate school enrollment, but most of these studies did not explore causal linkages between and among variables that might explain the dynamics underlying the apparent benefits to African-American students of HBCUs compared with PWIs.

WITHIN-COLLEGE EFFECTS

Taken as a whole, the research reviewed in the preceding section suggests that the impact of various institutional characteristics on persistence and educational attainment, although statistically significant and independent of other factors, tends to be small. As we concluded in our earlier review, it would appear that institutional characteristics may be too distal, too general, and too removed from students to produce large effects. These findings suggest that there may well be greater differences *within* than between categories of institutions (and within the institutions in any given category). Other forces, both more profound and more proximal, appear to be at work.

Conclusions from *How College Affects Students*

The pre-1990 literature clearly indicated that specific college experiences promote student persistence and educational attainment regardless of the characteristics of the institution attended. In addition to academic achievement (and consistent with theoretical expectations), the degree of a student's integration into campus social systems had positive net effects on attainment. Involvement in extracurricular activities and the extent and quality of students' peer interactions were particularly influential, although the impact was small. We speculated that the effects of social integration affirmed rather than changed initial educational aspirations.

The evidence was mixed concerning the direct influence of academic major on educational attainment, although it appeared that major departments do provide important academic, social, and occupational contexts that indirectly affect educational attainment. Stronger evidence indicated that living on campus (rather than commuting) was an important positive factor, probably because on-campus residence offers increased opportunities for peer interactions. Some evidence suggested fraternity or sorority membership also promotes persistence in the first two years of college, and residence in living-learning centers was clearly and positively influential, probably through their integration of students' academic and social lives. On two-year campuses, persistence and degree completion appeared to be more a function of academic than social integration.

Pre-1990 research found student orientation programs and first-year seminars designed to introduce students to their institution and to academic life promoted both persistence and degree completion, even when other factors were controlled. The effect probably derived from these programs' positive influence on students' initial social integration. The positive effects of high-quality academic advising also appeared to be more indirect than direct.

The pre-1990s evidence indicated that, net of other factors (such as academic ability), students receiving financial aid were as likely to persist as students not receiving financial aid, suggesting that aid programs tend to level the playing field for low-income students. Financial aid seemed to have greater impact at two-year and private institutions than at four-year and public colleges or universities, and scholarships had a stronger positive influence on persistence than other forms of aid. Net of other factors, working off campus, whether full- or part-time, tended to reduce the likelihood of persisting, whereas part-time work on campus tended to promote it.

Evidence from the 1990s

In this section, we turn to a synthesis of the post-1990 research literature examining college conditions and student experiences that influence persistence and educational attainment independently of the characteristics of the institutions students attend. These conditions or experiences may be more prevalent at some institutions than at others.

The volume of this literature is staggering. Because much of it is based on theoretical models of student persistence (Bean, 1980; Bean & Metzner, 1985; Pascarella, 1980; Tinto, 1975, 1987, 1993), we draw on the central constructs in these models to structure this review. The research of the 1990s falls generally into the following categories: academic performance; specific, academically related experiences (such as Supplemental Instruction, first-year seminars, academic support programs, advising, and undergraduate research experiences); financial aid; interactions with faculty members; interactions with peers; residence; learning communities; academic major; general academic and social integration; and intercollegiate athletics.

Academic Performance. Probably no other variable's relation to persistence or degree completion has attracted more attention than grade performance. Grades are hardly a perfect measure of learning and intellectual development in that they generally reflect a student's performance relative to other students rather than how much has been learned (Astin, 1993c). Moreover, although the concept of grades is familiar to all, the method of their calculation and the standards applied can vary enormously both within and across academic departments and institutions, muddying the meaning of a grade or grade-point average. In addition, grades are most likely confounded measures, reflecting a combination of a student's previous academic achievement, general intellectual capacities and abilities, academic skills (such as computer literacy and study and time management skills), and personal traits (such as motivation, self-discipline, and perseverance). Even so, the attention given grade performance in the research literature is warranted. Grade-point averages are the lingua franca of the academic instructional world, the keys to students' standing and continued enrollment, to admission to majors with enrollment caps, to program and degree completion, to admission to graduate and professional schools, and to employment opportunities.

Even given their limitations, however, college grades may well be the single best predictors of student persistence, degree completion, and graduate school enrollment. Grades are one of the most consistent predictors of these outcomes in both large, nationally representative studies and in the far more numerous single-institution studies. For example, using transcript and survey data from the High School and Beyond study of high school sophomores who were followed up 12 years after high school graduation, Adelman (1999) found both first-year grades and a measure of the subsequent trend in grades to be statistically significant, positive predictors of bachelor's degree completion beyond the effects of an array of other variables, including students' precollege characteristics, the selectivity and mission of the first institution attended, financial aid, and hours worked as well as selected college experience variables. Having first-year grades in the top two quintiles increased a student's likelihood of degree completion by two to three times over students with grades in the bottom three quintiles. Other studies, using different and more recent national samples of students, and whether descriptive (Berkner et al., 1996) or when controlling for students' background characteristics and college experiences (Astin, 1993c; Heller, 2001; Horn, 1998a; House, 1996b; Ishitani & DesJardins, 2002–2003), yield findings consistent with Adelman's.

The many single-institution studies consistently yield findings paralleling those of the larger national studies. Virtually without exception, students' grades make statistically significant, frequently substantial, and indeed often the largest contribution to student persistence and attainment. These findings hold true in the presence of a wide range of measures of students' precollege academic and sociodemographic backgrounds as well as college experiences. The positive and statistically significant net effects of grades on persistence and degree attainment, moreover, are consistently apparent even over varying periods of time.[5]

Perhaps more important from a practical and policy perspective, academic achievement during a student's first year of college may be a particularly powerful influence on subsequent retention and degree completion. The positive and statistically significant effects of grades on persistence and degree completion are evident whether the studies track persistence from the first to the second semester, to the second year, or over longer periods of time in a two-year institution[6] or into the second year or over longer periods in four-year colleges or universities.[7] As one might expect, given the magnitude of its net effect, causal models of the process indicate that the influence of first-year academic performance on persistence into the second year is both strong and direct. This finding has been replicated across three samples of students in different institutions in different parts of the country, including a nationally representative 18-institution study (Cabrera, Nora, & Castaneda, 1993; Cabrera, Nora, Terenzini, Pascarella, & Hagedorn, 1999; Nora & Cabrera, 1996).

Evidence from studies employing a promising new analytical approach called *event history analysis*[8] suggests, however, that the effects of grade performance (or theoretically, any independent variable) may vary over time. Consistent with studies of the importance of a student's first-year grades in predicting persistence into the second year, to later years, and to degree completion, a small number of investigations of the role of each successive year's grades on persistence over time among University of Minnesota students indicates that good grades reduce dropout behavior in the first year more than they do in subsequent years (DesJardins et al., 1999b; DesJardins, Ahlburg, & McCall, 1994) and that the effect of good grades simultaneously reduces the chances of stopping out and increases the probability of timely graduation (DesJardins, Ahlburg, & McCall, 2002b). A more recent event history analysis using nationally representative data from the High School and Beyond (sophomore cohort) survey found, however, that the effects of grades on degree completion in a 12-year period appear to be constant over time (DesJardins, McCall, Ahlburg, & Moye, 2002). The body of published research is too small to permit confident conclusions, but it seems reasonable to conclude that the effects of grades (or any other variable) might change over time. These approaches to such modeling variations over time constitute a promising step toward increasing the sophistication of models and theories and, hence, our understanding of how college affects students.

Programmatic Interventions. As the pressures have grown on public and private institutions to increase retention and degree completion, so has the research examining the effectiveness of programmatic interventions designed to promote both outcomes. In our earlier book, we summarized the then relatively modest number of studies indicating that underprepared students participating in such intervention programs earned grades on average that were about 10 percentile points higher than those of nonparticipants and also that participants persisted at rates about 8 percentage points higher than nonparticipants (see, for example, Clowes, 1992; Kulik, Kulik, & Shwalb, 1983). Kulik et al. examined four types of intervention programs: developmental studies and similar remedial programs, instruction in academic skills, advising and counseling programs, and comprehensive support services. Although specific programs are noteworthy, these categories provide a useful structure for a review of the literature of the 1990s. We also discuss first-year seminars and undergraduate research programs.

Developmental studies and other remedial programs. Although college grades probably reflect an amalgam of factors relating to performance and educational attainment, they are nonetheless susceptible to programmatic interventions. Developmental studies and other special programs are visible manifestations of college and university efforts to enhance the academic performance and persistence of underprepared students. These interventions vary considerably in content, structure, and duration, making synthesis of the research on their effectiveness difficult. The heterogeneity of these studies with respect to the specific interventions, sample sizes, and research and analytical designs further complicates synthesis and review.

Nonetheless, with a few exceptions (such as DesJardins, Kim, & Rzonca, 2002–2003; Hoyt, 1999; Zhao, 1999), the evidence consistently suggests that academic intervention programs are at least modestly effective in helping students overcome deficiencies in their precollege academic preparation and associated disadvantages. These remedial interventions appear to promote underprepared students' academic adjustment and persistence in the short term, such as semester to semester or into the second year at both two- and four-year institutions (Boylan & Bonham, 1992; Budny, 1994; Campbell & Blakey, 1995, 1996;

Easterling, Patten, & Krile, 1998; Garcia, 2000; Hector & Hector, 1992; Robbins & Smith, 1993; Weissman, Silke, & Bulakowski, 1997).

Perhaps more important, the research suggests remediation efforts also produce long-term benefits such as increased likelihood of persistence over periods of time ranging from two to six years as well as actual degree completion (Braley & Ogden, 1997; Easterling, Patten, & Krile, 1995; Easterling et al., 1998; Fullilove & Treisman, 1990; Weissman et al., 1997). In addition, remediation for academically underprepared students appears to be particularly effective during the first semester (Campbell & Blakey, 1996; Weissman et al., 1997). The evidence is generally consistent whether at-risk students who participate in developmental courses and activities are compared with similar at-risk students who do not or with students judged not to need remediation (for example, Weissman et al., 1997). Indeed, in some cases, students seen as needing remediation have subsequently persisted or graduated at higher rates than students not judged to need such support (Braley & Ogden, 1997; Easterling et al., 1998).

Instruction in academic skills. Supplemental Instruction (SI) is a distinctive intervention in the broad category of academic interventions aimed at enhancing academic performance and degree completion, and research on this approach dominates the empirical literature. Although similar in its overall goals to the academic remediation efforts of most developmental studies programs, SI differs in several important respects. Whereas conventional efforts target individual at-risk students, SI is available to all students in "historically difficult" courses (those with a record of a high proportion of low grades or withdrawals, typically more than 30 percent). Whereas conventional remediation efforts frequently call for intensive review of material covered in a course lecture, SI stresses interactive learning in groups with SI leaders who are "model students" and who have previously earned high grades in the course. These leaders attend all classes, take notes, and do class assignments. Under the supervision of academic advisers or other academic support personnel, the SI leaders serve as group facilitators in frequent sessions devoted to basic study skills and learning strategies (Center for Supplemental Instruction, 1998).

Given the extensive and consistent findings we reviewed in Chapter Three concerning the positive effects of Supplemental Instruction on the grades of participating students, one might expect similar benefits in persistence and graduation. And indeed that seems to be the case. Although only a handful of studies have been done, most at the University of Missouri at Kansas City (UMKC), the evidence indicates that SI participants are more likely than nonparticipants to persist at statistically significant levels from one fall to the next fall semester. For example, across a series of seven studies of SI courses offered at UMKC each fall from 1989 to 1995, participants in SI activities (group n of 386 to 795) persisted into the following fall semester at rates that ranged from 7 to 18 percentage points higher than nonparticipants (mean difference + 12.9 percentage points). All the differences, though statistically significant, were unadjusted for students' precourse characteristics (Center for Supplemental Instruction, 1998; National Center for Supplemental Instruction, 1997).

Similar advantages appear to accrue to SI participants in terms of higher degree completion rates. Martin, Arendale, and Associates (1993) over a seven-year period tracked a group of first-time, first-year students who entered UMKC in fall 1983. SI participants ($n = 124$) compared with nonparticipants ($n = 225$) completed their degrees at higher rates after four, five, six, and seven years, with an advantage of 10 to 12 percentage points in each year. In a more recent study of a similarly defined cohort that entered UMKC in fall 1989, SI-activity participants, when compared with nonparticipants in the same courses, again achieved higher graduation rates after four, five, six, and seven years. Although the differences in the four-year completion rates for this cohort were only about 4 percentage points (still statistically significant), the differences in cumulative graduation rates in succeeding years, all statistically significant, were again in the 10 to 15 percentage point range (Center for Supplemental Instruction, 1998). Ramirez (1997) found no statistically significant difference in the four-year graduation rates of "traditional" students, although at-risk SI participants graduated in four years at a rate nearly 20 percentage points higher than the rate of their nonparticipating peers. This finding is consistent with research showing that grade-related benefits of SI activities may be particularly significant for under-prepared students. More rigorously controlled analyses of SI-related benefits to students in terms of persistence and degree completion are needed.

Nonetheless, although the available evidence evokes caution, its overall weight leads to the conclusion that Supplemental Instruction probably has positive effects on the course-grade performance and persistence of students in high-risk courses who take advantage of SI opportunities. These benefits are clear in short-term outcomes (such as course grades and persistence into the next semester or year) but less compelling over the longer term. More—and more rigorous—studies of SI benefits are needed.

First-year seminars. Another distinctive approach to increasing academic performance and retention is the first-year seminar (FYS). Introduced by John N. Gardner at the University of South Carolina in 1972 as "University 101," the idea has since been adopted or adapted by nearly 95 percent of America's four-year colleges and universities (Barefoot, 2002). FYS courses operate like regular classes, having students meet with an instructor at regularly scheduled times, but these courses vary considerably both within and across institutions.[9] An FYS may be required or elective and offered to all new students or to targeted groups (such as at-risk students or students in a specific department, college, or school). The seminars also vary widely in content, duration, structure, pedagogies, and degree credit value, but all have the goal of promoting academic performance, persistence, and degree completion.

Despite the quarter-century-long history of the FYS concept, a body of research on the impact of such seminars did not begin to take shape until the late 1980s, although it has grown rapidly since then. Studies of first- to second-year persistence dominate this literature, and although our review of these studies is selective, with rare exceptions they produce uniformly consistent evidence of positive and statistically significant advantages to students who take the courses. Studies tracking the persistence rates of each cohort of "University 101" participants and nonparticipants at the University of South Carolina-Columbia between 1973 and 1996, for example, found that in each entering cohort participants were more likely to persist into their second year than were nonparticipants. In 15 of the 23 years, the differences were statistically significant, and in the cohorts where the differences were not significant, the persistence rates of FYS participants consistently exceeded those of nonparticipants (see also Fidler, 1991, 1999). With few exceptions (for example, Simmons, Wallins, & George, 1995; Wilkie & Kuckuck, 1989), other studies of first- to second-year persistence or of credit hours earned by FYS participants compared with nonparticipants yield evidence consistent with Fidler's (Barefoot, 1993; Barefoot, Warnock, Dickinson, Richardson, & Roberts, 1998; Cone, 1991; Fidler & Moore, 1996; Hoff, Cook, & Price, 1996; Murtuza & Ketkar, 1995; Shanley & Witten, 1990; Starke, Harth, & Sirianni, 2001; Tokuno, 1993).

Although we identified no studies in which conditional effects were formally tested, first-year seminars appear to benefit all categories of students. FYS participation appears to promote persistence into the second year for both males and females (Boudreau & Kromrey, 1994; Glass & Garrett, 1995), for both minority and majority students (Boudreau & Kromrey, 1994; Fidler & Godwin, 1994; Glass & Garrett, 1995; Shanley & Witten, 1990; Sidle & McReynolds, 1999; Starke et al., 2001; Strumpf & Hunt, 1993), for students of most ages and major fields (Glass & Garrett, 1995), for students living on and off campus (Fidler & Godwin, 1994), and (with two exceptions) for both "traditional admits" and at-risk students (Boudreau & Kromrey, 1994; Cone, 1991; Grunder & Hellmich, 1996; McIntyre et al., 1992; Starke et al., 2001). Robinson (1989) found no statistically significant advantage to FYS participation for at-risk students, and Simmons, Wallins, and George (1995) found that FYS participation promoted persistence into the second year among low-achieving students but not among under- or overachievers.

Administrators and policy makers may ask whether the gains in persistence and graduation rates are large enough to warrant investing resources in first-year seminars. Answering the cost-benefit question is beyond the purpose and scope of this chapter,[10] but we can suggest the *range* of gains reported in various studies while noting that we have not undertaken an exhaustive review of this considerable body of research or a formal meta-analysis.

Although few studies of persistence into the second year control for precollege differences between FYS participants and nonparticipants, these studies provide the most valid estimates of the size of the effect. Two single-institution studies matched participants and nonparticipants on such precourse characteristics as gender, race-ethnicity, high school achievement, and admissions test scores. Both estimated that FYS participants had a 7 percentage point advantage over nonparticipants in the likelihood of returning for a second year of college (Boudreau & Kromrey, 1994; Sidle & McReynolds, 1999). Strumpf and Hunt (1993), who monitored the persistence of randomly assigned groups of FYS participants and nonparticipants, estimated that participants reenrolled for their second year at a rate 13 percentage points higher than that of non-participants. With respect to degree completion, an informal examination of evidence of varying degrees of quality from more than 40 reports supports the estimate that FYS participants are 5 to 15 percentage points more likely than nonparticipants to graduate within four years. None of the studies on which these estimates are based, however, control for differences in students' precollege characteristics.

First-year seminars in most colleges and universities are an elective (National Resource Center for the First-Year Experience and Students in Transition, 2000), and students who choose to enroll in such courses may differ from those who do not in ways that relate to persistence. Most studies of the effectiveness of first-year seminars provide few controls for such potentially confounding factors as gender, race-ethnicity, socioeconomic status, or academic ability and achievement. When such variables are taken into account, the reported magnitudes of the advantages tend to shrink, although the benefits of FYS participation remain. Some of this evidence comes from studies in which participant and nonparticipant groups are "matched" on various combinations of precollege characteristics. These studies consistently find that FYS participation promotes persistence into the second year (see, for example, Boudreau & Kromrey, 1994; Fidler, 1991; Glass & Garrett, 1995) and over longer periods of time (Boudreau & Kromrey, 1994; Stupka, 1993). More recent studies employ various multivariate statistical procedures to control for academic ability and achievement and other precollege characteristics. Whatever the procedure, the research points to the same conclusion, indicating positive and statistically significant net effects of FYS participation (versus nonparticipation) on persistence into the second year (see, for example, Hyers & Joslin, 1998) or attainment of a bachelor's degree (Starke et al., 2001; Xiao & House, 2000).

We identified only one study that adopted a true experimental design (Strumpf & Hunt, 1993). Students entering the University of Maryland at College Park in the fall of 1986 who expressed an interest in taking an FYS were randomly assigned as participants ($n = 72$) and nonparticipants ($n = 75$). Such a procedure, in theory, creates two groups similar in all respects save their participation in the FYS. Strumpf and Hunt found that in each of four consecutive semesters (two full academic years), FYS participants were consistently more likely to persist at statistically significant rates.

But questions remain. A handful of studies control to varying degrees not only for students' pre-FYS course characteristics but also for other college experiences, and their findings suggest that factors other than FYS participation may be involved in students' persistence decisions. Sax and Gilmartin (2002), for example, in perhaps the most rigorous of these studies, analyzed data from more than 3,000 first-year students entering 43 institutions around the country. These authors made statistical adjustments for the effects of a wide array of demographic and other precollege characteristics, including measures of gender, ability, socioeconomic status, financial considerations, reasons for attending, and personality traits as well as institutional characteristics, sources of financial aid, and other first-year college experiences, such as college grades and contacts with faculty members. With such potentially confounding variables controlled, Sax and Gilmartin found that participation in an FYS had no statistically significant effect on enrollment the next year. Several other studies, which controlled for far fewer variables, produced results consistent with those of Sax and Gilmartin (Grunder & Hellmich, 1996; Sidle & McReynolds, 1999; Simmons et al., 1995).

The persistence-related processes or dynamics underlying the apparent success of the FYS remain largely unexamined. It is unclear, for example, whether the effects of participation on persistence and degree completion are direct or indirect, providing early socialization, improved study and time management skills, higher grades, and stronger interrelationships with faculty, staff, and peers, all of which are known to promote retention and educational attainment.

The evidence on this point, although only suggestive, is consistent. FYS participation appears to promote both persistence and college grade performance. With some exceptions (see also Cuseo, 2002; Hoff et al., 1996; Simmons et al., 1995), studies find a positive and almost always statistically significant relation between seminar participation and college achievement over varying periods of time, whether the studies leave students' precollege differences unaccounted for (Cone, 1991; Shanley & Witten, 1990; Stupka, 1993; Tokuno, 1993) or take into account various potentially confounding precollege differences between groups (Boudreau & Kromrey, 1994; Glass & Garrett, 1995; Grunder & Hellmich, 1996; Hyers & Joslin, 1998; Sidle & McReynolds, 1999; Starke et al., 2001).

Similarly, studies of first-year seminar participation point to a wide array of other positive and statistically significant effects for FYS participants (versus nonparticipants) in addition to higher persistence rates and better academic performance. These other effects, all positively related to persistence, include more frequent and more meaningful interactions with faculty members (Fidler, 1991; Keup & Barefoot, 2002; Maisto & Tammi, 1991; Starke, 1990; Starke et al., 2001) and with other students (Keup & Barefoot, 2002; Starke et al., 2001), more active involvement in extracurricular activities (Barefoot et al., 1998; Fidler, 1991; Starke, 1990; Starke et al., 2001), positive perceptions of self-as-learner (Barefoot, 1993), and satisfaction with the college experience (Barefoot, 1993; Starke et al., 2001).

Thus, it appears that the effects of FYS participation are *at least* indirect through enhancement of grades and various dimensions of academic and social integration, all of which, in turn, are related to retention and educational attainment. In short, the weight of evidence indicates that FYS participation has statistically significant and substantial, positive effects on a student's successful transition to college and the likelihood of persistence into the second year as well as on academic performance while in college and on a considerable array of other college experiences known to be related directly and indirectly to bachelor's degree completion. Causal linkages between and among these variables, however, are yet to be mapped.

Advising and counseling programs. Institutions of all sizes and types have long sought to enhance the quality and effectiveness of their academic advising programs. These efforts have taken many forms, including both pre- and postadmissions advising, "intrusive" advising, group advising, and a variety of enhancements in traditional advising programs.

Research consistently indicates that academic advising can play a role in students' decisions to persist and in their chances of graduating. Seidman (1991), for example, randomly assigned 278 new students entering a community college in the State University of New York system to two groups. The treatment group received both pre- and postadmissions advising, including meeting with an adviser to determine a course schedule, discussions about how to become academically and socially involved in campus life, and meeting with the adviser two subsequent times in the first semester to discuss progress and adjustment. Members of the control group went through the regular orientation process. Seidman found that students in the treatment group persisted into the second year at a rate 20 percentage points above that of their peers in the control group. Other studies of advising, employing various statistical techniques to take into account potentially confounding variables, provide evidence generally consistent with Seidman's (Beil, 1990; Elliott & Healy, 2001; Metzner, 1989; Peterson, Wagner, & Lamb, 2001; B. Smith, 1993; Steele, Kennedy, & Gordon, 1993; Trippi & Cheatham, 1991; Young, Backer, & Rogers, 1989).

With a few exceptions (Boyd et al., 1994; Boyd et al., 1991), a number of uncontrolled studies also indicate statistically significant and positive advantages of participation in advising programs (Austin, Cherney, Crowner, & Hill, 1997; Boyd et al., 1995, 1996; Glenn, Rollins, & Smith, 1990; Vowell, Farren, & McGlone, 1990; Walleri, Stoker, & Stoering, 1997; Yorke, 1998). Peer mentoring also appears to promote persistence (Anderson & Ekstrom, 1996; Schwitzer & Thomas, 1998; Smith & Associates, 1997; Thile & Matt, 1995; Twomey, 1991), although the evidence is limited in both volume and methodological rigor.[11]

Summer "bridge" programs are an early form of intervention intended to promote acclimatization and academic success and persistence among at-risk students. These programs have somewhat different goals than conventional summer orientation programs and are usually longer (a week or more versus a day or two) and more programmatically focused. Bridge programs vary in both content and structure, but in the main they target high school graduates who have been admitted for a fall semester. These programs usually bring students to campus during the summer for intensive academic and residential experiences, including courses or workshops designed to help the students develop time management and study skills, form peer networks, develop academic and career plans, familiarize themselves with the campus, and meet with faculty, other students, and academic support staff.

Fewer studies have looked at bridge programs than at the longer developmental studies programs offered during an academic year, but the findings are generally consistent in suggesting that bridge program participants are more likely than nonparticipants to persist into their second year (Chaney, Muraskin, Cahalan, & Goodwin, 1998; Garcia, 1991; Kleeman, 1991; Person & LeNoir, 1997; Reyes, 1997; Robert & Thomson, 1994; Santa Rita & Bacote, 1997). These summer programs appear to provide participants with a casual introduction to their institutions as well as an opportunity to develop friendships that offer both social and academic support during the bridge program and beyond (Garcia, 1991; Kleeman, 1991; Robert & Thomson, 1994).

Studies indicate that personal counseling also has a positive effect on persistence (Bishop & Walker, 1990; Sandler, 1999; Schwitzer, Grogan, Kaddoura, & Ochoa, 1993; Turner & Berry, 2000; Wilson, Mason, & Ewinig, 1997). After controlling for academic ability, Wilson, Mason, and Ewinig, for example, found a strong linear trend indicating that students' chances of persisting increased with the number of counseling sessions, at least up to six or seven sessions. Additional sessions, however, had little impact on persistence.

Whether the effects of such advising and counseling programs are direct or indirect is unclear. One study suggests a statistically significant direct effect (Peterson et al., 2001). Another reports finding a series of indirect effects on persistence through advising's positive influences on student grades, satisfaction, and intent to persist (Metzner, 1989). Whatever the causal connections, low-quality advising may be better than no advising at all (Metzner, 1989), and sooner is probably better than later (Campbell & Blakey, 1995, 1996).

Comprehensive support and retention programs. A number of colleges and universities, often with funding from state and federal programs, offer at-risk (and often all) students a broad array of services and programs intended to promote academic adjustment, persistence, and degree completion. The federal Student Support Services (SSS) program, one of the clusters of TRIO programs, is probably the best known and most widespread of these comprehensive programs and offers perhaps the best example of the range of services that can be provided. SSS provides nine supplemental academic programs to low-income, first-generation, and physically handicapped students. The program offers instruction in basic study skills; tutorial services; academic, financial, and personal counseling; career information; mentoring; special services for students with limited proficiency in English; laboratories (such as in math or writing); workshops (for example, in orientation, study skills, or career guidance); cultural events; and various handicapped services.

Research consistently indicates that such comprehensive programs have a statistically significant and positive effect on student persistence. In perhaps the most methodologically rigorous study we reviewed in this area, Chaney, Muraskin, Cahalan, and Goodwin (1998) studied the persistence behaviors of nearly 3,000 full-time, first-year SSS participants at 30 sites and about 3,000 students with similar characteristics at 20 non-SSS sites. Chaney and his colleagues found that participants in SSS programs were 7 percent more likely than nonparticipants to persist into their second year, particularly when the services were blended with other institutional services and even after adjustments for a wide variety of precollege demographic and academic background characteristics, educational goals and commitment levels, college-related and non-college-related experiences, and selected institutional characteristics. Instructional courses, peer tutoring, and workshops appeared to have the largest effects, although, as one might expect, the impact of each was related to the students' level of participation. Similar results were found when persistence into the third year at the same or another institution was the outcome measured. Given the somewhat smaller effect of SSS services on retention into the third year at any institution, the authors speculated that SSS programs might help build in students a sense of loyalty and belonging at their first institution. The study provides some evidence that comprehensive services programs not only may help at-risk students survive their first year of college but also may have longer-lasting effects by providing students with academic skills and integration into both the academic and social systems of their institutions.

Other studies support the conclusion that comprehensive support programs have positive and statistically significant net effects on student persistence and graduation (Astin, 1993c; Cunningham, Delci, & Goodman, 2001; H. Kim, 1996; Maack, 1998; Somers, 1995b, 1996a). Qualitative and less well-controlled quantitative studies also yield findings consistent with those reviewed in the preceding paragraph (Catalano & Eddy, 1990; Crosson, 1992; Glass & Bunn, 1998; Heverly, 1999; McPhee, 1990; Person & LeNoir, 1997; Walleri et al., 1997; West & Michael, 1998).

Undergraduate research programs. Experiential and inquiry-based learning have long interested advocates for education, notably John Dewey and Jerome Bruner. More recently, the idea of integrating research and teaching moved into the spotlight, especially since publication of the report of the Boyer Commission on Educating Undergraduates in the Research University (1998). The report urged, among other things, that universities adapt for undergraduate education the research-as-teaching model widely used at the graduate level. One offshoot has been a growth in undergraduate research programs, innovations intended to capitalize on conditions known to promote student learning. Undergraduate research programs are an amalgam of situational and behavioral factors intended both to provide a window on the intellectual life of the scholar and to promote students' active involvement in their own learning, increased and more meaningful interaction with faculty members, opportunities to apply course-related theory and skills in solving real problems, and a challenging intellectual activity. A few researchers have examined undergraduate research programs' effects on persistence, degree completion, graduate school enrollment, and degree aspirations.

Evidence on the effectiveness of such programs, just beginning to emerge, suggests the mix of student-faculty contact and active learning is relatively potent with respect to persistence and degree completion. Findings from several studies point to the positive influence of undergraduate research programs on persistence and degree completion (Jonides, von Hippel, Lerner, & Nagda, 1992; Nagda, Gregerman, Jonides, von Hippel, & Lerner, 1998; Rayman & Brett, 1995; Sax, 1994c; Verity et al., 2002). Nagda and his colleagues, for example, found that, even after adjusting for grade performance, admissions test scores, and race-ethnicity, most participants in an undergraduate research program demonstrated increased rates of persistence through to graduation. The effects were strongest for African Americans and for sophomores rather than first-year students. Well-controlled studies indicate that participation in research programs also elevates degree aspirations (Astin, 1993c; Astin & Astin, 1993; Heath, 1992) and the likelihood of enrolling in graduate school (Schowen, 1998; Walpole, 1997, 1998a; Zydney, Bennett, Shahid, & Bauer, 2002a; see also Zydney et al., 2002b). A study of an undergraduate research program at the University of Michigan suggests that program participants are significantly more likely than nonparticipants to pursue graduate education and postgraduate research activities. Among minority students who pursued postbaccalaureate study, program participants were more likely to enter schools of medicine and law than were similar students who participated in less structured forms of undergraduate research (Hathaway, Nagda, & Gregerman, 2002). Other studies report findings consistent with those from the Michigan study (Bauer & Bennett, 2003; Morley, Havick, & May, 1998). The differences between research program participants in these latter studies are not attributable to grades or, according to Morely et al., to other undergraduate experiences or family and peer encouragement.

Financial Aid. A large body of research focuses on the effects of financial aid on student decisions about whether and where to go to college.[12] Fewer studies examine the effects of financial aid on students' subsequent decisions to persist and graduate, but the evidence on this topic is still substantial.[13] The reason is not hard to discern: during the 2000–01 academic year, institutional, state, and federal sources dispersed a record $74 billion in student aid, a 7.1 percent increase over the preceding year and nearly double the amount (in constant dollars) distributed a decade previously (College Board, 2001). In 1999–2000, more than 73 percent of all undergraduates attending postsecondary institutions full-time for a full year received financial aid, averaging about $8,500 (Berkner, Berker, Rooney, & Peter, 2002).

Both theory (for example, Leslie & Brinkman, 1988; Paulsen & St. John, 2002; St. John, Paulsen, & Starkey, 1996; Tinto, 1993) and common sense suggest that economic circumstances play an important role not only in whether and where students go to college but also in how long they remain. Throughout the college search, choice, enrollment, and persistence process, students and often their families balance the anticipated educational and occupational return from attending college and earning a degree against its cost, including opportunity costs such as deferred income. Students meet these costs through a variety of mechanisms including institutional, state, and federal financial aid in the form of grants, scholarships, loans, and work-study as well as through family support, personal savings, and non-school-related work.

Estimating the effects of financial aid on student persistence and degree completion, however, is anything but straightforward (Heller, 2003). Apart from parental or family assistance and personal funds, students may receive aid in any of a number of combinations of amounts, forms (such as grants, scholarships, loans, work-study), and sources (personal, institutional, state, and federal). Funding levels and eligibility rules for state and federal programs can change frequently, and studying such a volatile mix over time may sometimes seem a fool's errand.

Looking at research published before 1990 on the impact of receiving (versus not receiving) financial aid, we concluded that, although the findings were "somewhat mixed" (Pascarella & Terenzini, 1991, p. 420), students who received financial aid were as likely to persist in college as those who did not, even after adjusting for academic ability.

Research since 1990 is more consistent in finding that students who receive financial aid are as likely as those who do not to persist in college from one year to the next and to graduate. Studies using the 1989–90 national Beginning Post-secondary Student Survey and the 1992 follow-up indicate that students who receive financial aid (compared with those who do not) are less likely to leave postsecondary education after two years and more likely to earn a degree or certificate. The impact of financial aid was particularly evident among students enrolled in two- or three-year programs and those from families with the lowest incomes. Among students at four-year institutions, the differences in persistence rates between aid recipients and nonrecipients were small, and females and males, as well as financially dependent and independent students, appeared to benefit equally from aid (Fitzgerald, Berkner, Horn, Choy, & Hoachlander, 1994). Four years later, the baccalaureate degree–seeking students in this same BPS:90 sample who received financial aid graduated at about the same rate as their peers who did not receive aid. In addition, aided students completed their programs faster (Cuccaro-Alamin, 1997).

Although the Fitzgerald et al. and the Cuccaro-Alamin studies did not take into account differences in students' academic abilities or other relevant characteristics, their findings are consistent with those in more controlled studies indicating that financial aid enhances persistence and degree completion, particularly among low-income students (Astin, 1993c; Cabrera, Stampen, & Hansen, 1990; Dynarski, 1999; Ishitani & DesJardins, 2002–2003; St. John, 1990; St. John, Kirshstein, & Noell, 1991; St. John & Masten, 1990; Wei & Horn, 2002). St. John and Masten, using data from the National Longitudinal Study of the High School Class of 1972, estimated that financial aid increased the odds of completing a bachelor's degree by about 11 percentage points. Controlled studies at the regional and state level (such as Daly, 1990), as well as those done on a single campus (such as Cabrera, Nora, & Castaneda, 1992; DesJardins, Ahlburg, & McCall, 2002a; DuBrock & Fenske, 2000; Jones & Moss, 1994; Mukuakane-Drechsel & Hagedorn, 2000; Nora, 1990; Somers, 1992, 1994, 1995b), lead generally to the same conclusions as the less well-controlled studies.[14] The findings of studies using the total amount of aid as the predictor variable are consistent with those using the simple receipt of aid as the primary independent variable (such as Somers, 1995b; St. John, 1990). Moreover, where researchers find that receipt of financial aid is negatively related to persistence, the evidence suggests that the aid was not so much ineffective as *insufficient* (Cofer & Somers, 1999a; Hippensteel, St. John, & Starkey, 1996; Kaltenbaugh, 1993; Somers, 1995a; St. John, Andrieu,

Oescher, & Starkey, 1994; St. John et al., 1996; St. John & Starkey, 1994). ("Unmet need" is discussed later in this chapter.)

Grants and scholarships. Although the evidence is both generally clear and consistent in indicating that receipt of financial aid reduces the economic barriers to enrollment and persistence for financially needy students, the research is less clear concerning which types of aid—such as grants and scholarships, loans, work-study, singly or in combination—have the greatest impact. Several studies, after controlling for academic performance and other relevant variables, find grants or scholarships (or packages including them) negatively related to both within-year and year-to-year persistence (Kaltenbaugh, St. John, & Starkey, 1999; Payne, Pullen, & Padgett, 1996; Somers, 1993, 1996a, 1996b; St. John & Oescher, 1992; St. John & Starkey, 1995b). DesJardins, Ahlburg, and McCall (2002a) found that, net of other relevant variables, grants (need-based awards) had no impact on persistence over a seven-year period, while scholarships (merit-based aid) of equal value had the largest impact in each year. "Vanity aid" for high-income students, net of other factors, appears to have little effect on within-year persistence (St. John et al., 1994).

More frequently, studies indicate that grant aid has a positive and significant, although modest, effect on persistence and degree completion. Several studies using nationally representative samples find that the beneficial effects of grants persist even when students' academic ability and other relevant background characteristics are taken into account (Astin, 1993c; Clotfelter, 1991; Cofer & Somers, 1999a, in press; DesJardins, Ahlburg, & McCall, 1997; Dynarski, 1999; Heller, 2003; St. John, 1990, 1991; St. John et al., 1991; U.S. General Accounting Office, 1995; Wei & Horn, 2002). By one estimate, after taking into account family income and size, academic ability, age, race-ethnicity, parental education, and full-time or part-time enrollment status and allowing for the time-variant effects of these variables, each $1,000 of grant aid (in 1998 dollars) increased educational attainment by about .16 years (Dynarski, 1999). Heller (2003) estimates that, after adjusting for demographic, academic, institutional, and cost factors, the odds of persisting into the second year are 6 percent higher for a student who receives a need-based grant of $1,200 than for a student who does not. Moreover, he also found that receipt of grant aid early in a student's college career was important in that student's persistence and attainment of a credential, whether a certificate or an associate or bachelor's degree. A $1,200 need-based grant and a $2,000 non-need-based grant both raised the likelihood that a student would persist or complete a program by 6 percent, even after controlling other relevant factors.

Grants may be especially beneficial for low-income students, particularly in the first year. The U.S. General Accounting Office (1995), after controlling for students' academic achievement and other background characteristics, estimated that an additional $1,000 in grant aid to a low-income student reduced the probability of that student's dropping out in the first year by 23 percent. But the odds were reduced by only 8 percent in the second year, and grants had no apparent effect on low-income students' persistence in the third year. Because most dropouts occur between the first and second years, the declining influence of grants on persistence may reflect a "floor effect." St. John, Hu, and Weber (2001) also found a decline over time in the effectiveness of grants-only aid in promoting persistence among students in Indiana public colleges and universities. Single-institution studies generally find that grants or scholarships enhance students' chances of persisting and graduating (Fenske, Porter, & DuBrock, 2000; Hollings, 1992; Lam, 1999; McDaniel & Graham, 2001; Payne et al., 1996; Schuh, 1999).

Work-study. Our earlier review identified only a few studies of the persistence-related effects of work-study (understood as either federal college work-study assistance or institutionally supported on-campus employment). These studies were fairly consistent in finding positive benefits associated with this kind of financial assistance. In addition to providing financial support, work-study also gives students opportunities to interact with administrative staff and faculty members, enhancing their students' social and academic integration.

Over the past decade, additional studies have appeared, but confident conclusions remain elusive. Several well-controlled studies using data from the National Postsecondary Student Aid Study of 1987 find that college work-study aid, whether in a package that includes either grants or loans or when considered net of the effects of other forms of aid (as well as other relevant student and institutional characteristics), is negatively related to fall-to-spring semester persistence (Kaltenbaugh et al., 1999; Paulsen & St. John, 2002; St. John & Starkey, 1995b). Clotfelter (1991), using the 1980 High School and Beyond (senior cohort) survey, reports no statistically significant relation between work-study aid and persistence or degree completion more than five years after enrollment.

Other studies, however, find statistically significant, positive, and frequently unique effects of work-study assistance on persistence and degree completion (Adelman, 1999; Beeson & Wessel, 2002; Cofer & Somers, 1998; DesJardins et al., 1997, 1999b, 2002a; Heller, 2003; Kodama, 2002; St. John, 1990; St. John et al., 1991; Wilkie & Jones, 1994). One of the goals underlying work-study programs is to let students learn and earn at the same time. Some evidence suggests that both persistence and learning are likely outcomes when students' employment, whether on or off campus, is related to their academic work or interests (Aper, 1994: Broughton & Otto, 1999; Fitzgerald et al., 1994; King & Bannon, 2002a).

Although these studies are consistent in finding that work-study has a positive impact on persistence, ambiguities remain, particularly as they relate to *when* the effects of work-study appear. St. John and his colleagues, for example, used the same database as Clotfelter (although with different sample specifications, variables, and analytical procedures) and, like Clotfelter, found no statistically significant relation between work-study and persistence into the second year. St. John et al. did, however, find work-study significantly and positively related to persistence into the third and fourth years. DesJardins and his colleagues, in contrast, report finding statistically significant and positive net effects of work-study on persistence but primarily in the first year or two of enrollment (DesJardins, Ahlburg, & McCall, 1997). They found that work-study's effects waned in the later years of the seven-year period (1986 to 1993) of their study, although in one set of analyses (DesJardins et al., 1999b) they found on-campus employment had a significant net effect in every year.

The overall weight of evidence suggests that work-study assistance, net of student characteristics and other forms of financial aid, is positively related to persistence and degree completion. But a more definitive conclusion requires further research, and the underlying causal mechanism also needs clarification. Is the positive effect of work-study related to the reduction of students' financial burdens, to greater opportunities for student engagement in the academic and social systems of the institution, or to both?

Loans. Student loans have long been prominent features of financial aid packages. In the 1990s, however, largely because of new loan program rules in the federal 1992 Reauthorization of the Higher Education Act, federal and state financial aid policies shifted significantly away from grants toward loans. In 1980, loans made up 41 percent of financial aid disbursed from all sources. Two decades later, the percentage had jumped to 58 percent (Witkowsky, 2002). Between 1990 and 2000, total student loan volume in real dollars more than doubled from $16.4 billion to $37.5 billion. The number of students taking out loans also more than doubled, from 4.5 million to 9.4 million (see also Berkner & Bobbitt, 2000; Center for Policy Analysis, 2001; Heller, 2001). By one estimate, nearly two-thirds (64 percent) of students graduating in 1999–2000 had some debt, up from 42 percent in 1992–93, and the average amount borrowed ($16,928) had nearly doubled over the same period (King & Bannon, 2002b).

Not surprisingly, interest in the effects of this policy shift on student persistence and degree completion has increased substantially over the past decade. The evidence, however, is mixed. Several studies report (net of other factors) a negative relation between borrowing and persistence into the next semester (Paulsen & St. John, 2002; Somers, 1996b; St. John & Oescher, 1992) or into the second year (Murdock, Nix-Mayer, & Tsui, 1995; Somers, 1996a). But research on the effect of debt on graduate school enrollment suggests that, net of individual and family characteristics, high debt levels have no consistent effect on graduating seniors' intentions to pursue postbaccalaureate study (McCormick, Nunez, Shah, & Choy, 1999; Weiler, 1991). The effects, moreover, appear to be independent of race or ethnicity (Ehrenberg, 1991a; Schapiro, O'Malley, & Litten, 1991). Noting that Schapiro et al. had studied graduates of highly selective institutions, which relatively few Black undergraduates attend, Ehrenberg (1991b) found that Black students at all income levels were much less likely than Whites to have taken out college loans. He concluded that financially dependent Black students' comparative reluctance to borrow and higher debt levels for financially independent Black students might, indeed, reduce the likelihood that Black college graduates would enroll in graduate school. Questions of causality remain, however: Does debt level shape students' graduate school enrollment decisions, or are students with high debt levels who are planning to enter financially lucrative occupations more willing to take on higher debt loads (Ehrenberg, 1991a; Weiler, 1991)?

More recent studies of baccalaureate degree recipients find that after adjusting for other relevant variables, students who borrow are less likely than those who do not to pursue enrollment in graduate or professional school (Choy, 2000b; Heller, 2001). The negative effect appears to be small, however, at least in the short term. Heller estimates that borrowing leads to a 0.2 percent decrease in the odds of graduate enrollment within four years of completing a bachelor's degree, net of race, income, parental education, age, the undergraduate institution sector, and such undergraduate characteristics as major field, degree aspirations, and grade-point average. As Heller notes, however, his study (and others that show no effects related to borrowing) examined a cohort of students who were enrolled or graduated before higher loan limits were authorized by the 1992 amendments to the Higher Education Act. Thus, more recent loan policies allowing greater borrowing, as well as higher tuitions and fees, may indeed promote higher debt levels—with potentially negative effects on persistence, graduation, and students' decisions about graduate school enrollment.

More frequently, and net of other variables, loans appear to be either positively related to persistence and graduation or to have no statistically significant effect on these outcomes (Choy & Premo, 1996; Clotfelter, 1991; Cofer & Somers, 1999a; Cuccaro-Alamin & Choy, 1998; DesJardins et al., 1997; Horn & Berktold, 1998; King, 2002; St. John, 1990, 1991; St. John et al., 1991; Wei & Horn, 2002).[15] But DesJardins (DesJardins et al., 1997, DesJardins, Ahlburg, & McCall, 1999a) found that although loans had no statistically significant effect on persistence during students' early years, borrowing reduced the chances of persistence in later years (see also St. John, 1991).

The effects of borrowing may be obscured by the fact that when loans are found to have a positive (or no) influence on persistence, they are often part of an aid package that also includes grants, work, or both (Cofer, n.d.; Cofer & Somers, 1999a; King, 2002; St. John, 1991; St. John et al., 1991; Wei & Horn, 2002). St. John, Hu, and Weber (2001) found the effects of loans-only aid on persistence to be statistically nonsignificant when other student characteristics and forms of aid were controlled. Moreover, the total amount of aid packaged in multiple forms often complicates analyses of the relative importance of the parts of the package, and some evidence suggests that the effects of any given form of aid vary during the course of a student's enrollment (for example, DesJardins et al., 1997; St. John et al., 1991).

As state and state financial aid policies have increasingly relied on loans for student support, concern has arisen about debt and its related consequences as factors in persistence decisions and degree attainment (St. John, 1990, 1991). In 1999–2000, nearly two-thirds (64 percent) of graduates completed their programs with debt averaging nearly $17,000, almost double the figure eight years earlier. During this period, the proportion of seniors graduating with debt in excess of $20,000 increased from 5 percent to 33 percent, with the greatest increases among low-income students (King & Bannon, 2002b).

It is important to differentiate between "debt" and "debt load"—with the former being the absolute amount owed and the latter term representing debt relative to an individual's ability to pay (King, 2002). Using annual salaries from 1993 graduates' primary jobs as the reference point, Heller (2001) estimated that one year after graduation most groups had loan repayment ratios in excess of the 8 percent recommended by banks. Three years after graduation the average balance had dropped below the 8 percent level for all groups.

Whether debt spurs or reduces an individual's chances of persistence and graduation remains unclear. Some studies (such as DuBrock & Fenske, 2000) find a positive relation between the amount of debt and persistence. Other studies, however, find that debt tends to reduce persistence (Cofer & Somers, 1998, 1999b; Kaltenbaugh et al., 1999; Somers, Cofer, Hall, & Vander Putten, 1999). Some evidence, moreover, indicates that the effects of debt may vary across student groups, although these studies did not formally test for interaction effects (Cofer & Somers, 1999b, in press; Somers et al., 1999). Thus, any conclusion regarding the effects of debt and debt load on both short- and longer-term persistence and graduation must await replication of these findings.

Unmet need and ability to pay. A number of scholars have begun to focus on unmet need and its impact on college access, choice, and persistence. Unmet need is defined as the cost remaining after financial awards, family contributions, and student earnings are subtracted from the student's institutionally determined total budget, including tuition, fees, and related costs of enrollment (Choy & Premo, 1996). Studies estimating unmet need suggest that the gap can be substantial, ranging from about $1,200 a year for students attending public two-year and four-year institutions to nearly $5,500 for students at private, four-year institutions. The gaps are largest among low-income students (Choy, 2000a).[16] The evidence is fairly consistent (Knight, 2002, is an exception) in indicating, as might be expected, that as unmet need increases, students' chances of persisting and graduating decline (Cibik & Chambers, 1991; Hippensteel et al., 1996; Kaltenbaugh et al., 1999; Murdock et al., 1995; Paulsen & St. John, 2002; S. Porter, 2002; Somers, 1994, 1995b; St. John, 1990; St. John et al., 1994).

A related line of inquiry explores the persistence-related effects of students' "ability to pay," the label given to a composite variable that usually includes measures of such factors as students' socioeconomic status, their perceptions of their and their family's ability to finance college, and satisfaction with the cost. Cabrera and his colleagues have explored this consideration at some length (Cabrera, Castaneda, Nora, & Hengstler, 1992; Cabrera, Nora, & Castaneda, 1992; Cabrera, Nora, Castaneda, & Hengstler, 1990; Cabrera, Stampen, & Hansen, 1990; Sandler, 2000a). Net of a variety of such precollege student characteristics as background, academic achievement, and parental and peer support for attendance, as well as financial aid and measures of academic and social integration and of institutional and goal commitment levels, Cabrera et al. find that students' ability to pay appears to be positively and significantly related to persistence and educational aspirations. That influence, however, appears to be more indirect than direct, primarily as it positively affects students' academic integration and subsequent institutional commitment.

Work. Whether as part of their financial planning for college or in response to a cost-aid gap, most students seek some form of employment during college. In a nationally representative sample of more than 41,000 undergraduates at 832 institutions during the 1995–96 academic year, researchers found that 80 percent worked, and half of these students worked to help pay for their education. The students, on average, worked 25 hours a week; 26 percent worked 35 hours a week or more. Among "students who work"[17] to help pay education-related expenses and who are enrolled full-time, 19 percent *also* worked full-time (35 or more hours per week). Another 26 percent worked 21 to 34 hours weekly. Thus, nearly half (45 percent) of the full-time students who were employed worked 21 or more hours a week (Horn, 1998b; Horn & Berktold, 1998).

The research on the effects of employment on persistence and degree completion consistently indicates that the more hours students work, the more likely they are to shift from full-time to part-time enrollment and the less likely they are to persist from one year to the next or to complete a bachelor's degree program. Not surprisingly, as the number of hours worked increases, so do student reports of problems with the number of courses they can take, course scheduling, choice of courses, access to the library, and academic performance (Horn & Berktold, 1998). The negative effects of hours worked on just about any criterion measure (such as persistence to the next year, graduation, or time-to-degree) remain in national studies both with and without controls for such factors as gender, race-ethnicity, age, attendance level (new versus continuing), full-time or part-time enrollment status, income, institutional sector, job location, and receipt and types of financial aid (Astin, 1993c; Berkner et al., 1996; Bradburn, 2002; Choy, 2000a; Cuccaro-Alamin, 1997; Cuccaro-Alamin & Choy, 1998; Fitzgerald et al., 1994; Gleason, 1993; Horn, 1994, 1998a; Horn & Berktold, 1998; King, 2002; King & Bannon, 2002a; Leppel, 2002; Nora, Cabrera, Hagedorn, & Pascarella, 1996; Stage & Rushin, 1993). Single-institution and state system studies produce findings consistent with those from the national samples (Ballard, 1993; Bers & Smith, 1991; Canabal, 1995; Cofer & Somers, 2001; Daly, 1990; Fralick, 1993; Furr & Elling, 2000; Grayson, 1998b; Guiterrez-Marquez, 1994; Harding & Harmon, 1999; House, 1996a; Lam, 1999; Sanchez, Marder, Berry, & Ross, 1992; B. Smith, 1993; Windham, 1995).

Based on the evidence from a number of studies, our earlier review concluded that on-campus employment had positive net effects on year-to-year persistence, timely graduation, bachelor's degree completion, and the probability of enrollment in professional or graduate school. As noted earlier in this chapter, we found little evidence concerning the effects of work-study to suggest that our previous conclusion was wrong. Horn and Berktold (1998) and Nora et al. (1996) are exceptions. After adjusting for gender, race-ethnicity, age, income, full-time or part-time status, institutional type, receipt of financial aid, and the number of hours worked, Horn and Berktold found the adjusted persistence rates of students working on and off campus to be virtually identical. Nora et al. also found that, net of other factors, whether a student worked on or off campus had no statistically significant effect on persistence into the second year. The one exception when that relation was examined by gender and race-ethnicity was the statistically significant and negative effect of off-campus employment on persistence among minority students.

The relation between hours worked and persistence or degree completion is not linear. Previous studies have indicated that working 20 or more hours per week (particularly off campus) reduces student persistence and degree completion. But as already suggested, on-campus employment may actually enhance the chances of persistence (Pascarella & Terenzini, 1991). Other studies in the 1990s suggest that the critical point may be closer to 15 hours than to 20. Horn and Berktold (1998), for example, found that net of other factors, working 14 or fewer hours weekly had a positive effect on persistence compared with working 15 to 33 hours a week (see also Fitzgerald et al., 1994; King, 2002). The nonlinear trend, moreover, may be U-shaped: students who do *not* work are more likely to withdraw than those who work 1 to 15 hours per week (Bers & Smith, 1991; Choy, 2000a; Horn, 1994; Horn & Berktold, 1998; King, 2002). Indeed, students who do not work may be as likely to interrupt their studies as students working 16 to 34 hours a week (Horn & Berktold, 1998).

These latter findings support the proposition that employment, under certain circumstances (particularly when it is limited in duration and on campus), can enhance student progress and degree completion.

Tuition and other charges. Numerous researchers have examined the effects of tuition and related charges on student decisions about whether and where to attend college (see Heller, 1997, and Leslie & Brinkman, 1988). Only in the past decade or so, however, have the roles of tuition and "net price" (usually construed as the difference between tuition and financial aid) attracted attention in how they shape student decisions not only about whether and where to go to college but also about whether to persist once enrolled. A few studies also explore the effects on educational attainment of net price calculated to include other cost factors such as room-and-board charges.

With a few exceptions (such as Cofer & Somers, 2000) most studies (also based on national samples) find that tuition charges are inversely related to student persistence (Cofer, n.d.; Cofer & Somers, 1998, 1999a; Hippensteel et al., 1996; Kaltenbaugh, 1993; Kaltenbaugh et al., 1999; Paulsen & St. John, 1997; St. John et al., 1994; St. John & Oescher, 1992; St. John, Oescher, & Andrieu, 1992; St. John et al., 1996; St. John & Starkey, 1994, 1995a, 1995b; St. John, Starkey, Paulsen, & Mbaduagha, 1995). The influence appears to hold, moreover, even when controls are in place for such potentially confounding variables as gender, age, race-ethnicity, degree aspirations, parental income and education, grade-point average, class year, residence on campus, institutional mission and control, and various forms and amounts of financial aid.

Although not resting on formal tests for interaction or conditional effects, some evidence indicates that the impact of tuition may vary among different categories of students. For example, studies have found that, net of other factors, the negative impact of tuition on persistence decisions may be greater on students enrolled in public versus private four-year institutions (Paulsen &

St. John, 1997), minority and lower-income students (Heller, 2000; Hippensteel et al., 1996; Kaltenbaugh, 1993; St. John et al., 1996; St. John & Starkey, 1994), traditional-age students enrolled in community colleges (Heller, 2000; St. John & Starkey, 1994), continuing (versus first-time) students (Heller, 2000), and students enrolled in proprietary versus not-for-profit institutions (St. John et al., 1995). Some evidence indicates that students respond not so much to a single net price figure (tuition minus aid) as to the totality of prices and subsidies presented to them (St. John & Starkey, 1995a).

With two exceptions (Heller, 2000; St. John, 1990), all of these studies draw on National Postsecondary Student Aid Study (NPSAS) data, which are cross-sectional and come from students at all class-year levels rather than from an entering cohort. Thus, these analyses of the effects of tuition are limited to fall-to-spring semester persistence. Consequently, although the consistency of the findings is noteworthy, the studies shed little light on how tuition might shape persistence decisions from year to year or beyond. Using High School and Beyond (HS&B:80) data, St. John found not only that the net effects of different forms of aid vary across year-to-year transition points but also that tuition charges are statistically significant (and negative) predictors of persistence only in the second- to third-year transition. Heller, basing his analyses on enrollment data for public institutions in the 50 states from 1976 to 1994, concluded that for most racial groups at most levels in public institutions, responsiveness to tuition price was greater for continuing than for first-time students. Both of these studies thus raise some doubt about the extent to which the relatively consistent findings of the negative effects of tuition on persistence can be generalized.

The conceptual and policy significance of these findings lies in their clear suggestion that financial considerations may have both direct and indirect dimensions, mediating the effects of other influences and affecting perhaps the nature and extent of the opportunities students have to become engaged in the academic and social systems of their institution and, consequently, their chances for persistence and degree completion. Astin (1993c) also reports a variety of indirect effects of financial aid on persistence and degree completion. He found, for example, that aid had positive and statistically significant net effects on such factors as grade-point average, majoring in certain fields, and satisfaction with the curriculum, instruction, and faculty members—all variables that have direct effects on persistence and educational attainment. The clear theoretical and policy implication of these findings is that while financial aid by itself may not be enough to ensure persistence, it nonetheless plays an important indirect role in educational attainment by shaping the nature of students' experiences once enrolled. That role is particularly striking for students whose financial resources fall short of meeting the costs of college attendance.

The evidence also suggests a complex causal network that we are only beginning to understand. Some of the recent research on the effects of financial aid and net costs has begun to explore the role of financial issues in what is increasingly viewed as a longitudinal process that begins some years before college matriculation and continues through the college years, culminating in withdrawal or degree completion. These models attempt to trace the flow of financial influences from the formation (or lack thereof) of college aspirations and the predisposition to enroll through the college search, application, and selection process and on into the college years. They also examine how students' financial circumstances shape the nature of their levels of engagement and interactions with the college environment in ways that lead ultimately to withdrawal or program completion (Paulsen & St. John, 2002; St. John et al., 1996). As the development, refinement, and validation of such models proceed, current thinking about financial aid policies and packaging practices may change.

Interactions with Faculty Members. Research reviewed in our earlier book indicates that student contact with faculty members outside the classroom appears consistently to promote student persistence, educational aspirations, and degree completion, even when other factors are taken into account. The nature of this relation appears to be a function of at least two processes. One is the socialization of students to the normative values and attitudes of the academy. The second is the bond between student and institution that appears to be facilitated and promoted by positive interactions with faculty members as well as with peers.

We found little evidence in the literature of the 1990s to contradict our earlier conclusions about the generally positive effects of nonclassroom student-faculty interactions on educational attainment. Not all studies find the frequency of contact between students and faculty outside of class positively related to persistence (see, for example, Grayson, 1998b; Ruddock, Hanson, & Moss, 1999) but most do. Astin (1993c), even when controlling for an array of students' personal, family, and academic background characteristics, college experiences, and the characteristics of the institutions they attend, found that "student-faculty interaction has significant positive correlations with *every* academic attainment outcome: college GPA, degree attainment (beta = .16), graduating with honors (beta = .12), and enrollment in graduate or professional school (beta = .11)" (p. 383; italics in the original). Other studies report similar conclusions, whether they draw on national samples (Avalos, 1994; Kuh & Hu, 2001) or single-institution samples (Belcheir & Michener, 1997; Johnson, 1997; Milem & Berger, 1997; Mohr, Eiche, & Sedlacek, 1998; Shields, 1994).

We also noted in our earlier book that, with the general exception of small and often selective liberal arts colleges, most student-faculty contact occurs in the formal setting of the classroom. How then to explain the consistent and apparently powerful influence of faculty contacts with students outside of class on student persistence and attainment? Several studies suggest that students' *perceptions* of faculty members' availability and interest in them may be enough to promote persistence. These studies indicate that students' perceptions of faculty members' concern for student development and teaching, as well as their availability to students, have positive and statistically significant effects on persistence, even when controlling for other factors (Halpin, 1990; Johnson, 1994; Mallette & Cabrera, 1991).

Studies of more formal, nonclassroom interactions between students and faculty members provide additional evidence of the positive benefits of such contacts on student persistence and degree completion. Faculty-student mentor programs, which vary widely in structure, content, duration, and kinds of students participating, appear to have positive net effects on student persistence and degree aspirations (Anderson, Dey, Gray, & Thomas, 1995; Campbell & Campbell, 1997; Gasman, 1997; Piotrowski & Perdue, 1998; Stith, 1994).

However, the causal direction of the link between student interactions with faculty members and persistence remains ambiguous. Does student-faculty contact lead to higher degree aspirations or persistence? Or are students who have stronger degree orientations or academic motivation than their peers more likely to seek interactions with faculty members? Kuh and Hu (2001), in a study of more than 5,000 students on the campuses of 126 four-year institutions, found that students who were better prepared than their peers and who spent more time studying were also more likely to interact with faculty members. Belcheir and Michener (1997) report similar findings. These studies, however, are more suggestive than conclusive. Most of the research rests on assumptions about causal directions; far fewer studies explicitly explore them.

Interactions with Peers. Peers constitute another powerful socializing agent in shaping persistence and degree completion (Astin, 1993c; Pascarella & Terenzini, 1991). Indeed, Astin asserts that "the student's peer group is the single most potent source of influence on growth and development during the undergraduate years" (p. 398). The precise nature of the peer influence remains ambiguous, however. Astin has suggested that the influence has both psychological (or individual) and sociological (or group) dimensions. From a psychological perspective, says Astin, students seek identification and affiliation with others thought to share their beliefs and who are like them in certain important ways. From the group or sociological perspective, peer influence follows from the group's power to confer or deny membership and the group's normative influence on members through its encouragement of conformity with the group's attitudes, beliefs, and behaviors.

Our earlier review noted that, after adjusting for students' precollege characteristics and other college experiences, the research was not clear about whether peer interactions and extracurricular involvement influenced persistence decisions. The few studies published since that review are generally clear and consistent in indicating that peer influence is a statistically significant and positive force in students' persistence decisions. Bank, Slavings, and Biddle (1990) found that the influence of both parents and peers on student persistence exceeded that of faculty members. The net influence of peers is discernible whether examining four-year college students' intent to persist (Eimers & Pike, 1997), actual persistence into the second year (Bank et al., 1990) or through four or more years (Astin & Astin, 1993), or degree aspirations (McCormick, 1997a; Pascarella, Wolniak, & Pierson, 2003; Tsui, 1995). Other studies point in various ways to the importance of peers and social climate in student decisions relating to persistence, degree completion, and graduate school attendance (Bonous-Hammarth, 2000; Gloria & Robinson, 1994; Grosset, 1991a; Huang, 1995; McGrath & Braunstein, 1997; Milem & Berger, 1997; Sax, 2001; C. Steele, 1997, 1999, 2000; Walpole, 1998a, 1998b).

Bank, Slavings, and Biddle (1990) also found that normative influences (the expectations and standards of behavior held by others that shape how one acts) appear to be stronger than modeling influences (pressures to copy the behaviors of others). Both Astin and Astin (1993) and Pascarella et al. (2003) suggest that modeling may be the underlying causal mechanism. In both of these studies, a contextual peer effect—the concentration of peers in particular majors or the average educational aspirations of peers—was a significant factor. These findings are consistent with the concept of *progressive conformity* (Astin & Panos, 1969), the idea that the dominant peer group both encourages homogeneity and discourages heterogeneity. This concept appears to drive changes in students' values, beliefs, and aspirations (Astin, 1993c) and may also be valuable in explaining students' persistence intentions and behaviors. In fact, McCormick provides evidence of the net effects of such "isomorphic adaptation" on students' educational aspirations, even after taking into account their precollege educational and occupational commitments (McCormick, 1997a, pp. 15–16; see also McCormick, 1996).

A growing number of studies examine the effects on persistence and degree completion of campus racial and ethnic diversity and students' perceptions of their campus's racial climate. Racial diversity appears to be positively related to students' inclination to socialize with others from a different racial group, to discuss racial issues, to participate in awareness workshops, and to take ethnic studies courses. The extent to which faculty emphasize diversity in their teaching and research and the overall institutional orientation to diversity also positively influence student persistence (Chang, 1996). Some evidence suggests that a campus's proportional racial mix (its structural diversity) is positively related to interracial interactions and racial discussions and that it indirectly promotes persistence and degree completion (Chang, 1999a, 2001). Cabrera, Nora, Terenzini, Pascarella, and Hagedorn (1999) also found evidence that perceptions of racial discrimination and prejudice in the classroom and on campus were negatively related to continued enrollment. Both studies, however, suggest that the racial climate effects are probably modest and more likely indirect than direct, operating through their influence on students' sense of belonging and satisfaction with their college experiences and their commitment to their institutions. Other research is generally consistent with these two studies in indicating that the social environment or climate effects, although important, are probably indirect (Bennett & Okinaka, 1990; Eimers & Pike, 1996, 1997; Gloria & Robinson, 1994; Nora & Cabrera, 1996).

Of particular interest is that perceived racial climate appears to affect the behaviors of minority and nonminority students more or less equally. Although the evidence is limited in scope, it comes from methodologically sound studies. Cabrera, Nora, Terenzini, Pascarella, and Hagedorn (1999), for example, studied

410 African-American and 1,300 White students at 18 four-year college and university campuses. After controlling for a variety of students' precollege personal, family, academic background characteristics, as well as for college experiences, students' perceptions of prejudice and discrimination were significantly and negatively (albeit indirectly) related to persistence into the second year. Other studies (Fogel & Yaffee, 1992, is an exception) also find student perceptions that prejudice or discrimination exists on their campus had negative effects on both minority and nonminority student persistence and educational aspirations (Eimers & Pike, 1996, 1997; Gilliard, 1996; Nora & Cabrera, 1996; Tafalla, Rivera, & Tuchel, 1993; Zea, Reisen, Beil, & Caplan, 1997). Some evidence, however, suggests that the dimensionality of students' perceptions of prejudice and racial-ethnic discrimination may vary across ethnic groups (Cabrera & Nora, 1994).

Perceptions of racial-ethnic prejudice or tension, particularly when seen in students' peers, have statistically significant and negative net effects on minority students' transition and adjustment to college as well as on their sense of belonging and attachment to their institutions. The phenomenon appears to be racially and ethnically blind, affecting Latino students (Hurtado & Carter, 1997; Hurtado, Carter, & Spuler, 1996; Jalomo, 1995; Velasquez, 1999), African-American students (Fisher & Hartmann, 1995; Fries-Britt & Turner, 2001, 2002; Gloria, Robinson Kurpius, Hamilton, & Willson, 1999; Hinderlie & Kenny, 2002; C. Steele, 1999, 2000), and Native American students (Healy, 2001; Huffman, 1991; Montgomery, Miville, Winterowd, Heffries, & Baysden, 2000; Murguia, Padilla, & Pavel, 1991; Tate & Schwartz, 1993).

Some formal components of the peer environment appear capable of counterbalancing or compensating for the negative influences of a peer environment that is perceived as unwelcoming, or even hostile, to students of color. These elements include an integrated living-learning community (C. Steele, 1997, 1999, 2000) and ethnic-racial student organizations, groups, or theme houses; all of these environments appear to have statistically significant and positive (although weak) net effects on the adjustment and persistence of students of color (Bennett & Okinaka, 1990; Gilliard, 1996; Healy, 2001; Hurtado & Carter, 1997; Murguia et al., 1991; Padilla, Trevino, Gonzalez, & Trevino, 1997; Person & Christensen, 1996; Smith & Associates, 1997; Thompson & Fretz, 1991; Trevino, 1992).[18]

Institutional staff members also appear to have a hand in shaping students' perceptions of a campus's overall climate, particularly those of students of color. Factors in student persistence appear to include friendly and courteous administrators (Baird, 1990b); effective communication of institutional rules and expectations, fair enforcement of rules, and involvement of students in decision making (Berger & Braxton, 1998); support and encouragement from administrators (Brown & Wright, 1998); supportive residence advisers and academic counselors (Hurtado et al., 1996); and administrators who define a hospitable racial climate (Gilliard, 1996).

Residence. Our earlier review and others (Blimling, 1989, 1993, 1997; Pascarella, Terenzini, & Blimling, 1994) have pointed to the remarkably consistent evidence that students living on campus are more likely to persist and graduate than students who commute. This relationship remains positive and statistically significant even when a wide array of precollege characteristics related to persistence and educational attainment are taken into account, including precollege academic performance, socioeconomic status, educational aspirations, age, and employment status.

In our current review, we found nothing to change our conclusion on this point. With few exceptions (for example, Grayson, 1998b), researchers have found that living in an on-campus residence hall increases the likelihood of persistence and degree completion whether students' precollege characteristics are controlled or not (Astin, 1993c; Astin et al., 1996; Ballard, 1993; Canabal, 1995; Christie & Dinham, 1991; Hollings, 1992; King, 2002; Ryland et al., 1994; Thompson, Samiratedu, & Rafter, 1993; Tsui, Murdock, & Mayer, 1997; Wolfe, 1993).[19]

Studies since 1990 exploring the causal mechanisms underlying the effects of residence halls are also consistent with earlier findings that point to the capacity of residence halls to facilitate students' social (and perhaps academic) involvement with other students, with faculty members, and with their institution. Blimling's (1993) review indicates that residential students (versus commuters) participate in more extracurricular activities, report more positive perceptions of the campus social climate, tend to be more satisfied with their college experience, report more personal growth and development, and engage in more frequent interactions with peers and faculty members. The evidence both here and elsewhere (Pascarella & Terenzini, 1991) indicates that these involvements and changes have a positive influence on persistence. Berger's (1997) path-analytic study offers the most recent primary evidence confirming the influence of social involvement on persistence. He found that social integration measures had a positive indirect effect on students' intent to reenroll for the next academic year and that student peer relations and subsequent institutional commitments had statistically significant and positive net effects on students' plans to attend in the future. Three different measures of residence hall living had strong positive and direct effects on student peer relations, particularly their level of interaction. Christie and Dinham (1991) and Wolfe (1993) report findings consistent with Berger's.

The pre-1990 studies that produced the strongest evidence of both the positive influence of residence halls and their underlying dynamics focused on living-learning centers (LLCs). Although these centers varied in programmatic structure, focus, and activities, their underlying thesis was that academically rich residential settings that included faculty participation and academic and cultural programs, as well as academic advising, mentoring, and on-site classes, would be more educationally potent environments than the environments found in conventional residence halls. The LLCs presumably blurred the boundaries between students' academic and social lives, and the evidence indicated clearly and consistently that they succeeded, even after controlling precollege academic achievement, gender, socioeconomic status, degree aspirations, and similar variables (Blimling, 1993, 1997; Pascarella & Terenzini, 1991; Terenzini, Pascarella, & Blimling, 1996).

Research in the 1990s, however, presents a somewhat less compelling picture. Kanoy and Bruhn (1996), after controlling for academic achievement, and Stassen (2000), after taking into account gender, race, high school achievement, and SAT scores, both found a marginal, statistically nonsignificant advantage from living in an LLC in terms of persistence into the second year when students in an LLC were compared with students in conventional residence halls. Another study, based on a small sample and controlling only for SAT verbal scores, suggests that living in an LLC may be inversely related to persistence (Goldman & Hood, 1995). Edwards and McKelfresh (2002) found a statistically significant and positive effect of residence in an LLC but only for non-White students. Hummel (1997; see also Hummel & Steele, 1996), however, found statistically significant and substantially higher four-year graduation (or fifth-year enrollment) rates among African-American students who as first-year students lived in a University of Michigan living-learning center compared with their peers who did not. Pike, Schroeder, and Berry (1997) found that living in a residential learning community had no direct effect on persistence into the second year but that such a residence had a statistically significant and positive *indirect* effect on persistence through its promotion of student-faculty interaction.

In each of these studies, the nature of the living-learning experience appears to have been less intensive and comprehensive than the LLC experiences studied prior to 1990. The centers examined in the earlier research often consisted of a specific building where students both lived and studied. Classes met in many of these centers, faculty members kept office hours there, and a faculty member might even have lived in the center. Academic and cultural programming specifically for center residents supplemented conventional courses. More recent living-learning programs, however, may be more modest (and less expensive). The living-learning experiences studied in the 1990s were confined to only some floors in a residence hall and restricted to specific major fields, or offered less frequent and less intensive contact with faculty members, or were limited to students in the same residence taking the same set of courses, or had only somewhat more academic-oriented programming than that offered in conventional residence halls.

Learning Communities. The learning community is a recent variant on the original LLC model (Gabelnick, MacGregor, Matthews, & Smith, 1990; Shapiro & Levine, 1999). That label covers numerous variations, including freshman interest groups and linked courses, but learning communities usually involve block scheduling and registration so that a group of students (who may or may not live the same residence hall) take the same two or three courses at the same time. The courses, moreover, are often thematically or substantively linked. With few exceptions, however, the literature is largely silent on the impact of these communities on student persistence and degree completion. The evidence indicates that learning communities have statistically significant and positive net effects on student persistence into the second semester (Tinto & Russo, 1994) and into the second year (Stassen, 2003; Tinto, 1997). Indeed, the research relating to the learning conditions these communities promote is largely the same as that noted earlier to be related to persistence and graduation. Johnson, Johnson, and Smith (1998a) report the results of a meta-analysis of more than 300 studies as indicating that cooperative learning environments promote both academic and social engagement and success. According to their review, learning communities foster development of supportive peer groups, greater student involvement in classroom learning and social activities, perceptions of greater academic development, and greater integration of students' academic and nonacademic lives. Some evidence also suggests that they foster a sense of "educational citizenship"—that is, a sense of responsibility for the learning of others as well as for one's own (Tinto, 1997; Tinto & Goodsell, 1993; Tinto, Goodsell, & Russo, 1993; Tinto & Russo, 1994).[20]

Together with the evidence summarized earlier on the positive links between first-year seminar participation and persistence, studies of cooperative learning and learning communities highlight students' classroom experiences as a factor in their persistence decision making. Although limited, some research also links other classroom activities and instructor skills and behaviors to institutional commitment and persistence. The evidence includes statistically significant and positive net effects of instructor organization, preparation, skill, and clarity (Braxton, Bray, & Berger, 2000), active learning activities (Hoit & Ohland, 1998), and classroom activities in general (Strauss & Volkwein, 2001b).

Although limited in volume, the evidence on the role of classroom activities and pedagogies in the persistence process is generally consistent with the proposition that learning communities promote persistence. Astin (1993c) found faculty use of active learning strategies negatively related to persistence, but most of the evidence points in the other direction. Braxton, Milem, and Sullivan (2000), for example, found that active instructional methods had positive, direct and indirect effects on first-year students' intentions to enroll the following year. Specifically, classroom activities requiring higher-order thinking had statistically significant and positive direct and indirect net effects on institutional commitment and intent to return. The study also found that classroom discussions promoted persistence, although the effect was indirect, through their positive impact on social integration. Group activities appeared not to be a factor in students' thinking about persistence. A meta-analysis of nine studies of the effects of working in small groups in science, math, engineering, and technology courses, however, indicates a statistically significant and positive advantage in terms of course persistence for students engaged in cooperative and collaborative activities compared with their peers who were not exposed to such instructional approaches (Springer, Stanne, & Donovan, 1999).

Academic Major. Students occupy multiple environments or communities during their college years, including their academic major. In our earlier review, we concluded that the effects of academic major on persistence, graduation, and graduate or professional school enrollment remained clouded, but more recent research on this topic disperses some of the mist. With few exceptions (Astin & Astin, 1993, is one), the largest cluster of studies finds that, net of other factors, students majoring in the sciences, mathematics, and engineering (SME) and/or business and health-related professions are more likely to persist and earn bachelor's degrees than their peers with majors in the social sciences, humanities, or education (Adelman, 1998a; DesJardins, Kim, & Rzonca, 2002–03; Fenske et al., 2000; Leppel, 2001). The former group of students, however, is apt to take longer than the latter to earn the bachelor's degree.[21]

Research in the 1990s on the role of the academic major field on students' enrollment decisions has produced more consistent findings than studies done earlier, but the nature of the underlying causal mechanisms remains obscure. In 1991, we suggested possible explanations for what were then inconsistent findings. One is related to the inherent multidimensionality and complexity of the educational attainment process: the fact that academic major, like the characteristics of institutions (such as size, type, and control), were too distal from the educational process and from students' decision making to have a consistent and noticeable effect. Net of the abilities, career goals and commitments, and other characteristics that students bring with them to college, we offered evidence to support the proposition that departmental conditions, such as faculty accessibility and the frequency of student-faculty interactions, faculty supportiveness, grading practices, and peer relations, are more proximal factors in students' persistence decisions and may, indeed, be the salient factors regardless of the department or discipline.

Research published during the 1990s supports that hypothesis. Both within and across the SME disciplines, studies of persistence point to the importance of classroom climate and activities and the practices, attitudes, values, and culture in these disciplines (Seymour & Hewitt, 1997), peer relations and the number of peers in different majors (Astin & Astin, 1993; Takahira, Goodings, & Byrnes, 1998), student characteristics and aspects of the general college environment (Sax, 1996b), and satisfaction with the major and its educational climate (Hilton, Hsia, Solorzano, & Penton, 1989). In addition, the percentage of science, math, and computer science credit hours taught by women has been shown, net of other factors, to be significantly and positively related to women's persistence into the second year (Robst, Keil, & Russo, 1998; Robst, Russo, & Keil, 1996). Among minority students, affective components relating to support services such as having minority faculty role models, receiving advice and support from students more advanced in their programs, and dedicated minority relations staff appear to promote persistence (Grandy, 1998). Holland and Eisenhart (1990) interviewed 23 women, both Black and White, and surveyed 362 others in studying the higher education experiences of women who entered two institutions in the early 1980s. Their study details how differential expectations and treatment of women by others, particularly peers, and gender relations guided in large measure by physical attractiveness shaped selections of major field and future careers.

A second set of hypotheses to explain the variability of the findings relating to academic major and persistence and degree completion focuses on the strength of the linkages among the various disciplines and the societal and economic contexts of the occupations for which students are preparing. The strength of some of these linkages is discussed in this volume's chapter on economic outcomes of college (Chapter Nine). Fields having a strong positive relation to educational attainment, such as medicine, law, and college teaching, usually require attending a graduate or professional school. In fields where the relation is negative, however, such as engineering, business, and technical fields, receipt of the baccalaureate degree may be sufficient to ensure immediate access to occupational prestige and financial well-being. Indeed, such incentives may actually discourage study beyond the bachelor's degree. Astin (1993c) reports evidence supporting this hypothesis, and Jackson, Gardner, and Sullivan (1993) found extrinsic and intrinsic job considerations, including salary expectations, were more influential in the decision making of persisters than nonpersisters.

General Academic and Social Engagement. Much of the research on persistence, degree completion, and educational attainment rests on theories delineating a set of interconnected constructs and dynamics presumed to underlie enrollment behaviors and educational attainment (Bean, 1980; Bean & Metzner, 1985; Rootman, 1972; Sewell & Hauser, 1975; Spady, 1970; Tinto, 1975, 1987, 1993). Although these theories vary in the constructs and dynamics specified as salient, each portrays a series of academic and social encounters, experiences, and forces that shape persistence and attainment. The evidence reviewed to this point could be said to have focused on special cases (such as academic performance, academic major, residence, or faculty and peer interactions) of the broader, theoretical frameworks presumed to be at work. These broader constructs and processes can be portrayed generally as the notions of academic and social engagement or the extent to which students become "involved" in (Astin, 1985) or "integrated" (Tinto, 1975, 1987, 1993) into their institutions' academic and social systems.

Tinto's (1975, 1987, 1993) theory of student departure is probably the most widely used framework guiding research into the complex persistence-related interconnections among students and their college experiences. In fact, Braxton (1999) accorded Tinto's theory "near paradigmatic stature" (p. 93) after Braxton and his colleagues (Braxton, Sullivan, & Johnson, 1997) identified more than 400 citations to Tinto's model by late 1994 as well as some 170 doctoral dissertations based on it and completed by early 1995.[22] A more recent estimate puts the number of citations at 775 (Braxton & Hirschy, 2004).

In their review of the large number of studies based to varying degrees on Tinto's model, Braxton, Sullivan, and Johnson (1997) identified 15 testable propositions specified by Tinto and then evaluated the empirical evidence relevant to each. They also examined whether the evidence, which was generally based on multiple regression or structural equation modeling techniques, varied for single- versus multi-institution studies, for men versus women, and for residential versus commuter campuses. They concluded that the evidence provided only "partial support" (p. 155) for the model overall, and that was true in residential, but not commuter, settings. The evidence specific to males and females provided only "frail support" (p. 156) for the model.[23]

Our review, although not specific to tests of one or more theoretical models, leads us to conclusions generally consistent with those of Braxton and his colleagues suggesting that students' institutional commitments exert an important and positive effect in shaping their persistence decisions, both planned and actual. This effect persists even in the face of controls for the precollege demographic and academic characteristics and the initial goal and institutional commitments students bring with them to college. The phenomenon appears to be general across a variety of settings. These findings are reported in studies done on urban commuter campuses (Cabrera, Castaneda, et al., 1992; Cabrera, Nora, et al., 1992, 1993; Cabrera, Nora et al., 1990; Dietsche, 1990; Mutter, 1992; Nora & Cabrera, 1993; Okun, Ruehlman, & Karoly, 1991) as well as on residential campuses (Allen & Nora, 1995; Beil, Reisen, Zea, & Caplan, 1999; Bray, Braxton, & Sullivan, 1999; Eimers & Pike, 1997; Hatcher, Kryter, Prus, & Fitzgerald, 1992; Thomas, 2000b; Willford, 1996).

Our review's findings are also consistent with those of Braxton, Sullivan, and Johnson (1997) and Astin (1993c) in suggesting that the level of student involvement and integration in any of the components of an institution's academic and social systems can be a critical factor in students' persistence decisions. With few exceptions (such as Axelson & Torres, 1995; Borglum & Kubala, 2000; Mutter, 1992), the evidence consistently indicates that student involvement—both generally and in an array of specific academic and social areas or activities—is related in some fashion to intended or actual persistence into the next academic year.

Braxton, Sullivan, and Johnson (1997) found moderate to strong evidence that students' academic and social engagement had positive, indirect effects on persistence through their influence on students' goal and institutional commitments. These effects remain even after statistical adjustments for a variety of precollege characteristics, abilities, and motivation. Numerous studies find a statistically significant and positive net effect of various forms and measures of academic and social integration on actual or intended persistence into the next year. The link between involvement and persistence is reported in studies based on nationally representative samples (Astin, 1993c; Horn, 1998a; Leppel, 2002; Thompson, 1990; Tinto, 1998) and in single-institution studies (Eaton & Bean, 1995; Ikenberry, Arrington, & McGraw, 1994; Kelly, 1996; Molnar, 1993; Nora, Attinasi, & Matonak, 1990; B. Smith, 1993; Thomas, 2000b; Witherspoon, Long, & Chubick, 1999). Some evidence also suggests that the earlier students become involved, the better (Gerdes & Mallinckrodt, 1994), particularly African-American students (Berger & Milem, 1999).

The question remains, however, whether those effects are direct, indirect, or both. Although most of these studies employ some form of multivariate analysis that controls for precollege characteristics, most do not adopt structural modeling techniques, and few include measures of *both* academic and social engagement *and* students' postmatriculation commitment levels to their institutions. Thus, their findings may provide an incomplete reflection of the relation between academic and social engagement and persistence. A handful of studies do include measures of all three constructs, but their evidence is inconsistent. Several find statistically significant and positive direct net effects of academic and social involvement on persistence (Dietsche, 1990; Liu & Liu, 2000; Willford, 1996). Thomas (2000b) reports both direct and indirect effects of academic integration on persistence into the second year, but only an indirect effect for social integration, through its positive effects on students' intention to persist. Pike, Schroeder, and Berry (1997) found no relation, direct or indirect, between social integration and persistence.

Several other studies suggest that the engagement-persistence relation may, in fact, be indirect (usually through institutional commitment). Beil, Reisen, Zea, and Caplan (1999), for example, used logistic regression techniques to study the enrollment behaviors of 512 first-year, full-time students at a midsize, predominantly White, private research university. They found that, when institutional commitment was not included in the model, measures of both academic and social integration were statistically significant, positive net predictors of persistence over a six-semester period. When a measure of commitment was added to the model, the engagement measures ceased to be significant, suggesting their effect is more indirect than direct. Other controlled studies yielded evidence generally consistent with that of Beil et al. (Braxton, Vesper, & Hossler, 1995; Bray et al., 1999; Cabrera, Castaneda, et al., 1992; Cabrera, Nora, & Castaneda, 1992; Cabrera, Nora, & Castaneda, 1993; Cabrera, Nora, Castaneda, & Hengstler, 1990; Eimers & Pike, 1997; Nora & Cabrera, 1996).

Some evidence suggests that academic and social integration are interrelated. Braxton, Sullivan, and Johnson (1997) found consistent evidence in two studies that the two forms of engagement may reinforce one another, although the specifics remain unclear. One study found each form of integration positively and directly related to the other, but the other study found a positive academic-to-social integration effect only among men and the reverse true among women. We did not identify any additional studies on this question that have been published since Braxton and his colleagues completed their review.

Whether one form of engagement is more important than another in the persistence process appears to vary with the students and type of institution under consideration. Both academic and social integration shape students' persistence decision making in a residential setting, although the evidence from two-year institutions is ambiguous (Braxton et al., 1997).

Questions involving causal linkages clearly have theoretical relevance, but they may be of less consequence for practical or policy purposes. In the final analysis, the differences across studies may reflect methodologies more than substantive issues because these studies vary considerably in their samples, model specifications, measures, and analytical procedures. Even so, it seems clear that various forms of academic and social engagement are central elements in the persistence decision-making process.

Intercollegiate Athletics.[24] Intercollegiate athletics, particularly the revenue-producing sports of football and men's basketball, have generated substantial interest both within the academy and outside of it concerning their effects on the institutions that sponsor intercollegiate teams and on the athletes who participate (Shulman & Bowen, 2001). This interest has spawned a number of studies since the mid-1980s, when the National Collegiate Athletic Association (NCAA) began monitoring and publishing the graduation rates of athletes compared with nonathletes at all Division I-A institutions. Although more research is available now than a decade ago, most of the evidence deals with graduation rates (by sport, gender, and race-ethnicity) unadjusted for differences in the precollege characteristics of student athletes and nonathletes (see, for example, National Collegiate Athletic Association, 2001, 2002). Our earlier review identified only one study (Pascarella & Smart, 1991) that examined the effects of athletic participation on educational attainment after controlling for various precollege characteristics.

Among the few controlled studies published since, the findings are mixed. Long and Caudill (1991) used the same nationally representative Cooperative Institutional Research Program database as Pascarella and Smart (1991), although with different sampling and variable specifications. Like the earlier study, Long and Caudill found that, net of other variables, intercollegiate athletic participation increased the probability of graduation within a nine-year period for both men (by about 4 percent) and women (no estimate given). The database in both studies did not permit disaggregation of the impact on educational attainment of participation in various sports. In another study of this same generation of students, Adelman (1994), using data in NLS-72 Postsecondary Education Transcripts Study, concluded that football and basketball players completed a bachelor's degree over a 12-year period at rates only slightly lower than athletes in "minor sports" (69.3 percent versus 71.5 percent, respectively) and substantially higher than nonathletes (52.0 percent); both differences are statistically significant. Varsity sport participation appeared to be somewhat more advantageous for African-American athletes: Black (as compared to White) major sport athletes who earned bachelor's degrees were more than twice as likely to complete graduate degrees. Evidence from a national cohort in the early 1980s also found that participation in intercollegiate athletics had statistically significant net effects on first- to senior-year increases in students' motivation to earn a college degree (Ryan, 1989).

More recent findings are difficult to interpret. Using a nationally representative sample of students and controlling for their background characteristics and initial degree aspirations, Briggs (1996) found that after four years, football and basketball players had significantly lower degree aspirations and degree attainment rates than their counterparts who played other intercollegiate sports. Shulman and Bowen (2001), however, in a study of athletes and nonathletes at 30 academically selective institutions, found that both male and female athletes participating in both high-profile and minor sports graduated at rates well above the national averages for collegiate athletes and also at higher net rates than nonathletes on their campuses (although athletes in all sports earned lower grades than their classmates). Male athletes are less likely than nonathletes to earn most kinds of advanced degrees (with the exception of MBAs). Some evidence suggests intercollegiate athletes may be less likely than nonathletes to stop out during their first four years yet still less likely than the general campus population to graduate in four years (DesJardins et al., 1994, 1997).

The nature of the forces underlying student athletes' persistence decision making remains obscure, although it seems likely that multiple factors are at work, including level of involvement, personal finances, and peer influences. The time required for participation in major sports at the intercollegiate level, often thought to be a significant influence, may in fact not be a factor. Briggs (1996) found no difference between the time that football and basketball players devoted to their sports compared with that of other athletes. Shulman and Bowen (2001) concluded that male and female athletes and other students heavily engaged in *any* sort of organized activity are, in fact, more likely to graduate than their less engaged peers. Some evidence suggests that persistence decisions, at least for players in revenue-producing sports, may be negatively affected by a high level of success in the men's football or basketball program in which they participate and by professional opportunities and the promise of significant financial rewards in the National Football League or National Basketball Association. But there is also reason to believe that the economic value of the degree to be earned from their institution can promote athletes' persistence to graduation (DeBrock, Hendricks, & Loenker, 1996). This latter finding held for all model specifications, sports, and genders and suggests that, although the economic opportunities in some sports appear to affect the persistence decisions of scholarship athletes adversely, alternative, traditional labor market opportunities also matter.

Peer influences—for better or worse—offer a third possible explanation. In this view, athletes are members of small, tightly knit groups dedicated to the achievement of specific goals, athletic and otherwise, and over time the goals and values of the individual slowly shift toward those of the peer group. The few studies done provide some support for this thesis. Pascarella and Smart (1991), for example, found that athletic participation, for both White and African-American males, had modest direct effects on degree attainment but also indirect effects in terms of social involvement, which, in turn, was positively related to graduation. Both Briggs's (1996) and Shulman and Bowen's (2001) findings support this hypothesis.

CONDITIONAL EFFECTS OF COLLEGE

Conclusions from *How College Affects Students*

In our earlier volume, we introduced this portion of our chapter on educational attainment with a discussion of conditional effects and limitations on the educational attainment research as it relates to different kinds of institutions and students. That introduction—with its caveats—is worth repeating (Pascarella & Terenzini, 1991, pp. 408–409):

> A substantial amount of research has suggested the possibility that different between- and within-college experiences may have a differential influence on educational attainment for different kinds of students. This body of research, however, has at least two problems that make it difficult to synthesize and even harder to draw firm conclusions from. First, most of the research erroneously infers conditional effects from differences found between various subgroups (men versus women, Blacks versus Whites, and so on) in the factors significantly associated with educational attainment. For example, a study that found grades a statistically significant influence on persistence for Blacks but not for Whites might conclude that grades are more important in the educational attainment process for Blacks than for Whites. Unfortunately, differences in sample size and simple chance sampling errors across independent samples can produce an artificial situation in which a variable has a statistically significant association with outcomes in one subsample but not in another. More often than not such differences are due to chance, and although there are statistical procedures that help one distinguish between chance and nonchance conditional effects, they were employed in only very few of the studies.
>
> A second problem, likely caused in part by the first, is the paucity of replicable conditional effects across different studies. The interpretation of chance differences as though they are real differences will often increase the probability of this phenomenon in a body of evidence. This further complicates the task of synthesizing the findings and formulating reasonable conclusions. Given these problems and in order to make sense of the many inconsistent findings, we used relatively stringent criteria for making conclusions about the robustness of conditional effects. First, we only considered conditional effects in individual studies to be nonchance if they were tested for statistical significance, or lacking this, if the difference in the magnitude of variable associations between samples was so large (a ratio of 1:2) that it was unlikely to be a chance difference. Second, the weight of evidence criterion we have employed throughout this book implies that greatest credence is given to those conditional effects that were more rigorously tested and were replicated across independent samples. We considered conditional effects that lacked replication to be only suggestive in nature. In this way we hoped to give some semblance of order to the extensive but highly inconsistent and disparate body of evidence.

Evidence from the 1990s

Institutional Characteristics by Student Characteristics. Earlier we examined the evidence relating to differences in the prospects for bachelor's degree completion for students who initially enroll in two-year versus four-year institutions. The evidence indicated that students starting at two-year colleges are at a disadvantage in their prospects for completing a baccalaureate degree compared with similar students entering a four-year institution. The question remained, however, whether that effect is general, applying more or less equally to all students, or whether the effect of attending a two-year versus a four-year institution varies depending on the characteristics of the student.

Some clarity on that point has emerged since 1991. Several studies, using independent samples and controlling for many of the same precollege student characteristics, find that the effects on educational attainment of initially enrolling at a two-year rather than a four-year institution are similar for all students, regardless of their racial or ethnic backgrounds. The evidence is consistent whether from two nationally representative cohorts of students tracked over a six-year period (Lee et al., 1993; Swanson, 2002) or from students who entered the City University of New York in the early 1970s and were followed up over a 14-year period (Crook & Lavin, 1989). Lee et al. also found no evidence of two-year versus four-year college conditional effects on enrollment in graduate school. Some evidence suggests that the cross-racial-ethnic group equivalency of two-year and four-year entrants' degree attainment may depend to some extent on the quality of the four-year institution in which the students ultimately enroll (Eide et al., 2000).

Studies of race-ethnicity-related effects of two-year versus four-year college attendance on educational aspirations lead to the same conclusions as the research on actual degree completion. They consistently find no differential race-ethnicity-related effects of two-year versus four-year college enrollment on students' degree plans (Lee et al., 1993; Pascarella et al., 1998b; Swanson, 2002; Whitaker & Pascarella, 1994).[25]

Whether a student enrolls in a two-year or a four-year institution may have a differential effect on that individual's educational plans and attainment, depending on what those plans were when the student entered college. The evidence on whether a relation in fact exists and what its causal nature may be, however, is incomplete, even contradictory. One study (Whitaker & Pascarella, 1994) suggests that having relatively high degree aspirations initially (compared with those of other entering students) is, net of other factors, more advantageous in terms of educational attainment after 14 years for students entering a four-year rather than a two-year institution. As initial aspirational levels decline, however, so do the attainment probability advantages of attending a four-year institution. Two other controlled analyses find that initially high educational aspirations are advantageous to students regardless of what kind of institution they attend and may be particularly important to the subsequent educational goal setting and attainment of community college entrants (Crook & Lavin, 1989; Pascarella et al., 1998b).

With respect to gender-related differential effects of two-year and four-year enrollment on educational attainment, the evidence is, with one exception (Swanson, 2002), consistent in indicating that any two-year versus four-year effects are similar for both males and females. Three studies using independent samples and similar (but not identical) sets of control variables all found no statistically significant net conditional effects of two-year versus four-year college attendance on the educational aspirations or attainment of women and men (Crook & Lavin, 1989; Pascarella et al., 1998b; Whitaker & Pascarella, 1994). Swanson (2002), however, reports evidence suggesting that women's educational aspirations may decline more rapidly than men's for each month they are not enrolled in a postsecondary institution and that women experience somewhat smaller gains than men from attending a four-year college. Moreover, and again excluding Swanson, this same set of studies found no differential effects from attending a two-year versus a four-year institution on students' educational aspirations or degree completion relating to age or social origins.

Using a nationally representative sample of students entering four-year institutions, Ethington (1997) found no conditional effects on educational attainment relating to students' socioeconomic status and the type of control, expenditures, percent graduate enrollment, or selectivity of the institutions they attended.

College Experiences by Student Characteristics. The literature of the 1990s adds little to our understanding of whether, and to what extent, particular college experiences have a differential influence on persistence or educational attainment for different kinds of students. Our earlier review turned up enough evidence to support only two general conclusions, both relating to students' levels of academic and social integration. The first conclusion was that a high level of social integration may compensate for a low level of academic integration, and vice versa. The second was that levels of social and academic engagement are most important for the persistence of students who enter college with traits that put them at risk of withdrawing or who have initially low levels of commitment to their institution or to completing a bachelor's degree. We have identified no studies published since that review that replicated either of these findings.

The closest we have come to identifying a replicated conditional impact concerns the apparently positive effect of living arrangement on persistence. In one study, after the effects of gender, race-ethnicity, and academic achievement had been taken into account, minority students in a living-learning residence had a significantly higher probability of persistence into the second year than minority students living outside the center, but living in such a center offered White students no advantage over living in regular residence halls. The finding suggests that, for students of color, the activities and environment of the living-learning residence may have neutralized the negative main effect on persistence of minority group membership (Edwards & McKelfresh, 2002). Similarly, a study of the interaction of precollege academic achievement and place of residence (on versus off campus) suggests that on-campus residence may be more effective in promoting persistence among students with average or below-average predicted success than among other students (Thompson et al., 1993).

Our review uncovered other studies that identified statistically reliable conditional effects (net of various potentially confounding factors), although the experiences and characteristics of the students studied differed across studies, and thus the specific findings await replication. These studies suggest that first-year academic performance, noted earlier in this chapter as a powerful factor in all students' persistence decisions, may be particularly important for minority (versus White) students (Zea et al., 1997). Some evidence also suggests that, net of other precollege characteristics and college experiences, extracurricular and peer involvements have a more powerful positive effect on first-generation students' educational plans than they do for their peers whose parents have had some college experience or who hold a four-year degree (Pascarella, Pierson, Wolniak, &

Terenzini, 2004). This same study found other significant net conditional effects indicating that volunteer work, employment, and participation in intercollegiate athletics had a more negative impact on the educational plans of first-generation students than on the plans of students whose parents have had some college exposure. Although not a replication in any sense, these two sets of findings are consistent with those pointing to the positive effects on attainment of various forms of academic and social engagement. They also suggest, however, that not all forms of involvement are positive, nor do they affect all students equally.

Some evidence points to the potentially important contextual—and compensatory—effect on longer-term educational plans that may be fostered by the initial educational plans or aspirations of students' peers. Pascarella, Wolniak, and Pierson (2003), in a multi-institutional and nationally representative study, found that net of other factors, the average degree plans of community college students' peers at the time they entered college were positively related to all students' subsequent degree plans, but the effect was much stronger on students with initially and relatively lower degree goals than on students with higher degree aspirations.

Institutional Characteristics and College Experiences. We identified only one study that explored the possibility of the differential impact of college experiences on educational attainment for students attending different kinds of institutions. Although it awaits replication before drawing any firm conclusions, Crook and Lavin's (1989) 14-year study of students entering the City University of New York in the early 1970s yielded some interesting findings. These investigators, after controlling for a wide array of students' precollege personal, family, and academic background characteristics, found that full-time employment, although not an obstacle to degree completion for community college starters, reduced the likelihood of graduation for students who began their college careers at four-year institutions. Crook and Lavin speculate that greater stringency in standards at the senior level may make it more difficult, at least initially, for students to balance their employment and academic roles. They also found that the liberal arts curriculum in the CUNY system's community colleges functioned as a transfer track. Community college students who followed a liberal arts curriculum were 13 percentage points more likely to earn a bachelor's degree than were similar students following a vocational course of study. At the senior level, however, students following a liberal arts curriculum enjoyed no particular advantage in their prospects for graduation when compared with their peers enrolled in more professionally or occupationally oriented programs.

LONG-TERM EFFECTS OF COLLEGE

Conclusions from *How College Affects Students*

As we noted in our earlier review, "The major long-term effect of college on educational attainment is manifest largely in the intergenerational transfer of benefits from parents to children" (Pascarella & Terenzini, 1991, p. 415). Even in the face of controls for such factors as family size, parental income and occupation, and the student's academic ability and achievement, parents' educational attainment reliably and positively shapes the educational attainment of their children. Moreover, the links between educational attainment and significant other factors, such as social and occupational status, income, and various quality-of-life dimensions, are positive and consistent. It seems reasonable to suggest that mothers and fathers who have benefited socially, occupationally, economically, and personally from their college education will want the same benefits for their children. As we said: "Thus does education beget education" (p. 415).

We also noted then that research linking the college enrollment and graduation of parents to the educational attainment of their children was more limited in volume than that dealing with the effects of parents' educational attainment more broadly.

Evidence from the 1990s

A substantial body of evidence concerning intergenerational transfer emerged in the 1990s, much of it from several of the large, nationally representative, longitudinal student databases developed for the National Center for Education Statistics. These databases have facilitated a number of studies of persistence and degree completion rates of students whose parents have no postsecondary educational experience (first-generation students) contrasted with those whose parents have had some exposure to postsecondary education or who have completed a baccalaureate or higher degree.

These studies make it clear that first-generation students (compared with their non-first-generation peers) come to college with different demographic characteristics, personal experiences, educational preparation (both in terms of academic skills and high school curriculum), lower degree aspirations, more self-doubt, and less knowledge of just about every aspect of postsecondary education enrollment and life (Berkner & Chavez, 1997; Choy, 2001; Horn & Nunez, 2000; Richardson & Skinner, 1992; Terenzini, Springer, Yeager, Pascarella, & Nora, 1996; York-Anderson & Bowman, 1991). For these students, "going to college" can be a difficult choice and experience, threatening to both them and their parents (London, 1989; Rendon, 1992, 1995; Terenzini, Rendon, et al., 1994). First-generation students not only reach the college threshold at a disadvantage in terms of most criteria related to persistence and degree completion but also are shadowed by these initial disadvantages in their postsecondary educational careers. The characteristics they bring to college expose first-generation students to a different set of college experiences than those encountered by comparable non-first-generation students. The children of parents with either some college experience or a bachelor's degree benefit from their parents' ability to guide their thinking and planning for college, including discussions about college and what it is like, attending programs designed to prepare students and parents for the college selection and application process, knowledge of financial requirements and sources of aid, motivation to visit various colleges, guidance toward an appropriate high school curriculum, and encouragement and support (Choy, 2002a; Horn & Nunez, 2000; Pascarella et al., 2004; Soller, 2001; Terenzini, Springer et al., 1996).

The educational attainment–related benefits to students of having parents with some college exposure or even a bachelor's degree are clear and consistent. Four years after high school, students with a college-educated parent are nearly nine times more likely than their first-generation peers to have had some postsecondary educational experience (44 percent versus 5 percent, respectively). Similarly, and at that same point in time, students whose parents have had some college are nearly twice as likely as first-generation students to earn a bachelor's degree (21 percent versus 11 percent), and students whose parents hold a bachelor's degree or higher are nearly five times more likely themselves to earn a baccalaureate degree (50 percent versus 11 percent) (Ingels et al., 2002; see also "Parental Educational Attainment," 1999). Six years after entering postsecondary education, first-generation students (compared with their peers who have a parent with a bachelor's degree) are nearly three times more likely to have earned a certificate (18 percent versus 7 percent, respectively) and two and a half times more likely *not* to have earned a baccalaureate degree (16 percent versus 41 percent). The odds of having earned an associate degree are about the same for both groups (Berkner, He, & Cataldi, 2002, Table 2.0-C).

The positive, persistence-related effects of having parents with college experience or a college degree are felt quickly: students with a college-educated parent who begin college at a four-year institution are less than half as likely as first-generation students to withdraw from that college before their second year (10 percent versus 23 percent, respectively) (Horn, 1998a). The difference remains even after adjustments are made for college grades, delayed college enrollment, working more than 35 hours per week, level of involvement in college, financial aid, attendance status, race-ethnicity, gender, socioeconomic status, and institutional control. The disadvantage of being a first-generation student entering a community college disappears, however, when those persistence-related factors are taken into account (Choy, 2001; Horn, 1998a).

Studies using nationally representative samples consistently show that the positive influence on degree completion of having parents with college experience or degrees persists over and above the effects of race-ethnicity, family income, college qualifications, and other factors associated with educational attainment (Berkner & Chavez, 1997; Nunez & Cuccaro-Alamin, 1998). The net effect, however, is modest. Nunez and Cuccaro-Alamin, after adjusting for full-time or part-time enrollment status, age, gender, race-ethnicity, type of institution attended, and measures of students' academic and social integration, estimated that students whose parents had some college exposure (compared with first-generation college students) still had a 7 percentage point advantage after five years (69 percent versus 62 percent, respectively) in their odds of earning some type of postsecondary education credential. Warburton and his colleagues (Warburton, Bugarin, & Nunez, 2001) report adjusted estimates consistent with those of Nunez and Cuccaro-Alamin. After taking into account student background characteristics, high school academic preparation, enrollment and employment status, and academic performance in college, Warburton et al. estimated that students with a college-educated parent (versus first-generation students) beginning their college careers in a four-year institution in 1995–96 were 4–5 percentage points more likely to be enrolled at their initial institution three years later, and 7–8 percentage points more likely to be "on the persistence track"[26] to a bachelor's degree. Thus, in terms of the odds that they will earn a bachelor's degree, first-generation students enrolling in a four-year institution are at a disadvantage throughout their college careers for reasons that are independent of other personal characteristics and college experiences.

Parents' education continues to influence their children's enrollment in graduate school or a first professional degree program.[27] Even after earning a bachelor's degree, first-generation students are less likely than their peers whose parents have had more than a high school education to be planning to attend graduate or professional school (Isaac, Malaney, & Karras, 1992) or actually to enroll (Nunez & Cuccaro-Alamin, 1998). Among students who have earned a bachelor's degree, those with a parent who also holds a bachelor's, or higher, degree are one-third more likely than first-generation students to enroll in graduate school (34 percent versus 25 percent). Even after adjusting for gender, race-ethnicity, age, college GPA, amount borrowed, and institutional control, the gap remains substantial (33 percent versus 26 percent for non-first-generation and first-generation students, respectively) (Choy, 2000b, 2001).

SUMMARY

Educational attainment may not be an educational outcome in and of itself, but education clearly has a powerful influence on a student's future occupational, social, and economic status as well as on other factors that affect quality of life. For that reason, the ways in which college shapes educational attainment are worth studying. And the evidence abounds. As in our earlier book, we have examined here not only the factors and dynamics involved in earning a degree or certificate (a typical measure of educational attainment) but also student persistence and the experiences students have along the way that influence whether they complete a postsecondary credential.

Between-College Effects

Where one begins a postsecondary career continues to affect a student's educational attainment beyond such precollege student characteristics as ability, socioeconomic status, and motivation. Community college proponents and critics have debated for decades whether these institutions divert or democratize educational opportunities—and the research published since 1990 suggests both camps are right. Consistent with the pre-1990 evidence and estimates, more recent studies indicate that beginning pursuit of a bachelor's degree at a two-year rather than a four-year institution reduces the chances of ultimately earning that degree by 15 to 20 percentage points. This and other evidence support the argument that community colleges may, indeed, "cool out" students, reducing their educational aspirations and their chances of attaining a baccalaureate degree. This evidence, however, rests on comparisons with similar students entering four-year institutions.

When the duration of attendance at various postsecondary settings is considered, time spent in a community college confers advantages compared with never attending school beyond high school or enrolling in a less-than-two-year setting. Such comparisons suggest that attending community college "warms" rather than "cools" educational attainment. The deciding event appears to be whether a community college student seeking a bachelor's degree actually transfers to a four-year institution. When that bridge is crossed, and net of other factors, these students' prospects for earning a bachelor's degree are about the same as the prospects of similar students who began their postsecondary studies in four-year institutions. Some evidence even suggests that community college transfers may enroll in more selective four-year institutions than would otherwise have been available to them had they applied for direct admission.

Evidence remains mixed regarding how enrollment in a public versus private institution and the institution's size affect the odds of persisting in college or completing a bachelor's degree. When looking at institutional retention and graduation rates or student persistence and degree completion rates, private institutions appear to have an advantage over public institutions that is consistent across studies. When controls are put in place for the characteristics of the students enrolling at the two kinds of institutions, however, the differences are more muted. In some studies, the private college or university advantage even disappears. Net of differences in the students enrolled, the advantage of attending a private institution is probably indirect, mediated by such other institutional characteristics as size, selectivity, emphasis on undergraduate education, and faculty and peer relations.

The size of an institution appears to be inversely related to student persistence and degree completion, but the influence is small and indirect. More likely, size shapes students' persistence decisions through its effects on their interactions with faculty members and peers and on their academic and social involvement.

Only the evidence from studies of institutional quality approaches the consistency of the findings relating to two-year and four-year institutions. Using entering students' admissions test scores, secondary school grades, or rank in class as measures of institutional "quality," research since 1990 indicates that institutional selectivity has a statistically significant, positive, and direct effect on persistence, educational aspirations, and degree completion. That effect persists, moreover, beyond effects attributable to characteristics of entering students and to other institutional traits. Even so, the effect of institutional selectivity is small and intertwined with the kinds of experiences students have while enrolled. The causal mechanisms underlying the role that institutional quality plays in students' aspirations and persistence decision making remain obscure.

Women attending a women's college (versus a coeducational institution) and African-American students attending a predominantly Black (versus predominantly

White) institution both appear to gain modest advantages. Both women at women's colleges and African-American students at predominantly Black colleges are more likely to persist and to graduate than similar students at coed or predominantly White institutions, respectively. Women and women's colleges, moreover, appear to derive additional human capital benefits in the form of higher educational expectations, egalitarian attitudes, and occupational aspirations and status. At both women's colleges and predominantly Black institutions, the effects may be more indirect than direct, influenced by more supportive faculty and peer relations and overall educational environment.

A noteworthy theme runs through the research findings on between-college effects: except for studies of the effects of two-year versus four-year enrollment on educational attainment, the effects of various institutional characteristics, although statistically significant and independent of other factors, are usually small and most likely indirect. Their influence appears to be mediated by other factors, most notably the kinds of experiences students have during their college years.

Within-College Effects

In studies of persistence and degree completion, perhaps no other variable has attracted more attention than grade performance. Although grades in many respects are a limited measure, the research is unwavering in finding that grade performance, even when controlling other factors, is a statistically significant and positive predictor of persistence and graduation. The influence of grade performance, however, appears to vary over time, being particularly important in the first year of college.

Since our earlier review, numerous studies have examined the effects of an array of programmatic interventions on persistence and degree completion. Developmental studies and similar remedial programs appear to be at least modestly effective in helping students overcome deficiencies in precollege academic preparation and other socioeconomic disadvantages. Supplemental Instruction, which targets "historically difficult" courses rather than individual students, also appears to enhance student persistence and degree completion.

Even more researchers have examined the outcomes of first-year seminars (FYS), particularly as they relate to persistence from the first to the second year. FYS effects may be both direct and indirect, operating through the seminars' consistently positive effects on grades in other courses. It also appears that the seminars promote various forms of academic and social integration. Although controlled studies of such seminars account for a small proportion of the total research, these studies consistently find persistence-related benefits even when student abilities, motivations, and other variables are controlled.

The diverse structures, components, targeted groups, and duration of comprehensive support and retention programs make synthesizing difficult, but it appears that such efforts, in the aggregate, are consistently effective in promoting student persistence. The beneficial effects, moreover, persist in the face of statistical controls for other factors. Academic advising, counseling, and summer bridge programs all appear to be effective to varying degrees. Some evidence suggests these and related support services may be most effective in the early college years and when blended with other institutional services.

Studies of the effects of financial aid on persistence and educational attainment are also numerous but less consistent in their findings. The most consistent evidence indicates that financial aid reduces (or eliminates) economic obstacles to obtaining a postsecondary credential: aided students are as likely (or even slightly more likely) than unaided students to persist and graduate. But which *forms* of aid, and in what kinds of packages, are most effective is less clear. Grants and scholarships have a net positive effect. The evidence concerning on-campus employment and loans (depending on size) is less consistent but generally indicates that such assistance has positive effects net of other factors and types of aid. Tuition, the number of hours worked off campus (when more than 15), and unmet need (the gap between college costs and financial aid and family and student contributions) are all inversely related to persistence and graduation.

As was clear in our earlier review, interactions with the major agents of socialization (faculty members and peers) play independent and positive roles in student persistence and educational attainment, with peers more influential than faculty members, even after taking other considerations into account. Both peer interactions in general and the settings in which they are most likely to occur appear to be important. At the same time, some evidence suggests that merely the perception that faculty members are accessible and concerned about student development and success can have a positive effect. In addition, living on campus, particularly in some form of living-learning residential community, also enhances persistence and graduation (although the evidence on this question since 1990 is less compelling than earlier research).

Less-residential or nonresidential learning communities promote both academic and social integration, and thus persistence, even when other factors are controlled. The academic major field appears to affect persistence, graduation, and graduate school enrollment, with students majoring in the sciences, engineering, business, and health-related professions more likely to graduate than similar students in other majors, as was reported in the pre-1990 literature. Students in programs that promise attractive employment and financial opportunities immediately after completion of the bachelor's degree, although more likely than students in other fields to persist to graduation, are less likely to pursue graduate study. The effects of the major field appear to be less a matter of the discipline than of the attendant economic opportunities as well as the culture and climate within a department. Racial diversity and the perceived climate on a campus for students of color also appear to affect persistence decisions, with the research indicating that perceptions of prejudice or discrimination are negatively related to persistence for both students of color and their White peers.

The research is clear that participation in intercollegiate athletics has a positive and significant effect on persistence and graduation. This conclusion is true not only for the revenue-producing sports of men's football and basketball but also for less visible intercollegiate sports, for both men's and women's sports, and when controls are in place for other potentially confounding factors. As in other areas of involvement and programmatic intervention, the underlying processes remain unclear. In the case of men's varsity sports, postcollege financial considerations and the peer culture appear to be among the forces at work.

In sum, the evidence consistently indicates that academic and social involvement in whatever form (but some more than others) exert statistically significant and positive net influences on student persistence and degree completion. Involvement per se is indisputably a factor, but it is less clear whether that influence is direct or indirect (through its effects on students' institutional commitments, as a number of studies suggest) or both. Despite a large number of studies designed to test one persistence model or another, the findings are inconsistent, and the causal linkages remain obscure.

Conditional Effects of College

Since 1990, researchers have paid more attention to conditional effects on educational attainment than did scholars in the two preceding decades, but replication of findings continues to be uncommon. An important exception is the consistent finding that the effect on educational attainment of attending a two-year versus a four-year institution is unaffected by a student's race-ethnicity or gender. The absence of any effect is reported across independent samples and when controlling for most of the precollege characteristics known to affect persistence and degree completion.

Our review unearthed few other replicated conditional effects. Some evidence suggests the possibility that living on versus off campus, particularly in a living-learning center, although beneficial in terms of graduation prospects for all students, may be particularly advantageous for students of color or for students with initially low or below-average predictions of success. These and other reported conditional effects, however, are more suggestive than conclusive and await replication.

Long-Term Effects of College

A relatively recent and consistent body of evidence suggests that "education begets education." The benefits of attending college in terms of educational attainment clearly pass from one generation to the next. Students whose parents have had some exposure to postsecondary education, or who have earned a baccalaureate or higher degree, derive clear benefits in their own educational attainment compared with students whose parents have had no formal education beyond high school (first-generation students). Four years after high school, graduates whose parents had some college exposure were nearly nine times more likely than their first-generation counterparts to have some college experience themselves and also were more likely to persist into a second year of college. Students whose parents have had some exposure to college are twice as likely as first-generation students to earn a bachelor's degree and are five times more likely to earn a bachelor's degree if their parents also hold one. The advantages students with college-educated parents enjoy over their first-generation peers persist over and above the effects of race-ethnicity, college qualifications, parents' income, and other factors associated with educational attainment. In addition, parents' education continues to play a role even after students have earned bachelor's degrees. After adjusting for gender, race-ethnicity, age, college grade point average, amount borrowed, and institutional control, students whose parents have had some exposure to college have a statistically significant advantage over their first-generation counterparts in enrollment in graduate and professional school.

Notes

1. Spanard (1990) provides useful reviews of the literature on reentry, persistence, and degree completion among adult students. Kasworm (1990) also reviews relevant research on adult students. A discussion of the literature relating to persistence and degree completion among adult and nontraditional students is beyond the scope of this chapter, but interested readers may want to look at the following studies: Ashar and Skenes (1993), Busby and Jackson (1995), Chartrand (1992), Choy (2002b), Cini and Fritz (1996), Cleveland-Innes (1994), Farabaugh-Dorkins (1991), Grayson (1997b), Grosset (1991b), Lynch and Bishop-Clark (1998), Mercer (1993), Naretto (1995), Ryder, Bowman, and Newman (1994), Sandler (2000b, 2001), Torres (1994), and Villella and Hu (1991).

2. Astin, Keup, and Lindholm (2002) estimated a net increase of three percentile points (+.08 of a standard deviation) above what was expected in bachelor's degree completion rates at 177 four-year institutions from the mid-1980s to mid-1990s. They attributed this increase to efforts during that period to reform America's higher educational system.

3. The seven risk factors include (1) delayed enrollment after high school graduation, (2) not having a high school diploma, (3) enrolling on a part-time basis, (4) being financially independent, (5) working full-time while enrolled, (6) having children younger than age 18, and (7) being a single parent. See Berkner, Cuccaro-Alamin, and McCormick (1996).

4. Seventy such colleges exist in the United States and Canada, according to the Women's College Coalition Web site, as of October 2002.

5. The varying persistence periods include those extending from one semester to the next (Montmarquette, Mahseredjian, & Houle, 2001; Ryland, Riordan, & Brack, 1994), one or two years (Beil, 1990; Cabrera, Nora, & Castaneda, 1992; DesJardins, Kim, & Rzonca, 2002–2003; Eimers & Pike, 1996; Kern, Fagley, & Miller, 1994; H. Kim, 1996; Mallette & Cabrera, 1991; McGrath & Braunstein, 1997; Mukuakane-Drechsel & Hagedorn, 2000; Perry, Cabrera, & Vogt, 1997; Pike, Schroeder, & Berry, 1997; Ruddock, Hanson, & Moss, 1999; B. Smith, 1993), and four or more years (Astin & Astin, 1993; DesJardins, Ahlburg, & McCall, 2002b; DesJardins, Kim, & Rzonca, 2002–2003; Guiterrez-Marquez, 1994; Lam, 1999; Murdock, Nix-Mayer, & Tsui, 1995; Ronco, 1995; Thompson, 1990; Trippi & Cheatham, 1991; Zhao, 1999).

6. See Baird (1990b), Bradburn (2002), Brooks-Leonard (1991), Burley, Butner, and Cejda (2001), Campbell and Blakey (1995), Clagett (1996), Cofer and Somers

(2001), Dolan and Schmidt (1994), Grosset (1991a), Kraemer (1995), Romano (1995), Webb (1989), Windham (1995), and Zhao (1999).

7. See Belcheir and Michener (1997), Bradburn (2002), DesJardins, Kim, and Rzonca (2002–2003), Glenn, Rollins, and Smith (1990), Grayson (1995b), Guyot (1997), Ikenberry, Arrington, and McGraw (1994), Johnson and Molnar (1996), McGrath and Braunstein (1997), Molnar (1993, 1996), Murtaugh, Burns, and Schuster (1999), and Zea, Reisen, Beil, and Caplan (1997).

8. This regression-like technique is used to study the occurrence and timing of events. Depending on the discipline, the procedure is also known as survival analysis (medicine), failure-time analysis (engineering), or duration or hazard modeling (economics). Whereas most applications of multiple regression or logistic regression analysis (the statistical procedures most commonly used in longitudinal panel studies) examine the effects of variables as if those effects were constant or "time invariant" during the period under study, event history analysis procedures allow the effects of the independent variables to vary over time. This procedure hypothesizes that the effect of any given variable may be greater at one time than another or, indeed, not present at all at some points. DesJardins (2003), Singer and Willett (1991, 1993), and Willett and Singer (1991) provide readable discussions of event history and survival analysis. Other examples of the application of these procedures in studies of the timing and other aspects of the persistence and degree attainment processes are provided by DesJardins (1996), DesJardins and Pontiff (1999), Murtaugh, Burns, and Schuster (1999), and Ronco (1994, 1995, 1996).

9. Seminars tend to fall into one of four categories: extended orientation or "college survival" courses (the most common form, making up an estimated 62 percent of all such courses); academic seminars with uniform content across sections (17 percent); academic seminars with content selected by the instructor and variable across sections (13 percent); and basic study skills, discipline-linked seminars, or other (8 percent) (see also Barefoot, 1992; National Resource Center for the First-Year Experience and Students in Transition, 2000). A series of online papers describing the results of a national survey of first-year seminars reports on the effectiveness of the different forms for selected outcomes (www.brevard.edu/fyc/fyi/essays/index.htm). Barefoot (2002) reports results of a survey of chief academic officers at 1,000 two- and four-year institutions describing first-year policies, procedures, and programs on their campuses.

10. Murtuza and Ketkar (1995) report one such attempt.

11. Cuseo (2003) provides an extensive review of the literature relating to academic advising and direct and indirect links to student retention.

12. Heller (1997) provides a review of this literature.

13. Murdock (1990) and St. John (1991) review the pre-1990 financial aid research literature as it relates to persistence and degree completion.

14. Findings from a number of studies that use national databases to examine persistence from one semester to the next (usually during the same academic year) are consistent with those examining persistence over longer periods of time (Cofer, n.d.; Cofer & Somers, 1998, 2000; Hu & St. John, 1999, 2001; Paulsen & St. John, 1997; Somers, Cofer, Hall, & Vander Putten, 1999; St. John, Hu, & Weber, 2001; St. John & Oescher, 1992; St. John et al., 1996). Results of similar term-to-term

studies of various groups of students on individual campuses also lead to the conclusion that receipt of aid enhances persistence (Somers, 1992, 1994, 1995b, 1996b).

15. See also Cofer (n.d.), Cofer and Somers (n.d.), Lam (1999), St. John, Hu, and Weber (2001), and Williams (1992).

16. See also Advisory Committee on Student Financial Assistance (2001), Choy and Premo (1996), and "Unmet (and Overmet) Financial Need of Undergraduates" (1999).

17. U.S. Department of Education (2002) describes the persistence patterns of "employees who study."

18. Tsui (1995) reports similar findings, indicating that, net of other factors, perceived gender egalitarianism and individual participation in multicultural workshops enhance graduate degree aspirations among women.

19. Blimling (1997) estimates that students in living-learning centers are about 2 percent more likely to persist than are their peers who live in conventional residence halls. This estimate is based on a meta-analysis of five studies, only one of which was done after 1990.

20. Lenning and Ebbers (1999), Tinto (1998, 2000a, 2000b), and Tinto, Russo, and Kadel (1994) provide reviews of this evidence and discuss its implications for practice.

21. Persistence and degree completion specifically in the sciences, engineering, mathematics, and technology fields have attracted substantial attention. Although a review of this research is beyond the scope of this volume, interested readers may wish to look at Adelman (1998a), Astin and Astin (1993), Hilton, Hsia, Solorzano, and Penton (1989), Hilton, Hsia, Cheng, and Miller (1995), Huang, Taddese, and Walter (2000), and Sax (1994c), all of whom provide analyses of this topic using nationally representative data sets. Seymour and Hewitt (1997) offer a detailed qualitative study of this topic. Other references include Civian and Schley (1996), Elias and Loomis (2000), Elliott, Strenta, Adair, Matier, and Scott (1996), Felder, Felder, Mauney, Hamrin, and Dietz (1995), Jackson, Gardner, and Sullivan (1993), Rayman and Brett (1995), Schaefers and Epperson (1994), and Schaefers, Epperson, and Nauta (1997).

22. Briefly, Tinto hypothesizes that students arrive at college with personal, family, and academic attributes that influence their initial levels of commitment to a college degree and to earning that degree at the institution where they are enrolling. These initial commitments, in turn, shape the experiences and interactions students have with their peers and faculty members, the major socializing agents on the campus, thereby influencing the extent to which they become integrated into the institution's academic and social systems. These levels of academic and social integration reshape students' goal and institutional commitment levels, ultimately affecting decisions about whether to withdraw or continue enrollment. A fuller description of Tinto's model is given in Chapter Two of this volume.

23. Our own "box score" of the findings reported by Braxton, Sullivan, and Johnson (1997) leads to a somewhat more positive evaluation. In the aggregate, and using the criteria and terms applied by Braxton and his colleagues, our count shows that 10 multi-institutional studies produced "moderate" or "strong" support for the 15 propositions and that single-institution studies produced "moderate" or "strong" support for 11 of the 15 propositions (see Braxton et al., 1997, Table 1,

p. 131). Thus, we are inclined to be somewhat kinder than Braxton and his colleagues; in our judgment, the evidence provides at least "moderate" support for the propositions implied in Tinto's model.

24. We identified only two studies that examined the persistence-related effects of student participation in intramural sports or recreation: Belch, Gebel, and Maas (2001) and Bradley, Bryant, and Milborne (1994). Both report a positive relation, but only Bradley et al. controlled for possibly confounding variables.

25. Swanson (2002) reports a statistically significant, positive effect among Hispanic students associated with enrollment in progressively higher-level institutions (less-than-two-year, two-year, and four-year) but no similar effect for other racial-ethnic groups.

26. Continuous enrollment in a four-year institution—that is, with no break of more than four months.

27. Medicine, chiropractic, dentistry, optometry, osteopathic medicine, pharmacy, podiatry, veterinary medicine, law, and theology.

CHAPTER NINE

Career and Economic Impacts of College

In this chapter we summarize the accumulated evidence on the career and economic impacts of college. Overall, the labor market impacts of postsecondary education remained substantial during the decade of the 1990s, and this fact has not been lost on students about to graduate from high school. For example, of the 2.7 million American high school graduates in 1996, nearly two-thirds (65 percent) went on to some type of postsecondary education ("College Continuation Rates for Recent High School Graduates," 1997). Moreover, the reasons for attending college appear to be strongly linked to a perception that a college degree gives decided economic and career advantages. According to the 1997 survey of American college freshmen by the Higher Education Research Institute at UCLA, nearly three-fourths said that getting a better job (74.6 percent) and making more money (73.0 percent) were the most important reasons for attending college (see also Flacks & Thomas, 1997; "Is College Still Worth the Cost?" 1998). We examine these labor market or occupational attainment impacts in considerable detail, but we also look at the evidence pertaining to other dimensions of career, such as career maturity, career progression and success, and job satisfaction.

By definition, of course, a large part of the evidence on the career and economic impacts of college concerns long-term or extended impacts. Consequently, we do not include a separate section on long-term effects in this chapter. Rather, we synthesize the evidence on such effects, where appropriate, into our other five sections.

CHANGE DURING COLLEGE

Conclusions from *How College Affects Students*

A consistent body of evidence suggests that students become significantly more mature, knowledgeable, and focused during college in thinking about planning for a career. Whether this is an effect of college or simply a development that occurs coincidentally with college attendance is difficult to determine. The simple fact of having to confront one's lifework may have a substantial impact on the increased maturity found in seniors' thinking and planning for a career.

Evidence from the 1990s

The small body of evidence from the 1990s is quite consistent with our 1991 conclusion that students become more mature, knowledgeable, and focused during college in thinking about a career. For example, Luzzo (1990, 1993) sought to determine if undergraduate class standing was related to scores on a standardized measure of career maturity. Career maturity was defined as the readiness of an individual to make informed, age-appropriate career decisions and cope with appropriate developmental tasks (Savickas, 1990). Although the statistically significant relationship was not particularly strong, Luzzo found that the more advanced one's undergraduate class standing, the higher one's level of career maturity. Although they employ different measures than Luzzo, similar results have been reported by Bowman and Tinsley (1991) for vocational realism, by Poe (1991) for stability of vocational identity and need for occupational information, by Van Haveren, Winterowd, and Fuqua (1999) for career decidedness, and by Flowers (2002b) for vocational purpose, organization, and commitment. Furthermore, there is also evidence to suggest that college seniors have a more accurate perspective about labor market realities than do students in the first two years of college. Two studies indicate that seniors have significantly lower and more realistic estimates of actual starting salaries for college graduates than either freshmen (Heckert & Wallis, 1998) or sophomores (Shepperd, Oullette, & Fernandez, 1996).

Despite the consistent evidence, interpreting such differences in career maturity, career identity, and vocational–labor market realism as an impact of college is problematic. Simple maturation or, as we suggested in our previous synthesis, the increased pressure on seniors to reach closure on career decisions may be equally valid as competing explanations for the findings.

In addition to focusing on the different dimensions of career maturity or career identity, other research has examined the extent to which college students are prepared to meet workplace requirements. This work was conducted by the Collegiate Employment Research Institute at Michigan State University (Gardner, 1998). A simulation-based assessment of a real workplace situation was developed that tapped individuals' competencies in such areas as applied problem solving, interpersonal effectiveness, and accountability. The instrument was normed on a group of recent college graduates evaluated as performing above average on a common job assessment instrument. Consistent with the evidence on career maturity, college seniors tended to have the highest overall workplace readiness scores while freshmen had the lowest. Gardner reports that the class-level differences in workplace readiness scores were modest, although no standard deviations were reported on which an effect size could be estimated. Irrespective of the size of the class-level differences in workplace readiness, however, attributing the differences to the college experience itself is hazardous. Because the study is cross-sectional in design, factors such as age and mortality of the least able students from upper-division samples might also explain the class-level differences.

The Gardner (1998) study not only reports the relative standing of freshmen, sophomores, juniors, and seniors in workplace readiness but also provides an absolute estimate. As already suggested, the workplace readiness assessment produced a normed score for employed college graduates who have been evaluated as performing above average on the job. This normed score was substantially above that of the average college seniors, suggesting that, although they are more proficient than those with less exposure to college, seniors may often lack an absolute level of job skills required for above-average job performance. Corroborating evidence is suggested in an additional survey of employers who first specified the absolute skill or performance levels new graduates should be expected to meet upon entry into their jobs and then indicated the level of preparedness of college graduates they observed. Students generally appeared to be well prepared in their academic and content areas, but they fell short in areas that were related to the context of work (for example, interpersonal skills, setting priorities) and applying their knowledge in work environments (Gardner, 1998; see also Candy & Crebert, 1991; O'Brien, 1997; Van Horn, 1995).

NET EFFECTS OF COLLEGE

Conclusions from *How College Affects Students*

Attaining a bachelor's degree has important implications for the type of job one obtains and for an individual's lifetime earnings. Our best estimates were that, net of an individual's background and other confounding influences, a bachelor's degree (compared with a high school diploma) conferred about a 34 percentile point advantage in occupational status or prestige, a 20 to 40 percent advantage in earnings, and a private rate of return of between 9.3 and 10.9 percent. The occupational status advantage that accrued to college graduates was not simply a function of the first job obtained. Rather, the significant occupational status differences between high school and college graduates were sustained over the occupational life span, even when the status of one's first job is taken into account. For both occupational status and earnings, there was a credentialing effect. One received a "bonus" for completing the bachelor's degree above and beyond the increment in job status or earnings received for every year of postsecondary education.

The fact that a bachelor's degree significantly enhanced the likelihood of entering relatively high-status managerial, technical, and professional occupations has implications not only for earnings but also for occupational stability. The very nature of jobs entered by college graduates (versus high school graduates) tended to make them less sensitive to employment fluctuations that occur with changing economic conditions. This may at least partially explain why college graduates were substantially less likely than high school graduates to be unemployed. Related evidence also suggested that college-educated individuals may have additional hedges against prolonged periods of unemployment in the form of increased accuracy of occupational information and efficiency in job search, increased regional mobility to take advantage of employment opportunities, and an increased network of personal contacts, some of which date back to college days.

Even though individuals derived substantial occupational status and earnings advantages from a bachelor's degree, irrespective of their background characteristics, the causal mechanisms underlying the ability of the degree to confer these advantages were not readily apparent. On the one hand, we found evidence to support a socialization or human capital explanation. That is, college imparts cognitive skills, values, attitudes, and behavioral patterns that make individuals more productive in complex technical, professional, and managerial occupations and therefore more highly paid. On the other hand, we also found evidence supporting a screening or certification explanation. This explanation posits that a college degree serves a screening or certification function so that those without a bachelor's degree are effectively barred from entry into high-status, high-income careers. If college-educated individuals are perceived by employers as more likely than high school graduates to possess the requisite competencies and values necessary for successful adaptation to complex technical and managerial positions, they will continue to secure higher-status and better-paying jobs irrespective of whether the competencies and values were acquired in college. Our reading of the total body of evidence was that both socialization–human capital and screening-certification may be part of any causal link between postsecondary education and occupational status and earnings. Neither hypothesis alone provided a completely satisfactory explanation.

College appeared to produce conflicting influences on satisfaction with one's work. College tends to have a modest, positive influence on job satisfaction by placing individuals in jobs with relatively high intrinsic (autonomy, challenge, interest) and extrinsic (income) rewards. Yet college tends to develop a capacity for critical judgment and evaluation that may make college-educated individuals more sensitive to the shortcomings of their jobs. Similarly, the college-educated are also quite likely to have higher expectations about the intrinsic rewards of their jobs than those with less education. The latter factors can lead to dissatisfaction in situations of "overeducation," where job demands do not require a college-level education.

Evidence from the 1990s

Evidence from the 1990s on the net career and economic impacts of college differs somewhat in focus from the evidence we reviewed from our 1991 synthesis. In our present synthesis, we found substantially less evidence on such topics as occupational productivity, job satisfaction, and job success but substantially more on the economic returns to different levels of postsecondary education. In reviewing this evidence, we have had the benefit of several excellent literature reviews (for example, Boesel & Fredland, 1999; Grubb, 1998; Paulsen, 1998), which has made the locating of studies and the development of this chapter substantially easier. Still, the body of evidence is extensive. Thus, in an attempt to provide some organizing structure we present the evidence in the following categories: occupational status, workforce participation, job satisfaction-performance, earnings, credentialing effects, private rate of return, and causal mechanisms.

Occupational Status. Occupational status can be generally regarded as a hierarchy of occupations that reflects their prestige or desirability. Not surprisingly, perceived occupational prestige or desirability in the United States has an overwhelming socioeconomic basis consisting largely of education and income (Stevens & Featherman, 1981). Usually, an occupation's status, or Socio-Economic Index (SEI) score, depends on the percentage of individuals working in that occupation who have completed a certain level of formal education or higher and the percentage with incomes at a certain level or higher. Because an occupation's SEI score is a function of its educational requirements, it would seem, on first consideration, that any association between formal education and occupational status is largely tautological. This probably overstates the case, however. The link between formal education and occupational status reflects a real social phenomenon that has implications for the cognitive complexity and desirability of the work, the social position of those who engage in the work, and their children's life chances (Jencks et al., 1979; Pascarella & Terenzini, 1991).

We uncovered only a small body of studies published in the 1990s that focused on the impact of postsecondary educational attainment on occupational status. The results of this research are quite consistent with the evidence from our previous synthesis, but the data sets analyzed are somewhat dated. Two studies (Knox, Lindsay, & Kolb, 1993[1]; Lin & Vogt, 1996) analyzed the 1986 follow-up of the National Longitudinal Study of the High School Class of 1972 (NLS-72), and one study (Kerckhoff & Bell, 1998) used the 1986 follow-up of the 1980 High School and Beyond (HS&B) data. An additional study by Lavin and Hyllegard (1991) analyzed a single-institution sample of 1970–1972 graduates followed up in 1984. What the evidence from these studies suggests is this: a bachelor's degree provides occupational status advantage over a high school degree of about .95 of a standard deviation (33 percentile points); an associate degree confers an estimated occupational status advantage over a high school degree of between .24 and .44 of a standard deviation (9 to 17 percentile points); and other amounts of postsecondary education or subbaccalaureate credentials such as a vocational degree or a license-certificate provide an estimated occupational status advantage over a high school diploma of between .12 and .22 of a standard deviation (5 to 9 percentile points). All of these occupational status advantages over those conferred by a high school degree are statistically significant and persist even in the presence of statistical controls in different studies for such influences as family socioeconomic status, sex, race, high school achievement, standardized test scores, educational aspirations, and occupational aspirations.[2] Thus, although a bachelor's degree appears to confer the largest incremental advantage in occupational status compared with a high school diploma, the evidence from the 1990s suggests that various forms of subbaccalaureate postsecondary education also provide modest but statistically significant occupational status advantages.

Workforce Participation. Consistent with the conclusions from our previous synthesis, evidence from the 1990s clearly suggests that the bachelor's degree not only increases the likelihood of entering relatively high-status technical and professional occupations but also increases the likelihood of holding a job that provides relative occupational stability. Compared with high school graduates, those with a bachelor's degree are substantially more likely to participate in the labor force and are substantially less likely to be unemployed (Blau, Ferber, & Winkler, 1998; Grubb, 1998; Office of Education Research and Improvement, 1996; Paulsen, 1998; U.S. Department of Education, 1992; Veum & Weiss, 1993). For example, data from the U.S. Bureau of the Census indicated that in 1996 about 84.7 percent of all bachelor's degree holders ages 25 to 64 were employed, or participated in the workforce, whereas the corresponding rate for those with a high school diploma was 74.6 percent. Conversely, the 1996 unemployment rate for bachelor's degree holders was 2.4 percent, about half that for those with a high school degree at 4.7 percent ("Employment and Unemployment Rates by Educational Attainment," 1997).

Although they are less dramatic in magnitude, similar differences exist between high school graduates and those with subbaccalaureate degrees or credits in postsecondary education (Blau et al., 1998; Grubb, 1998; Veum & Weiss, 1993). Using the same 1996 census data, the workforce participation rates were as follows: 82.3 percent for those ages 25 to 64 with an academic associate degree, 83.9 percent for those with a vocational associate degree, 79.4 percent for those with some postsecondary education credits but no degree, and 74.6 percent for those with a high school diploma. The unemployment rates were as follows: academic associate degree, 3.2 percent; vocational associate degree, 3.3 percent; some postsecondary education credits but no degree, 4.0 percent; and high school diploma, 4.7 percent ("Employment and Unemployment Rates by Educational Attainment," 1997).

Of course, such findings do not necessarily reflect the net impact of a postsecondary degree completed or postsecondary credits taken. They may simply represent employability-related differences in the intellectual or personal characteristics of individuals with varying levels of formal education. We uncovered two studies that addressed this issue with nationally representative data. Lewis, Hearn, and Zilbert (1993) analyzed the 1986 follow-up of the High School and Beyond database to determine if postsecondary vocational training influenced participation in the labor force and number of months employed. Net of controls for such factors as race, gender, academic ability test scores, secondary school grades, socioeconomic background, and high school program, neither participation in vocational training nor completing a vocational training program significantly influenced either measure of workforce participation. Consistent findings are reported by Surette (1997) in analyses of 12 years of data (1979 to 1990) for men from the National Longitudinal Study of Youth. Net of controls for ability test scores, labor market experience, and age, the completion of subbaccalaureate vocational training had only small and nonsignificant effects on both the probability of being employed and annual hours worked. However, both the number of community college credits completed and the number of four-year college credits completed had a significant, positive effect on the probability of employment. The number of four-year college credits completed and the completion of a bachelor's degree had significant, positive effects on annual hours worked. Thus, there is a modicum of support for the hypothesis that the relationship between amount of formal postsecondary education and workforce participation is causal and not simply attributable to the characteristics of individuals who acquire different amounts of postsecondary credits or degrees.

Job Satisfaction-Performance. Although it is possible that we may have missed some studies, our literature search for the present synthesis uncovered relatively little evidence on job satisfaction and job performance. What evidence we did uncover, however, is consistent with our previous synthesis in suggesting that postsecondary education tends to produce conflicting, or at least complex, influences on satisfaction with one's work. It is clear that having a college degree increases the likelihood that one will be engaged in work that not only provides higher levels of extrinsic rewards (for example, prestige and income) but also offers greater intrinsic rewards (complexity, autonomy, managerial authority, ideational content, nonroutine tasks, and sense of control over one's work) (Grubb, 1998; Hyllegard & Lavin, 1992; Kohn, Naoi, Schoenbach, Schooler, & Slomczynski, 1990; Ross & Reskin, 1992). Indeed, net of academic ability, socioeconomic background, race, and gender, increasing one's level of postsecondary education appears to increase the importance of such intrinsic work values (Knox et al., 1993). Having a college education tends to have a positive indirect effect on job satisfaction through its impact on such factors as job prestige and earnings, job autonomy, and nonroutine work. However, net of those factors, the direct effect of having a college degree on job satisfaction tends to be negative, possibly because education functions to raise workers' expectations (Ross & Reskin, 1992). There is also evidence indicating that when college graduates hold jobs that do not generally require a college degree, such "overeducation" can have a negative effect on job satisfaction (Jenkins, 1992). This negative effect may be due in part to college graduates' higher expectations of the intrinsic characteristics or returns of work than those of their actual job (Jenkins, 1992) and in part to the negative influence of overeducation on the extrinsic rewards of work, such as earnings (Verdugo & Verdugo, 1989).

We also uncovered little research on the influence of postsecondary education on job performance. Hill (1989) surveyed nearly 190 employers in Pennsylvania to determine the effects of postsecondary education on the performance of over 500 employees in six technical occupations: computer programmers, EDP equipment operators, electrical-electronic engineering technicians, mechanical engineering technicians, drafters, and surveying technicians. In the employee sample, 32 percent had a high school degree, 17 percent had a bachelor's degree, and 51 percent had some postsecondary education. With statistical controls for the number of employees in the company and the type of industry, workers with some postsecondary education or a bachelor's degree tended to display statistically significant performance advantages—performing better when starting work and requiring a shorter training period. They were also more likely to be promoted. Although such evidence suggests that postsecondary education improves job performance, it should be cautioned that the job classifications in the Hill study often do not usually require a bachelor's or even an associate degree. Whether the same results would hold in higher-level managerial or professional positions is not clear. We uncovered little consistent evidence in our 1991 synthesis to suggest job productivity differences when college-educated and non-college-educated individuals hold the same job, although the former may have greater career mobility. Furthermore, it is difficult to attribute the findings of Hill's study to the influence of postsecondary education. Because no controls were made for employee background characteristics, the findings could just as easily be attributed to differential recruitment. Compared with their counterparts who have high school degrees, those with exposure to postsecondary education may simply possess more of the personal characteristics that contribute to effective job performance to begin with.

Earnings. Earnings in the United States are strongly related to level of formal schooling or educational attainment. In the decade of the 1990s, a series of important studies attempted to determine if that relationship is causal or simply the result of individuals with greater personal earning capabilities (for example, intellectual ability) attaining higher levels of formal schooling. This research has tended to use either samples of identical twins (Ashenfelter & Krueger, 1994; Ashenfelter & Rouse, 1998a; Rouse, 1999) or naturally occurring randomized experiments such as age at the beginning of compulsory school attendance or the military draft lottery (Angrist & Krueger, 1991, 1993). As suggested by Ashenfelter and Rouse (1998b), the synthesis of these studies is remarkably consistent; it indicates that the earnings return to formal schooling is quite likely causal and is not attributable to the omitted correlations between schooling and personal attributes such as intellectual ability. Depending on the analytical approach taken, the typical economic return to each year of formal schooling completed is an advantage (or premium) of somewhere between 5 percent (Ingram & Neuman, 1999) and 16 percent (Ashenfelter & Krueger, 1994), with an average of about 9 to 10 percent (Ashenfelter & Rouse, 1998a; Rouse, 1999). Of course, this estimate is an average based on each additional year of schooling completed. Different levels of schooling and different credentials and degrees may vary in the net earnings premium they return to the individual. A substantial body of research in the 1990s has attempted to estimate the earnings premium to different postsecondary degrees and credentials as well as to years of postsecondary education when a degree or credential is not completed.

If one considers the premium to a bachelor's degree simply as the average earnings of individuals with a bachelor's degree relative to the average earnings of those individuals with a high school degree, expressed as a percentage, then it is reasonably clear that the premium to a bachelor's degree in the United States increased during the last part of the twentieth century (Boesel & Fredland, 1999; Bound & Johnson, 1992; Freeman, 1994; Grogger & Eide, 1995; Katz & Murphy, 1992; Levy & Murnane, 1992; Murphy & Welch, 1992a; Pencavel, 1991). This increase is clearly illustrated in *Current Population Survey* data from the Census Bureau for the average annual earnings of men and women 25 and older ("Is College Still Worth the Cost?" 1998). For the five-year period of 1967 to 1971, male and female bachelor's degree holders had an average annual earnings advantage (unadjusted for inflation) of 48.5 percent over their counterparts with a high school diploma. (In other words, for this five-year period the average annual earnings of those with a bachelor's degree were 1.485 times as large as those with a high school diploma.) In contrast, for the five-year period 1992 to 1996, men and women with a bachelor's degree had an average annual earnings advantage of 79.8 percent over men and women with a high school degree. The only aberration in this steady increase over time in the college premium has been a downtrend in the 1970s, which paralleled the arrival of the baby-boomer cohorts into the U.S. labor market (Berger, 1989; Boesel & Fredland, 1999; Murphy & Welch, 1992a, 1993). Indeed, for the five-year period from 1974 to 1979, college graduates as a group were only earning 43 percent more than those with a high school diploma ("Is College Still Worth the Cost?" 1998).[3, 4]

Of course, it is doubtful that the total earnings premium associated with a bachelor's degree (versus a high school degree) is entirely attributable to college attendance. Compared with high school graduates, individuals who attend and graduate from college may simply possess more of the cognitive skills and personal attributes that lead to success and high earnings in complex managerial and technical jobs to begin with. A body of research in the 1990s has attempted to estimate the net earnings premium of a bachelor's degree (versus a high school degree) by introducing various statistical controls for differences among individuals that might confound the relationship between level of formal education and earnings (Cancio, Silva, Evans, & Maume, 1997; Gray, Huang, & Jie, 1993; Groot, Oosterbeck, & Stern, 1995; Grubb, 1995b, 1996, 1997,

1998; Hollenbeck, 1993; Kane & Rouse, 1993, 1995a, 1995b; Knox et al., 1993; Leigh & Gill, 1997; Rivera-Batiz, 1998; Surette, 1997). The data sets employed in these analyses have been the National Longitudinal Study of the High School Class of 1972 (1986 follow-up); the National Longitudinal Study of Youth (1976 through 1983 high school graduates followed up in 1989, 1990, and 1993); the 1992 National Survey of Adult Literacy; the 1985 wave of the Panel Study of Income Dynamics; and the 1984, 1987, and 1990 cohorts from the cross-sectional Survey of Income and Program Participation, which includes individuals between the ages of 25 and 64. In these analyses, statistical controls were made for important confounding variables such as race, socioeconomic background, secondary school grades, ability (as measured by standardized test scores), age, job experience, job training, marital status, and the like (depending on the data set analyzed). Taking the results from these published and unpublished studies, we estimate that the average net annual earnings premium for a bachelor's degree (versus a high school diploma) is about 37 percent for men and about 39 percent for women. The hourly wage premium is about 28 percent for men and about 35 percent for women.[5, 6] Such average estimates fall at the upper end of our 1991 estimates of a net earnings premium for a bachelor's degree of between 20 and 40 percent. This finding perhaps reflects the increase in the size of the earnings premium for a bachelor's degree in the 1980s and 1990s.[7]

One of the greatest contributions of the literature of the 1990s has been its concern not only with the economic payoff of obtaining a bachelor's degree from a four-year institution but also with estimating the net earnings premium for different levels of subbaccalaureate education. The focus of this concern has been primarily on the payoff to an associate degree from a community college, but attention has also been paid to the returns to vocational certificates and to postsecondary credits or vocational training completed without a degree or certificate. The research was largely silent with respect to the economic returns to subbaccalaureate education in our previous synthesis. Not surprisingly, much of the important evidence in this area was uncovered in the same studies, cited earlier, that estimated the net premium to a bachelor's degree with nationally representative samples (Groot et al., 1995; Grubb, 1995a, 1995b, 1996, 1997, 1998; see also Grubb, 2002, for the published version of Grubb, 1998; Hollenbeck, 1993; Kane & Rouse, 1993, 1995a, 1995b; Leigh & Gill, 1997; Rivera-Batiz, 1998; Surette, 1997). Additional evidence on the net premium to subbaccalaureate education is provided in investigations by Grubb (1992a), Kerckhoff and Bell (1998), and Lin and Vogt (1996). Evidence yielded by the total body of studies comes from analyses of the 1986 follow-up of 22- to 24-year-olds in the 1980 High School and Beyond sample; the 1992 National Survey of Adult Literacy; the 1986 follow-up of the National Longitudinal Study of the High School Class of 1972; the National Longitudinal Study of Youth (1976 through 1983 high school graduates followed up in 1989, 1990, and 1993); and the 1984, 1987, and 1990 cohorts of individuals 25 to 64 years of age from the cross-sectional Survey of Income and Program Participation. Depending on the individual study, statistical controls were introduced for such factors as race, socioeconomic origins, secondary school grades and program type, ability (as measured by standardized test scores), marital status, age, job experience, job training, and the like.

With a few exceptions, the majority of the estimates of the net economic premium attributable to an associate degree were statistically significant. Aggregating the evidence across all of the studies just mentioned, we estimate that the average net annual earnings premium for an associate degree (compared with a high school diploma) is about 17.5 percent for men and about 27 percent for women. The hourly wage premium is about 13 percent for men and 22 percent for women.[8, 9] These estimates are somewhat smaller than the typical earnings premium for an associate degree, unadjusted for confounding influences. For example, Grubb (1996) provides the mean annual earnings for individuals age 25 to 64 in the years 1984, 1987, and 1990 of the Survey of Income and Program Participation, and corresponding earnings figures for the years 1995 and 1996 are provided by the *Current Population Survey* ("Is College Still Worth the Cost?" 1998). Across all five years, men with an associate degree had an annual earnings advantage of 27 percent over men with a high school degree, whereas the corresponding advantage for women with an associate degree was 40 percent. Still, the net economic returns to an associate degree from a community or two-year college represent substantial earnings advantages over a high school diploma for both men and women (Grubb, 1998; Paulsen, 1998). Furthermore, as suggested by Leigh and Gill's (1997) analyses of the National Longitudinal Study of Youth data through the 1993 wave respondents, the positive returns to an associate degree are essentially the same size for experienced adult workers who return to school as they are for continuing high school graduates.

There is also a small body of evidence that estimates the economic returns to postsecondary certificate programs. Certificate programs, as described by Grubb (1998), are usually one year in length and focus on occupational rather than academic preparation or general education. The certificate is a common credential in vocational and proprietary schools. Although the weight of evidence suggests that they can increase earning power, particularly for women, the average net economic returns to such certificates (compared with a high school diploma) appear to be somewhat less certain, and probably smaller, than the average net returns to associate degrees. As reviewed by Grubb (1998), analyses of the 1986 follow-up of the National Longitudinal Study of the High School Class of 1972 (Hollenbeck, 1993) and the 1992 National Survey of Adult Literacy (Rivera-Batiz, 1998) found only small and statistically nonsignificant effects of certificates for both men and women. In contrast, Grubb's (1997) analyses of the 1984, 1987, and 1990 cohorts of the Survey of Income and Program Participation found statistically significant, positive earnings effects of certificates for women across all three years. The effects for men were positive and statistically significant in 1984 and 1987 but small and nonsignificant in 1990. Results generally consistent with those of Grubb (1997) are also reported by Kerckhoff and Bell (1998) and Surette (1997). Analyzing the 1986 follow-up of the 1980 High School and Beyond data, Kerckhoff and Bell found a statistically significant, positive effect of a vocational license-certificate on the hourly wages of women but not on the wages of men. Surette's analyses of men only in the National Longitudinal Study of Youth found a small but statistically significant effect for the completion of vocational training. However, as Grubb (1998) points out, this might not be the same as completing a certificate.

Finally, the 1990s have seen a concern with estimating the net economic premium (compared with a high school diploma) of having different amounts of postsecondary education without completing a degree or credential (for example, Grubb, 1995a, 1997; Hollenbeck, 1993; Kane & Rouse, 1995b; Knox et al., 1993; Leigh & Gill, 1997; Lewis et al., 1993; Rivera-Batiz, 1998; Surette, 1997). As previously described, each of these investigations analyzes national samples and introduces statistical controls for salient confounding influences. This research has been concisely reviewed by several scholars (Boesel & Fredland, 1999; Grubb, 1998; Paulsen, 1998). Their syntheses of the evidence would suggest the following generalizations. First, individuals can potentially increase their earnings in the labor market by obtaining modest amounts of postsecondary education or vocational training without obtaining a degree or certificate. However, the average economic premium appears to be less certain and smaller in magnitude than that yielded by completing an associate degree or a vocational certificate. Second, the size of the premium depends substantially on what subject matter one takes. (As we shall see in the subsequent section of this chapter on within-college effects, this second point also holds for a bachelor's and an associate degree.) Third, a year of full-time enrollment can lead to a net increase in earnings over a high school diploma of about 5 percent or more, and the payoff for completing a year of academic credits at a community college appears to be at least equal to, if not larger than, the payoff for completing the same number of credits at a four-year college. Fourth, and finally, although there appears to be a statistically significant return to taking a year's worth of credits at a community college, it is unclear that any real benefit is derived from taking small numbers of community college credits (that is, one or two courses).[10]

Credential or Program Effects. In our 1991 synthesis, we uncovered a small body of evidence suggesting that one receives an earnings "bonus" for completing the bachelor's degree above and beyond the economic return for having the equivalent of four years of college (that is, 120 credits) but not completing a bachelor's degree. The economic literature often refers to this additional earnings increment associated with completing a degree as a *sheepskin effect* or a *credentialing effect* (for example, Arkes, 1999; Belman & Heywood, 1991; Jaeger & Page, 1996). Others (for example, Grubb, 1997, 1998) use the term *program effect* to indicate that a degree represents a coherent sequence of courses in a field of study or discipline as well as a program of general education. Regardless of the descriptive term employed, the research of the 1990s not only presents substantially more evidence on the credential or program effect attributable to obtaining a bachelor's degree but also estimates the corresponding credential-program effect linked to subbaccalaureate degrees and certificates.

Estimating the credential-program effect of different postsecondary degrees and certificates has been largely the concern of economists (Arkes, 1999; Belman & Heywood, 1991; Frazis, 1993; Grubb, 1996, 1997, 1998; Heywood, 1994; Jaeger & Page, 1996; Kane & Rouse, 1995a; Surette, 1997). This body of studies analyzed data from a range of nationally representative samples. These include the 1979 and 1986 follow-ups of the National Longitudinal Study of the High School Class of 1972; the 1989, 1990, and 1993 follow-ups of the National Longitudinal Study of Youth; the 1984, 1987, and 1990 cohorts of the National Survey of Income and Program Participation; and various iterations of the *Current Population Survey.* The usual analytical approach was to regress either hourly wages or annual earnings on a prediction model that specified highest degree or certificate obtained, number of years of postsecondary education completed if no degree was obtained, and depending on the specific study, statistical controls for important confounding influences (for example, tested ability, labor market experience, socioeconomic background, and the like).

Consistent with the conclusion from our 1991 synthesis, the weight of evidence from this research suggests that the individual who completes a bachelor's degree obtains a statistically significant earnings advantage over a similar individual with the equivalent of four years of college credits but no degree. The magnitude of this earnings advantage is more difficult to determine. However, across all studies our best estimate is that men with a bachelor's degree earn, on average, about 15 percent more than men with four years of college credits but no degree. For women, the corresponding earnings advantage is about 12 percent. Although the estimates are quite variable and not as consistent as those for the bachelor's degree, the weight of evidence would also suggest the presence of statistically significant credential-program effects for the associate degree. Combining the results from all studies using national samples that provide relevant evidence (Arkes, 1999; Grubb, 1997; Jaeger & Page, 1996; Kane & Rouse, 1995a; Surette, 1997), we estimate that men who finish an associate degree earn, on average, about 9 percent more than men with the equivalent of two years of postsecondary education but no degree. For women, the corresponding earnings advantage for completing an associate degree is about 11 percent.[11] We would caution, however, that these estimates, as well as those for a bachelor's degree, are somewhat rough and may not be particularly robust.

Finally, although it is not unequivocal, there is also a modicum of evidence from nationally representative samples to suggest a credential-program effect for completion of vocational training. For example, Grubb's (1997) analyses of the 1984, 1987, and 1990 cohorts of the National Survey of Income and Program Participation found that, across all three years, women who obtained a vocational certificate had an average earnings advantage of about 10 percent over women with one year of postsecondary credits but no credential. For men, the corresponding advantage was about 10 percent in 1984 but decreased to near parity or a slight disadvantage in 1987 and 1990. In contrast, Surette's (1997) analyses of the National Longitudinal Study of Youth through 1993 found that men who completed vocational training had a statistically significant 5 percent advantage in hourly wages over men with the required postsecondary credits but no degree. Our conclusion then is that the credential-program effect of completing vocational training, although likely real, is somewhat less certain and smaller in magnitude than the credential-program effect for either the associate degree or the bachelor's degree.

Private Rate of Return. Evidence establishing the net earnings premium of postsecondary degrees provides a perspective on only one part of the economic returns picture. Premium research focuses primarily on benefits, without considering the attendant costs. Yet postsecondary education often requires a financial investment on the part of the student in the form of tuition, books, and other educational fees. Moreover, for a substantial number of students, the time they invest in postsecondary education is a time during which they forgo income, or if they work part-time during college, at least part of the income that they would have earned had they entered the labor force immediately after high school. Such forgone earnings are sometimes referred to as the *opportunity costs* of attending college. Attempts to take the full range of costs into account when estimating the economic returns to postsecondary education has spawned a line of inquiry we will refer to as private (or internal) rate of return research.

Basically, private rate of return is an attempt to estimate one's percentage return on investment. Not surprisingly, the actual computation can get pretty complicated and esoteric because a number of assumptions must be considered, such as inflation on forgone earnings (for example, Alsalam & Conley, 1995; Becker, 1992; Cooper & Cohn, 1997; Geske, 1996; Leslie, 1990; McMahon, 1991). However, a simple way to visualize at least the fundamental concept of private rate of return to a bachelor's degree is to divide the difference between average posttax earnings of bachelor's degree holders and high school graduates by the sum of the private unsubsidized costs of education plus forgone earnings. For illustrative purposes, consider the following example using fictitious numbers for simplicity. Suppose that the average annual posttax earnings of all male bachelor's degree holders in the country in 1989 was $30,000 and the corresponding average posttax earnings of male high school graduates was $22,000. Therefore, a male with a bachelor's degree could expect to earn on average during his working life $8,000 more per year ($30,000 minus $22,000) than he would earn with only a high school degree. Let us also suppose that the average total unsubsidized costs of a college education (combining private and public institutions) in 1989, plus average forgone earnings if one did not work during college, were $60,000. If postsecondary education were considered an investment, such an arrangement would be the equivalent of purchasing a promise to receive an average of $8,000 annually during one's working life at a present cost of $60,000. If we divide $8,000 by $60,000, we see that the average annual yield of investing in a bachelor's degree is 13.3 percent. This 13.3 percent would be considered the private rate of return to a college degree.[12]

In our previous synthesis, we concluded that the average private rate of return to a bachelor's degree, based on studies covering the time period from 1940 to

1982, was somewhere between 11.8 and 13.8 percent. When this was adjusted for differences in intellectual ability between high school and college graduates, the private rate of return for a bachelor's degree fell to between 9.3 and 10.9 percent. The evidence we uncovered in our present synthesis suggests that this private rate of return to a bachelor's degree has remained stable or parallel to the earnings premium for a bachelor's degree, perhaps even increased in the late 1980s and early 1990s (Arias & McMahon, 2001; Cohn & Hughes, 1994). As with our literature review for *How College Affects Students,* we have had the benefit of a number of excellent reviews of the private rate of return findings in shaping our present synthesis (for example, Alsalam & Conley, 1995; Becker, 1992; Boesel & Fredland, 1999; Cohn & Hughes, 1994; Geske, 1996; Leslie, 1990; McMahon, 1991; Paulsen, 1998). Although they differ in the literature they review, all of these syntheses provide a rather consistent estimate of the average private rate of return to a bachelor's degree at around 12 percent, with a typical range from about 9 to 16 percent.

From one perspective, these estimates may be biased upward because they usually are not corrected for ability or intelligence. However, an interesting paper by Arias and McMahon (2001) uses recent studies of identical twins to estimate the average bias to ability and measurement error at about 12 percent. Applying their adjustment, our estimate of the average private rate of return to a bachelor's degree, controlling for ability, would be about 10.6 percent.[13]

From another perspective, however, the unadjusted estimates of the private rate of return to a bachelor's degree may underestimate the true private rate of return because they do not take into account other monetary returns such as health care, retirement, stock options, and support for continuing professional development. These and related fringe benefits tend to be more substantial in the kinds of jobs held by college graduates (Boesel & Fredland, 1999; Geske, 1996). There is also the issue of forgone earnings. Because so many students work while attending college, the assumption of many private rate of return estimates that students will forgo all earnings while obtaining their bachelor's degree seems untenable (Cohn & Rhine, 1989). Indeed, in analysis of the 1985 wave of the Panel Study of Income Dynamics, Cooper and Cohn (1997) found that when they took into account, along with other factors, the average earnings of a student while attending college, the private rate of return to a bachelor's degree ranged from 12.1 to 19.3 percent.

Even if one assumes that the private rate of return is what we estimate the average to be, 12 percent, such a rate of return compares quite favorably with other investments (Boesel & Fredland, 1999; Cooper & Cohn, 1997). As Boesel and Fredland point out, returns on the stock market have typically averaged around 11 percent, but unlike private rate of return, the stock market rates are nominal returns that disregard inflation. Moreover, if one considers the option value of a bachelor's degree (for example, the option of entering graduate or professional school) as well as the nonmonetary returns (for example, health benefits, working conditions, lifelong learning, enhanced life chances for children (see Leslie, 1990; Mathios, 1989; McMahon, 1998), then a college degree continues to be a reasonably informed and prudent investment.[14, 15]

Causal Mechanisms. Although the evidence is quite clear that bachelor's and associate degrees provide substantial occupational prestige and earnings premiums to individuals who obtain them, it is not always as clear just why this is the case. Determining the causal mechanisms underlying the positive link between postsecondary education and both occupational prestige and earnings has become a favorite indoor sport of both economists and sociologists. In our 1991 synthesis, we concluded that no single causal mechanism provided a completely satisfactory explanation and that a number of processes may be at work. We uncovered little evidence in the decade of the 1990s to suggest a fundamentally different conclusion.

As suggested by Bills (2000), there are at least seven distinct theories or explanations that economists and sociologists have offered for why those with the most schooling get the most desirable and best jobs. Because a detailed discussion of these theories is beyond the scope of this book, we confine our synthesis to the evidence regarding three of the major theories: human capital, signaling-screening, and credentialing. Human capital theory suggests that college graduates have more desirable jobs and earn more than high school graduates because postsecondary education provides the former with marketable skills and abilities relevant to job performance. Signaling-screening are two complementary mechanisms in that job seekers signal and employers screen (Bills, 2000). Postsecondary education may not so much influence the cognitive and personal traits related to job productivity as simply select for individuals who have such traits to begin with. Thus, a college degree can be used by job seekers to signal desirable intellectual and personal traits, irrespective of whether those traits are acquired as the result of postsecondary education. Employers can use a college degree as a relatively inexpensive screening device to select individuals who they believe possess intellectual skills and personal traits predictive of productivity for the best jobs. Finally, credentialism posits that employers may not select or reward individuals solely on the rational basis of potential or actual productivity. Rather, the factors that influence these decisions are shaped by such things as social class, snobbery, or as suggested by Bills (2000, p. 20), "widely shared societal assumptions about the appropriate relationship between schooling and job assignment." This would mean that those with postsecondary degrees could end up being overly positioned or rewarded in the labor market for reasons unrelated to individual productivity (Jencks et al., 1979).

Although we found evidence to support each of these explanations, none seems sufficient to account unambiguously for the relationship between educational attainment and labor market rewards. For example, the most straightforward explanation is probably human capital, and the underlying premise that postsecondary education provides skills that make individuals better employees has considerable logical appeal. It seems almost axiomatic that a bachelor's degree in such fields as engineering, accounting, nursing, and speech pathology, to name a few, indicates the completion of a course of study that actually provides knowledge and skills important to effective job performance. Not inconsistent with this view are Grubb's (1996, 1997) findings for both men and women that the economic returns to bachelor's and associate degrees tend to be more pronounced when one's academic major is closely related to one's job than when it is unrelated. Similar results are reported for two national samples of bachelor's degree recipients by Tsapogas, Cahalan, and Stowe (1994) and for graduates of single institutions by Callaway, Fuller, and Schoenberger (1996), Dutt (1997), and Fuller and Schoenberger (1991). Presumably, if the skills one acquires in one's program of study are applicable to the job requirements, the economic returns increase—a result generally compatible with human capital theory. However, as Grubb points out, this may also be explained by the fact that the academic majors that are linked to the highest economic returns are also the ones most likely to lead to related employment (for example, engineering, business, health).

Whether evidence suggesting a strong relationship between educational attainment and labor market success is simply the result of increasing one's human capital is nearly impossible to verify in the evidence we reviewed. For example, in their analyses of the 1986 follow-up of the National Longitudinal Study of the High School Class of 1972, Knox, Lindsay, and Kolb (1993) found an almost monotonic, positive relationship between amount of formal postsecondary education completed and both occupational status and earnings, even after controls were introduced for ability test scores, race, gender, and socioeconomic status. Similar findings are reported for earnings by Arkes (1999) in analyses of the 1993 wave of the National Longitudinal Study of Youth. One could reasonably view such findings through the lens of a human capital perspective and conclude that, net of ability, the greater one's acquisition of high-level knowledge and skills, as indicated by amount of exposure to postsecondary education, the greater one's returns in the labor market. Yet such evidence may merely suggest that years of postsecondary education or degrees signal important personal skills or attributes that employers value because they predict job productivity. For example, Arkes (1999) concluded that a bachelor's degree signals intellectual ability to employers. However, it was also the case that bachelor's and associate degrees provided an earnings premium above and beyond intellectual ability and the equivalent numbers of credit hours required. This suggests that these degrees may signal personal attributes to employers that they value as predictors of job productivity other than ability (for example, ambition, motivation, persistence).

Other evidence reported by Grubb (1993) is purported to support the screening-signaling hypothesis, at least in part. Grubb reasoned that if degrees signaled ability or other desirable traits to employers, then they would leave a stronger impact on earnings in salaried occupations, which are presumably screened, than on the earnings of those who were self-employed. Using the 1986 follow-up of the National Longitudinal Study of the High School Class of 1972, and controlling for such factors as ability, job experience, socioeconomic status, and high school grades, Grubb found mixed support for his hypothesis. Vocational associate degrees counted more in salaried (screened) than in self-employed (unscreened) positions, whereas generally the reverse was true for the bachelor's degree. Grubb concluded that the labor market for subbaccalaureate credentials works differently than it does for bachelor's degrees. Such a finding further underscores the difficulty one has in uncovering a single, or perhaps even a predominant, explanation for the education-earnings relationship.

Evidence supporting a credentialing explanation for the fact that the more highly educated have the most desirable and best-paying jobs rests largely on the evidence we reviewed in the previous section of this chapter on credential or program effects. As we saw in that section, the weight of evidence was reasonably clear that individuals receive an earnings bonus for completing a bachelor's or associate degree above and beyond the economic return of having the equivalent years of college (four or two, respectively) but not completing the degree. It is highly questionable that the final year of postsecondary education leading to either the bachelor's or the associate degree actually enhances individual productivity at a higher rate than the preceding years. Thus, through a credentialing lens, degrees may function as socially sanctioned gatekeepers by which those who have them gain easier access to higher-paying jobs and career paths than those who do not for reasons not necessarily related to productivity. Put another way, postsecondary degrees are less about conferring labor market skills, or signaling ability, than they are about conferring status that can be used in American society to gain entry into the most prestigious and rewarding occupations.

Of course, the earnings bonus or boost associated with completion of postsecondary degrees does not necessarily lead to the credentialing explanation. Completing a degree might signal personal traits such as perseverance or focus that are important to employers because they predict job productivity. Moreover, a degree may represent completion of a coherent, integrated program of study that is more predictive of job-relevant skills than simply completing an equivalent number of postsecondary credit hours.

What seems evident is that the causal mechanisms underlying the relationship between educational attainment and both occupational positioning and earnings are complex. They may function differently and with varying degrees of importance, in different career paths, at different times in one's career, in different jobs or labor market sectors, and with changes in the economy and the nature of work. It may be fruitless to search for a single, dominant explanation. Furthermore, the increased importance of computers and information technology—and how they influence fundamental notions of work and career— may be an additional wild card that shapes broad-based societal perceptions of competence and competitiveness in the labor market (Bassi, 1999).

A Final Word. In this section, we have attempted to summarize the evidence on the net effects of college on career and economic returns. Our estimates are based on the average returns that accrue to an individual, irrespective of the type of postsecondary institution attended or one's academic and nonacademic experiences once there (that is, major field of study, grades, extracurricular involvement, and the like). Consequently, they potentially mask variations in between-college and within-college effects. We turn to these in the next two sections of the chapter, starting with between-college effects.

BETWEEN-COLLEGE EFFECTS

Conclusions from *How College Affects Students*

The most investigated of all institutional characteristics was that of institutional quality, typically assessed in terms of student body selectivity (for example, average ACT or SAT score of entering students) or reputational and prestige indexes. Compared with other institutions, elite or selective institutions tend to enroll students with high occupational status aspirations to begin with, and their impact appears to be one of maintaining or perhaps slightly accentuating the status level or academic career orientation of initial choice. This net impact on career choice is quite small compared with that attributable to career choice at the beginning of college. It may be particularly true of students attending selective or prestigious institutions that the undergraduate experience is used more to implement than to choose a career.

Our earlier review found that attendance at a selective college modestly increases the likelihood that women will choose sex-atypical (male-dominated) majors and careers and that they will enter sex-atypical occupations. It also appeared that a degree from an elite institution confers a slight advantage in various dimensions of career mobility and success (for example, technical or supervisor responsibility, level of managerial attainment). However, with the possible exception that college selectivity may have more positive implications for attainment in the professions than in managerial or business occupations, the weight of evidence indicated that attending a selective or prestigious institution has little net impact on overall job status, job productivity, or job satisfaction.

Net of other factors, college quality (and particularly selectivity) has a small, positive, direct effect on earnings. The best estimate of the magnitude of this effect is that quality indexes account for between 1 and 1.5 percent of the variance in individual earnings above and beyond other factors. There was some evidence that this effect is nonlinear; only those colleges at the very top of the distribution of selectivity or academic reputation may significantly enhance earnings. Estimates of direct effects may underestimate the total positive impact of institutional quality measures on earnings. Institutional quality may also have a positive effect on earnings by enhancing educational attainment and attendance at prestigious professional schools. We concluded that the evidence is more supportive of a screening (as opposed to a human capital) explanation for the apparent impact of college quality on earnings.

Comparison of two-year and four-year institutions produced the most pronounced and consistent between-college effects on occupational status. Net of other factors, students who begin the postsecondary education experience in two-year colleges have significantly lower job status than those who start at four-year institutions. Most of this difference, however, appeared to be attributable to the adverse impact of two-year institutions on educational attainment. For individuals of equal educational attainment, whether they start at two-year or four-year institutions makes little difference in early occupational status, employment stability, or job satisfaction. Similarly, when individuals of equal background traits and educational attainment are compared, any direct earnings penalties for attending a two-year college are quite small early in the career, though they may increase slightly with longer work experience. It is likely, however, that initial attendance at a two-year college may have a discernible, negative indirect effect on earnings due in large measure to its inhibiting influence on educational attainment.

Although currently they are a nearly extinct institutional type, there was evidence in our previous synthesis indicating that men's colleges have independently enhanced male career choice and attainment in such areas as business, law, and the professions in general. Substantially more research, however, focused on the impact of women's (versus coeducational) institutions. The weight of evidence suggested that attending a women's institution rather than a coeducational one has little or no independent impact on a woman's career salience (interest in or commitment to a career), the status or prestige level of the job she obtains, her earnings, or the likelihood of her actually entering a sex-atypical career (globally defined according to the percentage of men in the field). That said, however, women's institutions appeared to enhance orientation toward a sex-atypical occupation during college, entrance in certain *specific* sex-atypical occupations (such as medicine and scientific research), and prominence or achievement in a specific occupational status level.

Net of other factors, attending a predominantly Black institution rather than a predominantly White institution appeared to have only a trivial impact on the occupational status of Black men or Black students generally. However, some evidence suggested that attendance at a Black college may enhance the early job status of Black women. There was little consistent evidence to suggest that college racial composition had a statistically significant net impact on the earnings of Black men or women.

Attending a large institution appeared to have a small, positive influence on occupational status and earnings independent of student background characteristics and the selectivity of the student body. There was parallel evidence to suggest that major research universities, most of which are large, also positively influence earnings, but it was difficult to separate this effect from institutional quality.

Institutional control appeared to have little consistent impact on career choice, occupational status, or women's entry into sex-atypical careers. However, public control appeared to enhance the likelihood of successfully implementing career plans for becoming an engineer or college teacher while reducing the likelihood of successfully implementing plans for law, business, medicine, or nursing. The major influence of liberal arts colleges may be in their enhancing of women's choice of sex-atypical majors and careers, although the evidence supporting this conclusion was not particularly strong. Net of other factors, attending a liberal arts college appeared to have little or no impact on occupational status.

The most consistent college environmental impact on career choice appeared to be that of *progressive conformity*. Progressive conformity hypothesizes that student career choice will be influenced in the direction of the dominant peer groups in an institution. A small amount of evidence indicates that irrespective of initial career choice, seniors tend to be planning careers consistent with the most typical academic majors in their institution. There is also evidence, though less of it, to suggest that independent of initial career choice, a student's likelihood of actually working in a particular occupation increases with the percentage of majors at his or her college corresponding to that occupation.

There was modest support for the expectation that transfer between four-year institutions has negative consequences for both early career occupational status and earnings. Most of this negative effect is indirect through the inhibiting influence of transfer on educational attainment.

Considering only four-year institutions, the weight of evidence suggested that any statistically significant between-college effects are quite modest in magnitude. This is particularly the case when compared with the general net effects of attending rather than not attending college.

Evidence from the 1990s

We uncovered a substantial body of studies conducted during the decade of the 1990s that focused on between-college impacts on career and economic returns. Much of this research is uneven in terms of methodological rigor, and perhaps in part because of these methodological problems it is difficult to find evidence consistent enough to permit unequivocal conclusions. Even in those areas where the evidence is relatively strong (for example, the impact of college selectivity on earnings), there are alternative findings or explanations that tend to muddy the waters. The same fundamental methodological problem that accompanies any estimate of between-college effects is particularly relevant in determining the between-college effects on career. Specifically, there is great variability in the cognitive abilities, socioeconomic backgrounds, career aspirations, and ambitions of students attending different kinds of postsecondary institutions (for example, Behrman, Kletzer, McPherson, & Schapiro, 1995; Behrman, Rosenzweig, & Taubman, 1994; Lewis & Kingston, 1989; Lillard & Gerner, 1999; Sazama, 1994). Furthermore, such individual student characteristics are likely to play a major role in different dimensions of career choice and success. For example, a number of economists have noted that the economic returns to cognitive skills (that is, the correlation between scores on standardized cognitive tests and earnings) has increased over the past several decades (for example, Hoxby & Long, 1999; Murnane, Willett, Duhaldeborde, & Tyler, 1998; Murnane, Willett, & Levy, 1995; Neal & Johnson, 1994). Similarly, one of the strongest predictors of eventual occupational attainment (for example, occupational status) is occupational aspirations or ambition when entering college (for example, Inoue & Ethington, 1997; Kingston & Smart, 1990; Stoecker & Pascarella, 1991; Whitaker & Pascarella, 1994). Consequently, the relationship between the type of college attended (selective versus nonselective) and any particular career outcome (earnings) is likely to be substantially confounded by differences in the career-salient characteristics of the students who attend different kinds of colleges.

Estimating between-college effects on career and economic returns is also complicated by other factors. For example, postsecondary institutions not only differ dramatically in the kinds of students they recruit and enroll but may also differ dramatically in what it costs the individual to attend them (Choy, 1999). For example, Morganthau and Nayyar (1996) point out that the average cost of attending an elite private college (an Ivy League, or similar, school) is about $1,000 a week, whereas the average cost of attending a public university is about one-fourth of that, or about $250 a week. Moreover, it is clearly the case that many measures of institutional "quality" (such as selectivity, academic reputation, prestige) are confounded by whether or not the institution is private. Even though the real costs of attending college may be less because of widespread financial aid in the form of student aid, grants, fellowships, tuition waivers, and the like, these differences in costs are still substantial and undoubtedly need to be taken into account when estimating the earnings' returns accruing to the graduates of different kinds of colleges.

A second factor is major field of study. As we will see in the section on within-college effects in this chapter, a student's major field of study is, unsurprisingly, a major determinant of his or her eventual occupation and earnings. However, it is evident that different types of colleges offer their students different kinds of academic majors. For example, as pointed out by Jacobs (1999), more selective, prestigious, private institutions tend to focus on academic fields of study that lead to more lucrative jobs (for example, engineering, business, science). Conversely, because of their state-oriented mission, less selective, public institutions may be expected, if not required, to offer academic majors that lead to less lucrative occupational paths (for example, education, social work, home economics). Thus, if academic field of study is not taken into account, it may be easy to attribute the earnings or occupational status differences of graduates to an institutional effect when it is really the result of one's major field of study.

Finally, the estimation of between-college effects on career and economic returns is also complicated by the fact that a substantial number of students in the American postsecondary system attend more than one college or university before earning their bachelor's degree (Adelman, 1998a). However, as opposed to such outcomes as learning, cognitive development, and values and attitudes, between-college impacts on career and economic returns do not necessarily assume a human capital or socialization influence (that is, that some colleges provide a higher-quality education than others). Rather, the impact of where one attends college may, in fact, simply reflect the extent to which completing a bachelor's degree from that particular institution signals personal traits that employers value as predictive of job performance or productivity, irrespective of where they were acquired (for example, high intelligence, ambition, social skills, and the like).

These considerations clearly make the estimation of between-college effects on career and economic returns complex and fraught with ambiguities. Nevertheless, we have attempted to synthesize this body of evidence into the following general categories: institutional quality, institutional control, Carnegie classification, institutional size, institutional racial composition, institutional gender composition, two-year versus four-year colleges, and impact of peers.

Institutional Quality. Research estimating the net impacts of institutional quality constituted at least 50 percent of the total body evidence we uncovered pertaining to between-college effects on career and economic returns. Not surprisingly, different studies operationally defined institutional quality in different ways. Included were such dimensions as academic expenditures per student, faculty-student ratio, percentage of faculty with Ph.Ds, tuition costs, reputational ratings, average faculty salaries, and selectivity (usually based on the average ACT or SAT scores of entering freshmen). An obvious problem, of course, is that all these various dimensions of institutional quality tend to be substantially and positively intercorrelated. For example, the most academically selective institutions tend also to have the highest reputational ratings, the highest faculty salaries, the highest expenditures per student, and because they also tend to be private, the highest tuition costs. As a result, and because of the vagaries of multiple regression procedures when the predictors are highly correlated, determining which quality dimensions are having the strongest impact is frequently problematic. Some researchers have dealt with this problem by creating a composite measure of institutional quality that combines several of the preceding dimensions. Most, however, have employed institutional selectivity (for example, the average ACT or SAT score of incoming students) as a single proxy measure for institutional quality. The research on the impact of institutional quality has focused on career choice, occupational status, career mobility and success, and earnings.

Career choice. What little evidence we uncovered suggests that institutional quality measures have only a mixed impact on students' career choices during college. For example, Cole, Barber, Bolyard, and Linders (1999) focused on the career choices of high-achieving arts and sciences majors (grade point averages of 2.8 or above) at 34 institutions: 8 Ivy League schools, 13 liberal arts colleges, 9 large state universities, and 4 historically Black colleges. Statistical controls were introduced for an extensive set of potential confounding influences such as race, specific freshman career interest, academic ability, college grades, interaction with faculty, influence of work experience, and the like. In the presence of such controls, attending an Ivy League institution (versus all others) had no significant impact on choosing law, medicine, or college teaching as a career. Attending an Ivy League school did modestly, but significantly, increase the likelihood that one would choose business as a career. However, this increase was essentially attributable to differences in senior-year business career choice between students at Ivy League schools and seniors at large public universities. In all four career choices (law, medicine, business, and college teaching), initial interest in a career as a freshman was, by far, the strongest predictor of senior career choice.

Tusin (1991) analyzed the 1971 to 1980 Cooperative Institutional Research Program data to determine why women choose elementary and secondary school teaching as a career. Net of a battery of potential confounding influences, including freshman-year career choice, institutional selectivity had a modest but statistically significant, negative influence on choosing elementary or secondary school teaching as a career. Such a finding may reflect the influence of faculty and peer cultures at selective institutions in shaping a student's career aspirations and choice. The normative press of the culture at selective, elite institutions may function to steer student aspirations toward career choices that are perceived as more lucrative and prestigious than teaching in elementary or secondary schools. At the same time, the effect could just as easily be attributable to the fact that more selective colleges and universities, particularly if they are private, are substantially less likely to offer education and teacher preparation as a major field of study.

Occupational status. Consistent with conclusions from our 1991 synthesis, we found little evidence to suggest that measures of institutional quality have more than a trivial and statistically nonsignificant, direct impact on overall occupational status. Analyzing the 1986 follow-up of the National Longitudinal Study of the High School Class of 1972, Knox, Lindsay, and Kolb (1993) introduced statistical controls for such factors as tested academic ability, race, gender, socioeconomic background, college grades, major field of study, educational attainment, and the like. In the presence of these controls, the selectivity of the institution attended had a small and nonsignificant effect on the occupational status of the job one held in 1986. Remarkably consistent results are reported by Avalos (1996), analyzing the 1994 follow-up of the Cooperative Institutional Research Program's 1985 freshman survey and by Dey, Wimsatt, Rhee, and Waterson (1998), analyzing the 1974–75 and 1992–93 follow-up of 1957 high school seniors from the Wisconsin Longitudinal Study. Both studies employed an analytical design similar to that of Knox et al. and introduced statistical controls for salient confounding influences. In the Avalos study, institutional selectivity failed to have a significant, direct impact on 1994 occupational status, and in the Dey et al. study, neither institutional prestige (for example, composite of selectivity, percent of students seeking a Ph.D., median high school grades of entering students, and ratio of high-ability applicants to total number of admitted students) nor institutional resources (for example, average faculty salary, faculty with Ph.Ds, number of library volumes) significantly influenced 1974–75 occupational status or 1992–93 occupational status.[16]

All three of the studies cited (that is, Avalos, 1996; Dey et al., 1998; Knox et al., 1993) focus on estimating the net *direct* influence of measures of institutional quality on overall occupational status. Although the clear weight of evidence suggests that this direct influence is trivial and not statistically significant, it is likely that institutional quality may, nonetheless, have at least a modest, positive indirect effect on occupational status. This indirect influence is attributable to the fact that (as we saw in Chapter Eight) dimensions of institutional quality such as student body selectivity positively influence educational attainment, which, in turn, is a strong determinant of the prestige of the job one holds. Unfortunately, the analytical models in the investigations by Avalos (1996), Dey et al. (1998), and Knox et al. (1993) do not permit us to estimate the magnitude or statistical significance of this indirect effect.

The failure of college quality measures to influence overall job status directly is consistent with our 1991 conclusions. However, also consistent with our 1991 conclusions is evidence to suggest that attending a selective college enhances occupational attainment in specific professions such as medicine and law. For example, Lentz and Laband (1989) found that even with controls for college grades, college courses taken, Medical College Admissions Test scores, race, and parental occupation and education, the academic selectivity of the college attended had a statistically significant, positive influence on admission to medical school. Similarly, Kingston and Smart's (1990) analyses of the 1980 follow-up of the 1971 Cooperative Institutional Research Program freshman survey found that attending one of the 74 most selective private colleges in the United States significantly increased one's likelihood of completing a high-status professional degree (that is, M.D., J.D., M.B.A.). This effect persisted even in the presence of statistical controls for such factors as race, sex, family background, high school achievement, precollege occupational aspirations, and self-estimates of academic ability and drive to achieve. Interestingly, in both studies this effect was nonlinear and generally accrued only to those students attending the most selective or elite institutions in the country. For Kingston and Smart, it was institutions having incoming freshmen with an average combined SAT score of 1175 or higher, whereas for Lentz and LaBand, it was institutions where more than 75 percent of the freshmen were in the top 10 percent of their high school class *and* scored over 1250 on the combined SAT. Such institutions, at most, educated about 1 or 2 percent of all four-year college students in the national postsecondary system. For the remaining 98 percent or so of all four-year college students, the selectivity of the institution they attended made little or no difference.

Career mobility and success. Consistent with the conclusions of our 1991 synthesis, we found a small body of evidence to suggest that attending a selective college confers a modest advantage in job attainment and career mobility. The evidence, however, is somewhat complex and suggests that college quality may signal an individual's ability to employers rather than conferring unique skills that make for better job performance. Data from graduates of accounting programs in 82 universities were analyzed by Colarelli, Dean, and Konstans (1991) to determine if institutional characteristics influenced job offers and early job productivity. Measures of institutional quality such as student body selectivity and institutional resources were both significantly and positively related to the number of job offers an individual received from the eight largest and most prestigious accounting-consulting firms in the region. However, after one year on the job, supervisors' ratings of job performance and promotability were unrelated to institutional resources and actually had a significant, negative association with institutional selectivity.

A more focused set of longitudinal studies by Spilerman and colleagues (Ishida, Spilerman, & Su, 1997; Spilerman & Lunde, 1991) investigated the educational factors that influenced job promotion prospects in a single large insurance company. Spilerman and Lunde (1991) introduced statistical controls for years of education, race, gender, age, seniority, and salary grade level and found that a measure of college selectivity had modest, but statistically significant, positive effects on promotion in the middle organizational ranks where college training would provide relevant job skills. The selectivity of the institution one attended had only a chance impact on the likelihood of being promoted at either the lowest or highest organizational ranks in the company. Generally consistent results were also reported by Ishida, Spilerman, and Su (1997) in what appears to be a further study of promotion in the same company. With controls for level of formal education, college major, age, race, sex, and seniority, institutional selectivity once again had a modest, but statistically significant, positive impact on promotion to the middle organizational ranks of the company (that is, senior management) but essentially only a chance effect on promotion at either lower or higher ranks (that is, administrative or vice presidential grades).

Although it is more prominent in the Spilerman and Lunde (1991) study than in the Ishida, Spilerman, and Su (1997) study, both investigations provide evidence to suggest that at the lower and middle ranks of the firm they studied, the impact of college selectivity on promotion varied with experience or seniority in the firm. The positive effect of college selectivity was greatest for employees who were recent or initial hires in the firm and at the early stages in their careers. As seniority in the firm increased, and direct measures of job performance became available, the selectivity of the college attended decreased in importance. Spilerman and his colleagues conclude from such evidence that given lack of direct information on job performance of new hires at the beginning of their careers, the firm's employers use college selectivity as a proxy or "signal" for the possession of intellectual and related skills that are important for job performance. However, if college selectivity signals higher intellectual or other skills related to effective job performance, it is not clear from either the Spilerman and Lunde or Ishida, Spilerman, and Su studies whether individuals acquire them from their experience in college or essentially enter college with them.[17]

Finally, there is also evidence of an indirect nature that speaks to the effect of college quality on career mobility. Robst (1995) analyzed data from 560 male heads of household between 18 and 64 years of age in the 1976, 1978, and 1985 waves of the Panel Study of Income Dynamics. His purpose was to estimate the net impact of college selectivity on the probability that an individual was employed in a job for which he was overeducated (that is, held a job in which his education was substantially higher than that generally required). With controls for years of education, work experience, number of years in one's current job, and scores on a 13-question sentence completion test, three institutional quality measures (that is, average ACT-SAT scores of the entering freshmen, educational and general expenditures per student, and a prestige rating) had modest, but statistically significant, negative effects on the probability of being overeducated. Moreover, college selectivity was also positively associated with the likelihood of moving from being overeducated for one's job in 1976 to being in a job in 1985 for which one was not overeducated. The findings of the Robst study, however, are likely confounded by the inability to control for men's precollege levels of career or occupational aspirations—strong predictors of both a man's eventual occupational level and the type of college he attends (Pascarella & Terenzini, 1991). Robst also candidly points out that it is questionable that a 13-item sentence completion test is an adequate measure of individual cognitive ability. In short, the presumed negative effects of college quality on overeducation may in fact be attributable more to the characteristics of the men who attend high-quality colleges.[18]

Earnings. Perhaps the largest single body of research on between-college effects on career and economic benefits concerns the impact of undergraduate institutional quality measures on individual earnings. Once again, institutional quality is operationally defined in different ways in different investigations, but student body selectivity appears to be the most common proxy. The typical study in this body of research analyzes data from a nationally representative sample, uses the natural logarithm of earnings as the dependent variable in order to adjust for positive skewness in the distribution of earnings, and introduces statistical controls for factors that potentially confound the relationship between the quality of the institution attended and an individual's earnings. These confounding factors include such variables as ability test scores, family socioeconomic background, race, sex, major field of study, educational attainment, and the like. On average, the studies we reviewed explained considerably less than half of the variance (R^2) in individual earnings, usually in the neighborhood of 25 to 35 percent. Unless one is willing to accept the view that two-thirds or more of the earnings differences among college graduates are attributable to luck, it seems reasonable to conclude that a number of important influences on earnings are not taken into account in the literature we reviewed.

This large percentage of unexplained variance does not necessarily mean that it is impossible to get a reasonably accurate estimate of the net effects of institutional quality on earnings. However, in analyzing the evidence we would argue that, in addition to such factors as race, sex, family socioeconomic factors, educational attainment, measures of labor market experience, and the like, obtaining an unbiased estimate of the net direct impact of institutional quality on individual earnings means that four additional influences need to be taken into account: cognitive or intellectual ability, ambition, major field of study during college, and the differential costs of attending different kinds of institutions. As previously pointed out in this chapter, cognitive ability and ambition are important considerations because they are not only highly correlated with attending a selective or elite institution (for example, Astin, 1993c; Dale & Krueger, 1999; Lillard & Gerner, 1999; Pascarella & Terenzini, 1991) but are also salient predictors of earning potential (Monks, 2000; Murnane et al., 1995;

Sweetman, 1994a, 1994b; Whitaker & Pascarella, 1994). Similarly, it is important to take into account major field of study because selective-prestigious institutions tend to offer academic fields of study that lead to the most lucrative jobs (Jacobs, 1999). Finally, failure to account for the substantially higher costs usually associated with attending a selective-prestigious (and often private) college can lead to inflated estimates of the actual net earnings benefits associated with attendance and graduation from such institutions (Behrman, Rosenzweig, & Taubman, 1996; Brewer, Eide, & Ehrenberg, 1999; Thomas, 1998, 2000a). Nearly all of the effects of college quality on earnings are derived from secondary analyses of preexisting data sets. The variables represented in most of these data sets simply do not permit one to introduce controls for all, or even most, of the important confounding influences. Consequently, as suggested by Kane (1998, p. 432) in a summary caution about research on college quality and earnings, "what looks like an effect of attending an elite college may really be an effect of unmeasured preexisting differences in academic or earning potential."

Our present synthesis is based on evidence from 27 individual published and unpublished studies that appeared between 1989 and 2003. These investigations analyze data from numerous independent data sets. The specific data sets and the studies that employ them were as follows:

1. The National Longitudinal Study of the High School Class of 1972–1979 and 1986 follow-ups (Arcidiacono, 1998; Brewer et al., 1999; Dale & Krueger, 1999; Hoxby & Long, 1999; James & Alsalam, 1993; James, Alsalam, Conaty, & To, 1989; Knox et al., 1993; Loury, 1997; Sweetman, 1994a, 1994b)

2. The High School and Beyond 1980 and 1982 cohorts followed up in 1986 and 1991, respectively (Brewer & Ehrenberg, 1996; Brewer, Eide, & Ehrenberg, 1996; Fitzgerald, 2000; Fox, 1993; Hilmer, 2000; Kane, 1998; Loury, 1997)

3. The National Longitudinal Survey of Youth, 1987–1989, 1993, and 1995 follow-ups (Daniel, Black, & Smith, 1996a, 1996b; Hoxby & Long, 1999; Monks, 2000)

4. The College and Beyond 1976 cohort followed up in 1995 (Bowen & Bok, 1998; Dale & Krueger, 1999)

5. The Baccalaureate and Beyond Study of 1992–93 graduates followed up one year later (Thomas, 1998, 2000a) and four years later (Thomas, 2003)

6. The National Center for Education Statistics Surveys of Recent College Graduates: 1985–86 graduates followed up in 1987 (Rumberger & Thomas, 1993), 1989–90 graduates followed up in 1991 (Tsapogas et al., 1994)

7. The National Science Foundation New Entrants Survey of 1992 graduates followed up in 1993 (Tsapogas et al., 1994)

8. The Occupational Changes in a Generation, 1972 data (Hoxby & Long, 1999)

9. The Cooperative Institutional Research Program data: 1972 freshmen followed up in 1980 (Kingston & Smart, 1990), 1985 freshmen followed up in 1994 (Avalos, 1996)

10. The Panel Study of Income Dynamics from 1975 to 1992 (Turner, 1999)

11. A survey of identical and nonidentical female twins born in Minnesota and followed up in 1993 at about age 45 to 46 (Behrman, Rosenzweig, et al., 1996)

The body of evidence yielded by these investigations suggests the following general conclusions. First, although there are some clear exceptions (Arcidiacono, 1998; Avalos, 1996; James & Alsalam, 1993; Knox et al., 1993; Thomas, 1998; Tsapogas et al., 1994), the weight of evidence suggests that measures of institutional quality, and particularly student body selectivity, have statistically significant, positive net impacts on subsequent earnings. Our best estimate is that, net of other influences (including both individual student characteristics and other institutional characteristics such as private control and size), attending a college with a 100-point higher average SAT score (or ACT equivalent) is associated with about 2 to 4 percent higher earnings in later life. (We note that this estimate is somewhat more conservative than other summaries [for example, Dale & Krueger, 1999; Hilmer, 2000], but this difference is likely attributable to the fact that we derive our estimates from a somewhat broader range of studies.) Moreover, when differential tuition costs are taken into account to adjust for the fact that the most selective institutions are typically private, the positive effect of attending a selective or elite institution on subsequent earnings is reduced but does not disappear (for example, Behrman et al., 1994; Brewer & Ehrenberg, 1996; Brewer et al., 1999; Sweetman, 1994a). Second, consistent with the conclusions from our 1991 synthesis, there is also evidence to suggest that the impact of institutional selectivity on earnings is nonlinear. Only those elite institutions at the very top of the selectivity distribution may have a substantial impact on earnings (for example, Fox, 1993; Hilmer, 2000; Kingston & Smart, 1990). Third, there is empirical support for the contention that the net impact of institutional selectivity or similar quality measures on earnings has increased over time. Investigations that consider the effects of college selectivity for different national cohorts in different time periods tend to find that its estimated impact on earnings is of a somewhat larger magnitude in more recent than in older cohorts (Brewer et al., 1996; Hoxby & Long, 1999; Loury, 1997; Turner, 1999). Finally, there is also evidence suggesting that, in addition to its statistically significant direct effect on earnings, college selectivity may also have a positive indirect effect due to its enhancement of educational attainment and graduate or professional school attendance (Arcidiacono, 1998; Eide, Brewer, & Ehrenberg, 1998). Because these studies do not control for either precollege educational or occupational aspirations, however, it is likely that this indirect effect is biased upward by some unknown amount.

Although most of the evidence on institutional quality and earnings employs various measures of selectivity as the primary quality indicator, there is also evidence to suggest that other quality indicators may be linked with earnings. Unfortunately, there is little in the way of evidence that is consistent across studies analyzing different samples. For example, with controls for other college characteristics as well as individual-level confounding variables, Daniel, Black, and Smith (1996a, 1996b) found that expenditures per student had a significant, positive effect on wages for men, though not for women. However, there is only mixed support for this finding in the work of Behrman, Rosenzweig, and Taubman (1996), Dale and Krueger (1999), and Fitzgerald (2000) and none at all in findings reported by James and Alsalam (1993) and Tsapogas, Cahalan, and Stowe (1994). Similarly, Tsapogas, Cahalan, and Stowe found that percent of faculty with Ph.Ds positively influenced earnings in one national sample they analyzed but not in the other. Moreover, there was little support for the unique, positive impact of percent of faculty with Ph.Ds in the earnings functions of Daniel, Black, and Smith (1996a, 1996b). Behrman, Rosenzweig, and Taubman did find that average faculty salaries at the institution attended positively influenced the subsequent earnings of women, but we uncovered no independent replication of their evidence.

Aside from various measures of institutional selectivity, we uncovered only one institutional quality indicator, faculty-student ratio, that was found to have a significant, positive net effect on earnings across independent samples. Both Behrman, Rosenzweig, and Taubman (1996) and Daniel, Black, and Smith (1996b) found that attending an institution with a high faculty-student ratio had a significant, positive effect on earnings, net of other factors. However, even here the overall findings are inconsistent. In their analyses of two independent national samples, Tsapogas, Cahalan, and Stowe (1994) found that an institution's faculty-student ratio had a significant net positive effect on earnings in one sample and a significant net negative effect on earnings in the other sample. Similarly, Fitzgerald's (2000) analyses of the 1991 follow-up of the 1980 High School and Beyond cohort reported that an institution's ratio of faculty to students had no net impact on women's earnings and a small, negative effect on the earnings of men.

Thus, the bottom line would appear to be that, when institutional quality is defined largely in terms of academic or student body selectivity, it has a generally consistent, positive effect on subsequent earnings. Our estimate is that each 100-point increase in the average SAT score (or ACT equivalent) of the entering students at a college increases earnings by about 2 to 4 percent, although earnings may be most clearly enhanced by attending an institution at the very highest or elite levels of the selectivity distribution. We would argue, however, that the body of research evidence on which we base this conclusion probably provides an inflated estimate of the impact on subsequent earnings of having a bachelor's degree from a selective institution. In large measure because they are generally conducting secondary analyses of existing data sets, nearly every investigation we reviewed in this body of research was unable to control for one or more salient confounding variables. This was the case for even the most meticulously conducted and methodologically rigorous studies. For example, Brewer and Ehrenberg (1996) considered cognitive ability and differential tuition costs, but they did not control for either undergraduate major or an individual's precollege ambition. Both Bowen and Bok (1998) and Fitzgerald (2000) introduced statistical controls for cognitive ability and major field of study but not for differential tuition costs or ambition. Most recently, Thomas (2003) controlled for cognitive ability and academic major and considered differential costs in the form of a debt-earnings ratio. However, he included no ambition measures in his prediction of earnings.

Measures of individual ambition are almost universally absent in investigations of the impact of college quality on earnings.[19] This absence should probably come as no great surprise because measuring ambition in a way that predicts one's future economic success is a nontrivial challenge. Unfortunately, the inability to specify an individual's ambition adequately in regression models does not prevent unmeasured or unobserved ambition from confounding the relationship between the selectivity of the college one attends and one's subsequent earnings. In short, elite, highly selective colleges may simply recruit and enroll students who would have a high earnings capacity no matter where they went to college.

This issue has been creatively addressed in an important study by Dale and Krueger (1999). They hypothesized that, given broad public awareness of the link between attending an elite college and career success, the selectivity of the colleges to which a student applies may signal unaccounted-for ambition and earnings capacity. They tested this hypothesis for a combined sample of men and women by reanalyzing data from the 1995 follow-up of the 1976 cohort of the College and Beyond data set. (Previous analyses of these data by Bowen and Bok, 1998, had yielded significant net positive effects of college selectivity on 1995 earnings.) A basic equation was developed that regressed the natural logarithm of 1995 earnings on predicted parental income, individual SAT score, sex, race, high school academic achievement, collegiate athletic participation, and college selectivity (average SAT score). In this equation college selectivity had a significant, positive effect on earnings. However, when measures of the average selectivity of the colleges to which one applied and the number of applications one made were added to this equation, the effect of college selectivity on earnings was reduced to a magnitude that was trivial and nonsignificant. Furthermore, this finding appeared to be robust. Almost exactly the same results were obtained when the same control for ambition was applied to a combined sample of men and women from the 1986 follow-up of the National Longitudinal Study of the High School Class of 1972—a more nationally representative sample than College and Beyond. When a measure of precollege ambition was taken into account in either sample, students who attended more selective institutions did not earn more than their counterparts who were accepted and rejected by comparable schools but attended less selective institutions.

Despite the volume of evidence concerning college selectivity and earnings reviewed here, we tend to agree with Dale and Krueger (1999, p. 29) that their "findings cast doubt on the view that school selectivity, as measured by the average SAT score of the freshmen who attend a college, is an important determinant of students' subsequent incomes." Put another way, extremely bright and ambitious students (that is, those with a high earnings capability) are more likely than other students to attend and graduate from highly selective colleges. Whether such elite institutions contribute significantly more to those students' earnings capabilities[20] than would less selective schools, however, is problematic.[21]

In addition to the problem of unmeasured ambition, there is also the question of which students are really receiving significant economic returns from attending a selective institution. There is at least some evidence to suggest that studies that fail to take into account a student's educational path—practically a universal characteristic of the existing body of research—overestimate the effects of institutional selectivity for what may be the majority of students. In an analysis of the 1986 follow-up of the nationally representative High School and Beyond sample, Hilmer (2000) estimated the net returns to undergraduate college selectivity for three groups of male graduates: direct attendees (those who initially enrolled at the institution and remained there through graduation), university transfers (those who transferred to the institution from another four-year college), and community college transfers (those who transferred to the institution from a two-year community college). With controls for such factors as race, high school and college grades, tested math and reading ability, college major, labor market experience, and having a postgraduate degree, but not ambition, the overall effects of college selectivity (average student SAT score) on earnings were trivial and nonsignificant for direct attendees. Four-year and community college transfers derived significant economic returns from selectivity but only if they transferred to, and graduated from, a four-year institution that had an average student SAT score of 1200 to 1400. Because four-year and two-year college transfer students made up only about a third of Hilmer's nationally representative High School and Beyond sample, his findings suggest that for the majority of male four-year college graduates (direct attendees), the selectivity of the college attended has little impact on their subsequent economic success.

Institutional Control (Private Versus Public). A small body of evidence speaks to the impact of attending a private versus a public institution on various aspects of a student's career. We have organized that evidence in terms of career choice, occupational status, earnings, and career eminence.

Career choice. There is some limited evidence that institutional control may have an impact on the prestige of one's career choice. In Astin's (1993c) analyses of the 1985 to 1989 Cooperative Institutional Research Program data, he attempted to estimate the effects of different institutional characteristics on college seniors' choice of various careers. With controls for initial career choice, other individual-level background traits, institutional characteristics, and measures of student academic and social involvement in college, attending a private university had a positive influence on seniors' choice of physician as a career.

Conversely, attending a private institution had a negative effect on choice of schoolteacher as a career.

Occupational status. We found little to suggest that attending a private (as compared to a public) postsecondary institution had anything more than a trivial and statistically nonsignificant influence on overall occupational status. Analyzing the 1986 follow-up of the National Longitudinal Study of the High School Class of 1972, Knox, Lindsay, and Kolb (1993) introduced statistical controls for race, sex, family background, tested academic ability, college grades, college major, educational attainment, institutional selectivity, and institutional size. In the presence of such controls, attending a private (versus public) institution as an undergraduate had only a small, chance influence on 1986 occupational status. Consistent results are reported by Dey, Wimsatt, Rhee, and Waterson (1998) analyzing the 1974–75 and 1992–93 follow-ups of the Wisconsin Longitudinal Study of 1957 high school seniors.

Earnings. We uncovered a substantial body of studies that attempted to estimate the unique impact of attending a private (versus public) institution on earnings. The specific data sets and studies that employ them are as follows:

1. The National Longitudinal Study of the High School Class of 1972, 1986 follow-up (Arcidiacono, 1998; James & Alsalam, 1993; James et al., 1989; Knox et al., 1993; Sweetman, 1994a, 1994b)

2. The National Center for Education Statistics Surveys of Recent College Graduates: 1985–86 graduates followed up in 1987 (Rumberger & Thomas, 1993), 1989–90 graduates followed up in 1991 (Tsapogas et al., 1994)

3. The National Science Foundation New Entrants Survey of 1992 graduates followed up in 1993 (Tsapogas et al., 1994)

4. The Baccalaureate and Beyond Study of 1992–93 graduates followed up one year later (Thomas, 1998)

5. The National Longitudinal Survey of Youth, 1987–1989, and 1993 follow-ups (Daniel et al., 1996b; Monks, 2000)

6. The High School and Beyond 1980 cohort followed up in 1986 (Fox, 1993)

7. The Cooperative Institutional Research Program data, 1985 freshmen followed up in 1994 (Avalos, 1996)

8. A survey of identical and nonidentical female twins born in Minnesota and followed up in 1993 at about age 45 to 46 (Behrman, Rosenzweig, et al., 1996)[22]

With two exceptions (Avalos, 1996; Behrman, Rosenzweig, et al., 1996), all of the studies cited here attempt to control not only for individual student characteristics (for example, race, sex, socioeconomic background, tested ability, and the like) but also for a measure of the academic selectivity of the institution attended. Thus, the estimates they report are for attending and graduating from a private institution, irrespective of its level of selectivity. About half of these studies find a small but statistically significant, positive effect on earnings accruing to students who receive their bachelor's degree from a private college. The other half find nonsignificant, but generally small, positive effects. Across all studies that provide requisite information, we estimate the average net earnings advantage associated with graduating from a private institution (irrespective of its level of selectivity) to be about 3 percent. Because of the designs of the studies, however, this estimate does not discount the differential tuition costs between attending private versus public institutions.[23] Were these differential tuition costs taken into account, the net earnings premium associated with attending a private institution would in all likelihood be considerably reduced, at least early in one's career. Thomas (1998), for example, shows how attendance at a private (versus public) institution leads to a statistically significant and substantially higher debt-to-earnings ratio for recent college graduates. The estimates also do not take into account individual precollege ambition or earnings capability, which might be differentially distributed across private and public institutions in much the same way it was differentially distributed across institutions differing in selectivity (Dale & Krueger, 1999).

There is also limited evidence to suggest that different types of private colleges may differentially influence earnings, even when their level of selectivity is held constant. For example, Sweetman (1994a, 1994b) found that only those private colleges that were not affiliated with a church had a significant, positive influence on earnings. James and Alsalam (1993) found that, at least for men, earnings were significantly enhanced by attending a private college only if the college was located in the northeastern United States. These findings, however, are based on single samples and await replication. Moreover, it is not clear if the private nonsectarian or private northeastern categories are really proxies for other institutional characteristics.

Career eminence. We uncovered one study (Wolf-Wendel, 1998) that estimated the effect of attending a private (versus public) institution on the career eminence or success of women. Career eminence was operationally defined as inclusion in one of several national *Who's Who* compilations: *Who's Who in America, Who's Who Among Black Americans,* and *Who's Who Among Hispanic Americans.* Institutions were the unit of analysis. With statistical controls that varied for different analyses but that typically included such institutional factors as selectivity, racial composition, and gender composition, obtaining a bachelor's degree from a private institution positively influenced career eminence for African-American and Latina women but had no significant effect on the career eminence of White women. Whether such findings for African-American and Latina women are attributable to socialization or recruitment effects, however, is somewhat difficult to discern from Wolf-Wendel's analyses. It was not possible for her to control for such factors as the average entering aspirations, career ambition, or even family background characteristics of African-American and Latina women who enrolled in private (versus public) institutions. Even with institutions as the unit of analysis, differences in these average entering student characteristics between private and public colleges may be a quite reasonable alternative explanation for her results. As suggested by the work of Dale and Krueger (1999), controls for institutional selectivity may not provide an adequate proxy for student ambition.

Carnegie Classification. A modest body of research in the 1990s attempted to estimate the effect of the Carnegie classification of institutions on earnings. The Carnegie classification (Carnegie Foundation for the Advancement of Teaching, 1994) places four-year institutions in the following general categories: *research universities* (I and II, depending on annual number of doctorates awarded and external research funding); *doctoral universities* (I and II, depending on range of doctoral programs and number of doctorates awarded); *comprehensive institutions* (I and II, depending on range of master's programs and master's degrees awarded; these institutions have no doctoral programs); *liberal arts colleges* (I and II, depending on selectivity); and *specialized institutions* (for example, medical, engineering, business, and the like). Unfortunately, these classifications are confounded by such factors as student body selectivity, private (versus public) control, institutional resources, and size. Consequently, findings based on the Carnegie classification might well represent proxies for other institutional characteristics. For example, in analyses of the 1986 follow-up of the National Longitudinal Study of the High School Class of 1972, Grubb (1992b, 1995b) sought to determine if the net economic returns to a bachelor's degree differed in magnitude for students graduating from different Carnegie classification institutions. Net of such factors as race, family income, high school grades, tested ability, and job experience, the returns (versus a high school degree) were relatively stable across the different institutional classifications, except for the categories having the most and least selective institutions.

Across all the studies we uncovered that considered the economic returns to earning a bachelor's degree from different Carnegie-type institutions, only specialized institutions (for example, those focusing on medical specialties, business, engineering, and the like) had a consistently positive net effect on earnings (Bellas, 1998; Monks, 2000; Tsapogas et al., 1994). Moreover, this positive effect remained statistically significant, even when measures of institutional selectivity were taken into account (Monks, 2000; Tsapogas et al., 1994). In all these studies, the comparison group was either liberal arts colleges I and II grouped together (Bellas, 1998; Monks, 2000) or liberal arts colleges II (Tsapogas et al., 1994). The average earnings advantage accruing to graduates of specialized institutions (versus graduates of liberal arts colleges) was about 19 percent.

Evidence with respect to the relative economic returns linked to a bachelor's degree from other Carnegie-type institutions is markedly less consistent. Monks's (2000) analyses of the 1993 follow-up of the 1979 cohort of the National Longitudinal Survey of Youth found that, even in the presence of controls for student background characteristics, work experience, and a measure of institutional selectivity, graduating from a Carnegie research university, doctoral university, or comprehensive (master's) university (versus a liberal arts college I or II) provided a positive and statistically significant advantage in earnings. There was little support for this, however, in analyses of the NCES Recent College Graduates Survey and the NSF New Entrants Survey (Tsapogas et al., 1994) and the 1991 follow-up of the High School and Beyond (HSB) 1980 cohort (Fitzgerald, 2000). With similar controls in place, including measures of institutional selectivity, there were no significant earnings differences in the NSF New Entrants Survey between liberal arts II graduates, on the one hand, and graduates of research, doctoral, or comprehensive universities, on the other. In the NCES Recent College Graduates Survey, the net returns to graduates of comprehensive I universities were significantly higher than those of liberal arts colleges II, but the net returns to graduates of research I universities were significantly lower. The waters are muddied even further by Fitzgerald's (2000) findings that women receive an early career earnings boost by graduation from a liberal arts I college, whereas an earnings penalty accrues to men who graduate from a private research I university.

Bellas's (1998) analyses of the 1993 Baccalaureate and Beyond study suggest that graduation from a research or doctoral university (versus a liberal arts college) has a modest, positive indirect effect through labor market experience and occupational classification. Because she could not control for institutional selectivity, however, it is unclear how much this indirect effect might be confounded.[24]

Although they do not place major focus on the Carnegie typology, three additional studies have estimated the economic premium associated with earning a bachelor's degree from an institution with a doctoral program. In these studies, doctoral program institutions were compared with all others, but like the studies reviewed in the preceding paragraphs that employed the Carnegie classifications, the results were inconsistent. Behrman, Rosenzweig, and Taubman (1996) found that receiving a bachelor's degree from a doctoral granting institution had a positive net influence on subsequent earnings, but both James, Alsalam, Conaty, and To (1989) and Hilmer (2000) report findings indicating that it did not. Furthermore, Hilmer also reports an additional finding suggesting that graduating from a research I university may have actually had a small, negative impact on subsequent earnings. In all three investigations, controls were introduced for institutional quality measures as well as individual-level student characteristics. Only the James et al. and Hilmer studies also included a direct measure of institutional selectivity, however.

Generally, then, when institutional selectivity is taken into account, it is questionable that either an institution's Carnegie classification or its doctoral-research orientation has a consistent, statistically significant link to an individual's subsequent earnings. The one exception to this finding appears to be graduation from a Carnegie-type specialized institution, and this exception is likely because such institutions frequently focus on preparing individuals for occupational fields characterized by high economic returns, such as medical specialization, engineering, and business.

Institutional Size. The evidence on institutional size was organized under two categories, occupational status and earnings.

Occupational status. We uncovered little evidence in the research of the 1990s to suggest that institutional size has anything more than a small and statistically nonsignificant impact on occupational status. Analyzing data from the 1986 follow-up of the National Longitudinal Study of the High School Class of 1972, Knox, Lindsay, and Kolb (1993) introduced controls for such individual- and institutional-level variables as race, sex, socioeconomic status, college grades and major, institutional selectivity, and private (versus public) control. In the presence of these controls, the size of the institution attended (operationally defined as student enrollment) had a small, positive, but statistically nonsignificant impact on 1986 occupational status. Generally similar results are reported by Dey, Wimsatt, Rhee, and Waterson (1998) in their analyses of the 1974–75 and 1992–93 follow-ups of the Wisconsin Longitudinal Study of 1957 high school seniors.

Earnings. A modest body of research has estimated the net effect of attending institutions of varying size (usually defined as student enrollment) on subsequent earnings. With the exception of two studies, which report weak evidence for a statistically significant, negative effect (Behrman, Rosenzweig, et al., 1996) or a very small, nonsignificant, negative effect (Hilmer, 2000), the evidence consists of studies reporting that institutional size either has a significant, positive net influence on subsequent earnings (Avalos, 1996; Dowd, 1999; James & Alsalam, 1993; Thomas, 1998) or a small and positive but statistically nonsignificant net influence on earnings (James et al., 1989; Knox et al., 1993; Tsapogas et al., 1994). Importantly, we believe, the studies that find a significant, positive impact of institutional size also introduce, in addition to controls for individual-level characteristics, controls for either institutional selectivity (Dowd, 1999), private control (Avalos, 1996), or both institutional selectivity and private control (James & Alsalam, 1993; Thomas, 1998). Indeed, Dowd found that graduates of large institutions (universities) that were substantially less selective actually had an earnings advantage of about 14 to 15 percent over graduates of the most elite liberal arts colleges, those with an average student body SAT score *greater than 1300.* We conclude that the weight of evidence suggests that, other things being equal, institutional size confers a small but statistically significant advantage in earnings. (The nature of the results reported by different studies makes determination of the magnitude of the effect problematic.) As suggested by Dowd, this positive effect of graduating from a large institution probably stems from economies of scale in providing diverse programs and major fields of study as well as more extensive job networks due to larger alumni groups. Furthermore, by means of the greater number of majors and preprofessional programs they offer, larger institutions usually have a wider range of links with occupational and economic groups in society. Other factors being equal, this may afford larger institutions superior status-allocating capacity than smaller institutions (Pascarella & Terenzini, 1991).

Institutional Racial Composition. In previous chapters in this book, we have seen that African-American students attending historically Black colleges (HBCs) not only make content knowledge and intellectual gains that are equal to, if not greater than, their counterparts attending predominantly White institutions (PWIs) but also are more likely to complete a bachelor's degree. Does graduation from HBCs confer any distinct advantages on African Americans in their careers?

Career preparation and occupational aspirations. A small body of evidence suggests that African-American students attending HBCs tend to believe they have made greater gains in preparation for a career and report a higher level of occupational aspirations than their counterparts attending PWIs. For example, DeSousa and Kuh (1996) asked African-American students attending an HBC and a PWI to indicate the gains they felt they had made during college in vocational and career skills (for example, acquiring knowledge and skills applicable to a job, gaining a range of information that might be relevant to a career). HBC students reported making gains on the scale that were about .58 of a standard deviation larger than African-American students at PWIs. Such a finding is consistent with that of Cole, Barber, Bolyard, and Linders (1999) who found that African-American students at HBCs scored significantly higher than their counterparts at PWIs on an index measuring the extent to which they focused on school as a means to an occupation versus getting a broad liberal arts education. The designs of these studies, however, make it difficult to determine if these differences in self-reported gains in vocational and career skills, and focus on college's instrumental value in preparing one for a career, are attributable to the influence of attendance at an HBC or PWI. They may merely reflect differences in the precollege career orientations of African-American students who choose to attend HBCs versus PWIs.

The unique influence of attending an HBC on African-American students' occupational aspirations has been addressed by Allen (1992) and Wenglinsky (1996). In Allen's study of African-American students at eight HBCs and eight PWIs, statistical controls were introduced for such factors as educational aspirations, class level, college and high school grades, sex, socioeconomic status, self-concept, and the like. In the presence of these controls, attending an HBC (versus a PWI) had a modest but statistically significant, positive, direct effect on a measure of the prestige and power dimensions of one's occupational plans. HBC attendance also had a modest, positive, indirect effect on occupational plans, transmitted through the positive effects of HBCs on students' social involvement during college. Although no controls could be introduced for prior educational or occupational aspirations, consistent findings are reported by Wenglinsky (1996) in analyses of the more nationally representative National Postsecondary Aid Study of 1990. Similarly, Astin (1993c) reported that attending an HBC had a significant, positive net influence on seniors' choice of physician as a career.

Occupational status, earnings, and career eminence. Evidence concerning the impact of graduating from an HBC (versus a PWI) on African Americans' actual occupational and economic attainments is mixed. For example, Ehrenberg and Rothstein (1994) analyzed data from the 1979 follow-up of the National Longitudinal Study of the High School Class of 1972 to determine if an HBC conferred an early occupational status or earnings advantage on African Americans. Controlling for gender, SAT scores, high school rank, educational attainment, parents' education and income, father's occupational status, and the unemployment level in one's state of residence, attending an HBC (versus a PWI) had only statistically nonsignificant effects on 1979 occupational status and 1979 earnings. Similar findings are reported by London (1998) for occupational status, though with a much smaller and focused sample.[25] However, analyzing data from the same sample, but with a later follow-up, Constantine (1994, 1995) reported findings suggesting that attendance at an HBC may indeed have a positive impact on African Americans' subsequent wages. She used two different samples to derive her estimates. In the first, she attempted to reproduce the analytical model of Ehrenberg and Rothstein by restricting the sample to African Americans in four-year institutions. Controlling for such influences as high school achievement, tested ability, sex, family background, athletic participation, and region of the country, she found that attendance at an HBC (versus a PWI) conferred a statistically significant advantage of about 11 percent in 1986 wages. When attainment of a bachelor's degree was added to the equation, the advantage dropped to about 8 percent and became nonsignificant, suggesting that part of the positive total impact of attending an HBC was indirect, transmitted through the positive effect of HBC attendance on African-American students' completion of a bachelor's degree.

In Constantine's (1995) second sample, she included all African-American students, irrespective of whether they enrolled in a four-year institution. She initially used background and other characteristics to predict, or model, three choices: no four-year college (that is, high school or two-year college), attendance at a four-year HBC, or attendance at a four-year non-HBC (PWI). Incorporating a term representing a correction for this choice or selection in her basic regression model yielded two important findings. First, the negative selection term suggested that the unobservable characteristics that led a student to select an HBC (over a PWI) were probably the ones that would have caused lower wages. Second, with this correction for selection taken into account, the estimated value-added in 1986 wages from attending an HBC (versus PWI) was actually about 38 percent.

Other research presents a less optimistic picture of the net impact of attending an HBC on African Americans' career and economic success. For example, Solnick (1990) examined the impact of attending an HBC on the job success of a sample of African-American college graduates employed by a large U.S. manufacturing firm. Three job success outcomes were predicted: starting salaries, salary growth, and promotion. With controls introduced for extensive personal and job characteristics, the resources of the colleges attended, and for possible attrition bias, African-American employees who were graduates of HBCs had a modest but statistically significant 4 percent advantage in starting salary over their counterparts who graduated from PWIs. Conversely, HBC graduates were significantly disadvantaged in both percentage of salary growth and the probability of being promoted within two years of being hired.

In his analyses of the 1997 follow-up of 1993 bachelor's degree recipients in the Baccalaureate and Beyond study, Thomas (2003) estimated the net impact of attending an HBC on both annual earnings and the debt-to-earnings ratio. Controlling for such factors as sex, race, family background, SAT scores, college grades and major, variables capturing labor market experience, and both the selectivity and private-public control of the institution attended, earning a bachelor's degree from an HBC (versus all other institutions) had no significant impact on the 1997 debt-to-earnings ratio. Graduates of HBCs did, however, have a statistically significant 23 percent disadvantage in 1997 earnings. Unfortunately, the sample used by Thomas includes individuals of all races, not just African Americans. Consequently, he is comparing graduates of HBCs, who presumably are nearly all African Americans, with graduates of all other institutions, irrespective of race. Thomas did, however, include dummy variables to represent African-American as well as Asian, Hispanic, and Caucasian (coded 0) racial categories. Thus, a reasonable interpretation of his findings is that for individuals in the same racial category (including African Americans), the average net effect of graduating from an HBC is a 23 percent disadvantage in 1997 earnings. Employing a similar sample and analytic design with the 1991 follow-up of the High School and Beyond 1980 cohort, Fitzgerald (2000) reported that graduation from an HBC had a statistically nonsignificant net effect on early career earnings of both men and women. Obviously, the effect of HBC graduation on African Americans' earnings would have been estimated more precisely with a sample limited to African Americans. Nevertheless, the findings of both Thomas and Fitzgerald are not irrelevant to the body of evidence.

In addition to the body of evidence concerning earnings, Wolf-Wendel (1998) sought to estimate the net impact of graduating from an HBC on the career eminence of African-American women. In the same study, she also estimated the impact on career eminence of Latina women attributable to earning a bachelor's degree from a primarily Hispanic-serving institution (that is, an institutional member of the Hispanic Association of Colleges and Universities—HACV). Institutions were the unit of analysis, and career eminence was defined as inclusion in one of two respective *Who's Who* compilations: *Who's Who Among Black Americans* and *Who's Who Among Hispanic Americans.* Net of statistical controls for institutional control and gender composition, African-American women graduates of historically Black colleges were significantly overrepresented in career eminence. Similarly, net of controls for institutional control, selectivity, and gender composition, graduating from a primarily Hispanic-serving institution had a significant, positive influence on the career eminence of Latina women. As with Wolf-Wendel's (1998) findings concerning graduation from a private college, however, there is the very real possibility that these findings are also confounded by the inability to control for such factors as the average career aspirations, ambition, and family backgrounds of students entering HBCs and Hispanic-serving institutions.

Overall, it is difficult to form a firm conclusion about the impact of attending a historically Black institution on African Americans' career and economic success. Historically Black colleges appear to enhance the career aspirations of African-American students, and there is some evidence that a bachelor's degree from an HBC is at least associated with one dimension of career eminence among African-American women. However, the weight of evidence with respect to the influence of graduating from an HBC on African Americans' occupational status, career mobility, and earnings is not totally convincing. The study of economic returns that follows African-American students furthest in their careers (Constantine, 1995) also yields the most positive estimates of HBC attendance on earnings or wages. Her findings are based on a single sample, however, and await replication.

Although the great majority of evidence on the effects of college racial composition on career and economic attainment focuses on historically Black colleges and African Americans, we uncovered four additional studies that estimated the impact of an institution's student-body racial composition on the earnings of non–African Americans as well as African Americans. Analyzing the four-year follow-up of the 1993 Baccalaureate and Beyond study, Thomas (2003) introduced statistical controls for an extensive set of individual-level and institutional-level characteristics. These included race, sex, family income, college grades, college major, tested ability, section of the country, and labor market experience at the individual level, and selectivity, private (versus public) control, and attendance at an historically Black college at the institutional level. In the presence of such controls, graduates of colleges with more diverse student bodies enjoyed a statistically significant earnings advantage relative to those from more racially homogeneous campuses. On average, a 10 percent increase in non-White students on campus led to a 3 percent increase in 1997 earnings, net of other factors. (Such results are quite similar to those found earlier for students majoring in business, education, and health-related fields by Rumberger & Thomas, 1993.) Thomas concludes that this finding may suggest that employers are recognizing and rewarding recent graduates' experiences with diverse populations, and these experiences are more likely to happen at institutions with diverse undergraduate student bodies (Gurin, 1999).

Consistent, if not totally comparable, findings are reported by Daniel, Black, and Smith (1996a, 1996b) in their analyses of the 1987–89 follow-up to the 1979 cohort of the National Longitudinal Survey of Youth. In their investigations, they created four categories representing the percent of African-American students at each institution: less than 5 percent, 5 to 7 percent, 8 to 17 percent, and more than 17 percent. Statistical controls were introduced for such individual-level influences as tested ability, home and family background, age, race, high school quality, college major, labor market experience, and industry of employment, and for a composite measure of college quality (for example, selectivity, spending per student, faculty with Ph.Ds, and the like) at the institutional level. Net of such controls, they found that men attending colleges with between 5 and 7 percent African-American students earned significantly more than those attending colleges with fewer than 5 percent African-American students. Furthermore, men attending colleges with between 8 and 17 percent African-American students had significantly higher earnings than men at schools with fewer than 8 percent or more than 17 percent African-American students. There was no significant difference in the magnitude of the effect of college racial diversity for African-American versus non-African-American men (Daniel et al., 1996b). Thus, even with controls for college quality and background characteristics, attending a college with a moderate level of racial diversity (percent African American) among its students significantly raised earnings for both African-American and non-African-American men and did so about equally.

The corresponding results for women were less clear (Daniel et al., 1996a). Net of background characteristics and institutional quality, African-American women who attended colleges with between 5 and 7 percent African-American students earned significantly more than their counterparts who attended colleges with less than 5 percent African-American students. The trends in the evidence also suggest they earned more than otherwise similar African-American women who attend colleges with more than 8 percent African-American students. Percent African-American students at the institution attended had only small and statistically nonsignificant effects on the earnings of non-African-American women.

Because it is unclear how many HBCs fell into the category of "more than 17 percent African-American students," it is difficult to draw a direct comparison between the findings of the Daniel, Black, and Smith (1996a, 1996b) studies and those that compare African-American students who attend HBCs with those who attend predominantly White institutions. Nevertheless, the results reported by Daniel, Black, and Smith suggest that, even if an African-American student does not attend an HBC, a modest percentage of other African Americans on campus may positively influence his or her subsequent earnings. Furthermore, taken together, the findings of Thomas (2003) and Daniel, Black, and Smith (1996b) suggest the intriguing possibility that non-African-American students, and particularly men, may derive potential benefits from experiences on a racially diverse campus that translate into subsequent economic advantages.

Institutional Gender Composition. As of the middle of the 1990s, there were fewer than 70 baccalaureate-granting women's colleges in the United States, and they granted slightly more than 2 percent of all bachelor's degrees awarded to women (College Entrance Examination Board, 1994; Ricci, 1994; Wolf-Wendel, 1998). Thus, in terms of both numbers of institutions and numbers of graduates, single-sex women's colleges could be considered only minor players in the overall national postsecondary system. In terms of the accomplishments and influence of their graduates, however, women's colleges are anything but minor. Graduates of women's institutions hold positions of leadership and eminence in such fields as government, business, the professions, and postsecondary education that are dramatically out of proportion to their small numbers (Astin & Leland, 1991; Forbes, 1998; Harwarth, Maline, & DeBra, 1997; Ledman, Miller,

& Brown, 1995; Tidball, Smith, Tidball, & Wolf-Wendel, 1999; Touchton, Shavlik, & Davis, 1993). The primary question for social scientists interested in the impact of college is whether the marked accomplishments of women's college graduates are the result of some unique socialization process that goes on in these colleges or merely reflect the recruitment of particularly talented and ambitious young women into those institutions. A substantial body of research has addressed this issue.

Acquiring career-related skills and attitudes. A number of scholars have been concerned with the extent to which attendance at a women's college influences career-related skills and attitudes. Because women's institutions provide more opportunities for women to exercise leadership skills as well as to interact with successful women faculty role models in a wide range of academic fields, it seems reasonable to hypothesize that attendance at a women's college would foster such outcomes as leadership skills, orientation toward success or accomplishment, and drive to achieve (for example, Miller-Bernal, 1993; Romano, 1996). With one exception (Astin, 1993c), however, the weight of evidence from the 1990s failed to support this hypothesis. For example, in a comprehensive and methodologically sophisticated investigation, Smith, Wolf, and Morrison (1995) used the 1986 to 1990 Cooperative Institutional Research Program data to compare women at 30 women's colleges with those who attended 173 private four-year coeducational institutions. With statistical controls for individual-level precollege variables and SAT scores, institutional selectivity, and measures of academic and social involvement during college, attending a women's college had only a small and statistically nonsignificant direct effect on seniors' self-ratings of leadership ability and a scale measuring success goals and outcomes (for example, to have administrative responsibility, to become an authority in one's field, self-rating of drive to achieve, and the like). Furthermore, the indirect effects of attending a women's college on the same two variables were trivial in magnitude. Quite similar findings, using other iterations of the Cooperative Institutional Research Program data and essentially the same general analytical procedures as Smith, Wolf, and Morrison (1995), have been reported by Kim and Alvarez (1995) for the acquisition of job-related skills and preparation for graduate or professional school, by McKinney (1997) for self-assessed leadership ability, by Langdon (1997) for leadership ability and drive to achieve, and by Tullier (1990) for career salience and range of perceived career options.

Choosing nontraditional majors and careers. Because women's colleges (compared with coeducational institutions) tend to provide a larger percentage of female faculty role models who function effectively in fields that are traditionally male-dominated and linked to high economic returns (for example, economics, mathematics, natural sciences), it also seems reasonable to hypothesize that the environments of women's institutions may be particularly effective in counteracting sex-stereotypic perceptions in women's career aspirations and development (for example, Riordan, 1994; Sebrechts, 1992; Solnick, 1995). Here, too, the evidence is mixed. On the one hand, we have the supportive findings of Sebrechts (1992) and Solnick (1995). Summarizing a report from the Women's

College Coalition, Sebrechts points out that women at women's colleges were three times as likely to earn a bachelor's degree in economics and one and one-half times as likely to earn bachelor's degrees in the life sciences, physical sciences, and mathematics as were women at coeducational colleges. Of course, such evidence could merely reflect precollege differences in the intended majors of women who enroll in women's and coeducational colleges. More pertinent to the actual impact of women's colleges is Solnick's study of changes in women's majors from entrance to graduation at eight women's and seven coeducational colleges. Depending on how broadly female-dominated majors (for example, education, social work, social sciences, and the like) are defined, about 40 percent to 75 percent of women at the eight women's colleges who began in such majors shifted to neutral or male-dominated fields (for example, mathematics, natural sciences, economics, and the like) during their college careers. This shift compared with only about 25 percent of women at the seven coeducational schools. Approximately 22 percent of women at both types of schools left male-dominated majors.

Other evidence, however, is less supportive of the notion that women's colleges actually enhance the likelihood that women will choose nontraditional majors and careers (Dickson, 1990; Touchton, Davis, & Makosky, 1991; Tullier, 1990). In contrast to Sebrechts (1992), Touchton, Davis, and Makosky (1991) summarized a report from the National Center for Education Statistics indicating that about the same percentage of women in women's colleges and coeducational colleges received bachelor's degrees in engineering, mathematics, and the physical sciences. Similarly, both Dickson (1990) and Tullier (1990) found that when women's and coeducational colleges of about equal selectivity were compared, senior women at both types of institutions were largely indistinguishable in their overall career choices and choice of a nontraditional (for example, male-dominated) career. The seeming contrast between these findings and those of Solnick (1995) may in part be explained by the fact that Solnick focused on major field of study, whereas Dickson and Tullier focused on actual career choice.

The evidence is also mixed with respect to the net impact of women's colleges on women's actual entrance into nontraditional careers. For example, in their analyses of the 1971 to 1980 Cooperative Institutional Research Program data, Stoecker and Pascarella (1991) attempted to estimate the net effect of attendance at a women's versus a coeducational college on women's entrance into a nontraditional or male-dominated occupation. Male-dominated occupations were operationally defined by the percentage of males in each occupational group, using data from the U.S. Bureau of Labor Statistics. With statistical controls for such confounding influences as individual-level background traits and aspirations, institutional selectivity and size, college major, college grades, marital status, and educational attainment, attending a women's college had only small and nonsignificant, direct and indirect effects on women's entry into male-dominated careers.

Generally if not totally consistent results are reported in a 1994 reanalysis of data indicating that graduates of women's colleges are substantially overrepresented in a specific male-dominated occupation: physician (Crosby et al., 1994). When different procedures and variables were employed to introduce previously absent controls for institutional selectivity, the effect of graduating from a women's college and becoming a physician either became nonsignificant or was substantially reduced in magnitude relative to other predictors. Furthermore, even with controls for institutional selectivity, it is quite possible that the relationship between attending a women's (versus coeducational) college and becoming a physician is still confounded by differences between the two institutional types in the percentages of women who aspire to a career as a physician when they begin college.

Other evidence is somewhat more supportive of the belief that women's institutions enhance the likelihood of women selecting a nontraditional career path. Sharpe and Fuller (1995) used the Doctoral Records File maintained by the National Research Council to examine the physical science and engineering doctorate productivity of the baccalaureate institutions of the cohort of women who completed a bachelor's degree between 1976 and 1986 and who earned a doctorate prior to 1992. Taking institutional size and Carnegie classification into account, the overall median physical science and engineering doctorate productivity was significantly higher for historically women's colleges than for coeducational institutions. Most of this effect was attributable to the overrepresentation of women's college graduates in earning a doctorate in chemistry. In both mathematics–computer science and physics–earth science, graduates of women's colleges demonstrated no significant advantage over their counterparts with a bachelor's degree from coeducational institutions. As Sharpe and Fuller point out, however, it is risky to attribute any of their findings to the impact of institutional socialization. It may simply be that women's colleges tend to enroll a higher proportion of women who aspire to careers in the physical sciences when they begin postsecondary education than do coeducational institutions. Without taking these precollege career dispositions into account, it is difficult to determine if the Sharpe and Fuller findings represent socialization or a recruitment effect.

Workforce participation. Analyses of two national data sets, the 1971 to 1980 Cooperative Institutional Research Program data (Stoecker & Pascarella, 1991) and the 1986 follow-up of the National Longitudinal Study of the High School Class of 1972 (Riordan, 1992; Rothstein, 1995), suggest that attendance at a women's college has little impact on the likelihood of women participating in the workforce. With controls for extensive individual-level background characteristics, institutional selectivity and size, marital status, college major, and educational attainment, both Stoecker and Pascarella (1991) and Rothstein (1995) found that the percent of undergraduate women at an institution had only small and statistically nonsignificant effects on the likelihood of a woman being employed. Riordan (1992) actually found that women's college graduates were less likely to be employed after obtaining a bachelor's degree than were women graduates of mixed-gender colleges. Moreover, in the Rothstein investigation, women's workforce participation was also uninfluenced by the percent of female faculty at an institution.

Occupational status and earnings. The weight of evidence with respect to the net impact of attending a women's college on occupational status and earnings is inconsistent and unconvincing. For example, in analyzing data from the 1986 follow-up of the National Longitudinal Study of the High School Class of 1972, Riordan (1992, 1994) found that, net of such influences as family socioeconomic status, tested ability, mental status, region of the country, and hours worked, attending a women's (versus a coeducational) college had a small but statistically significant, positive effect on the status or prestige of a woman's occupation in 1986. This, however, was not replicated in Riordan's (1993, 1995) analyses of the 1986 follow-up of the 1980 High School and Beyond cohort. With statistical controls similar to those employed in his analyses of the NLS-72 data, attendance at a women's college reduced the likelihood of being married and increased one's occupational aspirations but had only a small and statistically nonsignificant effect on the actual status of the job held by a woman in 1986. Similarly, in their analyses of the 1971 to 1980 Cooperative Institutional Research Program data, Stoecker and Pascarella (1991) found that attendance at a women's college had only small and nonsignificant direct and indirect effects on a woman's 1980 job status when the influence of salient individual- and institutional-level variables was taken into account.

The evidence pertaining to the impact of attendance at a women's college on subsequent earnings differs little from that pertaining to its effect on occupational prestige. Riordan's (1994) analyses of the 1986 follow-up of the NLS-72 data present the strongest evidence of a positive impact. Net of other influences, attending a women's college had a statistically significant, positive total effect on 1986 earnings. Most of this positive effect of attendance at a women's college was indirect, being transmitted through a direct, positive impact on 1986 occupational status, which, in turn, positively influenced earnings. There is a good chance, however, that this effect is biased upward, or inflated, because precollege (1972) occupational aspirations were not specified, and therefore not controlled statistically, in Riordan's regression models. Such precollege aspirations are important determinants of both subsequent occupational status and earnings. For example, using essentially the same database as Riordan (1994), both Inoue and Ethington (1997) and Whitaker and Pascarella (1994) found that precollege (1972) occupational status aspirations had a significant, positive effect on 1986 occupational status, even when precollege educational aspirations and subsequent educational attainment (among other variables) were taken into account. Occupational status aspirations also had a significant, positive effect on 1986 earnings, even in the presence of controls for educational aspirations, educational attainment, and occupational status (Whitaker & Pascarella, 1994). The importance of controlling for occupational aspirations is also underscored in Kingston and Smart's (1990) analyses of the 1971 to 1980 Cooperative Institutional Research Program data.

Additional evidence suggesting that attendance at a women's college may enhance subsequent earnings is provided in Dowd's (1999) 10-year follow-up study of graduates of 20 "highly prestigious" institutions. With controls for undergraduate major, ethnicity, financial aid, geographic region, marital status, and dependent children, women graduates of three highly selective liberal arts colleges actually had significantly lower earnings than their counterparts at five less selective universities. However, women graduates of four less selective liberal arts colleges, *three of which were women's colleges,* were not disadvantaged relative to the five comparison universities. In terms of impact on subsequent earnings, Dowd reasoned that the distinctive culture of women's colleges may have compensated for the institutional size disadvantage of liberal arts colleges relative to universities. (Recall our earlier review indicating a positive influence of institutional size on earnings.) Although such findings are intriguing, they are also based on an extremely small sample of institutions with quite limited generalizability. Moreover, the results may be confounded by the inability to control for precollege levels of career aspirations and ambition.

With the possible exception of Riordan (1994) and Dowd (1999), however, the weight of evidence is reasonably clear in suggesting that no statistically significant earnings benefit accrues to women who attend or graduate from a women's college versus a coeducational institution (Behrman, Rosenzweig, et al., 1996; Daniel et al., 1996a; Rothstein, 1995; Stoecker & Pascarella, 1991; Sweetman, 1994a, 1994b). These studies tend to analyze data from nationally representative samples such as the eight- and nine-year follow-ups of the 1979 cohort of the National Longitudinal Survey of Youth; the 1986 follow-up of the NLS-72 data; the 1986 follow-up of the 1980 cohort of the High School and Beyond data; and the 1971 to 1980 Cooperative Institutional Research Program data. An additional data set analyzed was a survey of identical and nonidentical female twins born in Minnesota and followed up in 1993 at about age 45 to 46. The studies usually make attempts to introduce statistical controls for all or some of the following: individual-level background traits (for example, tested ability, precollege educational or occupational aspirations, socioeconomic status); other institutional characteristics (for example, selectivity, size); college experiences (for example, academic major, grades); marital status and family obligations; educational attainment; and labor market experience (for example, work experience, sector of employment). With such controls in place, attending a women's college, or the percent of undergraduate women at the college attended, had no statistically significant, positive, direct or indirect influence on a woman's subsequent annual earnings or hourly wages. One of the studies we reviewed (Daniel et al., 1996a) suggests the possibility that attendance at a women's college actually confers a net earnings disadvantage on women. However, considering the evidence presented across the entire body of studies we uncovered, it is difficult not to conclude that women's colleges confer neither an earnings benefit nor an earnings penalty on women.[26]

Although they are each based on findings from a single study, and await replication, two other findings are worthy of mention. First, although Daniel, Black, and Smith (1996a) report that attending a women's college had a net negative effect on a woman's earnings, this was not the case for the economic productivity of a woman's spouse. Net of other influences, the percent of women at the institution attended had a significant, positive effect on the earnings of a woman's spouse. (Similar findings are reported by Riordan, 1992, for husband's occupational status, suggesting that the results of Daniel, Black, and Smith are not merely fortuitous or artifactual.) Second, Sweetman's (1994a, 1994b) analysis of the 1986 follow-up of the NLS-72 data found that, net of other factors, attending an all-male college (versus coeducational institution) conferred a 23 percent earnings advantage on White men.

Career eminence. We uncovered only one study (Wolf-Wendel, 1998) that estimated the net impact of attending a women's college on a woman's career eminence. Institutions (versus individuals) were the unit of analysis, and career eminence or success for women was defined as earning a bachelor's degree after 1965 and being listed in one of three *Who's Who* compilations—*Who's Who in America, Who's Who Among Black Americans,* and *Who's Who Among Hispanic Americans.* Separate analyses were conducted for three groups of women— White–European Americans, African Americans, and Latinas. Wolf-Wendel essentially was trying to predict the proportion of women baccalaureate graduates from four-year institutions included in these *Who's Who* compilations. Net of such institutional characteristics as selectivity, size, and private control, graduates of women's colleges were dramatically overrepresented in the three *Who's Who* compilations. Clearly, Wolf-Wendel's study is limited by the fact that she could not control for differences in the average levels of precollege aspiration and ambition among women attending women's and coeducational colleges. To some extent, her findings could simply reflect differential recruitment of ambitious women to women's and coeducational colleges rather than any unique career socialization that might occur at the former. Yet it is extremely difficult to argue with the magnitude of Wolf-Wendel's estimates of the impact of women's colleges. The standardized regression coefficients for institutional gender in her analyses vary between .27 and .59. Part of these large effects, of course, could be attributable to the use of institutions rather than individuals as the unit of analysis. Nevertheless, even if institutional-level controls could have been introduced for entering student ambition and aspirations, it is still questionable if Wolf-Wendel's estimates of the effects of women's colleges on women's career eminence would be reduced to statistical nonsignificance.

Two-Year Versus Four-Year Colleges. In the "Net Effects of College" section of this chapter, we reviewed the rather unsurprising evidence that, on average, completion of a bachelor's degree returned significantly higher levels of occupational status and earnings than did an associate degree. In this section, we review studies that focus on whether starting postsecondary education at a two-year versus a four-year college has important implications for one's career.

Persistence in mathematics, science, and engineering. We uncovered two longitudinal studies (Grandy, 1998; Hilton, Hsia, Cheng, & Miller, 1995) analyzing the same data that estimated the net impact of starting postsecondary education at a two-year versus a four-year institution. The sample, developed from data collected by the Educational Testing Service, consisted of 3,840 high-ability minority students (American Indian, African American, Mexican American, and Puerto Rican) who in 1985 scored at least 550 on the SAT mathematics test and who indicated that they planned to major in mathematics, science, or engineering (MSE) in college. (MSE majors were operationally defined as agriculture, architecture, biosciences, computer sciences, engineering, medical and dental professions, mathematics, and physical sciences.) The sample was followed up in 1990 to determine whether they persisted in mathematics, science, or engineering. MSE persistence in 1990 in the Hilton et al. study was defined as follows: receiving a bachelor's degree in MSE and being engaged in full-time MSE work, being enrolled full-time in an MSE graduate school (regardless of what the undergraduate major may have been), or having a bachelor's degree in an MSE field and being enrolled part-time in an MSE graduate program. In the Grandy study, MSE persistence in 1990 was defined as working or studying, full-time or part-time (graduate or undergraduate), in an MSE field. With statistical controls for such factors as tested verbal and mathematics ability, educational aspirations, family socioeconomic status, high school math and science experiences, gender, college grades, commitment to science during college, and the like, starting postsecondary education at a two-year (versus a four-year) college had a statistically significant, negative direct effect on 1990 MSE persistence in both studies and a statistically significant, negative (though reduced) total effect on MSE persistence in the Grandy study.

Job performance. We uncovered only one study (Banta & Associates, 1993) that compared the job performance of two-year and four-year college graduates. A consortium of institutions in Tennessee surveyed their alumni about their employment status and satisfaction. Employers were also identified and surveyed regarding salient employee traits. Although employers of four-year college graduates perceived that their employees had more of the characteristics they expected of a college graduate, no statistically significant differences in employer perceptions of two-year and four-year college graduates were found on global ratings of job performance, quality of general education preparation, or quality of education in the area of specialization. Because it is unclear that graduates of the two types of colleges were holding the same level jobs, however, it does not necessarily follow from this finding that employers regard both as equally competent employees.

Occupational status and earnings. A small body of research has estimated the net impact on subsequent occupational status and earnings of starting postsecondary education at a two-year community college versus a four-year institution. In terms of statistical significance, the findings with respect to occupational status are mixed, but they are quite similar in terms of the magnitude of the effect. Monk-Turner (1990) analyzed data from the National Longitudinal Survey of Labor Market Experiences on men and women who were full-time workers in 1978 and were between 24 and 34 years old. The dependent measure was occupational status or prestige as measured by the Socio-Economic Index, or SEI. In the presence of controls for age, a measure of mental ability, socioeconomic background, work experience, educational attainment, race, sex, marital status, and region of the country, starting postsecondary education at a two-year college (versus a four-year college) resulted in a statistically significant disadvantage in 1978 occupational status of 2.83 points. However, using the same dependent variable as Monk-Turner, analyses of the 1986 follow up of the National Longitudinal Study of the High School Class of 1972 (NLS-72) data by Whitaker and Pascarella (1994) led to a slightly different conclusion. Controlling for sex, race, family socioeconomic status, age, secondary school grades, and extracurricular involvement, 1972 self-esteem, 1972 educational aspirations, 1972 occupational aspirations, college grades, and educational attainment, starting at a two-year college was associated with a statistically nonsignificant disadvantage in occupational status of 1.13 points. Thus, across both studies the direct disadvantage in occupational status attributable to community college attendance was quite modest, about 2 SEI points or .10 of a standard deviation (four percentile points).[27]

In addition to estimating the impact of entering postsecondary education at a two-year versus a four-year college on subsequent occupational status, Whitaker and Pascarella (1994) also estimated the corresponding impact on 1986 earnings. To the controls used in their prediction of 1986 occupational status (for example, race, gender, socioeconomic status, 1972 aspirations, 1986 educational attainment, and the like), they added 1986 occupational status and hours worked per week. Net of these influences, starting postsecondary education at a community college, versus a four-year institution, had only a small and statistically nonsignificant effect on 1986 earnings. Moreover, even without controls for 1986 educational attainment, occupational status, and hours worked per week, the effect of attending a community college on 1986 earnings was still small and nonsignificant. Analyzing the same data, Adelman (1992, 1994) reports similar findings with respect to the impact of attendance at a community college on both earnings and home ownership.

Two-year college attendance and transfer institution "selectivity." Although it does not speak directly to the impact of initially attending a community college versus a four-year institution on career success or earnings, it is worth briefly reviewing the findings of an additional study that speaks to the academic selectivity of the four-year institutions that community college transfers attend. As we observed in reviewing the evidence, there are certainly legitimate questions about the magnitude of the impact of four-year college selectivity on an individual's economic success. Yet, of all the institutional characteristics considered, the selectivity of the undergraduate student body at a college probably had the most consistent, positive influence on a graduate's economic attainment. From this perspective, Hilmer's (1997) creative study is of some relevance. Analyzing combined data from the sophomores and seniors in the 1980 High School and Beyond study, Hilmer sought to determine if students who transferred from community colleges to four-year institutions ended up at four-year institutions that were higher or lower in selectivity (operationally defined as the average combined SAT verbal and mathematics score for the institution's 1984 freshman class). Educational path equations were developed that estimated the selectivity of the four-year institution attended based on a student's sex, ethnicity, high school program (college preparation or other), high school geographic region, family income, high school extracurricular activities, tested ability, number of institutions per 1,000 students, and fees charged by institutions in the student's home state. Taking these influences into account, he predicted that a student who initially attended a community college would transfer to a four-year institution that had an average student body selectivity 32 SAT points higher than the four-year institution he or she would have attended right out of high school. In short, the results suggested that students are able to attend more selective four-year institutions if they first attend community colleges. Additional findings suggested that the predicted institutional selectivity benefit was largest for community college students who came from poor families, were of low tested ability, or performed poorly in high school. Students whose family wealth, test scores, or high school grades were more than one standard deviation below the mean transferred to four-year institutions that were up to 75 SAT points higher than they would have attended right out of high school. Conversely, high-ability, high-income, and high-performing students lost little or nothing in institutional selectivity if they decided to transfer.

Impact of Peers. In our 1991 synthesis, we concluded that, when it came to career choice, the most consistent college environmental impact was *progressive conformity.* Progressive conformity posits that, other things being equal, a student's major field of study and career choice will be influenced in the direction of the dominant peer groups at an institution. Our present synthesis found considerable evidence in support of the progressive conformity hypothesis. Probably the most extensive and methodologically rigorous research done in this area has been carried out by scholars affiliated with the Higher Education Research Institute at UCLA (Astin, 1993c; Astin & Astin, 1993; Sax, 1994c, 1996a). These scholars have analyzed various longitudinal iterations of the Cooperative Institutional Research Program data and have generally introduced statistical controls for an extensive set of individual-level characteristics, such as tested ability, race, sex, expected major, high school experiences, family background, precollege career plans, and measures of the academic and social experience of college. In the presence of such controls, there is clear evidence that both major choice and career choice are influenced by the distribution of student majors at the institution attended.

For example, in their national study of the factors that influence students' interest in studying science, mathematics, and engineering (SME) and pursuing careers in those areas, Astin and Astin (1993) found that, even after entering student characteristics (including initial choice of major) and other environmental variables had been controlled, a student's final major in four areas—biological science, physical science, engineering, and social science—was significantly and positively influenced by the percent of undergraduate peers at his or her institution majoring in those areas. Similar findings have been reported by Astin (1993c) for senior-year career choice and by Sax (1996a) for enrollment in science, mathematics, and engineering graduate programs. Net of other factors, including precollege career choice, Astin (1993c) found that (1) a senior's career choice in business was positively influenced by the percentage of business majors at the institution, (2) a senior's career choice in engineering was positively influenced by the percent of engineering majors, (3) a senior's career choice as a lawyer was positively influenced by the percent of social science majors, (4) a senior's career choice to become a research scientist was positively influenced by the percent of natural science majors, and (5) a senior's career choice as a schoolteacher was positively influenced by the percent of education majors. Using a similar analytic design in her study of postcollege commitment to science careers, Sax (1996a) reported that enrollment in science, mathematics, and engineering graduate programs was significantly enhanced by attendance at an undergraduate institution where one's peers had a strong science orientation. Peer science orientation was operationally defined as the percent of students at an institution initially choosing a career as a scientific researcher or college teacher plus the average importance to peers of making a theoretical contribution to science as a life goal.[28, 29]

WITHIN-COLLEGE EFFECTS

Conclusions from *How College Affects Students*

The evidence was clear that certain major fields of study (for example, business, engineering, technical, or professional) tend to have a closer fit with the skills required in one's first job than do others (arts, humanities, and social sciences). It was not clear, however, that the job fit of one's major is a key determinant of job satisfaction.

We found little evidence across studies that academic major as usually categorized—humanities, social sciences, natural sciences, and so on—has more than a small and inconsistent pattern of effects on job status. This may be because traditional categorizations of major have only a marginal theoretical and functional fit with the structure of occupational status. There was some modest evidence to suggest that when academic majors are placed on a continuum in terms of how they are "targeted" toward occupations that stress prestige, supervisory authority, or income, they demonstrate a stronger impact on job status.

Although sparse, the evidence we found that college major independently influences the likelihood that women will enter sex-atypical careers was convincing. Net of other factors, a sex-atypical major (one that attracts a high percentage of men, such as business or mathematics) enhances the likelihood of a woman entering a sex-atypical career. Thus, academic major in college may be an important determinant of gender equality in the workforce. A student's major field of study, however, may have little to do with his or her job performance or long-term career mobility, although in the private sector this may depend on the employing company. Not a great deal of evidence pertained to these issues, but the evidence that did exist suggested that over the long run, in business at least, liberal arts majors do as well as (though not better than) those with a business or engineering degree.

According to clear and consistent evidence, major field of study has a significant impact on early career earnings that cannot be accounted for by differences in the characteristics of students selecting different majors. The majors that enhance earnings tend to be characterized by a relatively well-defined body of knowledge and skills, an emphasis on scientific or quantitative methods of inquiry, and often an applied orientation. Examples include such majors as engineering, business, several of the physical sciences, and preprofessional majors oriented toward medicine and dentistry. These majors tend to have close links to occupations with relatively high average earnings. Differences in the academic field of study chosen during college tend to explain part but not all of the lower earnings of women and racial minorities.

Nearly all of the studies on the influence of academic major on earnings focused on earnings during the early career. The evidence was less convincing that the same majors are linked with higher earnings in the later stages of one's career.

The evidence was consistent in suggesting that academic achievement during college has a small but statistically significant, positive impact on early occupational status. Part of this effect may be indirect, occurring because grades enhance educational attainment, a key determinant of job status. Though less extensive, there was similar evidence to suggest that college grades also enhance the likelihood of women entering sex-atypical careers. A substantial part of this influence may also be indirect, mediated through educational attainment.

It was estimated that without other factors being controlled, college grades account for no more than 2 or 3 percent of the variance in various noneconomic indexes of job performance and career mobility. Evidence from the most vigorously conducted study suggested that at least part of the link with career mobility may be causal. This did not appear to be the case for the link between college grades and job satisfaction, however, which we interpreted as spurious.

The weight of evidence from a large body of research indicated that academic achievement during college has a positive, direct impact on early career earnings that is independent of student background characteristics, the selectivity of the institution attended, and major field of study. Evidence with respect to a longer-term effect was less extensive and inconsistent. Any direct causal impact of grades on early career earnings appeared small, probably explaining no more than 1 percent of the differences in individual earnings. This might be increased by as much as one-third if the indirect effect of grades on earnings, through educational attainment, was also taken into account.

We found no consistent evidence to suggest that extracurricular involvement during college has more than a trivial net influence on the status of one's occupational choice, the actual occupational status of one's job, and one's earnings. There was some limited support, however, for the contention that social leadership involvement during college enhances the likelihood of women entering sex-atypical careers. With the exception of individuals in technical fields such as engineering, college graduates were consistent in indicating that extracurricular involvement, particularly in leadership roles, has a substantial impact on the development of interpersonal and leadership skills important to job success. It also appeared to be positively linked with managerial potential. Objective assessments, however, indicated only a trivial link between career mobility and both the extent of extracurricular involvement and involvement in leadership positions during college.

There was also little consistent evidence to suggest that intercollegiate athletic participation has anything but a trivial and statistically nonsignificant impact on occupational status or earnings, though it may enhance the social mobility of individuals from low socioeconomic backgrounds.

The existing evidence suggested that, net of other influences, working during college, particularly in a job related to one's major or initial career aspirations, enhances the level of professional responsibility attained early in one's career, the likelihood of women choosing a sex-atypical career during college, and women's plans for entering the workforce subsequent to college. However, the evidence with respect to the influence of work during college on subsequent earnings was inconsistent. This may be at least partially because the studies reviewed did not usually consider the degree to which work during college was related to an individual's postcollege employment.

The magnitude of faculty impact on student career choice appeared to vary with amount of informal contact or interaction. Net of other factors, including initial career choice, frequency of informal contact with faculty appeared to enhance women's interest in a career as well as their choice of a sex-atypical career. Similarly, it also appeared to have a net positive influence on orientation toward a scientific or scholarly career and, for some students, the status of their career choice. Although there were some problems in the designs of the extant studies, the weight of evidence also suggested that female faculty may be somewhat more influential career role models for women students than male faculty.

Evidence from the 1990s

A substantial body of literature in the decade of the 1990s has addressed within-college effects on dimensions of career and economic attainment. We have organized our synthesis of that literature into the following general categories: interventions to enhance career development, academic major, academic achievement, extracurricular and social involvement, work during college, academic involvement, and interactions with faculty.

Interventions to Enhance Career Development. There is voluminous literature on the career development of college students, most of it either tangential to or beyond the scope of this synthesis. However, there is a modest body of literature that estimates the impact of interventions designed to enhance students' career development during college. This literature is largely experimental or quasi experimental in design, but the nature of the interventions is not always clearly or comprehensively described. Similarly, the dependent measures employed appear to assess a considerable range of career development dimensions. Consequently, it is somewhat difficult to synthesize the findings.

Fortunately, we were able to uncover at least one meta-analysis of career development courses. Hardesty (1991) conducted a meta-analysis of 12 studies that attempted to evaluate the effectiveness of undergraduate career development courses that were offered for academic credit. Thus, these courses were usually at least a semester in length and combined a range of didactic, experiential, and counseling activities. In each of the studies, the outcome measure assessed either career maturity, career decidedness, or both. Essentially, level of career maturity represents an individual's ability to make a realistic career decision, while career decidedness appears to represent a person's level of certainty in their career choices. Across all relevant studies, students enrolled in the career development courses demonstrated improvement in career maturity that was between .43 and .44 of a standard deviation (17 percentile points) greater than similar students not exposed to the courses. For career decidedness, the improvement advantage for students in the career development courses averaged between .34 and .36 of a standard deviation (13 to 14 percentile points).

More recent literature would not appear to contradict Hardesty's (1991) major conclusion that career development courses or related interventions can significantly enhance dimensions of students' career development and maturity (for example, Eveland, Conyne, & Blakney, 1998; Mau, Calvert, & Gregory, 1997; Niles & Garis, 1990; Sullivan & Mahalik, 2000; Wei-Cheng, 1999; Zagora & Cramer, 1994). In some of these investigations, the intervention conditions consist of different computer-assisted or standardized career development programs such as "Career Decision Making," a computer-assisted instructional program that teaches theory-based strategies for choosing a career; the "Self-Directed Search," a vocational assessment and intervention designed to increase self-knowledge and the number of vocational options considered; "DISCOVER," a computer-assisted program providing information about the fit between personality and potential careers; and the "System of Interactive Guidance and Information Plus," an interactive system designed to help students clarify educational and career plans (Mau et al., 1997; Wei-Cheng, 1999). In other studies, the intervention is a combination of computer-assisted interventions and career counseling or instruction (for example, Eveland et al., 1998; Niles & Garis, 1990). Still other studies employ different group instructional-counseling workshop formats as the experimental treatment (for example, Sullivan & Mahalik, 2000; Zagora & Cramer, 1994). Generally, the results of these investigations suggest that students in the various career development interventions (or combinations of interventions) show significantly greater growth than students not exposed to the interventions on a range of important career development dimensions. These dimensions include career decision-making self-efficacy, level of vocational exploration and commitment, vocational identity, vocational construct integration, and number of occupations considered.

Not all of the studies report requisite statistical information for computing effect sizes. Moreover, given the differences across studies in the interventions employed and career development outcomes assessed, it is not clear what an average effect size would have represented. Consequently, we did not estimate an effect size for this more recent body of evidence.

It is also worth briefly discussing a creative study by Luzzo and colleagues (Luzzo, 1995; Luzzo, Funk, & Strang, 1996) that suggests that attributional retraining as developed by Perry and his colleagues (Perry, Menec, & Struthers, 1996; Perry & Penner, 1990; Perry & Struthers, 1994) can increase career decision-making self-efficacy among certain kinds of students. Recall from Chapter Three that attributional retraining is an intervention strategy designed to enhance motivation and achievement striving by changing how students think about the causes underlying their success or failure. There is evidence that attributional retraining is most effective in improving the learning of students who tend toward an external locus of attribution for success (that is, attribute it to luck). In the experiment by Luzzo et al., students were assigned either to a control condition or to an attributional retraining intervention. In the latter, students watched a brief attributional retraining videotape in which two college graduates persuaded students to attribute career-related difficulties to a lack of effort and to attribute successful career development to adequate effort and persistence. The dependent variable was career decision-making self-efficacy, or the extent to which a person feels confident in accomplishing tasks necessary to make good career decisions. Consistent with the effects of attributional retraining on learning, the career decision-making self-efficacy of students with an external locus of control increased significantly after receiving the intervention, while the career decision-making self-efficacy of students with an internal locus of control did not.

Academic Major. With the possible exception of a student's academic achievement during college, one's academic major or major field of study is the most studied of all within-college effects on career and economic attainments. As will become clear in our synthesis, undergraduate academic major can play a significant, if not always totally consistent, role in one's career. Moreover, academic major has important implications for gender equality-inequality in earnings.

Job-related skills. A small body of research has addressed the issue of whether different academic majors have a differential impact on the development of job-related skills (Smart, 1997; Smart, Feldman, & Ethington, 2000). Smart and his colleagues analyzed multi-institutional data from the 1986 to 1990 Cooperative Institutional Research Program sample and sought to determine if Holland's (1985) model of vocational choice was related to differential patterns of student growth. Holland's model postulates that students with different personality characteristics, career goals, and aspirations tend to select academic subenvironments (or major fields of study) consistent with these precollege characteristics and goals. In turn, these academic subenvironments tend to accentuate initial personality characteristics and career goals (for example, Huang & Healy, 1997;

Osipow & Fitzgerald, 1995; Smart & Feldman, 1998). Thus, from the perspective of Holland's theory, one would hypothesize that students in "enterprising" subenvironments (that is, majors in such fields as business, marketing, prelaw, industrial engineering, and public administration) would demonstrate greater gains in practical, job-related skills than students in other clusters of academic majors (for example, "investigative" majors, such as economics, natural sciences, experimental psychology, engineering; "artistic" majors, such as drama, English, philosophy, art, music; and "social" majors, such as history, political science, sociology, nursing, education). With statistical controls for students' precollege self-reported levels of competence, this is essentially what Smart and colleagues found. Seniors in majors in the enterprising subenvironment reported greater net levels of job-related skills and leadership growth (job-related skills, leadership skills, competitiveness, ability to work cooperatively, interpersonal skills) than did seniors in the other clusters of majors.

Workforce participation. There is little in the evidence from the 1990s to suggest that academic major has a statistically significant net impact on women's workforce participation (Bowen & Bok, 1998; Stoecker & Pascarella, 1991). Bowen and Bok analyzed the College and Beyond data, which followed up students about 19 to 20 years after entering college in 1976. Their operational definition of major consisted of the categories of social science, natural science, engineering, humanities, and other. With controls for such factors as race, SAT score, high school achievement, socioeconomic status, the selectivity of the institution attended, college academic achievement, educational attainment, marital status, and having children, undergraduate major had only a trivial impact on a woman's decision to work. Similar, if not totally comparable, results are reported by Stoecker and Pascarella in their analyses of the 1980 Cooperative Institutional Research Program follow-up of students who began college in 1971. Their operational definition of academic major was the percent of men in each respective field of study nationally in 1976. Net of such influences as socioeconomic status, secondary school academic and social accomplishment, precollege educational and occupational aspirations, measures of institutional selectivity, size, and gender distribution, and college academic achievement, marital status, and educational attainment, being in a sex-atypical or male-dominated major had a statistically nonsignificant impact on full-time labor force participation.

One possible reason why academic major had no significant impact on workforce participation in the Bowen and Bok (1998) and the Stoecker and Pascarella (1991) studies is that there was simply too great a period of time between the undergraduate experience and the follow-up—about 15 years for Bowen and Bok and about 5 years for Stoecker and Pascarella. It may simply be that the impact of academic major on workforce participation is manifest early in an individual's career (for example, Steinberg, 1994). Some indirect evidence for this possibility is suggested in studies by Bellas (1998) and Sagen, Dallam, and Laverty (1997). Bellas analyzed data from the first-year follow-up of the 1993 Baccalaureate and Beyond Longitudinal Study and sought to predict the number of job interviews and job offers received. Statistical controls were introduced for such factors as age, sex, race, marital status, institutional type, college grades, educational attainment, and work experience. In the presence of these controls, business-management and engineering majors received, on average, the most job interviews, while mathematics-computer-physical science majors and social science majors received the second most. Net of the same controls, plus number of job interviews received, majors in business-management and health professions received the most job offers, while engineers actually received the least. The rather counterintuitive nature of the latter finding, given the demand for engineers, may be explained by the fact that engineering majors received lucrative offers early in their job search. Thus, they may conclude their job search before some job interviews culminate in job offers (Bellas, 1998).

Sagen, Dallam, and Laverty (1997) take a somewhat different approach and attempt to predict success in securing employment appropriate to the bachelor's degree within two months following graduation from a large, midwestern research university. Employment appropriate to a bachelor's degree was determined by educational level in the *Dictionary of Occupational Titles*. Major was operationally defined in terms of four categories: specialized-hard (for example, engineering, computer science), specialized-soft (nursing, social work, education), broad professional (journalism and business), and general liberal arts (English, humanities). Statistical controls were introduced for such potentially confounding influences as ACT composite score, college grades, gender, work experience, coursework, volunteer activities, having a mentor as an undergraduate, and participation in student organizations. In the presence of such controls, one's academic major significantly influenced the likelihood of appropriate employment. Compared with general liberal arts majors, students in either the specialized-hard or specialized-soft majors were significantly more likely to have secured employment appropriate to a bachelor's degree. Students in broad professional majors were also advantaged in securing appropriate employment over general liberal arts majors, but the advantage was not statistically significant.

The findings of the Bellas (1998) and Sagen, Dallam, and Laverty (1997) studies are not totally consistent, in part perhaps because they address somewhat different outcomes. The evidence they provide, however, does suggest that one's major can have a significant net impact on getting a job and securing employment at a level appropriate to a bachelor's degree early in one's career. The clearest advantage in these areas would appear to accrue to students majoring in fields that have the most direct functional linkages with specific jobs or occupational sectors (for example, computer science, engineering, social work, nursing, and perhaps some specific business fields such as accounting).

Occupational status. Unlike the conclusion from our 1991 synthesis, we found evidence in the research of the 1990s to suggest that academic field of study did have a significant net impact on an individual's subsequent occupational status (Dey et al., 1998; Knox et al., 1993; Stoecker & Pascarella, 1991). In all of these studies, occupational status was operationally defined with the Socio-Economic Index (SEI). Dey et al. analyzed data from the 1974–75 and the 1992–93 follow-ups of the 1957 Wisconsin Longitudinal Study. With statistical controls for such influences as gender, socioeconomic status, academic ability, high school rank, the characteristics of the undergraduate institution attended, and educational degree attainment, students with undergraduate majors in engineering, the health-related fields (for example, premedical, predental, pharmacy, nursing), and mathematics-science tended to be in jobs in the 1974–75 follow-up that had the highest occupational status. Even when 1974–75 occupational status was added to the prediction equation, undergraduate majors in engineering and health-related fields continued to hold jobs with the highest occupational status in 1992–93.

With the exception of such fields as nursing, the findings of Dey et al. (1998) suggest that students majoring in fields of study that have been traditionally dominated by men (for example, engineering, mathematics, physical science, and technical preprofessional fields such as pharmacy, premedicine, and predentistry; see, for example, Jacobs, 1995, 1996a; Nelson and Dixon, 1997; Turner and Bowen, 1999) tend to be overrepresented in high-status occupations. Some generally corroborating evidence for this finding is reported by Stoecker and Pascarella (1991) in their analyses of the 1971 to 1980 Cooperative Institutional Research Program data and by Knox, Lindsay, and Kolb (1993), who analyzed the 1986 follow-up of the National Longitudinal Study of the High School Class of 1972. Recall that Stoecker and Pascarella operationally defined major as a continuous variable reflecting the percent of men in each respective field of study nationally in 1976. Net of controls for such factors as precollege demographic characteristics, educational and occupational aspirations, characteristics of the undergraduate institution attended, college grades, and educational attainment, the percent of men in a woman's major field of study had a modest but statistically significant, positive effect on the occupational status of the job she held in 1980. Similarly, Knox, Lindsay, and Kolb (1993) found that majoring in education or the liberal arts and sciences had a significant, negative effect on the occupational status of one's job compared with majoring in engineering, technical, and professional fields. This negative effect persisted even in the presence of statistical controls for academic ability, race, gender, socioeconomic status, the characteristics of the institution attended, college grades, place of residence, and educational attainment.

Career mobility and success. In our 1991 synthesis, we concluded, albeit cautiously, that a student's major field of study as an undergraduate may have little to do with his or her long-term career mobility in business. We also pointed out, however, that in the private sector this may well depend on the employing company. Although not particularly consistent across studies, the results of a very small body of research in the 1990s at least challenge our previous conclusion (Ishida et al., 1997; Solnick, 1990; Spilerman & Lunde, 1991). Spilerman and his colleagues conducted two studies of the factors that influenced job promotion prospects in a single large insurance company. In the first of these, Spilerman and Lunde (1991) sought to account for promotion within six salary grade intervals and introduced statistical controls for years of education, gender, age, race, and seniority. In the presence of these controls, employees who were mathematics-science-engineering majors as undergraduates had significantly higher rates of promotion in the middle organizational ranks than did employees who majored in the humanities or social services. At the highest organizational ranks of the company below vice president, both business-insurance majors and mathematics-science-engineering majors were significantly more likely to be promoted than were humanities or social sciences majors.

Somewhat different findings are presented by Ishida, Spilerman, and Su (1997) in a further analysis of the same data. This difference is probably due to the fact that they operationally defined promotion not within salary grade intervals but rather in terms of three major transitions: from clerical to administrative, from administrative to senior management, and from senior management to vice presidential grade. They also operationally defined major with a different set of categories. With controls for level of formal education, age, race, sex, seniority, and institutional selectivity, undergraduate social science and economics majors were significantly more likely than humanities majors to be promoted from administrative to senior management ranks. The probability of promotion from administrative to senior management ranks for both business and science-mathematics majors was not significantly higher than that of humanities majors. College major had no significant net impact either on the probability of promotion from clerical to administrative ranks or from senior management to vice presidential rank.

The waters are muddied still further by Solnick's (1990) study of the job success of 370 African-American college graduates employed by a large manufacturing firm. With controls for such factors as sex, marital status, college grades, timing of bachelor's degree, prior experience, salary grade, and the characteristics of the institution attended, undergraduate major (engineering, science, business, or other) had no significant impact on the probability of being promoted within two years after being hired. However, business majors were advantaged in percentage increases in wages over time.

It is difficult to form a conclusion about this body of evidence, except to say that, net of other factors, undergraduate college major can play a significant role in some aspects or levels of career mobility and success. It would appear, however, that the nature and magnitude of this impact depends on the type of company or firm being considered and its unique cultural norms and values, the particular period of time in one's career, the sector of the company in which individuals with certain undergraduate majors tend to be placed, and the level of promotion or advancement being considered. As in our previous synthesis, we found little evidence to suggest that undergraduate field of study plays a significant role in promotion to the very highest levels of corporate management or leadership (that is, vice president or above).

Job satisfaction. We uncovered two studies in the literature of the 1990s that estimated the impact of academic major on job satisfaction (Bowen & Bok, 1998; Fricko & Beehr, 1992). These studies take a very different approach to defining the relationship between academic major and job satisfaction. Analyzing the 1995 follow-up of the 1976 entering cohort from the College and

Beyond data, Bowen and Bok (1998) sought to determine the factors that predicted the likelihood of being "very satisfied" with their job. Statistical controls were introduced for an extensive array of potentially confounding influences, such as race, gender, SAT score, high school rank in class, socioeconomic status, the selectivity of the institution attended, college academic achievement, educational attainment, income, the labor market sector of employment (for example, profit, nonprofit, self-employed), and marital status. In the presence of these controls, one's undergraduate academic major (categorized as social science, natural science, engineering, humanities, and other) had only a trivial and statistically nonsignificant impact on being "very satisfied" with one's job.

Given the extended time period over which the Bowen and Bok (1998) study followed the 1976 entering cohort and the potential for extensive intervening influences, it is not particularly surprising that undergraduate academic major exhibited little impact on job satisfaction. In contrast, Fricko and Beehr (1992) followed up a sample of alumni from a single university who had been out of college for less than five years and had been in their present jobs for between one and two years. Moreover, instead of assessing the simple net relationship between academic major and job satisfaction, they were interested in how job satisfaction is influenced by the *congruence* between one's academic major and one's job. Major-job congruence was measured in two ways. The first was perceived congruence based on responses to the item: "My job is in the same field as my college major," answered on a seven-point scale ranging from "strongly agree" to "strongly disagree." The second was objective congruence based on the degree of match between the person's official major defined in Holland model codes and the person's job defined by the *Dictionary of Holland Occupational Codes*. With statistical controls for gender, the gender concentration in the job held (according to the U.S. Bureau of the Census), and salary, both perceived and objective measures of major-job congruence had statistically significant, positive effects on respondents' reported job satisfaction. In both regression specifications, the positive impact of major-job congruence on job satisfaction was about equal to or greater in magnitude than the positive impact of salary.

In our 1991 synthesis, we concluded that it was not clear that job fit with one's major was an important determinant of job satisfaction. Although it is based on a single-institution sample and, as far as we know, awaits replication, Fricko and Beehr's (1992) findings suggest that we need to modify our earlier conclusion.

Earnings. By far, the greatest volume of research on academic major and career attainment focuses on the impact of major field of study on subsequent earnings. In our present synthesis, we review evidence from 23 individual published and unpublished studies that appeared between 1989 and 2000. These investigations analyzed data from numerous data sets. The specific data sets and the studies that employ them were as follows:

1. The National Longitudinal Study of the High School Class of 1972 to 1979 and 1986 follow-ups (Arcidiacono, 1998; James et al., 1989;

James & Alsalam, 1993; Knox et al., 1993; Loury & Garman, 1995; Loury, 1997; Rothstein, 1995; Sweetman, 1994a, 1994b; Grubb, 1995b, 1998)

2. The High School and Beyond 1980 cohort followed up in 1986 (Fox, 1993; Hilmer, 2000) and in 1991 (Fitzgerald, 2000)

3. The Baccalaureate and Beyond Study of 1992–93 graduates followed up one year later (Thomas, 1998) and four years later (Thomas, 2003)

4. The College and Beyond 1976 cohort followed up in 1995 (Bowen & Bok, 1998)

5. The National Center for Education Statistics Surveys of Recent College Graduates: 1985–86 graduates followed up in 1987 (Rumberger & Thomas, 1993), 1989–90 graduates followed up in 1993 (Tsapogas et al., 1994)

6. The National Science Foundation New Entrants Survey of 1992 graduates followed up in 1993 (Tsapogas et al., 1994)

7. The Cooperative Institutional Research Program data: 1971 freshmen followed up in 1980 (Stoecker & Pascarella, 1991)

8. The 1987 and 1990 cohorts of individuals 25 to 64 years of age from the cross-sectional Survey of Income and Program Participation (Grubb, 1995b, 1997, 1998)

9. The 1993 follow-up of graduates of the class of 1982 at 20 prestigious colleges and universities (Dowd, 1999)

10. A sample of African-American employees of a large manufacturing firm who were hired between 1976 and 1982 (Solnick, 1990)

11. Two single-institution samples of graduates that estimate starting salary and subsequent salary (Dutt, 1997)

Drawing conclusions from this body of evidence is complicated by several factors. First, as might be anticipated, the studies use very idiosyncratic methods for operationally defining undergraduate field of study. Most use categorical (dummy) variables to indicate different majors (for example, physical sciences, social sciences, mathematics, humanities, education, and the like). However, there is only partial consistency in how major is categorized across studies. Some studies, such as Stoecker and Pascarella (1991), do not even use categories or clusters to define academic field of study but rather consider it a continuous variable defined by the percent of men in each specific major. Second, the studies vary substantially in the period of time over which individuals are followed in their careers. Some studies are concerned with the impact of academic major on starting salary or earnings early in one's career, whereas others follow up with individuals 10, or even 15, years after college graduation. Cross-sectional data, such as that from the Survey of Income and Program Participation, actually include information on full-time employees in nearly all age groups. Finally, the investigations vary to a substantial degree in the statistical controls they are able to introduce for potentially confounding influences. The typical study, however, introduces controls for such confounding influences as sex, race, socioeconomic background, tested academic ability, precollege aspirations, the selectivity and other characteristics of the undergraduate institution attended, college grades, educational attainment, and measures of work or labor market experience.

Despite these complications, it is still possible to offer the following generalizations from this body of evidence. First, consistent with our 1991 conclusions, it would appear that undergraduate major field of study has a substantial and statistically significant net impact on earnings that cannot be accounted for by other influences, including the background characteristics of students selecting different majors. With other factors controlled, there is typically between a 25 and 35 percent difference in the earnings of individuals who were in different fields of study as undergraduates. Also consistent with our previous synthesis, the largest earnings premiums accrue to majors characterized by a number of traits, including a relatively specific and well-defined body of content knowledge and skills, an emphasis on methods of inquiry that require a high level of quantitative or scientific skills, a generally close and direct functional link to occupations with relatively high average earnings, in many cases an applied orientation, and a history of being dominated by male students. Examples are engineering, business-accounting, several of the physical sciences, mathematics and computer science, and preprofessional majors in health sciences areas such as medicine and dentistry.[30] This general conclusion does not appear to be seriously affected by differences in the methodological rigor of the studies we reviewed. Moreover, although the net effect of academic major on earnings appears to be most definitive or pronounced in starting salary or early in one's career, the general pattern of economic returns to different majors appears to hold later in one's career.[31]

Second, there may be an exception to this general pattern for students attending particularly selective, prestigious institutions. For example, Dowd (1999) analyzed data from the 1993 follow-up of 1982 graduates of 20 of the nation's most selective colleges and universities. Statistical controls were introduced for ethnicity, region of the country where one held a job, marital status, number of children, and the selectivity of the institution attended. In the presence of these controls, female graduates from history and political science departments earned about as much as did female graduates of mathematics and physical science departments. Male history and political science majors actually earned somewhat more than their counterparts with mathematics or physical sciences majors. Dowd concludes, along with Eide and Waehrer (1998), that in elite institutions liberal arts disciplines may provide the "option value" of potential graduate or professional study. This functions to enhance longer-term earnings and alter the more typical or representative pattern of major field effects on the economic returns to college. Bowen and Bok's (1998) analyses of the College and Beyond sample yielded results for both women and men, but particularly the latter, that are generally consistent with those of Dowd. The College and Beyond sample they analyzed consisted of a 1995 follow-up of individuals who in 1976 enrolled in 28 of the country's most selective private and public institutions.

Third, although the great majority of studies focus on the economic returns to different college majors at the baccalaureate level, there is also a small body of research that estimates the returns to different fields of study at the subbaccalaureate level. Most of the evidence is provided by the work of Grubb (1995a, 1997, 1998). Analyzing data from two national data sets (the 1986 follow-up of the National Longitudinal Study of the High School Class of 1972 and the 1987 and 1990 cohorts of the Survey of Income and Program Participation), Grubb found that, net of other factors, there were substantial differences in the earnings of individuals with certificates or associate degrees in different areas of study. Generally, for men the economic returns were highest for majors in technical fields (for example, engineering-computers) and business, whereas the highest returns accrued to women with majors in business and health. Unlike the general trend for a bachelor's degree, however, obtaining an associate degree or certificate in some fields of study, such as education, the humanities, and the social sciences for men, often provided little consistent advantage in earnings over a high school diploma. Conversely, it is clear from Grubb's extensive analyses that returns to associate degrees and to bachelor's degrees overlap—largely due to an individual's field of study. For example, men can generally realize a larger economic premium by obtaining an associate degree in engineering, public service, or vocational-technical areas than they can from a bachelor's degree in the humanities or education. Similarly, women can generally get a greater earnings return from an associate degree in business or health than from a bachelor's degree in the humanities or education.

Fourth, a small, but consistent, body of evidence suggests that earnings are enhanced by the extent to which one's undergraduate major is related to, or congruent with, one's job. This finding generally holds at both the baccalaureate and subbaccalaureate levels. For example, analyzing data from the 1990 cohort of the Survey of Income and Program Participation, Grubb (1997) developed a categorical matching algorithm that links fields of study with census occupational codes. He then regressed 1990 earnings on years of formal education completed, plus the matching algorithm indicating if an individual's major was or was not related to his or her employment. At the bachelor's degree level, men in related employment had about a 17 percent advantage in earnings over men in unrelated employment. (Here, and in all subsequent estimates, we took the natural antilog, minus one, of the coefficients reported by Grubb and divided the larger by the smaller.) The corresponding advantage for women in related employment was about 43 percent. At the associate degree level, men in jobs related to their major had about a 15 percent advantage over men in unrelated employment, while the advantage for women was about 50 percent. At the subbaccalaureate certificate level, men in related employment demonstrated no earnings advantage over men in unrelated employment, but women in related employment had about a 29 percent advantage. Consistent findings are reported in analyses of three national samples by Kolb (1989) and Tsapogas, Cahalan, and Stowe (1994) and in analyses of single-institution samples by Callaway, Fuller, and Schoenberger (1996), Dutt (1997), and Fuller and Schoenberger (1991). The findings hold, no matter whether the study employs an objective or self-reported (perceptual) measure of major-job congruence or whether the study is predicting starting salary or earnings about five or more years into one's career. As we pointed out earlier in this chapter, however, part of this finding may be due to the fact that the majors most likely to lead to related employment (for example, engineering, business, health) are also linked to the highest earnings. Thus, the causal mechanism underlying this finding may be somewhat difficult to ascertain.

Gender differences in earnings. It is clear that one's undergraduate academic field of study plays a substantial role in determining one's earnings, particularly in the early stages of one's career. It is also clear, from a substantial body of evidence, that there have traditionally been pronounced differences in the pattern of majors populated by men and women (Adelman, 1990, 1991, 1998a; Alsalam & Rogers, 1991; Davies & Guppy, 1997; Dowd, 1999; Dutt, 1997; Jacobs, 1996b; Loury, 1997; National Center for Education Statistics, 1997; Nelson & Dixon, 1997; O'Shea, 1989; Sumner & Brown, 1996). Generally, men tend to be overly represented in fields of study that are closely linked to the highest-paying occupations. These lucrative fields of study include engineering, business, economics, mathematics-statistics, the physical sciences, and the like. Women, in contrast, tend to be overrepresented in fields of study that are linked to lower-paying occupations. These nonlucrative fields of study include the social sciences, humanities, nursing, education, English, journalism, and the like. Moreover, women are more likely than men to enter nonlucrative fields of study even after such influences as family structure, home environment, age, ethnicity, socioeconomic background, tested ability, and high school curricular track are taken into account (Davies & Guppy, 1997).[32]

Although it is not unanimous (for example, Turner & Bowen, 1999), the general view is that this gender segregation in major fields of study has been slowly diminishing in the last three decades (Adelman, 1998a; Blau, Ferber, & Winkler, 1998; Eide, 1994; Jacobs, 1995, 1996b). In turn, there is evidence suggesting that gradual convergence in the gender distribution across major fields of study may explain at least part of the decline in the earnings differential between college-educated men and women during the same period of time (for example, Blau et al., 1998; Eide, 1994; Light & Ureta, 1990; Loury, 1997). It is problematic, however, that parity in the distribution of men and women in academic fields of study would totally eliminate gender differences in earnings. Despite some exceptions (for example, Paglin & Rufolo, 1990), the weight of evidence is clear in indicating that differences in academic field of study chosen by men and women during college account for part, but not all, of the gender gap in earnings. When undergraduate academic major is taken into account, the difference in earnings attributable to gender usually becomes smaller (for example, Sweetman, 1994a, 1994b; Thomas, 1998, 2003), but it continues to be statistically significant and often substantial (Arcidiacono, 1998; Callaway et al.,

1996; Fox, 1993; Fuller & Schoenberger, 1991; Knox et al., 1993; Rumberger & Thomas, 1993; Solnick, 1990; Sweetman, 1994a, 1994b; Thomas, 1998, 2003; Tsapogas et al., 1994). This evidence is consistent with the conclusions from our 1991 synthesis.

Academic Achievement. In their discussion of the validity and fairness of alternatives to standardized cognitive tests in employment settings, Reilly and Warech (1993) argue that, for employers, academic achievement (hereafter grades) is a convenient, quantitative summary of a prospective employee's college performance. Employers, they assert, believe that grades measure motivation or conscientiousness as well as cognitive ability. As such, grades provide a reasonably useful predictor of training success in most types of jobs and of actual job performance—particularly in technical fields such as accounting or engineering (Reilly & Warech, 1993). Indeed, the evidence from research on individual differences suggests that the personal characteristics of cognitive ability and conscientiousness play a large role in career success (Roth & Clarke, 1998; Schmidt, Ones, & Hunter, 1992). As suggested by Roth and Clarke (1998), substantial correlational evidence links college grades with cognitive ability, while other evidence links grades with measures of conscientiousness (for example, Roth & Clarke, 1998; Schmitt, Ryan, Stierwalt, & Powell, 1995; Wolfe & Johnson, 1995). Consequently, it is not particularly surprising that the impact of grades on various dimensions of career and economic success has continued to be a significant focus for scholars in the decade of the 1990s. We synthesize this evidence in the following categories: workforce participation, the link between grades and adult success, job satisfaction, occupational status, and earnings.

Workforce participation. The evidence on college grades and workforce participation is mixed. There appears to be little support for the hypothesis that, net of other factors, grades directly influence the long-term likelihood that women will be in the workforce. For example, when statistical controls were introduced for such factors as precollege educational and occupational aspirations, high school grades, socioeconomic status, institutional selectivity and size, marital status, college major, and educational attainment, Stoecker and Pascarella (1991) found that college grades had no significant effect on women's likelihood of being full-time in the workforce about nine years after entering college. Using the same general analytic design, Bowen and Bok (1998) reported similar results. College grades did not significantly influence a woman's decision to work when measured about 19 years after entering college.

Of course, the fact that the Stoecker and Pascarella (1991) and Bowen and Bok (1998) studies considered workforce participation substantially after students entered, and presumably graduated, from college may in part explain why college grades had only a trivial and statistically nonsignificant impact. Studies that consider workforce participation within one or two years after obtaining a bachelor's degree report different results. For example, in analyses of two respective single-institution samples that followed up alumni during the first year after graduation, Grayson (1997a) and Sagen, Dallam, and Laverty (1997) introduced statistical controls for important student background characteristics and abilities. In the presence of these controls, college grades significantly and positively influenced the odds of being employed full-time (Grayson, 1997a) and being employed in a job appropriate to a bachelor's degree (Sagen et al., 1997). Another single-institution study of recent graduates conducted by Williams and Ball (1993) reports findings consistent with those of Grayson (1997a), although it is not clear that controls were in effect for potential confounding influences.

Link between college grades and occupational success. One approach to studying the impact of college grades on career and economic success has simply been to estimate the strength of the association between cumulative undergraduate grades and various measures of success in the workplace. There is no shortage of studies on this topic. Fortunately, since 1989 there have been a number of quantitative syntheses (or meta-analyses) of this evidence. Bretz (1989), synthesizing 39 studies, Dye and Reck (1989), synthesizing 72 studies, and Roth, BeVier, Switzer, and Schippman (1996), synthesizing 49 studies, have all estimated the link between undergraduate grades and various measures of job success. The measures of job success included supervisor's ratings of job performance, measures of output-productivity, salary, training success, and the like. Weighting the overall findings of each meta-analysis by the number of studies reviewed, we estimate that the average correlation between cumulative undergraduate grades and job success-performance was about .16. In other words, across all studies undergraduate grades accounted for about 2.6 percent of the variance in job success (that is, $.16^2$). Overall, this is not a particularly strong association. However, grades are a better predictor of performance as the links between education and jobs get closer. Examples would include such fields as business and engineering. Moreover, Roth, BeVier, Switzer, and Schippman (1996) also found that when the simple correlation between grades and job success was corrected for such factors as the reliability and range restriction of grades and job performance measures, the size of the correlation increased to between .23 and .36.

More recently, Roth and Clarke (1998) conducted a meta-analysis of 75 studies focusing on the relationship between undergraduate grades and earnings or salary. They found a simple correlation of .14 between grades and starting salary, which rose to .22 when the correlation was corrected for range restriction and the unreliability of grades. College grades had a simple correlation of .17 with current salary, which rose to .26 when the correlation was corrected for range restriction and the unreliability of grades. The correlation between grades and salary growth was negligible. Using the correlations derived by Roth and Clarke from their meta-analysis, one would conclude that undergraduate college grades are associated with between 2 and 4.8 percent of the variance in starting salary (that is, $.14^2$ and $.22^2$) and 2.9 and 6.8 percent of the variance in current salary. The lower estimates are quite consistent with the conclusions from our previous synthesis. The higher estimates are somewhat larger than our 1991 estimates, but that is probably due to the corrections for restricted range and unreliability of grades included in Roth and Clarke's work.

It is also worth noting that, consistent with the meta-analysis results on grades and job success, Roth and Clarke (1998) also found that in fields where there was a stronger connection between education and job skills, the correlation between grades and salary was larger. For example, in engineering the correlations were in the .35 to .45 range.

Of course, there is a significant problem with this body of evidence. That is, the simple correlation between college grades and various measures of job performance and success is likely confounded by other factors. Thus, only part of the association may be causal. Another body of research has attempted to estimate the actual net or causal impact of college grades on career and economic success. We turn now to a summary of that evidence.

Job satisfaction and job mobility. As with our previous synthesis, we found little evidence to suggest that undergraduate grades are causally linked with job satisfaction. Both Bretz (1989), analyzing a single-institution sample, and Bowen and Bok (1998), analyzing the multi-institutional College and Beyond sample, found that undergraduate grades had only a trivial and statistically nonsignificant relationship with measures of job satisfaction when salient confounding influences were controlled statistically. Similarly, we found little to suggest that undergraduate grades have a causal relationship with job mobility, at least when job mobility is measured by such things as salary growth or probability of promotion. Net of statistical controls for important confounding influences, both Bretz (1989) and Solnick (1990) found that undergraduate grades had only a negligible and statistically nonsignificant association with either salary growth or probability of promotion. These findings fail to support our 1991 conclusion that the association between grades and job success or mobility may be causal.

Occupational status. Consistent with the conclusion from our 1991 synthesis, the evidence from the 1990s suggests that college grades have a positive net effect on occupational status. The impact, however, may be as much indirect as direct. The evidence comes from analyses of two nationally representative data sets: the 1986 follow-up of the National Longitudinal Study of the High School Class of 1972 (Knox et al., 1993; Whitaker & Pascarella, 1994) and the 1972 to 1980 data from the Cooperative Institutional Research Program (Stoecker & Pascarella, 1991). All studies used the Socio-Economic Index (SEI) as the measure of occupational status. Knox, Lindsay, and Kolb introduced statistical controls for tested academic ability, race, gender, socioeconomic status, academic major, characteristics of the institution attended, and educational attainment. Net of such controls, undergraduate college grades had a small, but statistically significant, direct effect on 1986 occupational status. Using essentially the same analytic design but with a somewhat different subsample of the NLS-72 data, Whitaker and Pascarella found a modest, positive but statistically nonsignificant, direct effect of grades on 1986 occupational status. However, grades had a relatively substantial and statistically significant, indirect, positive effect on occupational status, mediated through the large, positive effect of grades on educational attainment. Consistent results are reported by Stoecker and Pascarella (1991). Net of the confounding influence of such variables as socioeconomic status, precollege educational and occupational aspirations, secondary school achievement, characteristics of the institution attended, college major, and educational attainment, college grades had a small, positive, but statistically nonsignificant, direct effect on women's occupational status. However, the indirect, positive effect of grades on occupational status, mediated through educational attainment, was larger than the direct effect and statistically significant. Our best estimate across all three studies is that, net of other factors, a one-unit increase in grades (for example, going from a B to an A) was associated with a direct increase in occupational status of only between .05 and .10 of a standard deviation. If the indirect effect of grades is added to this, however, the total positive effect of grades on occupational status is probably doubled (for example, .10 to .20 of a standard deviation).

Earnings. In our 1991 synthesis, we concluded that academic achievement during college had a small, positive effect on early career earnings. Evidence from the substantial body of research on this topic in the 1990s would tend to reinforce this conclusion. Moreover, there is also evidence from the research of the 1990s to suggest that grades significantly and positively influence earnings beyond the early career. In our present synthesis, we reviewed evidence from 27 individual published and unpublished studies that appeared between 1989 and 2000. These investigations analyzed data from a broad array of multi-institutional and single-institution samples. The specific data sets and the studies that employ them were as follows:

1. The National Longitudinal Study of the High School Class of 1972 to 1979 and 1986 follow-ups (Arcidiacono, 1998; Hollenbeck, 1993; James & Alsalam, 1993; James et al., 1989; Knox et al., 1993; Loury, 1997; Loury & Garman, 1995; Sweetman, 1994a, 1994b; Whitaker & Pascarella, 1994)

2. The Baccalaureate and Beyond Study of 1992–93 graduates followed up one year later (Thomas, 1998) and four years later (Thomas, 2003)

3. The High School and Beyond 1980 cohort followed up in 1986 (Hilmer, 2000) and 1991 (Fitzgerald, 2000)

4. The College and Beyond 1976 cohort followed up in 1995 (Bowen & Bok, 1998)

5. The National Center for Education Statistics Surveys of Recent College Graduates: 1985–86 graduates followed up in 1987 (Rumberger & Thomas, 1993), 1989–90 graduates followed up in 1991 (Tsapogas et al., 1994)

6. The National Science Foundation New Entrants Survey of 1992 graduates followed up in 1993 (Tsapogas et al., 1994)

7. The Cooperative Institutional Research Program data: 1971 freshmen followed up in 1980 (Stoecker & Pascarella, 1991), 1985 freshmen followed up in 1994 (Avalos, 1996)

8. The National Postsecondary Student Aid Survey of 1992–93 graduates followed up one year later (Bellas, 1998)

9. Seven single-institution or single-company data sets that followed graduates through their early career (Bretz, 1989; Callaway et al., 1996; Carvajal et al., 2000; Chesler, 1994; Fuller & Schoenberger, 1991; Jones & Jackson, 1990; Solnick, 1990)

Although varying across individual studies, statistical controls were usually introduced for such factors as tested academic ability or secondary school achievement, race, gender, socioeconomic status, institutional characteristics (where appropriate), academic major, educational attainment, and the like. As with our 1991 conclusion, the weight of evidence is consistent in suggesting that, net of other influences, undergraduate grades have a significant, positive impact on subsequent earnings. The effect is not just significant for starting salary or in the early career but also holds for studies that follow up individuals later in their career (for example, 13 to 19 years after enrollment in college). Across all studies that provided relevant information we estimate that, net of other influences, an increase in one grade group (for example, going from a B- to an A-) was associated with an average earnings premium or advantage of about 6.8 percent.[33] (In estimating this overall earnings premium, we took the average effect of different studies analyzing the same sample.) We found little to suggest that the magnitude of the earnings advantage was influenced in more than trivial ways by the methodological vigor of a study (for example, the comprehensiveness and salience of the control variables specified in the regression models). Furthermore, we found only negligible differences in the size of the effect for studies that considered starting salary or early career earnings compared with studies that considered earnings later in one's career.[34]

The preceding estimate reflects only the net direct influence of college grades on subsequent earnings. Similar to their influence on occupational status, it is also likely that grades exert an indirect, positive effect on earnings through their substantial impact on educational attainment (for example, Bowen & Bok, 1998; Stoecker & Pascarella, 1991). The great majority of studies did not permit us to estimate accurately the magnitude of this indirect effect. However, based on the few studies that did, we estimate that the indirect effect of grades on earnings, through educational attainment, might increase the total earnings premium associated with a one-grade-group increase to between 8 and 9 percent. Compared with our estimate of the net direct effect of grades on earnings, however, this estimate including the indirect effect is more tentative.

Extracurricular and Social Involvement. We uncovered only a small body of evidence in the literature of the 1990s that estimates the effects of extracurricular and social involvement on various dimensions of career or economic attainment. Most of the research focuses on extracurricular involvement and the development of career-relevant skills. However, there is also modest evidence relating to career aspirations, career choice, success in finding appropriate employment, and earnings.

Development of career-relevant skills. In a perceptive analysis of job training and education, Heckman (1999) has argued that, although educators tend to ignore it, a substantial amount of job-relevant skill formation takes place in informal, noninstructional settings. Consistent with the conclusion from our 1991 synthesis, there is considerable evidence in the literature we reviewed to support this contention, although nearly all of it is based on student self-reports or self-ratings of particular skills.

Probably the most comprehensive work in this area has been done by scholars analyzing various iterations of the nationally representative Cooperative Institutional Research Program data. For example, in his analyses of the 1985 to 1989 CIRP data, Astin (1993c) introduced statistical controls for an extensive battery of confounding influences, such as precollege self-ratings, academic ability, demographic characteristics, secondary school experiences, the characteristics and environmental dimensions of the institution attended, and other dimensions of social and academic involvement during college. In the presence of these controls, seniors' ratings of both their leadership skills and public speaking abilities were significantly and positively influenced by involvement in student clubs and organizations during college. Leadership abilities were also positively influenced by being elected to a student office and membership in a fraternity or sorority. Although the statistically significant effects are not totally consistent across different race and gender groups (possibly because of small sample sizes for non-White subsamples), generally similar results are reported by Antonio (1998) for the 1992 to 1996 iteration of the CIRP data and by Kezar and Moriarty (2000) for the 1987 to 1991 CIRP data. Net of important confounding influences, being active in a student organization or student government and membership in a fraternity or sorority tended to have modest, positive effects on seniors' self-ratings of their leadership ability and their ability to influence others. The importance of membership in Greek-letter fraternities and sororities for the development of leadership and interpersonal skills has also been identified in more focused samples by Kimbrough and Hutcheson (1998) and Sermersheim (1996) and in a qualitative investigation by McGovern (1997).

Independent of the impact of extracurricular-social involvement and Greek affiliation, there is also generally consistent evidence to suggest that involvement in diversity experiences during college enhances the development of career-relevant skills, at least from a student perspective. For example, Astin (1993c) found that socializing with students from different racial and ethnic groups positively influenced seniors' perceptions of their growth in job-related skills, while diversity activities had a positive net influence on growth in leadership skills. (Diversity activities included such things as discussing racial or ethnic issues, attending racial or ethnic workshops, and the like.) Once again, generally if not totally consistent results are also reported by Antonio (1998) and Kezar and Moriarty (2000) and at least partially by Hurtado (1999). Moreover, in their analyses of the National Study of Student Learning data, Whitt,

Edison, Pascarella, Nora, and Terenzini (1999a) found that a measure of students' nonclassroom interaction with peers, which included items about discussions with religiously, politically, nationally, and philosophically diverse students, had a positive impact on self-reported gains in preparation for a career. This effect persisted across all three years of their study and in the presence of controls for precollege-tested ability, demographic characteristics, institutional selectivity, patterns of coursework taken, and classroom experiences with peers.

Additional work by Gurin (1999) suggests that the positive impact of diversity experiences on the development of career-related competencies is not just limited to seniors' perceptions, at least for White students. Analyzing the 1994 follow-up of 1985 freshmen from the CIRP data, Gurin sought to determine the extent to which involvement in undergraduate diversity experiences affected perceptions by alumni in the workforce of how well their undergraduate education prepared them for their current jobs. Statistical controls were introduced for an extensive array of confounding influences, including SAT scores; high school achievement; sex; the ethnic diversity of one's high school and neighborhood; the selectivity, racial composition, and diversity emphasis of the institution attended; undergraduate grades; and the like. Net of these controls, diversity experiences in college such as attending a racial-cultural awareness workshop, discussing racial-ethnic issues, and socializing with students from a different racial-ethnic group each had statistically significant, positive effects on the extent to which White alumni in 1994 felt that their undergraduate education prepared them for their current jobs. Overall, the corresponding effects for African-American and Latino students tended to be statistically nonsignificant.[35] One substantive interpretation of Gurin's findings is that nonclassroom or informal diversity experiences during college are primarily important in preparing White students for effective functioning in a workforce that is rapidly becoming socially and ethnically heterogeneous. There may also be a methodological explanation, however. The relatively small size of Gurin's African-American and Latino samples, and the attendant lowering of statistical power, may have yielded the generally nonsignificant effects for those groups.

Although it does not always fall neatly into the category of extracurricular-social involvement in college, there is a small but reasonably consistent body of evidence to suggest that participation in voluntary or other service activities during college has a net positive impact on the development of career-related competencies. For example, Astin and Sax (1996, 1998) conducted a comprehensive evaluation of the Learn and Serve America Higher Education (LSAHE) program. The sample was composed of nearly 3,500 students at 42 colleges and universities with federally funded community service programs. Statistical controls were introduced for an extensive array of potentially confounding influences such as individual student characteristics at entry to college, including propensity to engage in service, structural characteristics of the institution attended (for example, size, type, selectivity), academic major, and the like. Net of these controls, service participation during college in each of four different settings (education, human needs, public safety, and environment) significantly and positively influenced students' self-reported growth in leadership skills. About 70 percent of the undergraduate service work was sponsored by student activities or student affairs, and only about 29 percent of the students performed their service work as part of a class or course. However, whether the service was sponsored by student affairs or was part of a course had little consistent effect on the findings.

A more comprehensive (12,376 students at 209 institutions) longitudinal study by Astin, Sax, and Avalos (1999) sought to determine longer-term effects of voluntary service participation on the development of career-related skills. Data were collected in 1985, when the students in the sample were freshmen; in !989, when they were presumably seniors; and again in 1994–95, approximately nine years after entering college. The independent variable was typical hours per week during the fourth year in college spent in volunteer work, while the dependent variable was 1994–95 self-reports of how well college prepared one for work. Statistical controls were introduced for a battery of entering freshman variables, including precollege service participation, educational attainment, 1989 values and attitudes, and hours spent in volunteer service after college (1994–95). In the presence of these controls, the estimate of hours spent as an undergraduate in volunteer work had a small but statistically significant, positive effect on 1994–95 alumni self-reports of how well college prepared them for work. (See also McKinney's [1997] analyses of a subsample of the same data.) Generally similar, if not totally comparable, results have been reported by Marx (1997) in an evaluation of a program designed to integrate internship experiences that appear to have substantial service components into a women's studies curriculum.

Career choice and aspirations. We uncovered little research in the 1990s that estimated the impact of extracurricular-social involvement on career choice and career aspirations. However, Astin's (1993c) analyses of the 1985 to 1989 Cooperative Institutional Research Program data suggest that certain dimensions of extracurricular involvement do contribute to choice of a career in business or law. Net of controls for a battery of confounding influences, including freshman career choice and academic major, being a member of a fraternity or sorority enhanced the likelihood of choosing a career in business or the law as a senior. Similarly, choice of a career as a lawyer was also enhanced by being elected to a student office. Conversely, some dimensions of extracurricular-social involvement tended to inhibit the choice of a career in business and nursing. Net of other factors, involvement in diversity activities (for example, discussing racial or ethnic issues, attending a racial or ethnic workshop) negatively influenced seniors' choice of a business career, while involvement in student clubs or organizations inhibited choice of a career in nursing. Analyses of the same 1985 to 1989 CIRP data, but with the addition of the 1994–95 follow-up, indicates further that involvement in volunteer-community service during college significantly enhanced the likelihood of entering a career with a social activist orientation (for example, social worker, school or college teacher, nurse, physician, lawyer). Net of confounding influences, including precollege career choice and career choice as a senior, performing volunteer work during college had a positive direct effect on Latino students' choice of a career having a social activist orientation. For White students, the corresponding influence was also positive but indirect, being mediated by career choice as a senior (Villalpando, 1996).

Allen's (1992) study of African-American students at eight predominantly White and eight historically Black institutions suggests that social involvement during college may also enhance career aspirations. Net of such influences as educational aspirations, high school and college grades, class standing, study time, sex, socioeconomic status, self-concept, and campus racial composition, a measure of extracurricular involvement during college had a small but statistically significant, positive effect on a measure of occupational aspirations that assessed job prestige and power.

Securing employment and earnings. Evidence presented by both Albrecht, Carpenter, and Sivo (1994) and Reardon, Lenz, and Folsom (1998) indicates that employers and corporate recruiters place considerable weight on student extracurricular involvement during college, particularly in leadership positions, in making hiring decisions. Consistent with this evidence is a single-institution finding from a longitudinal study conducted by Sagen, Dallam, and Laverty (1997). Recall from earlier in the chapter that they sought to determine the factors that influenced the likelihood of securing employment appropriate to a bachelor's degree within three months of graduating from college. Net of such controls as sex, field of study, work experience, college grades, ACT score, having an undergraduate mentor, and types of coursework taken, participation in student organizations had a modest, but statistically significant, positive effect on the odds of a graduate securing appropriate employment. Other evidence, however, is less supportive of the notion that extracurricular involvement enhances the likelihood of securing employment. Williams and Ball (1993) found that involvement in extracurricular activities during college had no significant relationship with the employment status of alumni surveyed a little over a year after graduation.

Evidence concerning the impact of extracurricular-social involvement on earnings is sparse and not totally consistent. Analyses of a small, single-institution sample by Fischer (1994) found that participating in student government as an undergraduate had a significant, positive effect on subsequent earnings from 12 to 17 years after college. This effect persisted in the presence of statistical controls for such factors as gender, educational aspirations, career goals, work during college, college grades, and measures of postcollege involvement. However, the sample was individuals who earned a master's degree or higher after graduating from college, so the finding may have somewhat limited generalizability. Indeed, Stoecker and Pascarella's (1991) analyses of the multi-institutional 1971 to 1980 Cooperative Institutional Research Program data found that a measure of student extracurricular-social involvement had only a trivial and statistically nonsignificant impact on women's subsequent earnings when competing influences were taken into account. Given the different samples and inconsistent findings, it is difficult to form any conclusion about the impact of extracurricular involvement on earnings other than that the evidence is not convincing.[36]

Work During College. We uncovered a small body of research from the decade of the 1990s that addresses the impact of different forms of employment during college on career and economic attainment. We synthesize this evidence based on the following categories: development of career-related skills, securing employment, and earnings.

Development of career-related skills. In his review of the literature on college students' career development, Jepsen (n.d.) has argued that students acquire human capital or job skills from a number of personal investments. One of these investments is work experience during college, often in the form of part-time jobs and internships. Consistent with Jepsen's argument, a small but generally consistent body of research supports the contention that employment during college enhances the development of career-related skills. Nearly all this evidence, however, is based on student self-reports. For example, in their analysis of the 1987 to 1991 iteration of the Cooperative Institutional Research Program data, Kim and Alvarez (1995) sought to determine the factors that influenced self-reported growth in women's acquisition of job skills during college. With controls in place for such factors as SAT scores, family background, race, educational aspirations, college environmental factors, college major, and other college experiences, involvement in a college internship program had a significant, positive effect on seniors' self-reported growth in job skills during college. Although other studies vary in sample characteristics and methodological rigor, the results they report for both male and female students are generally quite consistent with those of Kim and Alvarez (for example, Astin, 1993c; Broughton & Otto, 1999; Graham & Long, 1998; Hackett, Croissant, & Schneider, 1992; Kempner, Taylor, & West, 1990; Kuh, 1995). It would also appear that students' perceptions of job-related competence are optimally enhanced when their internship or employment experience during college is congruent with their career interests (for example, Kane, Healy, & Henson, 1992).

Securing employment. Employing data from a survey of the human resources department personnel of a large, national firm, Casella and Brougham (1995) point out why employment during college is valued by company recruiters. Approximately two-thirds of the human resources personnel surveyed indicated that, compared with those with no work experience, college graduates with work or internship experience during college produced higher-quality work, accepted supervision and direction more willingly, demonstrated better time management skills, and were better able to interact with coworkers on team projects. Over 90 percent of those surveyed indicated that work experience during college enabled graduates to make a more rapid transition from college to full-time employment. Results similar to those of Casella and Brougham are reported in a survey of employers from different companies by Reardon, Lenz, and Folsom (1998) and in data from the U.S. Department of Education, the Census Bureau, and the Bureau of Labor Statistics (O'Brien, 1997). With some exceptions (for example, Williams & Ball, 1993) and mixed findings (Callaway et al., 1996), the weight of evidence tends to support the contention that, net of important confounding influences, work or internship experiences during college significantly enhance the likelihood of gaining employment immediately after graduation (Grayson, 1997a; Knouse, Tanner, & Harris, 1999) and of gaining employment appropriate to a bachelor's degree (Sagen et al., 1997). Gleason's (1993) analyses of the High School and Beyond data also found that work during college was significantly and positively related to the number of months worked, and the average hours per week worked, in the first few years after college graduation. It is unclear, however, if this relationship was uncovered with the influence of important confounding factors taken into account. The positive impact of work experience during college on securing employment after graduation would appear to be maximized when the work experience is related either to one's major (Kysor & Pierce, 2000) or to one's chosen career (Sagen et al., 1997).[37]

Earnings. Evidence concerning the impact of employment or internship experiences during college on early career earnings is not totally consistent. For example, Fuller and Schoenberger (1991) sought to determine the factors that influenced starting salary for business college graduates from a single institution. With controls for specific academic major, college grades, age, and whether or not the job was related to the academic major, participating in an internship during college was associated with about an 11 percent advantage in starting salary for men and a 9 percent advantage in starting salary for women. Similar results with respect to the impact of work or internship experience during college on starting or early career salary have been reported by Gleason (1993) and Grayson (1998a). Other evidence, however, is less supportive of the link between work during college and early career earnings. Callaway, Fuller, and Schoenberger (1996), for example, found that internship experiences had a significant, positive effect on starting salary in one sample but a nonsignificant, though positive, effect on starting salary in a subsequent sample. Most recently, Kysor and Pierce (2000) found no statistically significant relationship between work and internship involvement during college and starting salary.

We uncovered little evidence to suggest that work or internship experiences enhance salary growth or earnings later in one's career (for example, Fuller & Schoenberger, 1991; Kysor & Pierce, 2000). Indeed, Fischer (1994) reports results suggesting that work on campus had a significant, negative net impact on later career earnings (12 to 17 years after graduation). Recall, however, that Fischer's sample was extremely small and of questionable generalizability (that is, alumni who had earned a master's degree or above).

Academic Experiences and Academic Involvement. The literature of the 1990s has produced a modest body of inquiry that estimates the impact of academic-classroom experiences on career development. This literature can be organized into the categories of cooperative learning, service learning, and academic involvement.

Cooperative learning. A small body of research suggests that cooperative learning experiences have a significant net positive influence on students' self-reported job-related skills. For example, Astin's (1993c) analyses of the 1985 to 1989 Cooperative Institutional Research Program data found that involvement in group class projects had a significant, positive effect on self-reported growth in both leadership abilities and job-related skills. These positive effects persisted even when statistical controls were made for such factors as precollege ability and demographic characteristics, the structural and environmental character-istics of the institution, and other measures of academic and social involvement during college. Results consistent with those of Astin are reported by both Antonio (1998), analyzing the 1992 to 1996 iteration of the Cooperative Institutional Research Program data, and Kezar and Moriarty (2000), analyzing the 1987 to 1991 iteration of the CIRP data. Employing analytical designs similar to Astin's, both studies found that working on group class projects positively influenced seniors' self-reported growth in leadership skills. Kezar and Moriarty also found that involvement in group class projects had positive net influences on seniors self-reported growth in both public speaking ability and ability to influence others. Similar findings have been reported in a well-conducted study of classroom cooperative group problem solving by Campbell, Bjorkland, and Colbeck (1998). Not surprisingly, related evidence indicates that cooperative-collaborative learning experiences have a net positive influence on self-reported ability to work effectively in groups (Cabrera, Colbeck, & Terenzini, 1998; Terenzini, Cabrera, Colbeck, Bjorklund, & Parente, 1999; Terenzini, Cabrera, Parente, & Bjorklund, 1998).

Astin's (1993c) comprehensive analyses of the 1985 to 1989 CIRP data also suggest that cooperative learning experiences in the classroom may significantly influence seniors' career choices. Participation in group class projects enhanced the likelihood of choosing a career in business or engineering but had an inhibiting influence on choice of a career in law, college teaching, or as a research scientist. These effects persisted even in the presence of controls for precollege variables, including initial career choice, measures of the structural and environmental characteristics of the institution attended, and other measures of academic and social involvement during college. One interpretation of these findings is that cooperative classroom experiences enhance choice of careers in which group problem solving or working cooperatively is valued (for example, business and engineering) and inhibit choice of careers where it may be less important (such as college teaching, research scientist). However, the findings might also reflect the distinctive classroom experiences in related clusters of coursework that usually lead to these particular career choices.

Service learning. Previously, we reviewed evidence indicating that involvement in voluntary service experiences was often seen by students and alumni as enhancing their career-related skills. There is also a small body of evidence suggesting that service experiences conducted as an integral part of formal coursework (that is, service learning) have impacts on dimensions of career development. Probably the most comprehensive investigation of this issue is a well-conducted study by Eyler and Giles (1999). Their sample included about 1,500 students from over 20 institutions. Some of the students were involved in service experiences as part of their coursework, while a control group was not. Among other outcomes, Eyler and Giles were interested in the effects of service learning (versus the control group) on such things as end-of-semester self-ratings of leadership skills and career skills. Statistical controls were introduced for self-ratings of each skill at the beginning of the semester as well as for family income, race, gender, age, and other college service. In the presence of these controls, involvement in service learning experiences had a small, but statistically significant, positive effect on end-of-semester self-ratings of leadership skills and a positive but nonsignificant impact on end-of-semester career skills (see also Dillon & Van Riper, 1993). Furthermore, net of the value placed on a career helping people at the beginning of the semester, as well as the other confounding influences already listed, participation in service learning also had a significant, positive effect on the extent to which a student valued a helping career at the end of the semester. Similar results are reported by Astin (1993c), who found that volunteer work increased the likelihood of seniors choosing a career as a physician.

Although less comprehensive in scope than the Eyler and Giles (1999) investigation, other studies provide evidence that also points to the potential impact of service learning on dimensions of career development. For example, Batchelder and Root (1994) found that students in course-based service learning made significant increases in a measure of occupational identity processing over the duration of the course. Occupational identity processing consisted of one's interest in exploring career alternatives as well as a willingness to invest personal or other resources in career development. Similar results have also been reported for the impact of curricular-based service learning (though not for service without a curricular base) on important career development tasks such as exploring alternative careers and majors and making plans for related summer employment (McElhaney, 1997).

Academic involvement. We uncovered a small but generally consistent body of evidence suggesting that the quality of effort or involvement students make in meeting the requirements of their formal academic program has an impact on their self-ratings of growth in career-related competencies and skills. For example, Davis and Murrell (1993) analyzed data from more than 2,000 students attending 11 colleges and universities to determine, among other outcomes, the factors that influenced student gains in vocational development during college. Vocational development consisted of gains in three areas: vocational training, career development, and specialized professional education. Net of statistical controls for family background, age, sex, college major, college grades, environmental characteristics of the institution attended, and social involvement during college, one's academic effort had a statistically significant and substantial positive impact on self-reported gains in vocational development. Academic effort was a scale that measured one's level of involvement in such areas as coursework and writing experiences. Other studies employed varying operational definitions of both academic effort and career-related competencies as well as analytical designs that differ in control of potential confounding influences. However, these studies' findings were generally, if not totally, consistent with those of Davis and Murrell (for example, Astin, 1993c; Kuh, Schuh, et al., 1991; Kuh & Hu, 2000; Polizzi & Ethington, 1996).

Interactions with Faculty. A modest body of research has attempted to estimate the net impact of various types of student interaction with faculty on the dimensions of career development and career attainment. This research appears to fall into the following categories: development of career-relevant skills, career choice, and occupational status.

Development of career-relevant skills. Analyses of three large-sample, multi-institutional data sets have yielded evidence relevant to the impact of student interaction with faculty on the development of job- or career-relevant skills. Two of the studies were longitudinal and analyzed different iterations of the Cooperative Institutional Research Program data on four-year college students (Astin, 1993c; Kim & Alvarez, 1995). The third appeared to be cross-sectional in design and analyzed data from a national sample of two-year college students (Polizzi & Ethington, 1996). All three investigations measured growth or gains in career-relevant skills with student self-reports.

Analyzing the 1987 to 1991 iteration of the CIRP data, Kim and Alvarez (1995) estimated the net effects of student background, institutional characteristics, and college experiences on women's self-reported growth in job skills during college. With statistical controls for such influences as SAT scores, degree aspirations, family background, institutional characteristics, and college major, three measures of women's relationships or interactions with faculty had significant, positive effects on self-reported growth in job skills. Two of these measures—the number of faculty who provided emotional support or encouragement and the number of faculty who provided role models—appeared to tap women's perceptions of the social-psychological accessibility of faculty. The third was working with a faculty member on his or her research. Similar, if not totally consistent, results were reported by Astin (1993c) in his analyses of the 1985 to 1989 CIRP data. Using an analytical design similar to that of Kim and Alvarez (1995), he found that students' self-reported growth in job skills was significantly enhanced through informal conversations with faculty. Polizzi and Ethington's (1996) evidence with community college students is more equivocal. Nevertheless, with controls for such influences as age, gender, grades, credit hours completed, and involvement in other areas, students' extent of interaction with faculty had a significant, positive impact on self-reported growth in career preparation for students in trade and industry fields of study. The corresponding effects for majors in business and health fields were in the same direction but not statistically significant.

Career choice. Consistent with the conclusions from our 1991 synthesis, the weight of evidence from the literature of the 1990s suggests that faculty play a potentially important role in student career choice through their contact or interactions with students in informal, and often nonclassroom, settings. Such contact may take various forms, including informal conversations with faculty outside of class, being encouraged by a professor to enter a specific career, working with a professor on his or her research, and the like. Indeed, the studies we review operationally define interaction with faculty in diverse ways, from scales that group a number of different dimensions of interaction to specific indicators such as having a faculty member as a role model.

Paradigmatic of the research on this topic are Astin's (1993c) analyses of the 1985 to 1989 CIRP data. With statistical controls in place for precollege career choice and other student background traits, characteristics of the institution attended, academic major, and involvement during college in other areas, a multidimensional scale measuring student-faculty contact and interaction in various settings had a significant, positive influence on a senior's choice of a career as a college teacher or a research scientist. Working with a faculty member on his or her research had a significant, positive effect on choice of a career as a physician. Employing similar analytical designs, generally corroborating results have been reported by Astin and Astin (1993) for choice of a career as a research scientist, by Cole, Barber, Bolyard, and Linders (1999) for choice of a career in academia by high-achieving minority students, and by Rayman and Brett (1995) and Sax (1996a) for postgraduation persistence in science careers (for example, enrolling in science graduate programs) by either men or women.[38] Across these investigations, career choices in college teaching, science, and scientific research were significantly enhanced by such factors as receiving encouragement from a faculty member, having informal conversations with faculty, having a faculty member as a role model,[39] working with a faculty member on his or her research, and a composite index of faculty-student interaction.

Although the weight of evidence we uncovered was relatively consistent in suggesting a significant, positive link between dimensions of student-faculty interaction and student choice of academic and scientific research careers, there is some ambiguity with respect to causal direction. Specifically, does student-faculty interaction increase the likelihood that one will choose an academic or scientific research career, or are students who have decided on such careers simply more likely to seek out interaction and research opportunities with faculty? Unfortunately, though competently conducted within the constraints of the data sets they analyze, the designs of the studies on this topic make it difficult to determine which alternative is the more likely.

Occupational status. We uncovered only one study that estimated the influence of student-faculty interaction on occupational status. Avalos (1996) analyzed data drawn from the Cooperative Institutional Research Program's national sample of 1985 freshmen, who were then followed up in 1989 and 1994. Occupational status was a revised measure of the Socio-Economic Index (SEI) used in most of the previous research on occupational status or prestige reviewed in this chapter. Student-faculty interaction was an eight-item measure that assessed such things as informal conversations with faculty outside of class, working with a faculty member on his or her research, being a guest at a professor's home, and the like. Controlling for such factors as parental education and income, precollege occupational status aspirations, and high school grades, the student-faculty interaction scale had a significant, positive, direct effect on the occupational status of alumni working full-time in 1994. However, when bachelor's degree attainment was entered into the equation, the positive effect of student-faculty interaction became smaller and statistically nonsignificant. Such a pattern of findings suggests that, although student-faculty interaction may ultimately enhance early occupational status, most of this influence is indirect, being mediated through the direct, positive effect of student-faculty interaction on bachelor's degree attainment.

A Final Thought: Within-College Versus Between-College Effects. In this chapter, we have attempted to review both between-college and within-college effects on career and economic attainment. An obvious question from this evidence is this: Does it matter more where you go to college or what you do in college? The answer to this question is obviously complex, and as we will see in the next section of this chapter, which reviews the evidence on conditional effects, it sometimes depends on who you are. Nevertheless, we would argue that, from a relative standpoint, what a student does during college will generally have a substantially greater impact on his or her subsequent career attainment than where he or she attends college. Consider, as just one example of this phenomenon, the evidence reported in analyses of the 1986 follow-up of the National Longitudinal Study of the High School Class of 1972 by James, Alsalam, Conaty, and To (1989) and James and Alsalam (1993). In both analyses, they attempted to predict the 1986 earnings of men with four sets of predictor variables: (1) an individual's background characteristics (for example, race, socioeconomic status, high school experiences, SAT-ACT scores), (2) college characteristics (for example, selectivity, enrollment, private-public, expenditures per student, size), (3) an individual's higher education experiences (for example, grades, mathematics, and computer science credits earned, dummy variables for college major, degree attainment), and (4) an individual's labor market experiences (for example, tenure in current job, career interruptions, marital status and number of children, hours worked per week). Both studies provide estimates of the unique increments of variance, or differences, in earnings associated with each set of variables. Controlling for the other three sets of variables, college characteristics (or between-college effects) explained estimated variance increments in 1986 earnings of between .4 percent and .5 percent. In contrast, individual college experience variables explained estimated net variance increments in 1986 earnings that were several times larger, between 2.9 percent and 7.9 percent. Although there are some exceptions to this (for example, Fitzgerald's [2000] results for women's earnings), most results are similar to those of James and her colleagues (for example, Bowen & Bok, 1998; Dowd, 1999; Knox et al., 1993; Thomas, 2000a; Tsapogas et al., 1994). This is not to say that between-college effects on career and economic attainment effects cannot be noteworthy (for example, Rumberger & Thomas, 1993). However, we would argue that the weight of evidence suggests that in most areas of career attainment they generally count less than within-college effects.

CONDITIONAL EFFECTS OF COLLEGE

Conclusions from *How College Affects Students*

Our 1991 synthesis led us to the following general conclusions concerning the conditional effects of college on career and economic attainment:

1. Non-White men appear to receive significantly greater job (or occupational) status returns from college than White men. (That is, the net difference in job status between non-White men with a high school degree and non-White men with a bachelor's degree is larger than the corresponding difference for White men.) Because most analyses in this area have employed male samples, it is not clear that the same conditional effect holds for women. However, we found little evidence to suggest that the impact of college on occupational status differs by gender.

2. When the criterion is earnings, the trend in the evidence suggests that since about 1970, a bachelor's degree has had a stronger positive influence on the earnings of Black and other non-White men than it has had on the earnings of White men.

3. The nature of any gender differences in the private rate of return to a bachelor's degree appears to depend on race. White men have typically had higher rates of return than White women, whereas the rate of return for Black or other non-White men has typically been lower than that for their female counterparts. With earnings as the criterion, the evidence is reasonably consistent in suggesting that irrespective of race, women derive greater economic benefits from postsecondary education than do men. Across both rate of return and simple earnings estimations, however, Black and other non-White women consistently derive the greatest relative benefits of all subgroups from postsecondary education.

4. The selectivity of the college attended appears to enhance job status more if one enters a professional occupation than if one pursues a business or managerial career.

5. The economic returns to a bachelor's degree are probably the same irrespective of one's academic aptitude or social origins.

6. The effects of institutional selectivity on earnings appear to be most pronounced for men from relatively high socioeconomic backgrounds and are less so for men from lower social origins. We found no compelling evidence, however, to indicate that the effect of college "quality" on earnings varies consistently for individuals from different

race or gender groups or for individuals with different levels of academic aptitude.

7. Good undergraduate grades appear to count more for entry into relatively high-status professions such as medicine and law and are more predictive of success in graduate business schools if they were earned at a relatively selective institution. This effect is, however, quite modest in magnitude.

8. The effect of undergraduate grades on earnings does not appear to depend on the selectivity of the institution in which they were earned.

9. There is evidence to suggest that the economic impact of college selectivity or prestige is more pronounced in the private employment sector and in managerial and professional occupations than in public sector or in blue-collar jobs. These conditional effects, however, await replication.

10. There appear to be gender differences in the impact of major field of study on early occupational status. The conditional effects are not easily reconcilable, however. One line of evidence indicates that women derive greater job status benefits from majoring in the natural or technical sciences than do men. Other evidence suggests that majors targeted toward income have a greater job status payoff for men. A series of findings also indicate gender differences in the impact of college major on earnings. However, the exact pattern of such differences is inconsistent.

Evidence from the 1990s

A substantial body of evidence has estimated the conditional effects of postsecondary education on different dimensions of career attainment. Consistent with the literature from our previous synthesis, the great majority of evidence concerns conditional effects on earnings—although there are also a few isolated studies that focus on occupational status, job satisfaction, and career choice. We attempt to synthesize this evidence in terms of four broad categories: postsecondary degree attainment, college characteristics, college experiences, and intergenerational effects.

Postsecondary Degree Attainment. Most of the research on the conditional effects of postsecondary degree attainment focuses on the varying impact of different postsecondary degrees or credentials for men versus women or for White versus non-White students. There is also a smaller body of evidence, however, that considers the impact of postsecondary degrees or credentials for individuals from different socioeconomic backgrounds or of different ages.

Postsecondary degree attainment by sex. Does a bachelor's degree have a greater economic payoff (compared with a high school diploma) for men or women? This issue has been addressed, either directly or indirectly, by a large number of scholars, analyzing both national and institutional samples (for example, Blau et al., 1998; Cancio et al., 1997; Cooper & Cohn, 1997; Dutt, 1997; Gray et al., 1993; Grubb, 1992b, 1995b, 1997, 1998; Gyimah-Brempong, Fichtenbaum, & Willis, 1992; Jaeger & Page, 1996; Kane & Rouse, 1995b; Knox et al., 1993; Miller, 1999; Murphy & Welch, 1992b; Pencavel, 1991). Generally, the evidence yielded by these investigations is inconsistent and leads us to conclude that, net of other factors, the earnings premium for a bachelor's degree is approximately the same for both men and women. To conclude this is not to imply that women with bachelor's degrees have the same earnings as their male counterparts. As we have seen earlier in this chapter, even when background factors and undergraduate major are taken into account, male college graduates still have higher average earnings than female college graduates. Rather, what the evidence suggests is that the net percent advantage in earnings of a male with a bachelor's degree over a male with a high school diploma is about the same as the percent advantage in earnings of a female with a bachelor's degree over a female with a high school degree. Indeed, our synthesis of the evidence on the net effects of college earlier in this chapter estimated the average earnings premium for a bachelor's degree to be about 37 percent for men and 39 percent for women.

A different picture emerges if one considers the relative effects of subbaccalaureate degrees for men and women. Evidence relevant to this issue can be gleaned from the findings of a number of scholars analyzing data from national samples (for example, Groot et al., 1995; Grubb, 1992a, 1995a, 1998; Hollenbeck, 1993; Kane & Rouse, 1995b; Kerckhoff & Bell, 1998; Leigh & Gill, 1997; Lin & Vogt, 1996; Rivera-Batiz, 1998). The overall weight of evidence from this body of research suggests that the earnings premium for an associate degree (compared with a high school diploma) is larger for women than it is for men. Across all the studies that provide relevant information, we estimate that the average net earnings premium linked to an associate degree for women is about 1.5 times as large as the corresponding premium for men. Although the evidence is not as extensive or as clear, it would also appear that women may be deriving a somewhat larger earnings premium from vocational certificates and the completion of vocational training than men (for example, Grubb, 1995a, 1997; Hollenbeck, 1993; Kerckhoff & Bell, 1998; Lewis et al., 1993; Rivera-Batiz, 1998).

A small body of research has estimated the differential effects of educational degree attainment on the occupational status returns to men and women. The evidence is consistent in suggesting that men may receive larger occupational status premiums from postsecondary degrees than women. For example, Knox, Lindsay, and Kolb's (1993) analyses of the 1986 follow-up of the National Longitudinal Study of the High School Class of 1972 data suggest that the average occupational status premium derived from a bachelor's degree (compared with a high school diploma) is larger for men than for women. Net of other factors, a bachelor's degree conferred a 23.32 point occupational status advantage for men but only a 14.04 point occupational status advantage for women. In other words, the net impact of a bachelor's degree on occupational status was about 1.7 times larger for men than for women. Similarly, analyses of two different national data sets—the 1986 follow-up of the NLS-72 sample (Lin & Vogt, 1996) and the 1986 follow-up of the 1980 cohort from the High School and Beyond sample (Kerckhoff & Bell, 1998)—suggest that an associate degree confers a larger occupational status premium on men than on women. Across both studies, the average occupational status advantage linked to an associate degree was about twice as large for men as it was for women.

Postsecondary degree attainment by race. It seems reasonably clear that racial differences in both work experience and earnings tend to diminish with increased levels of educational attainment (for example, "Calculating the Lifetime Economic Premium," 1998; Veum & Weiss, 1993). Data from the U.S. Census Bureau indicate that the median Black family income is only 61 percent of the median White family income, but among baccalaureate degree recipients, the median income of Black families rises to about 90 percent of the White level ("Taking Measure of the Additional Income Value of Higher Education," 1999). Such trends would suggest that non-White, and particularly Black, men and women are deriving a somewhat larger net average earnings premium from a bachelor's degree than are their White counterparts. This issue has been addressed directly or indirectly in a number of studies and literature reviews (for example, Becker, 1992; Belman & Heywood, 1991; Cancio et al., 1997; Geske, 1996; Jaeger & Page, 1996; Murphy & Welch, 1992b). Although not totally consistent, the weight of evidence, in fact, would appear to support the contention that the earnings premium for a bachelor's degree (compared with a high school diploma) is somewhat larger for Black than for White college graduates, particularly in the early career. Across all studies providing relevant information, we estimate that the average net earnings premium for Black bachelor's degree holders is about 1.2 times as large as the corresponding premium for Whites. This may, however, be attributable to particularly large returns to Black women (for example, Cooper & Cohn, 1997; Jaeger & Page, 1996), a finding consistent with the conclusions of our 1991 synthesis.

There is much less evidence with respect to racial differences in the returns to subbaccalaureate degrees, and the evidence that does exist is inconsistent. For example, Jaeger and Page (1996) found that Whites, and particularly White women, derive a somewhat larger earnings premium from associate degrees than do their Black counterparts. Conversely, Lin and Vogt (1996) reported an associate degree confers a larger earnings premium (but a smaller occupational status advantage) on Blacks than on Whites. It is difficult to draw a conclusion from this evidence.

Postsecondary degree attainment by socioeconomic status. A small body of research has addressed the issue of whether subbaccalaureate degrees and vocational training have differential economic returns for individuals from different socioeconomic strata (for example, Adelman, 1992; Lewis et al., 1993; Lin & Vogt, 1996; Sanchez et al., 1999). Sanchez, Laanan, and Wiseley's analysis of former students of California community colleges indicates that individuals from economically disadvantaged backgrounds experience earnings gains over the three-year period subsequent to completion of vocational certificates or associate degrees that are substantially larger than the corresponding gains accruing to students in general. Such evidence would suggest that completion of certificates and associate degrees from community colleges may be an effective way to overcome an initial socioeconomic disadvantage. Analyses of the 1986 follow-ups of the National Longitudinal Study of the High School Class of 1972 and the High School and Beyond samples, however, fail to offer much in the way of support for this contention. Findings by both Adelman, and Lin and Vogt, indicate that although associate degrees tend to enhance earnings significantly over a high school degree, the returns to individuals from lower socioeconomic levels may not be as large as the corresponding returns to individuals from higher socioeconomic origins. Thus, community college degrees and credentials may not be sufficient to narrow the income equity gap between different socioeconomic status groups. Lewis, Hearn, and Zilbert report similar findings for the impact of vocational training on the earnings of men (though not women) from the lowest socioeconomic status quartile.

Postsecondary degree attainment by age. We uncovered two studies that addressed the economic returns of postsecondary degrees for individuals of different ages. In their analyses of data on former California community college students, Sanchez, Laanan, and Wiseley (1999) found that younger students (under 25 years of age) experienced earnings gains over the three-year period subsequent to completion of vocational certificates or associate degrees that were substantially larger than the corresponding earnings gains of older students (25 years of age or older). However, as the authors point out, this may not be particularly surprising because older students already had higher earnings during their last year in college than did younger students. Consequently, the relative gain in earnings they might make for completing additional subbaccalaureate education is likely to be less than younger students with less work experience. Had factors such as prior salary level and work experience been taken into account, it is not clear how well this conditional effect would have persisted.

A somewhat different approach was taken by Bellas (1998) in her analyses of a one-year follow up of 1992–93 bachelor's degree recipients from the National Postsecondary Student Aid Survey. With controls for such factors as sex, race, marital status, college grades and major, institutional type, postbaccalaureate education, prior work experience, full- or part-time employment, and occupational classification, an individual's age had a positive effect on earnings. Although the findings would have been more convincing with controls for prior earnings, such evidence suggests that, at the very least, the earnings premium of a bachelor's degree does not diminish, and may in fact modestly increase, with age. However, it is likely that the later in one's working life one completes a bachelor's degree, the smaller the overall private rate of return to that degree.

College Characteristics. A modest body of research has addressed the conditional effects of college characteristics on career attainment. The great majority of this work estimates the effects of institutional quality measures (usually college selectivity) on earnings for White versus Black (or non-White) students or for men versus women. There are also isolated studies that consider the effects of institutional quality measures on earnings for students of different academic ability, different socioeconomic backgrounds, or who major in different academic fields of study. Finally, there is also evidence with respect to the effects of community college attendance on occupational status and earnings for different kinds of students.

Institutional quality by race. We uncovered eight studies that considered the differential effects of institutional quality measures on earnings for White and non-White (usually Black) students. Although institutional quality is operationally defined in various ways in this body of research, the most commonly used indicator is the academic selectivity of the undergraduate student body. The findings of this research are at least partially inconsistent. For example, both Loury (1997) and Bowen and Bok (1998) report evidence to suggest that Black students, and particularly Black women, derive larger subsequent earnings returns from attending an academically selective college or university than do their White counterparts. However, analyzing the same data sets but including additional controls, both Dale and Krueger (1999) and Kane (1998) found no significant difference between Black and White samples in the effects of institutional selectivity on earnings. With these exceptions, however, the remaining evidence indicates that Black or non-White students derive a somewhat larger earnings premium from "college quality" than do White students (Behrman, Constantine, Kletzer, McPherson, & Shapiro, 1996; Daniel et al., 1996a, 1996b; Monks, 1998). Our overall conclusion from this body of evidence is that Black or non-White students benefit economically from institutional quality or selectivity just as much as, and quite possibly more than, White students. (To the extent the latter condition is true, it would lead us to revise the conclusion of our 1991 synthesis.) Because of the differing operational definitions of college quality, and even college selectivity, employed in this body of research, however, we hesitate to estimate the size of the conditional effect.

Institutional quality by sex. Evidence with respect to the differential impact of institutional quality measures on the earnings of men and women is mixed. For example, Loury (1997) found that institutional selectivity had a stronger positive effect on earnings for women than men, whereas Monks (2000) and Rumberger and Thomas (1993) report that the effects of selectivity on earnings are largely the same for both men and women. Similarly, Fitzgerald (2000) suggests that institutional characteristics, most of which are proxy measures for institutional quality (for example, expenditures per student, faculty-student ratio) or selectivity, have stronger implications for the economic success of women than men. However, just the opposite is reported by Daniel, Black, and Smith (1996a, 1996b). Because these studies do not appear to differ appreciably in methodological rigor, we are left to conclude that institutional selectivity or quality has about the same average impact on the earnings of women as on the earnings of men. This conclusion is consistent with that from our previous synthesis.

Institutional quality by academic ability and socioeconomic status. Although they each are based on findings from a single sample, two other conditional effects suggest that the impact of institutional selectivity on subsequent earnings varies for students with different levels of academic ability or for students who come from different socioeconomic backgrounds. Specifically, attending a selective college may have its largest positive impact on earnings for individuals who have relatively low tested academic ability (Kane, 1998) or who come from families with very low parental income (Dale & Krueger, 1999). As tested academic ability or family socioeconomic status increases, the effects of institutional selectivity diminish. Although they await replication, such findings do not support the conclusions from our previous synthesis.

Institutional type by student characteristics. Though based on a single sample, and awaiting replication, there is also evidence to suggest that the labor market impacts of initially enrolling in a two-year versus four-year college vary for students with different levels of precollege occupational status aspirations (Whitaker & Pascarella, 1994). Students who entered postsecondary education with relatively high occupational status aspirations (as measured by the Socio-Economic Index, or SEI) benefited more in terms of early career occupational status and earnings if they initially enrolled in a four-year rather than a two-year institution. For their counterparts with relatively low occupational aspirations, initial attendance at a two-year or four-year institution had little net impact on the status of the jobs they obtained. However, students with relatively low occupational aspirations did tend to derive somewhat greater earnings returns from attendance at a two-year college. The latter finding suggests the possibility that initial community college attendance may play a compensatory role in the eventual economic success of individuals entering postsecondary education with low career aspirations or plans.

College Experiences. Nearly all of the research we uncovered with respect to the conditional effects of college experiences involved the varying impact of college grades and major field of study on earnings for men versus women or for White versus Black students.

Grades by sex. We uncovered six studies that permitted estimation of the differential effects of grades on earnings for men versus women (Carvajal et al., 2000; Fitzgerald, 2000; Fuller & Schoenberger, 1991; Jones & Jackson, 1990; Loury, 1997; Rumberger & Thomas, 1993). Across all studies, we estimated the net effect of grades on earnings for women to be approximately 1.3 times as large as the net effect of grades on earnings for men. This effect was approximately the same no matter whether the analyses were based on a multi-institutional, nationally representative sample or a single-institution sample. Moreover, the methodological rigor of the study appeared to have little impact on the results. Based on this evidence, we tentatively conclude that undergraduate college grades may have a modestly larger impact on subsequent earnings for women than for their male counterparts.

Grades by race. A small body of research permits us to estimate the differential effect of college grades on earnings for students from different social groups. The studies either compare the effect of grades on earnings for Black versus

White students (Loury & Garman, 1995) or for Black students versus all students (Bowen & Bok, 1998). Although the body of evidence is not extensive, it is consistent in suggesting that Black students derive larger economic benefits from good undergraduate grades than do either White students or non-Black students. For example, Loury and Garman found that the net effect of college grades on earnings for Blacks was about 2.5 times as large as the corresponding effect for their White counterparts. Similarly, Bowen and Bok found that the net effect on earnings of being in the top third (compared to the bottom third) of one's college class was 1.6 times as large for Black men as it was for all men (presumably including Black men). For Black women, the net effect on earnings of being in the top third of one's class was nearly 2.5 times as large as the corresponding effect for all women. Thus, although good grades in college appear to have a statistically significant economic payoff for individuals in general, there is at least a small body of replicated evidence to suggest that the payoff may be particularly large for Black men and women.

Academic major by sex. A substantial body of research has addressed the differential impact of academic major on earnings for men versus women (Bowen & Bok, 1998; Dowd, 1999; Dutt, 1997; Fitzgerald, 2000; Grubb, 1992b, 1995b, 1997, 1998; Loury, 1997; Rumberger & Thomas, 1993). Unfortunately, the studies employ different operational definitions of academic major, so synthesizing evidence across studies is somewhat problematic. Nevertheless, for students in four-year institutions, two reasonably clear patterns emerge. First, net of other factors, majoring in engineering has an impact on the subsequent earnings of women that, on average across studies, is about 1.5 times as large as the corresponding effect for men. Second, majoring in mathematics or the physical sciences has a net impact on the subsequent earnings of women that is about 1.75 times as large as the corresponding effect for men.[40]

Academic major by race. A small body of research has also considered the varying effects of academic major on earnings for individuals from different racial groups (Bowen & Bok, 1998; Loury, 1997). It is difficult to determine the magnitude of the conditional effect from the data provided. However, the results of both studies suggest that Black students receive a relatively smaller economic return from majoring in the social sciences (versus other majors) than do White students or other students who are not Black.

College characteristics by college experiences. In the section on between-college effects in this chapter, we reviewed evidence reported by Hilmer (2000) suggesting that any economic benefits of attending a selective college or university do not accrue to all individuals. Rather, they were realized primarily by those who transferred into a selective institution from another four-year college or university. Institutional selectivity had little or no importance for the subsequent earnings of individuals who entered a selective institution directly out of secondary school (direct attendees) and attended only one institution. Additional findings by Rumberger and Thomas (1993) further underscore the complexity that confronts us in attempting to understand the influence of measures of college quality on earnings. Their analyses found that different indicators of college quality (for example, selectivity, student-faculty ratio, percentage of faculty holding Ph.Ds, and the like) had significantly different impacts on early career earnings for individuals who were in different academic fields of study. For example, measures of college selectivity appeared to count more for students majoring in education, mathematics-science, and health-related fields than for their counterparts majoring in engineering, business, and the social sciences. As Rumberger and Thomas (p. 16) point out, "This suggests that it is hard to generalize about what institutional factors are important in explaining between-school differences in college earnings."

Rumberger and Thomas (1993) also report evidence to suggest that the effect of academic performance during college on early career earnings may also vary significantly in magnitude for individuals who were in different academic fields of study. Cumulative grades had a stronger positive impact on earnings for students majoring in business, education, and science-mathematics than for their counterparts majoring in engineering, social sciences, or health-related fields.

Intergenerational Effects. Does parental education influence the careers of children? We uncovered only one study that indirectly attempts to answer this question by estimating the factors influencing choice of a mathematics-science major during college (Maple & Stage, 1991). The results suggest a conditional effect based on race. Analyzing the 1984 follow-up of the High School and Beyond data, Maple and Stage sought to determine if there were differences in the pattern of influences on choosing a math-science major by race and sex. Net of such confounding influences as tested ability, high school grades, school and parental influence, attitudes toward mathematics, and initial choice of major, having a mother who was a college graduate had stronger positive effects on Black men and women majoring in mathematics or science fields than it did for their White counterparts.

SUMMARY

Change During College

The small body of evidence from the 1990s is consistent with our 1991 conclusion that students become more mature, knowledgeable, and focused during college in thinking about a career. Furthermore, there is also evidence to suggest that college seniors have a more accurate perspective about labor market realities and a higher level of overall workplace readiness than do their counterparts with less exposure to postsecondary education. It is hazardous to attribute these changes and class differences to the college experience itself, however. Simple maturation, the increased pressure on seniors to reach closure on career decisions, or the loss of the least able students from upper-division samples may be equally valid as competing explanations for the findings.

Although college seniors appear to have relatively higher levels of workforce readiness than those with less exposure to college, they may often lack an absolute level of job skills required for above-average performance. From an employer's perspective, college students appeared to be well prepared in their academic and content areas but fell short in areas that were related to the context of work (for example, interpersonal skills, setting priorities) and applying their knowledge in work environments.

Net Effects of College

The evidence from the 1990s would suggest the following general conclusions about the net effects of postsecondary education on career and economic attainment:

1. In general, a bachelor's degree provides a net occupational status advantage over a high school diploma of about .95 of a standard deviation (33 percentile points), an associate degree confers an estimated net occupational status advantage over a high school diploma of between .24 and .44 of a standard deviation (9 to 17 percentile points), and other amounts of postsecondary education or subbaccalaureate credentials such as a vocational degree or a license-certificate provide an estimated net occupational status advantage over a high school diploma of between .12 and .22 of a standard deviation (5 to 9 percentile points).

2. There is generally consistent evidence to suggest that as amount of postsecondary education increases, workforce participation increases and the likelihood of being unemployed decreases. Although sparse, and not totally consistent, there is a modicum of evidence supporting the hypothesis that the positive relationship between amount of formal postsecondary education and different indicators of workforce participation is causal and not simply attributable to the characteristics of individuals who have different amounts of postsecondary education.

3. Consistent with our previous synthesis, the small body of evidence we uncovered suggests that postsecondary education tends to produce conflicting, or at least complex, influences on satisfaction with work. Having a college education tends to have a positive indirect effect on job satisfaction through its impact on such factors as job prestige and earnings, job autonomy, and nonroutine work. Net of those factors, however, the direct effect of having a college degree on job satisfaction tends to be negative, possibly because education functions to raise workers' expectations. Having higher expectations of the intrinsic and extrinsic rewards of one's work may partially explain depressed levels of job satisfaction when college graduates hold jobs that do not generally require a college degree.

4. Some evidence suggests that when college-educated and high school–educated individuals hold the same job, the former display statistically significant advantages in job performance. Such findings,

however, may not reflect the impact of college. Rather, the job performance differences could be attributable to the fact that those with exposure to postsecondary education simply possess more of the personal traits that lead to effective job functioning to begin with.

5. Our synthesis of a large body of evidence, derived primarily from analyses of nationally representative samples, estimates the average net annual earnings premium for a bachelor's degree (versus a high school diploma) to be about 37 percent for men and about 39 percent for women. The hourly wage premium is estimated at about 28 percent for men and about 35 percent for women. Such average estimates fall at the upper end of our 1991 estimates of a net earnings premium for a bachelor's degree of between 20 and 40 percent. This finding perhaps reflects the increase in the size of the earnings premium for a bachelor's degree in the 1980s and 1990s.

6. A significant contribution of the literature of the 1990s is that it also permits us to estimate the net earnings premium for different levels of subbaccalaureate education. We estimate that the average net annual earnings premium for an associate degree (compared with a high school diploma) is about 17.5 percent for men and about 27 percent for women. The hourly wage premium is approximately 13 percent for men and 22 percent for women. Additional evidence suggests that the economic returns to an associate degree are essentially the same for experienced adult workers who return to school and for continuing high school graduates. Although the weight of evidence from a small body of research suggests that the completion of one-year vocational certificates can increase earning power, particularly for women, the average net economic returns to such certificates (versus a high school diploma) appear to be less certain, and likely smaller, than the average net returns to associate degrees.

7. Individuals can potentially increase their earnings by obtaining modest amounts of postsecondary education or vocational training without obtaining a degree or certificate. However, the average economic premium appears to be less certain and smaller in magnitude than the average economic premium yielded by an associate degree or certificate, and the size of the premium depends on what subject matter one takes. A year of full-time enrollment can lead to a net increase in earnings over a high school diploma of about 5 percent or more, and the payoff of completing a year of academic credits at a community college appears to be at least equal to the payoff of completing the same number of credits at a four-year college.

8. Consistent with the conclusion from our previous synthesis, the weight of evidence from the research of the 1990s suggests the presence of credentialing or program effects. The magnitude of these credentialing or program effects are more difficult to determine and may not be par-

ticularly robust. However, we estimate that men with a bachelor's degree earn, on average, about 15 percent more than men with four years of college credits but no degree. For women, the corresponding earnings advantage is about 12 percent. We estimate that men who finish an associate degree earn, on average, about 9 percent more than men with the equivalent of two years of postsecondary education but no degree. For women, the corresponding earnings advantage for completing an associate degree is about 11 percent. The credential-program effect of completing vocational training, although likely real, is less certain, more variable, and smaller in magnitude than the credential-program effect for either the bachelor's or associate degree.

9. Consistent with our previous synthesis, we estimate the private rate of return to a bachelor's degree at about 12 percent, with a typical range from about 9 to 16 percent.

10. The causal mechanisms underlying the relationship between postsecondary educational attainment and both occupational positioning and earnings are complex. They may function differently, and with varying degrees of importance, in different career paths, at different times in one's career, in different jobs or labor market sectors, and with changes in the economy and the nature of work. It may be fruitless to search for a single, dominant explanation. Moreover, how these underlying mechanisms may be influenced by the impact of computers and information technology on fundamental notions of work and career is not yet fully understood.

Between-College Effects

A large body of research conducted during the decade of the 1990s estimated between-college impacts on career and economic returns. The evidence from the body of research suggests the following general conclusions:

1. As with our earlier synthesis, estimations of the net impacts of various indexes of institutional quality formed the largest body of evidence pertaining to between-college effects on career and economic attainment. Although institutional student body selectivity was the most often employed proxy measure for institutional quality, the literature also operationally defined institutional quality in terms of such dimensions as academic expenditures per student, reputational ratings, faculty-student ratio, tuition, percentage of faculty with Ph.Ds, and the like. Consistent with the conclusions from our 1991 synthesis, we found little evidence to suggest that measures of institutional quality have more than a trivial and statistically nonsignificant, direct impact on overall occupational status. However, some evidence suggests that attending an institution in the upper 1 or 2 percent of the selectivity distribution enhances occupational attainment in specific high-status professions such as medicine and law. Attending a selective college confers a

modest advantage in job attainment and career mobility. The evidence is complex, however, and suggests that institutional selectivity positively influences promotion in the middle organizational ranks but has little impact at the highest ranks. The evidence further suggests that institutional selectivity signals the possession of intellectual and related traits that are important for job performance. However, it is not clear from the evidence if the individual acquires these traits from his or her experience in college or essentially enters college with them.

2. The weight of evidence suggests that measures of institutional quality, and particularly student body selectivity, have statistically significant, positive net impacts on subsequent earnings. When quality is defined as selectivity, attending a college with a 100-point higher SAT score or ACT equivalent is associated with a net increase of about 2 to 4 percent higher earnings in later life. However, the effect may not be linear, and only those elite institutions at the very top of the selectivity distribution may have an appreciable impact on earnings. Beyond institutional selectivity, it is difficult to find indexes of institutional quality that have consistent, positive effects on earnings across different studies. Although we are likely in the minority on this issue, we would argue that the body of research we reviewed probably provides an inflated estimate of the impact on earnings of having a bachelor's degree from a selective institution. Measures of individual ambition are almost universally absent in investigations of the impact of college quality on earnings. When a strong proxy for ambition is taken into account, along with other factors, the impact of college selectivity on earnings tends to become chance.

3. There is little empirical support for the hypothesis that attending a private (versus public) college has anything more than a trivial net influence on occupational status. Across all studies that provide requisite information, the average net earnings advantage associated with graduating from a private college (irrespective of its level of selectivity) is estimated at about 3 percent. Were differential tuition costs taken into account, however, the net earnings premium associated with attending a private college would in all likelihood be considerably reduced, at least early in one's career.

4. When institutional selectivity is taken into account, it is questionable that either an institution's Carnegie classification or its doctoral-research orientation has a consistent impact on an individual's subsequent earnings. The one exception to this appears to be graduation from a Carnegie-type specialized institution, and this is likely because such institutions frequently focus on preparing individuals for occupational fields characterized by high economic returns.

5. In contrast to the conclusion from our 1991 synthesis, the research from the 1990s suggests that institutional size has only a trivial and

nonsignificant impact on occupational status. However, consistent with our previous synthesis, the weight of evidence from the literature of the 1990s indicates that, independent of student background characteristics and of both institutional selectivity and private-public control, institutional size confers a small but statistically significant advantage in subsequent earnings. This positive effect of graduating from a large institution probably stems from economies of scale in providing diverse programs and major fields of study as well as a wider range of links with occupational and economic groups in society.

6. Overall, it is difficult to form an unequivocal conclusion about the impact of attending an historically Black college on the career and economic success of African Americans. Historically Black colleges appear to enhance the career aspirations of African-American students, and there is some evidence that a bachelor's degree from an HBC is at least associated with one dimension of career eminence among African-American women. However, the weight of evidence with respect to the influence of graduating from an HBC on occupational status, career mobility, and earnings is not totally convincing.

7. There is reasonably consistent evidence to suggest that non-African-American students, and particularly men, may derive potential benefits from experiences on a racially diverse campus that translate into subsequent earnings advantages. This may be attributable to the tendency for employers to recognize the importance of and to reward recent graduates' experiences with diverse populations, and these experiences are more likely to happen at institutions with diverse undergraduate student bodies.

8. We found only mixed and inconsistent evidence on the net impact of attending a single-sex college on women's acquisition of career-related skills, their likelihood of choosing nontraditional majors and careers, and their workforce participation. Similarly, the overall weight of evidence concerning the net impact of attending a women's college on occupational status and earnings is inconsistent and unconvincing. There is single-study evidence, however, to suggest that graduating from a women's institution may positively influence both women's subsequent career eminence and, interestingly, the likelihood of marrying a high-earning spouse.

9. Although sparse, the evidence from the 1990s indicates that initial attendance at a two-year (versus a four-year) college may decrease the likelihood of high-ability minority students persisting in mathematics, science, and engineering careers. Similarly, even when educational attainment is taken into account, initially attending a two-year college appears to have a very small, negative effect on subsequent occupational status. However, for similar individuals of equal educational attainment, initially enrolling in a two-year college does not necessarily

confer a significant earnings penalty. Moreover, there is evidence from a single study to suggest that students who initially enroll in a community college are able to transfer to more selective four-year institutions than they would have attended directly out of high school, and this effect was most pronounced for students who came from poor families, were of low tested ability, or performed poorly in high school.

10. Consistent with our 1991 synthesis, we found strong evidence from the research of the 1990s that the most consistent college environmental impact on career choice is progressive conformity. Progressive conformity posits that, other things being equal, a student's major field of study and career choice will be influenced in the direction of the dominant peer groups at an institution.

Within-College Effects

The extensive body of literature from the decade of the 1990s with respect to within-college effects on dimensions of career and economic attainment permits the following conclusions:

1. Generally consistent experimental and quasi-experimental evidence indicates that career development courses or related interventions (some of which are computer-based) can significantly enhance dimensions of students' career development and maturity.

2. Undergraduate major field of study appears to have a significant net impact on getting a job and securing employment at a level appropriate to a bachelor's degree early in one's career. The clearest advantage in these areas would appear to accrue to students majoring in fields that have the most direct, functional linkages with specific jobs or occupational sectors (for example, computer science, engineering, social work, nursing, accounting). Unlike the conclusion from our 1991 synthesis, evidence from the 1990s indicated that academic major did, in fact, significantly influence one's occupational status. Net of other factors, students majoring in fields of study that have traditionally been dominated by men (for example, engineering, mathematics, physical science, and technical-preprofessional fields) tend to be overrepresented in high-status occupations.

3. The results of a small body of research in the 1990s challenge our previous conclusion that undergraduate major may have little net impact on career mobility in business. It would appear, however, that the magnitude of this impact depends on the type of company being considered and its unique cultural norms and values, the particular time in one's career, sector of the company in which individuals with certain undergraduate majors tend to be placed, and the level of promotion or advancement being considered. As in our previous synthesis, there is little to suggest that undergraduate major plays a significant role in promotion to the highest levels of corporate leadership.

4. In contrast to our previous synthesis, we found single-study evidence suggesting that the degree of congruence between one's academic major and one's job had a net positive effect on job satisfaction that was similar in magnitude to the impact of salary on job satisfaction.

5. Consistent with our 1991 synthesis, one's undergraduate major leading to a bachelor's degree has a substantial net impact on earnings. With other factors controlled, there is typically a difference in the earnings of individuals in different majors of between 25 and 35 percent. The largest earnings premiums accrue to majors characterized by a relatively specific and well-defined body of content knowledge and skills, an emphasis on quantitative or scientific methods of inquiry, a generally close and direct functional link to occupations with relatively high average earnings, often an applied orientation, and a history of being dominated by men (for example, engineering, business-accounting, physical sciences, mathematics and computer science, and preprofessional majors in health science areas). Although the effect of major appears to be most definitive in starting salary or early in one's career, the same general pattern appears to hold later in one's career. A possible exception to the general pattern of major effects on earnings may occur at particularly selective or prestigious colleges. In these institutions, liberal arts majors may provide an "option value" of potential graduate or professional study that functions to enhance longer-term earnings.

6. Economic returns to associate and bachelor's degrees overlap—largely due to an individual's major field of study. For example, women can generally get a greater earnings return from an associate degree in business or health than from a bachelor's degree in humanities or education. Men can generally realize a larger economic premium from an associate degree in engineering, public service, or vocational-technical areas than from a bachelor's degree in the humanities or education. At both the baccalaureate and subbaccalaureate level, however, starting salary and early career earnings are enhanced by the extent to which one's undergraduate major is related to, or congruent with, one's job.

7. Generally, men tend to be overrepresented in academic majors that are closely linked to the highest-paying occupations, while the opposite tends to be true for women. Moreover, women are more likely than men to enter nonlucrative fields of study even after important background characteristics are taken into account. However, differences in academic major chosen by men and women fail to account for all of the gender gap in earnings among the college-educated.

8. College grades appear to have a net positive impact on the probability of being employed full-time and being employed in a job appropriate to a bachelor's degree in the early career. In contrast, the evidence that grades have a causal effect on either job satisfaction or job mobility is unconvincing. The latter finding calls into question a conclusion from our 1991 synthesis.

9. Consistent with our 1991 synthesis, the evidence from the 1990s suggests that college grades have a positive net impact on both occupational status and earnings. The total effect on occupational status of an increase of one grade group is estimated at between .10 and .20 of a standard deviation. The direct effect on earnings of an increase of one grade group was estimated at about 6.8 percent, whereas the total effect (the net direct effect plus the indirect effect through educational attainment) was estimated at between 8 and 9 percent.

10. Consistent with the conclusion from our 1991 synthesis, there is substantial evidence from the literature of the 1990s to suggest that extracurricular and social involvement during college, including Greek affiliation, has a net positive impact on student self-reports concerning the development of career-related skills. Similarly, both involvement in diversity experiences and voluntary service activities during college appear to enhance individuals' perceptions of how well college fostered their career skills and prepared them for their current jobs. However, evidence with respect to the net impact of extracurricular and social involvement on either securing employment early in one's career or subsequent earnings is unconvincing.

11. Work or internship experiences during college appear to have a positive net influence on the development of career-related skills and the likelihood of being employed immediately after college. The positive impact of work experience during college on securing employment after graduation would appear to be maximized when one's work experience is related either to one's major or to one's chosen career. In contrast, evidence with respect to the net impact of work during college on earnings and earnings growth during one's career is less consistent.

12. A modest body of evidence suggests that specific academic experiences and academic involvement have significant net impacts on dimensions of career development. Net of other factors, cooperative or group learning experiences appear to have a positive influence on self-reported growth in career-related skills such as leadership abilities, public speaking ability, ability to influence others, and ability to work effectively in groups. Similarly, service learning experiences appear to positively influence such dimensions of career development as self-ratings of leadership skills, the importance of a helping career, occupational identity processing, and salient career development tasks.

13. The weight of evidence suggests that extent of student-faculty interaction has a positive influence on the likelihood of students choosing academic and scientific research careers. However, there is some ambiguity about causal direction. Specifically, does interaction with faculty increase the likelihood that students will choose an academic or scientific research career, or are students who have decided on those careers simply more likely to seek out interaction with faculty? Evidence from

a single study suggests that, net of other factors, student-faculty interaction has a positive, indirect influence on an individual's early occupational status, mediated primarily through the direct, positive effect of student-faculty interaction on bachelor's degree attainment.

14. The weight of evidence would suggest that the net within-college effects on career and economic attainment tend to be larger than the corresponding net between-college effects. Put another way, as a general rule, what a student does during college will have a substantially greater impact on his or her subsequent career attainment than where he or she attends college.

Conditional Effects of College

A substantial body of research has estimated the conditional effects of postsecondary education on different dimensions of career attainment. Our synthesis of that research suggests the following general conclusions:

1. The weight of evidence suggests that the net earnings premium (that is, the percent advantage in earnings) for a bachelor's degree (versus a high school diploma) is approximately the same for men as it is for women. However, we estimate that the average net earnings premium linking to an associate degree for women is about 1.5 times as large as the corresponding premium for men. Although the evidence is not as extensive or clear, it would also appear that women may receive a somewhat larger earnings premium from vocational certificates and the completion of vocational training than men.

2. A small body of evidence suggests that the occupational status premium derived from postsecondary degrees (versus a high school diploma) is larger for men than women. The net advantage in occupational status linked to a bachelor's degree was about 1.7 times larger for men than women, while the corresponding advantage linked to an associate degree was about twice as large for men as for women.

3. We estimate that the average net earnings premium for African-American bachelor's degree holders (versus their counterparts with a high school diploma) is about 1.2 times as large as the corresponding premium for Whites. This may, however, be attributable to particularly large returns to African-American women, a finding consistent with the conclusions from our 1991 synthesis.

4. Although individuals clearly derive statistically significant economic advantages from completing associate degrees, such degrees may not always be sufficient to narrow the income equity gap between different socioeconomic status groups.

5. Evidence based on a single study suggests that the earnings premium of a bachelor's degree does not diminish, and may in fact modestly increase, with age. It is likely, however, that the later in one's working

life one completes a bachelor's degree, the smaller the overall private rate of return to that degree.

6. African-American or students of color benefit economically from institutional quality or selectivity just as much as, and quite possibly more than, White students. To the extent the latter condition is true, it would lead us to revise the conclusion of our 1991 synthesis. We found little consistent evidence from the 1990s that would lead us to change the conclusion from our previous synthesis that institutional quality or selectivity has about the same average impact on the earnings of men as on the earnings of women.

7. Attending a selective college may have its largest positive impact on earnings for individuals who have relatively (for selective institutions) low tested academic ability or who come from families with low parental income. Although they await replication, such findings do not support the conclusions of our previous synthesis.

8. Controlling for educational attainment and background characteristics, there is evidence from a single study to suggest that students with relatively low occupational aspirations tend to derive somewhat greater earnings returns from initial attendance at a two-year (versus a four-year) institution. This suggests the possibility that initial community college attendance may play a compensatory role in the later economic success of individuals entering postsecondary education with low career aspirations or plans.

9. We estimate the average net effect of undergraduate grades on earnings for women to be approximately 1.3 times as large as the corresponding effect for men. Although it is difficult to estimate the magnitude of the conditional effect, it would appear that, compared with other students, African-American men and women may derive a particularly large earnings payoff from good undergraduate grades.

10. Net of other factors, earning a bachelor's degree in engineering has an impact on earnings for women that is about 1.5 times as large as the corresponding effect for men. Similarly, majoring in mathematics or the physical sciences in a four-year program has a net impact on the subsequent earnings of women that is about 1.75 times as large as the corresponding effect for men. Thus, although women may be less likely to major in these fields of study, when they do so they appear to derive greater returns (versus other majors) than their male counterparts.

11. Although it is difficult to determine the magnitude of the conditional effect, replicated evidence suggests that African Americans receive a relatively smaller economic return from majoring in the social sciences (versus other majors) than do other students.

12. Other conditional effects suggest that any economic benefits linked to institutional quality or selectivity do not accrue generally to all stu-

dents. For example, institutional selectivity may count for students who transfer to a selective institution but have little impact on the earnings of students who enter a selective institution directly out of high school. Similarly, different measures of institutional quality may have different impacts on earnings for students in different academic fields of study. Such findings call into question generalizations about the impact of institutional quality on earnings.

13. Although based on a single study, there is also evidence to suggest that the positive impact of undergraduate grades on early career earnings differs in magnitude for students in different fields of study. Grades may count more in business, education, and science-mathematics than they do in engineering, social sciences, and health-related fields.

14. Finally, there is single-study evidence to suggest that the intergenerational effect of parental education on the career choices of children may vary by race. Having a mother who was a college graduate had stronger positive effects on African-American men and women majoring in mathematics-science fields than it did for their White counterparts.

Notes

1. The preliminary results of Knox, Lindsay, and Kolb (1993) were presented in a 1988 paper reviewed in our 1991 synthesis. However, we include it in our present synthesis because the 1993 publication reports somewhat different results based on somewhat different samples and analytical models.

2. See also Grubb (1998) for differences among individuals with different levels of formal education in managerial and professional occupations and Kohn, Naoi, Schoenbach, Schooler, and Slomczynski (1990) for evidence indicating a positive relationship between formal education and both job autonomy and nonroutine work.

3. Other estimates of the earnings premium for a bachelor's degree are provided by Boesel and Fredland (1999) and Katz and Autor (1998). The estimates differ somewhat in magnitude because of variations in samples and earnings indicators. For example, Katz and Autor take into account cohort demographic differences and use the Personal Consumer Expenditures deflator to obtain an inflation-adjusted log of weekly earnings for their estimates. However, the clear pattern of a generally steady increase in the college earnings premium over time, with a temporary decline in the 1970s and recovery in the 1980s, appears consistent across estimates (Boesel & Fredland, 1999).

4. Somewhat paradoxically, the increase in the economic premium for a college degree occurred during a demographic period when college-educated individuals were flooding the job market and were taking jobs that have not usually required a bachelor's degree (Boesel & Fredland, 1999; Boylan, 1993; Gray & Chapman, 1999; Heckler, 1992). There have been several attempts to explain this apparent contradiction. One is that it is college graduates who are lacking college-level literacy skills (prose, document, and quantitative) who are taking jobs with lower

educational requirements, and it is chiefly college graduates taking jobs requiring college-level literacy skills (for example, management analysis, financial adminis-tration) who are obtaining the major wage increases (Blackburn & Neumark, 1993; Pryor & Schaffer, 1997). A second explanation stresses job competition. The gap in the earnings of those with and without college degrees increased because expanding numbers of bachelor's degree holders in the labor market pushed those without college degrees, such as high school graduates, into even lower-paying jobs (Boylan, 1993; Gray & Chapman, 1999). Thus, it was not so much that the real wages of college graduates as a group increased substantially during the 1980s and 1990s. Rather, there was a dramatic deterioration in the real earnings of those with a high school degree (Gray & Chapman, 1999). A third explanation focuses on skill-based technological change in the workplace. In the 1980s and 1990s, there was a marked technological upgrading of jobs previously held by individuals with less than a bachelor's degree (Eck, 1993). This increase in the skill levels required by many "noncollege jobs" has had at least two conse-quences. First, there has been an increasing demand for, and economic premium paid to, highly skilled employees in these jobs. Second, many of these "noncol-lege jobs" have been turned into "college jobs" or "near-college jobs" (Boesel & Fredland, 1999).

5. Because the results of many of these studies use the natural log of earnings as the dependent variable, we estimated these percentages by taking the natural antilog of the regression coefficient for the dummy variable representing a bachelor's degree (versus a high school degree) and then subtracting 1.00. We employ this same adjustment in estimating the earnings premium for all levels of postsec-ondary education.

6. There is evidence from analyses of the National Longitudinal Study of Youth that the return to a bachelor's degree may be less for those who interrupt their school-ing (Light, 1995) or who complete college after age 31 (Monks, 1997). Because delayed or discontinued schooling is not usually accounted for in studies estimat-ing the net premium to a bachelor's degree, it would suggest that our summary estimates may be on the conservative side.

7. Despite this evidence, not everyone agrees that college has a substantial economic payoff for the individual. See McMenamin (1998) and Rubenstein (1998) for some well-reasoned counterarguments.

8. For corroborating evidence of the economic returns to an associate degree at the state or lower level, see Friedlander (1993), Sanchez, Laanan, and Wiseley (1999), Texas State Occupational Information Coordinating Committee (1995), Workforce Training and Education Coordinating Board (1996), and Yang and Brown (1998). Much of this evidence is also reviewed concisely by Grubb (1998).

9. There is some evidence that vocational associate degrees may provide greater returns than academic associate degrees, particularly for women (Grubb, 1995a; Kerckhoff & Bell, 1998). However, this did not seem to be the case in Grubb's analyses of the 1993 *Current Population Survey* data (reported in Grubb, 1998).

10. Leigh and Gill (1997) present evidence to suggest that the positive economic returns to community college credits or attendance without earning an associate degree are essentially the same in size for both continuing high school graduates and experienced adult workers who return to school.

11. For clear evidence of a credential-program effect for the associate degree with single-institution or state-level data, see Friedlander (1993, 1996) and Sanchez and Laanan (1998).

12. Another kind of rate of return is the return to society, or the "social" rate of return. This is usually calculated by means of pretax earnings (because from a societal point of view, taxes are counted in the national income) plus the costs that colleges and the government incur in educating students. Although the economic and other benefits that accrue to society from postsecondary education are certainly important, the purpose of this book is to synthesize the impact of college on individuals. Thus, we limit our synthesis to evidence on the private rate of return to college.

13. Using *Current Population Survey* data, Arias and McMahon (2001) estimate that the expected dynamic private rate of return in 1995 was about 13.3 percent or 11.7 percent adjusted for ability and measurement error. The expected dynamic rate of return is based on longitudinal trends rather than cross-sectional estimates.

14. Others have been more emphatic in suggesting that the private rate of return fails to capture the full returns to a bachelor's degree (Boesel & Fredland, 1999; Geske, 1996). Indeed, Boesel and Fredland argue that when all the returns to a bachelor's degree are considered, specifically earnings, other monetary benefits (for example, fringe benefits), and nonmonetary benefits (for example, health, working conditions, children's life chances), the actual return on obtaining a bachelor's degree may actually be twice the value of the standardized private rate of return.

15. There appears to be an absence of a systematic body of research on the private rate of return to the associate degree. One might hypothesize, however, that the private rate of return to the associate degree might be in the vicinity of, if not equal to, that of a bachelor's degree. Although the economic returns to an associate degree are not as large as those for a bachelor's degree, neither are the opportunity costs. For example, a recent study of college costs conducted by the American Council on Education (Hartle, 1998) reports that the average yearly tuition costs of a public community college are only about 44 percent of the average in-state yearly tuition costs of a four-year public university and only about 10 percent of the average tuition costs of a private four-year institution. In terms of average estimated total yearly costs, public community colleges were 60 percent of four-year public institutions and 24 percent of private four-year institutions.

16. There is also evidence on institutional quality and women's workforce participation, but it is mixed. Daniel, Black, and Smith (1996a) found that a composite quality measure combining selectivity and factors such as spending per student and percent of faculty with Ph.Ds positively influenced women's participation in the workforce. In contrast, Bowen and Bok (1998) found that women's workforce participation was essentially unaffected by the selectivity of the institution they attended, as did Rothstein (1995).

17. It is worth noting, for example, that Antonio's (1998) analyses of the 1992 to 1996 Cooperative Institutional Research Program data found that the development of leadership skills was essentially uninfluenced by the selectivity of the institution attended. Wolf-Wendel (1998) did find that selective institutions overproduced White women achievers but also underproduced Latino women achievers. Achievers were women included in various *Who's Who* compilations.

18. There is also evidence to suggest a positive relationship between attending elite schools (such as Ivy League or similar institutions) and various measures of career success and prominence such as becoming a Rhodes scholar, inclusion in various *Who's Who* compilations, high-level managerial and professional positions, and becoming a chief executive officer of one of the country's 100 largest corporations or financial firms (Hacker, 1997; Honan, 1993; Katchadourian & Boli, 1994; Youn, Arnold, & Salkever, 1998, 2000). The nature of this evidence, however, makes it difficult to determine if such prominence is attributable to the status-allocating "charter" of elite schools or if it simply reflects the extraordinarily talented and ambitious individuals who attend those schools (for example, Braxton & Berger, 1995). In an interesting argument, Hacker (1997) even suggests that considering the care that Ivy League and similar schools take in choosing the nation's most intellectually gifted and ambitious students, the question we should be asking is not why the graduates of these schools are overrepresented as CEOs of major corporations but rather why this overrepresentation is not even more pronounced than it is.

19. To their credit, Kingston and Smart (1990) make a substantial attempt to build measures of precollege ambition into their earnings predictions with the 1972 to 1980 Cooperative Institutional Research Program data. They were not, however, able to include a standardized measure of cognitive ability, nor did they account for differential tuition costs.

20. For example, by providing a higher-quality education or by signaling student traits.

21. Interestingly, when both the selectivity of the school attended and the average selectivity of the schools applied to are both in the equations, the estimated net effect of the latter is substantially larger than the former. This further suggests that the ambition of the students recruited to selective schools may have stronger effects on subsequent earnings than attendance at, or graduation from, the school itself.

22. Brewer and Ehrenberg (1996), Brewer, Eide, and Ehrenberg (1999), and Thomas (2003) also consider the effects of attending a private institution. Because their private-public categories are combined with levels of selectivity, however, it is difficult to determine which institutional characteristic is having the impact on earnings. Generally, students attending highly selective private institutions derive larger net earnings benefits than their counterparts at highly selective public institutions. None of the studies, however, is able to take into account individual precollege ambition, which might well be differentially distributed across private and public institutions (for example, Dale & Krueger, 1999).

23. Interestingly, there is also evidence to suggest that institutional tuition has a net positive influence on subsequent earnings (Dale & Krueger, 1999), even when institutional selectivity is taken into account along with individual-level confounding influences (Pascarella, Smart, & Smylie, 1992). However, it may be that institutional tuition level is essentially a proxy for attending a private institution. Analyses by Daniel, Black, and Smith (1996b) suggest that when both tuition level and attending a private college are part of an equation also containing controls for individual characteristics, neither institutional characteristic has a significant influence on wages.

24. Bellas (1998) also found that graduating from a research university significantly increased the number of one's job interviews, compared with graduating from a liberal arts college. There was no corresponding significant effect on the number of job offers one received, however.

25. Ehrenberg (1996, 1996–97) also presents evidence to indicate that although HBCs remain an important source for the undergraduate and law school educations of African-American lawyers and judges, it is no longer the case that HBCs educate the majority of them. Moreover, African-American lawyers who receive their undergraduate degrees from HBCs are underrepresented among the faculty of the country's most selective law schools, relative to African-American lawyers who received their undergraduate degrees from other institutions.

26. Rothstein (1995) also found that, although the percent of women faculty at an institution did not have a significant, direct influence on women's earnings, it may have had a small, positive indirect effect. This was largely because percent of women faculty at an institution positively influenced women's advanced degree attainment, which, in turn, had a positive, direct influence on women's earnings. It is not clear that this indirect effect was tested for statistical significance, however. Moreover, because a variable representing dominant institutional gender was also included in the regression specification, the effect of percent of women faculty on earnings may hold regardless of whether or not a woman attends a predominantly women's college.

27. Because Monk-Turner (1990) did not report a standard deviation for her occupational status measure, we estimated it with the standard deviation for the SEI supplied by Knox, Lindsay, and Kolb (1993).

28. To be sure, there is other evidence suggesting that different dimensions of an institution's peer environment have a net impact on major and career choice. For example, both Astin and Astin (1993) and Sax (1994c) found that the percent of peers holding outside jobs during college positively influenced persistence in, or recruitment to, science career choices. See Astin and Astin (1993) and Sax (1994c, 1996a) for greater detail concerning these findings. However, none of these specific dimensions of the peer environment seem to influence major and career choice with the same consistency or breadth as progressive conformity.

29. Other evidence consistent with the progressive conformity hypothesis is reported in studies indicating that the largest gains in students' self-reported vocational preparation are made at institutions with the strongest environmental emphasis on the development of vocational and occupational competencies (Kuh, Arnold, & Vesper, 1990, 1991).

30. Thomas (1998) also found that, in the presence of controls for demographic characteristics, family background, the characteristics of the institution attended, and labor market experiences, these majors also had a significant, positive effect on reducing the debt-to-earnings ratio of bachelor's degree recipients in the workforce about one year after graduation. The corresponding net effects about four years after graduation were generally in the same direction but not statistically significant.

31. Berger's (1992) analyses of the National Longitudinal Study of Young Men indicated that of five groups of majors, engineers had the highest salaries when they entered the workforce, followed in order by business, science, liberal arts, and education majors. Over time, and net of other factors, liberal arts majors had the fastest salary growth and engineers the slowest—suggesting that the earnings differentials of men in different fields of study narrow as they age. After 15 years of

experience, however, the rank ordering of the men in different fields was the same as when they entered the labor market. Thus, even after 15 years of experience, liberal arts majors did not catch up with engineers.

32. Controlling for the same variables, Davies and Guppy (1997) found that African-American and Hispanic students were just as likely to choose lucrative fields of study during college as other students.

33. Because grades have a net positive effect on early career earnings, it is not particularly surprising that they also have a significant impact on reducing a student's debt burden relative to his or her earnings. Thomas (1998) found this effect statistically significant for bachelor's degree recipients in the workforce about a year after college graduation. The same effect was not statistically significant about four years after graduation (Thomas, 2003).

34. Interestingly, there is also evidence to suggest that college grades have a significant, positive influence on seniors' expectations of starting salary, expected salary after 10 years, and expected salary after 20 years (Blau & Ferber, 1991).

35. There was a somewhat anomalous finding for African-American students indicating a negative effect for discussions of racial-ethnic issues. This finding perhaps suggests that when such discussions occurred for African-American students, it was often in a context of perceived prejudice or discrimination that may have negatively colored retrospective views of their undergraduate education.

36. We found little evidence with respect to the net influence of athletic participation on career or economic attainment. Adelman's (1990) analyses of the 1986 follow-up of the National Longitudinal Study of the High School Class of 1972 found a positive relationship between varsity athletic participation and both rate of employment and home ownership. However, it is unclear how much of this relationship might be confounded by other factors. Dale and Krueger's (1999) analyses of the 1976 cohort of the College and Beyond data found that, net of tested ability, gender, race, high school experience, and ambition, intercollegiate athletic participation was associated with a 10.8 percent premium in 1995 earnings. However, we are unaware of any study that replicates this finding.

37. Work during college may enhance one's chances of securing employment, but it would appear to diminish the likelihood that women who initially aspire to a career in science when they enter college will do so as seniors. Net of other factors, Sax (1994c) found that off-campus work during college significantly inhibited women's continued interest in a science career during college.

38. For an example of an innovative program designed to retain women in the sciences, and that includes, among other features, an emphasis on facilitating interactions between students and faculty, see Fisler, Hein, and Young (1999).

39. We found little evidence to support the notion that same-sex or same-race faculty role models are particularly important in influencing student career choice (Canes & Rosen, 1995; Cole et al., 1999).

40. Grubb (1997, 1998) has estimated the relative effects of academic major on the earnings of men and women who earned associate degrees. The evidence is not extensive, however, and it is difficult to detect a clear pattern of differences.

CHAPTER TEN

Quality of Life After College

In Chapter Nine, we synthesized evidence pertaining to the career and economic benefits associated with college attendance. In this chapter we review the accumulated evidence pertaining to the influence of postsecondary education on a range of nonmonetary benefits to the individual—health, happiness, community involvement, well-being of children, and the like. Economists, who have conducted much of the research on this topic, tend to use the terms *nonmarket* or *consumption* in referring to these benefits (for example, Cohn & Geske, 1992; Haveman & Wolfe, 1984).[1] We think a more general descriptor might be indicators of the quality of one's life. In our 1991 synthesis, nearly all the research in this area dealt with the impact of different levels of formal education on quality-of-life indicators. Consequently, our previous review was limited to the net effects of college. Similarly, the more recent literature of the 1990s has as its primary focus the net impact of different levels of education, but there is also a small body of evidence on between- and within-college effects on quality-of-life indicators.

NET EFFECTS OF COLLEGE

Conclusions from *How College Affects Students*

Problems in research design and the inability to control important confounding influences made causal attributions about the long-term impact of college on various quality-of-life indexes somewhat tenuous. It nevertheless remained true that college-educated individuals consistently rank higher than those with less education on a clear majority of the quality-of-life indicators considered. Compared to those with less education, the college-educated tend to have better overall health and a lower mortality rate, have smaller families and be more successful in achieving desired family size through informed and effective use of contraceptive devices, and spend a greater portion of time in child care, particularly in activities of a developmentally enriching nature (such as teaching, reading, and talking). They also tend to be more efficient in making consumer choices, save a greater percentage of their income, make more effective long-term investment of discretionary resources, and spend a greater proportion of discretionary resources and leisure time on developmentally enriching activities (reading, participation in arts and cultural events, involvement in civic affairs, and so forth).

It appeared likely that at least part of the impact of college on these indexes of life quality is indirect, being mediated through the socioeconomic advantages that tend to accrue to the college-educated. Having the economic resources to pay for desired goods and services is not without important consequences for the quality of one's life. At the same time, the positive link between educational level and many quality-of-life indexes remains even after economic resources are held constant. This suggests the possibility at least that college may also have a direct impact on quality of life by enhancing such characteristics as the ability to acquire new information and process it effectively, the ability to evaluate new ideas and technologies, the capacity to plan rationally and with a long-term perspective, the willingness to accept reasonable risk, and the developmental and cultural level of one's leisure interests and tastes. We pointed out, however, that the absence of controls for initial traits made it difficult to separate the direct impact of college from the confounding influence of preexisting differences between those who attend and those who do not attend college.

Even though college-educated individuals clearly rank higher on a broad array of quality-of-life indicators, they do not, on the average, express appreciably greater satisfaction with their lives than do those with less education. We suggested that this does not signify the absence of impact but rather that the impact of college has dimensions that function both to increase and to diminish expressions of satisfaction with one's life. On the one hand, the clear job status and economic returns to college are likely to have a positive impact on some dimensions of life satisfaction. On the other hand, one probable impact of college is that it tends to foster a more critical perspective in individuals. Consequently, as compared to those with less education, college-educated men and women may be more sophisticated, skeptical, analytical, and critical in their judgments of some facets of job satisfaction, marital satisfaction, and overall sense of well-being.

Evidence from the 1990s

The decade of the 1990s produced a substantial body of evidence with respect to the net effects of education on various quality-of-life indexes. Although it does not address all the elements of quality of life dealt with in our previous synthesis, the research from the 1990s that does exist yields evidence that is generally consistent with our 1991 conclusions. What is different about the literature from the 1990s is that on several quality-of-life indexes, the evidence permits a somewhat better understanding of the plausible causal mechanisms underlying the association with education. However, it is also the case that the majority of research treats education as a continuous variable (for example, years of formal education completed). Consequently, it is frequently difficult to determine the magnitude of the effect uniquely attributable to different amounts of postsecondary education. Rather, one often needs to infer, or extrapolate, the influence of postsecondary education from the overall effect of education. We synthesize evidence pertaining to the net influence of education on quality-of-life indexes under the following headings: subjective well-being, health, welfare of children, and community-civic involvement.

Subjective Well-Being. Consistent with the conclusion from our previous synthesis, the evidence from the 1990s clearly indicates that the causal relationship between formal education and different measures of subjective well-being, overall happiness, or satisfaction with life is complex. Nearly all the studies we reviewed indicate that, net of other factors such as age, sex, earnings, or health status, the direct effect of formal education on various indexes of subjective well-being or overall happiness in industrialized or developed countries tends to be small and statistically nonsignificant or, in some cases, even negative (for example, Clark & Oswald, 1994; Hartog & Oosterbeek, 1998; Ross & Mirowsky, 1989; Veenhoven, 1996). Part of this may be attributable to the positive impact of education in general, and postsecondary education in particular, on an individual's propensity and capacity to make measured, comprehensive, and critical judgments. Increased education may also lead one to interpret life satisfaction or happiness in more complex and qualitatively different terms. As a result, and consistent with the conclusions of our previous synthesis, educational attainment should perhaps be expected to have only a weak and inconsistent net positive impact on measures of life satisfaction or global happiness.

At the same time, the evidence is also quite clear in suggesting that educational attainment has positive net impacts on dimensions of life that, in turn, increase one's sense of life satisfaction or overall happiness. For example, Bowen and Bok's (1998) analyses of the College and Beyond data found that, net of other factors, educational attainment had a strong, positive influence on earnings 19 years after entering college. In turn, household income (a highly related correlate of earnings) had a strong, positive impact on the likelihood of being "very satisfied" with life. This effect persisted even in the presence of statistical controls for such factors as race, sex, tested ability, high school achievement, socioeconomic status, college major, college grades, college selectivity, employment sector, marital status, and dependent children. Similarly, net of other factors, educational attainment appears to have statistically significant, positive, direct effects on both one's sense of personal control over life and perceived social support, each of which, in turn, has positive net effects on sense of well-being (Ross & Mirowsky, 1989,

1992; Ross & Van Willigen, 1997). There is also evidence indicating that education has a net positive impact on perceived health status (Ross & Wu, 1995), which, in turn, has positive net impacts on overall sense of happiness (Hartog & Oosterbeek, 1998). Thus, although the direct impact of educational attainment on global happiness or life satisfaction is generally small and inconsistent, education appears to have important, positive, indirect impacts by means of its enhancement of economic affluence, sense of control over one's life, networks of social support, and perceived health status.

Health. Of all the quality-of-life indexes we consider in this chapter, none has been studied as much—in terms of its relationship to educational attainment—as health. The 1990s produced a substantial body of empirical work on this topic. It also produced several excellent literature reviews of the existing evidence that were of notable assistance in developing this part of our synthesis (for example, Grossman & Kaestner, 1997; Hartog & Oosterbeek, 1998; Leigh, 1998b; McMahon, 1998; Ross & Wu, 1995). Clearly, there is a strong, positive relationship between educational attainment and various measures of health, such as mortality rates, self-evaluation of health status, or physiological indicators of health, and this relationship persists no matter whether the units of observation are individuals or groups (Grossman & Kaestner, 1997). It is equally clear, however, that this relationship is potentially confounded by factors that may be linked to both educational attainment and health status (for example, economic and family circumstances, risk factors of one's work, access to medical care or health knowledge, personality traits, and the like). However, the late 1980s and the 1990s produced a substantial number of studies, analyzing primarily nationally representative data sets, that control for many of these confounding influences and clearly suggest the likelihood that educational attainment has a direct and/or indirect causal effect on good health (for example, Behrman, Sickles, Taubman, & Yazbeck, 1991; Behrman & Wolfe, 1989; Berger & Leigh, 1989; Desai, 1987; Grembowski et al., 1993; Grossman & Kaestner, 1997; Hartog & Oosterbeek, 1998; Haveman, Wolfe, Kreider, & Stone, 1994; Kahn, 1998; Kenkel, 1991; Leigh, 1990, 1998b; Menchik, 1993; Ross & Mirowsky, 1995; Sander, 1995a, 1995b, 1998).

Causal mechanisms. The exact mechanisms underlying this likely causal influence, however, may be numerous and complex (Leigh & Dhir, 1997). For example, taking a largely sociological or social-psychological perspective on the issue, Ross and Wu (1995) hypothesized that there were three major mechanisms through which education influences health. These were: (1) work and economic conditions (such as employment status, income and economic security, access to health insurance, fulfilling work; see, for example, Dewar, 1998; Ross & Mirowsky, 1995); (2) social-psychological resources (sense of control over one's life and social support networks; see, for example, Becker, 1993); and (3) health lifestyle (smoking, exercising, drinking, and health checkups; see, for example, Kenkel, 1991). In analyses of two national probability samples of U.S. households, and with statistical controls for sex, race, age, and marital status,

Ross and Wu found that years of formal education completed had statistically significant and direct, positive effects on measures of both self-reported health status and physical functioning-mobility in daily activities. With an additional control for self-reported health status the prior year, educational attainment also had a statistically significant and positive direct effect on improvement in health status over a one-year period. When added to the regression equations, measures of each of the three hypothesized mechanisms (that is, work and economic conditions, social-psychological resources, and health lifestyle) had significant, direct effects on physical functioning, health status, and improvement in health status. However, although reduced in magnitude by about half, the direct, positive effects of educational attainment on all three health outcomes remained statistically significant. Such findings suggest that part of the impact of education on health is indirect, mediated through its direct influence on work and economic conditions, social-psychological resources, and health lifestyle. Yet taken together, these three mechanisms fail to explain the total positive effect of education on health.

Economists provide a somewhat different, though not unrelated, perspective on the causal mechanisms underlying the link between education and health. For example, increased formal education is hypothesized to increase both *allocative* and *productive* efficiency (for example, Gilleskie & Harrison, 1998; Leigh, 1998b). Allocative efficiency addresses effects due to information. The better educated, and particularly those with exposure to postsecondary education, have more access to health knowledge and health information than the less well educated, and they are more likely to believe in it (Finnegan, Viswanath, Kahn, & Hannan, 1993; Leigh, 1998b). Productive efficiency implies that additional education permits the individual to derive better health status from the available information about different aspects of health, such as medical care, diet, smoking, alcohol consumption, exercise, avoidance of environmental and safety hazards, and the like (Gilleskie & Harrison, 1998; Leigh, 1990; Ng, 1989; Smith, 1997). That is, given equal access to the same information, the better educated are more likely to extract important knowledge and make decisions that produce good health than the less well educated. One might think of productive efficiency as the direct effect of education on health, whereas allocative efficiency reflects an indirect effect.

In addition to allocative and productive efficiency, economists also hypothesize a third causal mechanism through which education can increase health. They frequently refer to this as *time preference for the future* (for example, Becker, Grossman, & Murphy, 1991; Becker & Mulligan, 1997), though it might be thought of essentially as a willingness to delay present gratification for some future good. The evidence is fairly strong that education enhances this future orientation or capacity to delay gratification (Becker et al., 1991). (Indeed, the act of enrolling in a postsecondary institution itself suggests this future orientation, in that the individual must often forgo some portion of present earnings for the increased likelihood of a future advantage in career or economic attainment.) By enhancing future orientation, educational attainment leads to behaviors that have positive long-term effects on health, such as exercise, nonsmoking, moderate alcohol consumption, diet, and the like (for example, Ford et al., 1991; Ippolito & Mathios, 1990; Sander, 1995a, 1995b).

There is modest evidence to suggest that the indirect effects of allocative efficiency and future orientation function as causal mechanisms in explaining the positive link between education attainment and good health (for example, Gilleskie & Harrison, 1998; Kenkel, 1991; Leigh & Dhir, 1997; Sander, 1998). Where it is considered, however, the direct, positive effect of education, or productive efficiency, on measures of health status tends to remain statistically significant even when factors such as preventative health care, lifestyle choices (for example, exercise, smoking), and time preference are taken into account (Gilleskie & Harrison, 1998; Leigh & Dhir, 1997).

Our conclusion from this research is that there are a variety of causal mechanisms that potentially account for the direct and indirect effects of educational attainment on health. We agree with the conclusion of Leigh and Dhir (1997) that the search for a single causal mechanism to explain the correlation between educational attainment and health may be a largely fruitless exercise.

Education and risk factors for mortality and disease. The evidence is reasonably clear that increased educational attainment significantly lowers: the probability of mortality at any particular age (Guralnik, Land, Bluzer, Fillenbaum, & Branch, 1993; Kaplan & Keil, 1993), the likelihood of specific health problems, such as disability or frailty (Berger & Leigh, 1989; Leigh, 1998a; Leigh & Dhir, 1997) and arthritis (Leigh & Fries, 1991), the probability of mortality from cancer or cardiovascular disease (Bucher & Ragland, 1995), and the probability of having risk factors for cardiovascular and other diseases (Winkleby, Fortmann, & Barrett, 1990; Winkleby, Jatulis, Frank, & Fortmann, 1992). In some instances, it is possible to isolate the unique effects of postsecondary education on these outcomes. For example, Bucher and Ragland (1995) analyzed a sample of over 3,000 men in the Los Angeles and San Francisco areas who were middle-aged (39 to 59) in 1960–61 and were followed for a 22-year period. The sample was divided into two comparison groups—those who had attended or graduated from college and those who had a high school education or less. Compared to those with no exposure to postsecondary education, the college group had significantly lower risk factors for both coronary heart disease and cancer (that is, blood pressure, cholesterol levels, and cigarettes smoked per day). Moreover, even when these risk factors or age were controlled statistically, the college group had a significantly lower relative risk of mortality from all causes, and from coronary heart disease, than did the noncollege group. Similarly, Winkleby, Fortmann, and Barrett (1990) found that, even in the presence of controls for such factors as age, sex, income, and occupation, years of formal education had significant, negative impacts on four risk factors for disease: smoking, hypertension (high blood pressure), cholesterol level, and body mass index. On an overall risk score that combined these four factors, adjusted for age and sex, those with a bachelor's degree or more had the lowest score, followed by those with one to three years of college. The highest overall risk scores accrued to those with a high school education or less. Findings consistent with those of Bucher and Ragland, and Winkleby et al. are also reported by Burke, Bild, Hilner, Folsom, Wagenknecht, and Sidney (1996) and Hann and Asghar (1996) for clinical obesity, by Irabarren, Sidney, Sternfeld, and Browner (2000) for coronary heart disease, and by Mead, Witkowski, Gault, and Hartmann (2001) for women's health status.

Education and health habits. What has also become quite clear is that lifestyle choices or health-related behaviors (smoking, exercise, diet, alcohol consumption, and the like) play a major role in influencing both risk factors for disease and mortality rates. Although the estimates differ, there is general agreement that lifestyle behaviors account for a substantial percentage of mortalities in the United States (for example, McGinnis & Foege, 1993; National Center for Health Statistics [NCHS], 1992; Powell, 1988; Rogers & Powell-Gringer, 1991; U.S. Department of Health and Human Services, 1989). One of the main positive impacts of educational attainment on health is manifest in its influence on lifestyle or health-related behaviors. Net of confounding factors such as age, race, sex, marital status, income, and employment status, educational attainment tends to have significant, negative effects on cigarette smoking, alcohol abuse or dependency, and cholesterol level (Crum, Helzer, & Anthony, 1993; Darrow, Russell, Copper, Mudar, & Frone, 1992; Gilleskie & Harrison, 1998; Kenkel, 1991; Sander, 1998; Winkleby et al., 1990) and significant, positive effects on aerobic exercise, a healthy diet, and consumption of dietary fiber (for example, Ford et al., 1991; Gilleskie & Harrison, 1998; Ippolito & Mathios, 1990; Kahn, 1998; Kenkel, 1991).

Once again, some studies provide sufficient information to estimate the unique effects of postsecondary education on health-related behaviors. For example, both Sander (1995a, 1995b, 1998) and Zhu, Giovino, Mowery, and Eriksen (1996) present evidence based on national samples to suggest not only that exposure to postsecondary education reduces the probability of smoking cigarettes but also that those with a bachelor's degree, or four years of college, are the least likely of any educational group to smoke and the most likely to quit smoking. Net of other factors, Zhu et al. found that college graduates were about 2.8 times less likely to smoke than high school graduates and about 3 times more likely to quit smoking, if they had ever smoked, than high school graduates. Sander (1995a) reports that the net odds of quitting smoking are .49 and .59 for male and female college graduates, respectively, but only .40 and .45, respectively, for male and female high school graduates. Similarly, Kenkel's (1991) evidence suggests that having a bachelor's degree or more may be more important in reducing bad health habits (smoking) and promoting good health habits (aerobic exercise) than simply being highly knowledgeable about the impact of such behaviors on health.

The impact of postsecondary education on alcohol consumption is more complex, and this may be attributable, in part, to the fact that the relationship between alcohol consumption and health is not linear. Moderate alcohol consumption (compared with abstinence) is linked to lower risk of coronary heart disease, stroke, and hypertension, whereas very heavy drinking or alcohol abuse is associated with higher risk (Ross & Wu, 1995). Probably the most useful study of the effects of exposure to postsecondary education on alcohol abuse or dependency was conducted by Crum, Helzer, and Anthony (1993). Analyzing a subsample of data from individuals in 3,000 adult households, they introduced controls for such factors as age, sex, race, marital status, employment status, household composition, age of first intoxication, and history of previous psychiatric disorder. In the presence of these controls, individuals with an associate degree or above had the lowest risk estimate for alcohol abuse or dependency of any education group. Compared with this higher education group, those with 9 to 12 years of formal education had over 6 times the probability and those with a high school degree about 1.8 times the probability of alcohol abuse or dependency. Interestingly, however, those with some college, but less than an associate degree, had a risk probability for alcohol abuse or dependency that was three times greater than individuals with an associate degree or more. Thus, although completion of at least two years of postsecondary education appears generally to reduce the probability of alcohol abuse, simply attending college for a short period of time may not.[2]

Welfare of Children. In our previous synthesis, we reviewed evidence indicating that the more educated tend to have smaller families and make proportionally greater investments in child care of a developmentally enriching nature than parents with less formal education. Although a substantial amount of the evidence is based on simple correlations, unadjusted for confounding factors, the research from the 1990s reinforces and expands the conclusion that parental education, in general, functions to enhance the welfare of children. This impact may begin even before a child is born in the form of quality of prenatal care. In this regard, a study using the National Natality Survey by Rosenzweig and Schultz (1991) is enlightening. Controlling for such factors as predicted health status of the baby (that is, birth weight), father's income, medical services available in the area, race of mother and father, height and weight of mother and father, and area labor market conditions, the education of both mother and father had significant, positive effects on the mother's age at birth and the number of prenatal medical visits received and significant, negative effects on delay in prenatal visits, mother's likelihood of smoking during pregnancy, and number of births in the family. When factors such as mother's age, delay in prenatal care, and mother's smoking behavior during pregnancy were added to the previous controls, education of mother and father still had significant, positive effects on the likelihood of the expectant mother receiving medical services such as ultrasound or X-ray.

In addition to prenatal care and welfare, there is also evidence suggesting significant differences in the lives of children that relate to the level of parental education. For example, Wolfner and Gelles (1993) analyzed data from a national probability sample of households that had at least one child under 18 years living at home to determine the factors that lead to severe or abusive violence toward children. Severe or abusive violence was operationally defined as striking a child with an object. Net of statistical controls for race of parents, gender of the child, number of children in the family, and parental drug use, mother's education had no impact on use of severe or abusive violence against a child. However, net of the same factors, father's education had a significant, curvilinear relationship with the use of severe or abusive violence. Children in families where the father had at least some college or a college degree were at less risk of being subjected to severe or abusive violence than children in families where the father had some high school or a high school diploma. Interestingly, compared with children in homes where fathers had high school educations, children in homes where the father had no more than an elementary school education were also less at risk of being subjected to severe or abusive violence. Thus, although paternal exposure to postsecondary education may generally function to reduce abusive violence toward children, the net relationship between educational attainment and violence toward children is complex.

Additional evidence suggests that educational attainment is also correlated with other national indexes of children's quality of life. For example, the risk of childhood death by age two is inversely related to the educational level of parents (Rodriguez-Garcia & Goldman, 1994), and although about 18 percent of teenage pregnancies occur in families where parents have a high school diploma, the corresponding figure for families where the parents have completed college is only about 6 to 7 percent (Maynard & McGrath, 1997). Similarly, increased levels of parental education are positively associated with a higher probability of reading to a young child (ages three to five) every day (Federal Interagency Forum on Child and Family Statistics, 2002), greater parental involvement in a child's school (National Center for Education Statistics, 1999; Zill & Nord, 1994), and a greater probability of assisting a child with his or her homework ("Why College?" 1999). Finally, although only 10 percent of households where parents had a high school degree had access to online computer service in 1997, 38 percent of those where parents had a bachelor's degree or above had such access (Gladieux & Swail, 1999). Unfortunately, much of this evidence is based on simple correlations or associations, unadjusted for potential confounding influences. Thus, it is unclear just how much of the link between educational attainment and indexes of child welfare might be confounded by income, occupation, or other uncontrolled characteristics that lead individuals to obtain different levels of formal education. Nevertheless, such associations between educational attainment and children's quality of life or home environment are consistent with more internally valid evidence reviewed earlier.

Community-Civic Involvement. If one assumes that an individual's life is enriched through meaningful community and civic involvement, then such involvement might itself be seen as an additional index of one's quality of life. Although the evidence of the 1990s is not extensive, it is consistent with our previous synthesis in suggesting that increased educational attainment leads to higher levels of community and civic involvement. Much of this evidence comes from Knox, Lindsay, and Kolb's (1993) analyses of the 1986 follow-up of the National Longitudinal Study of the High School Class of 1972. In their analyses, statistical controls were introduced for race, sex, tested academic ability, family socioeconomic status, and previous level of involvement in either 1972 or 1974. In the presence of such controls, level of exposure to postsecondary education had statistically significant, positive effects on several dimensions of community-civic involvement. Individuals with a bachelor's degree (compared to those with a high school diploma) were 1.8 times as likely to be frequently involved in political activities, 2.4 times as likely to be an active participant in community welfare groups, 1.5 times as likely to be frequently involved in political discussions, 1.8 times as likely to be highly committed to community leadership, and 2.5 times as likely to vote in a national, state, or local election. Those with less than a bachelor's degree, but at least some exposure to college, were also between 1.7 and 1.6 times as likely to vote as their counterparts with a high school diploma. (The findings on voting behavior are consistent with those of other investigations, such as Institute for Higher Education Policy, 1997, and Kennamer, 1990.) The only involvement dimension on which a bachelor's degree had a significant net negative influence was organized volunteer work. Compared to those with a high school degree, individuals with a bachelor's degree were only about half as likely to be actively involved in organized volunteer work.

BETWEEN-COLLEGE EFFECTS

As noted earlier, in our 1991 synthesis, we reported essentially no between-college effects on quality-of-life indexes.

In contrast, we did uncover a very small body of research published in the 1990s that attempts to estimate such between-college effects. We synthesize this research within three basic topics: subjective well-being, community-civic involvement, and health.

Subjective Well-Being

In their comprehensive analyses of the College and Beyond sample, Bowen and Bok (1998) also addressed the net impact of attending a selective undergraduate institution on both job satisfaction and life satisfaction. In predicting the likelihood of being "very satisfied" with one's job in 1995 (about 19 years after entering college), they introduced statistical controls for race, sex, tested academic ability, high school academic achievement, socioeconomic status, college major, college grades, educational attainment, job sector (for-profit, self-employed, not-for-profit, and so on), family income, and marital-parental status. In the presence of these controls, attending a selective college had a significant, negative effect on the likelihood of being very satisfied with one's job. This is a somewhat unexpected finding because in Bowen and Bok's analyses, institutional selectivity enhanced earnings, which, in turn, has a typically positive influence on job satisfaction. One possible explanation is that selective institutions tend to foster a more critical perspective in students. However, in the absence of a control for this trait when the sample entered college, an equally plausible explanation is that academically selective institutions simply attract students with a more developed critical perspective to begin with.

Similar findings are reported by Bowen and Bok (1998) in predicting the likelihood of being "very satisfied" with one's life in 1995. In the presence of essentially the same statistical controls employed in the prediction of job satisfaction, institutional selectivity tended to have a modest, negative relationship with life satisfaction in the sample combining individuals from all racial categories. However, the negative effect appeared to be particularly strong for African Americans. Compared with their African-American counterparts graduating from the relatively lowest group of institutions in terms of selectivity, African Americans graduating from the most selective group were only slightly more than half (.55) as likely to report being very satisfied with their life. Once again, however, it is difficult to determine from the analytical design of Bowen and Bok's study if the negative influence of college selectivity on life satisfaction is a socialization effect of the institution attended or merely the result of differential student recruitment by schools varying in academic selectivity.

Community-Civic Involvement

Two separate studies, Bowen and Bok (1998), analyzing the College and Beyond data, and Knox, Lindsay, and Kolb (1993), analyzing the 1986 follow-up of the National Longitudinal Study of the High School Class of 1972, have estimated between-college effects on measures of community or civic involvement. In Knox, Lindsay, and Kolb's analyses, statistical controls were introduced for race, sex, tested academic ability, family socioeconomic status, educational attainment, undergraduate grades and major, and previous level of involvement in either 1972 or 1974. In the presence of such controls, institutional characteristics such as selectivity, enrollment, private-public control, and residential emphasis had only trivial and statistically nonsignificant effects on a wide range of community or civic involvement dimensions. These included the likelihood of voting in a national, state, or local election; the likelihood of being frequently involved in political activities; the likelihood of being an active participant in community groups, organized volunteer work, and youth organizations; and the importance of being a community leader.

Somewhat different results are reported by Bowen and Bok (1998) in predicting 1995 leadership positions in different dimensions of civic involvement for the College and Beyond sample entering college in 1976. In their analyses, they found that institutional selectivity tended to have a statistically significant, negative influence on the probability of taking a leadership role in youth or educational organizations (for example, Little League, scouting, PTA, school board) but a significant, positive effect on taking a leadership role in cultural or alumni activities (for example, museum board, cultural or historical societies, fundraising, or student recruitment for the college one attended). These significant effects persisted even in the presence of controls for such factors as race, sex, academic ability, socioeconomic status, college major and grades, educational attainment, job sector, and marital-parental status. Net of the same controls, college selectivity had only a small and statistically nonsignificant direct effect on leadership in social-community activities (for example, social service or social welfare volunteer work, community centers, civil rights groups). However, attending a selective college appeared to have a discernible, positive, indirect effect on leadership in social-community activities, mediated through intervening influences such as college major, educational attainment, and work and family variables.

One possible reason for the different results reported by Knox, Lindsay, and Kolb (1993) and Bowen and Bok (1998) is that the two studies employed somewhat different operational definitions of community or civic involvement. Knox, Lindsay, and Kolb tended to focus on active participation, whereas Bowen and Bok stressed leadership roles. Perhaps even more important, however, was that Knox, Lindsay, and Kolb were able to introduce a statistical control for prior level of involvement, whereas Bowen and Bok were not. Consequently, it is difficult to determine how much of the impact attributable to college selectivity in the Bowen and Bok study might be more appropriately attributed to differential recruitment of students with varying interests and propensities for leadership among institutions of different academic selectivity. Taking the findings from both studies into account, we conclude that the body of evidence with respect to the net impact of college selectivity on community-civic involvement is unconvincing.

Health

We uncovered only one study that directly estimates between-college effects on health. In analyses of data from a 1995 national telephone survey of adults ages 18 to 95, Ross and Mirowsky (1999) sought to determine if physical functioning and perceived health increase significantly with the selectivity of the college one attends. With statistical controls for years of education, age, sex, race, marital status, parental education, work and economic conditions, and social-psychological resources, the selectivity of the college attended had a very small, positive effect on both physical functioning and perceived health. Most of this effect was attributable to health-related behaviors (for example, exercise, weight, drinking, smoking). It is not clear from Ross and Mirowsky's analyses, however, if attendance at a selective college actually enhances health-related behavior. Selective institutions might simply recruit students with stronger social class–related propensities for healthy lifestyles to begin with. Furthermore, any positive effect of college selectivity on either physical functioning or perceived health was much smaller than the effect of years of formal education.

Although it does not speak directly to health after college, we uncovered an additional study that addresses between-college effects on binge-drinking behavior during college (Dowdall, Crawford, & Wechsler, 1998). Because alcohol abuse in the senior year of college is a strong predictor of alcohol abuse up to three years later (Gotham, Sher, & Wood, 1997), it seems reasonable that what influences drinking behavior during college may have implications for alcohol consumption in later life. Dowdall, Crawford, and Wechsler examined the self-reported binge-drinking behavior of nearly 10,000 women at 140 colleges and universities. Binge drinking was defined as having four or more drinks at any one time. Such binge drinking among women was markedly less likely at women's institutions than at coeducational institutions. For example, 7.5 percent of women at single-sex institutions reported being a binge drinker three or more times in the preceding two weeks. The corresponding percentage at coeducational institutions was 17.7 percent. In other words, a woman was about 2.4 times (17.7 divided by 7.5) as likely to be a binge drinker (at least by the study criterion) if she attended a coeducational college than if she attended a single-sex college.

One possible explanation for Dowdall, Crawford, and Wechsler's (1998) findings is that the unique environment of women's institutions creates a cultural norm that counters the social acceptability of binge drinking. For example, 55.6 percent of women at women's colleges agreed or strongly agreed with the statement "students here admire nondrinkers" compared with 45.3 percent of their counterparts at coeducational institutions. Similarly, 63 percent of women at women's colleges compared with 40.6 percent of women at coeducational institutions strongly disagreed that "you can't make it socially at this school without drinking." As with much of the research on the net impact of women's colleges, however, it is difficult to separate the differential socialization effect from the differential recruitment effect. The association between attending a women's institution and lower rates of binge drinking may simply reflect the fact that women's institutions are more likely to attract those who are not binge drinkers to begin with. Indeed, as Dowdall, Crawford, and Wechsler candidly point out, 29 percent of women attending coeducational institutions engaged in binge drinking during the last year in secondary school compared with only 21 percent of women attending women's colleges.

WITHIN-COLLEGE EFFECTS

Our 1991 synthesis reported essentially no within-college effects on quality-of-life indexes.

In our present synthesis, we did uncover a modest body of research that estimates within-college effects on quality of life after college. We synthesize this evidence within two basic topics: health and community-civic involvement.

Health

In the previous section of this chapter on college's net effects, we reviewed a substantial body of evidence indicating that educational attainment is strongly linked with good health as well as with lifestyle choices and behaviors that promote good health. There is additional evidence to suggest that health knowledge and good health habits in later life can be even further enhanced by purposeful instruction during college.

Pearman, Valois, Sargent, Saunders, Drane, and Macera (1997) estimated the impact of a college health and physical education course on selected health knowledge, attitudes, and behaviors of alumni. The one-semester course intervention carried academic credit and met in several 50-minute sessions per week. The content of the course included a balance of lectures and physical activity. Lectures covered the importance of exercise programs, nutrition, chronic diseases, and other wellness and lifestyle issues such as stress management and prevention of substance abuse. The physical activity sessions consisted of participation in aerobic exercise along with weight training or calisthenics. In addition, all students completed a comprehensive laboratory fitness assessment before and after the course. The course was required of all students at a private liberal arts college in the southeastern United States, and alumni of this institution were the experimental group. The control group consisted of alumni from another private liberal arts college in the same geographic region that had no similar course. The two institutions had similar admissions requirements and freshman class profiles (for example, SAT scores, socioeconomic status, high school grades). At each institution, samples of alumni from five graduating classes, covering a nine-year period (1985 to 1993), were surveyed about their health knowledge, attitudes, and behaviors. Compared with their counterparts who did not take the course, alumni exposed to the required course were significantly more likely to know their blood pressure, blood cholesterol, and recommended dietary fat intake; significantly more likely to exercise; and significantly less likely to smoke. The experimental group also had lower intakes of dietary fat, cholesterol, and sodium than those who were not exposed to the course. Clearly, there are internal validity issues with the design of the Pearman et al. study. Yet the evidence does suggest that purposeful health instruction during college can have extended health benefits beyond graduation, at least for young alumni. Such a conclusion is consistent with earlier evidence reported by Slava, Laurie, and Corbin (1984).

Other inquiry concerning within-college effects on dimensions of health has focused on whether the well-established link between fraternity-sorority (Greek) membership and alcohol abuse (Wechsler, 1996; Wechsler, Dowdall, Maenner, Gledhill-Hoyt, & Lee, 1998; Wechsler, Kuh, & Davenport, 1996) extends past graduation. A comprehensive investigation of students from 140 colleges by Wechsler, Davenport, Dowdall, Grossman, and Zanakos (1997) has suggested that living in a fraternity or sorority is a particularly strong predictor of binge drinking among students, no matter whether they are involved in intercollegiate athletics. Compared with other students, men and women living in fraternities and sororities were about four times as likely to engage in binge drinking during college. (Binge drinking was operationally defined as five or more alcoholic drinks in a row for men and four or more for women.) Moreover, this effect persisted even in the presence of statistical controls for such factors as binge-drinking behavior in high school, age, race, sex, parental alcohol use, college grades, time spent studying and socializing, number of friends, and both marijuana and tobacco use.

Whether Greek affiliation continues to predict the likelihood of binge drinking or alcohol abuse beyond college, however, is less certain. Perhaps the most useful evidence we uncovered on this topic is a focused, single-institution study by Sher, Bartholow, and Nanda (n.d.), which followed a sample of students for seven years. During each of the four years of college and three years after college (year seven), young adults completed measures of alcohol use, along with personality measures, alcohol expectancies, and environmental influences. Throughout the college years, Greeks consistently drank more heavily than non-Greeks, and statistically controlling for initial alcohol use did not eliminate this impact. This finding is generally consistent with that of Wechsler, Davenport, Dowdall, Grossman, and Zanakos (1997). However, when initial or baseline alcohol use was taken into account, Greek affiliation had no significant effect on postcollege drinking levels of either men or women. Moreover, the decrease in alcohol use between the college years and year seven was greater among Greeks than among non-Greeks. Thus, although the social norms of fraternities and sororities may lead to increased alcohol use among members during college, this influence may diminish rapidly once an individual is removed from that context and is confronted with more traditional adult roles such as employment or marriage (Sher et al., n.d.).

Community-Civic Involvement

Gurin's (1999) comprehensive study of diversity experiences during college, reviewed in earlier chapters of this book, also estimated the impact of those experiences on dimensions of community involvement. Recall that her study analyzed the 1985 to 1989 Cooperative Institutional Research Program data and included a further follow-up in 1994, nine years after the sample entered college. Statistical controls were introduced for such factors as SAT scores, high school grades, the ethnic diversity of the high school and home neighborhood, institutional selectivity, institutional control, and institutional structural diversity. In the presence of these controls, young White adults' 1994 self-reported involvement in community service activities was significantly and positively influenced by a range of diversity experiences during college. These experiences included having college friends of a different race, taking an ethnic studies course, attending a racial-cultural awareness workshop, and socializing with someone of another racial-ethnic group during college.[3] The corresponding effects for African-American and Latino young adults were much less extensive, although attending a racial-cultural awareness workshop did increase the probability of involvement in community service activities in 1994 for African Americans, and discussion of racial-ethnic issues had a positive influence on community involvement for Latinos. Unfortunately, it does not appear that Gurin was able to control for precollege community involvement or a suitable proxy variable for the likelihood of becoming involved. Thus, in this instance, it is difficult to determine the extent to which the association between involvement in diversity experiences during college and involvement in the community after college is genuinely causal. Gurin's results may simply reflect the possibility that students who enter college with a high propensity for involvement are more likely to do both.

SUMMARY

Net Effects of College

Consistent with the conclusion of our previous synthesis, the evidence from the 1990s indicates that the causal relationship between educational attainment and subjective well-being or satisfaction with life is complex. The direct effect of education tends to be small and statistically nonsignificant or, in some cases, even negative. This may be explained by education's impact on one's ability to make measured, comprehensive, and critical judgments. Increased education may also lead one to interpret subjective well-being or happiness in more complex and qualitatively different terms. At the same time, it is clear that educational attainment has positive net indirect impacts on life happiness or satisfaction by means of its enhancement of economic affluence, sense of control over one's life, networks of social support, and perceived health status.

The late 1980s and the 1990s produced a substantial body of evidence clearly suggesting that educational attainment has a direct and/or indirect causal effect on good health. The exact mechanisms underlying this likely causal influence, however, may be numerous and complex. They include work and economic conditions, health lifestyle, access to better health information, producing better health decisions from available information, and time preference for the future. The search for a single causal mechanism to explain the link between educational attainment and health may be a largely fruitless exercise.

The evidence is reasonably clear that increased educational attainment lowers the probability of mortality at any particular age; the likelihood of specific health problems, such as disability or frailty; the probability of mortality from cancer or cardiovascular disease; and the probability of having risk factors for cardiovascular and other diseases. Those studies that make it possible to isolate the unique impacts of different levels of formal education indicate that, compared to those with no exposure to postsecondary education, those who attend or graduate from college have significantly lower risk profiles (blood pressure, cholesterol levels, cigarettes smoked per day) for both coronary heart disease and cancer. Even with this risk profile and age controlled statistically, those who attend or graduate from college also have a significantly lower risk of actual mortality from all causes and from coronary heart disease.

One of the main positive impacts of educational attainment on health is realized through its influence on lifestyle or health-related behaviors. Net of important confounding influences, educational attainment in general tends to have significant, negative effects on cigarette smoking, alcohol abuse-dependency, and cholesterol level and significant, positive effects on aerobic exercise, a healthy diet, and dietary fiber intake. Compared to those with a high school education, individuals with a bachelor's degree are substantially less likely to smoke and substantially more likely to quit smoking if they ever did smoke. Moreover, having a bachelor's degree or higher may be more important in reducing bad health habits (for example, smoking) and promoting good health habits (for example, aerobic exercise) than simply being informed about the impact of such behaviors on health. The impact of postsecondary education on alcohol consumption is complex perhaps, in part, because the relationship between alcohol consumption and health is not linear. Although completion of at least two years of postsecondary education appears generally to reduce the probability of alcohol abuse or dependency, when compared with having lower levels of formal education, simply attending college for a short period of time may not reduce this probability.

Although part of the evidence is based on unadjusted correlations, the research from the 1990s reinforces and expands the general conclusion from our previous synthesis that parental education in general functions to enhance the welfare of children. Net of confounding influences, including income, parents' formal education increases the likelihood of a child receiving good prenatal care. There are also positive associations between increased parental formal education and the probability of parental involvement in a child's school, parental help with a child's homework, and a child's access to household computer resources. Conversely, parental formal education is inversely related to the risk of childhood death by age two and the probability of teenage pregnancy. Net of other factors, children in families where the father attended college had a lower probability of being subjected to severe or abusive violence than children in families where the father had some high school or a high school diploma.

Increased level of educational attainment leads to generally higher levels of community and civic involvement. Net of other factors, including prior levels of involvement, individuals with a bachelor's degree (compared to those with a high school diploma) are significantly more likely to be frequently involved in political activities, to be an active participant in community welfare groups, to be highly committed to community leadership, and to vote in a national, state, or local election. Those with some exposure to college, but less than a bachelor's degree, are also significantly more likely to vote than their counterparts with a high school diploma.

Between-College Effects

There is at least some evidence to suggest that the probability of being very satisfied with one's job and one's life are negatively influenced by attending a selective undergraduate college or university. One interpretation of this finding is that selective institutions tend to foster a more critical perspective in their students. However, the lack of a precollege control for such a perspective makes it plausible that academically selective institutions simply attract students with a more developed critical perspective to begin with. Evidence suggesting that institutional selectivity influences community-civic involvement is mixed, possibly because different studies employ different operational definitions of the dependent variable. Nevertheless, the study that reports little or no influence of college selectivity on community-civic involvement introduced a statistical control for prior involvement, whereas the study that reports a significant impact of selectivity did not. We conclude that the evidence on this issue is unconvincing.

Evidence suggests that binge-drinking behavior among women is significantly less likely at single-sex than at coeducational institutions. However, women who attend single-sex colleges were less likely than their counterparts at coeducational institutions to binge drink prior to entering college. Thus, it is not clear if this finding is the result of a socialization or a recruitment effect. There is also the suggestion that college selectivity may have a small, positive influence on perceived health and physical functioning, largely as the result of enhancing a healthy lifestyle. Here too, however, the possibility exists that this may be a recruitment effect.

Within-College Effects

There is a modicum of quasi-experimental evidence suggesting that health knowledge and good health habits after college can be enhanced by purposeful instruction during college. Alumni exposed to a one-semester health and physical education course during college that combined classroom and physical activity sessions had significantly higher levels of health knowledge and were significantly more likely to practice good health habits (for example, diet, exercise, nonsmoking) than alumni not exposed to the course. Clear evidence exists to indicate that being a member of a fraternity or sorority during college has a strong influence on binge drinking by both men and women during college, and this effect persists even in the presence of controls for important confounding influences, including binge-drinking behavior in high school. However, it does not appear to be the case that the effect of Greek affiliation on drinking behavior during college extends to the years immediately following college. When prior drinking behavior is taken into account, Greek affiliation has little impact on postcollege drinking levels for either men or women.

Single-study evidence indicates that involvement in racial-ethnic and other diversity experiences during college significantly increases the probability of involvement in community service activities in the years following college. The effect is particularly pronounced for young White adults. However, the design of the study makes it difficult to determine if the link between involvement in diversity experiences during college and community involvement after college is causal. The findings might reflect the fact that students who enter college with a high propensity for involvement are more likely to do both.

Notes

1. When used by economists, *nonmarket benefits* is a broader term that also includes social benefits. Like the rest of this book, however, this chapter focuses on benefits to the individual.

2. Considerable recent attention has been drawn to the incidence of student binge drinking (typically defined as five or more alcoholic drinks at any one time) in college and attendant dysfunctional behaviors associated with it (for example, DeBord, Wood, Sher, & Good, 1997; Engs, Diebold, & Hanson, 1996; Gross, 1993; Hanson & Engs, 1992; Prendergast, 1994; Presley, Meilman, & Lyerta, 1993; Wechsler, Dowdall, Maenner, Gledhill-Hoyt, & Lee, 1998; Wechsler & Isaac, 1992; Wechsler, Isaac, Grodstein, & Sellers, 1994). Most evidence estimates that somewhere between 24 percent and 44 percent of students binge drink on a regular basis, although the incidence is higher for men than women. Although tempting, in absence of a control group of those with less education, it is hazardous to attribute this to an impact of exposure to college. This is particularly so because most evidence we reviewed suggests that increased education generally reduces the probability of alcohol abuse or dependency. Moreover, evidence with respect to the relationship between heavy drinking and year in college is mixed (for example, Engs et al., 1996; Gross, 1993; Schall, Weede, & Maltzman, 1991; Wechsler, Dowdall, Davenport, Moeykens, & Castillo, 1995), and there is a strong tendency for heavy drinking in the last year of college to decrease significantly during the first three years after graduation (Gotham, Sher, & Wood, 1997).

3. Gurin's (1999) findings also suggest that involvement in diversity experiences during college increases both the likelihood of being actively involved in diversity experiences after college and the probability of interacting with racially and ethnically diverse friends, neighbors, and work associates after college. The results were, once again, particularly pronounced for White young adults.

CHAPTER ELEVEN

How College Affects Students

A Summary

In the preceding eight chapters, we reviewed the evidence on a wide range of specific college outcomes. We offer here a comprehensive summary of what is known about the impact of college on students. In developing this synthesis, we adopt a different organizational framework than was employed in Chapters Three through Ten. In each of those chapters, the evidence pertaining to a specific category or outcome—such as learning or psychosocial development—was, where appropriate, summarized in terms of six fundamental questions:

1. Do students change during the college years, and if so, how much and in what directions? (This is the "change" question.)

2. To what extent are these changes attributable to college attendance rather than to other influences, such as normal maturation or noncollege experiences? (This is the "net effects" question.)

3. Are these changes differentially related to the kind of institution attended? (This is the "between-college" effects question.)

4. Are these changes related to differences in students' experiences at any given institution? (This is the "within-college effects" question.)

5. Are these changes differentially shaped by individual student characteristics? (This is the "conditional effects" question.)

6. Is the influence of college durable? (This is the "long-term effects" question.)

In this chapter, we look at the evidence across the various outcome categories with respect to each of the six fundamental questions posed in the book. Thus, the focus is on the various impacts of college on a broad spectrum of outcomes rather than on how a specific outcome may be influenced by various elements of the college experience.

In addition to providing a comprehensive summary of our most significant conclusions, in this chapter we also look at the degree of consistency between the conclusions of the synthesis in our 1991 book, *How College Affects Students*, and the evidence from research published since then. Second, where possible we examine the extent to which the evidence supports major theories or models of student development and college impact.

CHANGE DURING COLLEGE

In our 1991 synthesis, we concluded that the college years are a time of student change on a broad front. Although the changes that occurred from freshman to senior year were generally the largest "effects" uncovered in our synthesis, the breadth of change was perhaps the most striking characteristic of the evidence. Students not only made statistically significant gains in factual knowledge and in a range of general cognitive and intellectual skills but also changed significantly on a broad spectrum of value, attitudinal, psychosocial, and moral dimensions. And the changes occurred in an integrated way, with change in any one area apparently part of a mutually reinforcing network.

Although the evidence from the 1990s on change during college is nowhere near as extensive as the evidence uncovered in our 1991 review, there is little that would lead us to revise our earlier conclusion that maturation during the undergraduate years is holistic in nature and embraces multiple facets of individual change. Indeed, although limited in volume, empirical evidence now exists to support what had previously been merely a proposition.

Research examining change during the undergraduate years reveals clear directions, summarized here, under the general topics of learning and cognitive change, psychosocial changes, attitudes and values, and moral development.

Learning and Cognitive Change

In our 1991 review, we concluded that students make statistically significant freshman- to senior-year gains on a variety of dimensions of learning and cognition. The dimensions along which gains occur and our estimates of the magnitude of the gains are shown in Table 11.1.

Studies of the "change" question during college in the areas of learning and cognition are much less extensive in the literature of the 1990s than in the literature that appeared before that time. However, with two possible exceptions, our current review uncovered little that would fundamentally alter our major conclusion in our earlier book that students not only make significant gains in subject matter knowledge during the undergraduate years but also become more

Table 11.1. Estimates of Freshman-to-Senior Gains, Pre-1990

Dimension	Effect Size (in Standard Deviation Units)
Verbal skills	.56
Quantitative skills	.24
Specific subject matter knowledge	.84
Speaking skills	.60
Written communication	.50
Piagetian (formal) reasoning	.33
Critical thinking skills	1.00
Reflective judgment-thinking (use of reason and evidence to address ill-structured problems; postformal reasoning)	1.00
Conceptual complexity	1.20

critical, reflective, and sophisticated thinkers. As might be expected, the learning outcome constructs and measures used differ somewhat between the two review periods. Thus, the following dimension labels do not correspond precisely with those discussed earlier, although the correspondence is close enough to permit general comparisons. Our estimates of the freshman-to-senior gains drawn from the literature of the 1990s are shown in Table 11.2.

The two notable differences between the conclusions from our 1991 synthesis and those from the literature of the 1990s concern quantitative-mathematics competencies and critical thinking skills. The research from the 1990s suggests that our previous synthesis may have underestimated typical student growth in quantitative-mathematics competencies in college and overestimated student acquisition of critical thinking skills during the undergraduate years. However, such a conclusion needs to be interpreted cautiously. The different estimates on these dimensions from the two syntheses could be attributable to use of different measurement instruments and different samples.

Our estimates of the gains made during the undergraduate years on various dimensions of academic learning and intellectual sophistication reflect only *relative* advantages of seniors over beginning students. As such, the estimates should be understood in the context of two additional, and important, findings from the research of the 1990s. The first suggests that college graduates as a group do not always perform particularly well in terms of *absolute standards* of knowledge acquisition or cognitive functioning. (For example, only about 50 percent of all college graduates appear to be functioning at the most proficient levels of prose, document, or quantitative literacy.) Such a finding suggests that documenting the proficiency of college graduates on *absolute standards* of subject matter knowledge and cognitive skills may be as important as knowing how much they change or grow during the undergraduate years.

Table 11.2. Estimates of Freshman-to-Senior Gains in the 1990s

Dimension	Effect Size (in Standard Deviation Units)
English (reading and literature, writing)	.77
Mathematics (general mathematics proficiency, algebra, geometry)	.55
Science (laboratory work and fieldwork, understanding fundamental concepts)	.62
Social studies (history, social sciences)	.73
Liberal arts competencies (for example, using science, using art, solving problems)	.80
Critical thinking skills	.50
Critical thinking disposition	.50
Reflective judgment-thinking	.90
Epistemological sophistication or maturity	2.00

The results of a second line of inquiry in the 1990s are cause for greater optimism. There is evidence to suggest that undergraduate students can retain as much as 70 to 85 percent of the subject matter content usually introduced in postsecondary settings. Of particular importance, it would appear that increasing the level of learning during college increases content retention subsequent to college.

Psychosocial Changes

Both our earlier and current syntheses reviewed changes in students' "self systems" (such as identity, self-concepts, locus of control) and "relational systems" (such as the nature of their relationships and interactions with people and institutions in their external world). The earlier research on identity formation generally indicated that students tended to gain in the clarity and sophistication of their identities and became more positive in academic and social self-concepts as well as in their self-esteem, but the shifts were neither large nor always linear. Changes in students' relational systems were more apparent, the largest being declines in authoritarianism and dogmatism (.70 to .90 SD). Modest increases were apparent in intellectual orientation (.33 SD), psychological well-being (.40 SD), general autonomy (.59 SD), and independence from family influences (.60 SD). The smallest shifts were increases in internal locus of control (.25 to .30 SD), independence from peer influence (.20 SD) and interpersonal relations (.16 SD), and a decline in ethnocentrism (.40 SD).

Since 1990, findings from both cross-sectional and longitudinal studies of identity formation and self-understanding are consistent with earlier research indicating students move during college toward more complex levels of identity, although, compared with learning gains, the degree of change is relatively slight, about .17 of a standard deviation by one estimate.

The sharpest departure from the pre-1990 research on identity development has been in the emergence of models of selected areas of identity development, specifically those relating to race-ethnicity and sexual orientation. Most of these post-1990 studies sought to validate the presence of hypothesized stages in the development of various dimensions of racial-ethnic identity or consciousness. Fewer studies explored changes across these dimensions or stages during the college years, and those that did, like earlier research, found little or no consistent evidence of such development. Research during the 1990s is more consistent in finding that "coming out" (revealing one's gay or lesbian identity) is a significant milestone in the formation of gay and lesbian identity and one that commonly occurs during the college years, perhaps because of the greater freedom and support gays and lesbians find in the college environment compared to home or secondary school.

In the aggregate, students gain during the college years in their academic and social self-concepts and overall self-esteem. The proportion of students showing such increases is small—about 3 and 5 percentage points in academic and social self-concepts, respectively. Those estimates, however, mask somewhat larger proportions of students who shift in opposite directions, some developing more positive academic self-concepts and others becoming more negative. These shifts are on the order of 10 to 18 percentage points in both directions for both self-concepts.

Gains in students' sense of independence and control over their lives and academic fortunes and in their interpersonal competence and leadership skills appear to accompany gains in self-concept and self-esteem. In the aggregate, the research on changes in the psychosocial aspects of students' lives during college creates an impression of holistic interconnections and change. Consistent with theory and logic, the empirical evidence suggests that changes in one psychosocial dimension accompany or reinforce—and perhaps even initiate—changes in other dimensions.

Attitudes and Values

The pre-1990 research found that, during college, students' cultural, aesthetic, and intellectual sophistication and interest in the visual and performing arts increased by about .25 to .40 of a standard deviation. The proportion that placed a high value on the intrinsic rewards of education grew by about 20 to 30 percentage points, and students came to attach a lower value to the extrinsic rewards of employment. In the aggregate, the research also indicated a general shift among college students toward the liberal end of the sociopolitical continuum, with students becoming less doctrinaire in their religious values over time and more likely to support gender equality and to be tolerant of the political, social, and religious views of others.

The most noteworthy shifts concerning attitudes and values were in the degree of change in students' social and political attitudes and in the topics of scholarly interest. The post-1990 research supports our earlier conclusions about changes in students' sociopolitical attitudes, knowledge of social and political issues, likelihood of voting, and engagement in political activities. The degree of "liberalization" in student views reported since 1990, however, was more limited than that of the preceding decades. The percentage of students on the far left or far right remained virtually unchanged from first to senior year, with shifts of about 4 percentage points to both left and right coming largely from middle-of-the-roaders. Some have suggested that these shifts toward the ends of the sociopolitical continuum reflect a political polarization among students. This phenomenon may also reflect, as Astin has suggested, a combination of greater conservatism among enrolling students and the tendency for students' attitudes and values to be influenced by those held by their peers. With a greater sociopolitical balance between left and right in the peer environment than was the case in the 1970s and 1980s, the degree of change that students show in the aggregate may be smaller.

Perhaps reflecting concern over perceived increases in students' social and political cynicism and disengagement, more scholarly attention has focused since 1990 on selected forms of social involvement, particularly volunteer community service. Compared with individuals who have no college experience, bachelor's degree holders are two to three times more likely to volunteer in their communities, although the degree of involvement varies considerably across the kinds of service rendered. Pre-1990 research examined attitudes and values relating to generalized concepts of social, racial, and political tolerance and support for individual rights, but more recent research has concentrated primarily on racial-ethnic attitudes, perhaps reflecting the increased diversity in higher education and the national spotlight trained over the past decade on federal affirmative action policies, particularly those relating to college admissions. The evidence finds more positive attitudes toward racial equality and tolerance among college students as well as greater awareness and understanding of other cultures, more interactions with students from other racial-ethnic and cultural backgrounds, reductions in racial "distance," and increases in students' commitment to promoting racial understanding.

Students also become more tolerant and supportive in their attitudes toward other "marginalized" groups during the college years. The average gains on measures of attitudes toward gender equity appears to be about a quarter of a standard deviation (about 10 percentile points), and although the few studies done were single-campus studies, they indicate that students develop greater knowledge and acceptance of nontraditional sexual orientations during college.

Moral Development

In our 1991 synthesis, we reported clear and consistent evidence that undergraduates increase significantly in their use of principled reasoning to judge moral issues. This finding held across different measurement instruments and even different cultures, although the relative magnitude of these gains was difficult to determine from the evidence presented. However, the most significant shift that occurred during college was from conventional to principled reasoning.

Our previous conclusion stands, although the research of the 1990s permits us to estimate the size of the effect. From the literature reviewed, it appears that the average gain of seniors over freshmen in principled moral reasoning is about .77 of a standard deviation. Furthermore, consistent with the conclusions from our previous synthesis, the research from the 1990s indicates that the main change taking place during the undergraduate years is from using moral reasoning that concedes to societal authority (conventional moral reasoning) to using reasoning based on the application of universal moral principles (principled moral reasoning).

Some Final Thoughts on Change During College

Our previous volume offered a number of general observations about documented changes during the undergraduate years that also apply to the present synthesis and are worth reiterating, at least briefly. First is the remarkable agreement across four comprehensive literature reviews (Feldman & Newcomb, 1969; Bowen, 1977; Pascarella & Terenzini, 1991; and the present synthesis) with regard to the changes that occur during college. All four syntheses indicate that consistent cognitive, attitudinal, value, and psychosocial changes have occurred among college students over the past 50 years. In our 1991 book (Pascarella & Terenzini, 1991, pp. 563–564), we concluded:

> Students learn to think in more abstract, critical, complex, and reflective ways; there is a general liberalization of values and attitudes combined with an increase in cultural and artistic interests and activities; progress is made toward the development of personal identities and more positive self-concepts; and there is an expansion and extension of interpersonal horizons, intellectual interests, individual autonomy, and general psychological maturity and well-being. Thus, it can be said that the nature and direction of freshman-to-senior changes appear to be reasonably stable and to some extent predictable.

Despite understandable differences in the estimated magnitude of changes across the four syntheses, we uncovered little in our present synthesis that would lead us to fundamentally alter our 1991 conclusion.

Second, throughout this book we have, where possible, estimated the magnitude of changes during the undergraduate years, although the possibilities for calculating these estimates vary across outcome categories. Although estimating effect sizes can provide useful information, it would be a mistake to focus solely on these numbers and to risk drawing conclusions based on the assumption that development happens along a continuum where all changes are equally important. Some developmental theorists would argue that growth does not occur in such an even and continuous fashion and that not all changes are of equal importance (such as King & Kitchener, 1994; Kohlberg, 1981a; Perry, 1970; Rest, 1986). Some shifts are critical to development no matter whether they reflect a large quantitative change on some continuous scale. For example, the shift during college from making judgments based on beliefs to relying on evidence is a key prerequisite to dealing effectively with ill-structured problems. Similarly, the shift from conventional to principled or postconventional reasoning during college represents a significant qualitative advance in moral development. On both these dimensions of development, the *qualitative* nature of the change may be of greater consequence than the size of a *quantitative* estimate of the change.

Third, the magnitude of change on any particular variable or set of variables during the undergraduate years may not be as important as the pronounced breadth of interconnected changes. The evidence indicates not only that individuals change on a broad developmental front during college but also that the changes are of a mutually consistent and supportive nature. The research literature may lack substantial empirical evidence that change in one area causes or permits changes in other areas, but it is clear from the evidence in both our 1991 and present syntheses that the changes coincident with college attendance usually involve the whole person and proceed in a largely integrated manner.

We also want to call readers' attention to at least two nontrivial problems endemic to any study of change during college. First, the evidence is based largely on studies that estimate typical or average change in a given sample (longitudinal studies) or typical or average differences between samples (cross-sectional studies). By focusing on average group shifts or differences, the findings of such studies tend to mask the presence of pronounced individual differences in patterns of change.

Second, as emphasized throughout this book, freshman-to-senior change during college does not necessarily represent the impact of college. Nearly all the studies of change discussed in our synthesis lacked a control group of students who did not attend college. Consequently, one cannot conclude that a shift of one standard deviation on some variable during college is really the result of college attendance. Part or even all of the change could be attributable to confounding influences, such as maturation, or even a practice effect associated with completing the same measurement instrument twice. In theory, similar individuals not attending college might exhibit the same degree of change as college students over the same period of time. In addition, just as the fact of change does not necessarily represent the impact of college, the absence of measured change does not necessarily indicate the absence of college impact. As suggested by Feldman and Newcomb (1969), one consequence of exposure to college may be to stabilize development on some dimensions at a certain level and to prevent reversion or regression. If such were the case on a specific trait, little or no freshman- to senior-year change would be evidenced. However, it may be that individuals who do not attend college regress or change in a negative direction on that same trait.

NET EFFECTS OF COLLEGE

Self-selection, not random assignment, determines who attends college, and so studies that seek to estimate the net or unique impact of college (as distinct from normal maturation or other noncollege sources of influence on change) employ some creative research designs or, more typically, statistical controls. Thus, the causal inferences one can draw from such studies are not of the same order of certitude as those drawn from randomized, "true" experiments. Nevertheless, we can construct a reasonably valid set of tentative conclusions about observed changes or outcomes that are attributable to attending college and not to rival explanations. As was true in our 1991 synthesis, the evidence supporting the net impact of postsecondary education on learning and cognition, moral reasoning, and career and economic returns is more extensive and consistent than the evidence concerning changes in attitudes, values, and psychosocial characteristics. This does not mean, however, that postsecondary education has a stronger net impact on the former outcomes than on the latter. Some of the observed differences may reflect variations in the extent and quality of the available evidence across areas of inquiry rather than significant differences in the actual impact of exposure to college.

Learning and Cognitive Changes

In our 1991 synthesis, we concluded that on nearly all dimensions with demonstrated freshman- to senior-year change, a statistically significant part of that change was attributable to attending college. Exposure to postsecondary education not only appeared to enhance significantly students' general verbal and quantitative skills as well as oral and written communication but also had a statistically significant, positive net effect on their general intellectual and analytic skills, critical thinking, their use of reason and evidence in addressing ill-structured problems (reflective judgment-thinking), and their intellectual flexibility. Further, these effects could not be explained by maturation or differences between those who attended and those who did not attend college in tested intelligence, academic ability, or other precollege characteristics. What was less clear in our previous synthesis was the magnitude of the net impact of college. The only learning and cognition outcomes for which we were able to estimate an effect size were general verbal skills (.26 to .32 of a standard deviation), general quantitative skills (.29 to .32 of a standard deviation), and critical thinking (.44 of a standard deviation) during the first year of college.

The studies done since 1990 on the net effects of college on learning and general cognitive skills do not make up a large literature, but the evidence we uncovered is consistent with the conclusions in our previous synthesis. What is new during the 1990s is our ability to estimate the magnitude of the net college effect for each outcome, as shown in Table 11.3.

As a rule, these estimated effects cannot be explained by rival hypotheses related to academic ability, sex, race, or (with the possible exception of reflective judgment-thinking) maturation.

Two additional points are worth noting. First, our estimate of the net impact of three years of postsecondary education on gains in critical thinking skills (.55 SD) is larger than our estimate of freshman- to senior-year change (.50 SD; see Table 11.2) and, to some extent, may reflect the confounding influence of research conducted with different critical thinking measures. However, the

Table 11.3. Estimated Magnitude of the Net Effect for Each Outcome

Dimension	Net Effect Size (in Standard Deviation Units)
General verbal and quantitative skills	.25
English	.59
Mathematics	.32
Science	.47
Social studies	.46
Critical thinking (first three years of college)	.55
Reflective judgment-thinking	.90

difference in estimates may also signal that our unadjusted estimate of freshman-to-senior change is overly conservative. Second, it is possible that our estimates of the net college effects on English, mathematics, science, and social studies are conservative. The instruments on which these net effects are based focus on assessing general education competencies that are usually taught in the first two years of college. Consequently, our estimated net effects in these content areas may not capture the full net effects of postsecondary education.

Psychosocial Changes

Little in our earlier review supported a confident conclusion about college's effects on changes in students' identities or ego stage development beyond what might be attributable to maturation. College-related changes were apparent in the pre-1990 research, however, in students' more positive academic and social self-concepts as well as their overall self-esteem, although these effects appeared to be indirect, mediated by certain college experiences. Net changes in self-esteem were small and interconnected with students' family background and precollege achievements. The research consistently indicated that at least some of the overall freshman- to senior-year declines in student authoritarianism, dogmatism, and ethnocentrism could be attributed to college effects independent of other forces.

The post-1990 research sheds little light on the effects of college on change in racial-ethnic or gay-lesbian identity, which may instead be attributable to maturation or to social forces related to racial-ethnic justice and gay-lesbian rights. In addition, in studies exploring identity, age and sociohistorical factors remain confounded with the period of college attendance.

The research on net college effects on students' academic and social self-concepts, in contrast, provides generally consistent evidence supporting earlier findings of positive changes independent of maturational or other factors. Studies of net college effects on self-esteem report mixed findings, making conclusions tentative. The research since 1990 also indicates statistically significant, if small, net gains in students' internal locus of control. The evidence is particularly strong concerning gains in students' sense of control over their academic performance. Similarly, solid evidence indicates that students grow in leadership skills to a degree unattributable to noncollege factors.

Attitudes and Values

Our earlier review found consistent evidence that the net effects of college tend to move students toward more open, liberal, and tolerant attitudes and values. We also concluded that these effects were more than reflections of changes in the larger society that took place over the sociopolitically turbulent two decades covered by the review.

The most notable difference between pre- and post-1990 research on sociopolitical attitudes is that the more recent evidence reveals few of the changes that were apparent earlier. Indeed, the small, unadjusted freshman- to senior-year shifts in sociopolitical orientations described earlier in this chapter virtually disappear when adjusted for students' precollege attitudes. The few statistically significant net changes tend to parallel societal attitudes. The evidence is clear that college has a net effect in at least one area: increased student civic and community involvement, although those impacts vary depending on the level of educational attainment and the area of community service.

The greater scholarly attention devoted to college's impact on students' racial-ethnic and multicultural attitudes is another noteworthy feature of the research published since 1990. Indeed, the more recent evidence seems conclusive in indicating that college attendance, independent of numerous other factors, promotes racial understanding and openness to diversity as well as the belief that racism remains a societal problem. Similarly, the evidence indicates freshman- to senior-year increases in student support for gender equity in salaries and employment opportunities as well as more skepticism about explanations offered in defense of rape.

Moral Development

In our 1991 synthesis, we concluded that individuals exposed to postsecondary education demonstrated significantly greater growth in the use of principled moral reasoning than individuals whose formal education ended with high school. Although it was not possible to estimate the magnitude of postsecondary education's net impact on growth in the use of principled moral reasoning, the difference persisted even in the presence of controls for maturation and for differences between those who attended and those who did not attend college in their levels of precollege moral reasoning, intelligence, and socioeconomic status.

Whether college has a statistically significant net impact on moral behavior was less clear, although two studies suggested a positive indirect effect in which college increases the likelihood of principled behavior by stimulating the growth of principled moral reasoning.

The conclusions from our present synthesis on this question concur with those from our 1991 synthesis. Postsecondary education appears to have a statistically significant and positive net effect on growth in the use of principled reasoning in addressing moral problems, although it is difficult to estimate the magnitude of that effect. Consistent with our previous synthesis, we also found extensive evidence of a positive relationship between level of principled moral reasoning and the likelihood of principled behavior in a wide range of settings. Principled reasoning alone, however, is probably insufficient to ensure principled behavior because it is only one of several influences on moral action. Other influences include moral sensitivity, moral motivation, and moral character, but few researchers have examined postsecondary education's impact on these other precursors of moral action.

Long-Term Effects of College

The bulk of the substantial body of research concerning the long-term effects of college focuses on estimating the enduring impact of attending versus not attending college. Consequently, we depart from the pattern of the preceding chapters and summarize the evidence on the long-term effects of college here rather than near the end of this chapter.

Consistent with our 1991 review, this synthesis indicates that postsecondary education has a broad range of enduring impacts. Attending college influences not only occupation and earnings but also cognitive, moral, and psychosocial characteristics as well as values and attitudes and various indices of the quality of life. Evidence also suggests that postsecondary education's influences extend beyond the individuals who attend college to the nature of their children's lives.

The long-term impact of postsecondary education manifests itself in at least two ways, one of which can be traced directly to college attendance or degree attainment (such as effects on job status and earnings) and the other acting indirectly through socioeconomic positioning and the interests, experiences, and opportunities made more likely by being a college graduate. Put another way, a significant part of the long-term effect of college arises out of the choices made by people who attend and graduate from college and the lifestyles they adopt. These indirect routes of influence are important in understanding the full long-term impact of college. Indeed, many college effects persist in large measure as a result of living in postcollege environments that support and further stimulate these effects.

Socioeconomic Outcomes

The evidence uncovered in our previous review limited any conclusions about the socioeconomic impacts of postsecondary education to the net impact of having a bachelor's degree versus a high school degree. We concluded that a bachelor's degree conferred average net advantages over a high school degree of about one standard deviation in occupational status (job desirability), 20 to 40 percent in earnings, and about 9 to 11 percent in return on personal investment in postsecondary education (private rate of return). These advantages persisted in the presence of statistical controls for confounding influences such as socioeconomic origins, tested intelligence, aspirations, and, in the case of private rate of return, costs of education and forgone earnings. Moreover, having a bachelor's degree continued to confer a statistically significant net advantage over a high school diploma in both stability of employment and career mobility and attainment. The actual magnitude of the advantages, however, was difficult to determine.

The evidence we uncovered in our present synthesis would not lead to significant revisions of our 1991 conclusions. What is new in the research of the 1990s is our ability in some areas to estimate separate net effects by gender and for levels of postsecondary education less than a bachelor's degree. Table 11.4 reports estimates of the net effects of postsecondary education on socioeconomic outcomes as indicated by the research of the 1990s.

Four additional points concerning the impacts of subbaccalaureate postsecondary education stand out. First, the earnings returns to an associate's degree appear to be essentially the same for experienced workers who return to school as they are for continuing high school graduates. Second, completion of one-year vocational certificates can increase earning power, particularly for women, but the average net earnings returns to such certificates (versus a high school diploma) appear to be less certain, and likely smaller, than the average net returns to associate's degrees. Third, individuals can potentially increase their earnings by obtaining modest amounts of postsecondary education without completing a degree or certificate, but the average economic premium appears to be less certain and smaller in magnitude than the average return yielded by an associate's degree or certificate. Finally, the economic payoff of completing a year of academic credits at a community college appears to be at least equal to the payoff of completing the same number of credits at a four-year college.

Although researchers have found discernible between- and within-college effects (summarized later in this chapter), it is clear from studies during the 1990s that the *average* occupational and economic returns to a bachelor's degree remained substantial. Similarly, although periodic fluctuations are to be expected, the private rate of return on investment in a bachelor's degree continued to be competitive with benchmark rates for alternative investments. Also, the *average* occupational and economic benefits attributable to earning an associate's degree also appear to be appreciable, although smaller in magnitude than those linked to a bachelor's degree.

The ways in which postsecondary education, and particularly a bachelor's degree, position an individual occupationally and economically represent an important long-term effect in and of itself but one that also has implications for other long-term impacts. One stems from the fact that jobs usually held by the college-educated tend to have a relatively high level of earnings, providing greater discretionary income and access to a range of material and nonmaterial resources and opportunities (such as books, magazines, computers, travel, cultural experiences, household help, medical care, additional education) that have potential impact on other long-term outcomes. A second implication stems from

Table 11.4. Estimates of the Net Effects of Postsecondary Education on Socioeconomic Outcomes

Dimension	Net Effect Size
Occupational status (men and women):	
Bachelor's degree	.95 SD advantage over a high school diploma.
Associate's degree	.24 to .44 SD advantage over a high school diploma.
Vocational degree or license-certificate	.12 to .22 SD advantage over a high school diploma.
Earnings (men):	
Bachelor's degree	37 percent advantage over a high school diploma.
Associate's degree	17.5 percent advantage over a high school diploma.
Earnings (women):	
Bachelor's degree	39 percent advantage over a high school diploma.
Associate's degree	27 percent advantage over a high school diploma.
Credentialing-program effects (men):	
Bachelor's degree	15 percent earnings advantage over four years of college credits but no degree.
Associate's degree	9 percent earnings advantage over two years of college credits but no degree.
Credentialing-program effects (women):	
Bachelor's degree	12 percent earnings advantage over four years of college credits but no degree.
Associate's degree	11 percent earnings advantage over two years of college credits but no degree.
Private rate of return (men and women):	Bachelor's degree confers about a 12 percent return on investment (over a high school diploma), with a typical range of 9 to 16 percent.
Stability of employment (men and women):	Increases with amount of postsecondary education, but size of effect is unclear.

the fact that the college-educated tend to hold jobs characterized by relatively higher levels of social interaction and self-direction than jobs held by those whose education ends with high school; the college-educated thus have important continuing influences on cognitive and noncognitive development initially shaped during the college years.

Learning and Cognitive Development

In our 1991 synthesis, we concluded that, despite some methodological weaknesses, the evidence from national samples indicated that college graduates had a substantially larger general knowledge base than did individuals whose education ended with high school. Similarly, in evidence from national surveys, alumni consistently reported that college had a substantial positive influence both on their specific and their general knowledge as well as on their ability to think critically and analytically.

Although the research published during the 1990s differs in form from the earlier literature and in some cases is less extensive, it provides substantial reinforcement for our 1991 conclusions. The evidence clearly indicates not only that the college-educated are more knowledgeable and more proficient at becoming informed than individuals with only a high school education but also that the undergraduate experience provides information and cognitive skills that increase the capacity for lifelong learning and continuing intellectual development. Learning and intellectual growth shaped by the undergraduate experience tend to continue along the same trajectories after college, although they depend to a substantial degree on the amount of intellectual stimulation and the availability of learning opportunities in postcollege life.

Compared to individuals with only a high school education, the college-educated have a number of advantages when it comes to learning opportunities and continuing intellectual stimulation in their lives. First, because of the nature of their occupations and level of earnings, the college-educated are likely to have greater access to resources and experiences that provide continued intellectual stimulation and opportunities for learning (such as books, magazines, computers, travel, concerts, continuing education courses). However, simply having more discretionary income or more intellectually stimulating work does not tell the whole story. The college-educated are more likely than those with a high school education to participate in activities that enrich their funds of knowledge and provide intellectual stimulation, such as using a public library, even when income, occupation, and other confounding influences are taken into account. This suggests that, in addition to fostering the *capacity* for lifelong learning, an important long-term impact of postsecondary education is its role in crystallizing a *personal disposition* for lifelong learning and intellectual development.

Psychosocial Changes

Pre-1990 research had little to say about the long-term effects of college on ego or identity development, although it found net effects of college on academic and social self-concepts that were still apparent nearly a decade after graduation. College's long-term effects appeared to be more indirect than direct, mediated by postcollege occupational success. Small but statistically significant, beneficial effects on self-esteem and internal locus of control also persisted up to 14 years after graduation. Net declines in authoritarianism experienced during college remained stable 10 years after graduation, and graduates reported both declines in stress and anxiety levels and increases in personal integration and overall psychological well-being.

Since 1990, college's net long-term impact on identity formation has remained largely unexplored, with research complicated by the conceptual and empirical confounding of identity formation with human development in the adult years. Studies of identity development among college graduates, almost exclusively qualitative, consistently suggest that shifts in identity begun in college probably continue to age 30 and beyond. It is impossible to attribute these continuing changes to college, however, because any college impacts remain confounded with normal maturation and sociohistorical developments. A small body of evidence suggests that college has positive and abiding net effects on students' self-concepts and internal locus of control, although not on self-esteem. Some studies indicate that college has a net long-term and positive impact on self-concepts and internal locus of control, respectively, but the findings are unreplicated and therefore tentative.

Attitudes and Values

Although few in number, pre-1990 studies consistently indicated that college effects related to attitudinal and value outcomes persist into the adult years. Despite differences in research designs, samples, analytical procedures, and historical periods, studies indicate that growth in sociopolitical liberalism during college appears to continue at a reduced rate into students' later years. The underlying dynamic may be the reinforcement of attitudes and values developed during college by family, friends, and colleagues who were similarly educated and who hold many of the same beliefs. Cultural, aesthetic, and religious attitudes and values developed during college remained stable in succeeding years. The research on changes in gender role attitudes reflected an emerging field of study and produced little evidence for any conclusions about long-term college effects.

Although the topics of scholarly interest during the 1990s shifted somewhat from the earlier period, research continues to support the conclusion that net college influences on students' attitudes and values have long-term impact. Educational attainment in general, and a bachelor's degree in particular, appear to promote significantly higher levels of community and civic involvement. Net of other factors, including prior levels of involvement, individuals with a bachelor's degree (compared to those with only a high school diploma) were 1.8 times more likely to be frequently involved in political activities, 2.4 times more likely to be an active participant in community welfare groups, 1.5 times more likely to be frequently involved in political discussions, 1.8 times more likely to be highly committed to community leadership, and 2.5 times more likely to vote in a national, state, or local election. Individuals with some exposure to post-secondary education but less than a bachelor's degree were also 1.7 times more likely to vote as their counterparts with only a high school diploma. Increases during college on measures of the value attached to the intrinsic rewards of both education and occupation (and the declines in the importance of extrinsic rewards) also persisted. The long-term impacts on occupational values were more apparent, no doubt because of the centrality of occupation in adult life.

College's impacts on sociopolitical and gender role attitudes appear to be greatest during the college years, with attitudes and values tending to stabilize after college. Studies done since 1990 buttress earlier conclusions that college's impact manifests itself in later life in at least two ways. First, college graduates tend to choose environments with similarly educated people, including spouses, family, close friends, and colleagues who share their points of view on social and political issues. Second, college not only shapes student values directly during the college years by contributing to their knowledge of society, the political process, and social issues, but also indirectly, by positioning graduates—affording them access to influential social networks and associational memberships by means of the social capital that education confers.

Moral Development

Our 1991 synthesis revealed strong evidence for postsecondary education having an enduring impact on the use of principled moral reasoning, at least through the first six years after graduation. Individuals attending college made greater gains in the use of principled reasoning during college than did individuals whose formal education ended with high school, and the gap between the two groups continued to widen in the years after college. This pattern could not be accounted for by initial differences in moral development or differential regression artifacts.

We did not find longitudinal evidence in the research of the 1990s that permitted long-term comparisons of trends in principled moral reasoning growth among individuals completing different levels of postsecondary education. However, the scant evidence we did uncover reinforces our previous conclusions that the developmental trends in principled moral reasoning put in motion by the postsecondary experience do not fade after college. Rather, the level of principled reasoning at the end of the senior year of college tends to persist or modestly increase during the years immediately following graduation. In part, this tendency may be attributable to an environment of continuing intellectual stimulation that often characterizes the occupational and lifestyle choices typical of, or more available to, college graduates.

Quality-of-Life Indices

In our 1991 review, problems in research design and the inability to control important confounding influences hindered causal attributions about the long-term impact of postsecondary education on various quality-of-life indices. Nevertheless, the college-educated consistently ranked higher than individuals with less education on a range of quality-of-life indices. The college-educated tended to have better overall health, a lower mortality rate, and smaller families and to spend a greater portion of time in child-care activities of a developmentally enriching nature (such as teaching, reading, talking). The college-educated also tended to be more efficient in making consumer choices, saved a greater percentage of their income, made more effective long-term investment of discretionary resources, and spent a greater proportion of discretionary resources and time on developmentally enriching activities (such as reading, participation in arts and cultural events, involvement in civic affairs). However, although college-educated individuals ranked higher on a broad array of quality-of-life indices, they did not, on average, report appreciably greater overall satisfaction with their lives than did persons with less education.

The research from the 1990s does not provide evidence on all the quality-of-life dimensions addressed in our previous synthesis, but it does yield findings in the areas of health, child welfare, subjective well-being, and job satisfaction that are consistent with our 1991 conclusions. Where the literature from the 1990s differs is that on several quality-of-life indices the evidence permits a better identification of the potential causal mechanisms underlying the significant, positive link with level of formal education. The majority of studies treat education as a continuous variable (such as years of formal education), making it difficult to estimate the magnitude of the net effect of different levels of postsecondary education. Thus, it is necessary to infer or extrapolate the impact of postsecondary education from the overall effect of education.

Researchers over the last two decades have produced an extensive body of methodologically sound research indicating that educational attainment has a positive causal impact on good health. The evidence is reasonably clear that, in the presence of statistical controls for salient confounding influences, increased educational attainment significantly lowers the probability of mortality at any particular age; specific health problems, such as disability or frailty; mortality from cancer and cardiovascular disease; and having risk factors for cardiovascular and other diseases.

Although it is difficult to estimate the magnitude of the effects, those studies that permit identification of the net influence of different levels of formal education indicate that, compared to those with no exposure to postsecondary education, individuals who attend or who graduate from college (earning a bachelor's degree) have significantly lower risk profiles (that is, blood pressure, cholesterol levels, cigarettes smoked per day) for both coronary heart disease and cancer. Moreover, even with risk profile and age taken into account, those who attend or who graduate from college, compared with those with no postsecondary education, have a significantly lower risk of actual mortality from all causes and from coronary heart disease.

The research suggests that a number of mechanisms underlie the likely causal influence of educational attainment on health, and their mutual interaction is probably complex. These mechanisms reflect both the direct and indirect effects of education and include work and economic conditions, health lifestyle, access to better health information, producing better health decisions from available information, and time preference for the future. The search for a single causal mechanism to explain the link between educational attainment and health may be a largely fruitless exercise.

One of the clearest impacts of educational attainment on health is realized through health lifestyle. Net of important confounding influences, educational attainment in general tends to have significant, negative effects on cigarette smoking, alcohol abuse-dependency, and cholesterol level and significant, positive effects on aerobic exercise, a healthy diet, and dietary fiber intake. For example, compared to individuals with only a high school education, those with a bachelor's degree are substantially less likely to smoke and substantially more likely to quit. Part of the explanation for this finding is that the college-

educated have better access to health information than do high school graduates. (Recall, for example, that postsecondary education increases the likelihood of library use, irrespective of occupation and income.) However, having a
bachelor's or higher degree appears to have a role in changing bad health
habits and promoting good health habits beyond simple knowledge about the
impact of such behaviors on health. This finding suggests two other causal
mechanisms that may be at work. First, the college-educated may be able to
produce better health decisions from the same information known to those
with only a high school diploma. Second, postsecondary education may reinforce a future orientation that underscores the long-term health consequences
of current behaviors.

Though not as methodologically rigorous as the body of research on educational attainment and health, correlational evidence from the 1990s supports
and expands the conclusion from our previous synthesis that parental education is positively linked to indicators of child well-being. For example, parents'
higher levels of formal education are positively associated with good prenatal
care, parental involvement in a child's school, reading to a child, helping with
homework, and providing access to computer resources. Conversely, parental
postsecondary education is negatively linked to the risk of a child's death by
age two and to the probability of teenage pregnancy.

Finally, with respect to the long-term impacts of postsecondary education on
job satisfaction and life satisfaction (or subjective well-being), our conclusions
from the research of the 1990s agree generally with those from our previous synthesis. Overall, we found the net total effect of education on both outcomes to
be small, probably because level of formal education has direct and indirect
impacts on both job satisfaction and life satisfaction that tend to be conflicting.
For example, having a college education tends to have a positive indirect effect
on job satisfaction through such factors as job prestige and autonomy, earnings,
and challenging work. However, the direct effect of a college degree on job satisfaction tends to be negative, possibly because postsecondary education fosters
a critical perspective and raises occupational expectations. Similarly, educational
attainment has positive, indirect impacts on life satisfaction or subjective well-
being by enhancing such factors as affluence and sense of control over one's
life. But the direct effect of education is often negative because education boosts
the capacity to make measured, comprehensive, and critical judgments. Higher
levels of education may also lead one to interpret subjective well-being or happiness in complex and qualitatively diverse terms.

Intergenerational Effects of College

An often overlooked element in the long-term impact of postsecondary education is the intergenerational transmission of benefits. In our 1991 synthesis,
we found evidence indicating that the net benefits of a college education are
not restricted to the person who attends college but are passed along to offspring. Net of confounding influences such as parental income and race, gender, and aspirations, having college-educated parents modestly enhanced a

person's educational attainment, job status, early career earnings and, for women, the likelihood of entering a financially lucrative, male-dominated occupation.

Researchers during the 1990s paid little attention to the intergenerational impact of college on the socioeconomic achievements of offspring, but it did provide new evidence suggesting that postsecondary education offers an intergenerational legacy in children's knowledge acquisition. Net of such confounding influences as race, sex, test scores, and parental socioeconomic status, having parents who attended college has a positive influence on a child's high school science and mathematics achievement as well as on college-level reading comprehension. This effect is likely attributable to the fostering of "learning capital" in offspring of the college-educated, much of it indirectly through the home environment. Little evidence suggests a similar intergenerational impact of parental postsecondary education on a student's general cognitive skills.

The intergenerational effects of college were clearer than ever in the research published since 1990 that examined differences in educational attainment among first-generation students and their peers whose parents have had some college exposure or earned a bachelor's or advanced degree. Four years after high school and net of other considerations, students whose parents had some college experience were nearly twice as likely as first-generation students to themselves earn a bachelor's degree (21 percent versus 11 percent), and students whose parents held a bachelor's degree or higher were nearly five times more likely to earn a bachelor's degree than were similar first-generation students (50 percent versus 11 percent).

BETWEEN-COLLEGE EFFECTS

In our 1991 review, we found that, across all of the outcomes considered, where students attended college had less impact than either the net effect of attending versus not attending college or of differences among individuals' experiences during college (within-college effects). The more recent evidence underlying the present synthesis reinforces this conclusion. Clearly, the 3,000-plus postsecondary institutions in the United States differ substantially in size, complexity, type of control, mission, financial and educational resources, research-teaching orientation of faculty, reputation and prestige, and characteristics of students enrolled. Yet, with some notable exceptions, the weight of evidence from the 1990s casts considerable doubt on the premise that the substantial structural, resource, and qualitative differences among postsecondary institutions produce correspondingly large differences in net educational effects on students. Rather, the great majority of postsecondary institutions appear to have surprisingly similar net impacts on student growth, although the "start" and "end" points for students differ across different institutions. Consistent with our 1991 synthesis (as well as with Bowen's 1977 review), the post-1990 research leads to the conclusion that similarities in between-college effects substantially outweigh the differences.

Overall, no single institutional characteristic or set of characteristics has a consistent impact across outcomes, but statistically reliable between-college effects are apparent in certain outcome areas. These between-college effects are more pronounced in the areas of career and economic attainment after college than they are in the developmental changes that occur during college (such as knowledge acquisition, cognitive development, changes in values and attitudes, and psychosocial development). These findings could be expected because in the areas of career and economic achievement, the status-allocating aspects of a college and what a degree from that college signals to prospective employers about the characteristics of its students may count as much as if not more than the education provided. Moreover, any estimation of between-college effects on the developmental changes that occur *during* college is complicated by recent evidence from nationally representative samples indicating that since the late 1980s, more than half of students who initially enroll at a four-year college ultimately attend two undergraduate institutions, and nearly 40 percent attend three or more. Thus, research findings concerning between-college effects may not generalize to the substantial numbers of U.S. students who attend more than one institution as undergraduates.

This final caveat aside, we uncovered considerably more evidence pertaining to between-college effects in the 1990s than we did in our previous review, and we turn now to a summary of those effects in the following categories: two-year versus four-year institutions, college quality, type, size, racial and gender composition, and college environment.

Two-Year Versus Four-Year Colleges

In our 1991 synthesis, we concluded that students who began their postsecondary education at a two-year community college were about 15 percent less likely to earn a bachelor's degree in the same time period as similar students who started at a four-year college. Thus, initial attendance at a two-year college appeared to have a negative, indirect impact on occupational status and possibly earnings. However, the impact was small and perhaps trivial for community college students who successfully transferred to a four-year college and completed their bachelor's degree in the same period of time as did four-year college students. Similarly, in comparing individuals of equal educational attainment, little evidence suggested that starting out at two-year colleges carried a penalty in terms of job stability, unemployment rate, or job satisfaction.

Although post-1990 findings do not conflict with the conclusions of our 1991 synthesis, the more recent research is clearly more comprehensive and addresses several uncharted areas with respect to the relative impact of beginning postsecondary education at a two-year versus a four-year college, suggesting the following conclusions:

1. When precollege ability, motivation, and other confounding influences were taken into account, students at two- and four-year colleges are essentially equal in first-year gains in reading comprehension,

mathematics, and critical thinking and in gains over two years of college in science reasoning and writing skills.

2. Community college students show greater gains in internal locus of attribution for academic success than do similar students at four-year institutions. That advantage, however, is not apparent only in the first year. The finding suggests not only that the effect may be variable over time but also that the impact is greatest when it is perhaps educationally most important—during the first year.

3. Community college students show greater gains than similar students at four-year institutions in their openness to both intellectual and racial-ethnic diversity. Community college students show a total advantage over their four-year counterparts of .21 of a standard deviation after one year and .22 of a standard deviation after two years. The small incremental increase in the total effect from the first to the second year indicates that the community college's impact is greatest in students' first year.

4. Consistent with pre-1990 estimates, beginning pursuit of a bachelor's degree at a two- rather than a four-year institution reduces the chances of ultimately earning that degree by 15 to 20 percentage points, even after statistical adjustments are made for students' precollege characteristics, including ability, socioeconomic status, and motivation.

5. The difference in bachelor's degree completion rates appears to lie in whether a community college student seeking a bachelor's degree actually transfers to a four-year institution. Once across that bridge, community college transfer students have about the same likelihood of earning a bachelor's degree as do similar students who began at a four-year college or university, although community college students tend to take longer to complete their degrees.

6. Evidence has emerged since 1990 tending to support the proposition that, even after adjusting for students' precollege characteristics, including degree plans, two-year college enrollment may reduce students' degree aspirations, perhaps by as much as 40 percent.

7. Net of other factors, initial attendance at a two- versus a four-year college appears to decrease the likelihood that high-ability minority students will persist in mathematics, science, and engineering careers.

8. Even when educational attainment is taken into account, initially attending a two-year college appears to have only a modest, negative effect on subsequent occupational status, and for similar individuals of equal educational attainment, initial attendance at a two-year college does not appear to confer a significant earnings penalty.

9. Net of other factors, students who initially enroll in a community college are able to transfer to more academically selective four-year institutions (defined by average entering student SAT scores) than they

could have enrolled in directly out of high school. This effect was most pronounced for students who came from poor families, who were low in tested ability, or who performed poorly in high school.

College Quality

In our 1991 review, we concluded that the net impact of college "quality" indices (most often defined in terms of institutional selectivity or prestige-reputation) depended in large measure on the type of outcome considered. Indices of institutional quality had less extensive impacts on developmentally oriented outcomes (learning, cognitive development, values, and psychosocial change) than on socioeconomic outcomes (educational attainment, occupational status, career mobility, earnings, and the like).

In the area of developmentally oriented outcomes, some weak to moderately consistent evidence indicated that college selectivity has a small, positive impact on aesthetic, cultural, and intellectual values; political and social liberalism; and secularism. Aside from these small effects, however, little consistent evidence suggested that college selectivity, prestige, or educational resources had any important net impact in such areas as learning, cognitive and intellectual development, the majority of psychosocial changes, the development of principled moral reasoning, or shifts in attitudes and values.

Clearer evidence supported the importance of institutional quality in career and socioeconomic attainments. Attending a selective or prestigious college had small, positive net effects on educational aspirations, plans for graduate or professional school, choice of an academic career, and choice of atypical careers among women. In addition to influencing aspirations and plans, attendance at an elite institution modestly enhanced a range of socioeconomic attainments, including bachelor's degree completion, graduate or professional school enrollment, entering sex-atypical careers for women, managerial status, occupational status in professional careers such as law and medicine, and earnings. Tempering the seemingly broad-based impacts of college selectivity or prestige on socioeconomic outcomes, however, were the facts that a substantial portion of the evidence was inconsistent, and the magnitude of the effect that could be attributed to college quality measures and not other influences was small.

As with our previous synthesis, evidence from the 1990s suggests that college "quality" has less important implications for intellectual and personal growth during college than for career and socioeconomic achievements. Net of important confounding influences, including tested precollege ability or cognitive level, we found that attending an academically selective institution has a negligible impact on knowledge acquisition or general cognitive development.

Similarly, we found little evidence of any appreciable effects of institutional selectivity on academic and social self-concepts, self-esteem, or other psychosocial dimensions once adjustments were made for other sources of influence. When institutional quality appears to be a factor at all, its impact is small and occasionally negative.

The same general pattern characterizes studies of admissions selectivity and changes in student attitudes and values. It appears not to matter much whether the outcome is sociopolitical dispositions, such as political identification, or social activism, liberalism, libertarianism, civic values, and views on gender roles. If admissions selectivity has any net impact at all, it is small and occasionally negative, inclining students on more selective campuses to perceive more racism on campus than do similar students on less selective campuses and tending to inhibit students' development of positive dispositions toward people from different racial-ethnic or cultural backgrounds.

Evidence with respect to the impact of college quality measures on socioeconomic outcomes is more pronounced, although still in some cases equivocal. The following generalizations appear warranted:

1. Institutional quality, as reflected in various measures of admissions selectivity, has a significant and positive direct effect on student persistence, educational aspirations, and degree completion, even after statistical adjustments for the characteristics of entering students and other institutional traits. But the effect of selectivity is small and intertwined with the kinds of experiences students have at college.

2. Attending a selective or prestigious institution appears to have only a trivial, direct impact on overall occupational status. However, attendance at an institution in the upper 1 or 2 percent of the selectivity distribution enhances degree attainment in specific high-status professions such as medicine or law.

3. Selective colleges confer a modest advantage in job attainment and career mobility, but only in relation to promotion in the middle organization ranks; graduating from a selective college apparently has little impact at the highest ranks. The evidence from this research further suggests that college selectivity signals intellectual and related traits in its students that are important for job performance. However, it is not clear if individuals attending selective institutions have these traits when they enroll or acquire them during college.

4. The weight of evidence suggests that, with controls in place for tested academic ability, socioeconomic origins, and undergraduate major, institutional quality and particularly student body selectivity have statistically significant, positive impacts on subsequent earnings. When quality is defined as selectivity, attending a college whose entering students average 100 points higher on the SAT (or the ACT equivalent) than enrollees at a comparison institution is associated with a net increase of as much as 4 percent higher reported earnings in later life. However, the effect of selectivity may not be linear, and only those elite schools at the very top of the selectivity distribution may confer an appreciable earnings premium. Aside from institutional selectivity, it is difficult to find indices of institutional quality that have consistent,

positive effects on earnings across studies. Moreover, the overall body of evidence may inflate estimates of the earnings premium attributable to a bachelor's degree from a selective college because studies usually lack adequate specifications for individual ambition. In addition, replicated evidence indicates that when ambition is taken into account, along with other factors, the impact of college selectivity on earnings tends to become negligible. Thus, a substantial part of the net earnings premium attributed to degrees from selective or prestigious colleges may in fact be due to the talents and motivations of the students they enroll.

College Type

In our earlier book, we concluded that estimating the net impact of different college types was complicated because type itself is often confounded with other institutional characteristics. For example, when considering the impact of selective liberal arts colleges, is the causal mechanism those institutions' private control, liberal arts curricular emphasis, or selective admissions? Nonetheless, modest evidence suggested that even when student body selectivity was held constant, private institutions appeared to have small, positive effects on educational aspirations and educational attainment, and liberal arts colleges tended to enhance the likelihood that women would choose sex-atypical majors and careers. Liberal arts institutions also appeared to stimulate increases in the value students attached to a liberal education and to intrinsic occupational rewards. Church-related colleges appeared to have negative net effects on measures of secularism and a positive influence on measures of humanitarian and altruistic social values. Aside from these effects, however, institutional categorizations such as the Carnegie classification revealed little difference in between-college impacts.

Post-1990 research also suggests that institutional type or Carnegie classification is not useful as a framework for understanding between-college effects. The literature of the 1990s says little about the net impact of institutional type on students' knowledge acquisition or general cognitive development, but some credible evidence suggests that small, private liberal arts colleges, including those that are religiously affiliated, may be particularly effective in fostering growth in principled moral reasoning.

Whether an institution is under public or private control appears to matter little with respect to students' psychosocial changes. Researchers have not examined whether type of control influences students' identity formation, and when institutional type appears to be a factor in shifts in students' academic and social self-concepts, the impact is small, and for students at public universities, usually negative.

Although more post-1990 studies explored the effects of type of control on shifts in students' attitudes and values, findings indicate that institutional type is at best a weak predictor of change when other student and institutional traits are taken into account. A few studies indicate that students at private colleges or universities show greater increases than similar students at public institutions on measures of their altruistic values and commitment to civic responsibility and community service. In addition, institutional type of control appears not to be a salient factor in net changes in student racial-ethnic or gender role attitudes or dispositions, educational or occupational values, or interest in the arts.

Studies consistently indicate that students attending private institutions have an advantage over their counterparts at public colleges and universities in terms of persistence and degree completion, although with controls in place for differences in the precollege characteristics of the students at each type of institution, the private institution advantage is muted or, in some studies, disappears. Net of other factors, the effects of attending a private college or university are probably indirect, influenced by such other institutional traits as size, selectivity, emphasis on undergraduate education, and faculty and peer relations.

Little empirical evidence suggests that attending a private (versus public) institution has any significant net influence on occupational status. Across all studies that provided the requisite information, the average net earnings premium associated with graduating from a private college (irrespective of its level of selectivity) is about 3 percent. If differential tuition costs are taken into account, this earnings premium would probably be substantially smaller, at least early in a graduate's career.

When academic selectivity is taken into account, neither an institution's Carnegie classification nor its doctoral-research orientation has a consistent impact on one's earnings. The sole exception appears to be for graduates of a Carnegie-type specialized institution, probably because such institutions usually focus on preparing students for occupational fields characterized by high earnings.

College Size

Our 1991 synthesis concluded that the net influence of institutional size (measured by enrollment) varied with the outcome being considered. Attending a large institution appeared to have small, positive direct effects on both occupational status and earnings, even when selectivity was taken into account. Conversely, large institutions had small, negative impacts on bachelor's degree completion, educational attainment, and development of social self-image during college. These impacts persisted irrespective of institutional selectivity but tended to be realized through indirect routes. Attending a large institution appeared to curb a student's level of social involvement during college, and social involvement was an important booster of such outcomes as educational attainment and self-concept.

In contrast to the conclusion of our 1991 synthesis, evidence from the 1990s suggests that institutional size has only a trivial and statistically nonsignificant net impact on occupational status. Consistent with our previous synthesis, however, the weight of evidence from the 1990s indicates that attending a large institution confers a small but statistically significant earnings advantage, even when controlling such factors as student body selectivity and private-public control. This positive effect of graduating from a large institution probably stems from major field and program diversity made possible by economies of scale as well as from numerous and wide-ranging links with occupational and economic groups beyond the campus.

The post-1990 research supports earlier findings that institutional size has little if any direct impact on psychosocial or attitudinal and value outcomes. Some evidence hints that large institutions have small, negative effects on over-all personal development, but it is more likely that institutional size has an indirect effect on psychosocial and attitudinal outcomes, acting through its effects on an array of student perceptions of their institutions, such as institutional priorities, faculty accessibility and interest in students, quality of instruction, and levels of satisfaction with various conditions and services on campus.

Institutional size is inversely related to student persistence and degree completion, although as in other areas, its impact is small and indirect. Size appears to shape students' enrollment decisions through its effects on student perceptions of institutional conditions, faculty and peer interactions, and students' academic and social involvement.

College Racial and Gender Composition

Although the evidence was not particularly compelling, our 1991 review concluded that attending a predominantly Black (versus a predominantly White) college appeared to have a modest, positive net impact on the cognitive development and educational attainment of African-American students in general and a small, positive impact on the occupational status and academic and social self-images of African-American women. These effects persisted even in the presence of controls for academic aptitude, socioeconomic origins, educational or occupational aspirations, and college selectivity. Similarly, moderately strong evidence suggested that single-sex colleges enhanced students' socioeconomic aspirations and career attainments, particularly for women. Net of college selectivity and individual background factors, attending a women's college appeared to enhance educational aspirations and attainment, choice of male-dominated careers, and the achievement of prominence in a field. Graduates of women's colleges were strongly overrepresented in the high-status, male-dominated occupations of medicine, scientific research, and engineering. However, research found little evidence that women's colleges had a net impact on occupational status and earnings.

The post-1990 research offers partial support for our previous conclusions, indicating that, despite relative disadvantages in financial and educational resources, historically Black colleges and universities (HBCUs) appear to be as proficient as primarily White institutions (PWIs), if not more so, in fostering the knowledge acquisition (such as reading comprehension, mathematics, science reasoning) and general cognitive growth (such as critical thinking) of African-American students. There was little evidence, however, that women's colleges had a stronger net impact on either the knowledge acquisition or general cognitive growth of women than did coeducational institutions.

The post-1990 evidence, although limited in volume, also supports our earlier conclusion that HBCUs and women's colleges, compared with predominantly

White schools and coed institutions, respectively, provide their students small, positive benefits in both academic and social self-concepts. HBCUs also appear to provide modest advantages in the overall personal development of their students. Net of other factors, however, there is little evidence that either HBCUs or women's institutions provide any advantage in self-esteem, internal locus of control, or leadership skill development. Women's colleges promote larger increases than coeducational institutions in their students' liberal political attitudes, desire to influence social conditions, civic values, and racial-cultural awareness and appreciation. Those differences are small, however, and the causal mechanisms are probably more indirect than direct, mediated by the peer environment and by student perceptions of the priorities their institutions give to social and multicultural objectives. African-American students at HBCUs compared with their peers at PWIs show greater gains on measures of the value they attach to learning for self-understanding.

Women at women's colleges (versus coeducational institutions) and African-American students at HBCUs (rather than PWIs) gain small to modest advantages in persistence and degree attainment. Women at women's colleges also appear to develop higher educational and occupational aspirations than women at coed institutions. At both women's colleges and HBCUs, however, institutional effects appear to be largely indirect, a function of HBCUs' more supportive faculty and peer relations and more supportive overall educational environment compared with those of coed and PWI campuses.

Overall, it is difficult to form an unequivocal conclusion from the literature of the 1990s about the impact of attending an historically Black college on the career and economic success of African Americans. Historically Black colleges appear to enhance the career aspirations of African-American students, and some evidence suggests that a bachelor's degree from an HBCU is linked with one dimension of career eminence among African-American women. However, evidence of the influence of HBCUs on African Americans' occupational status, career mobility, and earnings is inconsistent and, on occasion, conflicting.

Consistent evidence indicates that a racially diverse campus may produce subsequent earnings advantages for non-African-American students, particularly men. This outcome may reflect employers' willingness to recognize the importance of, and reward recent graduates' experiences with, diverse populations, and these experiences are most likely to occur at schools with racially diverse undergraduate student bodies.

Single-study evidence suggests that graduating from a women's institution positively influences a woman's subsequent career eminence as well as her likelihood of marrying a high-earning spouse. However, the 1990s produced inconsistent evidence concerning the net impact of women's colleges on the acquisition of career-related skills, the likelihood of choosing nontraditional majors and careers, and workplace participation. Similarly, as with our 1991 synthesis, the overall weight of evidence on the net impact of women's colleges on women's occupational status and earnings is inconsistent and thus unconvincing.

College Environment

Our 1991 volume reported the following five conclusions about the net impact of institutional environments:

1. Institutional environments that stress frequent student-faculty interaction and curricular flexibility facilitated knowledge acquisition as measured on standardized measures such as the Graduate Record Examination.

2. An emphasis on general education in the curriculum enhanced general cognitive growth on such dimensions as critical thinking and adult reasoning skills.

3. Environmental factors that maximize persistence and educational attainment include a peer culture in which students develop close on-campus friendships, participate frequently in college-sponsored activities, and perceive their college to be concerned about them individually as well as an emphasis on support services (including advising, orientation, and individualized general education courses that develop academic survival skills).

4. Environments that emphasize intrinsic motivations, student involvement in classroom discussions and course decision making, and overall student involvement with faculty in an academic community appeared to maximize overall psychosocial adjustment and maturity and minimize authoritarianism among students.

5. The most consistent college environmental impact on career choice is *progressive conformity,* where choices are influenced in the direction of the dominant peer groups. Irrespective of initial career choice, research uncovered a small but persistent tendency for seniors to plan to enter careers consistent with the most typical academic majors at their institutions and subsequently to do so.

The post-1990 research frequently developed operational definitions of institutional environments that had little in common with definitions used in the research underlying our 1991 synthesis. However, conclusions warranted by our present synthesis have several commonalities with those in our earlier review.

1. Although the specific findings do not replicate those of the research in our previous synthesis, the literature of the 1990s is consistent with earlier research in suggesting that studying institutional environments may be a more useful approach to understanding between-college effects on learning and cognitive development than is examining a school's structural characteristics (such as selectivity, private-public control, size, single-sex versus coeducational, and Carnegie type). Consistent evidence indicates that institutional environments with a scholarly or analytical emphasis foster both learning and general cognitive growth. Moreover,

such an emphasis was not determined by, nor merely a proxy for, institutional selectivity. Replicated evidence also suggests that critical thinking, analytic competencies, and general intellectual development thrive in college environments that emphasize close relationships and frequent interaction between faculty and students as well as faculty concern about student growth and development. This environmental emphasis appears to influence dimensions of general cognitive growth and do so independently of an institution's scholarly environment. Finally, evidence suggests that environments that support diversity and are relatively free of racial bias may facilitate learning among students of color.

2. Irrespective of size and selectivity, institutions with honor codes or honor systems enforced by students have significantly less anonymous self-reported academic dishonesty than do institutions without such honor codes, suggesting that a student culture of academic integrity inhibits cheating behavior. It is also possible that schools with visible honor codes attract students for whom academic integrity is a personal priority.

3. An institution's environment also appears to influence certain aspects of psychosocial change more than do its more formal, structural characteristics. An institution with structural diversity (that is, a racial-ethnic mix on campus) appears to enhance students' self-concepts, both academic and social. The impact, however, is indirect, operating through structural diversity's positive impact on the likelihood that students will encounter and interact with diverse people and ideas as well as through an institution's multicultural orientation such diversity reflects. The opportunities for involvement that women's colleges provide also promote students' positive social self-concepts, and the supportive personal environments of HBCUs appear to enhance their students' overall personal development.

4. Students' perceptions of the emphasis their institution places on diversity and multiculturalism, their beliefs about the sociopolitical dispositions of the faculty, and the peer environment, net of other factors, consistently and positively influence changes in a range of sociopolitical and civic attitudes and behaviors, including voting, "liberal" political orientations, commitment to social activism, respect for individual rights, and civic engagement. Student perceptions of the sociopolitical values and priorities of peers and faculty members also positively shape student racial-ethnic attitudes and openness to diversity. These liberal dispositions may fade, however, on campuses where students believe their peers place a high value on material possessions and social status.

5. Student perceptions that faculty members care about them and about teaching, as well as faculty accessibility to students, all promote persistence and degree completion even after adjustments for a variety of precollege characteristics, including ability. A normative peer environment also encourages persistence when it emphasizes community,

persistence, degree completion, and graduate school enrollment and provides students with both academic and social support. The perception that racial discrimination or prejudice exists in the classroom or on campus negatively affects continued enrollment among all students, regardless of race-ethnicity.

6. As in our 1991 synthesis, we again found strong evidence that the college environmental factor that most consistently influences career choice is progressive conformity. Irrespective of initial career choice, the dominant academic majors at an institution influence a student's major field of study and career choices.

Some Final Thoughts on Between-College Effects

Focusing on developmental changes that occur during college (such as learning, cognitive growth, moral reasoning, values, and psychosocial growth) reveals that even the statistically significant between-college effects found in the most methodologically sound studies tend to be small and of questionable practical importance. It may be that the aggregation of structural characteristics (such as selectivity, size, private-public control) or even environmental stimuli at the institutional level yields indices too remote from the actual social and intellectual forces that shape growth during college. With some exceptions, such as small, homogeneous liberal arts colleges, the majority of American postsecondary institutions have important social and intellectual subenvironments and peer cultures that exert more immediate and powerful impacts on individual students. Thus, it is reasonable to expect substantially greater diversity of impacts within than between institutions.

Where an individual attends college appears to play a consistently visible role in socioeconomic achievement. Attendance or graduation from a selective or prestigious institution may confer statistically significant advantages in various dimensions of career mobility and earnings, but with the possible exception of earnings, the magnitude of these advantages is not always consistent or clear. And even if we include earnings, part of what appears to be an institutional effect may still be a result of failing to adjust for ambition, aspiration, and other individual traits that impel socioeconomic achievement. Moreover, the evidence suggests that only a relatively small number of the most elite and selective institutions consistently confer economic and career advantages along with their diplomas. From the standpoint of *incremental* improvements in the chances for success, where one attends college probably confers a less pronounced and consistent average advantage than either that attributable to obtaining a bachelor's degree versus a high school diploma or that attributable to within-college experiences such as major field of study.

WITHIN-COLLEGE EFFECTS

The extensive post-1990 research literature on within-college effects, like the pre-1990 research, lacks a common set of conceptual or theoretical themes. Consequently, we have organized the synthesis of this large body of research around our own reading of the common threads, focusing first on commonalities and contrasts with our previous synthesis and then offering conclusions about the major determinants of within-college effects in the categories of residence, major field of study, academic experience, interpersonal involvement, extracurricular involvement, and academic achievement.

General Conclusions

The body of evidence from the 1990s on within-college effects has a number of features in common with the literature reviewed in our earlier synthesis. First, the types of within-college experiences that maximize impact depend to some extent on the kind of college attended. For example, a social environment that facilitates frequent informal student-faculty contact is more likely at a small, residential college than at a large university that has a mix of residential and commuter students. Even so, considerable variability in student-faculty contact is likely among small, residential colleges (as well as among other types of institutions), and nearly all of the important within-college impacts persist *irrespective* of the institutional context in which they occur.

In addition, many of the experiences that maximize the impact of college depend to some extent on the characteristics of the students who engage in them. For example, students who are most likely to engage in diversity experiences during college (such as interacting with racially diverse peers or attending racial-cultural awareness workshops) are also likely to be open to diversity at the time they enter college. The net impact of their involvement in diversity experiences during college most likely further strengthens their openness to diversity. Thus, many within-college effects appear to be essentially the accentuation of initial student characteristics and dispositions.

One of the most unequivocal conclusions drawn from both our previous synthesis and the research during the 1990s is that the impact of college is largely determined by individual effort and involvement in the academic, interpersonal, and extracurricular offerings on a campus. Students are not passive recipients of institutional efforts to "educate" or "change" them but rather bear major responsibility for any gains they derive from their postsecondary experience. This is not to say that an individual campus's ethos, policies, and programs are unimportant. Quite the contrary. But if, as it appears, individual effort or engagement is the critical determinant of the impact of college, then it is important to focus on the ways in which an institution can shape its academic, interpersonal, and extracurricular offerings to encourage student engagement.

The post-1990 research on within-college effects also differs from the research underlying our previous synthesis in several respects, particularly its greater emphasis on estimating the impacts of the academic experience. Researchers during the 1990s produced a substantial body of evidence on approaches to teaching that either did not exist in earlier decades or were in their nascent stages when we published *How College Affects Students* in 1991. Two important themes woven through many of these new pedagogies concern active student engagement in learning and learning in collaboration with faculty and peers.

A second significant addition of the literature of the 1990s has been the effort to estimate the impacts of specific extracurricular, interpersonal, or nonacademic experiences. Although more research has focused on instructional methods, post-1990 studies of the effects of fraternity or sorority membership, intercollegiate athletic participation, work during college, and interaction with racially diverse peers have provided a more complete understanding of the impacts of those experiences than we had a decade ago.

These two advances in the research of the 1990s constitute a growing body of empirical support for the proposition advanced in our earlier review that students change in holistic ways and that these changes have their origins in multiple influences in both the academic and nonacademic domains of students' lives. The research published since 1990 persuades us more than ever that students' in- and out-of-class lives are interconnected in complex ways we are only beginning to understand.

Residence

In our 1991 synthesis, we concluded that living on campus (versus living off campus or commuting) was the single most consistent within-college determinant of the impact of college. Net of important background traits and other confounding influences, living on campus had statistically significant, positive impacts on increases in aesthetic, cultural, and intellectual values; liberalization of social, political, and religious values and attitudes; development of more positive self-concepts; intellectual orientation, autonomy, and independence; tolerance, empathy, and ability to relate to others; and the use of principled reasoning to judge moral issues. Residing on campus also significantly increased the likelihood of persisting in college and earning a bachelor's degree. In addition, residing in an on-campus living-learning center bolstered the positive influence on persistence. Little evidence, however, suggested that living on or off campus influenced either knowledge acquisition or general cognitive growth. Living on campus, however, appears to foster change indirectly, by maximizing the opportunities for social, cultural, and extracurricular engagement.

Where students live during their college years figures less prominently in the post-1990 research on psychosocial and attitudinal and value changes. In studies that focus on residence as a variable of primary interest, some evidence indicates no appreciable net impact on self-esteem or locus of control, although living away from home appears to have positive effects on students' interpersonal skills. Living on rather than off campus does promote more positive and inclusive racial-ethnic attitudes and openness to diversity, researchers report, and as long as a student lives on campus, the type of housing may not matter. Consistent with our earlier review, post-1990 research finds the residential impact is strongest in those living settings purposefully structured to encourage students' encounters with people different from themselves and with ideas different from those they currently hold. These findings persist even after adjustments are made for student precollege characteristics, including a precollege measure of the psychosocial or attitudinal variable under study.

As in our previous review, we found little consistent post-1990 evidence that living on campus directly influences either knowledge acquisition or more general cognitive growth. We suspect that residing on campus may exert an indirect, positive influence on these outcomes, particularly on general cognitive growth, by facilitating academic and social engagement, but we uncovered no empirical test of this hypothesis.

The post-1990 research on the effects of residence on student persistence, degree completion, and educational attainment supports our earlier conclusion that students living on campus are more likely to persist to degree completion than are similar students living elsewhere. Post-1990 studies, however, achieved greater specificity in indicating that residence effects are primarily indirect rather than direct. Place of residence has a clear bearing on the extent to which students participate in extracurricular activities, engage in more frequent interactions with peers and faculty members, and report positive perceptions of the campus social climate, satisfaction with their college experience, and greater personal growth and development. Abundant evidence in both of our reviews indicates that such involvements positively influence persistence and that students who live in living-learning settings are more likely, net of other factors, to persist than are similar students in traditional housing arrangements. More recent research findings concerning living-learning centers are less compelling than earlier ones, however, perhaps reflecting a scaling back of this innovation of several decades ago.

Major Field of Study

The overall evidence from our 1991 synthesis indicated that a student's undergraduate academic major had its most visible impacts on cognitive and career outcomes, and the cognitive impact of major field of study was selective. Students tended to demonstrate the highest levels of learning in subjects most congruent with their major. Similarly, they tended to demonstrate the greatest proficiency on measures of general cognitive development when confronted with problems or examples taken from the content most typical of their academic major or the disciplinary emphasis of their coursework. Beyond these selective impacts, little consistent evidence suggested that a student's major had any significant impact on general intellectual or cognitive growth.

Pre-1990s research indicated the major field of study had potentially important implications for a student's eventual occupation and financial rewards. Majoring in engineering, business, some preprofessional programs, and selected natural sciences significantly increased the probability of a job with skill requirements consistent with that academic training and the concomitant advantages in early career earnings as well as entry by women into high-status, male-dominated occupations. The occupational impacts of an academic major, however, appeared to be strongest early in a career, decreasing over time and yielding in importance to general intellectual skills and the ability to learn on the job. Similarly, over the long term, the research showed, career mobility and occupational attainment levels of liberal arts majors in the business sector appeared to equal those of business or engineering majors.

Academic major appeared to have less impact on other outcomes. Some evidence indicated that majoring in the natural sciences, mathematics, or technical fields had small, positive effects on academic self-concept, but little evidence pointed to changes attributable to academic major in other areas of psychosocial growth, attitudes, or values. The evidence suggested that interpersonal climate and value homogeneity within a department may be more important than the structural characteristics of a discipline in shaping psychosocial and attitudinal changes.

Substantial post-1990 evidence concerning the effects of major field of study supports the conclusions in our 1991 synthesis, but findings in some studies suggest a need to revise some conclusions. In addition, research during the 1990s found new evidence on the impact of college major.

1. Research both pre- and post-1990 indicates that undergraduates tend to make the greatest knowledge gains and attain the highest level of academic skills in subject matter areas consistent with their major field of study and in disciplines in which they take the most courses. Additional post-1990 evidence suggests that the intellectual training in different fields of study leads to the development of different reasoning skills, a finding also consistent with our 1991 conclusion that academic major has a selective impact on cognitive growth.

2. As in 1991 and since, little consistent evidence suggests that a major field of study, in and of itself, leads to different effects on general measures of critical thinking. However, in considering specific coursework, replicated evidence indicates that exposure to natural science courses positively influences growth in critical-thinking skills. Evidence with respect to other coursework concentrations is inconclusive or awaits replication.

3. Different disciplines attract different kinds of students and then tend to accentuate initial differences among students across those various disciplines. For example, students in major fields categorized according to Holland's model as *investigative* (because of their emphasis on disciplinary exploration, understanding, and knowledge acquisition) show greater net gains in intellectual self-confidence, drive to achieve, and expectations of making a contribution to science than do similar students in other disciplinary areas. Similarly, students majoring in *enterprising* disciplines, which emphasize goal achievement or economic gain and leadership abilities, show greater net gains in those areas than students majoring in nonenterprising disciplines. Majoring in engineering and business have positive net effects on women's math self-concepts, and although the proportion of women in a particular major appears not to influence women's academic self-concepts, evidence suggests majoring in women's studies contributes to identity development in women.

4. In the aggregate, the evidence on the effects of major field on students' sociopolitical attitudes and values is inconclusive, being more field specific than general. Studies indicate that majoring in engineering or taking numerous quantitatively intensive courses has a negative net effect on increases in liberal sociopolitical stances, and students majoring in disciplines that emphasize social service and promoting the welfare of others show greater increases in those values than do students in other disciplines. Compared with other fields, majoring in business, nursing, science, or engineering is associated with smaller increases in positive racial-cultural attitudes and openness to diversity. In the main, the effects of major field may be more a function of the values and traits of the students choosing a discipline than of that discipline's specific content.

5. Both pre- and post-1990 research found that students majoring in the sciences, engineering, business, and health-related fields are more likely to graduate than similar students in other majors. Disciplines with high potential for attractive employment and financial opportunities immediately after graduation also bolster prospects of graduation, although students in these fields are less likely than similar students in other fields to go on to graduate school. A noteworthy contribution of the post-1990 literature is its clarification of some of the dynamics that underlie major field effects on educational attainment. Major field effects appear to be less a matter of the specific discipline than of two other factors: the economic opportunities associated with a discipline, and the culture and climate within a department, as evidenced in faculty values, faculty accessibility to students, the quality of student-faculty interactions, faculty support for students, and students' peer relations.

6. The undergraduate major students choose has a significant net impact on the probability of getting a job and securing employment at a level appropriate to a bachelor's degree early in their careers. The clearest advantages in these areas accrue to students majoring in fields having the most direct functional linkages with specific jobs or occupational sectors, such as computer science, engineering, social work, nursing, and accounting.

7. In contrast to the pre-1990 evidence, the research since that time indicates that academic major does, in fact, have a significant influence on occupational status. Net of other factors, individuals majoring in fields traditionally dominated by men (such as engineering, mathematics, physical science, and technical-preprofessional areas) tend to be overrepresented in high-status occupations.

8. A small body of evidence challenges our earlier conclusion that undergraduate major may have little net impact on career mobility in business. However, it is difficult to identify a clear pattern from the evidence. The impact appears to depend on the type of company considered and its unique cultural norms and values, the particular time in one's

career, the sector of the company in which individuals with certain majors tend to be placed, and the level of promotion or advancement considered. Consistent with our 1991 synthesis, little evidence suggests that undergraduate major plays a significant, independent role in promotion to the highest levels of corporate leadership.

9. Evidence from a single study suggests that the degree of congruence between students' academic major and their job has a positive influence on job satisfaction that is independent of salary level and similar in magnitude to salary level's impact on job satisfaction.

10. Consistent with our 1991 synthesis, the post-1990 research suggests that undergraduate major has a substantial impact on subsequent earnings. The evidence from the 1990s, however, permits estimation of the magnitude of this impact. After taking important confounding influences into account, researchers generally find a difference of 25 to 35 percent in subsequent earnings of students in the most and least lucrative majors. The largest earnings premiums continue to accrue to graduates of majors characterized by a relatively specific and well-defined body of content knowledge and skills, an emphasis on quantitative or scientific methods of inquiry, a generally close and direct functional link to occupations with relatively high average earnings, often an applied orientation, and a history of being dominated by men (such as engineering, business or accounting, physical sciences, mathematics and computer science, and preprofessional majors in health science areas). The impact of a major appears to be most pronounced early in graduates' careers, but the same general pattern appears to hold later in their careers as well.

11. A possible exception to the general pattern of the effects of major field of study on earnings may occur at particularly selective or prestigious institutions, where majoring in the liberal arts may provide an "option value" of potential graduate or professional study that enhances longer-term earnings.

12. Economic returns to holders of associate's and bachelor's degrees sometimes overlap, largely as a result of the individual's major field of study. For example, women can generally get a greater earnings return from an associate's degree in business or health than from a bachelor's degree in the humanities or education. Men can generally realize a larger economic premium from an associate's degree in engineering, public service, or vocational-technical areas than from a bachelor's degree in the humanities or education. At both the baccalaureate and subbaccalaureate levels, however, starting salary and early career earnings are enhanced by the extent to which undergraduate major is related to or congruent with the job.

13. Generally, men tend to be overrepresented in academic majors closely linked to the highest-paying occupations, whereas the opposite tends

to be true for women. Moreover, even after adjustments for important background characteristics, the research indicates that women are more likely than men to enter less lucrative fields of study. However, the evidence also reveals that differences between men and women in their academic majors fail to account for all of the gender gap in earnings among the college-educated.

The Academic Experience

Our 1991 synthesis supported five conclusions about the impact of students' academic experiences.

1. Other things being equal, the strongest evidence indicated that the greater a student's engagement in academic work or in the academic experience of college, the greater his or her level of knowledge acquisition and general cognitive growth. Less extensive evidence indicated that academic engagement reduced authoritarianism and dogmatism and increased autonomy and independence, intellectual orientation, and the use of principled moral reasoning.

2. Certain instructional and programmatic interventions not only increased active engagement in learning and academic work but also enhanced knowledge acquisition and some dimensions of both cognitive and psychosocial growth. Instructional strategies such as peer teaching and individualized learning approaches (for example, Personalized System of Instruction and computer-based instruction), based to a large extent on increasing active engagement in learning, appeared to enhance knowledge acquisition under experimental conditions. Evidence also indicated that inductive learning based on active involvement in concrete activities fostered growth in abstract reasoning, whereas instruction that emphasized active student discussion at a relatively high cognitive level and instruction that engaged students in active problem solving fostered critical thinking.

3. Academic experiences that purposefully provided for challenge and integration stimulated change in a wide variety of cognitive areas. These academic experiences included cognitive-developmental instruction and curricular experiences that required students to integrate learning from separate courses around a central theme.

4. Student learning showed an unambiguous link to instructor or teacher classroom behaviors. The two most salient dimensions of teacher behavior in predicting student learning were instructor skill (particularly clarity of presentation) and course structure-organization (such as class time structured and efficiently organized), both of which are learnable skills.

5. Tentative evidence suggested that, irrespective of a student's academic ability, the pattern and sequence of courses taken as an undergraduate

influenced not only mastery of material but also cognitive abilities. This research, however, was in its initial stages, leaving the mapping of consistent and replicable findings unresolved.

Post-1990s research focusing on the academic experience produced what may be the largest single body of new knowledge. Well-conducted experimental, quasi-experimental, and correlational investigations addressing the different aspects of a student's academic experience are so varied and numerous as to defy any tight organizational structure for discussion. Nevertheless, this large body of evidence warrants the following general conclusions:

1. The evidence from the 1990s prompts a modest revision in our previous conclusion that class size has no impact on the acquisition of subject matter knowledge. When learning is measured by course grade, the post-1990 research is reasonably clear that class size is negatively related to learning. When learning is assessed on standardized measures, however, little consistent evidence exists to suggest that class size has a negative influence, at least in the field of economics.

2. Although it is not always clear how the "control" or "traditional" method of instruction is operationally defined, we uncovered reasonably consistent experimental and quasi-experimental findings that a variety of innovative pedagogical approaches can improve subject matter learning. These approaches and the estimated average improvement in subject matter learning they produce when compared with control or traditional methods (expressed as part of a standard deviation) are shown in Table 11.5.

3. More focused classroom instructional techniques that appear to be effective tools for enhancing student learning include peer tutoring, reciprocal teaching, attributional retraining, concept-knowledge maps,

Table 11.5. Estimated Average Improvement in Subject Matter Learning, Compared with Traditional Methods, by Pedagogical Approach

Pedagogical Approach	Net Effect Size (in Standard Deviation Units)
Learning for mastery	.41 to .68
Computer-assisted instruction	.31
Active learning	.25
Collaborative learning	Unclear
Cooperative learning	.51
Small-group learning	.51
Supplemental Instruction	.39 (compared with nonparticipation)
Constructivist-oriented approaches	.14 to .40 (based on two studies)

and the one-minute paper. Methodologically sound research on problem-based learning and learning communities is in its nascent stages, but both approaches show promise.

4. A large body of evidence suggests that individuals who study using distance education approaches master course content with about the same level of proficiency as their counterparts in conventional on-campus settings. However, the absence of controls for students' self-selection into on-campus versus remote instructional sites undermines the internal validity of this research.

5. Replicated experimental or quasi-experimental evidence indicates that learning a computer programming language can provide an advantage of .35 of a standard deviation in general cognitive skills such as planning, reasoning, and metacognition. Similarly, consistent correlational evidence indicates that coursework requiring students to use computers; use of computers in learning activities such as data analysis, creating visual displays, and Internet searches; and use of electronic mail to practice argumentation all foster critical thinking and general reasoning skills.

6. Experimental and quasi-experimental evidence indicates that students learning in cooperative groups have an average advantage in developing problem-solving skills over their counterparts not in a cooperative learning format of .47 of a standard deviation. Moreover, net of other factors, cooperative or group learning experiences appear to influence positively self-reported growth in career-related skills such as leadership abilities, public speaking ability, ability to influence others, and ability to work effectively in groups.

7. The evidence suggests that critical thinking can be taught. Students who receive purposeful instruction or practice in critical thinking and problem-solving skills gain an average advantage of .23 of a standard deviation over similar students who do not receive such instruction. The absence of consensus across studies on what constitutes "instruction in critical thinking" may, at least partially, account for the modest magnitude of the effect.

8. Although the total body of evidence is relatively small and not particularly robust, it appears that growth in postformal reasoning may be facilitated by three loosely related innovative instructional approaches: reflective judgment–developmental instruction, active learning and team problem-solving instruction, and deliberate psychological instruction. On average, students exposed to these instructional approaches gain an advantage on measures of postformal reasoning of about .65 of a standard deviation over similar students not receiving such instruction.

9. The weight of evidence from both quasi-experimental and correlational research, although equivocal, indicates that service-learning experiences

enhance both course learning and dimensions of cognitive development. Quasi-experimental evidence concerning the impact of service-learning on principled moral reasoning is mixed. In addition, service-learning experiences appear to influence positively such dimensions of career development as self-ratings of leadership skills, the importance of a helping career, occupational identity processing, and salient career development tasks. The most effective service-learning approaches appear to be those that integrate service experiences with course content and provide for reflection about the service experience through discussion or writing.

10. The post-1990 research also links several aspects of students' academic experiences to some elements of psychosocial development. Service-learning courses help students clarify and define their identities and improve their self-esteem, internal locus of control, and interpersonal skills. Similarly, other academic experiences that actively involve students in their own learning also appear to yield certain psychosocial benefits. Taking diversity courses, tutoring, helping to teach a course, working with a faculty member on a research project, involvement in group projects for courses, exposure to active and collaborative pedagogical techniques, and the quality of instruction all promote to varying degrees students' identity formation, academic self-concept, self-esteem, internal locus of attribution for academic success, and general personal development.

11. Many of the academic experiences that influence psychosocial changes also promote shifts in attitudes and values. Although the evidence is sometimes mixed, service-learning courses appear to promote students' commitments to social justice, social activism, and changing social and political structures as well as to a sense of social responsibility and civic engagement. Taking diversity courses and participating in racial-ethnic or cultural workshops promote similar shifts in sociopolitical attitudes and dispositions to community and civic engagement. Diversity courses also increase student awareness of other ethnic groups and cultures, promote openness to diversity, and elevate the importance students attach to promoting racial understanding. Moderately consistent evidence also links several general classroom characteristics to increases in multicultural awareness and understanding. These classroom features include instructors who are women or persons of color, diversity-related content and research, and instructional practices that facilitate discussion of racial and cultural issues. Workshops targeted at particular social issues appear, net of other factors, to be effective in promoting increases in students' awareness, knowledge, and understanding of groups of different race-ethnicity or cultural origins, gender, and sexual orientation.

12. Although the volume and quality of the evidence varies, studies consistently show the effectiveness of several academic programs and

experiences specifically designed to promote student academic performance and persistence. These programs and experiences include first-year seminars, supplemental instruction, academic advising, summer "bridge" programs, undergraduate research programs, living-learning centers, learning communities, and active and collaborative pedagogies. However, student perceptions that prejudice or discrimination exists in the classroom, whether on the part of instructors or other students, have a negative net influence on persistence decisions.

13. Our previous synthesis noted that interventions focusing on moral dilemma discussion and personality development, with the instructor acting more as facilitator than information provider, had been found to be particularly effective in stimulating the use of principled moral reasoning. Quasi-experimental evidence from the 1990s suggests that instruction in philosophical methods of ethical analysis, as well as in dilemma discussion and personality development, further enhances growth in the use of principled moral reasoning.

14. Evidence from two independent longitudinal studies suggests that purposefully integrating ethical content into an undergraduate professional curriculum in nursing may foster growth in principled moral reasoning. Similarly, single-sample evidence indicates that a general education curriculum integrating moral and ethical decision making throughout a multidisciplinary six-course sequence bolsters the use of principled reasoning. Replicated quasi-experimental evidence also indicates that coursework that exposes students to diversity-related issues such as racism, sexism, and homophobia positively influences growth in moral reasoning.

15. Generally consistent experimental and quasi-experimental evidence indicates that career development courses or interventions (including computer-based ones) can significantly enhance dimensions of career development and maturity.

16. Modest quasi-experimental evidence supports the hypothesis that health knowledge and good health habits can be taught during college. Alumni who as students took a one-semester health and physical education course combining classroom instruction with physical activity sessions reported significantly higher levels of health knowledge and significantly more inclination to practice good health habits than alumni not exposed to the course.

17. Consistent with our previous synthesis, a large body of correlational research in the 1990s indicates that teacher behavior is an important influence on students' acquisition of course subject matter. Such factors as teacher preparation and organization, clarity, availability and helpfulness, quality and frequency of teacher feedback, and concern for and rapport with students continued to have significant, positive correlations with student mastery of course content. Furthermore,

although it awaits replication, correlational evidence, paired with extensive statistical controls, indicates that the overall extent of teacher organization and preparation at an institution positively influences general measures of learning and cognitive development (including reading comprehension and critical thinking) not tied to specific courses.

18. Our previous synthesis found experimental validation of the effects of teacher clarity on student mastery of course content. The literature of the 1990s offers additional experimental evidence validating the positive impact of both teacher expressiveness and enthusiasm and teacher organization on student content acquisition. Perhaps most important, each of the three teacher behaviors shown to facilitate knowledge acquisition in a course may be learned by college faculty.

19. Consistent with our previous synthesis, we found substantial post-1990 evidence indicating that, apart from courses taken and instruction received, both knowledge acquisition and general cognitive growth depend in large measure on an individual's level of academic effort and engagement. Other things being equal, the more students are psychologically engaged in activities such as use of the library, reading unassigned books, individual study, writing papers, and course assignments, the greater their knowledge acquisition and general intellectual growth. If the literature of the 1990s says anything, it is that, although colleges can fashion an undergraduate academic experience characterized by a plethora of learning opportunities, it is the extent to which students become engaged in and fully exploit these opportunities that largely determines the personal benefits they derive.

Interpersonal Involvement

Our 1991 synthesis concluded that the extent and content of interactions with the main agents of socialization on campus—namely, faculty members and students—played a large part in determining the impact of college on students. The influence of personal interaction with these groups was manifest in intellectual outcomes as well as in changes in attitudes, values, aspirations, and a number of psychosocial characteristics.

Net of student background characteristics, the extent of informal contact with faculty was positively linked with an array of outcomes, including perceptions of intellectual growth during college, increases in intellectual orientation, liberalization of social and political values, and growth in autonomy and independence. Contact with faculty also apparently fosters increases in interpersonal skills, gains in general maturity and personal development, educational aspirations and attainment, orientation toward scholarly careers, and women's interest in and choice of male-dominated careers. The most influential interactions appeared to be those that focused on ideas or intellectual matters, thereby extending and reinforcing the intellectual goals of the academic experience.

Interactions with peers also strongly influenced many aspects of change during college, including intellectual development and intellectual orientation; political, social, and religious liberalism; positive academic and social self-concept; interpersonal skills; use of principled moral reasoning; maturity and personal development; and educational aspirations and attainment. The degree of peer influence varied across outcomes, with some evidence suggesting that fellow students exerted greater influence on change in attitudinal and psychosocial areas than in learning or cognitive areas, where faculty influence appeared greater. The impact of peer interaction was greatest when peers challenged beliefs, attitudes, and values, forcing introspection, reflection, and re-evaluation.

Although not as extensive as the evidence supporting our previous synthesis, the post-1990 research underscores the importance of interaction with faculty and peers as a determinant of growth and change during college. The weight of evidence suggests that student-faculty interactions outside the classroom that reinforce and extend the intellectual ethos of the classroom or formal academic experience, or that focus on issues of personal growth, positively influence dimensions of general cognitive development such as postformal reasoning, analytic ability, and critical thinking skills. Similarly, single-sample evidence suggests that out-of-class interaction with faculty has a net positive influence on gains in principled moral reasoning.

The research is less clear with respect to the effects of student-faculty interactions on students' psychosocial dimensions, although some evidence suggests the faculty influence is greatest when student-faculty contacts are academically related. Faculty members also play a role in students' shifting sociopolitical dispositions, although the faculty influence is probably less powerful than that of peers. After adjustments for confounding influences, studies show faculty contact is positively related to increases in the importance students attach to influencing social values, contributing to their communities, changing political structures, voting, and promoting racial understanding.

In addition to reinforcing our earlier conclusions about the role student-faculty interaction plays in promoting persistence and educational attainment, perhaps the primary contribution of our current review is to shine a somewhat brighter light on the underlying processes. The post-1990 evidence supports earlier speculation that at least two dynamics are probably at work: the socialization of students to the normative values and attitudes of the academy and the bond between student and institution that positive student-faculty interactions appear to promote. Indeed, a few studies suggest that even students' *perceptions* of faculty availability and interest in them may be sufficient to promote persistence.

Consistent with our 1991 conclusions, post-1990 research suggests student-faculty out-of-class interaction may also play a role in students' careers. For example, student-faculty interaction appears to have a positive influence on the likelihood of students choosing careers in academic and scientific research, although some ambiguity exists with respect to causal direction. That is, does student-faculty interaction increase the likelihood that a student will choose an academic or scientific research career, or are students who have decided on such a career more likely to seek interaction with faculty? The same uncertainty afflicts the research on psychosocial development, attitudinal and value changes, and persistence. Are these within-college effects really a product of student contact with faculty members, or are students who are disposed to change or to persist more likely to seek contact with faculty members? Most studies assume the first proposition is more likely.

Both pre- and post-1990 research testifies to the importance of interactions with peers. However, an important additional contribution of the research of the 1990s has been a better understanding of the kinds of peer interactions that are most influential. The student-peer contacts that matter most appear to be those that expose the student to diverse racial, cultural, social, value, and intellectual perspectives. That is, students derive the greatest developmental benefits from engagement in peer networks that expose them to individuals different from themselves. Net of confounding influences, interactions with diverse peers have modest but consistently positive impacts on knowledge acquisition, dimensions of cognitive development such as critical thinking and complexity of thought, principled moral reasoning, and self-rated job skills after college.

Although less extensive than the pre-1990 evidence, the post-1990 research reinforces our earlier conclusions with respect to the influences of students' peer interactions on psychosocial outcomes. After adjusting for other influences, the research indicates that peer interactions promote positive academic and social self-concepts, self-confidence, and leadership skills. The effects of these interactions tend to be small, but interactions with peers of a different race-ethnicity may be particularly influential.

Virtually without exception, studies indicate that students' interactions with their peers have clear and statistically significant net effects on changes in various dimensions of sociopolitical, civic, racial-ethnic, and gender-role attitudes and behaviors. The post-1990 evidence is consistent with that in our earlier review, but it is both broader and more illuminating with respect to the mechanisms underlying student interactions and their effects. For example, a campus's structural diversity increases the likelihood that students will encounter peers with sociopolitical and cultural ideas different from their own and that these encounters will lead to more racially-ethnically diverse friendship groups and a greater frequency of discussions about race and ethnicity, all of which tend to promote openness to sociopolitical ideas and engagement in social and civic issues and activities as well as increased commitment to community service and to promoting understanding among people of different cultural origins. Personal interactions may also be an important mechanism in reducing negative attitudes toward gays and lesbians.

Extensive post-1990 evidence confirms our earlier conclusion that, in the aggregate, interaction with peers is probably the most pervasive and powerful force in student persistence and degree completion. The recent research suggests one dynamic at work is students' attraction to other students who are like themselves in various ways, including attitudes and values, and a second powerful influence is students' socialization to peer group norms through progressive conformity, which encourages students to adapt their goals and values to accommodate those of the peer group.

Extracurricular Involvement

Our 1991 synthesis uncovered a modest body of research concerning the net impact of extracurricular involvement. This research led to the conclusion that, with controls for important confounding influences, extracurricular involvement had modest, positive effects on institutional persistence and educational attainment, women's choice of nontraditional careers, and development of a positive social self-concept.

The evidence from the 1990s is decidedly more focused on the influence of several specific types of extracurricular involvement, including athletic participation, Greek affiliation, and work during college. Although small, the total body of evidence suggests that the impact of each of these extracurricular experiences is complex. For example, intercollegiate athletic participation, particularly for men in revenue-producing sports, appears to have an inhibiting influence on both general measures of learning (such as reading comprehension and writing skills) and cognitive development (such as critical thinking). However, little evidence suggests that participation in intercollegiate athletics had more than a chance impact on either principled moral reasoning or academic dishonesty, and only modest evidence supports the contention that athletic participation may encourage openness to diversity.

Several methodologically sound studies link intercollegiate sports participation to increases in social self-confidence and interpersonal skills. Male intercollegiate athletes, regardless of whether they participate in revenue-producing sports, show about the same net gains in locus of internal attribution for academic success as nonathletes. Contrary to widespread public opinion, intercollegiate sports appear to confer no advantage on athletes in terms of leadership skills, although athletes show somewhat greater net gains than nonathletes in civic values and community orientation. No differences are apparent between the two groups, however, in social and political dispositions in the postcollege years.

With some exceptions, the evidence indicates that intercollegiate sports also promote educational attainment, even with controls in place for other potentially confounding considerations. This conclusion holds for male and female athletes and for those in revenue-producing as well as less visible sports. Net of other factors and across all sports, male athletes are 4 percent more likely to graduate than male nonathletes; the advantage among women is less clear. The causal mechanism appears to involve a complex mix of level of involvement, peer influences, personal finances, and financial opportunities in sports as well as other occupational fields.

The impact of Greek affiliation is also complex and depends to some extent on the outcome being considered and at what point in the college career it is considered. For example, fraternity membership would appear to inhibit growth in general knowledge acquisition and critical thinking for men during the first year of college. After the first year, however, this negative effect essentially disappears.

Modest evidence suggests that Greek affiliation, in general, may inhibit growth in principled moral reasoning and increase the likelihood of both academic dishonesty and binge drinking during college. Interestingly, however, the effect of Greek affiliation on binge drinking during college does not extend to the postcollege years. When prior drinking behavior is taken into account, Greek affiliation has little impact on postcollege drinking levels for either men or women. Modest evidence supports the contention that fraternity or sorority membership can promote one's career. Net of other factors, Greek affiliation during college has a positive impact on the development of career-related skills.

Fraternities and sororities also have positive but small net effects on members' interpersonal skills, community orientation, and commitment to civic engagement. Membership has no appreciable impact on peer independence or locus of attribution for academic success, and it remains unclear whether the apparent negative influence of membership on social and political liberalism is real or a reflection of sociopolitical dispositions students bring to college. The research is clear, however, that fraternities and sororities have a net and negative influence on members' racial-ethnic attitudes and openness to diverse ideas and people. The post-1990 research is notably silent, however, on the net impact of fraternity or sorority membership on educational attainment.

Given the substantial number of undergraduates who now work during college, it is appropriate that the research of the 1990s began to estimate the impact of this experience. The small body of evidence we uncovered suggests that the influence of work depends on the outcome being considered. For example, little compelling evidence suggests that on- or off-campus work has any significant net impact on general measures of knowledge acquisition or cognitive growth during college. A small body of evidence indicates that off-campus employment during college has a negative influence on both principled moral reasoning and involvement in community service. However, work or internship experiences during college appear to have a positive net impact on the development of career-related skills and the likelihood of being employed immediately after college, particularly when the work experience is related to the major field of study. Evidence is inconsistent with respect to the impact of work during college on postcollege earnings or earnings growth.

The few studies that examined the net effects of employment on psychosocial and attitudinal outcomes indicate that part-time work on campus promotes positive academic self-concepts and increased social liberalism. Work also appears to enhance internal locus of attribution for academic success of community college students, although not their four-year counterparts. The net effects of employment on educational attainment depend to some extent on both the number of hours worked and whether the work is on or off campus. The more hours students work, the more likely they are to switch from full- to part-time enrollment and the less likely they are to persist as students from one year to the next or to complete a bachelor's degree. The relationship is not linear, however, and a most noteworthy contribution of the present review is in pinpointing when the number of hours worked shifts from being a positive influence to a negative one. Earlier evidence suggested that the shift occurred somewhere around 20 hours a week, but the more recent research puts that critical point closer to 15 hours. Indeed, the curve may even be U-shaped, with students who do not work at all being less likely to persist in college than those who do. The post-1990 research is only marginally clearer than what appeared earlier on the question of whether working on or off campus makes a difference. The answer is elusive: some studies suggest that on-campus work promotes persistence, whereas others indicate it does not. On balance, the evidence suggests that it does.

Academic Achievement

Our 1991 synthesis concluded that academic achievement, as indicated by grades, is among the most revealing indicators of students' successful adjustment to the intellectual and other demands of a course of study. Thus, it was not particularly surprising that undergraduate grades were perhaps the single best predictor of whether a student would earn a bachelor's degree, attend graduate school, or obtain an advanced degree. Academic achievement also reflects a number of personal traits that have implications for job productivity and success. These traits include requisite intellectual skills, personal motivation and effort, and willingness and ability to meet organizational norms. The independent impact of undergraduate grades on indices of occupational success was modest but persistent. Net of important confounding influences, the research indicated undergraduate grades are positively related to the status or prestige of the job one enters, career mobility, and earnings. Although we could not accurately estimate its magnitude, part of this effect was direct and part was indirect, being transmitted through the strong influence of grades on educational attainment.

The current review reinforces our earlier conclusion that grade performance is a critical predictor of persistence and educational attainment, even when other important predictors are controlled, including precollege characteristics (such as ability, secondary school achievement, and motivation), socioeconomic status, characteristics of the institution attended (such as selectivity and control), and other college experiences (such as academic major and social involvement). A noteworthy addition of the post-1990 literature to our understanding of the role of academic achievement is the finding that grade performance's salience varies over time, with good grades in the first year being particularly important to subsequent academic success and degree completion. Early academic achievement simultaneously reduces the chances of a student's stopping out and increases the probability of timely degree completion.

With one exception, the evidence of the 1990s supports or extends the conclusions from our previous synthesis. Net of important confounding influences, undergraduate grades appear to have a modest, positive impact on the probability of being employed full-time and of being employed in a job appropriate to a bachelor's degree in the early stages of one's career. In contrast, the evidence that grades have a causal impact on either job satisfaction or job mobility is unconvincing, and that finding calls into question the conclusion from our

1991 synthesis. Consistent with our previous synthesis, the evidence from the 1990s indicates that college grades have a positive net impact on both occupational status and earnings. The form of the evidence permitted us to estimate the magnitude of the impact on occupational status at between .10 and .20 of a standard deviation. Independent of important background traits and college experiences, including undergraduate major, the net earnings premium associated with an increase in one grade group was estimated at about 6.8 percent, whereas the total earnings premium (the net direct effect plus the indirect effect through educational attainment) was estimated at between 8 and 9 percent. Thus, other things being equal, good undergraduate grades provide modest but discernible career advantages.

CONDITIONAL EFFECTS OF COLLEGE

Our 1991 synthesis noted that, with only isolated exceptions, relatively little attention had been paid to the assessment of conditional effects. Researchers who did examine conditional effects found them most pronounced in two areas: learning and cognitive development and the socioeconomic outcomes of college. In the area of learning and cognitive development, reasonably strong evidence indicated that certain kinds of students benefited more from one instructional approach than another. Instruction appeared to interact with both personality traits and level of cognitive development. Students high in need for independent achievement or internal locus of control appeared to learn more when instruction stressed independence, self-direction, and participation. Conversely, students high in need for conforming or dependent achievement or who had an external locus of control appeared to benefit more from more highly structured, teacher-directed instructional formats.

Concerning socioeconomic outcomes, the clearest conditional effects involved race. Men of color, and Black men in particular, derived somewhat greater incremental occupational status benefits from a bachelor's degree than did White men. Similarly, between 1970 and 1990, men of color, and Black men in particular, appeared to receive somewhat greater incremental earnings benefits from a bachelor's degree than White men. Gender effects were less clear and for private rate of return were conditional on race. Among all groups, women of color appeared to receive the greatest economic return on investment from a bachelor's degree. In terms of incremental effects on earnings, a bachelor's degree was probably more valuable to a woman than to a man.

A final set of conditional effects in the pre-1990 research concerned the influence of college selectivity on occupational status and earnings. Scholars found that college selectivity had a positive impact on occupational status in professional careers (such as medicine and law) but was of questionable value in business or managerial careers. In terms of economic returns, college selectivity had a stronger impact on earnings for men from relatively high socioeconomic backgrounds than for men from relatively low socioeconomic origins.

The research of the 1990s devoted substantially more attention to estimating conditional effects. We uncovered many more statistically significant conditional effects, which appeared to cluster into three general types: student characteristics by net effects of college, student characteristics by between-college effects, and student characteristics by within-college effects. Unfortunately, as we noted in *How College Affects Students,* specific conditional effects do not always replicate well, particularly in correlational or nonexperimental research. In fact, most of the conditional effects we uncovered in the literature of the 1990s are based on a single finding and await replication. Because of their number, it is impossible to report and describe every statistically significant conditional effect found. In selecting what to report, we focused on replicated conditional effects, areas of research where investigators made concerted efforts to determine the presence of conditional effects, and conditional effects that have strong theoretical rationales or potentially important policy implications.

Student by Net Effects of College

The post-1990 evidence clearly indicates that the net effects of college differ in magnitude according to student sex and race.

1. Partially replicated evidence indicates that women may derive smaller learning or knowledge acquisition benefits from college than men. In the areas of science reasoning and mathematics, this difference remains even with statistical controls for patterns of coursework taken.

2. Women and men change to about the same extent during college in their level of identity development and locus of control, but women gain slightly more than men in self-esteem. Women also grow more than men in self-esteem from earning an advanced degree. Net gains in self-esteem are about the same for Whites and students of color.

3. In the aggregate, the social and political attitudes and values of men and women at college move to about the same degree toward the liberal end of the sociopolitical continuum. When the social issues involve gender or race, however, the shifts toward liberal social attitudes are more pronounced among women than men.

4. The weight of evidence suggests that the net earnings premium from a bachelor's degree (versus a high school diploma) is about the same for men and women, a finding somewhat at odds with our 1991 conclusion that a bachelor's degree benefited women more. However, the earnings premium linked to an associate's degree was about 1.5 times as large for women as for men, and it also appears that women receive larger earnings premiums than men from vocational certificates and completion of vocational training.

5. The advantage in occupational status attributable to a bachelor's degree (versus a high school diploma) is about 1.7 times as large for men as for women, whereas the corresponding advantage in occupa-

tional status linked to an associate's degree is about twice as large for men as for women.

6. Single-sample evidence suggests that African-American students may make smaller gains in critical thinking skills through the first and third years of college than do their White counterparts. Similarly, Latino students may derive smaller critical thinking benefits than White students from the first year of college.

7. Generally consistent with the conclusion from our 1991 synthesis, we estimate the net earnings premium for African-American bachelor's degree recipients to be about 1.2 times as large as the corresponding premium for White recipients. To some extent, this finding may be attributable to large returns for African-American women.

8. The intergenerational effect of parental education on the career choices of children may vary by race. Having a mother who is a college graduate had stronger positive effects on African Americans majoring in mathematics and science fields than it did for their White counterparts.

Student by Between-College Effects

Although generally based on single-sample findings, ample evidence from the 1990s indicates that the impacts of attending different kinds of postsecondary institutions vary in magnitude for different kinds of students.

1. Single-sample evidence suggests that students of color derive larger first-year reading comprehension and mathematics benefits at two-year colleges than at four-year colleges, whereas their White counterparts benefit more on these dimensions of learning from attending a four-year college. Similarly, students of color who are relatively older and from low socioeconomic backgrounds gain more in writing skills from attending a two-year college, whereas relatively younger White students from high socioeconomic backgrounds gain more in writing skills from a four-year college. Thus, the kinds of students appearing to derive the greater learning benefits from attendance at a community college tend to be students of color, older students, and less affluent students—all of whom are most likely to attend a community college (versus a four-year institution) in the first place.

2. Single-sample evidence indicates that at two-year colleges women may make significantly smaller gains in first-year critical thinking than do men. Conversely, at four-year colleges women appear to make significantly larger first-year gains in critical thinking than men.

3. Single-sample evidence suggests that an institution's environmental emphasis on being critical, evaluative, and analytical produces greater gains for Latino students on measures of first-year critical thinking skills than for other students. Conversely, elements of covert discrimination

in an institutional environment have a stronger negative effect on the critical thinking gains of Latinos than of other students.

4. Replicated evidence indicates that two- and four-year institutions have about the same impact on internal locus of attribution for academic success during the first two years of college regardless of a student's precollege locus of attribution, academic ability, or age. However, experiences at two- and four-year institutions do have a differential impact. Initial enrollment at a two- rather than a four-year institution may reduce students' degree aspirations and the likelihood of completing a bachelor's degree. Replicated evidence indicates that those effects are about the same for women and men and for both Whites and students of color.

5. The general level of openness to diversity among entering students on a campus and student perceptions that their institution supports diversity have more positive effects on the racial-ethnic attitudes of women and students of color than on men and White students.

6. Post-1990 research indicates that students of color, particularly African-American students, benefit economically from institutional quality or selectivity about as much as, or perhaps more than, White students. The impact of college quality measures on earnings was seen to be about the same for men and women.

7. Somewhat at odds with the conclusion of our previous synthesis, attending a selective college has its strongest positive impact on earnings for students with relatively low academic ability or from relatively low socioeconomic origins.

8. College selectivity may have a positive net effect on earnings for students who transfer to selective institutions but little or no impact on earnings for those who enter selective institutions directly out of high school. Similarly, institutional quality measures may have different impacts on earnings associated with different major fields of study. Such evidence suggests that any economic benefits linked to institutional quality or selectivity do not accrue homogeneously to all students. Thus, blanket statements about the impact of institutional quality or selectivity on earnings may be unwarranted.

Student by Within-College Effects

By far, the most numerous conditional effects we uncovered in the literature of the 1990s involved the interaction of student characteristics and various within-college experiences. This prompted conclusions in four general areas.

Student Learning Style. The most consistent evidence of conditional effects concerns student learning style and extends the findings of our 1991 synthesis into a more general conclusion about matching student learning style to appropriate methods of instruction or learning experiences. Replicated experimental and quasi-experimental evidence clearly indicates that college students demonstrate significantly higher levels of knowledge acquisition when instruction matches their preferred learning style than when it does not. Across all studies with college-level samples, we estimate that students receiving instruction matched to their learning style gain an advantage of .91 of a standard deviation over their counterparts who do not receive instruction accommodating their preferred learning style.

Gender, Race, Ability, and Parental Education. Although based largely on single-sample studies, the research of the 1990s suggests that many within-college effects vary in magnitude by gender, race, academic ability, and parental education.

- *Gender.* Engaging in volunteer work during college as well as coursework in the natural sciences and humanities may have stronger positive effects on measures of learning (such as reading comprehension) and general cognitive development (such as critical thinking) for men than for women. Men, however, appear to incur a greater deficit in first-year critical thinking growth from fraternity membership than women do from sorority membership. Women may derive greater cognitive growth (such as reflective thinking and critical thinking) than men from work experiences and living on campus during college, and women appear to derive greater economic returns from a bachelor's degree in engineering, mathematics, or the physical sciences, as well as from good undergraduate grades, irrespective of major. The positive impact on earnings linked to an engineering major (versus other majors) for women was about 1.5 times as large as the impact for men. Similarly, the positive economic impact linked to mathematics or physical science majors for women was about 1.75 times as large as the impact for men. Thus, although women have been seen to be less likely than men to enter these majors, they appear to derive greater incremental economic advantages versus other majors when they do.

  Similarly, women majoring in mathematics and science show greater first- to senior-year increases in math self-concepts than do men. Men majoring in disciplines that emphasize helping others, interpersonal skills, friendliness, and sensitivity to others experience greater gains in those areas than do men majoring in other fields. Women in these "social" fields, however, show no greater increases in such skills than do women who are not in those disciplines.

  A variety of college experiences appear to have about the same net impact on women's and men's openness to diversity. These experiences include living on campus, participating in racial-cultural awareness workshops, taking diversity courses, working, joining a fraternity or sorority, and interacting with peers.

- *Race.* The positive learning effects of studying with peers and using computers, as well as the positive economic effects of good undergraduate grades, appear to be somewhat larger for African-American students than for White students. Students of color may also derive greater knowledge acquisition benefits from cooperative learning approaches than do their White counterparts, and although fraternity membership appears to negatively influence gains in first-year knowledge acquisition and critical thinking among White men, it appears to have little or no impact on the learning and cognitive growth of men of color. Conversely, African-American students appear to receive smaller benefits in critical thinking skills from coursework in the natural sciences (versus other majors) than do White students and smaller economic returns from majoring in the social sciences (versus other majors) than do other students. Similarly, the positive effects on critical thinking skills of involvement in diversity experiences (such attending racial-cultural awareness workshops or making friends with someone of a different race) are significantly stronger for White students than for students of color.

  Students of color gain more in self-esteem than do similar White students both from taking more credits and from working. Minority students also gain in their openness to diversity more than Whites from fraternity or sorority membership. African-American men gain more in both academic and social self-concepts from intercollegiate sports participation than do similar White males. Finally, and after controlling for gender and ability, living-learning centers provide no persistence advantage to White residents, but such residential quarters do increase the likelihood of persistence among African Americans.

- *Tested academic ability.* The relative impacts of a variety of within-college experiences appear to vary in magnitude for entering students with different levels of tested academic ability. For example, replicated evidence suggests that high-ability students may be able to convert the use of different information technologies (such as hypertext and unstructured e-mail use) into greater learning and cognitive gains than can students of relatively low ability. Similarly, evidence suggests that high-ability students derive greater learning and cognitive benefits from social interaction with peers than do students with lower ability. In contrast, instructional approaches such as supplemental instruction, knowledge maps, and cooperative learning with knowledge maps may provide significantly larger learning benefits for students with relatively low academic ability or prior performance than for their counterparts with high ability or high prior performance.

- *Parental education.* A small body of single-sample evidence suggests that certain within-college experiences may be more important for first-generation college students than for students whose parents attended college. For example, first-generation students derived greater benefits in learning (as measured by reading comprehension) and general cognitive development (as measured by critical thinking skills) from full-time enrollment and the extent of their study effort than other students.

First-generation students also appear to derive greater benefits than other students in internal locus of attribution for academic success from several college experiences over the first three years of college, including coursework in various areas, academic effort, and extracurricular involvement. But not all college experiences are more beneficial to first-generation students than to others. The number of hours worked and doing volunteer work both negatively affected increases on measures of first-generation students' internal attributions for academic success while having no impact or a positive effect on other students. The clear disadvantages of being a first-generation student rather than having parents with some college experience or a bachelor's or advanced degree were summarized earlier.

Cooperative Learning. Single-sample evidence indicates that cooperative learning may have substantially more pronounced positive effects on higher or more complex levels of cognitive functioning than on lower or less complex levels of cognitive functioning.

Academic Achievement. Although undergraduate grades have a generally positive net effect on subsequent earnings, the magnitude of the effect may vary according to academic major. Grades appear to be of greater consequence for the subsequent earnings of students majoring in business, education, and science or mathematics than for their counterparts majoring in engineering, social sciences, or health-related fields.

Some Concluding Thoughts

At the end of our 1991 review, we recalled the story of the legendary bank robber Willie Sutton, who when asked why he robbed banks, allegedly replied: "Because that's where the money is." Like Sutton, we have gone where the "evidence" is in examining college impacts. That evidence, however, differs from the earlier literature in several important ways.

The 1990s saw significant expansion in the range of higher education outcomes, opening up whole new areas of study. When we concluded our earlier review, the Internet was in its infancy and the World Wide Web and various information technologies to promote learning in the classroom were nascent. Active and collaborative pedagogical alternatives to the lecture-discussion approach were relatively new and not yet widely adopted, and various curricular innovations were only beginning to attract widespread attention.

At the same time, changes in the demographic profile of America's undergraduates and related public policy issues, especially affirmative action, generated intense study of the educational impacts of racial-ethnic diversity in enrollment, curriculum, and students' lives. Both theoretical and policy interest in college access and program completion, particularly among low-income students, also increased. The upshot of these profound, perhaps transformational, developments has been a much larger and more varied research literature on college impacts, a literature that both inspires and intimidates.

In studying college impacts, post-1990 analysts were more mindful of differences among student groups, whether related to race-ethnicity, gender, ability, or socioeconomic status. In 1991, we wrote: "If there is a major future direction for research on the impact of college, it will be to focus on that growing proportion of students whom we have typically classified as nontraditional, although they are rapidly becoming the majority of participants in the American postsecondary system" (Pascarella & Terenzini, 1991, p. 632). The increased heterogeneity of American undergraduates, particularly in race or ethnicity, spurred—indeed, required—closer attention to what we have called conditional effects, or the possibility that any given college experience may have a different effect on different kinds of students. As a consequence, we know in far greater detail and with far greater precision how programmatic and policy interventions, as well as students' informal experiences, affect learning, change, and development.

Finally, research published during the 1990s reflects substantial gains in methodological quality. More studies draw on large, nationally representative databases, providing a firmer footing for generalizations about the impact of college on one or another outcome for many subsets of today's postsecondary students. In addition, the research overall reflects increased recognition of the complexity of the experience of "going to college" and greater readiness to explore those complexities by selecting theories, variables, and analytical procedures appropriate to the task. In sum, the post-1990 body of evidence significantly advances our knowledge about the effects of colleges and universities. Our final chapter delves into what this new body of knowledge may mean for theory and research, practice, and policy.

CHAPTER TWELVE

Implications for Research, Practice, and Policy

The research published over more than a decade contains a multitude of ideas to enhance higher education. A number of narrowly focused findings have implications for research and theory, practice, and both institutional and public policy, but we will concentrate here on the most salient implications of clusters of findings; some of these relate to a particular outcome, whereas others cut across outcome domains.

IMPLICATIONS FOR THEORY AND RESEARCH

Our review of the research published since 1990 suggests a number of future directions for theory development and research on the effects of college on students. The findings raise issues for theory and substantive areas of study as well as for research designs and analytical methods.

Theoretical Implications

Differentiating Change and Development. Chapter Two of both this volume and our earlier review noted the importance of differentiating between *change* and *development* in explaining research findings. *Change* refers simply to alterations over time in students' cognitive or affective characteristics. *Change* is a value-free term and may be quantitative or qualitative. The term implies no directionality. *Development*, in contrast, implies some ordered, perhaps hierarchical or evolutionary shift in fundamental, intraindividual patterns or processes. The term also implies progress toward a desirable educational end.

Much of the research published both before 1990 and since uses the two terms uncritically and synonymously. It is tempting to conclude that observed change reflects individual growth or development, an internal restructuring, development of an advanced set of inner rules or perspectives, or movement to an advanced level of maturity not found in the typical first-year student. Such conclusions are a particular temptation when the changes that occur are consistent with those posited by developmental models or theories.

Failure to distinguish between change and development can lead to subtle but important misinterpretations and misrepresentations of what is observed in college students' lives. The threat to interpretation arises when what we commonly refer to as development instead reflects an individual's response to the anticipated norms of new social settings or social roles. Different categories of people may be socialized to think and behave differently, and a substantial part of this categorization may have its basis in educational level. Thus, for example, college-educated men and women may manifest certain values, psychosocial traits, and perspectives not necessarily because of inner developmental restructuring but because they have been socialized to behave and think in ways consistent with dominant cultural norms for educated adults. (Feldman [1972] and Smart, Feldman, and Ethington [2000, pp. 16–20 and 236–246] provide an extended discussion of this issue.)

That is not to say that the changes observed in college students merely represent socialization to societal or cultural norms instead of important developmental steps. Rather, we emphasize the need to be wary of interpreting the effects of socialization as signs of development. Multiple influences, some internal and perhaps ontogenetic and others external to the individual, produce change during the college years. Theories can restrict as well as focus vision, subtly elevating the risk that a fundamental influence on change may be overlooked or mistaken for another, an error that in turn can lead to misspecified theories and ineffective practice and policy. Research that can differentiate and estimate the roles of these two processes, which may operate simultaneously, will add considerably to what we know about college impacts.

Interlaced Influences and Outcomes. One of the most striking features of the full corpus of the post-1990 research we reviewed is the broad scope of the dimensions of students' lives that change with exposure to college. Even after adjusting for other forces, and even if the exposure lasts for only a year or two, college changes students to a degree unattributable to normal maturation or other influences outside the academy. The clusters of changes listed in Table 12.1, moreover, are *clearly* not restricted to a few dimensions of students' lives. Rather, they suggest that people who go to college, compared with those who do not, learn better, know more, earn more. College adds value to their lives, enhances their self-esteem, and increases their understanding of others and their engagement in their communities. The college-educated are also more disposed to learning as a lifelong activity and tend to lead longer and healthier lives.

Table 12.1. Areas of Net Change Attributable to College Exposure

Academic and Cognitive	*Career and Economic*
Verbal skills	Employment
Quantitative skills	Occupational status
Content knowledge in various fields	Earnings
Critical thinking	Discretionary income
Reflective judgment	Job satisfaction
Principled moral reasoning	Return on personal investment in education (private rate of return)
Psychosocial	Employment stability
Academic self-concept	Job search abilities and skills
Social self-concept	Career mobility
Self-esteem	Socioeconomic positioning
Independence	
Sense of control over one's life	*Quality of Life*
Interpersonal skills	Future time orientation
Leadership skills	Health
	Longevity
Attitudes and Values	Attention to child care and development
Civic and community engagement	Efficient consumer choices
Racial understanding	Personal savings
Openness to diversity	Long-term investments
Support for gender equality	Discretionary resources and time spent on developmentally enriching activities
	Subjective well-being
	Disposition to lifelong learning

In addition, the evidence strongly suggests that these outcomes are interdependent, that learning is holistic rather than segmented, and that *multiple forces* operate in *multiple settings* to shape student learning and change in ways that cross the "cognitive-affective" divide. The research of the 1990s brings this interdependence into sharper focus and provides empirical support for our earlier suggestion that students change in two ways that are holistic. First, change in one outcome area appears to be accompanied by alterations in other dimensions of students' lives. Second, change in any given area appears to be the product of a holistic set of multiple influences, each making a distinct, if small, contribution to the change.

In addition, the research published since 1990 indicates that students' in- and out-of-class experiences are interconnected components of a complex process shaping student change and development in ways we are only beginning to understand. Numerous studies examining multiple sources of influence that shape change and learning in virtually every outcome area have found statistically significant and independent effects of classroom experiences and pedagogies, coursework, institutional environments and cultures, and an array of out-of-class activities. These combinations of academic and nonacademic elements are daunting in their complexity and in the challenges they present for future research and for educational program design and policymaking.

Such complexity suggests that studies focused narrowly on one or another discrete dimension of the college experience are likely to present only a partial picture of the forces at work. If other elements of these combinations are overlooked or dismissed in a study's design, they will remain confounded with the influence of particular interest, restricting or possibly invalidating interpretation of findings. Thus, for example, studies of impacts of selected pedagogies on students' development of critical thinking skills may overlook the opportunities students have to develop these skills in noncourse settings, such as in the residence halls, at work, or through their interactions with peers and faculty members. Similarly, studies of changes in student attitudes or values should not narrow their focus to the effects of, say, fraternity or sorority membership while leaving uncontrolled other out-of-class and academic experiences that may also influence attitude change. As discussed in the following section, such complex interactions across the multiple dimensions of students' college experiences have implications for public policy, institutional structures and operations, and curricular and pedagogical decision making.

Multidisciplinary Models. The interconnections among the forces influencing student change highlight the need to consider theoretical conceptions from multiple disciplines in designing studies of college impact. Pre-1990 research lacked multidisciplinary conceptual models and research designs that might more fully account for multiple sources of influence. Instead, psychological theories and models dominated the research on change during college. Important contributions also came from scholars trained in sociology, economics, and anthropology, but these disciplinary orientations to explaining college impacts were underrepresented in the pre-1990 literature.

In addition, the pre-1990 research on college effects, regardless of theoretical disposition, reflected little familiarity with the knowledge base outside the author's primary discipline, particularly in studies of students' psychosocial changes, where failure to differentiate change and development is most likely and potentially misleading. Thus, it remains unclear whether reported changes arose from developmental, psychosocial restructuring, or from socialization to the competencies and behaviors valued by important others. Such conceptual isolation was equally apparent in studies of persistence and educational attainment, where psychologists, sociologists, and economists applied their field's theories independently and with varying degrees of success and relevance for institutional programs and public policymaking.

The single-paradigm approach to studying college impacts has persisted throughout the 1990s. The literature reflects increased reliance on conceptual frameworks from a variety of disciplines, but many of the studies that are most clearly grounded theoretically embrace a single, discipline-specific conceptual approach. Furthermore, we encountered a number of studies done since 1990 that are largely atheoretical. Although researchers might claim to test one or another theoretical framework, too often the studies lacked any serious conceptual underpinnings to guide research design, variable selection, and analytical procedures. Theory-free studies offer little in the way of systematic understanding, and single-paradigm research restricts the range of analytical vision and the depth and validity of understanding. Both approaches limit the usefulness of findings for guiding development of effective academic and nonacademic programs, practices, and policies.

The picture, however, is brightening. Research since 1990 shows clear signs of increased attention to sources of influence in multiple areas of students' experience, if not to multidisciplinary theories, and to incorporating concepts from different disciplines into a particular study. Many other studies, however, would benefit from a coherent and explicit conceptual framework, delineating not only what variables are at issue but also how and why they are believed to relate to one another in a causal sequence or set of linkages.

New Substantive Directions

Our current review identified several shifts in the substantive directions for research. Although the post-1990 evidence does not often differ significantly from that uncovered in our earlier review, scholars during the 1990s opened a number of new lines of inquiry that are crucial to an accurate portrayal of the impact of postsecondary education on students.

Increasing Diversity. First, the research has begun to acknowledge the increasing diversity of students in the American postsecondary system. Despite a lingering tendency to focus on the most accessible students (such as those who attend college full-time, live on campus, and primarily are White), the literature of the 1990s made great strides toward a better understanding of the impact of the postsecondary experience on first-generation college students, commuters, part-timers, those who work during college, and students of color. This effort should expand, particularly in light of growing evidence that diversity in the faculty and student body is a potentially powerful force in shaping important cognitive and noncognitive outcomes.

Community Colleges. Second, in addition to paying more and closer attention to students largely marginalized in earlier studies, researchers during the 1990s expanded their vision to include community colleges, which many scholars had previously ignored. Consequently, the impact of community colleges on students is no longer an empirical "black hole." We have learned much about the impact of two-year institutions on cognitive, noncognitive, career, and economic outcomes and on educational attainment. Given that community colleges and other institutions that do not grant the baccalaureate degree enroll more than 40 percent of the students in America's colleges and universities, this line of research too should continue and expand.

New Academic Approaches. The expanded effort to understand the impact of the academic program, particularly teaching and instructional approaches, constitutes a third important line of inquiry. Interest in the impact of students' classroom experiences, visible in our previous review, blossomed over the past decade. We now have a much clearer and nuanced understanding of the cognitive impact of a wide range of instructional approaches and teaching behaviors, including active, collaborative, cooperative, and small-group learning as well as Supplemental Instruction, service learning, constructivist-oriented approaches, distance learning, attributional retraining, reciprocal teaching, concept maps, teacher expressiveness, and teacher organization. In short, the decade of the 1990s has provided experimental and quasi-experimental validation of an extensive repertoire of teaching behaviors and classroom activities with considerable curricular, pedagogical, and organizational implications.

New Information Technologies. Fourth, the explosion of new information technologies during the 1990s led to the extension and refinement of earlier findings on the cognitive effects of computer-assisted instruction, including hypertext, learning a computer language, use of information technologies in the classroom, and various unstructured and classroom applications of electronic mail. Immense potential remains in computer and information technologies to change the nature of teaching and learning fundamentally, presaging substantial future research. Salient lines of inquiry include how computers and information technologies influence students' cognitive processes, the role of the instructor, the psychosocial climate of teaching and learning, and the extent and nature of a student's interaction with peers and faculty. Similarly, the effects of various forms of technology-mediated distance education, particularly asynchronous instruction, loom as an immensely important area of study. Current research in this area is generally atheoretical and methodologically unsophisticated, although we readily acknowledge the considerable methodological challenges these topics present. Conventional research designs and data-collection methods are often ill suited to studying distance learners, and the enabling technologies for distance learning have such a brief shelf life that they and their related pedagogies can change even while a study is under way. Such volatility in the nature of technology-mediated instruction presents considerable challenges to researchers to develop creative designs and data-collection mechanisms.

Research Designs and Analytical Approaches

Our review suggests that several changes in the research designs and analytical approaches now in widespread use will enhance the practical and policy-related usefulness of the research on college students.

Change Versus Net Effects of College. Documentation of student change during college substantially exceeds the amount of evidence on the net effects or value added by college. *Net effects* refers to the changes in students during the college years that are attributable to the postsecondary experience and not to other, noncollege influences, such as normal maturation. The majority of the studies we reviewed make little or no effort to partition college impacts from other influences. Future research should devote less effort to documenting change or growth during the undergraduate years and concentrate more on the net or unique impacts of undergraduate education. Admittedly, net effects questions are considerably more difficult to address, but the answers are far more important and useful to practitioners and policymakers than knowing simply whether students change—for whatever reason—during their undergraduate years. The challenge requires research and sampling designs that include high school graduates who never entered college or who entered but did not complete college, using the degree of exposure to college as a predictor variable. It is essential to the design of effective educational programs, professional integrity, and public credibility that claims about the benefits of college be supported by evidence that separates college effects from noncollege influences.

The Importance of Estimating Effect Sizes.[1] If future research would be strengthened and become more useful by isolating net college effects, it would also benefit from estimating the size of these effects. The research of the 1990s put greater emphasis on reporting the *magnitudes* of college effects rather than just their statistical significance, but more studies should provide such information. Too often we could not estimate an effect size from research findings, particularly in the areas of psychosocial and attitude and value change, because the needed information, such as group means and standard deviations, was not reported. Still, compared with our 1991 review, our ability to estimate the magnitude of an effect from the literature reviewed in our current synthesis increased substantially.

Estimating effect sizes offers advantages for testing theory and for practical and policy applications. Statistical significance is sensitive to several factors, including sample size and unexplained variance. Statistically significant differences that may be detected in large samples may in fact be quite small and of little educational, administrative, or policy importance. Effect sizes provide a means for evaluating the strength of a relation and its substantive practical or policy relevance. When reviewing multiple studies, calculating effect sizes provides a common metric that not only sharpens conclusions but also facilitates program evaluation and refinement, policy formulation, and effective resource allocation. At the least, knowing the approximate magnitude of an intervention's effect is more useful to practitioners and policymakers than simply knowing that the observed change was not due to chance. If research results are to figure in programmatic, budgetary, and policy decisions, administrators and legislators need to know whether the impact of some intervention or aspect of the college experience is large enough to warrant attention, action, and resources.

Increased attention to estimating effect sizes opens the door to cost-benefit estimates of a broad array of outcomes, but cost-benefit studies are complex and often imprecise. Linking estimated effect sizes to dollar figures is a task that must be undertaken with great caution and sensitivity to the process and interventions under study and to the potential real-world implications of findings. In the end, the "benefits" portion of such equations comes down to judgments based on values, politics, and finances.

Where appropriate, future research on college impact should estimate the magnitude as well as the statistical significance of net effects. Doing so will lead to more parsimonious theories and conceptual models and will facilitate both better practice and better policymaking.

Better Measures of Between-College Effects. With a few exceptions, such as the research on earnings, the study of between-college effects has not been particularly productive or informative. Even in the studies with the best research designs and strongest statistical controls for important individual student characteristics, between-college effects tend to be quite small and inconsistent. More advanced multilevel statistical procedures such as hierarchical linear modeling may address this situation to some extent, but we believe a greater share of the problem lies in the global institutional characteristics on which most studies have relied.

Characteristics such as selectivity, type of control, Carnegie classification, average faculty salaries, and educational expenditures per student have major limitations. First, their use tends to mask considerable variability in subenvironments and subcultures in institutions. Second, such global characteristics are simply too distal from the classroom and out-of-class experiences that shape institutional impact on students in the most significant ways. Third, global characteristics, by and large, are features most institutions can do little about. Even if, say, public flagship universities wanted to become more selective in their admissions policies, it seems unlikely their state legislatures would agree to let them do so. Although the analogy may be overdrawn, the typical study of between-college effects is a little like tossing a stone into Lake Erie in Cleveland and trying to measure the ripple in Buffalo. If the ripple arrives at all, it is unlikely to be very dramatic.

Clearly, studies of between-college effects matter and should continue, but more useful insights into the college-effects process can be gained from measures that reflect institutional cultures—the community's collective values and campus *subenvironments,* particularly those created by the students themselves. Nevertheless, in terms of incremental payoff in understanding college's impact on students, studying within-college effects will likely yield greater returns than studying between-college effects.

However, even if measures of campus characteristics closer to students' daily lives are adopted, there is a student demographic trend, grown more pronounced over the past quarter century, that complicates the study of between-college effects. America's students have become highly mobile consumers of postsecondary education. By some estimates, half or more of America's college graduates attended more than one institution, and more than a third attended three or more institutions before completing their programs. Some students may enroll at two institutions simultaneously (Adelman, 1998a). Such national rates of multi-institutional attendance call into question both the interpretability and generalizability of studies that estimate institutional effects on educational outcomes. How can researchers estimate such effects when the impacts originate in two or more institutions and most likely over varying periods of time? Currently, researchers get around this issue by estimating institutional effects over comparatively short periods, such as the first year of college, or when following students over an extended period of time by analyzing samples of students who attended only one postsecondary institution. Such studies can provide valuable insights into the nature and magnitude of between-institution effects on educational outcomes, but the fact remains that the findings of the great majority of between-college effects studies may not generalize to the substantial numbers of American students who attend more than one undergraduate institution, perhaps even simultaneously. No solution to this conundrum is readily apparent, but the problem is unlikely to disappear. Indeed, it may grow larger.

The Timing of Change. Much of the research on college impacts concentrates on changes between the first and second year or between enrollment and graduation. Far fewer studies monitor change on an annual basis over a period of years. Thus, research findings rest on the assumption that change is probably linear (generally in the same direction) and monotonic (about the same magnitude at each intervening point) rather than discontinuous and episodic. Several studies published since 1990 tracked changes periodically over time, shedding light on whether change is steady and in the same general direction over time. Other studies, particularly in the area of educational attainment, have estimated whether the impact of a variable such as financial aid has the same effect on persistence in each year or whether the impact varies over time. For programmatic and policy purposes, it is important to know not only *whether* an intervention will make a difference but also *when* so that institutional efforts and resources can be invested where and when they are most likely to be effective.

Conditional Effects. Research during the 1990s, more so than earlier studies, explored conditional or interaction effects of college on students. Studies of conditional effects seek to determine whether a particular college characteristic or experience is general—that is, has the same effect on all students—or whether the impact varies according to one or more characteristics of the students involved, such as gender, race-ethnicity, ability, or socioeconomic status. To some extent, this new emphasis may be a response to the dramatic increase in diversity on American campuses in the 1980s and 1990s, a trend that is expected to continue. This greater concern with conditional effects is an acknowledgment that student diversity may play an important role in shaping the impact of college. As undergraduate students become more diverse in race, socioeconomic background, native language, age, academic preparation, and precollege social and intellectual capital, the likelihood increases that any given educational experience will not have the same impact on all of them. Indeed, such differential impacts are already apparent in the substantial number of statistically reliable conditional effects reported in the literature of the 1990s. Perhaps the important question to ask about the impact of postsecondary education is not which experiences are most influential but which experiences are most influential for which kinds of students. The increased ability to ask and at least partially answer such questions reflects a more mature science than was evident before 1990, but such progress always comes at a cost. Research into conditional effects can lead to complex explanations that are less tidy than those based on the assumption that an experience has the same effect for everyone. But in the end, more refined explanations are likely to lead to more informed and effective practice and policy.

Direct and Indirect Effects. The appendix to our 1991 review noted that multiple regression analysis was among the most useful forms of statistical analysis for studying the effects of college on students. But regression analysis is "largely predictive rather than explanatory in nature" (Pascarella & Terenzini, 1991, p. 675), providing limited information about connections between and among variables and about the causal patterns in which experiences combine to shape student change. We recommended wider use of one or another of the analyses that make up the family of procedures called *causal modeling* (with path analysis, structural equation modeling, and hierarchical linear modeling probably the best-known forms). Causal models aim at explanation rather than simply prediction. They permit not only the study of direct, unmediated causal effects of each independent variable but also *in*direct effects transmitted through (or mediated by) intervening variables.

Our current review indicated that in just about every outcome area in the research on the effects of college, some effects are or appear to be indirect rather than direct. Yet a variable that is a step removed from having a direct impact on some outcome can still be important to theory, policy, or practice. When indirect effects of variables remain unexplored, researchers risk underestimating or otherwise misrepresenting the nature and degree of a variable's impact on student change. The ramifications can be considerable. For example, although an institution's structural diversity appears to have comparatively little direct impact on educational outcomes, the racial-ethnic mix of students and faculty has an important indirect effect, affecting the likelihood that students of different races, ethnicities, and cultures on a campus will interact, influencing, in turn, a number of educational outcomes. Fortunately, compared with our earlier review, more studies now explore and test both direct and indirect effects, enhancing the usefulness of the research findings.

Qualitative Research Methods. We repeat the call we made in 1991 for research on the effects of college to use naturalistic and qualitative approaches more extensively. To be sure, the decade of the 1990s saw a marked increase in qualitative studies of college effects, and much of this inquiry made important contributions to our understanding. But traditional quantitative approaches continue to dominate the research, regardless of the topic area. Although quantitative approaches provide a powerful set of tools for estimating the impact of college on students, these tools are probably most useful in painting the broad outlines of the portrait. Rendering tone, tint, texture, and nuance may require the finer brushstrokes characteristic of qualitative approaches. Indeed, naturalistic and ethnographic inquiries may be particularly well suited to identifying and examining indirect and conditional effects. Finally, although qualitative research may be viewed as less demanding than quantitative approaches, that is not the case.

The impact of postsecondary education on students is an immense and complex field of study. It is unlikely any single methodological approach can capture that complexity.

IMPLICATIONS FOR PUBLIC POLICY

The post-1990 research holds implications for public policy in higher education that include campus diversity as a factor in student learning, similarities and differences in the effects of two- and four-year institutions, misconceptions about institutional quality, and issues of access and degree completion.

Diversity and Education

Few issues in higher education have received more public attention over the past decade than diversity on America's campuses. Most colleges and universities, both public and private, have made broad efforts over the past two decades to increase the representation of women and people of color among their students, faculty, and staff. These institutions also sought to introduce gender, racial, ethnic, and cultural diversity into their curricula and to create campus environments that welcome people from different cultural backgrounds and provide opportunities for diverse individuals to learn from and about one another.

Faculty salaries and personnel practices and policies affecting women and persons of color attracted attention at both public and private institutions, but legal challenges to race-conscious student admissions policies at public flagship universities captured the national spotlight. Critics of institutional affirmative action policies leveled charges of racial and ethnic favoritism, discrimination against Whites, watered-down curricula, lowered academic standards, compromised intellectual and institutional integrity, suppression of freedom of speech, and threats to academic freedom. Supporters countered that affirmative action went beyond efforts to rectify past injustices and that campus diversity was in fact an important educational instrument for promoting learning and preparing students for participation in a democracy in a diverse world. The U.S. Supreme Court resolved the dispute in 2003, at least temporarily, by ruling that racial-ethnic origin was a permissible consideration in admissions provided it was not applied mechanistically, but the educational effects of diversity in all its manifestations (such as enrollment mix, curricular content, programs and activities, interpersonal contacts) continue to be a central—and sensitive—issue on most campuses and in the public policy arena.

Our review of the research since 1990 indicates that what we have called "diversity experiences" are positively related to both cognitive and affective learning outcomes. The phrase refers to formal activities, such as enrolling in ethnic or gender studies or other diversity courses, having racially or culturally diverse instructors, and attending racial-cultural awareness workshops as well as to an array of more informal activities and experiences, such as developing diverse friendship groups, socializing with students from diverse racial-ethnic backgrounds, and discussing racial-ethnic or social justice issues.

The evidence consistently shows that diversity experiences have independent and positive net influences on a variety of cognitive and psychosocial outcomes. These outcomes include the acquisition of subject matter knowledge and increases in several dimensions of general cognitive functioning, including critical thinking, analytical competencies, complexity of thought, and problem-solving abilities. Diversity experiences also appear to have positive effects on a range of psychosocial outcomes, including academic and social self-concepts, self-esteem, locus of control, voting, community and civic engagement, support for individual rights, awareness of other cultures, commitment to promoting racial understanding, and openness to intellectual challenge and diversity. White students sometimes appear more likely to benefit from these experiences than do students of color, but some evidence suggests the learning benefits accrue to about the same degree to all students regardless of their racial-ethnic origins. Although we are only beginning to unravel the causal relations underlying most of the effects of diversity on educational outcomes, the evidence is mounting that structural diversity (the racial-ethnic representation among students and faculty on a campus) is a necessary if not sufficient condition for educational impact. It appears that as a campus's structural diversity increases, so do the odds that students will encounter that diversity in various formal and informal manifestations. These encounters, in turn, positively influence an array of educationally desirable outcomes.

Two-Year Versus Four-Year Institutions

In discussing the public policy implications of the findings in our earlier review, we identified several "equalities and inequalities in postsecondary educational outcomes" (Pascarella & Terenzini, 1991, p. 636). One of the inequalities dealt with two-year versus four-year institutions. The research consistently indicated that, even after adjusting statistically for a variety of personal, academic, and family background characteristics (including ability and degree aspirations), students entering four-year institutions were substantially more likely than community college entrants to complete a baccalaureate degree and to attend graduate school. The community college sector had greatly enhanced opportunities for historically disadvantaged groups to gain access to postsecondary education and to socioeconomic and other advantages compared with people who had only a high school diploma. But the evidence consistently indicated that the advantages were even greater for baccalaureate degree holders compared with two-year college graduates.

The research on educational attainment that has appeared since 1990 confirms earlier findings but only in part. Studies continue to report that, net of other relevant factors, beginning pursuit of a bachelor's degree at a two-year rather than a four-year institution reduces by about 15 percentage points the chances of ever earning that degree. We found evidence, moreover, supporting the argument that community colleges reduce the educational aspirations of their students. Enrolling in a community college rather than a four-year institution also appears to diminish the chances that high-ability minority students will persist in mathematics, science, and engineering careers. And even with educational attainment taken into account, attending a two-year college still appears to lead to employment in modestly lower-status occupations than does enrollment in a four-year institution. Finally, although the post-1990 literature suggests that students who attend a community college realize earnings benefits greater than those that accrue to similar individuals with only a high school diploma, that advantage, on average, is still less than the earnings benefit derived from a four-year college degree.

The post-1990 research, however, also paints a more complex and more positive picture than does pre-1990 research on differences in educational and occupational outcomes associated with two- versus four-year college enrollment. Indeed, studies published since 1990 indicate that in certain outcome areas, community college students derive benefits equal to or even greater than those realized by similar students at four-year colleges or universities. After one year of college, for example, and after adjusting for precollege ability, motivation, and other confounding influences, community college students gain to about the same degree as similar students at four-year institutions on measures of reading comprehension, math skills, and critical thinking skills. After two years, the two groups also showed increases of about the same degree in their science reasoning and writing skills. Moreover, although community college students in general reap these benefits, the gains are greatest among students of color, older students, and less affluent students—in other words, those most likely to attend a community college rather than a four-year institution in the first place. And for similar individuals of equal educational attainment, initial attendance at a two-year college appears to impose no significant penalty in earnings.

In addition to reaping many of the same learning and earning benefits as similar students at four-year institutions, community college students may come out ahead in other areas. For example, two-year college students gain significantly, if modestly, more than similar four-year students in both internal locus of attribution for academic success and in openness to intellectual challenge and racial-cultural diversity. The advantage in locus of attribution is noteworthy for three reasons. First, the finding reflects two-year students' greater increases in their sense of control over their academic performance—that is, their belief that academic success is more a function of hard work than luck or an instructor's grading practices or teaching abilities. Second, community college students appear to benefit most during the first year of college, when such gains may be most important to their subsequent persistence and academic performance.

Third, the benefits in terms of internal locus of attribution accrue about equally to all two-year students regardless of gender, race-ethnicity, ability, or age.

To the extent that attending a community college contributes to students' sense of control over their academic lives and to their openness to intellectual challenge, and thus to the possibility of higher performance and persistence, it may also lead to longer-term impacts. The evidence of the post-1990 research indicates that once students transfer from a two- to a four-year institution, their odds of completing a bachelor's degree are about the same as for similar entrants at four-year colleges, although transfer students may take somewhat longer to complete their degrees. In addition, some evidence suggests that, net of other factors, students who initially enroll in a community college are able to transfer to more selective four-year institutions than would have been open to them right out of high school. This opportunity appears to accrue particularly to low-income students, to students with low tested abilities, and to those who performed poorly in high school.

The overall picture, as noted, is considerably more complex than it initially appears. Some may say that community colleges appear to be doing what is expected of them and should be congratulated and then left to carry on. Such a perspective may derive more from the status structure in our national system of higher education, a hierarchy topped by a handful of research universities and elite liberal arts colleges that set the standard against which all other institutions are judged and supported. The characteristics common to these pace-setters have become the criteria for judgment: selectivity, research productivity, top-dollar faculty members, and largely residential undergraduate programs for students who, for the most part, are White, ages 18 to 22, in the middle or upper classes socioeconomically, and attend full-time. "The more an institution deviates from this set of standards, the lower it ranks in the status hierarchy, the less likely it is to be seen as providing a quality undergraduate education, and the more invisible it becomes to the American public. By the time we get to community colleges, with their open admissions policies, faculties rewarded essentially for teaching, and their disproportionate numbers of commuting, part-time, older, nonwhite, and working-class students, we're about off the radar screen in terms of public recognition" (Pascarella, 1997b).

A more positive conclusion would be that community colleges appear to be doing what is expected of them and in some cases having greater impact than four-year institutions, despite the wide variation in the abilities, preparation, and motivation of the students who enroll, despite being considered by many as second- or third-rate institutions, and despite being relatively underfunded in comparison with other public colleges and universities. The evidence of the parity between two- and four-year institutions in certain outcome areas is all the more significant given the relatively lower public and individual costs of a two-year rather than four-year institution. Viewed in such a light, at least one implication is that two-year institutions may well provide students (and taxpayers) with cost-effective routes to the bachelor's degree that do not sacrifice either intellectual rigor or competitiveness in the marketplace. Indeed, two-year institutions may even constitute role models for four-year institutions in how to work with students who are academically at risk and likely to drop out, particularly historically underrepresented students and those of low socioeconomic status.

A second implication is that the time may have come for policymakers and others in the higher education community to recognize two-year colleges' achievements in preparing students academically and personally and consequently to fund these institutions at levels commensurate with their importance and performance. The persistent gap in bachelor's degree completion rates between students who begin work toward a bachelor's degree at a community college and those who start at a four-year institution remains a cause for concern, but community colleges nonetheless appear to be providing a relatively good return on the investment of public funds. John Gardner (1961), secretary of the U.S. Department of Health, Education, and Welfare from 1965 to 1968, put it this way:

> We must recognize that there may be excellence or shoddiness in every line of human endeavor. We must learn to honor excellence (indeed to *demand* it) in every socially accepted human activity, however humble the activity, and to scorn shoddiness, however exalted the activity. As I said in another connection: "An excellent plumber is infinitely more admirable than an incompetent philosopher. The society which scorns excellence in plumbing because plumbing is a humble activity, and tolerates shoddiness in philosophy because it is an exalted activity, will have neither good plumbing nor good philosophy. Neither its pipes nor its theories will hold water." [p. 86]

Redefining Educational "Quality" and Rethinking Accountability

Our 1991 review led us to conclude that "across all outcomes . . . the net impact of attending (versus not attending) college tends to be substantially more pronounced than any differential impact attributable to attending different kinds of colleges" (Pascarella & Terenzini, 1991, p. 588). In the preceding section of this chapter, and at several other points throughout this review, we state the same conclusion: on just about any outcome, and after taking into account the characteristics of the students enrolled, the dimensions along which American colleges and universities are typically categorized, ranked, and studied, such as type of control, size, and selectivity, are simply not linked with important differences in net impacts on student learning, change, or development. Despite structural and organizational differences, institutions are more alike than different in their effects on students. After adjusting for differences in the characteristics of the students enrolled, the *degree of net change* that students experience at the various categories of institutions is essentially the same. That is not to say that any one institution resembles any other institution in its power to affect learning. Nor does it mean that students complete their education with about the same level of accomplishment across outcome areas no matter which school they attend. Rather, what the evidence indicates consistently, as it has for the past 30 years (Astin, 1993c; Astin & Lee, 1972; Bowen, 1977; Pascarella

& Terenzini, 1991), is that what happens to students after they enroll at a college or university has more impact on learning and change than the structural characteristics of the institution these students attend. What matters is the nature of the experiences students have after matriculation: the courses they take, the instructional methods their teachers use, the interactions they have with their peers and faculty members outside the classroom, the variety of people and ideas they encounter, and the extent of their active involvement in the academic and social systems of their institutions.

The clear implication of this evidence is that students and their parents are making college selections, and state and federal legislators are making public policy decisions, based on a flawed conception of educational quality that prompts misleading comparisons. As a result, decisions with high price tags for both individuals and the public treasury are based on a demonstrably invalid set of variables for describing college's impact on learning outcomes. Such a misguided perception of quality restricts unnecessarily both student choice and the ability of public institutions to compete meaningfully for public resources. In addition, efforts to reform the system or to improve institutional performance become a search for a silver bullet, for the solution that can be applied to all institutions regardless of fundamental differences in their missions, makeup, locations, curricula, resources, and clienteles.

In addition to knowing what things do *not* differentiate among colleges and universities in their abilities to promote student learning and growth, we also know what factors *do* differentiate among educationally effective institutions. These characteristics, summarized in Chapter Eleven, provide the themes of this book: student involvement in the academic and nonacademic systems of an institution, the nature and frequency of student contact with peers and faculty members, interdisciplinary or integrated core curricula that emphasize making explicit connections across courses and among ideas and disciplines, pedagogies that encourage active student engagement in learning and encourage application of what is being learned in real and meaningful settings, campus environments that emphasize scholarship and provide opportunities for students to encounter different kinds of people and ideas, and environments that encourage and support exploration, whether intellectual or personal. The challenge is to find creative ways to develop measures of institutional characteristics, educational experiences, and outcomes that can be aligned with the information requirement of public accountability and policymaking and to do so in ways that enable valid and fair comparisons.

Access and Program Completion

The research strongly suggests that if one of the purposes of public higher education policy is to make the benefits of college attendance and degree completion equally available to all, then we must begin to think of college attendance and completion as a more complex and longer-term process than we have previously. Public policy on postsecondary education has been largely concerned with student financial aid, and such legislation will continue to be a significant policy lever affecting higher education. Our review makes clear, however, that financial aid is only one element in college persistence and program completion and that a narrow public policy concentration on financial aid and access has several shortcomings.

First, most of the research on financial aid both pre- and post-1990 concentrates on the effects of aid on student decisions about whether and where to attend college. Financial aid levels the playing field somewhat for students of lower socioeconomic status in terms of persistence and degree completion, but the picture is incomplete. Despite considerable institutional, state, and federal investments in aid, the evidence also indicates that equal access to postsecondary enrollment does not translate into equal access to important learning-related college experiences and to opportunities to complete a degree.

Public policies that view financial considerations as the chief determinants of access to college assume parity in students' upbringing and earlier schooling and thus an equal opportunity to reach the gateway to higher education and realize its benefits. The evidence suggests the contrary (Terenzini, Cabrera, & Bernal, 2001). Significant gaps exist in the academic development and college-going rates between students from families of low socioeconomic status and their more affluent peers. And the gaps grow progressively wider at each step of the process: elementary and secondary academic preparation, high school completion, and applying to and enrolling in college (Cabrera & La Nasa, 2000). Research intended to support institutional and state policy efforts to promote student persistence and degree completion underscores that the path to a college degree begins well before the first year of college (Hossler, Braxton, & Coopersmith, 1989; Hossler, Schmit, & Vesper, 1999). "By the time students reach the twelfth grade, it is too late to . . . increase the numbers of students who are ready for college. In fact, it could be said that students begin to drop out of college in grade school" (Rendon, 1998, p. 61). According to the College Board, "For many students, in fact, . . . the die is cast by the eighth grade. Students without the appropriate math and reading skills by that grade are unlikely to acquire them by the end of high school" (Gladieux & Swail, 1998a, p. 16; see also Gladieux & Swail, 1998b). The socioeconomic and educational conditions that underlie these disparities require attention to the serious questions about the current organizational and functional boundaries between elementary and secondary schools on the one hand and colleges and universities on the other. At present, the two sectors are organized, funded, and operated as if the interests and effectiveness of one sector were independent of the other.

Discrete, unintegrated, and uncoordinated efforts to prepare students for college or to help them succeed once they enroll are likely to be only marginally successful (Adelman, 1999; Terenzini, Cabrera, & Bernal, 2001). Researchers, teachers, administrators, and, increasingly, policymakers are coming to recognize that choosing to attend college and succeeding once there are part of a complex interaction of family-, school-, and college-related factors. Additional efforts at kindergarten-through-college thinking, planning, and cooperation are worthy of support.

A second reason why the public policy concentration on removing financial barriers to college access is unnecessarily narrow is that it appears to rest on the assumption that if such barriers can be reduced or removed, everything else will take care of itself, and any social or moral imperative to provide equal access to the benefits of college will have been satisfied. The fixation on access, however, overlooks the fact that, as Adelman (1999) wrote: "Degree completion is the true bottom line for college administrators, state legislators, parents, and most importantly, students—not retention to the second year, not persistence without a degree, but completion" (p. v). Our review makes clear that finances are only one of the factors affecting student persistence and program completion, although their reach extends into a number of areas that influence persistence and degree completion. The emerging evidence suggests that financial considerations are part of a complex longitudinal process that begins long before students enter college, perhaps as early as the middle school years, shaping whether students have college aspirations as well as the nature of these aspirations and the ensuing college search and selection process.

Once students enroll in college, moreover, financial aid and net cost considerations may modify educational plans and affect students' levels of involvement in the academic and social domains of college. The links between involvement and persistence and educational attainment are well established. Unmet need (total costs minus all forms of aid), for example, can influence whether students borrow money or seek employment to fill the gap. In excess, either action can have educationally negative consequences. Students who defer college entry or interrupt their enrollment to work and save money before enrolling or returning sharply reduce their chances of completing their programs. Alternatively, unmet need may increase pressures on students to work while enrolled. Both delayed or interrupted enrollment and employment for more than 15 to 20 hours a week will necessarily reduce the degree of students' exposure to college, the time they have to study, and the time and opportunities they have to become involved in the wide array of college activities that facilitate their learning, change, and persistence. Thus, financial aid can determine not only whether and where students go to college but also the kinds of experiences they have while there, how much they will learn or change, the likelihood that they will persist and graduate, and, ultimately, whether they will reap the full intellectual, personal, social, occupational, and economic benefits of college. Moreover, the intergenerational legacies of education that are (or are not) passed on to succeeding generations mean that the impact of financial aid will extend beyond today's individual students to affect the odds that their children will attend college and complete a degree program.

Thus, public policymaking intended to extend access for all students to the full range of opportunities and benefits of college attendance and program completion should be developed to provide four types of support: (1) early interventions designed to raise the awareness of low-income middle school children and their parents of the possibilities of college attendance and to help them secure the necessary academic qualifications for admission and success once there; (2) financial aid in amounts and packages that will allow recipients to participate fully in the academic and nonacademic systems of their institutions; (3) services that will assist underprepared students to make a successful transition from secondary school or work to college and to succeed once there; and (4) incentives for colleges and universities to adopt the kinds of curricular arrangements and instructional approaches that our review indicates will increase involvement and student learning, change, and development in educationally desirable ways.

IMPLICATIONS FOR INSTITUTIONAL PRACTICES AND POLICY

Over the past decade, a quiet revolution has been under way in higher education in the United States and elsewhere. Until the decade of the 1990s, an educational model that put delivery of instruction, not student learning, at the center of the enterprise dominated American higher education (Barr & Tagg, 1995; Tagg, 2003). Under this model, higher education has been teacher-centered and teacher-directed. The model has driven organizational and reward structures, curriculum design, course scheduling, the nature and status of faculty work, the organizational bifurcation of "academic" and "student" affairs, and the nature of student-faculty interactions in and out of the classroom. Most importantly, the teacher-centered model has controlled what goes on (and what does not) in the classroom. Faculty members decide what will be learned, how, when, and where. Faculty members do the teaching, and learning is considered an essentially passive activity, requiring of students only the acquisition of knowledge, not their active participation in its discovery or construction. It has separated teacher from student, knowledge from experience, and curricular from cocurricular life (Baxter Magolda, 1992b).

The emerging model is learning-centered rather than teacher-centered (Barr & Tagg, 1995; Tagg, 2003). It redefines the purpose of colleges and universities to be learning and in so doing dramatically alters the roles of teachers and learners. Under this model, it is important not to be too quick to equate "teacher" with faculty member and "learner" with student. Rather, students teach and learn from one another, as well as from faculty, and instructors are learning guides and facilitators rather than knowledge dispensers.

From at least one perspective, the research published since 1990 provides considerable empirical support for the desirability of this evolution in higher education. The evidence indicates clearly that encounters with new and different ideas and with people different from themselves challenge students to learn. When students are actively engaged in learning, whether through classroom instruction or through out-of-class activities, change is likely to occur. The research consistently shows that learning is bound neither by time nor by place, that it occurs continuously in a variety of locations, often unpredictably, and that it is maximized when both the activities and outcomes have meaning for the learner. Finally, learning is not a solitary activity but is more likely relational and social, taking place when students engage in a task with others and in informal interactions with peers and faculty members.

Teaching and Learning

Perhaps the clearest implication of the post-1990 research on the effects of college is that educational settings and approaches defined by the teacher-centered and teacher-directed paradigm are, if not flawed, at least incomplete and demonstrably less effective than other approaches to education. The evidence strongly suggests that learning is holistic rather than segmented. As discussed earlier in this chapter, research indicates that a single learning experience may affect multiple dimensions of students' lives and, conversely, that multiple experiences in any of a variety of settings can influence a single learning outcome. Students develop academically and cognitively outside the classroom as well as inside it, and psychosocial changes can originate in or be enhanced by experiences inside the classroom as well as outside it.

Another finding of this review is that the most effective teaching and learning require opportunities for active student involvement and participation. As noted, the research indicates that encounters with people and ideas that challenge beliefs trigger learning, especially when students actively *engage* these challenging people and ideas. Knowledge acquisition, skill development, and psychosocial change are most likely when learners find meaning in both the activities and the outcomes of the college experience.

Nonetheless, it would be both premature and shortsighted to discard the lecture, which *is* an efficient means of transmitting information. Research provides ample evidence that the dominant teacher-student paradigm (of which the lecture is the centerpiece) is effective in promoting knowledge acquisition and cognitive skill development among college students. Moreover, an impressive body of post-1990 research identifies a number of pedagogical skills that teachers can acquire, such as clarity, expressiveness, and organization-preparation. Thus, conventional instructional approaches can be made even more effective than they now are. In short, the research indicates that faculty members, for the most part, know how to be effective classroom teachers and to promote student learning.

The post-1990 research also makes clear, however, that we now know a good deal about how to promote learning in ways that are even more effective than lecturing. With striking consistency, studies show that innovative, active, collaborative, cooperative, and constructivist instructional approaches shape learning more powerfully, in some forms by substantial margins, than do conventional lecture-discussion and text-based approaches.

The "take-home message" from this research is that college and university faculty can use a variety of vetted instructional behaviors and pedagogical approaches, from teachers teaching students to students teaching and learning from other students, and students "constructing" rather than receiving knowledge, with information technology and service experiences added to the mix. In our view, the national dialogue on teaching and learning will be more productive if lines are not narrowly drawn. The evidence implies neither an instructional hierarchy nor a need to replace one paradigm with another. Rather, researchers have turned the spotlight on ways to make the dominant model even more effective than it already is and have pointed out *additional* approaches to effective teaching and learning. The discussion should not be about replacing the old with the new but rather about enhancing the old and augmenting the current array of instructional tools. The challenge is to find ways to encourage the incorporation of these enhancements and new pedagogical approaches into our institutions.

Organizational Structures

The research we have reviewed also has implications for how colleges and universities organize and operate. Now the mission is to find creative ways to align better what we do with what we know about student learning and how to promote it.

The holistic nature of learning suggests a clear need to rethink and restructure highly segmented departmental and program configurations and their associated curricular patterns. Curricula and courses that address topics in an interdisciplinary fashion are more likely to provide effective educational experiences than are discrete courses accumulated over a student's college career in order to produce enough credits for a degree. Such interdisciplinary connections will require new organizational and curricular structures. The goals, where feasible, should be learning experiences that cut across disciplines. The guideposts should be the *interconnections* that are at the core of student learning, not convenient faculty-centered divisions of labor, discrete organizational units, or budget development and resource allocation models driven by credit hours.

Whatever form curricular and organizational reconfigurations might take, failure to incorporate and capitalize on students' out-of-class experiences risks increasing learning only at the margins. Learning-centered organizations will find ways to increase opportunities to link the formal and informal worlds of learning and instruction, guided by the educational philosophies, designs, and learning productivity of the living-learning centers. But the decline in the residential character of much of higher education and the increased heterogeneity of the student body will challenge imagination. How creative can colleges and universities be in eliminating the conceptual and organizational separation of student learning into cognitive and affective, academic and nonacademic? Can structures and practices be developed that recognize learning as ongoing, without regard to time and place? In some areas of intellectual development (including critical thinking), the breadth of student involvement in the intellectual *and* social experiences of college, rather than any particular type of involvement, matters most. The greatest impact appears to stem from students' *total* level of campus engagement, particularly when academic, interpersonal, and extracurricular involvements are mutually reinforcing and relevant to a particular educational outcome.

Institutional Policy

The need for new thinking suggests a set of implications for institutional policy. The kinds of changes outlined here would constitute shifts in the bedrock culture of America's colleges and universities. But culture shifts come slowly, requiring incentives to change as well as the institutionalization of these changes. Some disciplines and institutions are making important progress in rebalancing the attention accorded to teaching and to research when hiring, merit salary, promotion, and tenure decisions are made. Others, however, primarily large research universities, lag behind. Yet it seems unlikely that learning-centered cultures will emerge and take root without a redistribution of the financial and status rewards that guide hiring, promotion, and tenure decisions.

Better matching what we do and what we know about effective education requires not only looking to stimulate faculty members to rethink course designs and teaching methods but also seeking ways to prepare the next generation of faculty, the one now moving through our doctoral programs. What values and abilities are graduate students learning? Are they discovering how to facilitate learning in others? Or are they learning, as many of their mentors have, to value research more than teaching?

Similarly, when new Ph.D.s enter the professoriate, what criteria for success will they encounter in the academic marketplace? Will faculty who are doing the recruiting and hiring be looking for others like themselves, or knowing that it is easier to hire a good teacher than to retool a poor one, can they be persuaded to seek colleagues who are as adept in their teaching as in their scholarship? Will candidates, as part of the recruiting process, be asked to demonstrate their talent in the classroom as well as their scholarship?

Assessment of department-specific learning outcomes can be a useful vehicle of change. Assessment plans and activities developed and approved by faculty can provide an empirical foundation for systematic and ongoing rethinking, redesigning, and restructuring programs and curricula. For faculty members, trained to be skeptical about claims, evidence is the gold standard in the academy, and they are unlikely to adopt new ways of thinking or behaving without first being convinced that the new pedagogies and organizational structures are better than the old. In addition, the findings of assessment studies specific to faculty members' academic units will generate more interest and attention than general or institutionwide evidence.

Many instructional and organizational changes—such as those concerning doctoral education; revised hiring, promotion, and tenure criteria; organizational realignments; and incorporation of new pedagogies—do not require large infusions of cash. Indeed, some institutions have found creative ways to accomplish instructional goals by redistributing resources. But a big threat to changes in pedagogies and organizational practices and policies lies in current pressures to reduce operating costs and develop new revenue streams, such as research grants and contracts. Such pressures are powerful incentives for faculty members *not* to modify teaching practices or hiring, promotion, and tenure criteria. The popular belief that good researchers make good teachers has little support in the literature (Feldman, 1987; Marsh & Hattie, 2002). And pressures that equate research productivity with institutional quality can drive institutions in unexamined directions, subtly subverting the instructional dimension of an institution's mission.

Better teaching and greater learning are also unlikely to emerge without leadership and support both from an institution's president and from within the faculty, particularly from faculty who are widely respected and who are known to value student learning. In the end, rebalancing teaching and learning vis-à-vis research, production of knowledge, and generation of extramural funding presents a test of institutional will. At issue is whether colleges and universities of whatever mission, shape, or size will remain faithful to the one element common to their missions, to what defines them as institutions of higher education— the education of students.

Note

1. An effect size is usually estimated in standard deviation units by subtracting, for example, the mean of first-year students on some variable from the mean of seniors and then dividing that difference by the pooled standard deviation or, if that is not available, the standard deviation of the comparison or control group—in this case, first-year students (Hays, 1994). The procedure converts the difference in group means to standard deviation units. Although there is some disagreement over what constitutes a practically significant effect size, the consensus seems to be that those less than .30 are "small," those between .30 and .70 are "moderate," and those above .70 are "large" (Bowen, 1977; Cohen, 1988; Gall, Borg, & Gall, 1996; Sprinthall, Schmutte, & Sirois, 1991). An effect size in standard deviation units can be converted to its percentile point equivalent using the area under the normal curve, usually given in a table of cumulative normal probabilities and found in an appendix in most inferential statistics texts. For example, given an estimated effect size of, say, $+1$ standard deviation (a z-score of $+1.0$), the area under the normal curve extends from the 50th to the 84th percentile, indicating such an effect size is the equivalent of a shift of 34 percentile points.

REFERENCES

ACT. (2002). *National collegiate dropout and graduation rates.* Iowa City: ACT, Office for the Enhancement of Educational Practices.

Adams, M. (2002, Fall/Winter). Charting cognitive and moral development in diversity classes. *Diversity Digest, 6,* 21–23.

Adams, M., & Zhou-McGovern, Y. (1990, April). *Some cognitive developmental characteristics of diversity education.* Paper presented at the meeting of the American Educational Research Association, Boston.

Adams, M., & Zhou-McGovern, Y. (1994). *The sociomoral development of undergraduates in a "social diversity" course: Developmental theory, research, and instructional applications.* Paper presented at the meeting of the American Educational Research Association, New Orleans.

Adams, T. (1997). Technology makes a difference in community college mathematics teaching. *Community College Journal of Research and Practice, 21,* 481–491.

Adams, T., Kandt, G., Thronmartin, D., & Waldrop, P. (1991). Computer-assisted instruction vs. lecture methods in teaching the rules of golf. *Physical Education, 48,* 146–150.

Adelman, C. (1990). *A college course map. Taxonomy and transcript data: Based on postsecondary records, 1972–1984, of the high school class of 1972.* Washington, DC: U.S. Department of Education.

Adelman, C. (1991). *Women at thirtysomething: Paradoxes of attainment* (No. OR 91–530). Washington, DC: U.S. Department of Education, Office of Educational Research and Improvement.

Adelman, C. (1992). *The way we are: The community college as American thermometer* (No. OR 92–511). Washington, DC: U.S. Department of Education, Office of Educational Research and Improvement.

Adelman, C. (1994). *Lessons of a generation: Education and work in the lives of the high school class of 1972.* San Francisco: Jossey-Bass.

Adelman, C. (1998a). *Women and men of the engineering path: A model for analyses of undergraduate careers* (Document No. PLLI 98–8055). Washington, DC: U.S. Department of Education and National Institute for Science Education.

Adelman, C. (1998b, November). *Institutional effects in an age of multi-institutional attendance.* Paper presented at the meeting of the Association for the Study of Higher Education, Miami.

Adelman, C. (1999). *Answers in the toolbox: Academic intensity, attendance patterns, and bachelor's degree attainment.* Washington, DC: U.S. Department of Education, Office of Educational Research and Improvement.

Advisory Committee on Student Financial Assistance. (2001). *Access denied: Restoring the nation's commitment to equal educational opportunity.* Washington, DC: Author.

Agarwal, R., & Day, E. (1998). The impact of the Internet on economic education. *Journal of Economic Education, 29,* 99–110.

Alavi, M. (1994). Computer-mediated collaborative learning: An empirical evaluation. *MIS Quarterly, 18,* 159–174.

Albanese, M., & Mitchell, S. (1993). Problem-based learning: A review of literature on its outcomes and implementation issues. *Academic Medicine, 68,* 52–81.

Albrecht, D., Carpenter, D., & Sivo, S. (1994). The effect of college activities and grades on job placement potential. *NASPA Journal, 31,* 290–296.

Aleamoni, L. (1999). Student rating myths versus research facts from 1924 to 1998. *Journal of Personnel Evaluation in Education, 13,* 153–166.

Aleman, A. (1994, April). *The cognitive value of college women's friendships.* Paper presented at the meeting of the American Educational Research Association, New Orleans.

Aleman, A. (1997). Understanding and investigating female friendship's educative value. *Journal of Higher Education, 68,* 119–159.

Al-Hilawani, Y., Merchant, G., & Poteet, J. (1993). *Implementing reciprocal teaching: Was it effective?* Paper presented at the meeting of the Midwest Association of Teachers of Educational Psychology, Anderson, IN.

Allen, B., & Niss, J. (1990). A chill in the college classroom? *Phi Delta Kappan, 71,* 607–609.

Allen, D., & Nora, A. (1995). An empirical examination of the construct validity of goal commitment in the persistence process. *Research in Higher Education, 36,* 509–533.

Allen, W. (1992). The color of success: African-American college student outcomes at predominantly White and historically Black public colleges and universities. *Harvard Educational Review, 62,* 26–44.

Allen, W., Epps, E., & Haniff, N. (Eds.). (1991). *College in Black and White: African American students in predominantly White and in historically Black public universities.* Albany: State University of New York Press.

Allport, G. (1979). *The nature of prejudice.* Reading, MA: Addison-Wesley. (Originally published 1954.)

Almer, E., Jones, K., & Moeckel, C. (1998). The impact of one-minute papers on learning in an introductory accounting course. *Issues in Accounting Education, 13,* 485–497.

Alsalam, N., & Conley, R. (1995). *The rate of return to education: A proposal for an indicator.* Unpublished manuscript, prepared for the Organization for Economic Cooperation and Development, Washington, DC.

Alsalam, N., & Rogers, G. (1991). *The condition of education, 1991: Vol. 2. Postsecondary education.* Washington, DC: National Center for Education Statistics.

Alwin, D., Cohen, R., & Newcomb, T. (1991). *Political attitudes over the life span: The Bennington women after fifty years.* Madison: University of Wisconsin Press.

Alwin, D., & Krosnick, J. (1991). Aging, cohorts, and the stability of sociopolitical orientations over the life span. *American Journal of Sociology, 97,* 169–195.

American Association of Colleges and Universities. (2002). *Greater expectations: A new vision for learning as a nation goes to college* (National Panel Report). Washington, DC: Author.

Amundsen, C., Gryspeerdt, D., & Moxness, K. (1992, April). *Practice-centered inquiry: Developing perceptions and behaviors toward more effective teaching in higher education.* Paper presented at the meeting of the American Educational Research Association, San Francisco.

Anaya, G. (1992). *Cognitive development among college undergraduates.* Unpublished doctoral dissertation, University of California, Los Angeles.

Anaya, G. (1996). College experiences and student learning: The influence of active learning, college environments, and cocurricular activities. *Journal of College Student Development, 37,* 611–622.

Anaya, G. (1999a). College impact on student learning: Comparing the use of self-reported gains, standardized test scores, and college grades. *Research in Higher Education, 40,* 449–526.

Anaya, G. (1999b). *Accuracy of student-reported test scores: Are they suited for college impact assessment?* Unpublished manuscript, Indiana University, Bloomington.

Anaya, G. (1999c, April). *Within-college, curricular, and co-curricular correlates of performance on the MCAT.* Paper presented at the meeting of the American Educational Research Association, Montreal.

Anaya, G. (2001). Correlates of performance on the MCAT: An examination of the influence of college environments and experiences on student learning. *Advances in Health Science Education, 6*(3), 179–191.

Anderson, B., & Ekstrom, R. (1996, May). *Improving the retention of African-American undergraduates in predominantly White colleges and universities: Evidence from 45 institutions.* Paper presented at the meeting of the Association for Institutional Research, Albuquerque, NM.

Anderson, C. (1995). "How can my faith be so different?" The emergence of religious identity in college women. *Dissertation Abstracts International, 56,* 7A.

Anderson, G., Dey, E., Gray, M., & Thomas, G. (1995, November). *Mentors and proteges: The influence of faculty mentoring on undergraduate academic achievement.* Paper presented at the meeting of the Association for the Study of Higher Education, Orlando.

Anderson, J., & Bryjak, G. (1989). Out of the tower and into the street: University students and social justice issues. *Educational Research Quarterly, 13,* 47–56.

Anderson, L., Stoelb, M., Duggan, P., Hieger, B., Kling, K., & Payne, J. (1998). The effectiveness of two types of rape prevention programs in changing the rape-supportive attitudes of college students. *Journal of College Student Development, 39,* 131–141.

Angelo, T., & Cross, K. (1993). *Classroom assessment techniques: A handbook for college teachers.* San Francisco: Jossey-Bass.

Anglin, L., Davis, L., & Mooradian, P. (1995). Do transfer students graduate? A comparative study of transfer students and native university students. *Community College Journal of Research and Practice, 19,* 321–330.

Angoff, W., & Johnson, E. (1990). The differential impact of curriculum on aptitude test scores. *Journal of Educational Measurement, 27,* 291–305.

Angrist, J., & Krueger, A. (1991). Does compulsory school attendance affect schooling and earnings? *Quarterly Journal of Economics, 106,* 979–1014.

Angrist, J., & Krueger, A. (1993). *Estimating the payoff to schooling using the Vietnam era draft lottery* (NBER Working Paper No. 4067). Cambridge, MA: National Bureau of Economic Research.

Antonio, A. (1995, November). *Making social comparisons: Black and White peer group influence in college.* Paper presented at the meeting of the Association for the Study of Higher Education, Orlando.

Antonio, A. (1998, April). *Student interaction across race and outcomes in college.* Paper presented at the meeting of the American Educational Research Association, San Diego, CA.

Antonio, A. (1999, November). *Diversity and the influence of friendship groups in college.* Paper presented at the meeting of the Association for the Study of Higher Education, San Antonio, TX.

Antonio, A. (2000, April). *Developing leadership skills for diversity: The role of interracial interaction.* Paper presented at the meeting of the American Educational Research Association, New Orleans.

Antonio, A. (2001). Diversity and the influence of friendship groups in college. *Review of Higher Education, 25,* 63–89.

Antonio, A., & Lopez, J. (1999, November). *Does race matter in the frog pond? How friendship groups affect intellectual self-confidence and educational aspirations in college.* Paper presented at the meeting of the Association for the Study of Higher Education, San Antonio, TX.

Aper, J. (1994, April). *An investigation of the relationship between student work experience and student outcomes.* Paper presented at the meeting of the American Educational Research Association, New Orleans.

Aper, J. (1997). *An investigation of the relationship between student work experience and student outcomes.* Unpublished manuscript, University of Tennessee, Knoxville.

Appel, M., Cartwright, D., Smith, D., & Wolf, L. (1996). *The impact of diversity on students: A preliminary review of the research literature* (Research report). Washington, DC: Association of American Colleges and Universities.

Arambula-Greenfield, T. (1996). Implementing problem-based learning in a college science class. *Journal of College Science Teaching, 26,* 26–30.

Arcidiacono, P. (1998). *Option values, college quality, and earnings: Results from a dynamic model of college and major choice.* Unpublished manuscript, University of Wisconsin, Madison.

Arendale, D. (1994). Understanding the supplemental instruction model. In D. Martin & D. Arendale (Eds.), *Supplemental Instruction: Increasing achievement and retention* (pp. 11–21). San Francisco: Jossey-Bass.

Arendale, D., & Martin, D. (1997). *Review of research concerning the effectiveness of Supplemental Instruction from the University of Missouri-Kansas City and other institutions from the across the United States.* Kansas City: University of Missouri. (ERIC Document Reproduction Service No. ED 370 502)

Arias, O., & McMahon, W. (2001). Dynamic rates of return to education in the U.S. *Economics of Education Review, 20,* 121–138.

Arkes, J. (1999). What do educational credentials signal and why do employers value credentials? *Economics of Education Review, 18,* 133–141.

Armstrong, M. (1993). Ethics and professionalism in accounting education. *Journal of Accounting Education, 11,* 77–92.

Arnold, D., & Ponemon, L. (1991). Internal auditors' perceptions of whistle-blowing and the influence of moral reasoning: An experiment. *Auditing: A Journal of Practice and Theory, 10*(2), 1–15.

Arnold, J., Kuh, G., Vesper, N., & Schuh, J. (1991, November). *The influence of student effort, college environment, and selected student characteristics on undergraduate student learning and personal development at metropolitan institutions.* Paper presented at the meeting of the Association for the Study of Higher Education, Boston.

Arnold, J., Kuh, G., Vesper, N., & Schuh, J. (1993). Student age and enrollment status as determinants of learning and personal development at metropolitan institutions. *Journal of College Student Development, 34,* 11–16.

Arnold, K. (1993). Academically talented women in the 1980s: The Illinois Valedictorian Project. In K. Hulbert & D. Schuster (Eds.), *Women's lives through time: Educated American women of the twentieth century* (pp. 393–414). San Francisco: Jossey-Bass.

Asada, H., Swank, E., & Goldey, G. (2003). The acceptance of a multicultural education among Appalachian college students. *Research in Higher Education, 44,* 99–120.

Ashar, H., & Skenes, R. (1993). Can Tinto's student departure model be applied to nontraditional students? *Adult Education Quarterly, 43,* 90–100.

Ashenfelter, O., & Krueger, A. (1994). Estimates of the economic return to schooling from a new sample of twins. *American Economic Review, 84,* 1157–1173.

Ashenfelter, O., & Rouse, C. (1998a). Income, schooling, and ability: Evidence from a new sample of identical twins. *Quarterly Journal of Economics, 113,* 253–284.

Ashenfelter, O., & Rouse, C. (1998b). *Schooling, intelligence, and income in America: Cracks in the bell curve* (Working Paper No. 407). Princeton, NJ: Princeton University, Industrial Relations Section.

Askar, P., & Koksal, M. (1993). The contribution of computer-assisted instruction to freshman mathematics achievement. *College Student Journal, 27,* 203–207.

Astin, A. (1968). *The college environment.* Washington, DC: American Council on Education.

Astin, A. (1970a). The methodology of research on college impact (I). *Sociology of Education, 43,* 223–254.

Astin, A. (1970b). The methodology of research on college impact (II). *Sociology of Education, 43,* 437–450.

Astin, A. (1973). Measurement and determinants of the outputs of higher education. In L. Solmon & P. Taubman (Eds.), *Does college matter? Some evidence on the impacts of higher education.* New York: Academic Press.

Astin, A. (1977). *Four critical years: Effects of college on beliefs, attitudes, and knowledge.* San Francisco: Jossey-Bass.

Astin, A. (1984). Student involvement: A developmental theory for higher education. *Journal of College Student Personnel, 25,* 297–308.

Astin, A. (1985). *Achieving educational excellence: A critical assessment of priorities and practices in higher education.* San Francisco: Jossey-Bass.

Astin, A. (1991). *Assessment for excellence: The philosophy and practice of assessment and evaluation in higher education.* New York: Macmillan.

Astin, A. (1992). What really matters in general education: Provocative findings from a national study of student outcomes. *Perspectives, 22,* 23–46.

Astin, A. (1993a, March/April). Diversity and multiculturalism on the campus: How are students affected? *Change, 25,* 44–49.

Astin, A. (1993b). An empirical typology of college students. *Journal of College Student Development, 34,* 36–46.

Astin, A. (1993c). *What matters in college?* Four critical years *revisited.* San Francisco: Jossey-Bass.

Astin, A. (1996a). "Involvement in learning" revisited: Lessons we have learned. *Journal of College Student Development, 37,* 123–134.

Astin, A. (1996b, March/April). The role of service in higher education. *About Campus, 1,* 14–19.

Astin, A. (1998). The changing American college student: Thirty-year trends, 1966–1996. *Review of Higher Education, 21,* 115–135.

Astin, A., & Astin, H. (1993). *Undergraduate science education: The impact of different college environments on the educational pipeline in the sciences.* Los Angeles: University of California, Graduate School of Education, Higher Education Research Institute.

Astin, A., Keup, J., & Lindholm, J. (2002). A decade of changes in undergraduate education: A national study of system "transformation." *Review of Higher Education, 25,* 141–162.

Astin, A., & Lee, C. (1972). *The invisible colleges: A profile of small, private colleges with limited resources.* New York: McGraw-Hill.

Astin, A., & Panos, R. (1969). *The educational and vocational development of college students.* Washington, DC: American Council on Education.

Astin, A., & Sax, L. (1996). *How undergraduates are affected by service participation.* Unpublished manuscript, University of California, Los Angeles.

Astin, A., & Sax, L. (1998). How undergraduates are affected by service participation. *Journal of College Student Development, 39,* 251–263.

Astin, A., Sax, L., & Avalos, J. (1999). Long-term effects of volunteerism during the undergraduate years. *Review of Higher Education, 22,* 187–202.

Astin, A., Tsui, L., & Avalos, J. (1996). *Degree attainment rates at American colleges and universities: Effects of race, gender, and institutional type* (No. HE 029 589). Los Angeles: University of California, Higher Education Research Institute.

Astin, A., Vogelgesang, L., Ikeda, E., & Yee, J. (2000). *How service learning affects students.* Los Angeles: University of California, Higher Education Research Institute.

Astin, H., & Antonio, A. (1999). *The impact of college on character development* (Final Report supported by the John Templeton Foundation, Grant ID No. 468). Los Angeles: University of California, Higher Education Research Institute.

Astin, H., & Antonio, A. (2000, November/December). Building character in college. *About Campus, 5,* 3–7.

Astin, H., & Cress, C. (1998). *The impact of leadership programs on student development* (Technical report to the W. K. Kellogg Foundation). Los Angeles: University of California, Higher Education Research Institute.

Astin, H., & Leland, C. (1991). *Women of influence and women of vision.* San Francisco: Jossey-Bass.

Atkinson, D., Morten, G., & Sue, D. (1989). A minority identity development model. In D. Atkinson, G. Morten, & D. Sue (Eds.), *Counseling American minorities* (pp.35–52). Dubuque, IA: William C. Brown.

Attinasi, L. (1992). Rethinking the study of the outcomes of college attendance. *Journal of College Student Development, 33,* 61–70.

Austin, M., Cherney, E., Crowner, J., & Hill, A. (1997). The forum: Intrusive group advising for the probationary student. *NACADA Journal, 17,* 45–47.

Avalos, J. (1994, November). *Going beyond the decision: An analysis of the reasons for leaving college.* Paper presented at the meeting of the Association for the Study of Higher Education, Tucson, AZ.

Avalos, J. (1996). *The effects of time-to-degree completion, stopping out, transferring, and reasons for leaving college on students' long-term retention.* Unpublished doctoral dissertation, University of California, Los Angeles.

Avens, C., & Zelley, R. (1992). *QUANTA: An interdisciplinary learning community* (four studies). Daytona Beach, FL: Daytona Beach Community College. (ERIC Document Reproduction Service No. ED 349 073)

Axelson, R., & Torres, D. (1995, May). *Modeling first-semester integration and departure of community college students.* Paper presented at the meeting of the Association for Institutional Research, Boston.

Bach, S., Banks, M., Kinnick, M., Ricks, M., Stoering, J., & Walleri, D. (2000). Student attendance patterns and performance in an urban postsecondary environment. *Research in Higher Education, 41,* 315–330.

Baier, J., & Whipple, E. (1990). Greek values and attitudes: A comparison with independents. *NASPA Journal, 28,* 43–53.

Baird, L. (1988). The college environment revisited: A review of research and theory. In J. Smart (Ed.), *Higher education: Handbook of theory and research* (Vol. 4, pp. 1–52). New York: Agathon.

Baird, L. (1990a). A 24-year longitudinal study of the development of religious ideas. *Psychological Reports, 66,* 479–482.

Baird, L. (1990b). *Academic, personal, and situational factors in retention in community colleges* (Research Report No. 90–1). Lexington: University of Kentucky.

Baird, L. (1991, May). *What can studies of college environments contribute to institutional research?* Paper presented at the meeting of the Association for Institutional Research, San Francisco.

Baird, L. (1992, May). *Renovating the campus to enhance the intellectual life of the institution: Perspectives from research.* Paper presented at the meeting of the Association for Institutional Research, Atlanta, GA.

Baldizan, L., & Frey, J. (1995). Athletics and moral development: Regulatory and ethical issues. *College Student Affairs Journal, 15,* 33–43.

Baldwin, D., Adamson, T., Sheehan, J., Self, D., & Oppenberg, A. (1996). Moral reasoning and malpractice: A pilot study of orthopedic surgeons. *American Journal of Orthopedics, 25,* 481–484.

Ballard, K. (1993). The relationship of involvement in college activities to persistence towards bachelor's degree completion in nursing. *Dissertation Abstracts International, 54,* 828A.

Ballou, R., Reavill, L., & Schultz, B. (1995). Assessing the immediate and residual effects of the residence hall experience: Validating Pace's 1990 analysis of on-campus and off-campus students. *Journal of College and University Student Housing, 25,* 16–21.

Baltes, P. (1982). Life-span development psychology: Some conveying observations on history and theory. In K. Schaie & J. Geiwitz (Eds.), *Readings in adult development and aging.* Boston: Little, Brown.

Bandura, A. (1994). Self-efficacy. In V. Ramachaudran (Ed.), *Encyclopedia of human behavior* (Vol. 4, pp. 71–81). New York: Academic Press.

Bandura, A. (1997). *Self-efficacy: The exercise of control.* New York: Freeman.

Bank, B., Slavings, R., & Biddle, R. (1990). Effects of peer, faculty, and parental influences on students' persistence. *Sociology of Education, 63,* 209–225.

Banks, J. (1995). Multicultural education: Its effects on students' racial and gender role attitudes. In J. Banks & C. McGee Banks (Eds.), *Handbook of research on multicultural education* (pp. 617–627). New York: Macmillan.

Banta, T., & Associates. (1993). *Making a difference: Outcomes of a decade of assessment in higher education.* San Francisco: Jossey-Bass.

Barefoot, B. (1992). Helping first-year college students climb the academic ladder: Report of a national survey of freshman seminar programming in American higher education. *Dissertation Abstracts International, 53,* 1412A.

Barefoot, B. (Ed.). (1993). *Exploring the evidence: Reporting outcomes of freshman seminars* (Vol. 11). Columbia: University of South Carolina, National Resource Center for the Freshman Year Experience.

Barefoot, B. (2002). *Second national survey of first-year academic practices, 2002.* Brevard, NC: Policy Center on the First Year of College. [Available at: http://www.brevard.edu/fyc/survey2002/].

Barefoot, B., Warnock, C., Dickinson, M., Richardson, S., & Roberts, M. (1998). *Exploring the evidence: Reporting outcomes of first-year seminars* (Vol. II, Monograph No. 25). Columbia: University of South Carolina, National Resource Center for the First-Year Experience and Students in Transition.

Bargad, A., & Hyde, J. (1991). Women's studies: A study of feminist identity development in women. *Psychology of Women Quarterly, 15,* 181–201.

Barker, B., Frisbie, A., & Patrick, K. (1989). Broadening the definition of education in light of the new telecommunications technologies. *American Journal of Distance Education, 3,* 20–29.

Barker, R. (1968). *Ecological psychology: Concepts and methods for studying the environment of human behavior.* Stanford, CA: Stanford University Press.

Barker, R., & Associates. (1978). *Habitats, environments, and human behavior: Studies in ecological psychology and eco-behavioral science.* San Francisco: Jossey-Bass.

Barnes, L., Bull, K., Campbell, N., & Perry, K. (1998, April). *Discipline-related differences in teaching and grading philosophies among undergraduate teaching faculty.* Paper presented at the meeting of the American Educational Research Association, San Diego, CA.

Barr, R., & Tagg, J. (1995, November/December). From teaching to learning: A new paradigm for undergraduate education. *Change, 27,* 13–25.

Barrows, H. (1996). Problem-based learning in medicine and beyond. In L. Wilkerson & W. Gijselaers (Eds.), *Bringing problem-based learning to higher education: Theory and practice* (pp. 3–12). San Francisco: Jossey-Bass.

Barton, P., & LaPointe, A. (1995). *Learning by degrees: Indicators of performance in higher education.* Princeton, NJ: Educational Testing Service, Policy Information Center.

Basseches, M. (1984). *Dialectic thinking and adult development.* Norwood, NJ: Ablex.

Bassi, L. (1999). Are employers' recruitment strategies changing: Competence over credentials? In N. Stacey (Ed.), *Competence without credentials* (pp. 13–27). Washington, DC: U.S. Department of Education, Office of Educational Research and Improvement.

Batchelder, T., & Root, S. (1994). Effects of an undergraduate program to integrate academic learning and service: Cognitive, prosocial cognitive, and identity outcomes. *Journal of Adolescence, 17,* 341–355.

Bates, J. (1997). The effects of study abroad on undergraduates in an honors international program. *Dissertation Abstracts International, 58,* 4162A.

Battistani, R. (1996). The service learner as engaged citizen. *Metropolitan Universities, 7,* 86–98.

Bauer, K. (1992). Self-reported gains in academic and social skills. *Journal of College Student Development, 33,* 492–498.

Bauer, K. (1995). Freshman to senior year gains reported on the college student experiences questionnaire. *NASPA Journal, 32,* 130–137.

Bauer, K. (1996, May). *Year two of the longitudinal study of university undergraduates: Changes occurring from the freshman to sophomore year.* Paper presented at the meeting of the Association for Institutional Research, Albuquerque, NM.

Bauer, K. (1998, May). *Academic and social development of undergraduate students: Summary of findings for the UD longitudinal study, fall 1993–spring 1997.* Paper presented at the annual meeting of the Association for Institutional Research, Minneapolis, MN.

Bauer, K., & Bennett, J. (2003). Alumni perceptions used to assess undergraduate research experience. *Journal of Higher Education, 74,* 210–230.

Bauer, K., Mitchell, F., & Bauer, P. (1991). Students' perceptions of selected academic and personal characteristics acquired at community colleges. *College and University, 67,* 65–71.

Baxter Magolda, M. (1990). Gender differences in epistemological development. *Journal of College Student Development, 31,* 555–561.

Baxter Magolda, M. (1992a). Cocurricular influences on college students' intellectual development. *Journal of College Student Development, 33,* 203–213.

Baxter Magolda, M. (1992b). *Knowing and reasoning in college: Gender-related patterns in students' intellectual development.* San Francisco: Jossey-Bass.

Baxter Magolda, M. (1993, April). *The convergence of relational and impersonal knowing in young adults' epistemological development.* Paper presented at the meeting of the American Educational Research Association, Atlanta, GA.

Baxter Magolda, M. (1995). The integration of relational and impersonal knowing in young adults' epistemological development. *Journal of College Student Development, 36,* 205–216.

Baxter Magolda, M. (1998). Developing self-authorship in young adult life. *Journal of College Student Development, 39,* 143–156.

Baxter Magolda, M. (1999a). Constructing adult identities. *Journal of College Student Development, 40,* 629–644.

Baxter Magolda, M. (1999b, November). *The search for meaning in young adulthood: Implications for educational practice.* Paper presented at the meeting of the Association for the Study of Higher Education, San Antonio, TX.

Baxter Magolda, M. (1999c). The evolution of epistemology: Refining contextual knowing at twentysomething. *Journal of College Student Development, 40,* 333–344.

Baxter Magolda, M. (1999d). *Creating contexts for learning and self-authorship: Constructive-developmental pedagogy.* Nashville, TN: Vanderbilt University Press.

Baxter Magolda, M. (2000). Interpersonal maturity: Integrating agency and communion. *Journal of College Student Development, 41,* 141–156.

Baxter Magolda, M. (2001). *Making their own way: Narratives for transforming higher education to promote self-development.* Sterling, VA: Stylus.

Baxter Magolda, M., & Buckley, J. (1997, March). *Constructive-developmental pedagogy: Linking knowledge construction and students' espistemological development.* Paper presented at the meeting of the American Educational Research Association, Chicago.

Bean, J. (1980). Dropouts and turnover: The synthesis and test of a causal model of student attrition. *Research in Higher Education, 12,* 155–187.

Bean, J., & Metzner, B. (1985). A conceptual model of nontraditional undergraduate student attrition. *Review of Educational Research, 55,* 485–540.

Bebeau, M. (1994). Influencing the moral dimensions of dental practice. In J. Rest & D. Narvaez (Eds.), *Moral development in the professions: Psychology and applied ethics* (pp. 113–139). Hillsdale, NJ: Erlbaum.

Beck, S., Bennett, A., McLeod, R., & Molyneaux, D. (1992). Review of research on critical thinking in nursing education. *Review of Research in Nursing Education, 5,* 1–30.

Becker, G., Grossman, M., & Murphy, K. (1991). Rational addiction and the effect of price on consumption. *American Economic Review, 81,* 232–241.

Becker, G., & Mulligan, C. (1997). The endogenous determination of time preference. *Quarterly Journal of Economics, 112,* 729–758.

Becker, M. (1993). A medical sociologist looks at health promotion. *Journal of Health and Social Behavior, 34*(2), 1–6.

Becker, W. (1992). Why go to college? The value of an investment in higher education. In W. Becker & D. Lewis (Eds.), *The economics of American higher education* (pp. 91–120). Norwell, MA: Kluwer.

Becker, W., & Powers, J. (2001). Student performance, attrition, and class size given missing student data. *Economics of Education Review, 20,* 377–388.

Beckett, R. (1996). Critical thinking and self-efficacy in autodidactic learning: The effects of program type, self-esteem, and program characteristics. *Dissertation Abstracts International, 16,* 2551A.

Beeson, M., & Wessel, R. (2002). The impact of working on campus on the academic persistence of freshmen. *Journal of Student Financial Aid, 32,* 37–45.

Behrens, J. (1997). Does the White racial identity attitude scale measure racial identity? *Journal of Counseling Psychology, 44,* 3–12.

Behrens, J., & Rowe, W. (1997). Measuring White racial identity: A reply to Helms (1997). *Journal of Counseling Psychology, 44,* 17–19.

Behrman, J., Constantine, J., Kletzer, L., McPherson, M., & Shapiro, M. (1996). *Impacts of college quality choices on wages: Are there differences among demographic groups?* Williamstown, MA: Williams Project on the Economics of Higher Education.

Behrman, J., Kletzer, L., McPherson, M., & Schapiro, O. (1995). *How family background sequentially affects college choices: High school achievement, college enrollment and college quality* [Mimeo]. Philadelphia: University of Pennsylvania.

Behrman, J., Rosenzweig, M., & Taubman, P. (1994). Endowments and the allocation of schooling in the family and in the marriage market: The twins experiment. *Journal of Political Economy, 102,* 1131–1174.

Behrman, J., Rosenzweig, M., & Taubman, P. (1996). College choice and wages: Estimates using data on female twins. *Review of Economics and Statistics, 78,* 672–685.

Behrman, J., Sickles, R., Taubman, P., & Yazbeck, A. (1991). Black-White mortality inequalities. *Journal of Econometrics, 50,* 183–203.

Behrman, J., & Wolfe, B. (1989). Does more schooling make women better nourished and healthier? Adult sibling random and fixed effects estimates from Nicaragua. *Journal of Human Resources, 24,* 644–663.

Beil, C. (1990, May). *No exit: Predicting student persistence.* Paper presented at the meeting of the Association for Institutional Research, Louisville, KY.

Beil, C., Reisen, C., Zea, M., & Caplan, R. (1999). A longitudinal study of the effects of academic and social integration and commitment on retention. *NASPA Journal, 37,* 376–385.

Belch, H., Gebel, M., & Maas, G. (2001). Relationship between student recreation complex use, academic performance, and persistence of first-time freshmen. *NASPA Journal, 38,* 254–268.

Belcheir, M., & Michener, B. (1997, May). *Dimensions of retention: Findings from quantitative and qualitative approaches.* Paper presented at the meeting of the Association of Institutional Research, Orlando.

Belenky, M., Clinchy, B., Goldberger, N., & Tarule, J. (1986). *Women's ways of knowing: The development of self, voice, and mind.* New York: Basic Books.

Belfield, C., Bullock, A., & Fielding, A. (1999). Graduates' views on the contribution of their higher education to their general development: A retrospective evaluation for the United Kingdom. *Research in Higher Education, 40,* 409–438.

Bellas, M. (1998, April). *Investments in education: Do returns diminish with age?* Paper presented at the meeting of the American Educational Research Association, San Diego, CA.

Beller, J., & Stoll, S. (1992, Spring). A moral reasoning intervention program for student athletes. *Athletic Academic Journal,* pp. 43–57.

Beller, J., Stoll, S., Burwell, B., & Cole, J. (1996). The relationship of competition and a Christian liberal arts education on moral reasoning of college student athletes. *Research on Christian Higher Education, 3,* 99–114.

Belman, D., & Heywood, J. (1991). Sheepskin effects in the returns to education: An examination of women and minorities. *Review of Economics and Statistics, 73,* 720–724.

Bennett, C. (1995). Research on racial issues in American higher education. In J. Banks & C. McGee Banks (Eds.), *Handbook of research on multicultural education* (pp. 663–682). New York: Macmillan.

Bennett, C., & Okinaka, A. (1990, March). Factors related to persistence among Asian, Black, Hispanic, and White undergraduates at a predominantly White university: Comparison between first and fourth year cohorts. *Urban Review, 22,* 33–60.

Benton, S., Kiewra, K., Whitfall, J., & Dennison, R. (1993). Encoding and external-storage effects on writing processes. *Journal of Educational Psychology, 85,* 267–280.

Berg, D., Lonsway, K., & Fitzgerald, L. (1999). Rape prevention education for men: The effectiveness of empathy-induction techniques. *Journal of College Student Development, 40,* 219–234.

Berger, J. (1997). Students' sense of community in residence halls, social integration, and first-year persistence. *Journal of College Student Development, 38,* 441–452.

Berger, J. (1998). *Organizational behavior and student outcomes: A new perspective on college impact.* Unpublished manuscript, University of New Orleans.

Berger, J. (2000a). Optimizing capital, social reproduction, and undergraduate persistence. In J. Braxton (Ed.), *Reworking the student departure puzzle* (pp. 95–124). Nashville, TN: Vanderbilt University Press.

Berger, J. (2000b). Organizational behavior at colleges and student outcomes: A new perspective on college impact. *Review of Higher Education, 23,* 177–198.

Berger, J. (2002). The influence of the organizational structures of colleges and universities on college student learning. *Peabody Journal of Education, 77,* 40–59.

Berger, J., & Braxton, J. (1998). Revising Tinto's interactionalist theory of student departure through theory elaboration: Examining the role of organizational attributes in the persistence process. *Research in Higher Education, 39,* 103–119.

Berger, J., & Milem, J. (1999). The role of student involvement and perceptions of integration in a causal model of student persistence. *Research in Higher Education, 40,* 641–664.

Berger, J., & Milem, J. (2000a). Exploring the impact of historically Black colleges in promoting the development of undergraduates' self-concept. *Journal of College Student Development, 41,* 381–394.

Berger, J., & Milem, J. (2000b). Organizational behavior in higher education and student outcomes. In J. C. Smart (Ed.), *Higher education: Handbook of theory and research* (Vol. 15, pp. 268–338). New York: Agathon.

Berger, M. (1989). Demographic cycles, cohort size, and earnings. *Demography, 26,* 311–321.

Berger, M. (1992). Private returns to specific college majors. In W. Becker & D. Lewis (Eds.), *The economics of American higher education* (pp. 141–171). Norwell, MA: Kluwer.

Berger, M., & Leigh, J. (1989). Schooling, self-selection, and health. *Journal of Human Resources, 24,* 433–455.

Berkner, L., Berker, A., Rooney, K., & Peter, K. (2002). *Student financing of undergraduate education: 1999–2000* (Statistical Analysis Report No. NCES 2002–167). Washington, DC: U.S. Department of Education, Office of Educational Research and Improvement, National Center for Education Statistics.

Berkner, L., & Bobbitt, L. (2000). *Trends in undergraduate borrowing: Federal student loans in 1989–90, 1992–93, and 1995–96* (Statistical Analysis Report No. NCES 2000–151). Washington, DC: U.S. Department of Education, Office of Educational Research and Improvement, National Center for Education Statistics.

Berkner, L., & Chavez, L. (1997). *Access to postsecondary education for the 1992 high school graduates* (Statistical Analysis Report No. NCES 98–105). Washington, DC: U.S. Department of Education, Office of Educational Research and Improvement, National Center for Education Statistics.

Berkner, L., Cuccaro-Alamin, S., & McCormick, A. (1996). *Descriptive summary of 1989–90 beginning postsecondary students: Five years later, with an essay on postsecondary persistence and attainment* (Statistical Analysis Report No. NCES 96–155). Washington, DC: U.S. Department of Education, Office of Educational Research and Improvement, National Center for Education Statistics.

Berkner, L., He, S., & Cataldi, E. (2002). *Descriptive summary of 1995–96 Beginning Postsecondary Students: Six years later* (Statistical Analysis Report No. NCES 2003–151). Washington, DC: U.S. Department of Education, Office of Educational Research and Improvement, National Center for Education Statistics.

Bernal, M., & Knight, G. (Eds.). (1993). *Ethnic identity: Formation and transmission among Hispanics and other minorities.* Albany: State University of New York Press.

Bernardi, R. (1991). *Fraud detection: An experiment testing differences in perceived client integrity and competence, individual auditor cognitive style and experience, and accounting firms.* Unpublished doctoral dissertation, Union College, Schenectady, NY.

Bers, T., McGowan, M., & Rubin, A. (1996). The disposition to think critically among community college students: The California Critical Thinking Disposition Inventory. *Journal of General Education, 45,* 197–223.

Bers, T., & Smith, K. (1991). Persistence of community college students: The influence of student intent and academic and social integration. *Research in Higher Education, 32,* 539–556.

Berson, J., & Younkin, W. (1998, November). *Doing well by doing good: A study of the effects of a service-learning experience on student success.* Paper presented at the meeting of the Association for the Study of Higher Education, Miami.

Betz, N., & Schifano, R. (2000). Evaluation of an intervention to increase realistic self-efficacy and interests in college women. *Journal of Vocational Behavior, 56,* 35–52.

Beyler, J., & Raftery, S. (1998, April). *Reciprocal teaching: Applications for introductory college-level social sciences.* Paper presented at the meeting of the American Educational Research Association, San Diego, CA.

Biddle, B., Bank, B., & Slavings, R. (1990). Modality of thought, campus experiences, and the development of values. *Journal of Educational Psychology, 82,* 671–682.

Bieber, J. (1999). Cultural capital as an interpretive framework for faculty life. In J. Smart (Ed.), *Higher education: Handbook of theory and research* (Vol. 14, pp. 374–381). New York: Agathon.

Biggs, S., Torres, S., & Washington, N. (1998). Minority student retention: A framework for discussion and decision making. *Negro Educational Review, 49,* 71–82.

Billings, D., & Cobb, K. (1992). Effects of learning style preferences, attitude, and GPA on learner achievement using computer-assisted interactive video instruction. *Journal of Computer-Based Instruction, 19,* 12–16.

Bills, D. (2000). *Credentials, signals, and screens: Explaining the relationship between schooling and job assignment.* Unpublished manuscript, University of Iowa, Iowa City.

Bills, D. (n.d.). *Adult education and the socio-economic life cycle: How educational reentry transforms the status attainment process.* Iowa City: University of Iowa.

Bin, Y., & Lee, B. (1992). Effects of learning style in a hypermedia instructional system. In *Proceedings of selected research and development presentations at the convention of the Association for Educational Communications and Technology* (p. 5). Washington, DC: Association for Educational Communication and Technology.

Biner, P., Welsh, K., Barone, N., Summers, M., & Dean, R. (1997). The impact of remote-site group size on student satisfaction and relative performance in interactive telecourses. *American Journal of Distance Education, 11,* 23–33.

Bishop, J., & Walker, S. (1990). What role does counseling play in decisions relating to retention? *Journal of College Student Development, 31,* 88–89.

Black, B. (1994). Students' attitudes toward women: Do social work programs make a difference? *Affilia, 9,* 417–436.

Blackburn, M., & Neumark, D. (1993). Omitted-ability bias and the increase in return to schooling. *Journal of Labor Economics, 11,* 521–544.

Blau, F., & Ferber, M. (1991). Career plans and expectations of young women and men. *Journal of Human Resources, 26,* 581–607.

Blau, F., Ferber, M., & Winkler, A. (1998). *The economics of women, men, and work* (2nd ed.). Englewood Cliffs, NJ: Prentice-Hall.

Blau, P., & Duncan, O. (1967). *The American occupational structure.* New York: Free Press.

Blimling, G. (1989). A meta-analysis of the influence of college residence halls on academic performance. *Journal of College Student Development, 30,* 298–308.

Blimling, G. (1990). Developing character in college students. *NASPA Journal, 27,* 266–274.

Blimling, G. (1993). The influence of college residence halls on students. In J. Smart (Ed.), *Higher education: Handbook of theory and research* (Vol. 9, pp. 248–307). New York: Agathon.

Blimling, G. (1997). *The benefits and limitations of residential colleges: A meta-analysis of the research.* Paper presented at the Oxford Roundtable on Educational Policy. Oxford, UK: Oxford University.

Bloom, B. (1968). Learning for mastery. *Evaluation Comment, 1*(2), 1–12.

Blumberg, M., & Lester, D. (1991). High school and college students' attitudes toward rape. *Adolescence, 26,* 727–729.

Boesel, D., & Fredland, E. (1999). *College for all? Is there too much emphasis on getting a college degree?* (Research report). Washington, DC: U.S. Department of Education, Office of Educational Research and Improvement, National Library of Education.

Bohr, L. (1994–95). College courses which attract and generate good readers. *Journal of College Reading and Learning, 26*(2), 30–44.

Bohr, L., Pascarella, E., Nora, A., & Terenzini, P. (1995). Do Black students learn more at historically Black or predominantly White colleges? *Journal of College Student Development, 36,* 75–85.

Bohr, L., Pascarella, E., Nora, A., Zusman, B., Jacobs, M., Desler, M., et al. (1994). Cognitive effects of 2-year and 4-year colleges: A preliminary study. *Community College Review, 22,* 4–11.

Bonate, D., & Jessell, J. (1996). The effects of educational intervention on perceptions of sexual harassment. *Sex Roles, 35,* 751–764.

Bonawitz, M. (2002). *Analysis and comparison of the moral development of students required to graduate with an ethics course.* Unpublished doctoral dissertation, Florida Atlantic University.

Bonous-Hammarth, M. (2000). Value congruence and organizational climates for undergraduate persistence. In J. C. Smart (Ed.), *Higher education: Handbook of theory and research* (Vol. 15, pp. 339–370). New York: Agathon.

Bonsangue, M. (1991). *Achievement effects of collaborative learning in introductory statistics: A time series residual analysis.* Paper presented at the joint annual meeting of the Mathematical Association of America and the American Mathematical Society, San Francisco.

Bonsangue, M. (1994). An efficacy study of the calculus workshop model. *Research in Collegiate Mathematics Education, 1*(1), 1–19.

Bonwell, C., & Eison, J. (1991). *Active learning: Creating excitement in the classroom.* Washington, DC: ASHE-ERIC Higher Education Reports, George Washington University.

Borden, V. (2004, March/April). Accommodating student swirl: When traditional students are no longer the tradition. *Change, 36,* 10–17.

Borglum, K., & Kubala, T. (2000). Academic and social integration of community college students. *Community College Journal of Research and Practice, 24,* 567–576.

Borresen, C. (1990). Success in introductory statistics with small groups. *College Teaching, 38,* 26–82.

Boss, J. (1994). The effect of community service work on the moral development of college ethics students. *Journal of Moral Education, 23,* 183–198.

Bothan, G. (1998). Distance education: Effective learning or content-free credits. *Cause/Effect* [Online Journal], *21*(2). [Available at: http://www.educause.edu/ir/library/html/com9827.html].

Boudreau, C., & Kromrey, J. (1994). A longitudinal study of the retention and academic performance of participants in freshman orientation course. *Journal of College Student Development, 35,* 444–449.

Bound, J., & Johnson, G. (1992). Changes in the structure of wages in the 1980s: An evaluation of alternative explanations. *American Economic Review, 82,* 371–392.

Bourdieu, P. (1977a). Cultural reproduction and social reproduction. In J. Karabel & A. Halsey (Eds.), *Power and ideology in education* (pp. 487–511). New York: Oxford University Press.

Bourdieu, P. (1977b). *Outline of a theory of practice.* Cambridge, UK: Cambridge University Press.

Bourdieu, P. (1986). The forms of capital. In J. Richardson (Ed.), *Handbook of theory and research for the sociology of education* (pp. 241–258). Westport, CT: Greenwood Press.

Bourdieu, P., & Passeron, J. (1990). *Reproduction in education, society, and culture* (2nd ed.). London: Sage.

Bourne, E. (1978). The state of research on ego identity: A review and appraisal. Part 2. *Journal of Youth and Adolescence, 7,* 371–392.

Bowen, H. (1977). *Investment in learning.* San Francisco: Jossey-Bass.

Bowen, W., & Bok, D. (1998). *The shape of the river: Long-term consequences of considering race in college and university admissions.* Princeton, NJ: Princeton University Press.

Bowman, S., & Tinsley, H. (1991). The development of vocational realism in Black American college students. *Career Development Quarterly, 39,* 240–250.

Boyd, V., Friesen, F., Hunt, P., Hunt, S., Magoon, T., & Van Braunt, J. (1995). *A summer retention program for transfer-ins who were academically dismissed and applied for reinstatement: A replication* (Research Report No. 12–95). College Park: University of Maryland, Counseling Center.

Boyd, V., Friesen, F., Hunt, P., Hunt, S., Magoon, T., & Van Braunt, J. (1996). *A summer retention program for students who were academically dismissed and applied for reinstatement* (Research Report No. 13–96). College Park: University of Maryland, Counseling Center.

Boyd, V., Gurney, G., Hunt, P., Hunt, S., O'Brien, K., & Van Braunt, J. (1994). *A summer retention program for transfer-ins who were academically dismissed and applied for reinstatement* (Research Report No. 13–94). College Park: University of Maryland, Counseling Center.

Boyd, V., Hunt, P., Hunt, S., Magoon, T., Molla, B., & Van Braunt, J. (1991). *Suggesting at-risk students participate in retention-related activities* (Research Report No. 17–91). College Park: University of Maryland, Counseling Center.

Boyer Commission on Educating Undergraduates in the Research University. (1998). *Reinventing undergraduate education: A blueprint for America's research universities.* New York: Author.

Boyer, E. (1987). *The undergraduate experience in America.* New York: HarperCollins.

Boylan, H., & Bonham, B. (1992). The impact of developmental education programs. *Review of Research in Developmental Education, 9,* 1–3.

Boylan, R. (1993). The effect of the number of diplomas on their value. *Sociology of Education, 66,* 206–221.

Boyte, H. (2000). *Public engagement in a civic mission: A case study.* Washington, DC: Council on Public Policy Education.

Bradburn, E. (2002). *Short-term enrollment in postsecondary education: Student background and institutional differences in reasons for early departure, 1996–1998* (Descriptive Analysis Report No. NCES 2003–153). Washington, DC: U.S. Department of Education, Office of Educational Research and Improvement, National Center for Education Statistics.

Bradburn, E., Hurst, D., & Peng, S. (2001). *Community college transfer rates to 4-year institutions using alternative definitions of transfer* (Research and Development Report No. NCES 2001–197). Washington, DC: National Center for Education Statistics, Office of Educational Research and Improvement.

Bradburn, N., & Sudman, S. (1988). *Polls and surveys.* San Francisco: Jossey-Bass.

Bradley, J., Bryant, J., & Milborne, C. (1994). Comparing student participation in campus recreation to other aspects of campus life. In R. Clark, F. Dudenhoeffer, J. Gong, & S. Young (Eds.), *Navigating the tides of change: Strategies for success* (pp. 144–166). Corvallis, OR: National Intramural-Recreational Sports Association.

Brady, K., & Eisler, R. (1996, August). *Gender equity in the college classroom.* Paper presented at the meeting of the American Psychological Association, Toronto.

Braley, R., & Ogden, W. (1997). When failing indicates higher graduation potential. *College Student Journal, 31,* 243–250.

Brand, J., & Dodd, D. (1998). Self-esteem among college men as a function of Greek affiliation and year in college. *Journal of College Student Development, 39,* 611–615.

Braskamp, L., & Ory, J. (1994). *Assessing faculty work: Enhancing individual and institutional performance.* San Francisco: Jossey-Bass.

Braxton, J. (1993). Selectivity and rigor in research universities. *Journal of Higher Education, 64,* 657–675.

Braxton, J. (1999). Theory elaboration and research development: Toward a fuller understanding of college student retention. *Journal of College Student Retention, 1,* 93–97.

Braxton, J. (Ed.). (2000). *Reworking the student departure puzzle.* Nashville, TN: Vanderbilt University Press.

Braxton, J., & Berger, J. (1995). Reading for heuristics. *Educational Researcher, 24*(8), 32–33, 46.

Braxton, J., Bray, N., & Berger, J. (2000). Faculty teaching skills and their influences on the college student departure process. *Journal of College Student Development, 41,* 215–227.

Braxton, J., & Hirschy, A. (2004). Modifying Tinto's theory of college student departure using constructs derived from inductive theory revision. In M. Yorke & B. Longden (Eds.), *Retention and student success in higher education.* Buckingham, UK: Open University Press.

Braxton, J., Milem, J., & Sullivan, A. (2000). The influence of active learning on the college student departure process: Toward a revision of Tinto's theory. *Journal of Higher Education, 71,* 569–590.

Braxton, J., Sullivan, A., & Johnson, R. (1997). Appraising Tinto's theory of college student departure. In J. C. Smart (Ed.), *Higher education: Handbook of theory and research* (Vol. 12, pp. 107–158). New York: Agathon.

Braxton, J., Vesper, N., & Hossler, D. (1995). Expectations for college and student persistence. *Research in Higher Education, 36,* 595–612.

Bray, N., Braxton, J., & Sullivan, A. (1999). The influence of stress-related coping strategies on college student departure decisions. *Journal of College Student Development, 6,* 645–657.

Bretz, R. (1989). College grade point average as a predictor of adult success: A meta-analytic review and some additional evidence. *Public Personnel Management, 18,* 11–22.

Brewer, D., & Ehrenberg, R. (1996). Does it pay to attend an elite private college? *Research in Labor Economics, 15,* 239–271.

Brewer, D., Eide, E., & Ehrenberg, R. (1996). *Does it pay to attend an elite private college? Cross cohort evidence on the effects of college quality on earnings.* Santa Monica, CA: RAND Corporation.

Brewer, D., Eide, E., & Ehrenberg, R. (1999). Does it pay to attend an elite private college? Cross-cohort evidence on the effects of college type on earnings. *Journal of Human Resources, 34,* 104–123.

Bridgeman, B., & Lewis, C. (1994). The relationship of essay and multiple-choice scores with grades in college courses. *Journal of Educational Measurement, 31,* 37–50.

Briggs, C. (1996, October). *Differences in degree aspirations and attainment outcomes between football or basketball players and other intercollegiate athletes.* Paper presented at the meeting of the Association for the Study of Higher Education, Memphis, TN.

Brim, O., & Wheeler, S. (1966). *Socialization after childhood: Two essays.* New York: Wiley.

Bringle, R., & Hatcher, J. (1996). Implementing service learning in higher education. *Journal of Higher Education, 67,* 221–239.

Bringle, R., & Kremer, J. (1993). Evaluation of an intergenerational service learning project for undergraduates. *Educational Gerontology, 19,* 407–416.

Brint, S., & Karabel, J. (1989). *The diverted dream: Community colleges and the promise of educational opportunity in America, 1900–1985.* New York: Oxford University Press.

Briscoe, C., & LaMaster, S. (1991). Meaningful learning in college biology through concept mapping. *American Biology Teacher, 53,* 214–219.

Brodie, D. (1999, April). *Has publication bias inflated the reported correlation between student achievement and ratings of instructors?* Paper presented at the meeting of the American Educational Research Association, Montreal.

Broido, E. (2000). Constructing identity: The nature and meaning of lesbian, gay, and bisexual identities. In R. Perez, K. DeBord, & K. Bieschke (Eds.), *Handbook of counseling and psychotherapy with lesbian, gay, and bisexual clients* (pp. 13–33). Washington, DC: American Psychological Association.

Brooks, J., & Brooks, M. (1993). *In search of understanding: The case for constructivist classrooms.* Alexandria, VA: Association for Supervision and Curriculum Development.

Brooks, K., & Shepard, J. (1990). The relationship between clinical decision-making skills in nursing and general critical thinking abilities of senior nursing students in four types of nursing programs. *Journal of Nursing Education, 2,* 391–399.

Brooks-Harris, J., Heesacker, M., & Mejia-Milan, C. (1996). Changing men's male gender-role attitudes by applying the elaboration likelihood model of attitude change. *Sex Roles, 35,* 563–580.

Brooks-Leonard, C. (1991). Demographic and academic factors associated with first-to-second-term retention in a two-year college. *Community/Junior College Quarterly of Research and Practice, 15,* 57–69.

Broughton, E., & Otto, S. (1999). On-campus student employment: Intentional learning outcome. *Journal of College Student Development, 40,* 87–89.

Brown, D., & Pacini, R. (1993a). The Vassar classes of 1929–1935: Personality patterns in college and adult life. In K. Hurlbert & D. Schuster (Eds.), *Women's lives through time: Educated American women of the twentieth century* (pp. 93–116). San Francisco: Jossey-Bass.

Brown, D., & Pacini, R. (1993b). The Vassar classes of 1957 and 1958: The Ideal Student Study. In K. Hurlbert & D. Schuster (Eds.), *Women's lives through time: Educated American women of the twentieth century* (pp. 161–189). San Francisco: Jossey-Bass.

Brown, J., & Wright, D. (1998, March). *African-American students' persistence and educational attainment: A matter of person-environment interaction.* Paper presented at the meeting of the American Association for Higher Education, Atlanta, GA.

Brown, L. (1995). Lesbian identities: Concepts and issues. In A. D'Augelli & C. Patterson (Eds.), *Lesbian, gay, and bisexual identities over the life span: Psychological perspectives* (pp. 3–23). New York: Oxford University Press.

Brown, L., & Gilligan, C. (1992). *Meeting at the crossroads: Women's psychology and girls' development.* Cambridge, MA: Harvard University Press.

Bruffee, K. (1993). *Collaborative learning: Higher education interdependence, and the authority of knowledge.* Baltimore, MD: Johns Hopkins University Press.

Bryant, A., Choi, J., & Yasuno, M. (2003, November). *Understanding the religious and spiritual dimensions of students' lives in the first year of college.* Paper presented at the meeting of the Association for the Study of Higher Education, Portland, OR.

Bryant, J., & Bradley, J. (1993). Enhancing academic productivity, student development, and employment potential. *NIRSA Journal, 17*(3), 42–44.

Bucher, H., & Ragland, D. (1995). Socioeconomic indicators and mortality from coronary heart disease and cancer: A 23-year follow-up of middle-aged men. *American Journal of Public Health, 85,* 1231–1236.

Buczynski, P. (1991a). Longitudinal relations among intellectual development and identity during the first two years of college: A structural equation modeling analysis. *Research in Higher Education, 32,* 571–583.

Buczynski, P. (1991b). The relationship between identity and cognitive development in college freshmen: A structural equation modeling analysis. *Journal of College Student Development, 32,* 212–222.

Budny, D. (1994). Counselor tutorial program: A cooperative learning program for the high-risk freshman engineering courses. *Journal of the Freshman Year Experience, 6,* 29–52.

Buier, R., Butman, R., Burwell, R., & Van Wicklin, J. (1989). The critical years: Changes in moral and ethical decision making in young adults at three Christian liberal arts colleges. *Journal of Psychology and Christianity, 8,* 69–78.

Burgess, W. (1994). *The Oryx guide to distance learning.* Phoenix, AZ: Oryx Press.

Burke, G., Bild, D., Hilner, J., Folsom, A., Wagenknecht, L., & Sidney, S. (1996). Differences in weight gain in relation to race, gender, age, and education in young adults: The CARDIA study. *Ethnicity and Health, 1,* 327–335.

Burley, H., Butner, B., & Cejda, B. (2001). Dropout and stopout patterns among developmental education students in Texas community colleges. *Community College Journal of Research and Practice, 25,* 767–782.

Burmeister, S. (1995). The challenges of Supplemental Instruction (SI): Improving student grades and retention in high risk courses. In M. Maxwell (Ed.), *From access to success: A book of readings on college developmental education and learning assistance programs* (pp. 209–214). Clearwater, FL: H & H Publishing.

Burt, M. (1980). Cultural myths and support for rape. *Journal of Personality and Social Psychology, 32,* 217–230.

Busby, C., & Jackson, H. (1995). Student retention through communication: Applying D'Aprix's proactive communication model. *NASPA Journal, 32,* 98–105.

Bussema, K. (1999). Who am I? Whose am I? Identity and faith in the college years. *Research on Christian Higher Education, 6,* 1–33.

Byrne, B. (1984). The general/academic self-concept nomological network: A review of construct validation research. *Review of Educational Research, 54,* 427–456.

Cabrera, A., Castaneda, M., Nora, A., & Hengstler, D. (1992). The convergence between two theories of college persistence. *Journal of Higher Education, 63,* 143–164.

Cabrera, A., Colbeck, C., & Terenzini, P. (1998, November). *Teaching for professional competence: Instructional practices that promote development of group problem solving and design skills.* Paper presented at the meeting of the Association for the Study of Higher Education, Miami.

Cabrera, A., Colbeck, C., & Terenzini, P. (2001). Developing performance indicators for assessing classroom teaching practices and student learning: The case of engineering. *Research in Higher Education, 42,* 327–352.

Cabrera, A., & La Nasa, S. (2000). On the path to college: Three critical tasks facing America's disadvantaged. *Research in Higher Education, 42,* 119–149.

Cabrera, A., & Nora, A. (1994). College students' perceptions of prejudice and discrimination and their feelings of alienation: A construct validation approach. *Review of Education/Pedagogy/Cultural Studies, 16,* 387–409.

Cabrera, A., Nora, A., Bernal, E., Terenzini, P., & Pascarella, E. (1998, November). *Collaborative learning: Preferences, gains in cognitive and affective outcomes, and openness to diversity among college students.* Paper presented at the meeting of the Association for the Study of Higher Education, Miami.

Cabrera, A., Nora, A., & Castaneda, M. (1992). The role of finances in the persistence process: A structural model. *Research in Higher Education, 33,* 571–593.

Cabrera, A., Nora, A., & Castaneda, M. (1993). College persistence: Structural equations modeling test of an integrated model of student retention. *Journal of Higher Education, 62,* 123–139.

Cabrera, A., Nora, A., Castaneda, M., & Hengstler, D. (1990, November). *Determinants of persistence: The inclusion and testing of ability to pay factors in Tinto's Model of Student Attrition.* Paper presented at the meeting of the Association for the Study of Higher Education, Portland, OR.

Cabrera, A., Nora, A., Terenzini, P., Pascarella, E., & Hagedorn, L. (1998). *Campus racial climate and the adjustment of students to college: A comparison between White and African-American students.* Unpublished manuscript, Pennsylvania State University, University Park.

Cabrera, A., Nora, A., Terenzini, P., Pascarella, E., & Hagedorn, L. (1999). Campus racial climate and the adjustment of students to college: A comparison between White students and African-American students. *Journal of Higher Education, 70,* 134–160.

Cabrera, A., Stampen, J., & Hansen, W. (1990). Exploring the effects of ability to pay on persistence in college. *Review of Higher Education, 13,* 306–336.

Calculating the lifetime economic premium for college-educated Blacks. (1998, Summer). *Journal of Blacks in Higher Education, 20,* 60–61.

Callan, P. (1997). Stewards of opportunity: America's public community colleges. *Daedalus, 126,* 95–112.

Callaway, R., Fuller, R., & Schoenberger, R. (1996). Gender differences in employment and starting salaries of business majors during the 1980s: The impact of college-acquired characteristics. *Research in Higher Education, 37,* 599–614.

Camburn, E. (1990). College completion among students from high schools located in large metropolitan areas. *American Journal of Education, 98,* 551–569.

Campbell, J., & Blakey, L. (1995, November). *Using Astin's I-E-O model to assess the impact of early remediation in the persistence of underprepared community college students.* Paper presented at the meeting of the Association for the Study of Higher Education, Orlando.

Campbell, J., & Blakey, L. (1996, May). *Assessing the impact of early remediation in the persistence and performance of underprepared college students.* Paper presented at the meeting of the Association for Institutional Research, Albuquerque, NM.

Campbell, S., Bjorklund, S., & Colbeck, C. (1998, April). *Grouping in the dark: What college students learn about communication from participating in group problem-solving projects.* Paper presented at the meeting of the American Educational Research Association, San Diego, CA.

Campbell, T., & Campbell, D. (1997). Faculty-student mentor program: Effects on academic performance and retention. *Research in Higher Education, 38,* 727–742.

Campus Compact. (1999). *Presidents' declaration on the civic responsibility of higher education.* Providence, RI: Author.

Canabal, M. (1995). Hispanic and non-Hispanic White students attending institutions of higher education in Illinois: Implications for retention. *College Student Journal, 29,* 157–167.

Cancio, A., Silva, T., Evans, D., & Maume, D. (1997). Reconsidering the declining significance of race. *American Sociological Review, 61,* 541–556.

Candy, P., & Crebert, R. (1991). Ivory tower to concrete jungle: The difficult transition from the academy to the workplace as learning environment. *Journal of Higher Education, 62,* 570–592.

Canes, B., & Rosen, H. (1995). Following in her footsteps? Women's choices of college majors and faculty gender composition. *Industrial and Labor Relations Review, 48,* 486–504.

Carini, R., & Kuh, G. (2003). *2002 NSSE-RAND Cross-Validation Study: Some insights into the role of student engagement to learning.* Bloomington: Indiana University Center for Postsecondary Research.

Carlsen, D., & Andre, T. (1992). Use of a microcomputer simulation and conceptual change text to overcome student preconceptions about electric circuits. *Journal of Computer-Based Instruction, 19,* 105–109.

Carlson, J., Burn, B., Useem, J., & Yachimovicz, D. (1990). *Study abroad: The experience of American undergraduates.* Westport, CT: Greenwood Press.

Carlson, J., Burn, B., Useem, J., & Yachimovicz, D. (1991). *The experience of American undergraduates in Western Europe and the United States.* New York: Council on International Educational Exchange.

Carlson, J., & Schodt, D. (1995). Beyond the lecture: Case teaching and learning of economic theory. *Journal of Economic Education, 26,* 17–28.

Carnegie Foundation for the Advancement of Teaching. (1991). *Campus life: In search of community.* San Francisco: Jossey-Bass.

Carnegie Foundation for the Advancement of Teaching. (1994). *A classification of institutions of higher education.* Princeton, NJ: Carnegie Council for the Advancement of Teaching.

Carnevale, A., & Fry, R. (2000). *Crossing the great divide: Can we achieve equity when Generation Y goes to college?* Princeton, NJ: Educational Testing Service.

Carroll, D. (1989). *College persistence and degree attainment for 1980 high school graduates: Hazards for transfers, stopouts, and part-timers* (Survey Report No. CS 89–302). Washington, DC: U.S. Department of Education, Office of Educational Research and Improvement, National Center for Education Statistics.

Carter, D. (1999). The impact of institutional choice and environments on African-American and White students' degree expectations. *Research in Higher Education, 40,* 17–41.

Carter, D. (2001). *A dream deferred? Examining the degree aspirations of African American and White college students.* New York: Routledge Falmer.

Carter, D. (2002). College students' degree aspirations: A theoretical model and literature review with a focus on African-American and Latino students. In J. Smart (Ed.), *Higher education: Handbook of theory and research* (Vol. 17, pp. 129–171). New York: Agathon.

Carter, V. (1996). Do media influence learning? Revisiting the debate in the context of distance education. *Open Learning, 11,* 31–40.

Cartright, G. (1993). Do computers help students learn? *EDUTECH Report, 9.*

Carvajal, M., Bendana, D., Bozorgmanesh, A., Castillo, M., Pourmasiha, K., Rao, P., et al. (2000). Inter-gender differentials between college students' earnings expectations and the experience of recent graduates. *Economics of Education Review, 19,* 229–243.

Casas, J., & Pytluk, S. (1995). Hispanic identity development: Implications for research and practice. In J. Ponterotto, J. Casas, L. Suzuki, & C. Alexander (Eds.), *Handbook of multicultural counseling* (pp. 155–180). Thousand Oaks, CA: Sage.

Case, C., & Greeley, A. (1990). Attitudes toward racial equality. *Humboldt Journal of Social Relations, 16,* 67–94.

Casella, D., & Brougham, C. (1995). Work works: Student jobs open front doors to careers. *Journal of Career Planning and Employment, 55*(4), 24–27, 54–55.

Cash, R. (1993, May). *Assessment of study abroad programs using surveys of student participants.* Paper presented at the meeting of the Association for Institutional Research, Chicago.

Cashin, W. (1990). Students do rate different academic fields differently. In M. Theall & J. Franklin (Eds.), *Student ratings of instruction: Issues for improving practice. New Directions for Teaching and Learning,* No. 43 (pp. 113–121). San Francisco: Jossey-Bass.

Cashin, W. (1999). *Student ratings of teaching: Their uses and misuses.* Unpublished manuscript, Kansas State University, Manhattan.

Cashin, W., Downey, R., & Sixbury, G. (1994). Global and specific ratings of teaching effectiveness and their relation to course objectives: Reply to Marsh (1994). *Journal of Educational Psychology, 86,* 649–657.

Caskey, S. (1994). Learning outcomes in intensive courses. *Journal of Continuing Higher Education, 42*(2), 23–27.

Cass, V. (1979). Homosexual identity formation: A theoretical model. *Journal of Homosexuality, 4,* 219–235.

Cass, V. (1983–84). Homosexual identity: A concept in need of definition. *Journal of Homosexuality, 9,* 105–126.

Catalano, J., & Eddy, J. (1990). A national study of retention efforts at institutions with baccalaureate degree nursing programs. *NASPA Journal, 27,* 287–291.

Center for Policy Analysis. (2001). *Student borrowing in the 1990s* (ACE Issue Brief). Washington, DC: American Council on Education.

Center for Supplemental Instruction. (1998). *Review of research concerning the effectiveness of SI from the University of Missouri-Kansas City and other institutions across the United States.* Kansas City: University of Missouri-Kansas City, Author. [Retrieved March 20, 2000, from: http://www.umkc.edu/centers/cad/si/sidocs/sidata97.htm].

Centra, J. (1993). *Reflective faculty evaluation: Enhancing teaching and determining faculty effectiveness.* San Francisco: Jossey-Bass.

Chaney, B., Burgdorf, K., & Atash, N. (1997). Influencing achievement through high school graduation. *Educational Evaluation and Policy Analysis, 19,* 229–244.

Chaney, B., Muraskin, L., Cahalan, M., & Goodwin, D. (1998). Helping the progress of disadvantaged students in higher education: The federal Student Support Services program. *Educational Evaluation and Policy Analysis, 20,* 197–215.

Chang, M. (1996). *Racial diversity in higher education: Does a racially mixed student population affect educational outcomes?* Unpublished doctoral dissertation, University of California, Los Angeles.

Chang, M. (1997, November). *Racial diversity: A compelling interest for higher education.* Paper presented at the meeting of the Association for the Study of Higher Education, Albuquerque, NM.

Chang, M. (1999a). Does racial diversity matter?: The educational impact of a racially diverse undergraduate population. *Journal of College Student Development, 40,* 377–395.

Chang, M. (1999b, November). *The impact of an undergraduate diversity course requirement on students' level of racial prejudice.* Paper presented at the meeting of the Association for the Study of Higher Education, San Antonio, TX.

Chang, M. (2000a, November). *Is it more than about getting along? The broader educational implications of reducing students' racial biases.* Paper presented at the meeting of the Association for the Study of Higher Education, Sacramento, CA.

Chang, M. (2000b, Winter). Measuring the impact of a diversity requirement on students' level of racial prejudice. *Diversity Digest,* pp. 6–7.

Chang, M. (2001). The positive educational effects of racial diversity on campus. In G. Orfield (Ed.), *Diversity challenged: Evidence on the impact of affirmative action* (pp. 175–186). Cambridge, MA: Harvard Education Publishing Group.

Chartrand, J. (1992). An empirical test of a model of nontraditional student adjustment. *Journal of Counseling Psychology, 39,* 193–202.

Cheatham, H., Slaney, R., & Coleman, N. (1990). Institutional effects on the psychosocial development of African-American college students. *Journal of Counseling Psychology, 37,* 453–458.

Cheng, D. (2001). Assessing student collegiate experience: Where do we begin? *Assessment & Evaluation in Higher Education, 26,* 525–538.

Cheng, D., & Chen, S. (1999, May). *Factors affecting grading practices.* Paper presented at the meeting of the Association for Institutional Research, Seattle, WA.

Cheng, H., Lehman, J., & Armstrong, P. (1991). Comparison of performance and attitude in traditional and computer conferencing classes. *American Journal of Distance Education, 5*(3), 51–64.

Cherry, C., DeBerg, G., & Porterfield, A. (2001). *Religion on campus.* Chapel Hill: University of North Carolina Press.

Chesler, H. (1994). Tell them that a "pure" liberal arts degree is marketable. *Journal of Career Planning and Employment, 54,* 50–53.

Chickering, A. (1969). *Education and identity.* San Francisco: Jossey-Bass.

Chickering, A., & Gamson, Z. (1987). Seven principles for good practice in undergraduate education. *AAHE Bulletin, 39*(7), 3–7.

Chickering, A., & Gamson, Z. (1991). *Applying the seven principles for good practice in undergraduate education.* San Francisco: Jossey-Bass.

Chickering, A., & Reisser, L. (1993). *Education and identity* (2nd ed.). San Francisco: Jossey-Bass.

Chizmar, J., & Ostrosky, A. (1998). The one-minute paper: Some empirical findings. *Journal of Economic Education, 29,* 1–10.

Chmielewski, T., & Dansereau, D. (1998). Enhancing the recall of text: Knowledge mapping training promotes implicit transfer. *Journal of Educational Psychology, 90,* 407–413.

Choney, S., Berryhill-Paapke, E., & Robbins, R. (1995). The acculturation of American Indians: Developing frameworks for research and practice. In J. Ponterotto, J. Casas, L. Suzuki, & C. Alexander (Eds.), *Handbook of multicultural counseling* (pp. 73–92). Thousand Oaks, CA: Sage.

Choy, S. (1999). *College access and affordability.* Washington, DC: U.S. Department of Education, National Center for Education Statistics.

Choy, S. (2000a). *Low-income students: Who they are and how they pay for their education* (Statistical Analysis Report No. NCES 2000–169). Washington, DC: U.S. Department of Education, Office of Educational Research and Improvement, National Center for Education Statistics.

Choy, S. (2000b). *Debt burden four years after college* (Statistical Analysis Report No. NCES 2000–188). Washington, DC: U.S. Department of Education, Office of Educational Research and Improvement, National Center for Education Statistics.

Choy, S. (2001). Students whose parents did not go to college: Postsecondary access, persistence, and attainment. In J. Wirt, S. Choy, D. Gerald, S. Provasnik, P. Rooney, S. Watanabe, R. Tobin, & M. Glander (Eds.), *The condition of education 2001* (pp. xvii–xliii). Washington, DC: U.S. Department of Education.

Choy, S. (2002a). *Access & persistence: Findings from 10 years of longitudinal research on students.* Washington, DC: American Council on Education.

Choy, S. (2002b). Nontraditional undergraduates. In J. Wirt, S. Choy, D. Gerald, S. Provasnik, P. Rooney, S. Watanabe, & R. Tobin (Eds.), *The condition of education 2002* (pp. 25–39). Washington, DC: U.S. Department of Education, National Center for Education Statistics.

Choy, S., & Premo, M. (1996). *How low-income undergraduates financed postsecondary education: 1992–93* (Statistical Analysis Report No. NCES 96–161). Washington, DC: U.S. Department of Education, Office of Educational Research and Improvement, National Center for Education Statistics.

Christie, N., & Dinham, S. (1991). Institutional and external influences on social integration in the freshman year. *Journal of Higher Education, 62,* 412–436.

Christie, R. (1999). The net effects of institutional type on baccalaureate degree attainment: A study of the sophomore cohort of the 1980 NCES High School and Beyond data. *Dissertation Abstracts International, 59,* 3750A.

Chronicle of Higher Education. Almanac Issue. (1995, September 1). *42.*

Cibik, M., & Chambers, S. (1991). Similarities and differences among Native Americans, Hispanics, Blacks, and Anglos. *NASPA Journal, 28,* 129–139.

Cini, M., & Fritz, J. (1996). *Predicting commitment in adult and traditional-age students: Applying Rusbult's investment model to the study of retention.* Pittsburg, PA: Duquesne University.

Civian, J., & Schley, S. (1996, April). *Pathways for women in the sciences II: Retention in math and science at the college level.* Paper presented at the meeting of the American Educational Research Association, New York.

Clagett, C. (1996, May). *Correlates of success in the community college: Using research to inform campus retention efforts.* Paper presented at the meeting of the Association for Institutional Research, Albuquerque, NM.

Clark, A., & Oswald, A. (1994). Unhappiness and unemployment. *Economic Journal, 104,* 648–659.

Clark, B. (1960). The "cooling-out" function in higher education. *American Journal of Sociology, 65,* 569–576.

Clark, F., & Anderson, G. (1992). Benefits adults experience through participation in continuing higher education. *Higher Education, 24,* 379–390.

Clark, M., & Caffarella, R. (Eds.). (1999). *An update on adult development theory: New ways of thinking about the life course. New Directions for Adult and Continuing Education,* No. 84. San Francisco: Jossey-Bass.

Clark, R. (1991). When researchers swim upstream: Reflections on an unpopular argument about learning from media. *Educational Technology, 31,* 34–38.

Clark, R. (1994). Media will never influence learning. *Educational Technology, Research, and Development, 42,* 21–29.

Clark-Thayer, S. (1987). The relationship of the knowledge of student-perceived learning style preferences and study habits and attitudes to achievement of college freshmen in a small urban university. *Dissertation Abstracts International, 48,* 872A.

Cleveland-Innes, M. (1994). Adult student drop-out at postsecondary institutions. *Review of Higher Education, 17,* 423–445.

Cliburn, J. (1990). Concepts to promote meaningful learning. *Journal of College Science Teaching, 19,* 212–217.

Clotfelter, C. (1991). Financial aid and public policy. In C. Clotfelter, R. Ehrenberg, M. Getz, & J. Siegfried (Eds.), *Economic challenges in higher education* (pp. 89–123). Chicago: University of Chicago Press.

Clowes, D. (1992). Remediation in American higher education. In J. Smart (Ed.), *Higher education: Handbook of theory and research* (Vol. 8, pp. 460–493). New York: Agathon.

Cofer, J. (n.d.). *A comparison of persistence by income level: 1987 and 1996.* Unpublished manuscript, University of Missouri, St. Louis, Office of Finance and Administration.

Cofer, J., & Somers, P. (1998, April). *A comparison of the influence of debt load on the persistence of students at public and private colleges.* Paper presented at the meeting of the American Educational Research Association, San Diego, CA.

Cofer, J., & Somers, P. (1999a). An analytical approach to understanding student debt load response. *Journal of Student Financial Aid, 29,* 25–44.

Cofer, J., & Somers, P. (1999b, June). Deeper in debt: The impact of the 1992 Reauthorization of the Higher Education Act on within-year persistence. Paper presented at the meeting of the Association for Institutional Research, Seattle, WA.

Cofer, J., & Somers, P. (2000). Within-year persistence of students at two-year colleges. *Community College Journal of Research and Practice, 24,* 785–807.

Cofer, J., & Somers, P. (2001). What influences student persistence at two-year colleges? *Community College Review, 29,* 56–76.

Cofer, J., & Somers, P. (n.d.). *A comparison of persistence in two- and four-year colleges.* Unpublished manuscript. St. Louis: University of Missouri, Office of Finance and Administration.

Cohen, A., & Brawer, F. (1996). *The American community college* (3rd ed.). San Francisco: Jossey-Bass.

Cohen, J. (1988). *Statistical power analysis for the behavioral sciences* (2nd ed.). Hillsdale, NJ: Erlbaum.

Cohen, J., & Kinsey, D. (1994). "Doing good" and scholarship: A service-learning study. *Journalism Educator, 48,* 4–14.

Cohen, P. (1980). Effectiveness of student rating feedback for improving college instruction. *Research in Higher Education, 13,* 321–341.

Cohen, P., & Daganay, L. (1992). Computer-based instruction and health profession education. *Evaluation & the Health Profession, 15,* 259–281.

Cohen, R., & Alwin, D. (1993). Bennington women of the 1930s: Political attitudes over the life course. In K. Hulbert & D. Schuster (Eds.), *Women's lives through time: Educated American women of the twentieth century* (pp. 117–139). San Francisco: Jossey-Bass.

Cohn, E., & Geske, T. (1992). Private nonmonetary returns to investment in higher education. In W. Becker & D. Lewis (Eds.), *The economics of American higher education* (pp. 173–195). Norwell, MA: Kluwer.

Cohn, E., & Hughes, W. (1994). A benefit-cost analysis of investment in college education in the United States: 1969–1985. *Economics of Education Review, 13,* 109–123.

Cohn, E., & Rhine, S. (1989). Foregone earnings of college students in the U.S., 1970 and 1979: A microanalytic approach. *Higher Education, 18,* 681–695.

Cokley, K. (1999). Reconceptualizing the impact of college racial composition on African-American students' racial identity. *Journal of College Student Development, 40,* 235–246.

Colarelli, S., Dean, R., & Konstans, C. (1991). Relationship between university characteristics and early job outcomes of accountants. *Canadian Journal of Higher Education, 21*(3), 24–46.

Colbeck, C., Cabrera, A., & Terenzini, P. (2001). Learning professional confidence: Linking teaching practices, students' self-perceptions, and gender. *Review of Higher Education, 24,* 173–191.

Colby, A., Ehrlich, T., Beaumont, E., & Stephens, J. (2002). Moral and civic development during college. *peerReview, 4,* 23–26.

Colby, A., Ehrlich, T., Beaumont, E., & Stephens, J. (2003). *Educating citizens: Preparing America's undergraduates for lives of moral and civic responsibility.* San Francisco: Jossey-Bass.

Colby, A., Kohlberg, L., Gibbs, J., & Lieberman, M. (1983). A longitudinal study of moral judgment. *Society for Research on Child Development Monograph, 48*(1–2, Serial No. 200).

Cole, S., Barber, E., Bolyard, M., & Linders, A. (1999). *Increasing faculty diversity: The occupational choices of high achieving minority students* (Report to the Council of Ivy Group Presidents). Stony Brook: State University of New York, Department of Sociology.

College affordability concerns of college freshmen greatest in 30 years. (1996, May). *Postsecondary Education OPPORTUNITY,* No. 46, 1–6.

College Board. (2001). *Trends in student aid: 2001.* New York: Author.

College continuation rates for recent high school graduates reached record high in 1996. (1997, August). *Postsecondary Education OPPORTUNITY,* No. 62, 1–9.

College Entrance Examination Board. (1994). *The college handbook, 1993–94* (31st ed.). New York: Author.

Collier, P. (2000). The effects of completing a capstone course on student identity. *Sociology of Education, 73,* 285–299.

Collins, A., White, B., & O'Brien, T. (1992). The relationship of cognitive style and selected characteristics of vocational education teachers. *College Student Journal, 26,* 167–173.

Collins, J. (2002). *A true experiment comparing learning outcomes of a two-way interactive (audio and video) telecourse and a traditional face-to-face course.* Unpublished doctoral dissertation, University of Iowa, Iowa City.

Cone, A. (1991). Sophomore academic retention associated with a freshman study skills and college adjustment course. *Psychological Reports, 69,* 312–314.

Congos, D., Langsam, D., & Schoeps, N. (1997). Supplemental Instruction: A successful approach to learning how to learn college introductory biology. *Journal of Teaching and Learning, 2*(1), 2–17.

Conklin, K. (1990). Assessment of institutional effectiveness: Career student outcomes. *Community/Junior College Quarterly of Research and Practice, 14,* 349–357.

Connolly, F., Eisenberg, T., Hunt, N., & Wiseman, C. (1991). The consensor classroom and knowledge retention. *Educational Technology, 31*(10), 51–55.

Conrad, D., & Hedin, D. (1991). School-based community service: What we know from research and theory. *Phi Delta Kappan, 72,* 743–749.

Consortium for Student Retention Data Exchange. (2002). *2001–02 CSRDE report: Retention and graduation rates in 360 colleges and universities.* Norman: University of Oklahoma, Center for Institutional Data Exchange and Analysis.

Constantine, J. (1994). The "added value" of historically Black colleges. *Academe, 80,* 12–17.

Constantine, J. (1995). The effect of attending historically Black colleges and universities on future wages of Black students. *Industrial and Labor Relations Review, 48,* 531–546.

Constantinople, A. (1969). An Eriksonian measure of personality development in college students. *Developmental Psychology, 1,* 357–372.

Cook, L. (1991). Learning style awareness and academic achievement among community college students. *Community/Junior College Quarterly of Research and Practice, 15,* 419–425.

Cooper, D., Healy, M., & Simpson, J. (1994). Student development through involvement: Specific changes over time. *Journal of College Student Development, 35,* 98–102.

Cooper, J., & Robinson, P. (1997). *Annotated bibliography of science, mathematics, engineering, and technology resources in higher education.* Los Angeles: California State University, Dominguez Hills.

Cooper, J., Robinson, P., & McKinney, M. (1994). Cooperative learning in the classroom. In D. Halpern & Associates (Eds.), *Changing college classrooms: New teaching and learning strategies for an increasingly complex world* (pp. 74–92). San Francisco: Jossey-Bass.

Cooper, S., & Cohn, E. (1997). Internal rates of return to college education in the United States by sex and race. *Journal of Education Finance, 23,* 101–133.

Coopersmith, S. (1967). *The antecedents of self-esteem.* New York: W. H. Freeman.

Corman, J., Barr, L., & Caputo, T. (1992). Unpacking attrition: A change of emphasis. *Canadian Journal of Higher Education, 23,* 14–27.

Cornelius, A. (1995). The relationship between athletic identity, peer and faculty socialization, and college student development. *Journal of College Student Development, 36,* 560–573.

Cornelius, R., Gray, J., & Constantinople, A. (1990). Student-faculty interaction in the college classroom. *Journal of Research and Development in Education, 23,* 189–197.

Cottell, P. (1996). A union of collaborative learning and cooperative learning: An overview of this issue. *Journal on Excellence in College Teaching, 7,* 1–3.

Cram, S. (1998). *The impact of service-learning on moral development and self-esteem of community college ethics students.* Unpublished doctoral dissertation, University of Iowa, Iowa City.

Crandall, C., Tsang, J., Goldman, S., & Pennington, J. (1999). Newsworthy moral dilemmas: Justice, caring, and gender. *Sex Roles, 40,* 187–209.

Creighton, J., & Harwood, R. (1993). *College students talk politics* (Report prepared by The Harwood Group). Dayton, OH: Kettering Foundation.

Cress, C., Astin, H., Zimmerman-Oster, K., & Burkhardt, J. (2001). Developmental outcomes of college students' involvement in leadership activities. *Journal of College Student Development, 42,* 15–27.

Criner, L. (1992). Teaching thinking and reasoning: A study of critical thinking in adults. *Dissertation Abstracts International, 53,* 2643A.

Crook, D., & Lavin, D. (1989, March). *The community college effect revisited: The long-term impact of community college entry on BA attainment.* Paper presented at the meeting of the American Educational Research Association, San Francisco.

Crosby, F., Allen, B., Culbertson, T., Wally, C., Morith, J., Hall, R., et al. (1994). Taking selectivity into account: How much does gender composition matter? *National Women's Studies Association Journal, 6,* 107–118.

Cross, K. (1998, July/August). Why learning communities? Why now? *About Campus, 3,* 4–11.

Cross, K. (1999). What do we know about students' learning, and how do we know it? *Innovative Higher Education, 23,* 255–270.

Cross, L., Frary, R., & Weber, L. (1993). College grading: Achievement attitudes and effort. *College Teaching, 41,* 143–148.

Cross, W., Jr. (1971a). Discovering the Black referent: The psychology of Black liberation. In J. Dixon & B. Foster (Eds.), *Beyond Black or White.* Boston: Little, Brown.

Cross, W., Jr. (1971b). The Negro-to-Black conversion experience: Toward a psychology of Black liberation. *Black World, 20,* 13–27.

Cross, W., Jr. (1980). Models of psychological nigrescence: A literature review. In R. Jones (Ed.), *Black psychology* (2nd ed.). New York: HarperCollins.

Cross, W., Jr. (1991). *Shades of Black: Diversity in African-American identity.* Philadelphia: Temple University Press.

Cross, W., Jr. (1995). The psychology of nigrescence: Revising the Cross model. In J. Ponterotto, J. Casas, L. Suzuki, & C. Alexander (Eds.), *Handbook of multicultural counseling.* Thousand Oaks, CA: Sage.

Crosson, P. (1992). Environmental influences on minority degree attainment. *Equity & Excellence in Education, 25,* 5–15.

Croteau, J., & Kusek, M. (1992). Gay and lesbian speaker panels: Implementation and research. *Journal of Counseling & Development, 70,* 396–401.

Crow, S., Fok, L., Hartman, S., & Payne, D. (1991). Gender and values: What is the impact on decision making? *Sex Roles, 25,* 255–268.

Crum, R., Helzer, J., & Anthony, J. (1993). Level of education and alcohol abuse and dependence in adulthood: A further inquiry. *American Journal of Public Health, 83,* 830–837.

Cuccaro-Alamin, S. (1997). *Findings from Condition of Education 1997: Postsecondary persistence and attainment* (No. NCES 97–984). Washington, DC: U.S. Department of Education, Office of Educational Research and Improvement, National Center for Education Statistics.

Cuccaro-Alamin, S., & Choy, S. (1998). *Postsecondary financing strategies: How undergraduates combine work, borrowing, and attendance* (Statistical Analysis Report No. NCES 98–088). Washington, DC: U.S. Department of Education, Office of Educational Research and Improvement, National Center for Education Statistics.

Cullivan, K. (1990). *Issues of quality in short-term summer sessions.* Paper presented at the 41st Annual Conference of the North Central Conference on Summer Schools, Chicago.

Cummings, R., Dyas, L., & Maddux, C. (2001). Principled moral reasoning and behavior of preservice teacher education students. *American Educational Research Journal, 38,* 143–158.

Cunningham, C., Delci, M., & Goodman, I. (2001, April). *Undergraduate engineering women's participation in engineering support activities and their perception of the supportiveness of the engineering department.* Paper presented at the meeting of the American Educational Research Association, Seattle, WA.

Cupp, L. (1991, October). *Acquiring new perspectives: The impact of education on adult students in a traditional university.* Paper presented at the meeting of the American Association for Adult and Continuing Education, Montreal.

Cuseo, J. (1992). Collaborative and cooperative learning in higher education: A proposed taxonomy. *Cooperative Learning and College Teaching, 2*(2), 2–4.

Cuseo, J. (2002). *Gaining and sustaining support for the first-year seminar: Empirical evidence, logical arguments, and persuasive strategies.* Unpublished manuscript, Marymount College, Verdes, CA.

Cuseo, J. (2003). *Academic advisement and student retention: Empirical connections and systemic interventions.* [Retrieved February 13, 2003, from: First-Year Assessment (FYA) Listserv Series: http://www.brevard.edu/fyc/listserv/remarks/cuseorentation.htm].

Dale, P., Ballotti, D., Handa, S., & Zych, T. (1997). An approach to teaching problem solving in the classroom. *College Student Journal, 31,* 76–79.

Dale, S., & Krueger, A. (1999). *Estimating the payoff to attending a more selective college: An application of selection on observables and unobservables.* Unpublished manuscript, Andrew Mellon Foundation, Princeton, NJ.

Daly, B. (1990). The Kentucky retention model for community colleges. *Community College Journal for Research and Planning, 7,* 5–21.

Daniel, E. (2000). A review of time-shortened courses across disciplines. *College Student Journal, 34,* 298–308.

Daniel, K., Black, D., & Smith, J. (1996a). *College characteristics and the wages of young women.* Stanford, CA: National Center for Postsecondary Improvement.

Daniel, K., Black, D., & Smith, J. (1996b). *College quality and the wages of young men.* Stanford, CA: National Center for Postsecondary Improvement.

Dannefer, D. (1984a). Adult development and social theory: A paradigmatic reappraisal. *American Sociological Review, 49,* 100–116.

Dannefer, D. (1984b). The role of the social in life-span developmental psychology, past and future: Rejoinder to Baltes and Nesselroade. *American Sociological Review, 49,* 847–850.

Dansereau, D. (1995). Derived structural schemas and the transfer of knowledge. In A. McKeough, J. Lupart, & A. Marini (Eds.), *Teaching for transfer: Fostering generalization in learning.* Hillsdale, NJ: Erlbaum.

Dansereau, D., & Newbern, D. (1997). Using knowledge maps to enhance learning. In W. Campbell & K. Smith (Eds.), *New paradigms for college teaching* (pp. 125–147). Edina, MN: Interaction Books.

d'Apollonia, S., & Abrami, P. (1997a). Navigating student ratings of instruction. *American Psychologist, 52,* 1198–1208.

d'Apollonia, S., & Abrami, P. (1997b). Scaling the ivory tower, Part II: Student ratings of instruction in North America. *Psychology Teaching Review, 6,* 60–77.

d'Apollonia, S., Abrami, P., & Rosenfield, S. (1993, April). *The dimensionality of student ratings of instruction: A meta-analysis of the factor studies.* Paper presented at the meeting of the American Educational Research Association, Atlanta, GA.

Darrow, S., Russell, M., Copper, M., Mudar, P., & Frone, M. (1992). Sociodemographic correlates of alcohol consumption among African-American and White women. *Women and Health, 18,* 35–51.

D'Augelli, A. (1991). Gay men in college: Identity processes and adaptations. *Journal of College Student Development, 32,* 140–146.

D'Augelli, A. (1994a). Identity development and sexual orientation: Toward a model of lesbian, gay, and bisexual development. In E. Trickett, R. Watts, & D. Birman (Eds.), *Human diversity: Perspectives on people in context* (pp. 312–333). San Francisco: Jossey-Bass.

D'Augelli, A. (1994b). Lesbian and gay male development: Steps toward an analysis of lesbians' and gay men's lives. In B. Greene & G. Herek (Eds.), *Psychological perspectives on lesbian and gay issues: Vol. 1. Lesbian and gay psychology: Theory, research, and clinical implications* (pp. 118–132). Thousand Oaks, CA: Sage.

D'Augelli, A., & Hershberger, S. (1995). A multi-year analysis of changes in AIDS concerns and homophobia on a university campus. *Journal of American College Health, 44,* 3–10.

D'Augelli, A., & Patterson, C. (Eds.). (1995). *Lesbian, gay, and bisexual identities over the life span: Psychological perspectives.* New York: Oxford University Press.

D'Augelli, A., & Rose, M. (1990). Homophobia in a university community: Attitudes and experiences of heterosexual freshmen. *Journal of College Student Development, 31,* 484–491.

Davies, S., & Guppy, N. (1997). Fields of study, college selectivity, and student inequalities in higher education. *Social Force, 75,* 1417–1438.

Davis, J. (1966). The campus as frog pond: An application of the theory of relative deprivation to career decisions of college men. *American Journal of Sociology, 81,* 491–513.

Davis, T., & Murrell, P. (1993). A structural model of perceived academic, personal, and vocational gains related to college student responsibility. *Research in Higher Education, 34,* 267–289.

DeBord, K., Wood, D., Sher, K., & Good, G. (1997). *The relevance of sexual orientation to substance abuse and psychological distress among college students.* Unpublished manuscript, University of Missouri, Columbia.

DeBrock, L., Hendricks, W., & Loenker, R. (1996). The economics of persistence: Graduation rates of athletes as labor market choice. *Journal of Human Resources, 31,* 513–539.

DeClute, J., & Ladyshewsky, R. (1993). Enhancing clinical competence using a collaborative clinical education model. *Physical Therapy, 73,* 683–697.

DeNeve, K., & Heppner, M. (1997). Role play simulations: The assessment of an active learning technique and comparisons with traditional lectures. *Innovative Higher Education, 21,* 231–246.

DePree, J. (1998, Fall). Small-group instruction: Impact on basic algebra students. *Journal of Developmental Education, 22,* 2 ff.

Derryberry, W., & Thoma, S. (2000). The friendship effect: Its role in the development of moral thinking in students. *About Campus, 5*(2), 13–18.

Desai, S. (1987). The estimation of the health production function for low-income working men. *Medical Care, 25,* 604–615.

DesJardins, S. (1996). Using event history modeling to study the temporal dimensions of student departure from college. *Dissertation Abstracts International, 57A,* 3759A.

DesJardins, S. (2002–2003). Event history methods: Conceptual issues and an application to student departure from college. In J. Smart (Ed.), *Higher education: Handbook of theory and research* (Vol. 18, pp. 421–471). New York: Agathon.

DesJardins, S., Ahlburg, D., & McCall, B. (1994, May). *Studying the determinants of student stopout: Identifying "true" from spurious time varying effects.* Paper presented at the meeting of the Association for Institutional Research, New Orleans.

DesJardins, S., Ahlburg, D., & McCall, B. (1997, May). *Using event history methods to model the different modes of student departure from college.* Paper presented at the meeting of the Association for Institutional Research, Orlando.

DesJardins, S., Ahlburg, D., & McCall, B. (1999a, June). *Investigating factors related to timely degree completion.* Paper presented at the meeting of the Association for Institutional Research, Seattle, WA.

DesJardins, S., Ahlburg, D., & McCall, B. (1999b). An event history model of student departure. *Economics of Education Review, 18,* 375–390.

DesJardins, S., Ahlburg, D., & McCall, B. (2002a, in press). Simulating the longitudinal effects of changes in financial aid on student departure from college. *Journal of Human Resources, 37,* 653–679.

DesJardins, S., Ahlburg, D., & McCall, B. (2002b). A temporal investigation of the factors related to timely degree completion. *Journal of Higher Education, 73,* 555–581.

DesJardins, S., Kim, D., & Rzonca, C. (2002–2003). A nested analysis of factors affecting bachelor's degree completion. *Journal of College Student Retention, 4,* 407–435.

DesJardins, S., McCall, B., Ahlburg, D., & Moye, M. (2002). Adding a timing light to the "Toolbox." *Research in Higher Education, 43,* 83–114.

DesJardins, S., & Pontiff, H. (1999). *Tracking institutional leavers: An application* (AIR Professional File, No. 71). Tallahassee, FL: Association for Institutional Research.

DeSousa, D., & King, P. (1992). Are White students really more involved in collegiate experiences than Black students? *Journal of College Student Development, 33,* 363–369.

DeSousa, D., & Kuh, G. (1996). Does institutional racial composition make a difference in what Black students gain from college? *Journal of College Student Development, 37,* 257–267.

de Tocqueville, A. (1966). *Democracy in America.* New York: HarperCollins. (Originally published 1835.)

Dewar, D. (1998). Do those with more formal education have better health insurance opportunities? *Economics of Education Review, 17,* 267–277.

Dexter, D. (1995). *Student performance-based outcomes of televised community college distance education.* Unpublished doctoral dissertation, Colorado State University, Fort Collins.

Dey, E. (1990, April). *Evaluating college student retention: Comparative national data from the 1981–1984 entering freshman classes.* Paper presented at the meeting of the American Educational Research Association, Boston.

Dey, E. (1991, March). *Community service and critical thinking: An exploratory analysis of collegiate influences.* Paper presented at the meeting of the conference "Setting the Agenda for an Effective Research Strategy for Combining Service and Learning in the 1990s," Racine, WI.

Dey, E. (1996). Undergraduate political attitudes: An examination of peer, faculty, and social influences. *Research in Higher Education, 37,* 535–554.

Dey, E. (1997). Undergraduate political attitudes: Peer influence in changing social contexts. *Journal of Higher Education, 68,* 398–413.

Dey, E., & Astin, A. (1989). *Predicting college student retention: Comparative national data from the 1982 freshman class* (Research report). Los Angeles: University of California, Higher Education Research Institute.

Dey, E., Wimsatt, L., Rhee, B., & Waterson, E. (1998, November). *Long-term effect of college quality on the occupational status of students.* Paper presented at the meeting of the Association for the Study of Higher Education, Miami.

Diaz, H., Gonyea, B., Junck, D., & Ward, E. (1998, Spring). Assessment of student-athlete involvement in a university residence hall. *Journal of the Indiana University Student Personnel Association,* pp. 39–49.

Dickson, C. (1990). *Goals and career choices of Smith women vs. women at Trinity, Wesleyan, Hamilton, and Grinnell.* Unpublished manuscript, Smith College, Northampton, MA.

Dietsche, P. (1990). Freshman attrition in a college of applied arts and technology of Ontario. *Canadian Journal of Higher Education, 20,* 65–84.

Dillon, A., & Gabbard, R. (1998). Hypermedia as an educational technology: A review of the quantitative research literature on learner comprehension, control, and style. *Review of Educational Research, 68,* 322–349.

Dillon, P., & Van Riper, R. (1993). Students teaching students: A model for service and study. *Equity and Excellence in Education, 26*(2), 48–52.

Dober, R. (1992). *Campus design.* New York: Wiley.

Dolan, R., & Schmidt, R. (1994). Modeling institutional production of higher education. *Economics of Education Review, 13,* 197–213.

Dollar, R. (1991). College influences on analytical thinking and communication skills of part-time versus full-time students. *College Student Journal, 25,* 273–279.

Doran, M. (1994). *Effects of individual, cooperative, and collaborative learning structures using a computer simulation in accounting.* Unpublished doctoral dissertation, Arizona State University, Phoenix.

Dori, Y., & Yochim, J. (1994). Human physiology: Improving students' achievements through intelligent studyware. *Journal of Science Education and Technology, 3,* 263–269.

Dougherty, K. (1994). *The contradictory college.* Albany: State University of New York Press.

Douvan, E., & Adelson, J. (1966). *The adolescent experience.* New York: Wiley.

Douzenis, C. (1996). The relationship of quality of effort and estimate of knowledge gain among community college students. *Community College Review, 24,* 27–35.

Douzenis, C., & Murrell, P. (1992, May). *An analysis of students' experiences at selected community colleges in Tennessee: Findings from the Community College Student Experience Questionnaire.* Paper presented at the meeting of the Association for Institutional Research, Atlanta, GA.

Dowd, A. (1999, April). *Collegiate grading practices and the gender gap.* Paper presented at the annual meeting of the American Educational Research Association, Montreal.

Dowdall, G., Crawford, M., & Wechsler, H. (1998). Binge drinking among American college women: A comparison of single-sex and coeducational institutions. *Psychology of Women Quarterly, 22,* 705–715.

Downing, N., & Roush, K. (1985). From passive acceptance to active commitment: A model of feminist identity development for women. *Counseling Psychologist, 13,* 695–709.

Doyle, S., Edison, M., & Pascarella, E. (1998, November). *The "seven principles of good practice in undergraduate education" as process indicators of cognitive development in college: A longitudinal study.* Paper presented at the meeting of the Association for the Study of Higher Education, Miami.

Drew, D., Meyer, L., & Peregrine, P. (1996). Effects of study abroad on conceptualizations of national groups. *College Student Journal, 30,* 452–461.

Drew, D., & Weaver, D. (1991). Voter learning in the 1988 presidential election: Did the debate and the media matter? *Journalism Quarterly, 68,* 27–37.

Drouin, L. (1992). An investigation of the critical thinking ability of engineering students seeking a bachelor of science degree. *Dissertation Abstracts International, 53,* 1070A.

DuBrock, C., & Fenske, R. (2000, May). *Financial aid and college persistence: A five-year longitudinal study of 1993 and 1994 beginning freshmen students.* Paper presented at the meeting of the Association for Institutional Research, Cincinnati, OH.

Duckett, L., Rowan-Boyer, M., Ryden, M., Crisham, P., Savik, K., & Rest, J. (1992). Challenging misperceptions about nurses' moral reasoning. *Nursing Research, 41,* 324–331.

Duckett, L., & Ryden, M. (1994). Education for ethical nursing practice. In J. Rest & D. Narvaez (Eds.), *Moral development in the professions: Psychology and applied ethics* (pp. 48–66). Hillsdale, NJ: Erlbaum.

Dukes, R., Johnson, R., & Newton, H. (1991). Long-term effects of travel and study: The semester-at-sea program. *Psychological Reports, 68,* 563–570.

Dunn, K., Dunn, R., Deckinger, E., Withers, P., & Katzenstein, H. (1990). Should college students be taught how to do homework? The effects of studying marketing through individual perceptual strengths. *Illinois School Research and Development Journal, 26*(3), 96–113.

Dunn, R., Bruno, J., Sklar, R., Zenhausern, R., & Beaudry, J. (1990). Effects of matching and mismatching minority developmental college students' hemispheric preferences on mathematics scores. *Journal of Educational Research, 83*, 283–288.

Dunn, R., & Dunn, K. (1993). *Teaching secondary students through their individual learning styles.* Needham Heights, MA: Allyn & Bacon.

Dunn, R., Dunn, K., & Price, G. (1990). *Learning style inventory.* Lawrence, KS: Price Systems.

Dunn, R., Griggs, S., Olson, J., Beasley, M., & Gorman, B. (1995). A meta-analytic validation of the Dunn and Dunn learning-styles model. *Journal of Educational Research, 88*, 353–362.

Dunn, R., & Stevenson, J. (1997). Teaching diverse college students to study with a learning-styles prescription. *College Student Journal, 31*, 333–339.

Durham, R., Hays, J., & Martinez, R. (1994). Socio-cognitive development among Chicano and Anglo-American college students. *Journal of College Student Development, 35*, 178–182.

Durkheim, E. (1951). *Suicide.* (J. Spaulding and G. Simpson, Trans.). Glencoe, IL: Free Press. (Originally published 1897.)

Dutt, D. (1997). How much gender disparity exists in salary? A profile of graduates of a major public university. *Research in Higher Education, 38*, 631–646.

Dye, D., & Reck, M. (1989). College grade point average as a predictor of adult success: A reply. *Public Personnel Management, 18*, 235–241.

Dykstra, D. (1996). Teaching introductory physics to college students. In C. Twomey Fosnot (Ed.), *Constructivism: Theory, perspectives, and practice* (pp. 182–204). New York: Teachers College Press.

Dynarski, S. (1999). *Does aid matter? Measuring the effect of student aid on college attendance and completion* (NBER Working Paper No. W7422). Cambridge, MA: National Bureau of Economic Research.

Earle, J. (1996). Acquaintance rape workshops: Their effectiveness in changing the attitudes of first-year college men. *NASPA Journal, 34*, 2–18.

Easterling, D., Patten, J., & Krile, D. (1995, May). *The impact of developmental education on student progress: A three-year longitudinal analysis.* Paper presented at the meeting of the Association for Institutional Research, Boston.

Easterling, D., Patten, J., & Krile, D. (1998, May). *Patterns of progress: Student persistence isn't always where you expect it.* Paper presented at the meeting of the Association for Institutional Research, Minneapolis, MN.

Eaton, S., & Bean, J. (1995). An approach/avoidance behavioral model of college student retention. *Research in Higher Education, 36*, 617–645.

Eck, A. (1993). Job-related education and training: Their impact on earnings. *Monthly Labor Review, 116*(10), 21–38.

Edison, M., Doyle, S., & Pascarella, E. (1998, November). *Dimensions of teaching effectiveness and their impact on student cognitive development.* Paper presented at the meeting of the Association for the Study of Higher Education, Miami.

Edwards, K., & McKelfresh, D. (2002). The impact of a living-learning center on students' academic success and persistence. *Journal of College Student Development, 43*, 395–402.

Ehrenberg, R. (1991a). Decisions to undertake and complete doctoral study and choices of sector of employment. In C. Clotfelter, R. Ehrenberg, M. Getz, & J. Siegfried (Eds.), *Economic challenges in higher education* (pp. 174–210). Chicago: University of Chicago Press.

Ehrenberg, R. (1991b). The demographic distribution of American doctorates. In C. Clotfelter, R. Ehrenberg, M. Getz, & J. Siegfried (Eds.), *Economic challenges in higher education* (pp. 211–232). Chicago: University of Chicago Press.

Ehrenberg, R. (1996). *Historically Black colleges and universities and the training of African-American lawyers and leaders of the legal profession.* Unpublished manuscript, Cornell University, Ithaca, NY.

Ehrenberg, R. (1996–97). Are Black colleges producing today's African-American lawyers? *Journal of Blacks in Higher Education, 14*, 117–119.

Ehrenberg, R., & Rothstein, D. (1994). Do historically Black institutions of higher education confer unique advantages on Black students? An initial analysis. In R. Ehrenberg (Ed.), *Choices and consequences: Contemporary policy issues in education* (pp. 89–137). Ithaca, NY: ILR Press.

Ehrlich, T. (Ed.). (2000). *Civic responsibility and higher education.* Phoenix, AZ: American Council on Education and Oryx Press.

Ehrmann, S. (1995, March/April). Asking the right questions: What does research tell us about technology and higher learning? *Change, 27*(2), 20–27.

Eide, E. (1994). College major choice and changes in the gender wage gap. *Contemporary Economic Policy, 12*, 55–64.

Eide, E., Brewer, D., & Ehrenberg, R. (1998). Does it pay to attend an elite private college? Evidence on the effects of undergraduate college quality on graduate school attendance. *Economics of Education Review, 17*, 371–376.

Eide, E., Goldhaber, D., & Hilmer, M. (2000, December). *Can two-year college attendance lead to enrollment and degree completion at more selective four-year colleges?* Paper presented at the meeting of the American Economics Association, New Orleans.

Eide, E., & Waehrer, G. (1998). The role of the option value of attendance in college major choice. *Economics of Education Review, 17*, 73–82.

Eig, J. (1997, Spring). Supplemental instruction programs: An effective way to increase student academic success? *Journal of the Indiana University Student Personnel Association*, pp. 11–15.

Eimers, M., & Mullen, R. (1997, May). *Understanding transfer student success: Implications for policy at a multicampus university.* Paper presented at the meeting of the Association for Institutional Research, Orlando.

Eimers, M., & Pike, G. (1996, May). *Minority and nonminority adjustment to college: Differences or similarities?* Paper presented at the meeting of the Association for Institutional Research, Albuquerque, NM.

Eimers, M., & Pike, G. (1997). Minority and nonminority adjustment to college: Differences or similarities? *Research in Higher Education, 38*, 77–97.

Ekstrom, R., & Villegas, A. (1994). *College grades: An exploratory study of policies and practices* (College Board Report No. 94–1). Princeton, NJ: College Entrance Examination Board.

Elias, S., & Loomis, R. (2000). Using an academic self-efficacy scale to address university major persistence. *Journal of College Student Development, 41,* 450–454.

El-Khawas, E. (1995). *Campus trends, 1995.* Washington, DC: American Council on Education.

Elliott, K., & Healy, M. (2001). Key factors influencing student satisfaction related to recruitment and retention. *Journal of Marketing for Higher Education, 10,* 1–11.

Elliott, R., Strenta, A., Adair, R., Matier, M., & Scott, J. (1996). The role of ethnicity in choosing and leaving science in highly selective institutions. *Research in Higher Education, 37,* 681–709.

Ellison, C., & Powers, D. (1994). The contact hypothesis and racial attitudes among Black Americans. *Social Science Quarterly, 75,* 385–400.

Employment and unemployment rates by educational attainment 1970 to 1996. (1997, August). *Postsecondary Education OPPORTUNITY,* No. 62, 10–15.

Engs, R., Diebold, B., & Hanson, D. (1996). The drinking patterns and problems of a national sample of college students, 1994. *Journal of Alcohol and Drug Education, 41,* 13–33.

Engstrom, C., & Sedlacek, W. (1997). Attitudes of heterosexual students toward their gay male and lesbian peers. *Journal of College Student Development, 38,* 565–576.

Ennis, R. (1985). A logical basis for measuring critical thinking skills. *Educational Leadership, 43,* 44–48.

Ennis, R., Millman, J., & Tomko, T. (in press). *Cornell Critical Thinking Tests Level X & Level Z Manual* (4th ed.). Pacific Grove, CA: Critical Thinking Books and Software.

Erikson, E. (1959). Identity and the life cycle. *Psychological Issues Monograph, 1,* 1–171.

Erikson, E. (1963). *Childhood and society* (2nd ed.). New York: W. W. Norton.

Erikson, E. (1968). *Identity: Youth and crisis.* New York: W. W. Norton.

Erwin, T. (1997). *Definitions and assessment methods for critical thinking, problem solving, and writing.* Harrisonburg, VA: James Madison University, Center for Assessment and Research Studies.

Erwin, T., & Love, W. (1989). Selected environmental factors in student development. *NASPA Journal, 26,* 256–264.

Etaugh, C. (1986, August). *Biographical and personality correlates of attitudes toward women: A review.* Paper presented at the meeting of the American Psychological Association, Washington, DC.

Etemad, M. (1994, April). *The role of kinesthetics in learning: The importance of active engagement and the connected process of reflection.* (ERIC Document Reproduction Service No. ED 374 887)

Ethington, C. (1997). A hierarchical linear modeling approach to studying college effects. In J. Smart (Ed.), *Higher education: Handbook of theory and research* (Vol. 12, pp. 165–194). New York: Agathon.

Ethington, C. (1998, November). *Influence of the normative environment of peer groups on community college students' perceptions of growth and development.*

Paper presented at the meeting of the Association for the Study of Higher Education, Miami.

Ethington, C. (2000). Influences of the normative environment of peer groups on community college students' perceptions of growth and development. *Research in Higher Education, 41,* 703–722.

Evans, D. (1988). Effects of a religious-oriented, conservative, homogeneous college education on reflective judgment. *Dissertation Abstracts International, 49,* 3306A.

Evans, N. (2003). Psychosocial, cognitive, and typological perspectives on student development. In S. Komives & D. Woodard (Eds.), *Student services: A handbook for the profession* (pp. 179–202). San Francisco: Jossey-Bass.

Evans, N., & Broido, E. (1999). Coming out in college residence halls: Negotiation, meaning making, challenges, supports. *Journal of College Student Development, 40,* 658–668.

Evans, N., Forney, D., & Guido-DiBrito, F. (1998). *Student development in college: Theory, research, and practice.* San Francisco: Jossey-Bass.

Evans, N., & Wall, V. (Eds.). (1991). *Beyond tolerance: Gays, lesbians, and bisexuals on campus.* Alexandria, VA: American College Personnel Association.

Evans, S., & Dansereau, D. (1991). Knowledge maps as tools for thinking and communication. In R. Mulcahy, R. Short, & J. Andrews (Eds.), *Enhancing learning and thinking* (pp. 97–120). New York: Praeger.

Eveland, A., Conyne, R., & Blakney, V. (1998). University students and career decidedness: Effects of two computer-based career guidance interventions. *Computers in Human Behavior, 14,* 531–541.

Ewell, P. (1989). Institutional characteristics and faculty/administrator perceptions of outcomes: An exploratory analysis. *Research in Higher Education, 30,* 113–136.

Eyler, J. (1993). Comparing the impact of two internship experiences on student learning. *Journal of Cooperative Education, 29*(3), 41–52.

Eyler, J. (1995). Graduates' assessment of the impact of a full-time college internship on their personal and professional lives. *College Student Journal, 29,* 186–194.

Eyler, J., & Giles, D. (1997). The importance of program quality in service learning. In A. Waterman (Ed.), *Service learning: Applications from the research* (pp. 57–76). Hillsdale, NJ: Erlbaum.

Eyler, J., & Giles, D. (1999). *Where's the learning in service learning?* San Francisco: Jossey-Bass.

Eyler, J., Giles, D., & Braxton, J. (1995, November). *The impact of alternative models of service learning on student outcomes.* Paper presented at the National Society for Experiential Education (NSEE) conference, New Orleans.

Eyler, J., Giles, D., & Braxton, J. (1996, April). *The impact of service learning on students' attitudes, skills, and values: Preliminary results of analysis of selected data from FIPSE sponsored comparing models of service-learning projects.* Paper presented at the meeting of the American Educational Research Association, New York.

Eyler, J., Giles, D., & Braxton, J. (1997a). The impact of service learning on college students. *Michigan Journal of Community Service Learning, 4,* 5–15.

Eyler, J., Giles, D., & Braxton, J. (1997b, March). *Report of a national study comparing the impacts of service-learning program characteristics on postsecondary students.*

Paper presented at the meeting of the American Educational Research Association, Chicago.

Eyler, J., Giles, D., Lynch, C., & Gray, C. (1997, March). *Service learning and the development of reflective judgment.* Paper presented at the meeting of the American Educational Research Association, Chicago.

Eyler, J., Giles, D., Root, S., & Price, J. (1997, March). *Service learning and the development of expert citizens.* Paper presented at the meeting of the American Educational Research Association, Chicago.

Eyler, J., Giles, D., Stenson, C., & Gray, C. (2001). *At a glance: What we know about the effects of service learning on college students, faculty, institutions and communities, 1993–2000* (3rd ed.). (Doc. No. L054). Scotts Valley, CA: National Service Learning Clearinghouse.

Facione, N. (1997). *Critical thinking assessment in nursing education programs: An aggregate data analysis.* Millbrae, CA: California Academic Press.

Facione, P. (1990a). *The California Critical Thinking Skills Test: College level technical report 1: Experimental validation and content validity.* Millbrae, CA: California Academic Press.

Facione, P. (1990b). *The California Critical Thinking Skills Test: College level technical report 2: Factors predictive of critical thinking skills.* Millbrae, CA: California Academic Press.

Facione, P. (1991, August). *Testing college level critical thinking skills.* Paper presented at the meeting of the 11th Annual Conference on Critical Thinking and Educational Reform, Sonoma, CA.

Facione, P., & Facione, N. (1992). *Test manual: The California Critical Thinking Dispositions Inventory.* Millbrae, CA: California Academic Press.

Facione, P., Facione, N., Blohm, S., Howard, K., & Giancarlo, C. (1998). *The California Critical Thinking Skills Test: Test manual.* Millbrae, CA: California Academic Press.

Facione, P., Facione, N., & Giancarlo, C. (1994). Critical thinking disposition as a measure of competent clinical judgment: The development of the California Critical Thinking Disposition Inventory. *Journal of Nursing Education, 33,* 345–350.

Facione, P., Facione, N., & Giancarlo, C. (1996). The motivation to think in working and learning. In E. Jones (Ed.), *Preparing competent college graduates: Setting new and higher expectations for student learning. New Directions for Higher Education,* No. 96 (pp. 67–79). San Francisco: Jossey-Bass.

Facione, P., Sanchez, C., Facione, N., & Gainen, J. (1995). The disposition toward critical thinking. *Journal of General Education, 44,* 1–25.

Factors influencing senior students' gains in learning and development at the University of Missouri-Columbia. (1997, Fall). Student Life Studies Abstracts, No. 4. Columbia: University of Missouri.

Family income by educational attainment: 1956–1997. (1999, April). *Postsecondary Education OPPORTUNITY,* No. 82, 11–16.

Fantuzzo, J., Dimeff, L., & Fox, S. (1989). Reciprocal peer tutoring: A multimodal assessment of effectiveness with college students. *Teaching of Psychology, 16*(3), 133–135.

Fantuzzo, J., Riggio, R., Connelly, S., & Dimeff, L. (1989). Effects of reciprocal peer tutoring on academic achievement and psychological adjustment: A component analysis. *Journal of Educational Psychology, 81,* 173–177.

Farabaugh-Dorkins, C. (1991). *Beginning to understand why older students drop out of college* (AIR Professional File, No. 39). Tallahassee, FL: Association for Institutional Research.

Faryniarz, J., & Lockwood, L. (1992). Effectiveness of microcomputer simulations in stimulating environmental problem solving by community college students. *Journal of Research in Science Teaching, 29,* 453–470.

Fassinger, P. (1995). Understanding classroom interaction. Students' and professors' contributions to students' silence. *Journal of Higher Education, 66,* 82–96.

Fassinger, P. (1996). Professors' and students' perceptions of why students participate in class. *Teaching Sociology, 24,* 25–33.

Feagin, J. (1992). The continuing significance of racism: Discrimination against Black students in White colleges. *Journal of Black Studies, 22,* 546–578.

Feagin, J., Vera, H., & Imani, N. (1996). *The agony of education: Black students at White colleges and universities.* New York: Routledge.

Federal Interagency Forum on Child and Family Statistics. (2002). *America's children: Key national indicators of well-being.* Washington, DC: U.S. Government Printing Office.

Felder, R. (1995). Longitudinal study of engineering performance and retention: IV. Instructional methods. *Journal of Engineering Education, 84,* 361–367.

Felder, R., Felder, G., Mauney, M., Hamrin, J., & Dietz, E. (1995). A longitudinal study of engineering student performance and retention: Gender differences in student performance and attitudes. *Journal of Engineering Education, 84,* 151–163.

Feldman, K. (1972). Some theoretical approaches to the study of change and stability of college students. *Review of Educational Research, 42,* 1–26.

Feldman, K. (1987). Research productivity and scholarly accomplishment of college teachers as related to their instructional effectiveness: A review and exploration. *Research in Higher Education, 26,* 227–298.

Feldman, K. (1994a). A strategy for using student perceptions in the assessment of general education. *Journal of General Education, 43,* 151–167.

Feldman, K. (1994b). Introduction to the Transaction edition. In K. Feldman & T. Newcomb, *The impact of college on students.* New Brunswick, NJ: Transaction.

Feldman, K. (1996). *Reflections on the study of effective college teaching and student ratings: One continuing quest and two unresolved issues.* Unpublished manuscript, State University of New York, Stony Brook.

Feldman, K. (1997). Identifying exemplary teachers and teaching: Evidence from student ratings. In R. Perry & J. Smart (Eds.), *Effective teaching in higher education: Research and practice* (pp. 368–395). New York: Agathon.

Feldman, K., Ethington, C., & Smart, J. (2001). A further investigation of major field and person-environment fit: Sociological versus psychological interpretations of Holland's theory. *Journal of Higher Education, 72,* 670–698.

Feldman, K., & Newcomb, T. (1969). *The impact of college on students.* San Francisco: Jossey-Bass.

Feldman, K., Smart, J., & Ethington, C. (1999). Major field and person-environment fit: Using Holland's theory to study change and stability of college students. *Journal of Higher Education, 70,* 642–669.

Fenske, R., Porter, J., & DuBrock, C. (2000). Tracking financial aid and persistence of women, minority, and needy students in science, engineering, and mathematics. *Research in Higher Education, 41,* 67–94.

Ferdman, B., & Gallegos, P. (2001). Racial identity development and Latinos in the United States. In C. Wijeyesinghe & B. Jackson III (Eds.), *New perspectives on racial identity development: A theoretical and practical anthology* (pp. 32–66). New York: New York University Press.

Ferguson, E., & Hegarty, M. (1995). Learning with real machines or diagrams: Application of knowledge to real-world problems. *Cognition and Instruction, 13,* 129–160.

Fidler, P. (1991). Relationship of freshman orientation seminars to sophomore return rates. *Journal of the Freshman Year Experience, 3,* 7–38.

Fidler, P. (1999, July). *The USC Freshman Seminar today: Twenty-five years of outcomes results.* Paper presented at the 12th International Conference on the First-Year Experience, Edinburgh, Scotland.

Fidler, P., & Godwin, M. (1994). Retaining African-American students through the freshman seminar. *Journal of Developmental Education, 17,* 34–41.

Fidler, P., & Moore, P. (1996). A comparison of effects of campus residence and freshman seminar attendance on freshman dropout rates. *Journal of the Freshman Year Experience, 8,* 7–16.

Finger, W., Borduin, C., & Baumstark, K. (1992). Correlates of moral judgment development in college students. *Journal of Genetic Psychology, 153,* 221–223.

Finnegan, J., Viswanath, K., Kahn, E., & Hannan, P. (1993). Exposure to sources of heart disease prevention information: Community type and social group differences. *Journalism Quarterly, 70,* 569–584.

Fischer, N. (1994). *The long-term effects of undergraduate student involvement experiences on cognitive and affective outcomes for selected college graduates at a southern California university.* Unpublished doctoral dissertation, University of California, Los Angeles.

Fisher, B., & Hartmann, D. (1995). The impact of race on the social experience of college students at a predominantly White university. *Journal of Black Studies, 26,* 117–133.

Fiske, M., & Chiriboga, D. (1990). *Change and continuity in adult life.* San Francisco: Jossey-Bass.

Fisler, J., Hein, J., & Young, J. (1999, April). *Retaining women in the sciences: Evidence from Douglass College's Project SUPER.* Paper presented at the meeting of the American Educational Research Association, Montreal.

Fitzgerald, R. (2000). *College quality and the earnings of recent college graduates* (Research and Development Report No. NCES 2000–043). Washington, DC: U.S. Department of Education, National Center for Education Statistics.

Fitzgerald, R., Berkner, L., Horn, L., Choy, S., & Hoachlander, G. (1994). *Descriptive summary of 1989–90 beginning postsecondary students two years after entry*

(Statistical Analysis Report No. NCES 94–386). Washington, DC: U.S. Department of Education, Office of Educational Research and Improvement, National Center for Education Statistics.

Five-year institutional graduation rates by degree level control and academic selectivity 1983–1997. (1997, December). *Postsecondary Education OPPORTUNITY,* No. 63, 1–8.

Flacks, R., & Thomas, S. (1997, November). *College students in the nineties: Report on a project in progress.* Paper presented at the meeting of the Association for the Study of Higher Education, Albuquerque, NM.

Flanagan, O. (1982). Virtue, sex, and gender. *Ethics, 92,* 499–512.

Flowers, L. (2000). *Cognitive effects of college: Differences between African-American and Caucasian students.* Unpublished doctoral dissertation, University of Iowa, Iowa City.

Flowers, L. (2002a). The impact of college racial composition on African-American students' academic and social gains: Additional evidence. *Journal of College Student Development, 43,* 403–410.

Flowers, L. (2002b). Developing purpose in college: Differences between freshmen and seniors. *College Student Journal, 36,* 478–484.

Flowers, L., Osterlind, S., Pascarella, E., & Pierson, C. (1999). *How much do students learn in college? Cross-sectional estimates using the College Basic Academic Subjects Examination.* Unpublished manuscript, University of Iowa, Iowa City.

Flowers, L., & Pascarella, E. (1999a). Cognitive effects of college racial composition on African-American students after three years of college. *Journal of College Student Development, 40,* 669–677.

Flowers, L., & Pascarella, E. (1999b). Does college racial composition influence the openness to diversity of African-American students? *Journal of College Student Development, 40,* 405–417.

Flowers, L., & Pascarella, E. (1999c). The effects of college racial composition on African-American college students' orientations toward learning for self-understanding. *The Professional Educator, 22,* 33–47.

Flowers, L., Pascarella, E., & Pierson, C. (1999). *Information technology use and cognitive outcomes in the first year of college.* Unpublished manuscript, University of Iowa, Iowa City.

Fogel, J., & Yaffee, J. (1992, May). *Ethnic minority and Caucasian student experiences at the University of Utah and recommendations for institutional research.* Paper presented at the meeting of the Association for Institutional Research, Atlanta, GA. (ERIC Document Reproduction Service No. ED 349 874)

Forbes, C. (1997). Analyzing the growth of the critical thinking skills of college calculus students. *Dissertation Abstracts International, 58,* 2101A.

Forbes, J. (1998, Spring). The role of women's colleges in the leadership development of female students. *Journal of the Indiana University Student Personnel Association,* pp. 50–56.

Ford, E., Merritt, R., Heath, G., Powell, K., Washburn, R., Kriska, A., et al. (1991). Physical behaviors in lower and higher socioeconomic status populations. *American Journal of Epidemiology, 133,* 1246–1255.

Foster, J., & La Force, B. (1999). A longitudinal study of moral, religious, and identity development in a Christian liberal arts environment. *Journal of Psychology and Theology, 27,* 52–68.

Fowler, J. (1981). *Stages of faith: The psychology of human development and the quest for meaning.* New York: HarperCollins.

Fowler, J. (1991). Stages of faith consciousness. In F. Oser & W. Scarlett (Eds.), *Religious development in childhood and adolescence* (pp. 27–45). *New Directions for Child Development,* No. 52. San Francisco: Jossey-Bass.

Fowler, J. (1996). *Faithful change: The personal and public challenges of postmodern life.* Nashville, TN: Abingdon.

Fox, M. (1993). Is it a good investment to attend an elite private college? *Economics of Education Review, 12,* 137–151.

Fralick, M. (1993). College success: A study of positive and negative attrition. *Community College Review, 20,* 29–36.

Francis, K., & Kelly, R. (1990). Environmental fit and the success or failure of high-risk college students. *Educational Policy, 4,* 233–243.

Franklin, J., & Theall, M. (1992, April). *Disciplinary differences: Instructional goals and activities measures of student performance, and student ratings of instruction.* Paper presented at the meeting of the American Educational Research Association, San Francisco.

Franklin, M. (1993). *The effects of differential college environments on academic learning and student perceptions of cognitive development.* Unpublished doctoral dissertation, University of Nebraska, Lincoln.

Franklin, M. (1995). The effects of differential college environments on academic learning and student perceptions of cognitive development. *Research in Higher Education, 36,* 127–153.

Frazier, P., Valtinson, G., & Candell, S. (1994). Evaluation of a coeducation interactive rape prevention program. *Journal of Counseling and Development, 73,* 153–158.

Frazis, H. (1993). Selection bias and the degree effect. *Journal of Human Resources, 28,* 538–554.

Freeman, R. (1994). *Working under different rules.* New York: Russell Sage Foundation.

Fricko, M., & Beehr, T. (1992). A longitudinal investigation of interest congruence and gender concentration as predictors of job satisfaction. *Personnel Psychology, 45,* 99–117.

Friedlander, J. (1993). *Using wage record data to track the postcollege employment and earnings of community college students* (Research report). Santa Barbara, CA: Santa Barbara City College, Office of Academic Affairs.

Friedlander, J. (1996). *Using wage record data to track the postcollege employment rates and wages of California community college students.* Santa Barbara, CA: Santa Barbara City College.

Friedlander, J., & MacDougall, P. (1992). Achieving student success through student involvement. *Community College Review, 20,* 20–28.

Friedlander, J., Pace, C., & Lehman, P. (1990). *Community college student experiences questionnaire.* Los Angeles: University of California, Center for the Study of Evaluation.

Fries-Britt, S., & Turner, B. (2001). Facing stereotypes: A case study of Black students on a White campus. *Journal of College Student Development, 42,* 420–429.

Fries-Britt, S., & Turner, B. (2002). Uneven stories: Successful Black collegians at Black and White campuses. *Review of Higher Education, 25,* 315–330.

Frost, S. (1991). Fostering the critical thinking of college women through academic advising and faculty contact. *Journal of College Student Development, 32,* 359–366.

Frye, M. (1990). The possibility of feminist theory. In D. Rhode (Ed.), *Theoretical perspectives on sexual difference.* New Haven, CT: Yale University Press.

Fuller, R., & Schoenberger, R. (1991). The gender salary gap. Do academic achievement, internship experience, and college major make a difference? *Social Science Quarterly, 72,* 715–726.

Fullilove, R., & Treisman, P. (1990). Mathematics achievement among African-American undergraduates at the University of California, Berkeley: An evaluation of the Mathematics Workshop Program. *Journal of Negro Education, 59,* 463–478.

Furr, S., & Elling, T. (2000). The influence of work on college student development. *NASPA Journal, 37,* 454–470.

Gabelnick, F., MacGregor, J., Matthews, R., & Smith, B. (Eds.). (1990). *Learning communities: Creating connections among students, faculty, and disciplines. New Directions for Teaching and Learning,* No. 41. San Francisco: Jossey-Bass.

Gadzella, B., Ginther, D., & Bryant, G. (1996). *Teaching and learning critical thinking skills.* Paper presented at the meeting of the 26th International Congress of Psychology, Montreal.

Gadzella, B., Hartsoe, K., & Harper, J. (1989). Critical thinking and mental ability groups. *Psychological Reports, 65,* 1019–1026.

Gadzella, B., & Masten, W. (1998). Critical thinking and learning processes for students in two major fields. *Journal of Instructional Psychology, 25,* 256–261.

Gagne, E., Yekovich, C., & Yekovich, F. (1994). *The cognitive psychology of school learning* (2nd ed.). New York: HarperCollins.

Gaines, T. (1991). *The campus as a work of art.* New York: Praeger.

Gall, M., Borg, W., & Gall, J. (1996). *Educational research: An introduction* (6th ed.). White Plains, NY: Longman.

Gallos, J. (1995). Gender and silence: Implications of women's ways of knowing. *College Teaching, 43,* 101–105.

Galotti, K., Kozberg, S., & Farmer, M. (1991). Gender and developmental differences in adolescents' conceptions of moral reasoning. *Journal of Youth and Adolescence, 20,* 13–30.

Ganderton, P., & Santos, R. (1995). Hispanic college attendance and completion: Evidence from the High School and Beyond surveys. *Economics of Education Review, 14,* 35–46.

Garcia, P. (1991). Summer bridge: Improving retention rates for underprepared students. *Journal of the Freshman Year Experience, 3,* 91–105.

Garcia, V. (2000, April). *An exploration of the influence that perceptions of remediation have on the persistence of students in higher education.* Paper presented at the meeting of the American Educational Research Association, New Orleans.

Gardiner, L. (1994). *Redesigning higher education: Producing dramatic gains in student learning.* Washington, DC: Clearinghouse on Higher Education, George Washington University.

Gardiner, L. (1998). Why we must change: The research evidence. *Thought and Action, 14,* 71–88.

Gardner, H. (1983). *Frames of mind.* New York: Basic Books.

Gardner, H. (1987). The theory of multiple intelligences. *Annals of Dyslexia, 37,* 19–35.

Gardner, H. (1993). *Multiple intelligences: The theory in practice.* New York: Basic Books.

Gardner, J. (1961). *Excellence: Can we be equal and excellent too?* New York: Harper-Collins.

Gardner, P. (1998). Are college seniors prepared to work? In J. Gardner & G. Van Der Veer (Eds.), *The senior year experience: Facilitating integration, reflection, closure, and transition* (pp. 60–78). San Francisco: Jossey-Bass.

Garside, C. (1996). Look who's talking: A comparison of lecture and group discussion teaching strategies in developing critical thinking skills. *Communication Education, 45,* 212–227.

Gasman, M. (1997, April). *Mentoring programs for African-American college students and their relationships to academic success.* Paper presented at the meeting of the Conference on People of Color in Predominantly White Institutions: Different Perspectives on Majority Rules, Lincoln, NE.

Geasler, M., Croteau, J., Heineman, C., & Edlund, C. (1995). A qualitative study of students' expression of change after attending panel presentations by lesbian, gay, and bisexual speakers. *Journal of College Student Development, 36,* 483–492.

Geelhoed, R., Abe, J., & Talbot, D. (2003). A qualitative investigation of U.S. students' experiences in an international peer program. *Journal of College Student Development, 44,* 5–17.

Geller, W. (1991). *Attitudes toward gays and lesbians: A longitudinal study.* (ERIC Document Reproduction Service No. ED 340 970)

Gerdes, H., & Mallinckrodt, B. (1994). Emotional, social, and academic adjustment of college students: A longitudinal study of retention. *Journal of Counseling and Development, 72,* 284–288.

Geske, T. (1996). The value of investments in higher education: Capturing the full returns. In D. Honeyman, J. Wattenbarger, & K. Westbrook (Eds.), *Struggle to survive: Funding higher education in the next century* (pp. 29–48). Thousand Oaks, CA: Corwin.

Giancarlo, C., & Facione, P. (1997). *A longitudinal study of Santa Clara undergraduate students' disposition toward critical thinking.* Unpublished manuscript, Santa Clara University, Santa Clara, CA.

Giancarlo, C., & Facione, P. (2001). A look across four years at the disposition toward critical thinking among undergraduate students. *Journal of General Education, 50,* 29–55.

Gielen, U., & Markoulis, D. (1994). Preference for principled moral reasoning: A developmental and cross-cultural perspective. In L. Adler & U. Gielen (Eds.), *Cross-cultural topics in psychology* (pp. 73–87). Westport, CT: Greenwood Press.

Giesbrecht, N., & Walker, L. (2000). Ego development and the construction of a moral self. *Journal of College Student Development, 41,* 157–171.

Giles, D., Honnet, E., & Migliore, S. (1991). *Research agenda for combining service and learning in the 1990s.* Raleigh, NC: National Society for Internships and Experimental Education.

Giles, D. E., & Eyler, J. (1994). The impact of college community service laboratory on students' personal, social, and cognitive outcomes. *Journal of Adolescence, 17,* 327–339.

Gilleskie, D., & Harrison, A. (1998). The effect of endogenous health inputs on the relationship between health and education. *Economics of Education Review, 17,* 279–297.

Gilliard, M. (1996). Racial climate and institutional support factors affecting success in predominantly White institutions: An examination of African-American and White student experiences. *Dissertation Abstracts International, 57,* 1515A.

Gilligan, C. (1977). In a different voice: Women's conceptions of self and morality. *Harvard Educational Review, 47,* 481–517.

Gilligan, C. (1979). Woman's place in man's life cycle. *Harvard Educational Review, 49,* 431–446.

Gilligan, C. (1981). Moral development. In A. Chickering & Associates (Eds.), *The modern American college: Responding to the new realities of diverse students and a changing society* (pp. 139–157). San Francisco: Jossey-Bass.

Gilligan, C. (1982). *In a different voice: Psychological theory and women's development.* Cambridge, MA: Harvard University Press.

Gilligan, C. (1986a). Remapping development: The power of divergent data. In L. Cirillo & S. Wapner (Eds.), *Value presuppositions in theories of human development.* Hillsdale, NJ: Erlbaum.

Gilligan, C. (1986b). Reply by Carol Gilligan. *Signs: Journal of Women in Culture and Society, 11,* 324–333.

Gilligan, C., & Attanucci, J. (1988). Two moral orientations: Gender differences and similarities. *Merrill-Palmer Quarterly, 43,* 223–237.

Gilmore, J. (1990). *Price and quality in higher education* (Research report). Washington, DC: U.S. Department of Education, Office of Educational Research and Improvement.

Giraud, G. (1997). Cooperative learning and statistics instruction. *Journal of Statistics Education, 5*(3). [Available at: http://www.amstat.org/publications/jse/v5n3/giraud.html].

Gladieux, L., & Swail, S. (1998a). Financial aid is not enough: Improving the odds of college success. *College Board Review, 185,* 16–21.

Gladieux, L., & Swail, S. (1998b). Postsecondary education: Student success, not just access. In S. Halperin (Ed.), *The forgotten half revisited: American youth and young families, 1988–2008* (pp. 101–114). Washington, DC: American Youth Policy Forum.

Gladieux, L., & Swail, S. (1999). *The virtual university and educational opportunity: Issues of equity and access for the next generation.* Washington, DC: College Board.

Glascott, K., & Stone, S. (1998). *Distance learning in higher education: A comparative analysis of undergraduates' constructivist learning perceptions in traditional and interactive instructional television classes (IITV)*. Paper presented at the meeting of the American Educational Research Association, San Diego, CA.

Glass, J., & Bunn, C. (1998). Length of time required to graduate for community college students transferring to senior institutions. *Community College Journal of Research and Practice, 22,* 239–263.

Glass, J., & Garrett, M. (1995). Student participation in a college orientation course, retention, and grade point average. *Community College Journal of Research and Practice, 19,* 117–132.

Gleason, P. (1993). College student employment, academic progress, and postcollege labor market success. *Journal of Student Financial Aid, 23,* 5–14.

Glenn, D., & Eklund, S. (1991, April). *The relationship of graduate education and reflective judgment in older adults.* Paper presented at the annual meeting of the American Educational Research Association, Chicago.

Glenn, L., Rollins, N., & Smith, B. (1990). The retention and attrition of American College Test scholars. *Journal of College Student Development, 13,* 280–281.

Glenn, N. (1980). Values, attitudes, and beliefs. In O. Brim & J. Kagan (Eds.), *Constancy and change in human development.* Cambridge, MA: Harvard University Press.

Globetti, E., Globetti, G., Brown, C., & Smith, R. (1993). Social interaction and multiculturalism. *NASPA Journal, 30,* 209–218.

Gloria, A., & Robinson, S. (1994, August). *Factors influencing the academic persistence of Chicano/a undergraduates.* Paper presented at the meeting of the American Psychological Association, Los Angeles.

Gloria, A., Robinson Kurpius, S., Hamilton, K., & Willson, M. (1999). African-American students' persistence at a predominantly White university: Influences of social support, university comfort, and self-beliefs. *Journal of College Student Development, 40,* 257–268.

Glover, J. (1996, November). *Campus environment and student involvement as predictors of outcomes of the community college experience.* Paper presented at the meeting of the Association for the Study of Higher Education, Memphis, TN.

Goldfinch, J. (1996). The effectiveness of school-type classes compared to the traditional lecture/tutorial method for teaching quantitative methods to business students. *Studies in Higher Education, 21,* 207–220.

Goldman, B., & Hood, S. (1995). Residence hall longevity and transfer rates of living/learning residence hall students versus other residence hall students. *Journal of College and University Student Housing, 25,* 38–40.

Gonsiorek, J. (1995). Gay male identities: Concepts and issues. In A. D'Augelli & C. Patterson (Eds.), *Lesbian, gay, and bisexual identities over the life span: Psychological perspectives* (pp. 24–47). New York: Oxford University Press.

Good, J., & Cartwright, C. (1998). Development of moral judgment among undergraduate university students. *College Student Journal, 32,* 270–276.

Gorman, M., Duffy, J., & Heffernan, M. (1994). Service experience and the moral development of college students. *Religious Education, 89,* 422–431.

Gotham, H., Sher, K., & Wood, P. (1997). Predicting stability and change in frequency of intoxication from the college years to beyond: Individual-difference and role transition variables. *Journal of Abnormal Psychology, 106,* 619–629.

Gould, R. (1978). *Transformations: Growth and change in adult life.* New York: Simon & Schuster.

Graham, S. (1997). *Looking at adult growth in college: Examining the effects of age and educational ethos.* Unpublished paper, University of Missouri, Columbia.

Graham, S. (1998). Adult growth in college: The effects of age and educational ethos. *Journal of College Student Development, 39,* 239–250.

Graham, S., & Cockriel, I. (1989). College outcome assessment factors: An empirical approach. *College Student Journal, 23,* 280–286.

Graham, S., & Cockriel, I. (1996). Indexes to assess social and personal development and the impact of college. *College Student Journal, 30,* 502–515.

Graham, S., & Cockriel, I. (1997). A factor structure for social and personal development outcomes in college. *NASPA Journal, 34,* 199–216.

Graham, S., & Donaldson, J. (1996). Assessing personal growth for adults enrolled in higher education. *Journal of Continuing Higher Education, 44,* 7–22.

Graham, S., & Gisi, S. (1999). *The effects of instructional climate and student affairs on college student outcomes.* Paper presented at the meeting of the Association for the Study of Higher Education, San Antonio, TX.

Graham, S., & Gisi, S. (2000). The effects of instructional climate and student affairs services on college outcomes and satisfaction. *Journal of College Student Development, 41,* 270–291.

Graham, S., & Long, S. (1998). *The role of college involvement for adult undergraduate students.* Paper presented at the meeting of the American Educational Research Association, San Diego, CA.

Grandy, J. (1998). Persistence in science of high-ability minority students: Results of a longitudinal study. *Journal of Higher Education, 69,* 589–620.

Gray, J., & Chapman, R. (1999). Conflicting signals: The labor market for college-educated workers. *Journal of Economic Issues, 33,* 661–675.

Gray, K., Huang, N., & Jie, L. (1993). The gender gap in yearly earnings: Is it lack of education or occupational segregation? *Journal of Vocational Education Research, 18*(3), 1–14.

Gray, M., Geschwind, S., Ondaatje, E., Robyn, A., Klein, S., Sax, L., et al. (1996). *Evaluation of Learn and Serve America, Higher Education: First year report* (Vol. I). Washington, DC: RAND Institute on Education and Training.

Gray, M., Ondaatje, E., Fricker, R., & Geschwind, S. (2000, March/April). Assessing service learning: Results from a survey of "Learn and Serve America, Higher Education." *Change, 32,* 30–39.

Gray, M., Ondaatje, E., Fricker, R., Geschwind, S., Goldman, C., Kaganoff, T., et al. (1999). *Combining service learning in higher education: Evaluation of the Learn and Serve America, Higher Education program.* Santa Monica, CA: RAND Corporation.

Gray, M., & Taylor, A. (1989). A study of factors influencing student performance in mathematics on the Florida College-Level Academic Skills Test (CLAST). *Journal of Negro Education, 58,* 531–543.

Grayson, J. (1995a). Does race matter? Outcomes of the first year experience in a Canadian university. *Canadian Journal of Higher Education, 25*(2), 79–109.

Grayson, J. (1995b). *Race and first year retention on a Canadian campus* (Research report). Toronto, Canada: York University, Institute for Social Research.

Grayson, J. (1996). *Value added in generic skills between first and final year: A pilot project* (Research report). Toronto: York University, Institute for Social Research.

Grayson, J. (1997a). *Who gets jobs? Initial labour market experiences of York graduates* (Research report). Toronto: York University, Institute for Social Research.

Grayson, J. (1997b). Institutional failure or student choice? The retention of adult students in Atkinson college. *Canadian Journal for the Study of Adult Education, 11*, 7–30.

Grayson, J. (1998a). *Experiences of York graduates—Two years later* (Research report). Toronto: York University, Institute of Social Research.

Grayson, J. (1998b). Racial origin and student retention in a Canadian university. *Higher Education, 36*, 323–352.

Grayson, J. (1999). The impact of university experiences on self-assessed skills. *Journal of College Student Development, 40*, 687–699.

Greeley, A. (1991). Patterns of college women's development: A cluster analysis approach. *Journal of College Student Development, 32*, 516–524.

Green, D., & Diehn, G. (1995). Educational and service outcomes of a service integration effort. *Michigan Journal of Community Service Learning, 2*, 54–62.

Green, K. (1996, March/April). The coming ubiquity of information technology. *Change, 28*, 24–28.

Green, S., Dixon, P., & Gold-Neil, V. (1993). The effects of a gay/lesbian panel discussion on college student attitudes toward gay men, lesbians, and persons with AIDS (PWAs). *Journal of Sex Education and Therapy, 19*, 47–63.

Greenwald, A. (1997). Validity concerns and usefulness of student ratings of instruction. *American Psychologist, 52*, 1182–1186.

Greenwald, A., & Gillmore, G. (1997). Grading leniency is a removable contaminant of student ratings. *American Psychologist, 52*, 1209–1217.

Greer, A., Weston, L., & Alm, M. (1991). Assessment of learning outcomes: A measure of progress in library literacy. *College and Research Libraries, 52*, 549–557.

Gregor, S., & Cuskelly, E. (1994). Computer-mediated communication in distance education. *Journal of Computer Assisted Learning, 10*, 168–181.

Grembowski, D., Patrick, D., Diehr, P., Durham, M., Beresford, K., & Hecht, J. (1993). Self-efficacy and health behavior among older adults. *Journal of Health and Social Behavior, 34*, 89–104.

Griffin, M., & Griffin, B. (1995). *An investigation of the effects of reciprocal peer tutoring on achievement, self-efficacy, and test anxiety.* Unpublished manuscript, Georgia Southern University, Statesboro. (ERIC Document Reproduction Service No. ED 383 756)

Griffin, R. (1990). Energy in the eighties: Education, communication, and the knowledge gap. *Journalism Quarterly, 67*, 554–566.

Grimes, S. (1995). Targeting academic programs to student diversity utilizing learning styles and learning-study strategies. *Journal of College Student Development, 36,* 422–430.

Groccia, J., & Miller, J. (1996). Collegiality in the classroom: The use of peer learning assistants in cooperative learning in introductory biology. *Innovative Higher Education, 21,* 87–100.

Grogger, J., & Eide, E. (1995). Changes in college skills and their use in the college wage premium. *Journal of Human Resources, 30,* 280–310.

Groot, W., Oosterbeck, H., & Stern, D. (1995). *A sequential probit model of college choice and wages.* Berkeley: University of California, National Center for Research on Vocational Education.

Gross, W. (1993). Gender and age differences in college students' alcohol consumption. *Psychological Reports, 72,* 211–216.

Grosset, J. (1991a, May). *Patterns of integration, commitment, and student characteristics and retention among Black students from different socioeconomic backgrounds.* Paper presented at the meeting of the Association for Institutional Research, San Francisco.

Grosset, J. (1991b). Patterns of integration, commitment, and student characteristics and retention among younger and older students. *Research in Higher Education, 32,* 159–178.

Grossman, M., & Kaestner, R. (1997). Effects of education on health. In J. Behrman & N. Stacey (Eds.), *The social benefits of education* (pp. 69–123). Ann Arbor: University of Michigan Press.

Grossweiler, R., & Slevin, K. (1995). The importance of gender in the assessment of historical knowledge. *Research in Higher Education, 36,* 155–175.

Grubb, N. (1989). The effects of differentiation on educational attainment: The case of community colleges. *Review of Higher Education, 12,* 349–374.

Grubb, W. (1991). The decline of community college transfer rates: Evidence from national longitudinal surveys. *Journal of Higher Education, 62,* 194–222.

Grubb, W. (1992a). Postsecondary vocational education and the subbaccalaureate labor market: New evidence on economic returns. *Economics of Education Review, 11,* 225–248.

Grubb, W. (1992b). The economic returns to baccalaureate degrees: New evidence from the class of 1972. *Review of Higher Education, 15,* 213–231.

Grubb, W. (1993). Further tests of screening on education and observed ability. *Economics of Education Review, 12,* 125–136.

Grubb, W. (1995a). Postsecondary education and the subbaccalaureate labor market: Corrections and extensions. *Economics of Education Review, 14,* 285–299.

Grubb, W. (1995b). The economic returns to baccalaureate degrees: Corrections. *Review of Higher Education, 18,* 483–489.

Grubb, W. (1996). *Working in the middle: Strengthening education and training for the mid-skilled labor force.* San Francisco: Jossey-Bass.

Grubb, W. (1997). The returns to education in the subbaccalaureate labor market, 1984–1990. *Economics of Education Review, 16*(3), 231–245.

Grubb, W. (1998, August). *Learning and earning in the middle: The economic benefits of subbaccalaureate education.* New York: Columbia University, Teacher's College, Community College Research Center, Institute for Education and the Economy.

Grubb, W. (2002). Learning and earning in the middle, Part I: National studies of pre-baccalaureate education. *Economics of Education Review, 21,* 299–321.

Grunder, P., & Hellmich, D. (1996). Academic persistence and achievement of remedial students in a community college's college success program. *Community College Review, 24,* 21–33.

Grunig, S. (1997). Research, reputation, and resources: The effect of research activity on perceptions of undergraduate education and institutional resource acquisition. *Journal of Higher Education, 68,* 17–52.

Guerin, K. (1997, May). *Tracking student exit, transfer, and graduation: An event history analysis of competing risks.* Paper presented at the meeting of the Association for Institutional Research, Orlando.

Guimond, S. (1999). Attitude change during college: Normative or informational social influence? *Social Psychology of Education, 2,* 237–261.

Guimond, S., & Palmer, D. (1989). Education, academic program and intergroup attitudes. *Canadian Review of Sociology and Anthropology, 26,* 193–216.

Guimond, S., & Palmer, D. (1990). Type of academic training and causal attributions for social problems. *European Journal of Social Psychology, 20,* 61–75.

Guiterrez-Marquez, A. (1994, May). *A longitudinal model for assessing student outcomes at a community college.* Paper presented at the meeting of the Association for Institutional Research, New Orleans.

Gunn, C. (1993). Assessing critical thinking: Development of a constructed response sheet. *Dissertation Abstracts International, 54,* 2267B.

Guralnik, J., Land, K., Bluzer, D., Fillenbaum, G., & Branch, L. (1993, July 8). Educational status and active life expectancy among older Blacks and Whites. *New England Journal of Medicine, 329,* 111–116.

Gurin, G. (1971). The impact of the college experience. In S. Withey (Ed.), *A degree and what else? Correlates and consequences of a college education.* New York: McGraw-Hill.

Gurin, P. (1999). Expert report of Patricia Gurin: *Gratz et al., v. Bollinger et al., No. 97–75321 (E.D. Mich.), Grutter et al. v. Bollinger et al., No. 97–75928 (E.D. Mich.)* (pp. 99, 100). *The compelling need for diversity in higher education.* [Available at http://www.umich.edu/~urel/admissions/legal/expert/gurintoc.html].

Gurin, P., Dey, E., Hurtado, S., & Gurin, G. (2002). Diversity and higher education: Theory and impact on student outcomes. *Harvard Educational Review, 72,* 330–366.

Gurin, P., Peng, T., Lopez, G., & Nagda, B. (1999). Context, identity, and intergroup relations. In D. Prentice & D. Miller (Eds.), *Cultural divides: Understanding and overcoming group conflict* (pp. 133–170). New York: Russell Sage Foundation.

Guskey, T. (1985). *Implementing mastery learning.* Belmont, CA: Wadsworth.

Guskey, T., & Pigott, T. (1988). Research on group-based mastery learning programs: A meta-analysis. *Journal of Educational Research, 81,* 197–216.

Guy, J., & Frisby, A. (1992). Using interactive videodiscs to teach gross anatomy to undergraduates at the Ohio State university. *Academic Medicine, 67,* 132–133.

Guyot, G. (1997, April). *High school factors that predict GPA and attrition in college.* Paper presented at the meeting of the Rocky Mountain Psychological Association, Reno, NV.

Gyimah-Brempong, K., Fichtenbaum, R., & Willis, G. (1992). The effects of college education on the male-female wage differential. *Southern Economic Journal, 58,* 790–804.

Hacker, A. (1997). *Money: Who has how much and why.* New York: Scribner.

Hackett, E., Croissant, J., & Schneider, B. (1992). Industry, academe, and the values of undergraduate engineers. *Research in Higher Education, 33,* 275–295.

Hagedorn, L., Pascarella, E., Edison, M., Braxton, J., Nora, A., & Terenzini, P. (1999). Institutional context and the development of critical thinking: A research note. *Review of Higher Education, 22,* 247–263.

Hagedorn, L., Siadat, M., Fogel, S., Nora, A., & Pascarella, E. (1997). *Success in college mathematics: Comparisons between remedial and nonremedial first year college students.* Paper presented at the meeting of the American Educational Research Association, Chicago.

Hagedorn, L., Siadat, M., Nora, A., & Pascarella, E. (1997, March). Factors leading to gains in mathematics during the first year of college: An analysis by gender and ethnicity. *Journal of Women and Minorities in Science and Engineering, 3,* 185–202.

Hake, R. (1998). Interactive-engagement vs. traditional methods: A six-thousand-student survey of mechanics test data for introductory physics courses. *American Journal of Physics, 66,* 64–74.

Hall, D. (1992). The influence of an innovative activity-centered biology program on attitudes toward science teaching among preservice elementary teachers. *School Science and Mathematics, 95,* 239–242.

Hall, D., & McCurdy, D. (1990). A comparative study of a BSCS-style and a traditional laboratory approach on student achievement at two private liberal arts colleges. *Journal of Research in Science Teaching, 27,* 628–636.

Hall, M., & Stocks, M. (1995). Relationship between quantity of undergraduate science preparation and preclinical performance in medical school. *Academic Medicine, 70,* 230–235.

Hall, R., & Sandler, B. (1982). *The campus climate: A chilly one for women?* (Report of the Project on the Status and Education of Women). Washington, DC: Association of American Colleges.

Hall, R., & Sandler, B. (1984). *Out of the classroom: A chilly campus climate for women?* (Report of the Project on the Status and Education of Women). Washington, DC: Association of American Colleges.

Halpern, D. (1993). Assessing the effectiveness of critical thinking instruction. *Journal of General Education, 42,* 238–254.

Halpin, R. (1990). An application of the Tinto model to the analysis of freshman persistence in a community college. *Community College Review, 17,* 22–32.

Hann, N., & Asghar, A. (1996). Prevalence of overweight and associated factors among Oklahomans. *Journal of the Oklahoma State Medical Association, 89,* 353–361.

Hanniford, B., & Sagoria, M. (1994, April). *The impact of work and family roles on associate and baccalaureate degree completion among students in early adulthood.* Paper presented at the meeting of the American Educational Research Association, New Orleans.

Hansford, B., & Hattie, J. (1982). The relationship between self and achievement/ performance measures. *Review of Educational Research, 52,* 123–142.

Hanson, D., & Engs, R. (1992). College students' drinking problems: A national study, 1982–1991. *Psychological Reports, 71,* 39–42.

Hanushek, E. (1997). Assessing the effects of school resources on student performance: An update. *Educational Evaluation and Policy Analysis, 19,* 141–164.

Hardesty, P. (1991). Undergraduate career courses for credit: A review and meta-analysis. *Journal of College Student Development, 32,* 184–185.

Harding, E., & Harmon, L. (1999). *Higher education students' off-campus work patterns* (No. SIPP 99-01-2301). Olympia: Washington State Institute for Public Policy.

Harrison, P., Downes, J., & Williams, M. (1991). Date and acquaintance rape: Perceptions and attitude change strategies. *Journal of College Student Development, 32,* 131–139.

Hart, E., & Speece, D. (1998). Reciprocal teaching goes to college: Effects for postsecondary students at risk for academic failure. *Journal of Educational Psychology, 90,* 670–681.

Hart, J., Rickards, W., & Mentkowski, M. (1995, April). *Epistemological development during and after college: Longitudinal growth on the Perry scheme.* Paper presented at the meeting of the American Educational Research Association, San Francisco.

Hartle, T. (1998). Clueless about college costs. *The Presidency, 1*(1), 20–27.

Hartog, J., & Oosterbeek, H. (1998). Health, wealth, and happiness: Why pursue a higher education? *Economics of Education Review, 17,* 245–256.

Harwarth, I., Maline, M., & DeBra, E. (1997). *Women's colleges in the United States: History, issues, and challenges.* Washington, DC: U.S. Government Printing Office.

Hatcher, L., Kryter, K., Prus, J., & Fitzgerald, V. (1992). Predicting college student satisfaction, commitment, and attrition from investment model constructs. *Journal of Applied Social Psychology, 22,* 1273–1296.

Hatcher, L., Prus, J., Englehard, B., & Farmer, T. (1991). A measure of academic situational constraints: Out-of-class circumstances that inhibit college student development. *Educational and Psychological Measurement, 51,* 953–962.

Hathaway, R., Nagda, B., & Gregerman, S. (2002). The relationship of undergraduate research participation to graduate and professional education pursuit: An empirical study. *Journal of College Student Development, 43,* 614–631.

Hattie, J., Biggs, J., & Purdie, N. (1996). Effects of learning skills interventions on student learning: A meta-analysis. *Review of Educational Research, 66,* 99–136.

Hattie, J., & Marsh, H. (1996). The relationship between research and teaching: A meta-analysis. *Review of Educational Research, 66,* 507–542.

Hattie, J., Marsh, H., Neill, J., & Richards, G. (1997). Adventure education and outward bound: Out-of-class experiences that make a lasting difference. *Review of Educational Research, 67,* 43–87.

Haveman, R., & Wolfe, B. (1984). Schooling and economic well-being: The role of non-market effects. *Journal of Human Resources, 19,* 377–407.

Haveman, R., Wolfe, B., Kreider, B., & Stone, M. (1994). Market work, wages, and men's health. *Journal of Health Economics, 13,* 163–182.

Hayek, J., Carini, R., O'Day, P., & Kuh, G. (2002). Triumph or tragedy: Comparing student engagement levels of members of Greek-letter organizations and other students. *Journal of College Student Development, 43,* 643–663.

Hayek, J., & Kuh, G. (1998, November). *The capacity for lifelong learning of college seniors in the mid-1980s and the mid-1990s.* Paper presented at the meeting of the Association for the Study of Higher Education, Miami.

Hayek, J., & Kuh, G. (1999, November). *College activities and environmental factors associated with the development of lifelong learning competencies of college seniors.* Paper presented at the meeting of the Association for the Study of Higher Education, San Antonio, TX.

Hayes, E., & Flannery, D. (1997). Narratives of adult women's learning in higher education: Insights from graduate research. *Initiatives, 58,* 61–80.

Haynes, K., & Dillon, C. (1992). Distance education: Learning outcomes, interaction, and attitudes. *Journal of Education for Library and Information Science, 33,* 35–45.

Hays, W. (1994). *Statistics* (5th ed.). Orlando: Harcourt Brace.

Healy, S. (2001). *Persistence of Native American students at a comprehensive university.* Unpublished dissertation, Pennsylvania State University, University Park.

Heath, D. (1968). *Growing up in college.* San Francisco: Jossey-Bass.

Heath, T. (1992, October). *Predicting the educational aspirations and graduate plans of Black and White college and university students: When do dreams become realities?* Paper presented at the meeting of the Association for the Study of Higher Education, Minneapolis, MN.

Heckert, T., & Wallis, H. (1998). Career and salary expectations of college freshmen and seniors: Are seniors more realistic than freshmen? *College Student Journal, 32,* 334–339.

Heckler, D. (1992, July). Reconciling conflicting data on jobs for college graduates. *Monthly Labor Review,* pp. 3–12.

Heckman, J. (1999). Doing it right: Job training and education. *Public Interest, 135,* 86–107.

Hector, J., & Hector, M. (1992, April). *Impact of state-mandated developmental studies on college student retention.* Paper presented at the meeting of the American Educational Research Association, San Francisco.

Heilweil, M. (1973). The influence of dormitory architecture on resident behavior. *Environment and Behavior, 5,* 377–412.

Heller, D. (1997). Student price response in higher education: An update to Leslie and Brinkman. *Journal of Higher Education, 68,* 624–659.

Heller, D. (2000). Are first-time college enrollees more price-sensitive than continuing students? *Journal of Staff, Program, and Organization Development, 17,* 95–107.

Heller, D. (2001). *Debts and decisions: Student loans and their relationship to graduate school and career choice.* New Agenda Series. Indianapolis: Lumina Foundation.

Heller, D. (2003). *Informing public policy: Financial aid and student persistence.* Boulder, CO: Western Interstate Commission for Higher Education.

Helminiak, D. (1987). *Spiritual development: An interdisciplinary study.* Chicago: Loyola University Press.

Helms, J. (Ed.). (1990a). *Black and White racial identity: Theory, research, and practice.* Westport, CT: Greenwood Press.

Helms, J. (1990b). Introduction: Review of racial identity terminology. In J. Helms (Ed.), *Black and White racial identity: Theory, research, and practice.* Westport, CT: Greenwood Press.

Helms, J. (1990c). An overview of Black racial identity theory. In J. Helms (Ed.), *Black and White racial identity: Theory, research, and practice* (pp. 9–32). Westport, CT: Greenwood Press.

Helms, J. (1990d). Toward a model of White racial identity development. In J. Helms (Ed.), *Black and White racial identity: Theory, research, and practice* (pp. 49–66). Westport, CT: Greenwood Press.

Helms, J. (1993). I also said, "White racial identity influences White researchers." *The Counseling Psychologist, 21,* 240–243.

Helms, J. (1994). The conceptualization of racial identity and other "racial" constructs. In E. Trickett, R. Watts, & D. Birman (Eds.), *Human diversity: Perspectives on people in context* (pp. 285–311). San Francisco: Jossey-Bass.

Helms, J. (1995). An update of Helms's White and people of color racial identity models. In J. Ponterotto, J. Casas, L. Suzuki, & C. Alexander (Eds.), *Handbook of multicultural counseling* (pp. 181–198). Thousand Oaks, CA: Sage.

Helms, J. (1997). Implications of Behrens (1997) for the validity of the White Racial Identity Attitude Scale. *Journal of Counseling Psychology, 44,* 13–16.

Helms, J. (1999). Another meta-analysis of the White Racial Identity Attitude Scale's Cronbach alphas: Implications for validity. *Measurement and Evaluation in Counseling and Development, 32,* 122–137.

Helms, J., & Carter, R. (1990). Development of the White Racial Identity Inventory. In J. Helms (Ed.), *Black and White racial identity: Theory, research, and practice* (pp. 67–80). Westport, CT: Greenwood Press.

Helms, J., & Piper, R. (1994). Implications of racial identity theory for vocational psychology. *Journal of Vocational Behavior, 44,* 124–136.

Helms, J., & Talleyrand, R. (1997). Race is not ethnicity. *American Psychologist, 52,* 1246–1247.

Henderson, C. (1995). *College freshmen with disabilities: A triennial statistical profile* (Research report). Washington, DC: American Council on Education, HEATH Resource Center.

Henderson-King, D. (1993). The development of a feminist consciousness: Effects of exposure to feminism and emotional stance. *Dissertation Abstracts International, 54,* 5983.

Henderson-King, D., & Kaleta, A. (2000). Learning about social diversity: The undergraduate experience and intergroup tolerance. *Journal of Higher Education, 71,* 142–164.

Henderson-King, D., & Stewart, A. (1999). Educational experiences and shifts in group consciousness: Studying women. *Personality and Social Psychology Bulletin, 25,* 390–399.

Hensen, K., & Shelley, M. (2003). The impact of supplemental instruction: Results from a large, public, midwestern university. *Journal of College Student Development, 44,* 250–259.

Heppner, M., Humphrey, C., Hillenbrand-Gunn, T., & DeBord, K. (1995). The differential effects of rape prevention programming on attitudes, behavior, and knowledge. *Journal of Counseling Psychology, 42,* 508–518.

Herek, G. (1994). Assessing heterosexuals' attitudes toward lesbians and gay men: A review of empirical research with the ATLG Scale. In B. Greene & G. Herek (Eds.), *Lesbian and gay psychology: Theory, research, and clinical applications* (pp. 206–228). Thousand Oaks, CA: Sage.

Hesse-Biber, S., & Marino, M. (1991). From high school to college: Changes in women's self-concept and its relationship to eating problems. *Journal of Psychology, 125,* 199–216.

Hesser, G. (1995). Faculty assessment of student learning: Outcomes attributed to service learning and evidence of changes in faculty attitudes about experiential education. *Michigan Journal of Community Service Learning, 2,* 33–42.

Heverly, M. (1999). Predicting retention from students' experiences with college processes. *Journal of College Student Retention, 1,* 3–11.

Hexter, H. (1990). *Students who work: A profile* (Report No. 81–1502). Washington, DC: American Council on Education, Division of Policy Analysis and Research.

Heywood, J. (1994). How widespread are sheepskin returns to education in the U.S.? *Economics of Education Review, 13,* 227–234.

Higgins, R., Cook, C., Ekeler, W., Sawyer, R., & Prichard, K. (1993). *The Black student's guide to college success.* Westport, CT: Greenwood Press.

Hill, E. (1989). Postsecondary technical education, performance, and employee development: A survey of employers. *Economics of Education Review, 8,* 323–333.

Hill, K. (1995). Critical thinking and its relation to academic, personal, and moral development in the college years. *Dissertation Abstracts International, 56,* 4603B.

Hilligoss, T. (1992). Demystifying "classroom chemistry": The role of the interactive learning model. *Teaching Sociology, 20,* 12–17.

Hilmer, M. (1996). Essays on community college transfer students. *Dissertation Abstracts International, 57,* 4069A.

Hilmer, M. (1997). Does community college attendance provide a strategic path to a higher-quality education? *Economics of Education Review, 16,* 59–68.

Hilmer, M. (2000). Does the return to university quality differ for transfer students and direct attendees? *Economics of Education Review, 19,* 47–61.

Hilton, T., Hsia, J., Cheng, M., & Miller, J. (1995). *Persistence in science of high-ability minority students. Phase IV: Second follow-up* (Research report). Princeton, NJ: Educational Testing Service.

Hilton, T., Hsia, J., Solorzano, D., & Penton, N. (1989). *Persistence in science of high-ability minority students* (Research Report No. 89–28). Princeton, NJ: Educational Testing Service.

Hinderlie, H., & Kenny, M. (2002). Attachment, social support, and college adjustment among Black students at predominantly White universities. *Journal of College Student Development, 43,* 327–340.

Hippensteel, D., St. John, E., & Starkey, J. (1996). Influence of tuition and student aid on within-year persistence by adults in two-year colleges. *Community College Journal of Research and Practice, 20,* 233–242.

Hirumi, A., & Bowers, D. (1991). Enhancing motivation and acquisition of coordinate concepts by using concept trees. *Journal of Educational Research, 84,* 273–279.

Hodge, E., Palmer, B., & Scott, D. (1992). Metacognitive training in cooperative groups on the reading comprehension and vocabulary of at-risk college students. *College Student Journal, 26,* 440–448.

Hodge-Hardin, S. (1995). *Interactive television in the classroom: A comparison of student math achievement among three instructional settings.* Unpublished doctoral dissertation, East Tennessee State University, Johnson City.

Hofer, B. (1994). *Epistemological beliefs and first-year college students: Motivation and cognition in different instructional contexts.* Paper presented at the meeting of the American Psychological Association, Los Angeles.

Hofer, B. (1998–99). Instructional context in the college mathematics classroom: Epistemological beliefs and student motivation. *Journal of Staff, Program, & Organization Development, 16,* 73–82.

Hoff, M., Cook, D., & Price, C. (1996). The first five years of freshman seminars at Dalton College: Student success and retention. *Journal of the Freshman Year Experience, 8,* 33–42.

Hoit, M., & Ohland, M. (1998). The impact of a discipline-based introduction to engineering course on improving retention. *Journal of Engineering Education, 82,* 79–85.

Holland, D., & Eisenhart, M. (1990). *Educated in romance: Women, achievement, and college culture.* Chicago: University of Chicago Press.

Holland, J. (1985). *Making vocational choices: A theory of vocational personalities and work environments.* Englewood Cliffs, NJ: Prentice-Hall.

Holland, J. (1997). *Making vocational choices: A theory of vocational personalities and work environments* (3rd ed.). Odessa, FL: Psychological Assessment Resources.

Hollenbeck, K. (1993). Postsecondary education as triage: Returns to academic and technical programs. *Economics of Education Review, 12,* 213–232.

Hollings, A. (1992, May). *A follow-up of CIRP freshman survey respondents four years later: How did they do and how did they change?* Paper presented at the meeting of the Association for Institutional Research, Atlanta, GA.

Hollingsworth, P. (1995). Enhancing listening retention: The two-minute discussion. *College Student Journal, 29,* 116–117.

Honan, W. (1993, October 3). Yale inaugurates dean and economist as its 22nd president. *New York Times,* p. 36.

Horn, L. (1994). *Undergraduates who work while enrolled in postsecondary education: 1989–90* (Statistical Analysis Report No. NCES 94–311). Washington, DC: U.S. Department of Education, Office of Educational Research and Improvement, National Center for Education Statistics.

Horn, L. (1998a). *Stopouts or stayouts? Undergraduates who leave college in their first year* (Statistical Analysis Report No. NCES 1999–087). Washington, DC: U.S. Department of Education, Office of Educational Research and Improvement, National Center for Education Statistics.

Horn, L. (1998b). *Undergraduates who work: National postsecondary student aid study 1996* (Report No. NCES 98–137). Washington, DC: U.S. Department of Education, Office of Educational Research and Improvement, National Center for Education Statistics.

Horn, L., & Berktold, J. (1998). *Profile of undergraduates in U.S. postsecondary education institutions: 1995–96, with an essay on undergraduates who work* (Statistical Analysis Report No. NCES 98–084). Washington, DC: U.S. Department of Education, Office of Educational Research and Improvement, National Center for Education Statistics.

Horn, L., & Nunez, A. (2000). *Mapping the road to college: First-generation students' math track, planning strategies, and context of support* (Statistical Analysis Report No. NCES 2000–153). Washington, DC: U.S. Department of Education, Office of Educational Research and Improvement, National Center for Education Statistics.

Horn, L., & Premo, M. (1995). *Profile of undergraduates in U.S. postsecondary institutions: 1992–93, with an essay on undergraduates at risk* (Statistical Analysis Report No. NCES 96–237). Washington, DC: U.S. Department of Education, Office of Educational Research and Improvement, National Center for Education Statistics.

Horowitz, H. (1987). *Campus life: Undergraduate cultures from the end of the eighteenth century to the present.* New York: Knopf.

Horse, P. (2001). Reflections on American Indian identity. In C. Wijeyesinghe & B. Jackson III (Eds.), *New perspectives on racial identity development: A theoretical and practical anthology* (pp. 91–107). New York: New York University Press.

Hossler, D., Braxton, J., & Coopersmith, G. (1989). Understanding student college choice. In J. Smart (Ed.), *Higher education: Handbook of theory and research* (Vol. 5, pp. 231–288). New York: Agathon.

Hossler, D., Schmit, J., & Vesper, N. (1999). *Going to college: How social, economic, and educational factors influence the decisions students make.* Baltimore, MD: Johns Hopkins University Press.

House, J. (1996a, May). *Student progress, goals versus outcomes and second-term retention: The first two years of the fall 1992 credit-seeking cohort.* Paper presented at the meeting of the Association for Institutional Research, Albuquerque, NM.

House, J. (1996b, May). *College persistence and grade outcomes: Noncognitive variables as predictors for African-American, Asian-American, Hispanic, Native American, and White students.* Paper presented at the meeting of the Association for Institutional Research, Albuquerque, NM.

Howard, J. (1998). Academic service learning: A counternormative pedagogy. In R. Rhoads & J. Howard (Eds.), *Academic service learning: A pedagogy of action and reflection* (pp. 21–29). San Francisco: Jossey-Bass.

Hoxby, C., & Long, B. (1999). *Exploring rising income and wage inequality among the college-educated.* Unpublished manuscript, Harvard University, Cambridge, MA.

Hoyt, J. (1999). Remedial education and student attrition. *Community College Review, 27,* 51–72.

Hu, S., & Kuh, G. (2003). Maximizing what students get out of college: Testing a learning productivity model. *Journal of College Student Development, 44,* 185–203.

Hu, S., & St. John, E. (1999, November). *Does money matter across the four critical years? The effects of financial aid on student persistence in a public higher education system.* Paper presented at the meeting of the Association for the Study of Higher Education, San Antonio, TX.

Hu, S., & St. John, E. (2001). Student persistence in a public higher education system: Understanding racial/ethnic differences. *Journal of Higher Education, 72,* 365–387.

Huang, G., Taddese, N., & Walter, E. (2000). *Entry and persistence of women and minorities in college science and engineering education* (Research and Development Report No. NCES 2000–601). Washington, DC: Office of Educational Research and Improvement, U.S. Department of Education.

Huang, S., & Aloi, J. (1991). The impact of using interactive video in teaching general biology. *American Biology Teacher, 53,* 281–284.

Huang, Y. (1995, April). *Whose rite of passage? An investigation of the impact of race on undergraduate academic and social integration.* Paper presented at the meeting of the American Educational Research Association, San Francisco.

Huang, Y., & Healy, C. (1997). The relation of Holland-typed majors to students' freshman and senior work values. *Research in Higher Education, 38,* 455–477.

Hudec, S. (2002). *Inducing voluntary community service in undergraduates: The relative contributions of prior experience, coursework, and the dispositions of empathy and moral development.* Unpublished doctoral dissertation, New York University.

Hudson, W. (1996). Combining community service and the study of American public policy. *Michigan Journal of Community Service Learning, 2,* 82–91.

Huebner, L. (1989). Interaction of student and campus. In U. Delworth, G. Hanson, & Associates (Eds.), *Student services: A handbook for the profession* (2nd ed.). San Francisco: Jossey-Bass.

Huffman, T. (1991). The experiences, perceptions, and consequences of campus racism among Northern Plains Indians. *Journal of American Indian Education, 30,* 25–34.

Hulbert, K., & Schuster, D. (Eds.). (1993). *Women's lives through time: Educated American women of the twentieth century.* San Francisco: Jossey-Bass.

Hummel, M. (1997, January/February). Eliminating the achievement gap: The 21st Century Program. *About Campus, 1,* 28–29.

Hummel, M., & Steele, C. (1996). The learning community: A program to address issues of academic achievement and retention. *Journal of Intergroup Relations, 23,* 28–33.

Humphreys, D. (2000, Fall). National survey finds diversity requirements common around the country. *Diversity Digest,* pp. 1–3.

Hunt, S., & Rentz, A. (1994). Greek-letter social group members' involvement and psychosocial development. *Journal of College Student Development, 35,* 289–295.

Hurtado, S. (1990). *An analysis of student coursework and GRE performance.* Paper presented at the annual meeting of the American Educational Research Association, Boston.

Hurtado, S. (1992). The campus racial climate: Contexts of conflict. *Journal of Higher Education, 63,* 539–569.

Hurtado, S. (1994). The institutional climate for talented Latino students. *Research in Higher Education, 35,* 21–41.

Hurtado, S. (1997). *Linking diversity with educational purpose: College outcomes associated with diversity in the faculty and student body.* Unpublished manuscript, Harvard Civil Rights Project, Harvard University, Cambridge, MA.

Hurtado, S. (Ed.). (1999). *Linking diversity and educational purpose: How the diversity of the faculty and the student body impacts the classroom environment and student development.* Cambridge, MA: Harvard Publishing Group.

Hurtado, S. (2001). Linking diversity and educational purpose: How diversity affects the classroom environment and student development. In G. Orfield & M. Kurleander (Eds.), *Diversity challenged: Evidence on the impact of affirmative action* (pp. 187–203). Cambridge, MA: The Civil Rights Project, Harvard University, Harvard Education Publishing Group.

Hurtado, S., & Carter, D. (1997). Effects of college transition and perceptions of the campus racial climate on Latino college students' sense of belonging. *Sociology of Education, 70,* 324–345.

Hurtado, S., Carter, D., & Sharp, S. (1995, May). *Social interaction on campus: Differences among self-perceived ability groups.* Paper presented at the meeting of the Association for Institutional Research, Boston.

Hurtado, S., Carter, D., & Spuler, A. (1996). Latino student transition to college: Assessing difficulties and factors in successful college adjustment. *Research in Higher Education, 37,* 135–157.

Hurtado, S., Enberg, M., Ponjuan, L., & Landreman, L. (2002). Students' precollege preparation for participation in a diverse democracy. *Research in Higher Education, 43,* 163–186.

Hurtado, S., Mayhew, M., & Engberg, M. (2003, November). *Diversity in the classroom and students' moral reasoning.* Paper presented at the meeting of the Association for the Study of Higher Education, Portland, OR.

Hurtado, S., Milem, J., Clayton-Pedersen, A., & Allen, W. (1999). *Enacting diverse learning environments: Improving the climate for racial/ethnic diversity in higher education* (ASHE-ERIC Higher Education Reports, Vol. 26, No. 8). Washington, DC: George Washington University, Graduate School of Education and Human Development.

Hyers, A., & Joslin, M. (1998). The first-year seminar as a predictor of academic achievement and persistence. *Journal of the Freshman Year Experience and Students in Transition, 10,* 7–30.

Hyllegard, D., & Lavin, D. (1992, April). *Higher education and desirable work: Open admissions and ethnic and gender differences in job quality.* Paper presented at the meeting of the American Educational Research Association, San Francisco.

Hyun, M. (1996). Commitment to change: How college impacts changes in students' commitment to racial understanding. *Dissertation Abstracts International, 57,* 1978A.

Icerman, R., Karcher, J., & Kennelley, M. (1991). A baseline assessment of moral development: Accounting, business, and nonbusiness students. *Accounting Educators' Journal, 3,* 46–62.

Ignelzi, M. (1990). Ethical education in a college environment: The just community approach. *NASPA Journal, 27,* 191–198.

Ikeda, E. (2000). *How reflection enhances learning in service-learning courses.* Paper presented at the meeting of the American Educational Research Association, New Orleans.

Ikenberry, R., Arrington, M., & McGraw, C. (1994, May). *Analyzing factors that influence first- to second-year college persistence using institutional data files.* Paper presented at the meeting of the Association for Institutional Research, New Orleans.

Ikenberry, S. (1997). Values, character, leadership: Reexamining our mission. *Educational Record, 78*(3, 4), 7–9.

The influence of Greek affiliation on students' college experiences and educational outcomes. (1997). *Student Life Studies Abstracts, No. 3.* Columbia: University of Missouri.

Ingels, S., Curtin, T., Kaufman, P., Alt, M., & Chen, X. (2002). *Coming of age in the 1990s: The eighth-grade class of 1988 12 years later* (Statistical Analysis Report No. NCES 2002–321). Washington, DC: U.S. Department of Education, Office of Educational Research and Improvement, National Center for Education Statistics.

Ingram, B., & Neuman, G. (1999). *An analysis of the evolution of the skill premium.* Unpublished manuscript, University of Iowa, Iowa City.

Inkelas, K. (1999). *The tide on which all boats rise: The effects of living-learning participation on undergraduate outcomes at the University of Michigan.* Ann Arbor, MI: University Housing.

Inkelas, K., & Weisman, J. (2003). Different by design: An examination of student outcomes among participants in three types of living-learning programs. *Journal of College Student Development, 44,* 335–368.

Inkeles, A. (1966). Social structure and the socialization of competence. *Harvard Educational Review, 36,* 265–283.

Inlow, F., & Chovan, W. (1993). Another search for the effects of teaching thinking and problem-solving skills on college students' performance. *Journal of Instructional Psychology, 20,* 215–223.

Inman, P., & Pascarella, E. (1998). The impact of college residence on the development of critical thinking skills in college freshmen. *Journal of College Student Development, 39,* 557–568.

Inoue, Y., & Ethington, C. (1997). *The educational and occupational attainment process for American women.* Paper presented at the meeting of the Association for the Study of Higher Education, Albuquerque, NM.

Institute for Higher Education Policy. (1997). *Now what? Life after college for recent graduates.* Washington, DC: Author.

Institute for Higher Education Policy. (1999). *Distance learning in higher education.* Washington, DC: Author.

Institutional graduation rates by academic selectivity and low-income representation. (1999, October). *Postsecondary Education OPPORTUNITY,* No. 88, 11–16.

Institutional graduation rates by degree level, control, and academic selectivity [Entire issue]. (1996, March). *Postsecondary Education OPPORTUNITY,* No. 45.

Ippolito, P., & Mathios, A. (1990). Information, advertising, and health choices: A study of the cereal market. *Rand Journal of Economics, 21,* 459–480.

Iribarren, C., Sidney, S., Sternfeld, B., & Browner, W. (2000). Calcification of the aortic arch: Risk factors and association with coronary heart disease, stroke, and peripheral vascular disease. *Journal of the American Medical Association, 283,* 2810–2815.

Is college still worth the cost? The private investment value of higher education 1967 to 1996. (1998, March). *Postsecondary Education OPPORTUNITY,* No. 69, 9–16.

Isaac, P., Malaney, G., & Karras, J. (1992). Parental educational level, gender differences, and seniors' aspirations for advanced study. *Research in Higher Education, 33,* 595–606.

Ishida, H., Spilerman, S., & Su, K.-H. (1997). Educational credentials and promotion chances in Japanese and American organizations. *American Sociological Review, 62,* 866–882.

Ishitani, T., & DesJardins, S. (2002–2003). A longitudinal investigation of dropout from college in the United States. *Journal of College Student Retention, 4,* 173–201.

Ishiyama, J. (2002). Does early participation in undergraduate research benefit social science and humanities students? *College Student Journal, 36,* 380–386.

Jablonski, M. (Ed.). (2001). *The implications of spirituality for student affairs practice. New Directions for Student Services,* No. 95. San Francisco: Jossey-Bass.

Jackson, L. (1998). The influence of both race and gender on the experiences of African-American college women. *Review of Higher Education, 21,* 359–375.

Jackson, L., Gardner, P., & Sullivan, L. (1993). Engineering persistence: Past, present, and future factors and gender differences. *Higher Education, 26,* 227–246.

Jackson, L., Hodge, C., & Ingram, J. (1994). Gender and self-concept: A reexamination of stereotypic differences and the role of gender attitudes. *Sex Roles, 30,* 615–630.

Jacobs, J. (1995). Gender and academic specialties: Trends among recipients of college degrees in the 1980s. *Sociology of Education, 68,* 81–98.

Jacobs, J. (1996a). Gender inequity and higher education. *Annual Review of Sociology, 22,* 153–185.

Jacobs, J. (1996b). *Gender and access to higher education.* Unpublished manuscript, University of Pennsylvania, Philadelphia.

Jacobs, J. (1999). Gender and the stratification of colleges. *Journal of Higher Education, 70,* 161–187.

Jacoby, B., & Associates (Eds.). (1996). *Service-learning in higher education: Concepts and practices.* San Francisco: Jossey-Bass.

Jaeger, D., & Page, M. (1996). Degrees matter: New evidence on sheepskin effects in returns to education. *Review of Economics and Statistics, 78,* 733–740.

Jalomo, R. (1995). *Latino students in transition: An analysis of the first-year experience in community college.* Unpublished doctoral dissertation, Arizona State University.

James, E., & Alsalam, N. (1993). College choice, academic achievement, and future earnings. In E. Hoffman (Ed.), *Essays on the economics of education* (pp. 111–138). Kalamazoo, MI: W. E. Upjohn Institute for Employment Research.

James, E., Alsalam, N., Conaty, J., & To, D. (1989). College quality and future earnings: Where should you send your child to college? *American Economic Review, 79,* 247–252.

Jeffrey, C. (1993). Ethical development of accounting students, business students, and liberal arts students. *Issues in Accounting Education, 8,* 26–40.

Jehng, J., Johnson, S., & Anderson, R. (1993). Schooling and students' epistemological beliefs about learning. *Contemporary Educational Psychology, 18,* 23–35.

Jencks, C., Bartlett, S., Corcoran, M., Crouse, J., Eaglesfield, D., Jackson, G., et al. (1979). *Who gets ahead? The determinants of economic success in America.* New York: Basic Books.

Jenkins, C. (1992, April). *Overeducation: Job satisfaction.* Paper presented at the meeting of the American Educational Research Association, San Francisco.

Jensen, L., Kitchener, K., & Wood, P. (1999, August). *The role of need for cognition in the development of reflective judgment.* Paper presented at the meeting of the American Psychological Association, Boston.

Jepsen, D. (n.d.). *American college students' career development: A review of social science literature, 1987–1993.* Unpublished manuscript, University of Iowa, Iowa City.

Johnson, D., & Johnson, R. (1993a). *Cooperation among adults: Impact on individual learning versus team productivity.* Unpublished manuscript, University of Minnesota, Minneapolis.

Johnson, D., & Johnson, R. (1993b). Creative and critical thinking through academic controversy. *American Behavioral Scientist, 37,* 40–53.

Johnson, D., & Johnson, R. (1995). *Creative controversy: Intellectual challenge in the classroom.* Edina, MN: Interaction Books.

Johnson, D., Johnson, R., & Smith, K. (1996). *Academic controversy: Enriching college instruction through intellectual conflict.* Washington, DC: George Washington University, Graduate School of Education and Human Development.

Johnson, D., Johnson, R., & Smith, K. (1998a, July/August). Cooperative learning returns to college: What evidence is there that it works? *Change, 30,* 26–35.

Johnson, D., Johnson, R., & Smith, K. (1998b). *Active learning: Cooperation in the college classroom* (2nd ed.). Edina, MN: Interaction Books.

Johnson, G. (1994). Undergraduate student attrition: A comparison of students who withdraw and students who persist. *Alberta Journal of Educational Research, 15,* 337–353.

Johnson, J. (1991). *Evaluation report of the Community College of Maine interactive television system.* Portland: University of Southern Maine.

Johnson, J. (1997). Commuter college students: What factors determine who will persist and who will drop out? *College Student Journal, 31,* 323–332.

Johnson, L. (1995). The psychosocial development of academically talented college students: An exploratory investigation. *College Student Journal, 29,* 278–289.

Johnson, M., & Molnar, D. (1996, May). *Comparing retention factors for Anglo, Black, and Hispanic students.* Paper presented at the meeting of the Association for Institutional Research, Albuquerque, NM.

Johnstone, K., Ashbaugh, H., & Warfield, T. (2002). Effects of repeated practice and contextual-writing experiences on college students' writing skills. *Journal of Educational Psychology, 94,* 305–315.

Jones, B., & Moss, P. (1994). The influence of financial aid on academic performance and persistence in medical school. *Journal of Student Financial Aid, 24,* 5–11.

Jones, C., & Watt, J. (2001). Moral orientation and psychosocial development: Gender and class-standing differences. *NASPA Journal, 39,* 1–13.

Jones, E. (1993). *Critical thinking literature review.* University Park: Pennsylvania State University, National Center on Postsecondary, Teaching, Learning, and Assessment.

Jones, E. (1994). *Defining important skills for college graduates to achieve.* Paper presented at the meeting of the Sixth International Conference on Thinking, Boston.

Jones, E. (1995, April). *Defining essential critical thinking skills for college graduates.* Paper presented at the annual meeting of the American Educational Research Association, San Francisco.

Jones, E., Dougherty, B., Fantaske, P., & Hoffman, S. (1997). *Identifying college graduates' essential skills in reading and problem solving: Perspectives of faculty, employers, and policymakers.* University Park: Pennsylvania State University, National Center on Postsecondary, Teaching, Learning, and Assessment.

Jones, E., Hoffman, S., Moore, L., Ratcliff, G., Tibbetts, S., & Click, B. (1995). *National assessment of college student learning: Identifying college graduates essential skills in writing, speech and listening, and critical thinking* (Research and Development Report No. NCES 95–001). Washington, DC: U.S. Government Printing Office.

Jones, E., & Jackson, J. (1990). College grades and labor market rewards. *Journal of Human Resources, 25,* 253–266.

Jones, E., & Ratcliff, J. (1990). *Is a core curriculum best for everybody? The effect of different patterns of coursework on the general education of high- and low-ability students.* Paper presented at the meeting of the American Educational Research Association, Boston.

Jones, E., & Ratcliff, J. (1991). Which general education curriculum is better: Core curriculum or the distribution requirement? *Journal of General Education, 40,* 69–100.

Jones, J., & Brickner, D. (1996). *Implementation of cooperative learning in a large-enrollment basic mechanics course.* Paper presented at the meeting of the American Society for Engineering Education.

Jones, J., Simonson, M., Kemis, M., & Sorensen, C. (1992). *Distance education: A cost analysis.* Unpublished manuscript, Iowa State University, Ames.

Jones, S. (2002, September/October). The underside of service learning. *About Campus, 7,* 10–15.

Jones, S., & McEwen, M. (2000). A conceptual model of multiple dimensions of identity. *Journal of College Student Development, 41,* 405–414.

Jonides, J., von Hippel, W., Lerner, J., & Nagda, B. (1992, August). *Evaluation of minority retention programs: The undergraduate research opportunities program at the University of Michigan.* Paper presented at the meeting of the American Psychological Association, Washington, DC.

Jordan, J. (Ed.). (1997). *Women's growth in diversity.* New York: Guilford Press.

Jordan, J., & Denson, E. (1990). Student services for athletes: A model for enhancing the student-athlete experience. *Journal of Counseling and Development, 69,* 95–97.

Jordan, K. (1994). The relationship of service learning and college student development. *Dissertation Abstracts International, 55,* 3053A.

Josselson, R. (1973). Psychodynamic aspects of identity formation in college women. *Journal of Youth and Adolescence, 2,* 3–52.

Josselson, R. (1987). *Finding herself: Pathways to identity development in women.* San Francisco: Jossey-Bass.

Josselson, R. (1996). *Revising herself: The story of women's identity from college to midlife.* New York: Oxford University Press.

Kadel, S., & Keehner, J. (1994). *Collaborative learning: A sourcebook for higher education* (Vol. 2). University Park: Pennsylvania State University, National Center on Postsecondary Teaching, Learning, and Assessment.

Kagan, S. (1992). *Cooperative learning.* San Juan Capistrano, CA: Resources for Teachers.

Kahn, M. (1991). Factors affecting the coming-out process for lesbians. *Journal of Homosexuality, 21,* 47–70.

Kahn, M. (1998). Education's role in explaining diabetic health investment differentials. *Economics of Education Review, 17,* 257–266.

Kalof, L., & Cargill, T. (1991). Fraternity and sorority membership and gender dominance attitudes. *Sex Roles, 25,* 417–423.

Kaltenbaugh, L. (1993). The influence of prices and price subsidies on within-year persistence by African-American students. *Dissertation Abstracts International, 55,* 1843A.

Kaltenbaugh, L., St. John, E., & Starkey, J. (1999). What difference does tuition make? An analysis of ethnic differences in persistence. *Journal of Student Financial Aid, 29,* 21–31.

Kalunian, J. (1997, Fall). Correlations between global-mindedness and study abroad. *International Education Forum, 17,* 131–143.

Kamens, D. (1971). The college "charter" and college size: Effects on occupational choice and college attrition. *Sociology of Education, 44,* 270–296.

Kamens, D. (1974). Colleges and elite formation: The case of prestigious American colleges. *Sociology of Education, 47,* 354–378.

Kane, S., Healy, C., & Henson, J. (1992). College students and their part-time jobs: Job congruency, satisfaction, and quality. *Journal of Employment Counseling, 29,* 138–144.

Kane, T. (1998). Racial and ethnic preferences in college admission. In C. Jenkins (Ed.), *The Black-White test score gap* (pp. 431–456). Washington, DC: Brookings Institution.

Kane, T., & Rouse, C. (1993). *Labor market returns to two- and four-year colleges: Is a credit a credit and do degrees matter?* (Faculty Research Working Paper No. 93-38). Cambridge, MA: Harvard University, Kennedy School of Government.

Kane, T., & Rouse, C. (1995a). Comment on W. Norton Grubb, "The varied economic returns to postsecondary education: New evidence from the class of 1972." *Journal of Human Resources, 30,* 205–221.

Kane, T., & Rouse, C. (1995b). Labor market returns to two- and four-year colleges. *American Economic Review, 85,* 600–614.

Kanoy, K., & Bruhn, J. (1996). Effects of a first-year living and learning residence hall on retention and academic performance. *Journal of the Freshman Year Experience and Students in Transition, 8,* 7–23.

Kanoy, K., Wester, J., & Latta, M. (1990). Understanding differences between high- and low-achieving women: Implications for effective placement and teaching. *Journal of College Student Development, 31,* 133–140.

Kanter, S. (1989). The value of the college degree for older women graduates. *Innovative Higher Education, 13,* 90–105.

Kaplan, G., & Keil, J. (1993). Socioeconomic factors and cardiovascular disease: A review of the literature. *Circulation, 88,* 1973–1998.

Karabenick, S., & Collins-Eaglin, J. (1996). *Relation of perceived instructional goals and incentives to college students' use of learning strategies.* Paper presented at the meeting of the American Educational Research Association, New York.

Kardia, D. (1996). Diversity's closet: Student attitudes toward lesbians, gay men, and bisexual people on a multicultural campus. *Dissertation Abstracts International, 57,* 1090A.

Kasworm, C. (1990). Adult undergraduates in higher education: A review of past research perspectives. *Review of Educational Research, 60,* 345–372.

Kasworm, C. (1997). *Adult meaning-making in the undergraduate classroom.* Paper presented at the meeting of the American Educational Research Association, Chicago.

Katchadourian, H., & Boli, J. (1994). *Cream of the crop: The impact of elite education in the decade after college.* New York: Basic Books.

Katz, A. (2001). *The influence of intergroup dialogues on undergraduates' identity formation and moral development schemas.* Unpublished master's thesis, California State University, Long Beach.

Katz, L., & Autor, D. (1998). *Changes in the wage structure and earnings inequality.* Unpublished manuscript, Harvard University, Cambridge, MA.

Katz, L., & Murphy, K. (1992). Change in relative wages 1963–1987. *Quarterly Journal of Economics, 107,* 35–78.

Kaufman, M., & Creamer, D. (1991). Influences of student goals for college on freshman-year quality of effort and growth. *Journal of College Student Development, 32,* 197–206.

Kaufman, P., & Feldman, K. (2004). Forming identities in college: A sociological approach. *Research in Higher Education, 45,* 463–496.

Keegan, D. (1993). *Theoretical principles of distance education.* New York: Routledge.

Keeler, C., & Anson, R. (1995). An assessment of cooperative learning used for basic computer skills instruction in the college classroom. *Journal of Educational Computing Research, 12,* 379–393.

Keeley, S. (1992). Are college students learning the critical thinking skill of finding assumptions? *College Student Journal, 26,* 316–322.

Kegan, R. (1982). *The evolving self: Problem and process in human development.* Cambridge, MA: Harvard University Press.

Kegan, R. (1994). *In over our heads: The mental demands of modern life.* Cambridge, MA: Harvard University Press.

Keil, J., & Partell, P. (1998). *The effect of class size on student performance and retention at Binghamton University.* Paper presented at the meeting of the Association for Institutional Research, Minneapolis, MN.

Kelava, M. (1993). Comparison of bulimic characteristics, sex-role characteristics, and self-esteem between female students in coed and all-women's colleges. *Dissertation Abstracts International, 54,* 2756B.

Keller-Wolff, C., Eason, B., & Hinda, M. (2000, April). *From the student's perspective: The effect of college courses.* Paper presented at the meeting of the American Educational Research Association, New Orleans.

Kelley, L. (1994). *Utilizing a graduate follow-up survey to assess institutional effectiveness in the small liberal arts college.* Paper presented at the meeting of the Association for Institutional Research, New Orleans.

Kelly, L. (1996, May). *Implementing Astin's I-E-O model in the study of student retention: A multivariate time-dependent approach.* Paper presented at the meeting of the Association of Institutional Research, Albuquerque, NM.

Kember, D., & Gow, L. (1994). Orientations to teaching and their effect on the quality of student learning. *Journal of Higher Education, 65,* 58–74.

Kempner, K., Taylor, C., & West, J. (1990). *Educational and career outcomes for high school and community college students: The consequences of employment during school.* Paper presented at the meeting of the American Educational Research Association, Boston.

Kendrick, J. (1996). Outcomes of service learning in an introduction to sociology course. *Michigan Journal of Community Service Learning, 3*(1), 72–81.

Kenkel, D. (1991). Health behavior, health knowledge, and schooling. *Journal of Political Economy, 99,* 287–305.

Kennamer, J. (1990). Comparing predictors of the likelihood of voting in a primary and a general election. *Journalism Quarterly, 67,* 777–784.

Kennedy, P., & Siegfried, J. (1997). Class size and achievement in introductory economics: Evidence from the TUCE III data. *Economics of Education Review, 16,* 385–394.

Kenny, P. (1989). *Effects of supplemental instruction on student performance in a college-level mathematics course.* Paper presented at the meeting of the American Educational Research Association, San Francisco.

Kerckhoff, A., & Bell, L. (1998). Hidden capital: Vocational credentials and attainment in the United States. *Sociology of Education, 71,* 152–174.

Kerlinger, F. (1986). *Foundations of behavioral research* (3rd ed.). New York: Holt, Rinehart & Winston.

Kern, C., Fagley, N., & Miller, P. (1994, April). *Correlates of college retention and GPA: Learning and study strategies, testwiseness, attitudes, and ACT.* Paper presented at the meeting of the American Educational Research Association, New Orleans.

Kerwin, C., & Ponterotto, J. (1995). Biracial identity development: Theory and research. In J. Ponterotto, J. Casas, L. Suzuki, & C. Alexander (Eds.), *Handbook of multicultural counseling.* Thousand Oaks, CA: Sage.

Keup, J., & Barefoot, B. (2002). *A study of first-year seminars.* Unpublished manuscript, Higher Education Research Institute, University of California, Los Angeles.

Kezar, A., & Moriarity, D. (2000). Expanding our understanding of student leadership development: A study explaining gender and ethnic identity. *Journal of College Student Development, 41,* 55–69.

Kiewra, K. (1997). The matrix representation system: Orientation, research, theory, and application. In R. Perry & J. Smart (Eds.), *Effective teaching in higher education: Research and practice* (pp. 115–153). New York: Agathon.

Kiewra, K., DuBois, N., Christian, D., & McShane, A. (1988). Providing study notes: A comparison of three types of notes for review. *Journal of Educational Psychology, 80,* 595–597.

Kiewra, K., DuBois, N., Christian, D., McShane, A., Meyerhoffer, M., & Roskelley, D. (1991). Note-taking functions and techniques. *Journal of Educational Psychology, 83,* 240–245.

Kiewra, K., DuBois, N., Staley, R., & Robinson, D. (1992, April). *Outline versus matrix representations: Memory, integration, and application effects.* Paper presented at the meeting of the American Educational Research Association, San Francisco.

Kilgannon, S., & Erwin, T. (1992). Longitudinal study about the identity and moral development of Greek students. *Journal of College Student Development, 33,* 253–259.

Kim, B., D'Andrea, M., Sahu, P., & Gaughen, K. (1998). A multicultural study of university students' knowledge of and attitudes toward homosexuality. *Journal of Humanistic Education and Development, 36,* 171–182.

Kim, H. (1996, May). *Why students leave or stay: A land-grant research I university experience.* Paper presented at the meeting of the Association for Institutional Research, Albuquerque, NM.

Kim, J. (2001). Asian-American identity development theory. In C. Wijeyesinghe & B. Jackson III (Eds.), *New perspectives on racial identity development: A theoretical and practical anthology* (pp. 67–90). New York: New York University Press.

Kim, J.-B., Cohen, A., Booske, J., & Derry, S. (1998). *Application of cooperative learning in an introductory engineering course.* Paper presented at the meeting of the American Educational Research Association, San Diego, CA.

Kim, M. (1995). *Organizational effectiveness of women-only colleges: The impact of college environment on students' intellectual and ethical development.* Unpublished doctoral dissertation, University of California, Los Angeles.

Kim, M. (1996). *The effectiveness of women-only colleges for intellectual development for women students.* Paper presented at the meeting of the American Educational Research Association, New York.

Kim, M. (1998, November). *Organizational effectiveness of women-only colleges: Cultivating students' desire to influence social conditions.* Paper presented at the meeting of the Association for the Study of Higher Education, Miami.

Kim, M. (1999, November). *A comparative analysis of academic development among African-American students in historically Black versus predominantly White institutions.* Paper presented at the meeting of the Association for the Study of Higher Education, San Antonio, TX.

Kim, M. (2000, April). *Do women-only colleges promote students' cultural awareness and tolerance?* Paper presented at the meeting of the American Educational Research Association, New Orleans.

Kim, M. (2001). Institutional effectiveness of women-only colleges: Cultivating students' desire to influence social conditions. *Journal of Higher Education, 72,* 287–321.

Kim, M. (2002a). Cultivating intellectual development: Comparing women-only colleges and coeducational colleges for educational effectiveness. *Research in Higher Education, 43,* 447–481.

Kim, M. (2002b). Historically Black vs. White institutions: Academic development among Black students. *Review of Higher Education, 25,* 385–407.

Kim, M., & Alvarez, R. (1995). Women-only colleges: Some unanticipated consequences. *Journal of Higher Education, 66,* 641–668.

Kimbrough, W. (1995). Self-assessment, participation, and value of leadership skills, activities, and experiences for Black students relative to their membership in historically Black fraternities and sororities. *Journal of Negro Education, 64,* 63–74.

Kimbrough, W., & Hutcheson, P. (1998). The impact of membership in Black Greek-letter organizations on Black students' involvement in collegiate activities and their development of leadership skills. *Journal of Negro Education, 67,* 96–105.

King, A. (1990). Enhancing peer interaction and learning in the classroom through reciprocal questioning. *American Educational Research Journal, 27,* 664–687.

King, J. (2002). *Crucial choices: How students' financial decisions affect their academic success.* Washington, DC: American Council on Education, Center for Policy Analysis.

King, P. (1978). William Perry's theory of intellectual and ethical development. In L. Knefelkamp, C. Widick, & C. Parker (Eds.), *Applying new developmental findings. New Directions for Student Services,* No. 4. San Francisco: Jossey-Bass.

King, P. (1997). Character and civic education: What does it take? *Educational Record, 78*(3, 4), 87–93.

King, P. (2003). Student learning in higher education. In S. Komives & D. Woodard (Eds.), *Student services: A handbook for the profession* (pp. 234–268). San Francisco: Jossey-Bass.

King, P., & Kitchener, K. (1994). *Developing reflective judgment: Understanding and promoting intellectual growth and critical thinking in adolescents and adults.* San Francisco: Jossey-Bass.

King, P., & Kitchener, K. (2002). The reflective judgment model: Twenty years of research on epistemic cognition. In B. Hofer & P. Pintrich (Eds.), *Personal epistemology: The psychology of beliefs about knowledge and knowing* (pp. 37–62). Hillsdale, NJ: Erlbaum.

King, P., & Mayhew, M. (2002). *Moral judgment development in higher education: Insights from the Defining Issues Test.* Unpublished manuscript, University of Michigan, Ann Arbor.

King, P., Wood, P., & Mines, R. (1990). Critical thinking among college and graduate students. *Review of Higher Education, 13,* 167–186.

King, P. M., & Baxter Magolda, M. (1996). A developmental perspective on learning. *Journal of College Student Development, 37,* 163–173.

King, T., & Bannon, E. (2002a). *At what cost? The price that working students pay for a college education.* Washington, DC: State PIRGs' Higher Education Project.

King, T., & Bannon, E. (2002b). *The burden of borrowing: A report on the rising rates of student debt.* Washington, DC: State PIRGs' Higher Education Project.

Kingston, P., & Smart, J. (1990). The economic payoff of prestigious colleges. In P. Kingston & L. Lewis (Eds.), *The high status track: Studies of elite schools and stratification* (pp. 147–174). Albany: State University of New York Press.

Kirkvliet, J. (1994). Cheating by economics' students: A comparison of survey results. *Journal of Economic Education, 25,* 121–133.

Kitchener, K., & King, P. (1981). Reflective judgment: Concepts of justification and their relationship to age and education. *Journal of Applied Developmental Psychology, 2,* 89–116.

Kitchener, K., & King, P. (1990). The reflective judgment model: Transforming assumptions about knowing. In J. Mezirow & Associates (Eds.), *Fostering critical reflection in adulthood: A guide to transformative and emancipatory learning* (pp. 159–176). San Francisco: Jossey-Bass.

Kitchener, K., Wood, P., & Jensen, L. (1999). *Curricular, co-curricular, and institutional influence on real-world problem solving.* Paper presented at the meeting of the American Psychological Association, Boston.

Kitchener, K., Wood, P., & Jensen, L. (2000). *Promoting epistemic cognition and complex judgment in college students.* Paper presented at the meeting of the American Psychological Association, Washington, DC.

Klassen, P. (2001). *General education skills development: An analysis of students' general education skills development at College of DuPage utilizing three years of CAAP testing.* Glen Ellyn, IL: College of DuPage.

Kleeman, G. (1991, May). *Work in progress: Moving from a reactive to a strategic mode in retaining minority students.* Paper presented at the meeting of the Association for Institutional Research, San Francisco.

Klein, J., & Pridemore, D. (1992). Effects of cooperative learning and need for affiliation on performance, time on task, and satisfaction. *Educational Technology, Research, and Development, 40,* 39–47.

Klein, S., Kuh, G., Chun, M., Hamilton, L., & Shavelson, R. (2003). *The search for value-added: Assessing and validating selected higher education outcomes.* Paper presented at the meeting of the American Educational Research Association, Chicago.

Knefelkamp, L. (1974). *Developmental instruction: Fostering intellectual and personal growth in college students.* Unpublished doctoral dissertation, University of Minnesota, Minneapolis.

Knefelkamp, L., Widick, C., & Parker, C. (Eds.). (1978). *Applying new developmental findings. New Directions for Student Services,* No. 4. San Francisco: Jossey-Bass.

Knight, W. (1993a). *A mediating effect for general education gains? A simultaneous examination of the effects of general education requirements and institutional type on freshman to senior gains on the ACT COMP for a national sample.* Paper presented at the meeting of the Association for Institutional Research, Chicago.

Knight, W. (1993b). An examination of freshman to senior general education gains across a national sample of institutions with different general education requirements using a mixed-effect structural equation model. *Research in Higher Education, 34,* 41–54.

Knight, W. (1994). *Influences on the academic, career, and personal gains and satisfaction of community college students.* Paper presented at the meeting of the Association for Institutional Research, New Orleans.

Knight, W. (2002). *Toward a comprehensive model of influences upon time to bachelor's degree attainment* (AIR Professional File, No. 85). Tallahassee, FL: Association for Institutional Research.

Knight, W., & Zhai, M. (1996). *Distance learning: Its relationships with student achievement and faculty and student perceptions.* Paper presented at the meeting of the Association for Institutional Research, Albuquerque, NM.

Knouse, S., Tanner, J., & Harris, E. (1999). The relation of college internships, college performance, and subsequent job opportunity. *Journal of Employment Counseling, 36,* 35–43.

Knox, P., Fagley, N., & Miller, P. (1998). *Moral orientation in a sample of African-American college students.* Paper presented at the meeting of the American Educational Research Association, San Diego, CA.

Knox, W., Lindsay, P., & Kolb, M. (1992). Higher education, college characteristics, and student experiences: Long-term effects on educational satisfactions and perceptions. *Journal of Higher Education, 63,* 303–328.

Knox, W., Lindsay, P., & Kolb, M. (1993). *Does college make a difference? Long-term changes in activities and attitudes.* Westport, CT: Greenwood Press.

Koch, L. (1992). Revisiting mathematics. *Journal of Developmental Education, 16,* 12–18.

Kochenour, E., Jolley, D., Kaup, J., Patrick, D., Roach, K., & Wenzler, L. (1997). Supplemental Instruction: An effective component of student affairs programming. *Journal of College Student Development, 38,* 577–586.

Kodama, C. (2002). Marginality of transfer commuter students. *NASPA Journal, 39,* 233–250.

Kodama, C., McEwen, M., Liang, C., & Lee, S. (2001). A theoretical examination of psychosocial issues for Asian-Pacific American students. *NASPA Journal, 38,* 411–437.

Kohlberg, L. (1969). Stage and sequence: The cognitive-developmental approach to socialization. In D. Goslin (Ed.), *Handbook of socialization theory and research.* Skokie, IL: Rand McNally.

Kohlberg, L. (1971). Stages of moral development. In C. Beck, B. Crittenden, & E. Sullivan (Eds.), *Moral education.* Toronto: University of Toronto Press.

Kohlberg, L. (1972). A cognitive-developmental approach to moral education. *Humanist, 6,* 13–16.

Kohlberg, L. (1975). A cognitive-developmental approach to moral education. *Phi Delta Kappan, 56,* 670–677.

Kohlberg, L. (1981a). *Essays on moral development: Vol. 1. The philosophy of moral development: Moral states and the idea of justice.* New York: HarperCollins.

Kohlberg, L. (1981b). *The meaning and measurement of moral development.* Worcester, MA: Clark University Press.

Kohlberg, L. (1984). *Essays on moral development. The psychology of moral development* (Vol. 2). San Francisco: HarperCollins.

Kohlberg, L., & Candee, D. (1984). The relationship of moral judgment to moral action. In W. Kurtines & J. Gewirtz (Eds.), *Morality, moral behavior, and moral development.* New York: Wiley-Interscience.

Kohlberg, L., Levine, C., & Hewer, A. (1984). Moral stages: The current formulation of the theory. In L. Kohlberg (Ed.), *Essays on moral development: Vol. 2. The psychology of moral development* (pp. 212–319). San Francisco: HarperCollins.

Kohn, M., Naoi, A., Schoenbach, C., Schooler, C., & Slomczynski, K. (1990). Positioning in the class structure and psychological functioning in the United States, Japan, and Poland. *American Journal of Sociology, 95,* 964–1008.

Kolb, D. (1976). *The Learning Styles Inventory: Technical manual.* Boston: McBer.

Kolb, D. (1981). Learning styles and disciplinary differences. In A. Chickering & Associates (Eds.), *The modern American college: Responding to the new realities of diverse students and a changing society.* San Francisco: Jossey-Bass.

Kolb, D. (1984). *Experiential learning: Experience as the source of learning development.* Englewood Cliffs, NJ: Prentice-Hall.

Kolb, M. (1989). *Linking education and work: The effect of college major-occupation fit on earnings.* Paper presented at the meeting of the American Sociological Association, San Francisco.

Komives, S., & Woodard, D. (Eds.). (2003). *Student services: A handbook for the profession.* San Francisco: Jossey-Bass.

Korn, J. (1993, November). *Another dimension of campus date rape: Assessing college students' attitudes.* Paper presented at the meeting of the Association for the Study of Higher Education, Pittsburgh, PA.

Kozeracki, C. (2000). Service learning in the community college. *Community College Review, 27,* 54–70.

Kozma, R. (1991). Learning with media. *Review of Educational Research, 61,* 179–211.

Kozma, R. (1994a). A reply: Media and methods. *Educational Technology Research and Development, 42,* 11–14.

Kozma, R. (1994b). Will media influence learning? Reframing the debate. *Educational Technology Research and Development, 42,* 1–19.

Kozma, R., & Johnston, J. (1991, January/February). The technological revolution comes to the classroom. *Change, 23,* 10–20, 22–23.

Kraemer, B. (1995). Factors affecting Hispanic student transfer behavior. *Research in Higher Education, 36,* 303–322.

Kraemer, B. (1997). The academic and social integration of Hispanic students into college. *Review of Higher Education, 20,* 163–179.

Kraft, C. (1991). What makes a successful Black student on a predominantly White campus? *American Educational Research Journal, 28,* 423–443.

Krautmann, A., & Sander, W. (1999). Grades and student evaluations of teachers. *Economics of Education Review, 18,* 59–63.

Kremer, J. (1990). Construct validity of multiple measures in teaching, research, and service and reliability of peer ratings. *Journal of Educational Psychology, 82,* 213–218.

Kremer, J. (1991). Identifying faculty types using peer ratings of teaching, research, and service. *Research in Higher Education, 32,* 351–361.

Kritch, K., Bostow, D., & Dedrick, R. (1995). Level of interactivity of videodisk instruction on college students' recall of AIDS information. *Journal of Applied Behavior Analysis, 28,* 85–86.

Kronholm, M. (1996). The impact of developmental instruction on reflective judgment. *Review of Higher Education, 19,* 199–225.

Kube, B., & Thorndike, R. (1991, April). *Cognitive development during college: A longitudinal study measured on the Perry scheme.* Paper presented at the meeting of the American Educational Research Association, Chicago.

Kuh, G. (1992, April). *In their own words: What students learn outside the classroom.* Paper presented at the meeting of the American Educational Research Association, San Francisco.

Kuh, G. (1993). In their own words: What students learn outside the classroom. *American Educational Research Journal, 30,* 277–304.

Kuh, G. (1995). The other curriculum: Out-of-class experiences associated with student learning and personal development. *Journal of Higher Education, 66,* 123–155.

Kuh, G. (1999). How are we doing? Tracking the quality of the undergraduate experience, 1960s to the present. *Review of Higher Education, 22,* 99–119.

Kuh, G. (2003). Organizational theory. In S. Komives & D. Woodard (Eds.), *Student services: A handbook for the profession* (pp. 269–296). San Francisco: Jossey-Bass.

Kuh, G., Arnold, J., & Vesper, N. (1990, November). *Influence of collegiate environments on student learning.* Paper presented at the meeting of the Association for the Study of Higher Education, Portland, OR.

Kuh, G., Arnold, J., & Vesper, N. (1991, November). *The influence of student effort, college environments, and campus culture on undergraduate student learning and personal development.* Paper presented at the meeting of the Association for the Study of Higher Education, Boston.

Kuh, G., & Hall, J. (1993). Using cultural perspectives in student affairs. In G. Kuh (Ed.), *Cultural perspectives in student affairs work* (pp. 1–20). Lanham, MD: American College Personnel Association.

Kuh, G., Hayek, J., Carini, R., Ouimet, J., Gonyea, R., & Kennedy, J. (2001). *NSSE technical and norms report.* Bloomington: Indiana University, Center for Postsecondary Research and Planning.

Kuh, G., & Hu, S. (1998, November). *Unraveling the complexities associated with the increase in grades between the mid-1980s and the mid-1990s.* Paper presented at the meeting of the Association for the Study of Higher Education, Miami.

Kuh, G., & Hu, S. (1999a, April). *Learning productivity at research universities.* Paper presented at the meeting of the American Educational Research Association, Montreal.

Kuh, G., & Hu, S. (1999b, November). *Is more better?: Student-faculty interaction revisited.* Paper presented at the meeting of the Association for the Study of Higher Education, San Antonio, TX.

Kuh, G., & Hu, S. (2000, April). *The effects of computer and information technology on student learning and other college experiences.* Paper presented at the meeting of the American Educational Research Association, New Orleans.

Kuh, G., & Hu, S. (2001). The effects of student-faculty interaction in the 1990s. *Review of Higher Education, 24,* 309–332.

Kuh, G., Hu, S., & Vesper, N. (2000). They shall be known by what they do: An activities-based typology of college students. *Journal of College Student Development, 41,* 228–244.

Kuh, G., Pace, C., & Vesper, N. (1997). The development of process indicators to estimate student gains associated with good practices in undergraduate education. *Research in Higher Education, 38,* 435–454.

Kuh, G., Schuh, J., Whitt, E., Andreas, R., Lyons, J., Strange, C., et al. (1991). *Involving colleges: Successful approaches to fostering student learning and personal development outside the classroom.* San Francisco: Jossey-Bass.

Kuh, G., & Vesper, N. (1992, April). *A comparison of student learning at "involving" and metropolitan universities.* Paper presented at the meeting of the American Educational Research Association, San Francisco.

Kuh, G., & Vesper, N. (1997a). A comparison of student experiences with good practices in undergraduate education between 1990 and 1994. *Review of Higher Education, 21,* 43–61.

Kuh, G., & Vesper, N. (1997b, February). *Do environments matter? A comparative analysis of the impress of different types of colleges and universities on character development.* Tallahassee, FL: Institute on College Student Values.

Kuh, G., & Vesper, N. (1999, April). *Do computers enhance or detract from student learning?* Paper presented at the meeting of the American Educational Research Association, Montreal.

Kuh, G., Vesper, N., & Krehbiel, L. (1994). Student learning at metropolitan universities. In J. Smart (Ed.), *Higher education: Handbook of theory and research* (Vol. 10, pp. 1–44). New York: Agathon.

Kulik, C., & Kulik, J. (1991). Effectiveness of computer-based instruction: An updated analysis. *Computers in Human Behavior, 7,* 75–94.

Kulik, C., Kulik, J., & Bangert-Drowns, R. (1990). Effectiveness of mastery learning programs: A meta-analysis. *Review of Educational Research, 60,* 265–299.

Kulik, C., Kulik, J., & Shwalb, B. (1983). College programs for high-risk and disadvantaged students: A meta-analysis of findings. *Review of Educational Research, 53,* 397–414.

Kysor, D., & Pierce, M. (2000). Does intern/co-op experience translate into career progress and satisfaction? *Journal of Career Planning and Employment, 60,* 25ff.

Lacy, W. (1978). Interpersonal relationships as mediators of structural effects: College student socialization in a traditional and an experimental university environment. *Sociology of Education, 51,* 201–211.

Ladd, E. (1996). The data just don't show erosion of America's "social capital." *Public Perspective, 7,* 5–22.

Lam, L. (1999, May). *Assessing financial aid impacts on time-to-degree for nontransfer undergraduate students at a large urban public university.* Paper presented to the Forum of the Association for Institutional Research, Seattle, WA.

Lambiotte, J., & Dansereau, D. (1992). Effects of knowledge maps and prior knowledge on recall of science lecture content. *Journal of Experimental Education, 60,* 189–201.

Lamport, M. (1994). Student-faculty informal interaction and its relation to college student outcomes in Christian college settings: Research and implications. *Research on Christian Higher Education, 1,* 66–78.

Landrum, R., & Chastain, G. (1998). Demonstrating tutoring effectiveness with a one-semester course. *Journal of College Student Development, 39,* 502–506.

Lang, M. (1996). *Effects of class participation on student achievement and motivation.* Unpublished honors thesis, University of Western Ontario, London, Canada.

Langdon, E. (1997). *A study of the persistence of affective outcomes of women's college alumnae.* Unpublished doctoral dissertation, University of California, Los Angeles.

Langer, P., & Chiszar, D. (1993). Assessment of critical thinking courses. *Perceptual and Motor Skills, 77,* 970.

Lapsley, D., Rice, K., & FitzGerald, D. (1990). Adolescent attachment, identity, and adjustment to college: Implications for the continuity of adaptation hypothesis. *Journal of Counseling and Development, 68,* 561–565.

Lapsley, D., Rice, K., & Shadid, G. (1989). Psychological separation and adjustment to college. *Journal of Counseling Psychology, 36,* 286–294.

Laubscher, M. (1994). *Encounters with difference: Student perceptions of the role of out-of-class experiences in education abroad.* Westport, CT: Greenwood Press.

Lavin, D., & Crook, D. (1990). Open admissions and its outcomes: Ethnic differences in long-term educational attainment. *American Journal of Education, 98,* 389–425.

Lavin, D., & Hyllegard, D. (1991). *The value of college.* New Haven, CT: Yale University Press.

Lawrence, G. (1982). *People types and tiger stripes* (2nd ed.). Gainesville, FL: Center for Applications of Psychological Type.

Lawrence, G. (1984). A synthesis of learning style research involving the MBTI. *Journal of Psychological Type, 8,* 2–15.

Learner, R. (1986). *Concepts and theories of human development* (2nd ed.). New York: Random House.

Ledman, R., Miller, M., & Brown, D. (1995). Successful women and women's colleges: Is there an intervening variable? *Sex Roles, 33,* 489–497.

Lee, J. (2002a). Changing worlds, changing selves: The experience of the religious self among Catholic collegians. *Journal of College Student Development, 43,* 341–356.

Lee, J. (2002b). Religion and college attendance: Change among students. *Review of Higher Education, 25,* 369–384.

Lee, V., & Frank, K. (1990). Students' characteristics that facilitate transfer from two-year to four-year colleges. *Sociology of Education, 63,* 178–193.

Lee, V., Mackie-Lewis, C., & Marks, H. (1993). Persistence to the baccalaureate degree for students who transfer from community college. *American Journal of Education, 102,* 80–114.

Lehman, D., & Nisbett, R. (1990). A longitudinal study of the effects of undergraduate training on reasoning. *Developmental Psychology, 26,* 952–960.

Leigh, D., & Gill, A. (1997). Labor market returns to community college. *Journal of Human Resources, 32,* 334–353.

Leigh, J. (1990). Schooling and seat belt use. *Southern Economics Journal, 57,* 195–207.

Leigh, J. (1998a). Parents' schooling and the correlation between education and frailty. *Economics of Education Review, 17,* 349–358.

Leigh, J. (1998b). The social benefits of education: A review article. *Economics of Education Review, 17,* 363–368.

Leigh, J., & Dhir, R. (1997). Schooling and frailty among seniors. *Economics of Education Review, 16,* 45–57.

Leigh, J., & Fries, J. (1991). Occupation, income, and education as independent covariates of arthritis in four national probability samples. *Arthritis and Rheumatism, 134,* 984–995.

Lenehan, M., Dunn, R., Ingham, J., Signer, B., & Murray, J. (1994). Effects of learning-style intervention on college students' achievement, anxiety, anger, and curiosity. *Journal of College Student Development, 35,* 461–466.

Lenihan, G., Rawlins, M., Eberly, C., Buckley, B., & Masters, B. (1992). Gender differences in rape-supportive attitudes before and after a date rape education intervention. *Journal of College Student Development, 33,* 331–338.

Lenning, O., & Ebbers, L. (1999). *The powerful potential of learning communities: Improving education for the future* (ASHE-ERIC Higher Education Reports, Vol. 26, No. 6). Washington, DC: George Washington University, Graduate School of Education and Human Development.

Lentz, B., & Laband, D. (1989). Why so many children of doctors become doctors: Nepotism vs. human capital transfers. *Journal of Human Resources, 24,* 396–413.

Leonard, W. (1990). Computer-based technology for college science laboratory courses. *Journal of College Science Teaching, 19,* 210–211.

Leonard, W. (1992). A comparison of student performance following instruction by interactive videodisc versus conventional laboratory. *Journal of Research in Science Teaching, 29,* 93–102.

Leppel, K. (1998). The use of class-specific group exercises in undergraduate statistics, or "How many body piercings do you have?" *Journal on Excellence in College Teaching, 9,* 3–11.

Leppel, K. (2001). The impact of major on college persistence among freshmen. *Higher Education, 41,* 327–342.

Leppel, K. (2002). Similarities and differences in the college persistence of men and women. *Review of Higher Education, 25,* 433–450.

Leslie, L. (1990). Rates of return as informer of public policy. *Higher Education, 20,* 271–286.

Leslie, L., & Brinkman, P. (1988). *The economic value of higher education.* New York: American Council on Education.

Levesque, J., & Prosser, T. (1996). Service learning connections. *Journal of Teacher Education, 47,* 325–334.

Levine, A. (1994, July/August). Service on campus. *Change, 26,* 4–5.

Levine, A., & Cureton, J. (1998a). *When hope and fear collide: A portrait of today's college student.* San Francisco: Jossey-Bass.

Levine, A., & Cureton, J. (1998b, May/June). Collegiate life: An obituary. *Change, 30,* 12–17, 51.

Levinson, D. (1978). *The seasons of a man's life.* New York: Knopf.

Levinson, D., & Levinson, J. (1996). *The seasons of a woman's life.* New York: Ballantine.

Levy, F., & Murnane, R. (1992). U.S. earnings levels and earnings inequality: A review of recent trends and proposed explanations. *Journal of Economic Literature, 30,* 1333–1381.

Lewis, D., Hearn, J., & Zilbert, E. (1993). Efficiency and equity effects of vocationally focused postsecondary education. *Sociology of Education, 66,* 188–205.

Lewis, L., Farris, E., & Alexander, D. (1997). *Distance education in higher education institutions* (Statistical Analysis Report No. NCES 98–062). Washington, DC: U.S. Department of Education, Office of Educational Research and Improvement.

Lewis, L., & Kingston, P. (1989). The best, the brightest, and the most affluent: Undergraduates at elite institutions. *Academe, 75,* 28–33.

Lewis, M. (1993). Athletes in college: Differing roles and conflicting expectations. *College Student Journal, 27,* 195–202.

L'Hommedieu, R., Menges, R., & Brinko, K. (1988). *The effects of student ratings feedback to college teachers: A meta-analysis and review of research.* Unpublished manuscript, Northwestern University, Center for the Teaching Professions, Evanston, IL.

L'Hommedieu, R., Menges, R., & Brinko, K. (1990). Methodological explanations for the modest effects of feedback. *Journal of Educational Psychology, 82,* 232–241.

Li, G., Long, S., & Simpson, M. (1998). *Self-perceived gains in communication and critical thinking skills: Are there disciplinary differences?* Paper presented at the meeting of the Association for Institutional Research, Minneapolis, MN.

Li, G., Long, S., & Simpson, M. (1999). Self-perceived gains in critical thinking and communication skills: Are there disciplinary differences? *Research in Higher Education, 40,* 43–60.

Liao, Y.-K., & Bright, G. (1991). Effects of computer-assisted instruction and computer programming on cognitive outcomes: A meta-analysis. *Journal of Educational Computing Research, 7,* 251–268.

Lichtenberg, J., & Moffitt, W. (1994). The effect of predicate matching on perceived understanding and factual recall. *Journal of Counseling and Development, 72,* 544–548.

Lidren, D., Meier, S., & Brigham, T. (1991). The effects of minimal and maximal peer tutoring systems on the academic performance of college students. *Psychological Record, 41,* 69–77.

Light, A. (1995). The effects of interrupted schooling on wages. *Journal of Human Resources, 30,* 472–502.

Light, A., & Ureta, M. (1990). Gender differences in wages and job turnover among continuously employed workers. *American Economic Review, 80,* 293–297.

Light, R. (1990). *The Harvard assessment seminars: Explorations with students and faculty about teaching, learning, and student life* (First report). Cambridge, MA: Harvard University, Harvard Assessment Seminars.

Light, R. (1991). *The Harvard assessment seminars: Explorations with students and faculty about teaching, learning, and student life* (Second report). Cambridge, MA: Harvard University, Harvard Assessment Seminars.

Light, R. (2001). *Making the most of college: Students speak their minds.* Cambridge, MA: Harvard University Press.

Light, R., Singer, J., & Willett, J. (1990). *By design: Planning research on higher education.* Cambridge, MA: Harvard University Press.

Lillard, D., & Gerner, J. (1999). Getting into the Ivy League: How family composition affects college choice. *Journal of Higher Education, 70,* 706–730.

Lin, Y., & Vogt, W. (1996). Occupational outcomes for students earning two-year college degrees: Income, status, and equity. *Journal of Higher Education, 67,* 446–475.

Lincoln, C. (1991). The relation between college orientation and student effort: An exploratory study. *Dissertation Abstracts International, 51,* 4034A.

Lind, G. (1997). *Educational environments which promote self-sustaining moral development.* Konstanz, Germany: University of Konstanz.

Lipetzky, P., & Ammentorp, W. (1991, May). *Measuring the effects of student involvement in community colleges: A preliminary test of the Community College Student Experiences Questionnaire.* Paper presented at the meeting of the Association for Institutional Research, San Francisco.

Liu, R., & Liu, E. (2000, May). *Institutional integration: An analysis of Tinto's theory.* Paper presented at the meeting of the Association for Institutional Research, Cincinnati, OH.

Loeb, R., & Magee, P. (1992). Changes in attitudes and self-perceptions during the first two years of college. *Journal of College Student Development, 33,* 348–355.

Logan, C., & Salisbury-Glennon, J. (1999, April). *The effects of a learner-centered undergraduate community of learners on motivation and cognitive learning strategies.* Paper presented at the meeting of the American Educational Research Association, Montreal.

London, C. (1998, April). *A pilot study on the career advancement of Black graduates of predominantly Black versus predominantly White colleges.* Paper presented at the meeting of People of Color in Predominantly White Institutions, Lincoln, NE.

London, H. (1989). Breaking away: A study of first-generation college students and their families. *American Journal of Education, 97,* 144–170.

London, H. (1996, November-December). How college affects first-generation students. *About Campus, 1,* 9–13, 23.

Long, J., & Caudill, S. (1991). The impact of participation in intercollegiate athletics on income and graduation. *Review of Economics and Statistics, 73,* 525–531.

Longuevan, C., & Shoemaker, J. (1991). *Using multiple regression to evaluate a peer tutoring program for undergraduates.* Paper presented at the meeting of the California Educational Research Association, San Diego, CA.

Lopez, G. (1993). The effect of group contact and curriculum on White, Asian American, and African American students' attitudes (intergroup attitude, college students). *Dissertation Abstracts International, 54,* 3900B.

Lopus, J., & Maxwell, N. (1995). A cost-effectiveness analysis of large and small classes in the university. *Educational Evaluation and Policy Analysis, 17,* 167–178.

Lord, T. (1997). A comparison between traditional and constructivist teaching in college biology. *Innovative Higher Education, 21,* 197–216.

Lottes, I. (1991). Belief systems: Sexuality and rape. *Journal of Psychology and Human Sexuality, 4,* 37–59.

Lottes, I., & Kuriloff, P. (1994a). The impact of college experience on political and social attitudes. *Sex Roles, 31,* 31–54.

Lottes, I., & Kuriloff, P. (1994b). Sexual socialization differences by gender, Greek membership, ethnicity, and religious background. *Psychology of Women Quarterly, 18,* 203–219.

Lou, Y., Abrami, P., & d'Apollonia, S. (2001). Small group and individual learning with technology: A meta-analysis. *Review of Educational Research, 71,* 449–521.

Lou, Y., Abrami, P., Spence, J., Poulsen, C., Chambers, B., & d'Apollonia, S. (1996). Within-class grouping. *Review of Educational Research, 66,* 423–458.

Lounsbury, J., & DeNeui, D. (1995). Psychological sense of community on campus. *College Student Journal, 29,* 270–277.

Loury, L. (1997). The gender earnings gap among college-educated workers. *Industrial and Labor Relations Review, 50,* 580–593.

Loury, L., & Garman, D. (1995). College selectivity and earnings. *Journal of Labor Economics, 13,* 289–308.

Love, P. (2001). Spirituality and student development: Theoretical connections. In M. Jablonski (Ed.), *The implications of student spirituality for student affairs practice* (pp. 7–16). *New Directions for Student Services,* No. 95. San Francisco: Jossey-Bass.

Love, P. (2002). Comparing spiritual development and cognitive development. *Journal of College Student Development, 43,* 357–373.

Love, P., & Goodsell Love, A. (1995). *Enhancing student learning: Intellectual, social, and emotional integration.* ASHE-ERIC Higher Education Reports, No. 4. Washington, D.C.: George Washington University, Graduate School of Education and Human Development.

Love, P., & Guthrie, V. (Eds.). (1999). *Understanding and applying cognitive development theory. New Directions for Student Services,* No. 88. San Francisco: Jossey-Bass.

Love, P., & Talbot, D. (1999). Defining spiritual development: A missing consideration for student affairs. *NASPA Journal, 37,* 361–375.

Loviscky, G. (2000). *Construct validity of a managerial defining issues test.* Unpublished doctoral dissertation, Pennsylvania State University, University Park.

Lowe, N., & Bickel, R. (1993). Computer-assisted instruction in Appalachia's postsecondary schools. *Journal of Educational Research, 87,* 46–52.

Ludlow, L. (1996). Instructor evaluation ratings: A longitudinal analysis. *Journal of Personnel Evaluation in Education, 10,* 83–92.

Luebke, B., & Reilly, M. (1995). *Women's studies graduates: The first generation.* New York: Teachers College Press.

Lundberg, C. (2002, November). *Working and learning: The role of involvement for employed students.* Paper presented at the meeting of the Association for the Study of Higher Education, Sacramento, CA.

Lundeberg, M., & Moch, S. (1995). Influence of social interaction on cognition: Connected learning in science. *Journal of Higher Education, 66,* 312–335.

Luzzo, D. (1990). *Perceived control, social class, and gender: Correlates of college students' career maturity.* Unpublished doctoral dissertation, University of California, Los Angeles.

Luzzo, D. (1993). Predicting the career maturity of undergraduates: A comparison of personal, educational, and psychological factors. *Journal of College Student Development, 34,* 271–275.

Luzzo, D. (1995, April). *The impact of attributional retraining on the career development of college students.* Paper presented at the meeting of the American Educational Research Association, San Francisco.

Luzzo, D., Funk, D., & Strang, J. (1996). Attributional retraining increases career decision-making self-efficacy. *Career Development Quarterly, 44,* 378–386.

Luzzo, D., McWhirter, E., & Hutcheson, K. (1997). Evaluating career decision-making factors associated with employment among first-year college students. *Journal of College Student Development, 38,* 166–172.

Lynch, C. (1996). Facilitating and assessing unstructured problem solving. *Journal of College Reading and Learning, 27,* 16–27.

Lynch, J., & Bishop-Clark, C. (1998). A comparison of the nontraditional student's experience on traditional versus nontraditional college campuses. *Innovative Higher Education, 22,* 217–229.

Maack, S. (1998, May). *Ethnicity, class, generation in college, and family involvement: What makes a difference in student success?* Paper presented at the meeting of the Association for Institutional Research, Minneapolis, MN.

Mabry, J. (1998). Pedagogical variations in service learning and student outcomes: How time, contact, and reflection matter. *Michigan Journal of Community Service Learning, 5,* 32–47.

Macalister, H. (1999). Women's studies classes and their influence on student development. *Adolescence, 34,* 283–292.

Machtmes, K., & Asher, J. W. (2000). A meta-analysis of the effectiveness of telecourses in distance education. *American Journal of Distance Education, 14*(1), 27–46.

MacKay, K., & Kuh, G. (1994). A comparison of student effort and educational gains of Caucasian and African-American students at predominantly White colleges and universities. *Journal of College Student Development, 35,* 217–223.

MacKinnon-Slaney, F. (1994). The adult persistence in learning model: A road map to counseling services for adult learners. Journal of Counseling and Development, *72,* 268–275.

MacPhee, D., Kreutzer, J., & Fritz, J. (1994). Infusing diversity perspectives into human development courses. *Child Development, 65,* 699–715.

MacPherson, K. (1999). The development of critical thinking skills in undergraduate supervisory management units: Efficacy of student peer assessment. *Assessment and Evaluation in Higher Education, 24,* 273–284.

Magnusson, D. (1995). Individual development: A holistic, integrated model. In P. Moen, G. Elder, & K. Luscher (Eds.), *Examining lives in context: Perspectives on the ecology of human development.* Washington, DC: American Psychological Association.

Maisto, A., & Tammi, M. (1991). The effect of a content-based freshman seminar on academic and social integration. *Journal of the Freshman Year Experience, 3,* 29–47.

Malaney, G., Williams, E., & Geller, W. (1997). Assessing campus climate for gays, lesbians, and bisexuals at two institutions. *Journal of College Student Development, 38,* 365–375.

Mallette, B., & Cabrera, A. (1991). Determinants of withdrawal behavior: An exploratory study. *Research in Higher Education, 32,* 179–194.

Malone, D., Jones, B., & Stallings, D. (2001, April). *Transforming perspectives through service learning: Inspiring growth and mindfulness in undergraduates.* Paper presented at the meeting of the American Educational Research Association, Seattle, WA.

Mansfield, A., & Clinchy, B. (1990). *Young women's ways of knowing: A longitudinal study of epistemological development in different domains of knowledge over the college years.* Paper presented at the meeting of the American Educational Research Association, Boston.

Maple, S., & Stage, F. (1991). Influences on the choice of math/science major by gender and ethnicity. *American Educational Research Journal, 28,* 37–60.

Marchant, M. (1991). What motivates adult use of public libraries? *Library & Information Service Research, 13,* 201–235.

Marchant, M. (1994). *Why adults use the public library: A research perspective.* Englewood, CO: Libraries Unlimited.

Marcia, J. (1966). Development and validation of ego-identity status. *Journal of Personality and Social Psychology, 3,* 551–558.

Marcia, J. (1980). Identity in adolescence. In J. Adelson (Ed.), *Handbook of adolescent psychology* (pp. 159–187). New York: Wiley.

Marin, P. (2000). The educational possibility of multi-racial/multi-ethnic college classrooms. In American Council on Education & American Association of University Professors (Eds.), *Does diversity make a difference? Three research studies on diversity in college classrooms* (pp. 61–83). Washington, DC: Editors.

Marks, H. (1994). The effect of participation in school-sponsored community service programs on student attitudes and social responsibility. *Dissertation Abstracts International, 55,* 926A.

Markus, G., Howard, J., & King, D. (1993). Integrating community service and classroom instruction enhances learning: Results from an experiment. *Educational Evaluation and Policy Analysis, 15,* 410–419.

Marr, D. (1995). *An investigation of the construct validity of the long form of the Academic Profile.* Princeton, NJ: Educational Testing Service.

Marra, R., Palmer, B., & Litzinger, T. (2000). The effects of a first-year engineering design course on student intellectual development as measured by the Perry scheme. *Journal of Engineering Education, 89,* 39–45.

Marrison, D., & Frick, M. (1993). Computer multimedia instruction versus traditional instruction in postsecondary agricultural education. *Journal of Agricultural Education, 34,* 31–38.

Marsh, H. (1987). Students' evaluations of university teaching: Research findings, methodological issues, and directions for future research. *International Journal of Educational Research, 11,* 253–288.

Marsh, H., & Dunkin, M. (1997). Students' evaluations of university teaching: A multidimensional perspective. In R. Perry & J. Smart (Eds.), *Effective teaching in higher education: Research and practice* (pp. 241–320). New York: Agathon.

Marsh, H., & Hattie, J. (2002). The relation between research productivity and teaching effectiveness. *Journal of Higher Education, 73,* 603–641.

Marsh, H., & Hocevar, D. (1991). Students' evaluations of teaching effectiveness: The stability of mean ratings of the same teachers over a 13-year period. *Teaching and Teacher Education, 7,* 303–341.

Marsh, H., & Roche, L. (1993). The use of students' evaluations and an individually structured intervention to enhance university teaching effectiveness. *American Educational Research Journal, 30,* 217–251.

Marsh, H., & Roche, L. (1997). Making students' evaluations of teaching effectiveness effective: The critical issues of validity, bias, and utility. *American Psychologist, 52,* 1187–1197.

Martin, D., Arendale, D., & Associates. (1993). *Supplemental instruction: Improving first-year student success* (Vol. 7). Columbia: University of South Carolina, National Resource Center for the Freshman Year Experience.

Martin, L. (2000). The relationship of college experiences to psychosocial outcomes in students. *Journal of College Student Development, 41,* 292–301.

Martin, R., & Koppelman, K. (1991). The impact of a human relations/multicultural education course on the attitudes of prospective teachers. *Journal of Intergroup Relations, 18,* 16–27.

Martinez, J. C. (1988). Mexican Americans. In L. Comas-Diaz & E. Griffith (Eds.), *Clinical guidelines in cross-cultural mental health.* New York: Wiley.

Marttunen, M. (1997). Electronic mail as a pedagogical delivery system: An analysis of the learning of argumentation. *Research in Higher Education, 38,* 345–363.

Maruyama, G., & Moreno, J. (2000). University faculty views about the value of diversity on campus and in the classroom. In American Council on Education & American Association of University Professors (Eds.), *Does diversity make a difference? Three research studies on diversity in college classrooms* (pp. 8–35). Washington, DC: Editors.

Marx, F. (1997). *The WILL/Westhampton report.* Wellesley, MA: Wellesley College Center for Research on Women.

Mason, M., & Gibbs, J. (1993). Social perspective taking and moral judgment among college students. *Journal of Adolescent Research, 8,* 109–123.

Mather, P., & Winston, J. R. (1998). Autonomy development of traditional-aged students: Themes and processes. *Journal of College Student Development, 39,* 33–50.

Mathiasen, R. (1998). Moral education of college students: Faculty and staff perspectives. *College Student Journal, 32,* 374–377.

Mathios, A. (1989). Education, variation in earnings, and nonmonetary compensation. *Journal of Human Resources, 24,* 456–468.

Matney, M. M., & Wiley Kelly, K. L. (1997, November). *Political attitude shifts: Changes in college impact for students in the 1980s and 1990s.* Paper presented at the meeting of the Association for the Study of Higher Education, Albuquerque, NM.

Matthews, D. (1994). An investigation of students' learning styles in various disciplines in colleges and universities. *Journal of Humanistic Education and Development, 33,* 65–74.

Matthews, R., Cooper, J., Davidson, N., & Hawkes, P. (1995, July/August). Building bridges between cooperative and collaborative learning. *Change, 27,* 34–40.

Matthews, S. (1993, Summer). Supplemental instruction and biology. *Supplemental Instruction News,* pp. 1, 3.

Mau, W., Calvert, C., & Gregory, R. (1997). Effects of career interventions on vocational cognitive complexity. *Journal of Career Development, 23,* 279–293.

May, D. (1990). *Student development: A longitudinal investigation of the relationship between student effort and change in intellectual development.* Unpublished doctoral dissertation, Memphis State University, Memphis, TN.

Mayer, R. (1997). Multimedia learning: Are we asking the right questions? *Educational Psychologist, 32,* 1–19.

Mayer, R. (1999). Designing instruction for constructivist learning. In C. Reigeluth (Ed.), *Instructional design theories and models* (Vol. 2, pp. 141–159). Hillsdale, NJ: Erlbaum.

Mayer, R., & Anderson, R. (1991). Animations need narrations: An experimental test of a dual-coding hypothesis. *Journal of Educational Psychology, 83,* 484–490.

Mayer, R., & Anderson, R. (1992). The instructive animation: Helping students build connections between words and pictures in multimedia learning. *Journal of Educational Psychology, 84,* 444–452.

Mayer, R., & Gallini, J. (1990). When is an illustration worth ten thousand words? *Journal of Educational Psychology, 82,* 715–726.

Mayer, R., & Sims, V. (1994). For whom is a picture worth a thousand words? Extensions of a dual-coding theory of multimedia learning. *Journal of Educational Psychology, 86,* 389–401.

Mayer, R., Steinhoff, K., Bower, G., & Mars, R. (1995). A generative theory of textbook design: Using annotated illustrations to foster meaningful learning of science text. *Educational Technology Research and Development, 43,* 31–44.

Maynard, R., & McGrath, D. (1997). Family structure, fertility, and child welfare. In J. Behrman & N. Stace (Eds.), *The social benefits of education* (pp. 125–174). Ann Arbor: University of Michigan Press.

McAdams, C., & Foster, V. (1998). Promoting the development of high-risk college students through a deliberate psychological education-based freshman orientation course. *Journal of the Freshman Year Experience, 10,* 51–72.

McBride, R., & Reed, J. (1998). Thinking and college athletes: Are they predisposed to critical thinking? *College Student Journal, 32,* 443–450.

McBroom, W., & Reed, F. (1994). An alternative to a traditional lecture course. *Teaching Sociology, 22,* 328–332.

McCabe, D., & Bowers, W. (1996). The relationship between student cheating and college fraternity or sorority membership. *NASPA Journal, 33,* 280–291.

McCabe, D., & Trevino, L. (1993). Academic dishonesty: Honor codes and other contextual influences. *Journal of Higher Education, 64,* 522–538.

McCabe, D., & Trevino, L. (1996, January/February). What we know about cheating in college. *Change, 28,* 29–33.

McCabe, D., & Trevino, L. (1997). Individual and contextual influences on academic dishonesty: A multicampus investigation. *Research in Higher Education, 38,* 379–396.

McCabe, D., Trevino, L., & Butterfield, K. (1996). The influence of collegiate and corporate codes of conduct on ethics-related behavior in the workplace. *Business Ethics Quarterly, 4,* 461–476.

McCabe, D., Trevino, L., & Butterfield, K. (1999). Academic integrity in honor-code and non-honor-code environments: A qualitative investigation. *Journal of Higher Education, 70,* 211–234.

McCabe, L. (1994). The development of a global perspective during participation in Semester-at-Sea: A comparative global education program. *Educational Review, 46,* 275–286.

McCagg, E., & Dansereau, D. (1991). A convergent paradigm for examining knowledge mapping as a learning and recall strategy. *Journal of Educational Research, 84,* 317–324.

McCarthy, J., & Anderson, L. (2000). Active learning techniques versus traditional teaching styles: Two experiments from history and political science. *Innovative Higher Education, 24,* 279–294.

McCleary, I., & Egan, M. (1995). *Program design and evaluation: Two-way interactive television* (Vol. 4). University Park: Pennsylvania State University Press.

McClelland, K., & Auster, C. (1990). Public platitudes and hidden tensions: Racial climates at predominately White liberal arts colleges. *Journal of Higher Education, 61,* 607–642.

McComb, M. (1994). Benefits of computer-mediated communication in college courses. *Communication Education, 43,* 159–170.

McCormick, A. (1990, November). *Mobility of educational expectations: The effect of community colleges.* Paper presented at the meeting of the Association for the Study of Higher Education, Portland, OR.

McCormick, A. (1996). Changes in educational expectations after high school: Effects of postsecondary participation and institutional type. *Dissertation Abstracts International, 57,* 3420A.

McCormick, A. (1997a, November). *Changes in educational aspirations after high school: The role of postsecondary attendance and context.* Paper presented at the meeting of the Association for the Study of Higher Education, Albuquerque, NM.

McCormick, A. (1997b). *Transfer behavior among beginning postsecondary students: 1989–94* (Statistical Analysis Report No. NCES 97–266). Washington, DC: U.S. Department of Education, Office of Educational Research and Improvement, National Center for Education Statistics.

McCormick, A., & Horn, L. (1996). *A descriptive summary of 1992–93 bachelor's degree recipients 1 year later, with an essay on time to degree* (Statistical Analysis Report No. NCES 96–158). Washington, DC: U.S. Department of Education, Office of Educational Research and Improvement, National Center for Education Statistics.

McCormick, A., Nunez, A., Shah, V., & Choy, S. (1999). *Life after college: A descriptive summary of 1992–93 bachelor's degree recipients in 1997, with an essay on participation in graduate and first-professional education* (Statistical Analysis Report No. NCES 1999–155). Washington, DC: U.S. Department of Education, Office of Educational Research and Improvement, National Center for Education Statistics.

McCowen, C., & Alston, R. (1998). Racial identity, African self-consciousness, and career decision making in African-American women. *Journal of Multicultural Counseling and Development, 26,* 28–38.

McDaniel, C., & Graham, S. (2001). Student retention in an historically Black institution. *College Student Journal, 35,* 143–157.

McDonough, M. (1997). An assessment of critical thinking at the community college level. *Dissertation Abstracts International, 58,* 2561A.

McElhaney, K. E. (1997, November). *Outcomes of service learning: A comparative analysis of curricular-based alternative spring breaks.* Paper presented at the meeting of the Association for the Study of Higher Education, Albuquerque, NM.

McEwen, M. (1996). Enhancing student learning and development through service learning. In B. Jacoby (Ed.), *Service learning in higher education: Concepts and practices* (pp. 53–91). San Francisco: Jossey-Bass.

McEwen, M. (2003a). The nature and uses of theory. In S. Komives & D. Woodard (Eds.), *Student services: A handbook for the profession* (4th ed., pp. 153–178). San Francisco: Jossey-Bass.

McEwen, M. (2003b). New perspectives on identity development. In S. Komives & D. Woodard (Eds.), *Student services: A handbook for the profession* (4th ed., pp. 203–233). San Francisco: Jossey-Bass.

McGinnis, J., & Foege, W. (1993). Actual causes of death in the U.S. *Journal of the American Medical Association, 270,* 2207–2212.

McGovern, D. (1997, November). *It ain't easy being Greek: A qualitative study of the college experience.* Paper presented at the meeting of the Association for the Study of Higher Education, Albuquerque, NM.

McGrath, M., & Braunstein, A. (1997). The prediction of freshmen attrition: An examination of the importance of certain demographic, academic, financial, and social factors. *College Student Journal, 31,* 396–408.

McIntyre, R., Pumroy, D., Burgee, M., Alexander, S., Gerson, S., & Saddoris, A. (1992). Improving retention through intensive practice in college survival skills. *NASPA Journal, 29,* 299–306.

McKeachie, W. (1997). Student ratings: The validity of use. *American Psychologist, 52,* 1218–1225.

McKinney, K. (1997). *The long-term effects of college on leadership ability in men and women.* Paper presented at the meeting of the Association for the Study of Higher Education, Albuquerque, NM.

McLure, G., & McClanahan, R. (1999, June). *Assessing student perceptions of general education courses in 2-year and 4-year institutions.* Paper presented at the meeting of the American Association for Higher Education, Denver.

McMahon, W. (1991). Relative returns to human and physical capital in the U.S. and efficient investment strategies. *Economics of Education Review, 10,* 283–296.

McMahon, W. (1998). Conceptual framework for the analysis of the social benefits of lifelong learning. *Education Economics, 6,* 309–346.

McMenamin, B. (1998, December 28). Who needs college? *Forbes* [Available at: www.forbes.com].

McNeel, S. (1994a). College teaching and student moral development. In J. Rest & D. Narvaez (Eds.), *Moral development in the professions: Psychology and applied ethics* (pp. 26–47). Hillsdale, NJ: Erlbaum.

McNeel, S. (1994b). *Integrating psychology and philosophy in the teaching of ethics: A replication of Penn's direct approach.* Unpublished manuscript, Bethel College, St. Paul, MN.

McNeel, S., Abou-Zeid, B., Essenburg, T., Smith, R., Danforth, D., & Weaver, R. (1996). Business students: Are they really different? *Research on Christian Higher Education, 3,* 33–56.

McNeel, S., & Granstrom, S. (1995). *Principled reasoning, critical thinking, and spirituality.* Unpublished manuscript, Bethel College, St. Paul, MN.

McNeel, S., Schaffer, M., & Juarez, M. (1997). Growth in moral judgment among baccalaureate nursing students. *Research on Christian Higher Education, 4,* 29–45.

McPhee, S. (1990). Addressing the attrition of minority students on predominantly White campuses: A pilot study. *College Student Affairs Journal, 10,* 15–22.

McPherson, M., & Shapiro, M. (1991). *Keeping college affordable.* Washington, DC: Brookings Institution.

Mead, H., Witkowski, K., Gault, B., & Hartmann, H. (2001). The influence of income, education, and work status on women's well-being. *Women's Health Issues, 11,* 160–172.

Mehta, J. (1993). *Cooperative learning in computer programming at the college level.* Unpublished doctoral dissertation, University of Illinois, Chicago.

Menchik, P. (1993). Economic status as a determinant of mortality among Black and White older men: Does poverty kill? *Population Studies, 47,* 427–436.

Menec, V., Perry, R., & Hunter, A. (1996, April). *Predicting success in college: The effect of perceived control on grades in a science and social science course.* Paper presented at the meeting of the American Educational Research Association, New York.

Menec, V., Perry, R., Struthers, C., Schonwetter, D., Hechter, F., & Eichholz, B. (1994). Assisting at-risk students with attributional retaining and effective teaching. *Journal of Applied Social Psychology, 24,* 675–701.

Menec, V., Perry, R., Struthers, W., Schonwetter, D., & Hechter, F. (1992, April). *Enhancing the ABCs (affects, behavior, cognitions) in college students: An attributional retraining and instructional perspective.* Paper presented at the meeting of the American Educational Research Association, San Francisco.

Menges, R., & Brinko, K. (1986, April). *Effects of student evaluation feedback: A meta-analysis of higher education research.* Paper presented at the meeting of the American Educational Research Association, San Francisco.

Mentkowski, M., & Associates. (2000). *Learning that lasts: Interpreting learning, development, and performance in college and beyond.* San Francisco: Jossey-Bass.

Mentkowski, M., Rodgers, G., Deemer, D., Tamar, B., Reisetter, J., Rickards, W., et al. (1991, April). *Understanding abilities, learning, and development through college outcome studies: What can we expect from higher education assessment?* Paper presented at the annual meeting of the American Educational Research Association, Chicago.

Mercer, D. (1993). Older coeds: Predicting who will stay this time. *Journal of Research and Development in Education, 26,* 153–163.

Mercer, S., & Cunningham, M. (2003). Racial identity in White American college students: Issues of conceptualization and measurement. *Journal of College Student Development, 44,* 217–230.

Merisotis, J., & Phipps, R. (1999, May/June). What's the difference? Outcomes of distance vs. traditional classroom-based learning. *Change, 31,* 12–17.

Merriam, S. (Ed.). (2001). *The new update on adult learning theory. New Directions for Adult and Continuing Education,* No. 89. San Francisco: Jossey-Bass.

Merriam, S., & Caffarella, R. (1999). *Learning in adulthood: A comprehensive guide* (2nd ed.). San Francisco: Jossey-Bass.

Metzner, B. (1989). Perceived quality of academic advising: The effect on freshman attrition. *American Educational Research Journal, 26,* 422–442.

Meyer, J. (1977). The effects of education as an institution. *American Journal of Sociology, 83,* 55–77.

Meyers, C., & Jones, T. (1993). *Promoting active learning: Strategies for the classroom.* San Francisco: Jossey-Bass.

Michelson, W. (1970). *Man and his urban environment: A sociological approach.* Reading, MA: Addison-Wesley.

Milem, J. (1991, October). *The role of college peer groups and faculty reference groups in the development of student attitudes toward race.* Paper presented at the meeting of the Association for the Study of Higher Education, Boston.

Milem, J. (1992). *The impact of college on students' racial attitudes and levels of racial awareness and acceptance.* Unpublished doctoral dissertation, University of California, Los Angeles.

Milem, J. (1994). College, students, and racial understanding. *Thought & Action, 9,* 51–92.

Milem, J. (1998). Attitude change in college students: Examining the effect of college peer groups and faculty normative groups. *Journal of Higher Education, 69,* 117–140.

Milem, J. (1999a). The educational benefits of diversity: Evidence from multiple sectors. In M. Chang, D. Witt, J. Jones, & K. Hakuta (Eds.), *Compelling interest: Examining the evidence on racial dynamics in higher education* (Chapter 5). Palo Alto, CA: Stanford University, Center for Comparative Studies in Race and Ethnicity.

Milem, J. (1999b, January). *The importance of faculty diversity to student learning and to the mission of higher education.* Paper presented at the meeting of the Symposium and Working Research Meeting on Diversity and Affirmative Action, sponsored by the American Council on Education and the Spencer Foundation, Arlington, VA.

Milem, J., & Berger, J. (1997). A modified model of college student persistence: Exploring the relationship between Astin's theory of involvement and Tinto's theory of student departure. *Journal of College Student Development, 38,* 387–400.

Milem, J., & Hakuta, K. (2000). The benefits of racial and ethnic diversity in higher education. In D. Wilds (Ed.), *Minorities in higher education: Seventeenth annual status report* (pp. 39–67). Washington DC: American Council on Education.

Miller, J. (1994). Linking traditional and service-learning courses: Outcomes evaluation using two pedagogically distinct models. *Michigan Journal of Community Service Learning, 1,* 29–36.

Miller, J. (1997). The impact of service-learning experiences on students' sense of power. *Michigan Journal of Community Service Learning, 4,* 16–21.

Miller, J., & Groccia, J. (1997). Are four heads better than one? A comparison of cooperation and traditional teaching formats in an introductory biology course. *Innovative Higher Education, 21,* 253–273.

Miller, S. (1999). Shortcut: High school grades as a signal of human capital. *Educational Evaluation and Policy Analysis, 20,* 299–311.

Miller, T., & Winston, R., Jr. (1990). Assessing development from a psychosocial perspective. In D. Creamer & Associates (Eds.), *College student development theory and practice for the 1990s.* (ACPA Media Publication No. 49). Alexandria, VA: American College Personnel Association.

Miller-Bernal, L. (1993). Single-sex versus coeducational environments: A comparison of women students' experiences at four colleges. *American Journal of Education, 102,* 23–54.

Miller-Bernal, L. (2000). *Separate by degree: Women students' experiences in single-sex and coeducational colleges.* New York: Peter Lang.

Millis, B., & Cottell, P. (1998). *Cooperative learning for higher education faculty.* Phoenix, AZ: Oryx.

Mines, R., King, P., Hood, A., & Wood, P. (1990). Stages of intellectual development and associated critical thinking skills in college students. *Journal of College Student Development, 31,* 538–547.

Mitchell, S., & Dell, D. (1992). The relationship between Black students' racial identity attitude and participation in campus organizations. *Journal of College Student Development, 33,* 39–43.

Moes, P., Bussema, K., & Eigenbrood, D. (1999). The use of essay writing as an assessment of personal, affective, and cognitive growth in college students. *Research on Christian Higher Education, 6,* 49–73.

Moffatt, M. (1989). *Coming of age in New Jersey: College and American culture.* New Brunswick, NJ: Rutgers University Press.

Moffatt, M. (1991). College life: Undergraduate culture and higher education. *Journal of Higher Education, 62,* 44–61.

Mohr, J., Eiche, K., & Sedlacek, W. (1998). So close, yet so far: Predictors of attrition in college seniors. *Journal of College Student Development, 39,* 343–354.

Molla, B., & Westbrook, F. (1990). *White students attitudes about African-American students in a university setting* (Research Report No. 9–90). College Park: University of Maryland.

Molnar, D. (1993, May). *The impact of mission effectiveness on student retention.* Paper presented at the meeting of the Association for Institutional Research, Chicago.

Molnar, D. (1996, May). *The impact of institutional effectiveness on student retention.* Paper presented at the meeting of the Association for Institutional Research, Albuquerque, NM.

Money, S. (1997). The relationship between critical thinking scores, achievement scores, and grade point average in three different disciplines. *Dissertation Abstracts International, 58,* 3401A.

Monks, J. (1997). The impact of college timing on earnings. *Economics of Education Review, 16,* 419–423.

Monks, J. (1998). *The returns to individual and college characteristics: Evidence from the National Longitudinal Survey of Youth.* Unpublished manuscript, Consortium on Financing Higher Education, Cambridge, MA.

Monks, J. (2000). The returns to individual and college characteristics: Evidence from the National Longitudinal Survey of Youth. *Economics of Education Review, 19,* 279–289.

Monk-Turner, E. (1990). The occupational achievements of community and four-year college entrants. *American Sociological Review, 55,* 719–725.

Montgomery, D., Miville, M., Winterowd, C., Heffries, B., & Baysden, M. (2000). American Indian college students: An exploration into resiliency factors revealed through personal stories. *Cultural Diversity and Ethnic Minority Psychology, 6,* 387–398.

Montmarquette, C., Mahseredjian, S., & Houle, R. (2001). The determinants of university dropouts: A bivariate probability model with sample selection. *Economics of Education Review, 20,* 475–484.

Montondon, L., & Eikner, A. (1997). Comparison of community college transfer students and native students in an upper-level accounting course. *Community College Review, 25,* 21–38.

Monzon, R., & Maramba, D. (1998, November). *The effects of campus and family environments among Filipino American college students: A path analytic application of Tinto's model.* Paper presented at the meeting of the Association for the Study of Higher Education, Miami.

Moore, B., & Parker, R. (1989). *Critical thinking: Evaluating claims and arguments in everyday life* (2nd ed.). Mountain View, CA: Mayfield.

Moore, M., & Thompson, M. (1990). *Effects of distance learning: A summary of literature.* University Park, PA: American Center for the Study of Distance Education.

Moore, M., & Thompson, M. (1997). *The effects of distance learning* (rev. ed.). University Park, PA: American Center for the Study of Distance Education.

Moore, W. (1991a, April). *The Perry scheme of intellectual and ethical development: An introduction to the model and major assessment approaches.* Paper presented at the meeting of the American Educational Research Association, Chicago.

Moore, W. (1991b). *The measure of intellectual development: An instrument manual.* Farmville, VA: Center for the Study of Intellectual Development.

Moos, R. (1979). *Evaluating educational environments: Procedures, measures, findings, and policy implications.* San Francisco: Jossey-Bass.

Moos, R. (1986). *The human context: Environmental determinants of behavior.* Malabar, FL: Krieger.

Moran, J. (1989). Social work education and students' humanistic attitudes. *Journal of Social Work Education, 25,* 13–19.

Morganthau, T., & Nayyar, S. (1996). Those scary college costs. *Newsweek, 127,* 52–58.

Morley, R., Havick, J., & May, G. (1998). An evaluation of the Georgia Tech summer undergraduate program of research in electrical engineering for minorities. *Journal of Engineering Education, 87,* 321–325.

Morrison, J. (1999). The role of teaching in education today and tomorrow: An interview with Kenneth Green, Part II. *On the Horizon, 7*(1), 2–5.

Mortimer, J., & Simmons, R. (1978). Adult socialization. In R. Turner, J. Coleman, & R. Fox (Eds.), *Annual review of sociology* (Vol. 4). Palo Alto, CA: Annual Reviews.

Mose, D., & Maney, T. (1993). An experiment in distance learning of geology. *Journal of Computers in Mathematics and Science Teaching, 12,* 5–18.

Mourtos, N. (1997). The nuts and bolts of cooperative learning in engineering. *Journal of Engineering Education, 86,* 35–37.

Muir, D. (1991). "White" fraternity and sorority attitudes toward "Blacks" on a deep-south campus. *Sociological Spectrum, 11,* 93–103.

Mukuakane-Drechsel, T., & Hagedorn, L. (2000). Correlates of retention among Asian-Pacific Americans in community colleges: The case for Hawaiian students. *Community College Journal of Research and Practice, 24,* 639–655.

Mullane, S. (1999). Fairness, educational value, and moral development in the student disciplinary process. *NASPA Journal, 36,* 86–95.

Mullen, A., Goyette, K., & Soares, J. (2003). Who goes to graduate school? Social and academic correlates of educational continuation after college. *Sociology of Education, 76,* 143–169.

Multon, K., Brown, S., & Lent, R. (1991). Relation of self-efficacy beliefs to academic outcomes: A meta-analytic investigation. *Journal of Counseling Psychology, 38,* 30–38.

Munoz-Dunbar, R., & Snyder, C. (1993, August). *Hope: A cross-cultural assessment of American college students.* Paper presented at the meeting of the American Psychological Association, Toronto.

Murdock, T. (1990). Financial aid and persistence: An integrative review of the literature. *NASPA Journal, 27,* 213–221.

Murdock, T., Nix-Mayer, L., & Tsui, P. (1995, May). *The effect of types of financial aid on student persistence toward graduation.* Paper presented at the meeting of the Association for Institutional Research, Boston.

Murguia, E., Padilla, R., & Pavel, M. (1991). Ethnicity and the concept of social integration in Tinto's model of institutional departure. *Journal of College Student Development, 32,* 433–454.

Murnane, R., Willett, J., Duhaldeborde, Y., & Tyler, J. (1998). *The role of cognitive skills in explaining recent trends in the U.S. distribution of earned income.* Unpublished manuscript, Harvard Graduate School of Education, Cambridge, MA.

Murnane, R., Willett, J., & Levy, F. (1995). The growing importance of cognitive skills in wage determination. *Review of Economics and Statistics, 77,* 251–266.

Murphy, K., & Welch, F. (1992a). Wages of college graduates. In W. Becker & D. Lewis (Eds.), *The economics of American higher education* (pp. 121–140). Norwell, MA: Kluwer.

Murphy, K., & Welch, F. (1992b, February). The structure of wages. *Quarterly Review of Economics, 107,* pp. 285–325.

Murphy, K., & Welch, F. (1993). Occupational change and the demand for skill, 1940–1990. *American Economic Review, 834,* 122–126.

Murphy, M., & Davidson, G. (1991). Computer-based adaptive instruction: Effects of learner control on concept learning. *Journal of Computer-Based Instruction, 18,* 51–56.

Murray, H. (1991). Effective teaching behaviors in the college classroom. In J. Smart (Ed.), *Higher education: Handbook of theory and research* (Vol. 7, pp. 135–172). New York: Agathon.

Murray, H., Jelley, R., & Renaud, R. (1996). *Longitudinal trends in student instructional ratings: Does evaluation of teaching lead to improved teaching?* Paper presented at the meeting of the American Educational Research Association, New York.

Murray, H., & Lang, M. (1997). Does classroom participation improve student learning? *Teaching and Learning in Higher Education, 20,* 7–9.

Murray, H., & Renaud, R. (1995). Disciplinary differences in classroom teaching behaviors. In N. Hativa & M. Marincovich (Eds.), *Disciplinary differences in teaching and learning: Implications for practice. New Directions for Teaching and Learning,* No. 64 (pp. 31–39). San Francisco: Jossey-Bass.

Murray, H., & Smith, T. (1989). *Effects of midterm behavioral feedback on end-of-term ratings of instructor effectiveness.* Paper presented at the meeting of the American Educational Research Association, San Francisco.

Murray, J., & Adams, D. (1998). Developmental implications of undergraduate student attitudes concerning juvenile justice. *NASPA Journal, 35,* 245–253.

Murtaugh, P., Burns, L., & Schuster, J. (1999). Predicting the retention of university students. *Research in Higher Education, 40,* 355–371.

Murtuza, A., & Ketkar, K. (1995). Evaluating the cost-effectiveness of a freshman studies program on an urban campus. *Journal of the Freshman Year Experience, 7,* 7–26.

Musil, C. (Ed.). (1992). *The courage to question: Women's studies and student learning.* Washington, DC: Association of American Colleges.

Mustapha, S., & Seybert, J. (1990). Moral reasoning in college students: Effects of two general education curricula. *Educational Research Quarterly, 14*(4), 32–40.

Mutter, P. (1992). Tinto's theory of departure and community college student persistence. *Journal of College Student Development, 33,* 310–317.

Myers, I. (1980a). *Introduction to type.* Palo Alto, CA: Consulting Psychologists Press.

Myers, I. (1980b). *Gifts differing.* Palo Alto, CA: Consulting Psychologists Press.

Myers, I., & McCaulley, M. (1985). *Manual: A guide to the development and use of the Myers-Briggs Type Indicator.* Palo Alto, CA: Consulting Psychologists Press.

Myers-Lipton, S. (1994). *The effects of service-learning on college students' attitudes toward civic responsibility, international understanding, and racial prejudice.* Unpublished doctoral dissertation, University of Colorado, Boulder.

Myers-Lipton, S. (1996a). Effect of service-learning on college students' attitudes toward international understanding. *Journal of College Student Development, 37,* 659–668.

Myers-Lipton, S. (1996b). Effect of a comprehensive service-learning program on college students' level of modern racism. *Michigan Journal of Community Service Learning, 3,* 44–54.

Myers-Lipton, S. (1998). Effect of a comprehensive service-learning program on college students' civic responsibility. *Teaching Sociology, 26,* 243–258.

Myerson, J., Rank, M., Raines, F., & Schnitzler, M. (1998). Race and general cognitive ability: The myth of diminishing returns to education. *Psychological Science, 9,* 139–142.

Nagda, B. A., Gregerman, S. R., Jonides, J., von Hippel, W., & Lerner, J. S. (1998). Undergraduate student-faculty research partnerships affect student retention. *Review of Higher Education, 22,* 55–72.

Naretto, J. (1995). Adult student retention: The influence of internal and external communities. *NASPA Journal, 32,* 90–97.

Nash, D. (1991). The course of sojourner adaptation: A new test of the U-curve hypothesis. *Human Organization, 50,* 283–286.

National Center for Education Statistics. (1996). *Working while in college* (Report No. NCES 96–796). Washington, DC: U.S. Department of Education, Office of Educational Research and Improvement.

National Center for Education Statistics. (1997). *Women in mathematics and science* (Report No. NCES 97–982). Washington, DC: U.S. Department of Education.

National Center for Education Statistics. (1998). *Digest of education statistics, 1997.* Washington, DC: U.S. Department of Education, Office of Educational Research and Improvement.

National Center for Education Statistics. (1999). *Parent involvement in school-related activities* (Report No. NCES 1999–001). Washington, DC: U.S. Department of Education, Office of Educational Research and Improvement.

National Center for Health Statistics (NCHS). (1992). *Advance report of final mortality statistics, 1989.* Hyattsville, MD: Public Health Service.

National Center for Public Policy and Higher Education. (2000). *Measuring up: The state-by-state report card for higher education.* San Jose, CA: Author.

National Center for Supplemental Instruction. (1997). *Supplemental Instruction (SI): Review of research concerning the effectiveness of SI from the University of Missouri-Kansas City and other institutions from across the United States.* Kansas City: University of Missouri-Kansas City, Center for Academic Development.

National Collegiate Athletic Association. (2001). *2001 Graduation-rates report for NCAA Division I schools.* Indianapolis: Author.

National Collegiate Athletic Association. (2002). *2002 Graduation-rates report for Division I schools.* Indianapolis: Author.

National Education Goals Panel. (1992). *National Education Goals Panel report: Building a nation of learners.* Washington, DC: U.S. Government Printing Office.

National Resource Center for the First-Year Experience and Students in Transition. (2000). *2000 National survey of first-year seminar programming.* [http://www.sc.edu./fye/research/surveyfindings/index.html]

National Women's Studies Association Task Force for the Association of American Colleges. (1991). *Liberal learning and the women's studies major.* College Park, MD: National Women's Studies Association.

Neal, D., & Johnson, W. (1994). The role of premarket factors in Black-White wage differences. *Journal of Political Economy, 104,* 869–895.

Nelson, E., & Dixon, C. (1997). Gender differences in enrollment in high-prestige academic college majors. *Journal of the Freshman Year Experience & Students in Transition, 9,* 99–114.

Nelson, E., & Krieger, S. (1997). Changes in attitudes toward homosexuality in college students: Implementation of gay men and lesbian peer panel. *Journal of Homosexuality, 33,* 63–81.

Nelson, E., & Torgler, C. (1990). A comparison of strategies for changing college students' attitudes toward acquaintance rape. *Journal of Humanistic Education and Development, 29,* 69–85.

Nesdale, D., & Todd, P. (1993). Internationalizing Australian universities: The intercultural contact issue. *Journal of Tertiary Education Administration, 15,* 189–202.

Nesdale, D., & Todd, P. (2000). Effect of contact on intercultural acceptance: A field study. *International Journal of Intercultural Relations, 24,* 341–360.

Nettles, M., Perna, L., & Freeman, K. (1999). *Two decades of progress: African Americans moving forward in higher education.* Fairfax, VA: Frederick D. Patterson Research Institute.

Neuhauser, C. (2002). Learning style and effectiveness of online and face-to-face instruction. *American Journal of Distance Education, 16,* 99–113.

Nevins, K., & McNeel, S. (1992). Facilitating student moral development through faculty development. *Moral Education Forum, 17*(4), 12–18.

Newcomb, T. (1943). *Personality and social change: Attitude formation in a student community.* Orlando: Dryden Press.

Newcomb, T., Koenig, K., Flacks, R., & Warwick, D. (1967). *Persistence and change: Bennington College and its students after 25 years.* New York: Wiley.

Ng, Y. (1989). *The demand for medical care by gender: Additional evidence.* Unpublished manuscript, Department of Economics, University of South Carolina, Columbia.

Nickerson, C. (1991). Curricular design and levels of reflective judgment. *Dissertation Abstracts International, 52,* 2040A.

Nie, N., Junn, J., & Stehlik-Barry, K. (1996). *Education and democratic citizenship in America.* Chicago: University of Chicago Press.

Niles, S., & Garis, J. (1990). The effects of a career planning course and a computer-assisted career guidance program (SIGI PLUS) on undecided university students. *Journal of Career Development, 16,* 237–248.

Niles, S., Sowa, C., & Laden, J. (1994). Life role participation and commitment as predictors of college student development. *Journal of College Student Development, 35,* 159–163.

Nixon, H. (1997). Gender, sport, and aggressive behavior outside sport. *Journal of Sport & Social Issues, 21,* 379–391.

Nolin, M., & Chapman, C. (1997). *Adult civic involvement in the United States* (E.D. TABS Report No. NCES 97–906). Washington, DC: U.S. Department of Education, Office of Educational Research and Improvement, National Center for Education Statistics.

Nora, A. (1990). Campus-based aid programs as determinants of retention among Hispanic community college students. *Journal of Higher Education, 61,* 312–330.

Nora, A., Attinasi, L., & Matonak, A. (1990). Testing qualitative indicators of precollege factors in Tinto's attrition model: A community college student population. *Review of Higher Education, 13,* 337–356.

Nora, A., & Cabrera, A. (1993). The construct validity of institutional commitment: A confirmatory factor analysis. *Research in Higher Education, 34,* 243–262.

Nora, A., & Cabrera, A. (1996). The role of perceptions of prejudice and discrimination on the adjustment of minority students to college. *Journal of Higher Education, 67,* 119–148.

Nora, A., Cabrera, A., Hagedorn, L., & Pascarella, E. (1996). Differential impacts of academic and social experiences of college-related behavioral outcomes across different ethnic and gender groups at four-year institutions. *Research in Higher Education, 37,* 427–451.

Nora, A., & Rendon, L. (1990). Determinants of predisposition to transfer among community college students: A structural model. *Research in Higher Education, 31,* 235–255.

Nordvall, R., & Braxton, J. (1996). An alternative definition of quality of undergraduate college education. *Journal of Higher Education, 67,* 483–497.

Noser, T., Manakyan, H., & Tanner, J. (1996). Research productivity and perceived teaching effectiveness: A survey of economics faculty. *Research in Higher Education, 37,* 299–321.

Nucci, L., & Pascarella, E. (1987). The influence of college on moral development. In J. Smart (Ed.), *Higher education: Handbook of theory and research* (Vol. 3, pp. 271–326). New York: Agathon.

Nunez, A., & Cuccaro-Alamin, S. (1998). *First-generation students: Undergraduates whose parents never enrolled in postsecondary education* (Statistical Analysis Report No. NCES 98–082). Washington, DC: U.S. Department of Education, Office of Educational Research and Improvement, National Center for Education Statistics.

Nunn, C. (1996). Discussion in the college classroom: Triangulating observational and survey results. *Journal of Higher Education, 67,* 243–266.

O'Brien, C. (1997, December). Life after college: Employment, further education, lifestyle for recent grads. *AAHE Bulletin, 50,* 7–10.

O'Brien, E. (1993). Outside the classroom: Students as employees, volunteers, and interns. *Research Briefs, 4*(1), 1–12.

O'Brien, T., & Thompson, M. (1994). Cognitive styles and academic achievement in community college education. *Community College Journal of Research and Practice, 18,* 547–556.

Office of Education Research and Improvement. (1996). *Labor market outcomes of literacy and education* (Report No. NCES 96–793). Washington, DC: U.S. Department of Education.

Okada, T., & Simon, H. (1997). Collaborative discovery in a scientific domain. *Cognitive Science, 21,* 109–146.

Okun, M., Ruehlman, L., & Karoly, P. (1991). Applications of investment theory to predicting part-time community college student intent and institutional persistence/departure behavior. *Journal of Educational Psychology, 83,* 212–220.

Olcott, D. (1992). *Instructional television: A review of selected evaluation research.* Unpublished manuscript, Oregon State University, Corvallis.

Olsen, D., & Simmons, A. (1996, May). *Research productivity, classroom teaching, and faculty/student contact: An investigation of relationships.* Paper presented at the annual meeting of the Association for Institutional Research, Albuquerque, NM.

Olsen, S. (1990). *Examining the relationship between college core course areas and sophomore critical thinking test scores.* Paper presented at the meeting of the American Evaluation Association, Washington, DC.

Olsen, S. (1991, April). *Examining the relationship between college general education science-oriented course work and CAAP science reasoning skills.* Paper presented at the meeting of the American Educational Research Association, Chicago.

O'Neil, J., Egan, J., Owen, S., & Murry, V. (1992). The gender role journey measure: Scale development and psychometric evaluation. *Sex Roles, 28,* 167–185.

Opp, R. (1991). *The impact of college on NTE performance.* Unpublished doctoral dissertation, University of California, Los Angeles.

Opper, S., Teichler, U., & Carlson, J. (1990). *Impacts of study abroad programmes on students and graduates.* London: Jessica Kingsley.

Orfield, G., & Paul, F. (1992). *State higher education systems and college completion: Final report to the Ford Foundation.* New York: Ford Foundation. (ERIC Document Reproduction Service No. ED 354 041)

Ortiz, A., & Rhoads, R. (2000). Deconstructing Whiteness as part of a multicultural educational framework: From theory to practice. *Journal of College Student Development, 41,* 81–93.

Osborne, R., Hammerich, S., & Hensley, C. (1998). Student effects of service learning: Tracking change across a semester. *Michigan Journal of Community Service Learning, 5,* 5–13.

O'Shea, D. (1989, April). *Gender income differential among college educated persons in early career.* Paper presented at the meeting of the American Educational Research Association, San Francisco.

Osipow, S., & Fitzgerald, L. (1995). *Theories of career development* (4th ed.). Needham Heights, MA: Allyn & Bacon.

Osman, S., & Davis, C. (1999). Predicting perceptions of date rape based on individual beliefs and female alcohol consumption. *Journal of College Student Development, 40,* 701–709.

Ossana, S., Helms, J., & Leonard, M. (1992). Do "womanist" identity attitudes influence college women's self-esteem and perceptions of environmental bias? *Journal of Counseling and Development, 70,* 402–408.

Osterlind, S. (1996, April). *Collegians' scholastic achievement in general education: A national look.* Paper presented at the meeting of the American Educational Research Association, New York.

Osterlind, S. (1997). *Collegians' achievement in general education: A national look.* Washington, DC: George Washington University.

Osterlind, S., & Merz, W. (1990). *Technical manual for college basic academic subjects examination.* Chicago: Riverside.

Outcalt, C., & Skewes-Cox, T. (2002). Involvement, interaction, and satisfaction: The human environment at HBCUs. *Review of Higher Education, 25,* 331–347.

Pace, C. (1969). *College and University Environment Scales (CUES) technical manual* (2nd ed.). Princeton, NJ: Educational Testing Service.

Pace, C. (1979). *Measuring outcomes of college: Fifty years of findings and recommendations for the future.* San Francisco: Jossey-Bass.

Pace, C. (1984). *Measuring the quality of college student experiences.* Los Angeles: University of California, Graduate School of Education, Higher Education Research Institute, Project on the Study of Quality in Undergraduate Education.

Pace, C. (1987). *Good things go together.* Los Angeles: University of California, Center for the Study of Evaluation.

Pace, C. (1988). *Measuring the quality of college student experiences* (rev. ed.). Los Angeles: University of California, Center for the Study of Evaluation.

Pace, C. (1990). *The undergraduates: A report of their activities.* Los Angeles: University of California, Center for the Study of Evaluation.

Pace, C. (1995, May). *From good processes to good products: Relating good practices in undergraduate education to student achievement.* Paper presented at the meeting of the Association for Institutional Research, Boston.

Pace, C. (1997, November). *Connecting institutional types to student outcomes.* Paper presented at the meeting of the Association for the Study of Higher Education, Albuquerque, NM.

Pace, C., & Stern, G. (1958). An approach to the measurement of psychological characteristics of college environments. *Journal of Educational Psychology, 49,* 269–277.

Padilla, A. (1995). On the nature of Latino ethnicity. In A. Lopez (Ed.), *Historical themes and identity: Mestizaje and labels.* New York: Garland.

Padilla, R., Trevino, J., Gonzalez, K., & Trevino, J. (1997). Developing local models of minority success in college. *Journal of College Student Development, 38,* 125–135.

Paglin, M., & Rufolo, A. (1990). Heterogeneous human capital, occupational choice, and male-female earnings differences. *Journal of Labor Economics, 8,* 123–144.

Palinscar, A., & Brown, A. (1984). Reciprocal teaching of comprehension-fostering and comprehension-monitoring activities. *Cognition and Instruction, 2,* 117–175.

Palinscar, A., Stevens, D., & Gavelek, J. (1989). Collaborating with teachers in the interest of student collaboration. *International Journal of Educational Research, 13,* 41–53.

Palmer, B. (2000, Winter). The impact of diversity courses: Research from Pennsylvania State University. *Diversity Digest,* pp. 4–5.

Palmer, B., & Willits, F. (1996, October). *A hierarchical linear model of the long-term effects of education on sex-role attitude change.* Paper presented at the meeting of the Association for the Study of Higher Education, Memphis, TN.

Palmer, E. (1999). *An analysis of a diversity requirement: The effect of course characteristics on students' racial attitudes, gender attitudes, and self-perceived learning.* Unpublished doctoral dissertation, Pennsylvania State University, University Park.

Paradice, D., & Dejoie, R. (1991). The ethical decision-making process of information systems workers. *Journal of Business Ethics, 10,* 1–21.

Parental educational attainment and higher educational opportunity. (1999, January). *Postsecondary Education OPPORTUNITY,* No. 79, 1–9.

Parham, W. (1993). The intercollegiate athlete: A 1990s profile. *Counseling Psychologist, 21,* 411–429.

Parker, W., Moore, M., & Neimeyer, G. (1998). Altering White racial identity and interracial comfort through multicultural training. *Journal of Counseling & Development, 76,* 302–310.

Parker-Gwin, R., & Mabry, J. (1998). Service learning as pedagogy and civic education: Comparing outcomes for three models. *Teaching Sociology, 26,* 276–291.

Parks, S. (2000). *Big questions, worthy dreams: Mentoring young adults in their search for meaning, purpose, and faith.* San Francisco: Jossey-Bass.

Pascarella, E. (1980). Student-faculty informal contact and college outcomes. *Review of Educational Research, 50,* 545–595.

Pascarella, E. (1985). College environmental influences on learning and cognitive development: A critical review and synthesis. In J. Smart (Ed.), *Higher education: Handbook of theory and research* (Vol. 1, pp. 1–64). New York: Agathon.

Pascarella, E. (1989). The development of critical thinking: Does college make a difference? *Journal of College Student Development, 30*, 19–26.

Pascarella, E. (1997a). College's influence on principled moral reasoning. *Educational Record, 78*(3, 4), 47–55.

Pascarella, E. (1997b, January/February). It's time we started paying attention to community college students. *About Campus, 1*, 14–17.

Pascarella, E. (1999). New studies track community college effects on students. *Community College Journal, 69*, 8–14.

Pascarella, E. (2001). Using student self-reported gains to estimate college impact: A cautionary tale. *Journal of College Student Development, 42*, 488–492.

Pascarella, E., Bohr, L., Nora, A., Desler, M., & Zusman, B. (1994). Impacts of on-campus and off-campus work on first-year cognitive outcomes. *Journal of College Student Development, 35*, 364–370.

Pascarella, E., Bohr, L., Nora, A., Raganathan, S., Desler, M., & Bulakowski, C. (1994). Impacts of two-year and four-year colleges on learning orientations: A preliminary study. *Community College Journal of Research and Practice, 18*, 577–589.

Pascarella, E., Bohr, L., Nora, A., & Terenzini, P. (1995a). Cognitive effects of two-year and four-year colleges: New evidence. *Educational Evaluation and Policy Analysis, 17*, 83–96.

Pascarella, E., Bohr, L., Nora, A., & Terenzini, P. (1995b). Intercollegiate athletic participation and freshman-year cognitive outcomes. *Journal of Higher Education, 66*, 369–387.

Pascarella, E., Bohr, L., Nora, A., & Terenzini, P. (1996). Is differential exposure to college linked to the development of critical thinking? *Research in Higher Education, 37*, 159–174.

Pascarella, E., Bohr, L., Nora, A., Zusman, B., Inman, P., & Desler, M. (1993). Cognitive impacts of living on campus versus commuting to college. *Journal of College Student Development, 34*, 216–220.

Pascarella, E., Edison, M., Hagedorn, L., Nora, A., & Terenzini, P. (1996). Influences on students' internal locus of attribution for academic success in the first year of college. *Research in Higher Education, 37*, 731–756.

Pascarella, E., Edison, M., Nora, A., Hagedorn, L., & Braxton, J. (1995, April). *Effects of teacher organization/preparation and teacher skill/clarity on general cognitive skills in college.* Paper presented at the annual meeting of the American Educational Research Association, San Francisco.

Pascarella, E., Edison, M., Nora, A., Hagedorn, L., & Braxton, J. (1996). Effects of teacher organization/preparation and teacher skill/clarity on general cognitive skills in college. *Journal of College Student Development, 37*, 7–19.

Pascarella, E., Edison, M., Nora, A., Hagedorn, L., & Terenzini, P. (1995–96). Cognitive effects of community colleges and four-year colleges. *Community College Journal, 66*(3), 35–39.

Pascarella, E., Edison, M., Nora, A., Hagedorn, L., & Terenzini, P. (1996). Influences on students' openness to diversity and challenge in the first year of college. *Journal of Higher Education, 67,* 174–195.

Pascarella, E., Edison, M., Nora, A., Hagedorn, L., & Terenzini, P. (1998a). Does work inhibit cognitive development during college? *Educational Evaluation and Policy Analysis, 20,* 75–93.

Pascarella, E., Edison, M., Nora, A., Hagedorn, L., & Terenzini, P. (1998b). Does community college versus four-year college attendance influence students' educational plans? *Journal of College Student Development, 39,* 179–193.

Pascarella, E., Edison, M., Whitt, E., Nora, A., Hagedorn, L., & Terenzini, P. (1996). Cognitive effects of Greek affiliation during the first year of college. *NASPA Journal, 33,* 242–259.

Pascarella, E., Flowers, L., & Whitt, E. (1999). *Cognitive effects of Greek affiliation in college: Additional evidence.* Unpublished manuscript, University of Iowa, Iowa City.

Pascarella, E., Palmer, B., Moye, M., & Pierson, C. (2001). Do diversity experiences influence the development of critical thinking? *Journal of College Student Development, 42,* 257–271.

Pascarella, E., Pierson, C., Wolniak, G., & Terenzini, P. (2004). First-generation college students: Additional evidence on college experiences and outcomes. *Journal of Higher Education, 75,* 249–284.

Pascarella, E., & Smart, J. (1991). Impact of intercollegiate athletic participation for African-American and Caucasian men: Some further evidence. *Journal of College Student Development, 32,* 123–130.

Pascarella, E., Smart, J., & Smylie, M. (1992). College tuition costs and early career socioeconomic achievement: Do you get what you pay for? *Higher Education, 24,* 275–290.

Pascarella, E., & Terenzini, P. (1991). *How college affects students: Findings and insights from twenty years of research.* San Francisco: Jossey-Bass.

Pascarella, E., & Terenzini, P. (1998). Studying college students in the 21st century: Meeting new challenges. *Review of Higher Education, 21,* 151–165.

Pascarella, E., Terenzini, P., & Blimling, G. (1994). The impact of college residence halls on student development. In P. Mable & C. Schroeder (Eds.), *Realizing the educational potential of college residence halls.* San Francisco: Jossey-Bass.

Pascarella, E., Truckenmiller, R., Nora, A., Terenzini, P., Edison, M., & Hagedorn, L. (1999). Cognitive impacts of intercollegiate athletic participation: Some further evidence. *Journal of Higher Education, 70,* 1–26.

Pascarella, E., Whitt, E., Edison, M., Nora, A., Hagedorn, L., Yaeger, P., et al. (1997). Women's perceptions of a "chilly climate" and their cognitive outcomes during the first year of college. *Journal of College Student Development, 38,* 109–124.

Pascarella, E., Wolniak, G., & Pierson, C. (2003). Influences on community college students' educational plans. *Research in Higher Education, 44,* 301–314.

Paul, R. (1987). Teaching thinking skills: Theory and practice. In J. Baron & R. Sternberg (Eds.), *Teaching thinking skills: Theory and practice* (pp. 127–148). New York: Freeman.

Paul, R. (1992). *Critical thinking: What every person needs to survive in a rapidly changing world* (2nd ed.). Santa Rosa, CA: Foundation for Critical Thinking.

Paulsen, M. (1998). Recent research on the economics of attending college: Returns on investment and responsiveness to price. *Research in Higher Education, 39,* 471–498.

Paulsen, M., & St. John, E. (1997). The financial nexus between college choice and persistence. In R. Voorhees (Ed.), *Researching student financial aid* (pp. 65–82). New *Directions for Institutional Research,* No. 95. San Francisco: Jossey-Bass.

Paulsen, M., & St. John, E. (2002). Social class and college costs: Examining the financial nexus between college choice and persistence. *Journal of Higher Education, 73,* 189–236.

Paulsen, M., & Wells, C. (1998). Domain differences in the epistemological beliefs of college students. *Research in Higher Education, 39,* 365–384.

Pavelich, M. (1996). *Helping students develop higher-level thinking: Use of the Perry model.* Paper presented at the meeting of the Frontiers in Education Conference, Salt Lake City, UT.

Pavelich, M., & Moore, W. (1996). Measuring the effect of experiential education using the Perry model. *Journal of Engineering Education, 85,* 287–292.

Pavelich, M., Olds, B., & Miller, R. (1995). Real-world problem solving in freshman-sophomore engineering. In J. Gainen & E. Willemsen (Eds.), *Fostering student success in quantitative gateway courses. New Directions for Teaching and Learning,* No. 61 (pp. 45–54). San Francisco: Jossey-Bass.

Payne, B., Pullen, R., & Padgett, J. (1996). An examination of student attrition at a medium-sized southern university. *Psychological Reports, 78,* 1035–1038.

Pearman, S., Valois, R., Sargent, R., Saunders, R., Drane, J., & Macera, C. (1997). The impact of a required college health and physical education course on the health status of alumni. *Journal of American College Health, 46,* 77–85.

Pearson, C. (1991). *Barriers to success: Community college students' critical thinking skills.* Washington, DC: U.S. Office of Education. (ERIC Document Reproduction Services No. ED 340 415)

Pearson, F., & Rodgers, R. (1998). Cognitive and identity development: Gender effects. *Initiatives, 58,* 17–33.

Peled, O., & Kim, A. (1996). Evaluation of supplemental instruction at the college level. *The Learning Assistance Review, 1*(2), 23–31.

Pencavel, J. (1991). Higher education, productivity, and earnings: A review. *Journal of Economic Education, 22,* 331–359.

Penn, W. (1990). Teaching ethics—A direct approach. *Journal of Moral Education, 19,* 124–138.

Penny, M., & White, W. (1998). Developmental mathematics students' performance: Input of faculty and student characteristics. *Journal of Developmental Education, 22,* 2 ff.

Perry, R. (1991). Perceived control in college students: Implications for instruction in higher education. In J. Smart (Ed.), *Higher education: Handbook of theory and research* (Vol. 7, pp. 1–56). New York: Agathon.

Perry, R., Hechter, F., Menec, V., & Weinberg, L. (1992). *A review of achievement motivation and performance in college students from an attributional retraining per-*

spective (Occasional Monograph Series No. 1). Winnipeg, Canada: University of Manitoba, Centre for Higher Education Research and Development.

Perry, R., Hechter, F., Menec, V., & Weinberg, L. (1993). Enhancing achievement motivation and performance in college students: An attributional retraining perspective. *Research in Higher Education, 34,* 687–723.

Perry, R., & Magnusson, J.-L. (1989a). Causal attributions and perceived performance: Consequences for college students' achievement and perceived control in different instructional conditions. *Journal of Educational Psychology, 81,* 164–172.

Perry, R., & Magnusson, J.-L. (1989b). *Students' attributional style and effective teaching: Implications for instructional practice.* Paper presented at the meeting of the International Society for the Study of Individual Differences, Heidelberg, Germany.

Perry, R., Menec, V., & Struthers, C. (1996). Student motivation from the teacher's perspective. In R. Menges & M. Weimer (Eds.), *Teaching on solid ground: Using scholarship to improve practice* (pp. 75–100). San Francisco: Jossey-Bass.

Perry, R., & Penner, K. (1990). Enhancing academic achievement in college students through attributional retraining. *Journal of Educational Psychology, 82,* 262–271.

Perry, R., Schonwetter, D., Magnusson, J.-L., & Struthers, C. (1994). Students' explanatory schemata and the quality of college instruction: Some evidence for buffer and compensation effects. *Research in Higher Education, 35,* 349–371.

Perry, R., & Struthers, C. (1994, April). *Attributional retraining in the college classroom: Some causes for optimism.* Paper presented at the meeting of the American Educational Research Association, New Orleans.

Perry, S., Cabrera, A., & Vogt, W. (1997, November). *Career maturity and college student persistence.* Paper presented at the meeting of the Association for the Study of Higher Education, Albuquerque, NM.

Perry, W. (1970). *Forms of intellectual and ethical development in the college years: A scheme.* San Francisco: Jossey-Bass.

Perry, W. (1981). Cognitive and ethical growth: The making of meaning. In A. Chickering & Associates (Eds.), *The modern American college: Responding to the new realities of diverse students and a changing society* (pp. 76–116). San Francisco: Jossey-Bass.

Person, D., & Christensen, M. (1996). Understanding Black student culture and Black student retention. *NASPA Journal, 34,* 47–56.

Person, D., & LeNoir, K. (1997). Retention issues and models for African-American male athletes. In M. Cuyjet (Ed.), *Helping African-American men succeed in college* (pp. 79–91). *New Directions for Student Services,* No. 80. San Francisco: Jossey-Bass.

Peterson, M. (1996). A team-based approach to problem-based learning: An evaluation of structured team problem solving. *Journal on Excellence in College Teaching, 7,* 129–153.

Peterson, M., Wagner, J., & Lamb, C. (2001). The role of advising in non-returning students' perceptions of their university. *Journal of Marketing for Higher Education, 10,* 45–59.

Pettit, J. (1992, May). *Listening to your alumni in assessing learning outcomes.* Paper presented at the meeting of the Association for Institutional Research, Atlanta, GA.

Phinney, J. (1989). Stages of ethnic identity development in minority group adolescents. *Journal of Early Adolescence, 1–2*, 34–39.

Phinney, J. (1990). Ethnic identity in adolescents and adults: Review of research. *Psychological Bulletin, 108*, 499–514.

Phinney, J. (1992). The multigroup ethic identity measure: A new scale for use with diverse groups. *Journal of Adolescent Research, 7*, 156–176.

Phinney, J., & Alipuria, L. (1990). Ethnic identity in college students from four ethnic groups. *Journal of Adolescence, 13*, 171–183.

Phinney, J., Chavira, V., & Williamson, L. (1992). Acculturation attitudes and self-esteem among high school and college students. *Youth & Society, 23*, 299–312.

Piaget, J. (1964). *Judgment and reasoning in the child.* Totowa, NJ: Littlefield, Adams.

Pierson, C. (2002). *Volunteerism in college: Impacts on cognitive outcomes, learning orientations, and educational aspirations.* Unpublished doctoral dissertation, University of Iowa, Iowa City.

Pierson, C., & Pascarella, E. (2002, November). *Volunteerism in college: Impacts on cognitive outcomes, learning orientations, and educational aspirations during the first year.* Paper presented at the meeting of the Association for the Study of Higher Education, Sacramento, CA.

Pierson, C., Wolniak, G., Pascarella, E., & Flowers, L. (2003). Impacts of two-year and four-year college attendance on learning orientations. *Review of Higher Education, 26*, 299–321.

Pike, G. (1991a). Using structural equation models with latent variables to study student growth and development. *Research in Higher Education, 32*, 499–524.

Pike, G. (1991b, May). *Dimensions of academic growth and development during college: Using alumni reports to evaluate education programs.* Paper presented at the meeting of the Association for the Study of Higher Education, Boston.

Pike, G. (1992a). The components of construct validity: A comparison of two measures of general education outcomes. *Journal of General Education, 41*, 130–159.

Pike, G. (1992b). Using mixed-effect structural equation models to study student academic development. *Review of Higher Education, 15*, 151–177.

Pike, G. (1995). The relationships between self-reports of college experiences and achievement test scores. *Research in Higher Education, 36*, 1–22.

Pike, G. (1996). Limitations of using students' self-reports of academic development as proxies for traditional achievement measures. *Research in Higher Education, 37*, 89–114.

Pike, G. (1999a). The effects of residential learning communities and traditional residential living arrangements on educational gains during the first year of college. *Journal of College Student Development, 40*, 269–284.

Pike, G. (1999b, May). *The influence of fraternity or sorority membership on students' college experience and cognitive development.* Paper presented at the meeting of the Association for Institutional Research, Seattle, WA.

Pike, G. (2000). The influence of fraternity or sorority membership on students' college experiences and cognitive development. *Research in Higher Education, 41*, 117–139.

Pike, G. (2002). The differential effect of on- and off-campus living arrangements on students' openness to diversity. *NASPA Journal, 39,* 283–299.

Pike, G., & Askew, J. (1990). The impact of fraternity or sorority membership on academic involvement and learning outcomes. *NASPA Journal, 28,* 13–19.

Pike, G., Kuh, G., & Gonyea, R. (2003). The relationship between institutional mission and students' involvement and educational outcomes. *Research in Higher Education, 44,* 241–261.

Pike, G., Schroeder, C., & Berry, T. (1996, November). *The effects of residential learning communities on student success at a large research university.* Paper presented at the meeting of the Association for the Study of Higher Education, Memphis, TN.

Pike, G., Schroeder, C., & Berry, T. (1997). Enhancing the educational impact of residence halls: The relationship between residential learning communities and first-year college experiences and persistence. *Journal of College Student Development, 38,* 609–621.

Piotrowski, C., & Perdue, B. (1998). Factors in attrition of Black students at a predominantly Euro-American university. *Psychological Reports, 83,* 113–114.

Pirrong, G., & Lathen, W. (1990, May). The use of interactive television in business education. *Educational Technology,* pp. 49–54.

Pittman, V. (1991). Academic credibility on the "image problem": The quality issue in collegiate independent study. In B. Watkins & S. Wright (Eds.), *The foundations of American distance education: A century of collegiate correspondence study* (pp. 109–133). Dubuque, IA: Kendall/Hunt.

Placier, P., Moss, G., & Blockus, L. (1992). College student personal growth in retrospect: A comparison of African-American and White alumni. *Journal of College Student Development, 33,* 462–471.

Plomin, V. (1997). Students' perceptions of contributions to growth and development and quality of effort. *Dissertation Abstracts International, 58,* 1187A.

Poe, R. (1991). Developmental changes in vocational identity among college students. *Journal of College Student Development, 32,* 249–252.

Poindexter-Cameron, J., & Robinson, T. (1997). Relationships among racial identity attitudes, womanist identity attitudes, and self-esteem in African-American college women. *Journal of College Student Development, 38,* 288–296.

Polizzi, T., & Ethington, C. (1996, November). *Factors affecting gains in career preparation: A comparison of vocational groups.* Paper presented at the annual meeting of the Association for the Study of Higher Education, Memphis, TN.

Pollio, H. (1996). *The two cultures of pedagogy: Teaching and learning in the natural sciences and the humanities* (Teaching-Learning Issues No. 75). Knoxville: University of Tennessee.

Ponemon, L. (1992). Auditor underreporting of time and moral reasoning: An experimental-lab study. *Contemporary Accounting Research, 9,* 171–189.

Ponemon, L. (1993). Can ethics be taught in accounting? *Journal of Accounting Education, 11,* 185–209.

Ponemon, L., & Gabhart, D. (1990). Auditor independence judgments: A cognitive development model and experimental evidence. *Contemporary Accounting Research, 7,* 227–251.

Ponemon, L., & Gabhart, D. (1993). *Ethical reasoning in accounting and auditing.* Vancouver: Canadian General Accountants' Research Foundation.

Ponemon, L., & Glazer, A. (1990). Accounting education and ethical development: The influence of liberal learning on students and alumni in accounting practice. *Issues in Accounting Education, 5,* 195–208.

Pope, R. (1998). The relationship between psychosocial development and racial identity of Black college students. *Journal of College Student Development, 39,* 273–282.

Pope, R. (2000). The relationship between psychosocial development and racial identity of college students of color. *Journal of College Student Development, 41,* 302–312.

Pope-Davis, D., Vandiver, B., & Stone, G. (1999). White racial identity attitude development: A psychometric examination of two instruments. *Journal of Counseling Psychology, 46,* 70–79.

Pope-Davis, D. B., & Ottavi, T. M. (1994). The relationship between racism and racial identity among White Americans: A replication and extension. *Journal of Counseling and Development, 72,* 293–297.

Porter, O. (1990, April). *Undergraduate completion and persistence at four-year colleges and universities: Completers, persisters, stopouts, and dropouts.* Paper presented at the meeting of the American Educational Research Association, Boston.

Porter, S. (2002). *Including transfer-out behavior in retention models: Using the NSC EnrollmentSearch data* (AIR Professional File, No. 82). Tallahassee, FL: Association for Institutional Research.

Posner, H., & Markstein, J. (1994). Cooperative learning in introductory cell and molecular biology. *Journal of College Science Teaching, 23,* 231–233.

Potthast, M. (1999). Outcomes of using small-group cooperative learning experiences in introductory statistics courses. *College Student Journal, 33,* 34–42.

Powell, K. (1988). Habitual exercise and public health: An epidemiological view. In R. Dishman (Ed.), *Exercise adherence: Its impact on public health* (pp. 15–44). Champaign, IL: Human Kinetics.

Powers, D., & Ellison, C. (1995). Interracial contact and Black racial attitudes: The contact hypothesis and selectivity bias. *Social Forces, 74,* 205–226.

Prendergast, D. (1998). *Influences of college environments and the development of critical thinking skills in college juniors.* Unpublished doctoral dissertation, University of Illinois, Chicago.

Prendergast, M. (1994). Substance use and abuse among college students: A review of recent literature. *Journal of American College Health, 43,* 99–113.

Presley, C., Meilman, P., & Lyerta, R. (1993). *Alcohol and drugs on American college campuses: Uses, consequences, and perceptions of the campus environment* (Vol. 1). Carbondale, IL: Core Institute.

Price, W., Wilmes, D., & Turmel, M. (1994). General education assessment in introductory psychology. *Journal on Excellence in College Teaching, 5,* 121–133.

Private correlates of educational attainment. (1995, April). *Postsecondary Education OPPORTUNITY,* No. 34, 9–17.

Private correlates of educational attainment. (1997, July). *Postsecondary Education OPPORTUNITY,* No. 61, 1–17.

Pryor, F., & Schaffer, D. (1997, July). Wages and the university educated: A paradox resolved. *Monthly Labor Review,* pp. 3–14.

Putnam, R. (1995). Bowling alone: America's declining social capital. *Journal of Democracy, 6,* 65–78.

Qin, Z., Johnson, D., & Johnson, R. (1995). Cooperative versus competitive efforts and problem solving. *Review of Educational Research, 65,* 129–143.

Railsback, G. (1994). An exploratory study of the religiosity and related outcomes among college students. *Dissertation Abstracts International, 55,* 483A.

Raimondo, H., Esposito, L., & Gershenberg, I. (1990). Introductory class size and student performance in intermediate theory courses. *Journal of Economic Education, 21,* 369–381.

Rama, D., Ravenscroft, S., Wolcott, S., & Zlotkowski, E. (2000). Service-learning outcomes: Guidelines for educators and researchers. *Issues in Accounting Education, 15,* 657–692.

Ramirez, G. (1997). Supplemental instruction: The long-term impact. *Journal of Developmental Education, 21,* 2–4, 6, 8, 10, 28.

Rankin, S. (2003). *Campus climate for gay, lesbian, bisexual, and transgender people: A national perspective.* New York: National Gay and Lesbian Task Force Policy Institute.

Ratcliff, J. (1993). *What we can learn from coursework patterns about improving the undergraduate curriculum.* University Park: Pennsylvania State University, National Center on Postsecondary Teaching, Learning, and Assessment.

Ratcliff, J., & Jones, E. (1993). Coursework cluster analysis. In T. Banta (Ed.), *Making a difference: Outcomes of a decade of assessment in higher education* (pp. 256–269). San Francisco: Jossey-Bass.

Ratcliff, J., Jones, E., Guthrie, D., & Oehler, D. (1991). *The effects of coursework patterns, advisement, and course selection on the development of general learned abilities of college graduates* (Research report). University Park: Pennsylvania State University, National Center on Postsecondary Teaching, Learning, and Assessment.

Ratcliff, J., & Yaeger, P. (1994, April). *What are the coursework patterns most associated with the development of quantitative abilities of college students with low math skills?* Paper presented at the meeting of the American Educational Research Association, New Orleans.

Rau, W., & Sherman Heyl, B. (1990). Humanizing the college classroom: Collaborative learning and social organization among students. *Teaching Sociology, 18,* 141–155.

Rayman, P., & Brett, B. (1995). Women science majors: What makes a difference in persistence after graduation? *Journal of Higher Education, 66,* 388–414.

Reardon, R., Lenz, J., & Folsom, B. (1998). Employer ratings of student participation in non-classroom-based activities: Findings from a campus survey. *Journal of Career Planning and Employment, 58,* 36–39.

Reich, J., Rosch, J., & Catania, F. (1988, November). *The scholar: Integrating teaching and research in higher education.* Paper presented at the meeting of the Association for the Study of Higher Education, St. Louis, MO.

Reilly, R., & Warech, M. (1993). The validity and fairness of alternatives to cognitive tests. In L. Wing & B. Gifford (Eds.), *Policy issues in employment testing* (pp. 131–224). Norwell, MA: Kluwer.

Reiser, R. (1994). Clark's invitation to the dance: An instructional designer's response. *Educational Technology, Research, and Development, 42,* 45–48.

Reisman, S. (1993). A comparative study of multimedia personal computing and traditional instruction in a business school curriculum. *Information Resources Management Journal, 6*(4), 15–21.

Reisser, L. (1995). Revisiting the seven vectors. *Journal of College Student Development, 36,* 505–511.

Reiter, S. (1994). Teaching dialogically: Its relationship to critical thinking in college students. In P. Pintrich, D. Brown, & C. Weinstein (Eds.), *Student motivation, cognition, and learning* (pp. 275–310). Hillsdale, NJ: Erlbaum.

Renaud, R., & Murray, H. (1996). Aging, personality, and teaching effectiveness in academic psychologists. *Research in Higher Education, 37,* 323–340.

Rendon, L. (1992). From the barrio to the academy: Revelations of a Mexican-American "scholarship girl." In S. Zwerling & H. London (Eds.), *First-generation students: Confronting the cultural issues* (pp. 55–64). *New Directions for Community Colleges,* No. 80. San Francisco: Jossey-Bass.

Rendon, L. (1994). Validating culturally diverse students: Toward a new model of learning and student development. *Innovative Higher Education, 19,* 33–51.

Rendon, L. (1995). *Facilitating retention and transfer for first-generation students in community colleges.* University Park: Pennsylvania State University, National Center on Postsecondary Teaching, Learning, and Assessment.

Rendon, L. (1998, September). *Access in a democracy: Narrowing the opportunity gap.* (Report No. NCES 98-283). Washington, DC: U.S. Department of Education, National Center for Education Statistics.

Rendon, L., & Jalomo, R. (1993, November). *The in- and out-of-class experiences of first-year community college students.* Paper presented at the meeting of the Association for the Study of Higher Education, Pittsburgh, PA.

Rendon, L., Jalomo, R., & Nora, A. (2000). Theoretical considerations in the study of minority student retention in higher education. In J. Braxton (Ed.), *Rethinking the departure puzzle: New theory and research on college student retention* (pp. 127–156). Nashville, TN: Vanderbilt University Press.

Renn, K. (2000). Patterns of situational identity among biracial and multiracial college students. *Review of Higher Education, 23,* 399–420.

Renn, K., Dilley, P., & Prentice, M. (2003). Identity research in higher education: Commonalities, differences, and complementarities. In J. Smart (Ed.), *Higher education: Handbook of theory and research* (Vol. 18, pp. 191–261). Norwell, MA: Kluwer.

Rest, J. (1979). *Development in judging moral issues.* Minneapolis: University of Minnesota Press.

Rest, J. (1986). *Moral development: Advances in research and theory.* New York: Praeger.

Rest, J. (1994). Background: Theory and research. In J. Rest & D. Narvaez (Eds.), *Moral development in the professions: Psychology and applied ethics* (pp. 1–25). Hillsdale, NJ: Erlbaum.

Rest, J., & Narvaez, D. (1991). The college experience and moral development. In W. Kurtines & J. Gewirtz (Eds.), *Handbook of moral behavior and development* (pp. 229–245). Hillsdale, NJ: Erlbaum.

Rest, J., Narvaez, D., Bebeau, M., & Thoma, S. (1999). *Postconventional moral thinking: A neo-Kohlbergian approach.* Hillsdale, NJ: Erlbaum.

Rest, J., Thoma, S., & Edwards, L. (1997). Devising and validating a measure of moral judgment: Stage preference and stage consistency approaches. *Journal of Educational Psychology, 89,* 5–28.

Rewey, K., Dansereau, D., Dees, S., Skaggs, L., & Pitre, U. (1992). Scripted cooperation and knowledge map supplements: Effects on the recall of biological and statistical information. *Journal of Experimental Education, 60,* 93–107.

Reyes, N. (1997). Holding on to what they've got. *Black Issues in Higher Education, 13,* 36–40.

Reynolds, A., & Hanjorgiris, W. (2000). Coming out: Lesbian, gay, and bisexual identity development. In L. Perez, K. DeBord, & K. Bieschke (Eds.), *Handbook of counseling and psychotherapy with lesbian, gay, and bisexual clients* (pp. 35–55). Washington, DC: American Psychological Association.

Reynolds, A., & Pope, R. (1991). The complexities of diversity: Exploring multiple oppressions. *Journal of Counseling and Development, 70,* 174–180.

Reynolds, K., & Nunn, C. (1997, November). *Engaging classrooms: Student participation and the instructional factors that shape it.* Paper presented at the meeting of the Association for the Study of Higher Education, Albuquerque, NM.

Rhee, B., & Dey, E. L. (1996, October). *Collegiate influences on the civic values of students.* Paper presented at the meeting of the Association for the Study of Higher Education, Memphis, TN.

Rhoads, R. (1993, November). *A critical postmodern view of student identity.* Paper presented at the meeting of the Association for the Study of Higher Education, Pittsburgh, PA.

Rhoads, R. (1994). *Coming out in college: The struggle for a queer identity.* New York: Bergin & Garvey.

Rhoads, R. (1995a). The cultural politics of coming out in college: Experiences of male students. *Review of Higher Education, 19,* 1–22.

Rhoads, R. (1995b). Learning from the coming-out experiences of college males. *Journal of College Student Development, 36,* 67–74.

Rhoads, R. (1995c, November). *Gay student contraculture and resistance in a university community: Tension between solidarity/difference.* Paper presented at the annual meeting of the Association for the Study of Higher Education, Orlando.

Rhoads, R. (1997a). A subcultural study of gay and bisexual college males: Resisting developmental inclinations. *Journal of Higher Education, 68,* 460–482.

Rhoads, R. (1997b). Interpreting identity politics: The educational challenge of contemporary student activism. *Journal of College Student Development, 38,* 508–519.

Rhoads, R. (1998). In the service of citizenship: A study of student involvement in community service. *Journal of Higher Education, 69,* 278–297.

Ricci, R. (1994). Recruiting strategies for women's colleges. *College and University, 69,* 130–134.

Rice, K. (1992). Separation-individuation and adjustment to college: A longitudinal study. *Journal of Counseling Psychology, 39,* 203–213.

Rice, K., FitzGerald, D., Whaley, T., & Gibbs, C. (1995). Cross-sectional and longitudinal examination of attachment, separation-individuation, and college student adjustment. *Journal of Counseling and Development, 73,* 463–474.

Rich, R. (1989). *The effects of training adult poor readers to text comprehension strategies.* Unpublished doctoral dissertation, Columbia University, New York.

Richardson, R., & Skinner, E. (1992). Helping first-generation minority students achieve degrees. In L. Zwerling & H. London (Eds.), *First-generation students: Confronting the cultural issues* (pp. 29–43). *New Directions for Community Colleges,* No. 80. San Francisco: Jossey-Bass.

Riding, R., & Chambers, P. (1992). CD-Rom versus textbook: A comparison of the use of two learning media by higher education students. *Education and Training Technology International, 29,* 342–349.

Riggio, R., Fantuzzo, J., Connelly, S., & Dimeff, L. (1991). Reciprocal peer tutoring: A classroom strategy for promoting academic and social integration in undergraduate students. *Journal of Social Behavior and Personality, 6,* 387–396.

Riordan, C. (1990). *Girls and boys in school: Together or separate?* New York: Teachers College Press.

Riordan, C. (1992). Single- and mixed-gender colleges for women: Educational, attitudinal, and occupational outcomes. *Review of Higher Education, 15,* 327–346.

Riordan, C. (1993, April). *The value of attending a women's college in the 1980s: Educational, occupational, and other benefits. A study of the high school class of 1980.* Paper presented at the meeting of the American Educational Research Association, Atlanta, GA.

Riordan, C. (1994). The value of attending a women's college: Education, occupation, and income benefits. *Journal of Higher Education, 65,* 486–510.

Riordan, C. (1995, April). *Women's college in the 1980s: Educational climate, aspirations, and attainment.* Paper presented at meeting of the American Educational Research Association, San Francisco.

Rivera-Batiz, F. (1998). *A profile and analysis of students in vocational training: Literacy skills, demographics, and socioeconomic characteristics* (Research Report No. MDS-809). Berkeley, CA: National Center for Research in Vocational Education.

Robbins, S., & Smith, L. (1993). Enhancement programs for entering university majority and minority freshmen. *Journal of Counseling and Development, 71,* 510–514.

Robert, E., & Thomson, G. (1994). Learning assistance and the success of underrepresented students at Berkeley. *Journal of Developmental Education, 17,* 4–14.

Robinson, L. (1989). The effect of freshman transition-to-college/orientation courses on student retention. *College Student Journal, 22,* 225–229.

Robst, J. (1995). College quality and overeducation. *Economics of Education Review, 14,* 221–228.

Robst, J., Keil, J., & Russo, D. (1998). The effect of gender composition of faculty on student retention. *Economics of Education Review, 17,* 429–439.

Robst, J., Russo, D., & Keil, J. (1996, May). *Female role models: The effect of gender composition of faculty on student retention.* Paper presented at the meeting of the Association for Institutional Research, Albuquerque, NM.

Rodgers, R. (1980). Theories underlying student development. In D. Creamer (Ed.), *Student development in higher education: Theories, practices, and future directions* (ACPA Media Publication No. 27). Alexandria, VA: American College Personnel Association.

Rodgers, R. (1989). Student development. In U. Delworth & G. Hanson (Eds.), *Student services: A handbook for the profession* (2nd ed., pp. 117–164). San Francisco: Jossey-Bass.

Rodgers, R. (1990). Recent theories and research underlying student development. In D. Creamer (Ed.), *College student development theory and practice for the 1990s* (Media Publication No. 49). Alexandria, VA: American College Personnel Association.

Rodriguez-Garcia, T., & Goldman, P. (1994). *The health development link.* Washington, DC: Pan American Health Organization/WHO.

Roebuck, J., & Murty, K. (1993). *Historically Black colleges and universities: Their place in American higher education.* New York: Praeger.

Rogers, R., & Powell-Gringer, E. (1991). Life expectancies of cigarette smokers and nonsmokers in the United States. *Social Science and Medicine, 32,* 1151–1159.

Rokeach, M. (1960). *The open and closed mind: Investigations into the nature of belief systems and personality systems.* New York: Basic Books.

Romance, N., & Vitale, M. (1999). Concept mapping as a tool for learning: Broadening the framework for student-centered instruction. *College Teaching, 47,* 74–79.

Romano, C. (1996). A qualitative study of women student leaders. *Journal of College Student Development, 37,* 676–683.

Romano, R. (1995). First-year attrition and retention at a community college. *Journal of Applied Research in the Community College, 2,* 169–177.

Ronco, S. (1994, May). *Meandering ways: Studying student stopout with survival analysis.* Paper presented at the meeting of the Association for Institutional Research, New Orleans.

Ronco, S. (1995, May). *How enrollment ends: Analyzing the correlates of student graduation, transfer, and dropout with a competing risks model.* Paper presented at the meeting of the Association for Institutional Research, Boston.

Ronco, S. (1996). *How enrollment ends: Analyzing the correlates of student graduation, transfer, and dropout with a competing risks model* (AIR Professional File, No. 61). Tallahassee, FL: Association for Institutional Research.

Root, M. (1990). Resolving "other" status: Identity development of biracial individuals. *Women and Therapy, 9,* 185–205.

Rootman, I. (1972). Voluntary withdrawal from a total adult socialization organization: A model. *Sociology of Education, 45,* 258–270.

Rosenberg, M. (1979). *Conceiving the self.* New York: Basic Books.

Rosenshine, B., & Meister, C. (1994). Reciprocal teaching: A review of the literature. *Review of Educational Research, 64,* 479–530.

Rosenzweig, M., & Shultz, T. (1991). Who receives medical care? Income implicit prices and the distribution of medical services among pregnant women in the United States. *Journal of Human Resources, 26,* 473–508.

Ross, C., & Mirowsky, J. (1989). Explaining the social patterns of depression: Control and problem solving—or support and talking. *Journal of Health and Social Behavior, 30,* 206–219.

Ross, C., & Mirowsky, J. (1992). Households, employment, and the sense of control. *Social Psychology Quarterly, 55,* 217–235.

Ross, C., & Mirowsky, J. (1995). Does employment affect health? *Journal of Health and Social Behavior, 36,* 230–243.

Ross, C., & Mirowsky, J. (1999). Refining the association between education and health: The effects of quantity, credential, and selectivity. *Demography, 36,* 445–460.

Ross, C., & Reskin, B. (1992). Education, control at work, and job satisfaction. *Social Science Research, 21,* 134–148.

Ross, C., & Van Willigen, M. (1997). Education and subjective quality of life. *Journal of Health and Social Behavior, 38,* 275–297.

Ross, C., & Wu, C.-L. (1995). The links between education and health. *American Sociological Review, 60,* 719–745.

Roth, P., BeVier, C., Switzer, R., & Schippman, J. (1996). Meta-analyzing the relationship between grades and job performance. *Journal of Applied Psychology, 81,* 548–556.

Roth, P., & Clarke, R. (1998). Meta-analyzing the relationship between grades and salary. *Journal of Vocational Behavior, 53,* 386–400.

Rothman, S., Lipset, S., & Nevitte, N. (2003). Does enrollment diversity improve university education? *International Journal of Public Opinion Research, 15,* 8–26.

Rothstein, D. (1995). Do female faculty influence female students' educational and labor market attainments? *Industrial and Labor Relations Review, 48,* 515–530.

Rotter, J. (1966). Generalized expectancies for internal versus external controls of reinforcement. *Psychological Monographs, 80.*

Rotter, J. (1975). Some problems and misconceptions related to the construct of internal versus external control of reinforcement. *Journal of Consulting and Clinical Psychology, 43,* 56–67.

Rouse, C. (1995). Democratization or diversion? The effects of community colleges on educational attainment. *Journal of Business and Economic Statistics, 13,* 217–224.

Rouse, C. (1999). Further estimates of the economic return to schooling from a new sample of twins. *Economics of Education Review, 18,* 149–157.

Rowe, W., Behrens, J., & Leach, M. (1995). Racial/ethnic identity and racial consciousness: Looking back and looking forward. In J. Ponterotto, J. Casas, L. Suzuki, & C. Alexander (Eds.), *Handbook of multicultural counseling* (pp. 218–235). Thousand Oaks, CA: Sage.

Rowe, W., Bennett, S., & Atkinson, D. (1994). White racial identity models: A critique and alternative proposal. *Counseling Psychologist, 22,* 129–146.

Rowland, P., & Stuessy, C. (1988). Matching mode of CAI to cognitive style: An exploratory study. *Journal of Computers in Mathematics and Science Teaching, 7*(4), 36–40.

Rowley, S., Sellers, R., Chavous, T., & Smith, M. (1998). The relationship between racial identity and self-esteem in African-American college and high school students. *Journal of Personality and Social Psychology, 74,* 715–724.

Royse, D., & Riffe, H. (1999). Assessing students' values in an era of change. *Journal of Baccalaureate Social Work, 4,* 71–83.

Rubenstein, E. (1998). *The college payoff illusion.* New York: Hudson Institute.

Ruddell, R., & Boyle, O. (1989). A study of cognitive mapping as a means to improve summarization and comprehension of expository text. *Reading Research and Instruction, 29,* 12–22.

Ruddock, M., Hanson, G., & Moss, M. (1999, June). *New directions in student retention research: Looking beyond interactional theories of student departure.* Paper presented at the meeting of the Association for Institutional Research, Seattle, WA.

Rudenstine, N. (1999). *Why a diverse student body is so important.* [http://www.inform.umd.edu/Diversityweb/Profiles/divdbase/harvard/ilsc.html].

Ruiz, A. (1990). Ethnic identity: Crisis and resolution. *Journal of Multicultural Counseling and Development, 18,* 29–40.

Rumberger, R., & Thomas, S. (1993). The economic returns to college major, quality, and performance: A multilevel analysis of recent graduates. *Economics of Education Review, 12,* 1–19.

Rush, R., & Milburn, J. (1988). *The effects of reciprocal teaching on self-regulation of reading comprehension in a postsecondary technical school program.* Paper presented at the meeting of the National Reading Conference, Tucson, AZ.

Russell, T. (1995). *The "no significant difference" phenomenon as reported in 214 research reports, summaries, and papers.* Raleigh: North Carolina State University, Office of Instructional Telecommunications.

Russell, T. (1999). *The "no significant difference" phenomenon as reported in 248 research reports, summaries, and papers.* Raleigh: North Carolina State University, Office of Instructional Telecommunications.

Ryan, F. (1989). Participation in intercollegiate athletics: Affective outcomes. *Journal of College Student Development, 30,* 122–128.

Ryan, M., & Twibell, R. (2000). Concerns, values, stress, coping, health, and educational outcomes of college students who studied abroad. *International Journal of Intercultural Relations, 24,* 409–435.

Ryder, R., Bowman, R., & Newman, P. (1994). Nontraditional students: Perceived barriers to degree completion. *College Student Affairs Journal, 13,* 5–13.

Rykiel, J. (1995). The community college experience: Is there an effect on critical thinking and moral reasoning? *Dissertation Abstracts International, 56,* 3824A.

Ryland, E., Riordan, R., & Brack, G. (1994). Selected characteristics of high-risk students and their enrollment persistence. *Journal of College Student Development, 35,* 54–58.

Sabot, R., & Wakeman-Linn, J. (1991). Grade inflation and course choice. *Journal of Economic Perspectives, 5,* 159–171.

Sachdev, P. (1997). Cultural sensitivity training through experiential learning: A participatory demonstration field education project. *International Social Work, 40,* 7–25.

Saddlemire, J. (1996). Qualitative study of White second-semester undergraduates' attitudes toward African-American undergraduates at a predominantly White university. *Journal of College Student Development, 37,* 684–691.

Sagen, H., Dallam, J., & Laverty, J. (1997). *Effects of career preparation experiences on the initial employment success of college graduates.* Unpublished manuscript, University of Iowa, Iowa City.

Sanchez, J., & Laanan, F. (1998). The economic returns of a community college education. *Community College Review, 25*(3), 73–87.

Sanchez, J., Laanan, F., & Wiseley, W. (1999). Postcollege earnings of former students of California community colleges: Methods, analysis, and implications. *Research in Higher Education, 40,* 87–113.

Sanchez, J., Marder, F., Berry, R., & Ross, H. (1992). Dropping out: Hispanic students, attrition, and the family. *College and University, 67,* 145–150.

Sanday, P. (1990). *Fraternity gang rape: Sex, brotherhood, and privilege on campus.* New York: New York University Press.

Sander, W. (1995a). Schooling and quitting smoking. *Review of Economics and Statistics, 77,* 191–199.

Sander, W. (1995b). Schooling and smoking. *Economics of Education Review, 14,* 23–33.

Sander, W. (1998). The effects of schooling and cognitive ability on smoking and marijuana use by young adults. *Economics of Education Review, 17,* 317–324.

Sanders, J., & Wiseman, R. (1990). The effects of verbal and teacher immediacy on perceived cognitive, affective, and behavioral learning in the multicultural classroom. *Communication Education, 39,* 341–353.

Sandler, B., Silverberg, L., & Hall, R. (1996). *The chilly classroom climate: A guide to improve the education of women.* Washington, DC: National Association for Women in Education.

Sandler, M. (1999, November). *A structural model of student integration, finances, behavior, and career development: An elaborated framework of attitudes and persistence.* Paper presented at the meeting of the Association for the Study of Higher Education, San Antonio, TX.

Sandler, M. (2000a, April). *A focal examination of integration, commitment, and academic performance: Three subsystems from the integrated model of student persistence with sociostructural background variable effects.* Paper presented at the meeting of the American Educational Research Association, New Orleans.

Sandler, M. (2000b). Career decision-making self-efficacy, perceived stress, and an integrated model of student persistence: A structural model of finances, attitudes, behavior, and career development. *Research in Higher Education, 41,* 537–580.

Sandler, M. (2001, April). *Perceived stress and an elaborated structural model of adult student persistence: An examination of financial aid, financial satisfaction, intent to persist, and persistence.* Paper presented at the meeting of the American Educational Research Association, Seattle, WA.

Sanford, N. (1962). Developmental status of the entering freshman. In N. Sanford (Ed.), *The American college: A psychological and social interpretation of the higher learning.* New York: Wiley.

Sanford, N. (1967). *Where colleges fail: A study of the student as a person.* San Francisco: Jossey-Bass.

Santa Rita, E., & Bacote, J. (1997). The benefits of college discovery prefreshman summer program for minority and low-income students. *College Student Journal, 31,* 161–173.

Santhanam, E., Leach, C., & Dawson, C. (1998). Concept mapping: How should it be introduced, and is there evidence for long-term benefit? *Higher Education, 35,* 317–328.

Santilli, N., & Hudson, L. (1992). Enhancing moral growth: Is communication the key? *Adolescence, 27,* 145–160.

Saucier, B. (1995). Critical thinking skills of baccalaureate nursing students. *Journal of Professional Nursing, 11,* 351–357.

Saupe, J., Smith, T., & Xin, W. (1999, May–June). *Institutional and student characteristics in student success: First-term GPA, one-year retention, and six-year graduation.* Paper presented at the meeting of the Association for Institutional Research, Seattle, WA.

Savickas, M. (1990). The use of career choice measures in counseling practice. In E. Watkins & V. Campbell (Eds.), *Testing in counseling practice* (pp. 373–417). Hillsdale, NJ: Erlbaum.

Sawyer, R., Pinciaro, P., & Bedwell, D. (1997). How peer education changed peer sexuality educators' self-esteem, personal development, and sexual behavior. *Journal of American College Health, 45,* 211–217.

Sax, L. (1994a). The dynamics of tokenism: How college students are affected by the proportion of women in their major. *Dissertation Abstracts International, 55,* 484A.

Sax, L. (1994b, April). *The dynamics of "tokenism": How college students are affected by the proportion of women in their major.* Paper presented at the meeting of the American Educational Research Association, New Orleans.

Sax, L. (1994c). Retaining tomorrow's scientists: Exploring the factors that keep male and female college students interested in science careers. *Journal of Women and Minorities in Science and Engineering, 1,* 45–61.

Sax, L. (1994d). Mathematical self-concept: How college reinforces the gender gap. *Research in Higher Education, 35,* 141–166.

Sax, L. (1994e). Predicting gender and major-field differences in mathematical self-concept during college. *Journal of Women and Minorities in Science and Engineering, 1,* 291–307.

Sax, L. (1996a, November). *The impact of college on postcollege commitment to science careers: Gender differences in a nine-year follow-up of college freshmen.* Paper presented at the meeting of the Association for the Study of Higher Education, Memphis, TN.

Sax, L. (1996b). The dynamics of "tokenism": How college students are affected by the proportion of women in their major. *Research in Higher Education, 37,* 389–425.

Sax, L. (2000). Citizenship development and the American college student. In T. Ehrlich (Ed.), *Civic responsibility and higher education* (pp. 3–18). Phoenix, AZ: Oryx Press.

Sax, L. (2001). Undergraduate science majors: Gender differences in who goes to graduate school. *Review of Higher Education, 24,* 153–172.

Sax, L., & Astin, A. (1997). The benefits of service: Evidence from undergraduates. *Educational Record, 78,* 25–32.

Sax, L., & Astin, A. (1998). Developing "civic virtue" among college students. In J. Gardner & G. Van der Veer (Eds.), *The senior year experience: Facilitating integration, reflection, closure, and transition* (pp. 133–151). San Francisco: Jossey-Bass.

Sax, L., & Gilmartin, S. (2002). *A study of first- to second-year persistence.* Unpublished manuscript. Los Angeles: University of California, Higher Education Research Institute.

Sazama, G. (1994). A measure of equality of choice in higher education. *Economics of Education Review, 13,* 79–88.

Schaefers, K., & Epperson, D. (1994, August). *Women in engineering: Factors affecting persistence and attrition in college majors.* Paper presented at the meeting of the American Psychological Association, Los Angeles.

Schaefers, K., Epperson, D., & Nauta, M. (1997). Women's career development: Can theoretically derived variables predict persistence in engineering majors? *Journal of Counseling Psychology, 44,* 173–183.

Schaeffer, A., & Nelson, E. (1993). Rape-supportive attitudes: Effects of on-campus residence and education. *Journal of College Student Development, 34,* 175–179.

Schall, M., Weede, T., & Maltzman, I. (1991). Predictors of alcohol consumption by university students. *Journal of Alcohol and Drug Education, 37,* 72–80.

Schapiro, M., O'Malley, M., & Litten, L. (1991). Progression to graduate school from the "elite" colleges and universities. *Economics of Education Review, 10,* 227–244.

Scheck, C., Kinicki, A., & Webster, J. (1994). The effect of class size on student performance: Development and assessment of a process model. *Journal of Education for Business, 70,* 104–111.

Schiff, T. (1993a). Political identification and political attitudes of American college students. *Dissertation Abstracts International, 54,* 2487A.

Schiff, T. (1993b, April). *Students' political identification and attitudes on political issues: The influence of peers and faculty.* Paper presented at the meeting of the American Educational Research Association, Atlanta, GA.

Schilling, K. (1991). *Assessing models of liberal education: An empirical comparison.* Washington, DC: Fund for the Improvement of Postsecondary Education. (ERIC Document Reproduction Service No. ED 359 864)

Schlossberg, N. (1981). A model for analyzing human adaptation to transition. *Counseling Psychologist, 9,* 2–18.

Schlossberg, N., Waters, E., & Goodman, J. (1995). *Counseling adults in transition* (2nd ed.). New York: Springer.

Schlosser, C., & Anderson, M. (1994). *Distance education: Review of the literature.* Ames: Iowa State University, Research Institute for Studies in Education.

Schmidt, F., Ones, D., & Hunter, J. (1992). Personnel selection. *Annual Review of Psychology, 43,* 627–670.

Schmidt, P. (1998, October). University of Michigan prepared to defend admissions policy in court. *Chronicle of Higher Education,* p. A32.

Schmitt, M., Ryan, A., Stierwalt, S., & Powell, A. (1995). Frame of reference effects on personality scale scores and criterion related validity. *Journal of Applied Psychology, 80,* 607–620.

Schmitz, C. (1993). Assessing the validity of higher education indicators. *Journal of Higher Education, 64,* 503–521.

Schneider, C. (2001). Toward the engaged academy: New scholarship, new teaching. *Liberal Education, 87,* 18–27.

Scholnick, E. (1996). *A two-year longitudinal study of science and math students in the College Park Scholars Program.* Unpublished report, University of Maryland, College Park.

Schommer, M. (1990). Effects of beliefs about the nature of knowledge on comprehension. *Journal of Educational Psychology, 82,* 498–504.

Schommer, M. (1993). Comparisons of beliefs about the nature of knowledge and learning among postsecondary students. *Research in Higher Education, 34,* 355–370.

Schonwetter, D. (1993). Attributes of effective lecturing in the college classroom. *Canadian Journal of Higher Education, 23,* 1–18.

Schonwetter, D., Menec, V., & Perry, R. (1995, April). *An empirical comparison of two effective college teaching behaviors: Expressiveness and organization.* Paper presented at the meeting of the American Educational Research Association, San Francisco.

Schonwetter, D., Perry, R., Menec, V., Struthers, C., & Hechter, F. (1993, April). *Key factors for college student achievement, cognition, affects, and motivation: Student locus of control and quality of instruction.* Paper presented at the meeting of the American Educational Research Association, Atlanta, GA.

Schonwetter, D., Perry, R., & Struthers, C. (1994). Students' perceptions of control and success in the college classroom: Affects and achievement in different instructional conditions. *Journal of Experimental Education, 61,* 227–246.

Schowen, B. (1998). Research as a critical component of the undergraduate educational experience. In National Research Council (Ed.), *Assessing the value of research in the chemical sciences* (pp. 73–81). Washington, DC: National Academy Press.

Schrader, D. (Ed.). (1990). *The legacy of Lawrence Kohlberg.* San Francisco: Jossey-Bass.

Schroeder, C. (1980). Redesigning college environments for students. In F. Newton & K. Ender (Eds.), *Student development practices.* Springfield, IL: Thomas.

Schuh, J. (1999). Examining the effects of scholarships on retention in a fine arts college. *Journal of College Student Retention, 1,* 193–202.

Schuh, J., Triponey, V., Heim, L., & Nishimura, K. (1992). Student involvement in historically Black Greek-letter organizations. *NASPA Journal, 29,* 274–282.

Schumow, L. (1999, April). *Problem-based learning in undergraduate educational psychology: Contributor to student learning and motivation?* Paper presented at the meeting of the American Educational Research Association, Montreal.

Schuster, D., Langland, L., & Smith, D. (1993). The UCLA Gifted Women, Class of 1961: Living up to potential. In K. Hulbert & D. Schuster (Eds.), *Women's lives through time: Educated American women of the twentieth century* (pp. 211–231). San Francisco: Jossey-Bass.

Schwitzer, A., Grogan, K., Kaddoura, K., & Ochoa, L. (1993). Effects of brief mandatory counseling on help-seeking and academic success among at-risk college students. *Journal of College Student Development, 34,* 401–405.

Schwitzer, A., & Thomas, C. (1998). Implementation, utilization, and outcomes of a minority freshman peer mentor program at a predominantly White university. *Journal of the Freshman Year Experience and Students in Transition, 10,* 31–50.

Scott, P. (1996). Attributes of high-quality intensive course learning experiences: Student voices and experiences. *College Student Journal, 30,* 69–77.

Sears, J. (1991). *Growing up gay in the South: Race, gender, and journeys of the spirit.* New York: Harrington Park.

Sebrechts, J. (1992). Cultivating scientists at women's colleges. *Initiatives, 55*(2), 45–51.

Sebrell, K., & Erwin, T. (1998). *Assessment of critical thinking: One performance method analyzed.* Unpublished paper, Center for Assessment and Research Studies, James Madison University, Harrisonburg, VA.

Seidman, A. (1991). The evaluation of a pre/post admissions/counseling process at a suburban community college: Impact on student satisfaction with the faculty and the institution, retention, and academic performance. *College and University, 66,* 223–232.

Self, D., & Baldwin, D. (1994). Moral reasoning in medicine. In J. Rest & D. Narvaez (Eds.), *Moral development in the professions: Psychology and applied ethics* (pp. 140–153). Hillsdale, NJ: Erlbaum.

Seltzer, R., Frazier, M., & Ricks, I. (1995). Multiculturalism, race, and education. *Journal of Negro Education, 64,* 124–140.

Semb, G., & Ellis, J. (1992, April). *Knowledge learned in college: What is remembered?* Paper presented at the meeting of the American Educational Research Association, San Francisco.

Semb, G., & Ellis, J. (1994). Knowledge taught in school: What is remembered? *Review of Educational Research, 64,* 253–286.

Semb, G., Ellis, J., & Araujo, J. (1993). Long-term memory for knowledge learned in school. *Journal of Educational Psychology, 85,* 305–316.

Sergent, M., & Sedlacek, W. (1990). Volunteer motivations across student organizations: A test of person-environment fit theory. *Journal of College Student Development, 31,* 255–261.

Sermersheim, K. (1996). Undergraduate Greek leadership experiences: A proven method for gaining career-related and lifelong skills. *Campus Activities Programming, 29,* 56–60.

Serow, R., Ciechalski, J., & Daye, C. (1990). Students as volunteers: Personal competence, social diversity, and participation in community service. *Urban Education, 25,* 157–168.

Serow, R., & Taylor, R. (1990). Values as behavior among postsecondary students: An emphasis on transitional states. *College Student Journal, 24,* 6–13.

Sewell, W., Haller, A., & Portes, A. (1969). The educational and early occupational attainment process. *American Sociological Review, 34,* 82–92.

Sewell, W., & Hauser, R. (1975). *Education, occupation, and earnings: Achievement in the early career.* New York: Academic Press.

Seymour, E., & Hewitt, N. (1997). *Talking about leaving: Why undergraduates leave the sciences.* Boulder, CO: Westview Press.

Shanley, M., & Witten, C. (1990). University 101 freshman seminar course: A longitudinal study of persistence, retention, and graduation rates. *NASPA Journal, 27,* 344–352.

Shapiro, N., & Levine, J. (1999). *Creating learning communities: A practical guide to winning support, organizing for change, and implementing programs.* San Francisco: Jossey-Bass.

Sharma, M., & Mulka, J. (1993, March). *The impact of international education upon United States students in comparative perspective.* Paper presented at the meeting of the Comparative and International Education Society, Kingston, Jamaica.

Sharpe, N., & Fuller, C. (1995). Baccalaureate origins of women physical science doctorates: Relationship to institutional gender and science discipline. *Journal of Women and Minorities in Science and Engineering, 2,* 1–15.

Shaub, M. (1994). An analysis of the association of traditional demographic variables with the moral reasoning of auditing students and auditors. *Journal of Accounting Education, 12,* 1–26.

Shavelson, R., & Bolus, R. (1982). Self-concept: The interplay of theory and methods. *Journal of Educational Psychology, 74,* 3–17.

Shavelson, R., Burstein, L., & Keesling, J. (1977). Methodological considerations in interpreting research on self-concept: The interplay of theory and methods. *Journal of Educational Psychology, 74,* 3–17.

Shavelson, R., Hubner, J., & Stanton, G. (1976). Self-concept: Validation of construct interpretations. *Review of Educational Research, 46,* 407–441.

Sheehan, E., Ambrosio, A., McDevitt, T., & Lennon, R. (1990). An examination of change in reports of AIDS-related knowledge and attitudes in 1986 and 1988. *Psychological Reports, 67,* 723–729.

Sheehan, O., & Pearson, F. (1995). Asian international and American students' psychosocial development. *Journal of College Student Development, 36,* 522–530.

Sheehan-Holt, J., & Smith, M. (2000). Does basic skills education affect adults' literacy proficiencies and reading practices? *Reading Research Quarterly, 35,* 226–243.

Sheehy, G. (1976). *Passages: Predictable crises of adult life.* New York: Dutton.

Sheehy, G. (1995). *New passages: Mapping your life across time.* New York: Random House.

Shepperd, J., Oullette, J., & Fernandez, J. (1996). Abandoning unrealistic optimism: Performance estimates and the temporal proximity of self-relevant feedback. *Journal of Personality and Social Psychology, 70,* 844–855.

Sher, K., Bartholow, B., & Nanda, S. (n.d.). *Short- and long-term effects of fraternity and sorority membership on alcohol use: A social norms perspective.* University of Missouri, Columbia.

Sherman, S. (1994, August 22). Leaders learn to heed the voice within. *Fortune,* pp. 92–100.

Shields, N. (1994). Retention, academic success, and progress among adult, returning students: A comparison of the effects of institutional and external factors. *NACADA Journal, 14,* 13–24.

Shorter, L. (1993). Perceptions of the college experience by female commuters and residents at a predominantly women's university. *Dissertation Abstracts International, 3,* 2268A.

Shulman, J., & Bowen, W. (2001). *The game of life: College sports and educational values.* Princeton, NJ: Princeton University Press.

Shultz, S., Scherman, A., & Marshall, L. (2000). Evaluation of a university-based date-rape prevention program: Effect on attitudes and behavior related to rape. *Journal of College Student Development, 41,* 193–201.

Shumer, R., & Belbas, B. (1996). What we know about service learning. *Education and Urban Society, 28,* 208–223.

Sidle, M., & McReynolds, J. (1999). The freshman year experience: Student retention and student success. *NASPA Journal, 36,* 288–300.

Sigelman, L., & Welch, S. (1991). *Black Americans' views of racial inequality: The dream deferred.* Cambridge, UK: Cambridge University Press.

Sigelman, L., & Welch, S. (1993). The contact hypothesis revisited: Black-White interaction and positive racial attitudes. *Social Forces, 71,* 781–795.

Silverman, S., & Casazza, M. (1999). *Learning and development: Making connections to enhance teaching.* San Francisco: Jossey-Bass.

Simmons, G., Wallins, J., & George, A. (1995). The effects of a freshman seminar on at-risk under-, over-, and low achievers. *NACADA Journal, 15,* 8–14.

Simoni, J. (1996). Pathways to prejudice: Predicting students' heterosexist attitudes with demographic, self-esteem, and contact with lesbians and gay men. *Journal of College Student Development, 37,* 68–78.

Simpson, M., Hynd, C., Nist, S., & Burrell, K. (1997). College academic assistance programs and practices. *Educational Psychology Review, 9,* 39–87.

Singer, J., & Willett, J. (1991). Modeling the days of our lives: Using survival analysis when designing and analyzing longitudinal studies of duration and the timing of events. *Psychological Bulletin, 110,* 268–290.

Singer, J., & Willett, J. (1993). It's about time: Using discrete-time survival analysis to study duration and the timing of events. *Journal of Educational Statistics, 18,* 155–195.

Slava, S., Laurie, D., & Corbin, C. (1984). Long-term effects of a conceptual physical education program. *Research Quarterly of Exercise and Sport, 55,* 161–168.

Slavin, R. (1996). Research for the future: Research on cooperative learning and achievement: What we know, what we need to know. *Contemporary Educational Psychology, 21,* 43–69.

Smart, J. (1996, November). *Academic subenvironments and differential patterns of self-perceived growth during college: A test of Holland's theory.* Paper presented at the meeting of the Association for the Study of Higher Education, Memphis, TN.

Smart, J. (1997). Academic subenvironments and differential patterns of self-perceived growth during college: A test of Holland's theory. *Journal of College Student Development, 38,* 68–77.

Smart, J., Ethington, C., Riggs, R., & Thompson, M. (2002). Influences of institutional expenditure patterns on the development of students' leadership competencies. *Research in Higher Education, 43,* 115–132.

Smart, J., & Feldman, K. (1998). "Accentuation effects" of dissimilar departments: An application and explanation of Holland's theory. *Research in Higher Education, 39,* 385–418.

Smart, J., Feldman, K., & Ethington, C. (2000). *Academic disciplines: Holland's theory and the study of college students and faculty.* Nashville, TN: Vanderbilt University Press.

Smart, J., & Hamm, R. (1993). Organizational culture and effectiveness in two-year colleges. *Research in Higher Education, 34,* 95–106.

Smeaton, A., & Keogh, G. (1999). An analysis of the use of virtual delivery of undergraduate lectures. *Computers and Education, 32,* 83–94.

Smith, B. (1993). The effect of quality of effort on persistence among traditional-aged community college students. *Community College Journal of Research and Practice, 17,* 103–122.

Smith, B., & MacGregor, J. (1992). What is collaborative learning? In A. Goodsell, M. Maher, V. Tinto, B. Smith, & J. MacGregor (Eds.), *Collaborative learning: A sourcebook for higher education* (pp. 9–22). University Park: Pennsylvania State University, National Center on Postsecondary Teaching, Learning, and Assessment.

Smith, D. (1990). Women's colleges and coed colleges: Is there a difference for women? *Journal of Higher Education, 61,* 181–197.

Smith, D. (1992). Validity of faculty judgments of student performance: Relationship between grades and credits earned and external criterion measures. *Journal of Higher Education, 63,* 329–340.

Smith, D., & Associates. (1997). *Diversity works: The emerging picture of how students benefit.* Washington, DC: Association of American Colleges and Universities.

Smith, D., Morrison, D., & Wolf, L. (1994). College as a gendered experience: An empirical analysis using multiple lenses. *Journal of Higher Education, 65,* 696–725.

Smith, D., Wolf, L., & Morrison, D. (1995). Paths to success: Factors related to the impact of women's colleges. *Journal of Higher Education, 66,* 245–266.

Smith, J., & Griffin, B. (1993). The relationship between involvement in extracurricular activities and the psychosocial development of university students. *College Student Affairs Journal, 13,* 79–84.

Smith, K. (1992). Gender differences and the impact of college on White students' racial attitudes. *Dissertation Abstracts International, 53,* 3819A.

Smith, K. (1993, May). *The impact of college on White students' racial attitudes.* Paper presented at the meeting of the Association for Institutional Research, Chicago.

Smith, K., & Waller, A. (1997). Cooperative learning for new college teachers. In W. Campbell & K. Smith (Eds.), *New paradigms for college teaching* (pp. 185–209). Edina, MN: Interaction Books.

Smith, P., & Oakley, E. (1996). The value of ethics education in business school curriculum. *College Student Journal, 30,* 274–283.

Smith, S. (1998). Effect of undergraduate college major on performance in medical school. *Academic Medicine, 73,* 1006–1008.

Smith, V. (1997). Feedback effects and environmental resources. In J. Behrman & N. Stace (Eds.), *The social benefits of education* (pp. 175–218). Ann Arbor: University of Michigan Press.

Smith-Sanders, C., & Twale, D. (1997, March). *Impact of number and type of core curriculum hours on critical thinking.* Paper presented at the meeting of the American Educational Research Association, Chicago.

Smith-Sanders, C., & Twale, D. (1998, April). *Further study of the impact of number and type of core curriculum hours on critical thinking.* Paper presented at the meeting of the American Educational Research Association, San Diego, CA.

Snodgrass, J., & Behling, R. (1996). Differences in moral reasoning between college and university business majors and nonbusiness majors. *Business and Professional Ethics Journal, 15,* 79–84.

Sodowsky, G., Kwan, K., & Pannu, R. (1995). Ethnic identity of Asians in the United States. In J. Ponterotto, J. Casas, L. Suzuki, & C. Alexander (Eds.), *Handbook of multicultural counseling* (pp. 123–154). Thousand Oaks, CA: Sage.

Sokolove, P., & Marbach-Ad, G. (2000, April). *Out-of-class group study improves student performance on exams: Comparison of outcomes in active learning and traditional college biology classes.* Paper presented at the meeting of the American Educational Research Association, New Orleans.

Soller, J. (2001). The impact of college for women: Perspectives from the 1949 Texas State College for Women graduating class. *Dissertation Abstracts International, 62,* 4091A.

Solnick, L. (1990). Black college attendance and job success of Black college graduates. *Economics of Education Review, 9,* 135–148.

Solnick, S. (1995). Changes in women's majors from entrance to graduation at women's and coeducational colleges. *Industrial and Labor Relations Review, 48,* 505–514.

Solorzano, D. (1995). The baccalaureate origins of Chicana and Chicano doctorates in the social sciences. *Hispanic Journal of Behavioral Sciences, 17,* 3–32.

Somers, P. (1992). *A dynamic analysis of student matriculation decisions in an urban public university.* Unpublished doctoral dissertation, University of New Orleans.

Somers, P. (1993a). Are "mondo" scholarships effective? *Journal of Student Financial Aid, 23,* 48–49.

Somers, P. (1993b). Using student financial aid to influence enrollment and persistence in urban institutions. *Journal of Student Financial Aid, 23,* 51–59.

Somers, P. (1994). The effect of price on within-year persistence. *Journal of Student Financial Aid, 24,* 31–45.

Somers, P. (1995a). First- to second-semester persistence: A case study. *Journal of the Freshman Year Experience, 7,* 43–62.

Somers, P. (1995b). A comprehensive model for examining the impact of financial aid on enrollment and persistence. *Journal of Student Financial Aid, 25,* 13–27.

Somers, P. (1996a). The influence of price on year-to-year persistence of college students. *NASPA Journal, 33,* 94–104.

Somers, P. (1996b). The freshman year: How financial aid influences enrollment and persistence at a regional comprehensive university. *College Student Affairs Journal, 16,* 27–38.

Somers, P., Cofer, J., Hall, M., & Vander Putten, J. (1999, November). *A comparison of the persistence of African-American and White college students.* Paper presented at the meeting of the Association for the Study of Higher Education, San Antonio, TX.

Sommer, R. (1969). *Personal space: The behavioral basis of design.* Englewood Cliffs, NJ: Prentice-Hall.

Son, B., & Van Sickle, R. (1993, April). *Problem-solving instruction and students' acquisition, retention, and structuring of economics knowledge.* Paper presented at the meeting of the American Educational Research Association, Atlanta, GA.

Sorenson, N., & Jackson, J. (1997, Spring). Science majors and nonscience majors entering medical school: Acceptance rates and academic performance. *NACADA Journal, 17,* 32–41.

Spady, W. (1970). Dropouts from higher education: An interdisciplinary review and synthesis. *Interchange, 1,* 64–85.

Spanard, J. (1990). Beyond intent: Reentering college to complete the degree. *Review of Educational Research, 60,* 309–344.

Spaulding, S., & Kleiner, K. (1992). The relationship of college and critical thinking: Are critical thinkers attracted or created by college disciplines? *College Student Journal, 26,* 162–166.

Sperber, M. (2000). *Beer and circus: How big-time college sports is crippling undergraduate education.* New York: Henry Holt.

Spilerman, S., & Lunde, T. (1991). Features of educational attainment and job promotion prospects. *American Journal of Sociology, 97,* 689–720.

Springer, L. (1996). *Applying the contact hypothesis to research on intergroup relations among college students.* Unpublished doctoral dissertation, Pennsylvania State University, University Park.

Springer, L., Millar, S., Kosciuk, S., Penberthy, D., & Wright, J. (1997, March). *Relating concepts and applications through structured active learning.* Paper presented at the meeting of the American Educational Research Association, Chicago.

Springer, L., Palmer, B., Terenzini, P., Pascarella, E., & Nora, A. (1996). Attitudes toward campus diversity: Participation in a racial or cultural awareness workshop. *Review of Higher Education, 20,* 53–68.

Springer, L., Palmer, B., Terenzini, P., Pascarella, E., & Nora, A. (1997, March). *The impact of ethnic and women's studies courses on students' attitudes toward diversity on campus.* Paper presented at the meeting of the American Educational Research Association, Chicago.

Springer, L., Stanne, M., & Donovan, S. (1999). Effects of small-group learning on undergraduates in science, mathematics, engineering, and technology: A meta-analysis. *Review of Educational Research, 69,* 21–51.

Springer, L., Terenzini, P., Pascarella, E., & Nora, A. (1995a). Influences on college students' orientations toward learning for self-understanding. *Journal of College Student Development, 36,* 5–18.

Springer, L., Terenzini, P., Pascarella, E., & Nora, A. (1995b, April). *Do White students perceive racism toward minority groups on campus?* Paper presented at the meeting of the American Educational Research Association, San Francisco.

Springer, L., Terenzini, P., Pascarella, E., & Nora, A. (1996, October). *Changes in degree aspirations of African-American college students at predominantly Black and predominantly White institutions.* Paper presented at the meeting of the Association for the Study of Higher Education, Memphis, TN.

Sprinthall, R., Schmutte, G., & Sirois, L. (1991). *Understanding educational research.* Englewood Cliffs, NJ: Prentice-Hall.

St. John, E. (1990). Price response in persistence decisions: An analysis of the High School and Beyond senior cohort. *Research in Higher Education, 31,* 387–403.

St. John, E. (1991). The impact of student financial aid: A review of recent research. *Journal of Student Financial Aid, 21,* 18–32.

St. John, E., Andrieu, S., Oescher, J., & Starkey, J. (1994). The influence of student aid on within-year persistence by traditional college-age students in four-year colleges. *Research in Higher Education, 35,* 455–480.

St. John, E., Hu, S., & Weber, J. (2001). State policy and the affordability of public higher education: The influence of state grants on persistence in Indiana. *Research in Higher Education, 42,* 401–428.

St. John, E., Kirshstein, R., & Noell, J. (1991). The effects of student financial aid on persistence: A sequential analysis. *Review of Higher Education, 14,* 383–406.

St. John, E., & Masten, C. (1990). Return on the federal investment in student financial aid: An assessment for the high school class of 1972. *Journal of Student Financial Aid, 20,* 4–23.

St. John, E., & Oescher, J. (1992, April). *A comparison of four approaches for assessment of the influence of student aid: An analysis of within year persistence by traditional college-age students in four-year colleges.* Paper presented at the meeting of the American Educational Research Association, San Francisco.

St. John, E., Oescher, J., & Andrieu, S. (1992). The influence of prices on within-year persistence by traditional college-age students in four-year colleges. *Journal of Student Financial Aid, 22,* 27–38.

St. John, E., Paulsen, M., & Starkey, J. (1996). The nexus between college choice and persistence. *Research in Higher Education, 37,* 175–220.

St. John, E., & Starkey, J. (1994). The influence of costs on persistence by traditional college-age students in community colleges. *Community College Journal of Research and Practice, 18,* 201–213.

St. John, E., & Starkey, J. (1995a). An alternative to net price: Assessing the influences of prices and subsidies on within-year persistence. *Journal of Higher Education, 66,* 156–186.

St. John, E., & Starkey, J. (1995b). The influence of prices on the persistence of adult undergraduates. *Journal of Student Financial Aid, 25,* 7–17.

St. John, E., Starkey, J., Paulsen, M., & Mbaduagha, L. (1995). The influence of prices and price subsidies on within-year persistence by students in proprietary schools. *Educational Evaluation and Policy Analysis, 17,* 149–165.

St. Pierre, K., Nelson, E., & Gabbin, A. (1990). A study of the ethical development of accounting majors in relation to other business and nonbusiness disciplines. *Accounting Educator's Journal, 3,* 23–35.

Stage, F. (1993). Chanting the names of the ancestors. *Educational Researcher, 22*(6), 22–24.

Stage, F., Muller, P., Kinzie, J., & Simmons, A. (1998). *Creating learning centered classrooms: What does learning theory have to say?* (ASHE-ERIC Higher Education Reports, Vol. 26, No. 4). Washington, DC: George Washington University.

Stage, F., & Rushin, P. (1993). A combined model of student predisposition to college and persistence in college. *Journal of College Student Development, 34,* 276–281.

Stage, F., & Williams, P. (1990). Students' motivation and changes in motivation during the first year of college. *Journal of College Student Development, 31,* 516–522.

Stake, J., & Hoffmann, F. (2001). Changes in student social attitudes, activism, and personal confidence in higher education: The role of women's studies. *American Educational Research Journal, 38,* 411–436.

Stake, J., Roades, L., Rose, S., Ellis, L., & West, C. (1994). The women's studies experience: Impetus for feminist activism. *Psychology of Women Quarterly, 18,* 17–24.

Stake, J., & Rose, S. (1994). The long-term impact of women's studies on students' personal lives and political activism. *Psychology of Women Quarterly, 18,* 403–412.

Stanton, G., Floyd, B., & Aultman, H. (1995). Effects of distance learning on student outcomes in general education courses. *Journal on Excellence in College Teaching, 6,* 131–144.

Starke, M. (1990). *Retention, bonding, and academic achievement: The success of the college seminar* (Research report). Mahwah, NJ: Ramapo College.

Starke, M., Harth, M., & Sirianni, F. (2001). Retention, bonding, and academic achievement: Success of a first-year seminar. *Journal of the First-Year Experience, 13,* 7–35.

Stassen, M. (2000, May). *Living-learning communities: A comparative assessment of two models.* Paper presented at the meeting of the Association for Institutional Research, Cincinnati, OH.

Stassen, M. (2003). Student outcomes: The impact of varying living-learning community models. *Research in Higher Education, 44,* 581–613.

Stasson, M., Kameda, T., Parks, C., Zimmerman, S., & Davis, J. (1991). Effects of assigned group consensus requirement on group problem solving and group members' learning. *Social Psychology Quarterly, 54,* 25–35.

Stearns, S. (1996). Collaborative exams as learning tools. *College Teaching, 44,* 111–112.

Steele, C. (1997). A threat in the air: How stereotypes shape intellectual identity and performance. *American Psychologist, 52,* 613–629.

Steele, C. (1999, August). Thin ice: "Stereotype threat" and Black college students. *Atlantic Monthly, 284,* 44–54.

Steele, C. (2000, February). "Stereotype threat" and Black college students. *AAHE Bulletin, 52,* 3–6.

Steele, G., Kennedy, G., & Gordon, V. (1993). The retention of major changers: A longitudinal study. *Journal of College Student Development, 34,* 58–62.

Steinberg, G. (1994). The class of '90 one year after graduation. *Occupational Outlook Quarterly, 38,* 10–20.

Stern, G. (1970). *People in context: Measuring person-environment congruence in education and industry.* New York: Wiley.

Sternberg, R. (1985). Teaching critical thinking. Part 2: Possible solutions. *Phi Delta Kappan, 67,* 277–280.

Stevens, G., & Featherman, D. (1981). A revised socioeconomic index of occupational status. *Social Science Research, 10,* 364–395.

Stith, P. (1994, May). *Faculty/student interaction: Impact on student retention.* Paper presented at the meeting of the Association for Institutional Research, New Orleans.

Stoecker, J., & Pascarella, E. (1991). Women's colleges and women's career attainments revisited. *Journal of Higher Education, 62,* 394–406.

Storch, E. (2002). Fraternities, sororities, and academic dishonesty. *College Student Journal, 36,* 247–252.

Strage, A. (2000, April). *Service-learning as a tool for enhancing student outcomes in a college-level lecture course.* Paper presented at the meeting of the American Educational Research Association, New Orleans.

Strange, C. (2003). Dynamics of campus environments. In S. Komives, G. Hanson, & Associates (Eds.), *Student services: A handbook for the profession* (4th ed., pp. 297–316). San Francisco: Jossey-Bass.

Strange, C., & Banning, J. (2001). *Educating by design: Creating campus learning environments that work.* San Francisco: Jossey-Bass.

Strausbaugh, W. (2003). *The effect of institutional type, gender, academic ability, age, and class-level on the faith maturity of college students.* Unpublished doctoral dissertation, Pennsylvania State University, University Park.

Strauss, L., & Volkwein, J. (2001a, June). *Comparing student performance and growth in two- and four-year institutions.* Paper presented at the forum of the Association for Institutional Research, Long Beach, CA.

Strauss, L., & Volkwein, J. (2001b, November). *Predictors of student commitment at two-year and four-year institutions.* Paper presented at the meeting of the Association for the Study of Higher Education, Richmond, VA.

Strumpf, G., & Hunt, P. (1993). The effects of an orientation course on the retention and academic standing of entering freshmen, controlling for the volunteer effect. *Journal of the Freshman Year Experience, 5,* 7–14.

A student success story: Freshman interest groups at the University of Missouri-Columbia. (1996). *Student Life Studies Abstracts, 1.*

Stukas, A., Snyder, M., & Clary, E. (1999). The effects of "mandatory volunteerism" on intentions to volunteer. *Psychological Science, 10,* 59–64.

Stupka, E. (1993). *An evaluation of the short-term and long-term impact a student success course has on academic performance and persistence* (Unpublished report). Sacramento, CA: Sacramento City College.

Sue, D., & Sue, D. W. (1990). *Counseling the culturally different: Theory and practice.* New York: Wiley.

Sullivan, K., & Mahalik, J. (2000). Increasing career self-efficacy for women: Evaluating a group intervention. *Journal of Counseling and Development, 78,* 54–62.

Sumner, K., & Brown, T. (1996). Men, women, and money: Exploring the role of gender, gender-linkage of college major, and career-information sources in salary expectations. *Sex Roles, 34,* 823–839.

Surething, N. (1999, August). *Occupational ego identity statuses in college students.* Paper presented at the meeting of the American Psychological Association, Boston.

Surette, B. (1997). *The effects of two-year colleges on the labor market and schooling experiences of young men.* Washington, DC: Federal Reserve Board, Divisions of Research and Statistics and Monetary Affairs.

Svinicki, M. (1991). Practical implications of cognitive theories. In R. Menges & M. Svinicki (Eds.), *College Teaching* (pp. 27–39). San Francisco: Jossey-Bass.

Swanson, C. (2002). *Cooling-out and warming-up: The role of the postsecondary institutional environment in managing ambitions* (Unpublished manuscript). Chicago: University of Chicago, National Opinion Research Center.

Swanson, J., Tokar, D., & Davis, L. (1994). Content and construct validity of the White racial identity attitude scale. *Journal of Vocational Behavior, 44,* 198–217.

Sweetman, O. (1994a). *College choice: Does it make a difference?* Unpublished manuscript, University of Newcastle-upon-Tyne, Newcastle, UK.

Sweetman, O. (1994b). *College quality, ability and returns to education.* Unpublished doctoral dissertation, University of Iowa, Iowa City.

Swell, L. (1992). Educating for success: A program to enhance the self-concept of freshmen on a large college campus: An evaluation. *Canadian Journal of Higher Education, 22,* 60–72.

Swigart, T., & Ethington, C. (1998). Ethnic differences in estimates of gains made by community college students. *Community College Journal of Research and Practice, 22,* 703–713.

Szelenyi, K. (2002, November). *Diverse viewpoints on American college campuses: Do students benefit? An exploratory study.* Paper presented at the meeting of the Association for the Study of Higher Education, Sacramento, CA.

Tafalla, R., Rivera, R., & Tuchel, B. (1993). *Psychological factors related to minority persistence on a predominantly White campus.* San Antonio, TX: Minority Student Today: Recruitment, Retention, and Success.

Tagg, J. (2003). *The learning paradigm college.* Bolton, MA: Anker.

Takahira, S., Goodings, D., & Byrnes, J. (1998). Retention and performance of male and female engineering students: An examination of academic and environmental variables. *Journal of Engineering Education, 87,* 1–8.

Taking measure of the additional income value of higher education for African Americans. (1999). *Journal of Blacks in Higher Education, 24,* 72–73.

Tan, D. (1995). Do students accomplish what they expect out of college? *College Student Journal, 29,* 449–454.

Tanaka, G. (2002). Higher education's self-reflexive turn: Toward an intercultural theory of student development. *Journal of Higher Education, 73,* 263–296.

Taraban, R., & Rynearson, K. (1998, Spring). Computer-based comprehension research in a content area. *Journal of Developmental Education, 21,* pp. 10 ff.

Tate, D., & Schwartz, G. (1993). Increasing the retention of American Indian students in professional programs in higher education. *Journal of American Indian Education, 33,* 21–31.

Tatum, B. (1999). *"Why are all the Black kids sitting together in the cafeteria?" and other conversations about race* (rev. ed.). New York: Basic Books.

Tatum, B. D. (1992). Talking about race, learning about racism: The application of racial identity development theory in the classroom. *Harvard Educational Review, 62,* 1–24.

Taub, D. (1995). Relationship of selected factors to traditional-age undergraduate women's development of autonomy. *Journal of College Student Development, 36,* 141–151.

Taub, D., & McEwen, M. (1991). Patterns of development of autonomy and mature interpersonal relationships in Black and White undergraduate women. *Journal of College Student Development, 32,* 502–508.

Taub, D., & McEwen, M. (1992). The relationship of racial identity attitudes to autonomy and mature interpersonal relationships in Black and White undergraduate women. *Journal of College Student Development, 33,* 439–446.

Taube, K. (1997). Critical thinking ability and disposition as factors of performance on a written critical thinking test. *Journal of General Education, 46,* 129–164.

Taylor, C., & Howard-Hamilton, M. (1995). Student involvement and racial identity attitudes among African-American males. *Journal of College Student Development, 36,* 330–336.

Taylor, M. (1983). The development of the measure of epistemological reflection. *Dissertation Abstracts International, 44,* 1065A.

Taylor, S. (1998). The impact of college on the development of tolerance. *NASPA Journal, 35,* 281–295.

Teich, P. (1991). How effective is computer-assisted instruction? An evaluation of legal educators. *Journal of Legal Education, 41,* 489–501.

Telander, R. (1996). *The hundred yard lie: The corruption of college football and what we can do to stop it.* Urbana: University of Illinois Press.

Tennant, M., & Pogson, P. (1995). *Learning and change in the adult years: A developmental perspective.* San Francisco: Jossey-Bass.

Terenzini, P. (1996). Rediscovering roots: Public policy and higher education research. *Review of Higher Education, 26,* 5–13.

Terenzini, P., Cabrera, A., & Bernal, E. (2001). *Swimming against the tide: The poor in American higher education* (College Board Research Report No. 2001-3). New York: College Board.

Terenzini, P., Cabrera, A., Colbeck, C., Bjorklund, S., & Parente, J. (1999, November). *Racial and ethnic diversity in the classroom: Does it promote student learning?* Paper presented at the meeting of the Association for the Study of Higher Education, San Antonio, TX.

Terenzini, P., Cabrera, A., Colbeck, C., Parente, J., & Bjorklund, S. (2001). Collaborative learning vs. discussion: Students' reported learning gains. *Journal of Engineering Education, 90*, 123–130.

Terenzini, P., Cabrera, A., Parente, J., & Bjorklund, S. (1998). *Teaching engineering design: Do active and collaborative learning techniques work?* Paper presented at the meeting of the American Society of Engineering Education, Seattle, WA.

Terenzini, P., Pascarella, E., & Blimling, G. (1996). Students' out-of-class experiences and their influence on learning and cognitive development: A literature review. *Journal of College Student Development, 37*, 149–162.

Terenzini, P., Rendon, L., Upcraft, M., Millar, S., Allison, K., Gregg, P., et al. (1994). The transition to college: Diverse students, diverse stories. *Research in Higher Education, 35*, 57–73.

Terenzini, P., Springer, L., Pascarella, E., & Nora, A. (1995a). Influences affecting the development of students' critical thinking skills. *Research in Higher Education, 36*, 23–29.

Terenzini, P., Springer, L., Pascarella, E., & Nora, A. (1995b). Academic and out-of-class influences affecting the development of students' intellectual orientations. *Review of Higher Education, 19*, 23–44.

Terenzini, P., Springer, L., Yaeger, P., Pascarella, E., & Nora, A. (1994, November). *The multiple influences on students' critical thinking skills.* Paper presented at the meeting of the Association for the Study of Higher Education, Orlando.

Terenzini, P., Springer, L., Yaeger, P., Pascarella, E., & Nora, A. (1996). First-generation college students: Characteristics, experiences, and cognitive development. *Research in Higher Education, 37*, 1–22.

Terenzini, P., Yaeger, P., Pascarella, E., & Nora, A. (1996, May). *Work-study program influences on college students' cognitive development.* Paper presented at the meeting of the Association for Institutional Research, Albuquerque, NM.

Terry, E. (1992). Values systems change and the collegiate environment: The freshman experience. *NASPA Journal, 29*, 261–267.

Texas State Occupational Information Coordinating Committee. (1995). *Automated student and adult learner follow-up system: Final report for program year (1994–95).* Austin: Texas State Occupation Information Coordinating Committee.

Thile, E., & Matt, G. (1995). The ethnic mentor undergraduate program: A brief description and preliminary findings. *Journal of Multicultural Counseling and Development, 23*, 116–126.

Thistlethwaite, D., & Wheeler, N. (1966). Effects of teaching and peer subcultures upon student aspirations. *Journal of Educational Psychology, 57*, 35–47.

Thoma, S. (1994). Trends and issues in moral judgment research using the Defining Issues Test. *Moral Education Forum, 19*, 1–17.

Thomas, P., & Higbee, J. (1996). Enhancing mathematics achievement through collaborative problem solving. *Learning Assistance Review, 1*(1), 38–46.

Thomas, R. (2001). *Recent theories of human development.* Thousand Oaks, CA: Sage.

Thomas, R., & Chickering, A. (1984). *Education and identity* revisited. *Journal of College Student Personnel, 25*, 392–399.

Thomas, S. (1998, November). *Deferred costs and economic returns to college major, quality, and performance: Recent trends.* Paper presented at the meeting of the Association for the Study of Higher Education, Miami.

Thomas, S. (2000a). Deferred costs and economic returns to college major, quality, and performance. *Research in Higher Education, 41,* 281–313.

Thomas, S. (2000b). Ties that bind: A social network approach to understanding student integration and persistence. *Journal of Higher Education, 71,* 591–615.

Thomas, S. (2003). Longer-term economic effects of college selectivity and control. *Research in Higher Education, 44,* 263–299.

Thompson, C. (1990, April). *Predicting involvement and educational attainment: A study of Black students in Black and White colleges.* Paper presented at the meeting of the American Educational Research Association, Boston.

Thompson, C., & Fretz, B. (1991). Predicting the adjustment of Black students at predominantly White universities. *Journal of Higher Education, 62,* 437–450.

Thompson, J., Samiratedu, V., & Rafter, J. (1993). The effects of on-campus residence on first-time college students. *NASPA Journal, 31,* 41–47.

Thompson, M., & Smart, J. (1998). *Importance of alternative student competences: Differences among faculty in Holland's academic environments.* Paper presented at the meeting of the Association for the Study of Higher Education, Miami.

Thompson, M., & Smart, J. (1999). Student competencies emphasized by faculty in disparate academic environments. *Journal of College Student Development, 40,* 365–376.

Thompson, P. (1991). The effect of section size on student performance in a statistics course. *College Student Journal, 25,* 388–395.

Thompson, S. (1995). Techniques for assessing general education outcomes: The natural science core program at the University of Denver. *Dissertation Abstracts International, 56,* 2139A.

Thomsen, C. J., Basu, A. M., & Reinitz, M. T. (1995). Effects of women's studies courses on gender-related attitudes of women and men. *Psychology of Women's Quarterly, 19,* 419–426.

Thorndike, R., & Andrieu-Parker, J. (1992, April). *Growth in knowledge: A two-year longitudinal study of changes in scores on the college basic academic subjects examination.* Paper presented at the meeting of the American Educational Research Association, San Francisco.

Thorson, E. (1997). *Greek and non-Greek alums: Giving, community participation, and retrospective college satisfaction.* Columbia: University of Missouri, School of Journalism, Center for Advanced Social Research.

Tidball, M. (1985). Baccalaureate origins of entrants into American medical schools. *Journal of Higher Education, 56,* 385–402.

Tidball, M., Smith, D., Tidball, C., & Wolf-Wendel, L. (1999). *Taking women seriously: Lessons and legacies for educating the majority.* Phoenix, AZ: Oryx Press.

Tierney, W. (1992). An anthropological analysis of student participation in college. *Journal of Higher Education, 63,* 603–618.

Tierney, W. (1999). Models of minority college-going and retention: Cultural integrity versus cultural suicide. *Journal of Negro Education, 68,* 80–91.

Tierney, W. (2000). Power, identity, and the dilemma of college student departure. In J. Braxton (Ed.), *Reworking the student departure puzzle* (pp. 213–234). Nashville, TN: Vanderbilt University Press.

Tinto, V. (1975). Dropout from higher education: A theoretical synthesis of recent research. *Review of Educational Research, 45,* 89–125.

Tinto, V. (1987). *Leaving college: Rethinking the causes and cures of student attrition.* Chicago: University of Chicago Press.

Tinto, V. (1993). *Leaving college: Rethinking the causes and cures of student attrition* (2nd ed.). Chicago: University of Chicago Press.

Tinto, V. (1995). Learning communities, collaborative learning, and the pedagogy of educational citizenship. *American Association for Higher Education Bulletin, 47,* 11–13.

Tinto, V. (1997). Classrooms as communities: Exploring the educational character of student persistence. *Journal of Higher Education, 68,* 599–623.

Tinto, V. (1998). Colleges as communities: Taking research on student persistence seriously. *Review of Higher Education, 21,* 167–177.

Tinto, V. (2000a). What have we learned about the impact of learning communities on students? *Assessment Update, 12,* 1–2, 12.

Tinto, V. (2000b). Linking learning and leaving: Exploring the role of the college classroom in student departure. In J. Braxton (Ed.), *Reworking the student departure puzzle* (pp. 81–94). Nashville, TN: Vanderbilt University Press.

Tinto, V., & Goodsell, A. (1993). Freshman interest groups and the first-year experience: Constructing student communities in a large university. *Journal of the Freshman Year Experience, 6,* 7–28.

Tinto, V., Goodsell, A., & Russo, P. (1993). Building community among new college students. *Liberal Education, 79,* 16–21.

Tinto, V., Goodsell Love, A., & Russo, P. (1994). *Building learning communities for new college students: A summary of research findings of the Collaborative Learning Project.* Syracuse, NY: Syracuse University, School of Education.

Tinto, V., & Russo, P. (1994). Coordinated studies programs: Their effect on student involvement at a community college. *Community College Review, 22,* 16–25.

Tinto, V., Russo, P., & Kadel, S. (1994). Constructing educational communities: Increasing retention in challenging circumstances. *Community College Journal, 64,* 26–30.

Tjaden, B., & Martin, C. (1995). Learning effects of CAI on college students. *Computers and Education, 24,* 271–277.

Tokar, D., & Swanson, J. (1991). An investigation of the validity of Helm's (1984) model of racial identity. *Journal of Counseling Psychology, 38,* 296–301.

Tokuno, K. (1993). Long-term and recent student outcomes of the freshman interest group program. *Journal of the Freshman Year Experience, 5,* 7–28.

Tom, G. (1997). Cooperative learning in the marketing research course. *Journal of College Student Development, 38,* 194–195.

Toma, J. (1998, April). *Representing the university: The uses of intercollegiate athletics in enhancing institutional identity.* Paper presented at the meeting of the American Educational Research Association, San Diego, CA.

Toma, J., & Cross, M. (1996, November). *Intercollegiate athletics and student college choice: Understanding the impact of championship seasons on the quantity and quality of undergraduate applications.* Paper presented at the meeting of the Association for the Study of Higher Education, Memphis, TN.

Topping, K. (1996). The effectiveness of peer tutoring in further and higher education: A typology and review of the literature. *Higher Education, 32,* 321–345.

Topping, K., Hill, S., McKaig, A., Rogers, C., Rushi, N., & Young, D. (1997). Paired reciprocal peer tutoring in undergraduate economics. *Innovations in Education and Training International, 34,* 96–113.

Topping, K., Watson, G., Jarvis, R., & Hill, S. (1996). Same-year paired peer tutoring with first-year undergraduates. *Teaching in Higher Education, 1,* 341–356.

Torres, D. (1994, May). *Non-academic factors influencing attrition in non-traditional university students.* Paper presented at the meeting of the Association for Institutional Research, New Orleans.

Torres, V. (1999). Validation of a bicultural orientation model for Hispanic college students. *Journal of College Student Development, 40,* 285–298.

Torres, V. (2003). Influences on ethnic identity development of Latino college students in the first two years of college. *Journal of College Student Development, 44,* 532–547.

Toth, L. (1996). An examination of student achievement and select psychosocial factors in relation to the cluster course teaching method. *Journal of Instructional Psychology, 23,* 81–84.

Touchton, J., Davis, L., & Makosky, V. (1991). *Fact book on women in higher education.* New York: American Council on Education.

Touchton, J., Shavlik, D., & Davis, L. (1993). *Women in presidencies.* Washington, DC: American Council on Education.

Toutkoushian, R., & Smart, J. (2001). Do institutional characteristics affect student gains from college? *Review of Higher Education, 25,* 39–61.

Townsend, B., McNerny, N., & Arnold, A. (1993). Will this community college transfer student succeed? Factors affecting transfer student performance. *Community College Journal of Research and Practice, 17,* 433–443.

Trevino, J. (1992). Participation in ethnic/racial student organizations. *Dissertation Abstracts International, 53,* 4230A.

Trippi, J., & Cheatham, H. (1991). Counseling effects on African American college student graduation. *Journal of College Student Development, 32,* 342–349.

Troiden, R. (1989). The formation of homosexual identities. *Journal of Homosexuality, 17,* 43–73.

Trosset, C. (1998, September/October). Obstacles to open discussion and critical thinking: The Grinnell College Study. *Change,* pp. 44–49.

Tsapogas, J., Cahalan, M., & Stowe, P. (1994, May). *Academic institutional characteristics and the educational labor market outcomes of recent college graduates— An exploratory analysis.* Paper presented at the annual meeting of the Association for Institutional Research, New Orleans.

Tsui, L. (1995, November). *Boosting female ambition: How college diversity impacts graduate degree aspirations of women.* Paper presented at the meeting of the Association for the Study of Higher Education, Orlando.

Tsui, L. (1998a, November). *A review of research on critical thinking.* Paper presented at the meeting of the Association for the Study of Higher Education, Miami.

Tsui, L. (1998b). *Fostering critical thinking in college students: A mixed-methods study of influences inside and outside of the classroom.* Unpublished manuscript, University of California, Los Angeles.

Tsui, L. (1999). Courses and instruction affecting critical thinking. *Research in Higher Education, 40,* 185–200.

Tsui, L. (2000). Effects of campus culture on students' critical thinking. *Review of Higher Education, 23,* 421–441.

Tsui, P., Murdock, T., & Mayer, L. (1997, May). *Trend analysis and enrollment management.* Paper presented at the meeting of the Association for Institutional Research, Orlando.

Tudor, R., & Bostow, D. (1991). Computer-programmed instruction: The relation of required interaction to practical application. *Journal of Applied Behavior Analysis, 24,* 361–368.

Tullier, L. (1990). *Women's careers and women's colleges: The effects of college experience on female students' career plans and attributes.* Unpublished doctoral dissertation, University of California, Los Angeles.

Tuma, J., & Geis, S. (1995). *Educational attainment of 1980 high school sophomores by 1992: Descriptive summary of 1980 high school sophomores 12 years later* (Statistical Analysis Report No. NCES 95–304). Washington, DC: U.S. Department of Education, Office of Educational Research and Improvement.

Turner, A., & Berry, T. (2000). Counseling center contributions to student retention and graduation: A longitudinal study. *Journal of College Student Development, 41,* 627–636.

Turner, S. (1999, April). *Changes in the return to college quality.* Paper presented at the meeting of the American Educational Research Association, Montreal.

Turner, S., & Bowen, W. (1999). Choice of major: The changing (unchanging) gender gap. *Industrial and Labor Relations Review, 52,* 289–313.

Tusin, L. (1991). The relationship of academic and social self-concepts with women's choice of teaching as a career: A longitudinal study. *Journal of Research and Development in Education, 24,* 16–27.

Twale, D., & Sanders, C. (1999). Impact of nonclassroom experiences on critical thinking ability. *NASPA Journal, 36,* 133–146.

Twomey, J. (1991). *Academic performance and retention in a peer mentor program of a two-year campus of a four-year institution* (Research report). Alamogordo: New Mexico State University Press.

Twomey Fosnet, C. (Ed.). (1996). *Constructivism: Theory, perspectives, and practice.* New York: Teachers College Press.

U.S. Department of Education. (1992). *Digest of education statistics* (No. 92–097). Washington, DC: National Center for Education Statistics.

U.S. Department of Education. (2000). *The National Study of the Operation of the Federal Work-Study Program: Summary findings from the student and institutional surveys.* (Doc. No. 00–10). Washington, DC: Office of the Under Secretary, Planning and Evaluation Service.

U.S. Department of Education. (2002). *The persistence of employees who pursue post-secondary study* (Statistics in Brief No. NCES 2002–118). Washington, DC: National Center for Education Statistics.

U.S. Department of Health and Human Services. (1989). *Reducing the health consequences of smoking: 25 years of progress.* Rockville, MD: U.S. Department of Health and Human Services.

U.S. General Accounting Office. (1995). *Higher education: Restructuring student aid could reduce low-income student drop-out rate* (Research Report No. 95–48). Washington, DC: U.S. General Accounting Office, Health, Education, and Human Services Division.

Underwood, L., Maes, B., Alstadt, L., & Boivin, M. (1996). Evaluating changes in social attitudes, character traits, and liberal-arts abilities during a four-year program at a Christian college. *Research on Christian Higher Education, 3,* 115–128.

Unmet (and overmet) financial need of undergraduates. (1999, October). *Postsecondary Education OPPORTUNITY, 88,* 1–10.

Upcraft, M., Terenzini, P., & Kruger, K. (1999). Looking beyond the horizon: Trends shaping student affairs—Technology. In C. Johnson & H. Cheatham (Eds.), *Higher education trends for the next century: A research agenda for student success* (pp. 30–35). Washington, DC: American College Personnel Association.

Vaillant, G. (1977). *Adaptation to life.* Boston: Little, Brown.

Van Gennep, A. (1960). *The rites of passage.* (M. Vizedon & G. Caffee, Trans.). Chicago: University of Chicago Press.

Van Haveren, R., Winterowd, C., & Fuqua, D. (1999, August). *Career decidedness and negative career thinking by athletic status, gender, and academic class.* Paper presented at the meeting of the American Psychological Association, Boston.

Van Heuvelen, A. (1991). Overview: Case study physics. *American Journal of Physics, 59,* 898–907.

Van Horn, C. (1995). *Enhancing the connection between higher education and the workplace: A survey of employers* (Research report). New Brunswick, NJ: State Higher Education Executive Officers.

Van Soest, D. (1996). Impact of social work education on student attitudes and behavior concerning oppression. *Journal of Social Work Education, 32,* 191–202.

Veenhoven, R. (1996). Developments in statistical research. *Social Indicators Research, 37,* 1–46.

Velasquez, P. (1999, November). *The relationship between cultural development, sense of belonging, and persistence among Chicanos in higher education: An exploratory study.* Paper presented at the meeting of the Association for the Study of Higher Education, San Antonio, TX.

Velasquez, P. M. (1997, March). *Resisting the normative implications of Tinto: Student and institutional characteristics supporting the persistence of Chicanos in higher education.* Paper presented at the meeting of the American Educational Research Association, Chicago.

Vendley, G. (1998). Effect of a multiethnic, multicultural program on student participants. *NASPA Journal, 35,* 234–244.

Verdugo, R., & Verdugo, N. (1989). The impact of surplus schooling on earnings: Some additional findings. *Journal of Human Resources, 24,* 630–643.

Verduin, J., & Clark, T. (1991). *Distance education: The foundations of effective practice.* San Francisco: Jossey-Bass.

Verity, P., Gilligan, M., Frischer, M., Booth, M., Richardson, J., & Franklin, C. (2002, February). Improving undergraduate research experiences. *AAHE Bulletin, 54,* 3–6.

Vernon, D., & Blake, R. (1993). Does problem-based learning work? A meta-analysis of evaluative research. *Academic Medicine, 68,* 550–563.

Veum, J., & Weiss, A. (1993). Education and the work histories of young adults. *Monthly Labor Review, 116*(4), 11–20.

Villalpando, O. (1996, November). *The effects of college on the values and behaviors of Chicanos and Chicanas.* Paper presented at the meeting of the Association for the Study of Higher Education, Memphis, TN.

Villella, E., & Hu, M. (1991). A factor analysis of variables affecting the retention decision of nontraditional college students. *NASPA Journal, 28,* 334–341.

Visor, J., Johnson, J., & Cole, L. (1992a, Fall). Supplemental instruction and self-esteem. *Supplemental Instruction News,* pp. 1, 7.

Visor, J., Johnson, J., & Cole, L. (1992b). The relationship of supplemental instruction to affect. *Journal of Developmental Education, 16,* 12–18.

Visor, J., Johnson, J., Schollaet, A., Good-Majah, C., & Davenport, O. (1995). Supplemental instruction's impact on affect: A follow-up and expansion. In *Proceedings from the 20th Annual Conference on Developmental Education* (pp. 36–37). Chicago: National Association for Developmental Education.

Vital signs: The current state of African Americans in higher education. (1996). *Journal of Blacks in Higher Education, 14,* 61–65.

Vitale, M., & Romance, N. (1992). Using videodisc instruction in an elementary science methods course: Remediating science knowledge deficiencies and facilitating science teaching attitudes. *Journal of Research in Science Teaching, 29,* 915–928.

Vogelgesang, L. (2000a). The impact of college on the development of civic values and skills: An analysis by race, gender and social class. *Dissertation Abstracts International, 57,* 3087A.

Vogelgesang, L. (2000b). The development of civic values and skills: An analysis by race, gender, and social class. *Diversity Digest, 4,* 15–17.

Vogelgesang, L. (2001, November). *The impact of college on the development of civic values: How do race, gender, and social class matter?* Paper presented at the meeting of the Association for the Study of Higher Education, Richmond, VA.

Vogelgesang, L., & Astin, A. (2000). Comparing the effects of community service and service learning. *Michigan Journal of Community Service Learning, 7,* 25–34.

Volkwein, J. (1991, November). *Improved measures of academic and social integration and their association with ten educational outcomes.* Paper presented at the meeting of the Association for the Study of Higher Education, Boston.

Volkwein, J., & Carbone, D. (1994). The impact of departmental research and teaching climates on undergraduate growth and satisfaction. *Journal of Higher Education, 65,* 147–167.

Volkwein, J., Schmonsky, R., & Im, Y. (1989, May). *The impact of employment on the academic achievement of full-time community college students.* Paper presented at the meeting of the Association for Institutional Research, Baltimore.

Volkwein, J., Valle, S., Parmely, K., Blose, G., & Zhou, Y. (2000, May). *A multi-campus study of academic performance and cognitive growth among native freshmen, two-year transfers, and four-year transfers.* Paper presented at the forum of the Association for Institutional Research, Cincinnati, OH.

Vowell, F., Farren, P., & McGlone, E. (1990). Intrusive advising fosters improved retention of undergraduate college students: A longitudinal study. *College Student Journal, 24,* 103–110.

Wachtel, H. (1998). Student evaluation of college teaching effectiveness: A brief review. *Assessment & Evaluation in Higher Education, 23,* 191–211.

Wade, B. (1991, April). *A profile of the real world of undergraduate students and how they spend their discretionary time.* Paper presented at the meeting of the American Educational Research Association, Chicago.

Walberg, H. (1985). Synthesis of research on teaching. In M. Wittrock (Ed.), *Third handbook of research on teaching.* Washington, DC: American Educational Research Association.

Walker, A. (2002, April). *Learning communities and their perceived effect on students' academic abilities.* Paper presented at the meeting of the American Educational Research Association, New Orleans.

Walker, L. (1984). Sex differences in the development of moral reasoning: A critical review. *Child Development, 57,* 522–527.

Walker, L. (1991). Sex differences in moral reasoning. In W. Kurtines & J. Gewirtz (Eds.), *Handbook of moral behavior and development. Vol. 2: Research* (pp. 333–364). Hillsdale, NJ: Erlbaum.

Walleri, R., Stoker, C., & Stoering, J. (1997, May). *Building a community of learning: A comprehensive approach to assisting at-risk students.* Paper presented at the meeting of the Association for Institutional Research, Orlando.

Walpole, M. (1997, March). *College and class status: The effect of social class background on college impact and outcomes.* Paper presented at the meeting of the American Educational Research Association, Chicago.

Walpole, M. (1998a, April). *Social mobility and highly selective colleges: The effect of social class background on college involvement and outcomes.* Paper presented at the meeting of the American Educational Research Association, San Diego, CA.

Walpole, M. (1998b). Class matters: How social class shapes college experiences and outcomes. *Dissertation Abstracts International, 59A,* 3374A.

Walsh, J., & Reese, B. (1995). Distance education's growing reach. *T.H.E. Journal, 22,* 58–62.

Waltman, J., & Cook, C. (1997, November). *The impact of midsemester feedback on teaching effectiveness.* Paper presented at the meeting of the Association for the Study of Higher Education, Albuquerque, NM.

Warburton, E., Bugarin, R., & Nunez, A. (2001). *Bridging the gap: Academic preparation and postsecondary success of first-generation students* (Statistical Analysis

Report No. NCES 2001–153). Washington, DC: U.S. Department of Education, Office of Educational Research and Improvement, National Center for Education Statistics.

Warren, B. (1997–1998). Supporting large classes with supplemental instruction (SI). *Journal of Staff, Program, & Organizational Development, 15,* 47–54.

Watkins, G. (1998). Achievement and attitudes with CD-Rom instruction. *College Student Journal, 32,* 293–301.

Watson, L., & Kuh, G. (1996). The influence of dominant race environments on student involvement, perceptions, and educational gains: A look at historically Black and predominantly White liberal arts institutions. *Journal of College Student Development, 37,* 415–424.

Watson, L., Terrell, M., Wright, D., & Associates. (2002). *How minority students experience college: Implications for planning and policy.* Sterling, VA: Stylus.

Weast, D. (1996). Alternative strategies: The case for critical thinking. *Teaching Sociology, 24,* 189–194.

Weaver, H. (1989). *Research on U.S. students abroad: A bibliography with abstracts.* New York: Council on International Educational Exchange, Education Abroad Program.

Webb, M. (1989). A theoretical model of community college student degree persistence. *Community College Review, 16,* 42–49.

Webb, R. (2001). Motivated to lead: A longitudinal assessment of students attending a Christian liberal arts college. *Research on Christian Higher Education, 8,* 95–106.

Wechsler, H. (1996, July/August). Alcohol and the American college campus: A report from the Harvard School of Public Health. *Change, 28,* 20–25, 60.

Wechsler, H., Davenport, A., Dowdall, G., Grossman, S., & Zanakos, S. (1997). Binge drinking, tobacco, and illicit drug use and involvement in college athletics. *Journal of American College Health, 45,* 195–200.

Wechsler, H., Dowdall, G., Davenport, A., Moeykens, B., & Castillo, S. (1995). Correlates of college student binge drinking. *American Journal of Public Health, 85,* 921–926.

Wechsler, H., Dowdall, G., Maenner, G., Gledhill-Hoyt, J., & Lee, H. (1998). Changes in binge drinking and related problems among American college students between 1993 and 1997: Results of the Harvard School of Public Health college alcohol study. *Journal of American College Health, 47,* 57–68.

Wechsler, H., & Isaac, N. (1992). Binge drinkers at Massachusetts colleges: Prevalence, drinking style, time trends, and associated problems. *Journal of the American Medical Association, 267,* 2929–2931.

Wechsler, H., Isaac, N., Grodstein, F., & Sellers, D. (1994). Continuation and initiation of alcohol use from first to the second year of college. *Journal of Studies on Alcohol, 55,* 41–45.

Wechsler, H., Kuh, G., & Davenport, A. (1996). Fraternities, sororities, and binge drinking: Results from a national study of American colleges. *NASPA Journal, 33,* 260–279.

Wei, C. C., & Horn, L. (2002). *Persistence and attainment of beginning students with Pell Grants* (Statistical Analysis Report No. NCES 2002–169). Washington, DC: National Center for Education Statistics, U.S. Department of Education.

Wei-Cheng, M. (1999). Effects of computer-assisted career decision making on vocational identity and career exploratory behaviors. *Journal of Career Development, 25,* 261–274.

Weidman, J. (1984). Impacts of campus experiences and parental socialization on undergraduates' career choices. *Research in Higher Education, 20,* 445–476.

Weidman, J. (1985). Postsecondary "high-tech" training for women on welfare: Correlates of program completion. *Journal of Higher Education, 56,* 555–568.

Weidman, J. (1989). Undergraduate socialization: A conceptual approach. In J. Smart (Ed.), *Higher education: Handbook of theory and research* (Vol. 5, pp. 289–322). New York: Agathon.

Weidman, J., & Friedman, R. (1984). The school-to-work transition for high school dropouts. *Urban Review, 16,* 25–42.

Weiler, W. (1991). The effect of undergraduate student loans on the decision to pursue postbaccalaureate study. *Educational Evaluation and Policy Analysis, 13,* 212–220.

Weiler, W. (1993). Postbaccalaureate educational choices of minority students. *Review of Higher Education, 16,* 439–460.

Weimer, M., & Lenze, L. (1997). Instructional interventions: Review of the literature on efforts to improve instruction. In R. Perry & J. Smart (Eds.), *Effective teaching in higher education: Research and practice* (pp. 154–168). New York: Agathon.

Weiner, B. (1980). *Human motivation.* Austin, TX: Holt, Rinehart & Winston.

Weissman, J., Silke, E., & Bulakowski, C. (1997). Assessing developmental education policies. *Research in Higher Education, 38,* 187–200.

Weller, H. (1996). Assessing the impact of computer-based learning in science. *Journal of Research on Computing in Education, 28,* 461–485.

Weller, H. (1997, March). *What have we learned from eight years of research on computer-based science learning?* Paper presented at the meeting of the American Educational Research Association, Chicago.

Wellman, J. (1999). *Contributing to the civic good: Assessing and accounting for the civic contributions of higher education* (Working paper). Washington, DC: Institute for Higher Education Policy, New Millennium Project on Higher Education Costs, Pricing, and Productivity.

Wellman, J. (2002). *State policy and community college—Baccalaureate transfer* (National Center Report No. 02–6). San Jose, CA: National Center for Public Policy and Higher Education and the Institute for Higher Education Policy.

Wenglinsky, H. (1996). The educational justification of historically Black colleges and universities: A policy response to the U.S. Supreme Court. *Educational Evaluation and Policy Analysis, 18,* 91–103.

West, K. (1994). Enhancing critical thinking in the political science curriculum. *Dissertation Abstracts International, 55,* 725A.

West, K., & Michael, W. (1998, April). *Factors associated with attrition and retention of science and engineering undergraduates at a highly selective research institution.*

Paper presented at the meeting of the American Educational Research Association, San Diego, CA.

West, T. (1996). Make way for the information age: Reconstructing the pillars of higher education. *On the Horizon, 4*(4), 1, 4–5.

Wetzel, C., Radtke, P., & Stern, H. (1994). *Instructional effectiveness of video media.* Hillsdale, NJ: Erlbaum.

Whitaker, D., & Pascarella, E. (1994). Two-year college attendance and socioeconomic attainment: Some additional evidence. *Journal of Higher Education, 65,* 194–210.

Whitbourne, S., Jelsma, B., & Waterman, A. (1982). An Eriksonian measure of personality development in college students: A reexamination of Constantinople's data and a partial replication. *Developmental Psychology, 18,* 369–371.

White, J. (1999). *Outcomes of computer-based instruction in mathematics.* Paper presented at the meeting of the International Conference on College Teaching and Learning, Jacksonville, FL.

Whitmire, E. (1998). Development of critical thinking skills: An analysis of academic library experiences and other measures. *College and Research Libraries, 59,* 266–273.

Whitmire, E., & Lawrence, J. (1996, November). *Undergraduate students' development of critical thinking skills: An institutional and disciplinary analysis and comparison with academic library use and other measures.* Paper presented at the meeting of the Association for the Study of Higher Education, Memphis, TN.

Whitt, E. (1994). "I can be anything!" Student leadership in three women's colleges. *Journal of College Student Development, 35,* 198–207.

Whitt, E., Edison, M., Pascarella, E., Nora, A., & Terenzini, P. (1999a). Interaction with peers and objective and self-reported cognitive outcomes across three years of college. *Journal of College Student Development, 40,* 61–78.

Whitt, E., Edison, M., Pascarella, E., Nora, A., & Terenzini, P. (1999b). Women's perception of a "chilly climate" and cognitive outcomes in college: Additional evidence. *Journal of College Student Development, 40,* 163–177.

Whitt, E., Edison, M., Pascarella, E., Terenzini, P., & Nora, A. (2001). Influences on students' openness to diversity and challenge in the second and third years of college. *Journal of Higher Education, 72,* 172–204.

Whitt, E., Pascarella, E., Elkins Nesheim, B., Marth, B., & Pierson, C. (2003). Differences between women and men in objectively measured outcomes, and the factors that influence those outcomes, in the first three years of college. *Journal of College Student Development, 44,* 587–610.

Whitt, E., Pascarella, E., Pierson, C., Elkins, B., & Marth, B. (in press). *Sex and gender in college: Evidence of differences in experiences and outcomes.* Nashville, TN: Vanderbilt University Press.

Why college? Private correlates of educational attainment. (1999, March). *Postsecondary Education OPPORTUNITY, 81,* 1–24.

Widick, C. (1975). An evaluation of developmental instruction in a university setting. *Dissertation Abstracts International, 36,* 2041A.

Widick, C., Knefelkamp, L., & Parker, C. (1980). Student development. In U. Delworth & G. Hanson (Eds.), *Student services: A handbook for the profession* (pp. 75–116). San Francisco: Jossey-Bass.

Wiegmann, D., Dansereau, D., & Patterson, M. (1992). Cooperative learning: Effects of role playing and ability on performance. *Journal of Experimental Education, 60,* 109–116.

Wijeyesinghe, C. (2001). Racial identity in multiracial people: An alternative paradigm. In C. Wijeyesinghe & B. Jackson III (Eds.), *New perspectives on racial identity development: A theoretical and practical anthology* (pp. 129–152). New York: New York University Press.

Wilder, D., & McKeegan, H. (1999). Greek-letter social organizations in higher education: A review of research. In J. Smart (Ed.), *Higher education: Handbook of theory and research* (Vol. 14, pp. 317–366). New York: Agathon.

Wilder, D., McKeegan, H., Midkiff, R., Skelton, R., & Dunkerly, R. (1997). The impact of Greek affiliation on students' educational objectives: Longitudinal change in Clark-Trow educational philosophies. *Research in Higher Education, 38,* 151–171.

Wilder, D., Midkiff, R., Dunkerly, R., & Skelton, R. (1996). Higher educational impact on student objectives: Longitudinal change in Clark-Trow educational philosophies. *Research in Higher Education, 37,* 279–298.

Wilkie, C., & Jones, M. (1994). Academic benefits of on-campus employment to first-year developmental education students. *Journal of the Freshman Year Experience, 6,* 37–56.

Wilkie, C., & Kuckuck, S. (1989). A longitudinal study of the effects of a freshman seminar. *Journal of the Freshman Year Experience, 1,* 7–16.

Willett, J., & Singer, J. (1991). From whether to when: New methods for studying student dropout and teacher attrition. *Review of Educational Research, 61,* 407–450.

Willford, L. (1996, May). *The freshman year: How do personal factors influence academic success and persistence?* Paper presented at the meeting of the Association for Institutional Research, Albuquerque, NM.

Williams, D. (1990). Is the postsecondary classroom a chilly one for women? A review of the literature. *Canadian Journal of Higher Education, 20*(3), 29–42.

Williams, M. (1992). The effects of emergency loans on student retention. *Journal of Student Financial Aid, 22,* 39–44.

Williams, M., & Ball, D. (1993). How grads rank their own employability factors. *Journal of Career Planning & Employment, 53,* pp. 25 ff.

Williams, R. (1996). Assessing students' gains from the college experience at East Tennessee State University. *Dissertation Abstracts International, 57,* 970A.

Williams, W., & Ceci, S. (1997, September/October). "How'm I doing?" Problems with student ratings of instructors and courses. *Change, 29,* 12–23.

Williamson, J., & Mellott, R. (1997, August). *Students' attributions and attitudes regarding sexual aggression.* Paper presented at the meeting of the American Psychological Association, Chicago.

Williamson, V., & Abraham, M. (1995). The effects of computer animation on the particular mental models of college chemistry students. *Journal of Research in Science Teaching, 32,* 521–534.

Wilson, K., & Boldizar, J. (1990). Gender segregation in higher education: Effects of aspirations, mathematics, achievement, and income. *Sociology of Education, 63,* 62–74.

Wilson, K., Rest, J., Boldizar, J., & Deemer, D. (1992). Moral judgment development: The effects of education and occupation. *Social Justice Research, 5,* 31–48.

Wilson, R. (1986). Improving faculty teaching: Effective use of student evaluations and consultations. *Journal of Higher Education, 57,* 196–211.

Wilson, S., Mason, T., & Ewinig, J. (1997). Evaluating the impact of receiving university-based counseling services on student retention. *Journal of Counseling Psychology, 44,* 316–320.

Windham, P. (1995). The relative importance of selected factors to attrition at a public community college. *Journal of Applied Research in the Community College, 3,* 65–78.

Winkleby, M., Fortmann, S., & Barrett, D. (1990). Social class disparities in risk factors for disease: Eight-year prevalence patterns by level of education. *Preventive Medicine, 19,* 1–12.

Winkleby, M., Jatulis, D., Frank, E., & Fortmann, S. (1992). Socioeconomic status and health: How education, income, and occupation contribute to risk factors for cardiovascular disease. *American Journal of Public Health, 82,* 816–820.

Winston, R., & Sandor, J. (1984). *Academic advising inventory.* Athens, GA: Student Development Associates.

Winston, R., Jr., & Miller, T. (1987). *Student Development Task and Lifestyle Inventory manual.* Athens, GA: Student Development Associates.

Witherspoon, A., Long, C., & Chubick, J. (1999). Prediction of college student dropouts using EDS scores. *Journal of College Student Development, 40,* 82–86.

Witkin, H. (1962). *Psychological differentiation.* New York: Wiley.

Witkin, H. (1976). Cognitive style in academic performance and in teacher-student relations. In S. Messick & Associates (Eds.), *Individuality in learning.* San Francisco: Jossey-Bass.

Witkowsky, K. (2002, Fall). Debating student debt. *National CrossTalk,* pp. 1, 8–9.

Wittig, G., & Thomerson, J. (1996). *Supplemental instruction improves student retention and performance in biology.* Paper presented at the 89th meeting of the Illinois State Academy of Science, Bloomington.

Wolfe, J. (1993). Institutional integration, academic success, and persistence of first-year commuter and resident students. *Journal of College Student Development, 34,* 321–326.

Wolfe, R., & Johnson, S. (1995). Personality as a predictor of college performance. *Educational and Psychological Measurement, 55,* 177–185.

Wolfle, L. (1983). Effects of higher education on achievement for Blacks and Whites. *Research in Higher Education, 19,* 3–9.

Wolfner, G., & Gelles, R. (1993). A profile of violence toward children: A national study. *Child Abuse and Neglect, 17,* 197–212.

Wolf-Wendel, L. (1998). Models of excellence: The baccalaureate origins of successful European-American women, African-American women, and Latinas. *Journal of Higher Education, 69,* 141–186.

Wolf-Wendel, L., Baker, B., & Morphew, C. (2000). Dollars and $ense: Institutional resources and the baccalaureate origins of women doctorates. *Journal of Higher Education, 71,* 165–186.

Wolf-Wendel, L., Toma, D., & Morphew, C. (2000). *Winning through diversity: Lessons from intercollegiate athletics in creating community from difference* (Diversity on Campus: Reports from the Field Project Report). Washington, DC: National Association for Student Personnel Administrators.

Wolniak, G., Pierson, C., & Pascarella, E. (2001). Effects of intercollegiate athletic participation on male orientations toward learning. *Journal of College Student Development, 42,* 604–624.

Wood, A., & Murray, H. (1999, April). *Effects of teacher enthusiasm on student attention, motivation, and memory encoding.* Paper presented at the meeting of the American Educational Research Association, Montreal.

Wood, P. (1997). A secondary analysis of claims regarding the reflective judgment interview: Internal consistency, sequentiality, and intradivisional differences in ill-structured problem solving. In J. Smart (Ed.), *Higher education: Handbook of theory and research* (Vol. 12, pp. 243–312). New York: Agathon.

Wood, P. (2000, August). *Scaling and scoring of an objective measure of epistemic development.* Paper presented at the meeting of the American Psychological Association, Washington, DC.

Wood, P., & Chesser, M. (1994). Black stereotyping in a university population. *Sociological Focus, 27,* 17–34.

Woodruff, J., & Mollise, D. (1995). Course performance of students in weekly and daily formats. *Journal of Continuing Higher Education, 43*(3), 10–15.

Workforce Training and Education Coordinating Board. (1996). *Workforce training results: An evaluation of Washington State's workforce training system.* Olympia, WA: Workforce Training and Education Coordinating Board.

Wright, S. (1989). Selected correlates of intellectual development of college freshmen. *Dissertation Abstracts International, 50,* 3498A.

Wright, S. (1992). Fostering intellectual development of students in professional schools through interdisciplinary coursework. *Innovative Higher Education, 16,* 251–261.

Wright, S., Aron, A., McLaughlin-Volpe, T., & Ropp, S. (1997). The extended contact effect: Knowledge of cross-group friendships and prejudice. *Journal of Personality and Social Psychology, 73,* 73–90.

Xiao, B., & House, J. (2000, May). *The impact of a freshman orientation course on the bachelor's degree attainment process.* Paper presented at the meeting of the Association for Institutional Research, Cincinnati, OH.

Yang, X., & Brown, J. (1998, May). *Using unemployment insurance data and job record data to track the employment and earnings of community college students.* Paper presented at the meeting of the Association for Institutional Research, Minneapolis.

York-Anderson, D., & Bowman, S. (1991). Assessing the college knowledge of first-generation and second-generation students. *Journal of College Student Development, 32,* 116–122.

Yorke, M. (1998). Noncompletion of undergraduate study: Some implications for policy in higher education. *Journal of Higher Education Policy and Management, 20,* 189–201.

Youn, T., Arnold, K., & Salkever, K. (1998, November). *Baccalaureate origins and career attainments of American Rhodes scholars.* Paper presented at the meeting of the Association for the Study of Higher Education, Miami.

Youn, T., Arnold, K., & Salkever, K. (2000). *Pathways to prominence: Social origin, educational prestige, and career distinction of American Rhodes scholars.* Paper presented at the meeting of the American Sociological Association, Washington, DC.

Young, R., Backer, R., & Rogers, G. (1989). The impact of early advising and scheduling on freshman success. *Journal of College Student Development, 30,* 309–312.

Young, R., Belasco, J., Barr, A., Gallaher, P., & Webber, A. (1991). Changes in fear of AIDS and homophobia in a university population. *Journal of Applied Social Psychology, 21,* 1848–1858.

Zagora, M., & Cramer, S. (1994). The effects of vocational identity status on outcomes in a career decision-making intervention for community college students. *Journal of College Student Development, 35,* 239–247.

Zea, M., Reisen, C., Beil, C., & Caplan, R. (1997). Predicting intention to remain in college among ethnic minority and nonminority students. *Journal of Social Psychology, 137,* 149–160.

Zeilik, M., Schau, C., Mattern, S., Hall, K., Teague, W., & Bisard, W. (1997). Conceptual astronomy: A novel model for teaching postsecondary science courses. *American Journal of Physics, 65,* 987–996.

Zhang, Z., & Richarde, R. (1998, April). *Assessing college students' development: A repeated-measures analysis using a mixed model.* Paper presented at the meeting of the American Educational Research Association, San Diego, CA.

Zhao, J. (1999, June). *Factors affecting academic outcomes of underprepared community college students.* Paper presented at the meeting of the Association for Institutional Research, Seattle, WA.

Zhu, B., Giovino, G., Mowery, P., & Eriksen, M. (1996). The relationship between cigarette smoking and education revisited: Implications for categorizing persons' educational status. *American Journal of Public Health, 86,* 1582–1589.

Zietz, J., & Cochran, H. (1997). Containing cost without sacrificing achievement: Some evidence from college-level economics classes. *Journal of Education Finance, 23,* 177–192.

Zigerell, J. (1991). *The uses of television in American higher education.* New York: Praeger.

Zill, N., & Nord, C. (1994). *Running in place: How American families are faring in a changing economy and an individualistic society.* Washington, DC: Child Trends.

Zlotkowski, E. (1998). A new model of excellence. In E. Zlotkowski (Ed.), *Successful service-learning programs: New models of excellence in higher education* (pp. 1–14). Bolton: Anker.

Zlotkowski, E. (Ed.). (2002). *Service-learning and the first-year experience: Preparing students for personal success and civic responsibility.* Columbia: University of

South Carolina, National Resource Center for the First-Year Experience and Students in Transition.

Zorn, C. (1996). The long-term impact on nursing students of participating in international education. *Journal of Professional Nursing, 12,* 106–110.

Zuniga, X., Berger, J., Kluge, M., & Williams, E. (2001). *The effects of student engagement with diversity on socio-cognitive and behavioral outcomes.* Paper presented at the meeting of the American Educational Research Association, Seattle, WA.

Zuschlag, M., & Whitbourne, S. (1994). Psychosocial development in three generations of college students. *Journal of Youth and Adolescence, 23,* 567–577.

Zydney, A., Bennett, J., Shahid, A., & Bauer, K. (2002a). Impact of undergraduate research experience in engineering. *Journal of Engineering Education, 91,* 151–157.

Zydney, A., Bennett, J., Shahid, A., & Bauer, K. (2002b). Faculty perspectives regarding the undergraduate research experience in science and engineering. *Journal of Engineering Education, 91,* 291–297.

Name Index

Subject Index

impact on, 119–120; active, 101–102; collaborative, 102–104; using computers and IT for, 97–100; constructivist-oriented approaches to, 107–109; cooperative, 104–105; deep approach to, 186; distance, 100–101; focused classroom instructional techniques and, 110–114; institutional practices/policy to improve, 646–647; mastery, 96–97; PBL (problem-based learning), 108–109; pedagogical approaches to, 95–110; service, 358–359; small-group, 105–106; social and extracurricular effort-involvement impaction, 120–134; Supplemental Instruction program for, 106–107; surface approach to, 186; teacher behavior and impact on, 114–119. *See also* Changes in learning; College student learning

Learning communities: educational attainment/persistence and, 422–423; student learning and, 109–110

Learning cycle-inquiry approach to instruction, 173

Learning facilitation, 185–186

Learning styles: conditional effects on learning and, 138–140; within-college effects of college and, 622–623

Lesbian identity development, 29–33, 217–218. *See also* Attitudes toward homosexuality

LFM (learning for mastery), 96

"Lifelong openness to change" hypothesis, 332

Literacy rates, 69

LLCs (living-learning centers), 421–422

Loans (student), 411–413

Locus of control: between-college effects on, 235–236; conditional effects of college on, 253–255; during college, 223, 224–225; long-term effects of college on, 259–260; net effects of college on, 229–230

Long-term effects: on attitudes/values, 327–334, 342, 586–587; on cognitive skills/intellectual growth, 202–204, 211, 584–585; on learning, 142–144, 150, 584–585; on moral development, 365–366, 370, 440–441, 587; on psychosocial change, 255–261, 268–269, 585–586; on socioeconomic status, 582–584t

LSAHE (Learn and Serve America Higher Education), 516

LSAT (Law School Admissions Test), 78, 80, 85, 93, 94

M

Major. *See* Academic major

Managing emotions, 21–22

Marcia's theory of identity development among women only, 24

Mastery learning, 95–97

Mastery pattern, 39

Mathematics self-concepts, 220–221

MCAT (Medical College Admissions Test), 78, 83, 92, 93, 94, 469

MER (Measure of Epistemological Reflection), 162–163, 177

Methodology definitions, 12–14

MID (Measure of Intellectual Development), 163, 203

Minorities. *See* African-American students; Asian-American students; Latino students; Native American students; Racial differences

MJI (Moral Judgment Interview), 346, 347

Moral development changes: between-college effects on, 351–353, 367–368; conditional effects of college on, 364–365, 370; during college, 345–347, 366–367, 576–577; long-term effects of college on, 365–366, 370, 587; net effects of college on, 347–351, 367, 581–582; within-college effects on, 353–364, 368–370

Moral development interventions, 354–358

Moral development theory, 42–43

Moral reasoning/action: between-college effects on, 352–353; net effects of college on, 350–351

Mortality risk factors, 556–557

MSE (mathematics, science, and engineering) majors: educational attainment/persistence and, 424; impact of peers on, 495–496; two-year versus four-year colleges and, 492–493

N

NAEP (National Assessment of Educational Program), on long-term effects of college, 143–144

National Board of Medical Examiners Examination, 92

National Center for Education Statistics, 100, 488

National Center for Education Statistics National Household Education Survey (1996), 274

National Longitudinal Study of Youth, 136

National Longitudinal Survey of Labor Market Experiences, 493–494

Native American students, 25–29. *See also* Racial differences

The Nature of Prejudice (Allport), 309

NCAA Division I athletes, 192, 322–323

NES (National Election Study), 329

Net effect, 12, 632–633

Net effects: on attitudes/values, 286–293, 335–337, 581; on career/economic changes, 447–463, 535–537; on cognitive skills, 164, 167–168, 205–206; defining, 12, 632–633; on learning, 70–75, 145–146, 579–580; on moral development, 347–351, 367, 581–582; on psychosocial change, 227–231, 263, 580–581; on quality of life after college, 551–560, 566–567